I0836681

G° Washington

From the original painting by Chappel, in the possession of the publishers.

Johnson, Fry & Co. Publishers, New York.

Painted by — LANDING OF CHRISTOPHER COLUMBUS. — Alonzo Chappel.

NEW YORK,
JOHNSON FRY & COMPANY.
27 BEEKMAN STREET.

HISTORY

OF

THE WORLD

FROM THE

EARLIEST PERIOD TO THE PRESENT TIME.

COLLECTED AND ARRANGED FROM THE BEST AUTHORITIES.

BY

EVERT A. DUYCKINCK,

AUTHOR OF "NATIONAL PORTRAIT GALLERY OF EMINENT AMERICANS," "CYCLOPEDIA OF AMERICAN LITERATURE," ETC., ETC.

Illustrated with Highly Finished Steel Engravings
OF
HISTORICAL EVENTS AND PORTRAITS OF EMINENT MEN

FROM ORIGINAL PAINTINGS BY ALONZO CHAPPEL, PAUL DE LA ROCHE, GEROMÆ, COPLEY, WEIR, POWELL, AND OTHER EMINENT ARTISTS.

VOLUME IV.

New York:
JOHNSON, FRY AND COMPANY,
27 BEEKMAN STREET.

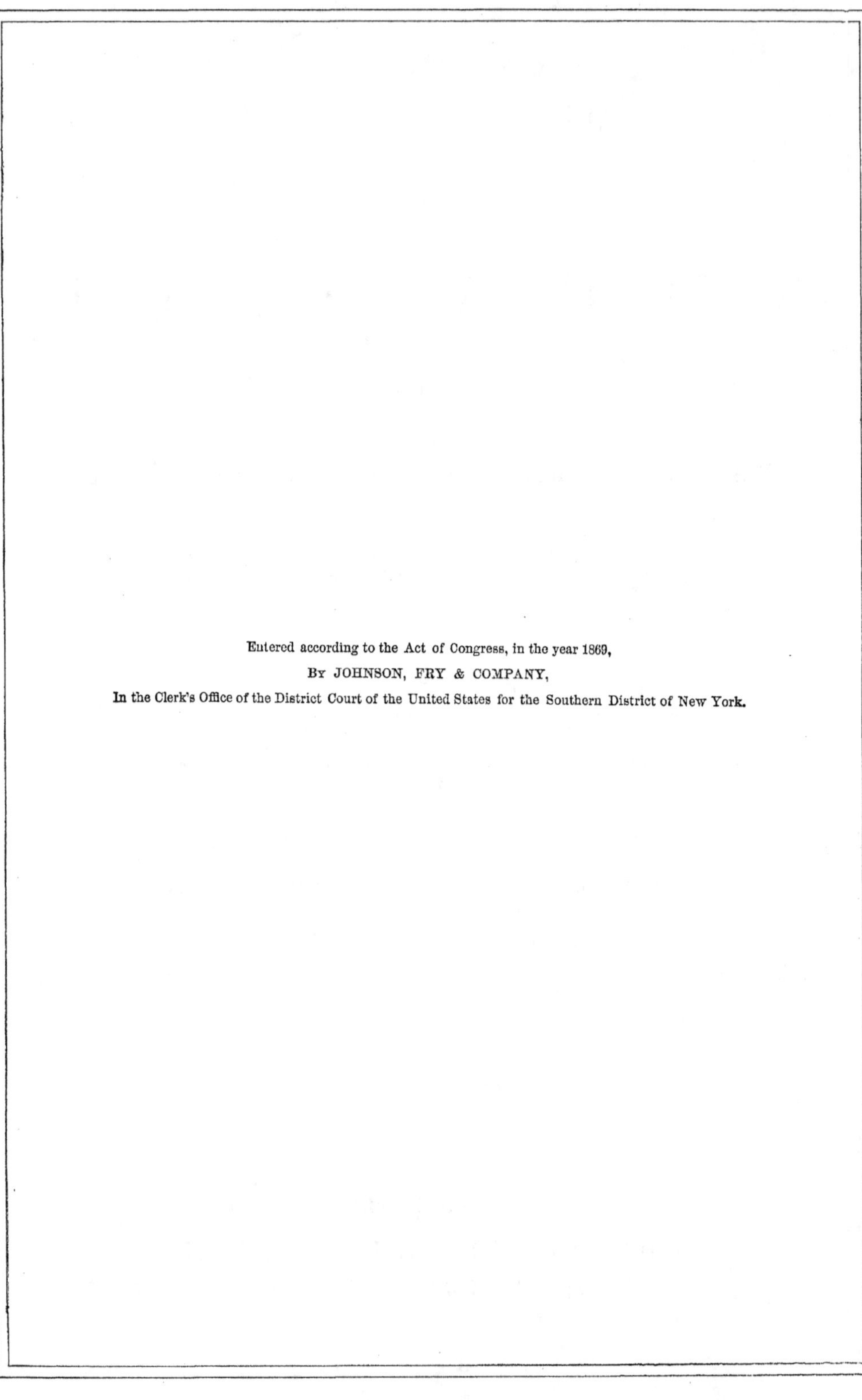

CONTENTS.

VOLUME FOURTH.

LIST OF ENGRAVINGS.

VOLUME FOURTH.

HISTORY OF THE WORLD.

AMERICA.

GENERAL VIEW.

THE continent of America extends from the 54th degree of south to the 71st of north latitude, its extreme length, from the Straits of Magellan to those of Behring, being 10,500 miles. The islands of Terra del Fuego reach one degree beyond its southern extremity into the Antarctic Ocean; and Greenland, which is connected by geographers with America, has been traced to the 78th degree of north latitude, and probably is prolonged much farther into the polar circle. The discoveries of Captains Parry, Ross, and Franklin, have given us much more exact ideas than we formerly possessed of the northern regions of America. The coast of the mainland has been traced almost completely from Behring's Straits to Fox's Channel on Hudson's Bay, and is found to run in a direction east and west, in an uneven line near the parallel of 70°. The bounds of continental America may therefore be considered as nearly determined on every side. The additional lights furnished by Captain Parry's, Dr. Kane's and other recent voyages render it extremely probable that a great archipelago of islands occupies all the space between the northern coast of the continent and the 80th parallel; and there is even some reason for believing that the country known by the name of Greenland is traversed from east to west by arms of the sea, like the regions on the west side of Baffin's Bay.

The new continent, when compared with the old, enjoys three important advantages. First, it is free from such vast deserts as cover a large part of the surface of Asia and Africa, and which not only withdraw a great proportion of the soil from the use of man, but are obstacles to communication between the settled districts, and generate that excessive heat which is often injurious to health, and always destructive to industry. Secondly, no part of its soil is so far from the ocean as the central regions of Asia and Africa. Thirdly, the interior of America is penetrated by majestic rivers, the Mississippi, Amazon, and Plata, greatly surpassing those of the old continent, in magnitude, and still more in the facilities they present for enabling the remotest inland districts to communicate with the sea.

In the physical arrangement of the parts of South and North America there is a remarkable resemblance. Both are very broad in the north, and gradually contract as they proceed southward, till they end, the one in a narrow isthmus, and the other in a narrow promontory. Each has a lofty chain of mountains near its western coast, abounding in volcanoes, with a lower ridge on the opposite side, destitute of any trace of internal fire; and each has one great central plain declining to the south and the north, and watered by two gigantic streams, the Mississippi, corresponding to the Plata, and the St. Lawrence to the Amazon. In their climate, vegetable productions, and animal tribes, the two great regions are very dissimilar.

The extent of the American continent and the islands connected with it is as follows:

North America, 7,400,000 square miles; South America, 6,500,000; Islands, 150,000; Greenland, and the islands connected with it lying north of Hudson's Straits, may be estimated at 950,000; total, 15,000,000 square miles. The American continent, therefore, with its dependent islands is fully four times as large as Europe, considerably larger than Africa, and about one fourth less than Asia, if we include with the latter Australasia and Polynesia. It constitutes about three-tenths of the dry land on the surface of the globe. A considerable portion is condemned to perpetual sterility by the rigor of the climate. If we draw a line from the head of Cook's Inlet, in latitude 61°, on the west side, to the straits of Bellisle on the east, so as to pass through Fort Churchill, on Hudson's Bay, we shall cut off a space rather exceedding one million and a half square miles, which may be considered as incapable of cultivation. At the south extremity of America, a small tract, extending 200 miles north of the straits of Magellan, though far within the limits of the temperate zone, is nearly in the same condition. These and the summits of the Andes are the only parts of the American continent which are rendered incapable of cultivation by the severity of the climate.

The vast chain of the Andes is distinguished by several peculiar features from all other mountains in the world. It has its principal direction nearly north and south, while all the great ridges of the old continent run from east to west; it is unparalleled in its prodigious length, in the richness of its mineral treasures, and in the number and magnitude of its volcanoes. The Andes, if we connect with them the Mexican Cordillera and the Rocky Mountains, extend from the Straits of Magellan in a line which may be considered as unbroken, to Point Brownlow on the shores of the Arctic Ocean, in the latitude of 70°, over a space equal to 10,000 miles in length, or two-fifths of the circumference of the globe. Their height, which attains its maximum within the tropics, declines towards both poles, but in such a mannner that, with a few exceptions, its higher summits ascend to the line of perpetual snow from one extremity to the other. It may thus be said to carry the temperature of the pole over the whole length of the American continent. The chain of the Andes is common to the two parts of America, and is in fact the link which connects them and makes them one continent.

South America is a peninsula of a triangular form. Its greatest length from north to south is 4550 miles; its greatest breadth 3200, and it covers an area, as already mentioned, of 6,500,000 square miles, about three-fourth of which lie between the tropics, and the other fourth in the temperate zone. From the configuration of its surface, this peninsula may be divided into five distinct physical regions, 1. The low country skirting the shores of the Pacific Ocean, from 50 to 150 miles in breadth, and 4000 in length. The two extremities of this territory are fertile, the middle a sandy desert. 2. The basin of the Orinoco, a country consisting of extensive plains or *steppes*, called Llanos, either destitute of wood or merely dotted with trees, but covered with a very high herbage during a part of the year. During the dry season the heat is intense here, and the parched soil opens into long fissures, in which lizards and serpents lie in a state of torpor. 3. The basin of the Amazon, a vast plain, embracing a surface of more than two millions of square miles, possessing a rich soil and a humid climate. It is covered almost everywhere with dense forests, which harbor innumerable tribes of wild animals, and are thinly inhabited by savages, who live by hunting and fishing. 4. The great southern plain, watered by the Plata and the numerous streams descending from the eastern summits of the Cordilleras. Open *steppes*, which are called Pampas, occupy the greater proportion of this region, which is dry, and in some parts barren, but in general is covered with a strong growth of weeds and tall grass, which feeds prodigious herds of horses and cattle, and affords shelter to a few wild animals. 5. The country of Brazil, eastward of the Parana and Araguay, presenting alternate ridges and valleys, thickly covered with wood on the side next the Atlantic, and opening into steppes or pastures in the interior.

The Andes skirt the shores of the Pacific Ocean, like a vast rampart opposed to its encroachments, along the whole line of the western coast, from 12° of north to 53° of south latitude. They derive their name, it is said, from *anti*, a Peruvian word signifying copper. Except at some points where they have been examined by scientific men, their structure is yet but imperfectly known; and hence they are often incorrectly exhibited on our maps. Though often described as a single chain, they generally consist of a succession of ridges, divided by high and narrow valleys; but these ridges, instead of running in parallel lines, generally ramify from central points in all directions, and thus present the appearance of a confused assemblage of small chains. Between the latitude of 33° and 6° south, they spread out their base to an extent of 300 miles, and even much farther, if we take in the smaller subordinate chains. In the intervals between the ridges are situated many lakes, of which the most considerable are Ondalgola, Pataipo, Hages, and the great lake of Titicaca, 200 miles in length. This lake, and the lake Parimé, in Guiana, are the only sheets of fresh water in South America which vie in magnitude with those singular reservoirs placed on the course of the St. Lawrence. From the latitude of 6° south to 2° north, the Andes contract their breadth, and form an elevated plateau. One part of this constitutes the Paramo or desert of Assuay, a plain at the height of 13,000 feet above the sea, and embracing a surface of 50 square miles, where snow-storms are frequent, and only a few alpine plants grow. Further north lies another range of table-land, from 9,000 to 9,440 feet in height, near the north extremity of which the town of Quito is situated. On this elevated plain are placed two lines of lofty summits, standing detached from each other, and crowned with diadems of perpetual snow.

The mean height of the Andes in Peru, or that of the continuous ridge, independent of projecting cones, is estimated by Humboldt at 11,000 or 12,000 feet: in Chili, the most elevated summits, at the latitude 33°, only reach the height of 15,000 feet, and the mean height of the chain is in some places as low as 8000; in Patagonia its height is unknown. Till lately, the loftiest summits were supposed to be in Quito, where Chimborazo attains the prodigious altitude of 21,440 feet, and the volcanic cones of Antisana and Cotopaxi have the elevations of 19,150 and 18,890 feet respectively; but Pentland is of opinion that the mountains of Quito are greatly surpassed in altitude by some of those of Upper Peru. The Andes here form two chains, which are separated by a large district of table-land, the northern extremity of which is occupied by the lake Titicaca. The eastern chain presents, between the 14th and 17th parallels, a range of snow-covered peaks, of which several have an elevation exceeding 20,000 feet. Among these, towards the north, in the latitude of 15° 30′, is Sorate, 25,250, and farther south Illimani, 24,450 feet in height. The former, therefore, is nearly 4000 feet higher than Chimborazo, but still 3000 feet lower than the loftiest summits of the Himalaya. The western chain is lower than the eastern, but one of its summits has an altitude of 18,800 feet. Pentland concludes from astronomical observations, that the eastern chain is 360 miles from the coast. The mineral wealth of the district has attracted a large population to this table-land, which, with the single exception of Thibet, is probably the highest inhabited soil on the face of the globe

Here are flocks, gardens, cultivated fields, and populous cities, suspended above the region of the clouds. La Paz, with 20,000 inhabitants, and Potosi, which had once 150,000, are situated in this plain, at the height of 12,190 and 13,500 feet above the level of the sea; and there are cottages near the mines at 15,700 feet, an elevation exceeding that of Mont Blanc. This table-land, from Cuzco to Potosi, was the primitive seat of the empire of the Incas, and the center of Peruvian civilization.

Three branches or transverse chains proceed from the Andes, nearly at right angles to the direction of the principal chain, and pass eastward across the continent, about the parallels of 18° of south, and 4° and 9° of north latitude. The most northern of these is "the Cordillera of the coast," which parts from the main trunk near the south extremity of the lake Maracaybo, reaches the sea at Porto Cabello, and then passes eastward through Caraccas to the Gulf of Paria. Its length is about 700 miles, and its medium height from 4000 to 5000 feet. The second transverse chain is connected with the Andes at the parallels of 3° and 4° north, and passing eastward, terminates in French Guiana, at no great distance from the mouth of the Amazon. Its mean height is estimated at 4000 feet above the level of the sea; but at about 70° and 75° west longitude, it sinks to less than 1000 feet, and at other points rises to 10,000. This chain divides the waters of the Orinoco and the rivers of Guiana from the basin of the Amazon, and is covered with magnificent forests. Its breadth is supposed to be from 200 to 400 miles, and it incloses amidst its ridges the great lake Parimé, in longitude 60°, and several of smaller size. On a table-land forming part of it, about the 67th degree of longitude, the Cassiquiari forms an intermediate channel which connects the rivers Orinoco and Amazon, so that, during the annual floods, a part of the waters of the former flow into the latter. The length of this chain is about 1500 miles. The third transverse chain, which bears various names, and is little known, crosses the continent between the parallels of 12° and 18°, connecting the Andes with the mountains of Brazil, and dividing the waters of the Amazon from those of the Plata. Its average height probably does not exceed 2000 or 3000 feet above the level of the sea.

The mountains of Brazil, which are of moderate height, and occupy a great breadth of country, form an irregular plateau, bristled with sharp ridges running in a direction approximately parallel to the eastern coast. They extend from 5° to 25° of south latitude, and their extreme breadth may be about 1000 miles. Itacolumi, about 250 miles northwest of Rio Janeiro, which is celebrated for its auriferous sands and gravel, and gives birth to three great rivers, the Parana, the St. Francisco, and the Tocantin, is considered the most elevated summit, and the stem of the whole group. It rises to the height of 5,700 feet above the level of the sea; and the ordinary elevation of the numerous ridges which branch off from it is supposed to be 3000 or 4000 feet.

The geology of the South American mountains, particularly the Andes, is distinguished, like their physical form and arrangement, by some remarkable peculiarities. The chain of the Andes may be considered as an immense dike, from two to three miles in height, and from one to three hundred in breadth. The first and most peculiar feature of this chain is, that it contains within its limits thirty active volcanoes, or nearly one-fifth of all that are known in the world. They are irregularly distributed in linear groups from Patagonia to New Granada. The most southerly or Chilian group extends from 43½° to 30° south latitude. After an interval of 8° without volcanoes, we have a second group, that of Bolivia, in Peru, extending from the 21st to the 15th degree of south latitude. About 14° beyond this, the third group, that of Quito appears, extending about 2° on each side of the equator. A fourth line or group, 500 miles in length, occurs in the isthmus, chiefly in the

State of Guatemala; and a fifth, consisting of five vents, crosses Mexico in an east and west direction. Some of these throw out smoke merely, some mud and water, and only a few produce eruptions of lava. They are of various elevations, up to 18,800 feet. Over nearly the whole chain earthquakes are extremely frequent, and at times fearfully destructive. The fundamental rock of the Andes is granite, or a rock of kindred nature, which, from being almost peculiar to the chain, has been termed Andesite. The Andes are rich in metals, abounding in mines of copper, silver, gold, etc. Crystalline schists occupy the greater part of Brazil and of Venezuela, and Guiana.. A deposit of fine mud, from 20 to 100 feet thick, is found on the banks of the Parana, and covers the plains called Pampas, from Buenos Ayres, nearly as far south as the river Colorado. It contains fossil remains of large mammalia in vast numbers, all of extinct species, and many of them even of extinct genera, including the Megatherium, Megalonix, Mastodon, etc.

The transverse chain of the coast of Caraccas consists partly of primitive and partly of secondary formations. The Cordillera of Parimé, so far as it has been examined, is entirely composed of primitive rocks, viz., granite, gneiss, mica slate, and hornblende; the Cordillera of Chiquito, which divides the Plata from the Amazon, is only known at its eastern extremity, where it joins the mountains of Brazil. These last consist of a great number of ridges, running in general south and north. Granite abounds in those nearest the Atlantic, but the prevailing rock everywhere else, as far westward as the mountains of Cujaba, in longitude 55°, is a quartzy mica slate, intermixed however with granite, gneiss, and quartz rock, and having portions of secondary sandstone resting on its sides or in its low valleys. This quartzy mica slate, in Brazil, is the matrix of the gold and diamonds; and the former is generally accompanied with platinum and iron.

In regard to the climate of America, it is to be noted that the trade winds help greatly to modify the state of the atmosphere over the land, both as to heat and humidity. Even in the parched steppes of Caraccas, the hottest known region in America, the temperature of the air during the day is only 98° in the shade, which rises to 112° in the sandy deserts which surround the Red Sea. At Calabozzo, farther east in the Llanos, the common temperature of the day is only from 88° to 90°; and at sunrise the thermometer sinks to 80°. The basin of the Amazon is shaded with lofty woods; and a cool breeze from the east ascends the channel of the stream, following all its windings, almost to the foot of the Andes. Hence this region, though under the equator, and visited with almost constant rains, is neither excessively hot nor unhealthful. Brazil, and the vast country extending westward from it between the Plata and the Amazon, is an uneven table-land, blest with an equable climate. At Rio Janeiro, which stands low, and is exposed to a heat comparatively great, the mean temperature in summer is only about 74°. Farther north, and in the interior, the mean temperature of the year falls below 65° or 67°. On the declivities of the Andes, and on the high plains of Upper Peru, the heats are so moderate that the plants of Italy, France, and Germany, come to maturity. Lower Peru, though a sandy desert, enjoys a wonderful degree of coolness, owing to the fogs which intercept the solar rays. At Lima, which is 540 feet above the sea, the temperature varies from 53° to 82°, but the mean for the whole year is only 72°. In the plains of La Plata, the mean temperature of the year is very nearly the same as at the corresponding north latitudes on the east side of the Atlantic. The range of temperature is probably greater in the basin of the Plata; but as we advance southwards, the diminishing breadth of the continent makes the climate approximate to that of an island, and the extremes of course approach each other In the Straits of Magellan the temperature of the warmest month does not exceed 43°

or 46°; and snow falls almost daily in the middle of summer.

Nine-tenths of North America lying under the temperate zone, the climate presents striking contrasts with that of the best known parts of the old world. The long narrow region denominated Central America, which connects the two great divisions of the continent, stretching from Panama to Tehuantepec, has in general a very humid atmosphere; but, for a tropical country, it is only moderately hot, as every part of it is within a small distance of the sea. At Vera Paz the rains fall during nine months of the year. Mexico is hot, moist, and unhealthy on the low coasts; but two-thirds of its area, comprising all the populous districts, consist of table-land, from 5000 to 9000 feet in height. In consequence of this singular configuration of its surface, Mexico, though chiefly within the torrid zone, enjoys a temperate and equable climate.

In the extensive region lying between the parallels of 30° and 50°, which comprehends three-fourths of the useful soil of North America, we have three well-marked varieties of climate, that of the east coast, the west coast, and the basin of the Mississippi. On the east coast, from Georgia to Lower Canada, the mean temperature of the year is lower than in Europe by 9° at the latitude of 40°, and by 12½° at the latitude of 50°, according to Humboldt's calculation. The summer is much hotter and the winter much colder. At Quebec the temperature of the warmest month exceeds that of the coldest by no less than 60½° of Fahr.; while at Paris, which is nearly under the same latitude, the difference is only 31°. The west coast of America, in the middle latitudes, has nearly as mild and equable a climate as the west coast of Europe. The climate of the great central valley, or basin of the Mississippi has a considerable affinity to that of the east coast. The climate of the interior exhibits in still greater excess those extremes of temperature which distinguish the eastern coast of this continent from the western, and from the shores of Europe. The northern most spot in America where grain is raised is on Red River, in latitude 50°. Wheat, and also maize, which requires a high summer heat, are cultivated here. Barley would certainly grow as far north as latitude 58¾°, where the heat of the four summer months is 4° higher than at Edinburgh. It is a peculiarity in the climate of America, that beyond the parallel of 50° or 52°, it seems to become suddenly severe at both extremities. At the one, summer disappears from the circle of the seasons; at the other, winter is armed with double terrors.

The mountains of North America will not detain us long. The branch of the Andes which divides the seas at the isthmus of Panama is very low the highest point of the railroad is only 300 feet above the sea. At the isthmus of Tehuantepec, a route was traced whose most elevated point was 702 feet. The most considerable elevations are on the south-west side of the isthmus; and twenty-one volcanoes are scattered over this limited space. From Puebla to Durango the Mexican mountains no longer present the appearance of a chain, but spread out to a table-land or elevated plain, from 5000 to 9000 feet in height, and from 100 to 300 miles in breadth. Across this plain, exactly at the 19th parallel, five volcanoes are distributed in a line running east and west. Two of these on the east side of the continent, with a group of four or five other cones lying between Jalapa and Cordoba, have an elevation exceeding 17,000 feet, and are the only mountains in New Spain that rise to the region of perpetual snow, which commences here at 15,000 feet above the level of the sea. Jorullo, the lowest of the five volcanoes, rose suddenly in the middle of a plain, in September, 1759, after fearful concussions of the ground, continued for fifty or sixty days. Near the tropic the Mexican Cordillera divides into three parts. One runs parallel to the eastern coast and terminates in New Leon. Another proceeds in a north-western direction, and sinks gradually as it approaches the Californian Gulf in Sonora. The third or central Cordillera traverses Durango and New Mexico, divides the sources of the Rio Gila from the Rio Bravo del Norte, and forms the eastern ridge or main trunk of the Rocky Mountains. From the southern point of California, a lower chain skirts the coast as far as the volcano of Mount St. Elias, in latitude 60°; and between this chain and the eastern several intermediate ones occur, the whole forming apparently an elevated plateau from 200 to 800 miles in breadth. Many of the summits of the Rocky Mountains are within the regions of perpetual snow; and several of their peaks have been found to measure 11,000, 11,320, 13,538, and 16,000 feet. In one of the valleys included in the plateau of the Rocky Mountains, measuring about 500 miles each way, is situated the great salt lake in Utah, in west longitude 112° and north latitude 41°. The lake, whose waters are intensely saline, is nearly 300 miles in circumference, and its shores, for a breadth of several miles, are covered with an incrustation of very pure salt.

If we run a line westward across the continent of North America at the latitude of Delaware Bay (38°), the geological formations present themselves in the following order:—1. Tertiary and cretaceous strata on the shores of the Atlantic; 2. Gneiss underlying these strata, and presenting itself on the eastern slope of the Alleghany or Appalachian mountains, but covered at parts by New Red Sandstone; 3. Palæozoic rocks, consisting of Silurian, Devonian, and carboniferous strata, curiously bent into parallel foldings. Upon these palæozoic rocks rest three great coal-fields—the Appalachian, that of Illinois, and that of Michigan, covering a large portion of the space between the Alleghanies and the Mississippi, and embracing collectively an area equal to the surface of Great Britain. From the Mississippi westward the country has not been thoroughly explored, but the Silurian, carboniferous, and secondary rocks, are said to extend to the base of the Rocky Mountains. Here the crystalline schists again present themselves, and not only form the crests of the two chains, but extend to the shores of the Pacific. Both in Oregon and California they have been greatly disturbed by eruptive rocks of many varieties. It is generally among the crystalline and palæozoic strata, where they have been penetrated by intrusive masses of igneous rock, that the precious metals have been found.

The superiority of America over the old world is conspicuous, in the number and magnitude of its navigable rivers. The Amazon alone discharges a greater quantity of water than the eight principal rivers of Asia, the Euphrates, Indus, Ganges, Oby, Lena, Amour, and the Yellow River and Kang-tse of China. The Mississippi, with its branches, affords a greater amount of inland navigation than all the streams, great and small, which irrigate Europe; and the Plata, in this respect, may probably claim a superiority over the collective water of Africa. But the American rivers not only surpass those of the old world in length and volume of fluid, but they are so placed as to penetrate everywhere to the heart of the continent. By the Amazon, a person living at the eastern foot of the Andes, 2000 miles of direct distance from the Atlantic, may convey himself or his property to the shores of that sea in forty-five days, almost without effort, by confiding his bark to the gliding current. If he wishes to return, he has but to spread his sails to the eastern breeze, which blows perennially against the stream. The navigation is not interrupted by a single cataract or rapid, from the Atlantic to Jaen, in west longitude 78°, where the surface of the stream is only 1240 feet above the level of its estuary at Para. The remotest and least accessible part of North America is the great interior plain extending from the Rocky Mountains to the Alleghanies and the lakes, between the parallels of 40° and 50°; but the Mississippi, Missouri, and St. Lawrence, with their branches, are so wonderfully ramified over this region, that when it is filled with civilized inhabitants, those who dwell in its inmost recesses, at the falls of the Missouri, for instance, 1700 miles from the Atlantic, will have a more easy communication with the ocean than the population of the interior of Spain and Hungary. There is little risk in predicting, that at no distant period, the Mississippi, the Amazon, and the Plata, will be the scenes of an active inland commerce, far surpassing in magnitude anything at present known on the surface of the globe. The Mississippi is navigable for boats from the sea to the falls of its principal branch, the Missouri, 1700 miles from the Mexican Gulf in a direct line, or 3900 by the stream; and the whole amount of boat navigation afforded by the system of rivers, of which the Mississippi is the main trunk, has been estimated as equal to 40,000 miles in length, spread over a surface of 1,350,000 square miles.

North America, like the Southern peninsula, naturally divides itself into five physical regions: 1. The table-land of Mexico, with the strip of low country on its eastern and western shores; 2. The plateau lying between the Rocky Mountains and the Pacific Ocean, a country with a mild and humid atmosphere as far north as the 55th parallel, but inhospitable and barren beyond this boundary; 3. The great central valley of the Mississippi, rich and well wooded on the east side, bare but not unfertile in the middle, dry, sandy, and almost a desert on the west; 4. The eastern declivities of the Alleghany Mountains, a region of natural forests, and of mixed but rather poor soil; 5. The great northern plain beyond the 50th parallel, four-fifths of which is a bleak and bare waste, overspread with innumerable lakes, and resembling Siberia both in the physical character of its surface and the rigor of its climate.

The indigenous population of America is estimated by Humboldt at 8,600,000, and presents man under many aspects, and society in various stages, from the regular but limited civilization of Mexico and Peru, to savage life in its most brutal state of abasement. At one extremity of the country we find the pigmy Esquimaux of four feet and a half in height, and at the other the Patagonian giants of seven feet. In complexion the variety is great, and may be said to embrace almost every hue known elsewhere on the face of the earth, except the pitchy black of the negro. About one-half of all the known languages is said to belong to America; and if we consider every little wandering horde a distinct community, we have a greater number of nations here than in all the rest of the world.

Physiologists are not at one in their accounts of the characteristics of the aborigines of the new world, nor are they agreed as to whether they should be considered one race or several. Blumenbach places them all under one class, except the Esquimaux. St. Vincent divides them into four races, or into five if we include the Esquimaux. Desmoulins reduces the species to two, the *Colombian* and the *American*; the former including all the North American tribes, with the Caribs, the Mexicans, and Peruvians, and other inhabitants of the Cordillera; and the latter the Brazilian Indians and Patagonians. None of these systems, when compared with facts, is very satisfactory. Dr. Prichard thinks that the mutual resemblance among the American nations has been exaggerated by some writers; yet it is certain that there is more of a common family character in their organization than in that of the indigenous population of Asia or Africa. "The Indians of New Spain," says Humboldt, "bear a general resemblance to those who inhabit Canada, Florida, Peru, and Brazil. We have the same swarthy and copper color, straight and smooth hair, small beard, squat body, long eye, with the corner directed upwards towards the temples, prominent cheek-bones, thick lips, and expression of gentleness in the mouth, strongly contrasted with a gloomy and severe look. Over a million and a half of square leagues, from Cape Horn to the river St. Lawrence and Behring's Straits, we are struck at the first glance with the general resemblance in the features of the inhabitants. We think we perceive them all to be descended from the same stock, notwithstanding the prodigious diversity of their languages."

The American aborigenes are distinguished by the form of the skull, which strongly resembles the Mongol type. The forehead recedes more than in any other variety of the human species; the cheek-bones are prominent, but not so angular as in the Mongol head; the occiput is rather flat, the cavity for lodging the cerebellum small, the orbits large and deep. The nose is generally aquiline, but in some tribes flat; and the nasal cavities are large. Compared with the head of the Negro, that of the American is much broader, and the teeth are less prominent: when placed by the side of the Caucasian head, it is seen to be smaller in size, less rounded and symmetrical, and less developed in the part before the ear. The skull is generally thin and light.

The varieties of color among the aborigines do not bear any visible relation to the temperature of the climate. A brownish yellow, or copper color, as it has been called, pervades nearly all the numerous tribes from the Arctic Ocean to Cape Horn, but still with many different degrees of intensity. The eastern nations of Chili have but a slight tinge of the brown color, and on the northwest coast, from latitude 43° to 60°, there are tribes who, though embrowned with soot and mud, were found, when their skins were washed, to have the mingled white and red which is the characteristic of the Caucasian race. In the hot country watered by the Orinoco, Humboldt found tribes of a dark, and others of a light hue, living almost in juxtaposition. It is remarkable, too, that the nations whose color approaches nearest to black are found in the temperate zone, namely, the Charruas of the Banda Oriental, in latitude 33° south, and the Cochimies, Pericus, and Guaycurus, spread over the peninsula of California. These people have skins of a very deep hue, but are not absolutely black; and they have neither the woolly hair of the negroes, nor their social and good-humored disposition. The Caribs and some Brazilian tribes have the yellowish hue of the Chinese, and the same cast of features. Among the nations dwelling on the west side of the Alleghanics, and near the northern lakes, there is also a considerable variety of complexion; but the brown or copper shade is found more or less in them all. In stature the variety is great. The North American tribes are generally above the middle size, and of a slender shape. The Brazilian nations and the Peruvians are short and squat. The Caribs of the Orinoco, and the tribes which rove over the Pampas west of the Plata, are tall and strong; and the Patagonians, a Chilian tribe, exceed in strength and stature all the other races in the known world.

Dr. Morton is of opinion that the most natural division of the aborigines is into two families, the *Toltecan* and the *American;* the former of which bears evidence of centuries of half-civilization, while the latter embraces all the barbarous nations of the new world, with the exception of the Polar tribes, which are evidently of Mongolian origin. In each of these, however, there are several subordinate groups, which may be distinguished as the *Appalachian*, the *Brazilian*, the *Patagonian*, and the *Fuegian*. The Appalachian branch includes all the nations of North America, except the Mexicans, together with the tribes of South America north of the River Amazon and east of the Andes. These nations are warlike, cruel, and unforgiving; and they turn with aversion from the restraints and culture of civilized life. The Brazilian branch is spread over a great part of South America, east of the Andes, including the whole of Brazil and Paraguay, between the River Amazon and 35° south latitude. In physical and other characteristics they differ but little from the Appalachian branch. The Patagonian branch includes the nations to the south of the Plata, as far as the Straits of Magellan; including also the mountain tribes of Chili. They are chiefly distinguished by their tall stature, handsome forms, and indomitable courage. The Fuegians, who call themselves *Yacannacunnee*, rove over the sterile wastes of Terra del Fuego, which is computed to be half the size of Ireland, and yet their whole number has been computed at only 2000. The physical aspect of the Fuegians is altogether repulsive. They are of low stature, with large heads, broad faces, and small eyes, and their mental operations are to the last degree slow and stupid.

The intellectual faculties of the American family appear to be decidedly inferior, when compared with those of the Caucasian or Mongolian race. They are not only averse to the restraints of education, but are for the most part incapable of a continued process of reasoning on abstract subjects. Their minds seize with avidity on simple truths, but reject whatever requires investigation and analysis. As to their social condition, they are probably in most respects the same as they were at the earliest period of their national existence. They have made few or no improvements in constructing their houses or their boats; their inventive and imitative faculties appear to be of very humble capacity; and they find great difficulty in comprehending the relations of numbers.

The Toltecan family embraced the civilized nations of Mexico, Peru, and Bogota extending from the Rio Gila in 33° north latitude along the western shore of the continent to the frontiers of Chili; and on the eastern coast, along the Gulf of Mexico, in North America. In South America, on the contrary, this family chiefly occupied a narrow strip of land between the Andes and the Pacific Ocean, bounded on the south by the great desert of Atacama. Farther north, however, in New Granada, were the Bogotese, a people whose civilization, like their geographical position, was intermediate between that of the Peruvians and the Mexicans. The arrival of the Spaniards reduced them to vassalage; and three centuries of slavery and oppression have left few traces of Mexican and Peruvian civilization, except what may be gleaned from their history and antiquities. It is in the intellectual faculties that the great difference between the Toltecan and the American families consists In the arts and sciences of the former we see the evidences of an advanced civilization; their architectural remains everywhere surprise the traveler and confound the antiquary. Among these are pyramids, temples, grottoes, bas-reliefs, and arabesques; while their roads, aqueducts, and fortifications, and the traces of their mining operations, sufficiently attest their attainments in the practical arts of life.

Of the languages spoken by the aborigines, Balbi has enumerated 423 which are, or at no distant period were, in use in America. Of these 211 belong to North, 44 to Central, and 168 to South America. Vater says that the number of languages in America exceeds 500. Under this great diversity of dialects, a remarkable analogy of structure has been detected in all those which are well known, and is believed to pervade the whole. The American languages are extremely complicated and artificial, and have extraordinary powers of combination; but as our space does not admit of entering into details, we must refer the reader to works specially devoted to this subject.

Though any attempt to reduce the aboriginal population under a few general classes, either on physical or ethnographical grounds, would be idle, a brief survey of the various nations, or families of nations, will enable us to form a more distinct idea of the whole.

All the northern coast of the new continent is tenanted by the Esquimaux, a dwarfish race, rarely exceeding five feet in height, and of the same stock with the Greenlanders, the Samoiedes, and the Laplanders. Near Mackenzie's River their territories commence at the 68th parallel, and extend to the Arctic Ocean. They live entirely by fishing, the whale and the seal being their most common food; they inhabit skin tents during their short summer, and in winter caves or houses built with snow in the shape of domes, within which a single rude lamp is kept perpetually burning. They are thought to be the only American race whose Asiatic origin is indisputable.

The Indians of the east coast belong almost entirely to three stems; and, before the arrival of the English colonists, occupied both sides of the Alleghany Mountains, from the Gulf of Mexico to Canada and New Brunswick. 1. The Delawares or Algonquins, comprehending the Ottogamies, Shawnese, Narragansetts, Chippeways, and other nations, to the number of thirty or forty, were spread over the space between the Mississippi and the Atlantic, as far north as Hudson's Bay; and all spoke dialects of one language. They preserved a tradition, to which some credit has been given, that they had migrated from the west many centuries before the white man crossed the Atlantic. 2. The Iroquois, often called the "Five Nations," and the "Six Nations," but comprehending fifteen tribes or more, among whom were the Mohawks, Oneidas, Hurons, and Senecas, all spoke dialects of one language. They lived on the south side of the great lakes, and finally obtained a complete ascendancy over the Algonquin race. 3. The Florida Indians included the Creeks, Seminoles, Choctaws, Chickasaws, Natchez, and Mobiles. Of these, the Cherokees and Creeks, in Alabama and Georgia, have made some advances in agriculture and the useful arts.

Tribes belonging to these three families occupied nearly all the region east of the Mississippi, from the Gulf of Mexico to Hudson's Bay, comprising more than a million of square miles. The Katawbas are said to have included twenty tribes, and nearly as many dialects. The Powhattans were a confederacy of thirty-three tribes, comprehending 10,000 persons. These nations have furnished brilliant models of the most shining qualities of savage life—a high sense of honor, according to their perceptions of duty, mutual fidelity among individuals, a fortitude that mocks at the most cruel torments, and a devotion to their tribe which makes self-immolation in its defence easy. On the other hand, they treat their wives cruelly, and their children with indifference. The apathy under the good and ill of life which the Stoic affected, is the grand element of the Indian's character. Gloomy, stern, and severe, he is a stranger to mirth and laughter. All outward expression of pleasure or pain he regards as a weakness; and the only feeling to which he ever yields, is the boisterous joy which he manifests in the moment of victory, or under the excitement of intoxication. He is capable of great exertions in war or the chase, but has an unconquerable aversion to regular labor. He is extremely improvident; eats enormously while he has abundance of food, without thinking of the famine which may follow; and, when liquors are supplied to him, wallows in the most beastly intoxication day after day. Most of the Indians believe in the existence of a supreme being, whom they call the Great Spirit; and of a subordinate one, whose nature is evil and hostile to man. To the latter their worship is principally addressed, the Good Spirit, in their opinion, needing no prayers to induce him to aid and protect his creatures. Human sacrifices are not unknown amongst them, but are rare. In most of the tribes there are jugglers or soothsayers, who pretend to discover lost property, and foretell the issue of hunting or warlike expeditions. By some tribes deities are supposed to reside in the sun and moon. They generally believe in a future state, in which the souls of brave warriors and chaste wives enjoy a tranquil and happy existence with their ancestors and friends, spending their time in those exercises in which they delighted when on the earth. Suicide is common among the women, in consequence of the cruel treatment they are exposed to; but the practice is viewed as immoral. Polygamy is allowed; and a number of wives is considered as adding to a man's consequence. Various modes of courting and marrying prevail; but among all the Indians, the presenting of gifts to the girl's father is an essential feature of the transaction, and shows that the wife is considered as procured by purchase. Deformed children, and lame or decrepit old persons, are sometimes destroyed; but the practice is uncommon. The Indian funerals are conducted with much decorum, and it is usual to mark the graves with a post, on which figures are carved expressive of the nature of the pursuits and achievements of the deceased.

Some nations of Indians wear little or no clothing; but the general dress of the men in the temperate and cold parts of the country, previous to the arrival of the Europeans, consisted of a cloak of buffalo skin hanging from the shoulders, a piece of skin used as an apron, and a pair of mocassins or loose boots, made of undressed skin also. The women wore a long robe of the same material, which was fastened round the waist; but among the tribes living near the whites, coarse woolens are now frequently substituted for the hides of wild animals, except for the mocassins. The habitations of the Indians are huts or cabins, generally of a circular form and small size, but sometimes of 30 or 40 feet in diameter, formed by stakes fixed in the ground, and covered with the bark of trees. Sometimes the spaces between the stakes are filled up with twigs, grass, and mud, and the roof is covered nearly in the same way. A hole in the top serves for the escape of the smoke, and the skins of wild beasts form the beds and seats. The custom of painting their bodies is nearly universal. They introduce the colors by making punctures on their skin; and the extent of surface which this ornament covers is proportioned to the exploits they have performed. Besides these ornaments, the warriors also carry plumes of feathers on their heads, their arms, or ankles. Their arms are the tomahawk, the war-club, knife, the bow and arrow; and, since they had intercourse with whites, many of them have muskets. Each tribe or community is governed by a chief and council, who are elective; but in matters of importance the whole warriors are consulted; and questions are not decided by the votes of a majority, but the resolution adopted must have the consent of every individual warrior. War is declared by sending a slave with a hatchet, the handle of which is painted red, to the nation they intend to break with. They generally take the field in small numbers. Each warrior, besides his weapons, carries a mat, and supports himself till he is near the enemy, by killing game. If they succeed in their attack, the scene of horror which follows baffles description. The savage fury of the conquerors, the desperation of the conquered, the horrid yells of both, and their grim figures besmeared with paint and blood, form an assemblage of objects worthy of pandemonium. Prisoners are usually murdered with tortures; the women are given to the warriors; and the boys and girls are made slaves.

Nearly all the Indian tribes raise maize, beans, and pumpkins, by the labor of their women, but only to a small extent, and as a resource against famine, their chief reliance being upon the chase. The buffaloes which wander over the prairies of the west, in herds of tens of thousands, are their great support; but deer, bears, and in time of need otters, beavers, foxes, squirrels, and even the most disgusting reptiles, are devoured. And last and worst, there is the horrid banquet on the flesh of their enemies, which is said to be still in use among some tribes.

The civilization attained by the aborigines, forms an interesting subject of inquiry. According to the Mexican annals, we learn that several nations belonging to one race migrated in succession from the north-west, and settled in *Anahuac* or Mexico. The Toltecs, the first of these, left their original seat, far to the west, in 544 of our era, and after a long journey invaded Mexico, then occupied by wandering hordes, in 641. This people, who penetrated to Nicaragua, if not to South America, were nearly destroyed after the lapse of some centuries; but were followed by the Chichimeks, a half-savage tribe, about 1170, and these a few years afterwards by the Anahuatlels, or seven tribes, including the Acolhuans, Tlascalteks and the Aztecs or proper Mexicans. All these people spoke dialects of one language, and had similar arts, customs and institutions. The town of Mexico or Tenochitlan was founded in 1325, and the series of Mexican kings which commenced in 1352 was continued through eight monarchs to Montezuma. When Cortes arrived, it embraced what are now the provinces of Vera Cruz, Oaxaca, Puebla, Mexico, and part of Valladolid, a surface of 130,000 square miles; but within this were comprehended three small independent states, Tlascala, Cholullan, and Zapeaca.

The Mexican nations derived their subsistence from agriculture, which, however, was conducted in the rudest manner, with very imperfect instruments. They cultivated maize, potatoes, plantains, and various other esculent vegetables. They raised cotton and understood the art of spinning and weaving it into cloth, of a texture which excited the admiration of the Spaniards. They had no iron, but showed considerable skill in fashioning the gold, silver and copper found in a native state, into domestic utensils and ornamental articles. Their carvings in wood were tolerably well executed, but the figures were disproportioned and uncouth. The same remark applies to their hieroglyphical drawings, which were far inferior in taste and design to those of the Hindoos, Japanese and Thibetians. For paper they employed sometimes the large leaves of the aloe, sometimes cotton cloth, or the skins of deer dressed. The written language of Mexico contained a few real hieroglyphics or symbols, purely conventional, to designate such objects as water, earth, air, day, night, speech, and also for numbers; but it was essentially a system of *picture-writing*, in which objects were represented by colored figures having a resemblance more or less exact to themselves. With all its necessary imperfections, this instrument was familiarly employed to a prodigious extent in deeds and instruments for effecting the transmission and sale of property. The government kept couriers for conveying intelligence from all parts of the empire; and the capital was watched and cleaned by a sort of police establishment. This is the bright side of Mexican civilization. On the other hand, it must be kept in view, that the Mexicans had no tame animals, no made roads, no money to serve as a universal medium of exchange in commercial transactions. The government was originally a perfect feudal monarchy, in which all power was monopolized by a numerous nobility and the priesthood. The great mass of the people were serfs, attached to the soil, and transferred with it from owner to owner by descent or purchase.

The religion of the Mexicans breathed a savage spirit, which sinks them, in a moral point of view, far below the hordes of wandering Indians. Their deities, represented by mis-shapen images of serpents and other hideous animals, were the creation of the darkest passions of the human breast, of terror, hatred, cruelty, revenge. They delighted in blood, and thousands of human sacrifices were annually offered at their shrines. The places of worship, called Teocallis, were pyramids composed of terraces placed one above another, like the temple of Belus at Babylon. They were built of clay, or of alternate layers of clay and unburnt bricks, but in some cases faced with slabs of polished stone, on which figures of animals are sculptured in relief. One or two small chapels stood upon the summit, inclosing images of the deity. The largest known, which is composed of four stories or terraces, has a breadth of 480 yards at the base, and a height of 55. These structures served as temples, tombs, and observatories; and it is remarkable that their sides are always placed exactly in the direction of the meridian.

The calendar of the Mexicans bespeaks a degree of scientific skill, and an accuracy of observation. which are not easily reconciled with their semi-barbarous habits, their general ignorance in other things, and the recent date of their civilization according to their own accounts. The Mexican Indian is grave, suspicious and taciturn; quiet and placid in his external deportment, but rancorous in his spirit; submissive to his superiors, harsh and cruel to those beneath him. His intellect is limited, and chiefly developes itself in imitative labors and mechanical arts. Slow, cautious and persevering, he loves, both in his acts and thoughts, to travel in a beaten track. The Toltec and Aztec races, when they established themselves in the country, diffused their own language partially from the lake of Nicaragua to the 37th parallel. They reclaimed by degrees, many of the neighboring savage tribes to a settled mode of life, and spread a feeble degree of civilization over a mixed mass of nations, speaking, according to Clavigero, thirty-five languages, of which Humboldt tells us that twenty still exist. The Aztec language is one of the most copious and polished of the American tongues, and abounds in words of the immoderate length of twelve or fifteen syllables. It is uncertain what was the number of subjects over whom Montezuma ruled. The ruins in the valley of Tenochtitlan, on which the capital stands, show that it must have been more populous before the conquest than now; but the population at present is diffused over an incomparably wider space; and upon the whole, there are no good grounds for believing that the number of civilized Indians was much greater when Cortez landed, than in 1803, when it amounted to 2,000,000.

The ancient empire of Peru, more extensive than that of Mexico, embraced the whole sea-coast from Pastos to the river Maule, a line of 2500 miles in length. Its breadth is uncertain; but as it included both declivities of the Andes, it must have extended in some cases to 500 miles, and the entire surface of the empire probably exceeded 500,000 square miles. The creating and maintaining of such an empire is a proof that the Peruvians had made no trifling progress in the useful arts and in the science of government. To keep in subjection so many remote provinces, there must have been an efficient force, rapid means of communication, considerable revenues and an organized magistracy capable of understanding and executing the plans of their rulers. It is clear that the ruling tribe, which was able to extend its dominion, and to a considerable extent its language, over a space of 2500 miles, must have possessed a marked superiority of some kind over the hordes that surrounded it. One of the most singular facts connected with the history of America is, that by far the largest empire it contained was formed by the most unwarlike people in it. The dominion of the Incas was founded entirely on policy, superstition, and the arts. It could only be by the intelligence and skill which civilization developes, that the Peruvians conquered tribes superior to themselves in courage; and it was by policy and superstition that the Incas tamed the rudeness of savage tribes, and held distant countries in subjection.

Agriculture was conducted with greater care and success in Peru than in Mexico. The lands capable of cultivation were divided into three shares. One was consecrated to the service of religion, the erection of temples and the maintenance of priests; the second was set apart as a provision for the support of the government; and the third and largest share, which was reserved for the people, was parcelled out, not among individuals, but among the hamlets and villages, according to the number and rank of the inhabitants; and a new division was made every year to meet any change that might arise in the circumstances of the parties. Their masonry was superior to that of the Mexicans. Like the ancient Egyptians, they understood mechanics sufficiently to move stones of vast size, even of thirty feet in length, of which specimens are still existing in the walls of the fortress of Cusco. They had the art of squaring and cutting blocks for building with great accuracy; and it is now known that they had hard chisels, made of copper, with a mixture of six per cent. of tin; a proof of considerable skill in the working of metals. The palaces or lodges of the Incas, of which there are many remains, had doors with slanting sides like the Egyptian; sloping roofs, which, it is supposed, were covered with rushes or stone slabs; no windows, but niches symmetrically distributed. Ancient stone structures, which are so rare in Mexico, are pretty abundant in Peru. The architecture of the Peruvians, like every thing else connected with their social state, displays a remarkable uniformity, not only of style, but of plan. "It is impossible," says Humboldt, "to examine a single edifice of the time of the Incas, without recognizing the same type in all the others which cover the ridge of the Andes, along an extent of 450 leagues."

The ancient public roads of Peru are justly considered as striking monuments of the political genius of the government. One of these extended along the sides of the Andes from Quito to Cusco, a distance of 1500 miles. It is about forty feet broad, and paved with the earth and stones which were turned up from the soil; but in some marshy places it is formed like the old Roman roads, of a compact body of solid masonry. A tolerably level line is preserved, by filling up hollows, cutting down small eminences, and winding round the sides of large ones. At proper distances zambos or storehouses were erected, for the accommodation of the Inca and his messengers. A similar road was made along the coast in the low country. Fissures a few yards in breadth were passed by bridges formed of beams laid horizontally; and an invention, at once bold and ingenious, afforded the means of crossing deep ravines, or the channels of rivers, which happened to intersect the route. This consisted of a suspension bridge, perfectly analogous in its principle to those now in use. It was formed of half a dozen cables of twisted osiers, passed over wooden supports, and stretched from bank to bank; then bound together with smaller ropes and covered with bamboos. Humboldt passed over one of these pendulous bridges, of 120 feet span; and Mr. Miers crossed one of 225 feet span, over which loaded animals might travel. The Peruvians manufactured a rude species of pottery; they understood the art of spinning, and, in an imperfect degree, that of weaving. They procured native gold by washing the gravel of rivers, and silver and perhaps copper, by working veins downward from the outcrop. They knew how to smelt and refine the silver ore; and they possessed the secret of giving great hardness and durability to copper by mixing it with tin. On the other hand, they had no money, no knowledge of iron or glass; and they were ignorant of the mode of mortising or joining beams, and of casting arches. They had no animals fitted for draught; but the llama, a small species of camel, which they had tamed, was employed to some extent as a beast of burden.

The political organization of Peru, which was artificial in a high degree, bears a general resemblance to that of the ancient Egyptians. The mass of the people were in a state of servitude, except a small number, who were free; above these in rank were the Curacas, or chiefs of districts, who formed a sort of nobility; and above the whole the family of the Incas, the members of which by intermarrying only with themselves formed a numerous and distinct caste. For the purposes of police and civil jurisdiction, the people were divided into parties of ten families, like the tythings of King Alfred, over each of which was an officer. A second class of officers had control over five or ten tythings, a third class over fifty or a hundred. These last rendered account to the Incas, who exercised a vigilant superintendence over the whole, and employed inspectors to visit the provinces, as a check upon mal-administration. Each of these officers, down to the lowest, judged, without appeal, in all differences that arose within his division, and enforced the laws of the empire, among which were some for punishing idleness, and compelling every one to labor. It is probable that the tythings and hundreds, as in England, would lose their numerical signification in course of time, and become mere local allotments. In the hamlets and villages, a person mounted a tower every evening, and announced where and how the inhabitants were to be employed next day. The taxes were paid in the produce of the fields; and magazines for receiving them were established in every district. Such is the account given by Acosta and Garcilasso of the civil institutions of Peru, which may be correct with regard to the oldest possessions of the Incas near Cusco, where their power had been long established; but it is not probable that such a complicated system was ever fully in operation in the more distant parts of the empire.

The government of Peru was a theocracy. The Inca was at once the temporal sovereign and the supreme pontiff. He was regarded as the descendant and representative of the great deity the sun, who was supposed to inspire his counsels, and speak through his orders and decrees. Hence even slight offences were punished with death, because they were regarded as insults offered to the divinity. The race of the Incas was held sacred. Among a simple-minded and credulous people, the claims of the Incas to a celestial origin seem to have been implicitly believed. They were blindly obeyed, and treated with a respect bordering on adoration, by the nobles as well as the common people. The Peruvians worshiped the sun, the moon, the evening star, the spirit of thunder and the rainbow; and had erected temples in Cusco to all these deities. That of the sun, which was the most magnificent, had its walls covered with plates of gold. The sacrifices consisted of the objects most prized by the people, of grain and fruits, of a few animals, and of the productions of their own industry. Sabaism, as it is the most rational of all the forms of idolatry, so it is generally the most mild; and doubtless this results from the tendency which it has to fix the thoughts on the marks of beneficence and wisdom which are displayed in the works of nature. The Peruvian temples were accordingly never polluted, like those of Mexico, with the blood of human victims; and the Incas even went farther, and signalized their zeal against such horrid rites, by suppressing them in all the countries they conquered. Though their history exhibits some bloody deeds, the general character of their government was the reverse of cruel. The severe punishments prescribed by their laws were rarely inflicted, and rebellion was scarcely known in their dominions.

According to the Peruvian annals, the origin of their laws and civilization seems to have come from without. About the year 1100, of our era, or perhaps a century later, Manco Capac, with his wife and sister Mama Ocello, appeared as strangers on the banks of the lake Titicaca. They were persons of majestic appearance, and announced themselves as "children of the sun," sent by their beneficent parent to reclaim the tribes living there from the miseries of savage life. Their injunctions, addressed to a people who probably worshiped the god of day were listened to by a few, who settled around them, and founded Cusco. By degrees other tribes were induced to renounce their wandering habits. Manco Capac instructed the men in agriculture and the arts, and Mama Ocello taught the women to spin and to weave. Laws, institutions, and religious rites, were added. The form of a civilized society arose, which was gradually extended by persuasion or conquest; the Incas having always planted their arts and religion wherever they established their authority. Huana Capac, the twelfth in succession from the founder of the dynasty, occupied the throne when the first party of Spaniards visited Peru in 1527; and the empire was then still in a state of progress; for this prince had conquered Quito at no distant date and nearly doubled the extent of his dominions.

The civilization of Peru being then probably exotic, it is an interesting question, whence was it derived? Various reasons have been given by learned writers for supposing that it came from China or from persons acquainted with Chinese arts and institutions; but the subject is too extensive to be entered into here.

The Quichua language or that of Peru was spread by the care of the Incas, over all the countries which they conquered, so far at least as to be understood, if not spoken by the great variety of tribes subject to their sway. It is understood at present as far as Santiago del Estero, 1200 miles of direct distance south-east from Cusco. This single fact proves both the long duration of their power, and the efficiency of their internal administration. It is said to be the most rich, polished, and harmonious of the South American languages, abounding in vowel sounds. It lacks, however, terms for abstract and universal ideas such as *time*, *space*, *being*, *substance*, *matter*, *body*, and even such as *virtue*, *justice*, *liberty*, *gratitude*. There are five dialects of the Quichua, which are spoken in Peru proper, and in Quito, New Granada and a considerable part of La Plata, and not only by the aborigines, but by many Spaniards of the higher classes. The Peruvians had no alphabetic writing. They possessed a very rude species of hieroglyphics, of which little use was made, and the quippus or knotted cords of various colors; but whether these last were employed to record events, or not it is difficult to say.

The Peruvians, according to Mr. Stevenson, are of a copper color, with a small forehead, small black eyes, and beautiful teeth. Their hair is black, coarse, and sleek, the body well proportioned, the stature rather diminutive. Their intellectual qualities are of the lowest order. The most prominent trait in their character is an imperturbable and incurable apathy. Though half-naked, they are as contented as the Spaniard in his most splendid raiment. Neither power nor dignity moves them; and they receive with the same indifference the office of alcalde and that of executioner. They are habitually slow in their motions, extremely indolent, timid, shy, and secretive. They prepare a fermented beverage called chicha, from maize, by a process known to them before the conquest, and at their festivals drink till their senses fail them, day after day. This bestial habit, however, is common to all the American nations, and is confined to the men, for the women are in general strictly sober. The Peruvian huts consist of stones laid upon one and other without any cement or mortar, thatched over with long grass or straw, affording no defence either from the wind or the rain. One small room contains the whole family; their bed a sheep-skin or two; their furniture one or two earthern pots. The principal food of the Peruvians is maize; but they raise also potatoes, wheat, beans, camates, yucas, pumpkins, and other vegetables. Christianity, imposed upon them in dogmas, by priests who take no pains to enlighten them, has scarcely gained admission to their understandings, and has no hold on their affections. They meet death with the same stupid indifference as the ordinary accidents of life, and rather decline than seek the assistance of a priest in their last hours. The oppression of the *mita*, or forced labor in the mines, with the introduction of the small-pox and the use of spirituous liquors, has destroyed prodigious multitudes of the Indians since the conquest. What their number was before that event it is impossible to tell; but judging from the extent of the Inca's dominions, he probably had not less thanthree or four millions of subjects. There are probably less than one million now in Peru.

In Chili there were several tribes who possessed nearly all the arts known to the Peruvians, but were distinguished from them by a finer physical constitution, and an unconquerable spirit. When the Spaniards arrived, Chili, according to Molina, was inhabited by fifteen tribes, independent of each other, who were spread over the country on both sides of the Andes, from atitude 30° to the Straits of Magellan. They all spoke dialects of one language, which is described as rich, harmonious, abounding in compound words, and having, like the other American tongues, very complicated grammatical forms. It has no affinity to the Quichua or Peruvian. The complexion of the Chilian tribes is, like that of the other American nations, a reddish brown; but they do not paint their bodies. The Chilians lived partly by hunting, but chiefly by agriculture, before they had any intercourse with Europeans. They cultivated maize, magu, guegen, tuca, quinoa, the potato, pumpkins, and some species of pulse; and to these they added, as food, the flesh of a small rabbit, and of the Chilihueque or Araucanian camel, of whose wool they are said to have manufactured cloth. Like the Peruvians, they understood the use of manure, practiced irrigation with considerable skill, and turned up the ground with a wooden spade or mattock. They had gold, silver, copper, tin, and lead, procured probably by washing; but they had few or no edge-tools of metal, as those found are almost always of basalt. They made baskets and mats, extracted salt from sea-water, and were able to give various dyes to their cloths. They lived in villages formed of houses standing at a distance from one another, under hereditary chiefs, but whose power was limited. It is remarkable that the Chinese mode of catching wild ducks on the rivers, by covering the fisher's head with a gourd, was practiced in Chili.

The Araucanians, the most intelligent, improved, and warlike of the Chilian tribes, occupy about 200 miles of the sea-coast, between the 37th and 39th parallels. They are of ordinary stature, but vigorously formed; bold, hardy, hospitable, faithful to their engagements, generous to a fallen enemy, ardent, intrepid, and enthusiastic lovers of liberty. Their vices are drunkenness, and a contempt of other nations, springing from pride. Araucania contains four tetrarchies, under four toquis or princes, who are independent of one another, but confederated for their joint security against foreign enemies. Each tetrarchy is divided into five provinces, ruled by five chiefs called *Apo-Ulmen;* and each province into nine districts, governed by as many *Ulmen*, who are subject to the Apo Ulmen, as the latter are to the toquis. These various chiefs compose the aristocracy of the country. They hold their dignities by hereditary descent in the male line, and in the order of primogeniture. The supreme power of each tetrarchy resides in a diet or great council of the ulmen, who assemble annually in a large plain, but no resolution of the diet is of any avail if it has not the hearty concurrence of the people. The Araucanians can raise altogether 6,000 to 7,000 men, besides a body of reserve. When war is declared by the great council, messengers bearing "arrows dipt in blood" are sent to all parts of the country, to summon the men to arms. Unlike many barbarous nations, which are immovably attached to their ancient customs, the Araucanians were not slow in copying the military arts and tactics of the Spaniards. Their troops now consist of infantry and cavalry; the former armed with pikes or clubs, the latter with swords and lances. They advance to battle in lines well formed, and fight with intrepidity. Their history affords a brilliant example of what a brave nation, animated by an enthusiastic love of liberty, can accomplish under the greatest disadvantages. After resisting the best troops and the best generals of Spain for 200 years, they at last compelled their proud enemies to acknowledge their independence. Combining the moral, intellectual, and physical qualities of the Araucanians, they were certainly the finest native race in the new world. They had nearly all the germs of civilization which belonged to the Mexicans and Peruvians; without the ferocity of the former, the apathy of the latter, or the slavish habits common to both; and without having their minds stupefied by that grovelling superstition which the rulers of these two nations seem to have considered as the only secure foundation of their authority. In true courage, in manliness and energy of character, they take precedence of all the American nations. The Araucanians believe in a supreme being, and in many subordinate spirits, good and bad. They believe also in omens and divination, but they have neither temples nor idols, nor religious rites; and discover upon the whole so little aptitude for the reception of religious ideas, that the Roman Catholic missionaries who are settled among them have had very little success in imbuing their minds with any knowledge of Christianity.

The other Chilian tribes are all much behind the Araucanians in civilization; but some, as the Puelches and the Tehuels, surpass them in strength and stature. Part of them live on horse flesh, part by keeping sheep and cattle, and part by hunting. Some of these tribes paint their faces. With regard to the height of the Patagonians, M. Lesson, an eminent French naturalist, has collected the authorities on the subject, and they appear to us to remove every rational doubt as to the fact of a race of men existing there, whose average stature is about six feet, and among whom men seven feet high are not at all uncommon. The Guaranis, in Brazil, at one time formed a numerous people, which seems to have been spread over a larger surface than any other now existing in America. Tribes, or remnants of tribes, whose relationship to the Guaranis is attested by the strong evidence of their language, are found diffused over the wide space between Orinoco and the embouchure of the Plata, over more than the half of South America. They are met with among the Andes of Peru, in the province of Chiquitos, in Mattogrosso, in Paraguay, in Minas Geraes; and the Omaguas, in the province of Quito, who, from their nautical habits, and the influence they obtained on the upper part of the Amazon, have been called the Phœnicians of the new world, are believed to be of the same race. They constituted the bulk of the native population of Brazil when the Portuguese gained possession of it, but were divided into many distinct tribes, quite independent of one another, and living, not in contiguity, but mixed with other nations. They are of low stature, of a square form, fleshy and ugly. Their color has a strong shade of the copper red, while that of the other Brazilian tribes inclines generally to the tawny or black. Their character, like their physical form, resembles that of the Peruvians. They are patient, torpid, mild, and passionless. Nearly all the Indians whom the Portuguese have civilized or converted belong to this race. Those whom the Jesuits civilized and collected into communities in the celebrated settlements of Paraguay belonged chiefly to the nation of the Guaranis. These missionaries are said to have borrowed the plan of the theocracy which they established here from that which the Incas had introduced into Peru. There is no doubt that the spirit of their system was the same; and considering that they were precluded from any other means of extending and supporting their authority than persuasion, their success was remarkable. The settlements were commenced about 1610, and were gradually extending over the country watered by the Parana and Uruguay, between the 27th and 30th degrees of south latitute, till the order of the Jesuits was suppressed in 1767. The incursions of the Portuguese compelled the Jesuits to take means for repelling force by force. All the male Indians of the proper age were accordingly armed with muskets, and disciplined as a militia. In 1732, the villages or parishes under the care of the missionaries contained a population of 141,000 souls. The Jesuits had another establishment of the same kind among the Chiriguas, a branch of the Guaranis, in the province of Chiquitos, containing 30,000 or 40,000 Indians; a third, of smaller size, in the province of Moxos; a fourth in California; and probably others. After the suppression of the order, all these were committed to the care of friars of other descriptions; and we believe they have universally fallen into decay

The problem as to the source whence America derived its population seems to present no difficulty, when the contiguity of the old and the new continent at Behring's Straits is known. The breadth of the sea here (latitude 66°) is only forty-five miles; the transit across is facilitated by two islands placed almost exactly midway between Asia and America; and in severe winters a firm body of ice joins the two continents. The climate, though rigorous, does not prevent the country on each side from being inhabited. The Aleutian Isles, besides, at the latitude of 53°, which run in a line like the piers of an immense bridge, from one continent to the other, present such easy means of communication, that few savage tribes a little familiar with sea-life could be long in Kamtschatka without threading their way across the Pacific to the peninsula at Alaska. Indeed, we have positive proof that America received part of its population from the north-east extremity of Asia; for the Esquimaux, living on the east side of Behring's Straits, speak a language which is radically the same with that of the Tschutskoi on the opposite shores. But in regard to other tribes who inhabit America, it is quite certain that they came by other routes.

Attempts to trace the descent of the aborigines from any particular people of the old world have not succeeded. We except the Esquimaux as above stated. Many analogies, however, in the physical character of the people, their rites, monuments, and superstitions, establish a connection between the Mexicans and some Asiatic nations. A general resemblance has been observed between the American nations and some tribes of Mongols and Mantchous, in the form of the skull, the brown color of the skin, the thinness of the beard, and the oblique position of the eye. Humboldt has shown that the Mexican calendar is identical in its principles, which are very artificial and complicated, with that which was in use among the Chinese, Japanese, Thibetians, Hindoos, and Tartars. Very possibly tribes belonging to the races of eastern Asia had separated from them while they were still living in the state of hunters, and, having crossed over Behring's Straits, had spread themselves by degrees over North America. Among some of these tribes, dwelling probably north of Columbia River, a few emigrants from China, Japan, or Chinese Tartary, at a comparatively late period, had been thrown by some of the accidents to which a seafaring life is liable, and bringing with them picture-writing, the art of building and weaving, a few mystical rites and traditions, and the calendar which was in use in their native country, had established their influence among the savages by address or force, and sown the seeds of civilization. After social life had made a few advances, the increasing numbers and power of the people would enable them to send off several swarms in succession to the eastward, and dispossess the earlier and ruder inhabitants of Anahuac and the plains of the Mississippi. The Toltecs were perhaps the first of these colonists; the Hurons, Iroquois, Chichimecks, and Aztecs (all of whom had hieroglyphics), must have been separated from the parent stock at a later period. To all appearance there was no race in America anterior to the Toltecs who possessed any germs of civilization, for the military works in Ohio can scarcely be referred to a period farther back than 800 or 1000 years from the present day. But for 2000 or 3000 years anterior to this the new continent had been overrun by tribes of hunters. This, we think, is clear; for while the analogies of physical character observed in the American nations, and in the structure of their dialects, show, on the one hand, that nine-tenths of them had sprung from one tribe, or a few tribes of one stock; the existence of 500 of these varieties of speech proves, on the other hand, that a very long period must have elapsed to admit of the subdivision of one, two, or even half-a-dozen of mother tongues into such a prodigious num ber of dialects. That the original seat of Toltec and Aztec civilization was not in Asia, but in the north-west parts of America, results from the non-existence of the cerealia and of tame cattle in the new world; and that the glimmering of knowledge which these people possessed had been kindled by the arrival of a few chance emigrants, perhaps at different periods, from China, Japan, or Chinese Tartary, seems equally certain, from the resemblance found in the calendars, the superstitions, and the cosmogonical traditions of the Asiatic and American races. In the great valley of the Mississippi and its mighty tributaries, the Ohio and Missouri, are the remains of the works of an extinct race of men, who seem to have made advances in civilization far beyond the races of *red men* there discovered by the first European adventurers. These remains consist chiefly of tumuli and ramparts of earth, inclosing areas of great extent, and much regularity of form. Some of them recall the barrows of Europe and of Asia, or the huge mounds and ramparts of Mesopotamia, as displayed at Babylon and Nineveh; while others remind us of the ruined hippodromes and amphitheatres of the Greeks and Romans. In that part of North America, the barrows are usually truncated cones; but in advancing farther south, they often assume the figure of four-sided pyramids in successive stages, with flattened tops, like the *Teocallis*, or temples of Mexico and Yucatan.

The barrows and ramparts are constructed of mingled earth and stones; and from their solidity and extent, must have required the labor of a numerous population, with leisure and skill sufficient to undertake combined and vast operations. The barrows often contain human bones, and the smaller tumuli appear to have been tombs; but the larger, especially the quadrangular mounds, would seem to have served as temples to the early inhabitants. These barrows vary in size, from a few feet in circumference and elevation, to structures with a basal circumference of 1000 or 2000 feet, and an altitude of from 60 to 90 feet, resembling, in dimensions, the vast tumulus of Alyattes, near Sardis. One in Mississippi is said to cover a base of six acres. The ramparts also vary in thickness, and in height from 6 to 30 feet, and usually inclose areas varying from 100 to 200 acres. Some contain 400; and one on the Missouri has an area of 600 acres. The inclosures generally are very exact circles or squares, sometimes a union of both; occasionally they form parallelograms, or follow the sinuosities of a hill; and in one district, that of Wisconsin, they assume the fanciful shape of men, quadrupeds, birds, or serpents delineated with some ingenuity, on the surface of undulating plains or wide savannahs. These ramparts are usually placed on elevations or hills, or on the banks of streams, so as to show that they were erected for defensive purposes, and their sites are judiciously chosen for this end. The area inclosed, therefore, bears no proportion to the relative labor bestowed on such ramparts; thus, in Ohio, an area of not more than 40 acres is inclosed by mounds of a mile and a half in circumference; and on the Little Miami, in the same State, is found an inclosure fully four miles round, that contains an area of about 100 acres. These remains are not solitary and few, for in the State of Ohio they amount to at least 10,000.

The inclosures in the form of animals are more rare than those now noticed, and seem nearly confined to Wisconsin. One of those represents a gigantic man with two heads, the size of which may be estimated, by the body being 50 feet long, and 25 feet across the breast. Another on a slope near Bush Creek, represents a tolerably designed snake, with an oval ball in its mouth; the undulating folds of its body and spiral of its tail extending to a length of 700 feet. The forms of quadrupeds and birds are also characteristically represented in these works. Those that have been explored contain human bones; and though the Indians deposit their dead within them occasionally, they have no tradition of their having belonged to their ancestors. The most probable supposition respecting them is, that each was the sepul chral monument of a different tribe, who have all disappeared from America.

As we advance southward, we find proofs of still greater refinement on the table-land of Anahuac or Mexico; and on descending into the humid valleys of Central America, the peninsula of Yucatan, and the shores of Honduras, we find striking remains of the semi-civilization of the races that inhabited those countries before the Spanish invasion. The barbarous policy of Cortez and other invaders, was to eradicate every trace of the former grandeur of the native races, thereby to enure them to a degrading servitude. The systematic destruction of the native works of art and gorgeous buildings in Mexico was relentlessly carried on for ages, to the infinite regret of the modern ethnographical inquirer. Little positive information on these subjects can be gleaned from the early Spanish historians of the conquest; and it was not until the publication of Humboldt's *Researches*, that anything was known of the state of the Great Mexican pyramid, or of the wonderful remains of Palenque and Papantla. More than a century ago, however, some Spanish adventurers penetrated the forest of Chiapas and discovered Palenque. Two Spanish travelers followed, and Mr. J. L. Stephens, in his "Incidents of Travel," added largely to our knowledge of these regions.

The most conspicuous ruins seem to have been temples or palaces, and almost invariably have a pyramidal form, in several stages, with wide intervening terraces, the ascent to which is by grand flights of steps. The chambers in those buildings have generally a length disproportioned to their width; they have no windows, but receive their light from the doors; just as the rooms do at this day in Barbary and some other eastern countries. The apartments are in two parallel rows, a narrow corridor or series of chambers runs along the front, and the apartments behind this receive their light only from the front rooms into which they open. Yet these interior apartments are often richly decorated with sculptures, ornamented with stuccos, and gaily painted red, yellow, white and black.

The ruins of Palenque, as may be seen in the researches of Humboldt, have the characters just mentioned. They are covered with hieroglyphics, and sculptures in relief, with ornamental cornices. The largest building stands on a terrace, faced with stone, measuring 310 by 260 feet; the building itself is 200 by 180 feet; its walls are 25 feet high. The stone has been originally covered with painted stucco, fronts the east, and contains 14 doors, separated by piers ornamented with stucco figures. In this building some of the figures are erect, while others sit cross-legged, in what we term the oriental fashion; one statue, 10½ feet high, was found at Palenque; and two fragments of two *torsos* and a head were also discovered that exhibited a severe but fair style of sculpture, that recals somewhat of the early style of Greek art.

The ruins at Copan, in Honduras, are of vast extent. Here a pyramidal structure remains, with an elevation of 150 feet measured along its slope, and this appears to be a principal temple, included with several smaller structures within a *sacred inclosure*, in the manner of the temples of ancient Egypt.

The similarity between the ruins at Copan and Palenque, and the identity of the hieroglyphic tablets in both show that the former inhabitants of Chiapas and Honduras had the same *written* language, though the present Indians of those provinces do not understand each other.

At Labphak, but more especially at Uxmal, both in Yucatan, are very magnificent ruins of the same kind. Several sculptured obelisks are here, also bearing on their principal face a figure of some deity probably, with a benignant countenance, represented in full, and the hands applied to the breast. The other sides of the obelisks are covered with hieroglyphical tablets, proving that the same race once inhabited the plains of Honduras, and the table-land of Anahuac. The principal building at Uxmal seems to have been a very magnificent pyramid in three stages or terraces, faced with hewn stone, and neatly rounded at the angles. The roofs here, unlike those of Palenque and Copan, are not stone arches, but are supported on bearers of a very hard wood that must have been brought from a distance of some hundred miles; and these beams too are covered with hieroglyphics. The flat roof of this building has been externally covered with a hard cement.

The ruins of Chichen, also in Yucatan, extend over an area of two miles in circumference. One of the best preserved buildings, with an ambit of 638 feet, is constructed in three terraces, which give it an apparent altitude of 65 feet. The buildings here, on the second terrace, have the façades highly sculptured, both above and below the horizontal fillet; and the doorways are enriched with mouldings, and *truss*-like ornaments supporting a drip-stone. The staircase here is 56 feet wide. The front apartments are 47 feet long and only 9 wide. There are three doors in the front, and in the central apartment are nine niches. The roofs are stone arches; and all has been once painted of various colors. It is worthy of notice, that the builders of those cities took great pains to supply them with one of the prime essentials of human comfort—abundance of good water, by means of wells and cisterns of excellent construction.

The remains, in all the forty-four ancient towns visited by Stephens, have a similar character; so that we can have no hesitation to ascribe them to the same nation, or to kindred races of men, who have certainly attained no inconsiderable civilization, although unacquainted with the use of iron, or even of bronze. They seem to have been farther advanced in the arts than even the inhabitants of the table-land of Mexico at the period of the Spanish conquest.

The discovery of a continent so large that it may be said to have doubled the habitable world, is an event so much the more grand and interesting, that nothing parallel to it can ever occur again in the history of mankind. America had of course been known to the barbarous tribes of eastern Asia for thousands of years; but it is singular that it should have been visited by one of the most enterprising nations of Europe five centuries before the time of Columbus, without awakening or securing the attention of either statesmen or philosophers. Iceland was discovered about 860, and colonized by the Norwegians in 874. About 50, or, according to other accounts, 100 years later, the same people planted colonies in Greenland, the ruins of which exist near the southern point of the peninsula. It is obvious that the same adventurous spirit which enabled these northern mariners to discover the southern extremity of the country, would not permit them to stop short without visiting what is now known to be the most habitable part of it—the western coast; and the fact has been established by an inscription in *Runic* characters, found on a stone four miles beyond Upernavik, at the 73d parallel. This was about the middle of the 14th century.

In 1001 an Icelander sailing to Greenland, was driven away by a tempest far to the south-west, where he saw a level country covered with wood. The wind abating, he turned his course homeward, and on his arrival gave such a flattering account of the country he had seen, as induced Lief, the son of the founder of the Greenland colony, to undertake a voyage thither. Lief and Biorn, who sailed together, first reached a rocky island, to which they gave the name of Helluland; then a low country, thickly wooded, which they called Markland; and some days afterwards they found trees loaded with fruits on the banks of a river. They spent the winter in the country; and one of them, who was a German, having found wild vines growing, they called it Vinland. They had some intercourse, and traded for furs, with a people who came in leathern boats, and were called *Skrælings*, from their dwarfish size. A colony was planted and remained for many years in the country, the situation being probably in the neighborhood of Rhode Island. Only a few unimportant particulars respecting the settlement are preserved; but it seems to have been abandoned or destroyed, like the Greenland colonies, of which it was an offset.

The Norsemen describe Vinland as a rich country, with a delightful climate. Helluland, Markland, and Vinland, were no doubt regarded as countries either connected with or similar to Greenland, the flattering descriptions of which given by the first discoverers were sadly belied by later experience. No reasonable doubt can exist, however, that the north-eastern portions of America (considering Greenland as a distinct country) were familiarly known to the Norwegians in the eleventh century.

The obscure allusions of Aristotle, Plato, and Seneca, to a country hid in the Western Ocean, must have derived fresh importance from the discovery of the Canary Isles, Madeira, and the Azores, in the early part of the fifteenth century. The love of maritime adventure was excited by these events; and among the active spirits who were attracted to nautical life by the career of distinction which was then opened up, was Christopher Columbus. Having received a good education, the study of the geographical systems then in vogue impressed him with a strong conviction that a voyage to India by a course directly westward was quite practicable, with the degree of nautical science which his contemporaries possessed.

Columbus was, however, without the fortune necessary to fit out ships; and when he attempted to interest some of the princes of those times in his project, he encountered neglects and difficulties which would have exhausted the patience of any mind less ardent than his own. At length, after many delays and discouragements, Ferdinand and Isabella of Spain supplied him with three small vessels, two of them only half-decked; and in this little armament, accompanied by 120 men, he set sail from the port of Palos on the 3d of August, 1492. He proceeded first to the Canary Isles, where he was detained three weeks in repairing one of his vessels. On leaving these isles he entered on an unknown sea, where all was chaos and mystery. The trade-wind, however, bore him steadily along, and the labor of the ships proceeded cheerfully, till the increasing length of the voyage, the failure of prognostics which had from time to time kept alive the hopes of the crew, and various circumstances interpreted by their superstition as evil omens, produced a mutinous spirit, which all the address and authority of Columbus would not probably have been able to quell, had the discovery of land happened one day later than it did.

It was on the 12th of October that the western world revealed itself to the wondering eyes of Columbus and his companions. What a triumph for this extraordinary man, who had treasured in his breast for twenty years, amidst neglect, discouragement, and ridicule, the grand truth, which his own in comparable skill, wisdom, and firmness, had now demonstrated in the eyes of an incredulous world! The spot which he first touched was Guanahani, or San Salvador, one of the Bahama Islands, 3650 miles from Teneriffe. After spending nearly three months in visiting Cuba, Hispaniola, and other isles, he returned to Spain. He made three other voyages, and in the second coasted along a part of South America, which he rightly judged to be a continent from the volume of water poured into the sea by the Orinoco; but he died ignorant of the real extent and grandeur of his discoveries, still believing that the countries he had made known to Europe belonged to that part of Eastern Asia which the ancients called India. Hence the name of West Indies, which the tropical islands and part of the continent have ever since received.

Without undertaking to go into details, we give a brief chronological notice of the more important discoveries and settlements made by the several nations of Europe in America.

1495. The first place in which the

Spaniards established their power was the large island of Hayti or Hispaniola, which was inhabited by a numerous race of Indians, of a mild and gentle character, a third part of whom are said to have perished within two or three years after the Spaniards conquered them.

1497. John Cabot, in the service of Henry VII. of England, discovered Newfoundland, and coasted along the shores of North America to Florida.

1500. Cabral, a Portuguese, visited the coast of Brazil, and discovered the mouth of the Amazon. It was probably colonized before 1515, as the first cargo of wood was sent from it to Portugal in that year.

1508. Vincent Pinzon is said to have entered the Rio de la Plata. It was in the same year that the Spaniards, finding the aborigines too weak for the labor of the mines in Hayti, first imported negroes from Guinea, and thus laid the foundation for the infamous traffic in slaves.

1511 Diego Columbus conquered the island of Cuba, with 300 soldiers, of whom he did not lose one.

1513. Balboa crossed the isthmus of Darien with 290 men, and discovered the Pacific Ocean.

1519. Hernando Cortes sailed from Cuba with 11 ships and 550 men, and landed on the coast of Mexico, which had been discovered in the previous year. The conquest of the empire was finished in 1521 by 950 Spaniards, assisted by a vast number of the Indians of Tlascala.

1531. Peru invaded by Pizarro, and conquered in little more than one year, with a force of 1000 men.

1534. James Cartier, a Frenchman, discovered the Gulf of St. Lawrence.

1535. Mendoza, a Spaniard, with 2000 followers, founded Buenos Ayres, and conquered all the country as far as Potosi, at which silver mines were discovered nine years after.

1537. Cortes discovers California.

1541. De Soto discovers the Mississippi; Chili conquered; Orellana sails down the Amazon to the Atlantic.

1578. New Albion (California) on the north-west coast of America discovered by Sir Francis Drake.

1587. Davis's Straits and Cumberland Islands discovered by John Davis.

1604. De Monts, a Frenchman, founded the first settlement in Nova Scotia, then called Acadie.

1607. After many ineffectual attempts during more than twenty years, the first permanent settlement of the English in North America was made this year, on the banks of James' River, in Virginia.

1608. Quebec founded by the French, who had had a small neglected colony in Canada since 1542.

1611. Newfoundland colonized by the English; a Dutch colony established on Hudson River. Manhattan, now New York, was founded in 1614.

1618. Baffin penetrates to the 78th degree of latitude, in the bay which bears his name.

1620. The first English colony established in New England, at Plymouth. It was in this year that the first negroes were imported into Virginia. They were brought by a Dutch vessel.

1635. A French colony established in Guiana.

1655. Jamaica conquered by the English.

1664. The Dutch colonies on Hudson River capitulate to the English.

1666. The Buccaneers begin their depredations on the Spanish colonies.

1682. William Penn establishes a colony in Pennsylvania. La Salle takes possession of Louisiana, in the name of the French king.

1698. A colony of 1200 Scots planted at Darien, and ruined in the following year, in consequence of the miserable jealousy of the English.

1733. Georgia colonized by the English.

1760. Canada, and all the other French settlements in North America, conquered by the English.

A few remarks may not improperly here be made on the colonial system introduced by the principal European nations who occupied extensive tracts of the new world. The English settlements extended from the 31st to the 50th degree on the east coast, and were divided into fifteen or sixteen provinces. The colonists had carried the love of liberty characteristic of their countrymen with them; and after many struggles with their British rulers, all the provinces, with one or two exceptions, were permitted to enjoy a form of government extremely popular. The executive power was vested in a governor appointed by the king. He was assisted by a council, which sometimes conjoined the functions of a privy council and a house of peers. The people were represented by a house of assembly, consisting of persons chosen by the freeholders in the country parts, and the householders or corporations of towns. The governor could levy no money without the consent of the house of assembly: the British parliament, however, claimed the privilege of imposing taxes upon the colonists, without consulting them. Against this assumption of power the local legislatures always protested as an infringement of their rights. The vessels of foreign states were not permitted to trade with the colonies; but the colonists were allowed to trade in their own ships with one another, with the mother country, and, to a limited extent, with foreign states. Their taxes, which were always small, were all consumed in defraying internal expenses; and, compared with any other people in the new world, they enjoyed an unexampled degree of commercial and political liberty. It was the growing prosperity of the colonies, and the increasing debt of the mother country, which induced the British ministers, for the first time, in 1764, to attempt raising a revenue in America, for purposes not colonial.

This unwise procedure of parliament having been persisted in led to a crisis, and ultimately to a collision between the colonies and the mother country. After a seven years' war, the Independence of the United States was secured in 1782. Further on we shall give the history of the Great Republic more at large.

The Spanish possessions in America, before the revolution, formed nine distinct governments, all constructed on the same plan, and independent of one another. Four of these, of the first rank, were vice-royalties, viz: Mexico, Peru, La Plata, and New Granada; and five were captain-generalships, viz: Yucatan, Guatemala, Chili, Venezuela, and the island of Cuba. The government was vested in the viceroy or captain-general, who was held to represent the king, and to enjoy all his prerogatives within the colony. But in these countries, as in others where the supreme power is apparently unlimited, it was indirectly restrained by the influence of the courts of justice, corporations, and other public bodies. The clergy, also, who were numerous and rich, necessarily possessed great influence among a superstitious people. The vices inherent in the colonial system existed in their utmost rankness in the Spanish American dominions. There was tolerable security for all classes except the miserable Indians, who were regarded and treated precisely as beasts of burden, out of whose toil and sufferings a provision as ample as possible was to be extracted, first to supply the wants of the royal treasury, and next to feed in idleness, and to satisfy the cupidity of a countless shoal of public officers and priests.

The memoir of Ulloa, with various other documents published since the revolution, depicts acts of extortion, perfidy, cruelty, and oppression practiced upon the Indians which have rarely been paralleled. Men rose to affluence in offices without salaries; and the priests rivalled the laymen in the art of extracting money from those whom they ought to have protected. As the sole aim of the Spaniards in the colonies was to enrich themselves, so the government at home made all its acts and regulations subordinate to the grand object of raising a revenue. Spain retained in her hands the whole trade of the colonies, and guarded her monopoly with the most severe penalties. The price of all European commodities was enhanced three, four, or sixfold, in America. The colonists were not allowed to manufacture or raise an article which the mother country could supply; they were compelled to root up their vines and olives; and for a long period one colony was not even permitted to send a ship to another. And the more effectually to crush all mental activity, natives of America could rarely obtain leave to go abroad, to seek in foreign countries what was denied them in their own. On the other hand the priests, sharing in the spoil, filled the minds of the people with childish superstitions, as a means of confirming their own power; and employed the terrors of religion to teach them patience under oppression.

The overthrow of Ferdinand, King of Spain, presented an opening for redress to the colonists, and by spontaneous efforts of the people "juntas of government" were formed, at Caraccas in April, 1809, at La Paz in Upper Peru in July, at Quito in August, at Santa Fe and at Buenos Ayres in May, 1810, and at Santiago in Chili in September the same year. In 1810, also, the first insurrection broke out in Mexico. The colonists unluckily had been too long the slaves of superstition and tyranny to be fit for conducting so bold an experiment; and after a struggle, which was generally short, but almost everywhere bloody, the juntas were all put down except in Colombia and Buenos Ayres. But in the stir and tumult of the contest, old prejudices had received a shock, and the seeds of political change had struck their roots too deep in the soil to be eradicated. A desultory war was carried on for six years between Buenos Ayres and Upper Peru, with little advantage on either side. At length, in 1817, the former State, which had assumed the style of an independent republic four years before, sent an army across the Andes to Chili, under General San Martin, and defeated the Spaniards at Chacabuco. A second victory, gained at Maipo in April, 1818, led to the entire subversion of the Spanish power in this colony. The war was now transferred to Peru, where the Spaniards continued to lose ground, till the decisive battle of Ayacucho put an end to their power in December, 1824, and in January, 1826, the Spanish flag no longer waved on any spot in the land of the Incas.

In New Granada and Venezuela the struggle was more bloody, variable, and protracted than in any other part of South America. From 1809, when juntas were established in Caraccas and Quito, to the surrender of Porto Cabello, in 1823, the vicissitudes of the war were numerous and extraordinary. The decisive victory of Carabobò, gained by the patriots in 1819, gave them an ascendancy which they never afterwards lost; but the Spaniards were only finally expelled in 1823.

In Mexico the revolutionary movement began at Dolores, in 1810, and soon wore a very prosperous appearance; but by one or two mischances, the force of the independent party was ruined in November, 1815, when Morelos, their able leader, was taken prisoner and executed. For six years after this period many guerilla bands maintained themselves in the provinces, and greatly annoyed the Spaniards; but they did not act in concert, and no congress or junta professing to represent the Mexican people existed. The celebrated Iturbide proclaimed a constitution, under the name of "the three guarantees," and put an end to the dominion of Spain in 1821, almost without bloodshed. Iturbide, who had nothing in view but his own aggrandizement, called a congress, which he soon dissolved, after getting himself proclaimed emperor. His usurpation kindled a spirit of resistance. He was exiled in 1823, made a new attempt on the liberties of his country in 1824, was taken prisoner, and shot within a few weeks after he landed.

Guatemala was the last portion of the American continent which threw off the Spanish yoke. In 1821 the persons in office assembled and formed a junta. Divisions arose, which were fomented by the intrusion of a Mexican army sent by Iturbide. This force, however, was beaten, and an elective assembly called, which declared the country independent, and established a constitution in July, 1823. Spain now retains none of her possessions in the new world but Cuba and Porto Rico.

The horrible cruelty of the Spaniards exceeds the power of the pen to depict. The executions in cold blood, the countless massacres, the treachery, perfidy, and contempt of the most solemn oaths and engagements, of which they were guilty, in every colony, and almost in every district, are, we believe, without a parallel in the modern civilized world, and strongly remind one of the barbarous and exterminating hostilities of the Jenghis Khans and Tamerlanes of Asia. The Indians were destroyed by thousands on the slightest provocation; and it has been estimated on good authority that the number of human beings destroyed by the sword in Spanish America between 1810 and 1825 was at least one million!

The government of Brazil was conducted by the Portuguese on a system extremely similar to that of the Spanish colonies. The monopoly which the mother country retained of the commerce of the colony was equally rigorous; the restrictions on its internal industry as severe; and the same means were employed to keep the people in a state of pupilage and ignorance. Down to 1806 a single printing press had never existed in Brazil. In 1807, the King of Portugal escaped from Napoleon and arrived in Brazil in January, 1808. He was received with joy by the colonists, who anticipated great benefits from his residence, of which they were not disappointed. Within a few months printing presses and newspapers were established, the ports were open to the trade of all nations, and the people were invited and encouraged to prosecute all those branches of internal industry from which they had till now been interdicted. Brazil was declared an independent kingdom in 1815, subject to the crown of Portugal, but entitled to its separate administration and its own laws. The revolutionary spirit pervading the Spanish colonies now found its way into Brazil, and produced an insurrection at Pernambuco in 1817. It was soon subdued, but received a new impulse from the constitutional systems suddenly introduced into Spain and Portugal in 1820. Don Pedro, who had been left by his father in Brazil, was asked to take the head of an independent government. In 1822 he was proclaimed emperor, and had his own title and the independence of Brazil acknowledged by his father three years afterwards. A representative system was at the same time introduced. An unlucky war now arose with Buenos Ayres, which weakened both countries; but it was at length terminated in 1828, by the recognition of the disputed territory as an independent State, under the title of the Banda Oriental, now Uruguay.

These changes having been thus effected, we may here briefly sketch the political arrangements which have followed, and other matters properly belonging to this general view of the New World. For details we refer the reader to the separate articles in the present volume devoted to the several States and nations of America.

America, with its isles, consists of twenty-one States, and various colonies belonging to six European powers. The States are, Brazil, Venezuela, New Granada, Ecuador, Peru, Bolivia or Upper Peru, Chili, the Argentine Republic, Uruguay, Paraguay, Patagonia, Costa Rica, Mosquitia, Guatemala, Honduras, Nicaragua, San Salvador, Mexico, United States, Hayti, Dominica. The colonies belong to Great Britain, Denmark, Sweden Holland, France, and Spain. Patagonia is hardly more than the geographical name of a district occupied by independent tribes of Indians; Mosquitia, or the Mosquito coast, is a small Indian State ruled by a native king; Hayti is a Negro State ruled by a black emperor; and Dominica is a republic on the eastern part of the island of Hayti.

Brazil is the largest State in South America, and enjoys the greatest combination of natural advantages. It is bounded on the south, west, and north, by La Plata, Paraguay, Uruguay, Bolivia, Peru, Ecuador, New Granada, Venezuela, and Guiana. Embracing an area of more than 3,000,000 miles, it is nearly as large as Europe, and is capable of supporting a much greater population. Its climate is probably cooler and more salubrious than that of any other extensive tropical country; and every part of its soil is rich and fruitful. Its commercial advantages are admirable. The Amazon with its numerous branches, the Parana, the Tocantin, the St. Francisco, and other streams, supply the most remote parts of the interior, with easy means of communication with the sea. Brazil possesses iron, copper, and probably all the other metals; but her mines of gold and diamonds are remarkably rich. Her most valuable productions for exportation are, cotton, sugar, coffee, hides, tobacco, vanilla, dyewoods, aromatic plants, timber, etc. Her commerce is much greater than that of all the Spanish colonies put together. The Brazilians are lively, irritable, hospitable, but ignorant, superstitious, and rather inclined to indolence. Their acquisition of independence, however, as above noted, has produced an extraordinary change in their industry, opinions, and modes of thinking. Lancasterian and other schools are spreading in all directions; the press brings forth new publications; and twenty-five journals existed in 1828, in a country where the art of printing was unknown in 1807. According to the constitution introduced by Don Pedro, the legislature consisted of a senate of fifty-two members, to hold their places for life, and a house of representatives of 107, elected by the people for three years; upon the acts of both of which bodies the emperor has a negative. The population of Brazil, according to a work published recently by the government, amounts to 11,780,000; of whom 1,400,000 are negro slaves; and 500,000 Indians.

The portion of South America next to the isthmus includes the United States of Columbia, or New Granada, Venezuela, and Ecuador. The territories of these three states are bounded on the south by Peru, on the south-east and east by Brazil and Guiana, on the other sides by the sea, and embrace an area of 945,000 square miles. The soil is fruitful, and the climate salubrious, except along the coast and in a few other low situations. The eastern part consists chiefly of the llanos or steppes of the Orinoco, which are very hot; the western, of the mountain ridges of the Andes, which support tracks of table-land where the blessings of a temperate climate are enjoyed, and the cerealia of Europe can be successfully cultivated. The tropical vegetation extends to the height of 4000 feet; from 4000 to 9000 is the region where wheat, barley, and leguminous plants thrive. Above the level of 9000 feet the climate becomes severe; and at 15,700 feet vegetation ceases. The situation of New Granada is highly favorable for commerce, and it has excellent ports on both seas. The Orinoco and the Amazon afford the inmost districts of Venezuela and Ecuador the advantages of water-carriage to the ocean. The Cassiquiari, an intermediate channel, by which the Orinoco *anastomoses* or connects with the Amazon (a remarkable hydrographical phenomenon), is within the limits of Venezuela. The territory contains much gold and silver; the former in alluvial deposits: it has mines of copper and mercury also, with platinum, iron and coal. The governments of these States are republican. The population of Columbia or New Granada is 2,900,000; of Venezuela, 2,200,000; and of Ecuador, 1,300,000.

The Argentine Republic, is, in point of natural advantages, the second state of importance of South America. It is bounded on the west by Chili; on the north by Bolivia, Paraguay and Uruguay; on the east and south by the sea, and embraces an area of 826,828 square miles. Nearly the whole territory of this republic consists of open plains destitude of timber, called *pampas*, extending from the Atlantic and the river Paraguay to the Andes. The eastern part of these plains exhibits a vigorous growth of herbage, intermixed with a forest of gigantic plants nine or ten feet high; in the middle they are covered with grass; and the western division, which extends to the foot of the Andes, consists of barren sandy plains, thinly sprinkled with shrubs and thorny trees. The openness and dryness of the country, however, render it healthy; and by the Parana, the Paraguay, and their branches, it possesses a great extent of natural inland navigation. It has mines of gold, silver, copper, lead, and probably iron. The force of this republic lies almost entirely in the wealth, intelligence, and commercial spirit of its capital, Buenos Ayres, which contains 120,000 souls, including a large proportion of foreigners. A small number of *estancias*, or grazing farms, are sparingly diffused over its boundless plains, the proprietors of which keep multitudes of horses and mules, flocks of sheep, and vast herds of cattle; the latter being chiefly valued for their skins. The population is estimated at 1,465,000.

Chili extends along the coast of the Pacific, from 25° to 44° of south latitude: its length is 1300 miles; its breadth varies from 30 to 120; and its surface is estimated to be 826,828 square miles. The country consists properly of the western slope or declivity of the Andes; for the branches of the mountains, running out in tortuous directions from the main trunk, reach to the sea-shore. It enjoys an excellent and healthful climate; severe cold is unknown in the inhabited parts. and the heat is seldom excessive. The useful soil bears a small proportion to the entire surface of the country, consisting merely of the bottom of the valleys. It has rich mines of gold, silver, and copper in the northern provinces; but very few of them can be worked, in consequence of the absolute sterility of the adjacent country. Its two northern provinces, occupying 450 miles of the coast, are nearly perfect deserts, and probably not one-fiftieth part of the country is fit for cultivation. But south of the river Maule the land is covered with fine timber, and bears crops of wheat and other grain, without the aid of any other moisture than what is supplied by the atmosphere. Chili has no manufactures, and is unfavorably situated for commerce. It has no navigable rivers, while its mountainous surface is an obstacle to the formation of roads; and its communications with all other parts of the world are circuitous and difficult. The population is about 2,000,000.

Peru is a continuation of the country which forms Chili, consisting of the western declivities of the Andes, from the 4th to the 22d degree of south latitude, with the addition of a considerable tract on the east side of the mountains, between the 4th and 15th parallels. There are few countries in the world which have a more singular physical character than the western part of Peru. It is a belt or zone of sands, 1700 miles in length, and from 7 to 50 in breadth, with considerable inequalities of surface. This long line of desert is intersected by rivers and streams, which are seldom less than 20 or more than 80 miles apart, and on the sides of which narrow strips of productive soil are created by means of irrigation. These isolated valleys form the whole habitable country. Some of the large rivers reach the sea; the smaller are either consumed in irrigating the patches of cultivated land, or absorbed by the encompassing desert, where it never rains, where neither beast nor bird lives, and a blade of vegetation never grew. No stranger can travel through one of these valleys without a guide, for the desert is trackless; and the only indications of a route are an occasional cluster of bones, the remains of beasts of burden that have perished. The country has two advantages—its mines of the precious metals, and a temperate and delightful climate, in consequence of the absence of rain, and the fogs which intercept the solar heat. Like Chili it has no navigable rivers, and nature has deprived it of means of forming good roads. The districts east of the

Andes, which have a hot climate, accompanied with a rich soil, will ultimately be the most valuable part of the country; but their secluded situation, and want of communication with other countries, must keep them long in a backward state. The government is republican. Peru comprehends a surface of 510,107 square miles; the capital, Lima, contains 121,400 inhabitants; and the entire population of the state is given as 2,500,000.

Bolivia lies eastward of Peru, and is bounded on the south by the Argentine Republic, and on the north and east by Brazil. It is of an irregular form, and comprehends a space of 535,769 square miles. The climate is pleasant and healthful, and the soil is generally dry, and in the eastern parts, as well as the elevated table-land, its aridity produces barrenness. Nature, however, as a compensation for its other disadvantages, has bestowed upon it some of the richest mines in the world. The country was erected into an independent state in 1825, and named Bolivia in honor of its liberator Bolivar. It has a small strip of barren territory, on the shores of the Pacific Ocean, between the 22d and 25th parallel; but it is, properly speaking, entirely an inland country, and more deficient in the means of communicating with foreign nations than any other state in America. It has a population of nearly 2,000,000.

Guatemala has a hilly surface, and is in most parts mountainous; the climate is warm and very moist. The mineral wealth of the country is not great; but this is compensated by the richness of its soil, and its excellent commercial position. This applies to Central America in general. The total area of the five States in Central America is 191,877 square miles. The population of Guatemala is 1,180,000; of San Salvador, 600,000; of Honduras, 350,000; of Nicaragua, 400,000; and of Costa Rica, 135,000.

About three-fourths of the surface of Mexico consist either of mountains or table-land, raised from 5000 to 10,000 feet above the sea. Owing to this extraordinary elevation, even those parts of the country which lie within the torrid zone (the low ground on the coast excepted) enjoy a dry, cool, and salubrious atmosphere; but this advantage is counterbalanced by the insufficient supply of moisture, and the rapid evaporation resulting from the same cause, which render the soil generally rather arid, and in many parts absolutely barren; by the smallness of the rivers, and the almost entire absence of inland navigation; and by the obstacles which the steep and rugged ascents from the coast present to land-carriage. Mexico is beside almost destitute of ports on the Atlantic side. It is extremely rich in the precious metals; and there are few regions upon which nature has lavished so great a variety of vegetable productions. The low ground on the east coast is admirably calculated for raising sugar; and no country is more favorably situated for growing the other great articles of West India produce: coffee, cotton, cocoa, indigo, and tobacco. The raising of *bread-stuffs*, as they are termed by the Anglo-Americans, wheat, maize, and barley, with potatoes, the cassava root, beans and pumpkins, fruit, etc., for domestic consumption, will necessarily be the chief branch of industry of the table-lands. The mines have never employed above 30,000 laborers; and their superior productiveness depends chiefly on two circumstances—the great abundance of the ore, which is only of poor quality, and the comparative facility with which they can be worked, owing to their being generally situated in fertile districts, where, provisions, wood, and all materials can easily be procured.

Mexico has her full share of the ignorance and superstition which belonged to Old Spain; and these evils, with her internal dissensions, and her rapacious, immoral, and intolerant clergy, have proved great obstacles to her improvement. That excessive inequality of fortune which corrupts both extremes of society was nowhere in the world more prevalent than in Mexico. The distinction of *castes*, which was maintained in the greatest rigor under the colonial system, has now disappeared, and power and office are open, not only legally but practically, to men of all colors. The African blacks form an extremely small proportion of the Mexican population; but there are very few of the whites, so called, who are free of a mixture of Indian blood. The population of Mexico is 8,218,100, of which it is estimated that 29 per cent. are whites, 27 per cent. mixed races, and 54 per cent. Indians. The total area is given, according to the latest estimate, at 773,144 square miles.

In regard to the gold and silver mines in America, it may be noted that Humboldt computed the whole produce of these mines from 1492 to 1803, to be 5,706,000,000 dollars, of which only 4½ per cent. was retained in America, and 5,445,000,000 dollars, or 95½ per cent., was remitted to Europe. A great auriferous deposit was discovered in Upper California in the end of 1847, just before its formal cession to the United States. It was known before that gold existed in the country; but the wonderful richness of the deposit was only discovered in 1847, in making a mill-race on American Fork, a small branch of the Sacramento. It soon became widely known, and attracted multitudes of persons, first from the neighboring districts, and by and by from all parts of the world. In connection with Humboldt's computation above, we give an estimate prepared by an officer of the Treasury at Washington, in answer to an inquiry as to the total produce of the gold and silver mines of the world (except Australia) since 1492.

America, exclusive of the United States		$6,877,833,800
California, received at Mint	$98,408,000	
California, foreign exports, manufactured, &c.	51,592,000	
Other U. States gold at Mint	15,855,000	
Ditto not brought to Mint	1,145,000	
Total United States		167,000,000
Total America		$7,044,833,800
Europe and Asia, exclusive of Russia		1,755,000,000
Russia		213,581,000
Total production, 1492 to 1852		$9,013,414,800

The United States were colonized a century later than Spanish America; but their rapid progress shows in a striking light how much more the prosperity of nations depends on *moral* than on *physical* advantages. The colonists had no gold mines, and a territory of only indifferent fertility, covered with impenetrable woods; but they brought with them intelligence, industry, a love of freedom, habits of order, and a strict morality. Armed with these gifts of the soul, they have converted the wilderness into a land teeming with life, and smiling with plenty; and they have built up a social system well calculated to promote the happiness and moral improvement of mankind. The republic is bounded on the north by Canada and British America, on the south-west by Mexico, and on the other sides by the Atlantic and Pacific Oceans. It now consists of thirty-seven states and nine *territories*, and embraces an area of 3,549,129 square miles. The agriculture of the United States partakes to some extent of a tropical character. The sugar-cane is cultivated in Louisiana, Florida, and other states, as high as the latitude of 31½°. Rice is obtained from the marshy coast lands of the South Atlantic and Gulf states. Cotton is raised in all the southern states within the 37th parallel, and tobacco in those within the 41st. Wheat succeeds in the middle and northern states, and maize or Indian corn thrives in every part of the Union. Agriculture is conducted with great skill and success; the grazing products are of large and increasing importance; and the manufactures are extensive in all the region north of the Potomac and Ohio Rivers. In the useful arts generally America is quite on a level with France and England; in the fine arts and the sciences she is not much behind. The internal commerce of the United States is conducted with extraordinary spirit. The capital expended on roads, canals, harbors, bridges, and other public works, is very great. The extent of foreign trade and the amount of shipping, place the United States among the very foremost commercial nations of the world. The population of the United States, according to the latest estimates is, 34,374,-900.

The United States are held together by a constitutional government, consisting of the legislative, judicial, and executive departments. The national government is supreme in all those things which have been entrusted to it; all other powers are reserved to the states respectively.

The legislatures consist in every case of two bodies, a house of representatives chosen for one or two years, and a senate for a period varying from two years to six; but both always by popular election, except in the case of the United States senate, which is chosen by the legislatures of the states. The President holds his office for four years, but is eligible for re-election.

The portion of the American continent called British America, extends from the Great Lakes to the Arctic Ocean, and from the Atlantic to the Pacific. It contains an area of 3,524,083 square miles, of which about one-half may be habitable, and one-seventh part tolerably fertile; but the districts which have been marked out into counties or townships, and in which settlements are begun, form a very small portion of this immense region. The entire population is estimated at 3,888,000.

Alaska, formerly Russian America, was purchased by the United States in 1867. It comprises the north-west angle of the continent, as far as the 141st meridian west from London, with a narrow strip of coast reaching as far south as 55½° of north latitude. It occupies a surface of about 500,000 square miles, of which the useful soil probably does not constitute a tenth part. There are a number of posts or factories stationed along the coast for conducting the trade in furs, which give these possessions their main value. New Archangel, in latitude 57.3° and longitude 135.20° west, is the head establishment. Owing to the rigor of the climate, this portion of America can never support more than a very limited population.

Hayti, called formerly Hispaniola and St. Domingo, was a colony belonging partly to France and partly to Spain, till 1791, when the blacks rose in arms, killed a number of whites and expelled the rest. The attempt of England in 1793, and of France in 1801, to conquer the island, both failed, and Hayti was at length acknowledged as an independent state, by all the great powers, including France. The island, which contains less than 20,000 square miles, is remarkably fertile; but its climate, like that of the West Indies generally, is rather unhealthful. The population is estimated at 708,000, and it is almost entirely composed of blacks and mulattoes. The island formed one state till 1844, when the eastern or Spanish portion revolted, and established its independence. It is now the republic of Dominica, or San Domingo, ruled by a president: the western portion, retaining the name of Hayti, constituted an empire, until 1859, when Faustin Soulouque was expelled and a republic proclaimed. After long negotiations, the French government agreed in 1838 to acknowledge the independence of Hayti, on condition of the latter paying 60,000,000 of francs, by small annual instalments continued for 30 years. The money was destined chiefly to indemnify the French proprietors who were chased from the island in 1791.

The multifarious nature of the subject prevents us from attempting any description of the West India colonies, insular and continental. The islands have been variously denominated, but the most convenient division seems to be the following:-1. The Great Antilles comprehending Cuba, Hayti, Jamaica, and Porto Rico; 2d. The Small Antilles, extending in a semicircle from Porto Rico to the coast of Guiana; 3. The Bahama Isles, about 500 in number, but only a small number of which are inhabited.

The British colonies are 18 in number, viz., 15 *insular*, Jamaica, Antigua, Barbadoes, Dominica, Grenada, Montserrat, Nevis, St. Kitts, St. Lucia, St. Vincents, Tobago, Tortola, Trinidad, Bahamas, Bermuda; and

3 *continental*, Demerara, Berbice, Honduras. The colonies contain a population of 1,384,000, of whom probably four-fifths are persons of color. In British Guiana there are 162,000 inhabitants.

The population of Cuba is given at 1,396,500; that of Porto Rico as 583,300. According to a recent Spanish writer, the different classes stand thus in Cuba: Whites and creoles 42 per cent., slaves 43, free persons of color 15 per cent.

The French colonies in the West Indies include Martinique, Guadaloupe, and some smaller isles, and on the continent Guiana. According to recent authority, the population of these colonies is 312,100 of whom about 195,000 are slaves.

The Dutch have Surinam on the continent, with the islands of Curaçoa, St. Eustatius, and St. Martin. The collective population of these possessions, is 192,500, of whom probably three-fourths are slaves.

The Danes have the small islands of Santa Cruz, St. Thomas, and St. Martin, containing a population of 38,300, of whom five-sixths are slaves. St. Bartholomew, another of the lesser Antilles, belongs to Sweden; population, 2,900.

In fine, the population of North America, according to the latest and best authorities is 46,671,600; of Central America, 2,690,600; and of South America, 28,072,600. The area of the entire continent of America with the islands is given on a previous page (p. 2.) as 14,950,000; other authorities make it about 15,700,000.

The American animals belonging to the Cuvierian Division of *Vertebrata* are very numerous. It is true that some of the larger quadrupeds have no living types in the new world. There are none to compare in size with the elephant, the rhinoceros, the hippopotamus, the giraffe, or the camel; but fossil remains of the mastodon, megatherium and megalonyx will vie in size with the largest quadrupeds of the old world.

In the class of Mammifera, America is very rich, as the following synopsis of the species in each order will show:— Quadrumana, 59; Carnivora, 89; Marsupialia, 21; Rodentia, 71; Edentata, 16; Pachydermata, 6; Ruminantia, 22; Cetacea, 18: — total, 302. Some of these are common to the old and the new worlds, and a few have been introduced by Europeans; but several, which were at one period considered as identically the same in both continents, have by more recent investigations been found to be only allied species. Some of the larger animals of Eastern Asia and North-Western America as the reindeer, make annual migrations over the Arctic Seas from one continent to the other; and many of the mammals inhabiting the sea no doubt may be considered as identical.

The quadrumana or ape tribes are found only at the southern extremity of the Continent. Among the carnivora are found the grizzly, white and other kinds of bears, dogs, foxes, skunks, weasel, panther, jaguar, seal, and walrus. Of the marsupialia, every kind of opossum is found. The rodentia includes the squirrel, marmot, beaver, porcupine, hare and mouse tribe. Of the edentata there are the sloth, armadillo, and ant-eater. Beside these there are vast fossil skeletons of the megatherium and megalonyx. The pachydermata include the boar and horse (both imported) and the peccari and tapir. In addition, we may note that America abounds in the fossil remains of the mastodon. Of the ruminantia there are numerous varieties of the deer, sheep, goat, bison, common ox (imported) and antelope. Among the cetacea may be noted the manati, dolphin, cachelot, and several varieties of the whale. The birds of America are very numerous in almost every great family, and between 500 and 600 species in North America and about the same number in South America have been described. Some, like the humming bird, toucan, wild turkey, etc., are peculiar to the new world. Serpents are unusually numerous, although only a small proportion are venomous. The rattlesnake is considered by far the most deadly of all. Of the testudinata there are a great variety; of the saurians, there are the cayman and alligator, and of the ranidae, the frog and toad. The varieties of fish in America are very numerous, including the salmon, sturgeon, mackerel, shad, trout, and many others.

The European animals which have been naturalized in America are the cow, horse, ass, hog, sheep, goat, dog; and these have multiplied to such a degree as to exceed the native quadrupeds greatly in numbers. The warm climate of the tropical parts of America has produced considerable changes in the habits and physicial qualities of most of these species. The hog, which generally wanders in the woods, and lives on the wild fruits and roots found there, has lost in a great measure its usual domestic habits, and assumed the character of the wild boar. The black cattle also, roaming at large in a country enentirely uninclosed, are found to fall off unless they receive a certain quantity of salt, in their food, which in some cases they procure from plants, in others from brackish water. By distributing salt to them at a certain regular hour, they are taught to assemble at their owner's residence, and are thus kept from becoming wild. The ass has undergone little alteration in America, and it has nowhere become wild. It is otherwise with the horse. Numbers of these animals in a wild state exist in Colombia, and many other parts of America, both South and North, where they wander over the plains and savannahs in troops. It is observed that the color of the animals living in this state returns to that bay chestnut which is considered as characteristic of the natural wild horse. The sheep thrives and multiplies in the temperate regions of America, and together with the dog and goat show little if any tendency to withdraw from their companionship with mankind.

NORTH AMERICA.

GREENLAND.

GREENLAND is the name given to that large insular body of land lying to the north-east of North America and for the most part comprehended within the Arctic circle. In early times it was supposed to form a part of the American continent; but the discoveries of modern navigators have proved, what indeed the very idea of a north-west passage from the Atlantic to the Pacific Ocean supposed, its insularity. And the latest discoveries, have morever, shown, or all but proved, the entire separation of the lands on the west side of Baffin's Bay from those of the opposite shores, so as to limit Greenland to the country on the eastern side of that great channel. From Cape Farewell in lat., 59° 49′ N., it stretches on the west side in a north-north-westerly direction through Smith's Sound, and then more easterly into a high northern latitude. On the other side the Greenland coast runs first north-north-easterly, then north-easterly, and finally (so far as yet traced), in a northerly direction, bending eastward in the 75th and 76th parallels of latitude. It expands from Cape Farewell, the southern point, up to latitude 70°, where it attains a width of about 600 miles, which is pretty evenly maintained to the northern extent of our researches on the eastern side. This side of Greenland has been denominated East or Old Greenland, the other West Greenland.

Greenland was first discovered by an Icelander named Gunbiörn, who was driven by storm upon this coast, about the beginning of the tenth century, and carried back intelligence of its existence to Iceland. Towards the end of the same century, an Icelandic chief named Eric Raude, or Eric the Red, having killed another powerful chief, and being obliged to quit the country, determined to follow up Gunbiörn's discovery. After having spent two or three years in exploring the country, he returned to Iceland, giving an exaggerated account of the freshness and verdure of the country, which he called Greenland. In consequence of this, a fleet of twenty-five sail was equipped and sent out, laden with persons of both sexes, cattle, and other necessaries for forming a settlement. Only about the half of the vessels reached their destination; but other adventurers setting out, not only from Iceland, but from Norway, the Orkneys, and other islands, in a few years a considerable colony was formed, and a regular trade established. Christianity was introduced about the eleventh century, and churches and convents were built. The colonists, though compelled to lead a life of severe privation and hardship, continued to increase and to extend to the north. The zeal of the early Scandinavians in pushing their settlements is attested by a curious monument discovered in 1824. It consists of a stone carved with Runic characters, which was found standing erect in the ground on the Island of Kingiktorsoak, under the parallel of 73°. The date on the monument is April, 1135.

For some centuries commercial intercourse

was kept up between Greenland and Norway; but about the beginning of the fifteenth century all intercourse ceased, and the colonists were cut off from the rest of mankind. Some 200 years afterwards, in 1721, Hans Egede, a clergyman from Vaagen, in Norway, accompanied by his wife and family, left his native country to settle as a missionary in Greenland. He landed at Baals River in N. Lat. 64°, and called the place Godthaab, or Good Hope. Since that time the Danes have established numerous settlements upon the western coast of Greenland, lying between 60° and 73° N. Lat. The whale fisheries have greatly contributed to the advancement of the colonies; and from the intimate intercourse which is now kept up with Europeans, their condition is at present more flourishing than at any former period.

There are, at present, thirteen Danish colonies in Greenland, besides some smaller establishments termed factories. For administrative purposes they are formed into two inspectorships, called respectively North and South Greenland. The former, which lies north of lat. 67°, comprises seven colonies, with a population between 3000 and 4000; the latter, which lies south of lat. 67°, comprises six colonies, with a population of 6000. The number of Danes is only 250; the rest are natives. The principal occupation of the inhabitants is the seal fishery, which is carried on extensively and successfully.

During the reign of Queen Elizabeth, Frobisher, a distinguished English navigator, made several voyages to this quarter of the globe. In 1577 he discovered the straits which have been called after him. In the year 1585, Davis, another able seaman, came in sight of high land, which he called Mount Raleigh, supposed to lie somewhere on the west of the straits bearing the discoverer's name. In 1610 Hudson discovered the straits and the bay which are called after him, in which he experienced a disastrous termination to his useful career. To certain rocky islands lying about the 64th parallel, he gave the name of Isles of God's Mercy. He also discovered two capes, one of which was called Digge's Cape, and the other Willoughby Cape. In 1616, Baffin, another navigator of note, discovered the large expanse northward of the Strait of Davis, now known as Baffin's Bay. Sailing in a little vessel only of about fifty-five tons burthen, he effected one of the most extraordinary voyages on record. Under the imperfect appliances of the age for navigation, Baffin, with one small vessel, circumnavigated to Smith's Sound, on the north of that bay or sea which, northward of "Hope Sanderson, the furthest land Master Davis reached, lying between 72 and 73 degrees," was an utterly unknown region,—thus adding some 1100 miles of discoveries, reckoned by the mere coasting line, to the knowledge of these ice-encumbered shores. For 200 years from the time of Baffin, knowledge of this great inlet had not been advanced. In the year 1818, however, the British Admiralty fitted out two expeditions for exploration, and especially for discovery of the north-west passage. We have not room for the details of these and subsequent expeditions to the ice-bound regions of the north in the neighborhood of the pole. We must refer the reader to the published accounts of the voyages of Captains Ross, Parry, Scoresby, and others, and particularly of our eminent fellow countryman Dr. E. K. Kane, 1853–55.

The mineral productions of the Arctic regions are of considerable interest. Only the shores of the country, however, have been examined, the interior remaining unexplored, on account of the perpetual ice and snow under which it is buried. The rocks, as far as they have been examined, are principally of the primitive formation, consisting of granite, gneiss, mica slate, hornblende slate, syenite, and clay slate. Among the secondary rocks is found the secondary sandstone, or coal formation, and containing impressions of plants. Specimens of the coal formation, collected by Captain Scoresby, were found to contain impressions of tropical plants; a very interesting fact, as connected with the change of temperature which the earth appears to have undergone. The most northern part of the coast of East Greenland examined by Captain Clavering was mountainous, and principally composed of trap rocks; lower down Captain Scoresby found the primitive rocks the prevailing ones. The west coast of Greenland is similar to that above described. The elevated parts of the country are for the most part covered with snow or ice; and in summer, although rivers appear, which are fed by the melting of the ice and snow, they are few and inconsiderable in size. There are also lakes, some of which are of considerable magnitude, and supplied from the same source as the rivers. Copper-ore is said to be abundant in various parts; and plumbago, iron-ore, and tin-stone, are found. The lands bordering on Baffin's Bay, and the islands lying at the northern extremity of it, are not much elevated above the level of the sea, the average height being 800 feet, and the highest elevations seldom exceeding 1500 feet.

The vegetation of a soil which for two-thirds of the year is bound together by intense frost and covered with snow several feet thick, cannot be supposed to present much variety or beauty. Even the hardy race of pine trees, if they make their appearance at all within the Arctic Circle, dwindle into stunted shrubs which only rise a few feet above the ground, throwing out lateral branches. But to supply this deficiency, and afford to the Esquimaux the means of making their arms and utensils, considerable quantities of drift timber are frequently thrown up on the barren shores. The most abundant plants are mosses and lichens; and these are not only copiously produced, but they possess a nutritious and salutary quality, which does not characterize those of the same species that grow in more temperate climates. Mushrooms and ferns also find the means of subsistence here; and there is a thick tufted juicy plant, of extreme fecundity, emphatically called scurvy-grass, on account of its acting as an antidote to scurvy. The different species of sorrel, are found flourishing under the snow at the very furthest limits of vegetation. Animal life is confined to the whale, seal, walrus, polar bear, reindeer, etc. The walrus and seal afford food and clothing, as well as fuel and light, to the inhabitants. Sea fowl are very abundant in the summer, as the auk, petrel, gull, eider-duck, etc. In the winter, the natives, thickly covered with skins, remain generally immured in their miserable huts; and crowding around the stove or lamp, contrive as far as possible, to doze away the long and tedious night. The inside of the hut, all openings in the walls of which are carefully stopped to exclude the piercing cold, becomes covered with a crust of ice; and if for an instant an aperture be made so as to admit the external air, the moisture within is precipitated in a shower of snow. After the sun has appeared above the horizon, the half-famished inhabitants venture forth in search of food about the shores of the sea. In June and July the sun is always above the horizon. The heat thus greatly augmented, gradually dissolves the perennial ice. The icy covering of the ocean breaks, and, separated into vast masses, is driven about, dissevered and dispersed by the winds and currents. In particular situations the snow and ice of successive years are cast into immense glaciers, the foundations of which being sapped by the sea, break off in prodigious masses, and floating far into the ocean, present to the mariner a bright but fearful spectacle, reflecting in varied tints the rays of light, yet threatening, if come in contact with, to crush to pieces the stoutest vessel. In these high latitudes, although the summer is short, the temperature is frequently oppressively sultry on land, which causes great humidity in the atmosphere, a characteristic of the arctic regions.

The Moravians have three settlements in South Greenland, Hernnhut, Lichtenfels, and Frederick-Stahl. All the other portions of the coast are under the charge of the Lutherans, whose missions enjoy the direct patronage of the government.

CANADA.

THE British Dominion of Canada, lying diagonally along the frontier of the United States from N. E. to S. W., is computed to be about 1500 miles in length from east to west, and from 200 to 400 in extent from north to south. Its area, according to the latest authorities, is estimated at 377,000 square miles. Formerly, the country was divided into two provinces, Upper and Lower Canada; by an act of Parliament, however, in 1841, it was constituted one province, with one legislature. The old terms, nevertheless, are to some extent kept up for electoral, judicial and other purposes.

Canada may be said to comprise one vast valley, through which the St. Lawrence takes its course, issuing from Lake Superior and flowing successively through Lakes Huron, Erie, and Ontario, until it falls into the ocean after a course of 2000 miles. This immense valley is on each side encompassed by different mountain ranges, sometimes nearly approaching the water, and at other times receding into the interior, and thus forming extensive plains, for the most part alluvial, and suitable for nearly every description of produce. The high table-land along the northern boundary of this valley separates the streams which take their rise within it and flow into its basin from those that take their rise in the almost unknown territory beyond, and which fall into Hudson's Bay. The high land along the southern boundary of the valley separates the streams which flow northwards into its basin from those that have their course southwards towards the Atlantic and Mississippi.

Commencing at the northern shore of the St. Lawrence, towards the mouth of that river, where the width is 90 miles, we find one of the walls of this vast valley which constitutes Canada rising boldly in mountainous form, close to the river, and continuing thus to form its rugged bank for upwards of 100 miles. One of the most remarkable of the heights of the northern bank is Cape Tourment, 30 miles below Quebec, overhanging the brink of the river; a still bolder and grander height is Cape Diamond, which rises to an elevation of 400 feet, and is crowned by the Citadel of Quebec. The city, overlooking a very excellent harbor, is about 400 miles from the mouth of the river. The St. Lawrence here contracts in width to about half a mile, with bold, rocky banks on either side. The general character of the country along the south side of the river, from Cape Rozière at its mouth to within 100 miles of Quebec, is rather rugged and hilly. Above Quebec, to the line of 45° N. Lat. (which is the southern boundary of Lower Canada) there is along the river's bank an extensive and fertile plain, and many prosperous and populous settlements. Montreal is in Lower Canada, nearly 200 miles above Quebec; it is situated upon an island of the same name, just below the confluence of the Ottawa and the St. Lawrence, and is at the head of ship navigation. Beyond, there is a great chain of river, lake, and canal navigation, which extends westward to Fond du Lac and Chicago, a distance of about 1400 miles. Montreal is the largest city in Canada, having a population of nearly 100,000.

Upper Canada, commencing about 80 miles up the St. Lawrence from Montreal on the north side of the river, extends for about 100 miles to Kingston, at the foot of Lake Ontario, and thence along the north shores of the great lakes, stretching to the head waters of the streams which flow into Lake Superior. The course of its navigable waters exceeds 2000 miles, and the shores of the great valley, through which these waters take their course embrace a country which has been aptly styled "the Garden of North

America." That portion of Upper Canada which has been set apart and divided for settlement, extends from its extreme eastern point, and reaches along the northern shore of the St. Lawrence, and upwards along the lakes to the shores of Lake Huron, — a direct course of about 700 miles. The breadth of settled country towards the north may be said to vary from 50 to 80 miles. Throughout the whole of this tract the soil is excellent, and is not surpassed by any other part of the American continent. It consists, generally speaking, of a fine dark loam, mixed with a vegetable mould, but it is in a great measure so varied as to present soils adapted to almost every species of produce. From the commencement of Upper Canada to the head of the Bay of Quinte, on Lake Ontario, the land is spread out into an almost uniform level of great beauty, which rises only a few feet from the banks of the St. Lawrence. It is in every direction well watered by numerous streams, which are generally navigable for boats and canoes, and at the same time present the most desirable situations for the erection of machinery. Farther into the interior, along the course of the Ottawa, which flows into the St. Lawrence a short distance above Montreal, and between the Ottawa and Lake Ontario, the face of the country is, in parts, here diversified by ridges and bold heights, and also by numerous streams and inland lakes. The Rideau canal, a work constructed by the government for military purposes, passing through this part of the interior from the town of Bytown, on the Ottawa, 120 miles above Montreal, through the country to Kingston—a distance of 135 miles—is almost one continued chain of natural lakes and streams. The chief link of these waters is Rideau lake, 24 miles in length, forming the summit level of the canal, and being 280 feet above the level of the Ottawa river, and 150 feet above Lake Ontario.

Lake Ontario, receives the waters of the upper lakes from the Niagara river, and discharges them into the St. Lawrence nearly 800 miles from the mouth of that river. The height of this lake above the sea is 232 feet. It is 180 miles in length, 50 miles in breadth, and 470 miles in circumference. It possesses several excellent harbors; and from its great depth of 500 feet, compared with the two lakes above it, it is not so easily moved by storms as Lake Erie, while it is quite exempt from the shallows, or *flats*, as they are called, of Lake St. Clair. All along the north shore of Lake Ontario, a distance of 180 miles, one extensive fertile plain presents itself, now and then agreeably sloping to the very edge of the lake, and bearing evidences of successful cultivation and progress. Several thriving towns are growing up rapidly along the shores of Ontario, the chief of which are Kingston at the foot of the lake, Toronto, thirty-five miles from the head, and Hamilton at the extreme head. Toronto, which is finely situated, is the largest city of Upper Canada, population nearly 51,000. The generally level stretch of well-cultivated plain which forms this northern shore of Lake Ontario is only partially broken by an inconsiderable ridge which runs through it, and which, coursing around the head of the lake, and crossing into the United States at the Falls of Niagara, forms the commencement of the extensive and fertile table-land which stretches westward from Lake Ontario, and, situated between Lakes Erie and Huron, forms the great western peninsula of Upper Canada.

The settled parts of this peninsula embrace about one-half of the settled parts of Upper Canada; and it is estimated to have at present a cultivated surface of upwards of 9,000,000 acres. The entire district has been styled "the Garden of Upper Canada." Hamilton, situated at the extreme head of Lake Ontario, nearly 1000 miles into the interior of Canada from the mouth of the St. Lawrence, is the chief port of this valuable country westward. Its situation is commodious and picturesque, being at the head of a fine bay, locked in by a strip of land from the main lake, with the exception of a navigable passage for steam and sailing vessels

Following the chain of waters westward, the traveler approaches the Niagara river, 33 miles long, connecting Lakes Ontario and Erie. The town of Niagara is situated near the mouth of the river; and the village of Queenstown at the foot of the table-land which stretches westward, is about four miles further up. Queenstown is about nine miles from the celebrated falls, and about 20 miles from Lake Erie. The fall of Niagara, which have been celebrated by all travelers as one of the greatest wonders of nature, are occasioned by the configuration of the country, which is one vast plain extending from the Ohio and Lake Erie westward beyond the Mississippi, and eastward to the Alleghany mountains. This plain after passing Lake Erie to the north, rapidly descends 340 feet to another plain, in the level of which lies Lake Ontario; and it is from the higher level of Lake Erie that the river Niagara is precipitated with such tremendous violence into the plain below. The rock over which the Niagara falls is in the form of an irregular semi-circle about three-quarters of a mile in extent. The river is here divided into two by Goat Island, the lower extremity of which is perpendicular, and in a line with the rock over which the water is precipitated. The cataract on the Canada side is called the Horse-Shoe, from its peculiar form, or the Great Fall; and the other, towards the south shore of the river, the American Fall. The perpendicular height of the Fall is about 160 feet, though it is quite probable that by a gradual retrocession, it will become much less in the course of a few years. The obstruction to navigation caused by the falls is obviated by the Welland canal, which unites Lakes Ontario and Erie, for the passage of vessels.

Lake Erie, which is situated 565 feet above the sea, and 333 above the level of Lake Ontario, is about 265 miles in length, from 30 to 60 miles in breadth, and between 600 and 700 miles in circumference. Its mean depth is 120 feet, being the shallowest of all the great lakes, and most easily frozen. Its waters are also, on account of its shallowness, more readily agitated by storms, causing its navigation to be therefore more dangerous during stormy weather. The shores of this lake present features very similar to those of Lake Ontario; the banks of Lake Erie being generally bolder and more elevated, and composed chiefly of clay and sand. The more fertile parts are at some distance from the banks, throughout the extensive plain of table-land beyond. There are several good natural harbors along the shore, formed chiefly by the mouths of deep creeks or streams, and protected from the action of storms and the current of the lake by strong projecting piers. The upper part of Lake Erie is distinguished by many beautiful islands, the largest of which is Pele, on which there is a lighthouse, and several farms. The shores along the upper part of the lake, especially towards the mouth of the Detroit river, have a smiling and luxuriant aspect. From the head of Lake Erie to the foot of Lake Huron, is a distance of between 80 and 90 miles, through a country of unsurpassed fertility. The Detroit river, about 27 miles in length, is interspersed with many islands, and several towns are situated along the Canada side of this river. Opposite Windsor, towards the upper part of the river, and where the banks narrow to about three-quarters of a mile, is Detroit, the chief city in the State of Michigan.

Lake St. Clair, which forms the connecting link, by means of the St. Clair and Detroit rivers, between Lakes Huron, Michigan, and Erie, is the smallest of all the lakes, and exceedingly shallow for the larger class of vessels passing through it. It is from 20 to 30 miles in length, and about the same in breadth. Its average depth is about 20 feet, but the principal channel used by vessels passing through it is much shallower, especially in dry seasons when the mud of its *flats* is stirred to the surface not unfrequently by large vessels.

Lake Huron, which is about 1000 miles in circumference, is the second in point of size of the great lakes, yielding only in this respect to Lake Superior. The surface of Lake Huron is about 30 feet above the level of Lake Erie, and 595 feet above the level of the Atlantic. The length may be estimated at 250 miles, and its breadth 160 miles, inclusive of the Georgian Bay, a large wing of the lake, extending along the north-eastern shore for a distance of about 100 miles. The mean depth of Lake Huron is 900 feet, and its greatest depth 1000 feet near the west shore. This lake is said to contain the almost incredible number of 32,000 islands, principally along the northern shore and at the north-western end, varying in size from mere rocky reefs and pinnacles to large and cultivable islands. The Great Manitoulin, the largest of the islands, is upwards of 75 miles in length, and varies in width from 3 to 23 miles. The waters of the lake are remarkably pure, clear, and cold; in these respects resembling Lake Superior. The surface of Lake Huron is about 32 feet lower than that of Lake Superior, and it is very nearly as deep as that lake. Numerous streams descend on all sides into the lake; and among its rivers may be mentioned the Maitland, Severn, and River Francais. The lake is rather subject to storms, and is deficient in good natural harbors: but it is admirably situated with respect to the other great lakes, and furnishes means of communication, through railroads and canals, in every direction.

The river or strait of St. Mary, connecting Lake Huron with Lake Superior, is between 30 and 40 miles in length, the rapids of which approach within about 18 miles of Lake Superior. The region in this direction seems much less fertile; the soil in many parts is light and sandy, while the lands close upon the banks lie for the most part low and flat. Here, however, is the chief seat of the great copper district of America; and the mines in Canada, along the shores of Lakes Huron and Superior, are perhaps entitled to rank among the most valuable resources of this great country.

Lake Superior is upwards of 400 miles in length and 130 in breadth, and the main entrance to the lake is marked by two rocky headlands, one upon either shore several miles apart. The shores of the lake, which are even now imperfectly explored, already prove to be abundant in mineral resources. Many associations are engaged in mining the seemingly inexhaustible treasures of virgin copper, which are found along the shores of this lake as well as Lake Huron. Lake Superior, which is the largest sheet of fresh water on the face of the globe, is the most remarkable of the great American lakes, not only from its magnitude, but also from its being in the most valuable mining district in North America, with the exception only of the gold deposits of California. The whole coast of the lake is rock-bound. Mountain masses of considerable elevation in some places rear themselves from the immediate shore, while steep precipices and frightful crags oppose themselves to the surges of the waters. The northern or Canadian shore of the lake is the most precipitous, and consequently most dangerous to the navigator. Good harbors for vessels of moderate capacity are comparatively few, but there are abundance of coves or boat-harbors formed by the countless indentations of the rocky coast. In remarkable contrast to Lake Huron, which is thickly studded with islands, there are very few islands in Lake Superior. The cold air from the lake, affects the vegetation near it shores, but further inland the temperature more resembles that of the settled parts of Canada. The native forest trees, and also the flowering plants, as well as the agricultural produce where clearings have been made, are believed to afford satisfactory evidence on this point. The forests are filled with excellent timber for building purposes; the white and yellow pines, particularly, being of large dimensions. The importance to Canada of the varied resources of the shores of the great lake, as well as its very valuable fisheries, can hardly yet be fully appreciated. The mines with their inexhaustible riches of silver and copper, were only discovered so lately as 1844; and although geological surveys have been made both by the United States and Canadian governments, yet much remains to be ascertained respecting this region.

The soil and climate of Canada are such that the country produces a great variety of grains and fruits. Besides wheat, barley, oats, rye, turnips, potatoes, hemp, flax, hops, which are all raised in abundance, Canada grows tobacco, rice, maize or Indian corn, etc. The full and steady heat of the summer matures with surprising rapidity the most valuable productions. The finest melons are grown in abundance in the open ground in Canada; and in some seasons peaches are so plentiful in the south-western parts of the country, along the shores of Lake Erie and the Detroit river, that they have seen sold for twenty-five cents per bushel. The vine is also cultivated in open gardens around parts of those favored shores, and grapes of perfect size and excellent flavor are produced. Apples, pears, plums, cherries, raspberries, currants, and strawberries are all grown in every part of Canada in perfection and abundance. Wild fruits also abound in great variety in the woods and elsewhere all over Canada. Almost all kinds of vegetables necessary or desirable for the table, grow luxuriantly in Canada, and are cultivated with very little trouble. Flowers grow in great variety and in rich profusion, favored by the soft genial atmosphere of a Canadian summer, and one of the most kindly soils. The woods in many places are literally carpeted with them. The forests of Canada abound in the finest and largest trees, adapted to almost every variety of purposes, useful or ornamental. Amongst the monarchs of these forests are the white and red pine, of which large quantities are annually imported into Britain from the St. Lawrence. Individual trees of the white pine are frequently found measuring 100 feet to the first branch, and occasionally trees reach 200 feet in height. The importance of these immense forests both to Canada and England, and even to the northern parts of the United States, is now beginning to be fully appreciated. In 1852, according to the official returns, the products of the Canadian forests exported from the country were valued at nearly $7,000,000. In 1851 it was computed that no less than 200,000 tons of sawn timber had been exported from Canada for the supply of the United States market on the Hudson river. Of the various districts of Canada where the clearing or cutting down of the forests is being now carried on most extensively, the valley of the river Ottawa may be classed among the first.

The two most noted and mischievous animals of the Canadian forests are the bear and the wolf. Both of these, however, now are almost exclusively confined to the more remote and unsettled parts of the country. In order to exterminate wolves, a premium is paid by government for the head of each animal presented to a local magistrate. The beaver is now seldom found within reach of white settlements. Foxes, silver-gray, red, and black raccoons, otters, martins, minks, and musk-rats still remain in diminished numbers. Abundance of squirrels also is found. The most valuable game in Canada are the elk and the stag. Wild turkeys of large size were, several years ago, comparatively plentiful in the western parts of Canada; and are still found there, but in diminished numbers. Among other animals known in Canada, besides several species of grouse, may be mentioned the woodcock, snipe, plover, and a species of hare. Pigeons are killed by thousands during the spring and autumn. Of ducks there are many varieties, and several of them very beautiful. These are found in large numbers in the marshy parts of lakes and rivers. The smaller kinds of birds are in many instances remarkable for beauty of plumage. In the list of these, native and migratory, may be mentioned the jay, several species of woodpecker, the scarlet tanager, bluebird, blackbird, the

American goldfinch, the kingfisher, humming-bird, etc. Among the finny tribes in the rivers and lakes, sturgeon is caught in the Canadian waters, frequently weighing from 80 to 100 lbs.; and the lake or salmon trout varies usually in size from 10 to 40 lbs. Large quantities of the finest species of the lake-trout family, known by the name of the siskawit, prized chiefly on account of its fatness, are annually caught by the fishermen of Lake Superior. This fish weighs from 5 to 20 lbs. Very fine salmon are also abundant in the waters of the St. Lawrence and the lakes. The smaller rivers and streams teem with the speckled trout. Perhaps the chief favorites of the Canadian waters are the white fish and maskelonge. The white fish is much esteemed for delicacy and richness of flavor. Among other varieties of fish we may mention pike, pickerel, bass, perch, and herrings. The fisheries of Canada are constantly growing in importance from year to year. Many thousands of barrels of salmon, white fish, and herrings are annually exported, at present, chiefly to the United States. Mackerel are also largely caught in the Gulf of St. Lawrence.

In regard to the extent and value of the cultivated land and agricultural products of Canada, its important and increasing trade, especially since the abolition of the British corn laws, and the relieving the colonies from the injurious effects of the navigation laws, as well as the numerous public works which display the energy and enterprize of the people, it is impossible to enter into details, or present statistical tables. We must content ourselves with giving a brief *résumé* of the political and civil history of Canada from its discovery to the present time.

If we except the ancient Scandinavian voyages, the discovery of the American continent may be ascribed to John and Sebastian Cabot, who, under the auspices of Henry VII., visited the coast of Labrador in June, 1497, nearly four months before Columbus came in sight of the main-land. To Gaspar Corterea., the next voyager in the course of the Cabots, is said to be due the discovery of the Gulf of St. Lawrence. Other parts of the country were from time to time discovered by various expeditions, French and English; but not until 1535 were these attended by any material results of extended knowledge of the country. In that year Jacques Cartier, under the auspices of Francis I. of France, entering the St. Lawrence, ascended the river to the spot where Montreal now stands, where there was then a circular Indian village surrounded by palisades, and situated amidst cultivated fields of Indian corn. In the year 1608 these and other discoveries were first turned to some practical account, when Champlain laid the foundation of the city of Quebec, and a French colony was established in the country. The settlement, however, continued to maintain a precarious existence, its administration being committed chiefly to trading companies, whose object was immediate gain, or to military governors who involved the colonists in perpetual feuds. For a century and a half the history of French colonization in the New World, occasionally relieved by the efforts and achievements of able and good men, is little else than a mere chronicle of bloody and harassing warfare with the native Indians, and latterly with the rival settlements of Great Britain. Some slight improvement, indeed, took place in the prospects of the colony in 1663, when Louis XIV., under the direction of his minister Colbert, erected Canada into a royal government with the laws and usages of France.

The treaty of Utrecht, in 1713, gave a short peace to Canada, and enabled the governor, Marquis de Vaudreuil, to direct his attention to the improvement of the province, the trade and agriculture of which continued to prosper under his wise and vigilant administration. War again breaking out between Great Britain and France, the colonies were involved in hostilities. It had been the policy of France to

Painted by | Entered according to act of Congress A.D. 1868 by Johnson, Fry & Co. in the clerk's office of the district court of the southern district of N. York. | Alonzo Chappel.

DEATH OF GENERAL WOLFE.

hem in the English settlements in North America by a chain of forts extending from the Gulf of St. Lawrence to the Gulf of Mexico. The jealousy of the English being kindled by this and other circunstances, it was resolved, in the course of the war, which was begun in 1755, to send an overwhelming force to North America, for the purpose of expelling the French from that quarter of the world. The Army under General Amherst having, however, made indifferent progress, an expedition against Quebec was despatched from England in 1759, the chief command of which was confided to Major-General Wolfe, who landing above Quebec on the 13th September, 1759, carried the heights of Abraham, and defeated the French under the Marquis of Montcalm, who, along with Wolfe himself, was killed in the action. Quebec submitted in a few days, and soon afterwards Montreal and the whole country, which was finally ceded to Great Britain by the peace of 1763. So much had the country suffered during the French sway, chiefly through the combined ravages of war and want, that in 1759 the population had only reached 65,000. The Roman Catholic religion was confirmed in all its rights and privileges to the French settlers; and the French laws were retained. The original inhabitants, thus conciliated, became the faithful subjects of the new sovereign; and when all the other American colonies rebelled against the tyranny of the mother country, they submitted to the imposition of the stamp act, and even took up arms to defend the country against an inroad of the American forces in 1775 under Generals Montgomery and Arnold. In 1791 the colony received a constitution, and was divided into Upper and Lower Canada; and the first parliament was held in Upper Canada in 1796. While the country was advancing in a career of prosperity, the war of 1812 broke out between the United States and Great Britain, and the frontier of Canada again became the scene of military operations. In the summer of that year the American forces under General Hull entered Upper Canada, and through that officer's incompetency, or, as some said, "treason," the greater part of Hull's troops were made prisoners by General Brock. Another body of American troops collecting on the Niagara frontier, passed over into Canada in October, and were after a severe struggle at the heights of Queenstown, compelled to surrender to General Brock, who was unfortunately slain in the action. The Americans renewed their attempts on the Niagara frontier with no better success than before. Early in 1813, however, they succeeded in taking possession of York and Niagara, and shortly afterwards the British were foiled in an attack on Sackett's harbor. In January, 1813, the American general, Winchester, was made prisoner, and a large part of his troops murdered by the Indian allies of the British. To counterbalance this success, Commodore Perry captured all the British vessels on Lake Erie; and General Proctor was defeated near Detroit. The British were consequently obliged to retire, and an American army advanced in three divisions towards Montreal; but no particular success attended their movement and the campaign closed. The campaign of 1814 was decidedly favorable to the Americans. They were repelled at first in attempting to invade Canada. But the capture of Fort Erie by General Brown was an important success; whilst Sir George Prevost, who attacked Plattsburg with a force of 11,000 men, was repulsed with great loss; and the British squadron fitted out on Lake Champlain was defeated by the American force under Commodore Macdonough. The British were making great exertions to recover their ascendancy both by sea and land, when the treaty of Ghent, signed in December, 1814, happily terminated the war, in which the loyalty of the Canadians, both of British and French extraction, was nobly vindicated.

The subsequent history of Canada was chequered by a course of dissensions between the provincial houses of assembly in Upper and Lower Canada and the respective executive governments, in which the home government also shared. The working of the system of provincial government, especially in the executive departments, had ceased to harmonize with public feeling, and acted in opposition to the expressed wishes of the popular branch of the legislature. Various abuses had crept into the administration, which were fostered by the high functionaries who held irresponsible offices, who guided the counsels of the successive governors more to their own advantage than to the interests of the province. The control and appropriation of the revenues and public offices were urgently demanded in Lower Canada, and were in part conceded; but many of the grievances remaining unredressed, disaffected leaders made use of them to goad the people to the brink of insurrection in 1836; the concessions of Lord Gosford and the home authorities being deemed insufficient. The disaffected of Lower Canada were joined by the malcontents of the upper province, and in the following year the whole of Canada broke out into open rebellion. On the 6th November, 1837, the city of Montreal was disturbed by a body of 250 members of a secret association called *Les Fils de la Liberté.* In various other parts of the country serious outrages were perpetrated. In the neighborhood of Toronto, a large body of insurgents, who were organizing an attack upon the town, were routed and dispersed by a force of militia under Sir Francis Head. Their leader, after many adventures, escaped into the United States in female attire. The influence of the disaffected had in the meantime extended itself across the American frontier, and numerous "sympathizers" passed into Canada with the view of assisting the rebels. This outbreak, which continued throughout 1837 and 1838, elicited plainly the loyalty of the great majority of the colonists; and as they were now in possession of the means to repel any assault, the numbers of the insurgents gradually melted away, and tranquillity was again restored. It was some time, however, before the rancor of party feeling was allayed and the colony once more assumed an aspect of progress and prosperity. The appointment of the Earl of Durham as governor-general and high commisioner in 1838, for the adjustment of the affairs of the colony—followed by that of Mr. Poulett Thompson, afterwards Lord Sydenham, in 1839—the success and vigor of his government—and the prudent administrations of subsequent governors, aided by discreet and able counsels of colonial ministers in the home government, together with the late recognition of colonial control of internal affairs—completely gained the confidence of the colonists, and opened the way for future uninterrupted prosperity. In 1849, a general amnesty was passed. Since that date, the legislature met every alternate four years in Toronto and Quebec, until 1859, when a removal was made to Ottawa, the new capital, situated on the Ottawa River and having a population of over 15,000.

During 1863 and 1864, long and ardent debates occurred in the Canadian parliament, under the governorship of Lord Monck, and several changes in the government occurred. A strong disposition was manifested towards adopting the federal principle, and the building up a united, combined Anglo-Saxon nationality. Previous to this, the maritime provinces, Nova Scotia, New Brunswick, and Prince Edward Island, had determined upon a Federal Union among themselves, Nova Scotia having taken the lead in the matter. A meeting of delegates from the several provinces was held at Quebec in October, and important resolutions adopted; these subsequently, on being communicated to the Home Government, were received with favor and a promise of help in all important matters. Some considerable trouble occurred on the frontiers, by the base conduct of certain of the rebels against the United States, availing themselves of the protection of a neutral country, to fit out raiding and plundering expeditions into the United States. Happily, the Canadian authorities and people acted with discretion during the rebellion, and manifested a desire to preserve amicable relations with our country.

In March, 1867, the Parliament of Great Britain passed an act which created the Dominion of Canada, and by proclamation it went into operation in May. The Constitution of the Provinces of Canada, Nova Scotia and New Brunswick were abrogated, and it was enacted that thenceforth they should be "federally united into one Dominion under the crown of Great Britain and Ireland, with a Constitution similar to that of the United Kingdom." Much discussion and difference of opinion have arisen as to the exact position and powers of the local legislatures in their relation to the General Legislature; but there seems to be good ground to hope for and expect the best results, seeing that the people of Canada are well aware that their true interests lie in furthering union, internal improvements, facilities of intercourse, and the like. The four Provinces of the Dominion are entitled, Ontario, Quebec, New Brunswick and Nova Scotia. The population of the Dominion is estimated at about 4,500,000; and in view of the encouragement given to education, the furtherance of social and moral culture, and the wise and judicious legislation for the good of the people, the steady progress of the Dominion of Canada may be regarded as assured for the future.

In the year 1870, a silly attempt on the part of the Fenians was made to invade Canada from the United States; but it proved to be a sorry failure, and our government at once interfered and put an end to so wild and wicked a scheme.

NEW BRUNSWICK.

NEW BRUNSWICK, one of the colonial possessions of Great Britain in North America, and one of the provinces of the Dominion of Canada, is bounded on the north by Quebec, on the east by the Gulf of St. Lawrence, on the south by Nova Scotia, and on the west by the State of Maine. It is 180 miles long from north to south and 150 broad; area, 27,704; population, about 212,000. The surface of New Brunswick may be divided in general into three regions. The southern region comprises the tract of land which stretches along the Bay of Fundy, and is divided into two unequal parts by the River Saint John. The whole coast of this region is bold and rocky, and the surface is much broken and diversified with rocks and ravines. To the west of the St. John the soil is deep and fertile, and covered with tall and dense forests. To the east of that river the soil is not so fertile, but there are many beautiful valleys, covered with forests mixed with corn-fields, and traversed by streams flowing into lakes at the bottom of the valleys, and ultimately joining the Saint John. The coast of the central region, along the Gulf of St. Lawrence, is low and sandy, covered with trees of a small size. For nearly twenty miles inland the country is flat, and consists of marshes and mosses; but in the interior it rises into gently-sloping hills and undulations, which extend westward as far as the St. John. The northern and north-western parts of New Brunswick are more mountainous than any of the other regions. A branch of the Alleghany Mountains traverses the north-west corner of the province, from the borders of Maine to the Bay of Chaleurs. The mountains are not of any great height; and while some are bold and precipitous towards the top, others are of a more rounded form, and many of the hills are clothed with wood to their summits. It is the forests that form the most striking feature of New Brunswick, and constitute not the least part of its value to the colonist. The principal trees are those belonging to the order of pines, which occupy most of the low-lying land in the province. Pines, larches, and spruces occur in great abundance; the oak, ash, maple, birch, poplar, and many other trees, are also found in New Brunswick, and afford inexhaustible supplies of timber. The province is well watered. Hardly any part of the country is destitute of some stream, of greater or less size; and in some parts of the interior a canoe can be conveyed with equal ease to the Bay of Chaleurs, the Gulf of St. Lawrence, or the Bay of Fundy. The largest river is the Aroostook, which rises in a lake of the same name in the State of Maine, flows first north-east and afterwards east, forming part of the boundary between Maine and Canada. It then enters New Brunswick, and flows south and south-east, till it falls into the Bay of Fundy at St. John's, after a course of 450 miles. The St. John is navigable for large steamers as far as Fredericton, 85 miles from the sea; but smaller vessels can ascend to the falls, about 140 miles further. The St. John receives many tributaries; and the Ristigouche, which marks the boundary between New Brunswick and Quebec, has a length of 100 miles, and falls into the Bay of Chaleurs. The Nipisigit also falls into this bay, having watered the north-eastern part of New Brunswick. The Peticodiac empties into the Bay of Fundy. The geological structure of the province resembles that of most other parts of North America. Coal constitutes the mineral wealth of New Brunswick; iron also is found abundantly, and copper on the banks of the Nipisigit.

The climate is subject to great extremes of heat and cold, the thermometer ranging at Fredericton from 35° below zero to 95° above. The soil is good, though agriculture has never received its due share of attention. The hay crop is the principal one; and the inhabitants are largely occupied in cutting and sawing wood for the lumber trade. The nature of the coasts of the province affords great facilities for fisheries; and the abundance of fish which is to be got here would render fishing a profitable pursuit. It is not, however, carried on to a very great extent; for though many of the inhabitants of the coast pursue this occupation, along with those of farming and lumbering, yet the demand for timber and the scantiness of the population give greater encouragement to other occupations; while the idleness of the people and the proximity of American fishermen prevent this employment from being prosecuted with as much activity as it might be. The principal seats of the fisheries are in the harbor of St. John's, and on the islands at the mouth of the Bay of Fundy. Cod, haddock, herring, and mackerel, are the principal fish got here; and the total value of the fisheries in the Bay, is estimated at about $300,000. The occupation of lumbering, in which a great part of the inhabitants are employed, though it is not favorable for the agricultural progress of the country, serves to clear out and open up the forests; and produces an active, hardy, and industrious set of men. The province is at present divided into fourteen counties, some of which, however, are but thinly peopled; and portions of land have been reserved for the aboriginal Indians, of whom there are about 1000 still remaining. The extent of land set apart for them is 61,273 acres.

The early history of New Brunswick is closely connected with that of Nova Scotia, of which it originally formed a part, when that province, then called Acadie or New France, was under the French dominion. The earliest attempt at colonization here was made in 1639; and in 1672 a number of French emigrants settled on the Miramichi and in other parts of the country. In 1713 New Brunswick was ceded to Great Britain, in terms of the treaty of Utrecht. The country was first settled by British colonists in 1764; and in 1784 New Brunswick was separated from Nova Scotia, and made a distinct province. It was originally peopled by several different Indian tribes; but the aborigines, as above stated, have now nearly all disappeared. The European inhabitants of the province consist to a large extent of descendants of royalists from the United States, who left their country at the American revolution, that they might remain under British sway.

The capital of New Brunswick is Fredericton, in the county of York, on the St. John, 85 miles from its mouth. It stands on a plain bounded on one side by the river, which is here three-fourths of a mile broad, and on the other by a range of hills, two miles long and half a mile wide; and it is regularly built, with long and straight streets. The most of the houses are of wood, but the public edifices are of stone, and some of them are very handsome. Population, about 8,000. St. John's, the principal commercial town in the province, is situated on a rocky promontory at the mouth of the St. John River, in north lat. 45. 20., west long. 66. 3. It is regularly and well built; but the streets are in some places very steep. There are many fine public buildings of stone, brick and wood, among which are a court-house, church and bank. The extreme point of the promontory is defended by two batteries; and here are also barracks and military stores.

NOVA SCOTIA.

NOVA SCOTIA, one of the provinces of the Dominion of Canada, in British America, is situated between north lat. 43. 25. and 46. 0., and west long. 61. 0. and 66. 30., and connected with the south-east part of the continent by an isthmus of only 8 miles in width. It is bounded on the north by the Strait of Northumberland, which divides it from Prince Edward's Island; on the north-east by the Gut of Canso, which interposes between it and the island of Cape Breton; on the south and south-east by the Atlantic Ocean; on the west by the Bay of Fundy; and on the north-west by New Brunswick. Its extreme length, from Cape Canso on the East to Cape St. Mary's on the west, is about 280 miles; but its breadth varies from 50 to about 100 miles; and it contains a superficies of 15,607 square miles (to which add that of Cape Breton, 3,120). From this, however, about one-fifth may be deducted for lakes, arms of the sea, and rivers; the greater part of the remainder is still uncleared, and covered with forests. Its population (including Cape Breton) is estimated to be 277,000.

The most remarkable characteristic of this peninsula is the numerous indentations along the coasts. The shores are lined with rocks, and studded with thousands of small islands; and close to these, and in the harbors, almost without exception, there is a considerable depth of water. All along the south-east shore there is a succession of excellent harbors; some of which will accommodate ships of the line. The principal inlets are Sheet Harbor, Halifax Harbor, Margaret's Bay, Mahon's Bay, on the Atlantic; St. Mary's Bay, Annapolis Basin, on the Bay of Fundy; Pictou Harbor on Northumberland Strait; St. George's Bay, on the Gulf of St. Lawrence; and Chidabucto Bay, on the Gut of Canso. The surface of the country is generally undulating and diversified. The interior is watered by numerous rivers, lakes and streams. The principal rivers are the Annapolis and the Shubenacadie, flowing into the Bay of Fundy; the East, West and Middle Rivers, into Pictou Harbor; the Avon, Mersey, etc. The climate is variable, though the winter is milder, and the summer less intensely hot, than at Quebec. In Nova Scotia and Cape Breton immense coal fields exist: the coal is of a bituminous character, and large quantities of gypsum are found in these coal formations. Varieties of copper, iron and lead ores are abundant. Fine specimens of agates, amethysts, and other stones are also found. Among the wild animals are the moose, bear, lynx, fox, porcupine, etc. Great numbers of birds, and vast shoals of fish are common to Nova Scotia, as well as its neighbors. The soil is of different qualities and various degrees of fertility. Wheat, barley, oats, potatoes, etc., are produced in abundance. The lands of the Atlantic coast are generally so rocky as to admit of cultivation only at much expense and labor; but after the stones are removed, the soil is by no means barren. The forests of Nova Scotia still constitute a new feature of the country. The trees are the same as those common to America, and the timber is generally large and lofty. Agriculture is carried on to a considerable extent in Nova Scotia. The cultivated ground consists partly of the rich alluvial marshes on the shore of the Bay of Fundy, and partly of the uplands in the interior of the country.

Sable Island, although distant about 85 miles from Nova Scotia, is considered as belonging to that province. It lies directly in the track of vessels bound to or from Europe, and has been the scene of numerous and melancholy shipwrecks. It is 25 miles in length, by about 1¼ in breadth, the eastern end being in lat. 43. 59. N., and long. 59. 45. W. It is a barren desert throughout, the soil consisting chiefly of sand, and the only vegetable productions being a coarse grass and some wild pease. An annual appropriation is devoted to keeping on the island a superintendent from Nova Scotia, with a party of men provided with provisions and other necessaries, for the purpose of affording assistance to any shipwrecked mariners, of whatsoever nation, who may be driven on its inhospitable shores.

The manufactures of Nova Scotia are few in number, consisting principally of coarse cloth, flannel, carpets, hats, paper, tobacco, leather, spirits, and agricultural implements. Ship building is also carried on to a considerable extent; but the chief occupation of the people is fishing. The total value of the fisheries is estimated to exceed $1,000,000. The exports consist principally of fish, sugar, molasses, rum, timber, etc.; the imports are flour, sugar, tea, etc.

The inhabitants of Nova Scotia consist of English, Scotch, Irish, Americans, Germans, Swiss, Acadian French, Indians, and freed Negroes. They mingle and live together in much harmony, and generally the social state of the province is improving. Its prosperity has greatly increased; and, instead of importing, it now exports provisions. Its fisheries, to which proper atention is at length paid, its rich and prolific soil, and its mines of coal and iron, are sources of wealth which were too long neglected by Great Britain. The province is divided into 18 counties, including Cape Breton, the population of which, as given above, is about 277,000. Halifax, it capital, has a population of about 30,000; other principal towns are Picton, Windsor and Annapolis.

Our limits admit of only a brief abstract of the history of Nova Scotia. Ancient authorities state that it was discovered by the Cabots in 1497; but it was not until 1604 that the French attempted to form settlements. They were, however, expelled from it in 1614 by the English colonists of Virginia, who claimed the country in right of the discovery of Sebastian Cabot. In 1621 Sir William Alexander obtained a grant of the whole peninsula, and it was named in the patent Nova Scotia, instead of Acadie, as the country was called by the French. In the meantime the latter obtained a footing in it a second time; and it was not until 1654, when a strong force was dispatched by Cromwell, that the French settlers were brought under subjection. In 1667 Nova Scotia was ceded to France by the treaty of Breda; but, after suffering during the war which broke out in 1701, as well as previously, it was finally ceded to England by treaty in the year 1711. From this period till 1749 it was neglected by Great Britain; but the designs of the French called the attention of government to the province. Encouragements were held out to settlers; Parliament gave a large grant; and about 4,000 adventurers, with their families, embarked for the colony. Halifax was immediately founded; but the French settlers, under the name of neutrals, were still very numerous; and with the aid of the Indians, they inflicted repeated injuries upon the British, until they were forcibly expelled by the latter. In 1758 a constitution was granted to Nova Scotia; and the capture of Louisburg, in the island of Cape Breton, during the same year, gave additional security to the colony, which now began to improve. By the treaty of Paris, in February, 1762, France resigned all further claims on any of her former possessions in North America, and nothing of any material importance has since occurred. New Brunswick and Cape Breton were separated from Nova Scotia, and formed into two distinct governments, in 1784, but the latter was re-annexed to Nova Scotia in 1819. For later information in regard to this province, see p. 47, where an account is given of the existing Dominion of Canada, of which Nova Scotia forms a part.

NEWFOUNDLAND.

NEWFOUNDLAND designates an island belonging to Great Britain, in the North Atlantic Ocean, off the east coast of North America, and forming the most of the eastern boundary of the Gulf of Saint Lawrence. It lies between north lat. 46. 38 and 51. 37, west long. 52. 44 and 59. 31; and is separated from Labrador by the Straits of Belleisle, about 12 miles broad; and on the south-west it approaches within 70 miles of North Point, in Cape Breton Island. Its form is generally triangular, but extremely irregular. Its area is about 36,000 square miles, its coast line is estimated at nearly 1000 miles in length, and it is apparently a mass of solid rock. Its population is estimated to be about 120,000. On its south-eastern quarter Newfoundland is formed into a peninsula of about 80 miles in length, by from 15 to 60 in breadth; the isthmus which unites it with the main-land being not more than four miles in breadth. This peninsula is called Avalon. To the N. of it, and on the eastern side of the island, lies Trinity Bay, which is separated from that of Bonavista by a narrow neck of land, the point of which is Cape Bonavista. A long neck of land also divides Trinity Bay from Conception Bay on the northern side of Avalon. This bay ranks as the first district in Newfoundland, as well on account of the spirit and enterprise of the inhabitants who people its shores, as from its natural advantages of large harbors, coves, and the like. About twenty miles from Cape St. Francis, the eastern boundary of Conception, are the bay and harbor of St. John's, the capital of Newfoundland: population about 24,000. A succession of bays indent the coast all round the peninsula of Avalon. Fortune Bay is from 60 to 70 miles deep, and from 20 to 30 broad, receiving many rivers from the island lakes, and containing numerous harbors, the principal of which is Fortune Harbor, on the eastern side. St. Pierre and Miquelon Islets are situated at the mouth of Fortune Bay. They were ceded to France in the year 1814, and the former contains a harbor which is the rendezvous of the French shipping, and the residence of the governor. From this point, all along the south side of Newfoundland to Cape Ray, which forms the north-east entrance of the Gulf of St. Lawrence, there are numerous bays, but none of size or importance. On the western side, formed by Cape Anguille and Cape St. George, is the Bay of St. George, a large and deep inlet of the sea, into which several rivers, emerging from lakes in the interior, empty themselves. Further to the north is the Bay of Islands, formed by three arms, into which several rivers discharge their waters. Boune Bay may next be named; as also St. John's Bay, which receives the waters of Castor's River. Pistolet Bay is beyond Cape Norman, the north-west point of the island, and Hare Bay is further south. White Bay is a very large inlet of the sea on the eastern side of the island. The Bay of Notre Dame and the Bay of Exploits are of great extent and contain a vast number of islands. Bonavista Bay contains several islands; to the south of it is Catalina Bay, containing Ragged Harbor, which completes the circuit of the island.

The interior of Newfoundland has as yet been very imperfectly explored. There appears to be a number of lakes and rivers, but it is poorly wooded and of a rocky and rather barren soil. The climate, though severe, is healthy; snow does not lie long on the ground, the summer is short, but in general mild and pleasant. The most remarkable feature is the fogs which prevail on the coasts of New foundland. Carriboo deer, beavers, foxes, wolves and bears abound; as well as the well-known Newfoundland dog. Beside, the cod-fish, trout, lobsters, mackerel, etc., are in great abundance. Herrings arrive in spring and autumn in prodigious numbers. The main importance of Newfoundland arises from its fisheries. The settlements are generally at the heads of the bays, particularly Conception Bay, thence to St. John's and southward to Cape Race. St. John's is situated 70 miles to the north of Cape Race, lat. 47. 35; W. long. 52. 48. It has an excellent harbor, formed between two mountains, the eastern points of which have an entrance called the Narrows. It is protected by various fortifications and could readily resist an invading enemy. The town itself consists chiefly of one long straggling street, extending nearly parallel to the shore on the north side of the port, from which branch out several narrow lines of houses, that can only be called lanes. The houses are chiefly built of wood, although diversified by some of brick and a few of stone; but they are somewhat irregularly placed, although the town has been much improved in this respect since the fire of 1846. The principal feature of the town consists in its multitudes of wharves and fishing stages, which entirely line the shore. The government wharf is a fine broad quay open to the accommodation of the public. St. John's has repeatedly and severely suffered from fires. In 1815 a great amount of property was destroyed by a visitation of this sort. Other conflagrations took place in 1817 and 1818; and in 1846 the town was again almost destroyed by fire. The trade of the place consists principally in the export of dried fish, and of seal, whale, and cod oil; and in the import of bread, flour, tea, sugar and other necessaries of life. The resident population is about 21,000 and the fishermen amount to about 6000. Total value of imports in 1855 was over $5,500,000: total value of exports, nearly the same amount.

When Newfoundland was first visited it was found to contain two distinct races of aborigines, the one termed Red Indian and the other Esquimaux; both are now nearly extinct. The island was discovered by John Cabot, June, 24, 1497. Sailing under the commission of Henry VII. in these seas, he descried a headland which, as a lucky omen, he called Bonavista, a name which it still retains. It was at that time inhabited by native Indians, three of whom he brought home, clothed in skins, and speaking a language which no person understood. It was afterwards visited by navigators from France and Portugal, who, reporting favorably of the abundance and excellency of its cod-fishery, European fishermen were soon attracted to its coasts. In 1536 an English vessel attempted to winter upon the island, but the crew nearly perished from starvation. Not deterred by this failure, however, nor by that of a former attempt, Sir Humphrey Gilbert, in 1583, landed on the island with 200 followers, and, under a patent of Queen Elizabeth, took quiet possession of the country. Being, however, desirous of prosecuting his discoveries, his crews became disaffected, and having separated into two parties, one of them returned home. Most of those who followed him were lost in a gale of wind off Sable Island, and the remainder perished along with himself on their voyage homewards. Subsequent attempts were made to explore and settle Newfoundland, but it was not until the year 1623 that the first colony was established under Sir George Calvert, afterwards Lord Baltimore. His son was made governor of the colony, which he named Avalon, and soon afterwards proceeding thither himself, it increased and flourished under his auspicies. Other individuals obtained grants of land; and, about the year 1654, fifteen settlements, comprehending 300 families, had been made on the island, nothwithstanding the constant bickerings between the English and French, the latter having established a colony at Placentia. On the breaking out of the war after the accession of William III., these assumed a more serious character, and, after various recriminations, St. John's was compelled to surrender to the French in 1696. The captors set fire to the fort and town, and destroyed most of the British settlement. To repair these losses, the English government despatched a squadron; but the cowardice of one commander, and the ignorance of another, frustrated the design. The re-establishment of peace put an end to hostilities for the time; but they were resumed in 1702, during which year several of the French settlements were destroyed, and a great many fishing-boats were burned or captured. In the following year an expedition miscarried, and this circumstance encouraged the French to attempt the conquest of the whole island in 1705. For this purpose 500 men were despatched from Canada to the assistance of the garrison of Placentia, who, though repulsed from St. John's, extended their ravages over the different settlements as far as Bonavista. In the year 1708 the French completely demolished the town of St. John's; and, shortly afterwards, Carbonia, the only settlement of consequence remaining in English hands, was partially destroyed. From this time until the conclusion of the peace of Utrecht, the French remained in quiet possession of Newfoundland; but, by this treaty, the island, with all the adjacent ones, was declared to belong to Great Britain, the French being only allowed the use of the two islets of St. Pierre and Miquelon. The revolutionary war in the United States occasioned fresh disputes as to the right of fishing upon the banks of Newfoundland. The New Englanders had hitherto enjoyed the right of taking fish, and on this being resisted, they retaliated, by refusing to supply the colony with many articles of provision upon which it depended. This dispute was settled by the treaty of Versailles in 1783, by which it was stipulated that the inhabitants of the United States should have liberty to take fish of every kind on the coast of Newfoundland, but not to dry or cure their fish upon the island. In 1809 Labrador and the Island of Anticosti were annexed to the government of Newfoundland. In 1854 the colonial government granted a charter to the Telegraphic Company, under Mr. Cyrus W Field's management, for the purpose of establishing telegraphic communications between Europe and America. Subsequently the land wires were completed between St. John's and the cable terminus at Cape Ray, and "The Atlantic Telegraph Company" was established in 1856 to extend the existing line to Ireland. Of the successful completion and extension of the vast enterprise of connecting the Old and the New Worlds by telegraphic cables and lines, we shall speak in another place.

UNITED STATES OF AMERICA.

THE United States occupy the vast portion of the continent of North America which stretches from the twenty-fourth to the forty-ninth degree of N. latitude, and from the sixty-ninth to the one hundred and twenty-fourth degree of west longitude. Its average breadth from N. to S. is about 1300 miles; its average length, E. to W. about 2400 miles; and its area, 3,549,129 square miles, *i. e.* nearly as great as the entire area of Europe. Among the natural features of the country none is more striking externally, or more directly connected with the pursuits and progress of the nation, than the immense proportion of navigable waters, exterior and interior; the shore line of the eastern coast being nearly 7000 miles, that of the southern 3400, and that of the western 2200, or 12,600 miles in all; while the lake line of the north is 1500 miles, and the extent of river navigation, north and south, east and west, is almost beyond the power of accurate computation.

The geographical divisions of the United States may be reduced to five in number, of which we subjoin a brief description. 1. The Atlantic slope is a long belt, extending westward from the Atlantic shore, beginning at the Gulf of St. Lawrence, and stretching to the Gulf of Mexico—nowhere wider than 200 miles, and in many places, particularly towards the north-east, having hardly any width at all. It is very plainly subdivided, where wide enough to be divided, into two portions, one a plain immediately upon the coast, the other a slope proper, from 50 to 300 feet in elevation, constituting in the Middle States what has been termed one of the most attractive and richest districts on the continent. 2. West of the Atlantic slope lies the mountainous tract, variously styled the Atlantic or the Appalachian system, which, like the slope with which it is generally parallel, begins at the St. Lawrence, and extends to the S. W. as far as Alabama, 1550 miles in length, and from 50 to 150 miles in width. The mean elevation of the various ridges composing this system is not more than 2500 feet, though some of the higher ranges attain an average altitude of 3500 or 4000 feet. The system is naturally divided into two groups, one in the N. E., consisting of the White, Green, and Adirondack Mountains, the highest peak being Mount Washington (6226 feet); the other in the S. W., consisting of the Alleghany, Blue, Cumberland, and other ranges, of which the highest point is Black or Mitchell Mountain (6470 feet). Allied with the Appalachian system, though separated from it by a great interval, is the Ozark range, between the Missouri and the Red River. 3. Next on the west, is the immense plain, partly tablelands, partly slopes, spreading westward to the Rocky Mountains, and from the Gulf of Mexico on the south to the nothern boundary of the United States. This vast continental area consists, so far as the United States are concerned, of three subdivisions. Least of the three is the basin of the St.

Lawrence and the lakes on the north. From this, southward and westward, opens the great basin of the Mississippi, partly forest, partly prairie land, with soil and climate the most favorable to material development, and promising, from the magnitude and variety of its physical resources, to become the chief district not only of the United States, but of the entire American continent. Westward from the Mississippi basin, the table-lands of the west, consisting of two plateaus, the lower or eastern attaining a mean height of 2500 feet, the higher or western one of 4000 feet, the western extremities, however, rising to 6000 feet as they reach the base of the Rocky Mountains. Both the plateaus, but especially the western, present wide expanses, almost entirely without tree or shrub, grassy in some parts, arid and actually desert in others, the dividing line between them and the fertile basin upon which they border being about the ninety-eighth meridian. 4. Next we find the Rocky Mountain system, vast, lofty, and irregular, partly volcanic, partly desert, the highest portion of the entire United States territory. It consists of three parallel divisions; a. The Chippewayans, or Rocky Mountains proper, a double, and, in some parts, a treble chain, the highest of which is the Wind River range, Fremont's Peak being 13,568 feet; b. An area of table-land, wide and elevated, the mean height 5000 feet, with salt and desert plains; c. A western chain, extremely broken, consisting of three principal ranges, the Sierra Nevada, the Coast, and the Cascade, the highest peak being one of the Cascade Mountains, St. Helen's (about 15,000 feet). 5. Lastly, the Pacific slope, an irregular and a narrow tract, about 100 miles in breadth, extends from the western chain of the Rocky Mountain system to the coast of the Pacific.

In the preliminary chapter to this volume, entitled a General View of America, we have already given some brief statements in respect to the geological formations, the zoology, early discoveries in the New World, and other matters of interest connected with North America. We have also considered at some length the question as to the aborigines of the western continent, their origin, customs, etc. We now propose to lay before the reader the civil and political history of the United States, in an orderly and consecutive narrative, and, measurably at least, proportioned to the greatness of the nation of which it treats.

The most simple and natural division of the history of the Great Republic is into three periods, viz., the colonial, the revolutionary or struggle for independence, and the constitutional period. The first commences with the earliest attempts at colonization in North America, from about A. D. 1500 to 1775; the second begins with the war in 1775, and reaches to the adoption of the constitution, in 1788; and the third extends from the organization of the Federal Government under the constitution to the present time.

CHAPTER I.

COLONIAL HISTORY: 1500—1775.

SUBSEQUENT to the great and noble achievement of Columbus, in 1492, there were various voyages of discovery made to the New World by the hardy navigators of England, France, Spain, and Portugal. Among the rest, De Soto, in 1541, discovered the Mississippi; but so far as colonization and settlement were concerned, all attempts, during the early half of the 16th century, failed entirely of success. It was not, in fact, till the beginning of the 17th century, that any thing like a permanent colony was planted in North America. Gilbert's voyages and efforts in 1579 and 1583 were a total loss; and Raleigh, who received from Queen Elizabeth an ample charter for the region of Virginia, after immense struggle and cost, from 1584 to 1590, was doomed to utter disappointment. All his plans and endeavors for effecting a settlement at Roanoke were wholly unproductive, and Raleigh gave up his proprietary rights in despair. Nothing had as yet been accomplished, and the century closed without a single English colony planted in the New World.

James I., King of England, granted in 1606, a charter of that portion of the continent between 34° and 45° north latitude, to the London Company and the Plymouth Company. The former was allowed to plant in the southern part, from Cape Fear to the Potomac; the latter in the northern part, from the mouth of the Hudson to Newfoundland. The intermediate region was open to either company, on certain easy conditions, for settlement. The government of the company was vested in a supreme council in England for all important matters; in other respects, the colonists were not to be restricted in any thing which tended to advance their interests and further the cause of trade and commerce The London Company entered zealously upon their work. In April, 1607, three ships and 105 emigrants entered Chesapeake Bay, and in the follow ing month the foundation of Jamestown was laid on the James river, about fifty miles from its mouth. Newport commanded the expedition, made up largely of so-called "gentlemen"; but the chief man of those who formed the council, and through whose efforts and ability, almost entirely, the colony was saved from ruin, and owed its success, was the famous Captain John Smith. This remarkable individual set about exploring the country in the vicinity of Jamestown; he visited Powhatan, the principal Indian chief in that region; and it was through the generous impulses of Pocahontas, Powhatan's daughter, that, on a memorable occasion, his life was saved. There was abundant need of all the energy, prudence and skill possessed by Smith. On the one hand, the Indians were displaying marks of decided hostility; on the other, the colonists were beginning to suffer seriously from the effects of heat, and lack of good food, and disease breaking out in their midst. Half of their number died within a few months, and the rest were in despair; but Smith resolutely opposed their purpose of abandoning the colony. Other emigrants arrived the next year, although not of the right sort, and Smith begged to have carpenters, gardeners, masons, and such like, sent thereafter. Progress was slow and discouraging, and the Company were but ill satisfied with the returns of their investment. Pocahontas proved a true and lasting friend to the white men, and a few years subsequently, in 1614, she was married to John Rolfe; she visited England with her husband and died there at the age of twenty-two.

Captain John Smith kept up the struggle as long as possible against faction and

Painted by W. H. Powell.

Entered according to act of Congress A.D. 1868 by Johnson, Fry & Co. in the clerks office of the district court of the southern district of N. Y.

DE SOTO'S DISCOVERY OF THE MISSISSIPPI.

disorder, but having been wounded accidently by a discharge of gunpowder, he was compelled to leave for England. He was treated with indifference and neglect, and never after revisited Virginia; but his name and services deserve perpetual honor. Soon after Smith's departure, in 1609, the colony went from bad to worse; the fearful "starving time" followed; and indolence, vice and want, together with Indian attacks, reduced the colonists from five hundred to sixty. Gates and Somers arrived in Virginia in May, 1610, with some partial relief; but so gloomy was the condition of affairs that they all resolved to abandon the settlement, and were on the point of doing so, early in June, when Lord Delaware, the new governor, arrived, and succeeded in arresting the dissolution of the colony. This excellent nobleman introduced order into affairs, required every man to work, and erected forts against the Indians. Lord Delaware was compelled to leave on account of ill health, and was followed in office by Sir Thomas Dale, who arrived in August, 1611, with about three hundred colonists, and a quantity of cattle, hogs, stores, etc.

Prospects began now to brighten, and new settlements were formed higher up the river. Dale labored judiciously and energetically till 1616, when he returned to England. Argall, a sort of half pirate, gave a good deal of trouble in the management of affairs; but George Yeardley happily became governor in 1619. He called together the first Colonial Assembly of Virginia, composed of the Governor, the Council and Deputies from the eleven plantations. These deputies were called burgesses, a name of some note in American history. Two years later, the Colony obtained a constitution and permament government, and Sir Francis Wyatt succeeded Yeardley. In 1622 the Indians attempted to massacre the whites, and nearly accomplished their object. This led to a savage system of retaliation, and the warfare thus began continued for about fourteen years.

King James I., a great lover of prerogative, and entirely misliking every thing that looked towards democratic freedom of speech, and the like, took umbrage at the course of the Virginia Company; and so, his majesty arbitrarily appointed a commission of investigation in 1624, and the next year had the company abolished. It had spent nearly $700,000 in the effort to establish the colony and make it remunerative; but could not withstand royal and ministerial power. We may mention here, that tobacco was a principal article of cultivation and trade; and that, in 1621, cotton seeds were planted as an experiment, which promised favorable results. We may also mention that, in 1620, a Dutch trading vessel brought into Jamestown a cargo of twenty negroes, who were purchased by the planters for slaves; from which beginning arose that mighty evil and bane of our country, the slave trade and slavery. God be thanked that slavery in this land is totally and forever abolished!

Turning our attention in another direction, we find that a brave Englishman, named Henry Hudson, sailed in the employ of the Dutch East India Company, on a voyage of discovery. This was in April, 1609. He reached the northern coast of America in due time, and early in September, entered Sandy Hook Bay. Passing through the Narrows, he voyaged up that noble river which perpetuates his fame, as far as the site of the present city of Albany. Descending the river, he embarked for Europe in October, and reached England in November. Here he was detained by a royal order, and dispatched on another voyage the next year; but he perished in the frozen regions of what is now known as Hudson's Bay.

The Dutch Company claimed the right of discovery, as having been made by their agent; and accordingly, in 1613, took possession of Manhattan Island, where the great city of New-York now stands. Trade was opened with the Indians; Adriaen Block penetrated through the East River and Long Island Sound; and a fort was erected on

Manhattan Island and also just below Albany. New Netherland was placed under the special charge of the Company, and in 1623, May became its first director. He was succeeded, in 1626, by Peter Minuit, who was active and vigorous during the six years of his government. Manhattan Island and also Staten Island were purchased of the natives, and forts and block houses erected for the protection of trade. Thus far the Dutch had in view immediate results, in the way of trade principally; and it was not till 1629 that a plan for colonization was adopted. This gave the privilege to any one planting a colony of fifty persons, on a tract sixteen miles in length within four years, of being called a "patroon" or lord, and enjoying the usual feudal prerogatives. The scheme met with favor, and desirable locations were secured on Delaware Bay and the south-west bank of the Hudson. Van Twiller succeeded Minuit in 1633; but did not meet with much success in his office. He brought over 100 soldiers, a school-master, and a minister, and favored the trade which had been commenced with the Indians, a number of years previously, on the Connecticut River. A fort was erected near where Hartford now stands, and when the sturdy Plymouth settlers disputed their rights, Van Twiller sent soldiers to drive away the Englishmen, but without success. The patroon privileges caused serious disputes and troubles, and as Van Twiller was accused of illegal or underhand procedures, he was recalled, and William Kieft was sent out as his successor, in March, 1637. The hardy and energetic Swedes undertook a settlement on Delaware Bay, in 1637, and soon after built a fort near its head. Kieft protested, and would have driven the Swedes out if he could; but emigration increased; a fort and residence of the governor were located near where Philadelphia now stands, and New Sweden seemed to be securely planted. We may mention here, however, that the Dutch built a fort at Newcastle, in 1651, which was attacked and destroyed by the Swedes. The Dutch then, under Stuyvesant, invaded New Sweden, and in 1655 it became wholly under their sway.

Leaving the Dutch and Swedes for the present, the founding of New England next claims the reader's notice. The Plymouth Company, spoken of on a previous page (see p. 56), met with very indifferent success in its efforts at colonization. In 1614, Captain John Smith explored the coast for the Company, from Penobscot to Cape Cod, made a map of the region, and gave it the name of New England. In 1619, the "Puritans," a body of menwho were averse, as a matter of conscience, to living under the religious rule of the English Church, and had been residing for years in Holland, resolved to embark for America, where they could regulate matters of religion according to their own sentiments. They asked to be allowed to settle in New Netherland, but were refused. They then determined to try and reach the northern part of the region next to the Virginia Company's districts, or the vicinity of the Hudson. It was in September, 1620, that they set sail, and after a long and dangerous voyage, they came in sight of the coast of New England, near Cape Cod. This was in November. They first organized themselves into a body politic under the sanction of a voluntary compact; appointed John Carver governor; and sent out an exploring party to find a good resting place on land. Winter speedily came on, and it was not till the 21st of December, 1620, that the Mayflower's company was landed on Plymouth Rock, and a settlement attempted. Hard and bitter was the trial to bear up against the piercing cold and furious storms of that ice-bound coast; and out of 101 souls, at least one-half was cut off before spring arrived. Carver died, and was succeeded by Bradford in 1621. Fortunately, no Indians appeared to molest the colony in its weakness. The Mayflower set sail for England, in April, and on further exploration the colonists found the three crested peninsula of Shawmut, where Boston now is.

Progress was slow and toilsome. The Wam

panoag Indians were friendly, but the Narragansetts were ill disposed and decidedly threatening. A palisade of timbers was formed around the village with three gates. They had no cattle, as yet, and only rude agricultural implements; and though fish were abundant, they were almost destitute of boats, wherewith to catch them. The settlement at Weymouth, failing of corn, began to plunder the natives, who resolved to massacre them; but Captain Miles Standish anticipated the Indians, and by needlessly killing some of them, laid the beginning of that spirit of hatred which was never quelled in the savage bosom. By degrees settlements were extended. Dover and Portsmouth in New Hampshire were founded in 1623. The next year as the joint stock system did not work well, each colonist at Plymouth began to plant on a tract for himself, which soon made corn abundant. At this date there were thirty-two dwelling houses and 184 inhabitants; in 1630 the number of the people was about 300. Distance from the mother country fostered the feeling of entire independence in action as well as thought, and the colonists exercised all the powers of government, even to capital punishment, when they deemed that necessary. Laws were enacted in General Assembly, and freedom to preach and pray was allowed to all who chose so to do — *i. e.* to all who agreed with Puritan views of doctrine and discipline.

John Endicott, with 100 followers, settled at Naumkeag or Salem, in 1628; and in the same year the Massachusetts Bay Company obtained a patent from Charles I., with liberal provisions, but containing no specific arrangements as to religion. A large number of the proprietors were members of the Church of England, and desired its form of worship and services; but that stern, unrelenting Puritan, John Endicott, with others of like stamp, resisted every such purpose, and shipped off to England, in 1629, two brothers named Browne, who were Churchmen, as "factious and evil conditioned." We shall see, by and by, how this spirit of old Endicott developed and strengthened into outrageous acts of tyranny and injustice.

Numerous and valuable additions were made to the colony, and together with Salstonstall, Dudley, Winthrop and others, more than 1000 emigrants arrived in 1630. Winthrop was chosen governor; Boston was founded; and townships formed at various neighboring points. Though professing much affection and esteem for "their dear mother the Church of England," they arranged their religious matters entirely to their own liking, irrespective of church and king. The winter of 1630 was very severe; more than 200 died before December; famine with all its terrors seemed at hand; and many of the emigrants lost heart and fled away back to their native land. In May, 1631, the General Court enacted that no one should have a vote who was not a member of some church. This stirred up no little ill feeling, since hardly one-fourth of the people were church members. It was in fact the first great attempt to establish a sort of theocracy, and it led to anything but a pleasant state of affairs. The ministers necessarily acquired potential influence, and interference with personal liberty as to amusements and the like, became a regular thing, and was resolutely carried out.

Dudley was made governor in 1634, in place of Winthrop, during whose four years of administration the colony had become firmly established. A fort had been built; mills had been brought into use; trade with the Virginians and Dutch had grown up, etc. Roger Williams's case at this date gave great trouble. The Puritans, in theory, were quite disposed to allow others that freedom of opinion which they claimed for themselves; but, in practice, they held that no opinion was to be tolerated which did not agree with their settled and established views. Now, Roger Williams was a man who, claiming what he termed "soul liberty," did not hesitate to differ, in many respects, from the ministers and leaders in the colony, and he set forth his views as to religious freedom, resolutely and persistently. This, of course, was not to be tolerated; and the summary measure of shipping him off to England (as had been done with the Brownes, p. 59) was resolved upon. Williams, however, fled in the depth of winter, and was received and kindly treated by the Narragansett Indians. He removed to Narragansett Bay, where he received from the Indians a free grant of a considerable tract of land, and in June, 1636, fixed upon the site of a town, which he named Providence, as being a refuge from persecution and wanderings. Here he was joined by others from Salem, among whom he freely distributed his lands, and towards whom he exercised that spirit of toleration which he claimed for himself. This was the beginning of Rhode Island, the smallest, but by no means the least distinguished of the United States.

Henry Vane, a man of some note, who had come over from England the year before, with a large body of emigrants, was, in 1636, elected governor. Soon after, new troubles of a religious kind arose, in which Governor Vane became deeply involved. There was, it seems, an excellent and pious woman in Boston, named Mrs. Anne Hutchinson, who avowed sentiments on doctrinal points which were even more offensive than those maintained by Roger Williams. In a state of enthusiasm, if not fanaticism, she went so far as to defy the ruling powers, denouncing some of the ministers as unsound, etc. Vane sided with Mrs. Hutchinson, and believed in her; but she was nevertheless tried, condemned and banished, in 1637; whereupon Vane left in disgust for England. Mrs. H. and a number of her followers settled in Aquiday, or Isle of Rhodes, in Narragansett Bay. Two years later, in 1639, Newport was founded on the southern side of the island, and universal toleration prevailed here, as in Providence under Williams. In 1644 a charter was obtained, which united the two under the name of Rhode Island and Providence Plantations.

The Dutch, as we have noted (see p. 58), tried to prevent the New Englanders from occupying the valley of the Connecticut (Indian name, meaning *Long River*); but without success. In 1635 and 1636, a large body of settlers pushed through the forests to the Connecticut, where Hartford, Windsor and other towns were founded. Saybrook also, at the mouth of the river, dates from this year, 1635.

The Pequod war broke out in 1636. This powerful tribe, who dwelt at and near the mouth of Thames River, was hostile to the white settlers, and had frequent difficulties and collisions with them. This soon led to a contest which speedily became one for life or death. The red men, exasperated by an attack on the Block Islanders under Endicott, in which great injury was done, retaliated, of course; and they resolved to exterminate, if possible, every white man in New England. Roger Williams, at great personal risk, persuaded the Narragansetts not to join the Pequods, and sent word of the Indian plot to Massachusetts. Early in the spring of 1637, determined to anticipate the attack of the savages, the men of Connecticut, less than 100 in number, under John Mason, who had served as a soldier in Flanders, set out for the work which was before them. About 80 Mohegans joined them in the perilous undertaking. The attack was made on the Pequod fort and village at night, and after a sharp fight, Mason had the torch applied to the wigwams, and the Pequods were entirely defeated. The colonists continued to war against this tribe with bitter tenacity, and during the summer completed the extermination of the "bloody heathen." Henceforth the name of Pequod was never heard.

The stringent regulations of Massachusetts in regard to religious matters, led to various emigrations on the part of those who disliked what they felt to be intolerance in the authorities. Davenport, in 1638, established the colony of New Haven; Wheelwright planted Exeter; Capt. Underhill went to Dover; others followed their example, and settlements began to spring up over the face of the country. Progress thus far had been steady, if not rapid. Trade increased; intercourse was mostly kept up by coasting; and there were now (1640), east of the Hudson, some fifty towns and villages, under twelve—soon after reduced to six—separate jurisdictions.

The progress of Virginia, after the accession of Charles I., (1625) was, on the whole, encouraging. Trouble with the Indians still existed, and tobacco was as yet the staple product. Various governors followed one another; Yeardley, Potts, Harvey and Wyatt, from 1625 to 1641; at which date Sir William Berkeley took the reins of government in hand. The code of laws was revised in 1632, and numerous excellent regulations were adopted, tending to promote good morals and industry in the community. The Virginians under Berkeley steadily adhered to the cause of royalty; but in 1652 a powerful expedition was sent by Parliament, which enforced submission in Virginia to its authority, their rights and privileges, however, being secured to the colonists. In 1644, Opechancanough, the successor of Powhatan and a bitter foe to the white men, made an attack, and succeeded in killing some 500 persons. Two years later, this relentless savage died of wounds in battle, and his successor made peace by giving up all the lands between the James and York Rivers. On the accession of Charles II. the burgesses re-elected Berkeley governor of Virginia. Steadily intent upon securing the liberty they enjoyed, they established the supremacy of the popular branch, the freedom of trade, religious toleration, exemption from foreign taxation, and the universal elective franchise.

The origin and early progress of Maryland are more than usually noteworthy. George Calvert, Lord Baltimore, a member of the Roman Catholic Church, obtained from Charles I. in 1632, a grant of a large tract of land on the Potomac, which, in compliment to the Queen, was called Maryland. He was a man of enlarged and comprehensive views, and he took care to secure in the charter of the new colony popular freedom in the management of civil affairs, and the most liberal toleration in regard to religion. Leonard Calvert, in 1634, arrived in the Chesapeake with about 200 colonists, mostly Roman Catholics, and built the little village of St. Mary's on the Potomac. The Virginians did not feel at all pleased with this, as they thought, encroachment on their territories, and Claybourne, especially, who was one of the council, manifested an untiring hostility towards the new settlement. The Colonial Assembly passed the first Statutes of Maryland, in 1639, in which and in subsequent enactments, toleration was firmly established. Claybourne, in 1643, stirred up insurrection in Maryland; but was finally driven out by Calvert, in 1646, and escaped to England. Owing to the troubles in the mother country, Maryland was claimed by different parties, and in 1650 there were four separate aspirants for chief control. In 1660, Philip Calvert became the acknowledged governor. The population at this date was about 10,000, and the colony gave promise of steady onward progress.

The affairs of New Netherland under Kieft (p. 58) did not advance successfully. He was quick tempered, not very wise, and no match for the Connecticut people, who were bent on expelling the Dutch from the region they had in possession and where they had planted several flourishing towns. Kieft, too, got into a war with the Indians. In February, 1643, he madly and wickedly caused the cutting off of a number of the Tappan Indians, who had taken refuge with the Dutch on being attacked by the Mohawks. Speedy and bloody retaliation followed. In every direction, near New Amsterdam, the whites were murdered, without mercy, and a piteous cry was raised against Kieft's government in an appeal sent to Holland in 1544. He was superseded in 1647 by Petrus Stuyvesant, a sturdy old soldier, but rather haughty and imperious.

The new governor undertook to settle difficulties and disputes, which were quite numerous, but he met with indifferent success. In 1647, there was a partial settlement of a boundary between the Dutch and the New Haven colonists; and in 1652, Stuyvesant summarily put a stop to action on the part of a convention of delegates who claimed a voice for the people in public affairs. More trouble and bloodshed occurred with the Indians in 1659, and there was an annoying dispute with Maryland on hand; but the real trial of Stuyvesant's life was the restless spirit of New England, and the determination of the English, at the earliest moment to seize upon the Dutch colony by force. This was done under the pretext of England's right to the whole region from Massachusetts to Virginia; and in 1664, Charles II. gave to his brother, the Duke of York, a charter for all the district between the Connecticut and the Delaware, ignoring the rights of New Netherland altogether. In the summer of the same year, a formidable expedition appeared in the harbor, and as the people refused to give aid, Stuyvesant had no alternative but to submit. The town and all the Dutch possessions passed quietly into the hands of the English; and henceforth New York became the name of the colony. Fort Orange on the Hudson capitulated, and the name Albany was given to it. The Dutch on the Delaware were also speedily reduced to submission.

New Jersey, lying between the Hudson and the Delaware, dates its origin from this year 1664. Lord Berkeley and Sir George Carteret were the proprietaries. Very favorable terms were offered to colonists, especially a Colonial Assembly, the sole power of taxation, religious freedom, etc. Various disputes arose within a few years as to quitrents, and in 1670, Carteret, the governor, was obliged to flee. He returned from England within two years with fresh powers. William Penn became one of the proprietaries this year, and by his arbitration the province was divided into East and West Jersey. The Quakers occupied the latter and soon became prosperous, and also obtained the good will of the Indians. In 1682, East Jersey was purchased by some Quakers, who obtained a new patent from the Duke of York in 1683. Andros, governor of New York, undertook to act in a lawless sort of manner towards Jersey; but the Quakers, guided by Penn, firmly asserted their rights. By an appeal to England the question was settled in their favor, and the colony gave promise of future solid growth.

In regard to New York, the early measures taken by the Duke gave but little satisfaction, and the merchants and others averred that they had gained nothing by the change from under the Dutch rule. In 1673, a Dutch fleet appeared in the harbor of New York; the town was surrendered, and the Dutch for a while held the place; but next year it passed back again by treaty into the hands of the English. The Duke of York sent over Edmund Andros to enforce his rights and claims and to insist upon obedience. Andros failed in an attempt on Connecticut, and also found the people of New York ill-disposed to submit to arbitrary, irresponsible power, especially in the laying of taxes. The Duke of York yielded at last to persistent remonstrances and appeals, and acceded to the calling of an assembly. On the 17th of October, 1683, the first popular Assembly met, and set forth their rights as freemen. The next year the Assembly met again, and adopted the charter of liberties and privileges; but as the Duke of York became King James II. in 1685, he refused to allow these privileges and rights recently granted. He ordered Dongan, the governor to resume the former arrangement of affairs, and to impose taxes without regard to the will of the people.

In the progress of New England History, an important step, taken in 1643, deserves notice here. This was the forming a confederation under the name of "The United Colonies of New England." It consisted of the Colonies of Massachusetts, New Plym outh, Connecticut, and New Haven; New Hampshire was included, coming in under the protection of Massachusetts. By the articles of confederation, each was pledged to the other to aid and assist in every matter, for defence or offence, tending to mutual safety and welfare. It was declared to be a perpetual union, and continued till James II. (1684–86) deprived the New England colonies of their charters.

Religious troubles and persecutions became rife at this date. Some of the Anabaptist sect, and a wild sort of a heretic named Gorton, were severely handled in 1637 and 1644; and the magistrates seemed to grow more and more stern and unrelenting. In 1648, Massachusetts set the first example of an execution for witchcraft, by putting to death Margaret Jones, charged with having "a malignant touch." Seven years later, Anne Hibbins suffered in the same way. Other and more shocking exhibitions of the spirit of persecution, necessarily consequent upon the fundamental principles of the Puritan theocracy, followed soon after, and they came about in this wise. The Quakers were a sect who took their rise in England about 1644, under the preaching of George Fox. They held to the notion of an internal revelation direct from Deity, superseding and rendering useless all external forms and ordinances of religion. They despised titles, ignored the ordinary civilities of life, and denounced pleasures of every sort, and especially the tyranny of rulers in high places, whether temporal or spiritual. They were overflowing with zeal, and manifested a fanatical desire to encounter persecution and outrage. Of course people of this sort would come at once into collision with Puritan rules and regulations. In July, 1656, two Quaker women arrived in Boston, having come from Barbadoes and being prepared to face the consequences. They were immediately arrested, imprisoned for five weeks, their trunks rifled, books burnt, and themselves expelled from the colony. Heavy fines were imposed upon all captains of vessels bringing in Quakers into Massachusetts; whippings were inflicted, ears were cropped, tongues bored, and the like; but still the Quakers came, and persevered in braving the authorities. It was war to the knife between ecclesiastical bigotry and insane fanaticism. In 1658, a decree of banishment was enforced on pain of death; but Robinson, Stephenson and Mary Dyer were bent upon martyrdom. The authorities did not flinch, though Winthrop and other good men pleaded earnestly against spilling the blood of those who were semi-lunatics at least. Robinson and Stephenson were hanged in 1659, and Mary Dyer, respited for a while, was also hanged on Boston Common in June, 1660. The magistrates entered upon a formal defence of their course, which was genrally condemned by the people. Others of the Quakers appeared, and even courted death, affirming that for every man executed five would come in his room. The authorities could not withstand the conviction that they were disgracing themselves and the cause of true religion by their action; and so they gave up hangings and the like; prisoners were discharged; if any returned they were to be whipped out of the bounds again; thus the mania, in due time, died out a natural death.

The labors of John Eliot, the Indian Missionary, form a pleasant offset to the above. He began his labors in 1646; learned the Indian dialect in New England, so as to translate the Bible for the benefit of the natives; and was prudent, zealous, gentle, and untiring in his devotion. Money was sent to him from England in 1661; his Indian Bible was printed at Cambridge, in 1663; a sort of Indian college was established the same year; and his whole life was spent in this service. He died in 1690, full of years and honors; and though it is true, that no permanent impression was made upon the natives, and that the sterner Puritans looked coldly upon his efforts, yet the name of John Eliot will always be remembered with thankfulness in the early annals of our country.

The progress of New England and the American Colonies generally, during Cromwell's rule in the mother country, was sure and steady in all the elements of material prosperity; and the men of that age, hardy, energetic, self-possessed, bred in the principles and under the influence of freedom, were becoming prepared, in God's Providence, for the period when they should assert and maintain their claims to independence of all but their own control. On the accession of Charles II. in 1660, New England entertained well-founded apprehensions of what might be the consequences to it. The Massachusetts folks determined, however, to hold on to their rights under the charter; to submit only so far as they were forced by compulsion; and while making a show of submission, to maintain their resistance to any and every act which they deemed injurious or prejudicial to their interests. The king's authority was acknowledged in general terms, and two agents were sent to England in 1662, to see what could be done in the emergency. Charles II. confirmed the charter, but required an acknowledgment of his prerogative, the oath of allegiance, toleration for the Church of England, and allowance of franchise to every freeholder. Evasive responses were made to these requisitions, and in 1664, Commissioners arrived in Boston to enforce the royal claims. They spent some two years in New England, but accomplished nothing. The Massachusetts leaders, profuse in expressions of loyalty, were unyielding in their determination to maintain their rights and privileges; and the king, on receiving the Commissioners' report in 1666, was preparing to force submission; but fortunately for the colony, he had his hands full at home—the plague and great fire in London occurred at this time, and for a few years New England was left undisturbed.

Connecticut and Rhode Island, more prompt than Massachusetts in acknowledging the royal authority, met with especial favor from the king. The younger Winthrop for the former, and Clarke for the latter, obtained very liberal privileges under the great seal for the obedient colonies. The provisions of their charters were confirmed, and freedom and toleration established on the broad platform of right and justice.

At this date, about fifty years from the landing on Plymouth Rock, the New England colonies numbered 120 towns, and between 60,000 and 70,000 inhabitants. Not only trade and commerce had increased, but the face of the country was become quite changed; so much so that the Indian tribes began to feel very restless and dissatisfied with the progress of the white men, and the consequent cutting off their hunting grounds in every direction. A leader only was wanting, in such a state of affairs, to induce the red men to make one desperate effort to stop the advance of civilization and the increase of the power of the white race. Philip, Sachem of the Wampanoags, was the man for the time. Brave, proud, of superior ability, and deadly in his hostility to the colonists, he was able to persuade all the tribes of New England to join in a confederacy in order to cut off their enemies. In 1675 King Philip's war began, and lasted for about two years. It was the most bloody and wide-spread conflict in which the colonies had ever been engaged. The lives which were lost, the terrible sufferings endured, especially by helpless women and children, the towns and settlements destroyed, were almost beyond description. The colonists not only met with these heavy losses, in this war, but contracted also a heavy debt in carrying it through; a debt, however, which they did not ask help from England to discharge. Philip was hunted down at last and shot, and his young son was sold as a slave in Bermuda.

In 1680, Edward Randolph came from England to enforce the acts of trade, which had been resisted, and to collect the royal customs. The magistrates refused submission altogether, and Randolph could effect nothing. Two years later he obtained a royal letter peremptorily demanding obedience.

The authorities obstinately persisted in the determination to which they had come; but it was to no purpose. A *scire-facias* was issued in England in 1684 and the charter of Massachusetts was declared to be forfeited. A temporary government was established; but in 1686 James II., the new king, sent Andros over to carry out the arbitrary and tyrannical designs of the last of the Stuarts. Connecticut and Rhode Island met with similar treatment. Andros dissolved the General Assembly in Rhode Island and demanded the charter of Connecticut. The document itself was saved, but Andros declared it to be forfeited. This state of things, however, was short-lived, since James II. was soon after compelled to abandon the English throne, and the accession of William and Mary wrought speedy and great changes in the position and prospects of the American colonies.

Sir William Berkeley, as we have seen (p. 61) was elected governor of Virginia in 1660, and apparently popular liberty was well established; but great changes occurred during the following twenty-five years. These were brought about by several causes. Virginia had been settled by a rather aristocratic class who had no high opinion of the people as a part of the ruling power in the land. There were indented servants and negro slaves, who, of course, could have no claim to the privileges of freemen; and the aristocratic class naturally obtained ascendancy in the management of public affairs. Berkeley was one of this class and rated the position of his order very highly; the Assembly kept themselves in office from year to year; part of the people were disfranchised; heavy taxes were laid; and all legislation was for the benefit of this ruling class in the community. Intolerance too, found opportunity for its exercise. Puritans, Baptists, and Quakers were fined and banished (though they did not kill any Quakers, as Massachusetts did); free schools and the printing press were denounced by Berkeley, and the whole aim of the party in power was to maintain the dominion of a body of wealthy planters over a submissive, ignorant commonalty, and a still lower class of white servants and negro slaves. Discontent soon manifested itself, and Nathaniel Bacon, a prominent planter, became the leader in efforts to obtain redress and secure to all their just rights and privileges. A bitter contest arose between Berkeley and Bacon, commencing with Indian troubles and disputes, and terminating only with the latter's death. Berkeley throughout displayed a bigoted and vengeful spirit. "Bacon's Laws," as they are called, were enacted by the Assembly (1676), and gave clear evidence of progress in the right direction. His sudden death, however, in 1677, put a stop to further reform, and Berkeley, "that old fool," as Charles II. called him, gratified to the full his malice by fines, exactions, cruel usage, and worst of all, by judicial murder of more than twenty persons. Culpepper and Effingham, two needy courtiers of Charles the spend-thrift, found opportunity, under a royal grant, to oppress the colonists and grind money out of them during the next seven or eight years. Popular liberty became nearly extinct, and James II. dissolved the Assembly just before he himself was ejected from the throne of England (1688).

Affairs in Maryland, as already stated (p. 61), were in a prosperous condition under Calvert, and Lord Baltimore obtained solid returns for the outlays he had made on the province (1676). Earnest efforts were put forth to secure something like a church establishment, as the great body of the colonists were Protestants, and some excitement and an outbreak followed (1681); but matters were soon put at rest. James II. was eager to take away the charter and bring ruin upon Maryland; but in this, as in the case of other colonies, he failed of success in consequence of the ignominious close of his own career.

About 1660, some adventurers from New England attempted a settlement near the mouth of Cape Fear River, but nothing permanent resulted. Charles II. in 1663 granted territory south of the Chesapeake, from Albemarle Sound to St. John's River, to a body of noblemen—the Earl of Clarendon, Duke of Albemarle, and others, as proprietaries, with all the rights, privileges and powers. The region was called Carolina. Settlements were made at Albemarle and Clarendon, and the prospect for the future was decidedly good. In order to establish a constitution suitable to the ideas and dignity of the noble proprietaries, John Locke was called upon for help (1670), and his "Grand Model" made evident the fact, that a man may be a great metaphysician and philosopher, and yet produce very absurd things for practical use among men. Such was the case with Locke's Grand Model, with its ranks of nobility, and its curious combination of impracticabilities. A fair trial of it was made; but nobody was satisfied; nobody could get along with the philosopher's scheme so far as the New World was concerned; and so, by and by, it virtually died out a natural death. This same year (1670), colonists under William Sayle, occupied a district between Ashley and Cooper Rivers. Yeamans succeeded Sayle two years later; and as the new settlement was at a distance from Albemarle a separate government was instituted; hence arose the distinction between *North* and *South* Carolina. Dutch and Huguenot emigrants arrived at this period, and added strength to the colony. The Indians, urged on by the Spaniards at St. Augustine, were hostile; and discontent, murmuring and hardships of various sorts followed. The proprietaries also were dissatisfied, not to say disgusted, at finding that they had to pay out money continually, instead of having it paid back to them; so that, for a number of years, frequent disturbances occurred from factions and quarrels not easy to be put at rest. James II. proposed to make short work of the charter here, as in other colonies, and ordered a *quo warranto* (1686); but still, despite all kinds of troubles, the Carolinas steadily and effectively advanced in population and general prosperity and in securing the rights and privileges of self-government.

Pennsylvania owes its name and foundation to the distinguished William Penn, the Quaker. He had for years been an efficient friend and helper to the members of his peculiar sect in New Jersey, and in 1681 he obtained an extensive grant of land west of the Delaware. The king owed him, on his father's account, some £16,000; but as money was an article not to be got from Charles II., Penn was glad to take the royal grant of land instead, in the hope that he might obtain a reasonable pecuniary return, and also furnish an asylum for the oppressed members of the Quaker sect in Europe or America. The terms proposed by Penn to settlers were liberal and even generous, and his course with regard to the Indians was such as to redound to his honor, for he was the first who treated the red man fairly and honestly, and recognized the fact that the natives had rights as well as the new comers. Three vessels with emigrants set sail, in July, 1681, for the shores of the Delaware, and in October, the next year, Penn himself landed in the New World. The freemen were called together, and laws and regulations of various kinds agreed upon and adopted. Philadelphia was founded in 1683, and grew rapidly. The success of Pennsylvania was certain, and was very gratifying, no doubt, to its large and liberal minded founder; but he, too, was called upon to suffer loss and meet with mortifying disappointment. In August, 1684, Penn returned to England, leaving twenty settlements and 7000 inhabitants in the colony; but his absence led to various encroachments on his rights as proprietary; he obtained only trifling returns, from quitrents, for his heavy outlays; the colonists gradually obtained possession of every thing; and when James II. fell, Penn suffered additional reverses, and he was deprived, in 1690, by order of the Privy Council, of all control in the affairs of Pennsylvania.

We may mention here, that French colonial enterprise thus far was much less successful than that of the English. The Indians were, nearly every where, bitterly hostile, despite the efforts of the Jesuit and other missionaries, and the company of New France, as it was called, gave up in despair in 1662. Marquette, in 1673, made his way to the Mississippi, "the great river," as the name imports, and floated on its waters a long way to the southward. La Salle followed, in 1678, exploring the great chain of lakes, Erie, St. Clair, Huron, and Michigan. Amid many severe trials and losses, La Salle persevered, and finally descended the Mississippi in a barge. In the name of France, he took possession of the mouth of the river, April 9th, 1682, and the name Louisiana was given to the newly acquired territory. La Salle's further efforts at colonization resulted disastrously, and he himself was murdered in March, 1687. Thus, at the date of James the Second's downfall, 1688, the French colonies in America were much weaker, and had much less of the elements of stability in them, than the English. Important consequences flowed from this fact, as we shall see, when the collision between England and France soon after occurred.

In New England the accession of William III., Prince of Orange, was hailed with great satisfaction by the people, and they proceeded at once to hasten forward measures of reform in opposition to the governors appointed by James II. Andros (p. 65) was arrested in Boston, and sent to England; the people of New York placed at the head of affairs Jacob Leisler, who, two years later, by a sort of judicial murder, was put to death under Sloughter, the new governor of the colony; Virginia, rather tardily, acknowledged William and Mary; and in Maryland a popular insurrection took place against Lord Baltimore, headed by John Coode, which lasted some three years. Almost immediately on the accession of William, he became involved in war with Louis XIV. of France. As a matter of course, the American colonies could not escape taking part in the contest. Both parties at first were eager for the strife. New England, not less than the French colonists, entertained schemes of conquest and advancement. The latter purposed to monopolize the western fur trade, secure uninterrupted passage through Lake Erie to the Mississippi, and cut off the English from the cod fishery on the banks of Newfoundland; while the former hoped, and apparently not without reason, to be able to deprive the French of all the advantages which they possessed, and even expel them entirely from the country. Both parties, too, nationally and religiously enemies, were prepared to engage in bloody strife with unpitying hearts and unmistakable ferocity. The war broke out in June, 1689, by an attack on Dover, and subsequently on other places. Count Frontenac was appointed governor of Canada and pushed forward hostilities with energy. Schenectady was destroyed by the French and Indians, in February, 1690, and Salmon Falls met with a similar fate. The people of New England and New York were terrified, but speedily resolved upon vengeance. A land and naval expedition against Canada was fitted out; Phipps commanded the ships, and Winthrop the troops; but the results were mortifying in the extreme. The land forces did not reach Canada at all, and Phipps, who expected to take Quebec by surprise, was compelled to return to Boston, in December, 1690, having accomplished nothing, except emptying the treasury and causing the first issue of paper money in the colonies to meet the emergency. Added to the sanguinary ravages of the French and Indians was the witchcraft delusion, that direful phenomenon in the history of Massachusetts. It prevailed during 1692 and 1693, especially at Salem, and was marked by cruelty and madness, and the fiercest displays of fanaticism and lawlessness which have ever disgraced the annals of any civilized nation in the world. The frontier warfare, meanwhile, continued, and the French and English, with the help of their savage allies, inflicted upon each other all the injuries of which they were capable; but with no special advantage to either party. The peace of Ryswick, at the close of 1697, brought the first intercolonial war to an end, leaving the possessions of the contending parties in about the same condition as when the contest began.

The disputes between France and England relative to the "Spanish succession" brought on a second intercolonial war, and involved the colonists not only with the French in the north, but with the Spaniards, also, in Florida. Active preparations were made in Canada, in 1702, for renewing the contest, and the settlements in Maine were furiously attacked. Massacres were perpetrated at Deerfield (1704) and Haverhill (1708) under De Rouville and the Indians. An expedition against Port Royal (Annapolis) was undertaken in 1710, and met with entire success. A much larger expedition, the next year, against Quebec, was a complete failure, and excited much indignation among the colonists. The struggle ended with the treaty of Utrecht, in 1713; but several important advantages had been obtained. These were, the entire possession of Hudson's Bay and the fur trade, the whole of Newfoundland (the French having certain privileges in the fisheries), and the territory of Acadie, which received the name of Nova Scotia.

The third intercolonial war took its rise from the effort on the part of Spain (1740) to maintain that jealous system of colonial monopoly which she had adopted in its utmost rigor, and in which she was imitated by the French and English. The latter had acquired, by the treaty of Utrecht, the privilege of transporting a certain number of slaves annually to the Spanish colonies, under cover of which a wide-spread system of smuggling had been introduced, against which the Spaniards vainly sought to protect themselves by the establishment of revenue cruisers. Some of these Spanish vessels had attacked English ships engaged in lawful traffic, and had committed several instances of barbarity, which had greatly moved the popular indignation, and excited a clamor for war, to which Walpole, the minister, was reluctantly obliged to consent. Soon after, a general European war broke out, under George II., and the colonies in America were, of course, involved in new struggles. The important fortress of Louisburg, on Cape Breton, was attacked by the New Englanders, aided by an English fleet, in 1745, and taken after a vigorously-conducted siege. It was, however, restored to France by the treaty of Aix-la-Chapelle, in 1748. For the present the struggle was closed; but the colonists never lost sight of Canada, and were determined upon expelling the French at the earliest possible moment.

Some years before the breaking out of the third intercolonial war, the colony of Georgia was planted in that waste and unproductive portion of Carolina between the Savannah and the Altamaha rivers (1732). Its origin was due to kindly and benevolent motives and desires, notwithstanding the errors of jndgment into which its founders fell; and the name of James Edward Oglethorpe will always be held in deserved honor and esteem. This philanthropic man was earnestly intent upon mitigating the evils connected with imprisonment for debt, and hoped also to provide seasonable relief for the struggling poor of England, who might desire to live soberly and industriously, and reap the fruits of their efforts. In conjunction with Lord Percival and other noblemen and gentlemen, Oglethorpe obtained a charter from Parliament of a part of Carolina, south of the Savannah, to be settled for the purposes just named. Liberal contributions were made by the nobility and clergy; parliament also made a grant; and the warmest interest was excited in favor of the plan. They who thought of political advantages, favored the project because of the service Georgia was likely to prove as a barrier on the south against the Spaniards; merchants were attracted by promises of wine and silk as staples for the new colony; Protestants looked hitherward as a refuge for their persecuted brethren on the continent; and those who desired to labor for the conversion of the Indians, had here a wide field opened to them for their self-denying labors. Savannah was founded in 1733; German, Scotch, and other emigrants settled in Georgia; efforts were made to provide defence against their hostile neighbors the Spaniards; but the progress of the colony was slow and unsatisfactory. After twenty years' striving, and the expenditure of parliamentary grants amounting to more than $600,000, the trustees gave up the charter, and thenceforth Georgia became a royal province (1752).

In this connection, we may here briefly note that Louisiana owed its origin to the persevering efforts of the French to establish an uninterrupted line of communication between Canada and the Gulf of Mexico. D'Iberville discovered the mouth of the Mississippi in 1699, and ascended as high as the Red River; but all attempts at colonization failed of anything like real success. In 1717, the whole population, white and black, amounted to only about 700. John Law, the Scotch adventurer, and the famous Mississippi Company, promised at this date untold wealth to be drawn from Louisiana; but the bubble burst in 1720, at which time the Royal Bank had paper in circulation amounting to 2,235,085,590 livres. The colony struggled on; the site of New Orleans was chosen by Bienville, the governor, in 1718; serious difficulties occurred, and sharp contests also, with the Spaniards and with the Indians; in 1732, the Mississippi Company gave up Louisiana to the king; and during the following twenty years, under De Vaudreuil as governor, the colony made fair progress, and advanced in prosperity.

After a brief interval, the struggle was renewed between the English and French colonists, the crisis having now been reached when it was to be decided which of the two were to be the masters in North America. The fourth intercolonial war began on the isthmus of Nova Scotia (1750), and a collision soon after occurred between the French in the Valley of the Ohio and the neighboring colonists in Virginia and Pennsylvania. This brings, for the first time, on the stage of history the illustrious GEORGE WASHINGTON, then just ripening into manhood. He was sent by Governor Dinwiddie, of Virginia, on a difficult and delicate mission to the French on the Ohio (1753), and acquitted himself of his task most satisfactorily. In the year 1755, a year before the formal declaration of war (the seven years' war in Europe), America was resounding with arms. The efforts of the English were not at first successful; Braddock was defeated in Western Pennsylvania, in July, 1755; Johnson won a barren victory at Lake George (1755); the forts at Oswego and Lake George were taken by Montcalm (1756–7); and not until a vigorous effort was made both by England and by her colonies, did the fortunes of the conflict turn. Then (1758), Louisburg and the Gulf of St. Lawrence were seized; and the next year Wolfe defeated Montcalm on the plains of Abraham, both heroes being killed at the same time, and Quebec fell into the possession of the English (1759). This decided the war, and peace soon followed. The treaty of Paris (1763) surrendered all the French possessions in America save the islands of St. Pierre and Miquelon off Newfoundland. New Orleans and the territory west of the Mississippi were transferred to Spain, who had been the ally of France in the last year of the war. All east of the Mississippi was ceded to England.

A large share of the victories achieved over the French in America was due, undoubtedly, to the exertions of the English colonists. They gave their best energies, their fortunes, and their lives to a cause which was as much theirs as it was the mother land's; and when they conquered, they felt that it was for the colonies as well as for England to profit by the victory. Not so, however, thought many Englishmen, especially among those in power. They asserted that the war had been waged mainly for England, and at the expense of England, and that the colonists owed a debt to the mother country, both pecuniary and political, which they must be led, or, if necessary, forced to discharge. Meanwhile, the colonies had increased in many ways; their physical and intellectual resources were enlarged, and if they were able to contribute more in the way of revenue to the mother country, they were also able to resist any undue demand of hers more effectually. The effect of the late wars was thus enhanced by the previous developments of peace and onward progress.*

It was in this same year (1763) that a wide spread combination among the Indians led to fearful ravages on their part. The Delawares and Shawanese, now occupying the banks of the Muskingum, Sciota, and Miami, provoked by being crowded rudely by the settlers fast pouring across the Alleghanies, and perhaps incited by the artful representation of French fur traders, made a simultaneous attack, in June, along the whole frontier of Pennsylvania and Virginia. The noted Pontiac, a man of superior ability, was the moving spirit of this confederation, and it tasked to the utmost the powerful influence of Sir William Johnson to keep the Six Nations from joining Pontiac against the white men. The English traders were plundered and slain, and the posts between the Ohio and Lake Erie, were surprised and taken. Only Niagara, Detroit, and Fort Pitt held out, the two latter being closely blockaded; and the troops which Amherst sent to relieve them did not reach their destination without severe encounters. General Gage, the new commander-in-chief, called for levies of troops to aid in putting an end to this war with the Indians, and in the course of the year the red men were brought to terms.

It was perhaps but natural that, under the circumstances, the English government should think seriously of attempting to draw revenue from the colonies by taxation. Under the ministry of William Pitt, England had obtained great glory over her enemies; but glory then, as now, was an expensive thing; the national debt was piled up to an enormous extent; and some measures must be taken to meet the difficulty. The colonists, on their part, as was but natural, looked suspiciously upon any scheme which had in view the trenching upon their inalienable right not to grant money except by or through their own representatives; and so they prepared themselves sturdily to resist every thing of the kind. As a part of the policy of the English ministry, is was proposed to maintain in America ten thousand regular troops as a peace establishment, for the defence of the colonies. Probably also there was had in view the importance of such a force as this, to help to sustain the authority of the crown in the colonies. So soon as peace was established, the successors of Mr. Pitt in the ministry, in accordance with the proposal of the Board of Trade some years before, determined to try the scheme of taxation by the supreme ordinance of Parliament. That Parliament had authority over the colonies, was admitted on all hands, but just what it was or how far it extended, was not quite so clear. Although the colonists had unwillingly yielded to the exercise of power by Parliament in *matters of trade*, still they had yielded submission, and had suffered legislation to extend to a number of other matters beside trade. Parliament had regulated colonial trade for the exclusive benefit of the mother country for a long time, and had appointed custom-house officers, and instituted admiralty courts in the colonies: it is true, these were systematically evaded and resisted; nevertheless, what had been done and submitted to, had given Parliament a sort of legal vested right in all points of the kind. But, let it be

* "Thus ended," says Mr. Irving, "the contest between France and England for dominion in America, in which, as has been said, the first gun was fired in Washington's encounter with De Jumonville (1754). A French statesman and diplomatist (Count de Vergennes), consoled himself by the persuasion that it would be a fatal triumph to England. It would remove the only check by which her colonies were kept in awe. 'They will no longer need her protection,' said he; 'she will call on them to contribute toward supporting the burdens they have helped to bring on her, and *they will answer by striking for independence.*'"—*Life of Washington*, I. 308.

noted, Parliament had never exercised the power of levying *taxes for revenue.* The minor matters of regulating the postage on letters, and certain duties on "enumerated articles," were mere trifles; and however the question might stand as to the power of Parliament to levy taxes upon the colonists, it was certain that it never yet had been attempted to be exercised. When the English ministry ventured to make the trial, the contest, almost at once, involved in itself the very essentials of life and liberty. That astute minister, Sir Robert Walpole, when a suggestion was made to him to levy a direct tax upon the colonies, had declined making so dangerous an experiment: "I shall leave this operation to some one of my successors, who may possess more courage than I, and have less regard for the commercial interests of England. My opinion is, that, if by favoring the trade of the colonies with foreign nations, they gain £500,000, at the end of two years, fully one half of it will have come into the royal exchequer, by the increased demand for English manufactures. This is a mode of taxing them more agreeably to their own constitution and laws, as well as our own." But there was not the same political sagacity in some of Walpole's successors; and they ventured to try what he had declined; they determined to tax the colonies. George Grenville enjoys the reputation of having given origin to the scheme which resulted in the well known Stamp Act. He became prime minister in 1764, and proposed several resolutions tending to develop his plan for taxing America, such as additional duties on imports into the colonies from foreign countries, on sugar, indigo, coffee, etc., it being openly avowed that the object had in view was, to "raise a revenue for defraying the expenses of defending, protecting, and securing his majesty's dominions in America." These resolutions passed the House without much debate or notice, it being resolved, without a division, "that Parliament had a right to tax the colonies." Among the resolutions proposed by Grenville, was one imposing "certain stamp duties on the colonies." The colonial agents sent copies of these resolutions to America, where they were denounced at once as unlawful and tyrannical in purpose and design. "If taxes are laid upon us without our having a legal representation where they are laid," was Samuel Adams's emphatic declaration, "we are reduced from the character of free subjects to the state of tributary slaves." Similar bold and uncompromising language was spread abroad throughout the colonies by means of the press, and remonstrances were addressed to Parliament of no doubtful or uncertain tenure. Grenville did not immediately press the measure, shrewdly hoping that the colonists would propose something else as an alternative, and so he would get the money he wanted; but, disappointed in this, for the Americans were quite as shrewd as he was, he brought the bill into Parliament, and it became a law in March, 1765.

Great were the excitement and indignation in the colonies when the action of Parliament was made known. Virginia and Massachusetts took the lead in passing strong resolutions, vindicating their rights, and in proposing the meeting of delegates in New York to consider and determine upon action necessary in the present exigency. On the 7th of October, committees from nine of the colonies met in New York, and after a three weeks' lively session agreed upon a Declaration of the rights and grievances of the colonies, in which they claimed all the privileges of Englishmen, as their birthright, and energetically denied the right of being taxed except with their own consent. Steps the most decided were taken in regard to any actual operation of the Stamp Act. It was treated virtually with contempt, and the people refused every where to use the stamps in legal or other proceedings; and what cut more deeply than all, they formed associations against importing British manufactures till the Stamp Act should be repealed. This latter step touched the manufacturing interest in England at once, and the result was that the merchants became as urgent as the colonists for repeal

Parliament met in January, 1766, and long and stormy debates ensued. Pitt distinguished himself on the occasion. It had been maliciously insinuated by Grenville that he had encouraged a rebellious temper in the colonists. The insinuation was not to be borne for an instant. Every one yielded at once to Pitt, who repelled the attack with characteristic intrepidity. "Sir, a charge is brought against gentlemen sitting in this House of giving birth to sedition in America. The freedom with which they have spoken their sentiments against this unhappy Act is imputed to them as a crime; but the imputation shall not discourage me. It is a liberty which I hope no gentleman will be afraid to exercise; it is a liberty by which the gentleman who calumniates it might have profited. He ought to have desisted from his project. We are told America is obstinate—America is almost in open rebellion. Sir, *I rejoice America has resisted;* three millions of people so dead to all the feelings of liberty, as voluntarily to submit to be slaves would have been fit instruments to make slaves of all the rest." After a long and eloquent speech, he advised the immediate and total repeal of the odious act. This was soon after done, the ministry and Parliament, however, previously declaring that "Parliament had, and of right ought to have, power to bind the colonies in all cases whatsoever." Legal authorities differed as to the real point at issue, viz., in regard to taxation. Lord Camden expressed himself in the clearest and most forcible manner: "My position is this — I repeat it; I will maintain it to the last hour — taxation and representation are inseparable. The position is founded in the law of nature. It is more; it is itself an eternal law of nature. For whatsoever is a man's own, it is absolutely his own. No man has a right to take it from him without his consent. Whoever attempts to do it, attempts an injury. Whoever does it, commits a robbery."

The news of the repeal of the Stamp Act was recei-ed in America with great satisfaction, and it was hoped that hereafter peace and concord would prevail; but England had begun the contest, foolishly and ignorantly, and though for the moment prevented from carrying out her real designs, yet she was none the less resolute and determined upon asserting and maintaining her absolute power over the colonies. Thoughtful men could not but notice the glaring discrepancy between giving up a claim and still affirming a power to maintain this same claim at any point of time when Parliament chose. Early in the following year (1767), Townshend proposed a scheme of taxation which, it was hoped, might be successful, on the principle maintained by Pitt as to the difference between a direct tax and commercial imposts for regulating trade. Hence, he proposed to lay a duty upon teas imported into America, together with paints, paper, glass and lead, which were articles of British produce; its alleged object being to raise a revenue for the support of the civil government, for the expense of a standing army, and for giving permanent salaries to the royal governors, with a view to render them independent of the colonial Assemblies. Pitt was at the time confined by sickness in the country, and the bill passed with very little opposition, and on the 29th of June, received the royal assent. In order to enforce the new act, and those already in existence, which, odious as they were to the Americans, had hitherto been continually evaded by them, a Board of Revenue Commissioners was to be established at Boston. The New York Assembly was also restrained from further legislative proceedings, until they manifested a more compliant humor than heretofore. Conduct of this kind stirred up anew excitement and indignation in America. The colonists could not, and would not, give up the *right*, which they felt to be on their side in this matter. Petitions were sent to the king, letters also to the prominent advocates in behalf of the colonies in England, and early in 1768 a circular letter was addressed by Massachusetts to the rest of the colonies, inviting them to engage in a common defence of their rights, concluding the letter with an expression of their "firm confidence in the king, their common head and father, and that the united and dutiful supplications of his distressed American subjects will meet with his royal and favorable acceptance." Everywhere the attitude of Massachusetts was looked upon with favor and earnestly seconded; the newly appointed custom house officers found it quite impossible to discharge their duties; impressment of seamen by a war vessel roused the deepest feeling; and troops from Halifax were brought into Boston to overawe the city and enforce obedience. A popular convention was held, delegates being sent from more than 100 towns, and the flame of liberty and resistance to tyranny was kept burning. Party lines, too, throughout the colonies began now to be strictly drawn. The partizans of the mother country were stigmatized as *Tories*, while the opponents of Parliamentary taxation took the name of *Whigs*—old names lately applied in England as designations for the king's friends and their opponents.

The vacillating course of the English ministry deserves to be specially noted. Weakness and folly seemed to characterize most of their plans with regard to America. Steadily bent upon obtaining revenue from the colonies, Parliament, at one moment, were for enforcing their laws; at the next, they gave way for their repeal. Doing and undoing, threatening and retracting, straining and relaxing, followed one after the other as occasion required. Anxious to establish the supremacy of Parliament, but afraid to stem the vigorous opposition of the colonies, they endeavored to pass such laws as would meet the wishes of the government, without rousing the resistance of the colonists. Had the British ministry been magnanimous enough to frankly and fully yield the point in dispute, as to the right of taxation without representation, the colonies, probably, would have met them in the same spirit with which they proposed to settle the matter. On the other hand, if England seriously contemplated the use of force, nothing could have been more unwise and inexpedient than to make partial concessions, to hesitate, and to employ only a show of force which irritated, without compelling obedience or even respect. Possibly, even now the differences might have been adjusted; but it was only a bare possibility; the colonists were daily becoming less and less disposed to yield, and the more the question was forced upon their attention, the more readily they began to entertain the idea of governing themselves and rejecting the domination of Parliament, three thousand miles away, on the other side of the ocean.

The contest was continued without abatement as months and years rolled on. A collision occurred (1770)—the "Boston Massacre"—between the soldiers and citizens, in which several of the latter were killed, stirring up a storm of indignation and thirst for vengeance, especially as this was the first blood shed in the dispute with England. Lord North, the new prime minister, tried the experiment of repealing all the duties imposed by Townshend's acts, except that on tea, this latter being retained in order to show that the right of taxation was still possessed by Parliament. The colonists resented this action, as they had resented similar action before; and an active correspondence and earnest mutual conference were kept up between the chief patriots and leading political bodies in the colonies. The excitement against Parliament was continued by popular meetings, and every thing tended to urge on the Americans to proceed to extremities. The attempt to force upon the colonies cargoes of tea, brought matters to a crisis. This article had largely accumulated in the warehouses, in England, of the East India Company; and it was hoped that the export duty being taken off, the colonists would not object to the odious imposition of three pence per pound, seeing that they in fact obtained the tea nine pence per pound cheaper than it was sold in England. But in this they reckoned without their host; and the colonists unanimously resolved not only not to use the tea at all, but also not even to permit it to be landed in America. Active steps for this purpose were immediately taken. The consignees were warned not to receive it when it came, or attempt to bring it into port any where. This was in the latter part of 1773. On the 16th of December, a town meeting was held in Boston to take action with reference to a ship recently arrived with a cargo of tea. Roused by the fervid eloquence of Josiah Quincy, the question was put to the assemblage:—"Will you abide by your former resolutions with respect to not suffering the tea to be landed?" A unanimous shout was the reply, and the excitement attained its utmost pitch. It was growing dark, and there was a cry for candles, when a man disguised as a Mohawk Indian raised the war-whoop in the gallery, which was responded to in the street without. Another voice suddenly shouted, "Boston harbor a teapot to-night! Hurra for Griffin's wharf!" The meeting instantly adjourned, and the people hurried down to the harbor to see the result. It was now six o'clock, but a fine, still evening. Some fifty men, in the guise of Mohawks, boarded the tea vessels, and while the dense crowd silently watched the proceeding, they drew up from the holds of the vessels three hundred and forty-two chests of tea, deliberately broke them open, and emptied their contents into the water. This occupied between two and three hours. No damage was done to any thing else, and when the tea had been destroyed, the crowd dispersed, without further noise or trouble, to their homes. A course equally decisive was pursued in New York, Philadelphia and Charleston, and in the last named city, though the teas were landed, care was taken to store them in damp cellars where they soon spoiled.

Direct collision with the mother country became now inevitable, and it was henceforth to be seen how far brave words would be supported by deeds. If blood *must* be shed, the colonists felt themselves equal to this last and searching appeal. The king was obstinate, and had no one near him to explain the true state of things in America, and admitted no misgivings except for not having sooner enforced the claims of authority. On the 4th of February, 1774, he consulted the American commander-in-chief, who had recently returned from New York. "I am willing to go back at a day's notice," said Gage, "if coercive measures are adopted. They will be lions while we are lambs; but, if we take the resolute part, they will undoubtedly prove very meek. Four regiments sent to Boston will be sufficient to prevent any disturbance." So little did George III. and his advisers understand or appreciate the spirit and energy of the Americans! As was to be expected, the ministry were very angry at what had been done, in Boston especially. The Boston Port Bill, by which that thriving mart of commerce was closed entirely, and other severe coercive acts were speedily adopted, and Parliament resolved to enforce these obnoxious measures at all hazards. The people of Boston were firm, patient, and stout-hearted; and the sympathy manifested on all hands was encouraging and cheering in a high degree. The House of Burgesses, in Virginia, acted in a spirited and decisive manner, and adopted a declaration of their views, in which a General Congress was strongly urged. Delegates were appointed, Washington being of the number; Massachusetts followed the important suggestion of Virginia, and also appointed delegates to the proposed Congress; the people generally began to take a lively interest in military drilling and exercises of every sort; and as the Governor was virtually shut up in Boston, the real administration of civil and political affairs was virtually carried on by popular convention.

The Continental Congress met in Philadelphia, September 5th, 1774. Fifty-three delegates appeared from twelve of the colonies, Georgia alone being unrepresented. It was a grave and reverend body, made up of the most eminent patriots in the land, Randolph, Henry, Lee, Rutledge, Adams, Jay, Washington, and others. A Declaration of Colonial Rights was drawn up, and expressed in clear and vigorous language the sentiments of all true-hearted Americans in regard to the questions at issue. Addresses were also adopted to the People of Great Britain, and to the Inhabitants of British America, together with a Petition to the King. This Congress adjourned at the close of October, after having made provision for another Congress to meet in the May following. The state of affairs in and around Boston grew more and more critical, and it became evident that direct collision between the soldiery and the people could not much longer be put off. Parliament and the ministry expressed themselves as outraged at the rebellious course pursued by the colonists, and avowed in unmistakable terms that they would compel these subjects of theirs into submission. Early in the year 1775, Pitt, now Lord Chatham, moved that the troops be removed from Boston, as a measure of conciliation; but though eloquently advocated, this proposal was rejected by a very large majority; and in an address to the king, Parliament declared "that as a *rebellion* actually existed in the Province of Massachusetts Bay, they besought his majesty to adopt measures to enforce the authority of the supreme legislature, and solemnly assured him that it was their fixed resolution, at the hazard of their lives and properties, to stand by him against his rebellious subjects." The Americans, meanwhile, were not idle. The Provincial Congress of Massachusetts met February 1st, 1775, at Cambridge, and about the middle of the month, adjourned to Concord. They entered with energy and spirit into measures and plans for resistance. They earnestly begged the militia, in general, and the minute-men, in particular, to be indefatigable in improving themselves in military discipline; they recommended the making of fire-arms and bayonets; and they dissuaded the people from supplying the troops in Boston with any thing necessary for military service. The Committee of Safety resolved to purchase powder, artillery, provisions, and other military stores, and to deposit them partly at Worcester, and partly at Concord. General Gage could not behold these movements with indifference, and the collision was certain to occur at no distant day. Having heard that military stores were collected at Concord, Gage resolved to seize upon them. He dispatched a body of 800 grenadiers on the night of April 18th, for this purpose. Instantly the country was alarmed through the activity of the men on watch, and the ringing of bells and firing of musketry gave evidence that the people were roused and ready for the struggle. Between four and five o'clock the next morning, the British troops reached Lexington, thirteen miles from Boston. Here about seventy of the minute-men were assembled, and were standing near the road; but their number being so small, they had no intention of making any resistance to the military. Major Pitcairn, who had been sent forward with the light infantry, rode towards them, calling out, "Disperse, you rebels! throw down your arms, and disperse!" The order was not instantly obeyed: Major Pitcairn advanced a little farther, fired his pistol and flourished his sword, while his men began to fire, with a shout. Several Americans fell; the rest dispersed, but the firing on them was continued; and, on observing this, some of the retreating colonists returned the fire. Eight Americans remained dead on the field. After this the troops advanced to Concord and destroyed all that they could lay hands on; but the end was not yet. The militia of the neighborhood advanced in arms, such as they had, and as blood had been shed, they attacked the retreating soldiers with vigor and spirit. Reinforcements poured in, and although Gage sent 900 men and two pieces of cannon, under Lord Percy, to support their comrades, yet the excitement in no wise abated. Men hastened in from all quarters; the troops were galled by incessant discharges of musketry; there was no respite whatever, and worn out with exhaustion they reached the end of their march soon after sunset, with 65 killed, 180 wounded and 28 made prisoners. The American loss was 50 killed and 34 wounded. Truly, as Washington said, in speaking of this matter, "if the retreat had not been as precipitate as it was — and God knows it could not well have been more so — the ministerial troops must have surrendered, or been totally cut off."

Deep and burning was the indignation throughout the length and breadth of the land when the news of the battle of Lexington was spread abroad, and within a few days Boston was besieged by the outraged people. The sword had been drawn, and it became evident to many, Washington especially, that the contest must be decided by the sword. Forts, magazines and arsenals, were speedily seized upon by the people in all directions. Troops were raised, nearly 20,000 men formed a line of encampment from Roxbury to the river Mystic, and General Ward was placed in command. Ethan Allen surprised and took Ticonderoga, in May, 1775, and Benedict Arnold did the same to Crown Point, thus securing possession of Lakes George and Champlain, and obtaining artillery, powder, etc. The second Continental Congress met, May 10th, at Philadelphia. It was, and was felt to be, a time of no ordinary trial, amid embarrassments and difficulties of the gravest character; but this assemblage of patriots was equal to the emergency. Besides issuing various state papers, it was voted that the colonies ought to be put in a posture of defence; and Congress ordered the enlistment of troops, the construction of forts at various points, the provision of arms, ammunition and military stores, etc. In order to meet the expense of these various measures, they authorized the emission of notes to the amount of $3,000,000, bearing the inscription of "The United Colonies;" the faith of the confederacy being pledged for their redemption. The Massachusetts Convention had requested Congress to assume the direction of the forces before Boston; and it was now resolved to raise ten additional companies of riflemen in Pennsylvania, Maryland, and Virginia, to be paid out of the public funds. Committees were appointed to prepare reports on subjects connected with the defence of the country, and a commander-in-chief was appointed, Washington being unanimously chosen. This was on the 15th of June, and Washington was at his post at the beginning of July. Additional troops, under Burgoyne, Clinton and Howe had arrived in Boston, and Gage resolved speedily to assume the offensive. Apprehending this, Col. Prescott was sent at nightfall with about 1000 men to take possession of Bunker's Hill. By some mistake, he advanced to Breed's Hill, which overlooks and commands Boston. The next morning the British general was astonished at the daring of the Americans, and resolved at once to have them dislodged. Three thousand picked men, led by Howe and Pigot, marched out in the afternoon of June 17th, 1775, and with studied contempt for their opponents, undertook to advance directly up the hill in front of the works; but they paid dearly for that experiment; for, although the Americans were fatigued and hungry and unsupported by reinforcements, they faltered not. The British troops were allowed to advance in silence almost to the very works, when a deadly discharge mowed them down, every shot telling upon the enemy. Again and again the assault was renewed, and each time, under the leadership of such men as Putnam, Stark, Prescott, and others of like stamp, it was met with the same heroic spirit; and, although it is true that the Americans were compelled at last to retire, and victory in that sense belonged to the British, yet it was a victory dearly bought, and more of a defeat, in fact, than a victory. The British loss was 1054; that of the Americans about 450.

On Washington's arrival in camp, he

BATTLE OF BUNKER HILL.

From the celebrated Picture by Trumbull.

found the army greatly needing discipline, drill, etc., and he had numerous and continual trials of patience and forbearance to encounter. The actual force was now about 14,000, and it was so posted as to keep Gage and some 11,000 troops shut up in Boston, and deprived of all supplies from the country. Congress, meanwhile, was occupied in its proper work. A bold and forcible Declaration was issued, setting forth the necessity of the Colonies taking up arms. Several addresses also were issued, as in the previous year, and once more a petition was made to the King; but it was the last. Earnest efforts were put forth to secure the aid, or at least the neutrality of the Indians; but with no success. Early in July, Georgia cast in her lot with the other colonies, and chose delegates to Congress; after which the style of "The Thirteen United Colonies" was assumed, and by that title the English provinces, confederated and in arms, were thenceforth designated. With this action, the position of the colonies in regard to the mother country, may properly be considered as fixed, and our first chapter be brought to its close. In reality, it was wholly useless to suppose that any settlement of the contest, but by the sword, was now possible. In words, it is true, and no doubt in good faith on the part of many of the people, who dreaded the issue of a bloody war, there was still a profession of loyalty to the King, and this singular contradiction of men, profuse in language of loyalty to George III., but arrayed in arms against Parliament and the government of this same king, was exhibited for some time longer, in fact for nearly a year beyond this date; nevertheless, the days of Colonial dependence had reached their termination; the great struggle for national life and freedom was now begun. In our next chapter we shall give a succinct narrative of the Revolutionary struggle, during the following seven years of war and bloodshed, and the further struggles and trials to which our fathers were subjected before the Constitution was adopted and went into operation.

CHAPTER II.

THE REVOLUTION, OR STRUGGLE FOR INDEPENDENCE: 1775—1788.

The trials of Washington at this date were very severe and vexatious, especially as the pernicious mistake was made of enlisting men for a year instead of for the whole time that the contest with England might last. Congress was willing and ready to sanction and aid his exertions; but the labor of inventing, combining, organizing, establishing, and sustaining a proper military system necessarily fell upon him. To this end he kept up an unremitted correspondence with Congress during the whole war. His letters were read to the House in full session, and almost every important resolution respecting the army was adopted on his suggestion or recommendation, and emanated from his mind. He was thus literally the centre of motion to this immense and complicated machine, not more in directing its operations than in providing for its existence, and preserving from derangement and ruin its various parts. His perplexities were often increased by the distance at which he was stationed from Congress, the tardy movements of that body, and the long time it took to obtain the results of their deliberations. By a constant watchfulness and forethought, and by anticipating the future in his communications, he contrived to lessen this inconvenience as far as it could be done. Besides this severe task upon his energies, the commander-in-chief was obliged to correspond very extensively with various public bodies throughout the colonies, and as far as possible stimulate their zeal, rouse their patriotism, and prevail upon them to give immediate and efficient aid. And this, too, despite the necessity which he felt laid upon him to refuse to detach troops at various points to protect the sea coast from the ravages of the English navy. In order to anticipate British hostility against the Colonies by way of the north, an attack on Canada was resolved upon. Two expeditions were accordingly organized and dispatched, one by the way of Lake Champlain, under General Schuyler, the other by the way of the River Kennebeck, under the command of Arnold. General Lee, with twelve hundred volunteers from Connecticut, was also directed to repair to New York, and with the aid of the inhabitants, fortify the city, and the Highlands on the Hudson River. The enterprise against Canada resulted in the taking of Montreal by the forces under General Montgomery, November 3d, 1775; an assault was made upon Quebec, on the last day of the year, at which the brave Montgomery was killed; and though a desperate struggle ensued in order to retain foothold in Canada, yet lack of men and necessary supplies was so great, and the increase of British troops so steady and large, that the Americans, during the spring of 1776, were driven out of Canada entirely. Washington was again compelled to call upon Congress to give immediate attention to the condition of the army and its increase, which call was responded to, of course, and a force of 20,000 to 30,000 was confidently expected to be raised. The commander-in-chief desired very much to act on the offensive against Boston, but was dissuaded by his officers. English vessels of war committed frequent and disgraceful outrages along the coast, which necessarily led to a determination to make reprisals. Several privateers were fitted out, under authority of Congress, and did good service; and in December, 1775, Congress resolved to have prepared thirteen ships of various sizes and capacities, a movement whereby was laid the foundation of that famous navy whose career fills a glorious page in our annals.

The course which Parliament was likely to pursue at its session in the latter part of 1775 was looked to with anxiety and deep concern, and on their action, it was felt, was to be based in great measure the future of the colonists. The petition to the king was rejected peremptorily and with virtual contempt, and it was voted that 25,000 men be employed in subduing America. Of these about 18,000 were Hessians, the sending of whom stirred the blood of the people to its very depths. An act was passed prohibiting trade and commerce, and confiscating all property seized in vessels, and treating the crews taken, not as prisoners, but as slaves. The crisis had been reached, and Americans henceforth had the alternative set clearly before them, either to resolve to be free, and peril their lives and their all in support of this resolve, or to submit quietly to become mere slaves of British arrogance and despotism. Dunmore's high-handed proceedings in Virginia, Conolly's scheme for engaging the Indians to murder the colonists, the course of Tryon and the tories in New York, only added fuel to the flame. It was a singular spectacle, indeed, at this conjuncture of affairs, as we have before pointed out, in that professions of loyalty were still persisted in by many; by a sort of transparent fiction, the king's name was spoken with reverence, and the very resistance to the king's troops was done in the king's name; and there were those who thought that they could keep on petitioning, and keep on resisting, hoping that, in some strange way or other, by and by matters would all come out right; but plainly, this was little else than child's play and folly; the work now to be done required men, men of nerve and steadiness, men who could clearly grasp the full idea of *independence*, and could take their stand upon this to do or die. The action taken by the peo-

DRAFTING THE DECLARATION OF INDEPENDENCE.

THE COMMITTEE ... FRANKLIN, JEFFERSON, ADAMS, LIVINGSTON & SHERMAN.

From the original Painting by Chappel, in the possession of the Publishers.

Johnson, Fry & Co. Publishers, New York

ple with respect to colonial government, the lofty sentiments of the judiciary expressed in public charges, and the course pursued by several of the colonies in instructing their delegates to advocate entire independence of Great Britain, all hastened on the great and decisive step. The great question of independence was brought *directly* before Congress, by Richard Henry Lee, one of the delegates from Virginia. On the 7th of June, 1776, he submitted a resolution, declaring, "that the United Colonies are and ought to be free and independent States; that they are absolved from all allegiance to the British crown; and that all political connection between them and the state of Great Britain is, and ought to be, totally dissolved." The resolution was postponed until the next day, and every member enjoined to attend, to take the same into consideration. On the 8th, it was debated, in Committee of the Whole, and adopted by a majority on the 10th. In order, however, to give time and secure unanimity, the discussion was deferred to the beginning of July, when the Committee appointed to draft a declaration, consisting of Jefferson, Adams, Franklin, Sherman and Livingston, brought in their report. The Declaration was written by Jefferson, and after being further discussed and amended, was unanimously adopted on the 4th of July. On the 2d of August, all the members of Congress (except one) signed the Declaration; the number of the signers was 56. We give this important document in full, as worthy a fixed place in every History of the United States.

The Unanimous Declaration of the Thirteen United States of America, in Congress Assembled.

"When, in the course of human events, it becomes necessary for one people to dissolve the political bands which have connected them with another, and to assume among the powers of the earth the separate and equal station to which the laws of nature and nature's God entitle them, a decent respect to the opinions of mankind requires that they should declare the causes which impel them to the separation.

"We hold these truths to be self-evident: that all men are created equal; that they are endowed by their Creator with certain unalienable rights; that among these are life, liberty, and the pursuit of happiness; that, to secure these rights, governments are instituted among men, deriving their just powers from the consent of the governed; that, whenever any form of government becomes destructive of these ends, it is the right of the people to alter or to abolish it, and to institute new government, laying its foundation on such principles, and organizing its powers in such form, as to them shall seem most likely to effect their safety and happiness. Prudence, indeed, will dictate, that governments long established, should not be changed for light and transient causes; and, accordingly, all experience hath shown, that mankind are more disposed to suffer, while evils are sufferable, than to right themselves by abolishing the forms to which they are accustomed. But when a long train of abuses and usurpations, pursuing invariably the same object, evinces a design to reduce them under absolute despotism, it is their right, it is their duty, to throw off such government, and to provide new guards for their future security. Such has been the patient sufferance of these colonies, and such is now the necessity which constrains them to alter their former systems of government. The history of the present King of Great Britain is a history of repeated injuries and usurpations, all having in direct object the establishment of an absolute tyranny over these states. To prove this, let facts be submitted to a candid world:—

"He has refused his assent to laws the most wholesome and necessary for the public good.

"He has forbidden his governors to pass laws of immediate and pressing importance, unless suspended in their operation till his assent should be obtained; and when so suspended, he has utterly neglected to attend to them.

"He has refused to pass other laws for the accommodation of large districts of people, unless those people would relinquish the right of representation in the legislature; a right inestimable to them, and formidable to tyrants only.

"He has called together legislative bodies at places unusual, uncomfortable, and distant from the depository of their public records, for the sole purpose of fatiguing them into compliance with his measures.

"He has dissolved representative houses repeatedly, for opposing, with manly firmness, his invasions on the rights of the people.

"He has refused, for a long time after such dissolutions, to cause others to be elected; whereby the legislative powers, incapable of annihilation, have returned to the people at large for their exercise; the state remaining, in the mean time, exposed to all the dangers of invasion from without, and convulsions within.

"He has endeavored to prevent the population of these states; for that purpose, obstructing the laws for naturalization of foreigners, refusing to pass others to encourage their migrations hither, and raising the conditions of new appropriations of lands.

"He has obstructed the administration of justice, by refusing his assent to laws for establishing judiciary powers.

"He has made judges dependent on his will alone, for the tenure of their offices, and the amount and payment of their salaries.

"He has erected a multitude of new offices, and sent hither swarms of officers to harass our people, and to eat out their substance.

"He has kept among us, in times of peace, standing armies, without the consent of our Legislatures.

"He has affected to render the military independent of, and superior to, the civil power.

"He has combined with others to subject us to a jurisdiction foreign to our constitutions, and unacknowledged by our laws; giving his assent to their acts of pretended legislation:—

"For quartering large bodies of armed troops among us;

"For protecting them, by a mock trial, from punishment for any murders which they should commit on the inhabitants of these states;

"For cutting off our trade with all parts of the world;

"For imposing taxes on us without our consent;

"For depriving us, in many cases, of the benefits of trial by jury;

"For transporting us beyond seas, to be tried for pretended offences;

"For abolishing the free system of English laws in a neighboring province, establishing therein an arbitrary government, and enlarging its boundaries, so as to render it at once an example and fit instrument for introducing the same absolute rule into these colonies;

"For taking away our charters, abolishing our most valuable laws, and altering, fundamentally, the forms of our governments;

"For suspending our own legislatures, and declaring themselves invested with power to legislate for us in all cases whatsoever.

"He has abdicated government here, by declaring us out of his protection, and waging war against us.

"He has plundered our seas, ravaged our coasts, burnt our towns, and destroyed the lives of our people.

"He is, at this time, transporting large armies of foreign mercenaries to complete the works of death, desolation, and tyranny, already begun with circumstances of cruelty and perfidy, scarcely paralleled in the most barbarous ages, and totally unworthy the head of a civilized nation.

"He has constrained our fellow-citizens, taken captive on the high seas, to bear arms, against their country, to become the execu tioners of their friends and brethren, or to fall themselves by their hands.

"He has excited domestic insurrections among us, and has endeavored to bring on the inhabitants of our frontiers the merciless Indian savages, whose known rule of warfare is an undistinguished destruction of all ages, sexes, and conditions.

"In every stage of these oppressions, we have petitioned for redress in the most humble terms. Our repeated petitions have been answered only by repeated injury. A prince, whose character is thus marked by every act which may define a tyrant, is unfit to be the ruler of a free people.

"Nor have we been wanting in attentions to our British brethren. We have warned them, from time to time, of attempts by their legislature to extend an unwarrantable jurisdiction over us. We have reminded them of the circumstances of our emigration and settlement here. We have appealed to their native justice and magnanimity, and we have conjured them by the ties of our common kindred, to disavow these usurpations, which would inevitably interrupt our connections and correspondence. They, too, have been deaf to the voice of justice and of consanguinity. We must, therefore, acquiesce in the necessity which denounces our separation, and hold them, as we hold the rest of mankind, enemies in war, in peace friends.

"We, therefore, the representatives of the United States of America in general Congress assembled, appealing to the Supreme Judge of the world for the rectitude of our intentions, do, in the name and by authority of the good people of these colonies, solemnly publish and declare, that these United Colonies are, and of right ought to be, FREE and INDEPENDENT STATES; that they are absolved from all allegiance to the British crown, and that all political connection between them and the state of Great Britain is, and ought to be, totally dissolved; and that, as free and independent states, they have power to levy war, conclude peace, contract alliances, establish commerce, and do all other acts and things which independent states may of right do. And for the support of this declaration, with a firm reliance on the protection of Divine Providence, we mutually pledge to each other our lives, our fortunes, and our sacred honor."

The Declaration of Independence was, in every point of view, wise and well timed. Every consideration of sound policy as well as justice, demanded that the war should no longer be a contest between subjects and their acknowledged sovereign, and it was of the first consequence, that the position assumed by our fathers, on this memorable occasion, should have all the moral force arising from the fact that they now stood before the world as a free and independent people, resolved to peril their lives and their all in defence of the liberties which were their birthright and their inalienable possession. So thought Washington and so did he express himself in ordering the Declaration to be read at the head of each brigade of the army. Previously to this date, however, it is proper to mention, Washington, by occupying Dorchester Heights, had compelled General Howe, the new British Commander-in-chief, to evacuate Boston, March 17th. Putnam was sent to New York to provide against the approach of the enemy, and Lee was dispatched south. Early in June, Sir Henry Clinton with a fleet of vessels and a large force, demanded the surrender of Charleston. This being refused, he made a furious assault upon the city, but to no purpose; the heroic defenders repulsed the British; and at the close of the month, the squadron set sail for New York. Under Washington's directions, efforts were made to put this latter city in a state of defence, without however accomplishing to any extent the desired end. Admiral Lord Howe arrived with reinforcements at the end of June, and landed on Staten Island. Offers were made by him and Gen. Howe, as commissioners, calling upon the people to submit to their gracious king and master; Congress published these offers in all the newspapers, being satisfied that the effect would be decidedly in favor of the cause of independence. An attempt also was made to open negotiations with Washington; but this, too, failed of producing any result. Gen. Carleton in Canada was actively engaged in an endeavor to push forward and effect a junction with the British troops at and near New York. A battle was fought on Lake Champlain, in October, where Arnold displayed his usual reckless daring and spirit; and the result was, that, though Carleton took Crown Point, he was unable to effect anything against Ticonderoga, and so went into winter quarters. Gen. Howe, at the close of August, 1776, attacked the Americans on Long Island. With a force of 10,000 men and forty cannon, he fell upon Washington's army, and gained a complete victory. The troops fought well; the contest was bitter and severe; but in the end discouraging to only half-disciplined men. A retreat was safely effected from Brooklyn, and the army took post at Harlem Heights. Howe advanced cautiously and pressed the Americans more and more. Some of the militia behaved scandalously at Kip's Bay, and it was almost by miracle that the Commander-in-chief was not taken or killed, so chagrined and indignant was he at their pusillanimous conduct on this occasion. But the troops made up for this momentary panic afterwards. Washington retreated from New York, which was taken by the British and held all through the war. Sickness among the troops, insubordination, a spirit of plundering, and a sad lack of needful provisions of all kinds, deeply affected Washington, and on the 24th of September, he wrote to Congress, in energetic, plain terms, as to what the present crisis demanded. A reorganization and increase of the army was ordered, the pay of the officers and soldiers was increased, etc., and earnest attempts were made by the Commander-in-chief to meet the difficulties of his position. Trouble, however, followed trouble; an engagement at White Plains was indecisive; Fort Washington and its garrison were taken by the British; the Americans began to retreat through the Jerseys; there was no help for it; Howe had more than three times as many troops as Washington, and all in good condition and with abundant supplies; and every thing seemed to foreshadow speedy ruin to the patriot cause. Howe issued another proclamation, and the tories or loyalists displayed a mean and contemptible spirit of persecution and cruelty. Washington continued to retreat, the enemy at times being almost in sight; and, as if this were not enough, Gen. Lee, with a spirit of self-will and recklessness inexcusable, allowed himself to be taken prisoner on the 13th of December, causing thereby great exultation to the British Commander. On the 20th of December, Washington crossed the Delaware, and escaped for the time the pursuit of Howe. Clinton, who had been sent against Rhode Island, was at this same date completely successful, and seriously interfered with the sending of reinforcements to Washington. And thus the year 1776 came to its close. Gloomy enough was the prospect, and hard was the lot of the Commander-in-chief in these days. All the forces he could collect numbered only about 7000 men, and these in part raw troops; while Howe had 27,000, well armed and disciplined, confident of success, and ready, it was believed, to cross the Delaware so soon as the river was frozen over and fit for the purpose. Painful, indeed, were the trials and perplexities, and humiliations which waited upon Washington's every step, and his soul was racked with the cares and burdens laid upon him. But trials are not sent without design. The great and noble leader was formed of that material which is purified and strengthened by trial. Bravely did he endure; profoundly learned and wise did he become by endurance; and no man of his day ever attained such vast influence as he did by the irrefragable proofs which he exhibited of the purity, integrity, and decision of his character and conduct.

At the beginning of the year 1777, Congress renewed the efforts already undertaken to induce foreign powers to yield assistance to America. Especially was it important to secure the alliance of France, and the commissioners, Franklin being of the number, were directed to use every exertion and offer every inducement to bring about an active coöperation; but the French ministry were cautious in the matter; they were not prepared as yet to go to war with England, which would of course result from espousing the cause of the colonies; but indirectly, they favored the Americans in various ways; captures made at sea were allowed to be brought into and disposed of in French ports; supplies, ammunition, and the like were allowed to be shipped, etc. Just at the close of the year, 1776, Washington addressed an earnest and forcible letter to Congress in regard to the army and its necessities: the effect of this communication was that Congress conferred powers on him which made him, in fact, a military dictator. The following was the resolve passed by Congress: "That Gen. Washington shall be, and he is hereby, vested with full, ample, and complete powers to raise and collect together, in the most speedy and effectual manner, from any and all of these United States, sixteen battalions of infantry, in addition to those already voted by Congress; to appoint officers for the said battalions of infantry; to raise, officer, and equip three thousand light horse, three regiments of artillery, and a corps of engineers, and to establish their pay; to apply to any of the states for such aid of the militia as he shall judge necessary; to form such magazines of provisions, and in such places as he shall think proper; to displace and appoint all officers under the rank of brigadier-general, and to fill all vacancies in every other department of the American armies; to take, wherever he may be, whatever he may want for the use of the army, if the inhabitants will not sell it, allowing a reasonable price for the same; to arrest and confine persons who refuse to take the continental currency, or are any otherwise disaffected to the American cause; and return to the states, of which they are citizens, their names, and the nature of their offences, together with the witnesses to prove them." Well was it for our country's cause that powers so vast, and so liable to misuse, were placed in the hands of George Washington! Anxious to do something in order to revive the drooping spirit of the people, the commander determined to strike a blow which should be felt, and Cornwallis's careless and almost contemptuous disregard of the Americans, afforded the opportunity. The British cantonments were arranged at distances, one from the other, and no apprehensions were for a moment entertained in respect to the feeble and fleeing foe. On Christmas night, however, Washington crossed the Delaware, attacked, defeated, and captured 1500 Hessians at Trenton; was joined by Cadwallader, with reinforcements, at the beginning of January, 1777; skillfully evaded Cornwallis and made an attack on Princeton, whence he retired to Morristown; and by constant activity and frequent surprises of the British troops, he virtually wrested the Jerseys out of their hands, and produced a powerful effect upon the minds of enemies as well as friends by his unwearied zeal and excellent generalship. On the 25th of January, Washington issued a counter proclamation to that of Howe (p. 81), requiring a proper submission to authority on the part of all the people, and ordering that all those who trusted in British protection should at once betake themselves within the enemy's lines, or suffer the consequences. The proclamation was well timed and effective to a high degree, especially as the promises of protection on the part of the British commander were found to be worthless. The rude and insolent soldiers had no scruples as to plundering and maltreating any body, whether tory or American, and the outrages and barbarity and horrible excesses of these men—if they may be called men—roused every where, abroad as well as at home, the bitterest indignation and a fixed determination, on the part of the sufferers, to expel these infamous robbers. But truth requires that it be stated here, that excess and outrage were not confined to the British troops. Love of pillage contaminated the Americans, too, and they too often joined in plundering the Jersey people under pretext that they were loyalists or tories: Washington was greatly pained at all this, and issued an order to the army, denouncing the severest punishment against all who were guilty of such abominable conduct. Added to these trials, we may mention, were those of the prisoners in the hands of the British. No language can possibly depict the horrible brutality of treatment which prisoners in New York at this date suffered; destitution of even common necessaries, exposure to the bitterly inclement weather, ravages of disease, deaths by the score, and all this sanctioned by the British general in command. Alas, what can be said of such savage treatment! What must war be, when it leads to such results! Nevertheless, the people faltered not, and as some good comes out of evil almost always, so now these cruelties of the enemy nerved the hearts of our fathers to do or die; death was far preferable to the tyranny and insolence of masters like these.

Early in the spring, the British made a sudden and successful attack on Peekskill, where was a depot of army stores; and in the latter part of April, they assaulted Danbury, Connecticut, with the same end in view, and were equally successful. As an offset to this, however, Colonel Meigs crossed the Sound from Connecticut, attacked Sag Harbor, burned a dozen brigs and sloops, destroyed the British stores, and returned without loss to Guilford, bringing a number of prisoners. General Howe, who was waiting for reinforcements, was very inactive at this date, and Washington had to lay his plans to meet the enemy when he was ready to strike. Having attempted to draw Washington into a general engagement, but without success, Howe evacuated New Jersey, and embarked a large force for the Chesapeake, in August, intending to march on Philadelphia. At this time, Washington met Lafayette, who had crossed the ocean to take part in the struggle for liberty, and who ever manifested the most enthusiastic love and reverence for the commander-in-chief. If he had been allowed to follow his own mature judgment, Washington would not have ventured a general engagement with the enemy; he knew too well that his troops were not in a condition to cope with the British veterans; but, under the circumstances, as the safety of Philadelphia was concerned, and it was important to make a strenuous effort to save the city, he deemed it best to meet the enemy. The battle of the Brandywine was the result, in which the American loss was very heavy: this was followed by other movements; Congress conferred additional powers on Washington; and with firm and steady demeanor and resolve left Philadelphia, on the 18th of September, and proceeded to Yorktown, where they remained for eight months, until Philadelphia was evacuated. Howe entered the city on the 26th. Early in October, Washington attacked the enemy at Germantown with vigor and spirit, and came very near gaining a victory. On the 21st of October, Count Donop was sent by Howe to reduce Redbank, which formed part of the obstructions to the navigation of the Delaware; but the expedition failed, and Donop was killed. Still further efforts were made to clear the river, which was all-important to Howe and his position in Philadelphia. Fort Mifflin was attacked on the 15th of November, and after a brave defence was deserted by the garrison, who escaped in safety. The American shipping was necessarily destroyed and the Delaware opened to the British. Howe tried to persuade Washington again to a general engagement, but to no purpose, and so he returned to Philadelphia. As yet, he had gained nothing by the campaign, except comfortable quarters in the capital of Pennsylvania. Washington soon after went into winter quarters at Valley Forge, about twenty miles from Philadelphia.

The campaign of the present year, 1777,

in the North, was one of great importance in its results to the American cause. General Burgoyne had been appointed to the command in Canada, superseding General Carleton (p. 82). He was a vain, self-important man, and entertained to the full the exaggerated notions of the immeasurable superiority of the British troops over the Continentals. He expected to be able to march directly forward to victory, and to a speedy settlement of the questions at issue. Following the directions of his masters at home, Burgoyne first employed the Indians to aid him with the scalping-knife and the tomahawk, and then entered upon vigorous operations against the Americans at Ticonderoga. General St. Clair was in command, and had about 2000 men under him, the larger part of the force having joined the Commander-in-chief in New Jersey. Not being aware of the large body of British troops now approaching, St. Clair endeavored to resist Burgoyne's advance; but it was to little purpose; he was beaten at every point, on water and land, and after having suffered loss of stores, men killed and made prisoners, and in the greatest possible distress, he reached Fort Edward and joined General Schuyler, about the middle of July, 1777. It can readily be imagined what consternation was produced in America by this rapid success of Burgoyne; and on the other hand, what exultation was thereby afforded to the enemies of the Republic. Burgoyne himself was extremely elated, and he was so puffed up by success, and the opening of his dashing campaign, that, forgetting that he had not yet reached the end, his further proceedings materially facilitated his own ruin. There were some sixteen miles of forest yet to be traversed, and Burgoyne delayed for his baggage and stores; General Schuyler, meanwhile, lost not a moment in throwing every obstruction possible in the enemy's way, in rousing up the spirit of the people, obtaining new recruits, sending a regiment into Vermont to make a diversion, and in fact, adopting measures which ultimately paved the way to victory at Saratoga. Washington, of course, afforded every assistance in his power to further and complete the plans of Schuyler. Burgoyne was some weeks in finding his way through the forest and reaching Fort Edward, from which the Americans deemed it best to retreat; and he began now to experience somewhat of those difficulties which finally compelled him to surrender. Stores and supplies began to fall short, and the further he advanced, the more difficult it became to obtain the necessary sustenance of his army. Having learned that the Americans had considerable stores, etc., at Bennington, some twenty-five miles east of the Hudson, he dispatched, on the 13th of August, a force under Colonel Baum to secure these stores. The enterprise, however, signally failed, and brave old Stark of New Hampshire, with the militia, hastily gathered through his influence, gained an advantage of the utmost consequence in foiling Burgoyne's aims. Aided by the troops of Warner, Stark, on the 16th of August, a bright and sunny day, sent forward two columns to storm the entrenchments of the enemy on the Wollamsac River. When the firing had commenced, he threw himself on horseback and advanced with the rest of his troops. As soon as the enemy's columns were seen forming on the hill-side, he exclaimed, "See, men! there are the red-coats; we must beat to-day, or Molly Stark's a widow." The militia replied to this appeal by a tremendous shout, and the battle which ensued, as Stark states in his official report, "lasted two hours, and was the hottest I ever saw. It was like one continual clap of thunder." The Indians ran off at the beginning of the battle; the tories were driven across the river; and although the Germans fought bravely, they were compelled to abandon the entrenchments, and fled, leaving their artillery and baggage on the field. Baum was killed in the encounter, about 800 prisoners were taken, and Burgoyne was not only deprived of all chance of obtaining supplies by lateral excursions, but found that he was in a fair way of being hemmed in, so that he could neither advance nor retreat. Early in the month, St. Leger had been detached by Burgoyne against Fort Stanwix, situate near the source of the Mohawk River; but he was no more successful than Baum. The Indian allies afforded him but little real help, and finally went off altogether, and when on the 22d, St. Leger began his retreat from before the fort, these wild red men displayed their real nature, and how little reliance could be placed upon them. The British troops were exposed to greater danger from Indian fury than from the pursuit of the Americans. During the retreat, they robbed the officers of their baggage and the army generally of their provisions and stores. Not content with this, they first stripped off their arms, and afterwards murdered with their own bayonets, all those who from inability to keep up, from fear, or other cause, were separated from the main body. The confusion, terror, and sufferings of this retreat found no respite till the royal troops reached the Lake on their way to Montreal.

Much to the chagrin of General Schuyler, Congress, on the 4th of August, appointed General Gates to command in his place. Unfortunately, Schuyler was very unpopular with the New England people, and although it was ungracious in the extreme, yet in view of the question of expediency, it was probably a wise step for Congress to take, especially as Gates stood high in the esteem of many for military skill and generalship. The new commander reached the field at the close of the month, and gladly availed himself of Schuyler's judicious preparations. Burgoyne, on his part, loth to give up and retire, was every day expecting news of Clinton's approach from New York, in order to aid him from the south; this general, delayed by the arrival of ships from England, was unable to attempt anything before the beginning of October; and even then, when he sailed up the Hudson and attacked successfully and stormed the forts in the Highlands, he, for some unexplained reason, did not push forward, and endeavor to relieve Burgoyne, but contented himself with uselessly and cruelly burning and destroying villages on the route, and with returning ingloriously to New York. Thus Burgoyne was left to his fate, which was rapidly drawing on. He crossed the Hudson in the middle of September and encamped on the heights of Saratoga, a fatal mistake for him, as he soon after found out. Gates, who had been reinforced, marched to and encamped near Stillwater, being only about twelve miles from Burgoyne. A battle resulted a few days later, which was severely contested, although, on the whole, decidedly in favor of the Americans. Burgoyne, on the 7th of October, finding that he must either starve or fight, resolved to try his fortune in another battle. About two o'clock, P. M., the fighting began; it raged with unabated fury during the rest of the day, and ended at night with the loss of Burgoyne's field-pieces, most of his artillery corps and numerous prisoners. During the night, the English general changed his position, after immense toil and fatigue through the rain and mud, and as a last resort, endeavored to retreat to Fort George. But it was too late; the troops were exhausted, and no supplies could be obtained; nothing was left but capitulation. Accordingly, on the 14th, Burgoyne made proposals to this end, and on the 17th the terms were finally arranged. They were substantially all that could be expected and are usual in such cases; the troops were to be allowed to return to Europe, on condition of not serving again in America during the war; and the treatment of the prisoners was generous and considerate in the extreme, when it is remembered how the British acted towards the Americans who fell into their hands (p. 84). We are sorry to say that Congress displayed a decided unwillingness to carry out the agreement as to the troops returning to England, where they would take the place of others to be sent against America; and so, on various pretexts, Congress finally refused to allow their embarkation at all. "We shall not undertake to decide," says an able writer, "whether the fears manifested by Congress had a real foundation, and we shall abstain as well from blaming the imprudence of Burgoyne, as from praising the wisdom, or condemning the distrust of Congress. It is but too certain, that in these civil dissensions and animosities, appearances become realities and probabilities demonstration. Accordingly, at that time, the Americans complained bitterly of British perfidy, and the English of American want of faith." General Gates, neglectful of evident propriety, did not communicate the news of victory to Washington, but sent his aid-de-camp directly to Congress, who received the announcement with joy, ordered a gold medal to be struck, etc.

From the very beginning of the struggle, it had been evident that, in order to enable Congress to act with vigor and efficiency, there must be some solid basis of union agreed upon. The subject had been broached several times, and efforts made to fix upon some definite articles of Confederation; but thus far without result. It was plain, however, now, that something must be done, for Congress had no powers or rights, except in so far as the states chose to recognize them, by carrying out its resolves. As a government, it was certain that Congress could not efficiently discharge the duties expected from its position: inherent defects attached to the revolutionary government, and it was fast breaking down, as well from the want of executive authority over the people of the whole country, as from the futility of any federative union among sovereign states, which leaves the execution of the measures adopted in general council, to the separate members of the Confederacy. Early in October, 1777, the question was taken up and discussed, day by day, until the middle of November, when "Articles of Confederation and Perpetual Union" were adopted for recommendation to the states, accompanied by a calm, earnest forcible Circular Letter. We may mention, in this connection, that on the 9th of July, 1778, delegates from eight of the states signed the ratification of the Articles; North Carolina and Georgia, a few weeks later; New Jersey, Nov. 26th; Delaware, May 5th, 1779; Maryland, March 1st, 1781; Congress thereupon met under the Confederation on and after March 2d, 1781.

Washington, as previously stated, went into winter quarters at Valley Forge, Dec. 1777 (p.84). Of the sufferings and anguish to which the army was exposed; of the cruel hardships, diseases, and unutterable trials of that bitter winter; of the frightful number of deaths, and the utter prostration of thousands in those gloomy days, we do not feel ourselves able adequately to speak. On the 1st of Febuary, 1778, 4000 of the troops, almost half of the army, were incapable of any kind of service for want of clothing; and had the British general been a man of enterprise and attacked Washington in this time of distress, disastrous consequences must have followed. Our great leader was authorized to seize upon provisions wherever he could find any in that region, and he required the farmers to thresh out their grain and furnish supplies by the beginning of March; but these could not be forced into such measures, and they resisted in every way in their power. Paper money was virtually worthless and the farmers preferred getting pay in gold from the British in Philadelphia. A large number of the officers also resolved to abandon the service, seeing that Congress was quite apathetic in regard to their sufferings and distresses. Washington spared no efforts to induce Congress to secure half pay to the officers after the war, either for life or for a definite term. Strange to say, this measure of simplest justice was looked coldly upon and delayed so long that its good effect was in great degree lost. It is no new thing in history for good and great men to meet with detraction and ingratitude, and therefore we are not surprised that Washington found those who were willing to make invidious statements as to his campaign of constant retreat, his losses in respect to New York and Philadelphia, his apparent inactivity and want of fire and decision, and such like; and further, that more than one was ready to point to the hero of Saratoga, and insinuate that *he* was the man for the position in the present crisis. Anonymous letters were sent round, to Patrick Henry and others, with the intention of ruining Washington's reputation, and if possible compelling him to resign. "Conway's Cabal," as the combination of men linked together for this end was called, was favored by a number of those in and out of Congress, Gates, Mifflin, Samuel Adams, etc., being of this number; but Washington was not the man to be moved from the path of duty by such means; despite the calumnies of these, as well as of later days, he persevered, and gave all his energies to the cause in which his very life was bound up.

The capture of Burgoyne gave a new feature to American affairs abroad. The British parliament, on the one hand, tried the futile experiment of passing conciliatory bills, which contained proposals that at one period would have proved satisfactory, but were now too late, since the Americans were determined to have independence, and nothing short of it; the French ministry, on the other, clearly saw that now was the time for them to act. Accordingly, in December, 1777, the American commissioners were informed of the purpose of France, and early in February, 1778, a treaty of commerce was signed, together with a treaty of defensive alliance against England. As may be imagined, the news of this treaty was received with great rejoicings in the United States; and all the efforts of the British commissioners, sent out under Lord North's conciliatory bills, were nugatory, and in October, 1778, they returned to England, baffled and disappointed. The first attention of the British army in Philadelphia was given, early in the spring, to the obtaining supplies; and foraging expeditions were sent out, and were generally successful. It was noted, however, that the British troops were becoming more savage and cruel than heretofore, and that consequently the prospect ahead was rather gloomy and depressing. A French fleet being expected to reach America at an early day, Sir Henry Clinton evacuated Philadelphia on the 18th of June, purposing to march through New Jersey to New York. His army was in number about 33,000; Washington's force was 15,000, with the probability that it could be raised to 20,000 effective men. The Commander-in-chief was disposed to try offensive operations; but the council of war, Lee being very urgent on the subject, strongly disapproved this course Active measures were taken for hindering the march of the British, by breaking down bridges, felling trees across the road, etc Clinton's march consequently was very slow and cautious. Washington, who followed him, and found that he was taking the road by Monmouth toward Sandy Hook, determined to risk an attack, and took his measures accordingly. He sent forward a thousand men under Wayne and Lafayette, intending to advance to their support with all speed; Lee took the command of this force, and, on the morning of June 28th, was ordered to move to the attack; on coming up to support the advance, Washington was shocked to find the troops retreating by Lee's orders. He demanded what all this meant, and Lee answered sharply and rudely; still he was willing to fight as the commander-in-chief required. With great spirit Washington urged on the attack, and supported by Greene, Wayne, Lord Stirling and other brave officers, his enthusiasm roused the troops, despite the intense heat of the day, to do their best. Night put a stop to the battle, and the Americans purposed to renew it in the morning; Clinton, however, withdrew in the darkness, and escaped further attack. The battle of Monmouth, though not a complete victory, was a great success, and Congress unanimously voted a resolution of thanks to Washington for what he had accomplished. As for Lee, he was tried by court-martial at his own request, and found guilty of disobedience of orders and disrespect to the commander-in-chief; he was suspended from all command for a year, and, deeply chagrined, left the army never to join it again.

A French fleet, which had set sail in April, arrived off the coast of Virginia early in July. Count D'Estaing was in command, and he expected to find the British still in Philadelphia, in which case it was probable they could be attacked with success; but, as they had left that city, D'Estaing sailed for New York, where the pilots refused to undertake the carrying the vessels in; from thence he sailed for Rhode Island, which he reached on the 29th. In conjunction with the French fleet, General Sullivan was charged with the reduction of the British force in Newport and vicinity, and there was every prospect of success; but, unfortunately, as Lord Howe had followed with some ships from New York, the Frenchman was seized with a desire to meet his lordship on the ocean. So, on the 10th of August, he sailed out, and consumed the day in manœuvring against the enemy; on the second day, a most tremendous storm occurred; nothing resulted of moment to either party; Howe went back to New York, and D'Estaing, on the 20th, returned to Newport with his fleet in a shattered condition. Sullivan had already commenced operations, and if the French had given the expected aid, an important victory would have been gained, beyond doubt; but D'Estaing had made up his mind to go to Boston to refit and repair damages; remonstrances and entreaties produced no effect; the fleet took its departure, and the expedition against the British failed, Sullivan escaping just in time before Clinton arrived with reinforcements. The French minister, M. Gerard, was received by Congress with proper honors, August 6th, 1778; a month or so later Dr. Franklin was sent as minister to France. The course pursued by D'Estaing was felt to be particularly aggravating at a critical moment, and some considerable complaint was made and ill language used respecting the new allies of the Americans; in fact, it put all of Washington's discretion and prudence to the test to quiet and soothe the irritation existing on both sides. As we have before noted, the disposition towards a more than usual savagery found place among the British at this date, and so odious did it become, in the destruction of Wyoming, with its horrors, the cold-blooded bayonetting of troops on foraging expeditions, etc., that Congress was compelled to recommend retaliation. This was done, on the 30th of October, in plain and emphatic words. As a matter of policy, nothing could have been worse, as Mr. Sparks well points out: "This was strangely misunderstood by the British, or more strangely perverted, at every stage of the contest. They had many friends in the country, whom it was their interest to retain, and they professed a desire to conciliate others; yet they burned and destroyed towns, villages, and detached farm-houses, plundered the inhabitants without distinction, and brought down the savages, with the tomahawk and scalping-knife, upon the defenceless frontier settlements, marking their course in every direction with murder, desolation, and ruin. The ministry approved and encouraged these atrocities, flattering themselves that the people would sink under their sufferings, bewail their unhappy condition, become tired of the war, and compel their leaders to seek an accommodation. The effect was directly the contrary in every instance. If the British cabinet had aimed to defeat its own objects, and to consolidate the American people into a united phalanx of opposition, it could not have chosen or pursued more effectual methods." Admiral Byron succeeded Lord Howe in command of the British fleet; he arrived in September with additional ships, and the following month sailed for Boston against D'Estaing; but, having met with a violent storm, before he recovered from its effects, the French commodore, November 3d, set sail for the West Indies. British troops were dispatched to operate against the South, which resulted, just at the close of the year, in the capture of Savannah by Col. Campbell, an officer, by the way, who, acting with judgment and wise regard for the people and their rights, accomplished far more for British interests than had been effected by all the cruelty and outrage in the North. Border warfare was carried on vigorously, and in several instances the savages met with severe handling; and Col. Clarke did excellent service in penetrating to the settlements on the Mississippi, capturing Kaskaskias with important papers, punishing the Indians, pushing forward, and early in 1779, taking Detroit and Governor Hamilton, one of the most violent of those engaged in setting the savages on, and thus saving the western frontiers of Virginia from Indian inroads, as well as teaching the red men some useful lessons.

Washington, finding the campaign virtually at an end in the Northern and Middle States, put his troops into winter quarters, extending his line of cantonments around New York, from Long Island Sound to the Delaware, and having them so arranged as to be able to help each other in case of need. The men were lodged in huts, but, in consequence of the French alliance, were more comfortably clothed than the previous winter (p. 87). Unhappily, at this date, there were manifested in Congress petty jealousies and party feuds, which materially interfered with Washington's plans and hopes. There was also, too, a disposition on the part of the people to think that no further sacrifices were necessary, the French having now become their allies. The recruiting of the army proceeded but slowly, and the greatest difficulty was experienced in providing for its wants. The dire necessity that existed for fresh emissions of paper money had led to a train of deplorable consequences. All attempts to sustain its value had proved abortive; a single dollar in cash was worth eight, and sometimes twenty, of the colonial bills; and the mischief was still further increased by the immense quantity of forged notes introduced by the tories. Prices, as a matter of course, rose enormously, and a wide field was open to the operations of speculators and contractors, a body of whom had grown up and enriched themselves amidst the distresses of their country. None were greater sufferers than the army by this state of things; supplies were so high that, in Carolina, a single pair of shoes cost $700 in paper, and the pay of privates and officers was insufficient for more than bare necessaries. "I would to God," said Washington, speaking of these speculating wretches, "that some one of the more atrocious in each state was hung in gibbets upon a gallows five times as high as the one prepared for Haman. No punishment, in my opinion, is too severe for the man who can build his greatness upon his country's ruin." About Christmas, the commander-in-chief went to Philadelphia to consult with Congress as to the coming campaign. More than a month was spent in this way, and the general plan arranged was to act principally upon the defensive, especially while the financial condition of affairs was so disheartening. Baron Steuben, we may mention, was of great service in promoting drill and discipline in the army; and the navy, though, from the nature of the case, not able to accomplish great things, still was very effective in many ways, and the names of Biddle, Paul Jones, Barry and Talbot furnish an honorable record for all time.

At the opening of 1779, Gen. Lincoln took command at the South, and entered with vigor upon the duties of his post. He found the troops badly conditioned and wretchedly furnished, in number less than 4000; while Prevost, the British commander, had a larger force and in excellent condition. The operations on neither side were of any great moment. Prevost made an irruption into South Carolina, marked by the usual disgraceful plundering and cruelty; Lincoln endeavored to punish the enemy who had threatened Charleston; the battle of Stono Ferry was fought June 20th, without material result; and the hot weather put a stop for the present to further efforts. National vigor, during 1779 and 1780 seemed to be wholly relaxed, and it required all Washington's energies and patience to struggle against the pernicious consequences of such a state of affairs. The officers of the New Jersey brigade on one occasion refused to march, owing to the utter disregard of the legislature of their just demands for support, and nothing but the wisdom and firmness of the Commander-in-chief prevented a mutiny with all its fatal results. The scarcity of food, during these years, imposed upon Washington the necessity of taking by force what was wanted from the people, and he, whom the inhabitants hitherto regarded as their protector, had now the hard alternative before him either to disband his troops, or to support them by force. The army looked to him for provisions; the inhabitants for protection of their property. To supply the one and not offend the other, seemed little less than an impossibility. To preserve order and subordination in an army like that under Washington, even when well fed, paid, and clothed, would have been a work of difficulty; but to retain them in the service and sustain proper discipline, when destitute not only of the comforts, but often of the necessaries of life, required address and abilities of such magnitude as are rarely found in any one man. In the midst of difficulties of this grave character, Washington not only kept his army together, but guided himself with so much discretion as to command the approbation, as far as was possible, both of the army and of the people. Clinton in June, 1779, advanced up the Hudson, compelled the Americans to abandon Stony Point and Fort Lafayette on Verplanck's Point opposite, and then, in July, sent Tryon on a predatory raid into Connecticut. This was performed with great gusto, and resulted in spreading fire and desolation over a large number of towns and villages. Stony Point was retaken July 16th, at the point of the bayonet under Gen. Wayne; but it was subsequently abandoned. Indian ravages had been so frequent and destructive, that it was determined to send a force sufficiently large, in order to punish them with such severity as to compel them through fear to desist. Accordingly, 3000 men were assembled at Wyoming, in August, under Gen. Sullivan, and received instructions from Washington "to lay waste all the settlements round, and to do it in such an effectual manner that the country may be not merely overrun, but destroyed." Sullivan began his march at once, and carried out his instructions to the full; so that hereafter the savages were much less willing to join the tories, and plunder and murder the Americans.

At the South, early in September, 1779, D'Estaing arrived off Savannah, and in October gave assistance to Lincoln towards an assault on the city; but the combined assault failed, and the French fleet sailed away. Such was the issue of the Count D'Estaing's campaign upon the coasts of North America, a campaign in which the allies had placed such sanguine hopes. After failing in the expedition against the British in the Delaware, he twice abandoned Newport at the most critical moment. Finally, under the walls of Savannah, he showed himself at first too circumspect; he delayed the attack, and afterwards precipitated an assault which resulted in discomfiture. It is but fair, however, to bear in mind that, although none of the great results which were expected, followed from D'Estaing's assistance to the Americans, yet the French fleet most materially aided the cause, by deranging the plans of the British, by causing the evacuation of Rhode Island, and by delaying the expedition of Clinton against the south. Unable to enter upon any active operations, for the reasons before stated, Washington again went into winter quarters, with a consciousness how greatly public virtue had declined, and how dark and gloomy was the prospect, and sustained only by a trust in God's good providence for the future of our land.

Sir Henry Clinton embarked for the South

with about 8000 men, and after a very stormy passage, reached Georgia on the last day of January, 1780. He determined to make an attack on Charleston at the earliest moment. That city was in rather a poor state of defence, Gen. Lincoln not having more than one third the troops necessary, and which had been promised, for sustaining a siege. Clinton made regular approaches during March and April, and although Governor Rutledge did all in his power to raise additional forces from the militia, yet it was to no purpose; the British succeeded in investing the city entirely and cutting off supplies; so that there was no alternative; Charleston was surrendered May 12th. It was a heavy blow to the American cause, and Clinton and Cornwallis adopted measures which were impolitic to a high degree, and in the end resulted in favor of independence and liberty. Clinton, in his proclamation, June 3rd, went upon the theory that the people were merely subdued rebels, and that any favors he might show them were the fruits of royal clemency. Several expeditions in different directions, which were all successful, materially increased this feeling of superiority and this disregard for the rights of the citizens, and the haughty and insolent behavior of the British officers, and their helpers the tories, stirred up a desire for revenge; in due time, this desire met with its accomplishment. The exploits of Sumpter and Marion, in carrying on a harassing partisan warfare, aided materially in rousing up the people to resist and try to expel the invaders. A force under De Kalb was sent to Carolina, and this was increased by the Virginia militia, and such other as were in North Carolina. The depressing effect of the fall of Charleston was in measure recovered from, and when, in the latter part of July, Gates was sent as commander, it was confidently expected that he, who had gained so great glory and renown at Saratoga, would gather fresh laurels at the South. This expectation, however, was doomed to a grievous disappointment; for Gen. Gates committed a mistake at the outset, by insisting upon advancing in a straight route through a barren region, instead of diverging from the direct road and keeping his troops in good condition. Heat and insufficient and improper food did their work, and the army suffered sadly from disease and attendant trials. Cornwallis was compelled, in this state of affairs, arising out of the approach of Gates and the renewed spirit of opposition on the part of the people, either to retreat or fight. He chose the latter, and the battle of Camden, on the 16th of August, was the result. Gates was entirely defeated, and escaped with a bare remnant of his troops; he left the army from this date, and Gen. Greene, on Washington's nomination, was appointed his successor, and reached headquarters on the 2nd of December. Cornwallis, elated with victory, and impressed with the necessity of sharpness with the rebellious Southerners, addressed a letter to the commandant of the British garrison at Ninety-six, as follows: "I have given orders that all the inhabitants of this province, who had submitted, and who have taken part in this revolt, should be punished with the utmost rigor; that they should be imprisoned, and their whole property taken from them or destroyed. I have likewise directed that compensation should be made out of these estates, to the persons who have been injured or oppressed by them. I have ordered, in the most positive manner, that every militia-man, who has borne arms with us, and afterwards joined the enemy, shall be immediately hanged. I desire you will take the most vigorous measures to punish the rebels in the district you command, and that you obey, in the strictest manner, the directions I have given in this letter relative to the inhabitants of the country." Similar orders were dispatched to the commanders of other posts. At the close of September, Cornwallis, who had left Camden, reached Charlotte in North Carolina, and set out against Salisbury. His victorious career, however, was arrested by the defeat of Major

Ferguson at King's Mountain. This officer had been very active in marshalling the tories to support the British cause, and the hardy mountaineers of Western Virginia and North Carolina resolved that he should be cut off. They mounted and pursued him with unflagging zeal and rapidity; and when they came up with his forces on the confines of North and South Carolina, they began the attack immediately, utterly routed Ferguson, hung up ten of the most obnoxious tories on the spot, and then returned home. Cornwallis at once began his retreat; this he accomplished by the end of October, having been harassed all the way by bands of partisans, who intercepted convoys and kept the enemy in continual alarm.

At the North, meanwhile, the early months of the year 1780, were spent in desultory operations, Washington being unable from lack of men and means, to undertake anything of moment. Lafayette returned from France at the end of April, bringing the good news that efficient aid would soon arrive in behalf of the Americans. On the 10th of July, the French fleet entered the harbor of Newport, the troops being under the command of Count De Rochambeau. Washington strongly wished to make an attack on New York, which would have taken place, had not the British received reinforcements before his plan could be carried into effect. The commander-in-chief was mortified and distressed at these abortive results of all his efforts; but there was no remedy but patience. At this date, the deeply laid scheme of treachery of Benedict Arnold was unfolded, and it is all the more remarkable in our history, because it is the only instance of the kind, despite the trials and temptations to which those struggling for independence were exposed. Arnold was one of those reckless, daring, unscrupulous men, who seem to be the natural product of war and civil commotion. He was a gambler and debauchee, and resorted to many of the meanest practices of the profligate scoundrel. He was held to be very brave, and was so, if his dashing exploits already noted (p. 82), are to be considered as proofs; but he was also arrogant, fond of show, dissolute and ready to do any thing, however low and contemptible, in order to keep up appearances and indulge in licentious habits and practices. This man, desperately in debt, and with no other available means of relief, offered to sell himself and his country for gold out of British coffers. For more than a year, he was engaged in perfecting his plan, and kept up a secret correspondence with Major André, Clinton's adjutant-general in New York. Under pretext of desiring active service, Arnold got himself appointed to the command of West Point, and leaving Philadelphia, arrived at the Point early in August. Washington was absent, on a visit to Hartford to meet the French officers, and the opportunity was seized in order to consummate the foul treachery. André came up the river in a sloop of war, the Vulture which anchored in Haverstraw Bay, and spent a night in conference with Arnold. He accompanied the traitor to the house of one J. H. Smith, within the American lines, and received a full account of the force at West Point, with plans, etc., and then, with a pass from Arnold to cross the lines, he set out on his return. Arnold, meanwhile, went back to his headquarters at Robinson's house, opposite West Point. Disappointed at not being able to get on board the Vulture, André was compelled to run the risk of returning to New York by land. He put on a citizen's dress, and accompanied by Smith, he crossed the river at King's Ferry, and took the road towards the city. At the outposts he was carefully scrutinized but not detained, being advised, however, as it was now dark, to remain all night, inasmuch as "the neutral ground," a tract of about thirty miles in extent along the Hudson, between the American and British lines, was infested with marauders. André reluctantly assented, and the next morning, very early, was again in the saddle. Parting with Smith, he hastened on, and considered himself now out of danger. About ten o'clock, on this eventful day, September 23rd, when André was about half a mile north of Tarrytown, three armed militia men sprang out from the road side, seized his bridle, and demanded where he was going. André, supposing himself among friends, said, "I hope you belong to our party." "What party?" was asked by one of the men. "The lower party." Being answered in the affirmative, André avowed himself a British officer, on pressing business; but immediately after, perceiving the blunder he had made, he showed Arnold's pass, and urged them not to detain him a moment. The men, John Paulding, David Williams, and Isaac Van Wart, refused his request, and causing him to dismount, they took him one side among the bushes, and searched him. Having pulled off his boots and stockings, they found next to the soles of his feet, the papers which Arnold had written out, respecting West Point, its defences, the state of the force, etc. André offered the men large sums of money, if they would release him; but, providentially for the cause of our country, they rejected the glittering bribe, and a few hours afterwards, he was delivered up to Lieutenant-Colonel Jameson, who was in command at North Castle, the nearest military post. This officer, astounded at sight of the papers, "lost his head," as the French have it, and with most unaccountable stupidity, resolved to send a letter with André to the traitor Arnold, himself! Happily, however, he dispatched an express with the papers to meet Washington, supposed to be on the road returning from Hartford. By the earnest expostulation of Major Tallmadge, Jameson did detain André as a prisoner, but persisted in sending his letter to Arnold, and giving him the very information which enabled him to escape the punishment due to his detestable crime. André aware of what had been done with the papers found on him, wrote a note to Washington, dated Sept. 24th, revealing his name and rank, and claiming that he was not a spy, but had got within the American lines unknowingly The Commander-in-chief, meanwhile, reached Fishkill on the afternoon of the 24th, where he spent the night, setting off again early the next morning, with the purpose of breakfasting with Arnold at Robinson's house. Delaying for a while, in examining some redoubts, word was sent to the house to explain the cause of not being quite in time, and so Arnold and family sat down to breakfast. While they were at table, that most singularly ill-timed letter of Jameson was brought in; Arnold read it, but did not lose presence of mind—he was too well skilled in dissimulation for that—left the table in some hurry, under the plea that he was needed at West Point, rode hastily to the river, entered a six-oared barge, stimulated the men by promises of drink, to extra exertion, held up a white handkerchief as he passed Verplanck's Point, and was soon in safety on board the Vulture. We need not dwell on the details of what followed. The unfortunate André was tried by court-martial, convicted as a spy, condemned to death, and despite the utmost exertions of Clinton and others, was hung on the 2nd of October. And as for Arnold, he received the reward of his treachery, and prepared to execute the commands of his masters, despised and scorned, although used by those who had bought him.

It was, as we have just noted, a matter of regret and mortification to Washington that the campaign reached its close without result, and further operations were impossible during the winter of 1780–1; a letter to a friend at this date is worthy of being quoted, as expressive of his sentiments and views respecting the then condition of affairs: "We are now drawing to a close an inactive campaign, the beginning of which appeared pregnant with events of a very favorable complexion. I hoped, but I hoped in vain, that a prospect was opening, which would enable me to fix a period to my military pursuits, and restore me to domestic life. The favorable disposition of Spain; the promised succor from

France; the combined force in the West Indies; the declaration of Russia (acceded to by other powers of Europe, humiliating to the naval pride and power of Great Britain); the superiority of France and Spain by sea, in Europe; the Irish claims, and English disturbances; formed in the aggregate an opinion in my breast, which is not very susceptible of peaceful dreams, that the hour of deliverance was not far distant: for that, however unwilling Great Britain might be to yield the point, it would not be in her power to continue the contest. But, alas! these prospects, flattering as they were, have proved delusory; and I see nothing before us, but accumulating distress. We have been half of our time without provisions, and are likely to continue so. We have no magazines, nor money to form them. We have lived upon expedients, until we can live no longer. In a word, the history of the war is a history of false hopes and temporary devices, instead of system and economy. It is in vain, however, to look back; nor is it our business to do so. Our case is not desperate if virtue exists in the people, and there is wisdom among our rulers. But to suppose that this great revolution can be accomplished by a temporary army; that this army will be subsisted by State supplies; and that taxation alone is adequate to our wants, is, in my opinion absurd."

The persistence of England in what she claimed as her due, "the right of search," led to an *armed neutrality* among the European powers; and indirectly America was benefitted by this, since the necessity of contending with numerous other enemies prevented the sending an overwhelming force into the United States, so as to crush out all opposition. Reinforcements, it is true, were sent, and hopes were entertained of ultimate success; but, on the other hand, France continued her aid to our suffering country, and Count de Grasse was directed to repair with his fleet to our coast, and coöperate with Rochambeau and Washington, a measure, as we shall see, which subsequently proved of the highest importance to the cause of independence. The condition of affairs was depressed in the extreme. The paper money issued by Congress had become worthless; it was no longer made a legal tender, or received in payment of taxes; and had not measures been taken, of some effectual kind, to get money, it would have been next to impossible to raise or maintain an army against the foe. Happily, Congress prevailed upon Robert Morris of Philadelphia, to become treasurer, a man of pure morals, ardent patriotism and first-rate ability as a financier. The zeal and genius of Morris soon produced the most favorable results. By means of the "Bank of North America," to which, in the course of the year, he obtained the approbation of Congress, he contrived to draw out the funds of wealthy individuals. By borrowing in the name of the government from this bank, and pledging for payment the taxes not yet collected, he was enabled to anticipate them, and command a ready supply. He also used his own private credit, which was good, though that of the government had failed; and, at one time, bills signed by him individually, were in circulation, to the amount of $581,000. Abroad, through Franklin's exertions, Louis XVI. gave over $1,000,000, and loaned nearly $750,000, to the United States in their emergency, and Holland also, on the guarantee of France, loaned $1,850,000 (10 millions of livres). These funds thus obtained were expended with the utmost prudence, and the prospect of improvement in public credit and administration of affairs grew brighter. A dangerous outbreak in the army manifested the critical condition in which Washington and the patriot defenders of our country were placed. On the 1st of January, 1781, some 1300 of the Pennsylvania line paraded under arms, refused to obey orders, and committed various outrages. Want and suffering had led to this. They had enlisted for three years or the war, and now demanded, as the three years were ended, to be paid and released. It was with great difficulty that Gen. Wayne by his firmness and moderation, succeeded in quieting the mutineers and arranging matters satisfactorily for the future. Washington looked with anxiety upon this alarming movement, and took measures to repress the spread of any spirit of the kind; and when some weeks later a part of the New Jersey brigade rose in arms, the commander-in-chief sent a sufficient force from the Highlands to put it down at once; two of the ringleaders were shot, and no further attempts at mutiny occurred. Arnold, with the true spirit of a renegade, endeavored to show his zeal in behalf of the enemies of his country. It was in Virginia, at Richmond and its vicinity, that he displayed his malice in ravaging and plundering; and the spring of 1781 was spent in efforts to resist the British inroads, and, if possible, to attack and seize upon Arnold, so as to visit upon him the punishment due to the traitor.

At the close of the year, 1780, as we have already noted (p. 92), Gen. Greene took command in the south. His position was difficult and critical; for, having an entirely insufficient force to meet and cope with Cornwallis, he was compelled to be constantly on the alert and guard against surprise and sudden attack. Morgan, with a part of the troops, about 600 in number, was detached to watch the enemy on the frontier of South Carolina, and did excellent service for the good cause. Tarleton, the famous cavalry officer, and noted for his cruelty, was sent to meet Morgan, no doubt being entertained of his success. The battle of the Cowpens, near Broad River, was the result, fought on the 17th of January; and so aroused and indignant were the American troops, that they attacked the enemy with tremendous force and energy, and routed them completely. Over 200 were killed, and 600 made prisoners, while Morgan's loss was only 12 killed, and 61 wounded. This victory at the Cowpens was certainly one of the most brilliant that had ever been achieved by American arms; and seldom has a battle, in which the number of combatants was so small, produced such important consequences; for the loss of the light infantry not only considerably diminished the force, but also crippled the movements of Cornwallis during the rest of the campaign. The British commander now set out in pursuit of Gen. Greene, who displayed military ability of a high order, in the conduct of his retreat. Cornwallis was unable to effect anything, although he pursued the Americans more than 200 miles, and, although they were subjected to great exposure and hardship; many of them were in rags, and many bare-footed, and not infrequently the road was marked by the blood from their wounded feet; yet, they endured all for their country's sake. Greene, having received some reinforcements, determined to attack Cornwallis, at Guildford Court House. The battle was fought on the 15th of March, and was sharply contested; but, though Greene was obliged to retire from the field, he did so in good order, and the British gained no permanent advantage. We need not enter into details of movements on the part of Greene or the enemy. In Georgia, as well as Carolina, that able general was constantly engaged in watching the British, in pursuit or retreat, and in frequent encounters, the benefit of which, on the whole, was on the side of the Americans. On the 16th of July, he reached the high hills of Santee, and remained there till the 22d of August. Early in September, he attacked the British at Eutaw Springs, 60 miles north of Charleston, having about 2000 men, mostly militia, in the field. Never was a battle more hotly contested, and it was one of the most bloody for the numbers engaged; but victory did not belong to either side; the British retired and moved towards Charleston, and the Americans returned to their former position. With this battle the war was virtually closed in South Carolina. Cornwallis, who was in Virginia, sent expeditions against Charlotteville, where Lafayette was in command, and Point of Fork, where Baron Steuben had a body of troops; both expeditions were successful to a large extent. Cornwallis, during the summer, entrenched himself at Yorktown, on the York River, opposite Gloucester, and expected reinforcements from Clinton, in New York. That general, however, learning that Washington was resolved to attack New York, if the French fleet would co-operate, and he could increase his force sufficiently, did not feel it safe to dispatch troops to Virginia, and so Cornwallis was left to do the best he could. Washington, finding that it was inexpedient to besiege New York, from lack of troops, suddenly changed his plan of operations, and determined to take Cornwallis in the snare he seemed to be preparing for himself. Accordingly, by great skill and discretion, he kept Clinton in fear lest New York should be attacked, and prevented his sending help to Virginia; and it was not till too late that the British commander was astounded by the conviction that the allies had fixed upon Virginia for the theatre of their combined operations. At the close of August, the troops marched rapidly to the South, where, on conference with Count De Grasse, in September, Washington entered upon the siege of Yorktown. The allied force was about 11,000, and with a good supply of artillery, they formally invested Yorktown early in October, and the result was that the British, finding their case desperate, surrendered on the 19th of October, 1781. The number of prisoners was about 7000; and Clinton, who reached the Capes of Virginia on the 24th, on learning the news, returned immediately to the North.

With the capture of Cornwallis, it became evident that the Americans were not to be overcome by force, and England speedily began to desire to put an end to the further contest. Attempts were made by the new British ministry to arrange respecting a peace, by sending Gen. Carleton to America in the spring of 1782. Washington, meanwhile, anxious as to the position of affairs, warmly urged Congress to provide for another campaign, and his judicious advice was followed by that body, who called upon the States to furnish their quotas at an early day, and persuaded the commander-in-chief to write two circular letters to the governors of all the States, at the beginning of 1782. Financial matters were in a sad condition, and there was an almost universal indisposition to either provide for or undertake further military operations. The spring and summer passed away in inactivity; Carleton kept himself quiet in New York, and Washington watched patiently and hopefully the progress of affairs; at the South, some desultory operations, but of no special moment, occurred. Negotiations in regard to peace were carried forward at Paris, and, though George III. with his usual stubbornness tried hard to put off the certain issue, yet, by the firmness of the American envoys, Franklin, Jay and Adams, and their French allies, the recognition, in full and complete, of the independence of the United States was secured. On the 30th of November, the provisional treaty was signed at Paris by both parties, in due form, and early the following year was approved and ratified by Congress. The definitive treaty of peace was arranged during the year; it was signed on the 3d of September, 1783, and ratified by Congress early in January, 1784.

It was a perilous time which had now arrived, when the war was virtually ended, and both officers and men took into account what they had suffered, what destitution had been brought upon them, and how small was the prospect of relief, even in the way of simple justice, to be expected from Congress or the State legislatures. Washington was greatly distressed at what occurred in the army, and though he both sympathized with his companions in arms, and knew their sufferings and their just claims, he could not, of course, for a moment give his sanction to a mutinous spirit or any illegal mode of procedure in order to gain certain ends. There were those, in 1782, who thought that the army must take the remedy in their own hands, and so in a letter, ably and skilfully written, May 2d, the commander-in-chief was asked to take the head of affairs and become a *king!* Washington's answer was an indignant and stern rebuke at the very thought of such a proposition, which, he declared, he "viewed with abhorrence." At the same time, in writing to the Secretary of War, he used language worthy of being quoted as demonstrating his earnest sympathy and regard for both officers and men: "I cannot help fearing the result, when I see such a number of men, goaded by a thousand stings of reflection on the past, and of anticipation on the future, about to be turned into the world, soured by penury, and what they call the ingratitude of the public; involved in debts, without one farthing of money to carry them home, after having spent the flower of their days, and, many of them, their patrimonies, in establishing the freedom and independence of their country; and having suffered everything which human nature is capable of enduring on this side of death. I repeat it, when I reflect on these irritating circumstances, unattended by one thing to sooth their feelings, or brighten the gloomy prospect, I cannot avoid apprehending that a train of evils will follow, of a serious and distressing nature. You may rely upon it, the patience and long-suffering of this army are almost exhausted, and there never was so great a spirit of discontent as at this instant." The officers sent a petition to Congress at the close of the year, asking, in urgent terms, for justice at least, and speedy relief; that body contained some men of truly national spirit, and who desired to do what was right in this emergency; but the majority, we are sorry to say, felt otherwise, and with that sectional spirit prevailing, they opposed everything like national action, and wished to place all matters of the kind in the hands of State legislatures for settlement. Nothing consequently was done, and the crisis arrived. On the 10th of March, 1783, a meeting of the officers was called, and the famous "Newburg Addresses" were prepared, addresses indicating great skill on the part of the framer of them, but at the same time advocating principles and a course which Washington could neither approve nor adopt. He accordingly, as a matter of duty, interfered; was present at the meeting called by him for the 15th, and by his great personal influence, his calm reasoning, his urgent appeals to their patriotism, he frustrated the evil which was threatening. "Truly," as Mr. Curtis says, "even at this distant day, the peril of that crisis can scarcely be contemplated without a shudder. Had the commander-in-chief been other than Washington, had the leading officers by whom he was surrounded been less than the noblest of patriots, the land would have been deluged with the blood of a civil war. But men who had suffered what the great officers of the Revolution had suffered, had learned the lessons of self-control which suffering teaches. The hard school of adversity in which they had passed so many years, made them sensible to an appeal, which only such a chief as Washington could make." At the urgent remonstrance and unwearied, watchful perseverance of the commander-in-chief, Congress at last, on the 22d of March, passed certain resolves on the subject to meet the just claims of the officers, and early in July, the accounts of the army were finally made up and adjusted. The army was disbanded at the beginning of November; the British under Carleton evacuated New York on the 25th; and Washington resigned his commission into the hands of Congress, Dec. 23d, 1783. The next day he reached the coveted retirement of Mount Vernon, from which he had been absent nearly nine years.

Thus, so far as military operations were concerned, the independence of our country was secured. But the condition of the country was such, there was so general a prostration of affairs, so many disputes, jealousies, bickerings, so many false and pernicious notions rife in the community, that the prospect ahead was gloomy enough, and might well cause the hearts of our patriot fathers to be sad and heavy as to the ultimate result. The history of the years between the treaty of peace and the adoption of the Constitution is a history of dangers and trials which words cannot describe. Trade and commerce were literally in ruins; agriculture was destroyed; the mechanic arts had neither place nor support; a mountain of debt was pressing the people down; and worse than all, they were on the very brink of anarchy and political destruction. Many a dark foreboding filled the minds of Washington and his compeers, and they beheld, with the deepest concern, the unhappy state of the country at large. Congress was totally inefficient. There was, in fact, no government. The separate independent State sovereignties, however efficient within their respective boundaries, were utterly incapable of furnishing or maintaining a government for the whole. There was, as yet, no nationality. The smaller States looked suspiciously upon the larger; and these in their turn both felt and were disposed to use their superior power and influence for State aggrandizement and State control. It soon became a question of importance, whether there was to be any country at all; whether the people of the United States were to be one people, or many; whether there was to be union, efficiency, energy at home, and respect and confidence abroad; and whether there was to be a national government, a national character, and a national integrity and honor. The Articles of Confederation, under which the war had been prosecuted in the latter years of the Revolution, though professing to be articles of perpetual union, were possessed of no power to effect and maintain union. Congress had exclusive power for a number of purposes, but had no ability to execute any of them. They were empowered to make and conclude treaties; but they could only recommend the observance of them. They could appoint ambassadors; but they could not defray their expenses. They could borrow money in their own name, on the faith of the Union; but they could not pay a dollar. They could coin money; but they could not import an ounce of bullion. They could make war, and determine upon the number of troops necessary; but they could not raise a single soldier. In fact, they could declare everything, but could do nothing. At the same time the Confederation had accomplished something. It had given an impulse, at least, towards nationality, and it had rendered good service, in obtaining a cession of the public lands, and carrying the war forward to its conclusion. But it had no authority to compel obedience. It had been miserably ineffective in obtaining the means for feeding, clothing, and paying its troops. It had been compelled to resort to temporary expedients, entirely at variance with order, economy, energy, and strict adherence to public faith and honor. It found itself, at the close of the war, without command of means to meet its obligations to that noble band of men, who had fought, and bled, and suffered unutterable miseries, in their country's behalf; without means to pay its citizens and foreigners, who had generously loaned their money; and without means to compensate any of those who had contributed property and personal service to the common cause. Its last hope of being able to do justice, hung upon the possibility of being able to obtain the assent of thirteen distinct legislative bodies, the dissent of either one of which would defeat any measure of Congress, and subject it to the disgrace and the pernicious effects of broken faith and national bankruptcy.

At this day it is probably impossible for us to realize the strange fact, that with all these, and many similar defects staring men in the face, they should have been so wedded to the notion of State sovereignty, and State efficiency, as to be reluctant, to the last degree, to attempt anything in the way of adequate remedies for the evils which threatened our national existence. For years, efforts were made by the wisest and best men in the country, to procure an indispensably necessary enlargement of the powers of the Continental Congress; but State jealousies predominated, State interests clashed, and every effort failed (1785). The Confederation, without resources, and without powers, was fast expiring of its own debility. It lost, not only its vigor, but the respect which it once claimed. It was in the last stages of its decline; and now the only question remained, whether it should dissolve, and even the semblance of a government be lost, or whether there should not be a brave effort made by the patriots and statesmen of the day, to form a more efficient government, before the great interests of the United States were buried beneath its ruins.

Early in 1783, Congress had declared that it was indispensably necessary that they should possess power to levy duties, and provide for the public expense by direct taxation. Under the Articles of Confederation (p.—) they had no such power; they could only issue *requisitions* on the States, which were complied with, or disregarded, or rejected, as the sovereign States pleased. They asked to be vested with power to levy duties on wines, teas, sugars, etc, these duties to be applied to the payment of the interest and principal of the public debt, for the term of twenty-five years. They also required the States to secure regularly and certainly their proportion of $1,500,000 annually, exclusive of duties. The design of the revenue system of 1783, was to see that justice was done to the creditors of the United States, and to strengthen and consolidate the government by the efforts which would be necessary to carry out national measures of so great moment. It was a wise and judicious movement, undoubtedly; for it had a most salutary effect in familiarizing the public mind with the important idea of the creditors looking to the general government for the payment of their dues, and not to the separate States; and it prevented the almost certain result that would have followed any attempt to rely upon the States, viz., of partial payment, of bankruptcy, or of entire repudiation. The scheme, it is true, was never adopted; yet, the influence of this revenue system was very great in saving the Union, at the time, from speedy dissolution, and in directing the attention of the States, to the necessity of giving to it additional powers with respect to commerce and kindred national objects. The arrangement which was completed, with regard to the pay due to the army, we have spoken of on a previous page (p 98); this, together with the proposal of the present plan of obtaining revenue for the general government, were, during the four years that followed, serviceable to a high degree, in making evident the necessities which existed, and in directing the thoughts of men, to the mode best adapted to the meeting these necessities, and the preserving our country from intestine discord and ruin. That part of the financial plan, which required from the States a pledge of internal revenues for twenty-five years, met, as was but natural, with the greatest opposition. Congress, satisfied, at length, that a general compliance with this part of the system was not to be expected, confined their requests to that relating to duties on imports. Under the influence of the urgent and solemn representations made by Congress, of the deplorable condition of the United States, in regard to its ability to maintain public faith at home and abroad, all the States, before or during the year 1786, complied with this part of the system, New York being the sole exception.

The subject of our foreign commercial relations occupied the attention of Congress at an early day. Beside England, it was held to be important to have treaties of this kind with Spain, Prussia, Russia, etc. But difficulties were interposed, especially in the case of Great Britain. The rulers of that country seem to have been possessed of very narrow, petty, jealous feelings and views, and in their fear of rivalry in matters of navigation and commerce, they were willing to take ground and do acts which stirred up ill will, and had an effect upon the sentiments of the nation for a long time, so far as the British were concerned. But commercial and revenue difficulties were not the only ones that harassed and annoyed the national government. Scarcely had the war of the Revolution been brought to a close, when the United States and Great Britain reciprocally charged each other with violations of the treaty of peace. A serious difference of opinion prevailed, on the construction of that part of the seventh article, which stipulates against the "destruction, or carrying away of any negroes, or other property of the American inhabitants." In addition to this circumstance, the troops of his Britannic majesty still retained possession of the posts on the American side of the great lakes. This gave them a decided influence over the warlike tribes of Indians in their neighborhood, and was a point on which the United States were peculiarly sensitive. On the other hand, the United States were charged with infringing the fourth, fifth, and sixth articles, which contain agreements respecting the payment of debts, the confiscation of property, and prosecution of individuals, for the part taken by them during the war. Congress, in January, 1784, passed a resolution, and transmitted it directly to the States, on the subject of confiscated property. This was recommendatory; but the collection of debts was expressly stipulated in the treaty; and a neglect, or hindrance in this particular, caused much complaint, and produced no little irritation on both sides. At the commencement of the war, £3,000,000 sterling were due from the inhabitants of the colonies to British merchants. When peace came, it was found that the laws of five States, either prohibited the recovery of the principal, or suspended its collection, or prohibited the recovery of interest, or made land a good payment in place of money. These and other laws of course produced trouble, and Congress could only recommend, not enforce, their repeal. After the lapse of three years from the signature of the preliminary articles, and of more than two years from that of the definitive treaty, the military posts in the Western country were still held by British garrisons, avowedly on account of the infractions of the treaty on the part of the Americans. In this complication of affairs, it was deemed advisable to send a minister-plenipotentiary to Great Britain. John Adams was selected, and reached London, in May, 1785. The not overwise old king, George III., still felt very sore at being compelled to give up all claim to the United States; and so, he and his courtiers treated the American minister in a rather shabby manner, with a sort of supercilious neglect and indifference, which cut deeply into the sensitive feelings of the representatives of the new and great nation which was about rising in the western world. Trifling insults, on such occassions, count for far more than they are worth; and both Mr. Adams and Mr. Jefferson (who was also at London) being subsequently presidents of the United States, it is not easy to estimate how great influence the conduct of the king and others had in fixing sentiments of ill-will in the minds of these men, and through these in the mind of the people at large. Mr. Adams was unable to accomplish anything, and the British still continued to hold the western posts and keep up an irritable feeling in general. Spain, too, was pertinacious in regard to the Mississippi, manifesting a desire to interfere with its free navigation; in 1786, the question of right was held in abeyance, and a commercial treaty concluded; and two years later, the whole matter in dispute was handed over to the new government under the Constitution, then about to go into operation.

In 1783, Congress urged upon the States who had not yet attended to its previous requests, to make speedy cession of their territorial claims, as well for hastening the extinguishment of the public debt, as for establishing the harmony of the United States. Virginia completed the cession of her claims in March, 1784, and Congress made provision for a temporary government of that fertile region, and the admission into the Union of new States formed out of it. New York followed; then Massachusetts and Con necticut; South Carolina, in August, 1787, granted to the United States, all her right to the country west of the ridge or chain of mountains which divides the eastern from the western waters. The United States thus became possessed of all the land north-west of the Ohio; and the establishment of a government for the inhabitants already settled as well as those who were hastening thither, became immediately necessary. On the 13th of July, 1787, Congress established the celebrated Ordinance for the government of the North-Western Territory, which superseded the resolve of 1784; a piece of legislation by the way, which Mr. Curtis, the historian of the Constitution, lauds in the highest terms, and which deserves all the praise which has been bestowed upon it. The position of the older States, however, engrossed a large share of public attention. As we have before noted, matters were becoming more and more critical, and were fast hastening to that pass that something effectual must be done, or the Union would inevitably perish. In this conjuncture, it happened that certain measures taken in Virginia, opened the way, through Washington's advice and influence, for the great movement which resulted ultimately in the Federal Constitution. Commercial regulations were what were had in view simply, but the report of the Commissioners led to the further assembling of gentlemen from other States at Annapolis, in September, 1786, who, in their report, urged the appointment of delegates to meet, in the following May, at Philadelphia, so as to revise the Constitution of the Government, and make it adequate to the exigencies of the Union. A letter was also sent to Congress, accompanied by a copy of this report to the States. This body, at first, looked rather doubtfully upon the movement; but still, it was felt that the crisis had come, and that deplorable results must follow further apathy and neglect. In February, 1787, after a preamble setting forth the probable value of a Convention, it was "*Resolved*, That, in the opinion of Congress, it is expedient, that on the second Monday in May next, a Convention of delegates, who shall have been appointed by the several States, be held at Philadelphia, for the sole and express purpose of revising the Articles of Confederation, and reporting to Congress and the several legislatures, such alterations and provisions therein, as shall, when agreed to in Congress, and confirmed by the States, render the Federal Constitution adequate to the exigencies of government, and the preservation of the Union." Acting under this authority, all the States except Rhode Island, appointed delegates to the Federal Convention. It may be doubted, however, whether necessary action would have taken place, even at this time, had not the alarming condition of affairs in the New England States, during the latter part of 1786 and opening of 1787, roused Congress and the people to a sense of the immediate danger which existed, of the whole country running into anarchy and ruin. The immense burden of debt, especially in Massachusetts, and the relaxation of principle, the scarcity of money, etc., were primary causes of insurrection in Massachusetts. Wild and extravagant notions of liberty led to various excesses. Proceeding from inflammatory words to actions, the disaffected citizens of Massachusetts armed themselves, surrounded the court-houses in several counties, and completely obstructed the sessions of the courts. Some fifteen hundred insurgents acted in this manner at Northampton. The governor issued a proclamation, early in September, calling upon the officers and citizens of the commonwealth to suppress all such treasonable proceedings; but in the excited state of the community, it had little effect. The week succeeding the proclamation, a body of more than three hundred insurgents posted themselves at the court-house in Worcester, and compelled the courts to adjourn. Similar riotous proceedings took place in other counties. One step led to another. The weakness of the government, and the attempts made by it to suppress the insurrection by persuasion and promises rather than by force, induced a large body of men to organize, under arms, in order to force the State to comply with its demands. Minot, the historian of the Insurrection, states, that in the month of December, 1786, in the counties of Worcester and Hampshire, some fifteen hundred men were embodied, and were headed by one Daniel Shays, who had been a captain in the continental army.

Washington, as may well be believed, was deeply concerned in the alarming condition of affairs at this date. Writing to Henry Lee he says: "You talk, my good sir, of employing influence to appease the present tumults in Massachusetts. I know not where that influence is to be found, nor, if attainable, that it would be a proper remedy for these disorders. INFLUENCE IS NOT GOVERNMENT. Let us have a *government*, by which our lives, liberties, and properties will be secured; or let us know the worst at once. Under these impressions, my humble opinion is, that there is a call for decision. Know precisely what the insurgents aim at. If they have *real* grievances, redress them, if possible, or acknowledge the justice of them, and your inability to do it in the present moment. If they have not, employ the force of government against them at once. If this is inadequate, *all* will be convinced that the superstructure is bad, or wants support. To be more exposed in the eyes of the world, and more contemptible, is hardly possible. To delay one or the other of these expedients, is to exasperate on the one hand, or to give confidence on the other, and will add to their numbers; for, like snowballs, such bodies increase by every movement, unless there is something in the way to obstruct and crumble them before their weight is too great and irresistible. These are my sentiments. Precedents are dangerous things. Let the reins of government, then, be braced with a steady hand, and every violation of the Constitution be reprehended, If defective, let it be amended, but not suffered to be trampled upon while it has an existence."

Early in 1787, Governor Boudoin of Massachussetts ordered out 4000 militia, and placed them under command of General Lincoln. They marched promptly to the scene of action, and pressing the insurgents closely, they at length, in February, succeeded in dispersing the rebel force, driving their leaders out of the State, and quelling this dangerous rebellion. Perhaps nothing short of the stern necessity which existed, of providing against the peril of a renewal of such scenes as these just narrated, and of losing the navigation of the Mississippi, and the western settlements, and also the necessity of reanimating the languishing, and almost annihilated commerce of the country, could have succeeded in bringing Congress and the various States to the conviction, that a Convention was not only the best, but, in fact, the only practicable mode of accomplishing the end universally desired. This important body, made up of the best talent of the country, assembled in May, 1787, at the State House in Philadelphia, and on the 25th, when nine States were represented by twenty-nine delegates, proceeded to organize for business. Washington was chosen president, and the Convention entered zealously upon their work. Details, obviously, cannot be gone into. The sessions were held with closed doors; but we know that the grave and momentous topics which engaged the attention of the Convention, were discussed freely and fully, with eloquence, learning, judgment and patriotism. There does not appear to have been much difference of opinion in the Convention, as to the propriety and importance of establishing the national government, in its three grand divisions of a supreme legislative, executive and judicial authority. In respect, however, to the arrangement and harmonizing these three great co-ordinate departments, the relative weight of the several States in these departments, and the powers with which each should be invested, there were very serious differences of sentiment, and the questions were debated with great earnestness and force of argument. It having been determined, that the legislature should be divided into two branches—viz., a House of Representatives and a Senate, the question immediately came up as to the votes of the States in these branches. The larger and the smaller States, it was supposed, had diverse interests, and the latter feared that the former would not respect the rights of the others. The smaller States, after some discussion, yielded the point in regard to the House, consenting that the number of members from each State should be in proportion to the whole number of white or other free citizens in each, including those bound to service for a term of years, and three-fifths of all other persons. But they absolutely refused to agree to anything less than an equal vote in the Senate. This point was a very difficult one to manage; the Convention, at one time, seemed to be at a standstill; and had not a spirit of compromise and mutual concession prevailed, after long and ardent disputation, it is impossible to tell what dreadful evils would have followed. Happily, however, the question was settled, and the equal vote in the Senate secured to all the States. It is not necessary that we should enlarge upon the other difficult and delicate topics which occupied the attention of the Convention; such as the powers granted to Congress; the restrictions on the powers of the States; the organization and powers of the Executive; the formation of the supreme judiciary; the importing of slaves; the powers of Congress relative to navigation acts; etc. The same spirit of compromise, as spoken of above, was continually called into action; and the members of this august assemblage found, that mutual concessions were absolutely requisite, and that no one of them was able to obtain such a Constitution, in all, or even most respects, as he had hoped for or expected. Having provided for amendments and agreed upon a final draft of the Constitution, the Convention ordered that the ratification of nine States should be sufficient for the establishment of the new government among the States so ratifying the same. A letter to Congress was prepared by Washington, as president of the Convention, to accompany the Constitution, and the Convention thereupon adjourned, September 17th, 1787.

Congress resolved immediately to submit the action of the Convention to the people in the several States, by means of delegates duly chosen for this purpose in each State. Debates were ardent and not free from bitterness, and the talent arrayed against was not less than that pledged in favor of the Constitution. It was, however, adopted unanimously, by the Conventions held in Delaware, New Jersey, and Georgia; and by large majorities in Pennsylvania, Connecticut, Maryland, and South Carolina. Rhode Island refused to call a Convention; and in several of the more important States it was, for a time, a matter of doubt, whether they would assent to the Constitution without previous amendments. The imminent danger, however, in which the country was placed, without a government, without funds, deeply in debt, treated with contempt abroad and threatened with anarchy at home, compelled men to action, which, under other circumstances, they almost certainly would not have taken. At the beginning of 1788, Massachusetts held a Convention, and after a month's discussion and uncertainty, with the proposal of amendments, the Constitution was adopted by a vote of 187 to 168. Virginia, New York and North Carolina held Conventions during the summer of 1788, and in these the most persistent and powerful opposition was made. The ablest men in the country took part in these discussions, and for a time the result was in abeyance; but, happily the patience, perseverance, skill and wisdom of such men as Hamilton, Madison, Randolph and others prevailed, and Virginia, in June, and New York, in July, ratified the Constitution.*

* For convenience of reference, we subjoin the dates of the Ratification of the Constitution, by the thirteen original states:—Delaware, December 7th, 1787; Pennsylvania, December 12th, 1787; New

New Hampshire being the ninth State in order which had ratified the Constitution, it was laid before Congress, July 2, 1788, and steps were taken immediately for its going into operation in the spring of 1789. At this point we bring the present chapter to a close, and shall proceed in the next to give a narrative of our history and progress under the Constitution.

CHAPTER III.

CONSTITUTIONAL HISTORY OF UNITED STATES: 1789—1867.

The Constitution of the United States was adopted after long and earnest discussion, and it was received in various portions of the country with no little doubt and apprehension. Its successful working, therefore, was but problematical in the estimation of many; and there were those, who, from the outset, disliked its aim and provisions, and determined to oppose its operation in every way which they could. Yet, seeing that it had been adopted by eleven of the States, it was certain that a trial of its merits must be had, notwithstanding the doubts and fears and vaticinations of ill on the part of its opposers. But, although there was this difference of opinion as to the new Constitution and its value, there was not any where any hesitation as to the man under whose auspices the test was to be applied, which was to demonstrate whether the Constitution was, or was not, what its friends or its opposers asserted. That man—the spontaneous impulse of every American heart prompted the utterance—was George Washington. Every one knew, it is true, his reluctance to leave the retirement of his home; every one knew, likewise, that his patriotism triumphed over all personal considerations; and the instinctive feeling of the whole country taught them, that there was no man so absolutely necessary, in the present crisis, as Washington, whose ability, wisdom, prudence, and character, alone could enable him, with any prospect of success, to sustain the difficulties and dangers of the new and untried position of the president of the United States of America. He could not but be made aware of public sentiment on the subject in many ways, and he was assured that, unless he gave his name and presence, the great experiment now to be tried might fail entirely.

During the winter of 1788–9, the election of members of the First Federal Congress went busily forward. Some of the ablest and best men in the land were chosen; among whom were Madison, Sherman, Ames, and others in the House of Representatives; and Langdon, King, Ellsworth, Morris, etc., in the Senate. The presidential electors met in the several States early in February, 1789, and gave in their ballots. The 4th of March was the day appointed for opening of these, but bad roads and other delays put off the opening till the 6th of April. The whole number of votes was sixty-nine. Washington received them all, without a single exception; and John Adams received thirty four. This, although not a majority of the whole, designated him, as, "after the choice of the president, the person having the greatest number of votes of the electors;" and consequently John Adams became the first vice-president. John Jay, R. H. Harrison, and John Rutledge, with others, received a

Jersey December 18th, 1787; Georgia, January 2d, 1788; Connecticut, January 9th, 1788; Massachusetts, February 6th, 1788; Maryland, April 28th, 1788; South Carolina, May 23d, 1788; New Hampshire, June 21st, 1788; Virginia, June 26th, 1788; New York, July 26th, 1788; North Carolina, November 21st, 1789; Rhode Island, May 29th, 1790.

number of votes. Official information was immediately communicated to Washington and Adams, and preparations were made for the solemn inauguration of the new government. Some liberal-spirited merchants of New York contributed over $30,000, and the "Federal Hall," the site of which is now occupied by the U. S. Treasury and Mint, was put in suitable order for the great uses to which it was to be devoted. Washington was officially notified of his election on the 14th of April, and though reluctant and self-distrustful, yet as it was the path of duty, he promptly set out for New York. The record in his diary deserves to be here quoted: "About ten o'clock, I bade adieu to Mount Vernon, to private life, and to domestic felicity; and with a mind oppressed with more anxious and painful sensations than I have words to express, set out for New York, in company with Mr. Thomson and Colonel Humphreys, with the best disposition to render service to my country in obedience to its call, but with less hope of answering its expectations." Washington's journey to New York was like a triumphal procession; every where on the road, every thing was done to manifest the love and veneration of the people; and he was received in the city, April 23rd, with all the marks of honor which could possibly be bestowed by Congress, the civic authorities, and the citizens.

The inauguration took place on the 30th of April, Chancellor Livingston administering the oath of office, and the new president then delivered in the Senate Chamber his inaugural address. It was a document characterized by modesty, dignity, wisdom and sound judgment, and we regret that our limits do not admit of giving it in full. His concluding words were, "an humble supplication to the benign Parent of the human race, that since he has been pleased to favor the American people with opportunities for deliberating in perfect tranquillity, and dispositions for deciding with unparalleled unanimity on a form of government for the security of their Union, and the advancement of their happiness; so His divine blessing may be equally conspicuous in the enlarged views, the temperate consultations, and the wise measures on which the success of this government must depend." The great and good man who now occupied a position of the gravest responsibility, found that there was indeed much reason for anxiety, as he carefully and accurately informed himself of the actual position of affairs at home and abroad. Agitation and excitement, had not yet subsided. Political animosities were rife in the community. The treasury was exhausted. Debts pressed heavily in all directions; and restlessness and discontent found place among too many ot the citizens. Among those in the First Congress, who were opposed to the Constitution, were a number clamorous for a new Convention; and even the most moderate called urgently for amendments of what had been ratified. Two States, North Carolina and Rhode Island, still refused to accede to the Constitution, a course which was equally annoying and embarrassing. The military force of the United States was less than six hundred men; while not only difficulties existed with Spain and Great Britain, on a variety of points, but the northern Indians between the Lakes, the Mississippi and the Ohio, numbered five thousand men, more than a third of whom were at open war with the United States; and the Creeks, in the south-west, who could bring six thousand fighting men into the field, were at war with Georgia. The commerce of the country was more restricted, than when it had formed part of the British empire. A treaty had been formed with the Emperor of Morocco, but Algiers, Tunis, and Tripoli, plundered the unprotected vessels of America, and enslaved all who fell into their hands. With neither money to purchase exemption, nor a naval force to command respect, the position of our commerce in the Mediterranean required immediate attention. The jealousy of Spain was but too apparent, and her attempts to impose restric

LIVINGSTON. St. CLAIR. OTIS. KNOX. SHERMAN. WASHINGTON. STEUBEN. ADAMS.

INAUGURATION OF WASHINGTON.

From the original Painting by Chappel, in the possession of the Publishers.

Johnson, Fry & Co. Publishers, New York.

tions on the free navigation of the Mississippi roused the whole Wes . The utmost watchfulness and prudence on the part of the executive were demanded in the emergency. Relations with Great Britain also were far from satisfactory. Old differences and grudges still existed. England was in no humor for conciliation, and the United States were somewhat captious and easy to take offence. The British government steadily refused to negotiate a commercial treaty on anything like favorable terms; and when an attempt to arrange a treaty with Portugal failed, it was charged upon England that she was the cause of this and other like trouble. With France, however, and the powers of Europe generally, friendly relations existed, and the prospects of trade and commerce were bright and encouraging.

The establishment of a system whereby an adequate revenue should be obtained for the discharge of national obligations was so manifestly of the first concern, that Madison proposed, very early in the session, the adoption of that system of imports, by which it had been attempted, without success, under the Confederation, to obtain a revenue to meet the demands of the nation's creditors at home and abroad. The plan proposed by Mr. Madison was, to lay specific duties, or duties according to quantity, on certain articles, such as spirituous liquors, wines, tea and coffee, sugar and molasses, and pepper; and on all other importations, an *ad valorem* duty, or percentage upon their actual value. It also included a tax upon the tonnage of vessels; American vessels being charged at a lower rate than those of other countries, and a discrimination being made in favor of those nations which had entered into commercial treaties with the United States. The debates on this whole subject, in the House, were very animated, and great variety of opinion was expressed. No part of the system was discussed more earnestly and warmly, than that which proposed to make a discrimination in favor of those nations with whom the United States had formed commercial treaties; and in the course of the debate, opinions and feelings with respect to foreign powers were disclosed, as Marshall states, which, strengthening with circumstances, afterwards agitated the whole American continent. The House, by a small majority, voted to make this discrimination; but the Senate refused to agree to the proposal, and expunged the discrimination in favor of the tonnage and distilled spirits of those nations having commercial treaties with the United States. After a conference, the House reluctantly gave way, and the discrimination was negatived.

In order to carry forward the executive affairs of the country, three departments were established, viz., that of foreign affairs, since denominated the department of state; that of the treasury; and that of war; to which last was added whatever might appertain to the naval concerns of the United States. In framing the acts establishing these departments, a debate sprang up, which caused much excitement; for the question then discussed, was at the time, and is still, believed to have involved principles of the utmost moment to the stability, well-being, and proper working of the federal government. The Constitution declared that, "by and with the advice and consent of the Senate," the president should have power to appoint the necessary officers in the various departments named in the second Article; but it was entirely silent on the very important point, as to where the power of removal was lodged. This matter, it may be here stated, does not appear to have been agitated at all in the Federal Convention. Immediately the members of Congress took sides on the question. On the one hand, it was urged, that, as the advice and consent of the Senate were necessary to the appointment, so, by parity of reasoning, the same advice and consent were necessary to the removal of executive officers; on the other, it was said, with great force, that, as the president was sworn to see the laws faithfully executed, so it was imperative, that he should be untrammelled in the removal, for what seemed to him good cause, of any and every executive officer. On the one side, it was asserted, that this was a dangerous prerogative, since it reduced all executive officers to a dependence upon the caprice or otherwise of the president; on the other, it was urged, that secrecy and dispatch were often necessary, and it would be impracticable to wait upon the Senate being convened, and further, that as power must be placed somewhere, it was safer to allow it to be exercised by one of the high character and integrity, which it was fair to presume the president of the United States would always possess. The question was finally settled in the House by a majority of twelve, first, by an amendment to the second clause in the bill, so as clearly to imply the power of removal to be solely in the president, and then by striking out the whole clause which had been under debate, thus leaving the president to exercise the power as a constitutional privilege. When the question first came before the Senate, in July, 1789, on the bill establishing the department of foreign affairs, some of the members were absent, and that body was equally divided, nine against nine, and the casting vote was given by John Adams, the vice-president. On a subsequent bill, there was a majority of two in favor of the same construction. That it might not be considered a grant of power by Congress, the law was so worded as to imply a constitutional power already existing in the president; the expressions being, "that whenever the secretary shall be removed by the president of the United States," &c. There can be no doubt that this is a grave question, and also not altogether easy of solution. A great deal has been said on the subject by men eminent for their knowledge and their patriotism, and it is still open to dispute, whether or not the first Congress decided wisely and rightly on this important question.*

A very large number of amendments to the Constitution, over 200 in all, were brought forward in the House. About 50 of these seemed to be worthy of some notice. After debate and inquiry, the number was reduced to seventeen, and finally, by the Senate, to twelve, ten of which were subsequently approved by the State legislatures, and thus became integral parts of the Constitution. The national judiciary was arranged by the passage of a bill, establishing a supreme court, and circuit and district courts. The district courts were to consist of one judge in each state. The States were divided into circuits, in each of which one of the judges of the supreme court, and the district judge of the State, in which the court was held, constituted the circuit courts. In certain cases this court had original jurisdiction, and also took cognizance of appeal from the district courts. The supreme court was composed of a chief justice, and five associate judges, and was to hold two sessions annually, at the seat of government. This court had exclusive jurisdiction in certain cases, and appellate jurisdiction from the circuit courts, and also from the State courts, in cases where the validity of treaties and the laws of the United States were drawn into question. This organization of the national judiciary has remained substantially the same to the present time. At the close of September, 1789, Washington made choice of Jefferson for secretary of state, Hamilton, secretary of the treasury, Gen. Knox, secretary of war, and Edward Randolph, attorney-general. John Jay was appointed chief-justice, and with him were associated men of equally high character and ability, as associate-justices, viz., W. Cushing, of Mass., J. Wilson, of Penn., R. H. Harrison, of Maryland, John Blair, of Va., and John Rutledge, of S. C. On the 29th of September, Congress adjourned to meet on the first Monday in January, 1790.

On the re-assembling of Congress, Hamil-

* In this connection, we may state that, in March, 1867, a tenure-of-office bill was passed, by which it was set forth that the consent of the Senate was necessary to the displacement as well as the appointment of officers.

ton, who had been directed to prepare a plan for the support of the public credit, brought in his report, which was submitted to the House Jan. 15th. The national debt, it is to be borne in mind, had its origin principally in the Revolution, and was of two kinds, foreign and domestic. The total amount, according to the estimate of the secretary of the treasury, was about $54,000,000. Of this sum the foreign debt, which was due mostly to France and the Hollanders, amounted to nearly $12,000,000, including the interest; and the domestic debt, including a large amount of interest, reached to the amount of about $42,000,000. Besides these, there was another species of debt, which had been contracted by the several States, during the war, and for the purposes of the war, such as erecting works of defence, furnishing provisions, clothing, munitions of war, and the like, for the army, advancing pay and bounties, etc. These State debts were estimated at about $25,000,000. The report of the secretary was full, lucid, and comprehensive, and it entered at large into the momentous question which was then to be settled; for Hamilton was no ordinary statesman, and whatever might be the result of the plans he proposed, no one could doubt that they were urged with arguments of great power, and with a courage and consistency, that extorted praise from his most determined opponents. That the foreign debt should be paid strictly according to the terms of the contract, no one pretended to deny; but with respect to the domestic debt, wide differences of opinion prevailed. Hamilton argued, that the national faith and honor demanded the payment of the debt due to citizens and others holding the public pledges for such payments. He also declared himself in favor of the assumption of the State debts, and earnestly opposed making any difference between the creditors of the Union and those of the States. In regard to the foreign debt there was no difference of opinion, and provision was made at once as recommended, but there was a very animated debate as to the appropriating permanent funds for the payment of interest on the domestic debt, and for the gradual redemption of the principal. After full discussion, though opposed by men like Madison, Hamilton's plan was adopted. The subject of the State debts next came up, and the proposition to assume them roused up deep passions and hatreds. The debts of the several States were very unequal, from the nature of the case. Those of Massachusetts and South Carolina amounted to more than $10,500,000; while the debts of all the other States were estimated at between $14,000,000 and $15,000,000. Naturally, these differences led to mean and invidious comparisons, which were unworthy the national legislature and its halls. The first proposition on this subject in the House of Representatives, was to assume the whole of these debts. This was at first adopted, in committee of the whole, by a small majority. Afterwards, when the members from North Carolina took their seats, the subject was recommitted, and negatived by a majority of two—thirty-one to twenty-nine. Propositions were afterwards made, to assume specific sums from each, but were negatived. These various propositions occasioned long and violent debates among the members from different States, and led to an inquiry into the origin of the State debts, and to a comparative view of the different exertions and expenses of the States themselves, in their struggle for independence. The House finally sent the bill to the Senate, with a provision for those creditors only, whose certificates of debt purported to be payable by the Union. In this position of affairs, the assumption of the State debts would almost certainly have been negatived by Congress, had there not been put in practice one of those manœuvres not infrequent in legislative bodies; we refer to that "giving and taking" arrangement, by which one party agrees to support the measures of another, provided its measures are in turn supported by the other party. The case in hand was briefly as follows: There was no little dispute as to the permanent site of the capital of the United States. Various localities were named and had their advocates; but no one had as yet been able to obtain the assent of a majority. At length a compact respecting the temporary and permanent seat of government was entered into between the friends of Philadelphia and the Potomac, stipulating that Congress should hold its sessions in Philadelphia for ten years, during which time buildings for the accommodation of government should be erected at some place on the Potomac, to which the government should remove, on the expiration of that time. This compact having united the representatives of Pennsylvania and Delaware with the friends of the Potomac, a majority was obtained in favor of both situations; and a bill brought into the Senate in conformity with this arrangement, passed both Houses by small majorities. This having been done, and the site of the federal city fixed, two of the Potomac members, who heretofore were opposed to the assumption, now changed their votes, and declared themselves in its favor; and thus the majority was changed. The amendment which had been negatived, was now carried, and $21,000,000 of the State debts were assumed in specified proportions. The Senate gave a majority of two in its favor, and the House concurred, by a majority of six.* The national debt having thus been brought into a tangible shape, the measures necessary for its payment were taken at as early a date as practicable. The general effect upon the whole country was very marked. Increase in the money capital invigorated commerce, roused the active energies of the people, and stimulated anew agricultural and other pursuits. Politically, however, according to Mr. Sparks, the funding system had an unhappy influence (p. 109). It widened the breach of parties, produced irritations, and excited animosities. Washington expressed no opinion while the matter was in debate in Congress, but he approved the act, and was, no doubt, from conviction, a decided friend to the measure.

The question of the slave-trade was brought up, on a petition written by Dr. Franklin, just before his death, praying for the abolition of slavery. The subject was discussed at great length, and with much warmth on both sides; and toward the close of March, 1790, it was resolved, "that Congress have no authority to interfere in the emancipation of slaves, or in the treatment of them within any of the States." Laws were passed in respect to naturalization of aliens, patent rights, the mercantile marine, Indian affairs, etc., and Congress adjourned on the 12th of August. The third session was held in Philadelphia, and opened on the 6th of December. Previously to this, however, Washington had been anxiously occupied with foreign affairs. England, especially, (p. 107) continued to manifest the same unwillingness to deal fairly and liberally towards our country, and with her usual shortsightedness as to her *real* interests, she declined overtures presented by the chief magistrate and only deepened the ill-will already existing in the American mind. The Indians on the frontiers were, nearly all of them, hostile to the United States, and this enmity was kept alive by foreign influence. British agents were at work in the North, and the Spaniards kept exciting the Creek Indians in the South. Washington made another effort to quiet the Creeks, and was enabled to prevail upon their chiefs to visit New York, and early in August, 1790, agree upon terms of peace. The Indians in the North-west, however, continuing hostile, an expedition was sent against them under General Harmar, who attacked them on the Scioto and Wabash; he was at first successful, but was subsequently defeated near Chilicothe.

* The debts were apportioned among the States as follows:—New Hampshire, $300,000; Massachusetts, $4,000,000; Rhode Island, $200,000; Connecticut, $1,600,000; New York, $1,200,000; New Jersey, $800,000; Pennsylvania, $2,200,000; Delaware, $200,000; Maryland, $800,000; Virginia, $3,200,000; North Carolina, $2,200,000; South Carolina, $4,000,000; Georgia, $300,000.

Two important measures were brought forward and vehemently discussed during this session of Congress, viz., the tax on ardent spirits distilled in the United States, and a national bank. The Secretary of the Treasury stated, that additional revenue was necessary for meeting national obligations, and he recommended for this purpose, an additional impost on foreign distilled spirits and a duty on spirits distilled within the United States. A sharp and even angry debate ensued, the Southern and Western members being particularly warm in their opposition. As, however, they were unable to suggest any other feasible mode of meeting the difficulty, the bill passed in January, 1791, by a vote of 25 to 21. A few days afterwards, the bill to incorporate the subscribers to the Bank of the United States, having been sent from the Senate, was read the third time, and the question was now on its passage. A strong opposition, however, sprang up at this point, and the debate for the week following was of the most ardent and determined character, and called forth the ablest efforts of such men as Madison, Giles, and others *against*, and of Ames, Boudinot, Gerry, and others *for* the bill. The argument turned mainly upon the constitutional authority of Congress to pass an act incorporating a national bank. On the one hand, it was contended, that Congress had no such power, under the Constitution, as would enable them to create this or any other corporation; and also, that so large a moneyed institution would, in its effects, be extremely injurious to the community. On the other hand, it was argued, that the establishment of a bank, though not named in the Constitution, was among the powers contemplated by that instrument, which gave Congress authority to make all laws *necessary* and *proper* for carrying into execution the powers expressly granted. The advocates of the bank claimed, that it was equally necessary and proper, and that similar institutions had been required in all well regulated communities for the management of the finances, and for the attainment of the great ends of civil government. The opponents of the bank denied its necessity or utility, and asserted that the construction of the Constitution, given by the gentlemen on the other side, was too broad and dangerous to be admitted, they maintaining, that no means were to be held "necessary" for the purpose of carrying into execution the specified powers, except those, without which, the powers granted would be nugatory, or the ends contemplated absolutely unattainable. On the 8th of February, 1791, the bill was passed by a vote of 39 to 20. The capital stock of the bank was $10,000,000, of which $2,000,000 were subscribed for the benefit of the United States, and the residue by individuals. One-fourth of the sums subscribed was to be paid in gold and silver, and three-fourths in the public debt. By the act of incorporation, it was to be a bank of discount as well as deposit, and its bills, which were payable in gold and silver, on demand, were made receivable in all payments to the United States. The bank was located at Philadelphia, with power in the directors, to establish offices of discount and deposits only, wherever they should think fit, within the United States. The duration of the charter was limited to the 4th of March, 1811; and the faith of the United States was pledged, that during that period, no other bank should be established under their authority. One of the fundamental articles of the incorporation was, that no loan should be made to the United States, for more than $100,000, or to any particular State for more than $50,000, or to any foreign prince, or State, unless previously authorized by a law of the United States. The books were opened for subscriptions, in July, 1791, and, in two hours' time, the whole number of shares offered was taken up. The Cabinet of Washington were divided on the constitutionality of the question, Jefferson and Randolph being opposed, Hamilton and Knox in favor. The president required written statements from each, and then, after due deliberation, signed the bill. It was undoubtedly a measure which made a deep impression on many members of the national legislature, and contributed not a little to the complete organization of those distinct and visible parties which, in their long and dubious conflict for power, subsequently shook the United States to their very centre. Vermont was admitted to the Union, February 18, 1791; the census of 1790 showed an entire population of nearly 4,000,000; a United States mint was formed; an increase of the army was ordered; various appropriations were made; and the first Congress reached its close, March 3d, 1791.

Washington, in the autumn of 1789, made a tour in his own carriage, through the Eastern States; nearly two years later, he visited the Southern States; in both cases noting with deep interest the condition of the country, and receiving everywhere evidences of the love and veneration of the people. On the 25th of October, 1791, the Second Congress began its first session. Numerous topics of interest were brought before this body by the President, and the session was a busy one, reaching to May, 1792. The Indians in the North-west were very hostile and needed to be looked after with energy and force. General St. Clair was appointed commander-in-chief of the troops. He marched against the Indians, but early in November was defeated with terrible slaughter. Additional troops were ordered, and General Wayne was appointed commander; but the enlistments were very slow, and efforts again were made, in 1792, to obtain peace. Thomas Pinckney was appointed minister to England, and Gouverneur Morris to France; W. Short was sent to the Hague, and with Mr. Carmichael was instructed to effect, if possible, a treaty with Spain. Party organizations were becoming every day more and more fixed and settled, and the bitterness, unfairness, injustice and meanness of party and party spirit began to be more and more evident. Not only in Congress, but in the Cabinet of the President, had they already become very troublesome and annoying. Jefferson and Hamilton were almost always on different sides. Their views of politics were irreconcilable. Hamilton favored always what were called federal views and principles, *i. e.*, a strong government, a national government, a policy which should make the Americans one people, under one head, and that a vigorous, energetic, strongly supported head. Jefferson, on the other hand, was the coryphæus of the republican party, as it was then called. He was apprehensive of any state of affairs which placed strength and power in the hands of the national government. He had no fears arising out of its ever being too weak. He thought highly of State sovereignty and power, and was ready to favor any policy which limited the exercise of powers vested in the government of the United States. Jefferson's predilections were toward France and against England, and he was deeply interested in the struggles of the people to establish a republic, notwithstanding the excesses and horrors of the French Revolution. Hamilton greatly preferred a fixed, settled government and institutions like those of England, and dreaded the awful scourge of rebellion and anarchy. The disputes in the Cabinet were mortifying to the President; he wrote to both the secretaries, begging for peace and unanimity; but all his efforts to reconcile them were in vain. Both federalists and republicans had their newspapers, and both used them in the way in which party papers are and always have been used not only as advocates of party policy, but as mediums of calumny, abuse and assaults on personal character. In the autumn of 1791, Mr. Hammond arrived as British minister, but his course gave no satisfaction, or helped at all towards a commercial treaty. The second session of Congress began November 5th, 1792, and it was speedily evident that party virulence was on the increase. The Secretary of the Treasury being called on by resolution, proposed a plan for the redemption of the public debt, but the opposition in the House deferred its consideration by various methods. Mr. Giles, in January, 1793, moved resolutions inculpating Hamilton in the management of the treasury, as to loans, etc. Hamilton sent in three successive reports, in which he gave a full exposition of his views and conduct in the treasury department. It was plain that he felt aggrieved at this attack upon his reputation; and he did not hesitate to use language of great plainness and severity, observing, in conclusion; "Thus have I not only furnished a just and affirmative view of the real situation of the public accounts, but have likewise shown, I trust, in a conspicuous manner, fallacies enough in the statements, from which the inference of an unaccounted for balance is drawn, to evince that it is one tissue of error." Mr. Giles, at the end of February, brought in a series of nine resolutions, charging Hamilton with various misdemeanors; but the resolutions, after an acrimonious debate, were rejected by a large majority and Hamilton was thus entirely exculpated. The Second Congress came to end, March 2, 1793; and Washington's first term of service expired at the same date.

Long previously to this, Washington had resolved to retire from office at the close of his four years' labors; but, so grave was the apparent crisis in public affairs, so absolutely necessary was it to have the weight of character, the dignity, the unspotted patriotism of this great and good man in the position of president, that on all sides, from Jefferson, the leader of the republicans, no less than from Hamilton and others like him, appeals the most urgent were addressed to him, begging him, by every consideration, not to refuse still further to serve his country in this her hour of need. Washington yielded again to that call which he dared not disobey; and so he was again unanimously chosen president; John Adams was also re-elected vice-president.

Washington entered upon his second term of office, March 4th, 1793, at a time when his impartial honesty and firmness were especially needed. The state of things in Europe was such that some definite line of policy was a matter of necessity to our country. Naturally, the American people sympathized warmly with France, and despite the horrors of the French Revolution, looked eagerly and hopefully for good results; naturally, too, there were many Americans who were ready to join her in the contest against Great Britain especially, and to engage in privateering expeditions against the commerce of the belligerent powers, regardless of the consequences to themselves or their country. It was plain, however, to the President, that sound judgment should prevail, and not impulse or feeling. He foresaw that the storm which was gathering in Europe, must soon reach the United States, and he felt it his duty, as far as possible, to prevent its desolating effects here. In the mighty conflict which was to ensue, a conflict in which all the great European powers either were or must necessarily be engaged, he was satisfied the best interests of his country demanded a state of neutrality; and he was convinced that this course might be pursued without a violation either of national faith, or national honor. Neutrality, however, he knew, to be just, must be impartial; and he was sensible, that from the state of public feeling in America, it would be extremely difficult to preserve a state of strict neutrality, or to avoid collisions with some of the contending powers, particularly France or Great Britain. Aware of the importance and delicacy of the crisis, he submitted certain questions to the Cabinet, in April. The result was in favor of issuing a proclamation of neutrality, which was accordingly done, "forbidding the citizens of the United States to take part in any hostilities on the seas, either with or against the belligerent powers, and warning them against carrying to any such powers, any of those articles deemed contraband, according to the modern usages of nations, and enjoining them from all acts and proceedings inconsistent with the duties of a friendly nation towards those at war." This measure, which Washington determined upon, after mature deliberation, was undoubtedly one of the most important of his administration. It laid the solid basis of that system which our country has steadily pursued, in its intercourse with foreign nations, and to which a large share of its prosperity is to be ascribed. In fact, it was a measure essential to the independent existence and character of the United States; and it is greatly to the honor of the President, that he dared to do what he knew to be right and just, in the very face of popular clamor, and at the risk of personal abuse and defamation. As we look back upon the past, it seems almost incredible that Washington's good name could have been so foully aspersed as it was, by violent, unscrupulous partizans of that day; but so it was, and the anti-federal party embraced the opportunity of assaulting the motives and character of the President, whose views, it was known, were more in accordance with the principles denominated federal than the opposite. No American of the present day, when Washington's name and fame constitute a precious treasure, can credit what was uttered and published to the world, except by actual perusal of the political, vile slanders against him in the party papers of that stormy period.

Early in April, 1793, M. Genet arrived at Charleston, being the new minister to the United States from the French republic. Professedly, his course was to be a fair and just one; but, as was subsequently discovered from his direct instructions, which he published, he was in reality to act quite otherwise. While distinctly avowing that France did not desire the United States to become a party to the war with Great Britain, the main object of his mission, as afterwards disclosed, was to take every step possible to induce the Americans to make common cause with the French against all Europe. Genet's reception was very enthusiastic, and he began at once to issue letters of marque, and fit out privateers against other nations, especially England and English commerce. Captures which were made by these cruisers were brought into port, and the French consuls were actually assuming to hold courts of admiralty, etc.! Notwithstanding this audacious course of Genet, he was received by the President with due courtesy and consideration; and in conversation, he gave most explicit assurances that France had no wish to engage the United States in the war against Great Britain and other European powers. The British minister made numerous and well founded complaints, and Washington determined to sustain the ground he had taken in his proclamation of neutrality. The madness and folly of Genet, and the infamous violence and abuse of the party press, did not provoke Washington to unseemly language or undue severity. Genet's meanness and insults, however, became intolerable after a while, and self-respect required that his recall be insisted upon. This was done, in a letter to Mr. Morris, at Paris, August 16th, with the correspondence to be laid before the French government. Genet was furious, when he learned what had been done, and he wrote a passionate letter to Jefferson, in which, while abusing the government as a whole, he by no means spared the Secretary of State himself. Marshall, in his Life of Washington, has given a full and exact account of the various steps which were taken both by Genet and the Executive; the singular persistence of the former, in his attempts to set at defiance the government; the large encouragement he received from partizans of France, and opponents of the administration; the intemperate and arrogant letter, which he addressed to the President, and circulated through the newspapers; the flagrant outrage committed against the neutrality of the United States, by the French consul in Boston; Genet's schemes for at tacks on Florida and Louisiana, and such like: the reader will do well to refer to the invaluable work of Chief Justice Marshall.

Relations with England were still in a very annoying and perplexing condition. Negotiations with Mr. Hammond (p. 112) proceeded slowly and unsatisfactorily. The posts on the frontier were still held, contrary to the treaty of peace, and there was no doubt of British interference with the Indians in the North-west. With the insolence of superior power, British vessels of war stopped American ships, searched them, and impressed American seamen within the acknowledged jurisdiction of the United States; and privateers from the Bermudas committed depredations on American commerce with impunity, and even the sanction of the admiralty courts in those islands. The French government having, in direct contravention of the treaty, authorized, in May, 1793, the arrest of neutral vessels laden with enemies' goods, or with provisions destined for an enemy's port, Great Britain retaliated, with a design of distressing France, by issuing two orders in council, the one in June, the other in November, which operated with peculiar force upon the commerce of the United states. By the first order, British cruisers were directed to stop all ships loaded with corn, flour or meal, bound to any French port, and send them to some convenient port, where the cargoes might be purchased on behalf of the British government. By the second, ships of war and privateers were charged to detain all vessels laden with goods, produced in any colony belonging to France, or with provisions for any such colony, and to bring them for adjudication to the courts of admiralty. Outrage such as this upon the rights of neutrals, gave occasion to earnest and indignant remonstrance on the part of the United States, and the orders in council were denounced as unjust in principle, and injurious to a high degree in their effects. Algerine piracies at this date assisted in increasing the ill-will towards Great Britain; for it was felt, as a moral certainty, that England gave encouragement to the depredations of these infamous pirates, and was quite willing that our country, having no navy, should suffer the consequences. With Spain likewise, there was an uncomfortable feeling of discontent, and hostilities seemed to be impending. The question of the Mississippi was again agitated violently in the West, and Washington was anxiously on the alert.

The Third Congress began its first session December 2d, 1793. The opening speech of Washington called attention to many and important topics requiring prompt and energetic action. The state of our relations with both England and Spain was very critical, and it was evident that something must be done. Jefferson, in compliance with a resolution of the House three years before, now made an elaborate report as to the condition of American commerce, its privileges, the restrictions imposed, measures necessary for improvements, etc. It was his last official act, and at the close of December, 1793, he left the Cabinet, Randolph being put in his place. Madison, at the beginning of 1794, offered certain resolutions in the House on this subject, which were long and keenly debated. The first, which contained the general principle of Madison's commercial policy, viz., discriminating duties in favor of those nations with whom the United States had treaties of commerce, was carried by a small majority. The other resolutions were postponed till later in the session. The Algerine pirates, having committed large depredations on American commerce by capturing 11 ships and making 100 prisoners into slaves, it was resolved, early in January, to provide a naval force against them. This action was bitterly opposed by the anti-federalists, but was finally adopted. British aggressions and injustice roused a fresh hostility, and steps were taken to put our seaports in a state of defence. The opponents of the administration urged, as sufficient, commercial restrictions, while Washington and the government favored stronger measures, such as increasing the army, calling upon the States for 80,000 militia, laying an embargo, etc. This latter measure was adopted, and the embargo was laid March 26th, extending to May 25th, 1794. Proposals were made in Congress to sequestrate all debts due British subjects, and to prohibit all intercourse with Great Britain. By news received from Mr. Pinckney in England, it was ascertained that British cruisers were ordered to bring in those neutral vessels only which were laden with cargoes the product of the French islands, and were on direct voyage from these islands to Europe. It seemed plain from this that the British government did not desire to push matters to an extremity with the United States at this juncture. Washington, steadfast in his adherence to the principles he had always avowed, was neither to be enticed nor driven from the path of right, by popular applause, or popular abuse. As a truly brave, as well as good man, he looked upon war as only a last resort; and he knew that peace was above all things important, not only to the prosperity of the country, but also to prevent such entangling alliance with France, as would involve the United States in difficulties and perplexities of a very serious character. It was his conviction, that the differences between our country and England had not yet reached a point wherein it would be dishonorable to attempt a settlement, except by the sword; and so he resolved upon that decisive measure, which alone seemed to afford any hope of successfully terminating the disputes and differences between the two nations. On his nomination, John Jay, chief justice of the United States, was sent as envoy-extraordinary to England, to obtain redress from that government, and effect a commercial treaty, if possible. In opposition to this movement, a non-intercourse bill was passed in the House, but defeated in the Senate by the casting vote of John Adams. In order to provide for what must follow in case negotiations failed, the country was placed in a state of defence; and in order to meet the additional expenses, various taxes were laid on carriages, auction sales, snuff, etc. Congress, also, took measures effectually to prevent any repetition of violating the laws and sovereignty of the United States, by foreigners or acts of their own citizens. Heavy penalties were affixed to every violation of the kind; but, as just noted, the casting vote of the vice-president passed this bill also. After a stormy and active session, Congress adjourned, June 9th, 1794. Gouverneur Morris, the minister to France, was superseded at the French court by James Monroe, May 28th, he being a republican, and likely to do good service in France, where Mr. Morris had met with shabby treatment because he could not sanction the excesses of the French Revolution. It was high time to come to some understanding with the government of the republic, for there had been committed so many outrages against the Americans, that it would be impossible to have matters go on in this way and escape national disgrace.

In February, 1794, M. Fauchet came to the United States to take Genet's place, and for a while matters appeared to be conducted fairly and honestly; but it soon after became evident that French emissaries were exciting trouble and discord in the west, especially in Kentucky, where a lawless spirit was prevailing, and menaces put forth against the government. Gen. Wayne (p. 112), who had endeavored to make peace with the Indians, finding this impossible, attacked them on the Maumee, Aug. 20th, and gained a decisive victory. As their hostility was not abated, their whole country was laid waste, and forts erected in the heart of their settlements, to prevent their return. In Western Pennsylvania there was so strong opposition made to the excise laws, that it broke out into actual insurrection. The revenue officers were maltreated, and their lives threatened, and the marshals were unable to execute process on the delinquents. The crisis was imminent, and the president met it at once. Early in August, he issued a proclamation, commanding the insurgents to disperse before the 1st of September, and warning all persons against aiding, abetting or comforting the perpetrators of these treasonable acts, and requiring all officers, and other citizens, according to their respective duties and the laws of the land, to exert their utmost endeavors to prevent and suppress such dangerous proceedings. On the same day a requisition was made on the governors of New Jersey, Pennsylvania, Maryland and Virginia, for their quotas of militia, amounting in all to above 12,000 men. Anxious, however, to avoid collision and blood-shed, Washington sent commissioners to endeavor to persuade the insurgents to yield, but it was without success. He then issued a second proclamation, Sept. 25th, stating that he should use the power placed in his trust, and compel obedience. The militia behaved well, and in October were marched into the insurgent district. But happily, no open opposition was ventured upon. Some of the leaders were seized, tried and convicted, but were afterwards pardoned by the president. Thus "the Whiskey Rebellion," as it was called, was suppressed without a drop of blood shed, and the power and authority of the government were established. The pernicious influence of combinations of men, calling themselves "democratic societies," was severely commented on by Washington, and while the friends of the government rejoiced, and were elated by the ease with which this rebellion had been quelled, the republicans, with Jefferson prominent among them, sneered at the needless expense incurred, and denounced and ridiculed the sentiments of the president as to the democratic societies, &c.

Congress met, November 19th, 1794, and were addressed by Washington, in a longer speech than usual, on the exciting topics of the day, and urging them to be active and zealous in regard to various matters now before them. The answer of the Senate was a cordial approval of the course of the president; but in the House, the opposition was strong enough to prevent any expression of the kind. On the 21st of January, 1795, the comprehensive and able plan of the secretary of the treasury, for the *support of public credit*, was submitted to Congress, and on the 2d of February, he submitted an additional one, for the *improvement of the revenue*. Details here cannot be gone into, but we may state that an act was passed substantially in accordance with Hamilton's views. The funds, appropriated for the reimbursement and redemption of the debt, were by law vested in the commissioners of the sinking fund, in trust for that object, and the faith of the United States was pledged, that the funds should inviolably so remain appropriated and vested, until the whole debt should be paid. These funds were to be applied to the payment of eight per cent. per annum, on account of the principal and interest of the six per cent. and deferred stock, and the surplus to the payment of the other debts, foreign and domestic. The total amount of the unredeemed debt of the United States, (including the unassumed debt,) in the year 1795, was $76,096,468 17 cts. (The six per cent. stock was fully paid in 1818, the deferred in 1824.) Hamilton resigned at the end of January, 1795, and was succeeded by Oliver Wolcott. The Third Congress came to an end, March 3d. On the 7th, Washington received a copy of the treaty with England, entered into by Mr. Jay (p. 116). This distinguished envoy left New York in May, 1794, and on reaching England, entered at once upon negotiations with Lord Grenville; and the result was in substance as follows:—The western posts were to be surrendered to the United States, on or before the 1st of June, 1796; but no compensation was made for negroes carried away by the British, after the peace of 1783. The United States were to compensate British creditors for losses occasioned by legal impediments to the collection of debts, contracted before the Revolutionary War; to be settled and adjusted by commissioners; and Great Britain was to make compensation to American merchants for illegal captures of their property, to be adjusted also in the same mode. Provision was also made for ascertaining more accurately the boundaries between the United States and the British North American possessions. It was ex pressly provided that there was to be no sequestration of private debts or obligations. Both parties had liberty to trade with the Indians, in their respective territories in America, and the Mississippi was to be open to both nations. The first ten articles covering these points, were made permanent; the other eighteen were limited to twelve years. A direct trade was permitted between the United States and the British West India Islands, in American vessels not above the burden of seventy tons, and in goods or merchandize of the growth, manufacture, or produce of the States, and in the production of the islands; but the United States were restrained from carrying molasses, sugar, coffee, cocoa, or cotton, either from the islands, or from the United States, to any part of the world. A reciprocal and perfect liberty of commerce and navigation between the United States and the British dominions in Europe, was established, neither to be subject to higher duties than other nations, the British government reserving the right of countervailing the American foreign duties. And American vessels were freely admitted into the ports of the British territories in the East Indies, but not to carry on the coasting trade. Mr. Jay was unable to obtain a stipulation that free ships should make free goods; neither was he successful in arranging as to provisions becoming contraband, or in regard to suspension of privateering in case war were to occur between England and the United States; but, on the whole, the treaty was the best attainable, and in his judgment, for the interest of our country to accept. Washington had hoped to receive a treaty more to his satisfaction, and more fair and liberal in its terms, and so he hesitated in regard to signing it. The Senate was called together early in June, and after two weeks' discussion, approved the treaty by a bare majority, 20 to 10. Meanwhile, one of the Virginia Senators, S. T. Mason, in violation of the obligation of secrecy, and the evident demands of propriety, sent a copy of the treaty to the "Aurora," a violent partisan paper in Philadelphia. On the 2d of July it was published, and spread before the community, without the authority of the executive, and without any of the official documents and correspondence necessary to a fair appreciation and understanding of its various provisions. Tremendous was the storm raised by this occurrence, among those who hated England and adored France; and, as Jefferson's admiring biographer says, "the entire Democratic party, from one end of the Union to the other, exclaimed with one voice, that the treaty had tamely and basely surrendered the honor, rights, and interests of the United States at the feet of their most deadly enemy!" Meetings were held in the large cities and towns; denunciatory resolutions adopted; fierce invectives indulged in; inflammatory appeals issued; even mobs were gathered, and personal violence practiced; the foulest abuse was heaped upon the president because he refused to be guided by popular clamor; and yet, despite the fierce menaces and malignant tirades of unscrupulous politicians and demagogues, the treaty was signed on the 11th of August, 1795, and in due time its good results were plainly evident. It saved the country from a war, when war was especially to be deprecated; it began, and rapidly developed, that commercial enterprise which has yielded such vast returns; and it demonstrated the sound wisdom and uprightness, and pure patriotism of Washington. Jefferson, it is true, denounced Jay's treaty, as "an execrable thing," and subsequently did all that he could to get the House of Representatives to interfere, and "rid us of this infamous act;" but the third president, as Jefferson by and by became, was not the man whom history will ever put in comparison with the first, at a date when, so far as human wisdom can determine, no living man could have saved our country from ruin and fatal entanglement but George Washington.

A treaty with Spain was settled upon in October, and the free navigation of the Mississippi secured. Those piratical scoundrels, the Algerines, were paid $1,000,000 to release captives, etc. The Fourth Congress began on December 7th, and entered upon its work with strong party feeling active among its members. Monroe had been sent to France (p. 116), and seemed to have adapted himself to the taste, etc., of the people; and when Adet came to the United States in the summer of 1795, he expected that the French flag should be placed (as the American was in Paris), in the legislative halls; but that preposterous idea was at once but quietly put aside. In Febuary, 1796, Washington proclaimed the British treaty as complete, and enjoined its exact observance. This gave rise to a long and earnest discussion in the House, as to where the treaty-making power was constitutionally lodged, and what the House now ought to do. Madison, Gallatin, Giles, and others, on the one side, and Smith, of South Carolina, Hillhouse, Harper, etc., on the other, thoroughly ventilated the subject. On a call being made upon the President, Washington refused the call, as an intrusion upon his constitutional prerogative. He was sharply criticized and pretty freely abused by various members, and the House, having determined that it had a right to discuss the laws needful to carry out fully any treaty, there followed a debate of marvelous power and greatness. This was in the latter part of April, and the result was, that the House finally agreed to pass the laws, by a vote of 51 to 48. After some further business, the session closed, June 1st, 1796.

The conduct of the French Directory at this date was especially annoying and vexatious. Undertaking to affirm that our country had no right to act with regard to her own interests, but only as France thought best, a haughty and overbearing tone was indulged in by the government; and in July, 1796, a decree was issued, declaring that "all neutral or allied powers shall, without delay, be notified, that the flag of the French republic will treat neutral vessels, either as to confiscation, as to searches, or capture, in the same manner as they shall suffer the English to treat them." Spain was guilty of intriguing in the West to produce dissension among the people; Holland was also compelled to follow the leading of France. The President, in view of what had taken place, was not satisfied with Monroe's course in France; he felt that Monroe did not faithfully carry out his instructions, but was doing injury rather than good; so he determined to send General Pinckney to France in Monroe's place. This was done in the autumn of 1796; and Monroe and the French Directory, the latter being rather supercilious about it, parted company. Pinckney was treated with great contempt by the Directory, and had to leave the country in February, 1797. Monroe's defence of his career, on his return home, was only partially satisfactory to his countrymen.

The great and good man at the head of government, who had for years been (as he himself says) spoken of "in such exaggerated and indecent terms as could scarcely be applied to a Nero, to a notorious defaulter, or even to a common pickpocket," resolved to retire from public life at this date. He was urged to remain in office, but he felt that he had made all the sacrifice that could justly be demanded, and consequently he adhered to his resolve. In Sept., 1796, he sent forth his noble, wise, and patriotic Farewell Address, which we regret that we cannot spread out in full on our pages. It was received everywhere throughout the land with reverence and regard, and Americans have ever since looked upon it as a precious legacy from the father of his country. The federalists and republicans took up respectively John Adams and Thomas Jefferson for president, and the contest was ardently and even bitterly carried forward. Adet the French minister, with outrageous impertinence, undertook to interfere in the election; but he went too far, and disgusted Americans generally with the insolence and fanfaronade of his printed letter and appeal. Congress met. in December, 1796, and Wash ington delivered his last public speech. It was full of interesting and important information and suggestions as to the need of a navy, as to agriculture, manufactures, the revenue, etc. The depredations of the French on American commerce, were carried on with unblushing audacity, and the president sent a special message to Congress on this subject. In this the whole matter was thoroughly gone into, and the policy of the government set forth and fully justified. But Congress was too deeply interested in party matters and the approaching election, to attend to the urgent representations and appeals of the president. John Adams was elected president by 71 votes; Jefferson received 68, Pinckney 59, and others smaller numbers. Washington's earnest desire for rest and repose were evident: in a letter to Gen. Knox, March 3d, 1797, he said: "To the wearied traveller, who sees a resting-place, and is bending his body to lean thereon, I now compare myself; but to be suffered to do *this* in peace, is too much to be endured by *some*. To misrepresent my motives, to reprobate my politics, and to weaken the confidence which has been reposed in my administration, are objects which cannot be relinquished by those who will be satisfied with nothing short of a change in our political system. The consolation, however, which results from conscious rectitude, and the approving voice of my country, unequivocally expressed by its representatives, deprive their sting of its poison, and place in the same point of view both the weakness and malignity of their efforts."

On reviewing the eight years of public life of the illustrious first president, there can hardly remain a doubt in the minds of any Americans, of the ability, wisdom, and energy with which he discharged his weighty responsibilities. Notwithstanding the violence and malignancy of party spirit, and the furious assaults to which his administration was subjected, Washington had firmly settled the practical working of the Constitution of the United States. "In the midst of the most appalling obstacles, through the bitterest internal dissensions, and the most formidable combinations of foreign antipathies and cabals, he had subdued all opposition to the Constitution itself; had averted all dangers of European war; had redeemed the captive children of his country from Algiers; had reduced by chastisement, and conciliated by kindness, the most hostile of the Indian tribes; had restored the credit of the nation, and redeemed their reputation of fidelity to the performance of their obligations; had provided for the total extinguishment of the public debt; had settled the Union upon the immovable foundation of principles; and had drawn around his head for the admiration and emulation of after times, a brighter blaze of glory than had ever encircled the brows of hero or statesman, patriot or sage."

On the 4th of March, 1797, John Adams was inaugurated president of the United States. He retained the cabinet as it was, although ere long dissension found place there. It was unfortunate for the second president that he was rather quick tempered, impatient, fond of popular applause, and given to suspect Hamilton of a constant interference, as far as might be, with his plans and purposes. Relations with France were perplexing and threatening. Pinckney, as we have said, (p. 119), was grossly insulted by the French Directory, and virtually driven out of France. Outrage of this kind, and the systematic plundering of our commerce by French vessels, rendered it imperative to take some action on the subject without delay. Accordingly in March, the president called a special session of Congress for May 15th, 1797. Mr. Adams's speech was dignified and firm, and while it expressed earnest desire for accommodation and peace, it urged Congress to provide for war, possibly, with France. John Marshall and Elbridge Gerry were sent as envoys to join Pinckney on a special mission to France, to try to settle difficulties. Acts were passed by Congress, prohibiting citizens of the United States from privateering against nations in amity with the United States; forbidding the export of arms and amunition, and encouraging the import of them, for a limited and specified period; providing for the further defence of the ports and harbors of the country; providing a naval armament; authorizing a detachment of the militia; and concerning the registering of American ships. Other bills, relating to the provisional army, the increase of the artillery, the organizing of the militia, preventing the arming of private ships, and the volutary enlistment of United States' citizens into the service of foreign states, except under certain restrictions, together with some bills for providing for the expenses, both ordinary and extraordinary, were either put off till the next session, or failed to pass in one or both Houses. On the 10th of July, Congress adjourned to meet in November. Our envoys arrived in Paris, in October, and endeavored to enter promptly upon their work. But, it is painful to state, in the words of Marshall, that "history will scarcely furnish the example of a nation not absolutely degraded, which has received from a foreign power such open contumely and undisguised insult, as were, on this occasion, suffered by the United States, in the persons of their ministers." On the 8th of October, the envoys waited upon Talleyrand, the minister for foreign affairs, and delivered their letters of credence. This wily and unscrupulous diplomatist, who, like most of his compeers of that day, displayed quite as much ignorance as insolence in dealing with American interests, coolly informed the envoys, that, by order of the Directory, he was preparing a report upon the existing relations of the United States with France, and that, when it was finished, he would tell them what steps were to follow! But the demand of the Directory was speedily made known, and it was, in one word, MONEY. Talleyrand's cupidity, the Directory's cupidity, the national cupidity, must be satisfied. Give money, plenty of money, was the cry; give money, and we will soon settle matters; refuse to give, and we will visit upon you the displeasure of victorious France. Talleyrand wanted only some $250,000 for his private disposal. The Directory would prove gracious if some $13,000,000 were loaned, that is, given to them; and they seemed to have supposed that the American people, like whipped curs, would submit to such mean and debasing propositions! Not to dwell upon this matter, we may say in few words that the mission was a failure, so far as obtaining justice or even decent treatment was concerned, and the envoys returned home.

Congress re-assembled, November 23d, 1797, and were called upon immediately to consider the necessity of vigorous measures for retaliating long and persistently continued injuries on the part of France. The spirit of the country was roused on learning the disgraceful terms proposed by the Directory, and the outrageous decree of January 8th, 1798, condemning as prizes all neutral vessels having on board merchandize and commodities produced in England. Pinckney's expression, "Millions for defence, not a cent for tribute," became a rallying cry, and "Hail Columbia" exerted an inspiriting influence throughout the Union. The regular army was strengthened, and an act passed for raising a provisional army. Washington, whose interest was as deep as ever in his country's welfare, was appointed commander-in-chief early in July, 1798, and, though reluctantly, accepted the position. Congress in April established the navy department, the republicans opposing the bill warmly. The United States, 44, was launched at Philadelphia, being the first vessel got into the water under the present organization of the navy. The whole force authorized by law, on the 16th of July, consisted of 12 frigates; 12 ships of a force between 20 and 24 guns inclusive; and six smaller sloops, besides galleys and revenue cutters; making a total of 30 active cruisers. An act was passed to declare the treaties with France no longer obligatory, as they had been repeatedly violated by the French government. It was during this session of Congress, that those acts were passed which caused John Adams's administration to be stigmatized in the severest terms, and which, no doubt, hastened the downfall of the federal party; we refer to the acts of the 18th of June, 1798, amending the previous naturalization laws, and requiring a residence of fourteen years in order to become a citizen; that of June 25th, entitled "an act concerning aliens;" that of July 6th, concerning alien enemies; and that of July 14th, "in addition to the act for the punishment of certain crimes against the United States." The last three of those acts are what are commonly known as the *alien and sedition laws.* By the acts respecting aliens it was provided that a register of resident aliens should be kept; and they were required to report themselves at certain times; it was also made lawful for the president to order all such aliens as he judged to be dangerous to quit the United States, under penalty of imprisonment. The sedition law, as it is called, provided that *unlawful* combinations against the government or laws of the United States, or intimidation of any officer of government, should be punished by a fine not exceeding $5,000, and imprisonment for not more than five years; and the publication of libels against the government should be punished with severity of fine and imprisonment not much less: the operation of this law was limited to two years. These acts were passed with only small majorities, and they afforded excellent capital for Jefferson, who stood at the head of the republican party, to stir up vigorously his adherents against Adams and the federalists.

In view of the position of affairs, it need not be wondered at that laws of this kind were passed. The country swarmed with spies and secret agents. Foreign emissaries and fugitives from justice were actively employed in stirring up internal dissensions. There were some thirty thousand Frenchmen in the United States, numbers of whom were in the pay of the Directory, and busily at work to accomplish its ends. The number of British subjects was still greater, and these with thousands of the United Irishmen, and of German emigrants, were organized into associations hostile to the government. In point of numbers, and in daring, factious disregard of the laws, these aliens were naturally a source of alarm to all classes of Americans who had the welfare of their country at heart. "They abused the freedom of the press by traducing the characters of the administration and its supporters, in the vilest manner, and by instigating the resistance of the people against the government and laws of the Union. The alien acts produced good results at once, by causing the sudden departure of numbers of the most notorious of them; and the acts were never put into execution. The sedition law was more objectionable on almost every account, in a country such as ours, where the freedom of the press runs into lawless license and unmeasured abuse of all public men and acts; it is better perhaps, to endure the evils we see and know, than by sedition laws, to run ourselves into evils that we know not and probably could not endure. Congress ended its active and busy session on the 19th July, 1798. The republicans under Jefferson and Madison, his right hand man, were busily at war upon the administration, its policy and acts, and, deeming the alien and sedition laws violations of the Constitution, determined upon their line of action. Jefferson (though secretly and with wise forecast as to his personal interest) wrote the famous Kentucky Resolutions, which were introduced into the legislature of that state November 10th, 1798. These Resolutions are nine in number, of great length, and assert and defend the doctrine of absolute State sovereignty and the power of *Nullification* by each and every State, a doctrine which has never been accepted by the American people as yet, and almost certainly never will be. Madison, on the other hand, devoted as he was to Jefferson, prepared at his earnest solicitation what are known as the Virginia Resolutions. These are six in number, and assert State rights strongly; they also declare the alien and sedition laws *unconstitutional*, and call upon the other States to join Virginia in measures to secure rights etc., under the Constitution. It will be observed that Jefferson wished to go much further than the Virginia Resolutions contemplated. He desired that the State legislatures should not only declare the alien and sedition laws absolutely null and void, but that they should *make* them so, by resisting forcibly their execution, and, if need be, by seceding from the Union. Madison was not prepared for any such extreme step, and at a later period of his life he repudiated explicitly the doctrines of those who believed in the right and power of a State to nullify the acts of the general government.*

Congress assembled for its third session, December 8th, 1798, and the answers to the president's speech showed evident disposition to sustain him in the present conjuncture. Its acts, also, were mostly to this effect. Washington, though somewhat embarrassed as to the selection of officers for the army, was nevertheless very active and earnest in concerting, with Hamilton, second in command, and Pinckney, major-general, arrangements for raising and organizing the army. It is true, he did not believe France would venture upon invasion, but he held it as a principle always to be prepared. Pickering, secretary of state, presented, in January, 1799, an elaborate report on the correspondence, etc., relative to the French mission, in which he dealt with "the unparalleled effrontery of M. Talleyrand" in a rather sharp manner, and made plain the fact that the Directory had acted with bad faith all the way through. The officers and men in our infant navy behaved with that gallantry and skill which have always characterized this arm of the service. The victory of Truxtun, in the Constellation, Feb. 9th, over l'Insurgente, a French frigate, was justly regarded with pride by Americans, and the numerous other instances in which our navy, small as it was, did good service in protecting our commerce and punishing French depredations, not only encouraged the people, but induced Congress to give it additional attention. France, probably, never intended to go to war with the United States. All that she wanted, she expected to get by the peculiar line of conduct she adopted; letting loose a horde of pirates against the commerce of America; bullying her ambassadors in the hope of tribute; and tampering with the factious adherents that she was able to claim in the United States. France felt not the least concern respecting the immorality of her schemes; her foreign minister, with his detestable maxim, that *the use of language is to conceal, not reveal, our thoughts*, was equal to any amount or species of diplomatic duplicity. It should also be noted that our country had no disposition to allow gratitude for former favors to involve her in a sort of vassalage, and consequently the piracies and insults of France were very summarily dealt with, and Adams, as president, represented the real spirit of Americans in refusing everything like tribute, and all further intercourse, until assurances should be given that our minister would be treated with proper respect and consideration. If the President had adhered firmly to this line of policy, very possibly the federal party might have remained longer in power.

In the present state of the public mind, deeply outraged by the continued and gross insults and injuries which the profligate government of France heaped upon our country and her commerce, and fully roused to the point of firm, united resistance, the federalists, as a body, resolved to maintain the dignified attitude which had been assumed, and to insist that overtures should be made by France for an amicable settlement of difficulties and disputes between the two nations. They thought that they had a right to exact of the president that he should carry out this national policy, and not subject them to the disgrace and ruin which must follow from a change in the course which they deemed wisest and best to pursue. But

* See Madison's *Letter to Edward Everett*, under date of August, 1830, on the subject of Nultification, the acts of the Virginia legislature, etc.

Adams thought differently. He suddenly adopted a plan of action which astonished the federalists, and clearly presaged the approaching supremacy of the republicans. The president, without that assurance from Talleyrand, which it was thought he ought to have insisted upon, nominated, on the 18th of February, 1799, Mr. Vans Murray, then at the Hague, as minister plenipotentiary to France. Jefferson, writing to Madison, with his usual astuteness, pointed out that Adams's measure, so sudden and so astonishing, "silenced all arguments against sincerity of France, and rendered desperate every further effort towards war." Remonstrance was of no avail with Adams; but he was persuaded to send two others, Ellsworth (chief justice) and Gen. Davie, of N. C., to join Murray in his mission. The departure of the envoys was delayed through the spring and summer, although Adams was desirous to hurry them off; his cabinet did not agree with him in the policy of the measure, and as the Directory was overthrown, and it was clear that a change of government was about to take place in France, they did all they could to prevent the departure of Ellsworth and Davie. It was of no use, however; Adams insisted, and ordered the frigate United States to convey the envoys to their destination, early in November, 1799. In Pennsylvania, in the spring of this year, a man named Fries was at the head of an insurrectionary movement; but he was easily put down; he was convicted of treason and sentenced to death, but subsequently pardoned by Adams. The case of another person, named Nash or Robbins, who had been given up to the British and hung as guilty of mutiny some years before, was brought up in Congress and warmly debated. It was early in March, that Marshall delivered that profound and learned speech which, as Story says, "silenced opposition, and settled then and forever the points of national law upon which the controversy lingered." The resolutions of censure were negatived by a vote of 62 to 35. Intercourse was reopened with St. Domingo; a treaty of amity and commerce was concluded with Prussia; the legislature of Kentucky, getting little or no sympathy from the other States (p. 122), reaffirmed its nullification views and declarations; and Virginia, by a report from Madison, asserted again the views which had been before set forth.

The Sixth Congress assembled December 2, 1799. The federalists still were the stronger party, and after Adams's opening speech, were prepared to enter vigorously upon the work to be done by the national legislature. But suddenly there came a blow upon the whole country, which was felt throughout the length and breadth of the land, and which for the time affected every American heart with grief. We refer to the *death of Washington.* He had returned to Mount Vernon, and was busily occupied in the affairs of home and anxiously watching the course of events. On the 12th of December he was several hours on horseback; the weather was wet and cold; he became chilled through with the mingled sleet and rain; and the same night was attacked with inflammation of the wind-pipe, with chills, fever, and the usual accompaniments. Every thing that medical skill and devotion could accomplish was done, but he sank rapidly, saying to Dr. Craik, at the last, "I die hard, Doctor, but I am not afraid to die; my breath cannot last long." Between ten and eleven at night, December 14th, he expired, being in the 68th year of his age, and in full possession of his mental faculties. On Wednesday, December 18th, his mortal remains were placed in the family tomb at Mount Vernon. And thus GEORGE WASHINGTON died, in the fullness of his days, quietly, calmly, and as a Christian man should die. His mission was accomplished; his work was done; there was no higher honor that he could receive; there was nothing left for him to do, but to die as he had lived, one of the noblest, most upright, purest-minded heroes, patriots, and statesmen with which God has ever been pleased to bless this world of ours. His death only was needed, to render his fame imperishable wherever the light of Christian civilization has dawned upon mankind. Every where the people mourned "with a great and very sore lamentation," for the death of Washington. This mourning was manifested by every token which could indicate the sentiments and feelings of Americans. Orators, divines, journalists, in short all who could write or speak, responded to the general voice of the country, and employed their talents to solemnize the event, and to honor the memory of the great and the good Washington. It was meet, that the close of one century should be marked by the death of that noblest patriot and statesman which it had produced, and that another should commence filled with his glorious memory, and with the elevating example which he set, not for his countrymen only, but for all time and for all people.

Although the death of Washington calmed for a period the waters of political strife, yet it was for only a brief season. The federalists were divided among themselves, and the republicans though in the minority were active, well-organized, and waiting for the favorable moment when victory might be within their grasp. During a considerable part of the present session of Congress, party intrigue was working its approaches to the election. Private conferences, secret caucuses, less secret meetings, correspondence by post and messenger, (Jefferson continually fearing that the seals of his missives might be broken), promises, counter-promises, bargains, suspicions, schemes, and tricks,—the proceedings can easily be imagined, they have often been repeated. In January, 1800, the president urged the formation of a military academy, but no action was taken. There was, however, action in regard to financial matters, duties on various articles, the taking the census in 1800, removing to the new seat of government, providing a territorial government, etc. Late in the session, measures were taken with respect to the sale of the public lands, the importance of which, in a financial point of view was very evident, and on the 10th of May, an act was passed laying the foundation of the land system as it has since existed. On the 14th of May Congress adjourned, being the last occasion on which it met in Philadelphia. Troubles in the Cabinet (p. 124) kept on increasing. McHenry and Pickering were removed from office, Marshall taking Pickering's place as secretary of state. Truxtun (p. 123) again performed glorious acts in the Constellation; and Bainbridge, who had been sent with the *tribute* to those rascally pirates of Algiers (September, 1800), behaved with great discretion and prudence, although he was compelled to do some work for the dey which that public robber dared not put into the hands of his own freebooters. The American envoys (p. 124) reached Paris, March 2, 1800. Napoleon was now at the head of affairs, and negotiations were entered upon at once; but the proposals on both sides were unacceptable, each to the other; and the result at last reached was a "Convention," (September 3d), leaving disputed matters to be settled in the future, and agreeing upon various points relative to commercial intercourse, etc. The results of the mission did not give that satisfaction to the people at large which had been hoped for and expected. Politics in the State of New York were narrowly watched at this date. Both parties strove for the mastery, Hamilton being the leading spirit on the federal as Aaron Burr was on the democratic side. A proposal was made to Governor Jay to take certain steps in order to secure the election of the federal ticket; but he refused entirely; and the republicans obtained their desires. The federalists, in caucus, fixed upon Adams and Pinckney, though a strong minority were determined to defeat Adams; and the other party without any division of sentiment fixed upon Jefferson and Burr, the latter of whom had been very useful and deserved reward. In June, 1800, the public offices, etc., were removed to the city of Washington, at that time hardly more than a village. The second census resulted as follows:—Total in the free States, 2,684,609; in the slave States, 2,621,316; grand total, 5,305,925. Hamilton, who was resolute in determining to prevent Adams's re-election, loved the president quite as little as that high functionary loved him. He had demanded of Adams a retraction of certain charges, to which demand no attention was paid; and so, he published a famous "Letter" concerning Adams. As a political move, it was a gross blunder, and the republicans gained far more than could be afforded to be lost by Hamilton and those who agreed with him in attacks on John Adams. As the time for choosing electors drew on, new intrigues, as a necessary consequence, were set on foot, compromises proposed, etc.

Congress assembled November 17th, 1800, and the president's speech was delivered on the 22d. It was well received by the two Houses, and promises were made by both as to industry, dispatch, and the like. The principal events which marked this session were the act respecting the judiciary, and the election of a president by the House of Representatives. A number of new judges, and a rearrangement of their duties were determined, and this gave Adams the opportunity of appointing several federalists to office just at the end of his official life. Jefferson bitterly resented this, but could not prevent it. Ellsworth resigned the chief-justiceship, and Adams nominated John Marshall to fill the vacancy, January 27th, 1801; in view of the career of this eminent jurist, for nearly thirty-five years in that important chair, we cannot but be thankful that he was appointed at the time he was. Burr, the active and unprincipled politician, was very successful in advancing the interests of his party; and so madly bitter and malignant were some of the federalists towards Jefferson, that they actually contemplated taking Burr and giving all their influence towards putting him in the presidential chair. Hamilton strongly deprecated such an idea. Speaking of Burr, he said: "Every step in his career proves, that he has formed himself upon the model of Catiline, and he is too cold-blooded and too determined a conspirator ever to change his plans." Even with these warnings sounding in their ears, the blinding rage of party animosity nearly led to the rejecting of Jefferson and the elevation of Aaron Burr. Badly as men may think and speak of the third president and his career, it will hardly be denied that it was a mercy which spared our country from the rule of the bold, bad man who was at this time placed in the vice-president's chair. On the 11th of February, 1801, the electoral votes were opened by Jefferson, president of the Senate. Total for Adams, 65; for Pinckney, 64; for Jefferson and Burr, each, 73. By this result the House was compelled to choose between the two latter which was to be president. Balloting began February 11th, nine States being necessary for a choice. Jefferson received 8, Burr 6, on the first ballot, two States being divided. Day after day (one too being Sunday) the balloting went on, with the same result, until the 17th; the federalists were compelled to choose between the two, both of whom they feared and distrusted. At length Bayard, of Delaware, obtained from Jefferson some vague promises as to what he would do, and then acting with five others, they voted blank on the 36th ballot; this gave ten States for Jefferson, Burr receiving only four. And thus was accomplished what the third president exultingly called the "Republican Revolution of 1801." The few weeks of power belonging to Adams were dreary enough to him, and early on the 4th of March he left Washington, and bade adieu to public life. Remembering the many and valuable services of his career before he became president, we may pass over in silence that which some writers criticise with unmitigated severity and bitterness. The federal party fell with him, and Jefferson came into power; it remained to be seen how the attainment of his ambition would affect his future career, and the welfare of our country, in this period of her history.

On the 4th of March, 1801, the third president of the United States appeared in the Senate chamber, and delivered his inaugural address. It is a document written evidently with great care, rather florid in style, but containing much political wisdom and shrewdness. An extract or two may be given in this place:—"Called upon to undertake the duties of the first executive office of our country, I avail myself of the presence of that portion of my fellow-citizens which is here assembled, to express my grateful thanks for the favor with which they have been pleased to look towards me, to declare a sincere consciousness, that the task is above my talents, and that I approach it with those anxious and awful presentiments, which the greatness of the charge, and the weakness of my powers, so justly inspire. . . . . When I see the hopes of this beloved country committed to the issue and the auspices of this day, I shrink from the contemplation, and humble myself before the magnitude of the undertaking. Utterly, indeed, should I despair, did not the presence of many, whom I here see, remind me, that, in the other high authorities provided by our Constitution, I shall find resources of wisdom, of virtue, and of zeal, on which to rely under all difficulties. . . . . All will bear in mind this sacred principle, that though the will of the majority is in all cases to prevail, that will, to be rightful, must be reasonable; that the minority possesses their equal rights, which equal laws must protect, and to violate which would be oppression. . . . . Every difference of opinion is not a difference of principle. We have called by different names brethren of the same principles. *We are all republicans: we are all federalists.* . . . Enlightened by a benign religion, professed indeed and practiced in various forms, yet all of them inculcating honesty, truth, temperance, gratitude, and the love of man; acknowledging and adoring an overruling Providence, which, by all its dispensations, proves, etc. . . . Without pretensions to that high confidence you reposed in our first and greatest revolutionary character, whose pre-eminent services had entitled him to the first place in his country's love, and destined for him the fairest page in the volume of faithful history, I ask so much confidence only as may give firmness and effect to the legal administration of your affairs." The oath of office was then administered by John Marshall, and the next day the Senate confirmed the nominations for his cabinet. These were James Madison, secretary of state; H. Dearborn, secretary of war; L. Lincoln, attorney-general; S. Dexter, of the treasury; B. Stoddert, of the navy; the two last were in May superseded by A. Gallatin and R. Smith.

Jefferson, immediately on his entrance upon office, found himself in a perplexing position. The party who had placed him in this coveted chair had got the idea that they were entitled to the rewards of exertion, and that all the patronage of the government was to be bestowed upon them exclusively. The present holders of office,—most of them, by the way, having been appointed by Washington,—were of course to be removed, and the many friends and supporters of the new dynasty were to be put in their places. The democracy were clamorous for the spoils; the federalists were anxiously waiting the result which the president and dominant party had reached on this question. Indiscriminate removals, the astute president felt, would be very unwise and very bad policy; and yet nothing short of a large excision would be tolerated by his adherents. An able writer, noticing the fact that it was natural for the republicans to expect a fair share in the offices under government, states what is worth remembering:—"He set the first example of a president removing men from office because their political opinions differed from his own." It is worth remembering, too, that "by the frequent exercise of the power of removal for this cause alone, more strength must be given to the national government, and especially to the executive—that branch which freemen should watch with most jealousy—than by the most latitudinarian construction of the Constitution which any federalist was ever disposed to give to it." Jefferson understood exactly the difficulty of his position; and so he was in favor of being cautious in his movements, "balancing" (as he says) "our measures according to the impression we perceive them to make." He announced to his friends that he was resolved to remove all who had been appointed by Adams after the election was known, and the attorneys and marshals of the federal court. And he kept his word in this at least. To a remonstrance from New Haven, he stated that he was bound to give his friends a fair share in the offices in his hands; when he should have accomplished this, he says, "I shall return with joy to that state of things, when the only question concerning a candidate shall be, Is he honest? Is he capable? Is he faithful to the Constitution?" We may remark, however, in this connection, that that millenial condition of affairs was never reached in Jefferson's days, nor has it been at any time since. The president also announced that he should communicate with Congress simply by message, no answers being expected; that the army and navy (particularly the latter) were to be reduced; the utmost economy to be practiced, etc. Jefferson sent a special messenger to France, with the treaty duly ratified (p. 125), and appointed R. R. Livingston minister plenipotentiary. Although the new party just come into power had no love for the navy, and a law had been passed for dismantling and selling ships, etc., yet an impudent demand from Tripoli compelled Jefferson to use the naval arm. Commodore Dale, with three frigates and a sloop of war, was dispatched to look after these pirates of the Mediterranean. The Pasha of Tripoli demanded money, ships, etc., or he would declare war, and as the money did not come at the date he required, in May, 1801, he cut down the flag-staff of the American consulate, and threatened dire vengeance. Thus our concessions to one nest of pirates, in 1795, preferred as an alternative to completing and sending out the six frigates that had been conditionally authorized by the act of Congress of the year before, to impose by force of arms, our own terms, naturally provoked and encouraged the cupidity and insolence of another. Dale arrived at Gibraltar, July 1st, where he found the Tripolitan admiral with two vessels. Leaving a ship to watch them, he proceeded to Algiers and Tunis, and pretty thoroughly lowered the insolent tone of these pests of commerce by the mere sight of his broadside. Lieut. Sterret, in the Enterprise, a 12-gun schooner, met a Tripolitan ship of 14 guns, and after a three hours' running fight captured her, and not being allowed to carry her in, set her adrift with some 30 out of 80 surviving, and an old sail and spar, so that she might get home. The pirates were a long time in getting there, and when they arrived the reis or commander was mounted on a jackass, paraded through the streets, and received the bastinado. After rendering most effectual service to our commerce in this quarter, Dale left two vessels in the Mediterranean, and in obedience to orders returned home at the close of November.

The Seventh Congress met December 7th, 1801. The republican or democratic party had a majority in both Houses, and Jefferson, according to his notion of reform, sent in his first message; this plan has ever since been followed; but it may be doubted whether the former plan had not several advantages which made it worth continuing. The message was long, well-written, and full of material on which Congress was to act. It was assailed by the federalists, as may be supposed, with no gentle hand. "The points deemed most exceptionable (as Jefferson's biographer says), or at least most vulnerable to attack, were the reduction of the army and navy, the revision of the judicial system, and the proposed facility to naturalization.

all of which they attributed either to false or visionary notions of government, or to an unprincipled sacrifice of the best interests of the nation to popular prejudices." By the president's urgent desire, an immediate attack upon the judiciary system (p. 126) was resolved upon. Jefferson asserted that the federalists "had retired into the judiciary as a stronghold. There the remains of federalism are to be preserved and fed from the treasury; and from that battery all the works of republicanism are to be beaten down and erased. By a fraudulent use of the Constitution, which has made judges *irremovable*, they have multiplied useless judges merely to strengthen their phalanx." Such was the violent language of Jefferson in regard to matters out of his reach. Would he have been so violent, had the judges (like the chief justice) been, not federalists in political sentiments, but democrats? We trow not. A bill to repeal the law before mentioned (p. 126) was brought in early in January, 1802, and warmly debated by Bayard, Morris, Giles, etc. The vote in the House in favor of repeal, was fifty-nine to thirty-two; in the Senate the republicans had only one majority on this question. As Jefferson's biographer says, "the course taken by the majority of the legislature, in the repeal of the judiciary act, did not receive the unanimous support of the republican party. To those who regarded the independence of the judges as a cardinal principle in free governments, the repeal appeared to be contrary to the spirit and meaning of the Constitution; as, if the judges could be deprived of their offices by the abolition of the courts, the provision in the Constitution, by which they were to hold them *during good behavior*, was rendered nugatory; and the judiciary were virtually rendered dependent on the legislature. Nor were there wanting moderate men in the republican ranks who believed the repeal of this law to be as clear an infraction of the Constitution as the sedition law had been. The number of these was, however, too small to produce effect; and their disapprobation, together with the louder voice of the opposition, was drowned in the popular huzzas, which were everywhere heard for the new administration." Congress, at this session, abolished the internal taxes and passed an act for the redemption of the public debt by the yearly appropriation of $7,300,000 to the sinking fund. But, it ought to be noted, that the act now passed was only nominal in its operations; new loans were effected, and reduction of the debt was rather in theory than in fact, as the appropriations for expenses for 1802 were more than equal to the receipts of the previous year. Ohio was admitted into the Union in April, 1802, having about 50,000 inhabitants; and on the 7th of May the session of Congress reached its close.

In the spring of 1802, it became known that Spain had ceded the province of Louisiana to France. Great excitement arose out of this at once, and the prospect of collision with France seemed near at hand. The Spanish authorities, in violation of the treaty, prohibited the Americans from further use of New Orleans as a place of deposit. This measure roused up thoroughly the people of the west, and sooner than submit to imposition in regard to the Mississippi, they were ready to organize and assert their rights by force of arms. About the middle of December, 1802, the second session of Congress began. The president's message was full of important material for consideration and action. Early in Jan., 1803, resolutions were offered in the House, calling for the papers on the subject of the cession of Louisiana to France, and asserting our right to the Mississippi; but the majority refused to pass these resolutions and substituted others, virtually committing the management of the whole matter to Jefferson. He, ever suspicious of the federalists, seemed to think that the object of the opposition was, to force the country into a war with Spain, "in order to derange our finances," or if that could not be done, "to attach the western country to them, as their best friends, and thus get again into power." Which latter supposition may have some show of reason; although other and nobler motives, we think, might account for their actions in the matter. With a view of carrying his pacific policy into effect, the president, on the 10th of January, appointed James Monroe minister plenipotentiary to France, to act with Mr. Livingston, in the purchase of New Orleans and the Floridas; for, as he observed, in writing to Monroe upon the appointment, "the measures previously pursued by the administration being *invisible*, did not satisfy the minds of the western people; consequently something *sensible* had become necessary." Napoleon, beyond doubt, intended to take possession of the province he had acquired from Spain; and had he done so, almost certainly it would have been conquered by Great Britain, and thus we should have had to fight the matter out with England. How singular are the changes produced in the history of the world by what seem to be very slight and insufficient causes! The military colony of twenty thousand men was on the eve of embarkation, and Napoleon had resolved to make this colony, in the centre of the western hemisphere, the stand for a lever to wield at his pleasure the destinies of the globe. A petty squabble with England about the Island of Malta, deranged his plans, and he formed another resolve, viz., to rival Julius Cæsar, by the invasion and conquest of England. In order to do this, he could not spare his veterans to run the risk of a voyage across the Atlantic; for England was mistress of the seas, and could certainly have wrested Louisiana from him. Napoleon, therefore, abandoned his projects of conquest and glory in America, and as money was all important to enable him to carry forward his schemes, he suddenly resolved to offer Louisiana for sale to the United States. It was, indeed, a propitious turn in the tide of events for the administration of Jefferson; for war with France would have been inevitable, if Napoleon had attempted to hold the province, and however just the cause of the United States would have been, it would have given a direction to national affairs adverse to the whole system of Jefferson's policy, and in all probability would have proved fatal to the popularity and success of his administration. In Congress, later in the session, other motions were presented respecting this important business; for the western states began to show symptoms of increasing impatience, under so serious a restriction to their trade as the interdiction of the right of deposit at New Orleans. Mr. Ross, of Pennsylvania, in the Senate, proposed, on the 14th of February, that the president should call out some fifty thousand militia, and occupy New Orleans; and that $5,000,000 should be appropriated to that retaliatory measure. But Mr. Breckenridge, of Kentucky, was more successful in his resolutions, raising the numbers of the militia, or of volunteers, to eighty thousand, but not defining the work they should be set to do, nor appropriating any specific sum of money, as the service was contingent merely. The president also asked and obtained an appropriation of $2,000,000, under the head of "foreign intercourse," as the commencement of a fund for effecting the purchase of New Orleans and the Floridas.

Napoleon at first offered Louisiana to Mr. Livingston for fifty millions of francs, and when Monroe arrived at Paris in April, negotiations were rapidly pushed forward. Marbois, who was acting for Napoleon, now asked eighty millions of francs, to which our ministers agreed, on condition that twenty out of the eighty millions should be assigned to the payment of what was due from France to citizens of the United States. The treaty was concluded April 30th, and signed by the American and French ministers four days afterwards. Napoleon was not only glad to get money, but he liked to spite England all he could, remarking at the time, "I have given to England a maritime rival that will, sooner or later, humble her pride." Jefferson, though greatly pleased with the successful result of his negotiations, still felt, as he himself said, in a letter, that he "had done an act beyond the Constitution." He supposed that an amendment would be needed to ratify his course; at the same time, like an astute politician as he was, he warned his adherents in Congress to say as little about the matter as possible. Congress was called together in October, and the treaty was ratified on the 20th by the Senate, by a vote of 24 to 7; and two days later officially communicated to the House as complete. The republicans had the majority in Congress, and though the federalists set themselves against the treaty, and urged strongly the unconstitutionality of the acquisition of foreign territory, they were not able to effect anything. In respect to this point and also another in the treaty, by which, for a period, preference was given to the ports of Louisiana over those of other States, it is confessed by Jefferson's biographer, that "the republican party now found that the very strict construction of the Constitution, for which they had contended when in the opposition, was not suited to them when in the exercise of power; and which, if pushed to that extreme of nicety, which some affected, would often defeat the main purposes for which the Constitution was established." Eighty-nine, therefore, voted in favor of the general resolution for carrying the treaty into effect, against twenty-three opponents; and the resolutions for a provincial government over the ceded territory, and for providing the purchase money, were passed without a division. On the 20th of December, 1803, formal possession was taken of the country, Gov. Claiborne, of Mississippi, and Gen. Wilkinson being the commissioners in behalf of the United States. J. Q. Adams, in speaking of this point, says: "The renewal of the European war, and the partialities of Mr. Jefferson in favor of France, enabled him to accomplish an object which greatly enlarged the territories of the Union —which removed a most formidable source of future dissensions with France—which exceedingly strengthened the relative influence and power of the State and section of the Union, to which he himself belonged, and which in its consequences changed the character of the Confederacy itself. This operation, by far the greatest that has been accomplished by any administration under the Constitution, was consummated at the price of fifteen million of dollars in money, and of *a direct, unqualified, admitted, violation of the Constitution of the United States.* According to the theory of Mr. Jefferson, as applied by him to the alien and sedition acts, it was absolutely null and void. It might have been nullified by the legislature of any one State in the Union, and if persisted in, would have warranted and justified a combination of States, and their secession from the Confederacy in resistance against it. That an amendment to the Constitution was necessary to legalize the annexation of Louisiana to the Union, was the opinion both of Mr. Jefferson and of Mr. Madison. They finally acquiesced, however, in the latitudinous construction of that instrument, which holds the treaty-making powers, together with an act of Congress, sufficient for this operation. It was accordingly thus consummated by Mr. Jefferson, and has been sanctioned by the acquiescence of the people." The interest taken by the president in the great west, led to the sending out the exploring expedition under Lewis and Clarke. It consisted of 28 individuals in all, and in May, 1804, left the banks of the Mississippi. This brave band penetrated, by the Columbia River, to the Pacific Ocean; were absent more than two years; and on their return, received a high eulogy from the president for the valuable results of their expedition to geography, character of the country and people, etc.

The Eighth Congress, as stated above, met in the middle of October, 1803, and took up the subject of an amendment to the Constitution, relative to the election of president and vice-president, so as to designate the person voted for as president or as vice-pres ident, instead of the existing article, which required the electors to vote for two persons for these offices, of whom the one who had the highest number of votes was to be president. The amendment, though urgently opposed by the federalists, was finally carried by the requisite two thirds vote, and during the year 1804 was ratified by the State legislatures. The bankrupt law, passed under Adams's administration, was repealed by Jefferson's intervention; and now that the third president was in power he expressed his intense hostility, shared by the democrats generally, against the U. S. Bank. His biographer, however, rates Jefferson's notions of danger to the country from the bank as of small value; in which we entirely agree with him. Judge Pickering, of New Hampshire, was convicted and removed, in the spring of 1803, and Judge Chase of Maryland was impeached, but not tried till February, 1805, when he was acquitted. Congress adjourned, March 27th, 1804, after a long and busy session. Among other things done, we may mention that the salaries of the principal officers of government were increased; additional duties were imposed on imports, to defray the expenses of naval operations in the Mediterranean; a naturalization law was passed, which required a residence of five years instead of fourteen; and two separate governments were established in the newly acquired territory of Louisiana, to be organized as the president might deem expedient.

Naval affairs in the Mediterranean were conducted with as much success as was possible, under the mean and inadequate views of this administration in regard to the necessity of our having a strong force in the region of the pirates. During the latter part of 1802 and 1803, Chauncey, Rodgers, Porter, and others, sustained the reputation of their countrymen for bravery and skill, and met with numerous successes; but Commodore Morris had no guns sufficient in calibre to bombard Tripoli, which was the only mode of treatment that the pasha thoroughly appreciated. Morris was recalled and Preble put in command. Bainbridge, in the Philadelphia, with 315 men, ran on the shoals of the harbor of Tripoli, and were all made prisoners; but Decatur, in February, 1804, succeeded in setting fire to and destroying the ship. Preble tried to bombard Tripoli, but without success; and in September, was superseded by Barron. Through the combined efforts of Mr. Eaton and Hamet, brother of the pasha, an expedition by land was undertaken, and Derne was taken in April, 1805. Peace soon after was concluded, the usual intrigues, delays and prevarications preceding. This was in June. By it no tribute was to be paid in future, but $60,000 were given by the United States for the ransom of prisoners in Tripoli. Tunis next needed a lesson. Accordingly, Rodgers, now in command, anchored, August 1st, 1805, in Tunis Bay. The bravado and insolence of the bey were now only contemptible; and Rodgers brought matters to a speedy settlement. The bey having expressed a wish to send an ambassador to the United States, Decatur, in September, carried a Tunisian officer to Washington. The fellow had the assurance to talk about tribute, but he met with a very decided refusal; and the bey, wiser by experience, deemed it inexpedient to take any hostile steps in consequence. A small squadron was kept up in the Mediterranean, in order to warn the Barbary powers against the venturing to renew their attacks upon American commerce.

In 1804, we are told by Jefferson's biographer, that his administration was at "the meridian of its popularity, and an unexampled quiet reigned over the land." The federal party seemed to have become virtually extinct, and the republicans carried every thing before them. This peaceful state of things, however, was delusive to a large extent, and "even then causes were at work which greatly agitated the last years of his administration, both in its domestic and foreign relations." The presidential election was near at hand, and the caucus in Congress agreed, as a matter of course, upon Thomas Jefferson for reëlection. Aaron Burr, disliked and distrusted by those whom he had served so efficiently, had lost the confidence of the republican party, and they dropped him without scruple. George Clinton, of New York, a fast friend of Jefferson, was selected by the caucus as their candidate for the vice-presidency. Burr now resolved to become Governor of New York, if possible, and entered upon a fierce contest against Lewis, the regular nominee. Lewis was supported by the great mass of the democrats, Burr by a section of that party, consisting chiefly of the younger and more ardent, or less scrupulous members of it. Many of the federalists also sided with Burr, just as on former occasions. Thus both parties were split; for Hamilton, and those who looked up to him as their political leader, opposed them with the utmost ardor. Hamilton, indeed, could do no otherwise, knowing Burr so well as he did, and so thoroughly distrusting him (p. 126). The most atrocious libels were daily circulated by the press, and every kind of party malignity and meanness resorted to. Burr failed this time; and so he resolved to have the life of the man whose powerful influence was arrayed against him. He based his demand for satisfaction on the ground that a Dr. Cooper had said that Gen. Hamilton entertained and expressed a very despicable opinion as to Burr! Hamilton was foolish enough to answer Burr's letter, saying that he was ready to avow or disavow any positive, definite statement. This gave Burr the advantage, and he insisted immediately on a definite reply; but Hamilton declined answering this note. Burr now had the way clear for gratifying his ardent longing for revenge. On the 25th of June, the challenge was ready, and Van Ness, Burr's friend, delivered it. Hamilton tried to avoid the duel by the aid of Judge Pendleton; but in vain. Burr had determined to kill him, if possible, so he urged on matters in the most offensive and insulting manner. Some delay occurred, because Hamilton wished to discharge certain duties to his clients, and also to arrange his affairs in view of what he seemed to have a prevision must be the fatal termination of the encounter. He prepared his will, and wrote out his views as to this expected meeting, declaring himself as abhorring the shocking practice of duelling, yet, strangely insisting that he must violate his sacred principles of right and duty, and meet Burr,—in order to be murdered. Fatal inconsistency! Unhappy yielding to the base and barbarous notions of honor too prevalent then and since! How strange it seems that Hamilton, with his clear, piercing intellect, and with his sincere desire to be a Christian, and live and die as a Christian should live and die, should have been so blinded as to consent for a moment to violate the laws of God as well as of man, by going to be shot at by Aaron Burr! On the morning of the 7th of July, 1804, the parties met at Weehawken, opposite New York. Burr, eager for blood, discharged his pistol the instant the word was given; Hamilton, mortally wounded, aimlessly drew the trigger of his pistol, and fell heavily on his face. Burr, uninjured, and his companion in crime, Van Ness, immediately departed; and Dr. Hosack, Pendleton, and the boatmen who had conveyed Hamilton to the field of death, bore him back again to lie in agony untold —for his wife and seven children shared in that mortal stroke—till the next day, in his friend Bayard's house, and then to die. Funereal honors in abundance were paid to him, and it was felt that, since the death of Washington, no blow so severe as this had fallen upon our country. Not too strongly did Fisher Ames declare, that "his soul stiffened with despair when he thought what Hamilton would have been," remembering what he was when this sad calamity came upon him.

Congress assembled for its second session, Nov. 5th, 1804. The president's message was devoted largely to our foreign relations, to the revenue, and to the gunboat scheme, a sort of pet of Jefferson's, but greatly ridiculed by others. The republican majority in Congress was now so considerable, that "freedom of debate" was nearly impossible; every affair of importance being determined by the supporters of the administration in private caucus, before it was brought under the notice of the legislature. The consequence of such a procedure was, necessarily, that Congress was more largely influenced by party considerations and party pledges, than by the force of sound reason and fair discussion. During the autumn of 1804, the presidential election took place: Jefferson and Clinton received 162 votes, while Pinckney and King received only 14, thus demonstrating the strength of the republican party. On the 3d of March, 1805, Congress closed its second session, and the first term of Jefferson's service also reached its conclusion. It is needless to say that the gratulations of his friends were well nigh innumerable and unbounded in extent.

The next day Jefferson's second term began, and he delivered the usual inaugural address. His course thus far, as Tucker puts it, during which he had held the helm, had been singularly prosperous; and if he had not always met with a smooth sea, he had been able to continue his course over it by the strong gale of his popularity; but from this time he met with adverse winds and opposing currents which greatly impaired the comfort of the voyage, and in some degree its success. The Ninth Congress met Dec. 2d, 1805, for its first session. The president's party was largely in the majority, but there were evidences of discord already. This was speedily shown by the action of the committee, John Randolph, chairman, on a special message sent in by Jefferson respecting relations with Spain. The Spanish authorities, who were always haughty and overbearing, where they dared to be so, never liked what the United States had done in purchasing Louisiana, and behaved in a very ugly manner about the boundaries of the province on the east next to Florida. Spain seemed to desire war, and it was very imminent at this date by the insolent claims and conduct of the Spaniards. Monroe was sent to join Pinckney in going to Madrid to effect a settlement of difficulties; but after nearly five months' fruitless endeavors, they gave up the mission in despair. It was found also, that Napoleon behaved with his usual unscrupulousness in the matter, and as he had gained his end and got the money, he cared for nothing else. Randolph's report was brought in, January 3d, 1806, in which the hope was expressed that Spain would not proceed to extremities, yet, in consequence of the insulting character of Spanish proceedings, the committee submitted a resolution, "that such a number of troops as the president should deem sufficient to protect the southern frontier from insult, should be immediately raised." This was not what Jefferson wished: his desire, as privately intimated, was for money, not troops. War was very repugnant to his views, and he thought much more could be accomplished with money than by fighting about Louisiana and Florida. Randolph sturdily opposed everything of the sort, as derogatory to the dignity and independence of our country, and not unlike putting ourselves under *tribute* whenever France, or any other European nation saw fit to exact it. At the president's wish, a resolution was passed, after two weeks' debate, appropriating $2,000,000 to meet "extraordinary expenses of foreign intercourse," the Senate being informed that the object was to enable Jefferson to purchase the Spanish territories east of the Mississippi. John Randolph was very indignant at all this, declaring that "the doors were closed, and the minority, whose motives were impeached, and almost denounced, were voted down without debate." The president sent Armstrong and Bowdoin to endeavor to effect an amicable settlement with Spain. We may mention, in this connection, that, probably nothing but the destruction of the Spanish navy at Trafalgar, October 21st, 1805, prevented a war between Spain and the United States. General Wilkinson was actually ordered to meet hostilities by hostilities, so pressing and menacing were the Spanish advances in the south, and so little had been effected by negotiations. In fact, nothing of moment was accomplished during Mr. Jefferson's administration; for the American envoys at Paris, ere long were irreconcilably at variance, and the progress of negotiation was virtually at a standstill. Relations with England were also very unsatisfactory at this date. The rapid increase in commerce of the United States, as a neutral nation, under existing neutrality laws, was looked upon by Great Britain with no favorable eye, and she resolved to put a stop to it. To use the language of J. Q. Adams, now, "suddenly, as if by a concerted signal, throughout the world of waters which encompass the globe, our hardy and peaceful, though intrepid mariners, found themselves arrested in their career of industry and skill; seized by British cruisers; their vessels and cargoes conducted into British ports, and by the spontaneous and sympathetic illumination of British courts of vice-admiralty, adjudicated to the captors, because they were engaged in a trade with the enemies of Britain, to which they had not usually been admitted in time of peace. Monroe had scarcely reached London, when he received a report from the consul of the United States, at that place, announcing that about twenty of their vessels had, within a few weeks, been brought into the British ports in the channel, and that by the condemnation of more than one of them, the admiralty court had settled *the principle*." But this was not all. England, with the insolence of power, claimed what has forcibly been termed the "right of man-stealing from the vessels of the United States." British naval officers boarded our ships, and, down to the beardless midshipmen, seized upon any seaman whom they chose to take for a British subject. In this high-handed manner, not less than 3,000 American sailors had been forced to serve in the British navy. This infamous course was protested against on all occasions; but we were too weak then to defend ourselves, and with Jefferson's fantastical notions on the subject of the navy, if he had continued in office, we always should have been too weak to do anything. It took a number of years to bring our maritime force into a right condition, and then we taught the so-called "Mistress of the Seas" a lesson which she has never forgotten. Congress had these subjects before them, but accomplished nothing; party divisions, criminations, and recriminations, some favoring England, some France, put matters in a very unpleasant shape, and rendered the president's position far from comfortable. Added to all this, were other matters, which excited the country generally, and opened up discussions as to the Constitutional rights of the national legislature. One of these was, in respect to appropriations of public money for promoting internal improvements. An act was passed, in March, for constructing a national road from Cumberland, Maryland, to the State of Ohio. Not only was this bill, appropriating $30,000 of the public money to this service, signed by Jefferson; but bills were also approved appropriating various other sums to the making three other roads in the Southern States. Another question keenly debated was that which related to imposing a tax of ten dollars on every slave imported into the United States. Southern members did not like the having to pay a tax on slaves as property, and the bill failed of success. Congress adjourned April 21st, 1806, after a rather stormy session. The republican party was divided into at least two parts, and a considerable portion opposed Jefferson's policy on various points. Further trouble, too, arose out of the question as to who was to be the successor of Jefferson. On the whole, Madison seemed to have the best claim; but Randolph and others urged Monroe as a candidate. The president had his ability and skill severely tried in reconciling these gentlemen, and arranging matters so as not to have a "split" in the party. From some of Jefferson's letters at this date, it is evident that he had become tired out with the cares of office and the annoyances inseparable from his position.

The projects of Aaron Burr at this time occupied a large share of public attention. This ambitious but unprincipled man, cast off by the party which had placed him in the vice-president's chair, and looked upon with horror and deep indignation by a community which remembered that the blood of Hamilton was yet wet upon his hands, turned away in rage and disappointment from his native region, and sought in the great valley of the Mississippi some adventure adequate to his ability and his ambition. Schemes of conquest, and elevation to the height of political power, seem to have filled his mind; and we can well believe that Burr would let no scruples interfere with carrying out his plans. What these were, it is not easy, perhaps not possible, to say; indeed, it is quite probable, that he himself had no clear conception of what he purposed doing, but, like many another unprincipled adventurer, meant to be governed a good deal by circumstances and opportunities. Rumors ere long reached the north and east, that he was planning and organizing some vast expedition, the precise object of which no one could tell. Whether it was his design to make war on the Spanish province of Mexico; whether, knowing the discontents which existed in the west, he hoped to be able to separate this portion of the country from the Union; or whether, in the ruined condition of his fortunes, he hoped to repair them by some bold movement which promised a golden return; all was matter of conjecture; while, at the same time, there was none who doubted for a moment that he was equal to any undertaking, any desperate adventure, whether of foreign aggression or domestic treason. Jefferson, who hated Burr, was actively occupied in trying to find out his plans and to prevent the traitor from carrying them out, and he issued orders to seize on any boats or stores of Burr, and arrest persons engaged in his service.

Congress met for its second session, Dec. 1st, 1806, and the president sent in his message the next day. He spoke at large of "foreign relations," of Burr and his expedition, of the prosperous state of the finances, etc. He also used language respecting the slave trade, worth quoting: "I congratulate you, fellow citizens, on the approach of the period, at which you may interpose your authority constitutionally, to withdraw the citizens of the United States from all further participation in those violations of human rights, which have been so long continued on the unoffending inhabitants of Africa, and which the morality, the reputation, and the best interests of our country, have long been eager to proscribe. Although no law you may pass can take prohibitory effect till the first day of the year 1808, yet the intervening period is not too long to prevent, by timely notices, expeditions which cannot be completed before that day." In January, 1807, Congress called upon the president for information as to Burr's movements, etc. A long message was sent in, stating what had been done as to Burr, and also that one of the persons arrested by General Wilkinson had been liberated by *habeas corpus*; whereupon the Senate, with singularly hot haste, passed a bill "suspending the writ of *habeas corpus* for three months," and communicated their action to the House. It was a startling request this, to ask the House of Representatives to agree to place the liberty of the citizens of the entire Union in the hands of Thomas Jefferson, because Aaron Burr, "with about ten boats, navigated by about six hands each, without any military appearance," had passed down the Ohio, determined to overthrow and destroy the government of this great Republic, and to build up for himself, an empire upon its ruins! And the House, by a vote of one hundred and thirteen to nineteen, treated the proposition with very summary condemnation. Into the particulars of "Burr's conspiracy" we need not enter. He professed to be on his way to settle in Louisiana, but quite likely he meant to seize upon New Orleans, invade Mexico, engage in land piracy, etc. He was apprehended, March 26th, 1807, and conveyed to Richmond for trial. The miserable party-spirit of the day led the federalists to wish to get Burr off, so as to spite the president; while on the other hand, Jefferson allowed his hatred of Burr to cause him to say and do things, which, now that his correspondence is published, are nothing less than disgraceful. After various preliminary matters in getting ready to enter upon the important trial, the court assembled on the 3d of August, Chief-justice Marshall presiding. Nearly two weeks were occupied in endeavoring to get a jury, and the charges were, that Burr had excited insurrection, rebellion, war, etc. Unfortunately, no sufficient evidence could be obtained of Burr's guilt, and he escaped conviction. No one doubted that he was really and truly a traitor, and the conduct and decision of the Chief-justice were severely commented upon by those partizans who thought and asserted that he was bound to accomplish a very different result from that to which the trial was brought. Burr soon after sailed for England and his name and character were consigned to perpetual infamy.

On a previous page (p. 133), we have alluded to the pet scheme of Jefferson in regard to the gun boats which he wished to have in place of the navy, and thereby exposed himself to the ridicule and contempt of the larger part of the community. Early in 1807, he was called on for information as to the efficacy of gun-boats in protecting harbors, etc., and he sent in a message to Congress on the subject. He stated that 200 gun-boats would be required for the various harbors; that seventy-three were already built or building; and that the remainder would cost from half a million to $600,000. An appropriation was made by the dominant party in Congress of $150,000 to build thirty gun-boats; and subsequently a law was passed authorizing the construction of 188 gun boats, which, with those already built, would make the whole number 257. The whole scheme, however, was an absurd one, as Jefferson's friends knew very well, and the result was, as his biographer and admirer states, that "the public, pinning its faith on experienced men (in the navy and maritime affairs), remained incredulous; and when, soon afterwards, many of the new marine were driven ashore in a tempest, or were otherwise destroyed, no one seemed to regard their loss as a misfortune, and the officers of the navy did not affect to conceal their satisfaction; nor has any attempt been since made to replace them." A law was passed, prohibiting the African slave trade, after January 1st, 1808, under very severe penalties. The debates were long and fiery, and produced great excitement. Various stringent regulations were made; but the question of slavery itself was left untouched. It deserves, however, to be noted here, as a matter of justice to our country, that this action of Congress was in advance of that taken by any other nation in the civilized world, and that, though we were justly liable to the reproach so freely bestowed for the continuance of slavery down to the period when emancipation was effected in the United States (1863), nevertheless, the United States, in 1820, were the first to declare the slave trade to be piracy and punishable accordingly. On the 3d of March, 1807, the Ninth Congress closed its second session.

The deadly struggle between England and Napoleon seemed calculated to force the United States out of their position of neutrality. Ever since the annihilation of the navies of Spain and France by the decisive victory at Trafalgar, Great Britain had strenuously exerted her gigantic powers to retain in her own hands solely, the trade of Europe. In May, 1806, she had declared the whole coast of Europe, from the Elbe in Germany, to Brest in France, (about a thousand miles of sea-coast), to be in a state of blockade, which subjected American vessels attempting to enter the continental ports, to capture and condemnation. Napoleon, on his part, having by his deadly blows, at Austerlitz and Jena, laid the continental powers prostrate, perceived no way of securing and extending his conquests, especially against the one nation that had successfully resisted his might, except that which he entitled the "Continental System," the first effort to realize which was the famous "Berlin Decree," issued Nov. 21st, 1806. From the terms of this decree, it was evident that the neutral trade of America would be affected (to the full extent of Napoleon's power to enforce so prodigious an edict), quite as injuriously as it had been by the imperious maxims of Great Britain. And although Armstrong, the American minister at Paris, obtained from the French minister of marine and colonies, what seemed to be an express statement, that the terms of the treaty of 1800 would still determine the relations of France to American commerce, it was too evident that Jefferson's view, that the flag should cover the goods, would not be allowed in the internecine warfare that the Emperor of France was now waging with England. The treaty which had been made by Monroe and Pinckney with England, on the last day of the year 1806, in several respects was more favorable than Jay's treaty (p. 117); but it did not satisfy the president; it left the question of impressment open; and further, in consequence of Napoleon's decree, the British government announced, that it held itself at liberty to adopt countervailing regulations, if it saw fit, without regard to the treaty. Jefferson's course, in this condition of affairs, in refusing to submit the treaty to the Senate, was looked upon as a high-handed measure, and he was denounced, by the federalists especially, and the commercial classes; he was also twitted with his manifest preference for France and hatred of England; but the party stood by him and supported his course. Monroe and Pinckney were not pleased at the treatment of their labors, and when, in October, 1807, they attempted to open anew negotiations, Mr. Canning quietly told them that any such procedure was wholly "inadvisable." As aiding to increase the ill feeling already existing against England, we may mention here that the assault on the Chesapeake, Commodore Barron, by a British frigate, the Leopard, in the latter part of June, was a most outrageous affair, and i stirred up the people everywhere to the very highest point of indignation and desire for vengeance. The president issued a proclamation, July 2d, interdicting all armed British vessels from the harbors and waters of the United States; and had almost any one else but Jefferson been president, war with England would have begun at once, instead of putting it off for four or five more years, in which to endure the insolence and vindictiveness of Great Britain.

The Tenth Congress was summoned together, October 22, 1807, and Jefferson, in his message, enlarged upon existing difficulties with England, but passed over the infamous tyranny and injustice of France; an l so he recommended gunboats, etc., again. Feeling in Congress was growing warm; and when, in December, a confidential message was sent in, recommending "an inhibition of the departure of our vessels from the ports of the United States," the wishes of the president were speedily gratified. A bill laying an embargo was passed in the House, December 22d, by a vote of 82 to 44; the Senate voted to the same effect, 22 to 6; and all American vessels were thenceforward prohibited from sailing for foreign ports, all foreign vessels from taking out cargoes, and all coasting vessels were required to give bonds to land their cargoes in the United States. The embargo was violently denounced by the opposition, and a portion of the democrats, or administration party, as useless, so far as compelling either France or England to yield an inch; they were both determined, if possible, to drive our country to join one or the other, and, of course, go to war with one or the other. Indeed, as Cooper rather dryly says, "with a foreign trade that employed 700,000 tons of American shipping alone, Congress passed a law declaring an unlimited embargo for all the purposes of foreign commerce, on every port in the Union; *anticipating a large portion of the injuries that might be expected from an open enemy, by inflicting them itself!*" In this fearful struggle which was going on in Europe, England showed no disposition to yield. "Orders in Council" were issued, November 11th, in retaliation for the "Berlin Decree." By these orders, all neutral trade was prohibited with the ports of France and her allies, or of any country at war with Great Britain, and with all other European ports from which the British flag was excluded, unless such trade should be carried on through her ports, under her licenses, and paying duties to her exchequer. Napoleon, on the other hand, fulminated his "Milan Decree," on the 17th of December, 1807, and seized upon this pretext to complete his system of blockade and confiscation, by which he hoped effectually to cut off the commercial and financial resources of Great Britain. By this decree it was declared, that every vessel which should submit to be searched by a British ship of war, or which should touch at a British port, or pay any impost whatever to the British government, should be *denationalized*, and subject to seizure and condemnation. The two great belligerent powers thus mutually rivalled each other in the work of destroying the commerce of the only remaining neutral State which their indiscriminate violence had left out of the circle of hostility. At the close of 1807, England sent Mr. Rose as special minister to the United States to settle the difficulty arising out of the assault on the Chesapeake; but he took such ground on his part, and Jefferson insisted on opening up the question of impressments, etc., on behalf of the United States, that the mission was a failure, and Mr. Rose returned to England. The president sent to Congress a variety of papers, messages, and the like, in February and March, 1808, which received due attention and action. The president was authorized to suspend the embargo, if he pleased, and the session closed, April 25th.

Jefferson, who had found that power and elevation do not always confer happiness or peace, refused to be a candidate for re-election, and said, quite pathetically, in a letter, "Never did a prisoner, released from his chains, feel such relief as I shall on shaking off the shackles of power." As stated on a previous page (p. 135), Madison was in the legitimate order of succession, and he was nominated accordingly. The federalists were too weak to accomplish anything, but they put forward Pinckney and King again. The result was, we may here mention, that Madison received 122 votes out of 176, and Clinton, for vice-president, received 113. Our limits do not admit of details respecting the acts, supplementary, suspensory, and explanatory, by which the embargo was made more rigid, or alleviated, as occasion seemed to require; or respecting the violence of the debates in Congress, and the duels which arose out of expressions which appeared to apply to persons, rather than to principles, or politics. It is sufficient to quote the sarcastic language of John Quincy Adams, in speaking of the mighty belligerents, and what was done to meet the emergency: "Jefferson met them with moral philosophy and commercial restrictions, with dry-docks and gun-boats—with non-intercourses and embargoes, till *the American nation were told that they could not be kicked into a war*, and till they were taunted by a British statesman in the imperial parliament of England, with their five fir frigates and their striped bunting. Jefferson pursued his policy of peace till it brought the nation to the borders of internal war. An embargo of fourteen months' duration was at last reluctantly abandoned by him, when it had ceased to be obeyed by the people, and State courts were ready to pronounce it unconstitutional." If it did any good, it was small in comparison with the harm and mischief which flowed from it, and the permanent injury which it did to the commerce of our country. Congress reassembled, November 7th, 1808, and Jefferson sent in his last message, a long, carefully prepared, and important paper. Debates, reports, etc., about the embargo occupied the main attention of Congress. This measure, as we have said above, was a failure. Neither England nor France had been moved at all by it. Neither "decrees" nor "orders" had been repealed. France cared not a rush for America's interests. Great Britain was still supreme on the sea—invincible. Our country was the poorer by some $50,000,000 of exports, the treble of what war would have cost us, as Jefferson himself admitted just as he went out of office. At the close of November three resolutions were proposed in the House, viz.: 1st. That the United States cannot, without a sacrifice of their rights, honor, and independence, submit to the late edicts of England and France. 2d. That it is expedient to prohibit the admission of either the ships or merchandise of those belligerents into the ports of the United States. 3d. That the country ought to be immediately placed in a state of defence. The first two passed by a large vote; the last unanimously. In the Senate, a motion to repeal the embargo act was lost by twenty-five against six; at the same time, as Tucker puts it, a large portion of the dominant party "entertained strong hopes that some course would be taken during the present session, by which the industry and enterprise of the country would be again put into activity, its vessels be once more suffered to venture on the ocean, and, perhaps, be permitted to arm in their own defence, if not to make reprisals. Indeed, there was no one who did not admit that war would be preferable to the continuance of the embargo beyond a a time not very distant; and every day was adding to the number of those who believed that time already arrived." Early in January, 1809, Jefferson was armed with new powers for enforcing the embargo, which stirred up more ill blood, and led to his being charged with ambitious longings for arbitrary power at home, while he was entirely submissive to the will of Napoleon abroad. Fearing the danger which threatened from New England, Congress, at the end of February, repealed the embargo as to all nations except France and England. This measure was called the non-intercourse law. The Tenth Congress came to an end on the 4th of March, and at the same time Jefferson's public life reached its close. Of course, the third president received numerous testimonials of the high estimate in which he was held by his friends and admirers. Jefferson always has had admirers, and probably always will have; but he has had also many and bitter enemies. It will probably always remain uncertain among Americans as to what precisely his deserts are. If he were not the profound statesman and large-hearted patriot his friends claimed him to be, he was undoubtedly in possession of vast influence, and wielded it with consummate skill, for eight eventful years. If he were not a mere party leader, as his enemies openly and constantly asserted, it is undeniable that he never lost sight of the interest and the advancement of the party at whose head he was placed. Let the reader judge for himself after carefully weighing the facts which are on record, and the principles which Jefferson avowed in his writings.

On the 4th of March, 1809, James Madison delivered his inaugural address, and took the oath of office. His address was reasonably short, and in good tone and temper. His cabinet consisted of R. Smith, of Maryland, secretary of state; Albert Gallatin, secretary of the treasury; W. Eustis, secretary of war; Paul Hamilton, secretary of the navy; and C. A. Rodney, attorney-general. Madison came into power at a critical period. Matters had reached such a state that the opinion prevailed largely abroad, that our countrymen would submit to any indignities sooner than defend themselves in a manly way. England had never been satisfied with the result of the Revolutionary War. She had ever since acted in an overbearing, offensive, and unhandsome style towards the growing Republic of the west; and she had put forth claims and assertions, which it was impossible for any free people to submit to and retain its self-respect. And France, under the grasping ambition of Napoleon, wished to treat the United States as a sort of ward of hers, as one bound to be subservient, and to be deeply impressed with sentiments of gratitude and admiration for past favors and present smiles of approval. The country, it is true, was in no fitting condition to go to war. Jefferson's policy had nearly destroyed the navy, and preparations for defence against invasion were scandalously insufficient. War would be carried on under every disadvantage, as regards finances, and the like. Yet, as neither England nor France would do what was right by peaceable means, our fathers were resolved to assert and maintain their rights by force of arms; and, though war did not break out immediately, it was evident that war must come before long. Mr. Erskine was the British minister at Washington at this date, and was laudably anxious to effect a settlement of difficulties between the United States and Great Britain. Negotiations were rapidly pushed forward, and on the 19th of April the president issued a proclamation, announcing the intended withdrawal of the offensive "orders," on the 10th of the following June, and the renewal of the trade with Great Britain on the same day. The news of this arrangement was received throughout the Union with the highest degree of gratification; and the general exultation furnished decisive evidence of the strong desire of all classes of persons to be at peace with Great Britain. Fresh activity was roused at once, and American vessels, in unusually large numbers, gladly ventured forth to avail themselves of renewed commercial intercourse with England.

The Eleventh Congress assembled for special session, May 22d, 1809, and remained together till June 20th, without accomplishing much of any moment to the welfare of the country. Madison's message related to urgent matters in regard to our foreign relations, and expressed hope of brighter days near at hand. The Pritish government, however, not at all pleased with Mr. Erskine's conduct, peremptorily refused to carry into effect the arrangement agreed upon between him and the secretary of state. The news of this result reached the United States just after the adjournment of Congress; whereupon the president, issued another proclamation, August 10th, declaring the non-intercourse act to be revived, and in full force. It is hardly possible to imagine the irritating effect upon the community produced by this sudden dashing of the hopes and expectations of commercial advantages. "Free trade and sailor's rights!" was an exclamation heard on every hand; the impressment of our seamen, and the violations of our flag, were discussed and denounced vehemently at public meetings and elsewhere; and had Madison then come forward boldly, and put the contest with Great Britain to the issue of the sword, there can be no doubt that the war would have met with popular favor and support. But he was too cautious and peace-loving, to hasten matters and precipitate the crisis which was evidently not far distant; and whatever judgment may be pronounced upon his policy, it is but right and just to give the due meed of praise to the purity of his motives. The federalists took occasion to censure the administration because of this ill turn of affairs; and at the same time many of the republicans held that the policy of the executive was too lukewarm and conciliatory towards England. Early in October, Mr. Jackson arrived as minister in place of Mr. Erskine. He seems to have had very high notions of his own consequence, and took the supercilious tone in his intercourse with the secretary of state. He even dared to make dishonorable insinuations in regard to what had taken place with Mr. Erskine; whereupon he was informed that, as he did not know his proper place, no further intercourse could be had with him. Congress assembled, November 29th, 1809, and the president sent in his message the next day. In it he gave a clear view of the existing state of our foreign relations; called the attention of Congress to the state of the national defences; recommended the "giving to our militia, the great bulwark of our security, and resource of our power, an organization the best adapted to eventual situations, for which the United States ought to be prepared;" assured the House that no loan had been found necessary, but that a deficiency in the revenue for the ensuing year was to be expected; and concluded his message with words of encouragement and congratulation: "In the midst of the wrongs and vexations experienced from external causes, there is much room for congratulation on the prosperity and happiness flowing from our situation at home. . . . . . Recollecting always, that for every advantage which may contribute to distinguish our lot from that to which others are doomed by the unhappy spirit of the times, we are indebted to that Divine Providence whose goodness has been so remarkably extended to this rising nation, it becomes us to cherish a devout gratitude, and to implore from the same omnipotent source, a blessing on the consultations and measures about to be undertaken for the welfare of our beloved country." Both Houses passed resolutions in support of the course pursued towards the British envoy, who was soon after recalled; but his conduct met with no censure at home, and no apology was offered to the American government. Congress adjourned May 12th, after a session of more than five months, and accomplishing almost nothing towards sustaining the honor and rights of the nation. Napoleon resented the passage of the non-intercourse act of March, 1809, and immediately issued a new decree, at Rambouillet, aimed especially at American commerce. About 150 vessels, captured by the French, were condemned and sold, and every American ship entering a French port was declared confiscated. This outrage was taken quite meekly by our government, and Napoleon, early in August, 1810, announced the recall of the "decrees" of Berlin and Milan, on November 1st, following, provided that the British "orders in Council" should also be revoked, or the United States should cause their rights to be respected by the English. Napoleon's minister indulged himself in language which was as ridiculous as it was impudent: *e. g.*, "His Majesty loves the Americans. Their prosperity and their commerce are within the scope of his policy. The independence of America is one of the principal titles of glory to France. Since that epoch the Emperor is pleased in aggrandizing the United States," etc. The British government, on their part, refused to rescind the orders in Council, which led to a proclamation interdicting all commercial intercourse with England. As for Napoleon, with his usual lack of veracity and sincerity, he not only declared the Berlin and Milan decrees fundamental laws of his empire, but also gave notice that no remuneration or redress was to be expected for plundering our ships by French armed vessels. Further trouble arose in a new quarter. West Florida having, in September, 1810, declared herself independent of Spain, asked to be annexed to the United States, and the president authorized its becoming a part of the Territory of Orleans. Naturally enough, England, now the ally of Spain against France, took this procedure on the part of the United States with very ill grace, and looked upon it as, in part, a blow aimed at herself. And we can believe that she endeavored to carry out her policy towards the United States with fresh alacrity and zeal, and that the annoying, insulting, and outrageous conduct of the commanders of her ships of war stationed before the principal harbors of the United States, met with her entire approbation.

Congress assembled December 5th, 1810, and were furnished the next day with a long and important message from the president. The occupancy of West Florida gave rise to an ardent debate; and when the inhabitants of the Territory of Orleans petitioned to be admitted as a State into the Union, the federalists strenuously resisted the measure on constitutional grounds, Josiah Quincy even going so far as to declare that if this bill passed, the Union would necessarily be dissolved thereby. The bill, however, was finally adopted by a large majority. The question, as to the renewal of the charter of the Bank of the United States came up in the House early in January, 1811; it was ably debated, but the whole subject was indefinitely postponed on the 24th. In the Senate, a bill was introduced by Mr. Crawford, February 5th, for the renewal of the charter. After long and labored discussion, the question was taken on the 20th, and a tie resulting, the casting vote was given by George Clinton, vice-president, in the negative. Argument and entreaty were alike vain. Not even a temporary extension of the bank's existence was allowed; and its affairs were placed in the hands of trustees in order to bring them to a final settlement. Not only the members, but the whole country took a deep interest in the proceedings of Congress. The vacillating and insidious course of the French government, and the persistency of England in enforcing her lawless edicts and regulations against the commerce of the United States, kept alive the irritation and excitement in the community, and greatly aggravated the violence of party assaults and recriminations. As having reference to the appeal to arms, which many saw clearly must be made soon, the president was authorized to negotiate a loan of $5,000,000; and it was felt quite generally, that all further expedients would prove inefficient.* Soon after the adjournment of Congress, March 3d, 1811, a rencontre happened on the water, which roused the feelings of the people to a high pitch of patriotic eagerness for battle with England. Ever since the disgraceful attack on the Chesapeake (p. 138), the officers of the navy seemed to have longed for an opportunity of wiping out what they considered the stigma on the service by that affair, and the whole maritime force of the nation was kept at home. The English, says Cooper, increased their cruisers on the American coast, in proportion as the Americans themselves did, though their vessels no longer lay off the harbors, impressing men and detaining ships. Still they were numerous; cruised at no great distance; and by keeping up constant communications between Bermuda and Halifax, may be said to have intercepted nearly every ship that passed from one hemisphere to the other. Early in May, word was brought to Commodore Rodgers, on board the President, forty-four, that a man had been impressed from an American brig by an English vessel of war, off Sandy Hook. The President was promptly put in readiness to inquire into the facts, and on the 16th of May, at noon, made a sail about six leagues from the land, to the southward of New York city. It was soon perceived that she was a vessel of war, and in the course of the afternoon Rodgers came within hailing distance. Instead of answering, a shot was fired by the Little Belt (such was her name), which entered the mainmast of the President. Of course this led to firing in return, and it soon became evident that the Little Belt was no match for the President. She was entirely crippled, 31 killed and wounded, while Rodgers' ship was unhurt and only a boy wounded. This affair produced much excitement, embittering the feeling of hostility in England, and led to much censure of Commodore Rodgers. Another affair on the water soon after showed the state of feeling existing. The United States, Commodore Decatur, met two British ships near New York, and a gun was fired during the hailing, said to have been accidentally discharged, but more probably by design; happily, the commanders acted with prudence, and no battle resulted, although many desired a fight. Mr. Foster, the newly appointed British minister, arrived in the United States, in June, 1811, and speedily entered upon his duties. Long and import-

* The third census of the United States gave the following result; number of free whites, 5,862,073; number of slaves, 1,191,364; all others, except Indians not taxed, 186,377; making a total population of 7,239,814.

ant correspondence ensued, in which it was evident that Great Britain was not yet prepared to recede from the stand she had taken, and deal justly and rightly with America. Reparation was offered for the attack on the Chesapeake, by which the act was to be formally disavowed, etc. But with respect to the vital questions which sprang out of the orders in Council, and the claim to impressment, Mr. Foster was not at liberty, even if disposed, to afford satisfaction. These odious and insulting orders and claims continued to be enforced, and the nation was rapidly verging to the point of armed resistance against England. Dispatches from abroad showed, that no less than twenty-six vessels had been condemned in the court of admiralty, and that others were about to share the same fate. All the evils of war, nearly, had already fallen upon the United States; while England was enjoying the advantages of war without the cost. In fact, as it was estimated, her cruisers had captured nine hundred American vessels, since the year 1803. The larger part of the country, except New England, was in a state of exasperation and ready to go to war; but Madison held back, and his cabinet were at variance on the subject. James Monroe took the place of Smith as secretary of state, and Pinckney became attorney-general. In the north-west the Indians were becoming excited and dangerous, through the influence of British emissaries, and Tecumseh, a Shawnee chief, seemed desirous to emulate the doings of the noted Pontiac (p. 70), and organize a confederacy against the white men. He and his warriors met General Harrison, governor of Indiana Territory, in August, 1810, at a council at Vincennes, but with no result except to incite them to war and bloodshed. The following spring, matters came to a crisis; the people were greatly alarmed and called for help, and in November, Harrison marched to their relief. On his approach near the Indian town, the principal chiefs came out with offers of peace and submission, and requested Harrison to encamp for the night; but, as he suspected, this was only a treacherous artifice. At four in the morning, the camp was furiously assailed, and a bloody contest ensued; the Indians were however repulsed. The loss on the part of the Americans was sixty-two killed, and one hundred and twenty-six wounded; a still greater number fell on the side of the red men. In fact, this was one of the most desperate and hardly contested battles ever fought with the Indians. Tecumseh was present, and Harrison, having destroyed the so-called prophet's town, and established forts, returned to Vincennes, and received much praise for his successful conduct of the expedition.

The Twelfth Congress assembled, Nov. 4th, 1811, and Henry Clay was elected speaker. The president, in his message, enlarged upon the critical condition of affairs, especially in regard to the unfriendly and hostile spirit of England, and the failure on the part of France to repair wrongs committed by her and do the United States justice. He urged the necessity and "the duty of putting the United States into an armor and an attitude demanded by the crisis and corresponding to the national spirit and expectations;" he recommended adequate provisions in men, ships, and all the materials of warlike preparations, and for appropriations suitable to the emergency. Laws to regulate the mercantile marine, and suppress smuggling, were also called for; and the finances were said to be in a favorable condition. The tone of the message was thought to be rather tame, and the western and southern members determined upon more energetic measures. The committee on foreign relations recommended six resolutions: — 1st. To fill up the ranks of the present military establishment by the aid of a bounty. 2d. To raise an additional force of ten thousand men by the like means. 3d. To authorize the president to accept the services of fifty thousand volunteers. 4th. To give like authority to order out such detachments of militia as the public service may require. 5th. To cause the public vessels not now in service to be fitted out imme diately. 6th. To permit merchant ships, owned and navigated wholly by American citizens, to arm in self-defence. An earnest debate followed; the first five of the resolutions were adopted by large majorities, and the sixth was laid on the table. The feeling manifested in the Senate was equally strong, and every indication pointed towards war. The British minister undertook to defend the course of his government; but the secretary of state, in his reply, Jan. 14th, 1812, expressed the conviction that it was impossible to see anything in the conduct of England "but a determined hostility to the rights and interests of the United States." The position of the president at this time was far from agreeable. He was averse to war, quite as much so as Jefferson, who preferred using money and diplomacy (p. 134); his cabinet were not the men to carry forward matters in such a crisis; the army amounted to almost nothing, and the navy had nearly been destroyed by Jefferson and the democrats; and the finances were in no sort of condition to enter upon war. Moreover, Madison wished to be honored as his predecessor had been by a re-election; and so when he was waited upon by some of the more ardent of the party, and significantly informed that he might be dropped, and De Witt Clinton put in the presidential chair unless he acceded to their wishes, he agreed to the proposal and undertook to push onward the struggle with England. Mr. Gallatin, secretary of the treasury, was called upon to devise ways and means to meet the expenses incident to such a state of things as was now virtually at hand. On the 10th of January, 1812, he sent in a reply to the application for information, in which he expressed his opinion, that in case of war, the imposts would not yield more than $2,500,000. The duties on tonnage, merchandise, etc., he estimated at $6,000,000, leaving a deficiency of $3,600,000 to meet the expenditures of 1813. An annual loan, he thought of $10,000,000 would be required during the war, and to meet the interest on this, the deficiency in the revenue, he recommended the raising $3,000,000 by a direct tax and $2,000,000 by indirect taxes, such as licenses, excise, stamps, etc. He concluded that there would probably be no difficulty in effecting the loans suggested, and recommended that they be made irredeemable for ten years. Towards the close of February, the House acted upon this subject, and a loan of $11,000,000 was determined upon by a vote of ninety-two to twenty-nine. As the loan did not fill up very rapidly, we may mention that the issue of $5,000,000 of treasury notes was directed, and the impost was doubled. There was no other security for notes or loans than the surplus of the $8,000,000 a year theretofore pledged by way of sinking-fund to redeem the national debt, then amounting to $55,000,000. And these, as has been said "were the only acts of the war-declaring Congress for invigorating the money-sinew of the war."

Early in April, 1812, an embargo was laid on all vessels then in port or thereafter arriving. The president still hoped to be able to avoid the last resort; but the ruling spirits in the party were resolved upon war. Various other measures of a warlike tendency were adopted, such as prohibiting exportation of specie, organizing corps of artificers, etc. On the 8th of April, Louisiana was admitted into the Union. Napoleon, pursuing his usual reckless course of injustice, treated Mr. Barlow, our minister, with virtual contempt, and would neither redress, nor promise to abstain from injuries to our commerce; and in England, despite the sufferings of the manufacturing interests, and immense taxation, the ministry persisted in refusing to revoke the odious orders in Council. When it was too late, however, at the end of June, 1812, the government *did* revoke the orders, but to no purpose; war was already declared. Mr. Foster addressed a letter to the secretary of state, in which he reviewed the existing controversy, and, in substance, announced that England would not recede from the ground she had assumed. Matters had now reached their crisis; something besides talking must now be resorted to; and the president determined upon his course. On the 1st of June, 1812, Madison transmitted to Congress a confidential message, of considerable length, which presented, clearly and forcibly, the various grounds on which war was held to be necessary under the existing state of affairs. We regret that we have not space to give this important document in full; for it will repay perusal. The committee on foreign relations reported on the message within a few days, and declared that the encroachments, insults, and claims of England had become intolerable, and that an appeal to arms was absolutely necessary. The federalists and a portion of the democrats opposed with all their might the declaration of war; but it was settled against them on the 4th of June, by a vote of 79 to 49. In the Senate, there was a long and hot debate for nearly two weeks, and on the 17th the bill was carried by a vote of 19 to 13.* Immediately the act was drawn up in the following terms:—"An Act declaring war between the United Kingdom of Great Britain and Ireland, and the dependencies thereof, and the United States of America and their territories. Be it enacted, etc. That WAR be, and the same is hereby declared to exist between the United Kingdom of Great Britain and Ireland, and the dependencies thereof, and the United States of America and their territories; and that the president of the United States be and is hereby authorized to use the whole land and naval force of the United States to carry the same into effect, and to issue to private armed vessels of the United States commissions, or letters of marque and general reprisal, in such form as he shall think proper, and under the seal of the United States, against the vessels, goods, and effects of the government of the same United Kingdom of Great Britain and Ireland, and the subjects thereof." On the 19th, the president issued his proclamation, announcing the fact, and calling upon the people to sustain the government in the work now entered upon. Congress, on the 26th, passed an act for letters of marque, etc., from which much advantage was expected to be attained by our enterprising countrymen. On the 6th of July, this very long session came to an end; and on the 9th, the president issued a proclamation (which Congress had recommended), appointing the third Thursday in August as a day of humiliation and prayer; which day, we may mention, was duly observed throughout nearly the whole land.

For a second time our country was in arms against England, and, smarting under a sense of wrong and insult persisted in for so many years, she was roused up fully to enter upon the deadly conflict. Certainly, in many respects, the United States were far more capable now than at the Revolution, of maintaining the fight in behalf of liberty and justice. Americans now had grown and increased in national pride, and held themselves to be the equals of any nation in the world. And, however absurd it might have seemed, on a review of the relative power and position of England and the United States, for the latter to venture single-handed upon such a struggle as this, Americans did not hesitate. With a sort of self-reliant audacity, they counted themselves a host, and deemed no odds sufficient to fright them from the tented field and the bloody conflict. There were unquestionably zeal and spirit enough in our countrymen for this emergency. There was courage enough, strong hands and stout hearts enough; but it must be confessed, there was no adequate preparation for the

* Of the seventy-nine members of the House who voted for the declaration of war, forty-six resided south, and thirty-three north of the Delaware; of the nineteen senators who voted for the war, fourteen resided south and five north of the Delaware. New England opposed the war; Massachusetts (including Maine), New Hampshire, Rhode Island, and Connecticut, with a large part of New York, and the majority of New Jersey, deprecated hostilities; the west and south, with the large central States of Virginia and Pennsylvania, warmly supported the declaration; Vermont was the only New England State in favor of the war.

contest with so powerful an enemy as England. Neither in men nor in officers; neither in the executive, nor his cabinet; neither in the financial provisions, nor in regard to the nature and character of the war, was there the proper foresight, the just conception, the needful training, the fitting ability for the vigorous and successful prosecution of hostilities against the neighboring colonies of England by land, or her vast and terrible array of ships of war on the sea. The haughty mistress of the ocean had her thousand floating castles, bearing aloft the royal flag, and innumerable cruisers and privateers; while the entire naval force of the United States, in ordinary or in building, was only eight frigates and twelve sloops! But, bad as this was, it was not the worst feature in the then position of affairs. The rage of party feelings; the unhappy discords of democrats and federalists; the singularly bitter and determined opposition of New England men, their legislatures, men of wealth and talent and position; — these and the like gave sad indications of trials and troubles to be encountered in carrying on the war. In the middle and southern States the majority were in favor of the war; but it was in the west that there was real enthusiasm on the subject; and the stalwart denizens of that section of our country were ready, to a man, to fight for the cause of liberty and equal rights. With them, enthusiasm and the love of country glowed in every bosom, and they were eager for the call to the battle-field. Conscious of the dangers to which the frontier was exposed from savage incursions; fully persuaded that England was engaged in the mean and detestable occupation of inciting the Indians to murderous hostility; and with imaginations fired with the prospect of conquering Canada, and expelling the enemy from the continent; the people of the west entered heart and soul into the contest; and suffered not a doubt to enter their minds that victory would crown their patriotic efforts. The appointment of officers for the army was a matter of great perplexity to the president; for there was so little material to choose out of, so little of any value, that it became a hard task to decide upon whom to place the responsibility of command. Dearborn was made commander-in-chief, and with him were associated as brigadier-generals, James Wilkinson, Wade Hampton, William Hull, and Joseph Bloomfield. The president also appointed Thomas Pinckney a major-general. In the case of these officers it was soon after discovered, that age and long cessation from military toils and activity would seriously interfere with their being able to prosecute hostilities with vigor and reasonable prospect of success. Then, too, although Congress had authorized the enlistment of twenty-five thousand men, it was found impossible to fill up the ranks from the few who felt any necessity of enlisting. The regulars amounted to about 5000 men, but were scattered over the country. The president was empowered to receive 50,000 volunteers, and to call out 100,000 militia; but these were unreliable troops at best, and, moreover, some of the State authorities refused to obey the president's demand for militia.

The invasion of Canada, as above stated, was a favorite project, and it was supposed that there could be little or no doubt as to the result. Hull, commander of the northwestern army, was to begin the attack, with about 700 regulars and 2,000 Ohio militia. He was to have also the co-operation of the army of the centre, on the Niagara frontier, consisting of some 2,000 regulars and over 2,000 militia. If Hull had possessed any military capacity, and been properly supported at Washington, he might very possibly have succeeded; but as he was one of the poorest specimens of a general, and as the war department was wretchedly managed at the capital, it need excite no wonder that the expedition resulted in nothing but defeat and disgrace. The particulars are of little moment. Hull set out for Detroit about the middle of June; reached that point early in July; received news of the declaration of war, through the mail, on the 2d of July; and, as his troops were anxious to do something, he crossed into Canada on the 12th, and sent out a proclamation full of bold words and such like, but wholly unsupported by bold action. He hesitated about attacking Malden, thought he would wait for his "big guns," and let the precious moment slip away. Instead of liberating Canada, he remained, week after week, in a state of inactivity as mortifying as it was inexplicable, not doing a single thing to justify either the invitations or the menaces of his proclamation; so that, whatever ardor had fired his troops was cooled greatly, and distrust and contempt expelled confidence and attachment from the hearts of the Canadians. The enemy meanwhile were not idle. Malden was reinforced; the supplies were almost entirely cut off; and Hull was getting deeper and deeper into the mire. Mackinaw fell into the hands of the British, July 17th, and Hull, when he heard the news, was panic stricken, and returned, early in August, to Detroit. The English force, under Prevost, Brock and Tecumseh (p. 144), displayed activity, and gained several victories over portions of Hull's force. Miller at Maguaga repulsed the enemy; but Heald evacuated Chicago, was overcome by the savages and conquered, and Cass and McArthur, who had gone to the relief of Brush, lost their way, and accomplished nothing. Gen. Brock, on the 15th of August, summoned Hull, at Detroit, to surrender, and this being refused, he opened his batteries on the town and fort. Hull's vacillation and timidity appeared to the officers to be disgraceful, and the result seemed to show that they were right in wishing to deprive him forcibly of his command. The British, on the 16th, marched to the attack on Detroit. Hull's force was drawn up in battle-array outside the fort, the artillery was well planted, and the Americans had no fear of meeting the enemy; but when the British were about five hundred yards distant, the astounding command was given for the troops to retire within the fort! The scene which followed beggars description; and poor Hull, anxious only to escape from his present pitiable condition, ordered a white flag to be hung out on the walls of the fort! Not a blow was struck, not a gun was fired, not a word of consultation was had with his officers, not a single stipulation for the honor of his troops; but an unconditional giving up of all to the enemy. The fortress, the garrison, and munitions of war, the detachment under Cass and M'Arthur, and even the soldiers under Captain Brush, were included in the capitulation. Brock's force was in all about 730, with 600 Indians; while Hull surrendered 2,500 men, of whom 1,200 were militia. The amazement and indignation of the whole country, at Hull's surrender, cannot adequately be depicted in words, and charges of not only cowardice and disgraceful inefficiency, but also of treason and collusion with the enemy, were freely bestowed upon the unhappy general. His official report, under date of Aug. 26th, was sent to Washington, and puts the best face possible on the whole matter. He was tried by court-martial, condemned and sentenced to be shot; but this extreme penalty was remitted by the president, while at the same time his name was stricken from the roll of the army.

These disasters in the north were very mortifying to our countrymen; but singularly enough, brilliant success came from an unexpected quarter to American arms. England had always been counted supreme upon the ocean, and her navy had gained so many illustrious victories, that it was thought to be impossible that any reverses could befall her conquering ships of war. Least of all was it supposed, that the United States, who possessed no navy, and who had at best but a few frigates and smaller vessels, would dare to encounter in battle the lordly masters of the sea. But it was speedily demonstrated to England, as well as to the world, that the gallant little navy of the United States was as able as it was willing to meet the enemy, and to teach them some lessons of value and moment. On the 19th of August, 1812, only three days after the disgrace at Detroit, Captain Hull, in the Constitution, brought unequalled glory upon that name which his uncle had rendered a bye-word in the United States, and proved to the world what the American navy was capable of performing in a fair fight with their haughty enemy. In the afternoon of the 19th, the Constitution discovered and gave chase to a large English frigate, the Guerriere, thirty-eight, Captain Dacres, who had professed himself to be extremely desirous of meeting with an American ship of war, and did not doubt, he said, that he would obtain an easy victory. Captain Hull gave strict orders not to return the enemy's fire, until they were so near that every shot was certain to take effect. When in the position he desired, Hull opened upon the Guerriere, with broadside following broadside, very rapidly and with tremendous force. In half an hour's time, the Guerriere was little better than a wreck, and Captain Dacres, having lost over a hundred men in killed and wounded, surrendered to the victorious Hull. The loss of the Constitution was only seven killed and seven wounded. As it was impossible to get the Guerriere into port, she was set fire to, and blown up in fifteen minutes. Great indeed were the exultation and enthusiasm caused by this victory; while in England unbounded astonishment and the deepest mortification fell upon those who boasted of British invincibility on the ocean, and "had publicly predicted that before the contest had continued six months, British sloops of war would lie alongside of American frigates with comparative impunity." Other victories followed that of Hull in the Constitution. On the night of the 16th of October, the British sloop of war Frolic, eighteen, convoying six merchant ships, fell in with the United States sloop-of-war Wasp, eighteen, Captain Jones. The engagement which ensued was fierce and bloody. The Wasp was much injured in her spars and rigging, brt on boarding the Frolic found the deck covered with only the dead and wounded. Thirty were killed and fifty wounded. The Wasp had only five killed and five wounded. Lieutenant Biddle lowered the English flag with his own hands, after a contest of forty-three minutes' duration. Both the Frolic and Wasp were, however, taken, a few hours later, by the Poictiers, a seventy-four. This victory dissipated effectually the notions of British invincibility at sea; but the most valuable result, perhaps, was the testimony afforded to the superiority of cool and scientific gunnery in naval combat. Sea-fights had been for the most part decided by mere animal courage and brute force. The only science shown had been in the handling of the ships, and the manœuvring of the fleets. Our naval officers, not neglecting this department of strategics, *took aim* when they discharged their guns, and brought these engagements to a speedy decision by not aimlessly squandering their shot. No amount of courage, backed mostly by noise and smoke, —and artillery badly aimed, or not aimed at all, is no more,—could stand against the heavy metal, flying true to its mark, of the American guns. A week or so later, Commodore Decatur added to his laurels by another victory. He was now in the United States, and happening to fall in with the Macedonian, a combat immediately ensued, and lasted for about an hour, when the Macedonian struck, having suffered very severely. The Constitution (Bainbridge being now in command), on the 28th of December, met with the Java, 38, and after a fight of less than an hour, the British ship became a complete wreck, and was blown up. The indignation caused by what was called "Hull's treason," led to various efforts on the part of volunteers, who flocked in, in numbers, from Ohio and Kentucky. Gen Harrison was placed in command in the latter part of September, 1812. The main division of the army, consisting of three thousand men, under Harrison in person, was at this time at the River St. Mary's. Another division, under General Winchester, consisting of two thousand, had penetrated on the road to Detroit, as far as Fort Defiance; but they were in want of provisions, and had sent to Harrison for relief. That general immediately marched with a considerable part of his troops, and on the 3d of October, joined General Winchester at Fort Defiance. He ordered a body of militia, under Tupper, to dislodge the enemy at the Rapids of the Miami, but this enterprise failed. Further westward, during September, nearly four thousand men, chiefly mounted riflemen, under command of General Hopkins, gathered at Vincennes, on the Wabash, for the purpose of chastising the Indians on the Illinois and Wabash Rivers. Earlier in the month, Captain Zachary Taylor had displayed his ability in defending Fort Harrison on the Wabash. On the 4th of September, the fort was attacked by several hundred Indians with great fury. Captain Taylor's force, though numbering fifty, consisted in fact of only eighteen effective men, the rest being incapable of duty in consequence of sickness; nevertheless, with great intrepidity and steadiness the assault was repelled, and the Indians retired in disgust. The army under Gen. Hopkins reached Fort Harrison about the 10th of October, and on the 14th crossed the Wabash, and proceeded on the march against the Kickapoo and Peoria towns; but the insubordination of both officers and men rendered the expedition futile. Other expeditions, on a minor scale, met with better success, and served to secure the frontier against the scalping knife and the midnight assaults of the savages. Military operations in the north next require notice. Volunteers and new recruits marched to the borders of Canada, and towards the close of the year the forces were chiefly concentrated in two bodies; one near Lewiston, consisting of some regulars newly enlisted, and militia, amounting to four thousand men, under General Van Rensselaer, of New York; the other in the neighborhood of Plattsburg and Greenbush, under the commander-in-chief, General Dearborn. Bodies of regulars were distributed at Black Rock, at Ogdensburg, and Sackett's Harbor, with officers of experience, for the purpose of drilling the raw troops as they arrived; and it was expected, that an invasion of Canada might be made before cold weather set in. Such officers as Pike, Boyd, and Scott were very diligent in training and disciplining the army; and with a force of between eight and ten thousand men, along the frontier, it was not unreasonable to look for some effective result in the proposed invasion of Canada. Van Rensselaer's headquarters were at Lewiston, on the Niagara River, opposite to which stood Queenstown, a fortified British post. The troops were eager for the attack. Accordingly, at four in the morning of the 11th of October, in the midst of a dreadful northeast storm and heavy rain, an attempt was made to pass the river; but, owing to the darkness of the night, and various unforeseen accidents, the passage could not be effected. The troops being still more impatient, another attempt was made, early on the morning of the 13th, under cover of the American batteries. The force designated to storm the heights, was divided into two columns; but, by some mismanagement or carelessness, there were not boats enough to carry them all over at once, and they were forced to cross in detachments. Colonel Fenwick's artillery was to follow, and then the other troops in order. The British, meanwhile, anticipating attack, had been reinforced, and at daylight opened fire upon the Americans. Captain Wool and his men behaved with great bravery, and after a severe fight the British were driven down the hill. Being again attacked by fresh troops of the enemy, they again drove the British back, Gen. Brock being mortally wounded. But the victory was not yet complete. The enemy, reinforced by Indians, advanced to the attack, but our men, under Scott and Christie, compelled them, at the point of the bayonet, to retreat. Had these brave officers and men been properly supported, a complete triumph would have crowned our arms. But, when Van Rensselaer crossed to expedite reinforcements, he was astounded to find that not a man out of 1,500, who had been boasting of their prowess, was willing to go over and join in the fight! Remonstrance and entreaties were unavailing; and so, the consequence resulted which it was impossible to prevent. Late in the afternoon, the British renewed the attack; it was met with spirit; but they had been fighting all day, and were nearly all killed or wounded; surrender was of course a necessity. A Gen. Alexander Smyth next made a vainglorious setting forth of what he could do. Having succeeded Van Rensselaer in the command, he managed to get together several thousand volunteers, with Gen. Porter to aid in the expedition. It was a clumsily managed affair, so far as Smyth was concerned. There were brave men in the army as well as brave officers, and on the 1st of December, 1812, a distinct effort was made to cross into Canada; but Smyth recalled those who had set out, ordered the volunteers to return home, and the regulars to go into winter quarters. Porter posted Smyth as a coward, and a duel resulted, wherein, having fired at one another, their nice sense of honor was soothed; the public were congratulated on the happy issue; Ingersoll dryly says, "the public would have preferred a battle in Canada." Some other efforts, under Brown, Pike, Lyons, etc., to do something, were on the whole successful. But the senile conduct of Gen. Dearborn capped the climax of the military misdeeds of 1812. He certainly had numerous difficulties to contend against; the government was disgracefully remiss in regard to supplies and support generally; and there was a sad lack of officers worth anything, and of men disciplined into soldiers; all this is true enough, but it will not serve to excuse his idleness and inactivity, and neglect to avail himself of the plainest advantages within his reach. He had 3,000 regular troops, and 3,000 militia; while the British force in Canada was not more than half that number. On the 20th of November, he sent Bloomfield to Canada to achieve some deed of daring. The British got news about the invasion three days before it took place, and as Col. Pike was leading the advance, the enemy fell in with him. It was a curious sort of fight which followed, and, as Ingersoll puts it, "each party's object was to get away from the other. Where Gens. Dearborn, Chandler and Bloomfield were during this wretched foray, did not then appear, nor can be now told; and on no occasion did Gen. Dearborn ever lead his troops into action." On the whole, then, making all due allowances for failure in this campaign, there were nevertheless encouraging results attained with reference to the future. The great body of the army was in no wise lacking in bravery; and numerous officers gave earnest of their future success. Miller, Scott, Christie, Wadsworth and Wool, gained honor for themselves and their country; and Maguaga and Queenstown will bear comparison with the heroic deeds of other days in our history.

The United States having entered upon this war with reluctance, efforts were made in the year 1812 to arrest hostilities. Proposals were made for an armistice, so as to allow of a settlement of difficulties; but the English government haughtily declined, being resolved to maintain the right (as they called it) of impressment. A correspondence took place in October, between Monroe, secretary of state, and Admiral Warren, in which Monroe distinctly affirmed that impressment would on no terms, and under no circumstances, be submitted to. Still, being desirous of peace, when the Emperor of Russia, in 1813, offered his mediation, it was cordially accepted; but England refused everything of the kind. The presidential contest, in the autumn of 1812, resulted in the election of Madison for president, and the election of Gerry for vice-president, by votes of 128 and 131. Clinton and Ingersoll, the candidates of the other section of the democrats, received 89 and 86 votes for president and vice-president. Congress assembled on the first Monday in November, and the next day the president sent in his message. It was a long and carefully prepared document—calm, but decided in tone—and strongly patriotic in its sentiments. Most of the time of the session was taken up in giving attention to the army and navy, and in providing means for carrying on the war. Twenty new regiments were authorized, with ten companies of rangers, additional officers, etc.; and four 74-gunships, six frigates, and six sloops of war were ordered to be constructed. A law was passed, in February, 1813, providing for a loan of $16,000,000, which, with the issues of treasury notes, and other loans, made the gross sum of $37,000,000, borrowed by this Congress for carrying on hostilities, but without providing for the redemption of the debt by the imposition of additional taxes. In January, 1813, the committee on foreign relations made their report, using strong and severe language against England, and urging vigorously that the "practice of impressment" is one against which our country will fight until it be given up. On the 24th of February, the president sent a message, denouncing the mean and wicked efforts by which the British were trying to sever New England from the Union, by offering trade licenses, etc. The Twelfth Congress came to an end, March 3d, 1813. The next day Mr. Madison entered upon his second term of office, with the usual ceremonies; his inaugural was brief, but not lacking in energy and earnestness, in defence of the war against England. Some changes in the cabinet took place: W. Jones took the place of Hamilton, as secretary of the navy; and General Armstrong succeeded Eustis in the war department. The campaign of 1813 was looked forward to with anxiety, and it was hoped that some of the disgrace of the previous year might be wiped out.

Harrison was in command in the northwest (p. 149), and had sent Winchester, at the very beginning of the year, to get possession of the Rapids of the Miami, in which he succeeded. Hearing of the state of things at Frenchtown, a detachment of 660 men was sent to relieve the inhabitants; and this also was successful; but the troops were only 18 miles from Malden, whence the British might speedily be expected, and so Winchester, on the 19th of January, set out with 250 men, to reinforce Lewis and Allen. Strange to say, the most singular and culpable carelessness was manifested, in respect to providing for sudden attack by the enemy. Approach was made in the night, and early on the morning of the 22d, a violent assault resulted, from the English and Indians. The detachment was driven back; Lewis and Winchester were made prisoners, and Allen was shot. The British commander, Proctor, finding that he had Winchester a prisoner, determined to obtain the surrender of the rest of the force by fraud and falsehood. He assured Winchester, that nothing but an immediate surrender could save the Americans from an indiscriminite massacre by the Indians, and he gave his pledge, that if they would promptly lay down their arms, they should be protected from massacre; if this were not done, Proctor declared that he would set fire to the village, and would not be responsible for the conduct of the savages. Winchester, intimidated by this threat, sent an order to the troops under Major Madison, to surrender; which order was reluctantly obeyed, with the distinct understanding, that the lives, persons, and effects of the prisoners should be protected and properly cared for. At this time, the killed, wounded, and missing, of the little army, including those that had been outside of the pickets, amounted to more than three hundred men; those under Madison, who capitulated at Winchester's bidding, numbered thirty-five officers, and above four hundred and fifty men. The barbarities which followed were of the most shocking character, and Proctor and his companions steeped themselves in infamy. Our officers and men were murdered in cold blood; every indignity was heaped upon them; and the pledged word of Proctor only displayed what a liar and a scoundrel he was capable of being. Harrison now constructed a stronghold at the Rapids, and named it Fort Meigs; but the miserable work Winchester had made prevented his attacking Malden this season. Early in April, 1813, Harrison learning that the enemy were about undertaking a siege of the fort, made his preparations accordingly. On the 1st of May, the British batteries opened fire, which was returned with spirit by the besieged. On the 5th, a brilliant sally was made, and the enemy driven back, their cannon spiked, etc. Proctor soon after retreated. In June an offer was made by the Indians, in Ohio, to follow Harrison into Canada. The government had heretofore declined using the Indians; but, as it was necessary to have them, as friends or enemies, it was deemed best to accept their offer, on the express condition, that they should spare their prisoners, and not assail defenceless women and children.

Operations on the northern frontier were carried on with varied success. Incursions were made by the British quite frequently, whereupon Major Forsythe, in command at Ogdensburg, resolved to retaliate. This he did to excellent purpose, early in February, having taken fifty-two prisoners, together with a large amount of public property. On the 21st, Ogdensburg was attacked by the British; our men fought bravely, but were compelled to retire, and abandon their artillery and stores to the enemy. General Pike, a brave and energetic officer, was diligently occupied at Sackett's Harbor in disciplining the recruits as they arrived, a work of great difficulty and requiring the utmost patience and perseverance. Great exertions had also been made by Commodore Chauncey to build and equip a squadron on the lake, which should enable the Americans there to cope with the British; and in the course of the spring he had under him two sloops and eleven schooners, manned with crews who doubted not their ability to contend successfully with their enemies. Chauncey was ordered by the navy department to co-operate with General Dearborn in any operations he might direct. Accordingly, on the 25th of April, with sixteen hundred men on board, the flotilla sailed from Sackett's Harbor, for the purpose of making an attack on York (now Toronto), the capital of Upper Canada. General Pike was in command, and on the 27th the fleet safely reached its destination. The British tried to prevent the landing of our men, but unsuccessfully. The attack was gallantly made, and the British driven back, when just as they were near the enemy's main works, a magazine exploded, killing Pike, and 100 of our men. The British having destroyed all they could, retreated, except the militia in York. The victory was opportune, and the amount of stores, etc., captured was valued at fully $500,000. Early in May, York was evacuated, and it was determined to attack Forts George and Erie: the attack was successfully made on the 27th, and the British driven out. At this same date, Prevost, the British commander, made a desperate effort to take Sackett's Harbor; but he was repulsed. Early in June, Generals Winder and Chandler were sent against the British, under Vincent, who held a strong position at the head of Burlington Bay. Our troops encamped at Stony Creek, where they were attacked at night by the enemy; an irregular conflict ensued, in which Winder and Chandler were made prisoners. The impression at the time was, that culpable negligence had been manifested by the leaders of this expedition. Two weeks later Colonel Boerstler, with 600 men, marched against Beaver's Dam, but he was entrapped on the way and surrendered without a struggle. Subsequent to this, during June and July, 1813, the contest was little else than a war of posts. General Boyd, we may mention, induced by the same considerations previously noted above, determined to accept the services of the Seneca warriors under Cornplanter, an intelligent and educated chief. The same stipulation, however, in regard to the unresisting and defenceless was expressly insisted on, and we believe was observed by the Indians during the war. On the 11th of July, the British made an attack on Black Rock, but were driven back, losing nine of their men and Colonel Bishop, their commander. On the 28th of July, an expedition was undertaken against York, which had been re-captured by the enemy after the battle of Stony Creek. Three hundred men, under Colonel Winfield Scott, embarked in Commodore Chauncey's fleet, and suddenly landing at that place, destroyed the public stores and property, released a number of Colonel Boerstler's men, and returned to Sackett's Harbor, with only a trifling loss. General Dearborn, on account of age and infirmities, retired from the service, and General Wilkinson was appointed to the command of the army of the centre. Such armed barges and schooners as the Americans had been able to collect on Lake Champlain, were taken by the enemy, who then attacked Plattsburg, and destroyed the public buildings and private property, and carried off rich booty. This, and similar acts, stirred up deep feeling in the bosoms of our countrymen. In Europe, the declining power and greatness of Napoleon were already producing their effect, and the state of things was verging to the point which gave England an opportunity to devote more attention to the war in America. The naval victories of the United States had not only mortified British pride, but had also naturally excited a strong desire to punish so audacious a competitor on the ocean. Early in the year 1813, it was known that a British squadron had arrived at Bermuda, with a body of troops on board, and a large supply of bombs and other means of attacking the cities and towns on the seacoast. As in the Revolution, it was determined to devastate and lay waste towns and villages, in every accessible direction. The necessary effect in this, as in other cases, was to rouse the spirit of the people; and in the result, we find, that the outrages of the British, under Cockburn and his ass'stants, stirred up intense indignation, and incited the Americans to deeds of revenge. Early in February, a squadron appeared in Delaware Bay, which destroyed many vessels, and blockaded the Bay. On the 10th, Lewiston, Delaware, was bombarded, but it was in the Chesapeake that Cockburn acquired principal notoriety and disgrace, by his piratical excursions, his robbing houses, plundering families, destroying public property, and inflicting insults and injuries on women and children. Frenchtown was assaulted and plundered. Havre de Grace, early in May, shared the same fate; as did also Georgetown and Fredericktown. Admiral Warren having arrived with additional ships, much alarm was felt in the neighbouring region. Baltimore, Annapolis, and Norfolk were threatened; and on the 22nd of June, an assault on the last named place was undertaken. The British were met by our troops at Craney Island, and bravely repulsed. Angered at this, Cockburn resolved to destroy Hampton, which he did, advancing against it by water and land. Contemporary accounts are filled with the shocking and detestable conduct of the lawless and inhuman invaders. During the summer other places, as Washington, Annapolis, Baltimore, etc., were threatened, but with no material result. Cockburn, in July, proceeded further south, and exercised his peculiar ability in marauding expeditions on the coast of North Carolina, where, beside the usual plunder, he inveigled a number of slaves on board his ship, and afterwards sold them in the West Indies.

At the north, attacks on the coast were conducted by the blockading force whenever practicable, but in a manner much more to the credit of the British name. This was due, no doubt, to Commodore Hardy, who was in command north of the Chesapeake, and seems to have despised the savagery of Cockburn. The city of New York was strictly blockaded. The frigates United States and Macedonian, and the sloop Hornet, attempted to sail on a cruise from that port about the beginning of

May, but finding the force at the Hook much superior to theirs, they put back and passed through Hell Gate, with the intention of getting out by the Sound. In this they were also frustrated; and on the 1st of June, after another attempt, they were chased into New London. Six hundred militia were immediately called in from the surrounding country, for the protection of the squadron; and Commodore Decatur landing some of his guns, mounted a battery on the shore, and at the same time so lightened his vessels, as to enable them to ascend the river out of the reach of the enemy. This town was so well fortified, however, that no attempt was made upon it, although the blockade was kept up for several months. Incensed by the depredations committed on our coasts by the blockading squadrons, Congress passed an act, by which a reward of half their value was offered for the destruction of ships belonging to the enemy by means other than those of the armed or commissioned vessels of the United States. This measure was intended to encourage the use of *torpedoes*, of which Bushnell was the inventor during the Revolution. In the latter part of July, attempts were made, without success, to blow up a seventy-four in Lynnhaven Bay; but on the last occasion, the torpedo exploded only a few seconds too soon. Complaint was made, by Hardy and others, against this mode of destroying an enemy, as unmanly and dishonorable; but, as has been well remarked, no one was able to show why it was more dishonorable or unfair than the resort on land to surprises, ambushes and mines.

Naval affairs of 1813 next demand attention. At the close of January, Lawrence in the Hornet left San Salvador and shaped his course to Pernambuco. On the 4th of February, he captured an English brig, and on the 22d, while under way for Demerara, he came across the Peacock, a vessel somewhat his superior in force. A contest was at once commenced. It was brief but decisive in favor of the Hornet; so sharp and rapid were the broadsides of Lawrence, that the Peacock soon became a wreck and sunk. The officers of the lost vessel expressed their special thanks to the victor for his generous treatment while they were his prisoners. Towards the close of April, (while at Boston), Lawrence was appointed to the Chesapeake. He accepted the post with reluctance, for the Chesapeake was looked upon as an unlucky ship, a circumstance of much moment with sailors, and her crew was ill assorted and in a disaffected and complaining state. He entered with alacrity, however, upon the duties of his post, and, had time been allowed him, he might have rendered the Chesapeake worthy of a better fate than that which befell her and her gallant commander. The British had taken pains in every way possible to improve their ships of war, especially in drilling the crews, in ball practice, and the like, in order to be able to meet the Americans to more purpose and regain their supremacy. Captain Broke, in the Shannon, 32, but mounting 52 guns, had acted on the wishes of his government, and had his crew in capital order for a fight. On the 1st of June, the Chesapeake, though by no means in a proper state of fitness, sailed out to meet the Shannon. A fierce battle ensued, and the Chesapeake seriously damaged in her rigging, fell foul the Shannon and was boarded by the enemy and taken. Lawrence was wounded early in the action, and soon after fell with a ball through his body. It was one of the most sanguinary actions that ever occured. It lasted only 15 minutes, and yet in that time, forty-eight were killed and ninety-eight wounded on board the Chesapeake, and twenty-four killed and fifty-nine wounded on board the Shannon. Lawrence's dying words, "DON'T GIVE UP THE SHIP," became consecrated in the eyes of his countrymen, and have many a time since been used to animate the spirits of our brave seamen. The effect of the capture of the Chesapeake was wonderful in England, and hardly less so in the United States. The English rejoiced over it with very disproportioned exultation, as if their invincibility were entirely re-established; while the Americans, who had foolishly got the notion that they were unconquerable on the ocean, fretted and felt mortified, almost as if they had lost every thing. The truth seems to be, that, under all the circumstances, the victory was nothing more than Broke ought to have gained; and the honors that were heaped upon him for this exploit, were virtual confessions of American superiority on the water, and went a good way towards consoling our people for the loss of the Chesapeake. On the 14th of August, the British sloop of war Pelican captured the Argus after a brief struggle. As an offset to this the brig Enterprize, on the 4th of September, came across the British brig Boxer, and after an action of forty minutes, gained a complete victory. There was also a large amount of privateering carried on and with much success, showing the native adaptability of our countrymen for naval affairs. The cruise of the Essex under Capt. Porter, was remarkable for its daring and success. Porter left the United States in Oct., 1812, and proceeded to the coast of South America to meet Bainbridge in the Constitution. Having missed this meeting, Porter resolved to take the Essex around Cape Horn, and both look after the interests of American whalers, and capture any British ships he could find in the Pacific. At Valparaiso, on the 13th of March, 1813, he was welcomed as a friend by the new government of Chili; his first exploit was the rescue of two American vessels which had been taken by a Peruvian privateer. In April, he made three prizes of armed whalers, and one of them he manned and equipped with sixteen guns to sail as consort to his own vessel. Nine other vessels also fell into his power; making twelve prizes in the course of this year. Four thousand tons of shipping were thus captured by him; and four hundred prisoners made, many of whom consented to serve under him; and but for his presence in those seas, the American whalers would have experienced the same fate, and been taken by the enemy. In the autumn of the year 1813, hearing that some British vessels had been sent in search of him, he proceeded to the Marquesas, and refitted in the Bay of Nouaheevah, before attempting to make his way back to America.

On the 24th of May, 1813, Congress assembled for an extra session. Henry Clay was elected speaker, and Daniel Webster was among the active members in the opposition. The president's message was a *résumé* of the phases of the war, hopes were held out of a restoration of peace, etc. The principal difficulty just now before the government was the laying of additional taxes in order to provide revenue; and the president expressed his strong conviction that the people would cheerfully contribute in this way to bringing the war to a decisive end. The principal work of the session was the providing means of relieving the government from financial embarrassment. Necessity compelled the adoption of unpopular measures, The existing duties on imports were doubled, and the assessment and collection of direct taxes and internal duties were also provided for Acts were passed imposing duties on refined sugars, salt, carriages, auction sales, licenses for distilleries, and for retailing wine, spirit, and foreign goods, with stamp duties on bank notes, bills of exchange, and other notes; (which were expected to produce $2,000,000 yearly); and a direct tax on houses, lands, and slaves at their assessed value, amounting to $3,000,000 a year. But the advantages expected from this resumption of the system of internal taxation, which Jefferson had denounced, could not be enjoyed before the following year; and for the current year, another loan of $7,500,000 was authorized. The treasury notes, five millions of which had been issued, were, however, at a great discount; and although the former loan had been taken at par, for six per cent. stock, this second loan apparently taken at the same rate, was all paid in depreciated currency. The finances were, in fact, in a very serious state of embarrassment. The banks had suspended specie payments, excepting a few in New

England; and there was a sad lack of clothing, etc., for the militia and for the army in general. Nevertheless, the people bore cheerfully these impositions, and adhered to their determination to sustain the government in carrying through the war. Congress adjourned, August 2d, 1813, after an active and busy session.

In the south-west, at this date, affairs were assuming a shape calculated to excite great alarm and anxiety. Among the Creeks, Tecumseh, that implacable foe of the white man, had used all his influence to stir up the dormant feelings of hatred and revenge. Every art was employed by him to incite them to attack the United States in the south, whilst he and his allies, the British, assaulted them in the north. The war spirit grew stronger and stronger, despite the efforts of those who saw and knew that the ultimate result of war must be the red man's destruction. Murders were committed on the frontiers, and the governor of Tennessee was empowered to call out 10,000 militia to punish the aggressors; but the war party prevailed and crushed out all opposition, by murdering the friendly chiefs among the Creeks, and by deeds of savage violence and vindictiveness in every quarter. The Choctaws were urged to join them, but refused. Throughout the white settlements on the Tombigbee and Alabama Rivers, the liveliest alarm prevailed, and with good reason, as was soon after proven. Arms and ammunition having been furnished them, the Creeks resolved to attack Fort Mimms, on the Alabama, not far from Mobile, in the summer of 1813. It was one of the stockaded forts on the river, and was held by Major Beasley, with 180 men. Besides these, there were many of the frightened inhabitants in the fort, and Beasley was ordered to use the utmost caution and vigilance. By some strange fatuity and delusion, Beasley acted as if there was no danger to be feared. He was several times warned expressly during August, but paid no heed to these intimations of the approach of the deadly savage. On the 30th of August, towards noon, the Indians advanced through an open field, to within thirty yards of the fort, before they were discovered, so well devised, bold and fortunate was the plan of these furious enemies of the pale faces. The gate, too, was wide open, and raising their wild yell, they rushed into the fort. It was literally a massacre that which followed. The troops fought bravely, but they were no match for the Indians, who outnumbered them by the hundreds. A few managed to fight their way out; but there were more than 350 who perished in the flames or were murdered after all resistance had ceased. No wonder, gloom and consternation took possession of the whole south-western frontier. Every fort was crowded with fugitives, and Mobile, which General Wilkinson had seized in the month of April, was now a most welcome harbor of refuge to multitudes, whom terror at the news of the tragedy at Fort Mimms drove from their homes. The whole region was in a deplorable state, and the distress of the people during the sickly season, in September, was extreme. The number and fierceness of the Indians were frightful, and every station, every block-house, and every fort was assailed by the open foe, or by lurking bands of savages. In this emergency, the people of the States of Georgia and Tennessee, aided by those in South and North Carolina, promptly undertook to face the enemy. The Choctaws, who had refused to join the Creeks, were now persuaded to take part against them; and about the middle of November, Gen. Claiborne advanced towards Weatherford's Bluff, on the Alabama, for the purpose of erecting a stockaded depot for the use of the Tennessee troops now under march along the line of the Coosa; by the end of the month the fort was completed and put into use. Gen. Floyd, from Georgia, advanced in November into the Creek country, with about 2,500 men. Tennessee, however, furnished the most important assistance; and early in October, one column, of 2,000 choice volunteers, under Gen. Jackson, set out from Nashville; another column, of about equal strength, advanced from East Tennessee, under Gen. Cocke. On the 2d of November, Gen. Coffee was detached, with 900 men, against Tallushatches, a Creek town, where, although the Indians fought obstinately, he gained a victory of considerable importance. Four days later, Jackson set off to relieve a town of the friendly Creeks. Marching all night, he came upon the enemy early in the morning, and the battle commenced. The Indians being repulsed on all sides, attempted to escape, but found themselves enclosed; and had not two companies of militia given way, whereby a space was left open through which a considerable number escaped to the mountains, they would all have been taken prisoners or destroyed. In the pursuit many were sabred or shot down. In this action, the American loss was fifteen killed, and eighty wounded. That of the Creeks was not much short of three hundred killed, their whole force exceeding a thousand. "In a very few weeks," wrote Jackson, "if I had a sufficiency of supplies, I am thoroughly convinced I should be able to put an end to Creek hostilities." Gen. White, on the 18th of November, 1813, entered a Hillabee town, and, out of 300, killed 60 warriors and took the rest prisoners; he also burned several villages, and returned without losing a single man. At the close of November, Gen. Floyd obtained a victory at Autossee, on the Talapoosa. This was considered the Creek metropolis, and the warriors fought with desperate fury; but the artillery and the bayonet were too much for them. Their loss was very heavy, and their town with all its valuables was burned. In December, Claiborne advanced into the Creek country, and on the 23d attacked Ecchanachaca, "Holy Ground," on the Alabama. This was Weatherford's stronghold; but the Indians were defeated, and the town and country were devastated. Several severe encounters were had with the Creeks early in 1814, and almost always with success. Gen. Jackson, in March, having gathered a force of about 4,000, together with 1,000 Indian auxiliaries, resolved to bring the war to a close by an attack upon the last stronghold of the Creeks. This was at the bend of the Talapoosa, named Horse Shoe Bend. It was a fortified position, of great strength, and was defended by the Indians with the bravery of desperation; but the valor and discipline of our troops prevailed; the Creeks were entirely defeated and cut to pieces. Gen. Jackson brought the war to an end, and imposed severe terms in the treaty which was made, so as to prevent future outbreaks.

Turning again to the north-west, we find that Perry was actively employed in forwarding preparations to compete with the British on Lake Erie. Proctor, meanwhile, aware of the spirit and determination of the Americans, undertook, on the 1st of August, 1813, to invest Fort Stephenson, at Lower Sandusky, on the Sandusky River. He had about 500 men and 3000 Indians; while Major Croghan, in the fort, had only one gun and 160 youthful and inexperienced troops. Proctor demanded a surrender, in haughty terms, but was answered with great spirit by Croghan, that "the fort should not be given up while a man was able to fight." The assault was fierce and urged on with all the energy of the British; but our brave men stood manfully in their defence, and drove the enemy back: these retreated down the river, having abandoned considerable baggage and military stores. Perry, despite all obstacles and hindrances pushed forward his preparations, and by the 2d of August the fleet was equipped; on the 4th he sailed after the enemy, but not meeting him, returned on the 8th. Getting reinforcements, he sailed out again and cruised off Malden. His fleet consisted of nine vessels, 54 guns and two swivels. The English commodore, Barclay, had a fleet of six vessels, 63 guns, 4 howitzers, and two swivels, and on the 10th of September resolved to attack Perry. The union jack was hoisted about eleven o'clock, having for its motto

the dying words of the lamented Lawrence, 'DON'T GIVE UP THE SHIP!" It was received with repeated cheerings by the officers and crews. And now having formed his line, Perry bore for the enemy; who likewise cleared for action and hauled up his courses. A little before noon, the British opened fire upon the Lawrence, Perry's flag-ship, and as he could not return the fire for some little time, owing to his guns being of insufficient range, the Lawrence was speedily reduced almost to wreck, and Perry resolved to make a bold movement so as not to be defeated. He determined to abandon the Lawrence and hoist his flag on board the Niagara, which was then in the thickest of the fight. Leaving Lieutenant Yarnall in the Lawrence, he hauled down his inspiriting colors, and taking them under his arm, gave orders to be put on board the ship where Captain Elliot was in command. Perry went off from the ship in his usual gallant manner, standing up in the stern of the boat, until absolutely pulled down among the crew. Broadsides were leveled at him, and small arms discharged by the enemy, two of whose vessels were within musket shot, and a third one nearer; the balls struck around him and flew over his head in every direction; but the same Providence that watched over the heroic commodore throughout the battle, brought him safely to the Niagara, where the flag was again hoisted with exultation. Signal was now made for close action, and the fight was severely contested. Three hours the engagement lasted, and the victory was decisive and complete; although the carnage was fearful. Perry's dispatch to Gen. Harrison was brief and pithy: it was dated, September 10th, on board the Niagara: "Dear General:—We have met the enemy, and they are ours; two ships, two brigs, one schooner and a sloop." The results of this victory were instantaneous and of the first consequence. It had been won by a squadron of American vessels over a British squadron, in which it differed materially from other maritime successes achieved during the war. But that was not the chief matter of exultation; the Americans were now masters of Lake Erie, and had it in their power at once to intercept the whole coasting trade, by which Proctor's troops and Indians were supplied with provisions, and to land any force they chose in his rear, and entirely cut him off from Kingston and York. Abandoning, therefore, and destroying all his fortified posts beyond the Grand River, Proctor commenced a retreat at once, accompanied by Tecumseh and his Indians. Part of the prizes and part of his squadron Perry now employed as transports, and twelve hundred of Harrison's troops were without delay carried over to Canada, where on the 23d of September, they took possession of Malden, which had been deserted and dismantled. Detroit was next recovered, on the 27th; and there Colonel Johnson's regiment of mounted rifles joined the expedition, which was the more welcome, because Proctor had driven off all the horses of the country, to prevent pursuit. Perry's squadron now attended the march of the army with supplies, and all needful aid for its rapid advance, while the British, almost starving, toiled through wretched roads and dreary forests. On the 4th of October, Harrison came up with the British rear, and succeeded in capturing nearly all their stores. Proctor's only alternative now was to fight, and he took position on the Thames. His force numbered about 2000, of whom fully half were Indians; while Harrison had with him some 3000 men and the sharp-shooters of Kentucky and Ohio. The fight began on the 5th of October, 1813, and the Indians under Tecumseh displayed the utmost fury and determination. But Harrison's troops, especially the mounted riflemen under Johnson broke the British line and routed them beyond possibility of recovery. Proctor fled, but Tecumseh resisted to the last moment, when he was killed, and the victory soon after was complete. Harrison, at the close of October, took about 1200 of his men, and went to Buffalo, to reinforce the army of the centre and aid in the invasion of Canada. On the same day that

Proctor was defeated on the Thames, six British schooners, having on board two hundred and fifty soldiers, proceeding from York to Kingston, without convoy, were captured by Chauncey, on Lake Ontario. These repeated losses, coupled with the alarming intelligence received at the same time of great preparations for a general invasion of Lower Canada, made Prevost wisely determine it to be impossible to continue any longer the investment of Fort George; and the siege was accordingly raised a few days later. The retreat was conducted in an orderly manner, and the British took post at Burlington Heights, where Proctor, with those who had fled with him, soon after joined them, making the entire force about fifteen hundred.

Wilkinson was in command of the army of the centre, and he was urged by the secretary of war to push forward the invasion of Canada, and reap the fruits of Perry's great victory. His force at Niagara amounted to 8000 regulars, besides the 1,200 under Harrison, just arrived. Hampton was in command of the army of the north, then encamped at Plattsburg, on Lake Champlain; his force amounted to about 4000 men. The outline of the plan adopted was: to descend the St. Lawrence, passing the British outposts without attempting their capture; to form a junction with Hampton, at some designated point on the river; and then with the united forces to proceed to the Island of Montreal. Various difficulties delayed any movement till the beginning of November, when Chauncey took position in the St. Lawrence near French Creek. The enemy attacked the advance, under General Brown, but to no purpose. On the night of the 6th, the flotilla passed the British fort, Prescott, in safety, and early the next day arrived at French Creek, the place of destination. Word was sent to Hampton, requiring coöperation. The British commander was active and watchful, and did all in his power to impede Wilkinson's progress. A sharp engagement took place on the 11th of November at Chrsytler's field, near Williamsburg, in which neither party gained any particular advantage. Hampton sent word to Wilkinson that he should not join him at St. Regis, as directed, but would meet him lower down the St. Lawrence. Hampton had made an ineffectual attempt before this to do something on his own account, but without any success; and as he refused to join Wilkinson, it was held that the campaign was really at an end. The army went into winter quarters, and both Hampton and Wilkinson received sharp and severe censure for the failure of the Canada invasion. General Harrison, who had reached Buffalo in October, set out to follow Wilkinson, and did not get the order to remain where he was until after his departure. M'Clure, who was in command at Fort St. George in October, on receiving news of the approach of the British, early in December removed his stores, destroyed the fort, and set fire to the village of Newark, leaving the miserable inhabitants, including more than 400 women and children, to the accumulated horrors of famine, and a Canadian winter. And, as if this cruelty were not enough, he fired red-hot shot into Queenstown from Fort Niagara, so as to deprive the enemy of any shelter there. Our government disowned at once this stupidly needless cruelty; but the British made it a pretext for subsequent outrage, in every part of the country. Fort Niagara was taken by surprize on the 10th of December, and the garrison of 300, mostly on the sick list, were put to the sword. The enemy now proceeded to lay waste the frontier with almost savage vindictiveness. Lewiston, Manchester, the Tuscarora villages, Black Rock, and Buffalo, were set on fire, and in great measure destroyed. Thus the year 1813 came to its close; and though marked by many mortifications and disappointments, still had some degree of consolation in it, in the successes of Harrison, Perry, Jackson, and others. There was no disposition to yield to the haughty enemy on any but honorable terms, and the national legislature displayed the true spirit of our people in carrying forward the war to its legitimate end.

The Thirteenth Congress began its second session, December 6th, 1813. The president, in his message, expressed his regret at the failure of the efforts to negotiate a peace by the mediation of Russia. He next spoke of the events of the war thus far; of Perry's victory, of Chauncey's activity and zeal, of Harrison's success at the Thames, of Jackson's conduct of the Creek war to a thorough conclusion, and of the necessity of the measures he had taken to retaliate the course pursued by the British in taking our naturalized citizens and arraigning them as traitors. The report upon the state of the treasury showed $7,000,000 in hand out of the receipts for the preceding year, amounting to above $37,500,000, nearly $24,000,000 of which were the produce of loans. Further sums, it was stated, would be necessary to be obtained in the same way during the ensuing year, and the president had no doubt that the patriotism of the people would meet all needful demands. Early in the session, the embargo and non-importation system was revived and extended. An embargo was laid on all ships and vessels in the United States, with very severe provisions; it was, however, repealed in April, 1814. Laws were passed for the increase of the army and navy, and provision made for the payment of bounties and pensions. A loan of $25,000,000, in addition to the former loans, was authorized at this time for the prosecution of the war. There were also ordered to be re-issued $10,000,000 of treasury notes. For the expenditure was estimated at $45,000,000; and the new taxes could not yield more than $3,500,000, while the income derived from the customs and the sale of public lands did not much exceed $6,500,000. A scheme for establishing a Bank of the United States was again set on foot. The proposal came from New York, and it was discussed in one form and another for two months, but finally was lost.

The year 1814 opened with no very encouraging prospects. The resources of the country were almost exhausted; the finances were depressed and deranged; party feuds were prevalent, and the breaking up of the Union seriously contemplated; and yet the spirit of those who favored the war did not fail, and they were ready to persevere under all difficulties. Great Britain, now that Napoleon's career was near its close, was at liberty to direct her energies to the speedy settlement of the war with the United States. With singular ignorance of the real condition of things, and the unyielding patriotism of the people, England expected to be able to strike a few decisive blows, and reduce the United States to prompt, and even abject submission. The peace of Paris was scarcely ratified, before fourteen thousand of those troops, which had gained so much renown under the Duke of Wellington, were embarked at Bordeaux for Canada; and about the same time a strong naval force, with an adequate number of troops, was collected, and dispatched for invading different parts of the coast of the United States. During January and February nothing was done. Towards the latter end of March, Wilkinson determined to erect a battery at Rouse's Point, where had been discovered a position from which the enemy's fleet, then laid up at St. John's, might be kept in check, and their contemplated movement on Lake Champlain impeded or prevented. The breaking up of the ice on the lake at an earlier period of the season than usual, defeated his plan. A body of the enemy, some two thousand in number, on discovering his design, had been collected at La Colle Mill, three miles below Rouse's Point, for the purpose of opposing him. With a view of dislodging this party, Wilkinson, at the head of between 3000 and 4000 men, crossed the Canada line, March 30th. Having dispersed the skirmishing parties, he reached La Colle Mill, a large fortified stone house. The attack was unsuccessful, and as Wilkinson was rarely anything else but unsuccessful, he was suspended from command. Early in May, the greater part of the British force was collected at St. John's and Isle Aux Noix in order to secure the entrance of their squadron into Lake Champlain, on the breaking up of the ice. M'Donough had been laboring for months past to increase his naval force, so as to make it equal to that of the British. The enemy attempted to destroy his vessels, but without success. Active preparations were also making on Lake Ontario, and Chauncey endeavored to keep himself in readiness to meet the enemy at the earliest moment. Oswego was attacked by the British, but to no great purpose, for the valuable stores, etc., were all safely removed; and, while Major Appling, with the stores, was under way for Sackett's Harbor, the British were caught completely in an ambuscade at Sandy Creek. In the west, the enemy had been able to hold possession of Fort Mackinaw, a position of importance to them. Efforts were made to recover it, but without success. At the close of February, Capt. Holmes met a British party on the River Thames, and though attacked with fury, was able to drive off the enemy with great loss on their part. Gen. Brown, aided by Scott and Ripley, was busily occupied during the spring in drilling and disciplining his troops for the work which was before them. In June, Brown marched his army to Buffalo, having about 3,500 men, and on the 3d of July invested Fort Erie, which surrendered at once. He now determined to attack the British General Riall, entrenched at Chippewa, not far from Erie. Scott was ordered to advance with the artillery, and Ripley followed. Very early in the morning of the 6th of July, the action commenced, the Canadian militia and Indian allies attacking the American volunteers, the redoubted marksmen of Kentucky, who stood their ground so bravely, and dealt such deadly shots into the ranks of the enemy that not till some of the regulars came up were they driven back. The intrepidity of our troops was worthy of great praise, and showed the effect of drilling under good officers. The fight was severely contested, the British losing in all over 500 killed, wounded, and missing; the American loss was 328 in killed, wounded, and missing. The result of this battle was especially gratifying to the people, for it served to prove, that nothing but discipline was wanting on land, to give our soldiers the same capability, which had been so gallantly maintained by our sailors, of meeting and conquering the veteran troops of England. The battle was fought manfully on both sides, and, as above shown, was unusually sanguinary. General Brown sent Ripley forward two days afterwards to open a road and build a bridge over the Chippewa River. Riall, unable to prevent this, fell back upon Queenstown, and the next day fell back still further, General Brown following. He was prepared to advance on Forts Niagara and George; but Chauncey having been ill, and so unable to co-operate with his naval force, Brown withdrew from his advanced position, and determined to follow and attack the British at Burlington Heights. Riall took position at Queenstown, which had been abandoned by our troops, and Brown resolved to move without delay against him. Late in the afternoon of July 25th, Scott led his brigade out of camp, and proceeding along the Niagara road, discovered Riall on an eminence near Lundy's Lane, a position of great strength, where he had planted a battery of nine pieces of artillery, two of which were brass 24-pounders. Scott pressed forward, and the engagement began and raged furiously for an hour. Both sides waited only for reinforcements, and when they arrived the battle was renewed. The brave Colonel Miller and his men assaulted the height on which the British artillery were placed, and swept the enemy from their very guns. Jessup turned the British flank, and did great execution; but the great point of contest was the height where the artillery was placed. Again and again did the British endeavor to retake the height; but they were repulsed every time with fearful slaughter. Ripley was in command for a while, Brown and Scott both being severely wounded, and made some efforts to bring away the cannon from the height, but unfortunately did not succeed in doing so, and on being summoned to camp, left them to the enemy to retake. This famous battle (known as the battle of Niagara, or of Bridgewater, or of Lundy's Lane) was the most severely contested, and, in proportion to the numbers engaged, the most destructive to human life, of any that had ever been fought in America. The British force numbered something short of five thousand, including militia and Indians. The American army was, in number, less than three thousand; yet, on each side, nearly nine hundred men were killed, wounded, and missing. The proportion of officers killed and wounded was unusually large, and showed clearly that, so far as the American army was concerned, our countrymen were as able as they were willing, to meet even the veteran troops which had gained laurels on the battle-fields of the old world. The next morning Ripley was ordered to go and bring away the cannon, as trophies of victory; but this he was unable to do, as the British had regained possession of the eminence, and so he retreated to Fort Erie. Both sides claimed the victory; the Americans, because they had driven the enemy from his position, and captured the guns; the British, because they had recovered the guns again, and because, the next morning, Ripley did not attack them, but retreated. General Gaines entered on command at Fort Erie, August 4th, 1814, and was very active in preparing for the contest which the enemy was threatening. For a week or more, cannonading was kept up by batteries on both sides; but on the 14th the British determined to assault the fort in the night. This was done, and a terrible struggle ensued; but early the next morning the enemy were repulsed with very heavy loss. The siege was continued; the British pushed forward their work; frequent skirmishes ensued; and on the 17th of September, a brilliant sortie was made from the fort, and the enemy retreated to his entrenchments.

Early in the spring, the northern sea-coast was attacked by the British at various points. The Connecticut River was entered above Saybrook and much shipping destroyed. The harbors of New York, New London and Boston continued to be blockaded, and the whole coast lay open to the ravages of the enemy. In July, 1814, Commodore Hardy, with eight ships and 2,000 men, seized upon Eastport, and declaring it and the vicinity to be the property of the British king, required the people to take the oath of allegiance, etc. Hardy, on the 9th of August, resolved to attack Stonington; but the brave people of that town nobly stood forward in defence of their homes, and so Hardy's efforts were repulsed. On the 1st of September, a squadron of over twenty vessels entered the Penobscot and took possession of Castine and Belfast. They took possession of this region also, and declared it to belong to the king; and entered upon preparations for an expedition to retaliate for the American invasion of Canada. Plattsburg had very few troops at this time to defend it; but Prevost, the British commander, had about 10,000 men ready to make an immediate attack, and, had his naval force been equal to his land troops, the danger of defeat to our force would have been imminent. Gen. Macomb at Plattsburg lost no time in placing the works in a state of defence, and constant skirmishes were had with the enemy. Macomb, finding the village of Plattsburg to be no longer tenable, destroyed the bridge over the Saranac, and erected breastworks to oppose the advance of the British, who had encamped on the ridge west of the town. The enemy delayed the assault till the arrival of their flotilla, intending to conquer on land and water at the same time. About eight in the morning of Sunday, the 11th of September, the British fleet, under command of Captain Downie, appeared round Cumberland Head, and at nine o'clock anchored in a line ahead, about three hundred yards distant from Commodore M'Donough's vessels, which were drawn up to receive them. Long and hotly contested was the battle of Lake Champlain; it raged for more than two hours; but the victory was decidedly in the hands of M'Donough and his brave co-workers. On land, Prevost urged on the attack with vigor and skill. Three fierce attempts were made by the British to cross the Saranac, and crush the Americans by assault; but they were bravely met, and failed in accomplishing their purposes. When the shouts of our countrymen announced that the British fleet had surrendered, Prevost felt that it was useless to protract the contest. Although the firing was kept up till dark, his plans were completely frustrated. Now that the Americans had the command of Lake Champlain, the possession of their works on the land could not serve him in any further design; and in the mean time, he was exposed to danger, which increased with the hourly augmentation of the American force. He determined therefore to raise the siege. Under cover of the night he sent off all the baggage and artillery for which he could obtain means of transportation; and precipitately followed with all his forces, leaving behind him the sick and wounded. A large quantity of provisions, ammunition, and implements of war was left by the enemy, on their retreat; subsequently, other valuable stores were found hidden in marshes or buried in the ground. In the west, during the summer, an expedition was undertaken to recover Mackinaw; but it did not meet with success. Gen. Harrison resigned his commission, and Gen. M'Arthur, who took command, gained an important victory over the British at the River Thames, early in November.

The British squadron on the coast continued their system of petty plundering and devastating, wherever they found opportunity. Especially was this plan pursued on the waters of the Chesapeake, where Cockburn was in command; and numerous and disgraceful inroads were made under his direction, or with his entire sanction. A flotilla for the defence of the inlets and smaller rivers of the bay, consisting of a cutter, two gunboats, and nine barges, was placed under command of Commodore Barney, who, during the month of June, performed a number of gallant exploits in the discharge of his responsible duties. Every attempt of the enemy to capture the flotilla failed, Barney at times running up small creeks out of reach of the British guns; at other times, silencing them by superior skill and accuracy in firing. Cockburn had menaced Washington the year before; but it was not supposed that any serious attack would be made. Nevertheless, the English authorities seemed to have determined to strike a blow or two which should tell with tremendous effect, and compel the Americans to sue for peace on any terms. The invasion and destruction of Washington was one of these. At the close of June, 1814, the president recommended forming a camp of 3,000 men near the Potomac, and embodying 10,000 men at Washington. Steps were taken at once to carry into effect so judicious a measure; and requisitions were made on Maryland, Pennsylvania and Virginia for 15,000 militia, of which it was thought certainly 10,000 would take the field. A thousand regulars, it was reported, could be counted on, and Barney's men, if necessary, could be taken from the flotilla. This looked well, on paper at least; but the actual result was very different. Gen. Winder was appointed to the command; but as everything was to be done, fortifications erected, troops collected, plans matured, etc., he soon discovered how little support was likely to be got in readiness for the defence of the capital. The call for militia failed woefully, and early in August, Winder found that he had about 1,000 regulars, and less than 2,000 militia; and with such miserably insufficient preparation the veteran troops of England in large force were to be met and repulsed! Ingersoll's account of the state of things at Washington is graphic indeed:—"There were no funds; though the city banks proffered a few hundred thousand dollars of their depreciated, and in a very few days unconvertible paper—as, with the fall of Washington, all banks south of New England stopped payment in coin. There were no rifles; not flints enough; American gunpowder was inferior to English; there was not a cannon mounted for the defence of the seat of government; not a regular soldier there; not a fortress, breastwork, or military fortification of any kind, within twelve miles. The neighboring militia of Maryland and Virginia were worn down by disastrous and mortifying service, routed and disheartened. The proportion of regular troops, all of them mere recruits, never tried in fire, was like that of coin to paper, in the wretched currency; so small an infusion of precious metal, that there was scarcely any substance to rely upon." Admiral Cochrane's fleet of 21 sail of the line joined Cockburn on the 16th of August. The enemy's force was divided into three parts, so as to threaten different points; but the main object was the attack on Washington. The Patuxent was ascended as far as Benedict, 40 miles southeast of the capital, and the troops debarked, on the 20th of August, under Gen. Ross. Barney's flotilla was blown up on the approach of the enemy in launches and barges. Ross's force was about 4,500, and he advanced slowly and tediously; no resistance was made; not a step taken to retard his advance; and the inhabitants of both country and town, panic-stricken, seemed to disappear in mass before the truculent invaders.

General Winder had about 3,000 men, mostly militia; his camp was about twelve miles, and early on the 22d of August an advance corps, for the first time, beheld the enemy; but Winder dared not fight with his raw and undisciplined troops. Thus, Ross, who had left his shipping with great uneasiness, was allowed, without cavalry, with hardly a piece of cannon, to advance unmolested, through a settled country abounding in defiles, ravines, streams and woods, of which our men took no advantage, but kept retreating without a blow in defence of their homes and firesides. Having received some reinforcements, Winder resolved to make a stand at the heights of Bladensburg, although the laxity of discipline, insubordination, and turbulence in the camp argued ill for prospective success. The enemy advanced to the attack on the 24th of August, and in a brief space cleared the woods of skirmishers, who fell back upon Winder's first line, and threw it into disorder; and when the line was ordered to retreat by the commander, it gave way and fled in the utmost confusion. The second line stood its ground for a while, and even drove back the enemy; but the British having crossed the narrow stream, and advanced to the charge, the whole line wavered, broke, and rushed from the field. Barney and his sailors alone offered any resistance, and they stood to their guns to the last moment. The British were so fatigued that they could not pursue the panic-striken Americans, but laid down for rest on the field of battle, and, in the cool of the evening, set out towards Washington. Meanwhile, a Virginia regiment which had come up, halted about two miles from the city; but Winder ordered them to retreat nearer, and then into the capital, and thence to the heights of Georgetown. For the 7th time that day, a retreat was once more commanded, and it was performed amid execration, a deep and bitter sense of degradation, and a spirit of insubordination, which threatened utter demoralization. At the first alarm, the navy yard, and all its contents were destroyed; and when fugitives from Bladensburg arrived, every body was frightened nearly to death, and began to run away. The president and public official lost not a moment; some few of the public records were saved by the clerks; but before the British arrived, the capitol was given over to outrage and plunder by slaves and ruffians. About eight in the evening, Ross and Cockburn entered the city, now entirely deserted by its eight or ten thousand inhabitants. A solitary musket was fired from a house, and the general's horse was killed. That was enough: instantly the savage work of these vandals began; the house was demolished at once; the capitol set on fire; the library of Congress destroyed; public documents of moment burned up; the president's house and the offices of the state and treasury departments shared the same fate. During the night a tremendous storm and tornado arose, and the lightning's flash and the thunder mingled with the flames of the capitol, and the explosion of depots of gunpowder. The next morning the ruthless invaders continued their work. The war-office was burned. The printing office of "The National Intelligencer" was sacked, under Cockburn's personal direction, and the letter thrown into the street. The great bridge across the Potomac was set on fire and destroyed. Two rope-walks, near the navy yard, were burnt, and by accident a torch was flung into a dry well in the arsenal at Greenleaf's Point, which had been used as a receptacle for old cartridges, waste powder and other combustibles. A terrible explosion instantly ensued, the houses and buildings near were shattered and thrown down, and a great number of soldiers lost their lives, or were frightfully mutilated. There was also some injury done to private houses and stores by the invaders, but principally owing to the interference of General Ross, who seems to have had grace enough to be ashamed of the contemptible work in which he was engaged, the depredations were not so numerous as Cockburn would have made, had he been allowed his own way entirely.* Notwithstanding the pusillanimous conduct of the Americans, the British were very anxious to get away back to their shipping. The hurricane came on more furious than ever, and the rain fell as in a deluge. Some thirty or forty soldiers perished under the ruins of fallen walls and buildings. Leaving the post office and patent office, and everything else marked out for destruction, the invaders, as soon as the darkness of the night admitted, hastily set out on their retreat. The wounded they could hardly undertake to remove; it was hence determined to leave them behind, and the care of them was assigned to Commodore Barney, who had been wounded and taken at Bladensburg, and who, with the other prisoners, was released upon parole, for this purpose. The watchfires having all been trimmed, in perfect silence, the enemy retreated; and on the 29th and 30th, they re-embarked at Benedict, to enter upon other schemes of rapine and outrage. It must always remain a marvel why this vandal-like inroad should have been permitted by our countrymen; yet, where so many are to blame, it is difficult, if not impossible, to discriminate and fix the stigma upon those who rightly deserve it. Beyond doubt, the British government thoroughly disgraced itself by ordering such an expedition, so utterly useless under any impression that our countrymen were in this way to be subdued. So far from such a result being reached, this course of the enemy roused up afresh the spirit of the country—unanimity prevailed—the war became popular, and everywhere active preparations were made to place the seaboard cities and towns in a state of defence. The enemy's ships, under Gordon, ascended the Potomac three days afterwards. Fort Warburton had been blown up, in a panic, at the very name of the approaching foe. On the 29th Alexandria was reached, and the inhabitants bought off these pirates on the best terms possible. Everything that could be laid hands on was seized by Gordon, and he made off down the river with a fleet of prize vessels and a rich booty. Sir Peter Parker, who went up the Chesapeake, was not so fortunate as his fellow invaders. On the 30th of August, he landed at Moore's Fields, intending to take by surprise a body of militia there under Colonel Reed, but he was disappointed; our men bravely resisted the enemy, and finally repulsed them. Parker was wounded and died a few days afterwards. Having suc-

* The value of the public property destroyed at Washington exceeded $2,000,000. We have no estimate of the loss which was sustained by private ndividuals, in this disgraceful incursion.

ceeded so well in plundering Washington, the British resolved next to try Baltimore. Happily the panic had now subsided, and the people went vigorously into the work of preparing to meet the ruthless enemy. Fort M'Henry, about two miles from Baltimore, on the river, was the main reliance against the ships of the British, and it was garrisoned with 1,000 men, under Major Armistead. Cochrane, on the 11th of September, 1814, appeared at the mouth of the Patapsco, about fourteen miles from Baltimore, with some fifty sail. The next day about 6,000 troops landed at North Point, Ross in command, and advanced towards the city. They marched forward for some miles without opposition, but about one o'clock came up with our troops. General Ross was killed, and after a severe struggle of more than an hour, General Stricker retired before the enemy. The next morning the British resumed their march, and about noon concentrated in front of the American line, apparently for an attack that evening. The attack on Fort M'Henry, meanwhile had been commenced. About sunrise, on the 13th, the British had brought sixteen ships within two miles and a half of the fort, and the assault was begun by five bomb-vessels, which had anchored at the distance of two miles. These, being out of the range of the guns of the fort, maintained an incessant bombardment; yet, despite the bombs and rockets every moment falling in and about the fort, the garrison wavered not; every man stood to his post without shrinking. Some of the enemy's vessels approaching nearer, a tremendous fire was opened upon them, and they hastily retired. During the night, whilst the enemy on land was retreating, and whilst the bombardment was the most severe, two or three rocket-vessels and barges succeeded in getting up the Ferry Branch; but they were soon compelled to retire. At seven o'clock the next morning, the bombardment was given over, fifteen hundred shells having been thrown, but with comparatively little injury to the fort and its defenders. Only four were killed and twenty four wounded in this assault on Fort M'Henry. Cochrane and the commander of the British troops began their retreat that night, and the admiral retired with his fleet to the West Indies.

The president returned to Washington as soon as possible after the British retreated, and called Congress together on the 19th of September. They met on that day, and the message was sent in and read to both Houses. Moderate in length, but firm, almost defiant in tone, the message reviewed succinctly the existing state of things, and the measures which seemed to be required under the circumstances. The various successes of our arms on land and sea were dilated upon and the disgraceful mode of warfare which the British had recently adopted, was vigorously denounced. The necessity of filling the ranks of the regular army was adverted to, as more economical than employing the militia to any great extent, the president at the same time strongly urging that the militia be classed and disciplined for more efficient service. The financial statement of the three quarters of a year that had elapsed since the last preceding account, showed $32,000,000 received, all from loans except about $11,000,000, and $34,000,000 disbursed, leaving nearly $5,000,000 in the treasury. But it was added, that "large sums" would be required to meet the demands already authorized by Congress, and those arising from "the extension of the operations of war." The president did not attempt to disguise the fact that the situation of the country called for active and vigorous efforts on the part of all; he knew well the power and vindictive spirit of the enemy, but he was willing to rely on the courage and constancy of the people, and he believed that they would endure unto the end. Some discussion arose as to the removal of the government to Philadelphia, but it was not carried. The British having burned the library of Congress, Jefferson offered to sell his library to Congress, as the nucleus of a new one, and it was accordingly purchased, although the third president's enemies had by no means forgotten him, and voted against the purchase. Changes in the cabinet occurred. Armstrong, who was sharply censured because Washington had been plundered, threw up the war department, and Monroe took his place, Sept. 27th, holding at the same time the state department until March, 1815. A. J. Dallas was made secretary of the treasury, and B. W. Crowninshield secretary of the navy. In our estimate of the measures of this session, we must not only remember that it was the last of the thirteenth or war Congress, but also that active efforts were in progress for the negotiation of peace, the American commissioners being at Ghent awaiting the arrival of the envoys from England. And further, it deserves to be noted, that at this period the disaffection of the eastern States attained its highest pitch, and the "Hartford Convention," of which we shall speak further on, was the sign, or the menace, of something terrible in the future; possibly even a dissolution of the Union, with its portentous consequences. The finances claim our first notice. The report presented at the beginning of the session was deplorable; the loan had failed utterly; of $6,000,000 advertised for in the preceding month, only some $2,500,000 could be obtained, and that at a loss of twenty *per cent.* Mr. Dallas, the new secretary, did not waste time in suggesting additional taxation, but carried it. The direct tax was doubled forthwith; all duties were raised; new internal duties imposed; postage was increased 50 per cent.; and a national bank was recommended with $50,000,000 capital, to be under government control, and to loan at once to the government $30,000,000. The bank scheme was debated in the House for eleven days; Webster opposed it; Calhoun advocated it; and it failed, as on a former occasion (p. 161). In December, another bank scheme was discussed, referred, etc., and finally adopted, Jan. 7th, 1815. The president vetoed the bill, as insufficient, and although debated, reported on, and referred, it was at last postponed by a single vote. Monroe, for the war department, proposed a plan for augmenting the army, in order effectively to carry on the next campaign; it was to raise an army of 100,000 men by draft for the rank and file; but the plan was denounced terribly, and was rejected. A bill authorizing the president to call out the militia of any State, if the governor refused to do so, was carried in the House, but failed in the Senate by one vote.

Commodore Porter (p. 156) gave a thorough overhauling to the Essex, in November, 1813, and on the 12th December sailed for the coast of Chili. He reached Valparaiso on the 12th of January, 1814, not without hope of yet gaining some victory over the enemy. While there, two British war vessels appeared, and he was blockaded, greatly to his annoyance. The British captain was too wary to engage the Essex with one of his vessels, and Porter, on the other hand, did not quite like to fight both vessels at the same time. Wearied out, however, with the tedious blockade, Porter resolved, on the 28th of March, to run out of the harbor between the British vessels and the shore. Unfortunately, in doubling the headland which closes it in, he lost his maintopmast, together with several of his men, who fell into the sea and were drowned. There was no alternative now but to regain the port, or to fight both the enemy's ships, under the additional disadvantage of being crippled. Finding it impossible to get back to the common anchorage, Porter ran close into a small bay about three-quarters of a mile to leeward of the battery, on the east of the harbor, and anchored within pistol-shot of the shore. He supposed the enemy would regard this as neutral ground, and went to work at once to repair; but it soon became apparent that the British were not going to allow so capital an opportunity of attack to slip away. Porter did all that was possible under the circumstances. The Phœbe and Cherub, the English ships, took their position as suited them, and were enabled to fire upon the Essex according as they wished, while Porter could not bring his broadside to bear, or prevent the terrible fire of the enemy. The fight lasted for two hours and a half, and was one of the most destructive to human life of which we have any account. Porter tried to run the Essex on shore and burn her, but failed in this, and surrendered. He and his companions were allowed to return home on parole. The sloop-of-war, Peacock, met a British brig, Epervier, of the same number of guns (April 29th), and, after forty-two minutes' fight, took the Epervier. The Wasp, 18, at the close of June, 1814, in cruising off the English channel, met the Reindeer, 18, and, after a sharp fight, captured the Reindeer, then a mere wreck. On the 1st of September, the Wasp also captured the Avon, which sank almost immediately. The Wasp continued her cruise, but was never afterwards heard of. Decatur started from New York, in the President, in January, 1815, determining, if possible, to get past the blockading squadron; but, striking on the bar, he was delayed, and at dawn was discovered by the enemy. Three vessels at once set out in pursuit, and Decatur endeavored to escape along the coast of Long Island; but, late in the afternoon, the Endymion gained on the President so much as to begin the fight; it lasted two hours, by which time the Endymion, almost a wreck, fell astern, and two other fresh ships came up. In view of all the circumstances, Decatur felt it his duty to surrender. The Constitution, "Old Ironsides," Captain Stewart, sailed from Boston, December 17, 1814, and, in February, 1815, in the vicinity of Lisbon, discovered two English ships, the Cyane and the Levant. Stewart attacked them both, and, after a severe fight, captured both. In March, Stewart took the Cyane to the United States. The Hornet and Peacock, who were to accompany Decatur, managed to get out of New York, and sailed for the Indian Ocean. Off the Cape of Good Hope, the Hornet fell in with the Penguin, March 23d, and, after a furious contest, captured the enemy. The Hornet was chased by a British 74, and barely escaped. The Peacock, on the 30th of June, met the Nautilus, and began an engagement which speedily ended in the surrender of the Nautilus. The vessel was given up the next day, on learning that peace had already been made. "Thus," as Alison says (no lover of the Americans, by the way), "terminated at sea this memorable contest, in which the English, for the first time for a century and a half, met with equal antagonists on their own element; and in recounting which, the British historian, at a loss whether to admire most the devoted heroism of his own countrymen, or the gallant bearing of their antagonists, feels almost equally warmed in narrating either side of the strife."

Gen. Jackson, of whose movements we have spoken on a previous page (p. 158), had about 2,000 men under him at Mobile, and determined to prevent the British getting any help from the Spaniards in their projects against the south. In the latter part of August, learning that the enemy were at Pensacola in force, Jackson called for the militia and volunteers from Tennessee and Kentucky, and added very materially to his means of repulsing British designs. The enemy kept up a system of petty plundering, and tried hard to enlist the Baratarian pirates under Lafitte; they now resolved to attack Mobile. Jackson fortified Fort Bowyer, in Mobile Bay, which was assaulted, Sept. 15th, 1814, by the enemy, but to no purpose; they were driven off with great loss. In this campaign, as is noted by a great admirer of Jackson, he acted without specific, if indeed any, orders, sometimes almost against orders, performing exploits of warfare and civil administration, which paved his way to the presidency. Discovering that the British had returned to Pensacola, Jackson resolved to occupy that place. Accordingly, he advanced against it with about 3,500 men, and having reached it

Nov. 6th, stormed it the next day. The assault was short, sharp and decisive, and the British the next day blew up the fort at Barancas. Two days later, Jackson restored the town to the Spaniards, and returned to Mobile. Thence, in December, he entered upon preparations for the defence of New Orleans against the enemy, who purposed here striking a blow of the most effective and destructive kind. The condition of affairs in the city was of the most discouraging character, and probably almost any man but Jackson, whose will was iron, and who was immovable when he had made up his mind, would have given up in despair; the population was a mixed one and largely worthless; profligacy abounded; slaves were in great numbers; there were no stores or munitions of war; there was discord, indolence, cowardice and treachery; Jackson, too, was not in good health; the city was without fortifications; military stores could not be obtained readily; the troops had not yet arrived, and might be delayed still longer; all these give us something of a glimpse of the trials under which the defence of New Orleans was to be conducted. But Jackson was not to be daunted; he called out the blacks; he summoned gangs of slaves to erect fortifications in the marshes; and he actually took the Baratarian pirates into service. It is not necessary here to dwell upon the many and valuable defences with which nature has surrounded New Orleans against an attack from sea; its peculiar situation; the difficult navigation of its large river; the vast lagunes, with their intercommunicating creeks and channels; and the impassable swamps which breed pestilence around it; each of these served as an obstacle to the foe, and enabled Jackson to provide against his approach. The banks of the Mississippi were fortified, so as to prevent the enemy's vessels from ascending, and a battery was erected at the Rigolets, or pass leading from Lake Borgne into Lake Ponchartrain, so as to oppose his passage in that direction. A strong battery and a garrison were placed at the mouth of the bayou St. John, which forms the chief communication from the city into Lake Ponchartrain; and a flotilla, consisting of five gunboats, a schooner, and a sloop, was stationed at the Bay of St. Louis, sixty miles to the north-east of New Orleans. About the 9th of December, the British squadron, of some forty sail, appeared off Ship Island, and soon after succeeded in driving away the flotilla and destroying the gunboats which, it had been hoped, would successfully hinder the enemy's advance. Some alarm was excited in the city by the news of this misfortune; and Jackson, finding that matters were not going on as he wished, took the law into his own hands, and by proclamation, Dec. 16th, put the city and environs under strict martial law. This was no empty formality with him, and he gave members of the legislature and other persons fonder of talking than doing, clearly to understand that he was master and would be obeyed. Being much pressed to inform the legislature of his plans, he averred, after his peculiar manner, that he would cut the hair off his head, if he thought it had divined his intentions; and added, rather grimly, "You may expect a warm session, if I am driven from my lines into the city!" Domiciliary visitations, in search of arms, and of anything else that could be used for the defence of the city; the enrollment of all men capable of bearing arms; the prohibiting of any one from going abroad after nine o'clock at night, except by special permission; these measures, and others even more insupportable, did undoubtedly look very much like "despotic severity;" but martial law, it is to be remembered, includes any and every step, which appears to him who proclaims it, requisite for securing the object he has in view; and Jackson, as we shall see further on, was never afraid of assuming responsibility when he had resolved upon his course. Gens Coffee and Carroll, with about 3,500 Tennessee and Kentucky troops, opportunely arrived at New Orleans, on the 23rd of December, and were immediately put on duty to guard the defences of the city. On the same day, the first division of the British troops, under General Keane, effected a landing in the midst of a huge wilderness of reeds beside one arm of the Mississippi, and at once advanced towards the city. One party of this division succeeded in capturing the whole of the most advanced American piquet, at the mouth of the bayou Bienvenu, and thus they were enabled to move forward without the least impediment. About noon-time, having left the swamp for the cultivated region, they surprised another outpost, but one young man managed to escape, and was the first to announce at New Orleans the arrival of the enemy, now only some six or seven miles distant. Keane and his men, instead of advancing, set about enjoying themselves with good cheer of all kinds which they could lay hold of; but about half past seven in the evening, they were astounded on seeing a large vessel in the river, which, having anchored, poured in a terrible broadside of grape-shot. Nor was this all; while endeavoring to escape this dreadful fire, a simultaneous yell and discharge of musketry came down upon them. Coffee and Jackson were there, and the enemy were very severely handled. Jackson fell back, about four the next morning, to a position two miles nearer the city, where he purposed to make a final stand. By the 27th of December, all the forces had arrived, and Pakenham and Gibbs, the commanders, were ready to test their capability of overcoming the Americans. They succeeded in destroying the vessel which had annoyed them so severely, and the way was now clear to advance upon the city. Jackson, meanwhile had not been idle. In these and the immediately following days and nights, sleepless himself, and allowing few if any around him to sleep, until an available position for defence had been secured, he had constructed a lengthened rampart about four miles below New Orleans, of the most formidable description for his purpose. Beside the earth, which was thrown up out of the deep ditch in front, bales or bags of cotton, brought from the city, were unsparingly used. The line extended from the Mississippi to a low swamp, about a mile off, and the ditch was filled with water nearly to the top. In the river, the gunboat Louisiana protected the right flank; and a work, mounting twenty guns, on the opposite bank, added yet more to the strength of the position. The levee, or embankment of the river, also was by Jackson's direction cut through, both above and below the position of the British, thus embarrassing their movements both in front and in the rear.

Pakenham, on the 28th of December, advanced up the levee with the intention of driving the Americans from their entrenchments; and commenced the attack, at the distance of half a mile, with rockets, bombs, and cannon. After some seven hours' fighting, the British, having been very warmly received, were glad to retire. The attempt was renewed on the first day of the new year, 1815, but although the force was large and had a battery of over 30 cannon, the enemy met with no better success than before. It was now thought best to deepen the canal between the Mississippi and the bayou Bienvenu, so as to have the use of the boats to ferry troops across. This took nearly a week, but finally the assault was fixed upon to be made very early in the morning of the 8th of January. Jackson had completed his line of defence, on the left bank of the river, and had it manned by some 3000 infantry and artillerists; there was also a ditch of five feet of water, and he had eight batteries judiciously posted, mounting in all 12 guns. On the opposite bank there was a battery of 15 guns, held by Kentucky troops. On the night of the 7th, the British under Col. Thornton crossed the river and carried the works just noted, thus securing an important position. Pakenham, at day-break on the 8th of January, ordered the first column to the assault. It was bravely undertaken and pushed forward; but our men stood with equal bravery in defence of their country and her rights; and the slaughter of the enemy was terrible. Shattered and disordered, they broke and fled. Pakenham endeavored to rally the panic-stricken and disheartened troops. Waving his hat and calling on them to follow, he reached the edge of the ditch,—but only to fall dead in front of his men. Generals Gibbs and Keane succeeded in bringing the troops a second time to the charge; but the second approach was more fatal than the first. The continued roll of the American fire resembled peals of thunder; it was such as no troops could withstand. The advancing columns again broke; a few platoons reaching the edge of the ditch, only to meet certain destruction. An attempt was made, by their officers, to lead them to the attack a third time, but entirely without success. Generals Gibbs and Keane were carried from the field, the latter severely, the former mortally wounded. The narrow field of strife between the British and the American lines was strewed with the dead. So dreadful a carnage, considering the length of time and the numbers engaged, has seldom been recorded; for there, on that blood-stained field, lay two thousand men in dead and wounded; while of our countrymen, who dealt such terrible destruction to the invaders from behind those ramparts, there were less than 20 in killed and wounded.* Gen. Lambert, who was now in command, made preparations for a speedy retreat; two days' truce was allowed to bury the dead; and then the invaders got away as quickly as possible to their ships.

Whilst these matters were going on at the south, the close of 1814 in New England, illustrated very forcibly the strength and tenacity of the opposition which had all along been manifested to the war in that section of our country. As we have stated several times already, the people of New England, as a body, looked with no favor upon the war, and were not disposed to yield it any countenance or support. They felt keenly the burden imposed upon them by the ruin of their commerce, the disorganized currency, the destruction of their resources, the inroads of the enemy, and the like; and when the "conscription" system, as it was called (p.167,) was proposed, and the British threatened to carry fire and sword into every town, and village, and hamlet, which was accessible to their ships and boats, it need cause no surprise that a popular excitement arose, and that it was thought necessary for the New England maritime states to consult upon measures absolutely called for, as they thought, by the perilous emergency. At the meeting of the Massachusetts legislature in the summer, it was agreed to call together delegates at Hartford, in December, to consider upon the state of the country and report as to measures needful to obtain redress of grievances. Connecticut, Rhode Island, New Hampshire and Vermont sent delegates, and on the 15th, the members assembled, 26 in all. For three weeks, with closed doors, the Convention was occupied in its work; and the result of their consultations and labors we have in the long reports, the resolutions and the secret journal of the Convention, published by Mr. Dwight, the secretary. For particulars as to this Convention, we must refer our readers to the volume just named; the speedy return of peace removed many of the difficulties complained of; and the Hartford Convention, while it has its defenders, is generally looked upon with disfavor and even scorn and contempt.

The British government appointed commissioners to negotiate a peace with the United States, who proceeded to Ghent early in August, 1814, and met our commissioners, Messrs. Clay, Adams, Bayard, Gallatin, and Russell. The discussions were tedious enough, and at times it seemed as if no conclusion would ever be reached; but after long delays and disputation, concessions ha·

* The English accounts vary largely from the statement in the text. They say that Jackson had 12,000 men, while the British force was not half that number. The American account gives Jackson's force as 4698, and Pakenham's as not short of 12,000.

ing been made on both sides, and the subject of impressment having been dropped, the treaty was concluded on the 24th of December, and immediately transmitted to London and Washington. It was duly ratified and confirmed on the 17th of February, 1815, and the next day was publicly proclaimed by the authority of the president. Meanwhile, Congress, in uncertainty as to the result of the negotiations, endeavored to provide for carrying on the war. The secretary of the treasury gave a sad picture of financial distress, at the opening of 1815; nevertheless, new taxes were proposed, treasury notes emitted, acts passed for increasing the army and navy, etc. The president recommended that steps be taken in accordance with the then position of affairs, and Congress entered zealously upon the work. Various acts relating to a state of war were repealed. A loan of $18,500,000 was authorized, for the purpose of retiring the outstanding and depreciated treasury paper; and $25,000,000 of notes, part of which were to be for sums under a hundred dollars, and not to bear interest—the rest for larger amounts in the old fashion; and both kinds might be paid for taxes, etc., or funded at the option of the holder, those without interest at seven per cent., and the others at six. The army was reduced to a peace footing of 10,000 men, and provision was made for a progressive increase of the navy. A day of thanksgiving for the return of peace was appointed, and on the 3d of March, Congress brought its session to a close.

Peace was very welcome, indeed, as all alike felt, but in its effects upon the community it was very various, and wrought sudden and great changes. Some were ruined; others immediately began to grow rich; domestic manufactures were at once depressed, and could not, without protection, compete with the workshops of England. The subject was largely and widely discussed throughout the country, and with the increase in value of cotton and tobacco especially, trade and commerce began to revive, and the people to recover again from the great depression caused by the war. A commercial convention was arranged between England and the United States, which contained some advantages, but was by no means satisfactory in its main conditions. So soon as peace was concluded, it was found necessary to give immediate attention to the impudent and insolent Algerine pirates (p. 132). Tribute—strange as it may sound—had been paid year after year, to the value of over $20,000 a year, to the dey, and when the war of 1812 broke out, he began anew his outrages on American vessels, and especially ordered the American consul to pay him immediately some $27,000 which he claimed, or else this robber on a large scale would seize upon everything, and make slaves of every American in his reach. In May, 1815, however, Bainbridge sailed to the Mediterranean, preceded by Decatur, with several vessels of war. On the 17th of June, Decatur fell in with an Algerine pirate, 46, and in twenty-five minutes captured the vessel; a brig also was taken two days afterwards; and Decatur, on the 28th, proceeded to Algiers. Here he brought matters to a speedy settlement, the dey being astounded at finding that the United States now would not submit for a moment to any further insolence or barbarity. In July and August, Decatur visited Tunis and Tripoli, and compelled these fellow-robbers with the Algerines, to know and understand what must be law for the future on the subject of attacking our commerce and enslaving Americans. Various wrongs and outrages which had taken place since 1812, were, on Decatur's peremptory demand, redressed to the full extent.

The Fourteenth Congress began its first session, December 4th, 1815. The president's message was full of valuable and important material for legislative consideration, especially that part which related to the finances and the revival of public credit. The secretary of the treasury, Mr. Dallas, recommended the reduction of the direct tax by one half, and the retention of the duty on stamps, and of that on refined sugars, whilst other taxes were marked for abolition or reduction. But the principal recommendation was, the establishing a national bank. A moderately productive tariff was, after full discussion, agreed upon; and a long and careful consideration was given to the bank question. Clay and Calhoun strongly favored the plan; Webster and others equally strongly opposed it. The bill was passed by the House, March 14th, 1816, by a vote of 80 to 71, and on the 3d of April was approved by the Senate, by a vote of 22 to 12. The president gave it his sanction at once; although in this he was acting contrary to the usual democratic party policy. The principal features of the new bank were as follows: Its charter was extended to twenty years. Its capital was fixed at $35,000,000, one-fifth of which the government was to subscribe; the rest, in $100 shares, was to consist of gold and silver, to the extent of a quarter, and the other three-quarters of funded debt. The subscriptions of every kind were made payable in four instalments, and as soon as the first instalment was paid, the bank was to be organized, and operations were to be commenced. The location of the bank was to be at Philadelphia, but branches might be established in the States by the directors, to be under the control of thirteen persons appointed by the directors. The management of the institution was vested in a board of twenty-five directors, one-fifth appointed by the government, the rest elected yearly by the stockholders, some being changed at each election, on the principle of rotation. The directors were to choose one of their number a president, annually; but resident citizens alone were eligible as directors. Its notes were made receivable in all payments to the United States; and it was to hold the public money, and in return, to transmit and pay the public money without any kind of charge. Specie payments were not to be suspended, unless by the authority of Congress, or of the president of the United States; and $1,500,000 were to be paid in instalments at the end of two, three, and four years, as a bonus for the charter of the bank. Congress, having passed a resolution to prevent, for the future, the District of Columbia being a depot for the slave trade of the neighboring slave States, adjourned on the 30th of April.

At the republican or democratic caucus for nomination, James Monroe and Daniel D. Tompkins became the regular candidates; and at the election, in the autumn, these received 183 votes, being a large majority over all the opposing candidates. Earnest efforts were made by the secretary of the treasury, acting under authority of Congress, to compel the State banks to resume specie payments, and it was proposed that the Bank of the United States should go into operation, if possible, on January 1st, 1817. Congress began its second session, December 2d, 1816, and the president sent in his last message. It was an interesting document, and contained suggestions of value and moment in regard to the judiciary, a national university, the peace establishment. As to the finances, the president spoke encouragingly, and looked for efficient aid in the newly established bank. Congress took matters in hand with zeal and spirit, and one act of great importance was passed, providing for the paying off the national debt by annual instalments of $10,000,000; this debt, at date, amounted to over $120,000,000. Internal improvements were again a subject of discussion, Calhoun and Clay being the principal advocates for this use of a portion of the public money. The bill passed both Houses; but the president vetoed it, and it was lost. On the 11th of December, 1816, Indiana was admitted into the Union; and on the 3d of March, 1817, the session closed, and James Madison laid down the office he had held for the eight preceding years.

On the 4th of March, James Monroe, the fifth president of the United States, went through the imposing ceremony of inauguration. His address was unusally long, and in it he gave a clear exposition of the principles on which he meant to proceed in the discharge of the duties of his position. John Quincy Adams was made secretary of state; W. H. Crawford secretary of treasury; Calhoun and Wirt subsequently became secretary of war and attorney-general. In these appointments, Monroe, contrary to Jackson's advice, had distinct reference to the political sentiments and views of his cabinet. During the summer the president made a tour through the eastern, middle and western States, and reached Washington on the 18th of September. The Fifteenth Congress commenced on the 1st of December; and the next day, Monroe sent in his first message. It began with congratulations upon the general condition of the country, and spoke of the various steps which had been taken in regard to arrangements with the British government, naval armaments on the lakes, the north-eastern boundary, the fisheries, the relations with Spain, etc. The internal concerns of the country were represented as peculiarly gratifying. "After satisfying the appropriations made by law for the support of the civil government, and of the military and naval establishments, embracing suitable provision for fortifications and for the gradual increase of the navy, paying the interest of the public debt, extinguishing more than $18,000,000 of the principal, within the present year, it is estimated that a balance of more than $6,000,000 will remain in the treasury on the 1st day of January next, applicable to the current expenses of the ensuing year." The receipts for the next year were estimated at $24,500,000 and the out-goings at nearly $22,000,000; so that there would be an excess of revenue beyond expenditure amounting to nearly $2,750,000, exclusive of the balance expected to be in the treasury at the beginning of the year. The financial prospects of the country were, consequently, considered as full of encouragement and promise for the future.

Among the matters to which Congress gave early attent'on was the abolition of internal taxes, recommended by the president. The duties on licenses to distillers and others, on sales by auction, pleasure carriages, stamps, and refined sugar, were, by one act, removed. The duty on salt was also marked for repeal; but, prosperous as the finances seemed, it was thought best not to give this up, as a deficiency might occur. The debates showed that the state of the country was rather highly colored in the message. Retaliatory measures were talked of toward England, but not much of anything done; and some changes in the tariff were made; but the tariff was strongly opposed in the commercial sections of the country, and so nothing special was accomplished at this time. Internal improvements were again discussed, but as it was known that Monroe would veto any bill in their favor, the whole subject was postponed to a future day. Mississippi was admitted into the Union, December 10th, 1817, and the initiatory steps needed for the same purpose were taken by the territories of Illinois and Missouri. A bankrupt law, negotiations with Spain, the Seminole war, etc., came up, bnt we have no room for details.

A set of pirates and adventurers on Amelia Island and at Galveston, Texas, had given much trouble in East Florida, and had been forcibly driven out by the United States; Spain was unable to exercise any authority, and the territory was pretty much given over to outlaws, smugglers, and the like. The Seminole Indians had committed outrages on the borders of Georgia, and in December, 1817, a boat was attacked, laden with supplies, on the Appalachicola, and more than forty persons killed. The government immediately gave orders to advance into Florida, and Jackson was directed to take the lead in the movement and call out the militia. Early in January, 1818, Jackson, at the head of a formidable band of Tennessee volunteers, set out for the seat of war. Before the end of the month, he concluded a treaty with that part of the Creek nation which was friendly to the United

States; and secured their assistance against the Seminoles. On the 1st of March, he reached Fort Scott, on the Appalachicola; having now under his command above 4,000 men, a force exceeding in number the whole of the nation he was about to attack, including both women and children. Provisions running short, he hastened southward without delay, employing his Indians to scour the whole country round the line of march, by which means he secured a great number of prisoners from the enemy. On the site of the stronghold which the negroes had held, and been dispossessed of in 1816, Jackson built a fort, and named it Fort Gadssen; and this he made use of as a depot for supplies. At the beginning of April, a number of Creek towns were stormed and destroyed, and many shocking evidences of savage barbarity were discovered. The American commander was not a man easily deterred by difficulties or scruples. Having no doubts in his mind of the complicity of the Spaniards and of their furnishing supplies to the Seminoles, he marched forward, without delay, to St. Mark's, a small Spanish post, with a fort, at the head of Appalachicola Bay. After a feeble resistance, the fort surrendered, and was occupied by American forces. This action was directly contrary to what the instructions of the government required, but nevertheless, Jackson went on. While here he took prisoner, a Scotch trader, from New Providence, named Alexander Arbuthnot, and soon after Robert C. Ambrister, a native of the same province. Both were engaged in active trade with the Indians, and were charged with stimulating them to hostilities. Jackson without hesitation had them both tried by a court martial, April 20th, and they were executed immediately. He then marched on Pensacola, which surrendered without a blow; after which he bombarded the fortress Barancas. The Spanish authorites were sent to Havana and the province occupied by American troops. Jackson then returned to Nashville, leaving Gen. Gaines in command. These proceedings of Jackson caused great excitement throughout the country, and were looked upon by many as of a very high-handed character, while others justified them as eminently wise, energetic and decisive.

Congress met, according to adjournment, Nov. 16th, and the message of the president contained a full and interesting summary of affairs. The Bank of the United States, from the establishment of which great expectations of advantage had been formed, did not accomplish all that the people desired. The consequence was, that loud complaints were made, and charges of mismanagement were freely circulated against the directors of the bank. At the time when Congress assembled, and the president presented his flattering picture of the state of things in the United States generally, the bank was evidently getting into an exceedingly unsatisfactory condition; and the greatest fears were every where entertained in consequence. A committee of inquiry was appointed, with John C. Spencer at the head, who ascertained some of the immediate causes of this; in substance, they were, a series of outrageous stock-jobbing operations, by which speculators, aided by the officers of the bank, engaged in gambling and cheating on a large scale. There was imminent danger of bankruptcy, and had not the committee recommended stringent measures, doubtless the bank would have failed and ruin to thousands followed. A new board of direction was chosen, and Langdon Cheves, whose reputation as a financier stood deservedly high, was appointed president. Under his able and vigilant control, matters speedily assumed a brighter aspect. The stock found its way into the hands of real capitalists, and rose again in value to $120 per share. The affairs of the institution were minutely examined, and a careful and trustworthy statement was published, which quite reassured the minds of the shareholders. The most prudent measures, in borrowing specie, curtailing discounts, arranging the relations of the branches, and prosecuting defaulters, were adopted; and not only was bankrupcy averted, but the establishment, after a short season of uncertainty and unpopularity, began to recover from its losses, and to regain and to deserve the confidence of the mercantile world.

Early in the session, the president sent into both Houses the papers relating to the Seminole war. Some three weeks at the beginning of the year 1819, were spent in debates as to whether Jackson ought to be censured or applauded; the latter was finally the conclusion, as was to be expected, for the qualities displayed were just the sort to gain popularity in a country and among a people like ours. Illinois was admitted into the Union, Dec. 3d, 1818; and Missouri and Arkansas applied for admission in February, 1819. Mr. Tallmadge, in the House, proposed to fix a limit to the existence of slavery in the new State of Missouri, prohibiting the introduction of slaves, and gradually emancipating those then in bondage. The discussion soon became warm and urgent on both sides of the slavery question; but the proposal of Mr. Tallmadge was carried, and the bill was sent to the Senate. The Senate refused to concur in the clauses against slavery, by a vote of twenty-two to sixteen. The House insisted on retaining the clause prohibiting slavery generally; but neither receding on this point, the bill was lost. The whole subject was consequently laid over till the next Congress, when, as we shall see, the "Missouri Question" gave rise to scenes of excitement and discord hardly to be paralleled in our annals. Alabama was admitted as a slave State, Dec. 14th, 1819.

Notwithstanding the unpleasant posture of affairs caused by Gen. Jackson's march into Florida, negotiations were pushed forward with the Spanish minister, and a treaty was concluded and signed, Feb. 22d, 1819, by which Florida was ceded to the United States for $5,000,000. The treaty, however, was not to be made public until ratified by Spain; and the money was to be paid to citizens of the United States, on account of spoliations by Spain on citizens of the United States. A bill was passed authorizing the president to take possession of East and West Florida. The Spanish king protracted the matter unduly, and it was not finally ratified till Oct. 24th, 1820. American commerce, as we have noted before, suffered greatly by spoliations of the belligerent powers of Europe during the struggle between Napoleon and those who made head against him. Efforts accordingly were made to obtain redress by sending special envoys to Europe; but it was to no purpose. Naples, Holland, Denmark and France, though urgently pressed, evaded the issue and refused to make indemnity.

The slavery question, at this date, now beganto assume grave and somewhat fearful importance, and popular feeling was greatly roused on this subject. Interest as well as principle; prejudice as well as conscientiousness; sectional feuds and jealousies as well as patriotism and love of the Union, moved the minds of men and guided their course of action; and before Congress assembled, it became evident that the old battle was to be renewed, with circumstances of bitterness and savageness added to the contest. The Sixteenth Congress began its first session, Dec. 6th, 1819. Henry Clay was re-elected speaker of the House. The president's message was full of material for the consideration and action of Congress, such as the commercial convention with England, the encouraging of domestic manufactures, coast fortifications, etc. The "Missouri Question" formed the engrossing theme of the session, and the contest began almost immediately. The best talent and political skill and ability were brought to bear upon the issue; whether slavery should be restricted within certain bounds and its progress put an end to, or whether it should be permitted to have free scope and to spread wherever its advocates and supporters could carry it. The position of things at the time helped on the excitement. The south, jealous of the advancing progress of the free States, had insisted all along that Congress should admit a slave State as often as they admitted a free State; and this practice had been followed. Alabama had been the last admitted, and that was a slave State; so that now the advocates of the other side claimed that Missouri, according to rule, ought to come in as a free State. At this date, there were only ten slave States, whilst the free numbered twelve; another, which was free, was soliciting admission; so that unless Missouri could be secured, the southern members felt that slavery was threatened with extinction by the action of Congress, in opposition as they averred, to the original compromise of the Constitution. Besides, the following year the census was to be taken, and a new distribution of the Representatives would be made: already there were a hundred and five members from free States, opposed to only eighty from slave States; so that if Missouri were not secured amongst the latter, the opponents of slavery would have so undoubted a majority in both Houses of Congress as to enable them to do what they pleased, whether the south liked it or not. Whilst, to add to this embroilment, the presidential election was approaching, and if Missouri were not admitted, there would be votes lost or gained for some of the candidates. On the side of the south it was argued, as on former occasions, that Congress had no right to impose restrictions on this subject; that the Constitution recognized slavery as existing and as entitled to protection; that the slaves, as a class, were contented, happy, and well provided for; that even admitting slavery to be an evil, its abolition at the south would be a greater calamity than its continuance; that the addition of Missouri to the Union would not increase the number of slaves, but only diffuse them over a larger space; and in many like ways, with eloquence, zeal and earnestness, the southern men plead for the cause to which they were devoted. The opponents of slavery extension were equally zealous and urgent. They argued that it was plain that slavery was really discountenanced and disliked by the people generally; that it was an anomaly, an abortion, in a country which claimed to be free; that from the first it had been looked upon by our statesmen and patriots, as an evil entailed upon us, but to be got rid of as soon as possible; that the proposition to extend the evils of perpetual bondage over the vast public domain was horrible and revolting; and that Congress certainly had and ought to exercise the power of legislation on this subject. These and similar arguments were urged by northern and western members; and it was felt that the question must now be decided one way or the other. Additional excitement was caused in the Senate by uniting the bill for the admission of Maine to that for the admission of Missouri. The strife raged until the beginning of March, 1820, when it was felt that a conclusion must be soon reached, or neither Maine nor Missouri could take part in the forthcoming election. Accordingly a committee of the two Houses recommended a compromise, which was finally effected; by which all the territory north of the line 36° 30′ was to be forever free from slavery. The vote in favor of this line, in the House, was, 134 in favor, only 42 against. A bill for the admission of Missouri was passed March 6th, 1820; the bill admitting Maine was passed three days earlier.

Congress, notwithstanding its long discussions on the Missouri compromise question, was not neglectful of other matters. Action was taken in regard to a bankruptcy law, a revision of the tariff, a national currency, public land sales, etc. On the 15th of May, Congress adjourned to meet again in November. The fourth decennial census was taken in Aug., 1820: whites, 7,872,711; free colored, 233,566; slaves, 1,543,688; total population, 9,649,965. Senator Benton has much to say of the "gloom and agony" of the years 1819, 1820; suspended specie payments, no help from United States Bank, no price for property or produce, no employment for honest labor, no medium of exchange but bits of dirty paper, distress the universal cry, and relief the universal demand; these, and the like, formed a crisis in affairs which required all the wisdom, energy and zeal of patriots and rulers to meet. Congress reassembled, Nov. 13th, 1820, and as Mr. Clay declined the speaker's chair, a contest of several days' duration occurred, which resulted in electing Mr. Taylor, of New York. The president's message gave a view of public affairs much less gloomy and discouraging than that alluded to above, and Congress entered zealously upon the work before it. The Missouri question came up again, and the strife was again renewed. It appears that the new State, in forming its constitution, had inserted a clause (through Benton's agency) prohibiting free blacks from so much as entering the State, under any pretext whatsoever. The Senate, after a sharp debate, was willing, Dec. 11th, to sanction the State constitution, notwithstanding the objectionable clause; but in the House, the question was not so easily settled. The attempt to carry a resolution in favor of the admission of Missouri was rejected by a vote of ninety-three to seventy-nine. The next step was a resolution for admitting Missouri, provided the obnoxious provision in her constitution be expunged. The resolution was, on the 15th of January, 1821, referred to the committee of the whole, as was also the resolution from the Senate. For some weeks the question rested in the House, various amendments having been proposed, and numerous schemes devised to get rid of the difficulty, and if possible harmonize the conflicting views and opinions of members of Congress. Early in February, a resolution was proposed, calling upon Missouri to expunge the objectionable clause, as contrary to the Constitution of the United States, by a certain day, and then to be admitted into the Union. This proposition was, however, rejected; whereupon, under Henry Clay's guidance, a select committee was appointed to consider and report on the subject. Finally, a joint committee, on the 26th of February, reported a resolution, by which, in a round-about sort of way, were secured, in Missouri, all the rights and privileges to which any citizen of any State is entitled under the Constitution. The House voted in its favor, 87 to 81; the Senate 28 to 14. The presidential election resulted in the reelection of Monroe and Tompkins by almost unanimous vote. The financial distress of the country necessarily occupied a large share of the attention of Congress. The treasury was much embarrassed; a new loan of $5,000,000 was authorized; reduction of salaries was proposed, but lost of course; the army was reduced; half the appropriation for the navy was withdrawn; and various public works held in a state of suspension. Several measures of importance, in regard to the Florida treaty, the public-land debtors, a national system of education, etc., were brought forward and to some extent acted upon. On the 3d of March, Congress reached its close, and at the same date Monroe's first term of service expired.

The inauguration took place on the 5th of March (the 4th being Sunday), in presence of the usual assemblage. The address was a very long document, quite unostentatious, and, in a business-like way, recited the principal incidents of his first administration, and indicated the resources of the country. The fortification of the sea-coast, and the augmentation of the navy; neutrality with regard to the new States in South America, and their contests with foreign powers; negotiations with Great Britain, France, and other European nations; the removal of the Indian tribes westward; the brilliant prospects of our country in the future; these, and the like, formed the staple of the inaugural. On the 10th of March, Monroe appointed Jackson Governor of Florida, the newly-acquired territory. In June, Jackson arrived in Florida and took formal possession. The proceedings of the new governor were, as might have been expected, characteristic of the man, his energy, and executive ability, mixed up with his prompt settlement of questions on his own judgment, without caring much for what others said or did. The Spanish authorities and various officers took offence at the summary demands of Jackson; but the governor made short work with them all; he would have nothing but obedience; and when the chief justice interfered with a *habeas corpus*, Jackson treated him and it with contempt. The energetic governor held his position for another year, when, the American population having increased to 5000 males, Florida was organized as a territory, in the first grade of territorial government.

The Seventeenth Congress began its first session, December 3d, 1821. The president, in his message, gave an encouraging view of public affairs, showing that there was a surplus in hand, by help of the $5,000,000 loan; nevertheless, he recommended a moderate additional duty on certain articles. Jackson and his disputes and troubles came before the House, in January, 1822, but there was no action taken; somehow, nobody cared to record himself as casting censure on a man who was, ere long, to be president of the United States. A general bankrupt law was again proposed, and warmly urged on various grounds; but being opposed by the southern and western members, it was lost by a vote of 99 to 72. The tariff question gave rise to much discussion, and the standing committee on manufactures reported against the expediency of further protection to home manufactures. Provision was made for receiving subscriptions to a loan of $26,000,000, at five per cent., for the purpose of meeting the public debt at six and seven per cent., then falling due. Aid to the Cumberland road was voted; but the president vetoed it, as unconstitutional to make appropriations for public improvements. Congress adjourned, May 8th, 1822.

New political combinations occurred at this date, and there were already six candidates for the presidential chair. J. Q. Adams seemed to be in the regular order of "succession;" Andrew Jackson, the hero of New Orleans; Henry Clay, the statesman and orator; W. H. Crawford, W. Lowndes, and J. C. Calhoun, representatives of sectional and local politics; of these, Jackson was the idol of what may be called the new or advanced democracy. A commercial convention was entered into with France; and with England it was agreed that there should be a reciprocal trade between her colonies and the United States. Privateering in the West India waters had become daring to a high degree, and called for summary punishment. Commodore Porter (p. —), was placed in command of the squadron, in 1823, and by his vigorous measures speedily routed the pirates, although there was great loss of life from yellow fever. Porter, not long after, got into trouble, was tried by court-martial, and suspended for six months, entered the Mexican service, etc. Captain Warrington took his place in command of the squadron.

In the message of Monroe, at the opening of the Eighteenth Congress, December 1st, 1823, the matter of chief interest was in relation to foreign powers, and their course of policy as respected the continent of America. Naturally, our countrymen looked with interest and sympathy upon the struggles of the South American people to free themselves from the dominion of foreign powers. Spain was making vigorous efforts to subdue her rebellious colonies, and was endeavoring to obtain help from the allied sovereigns to this end. In the message, Monroe stated, that amicable negotiations were in progress with Russia and England, to settle their respective rights and interests on the northwest coast. "In the discussions to which this interest has given rise," he adds, "and in the arrangements by which they may terminate, the occasion has been judged proper for asserting, as a principle in which the rights and interests of the United States are involved, that the American continents, by the free and independent condition which they have assumed and maintain, are henceforth not to be considered as subjects of future colonization by any European powers"

Towards the close of the message the president said: "In the wars of the European powers, in matters relating to themselves, we have never taken any part, nor does it comport with our policy so to do. It is only when our rights are invaded, or seriously menaced, that we resent injuries or make preparation for our defence. With the movements in this hemisphere we are, of necessity, more immediately connected, and by causes which must be obvious to all enlightened and impartial observers. The political system of the allied powers is essentially different in this respect from that of America. This difference proceeds from that which exists in their respective governments. And to the defence of our own, which has been achieved by the loss of so much blood and treasure, and matured by the wisdom of our most enlightened citizens, and under which we have enjoyed unexampled felicity, this whole nation is devoted. We owe it, therefore, to candor, and to the amicable relations existing between the United States and those powers, to declare, that we should consider any attempt on their part to extend their system to any portion of this hemisphere as dangerous to our peace and safety. With the existing colonies or dependencies of any European power we have not interfered, and shall not interfere. But with the governments who have declared their independence, and maintained it, and whose independence we have, on great consideration, and on just principles, acknowledged, we could not view any interposition for the purpose of oppressing them, or controlling in any other manner their destiny, by any European power, in any other light than as the manifestation of an unfriendly disposition toward the United States. . . . . . Our policy in regard to Europe, which was adopted at an early stage of the wars which have so long agitated that quarter of the globe, nevertheless, remains the same; which is, not to interfere in the internal concerns of any of its powers; to consider the government, *de facto*, as the legitimate government for us; to cultivate friendly relations with it, and to preserve those relations by a frank, firm, and manly policy; meeting, in all instances, the just claims of every power, submitting to injuries from none. But, in regard to these continents, circumstances are eminently and conspicuously different. It is impossible that the allied powers should extend their political system to any portion of either continent without endangering our peace and happiness; nor can any one believe that our southern brethren, if left to themselves, would adopt it of their own accord. It is equally impossible, therefore, that we should behold such interposition, in any form, with indifference. If we look to the comparative strength and resources of Spain and those new governments, and their distance from each other, it must be obvious that she can never subdue them. It is still the true policy of the United States to leave the parties to themselves, in the hope that other powers will pursue the same course." In such words was set forth the somewhat famous "Monroe doctrine." It originated with J. Q. Adams, and was adopted by the president. However questionable it might be considered for the president to avow so openly and fully sentiments like these, committing the United States to a policy as novel as it was bold, the people of the Union adopted them at once; and though foreign powers were startled somewhat, and a little disposed to complain, the line of policy then marked out has ever since been that by which our government has regulated its conduct on this important subject.

Amendments of the Constitution, for political purposes, were proposed and discussed, and schemes and plans of demagogues, with manœuvres and intrigues of all kinds, were actively at work. The revision of the tariff occupied a very large share of the attention of Congress. Clay and Webster displayed their unrivalled eloquence, and powers as debaters, although on different sides. The agricultural and manufacturing interests in the east and the west were united in support of the principle of a protective tariff; and constituted a small majority in both Houses. The commercial and navigating interests of the North, joined with the large planters of the South, constituted a powerful, intelligent, and persevering minority, opposed to any tariff except for purposes of revenue. For some ten weeks was this question debated; and at last, on the 16th of April, 1824, the bill passed the House by a majority of five, and the Senate accepted it, but amended its details considerably, the majority there being but four. It passed the Senate on the 15th of May, and, after a conference with the House, was finally adopted and approved by the president.

Greece at this date was struggling for independence, and Webster roused the sympathy of the whole country by one of his greatest speeches. Meetings were held; subscriptions liberally made; money, clothing, etc., shipped to Greece; and in some instances, Americans went to fight with the Greeks against their oppressor. Congress adjourned, after a very long and busy session on the 27th of May.

During the summer of 1824, the illustrious Lafayette revisited America. He reached New York, August 15th; was enthusiastically received; travelled through the country during the autumn; spent most of the winter in Washington; visited the South in February and March, 1825, and returning to the North took part in laying the cornerstone of the Bunker Hill monument, and in celebrating the 4th of July in New York. Congress voted to him $200,000 and a township of land in Florida, and on the 7th of September words of farewell were spoken, and Lafayette set out on his return to France.

The contest for the presidency was actively carried on during the summer and autumn of 1824, and the friends and supporters of each candidate were not without hopes of ultimate success. Jackson, Adams, Crawford, and Clay, were now before the people, and the result of the electoral vote was as follows:—for Andrew Jackson for president, 99 votes; for J. Q. Adams, 84; for W. H. Crawford, 41; for Henry Clay, 37. As no one of the candidates received an absolute majority, (131 votes), the election consequently devolved upon the House of Representatives.

Congress assembled, December 6th, 1824. Monroe sent in his last annual message, which contained much of interest and value. Little business, however, was transacted during the session. The presidential election was the chief point of interest, and canvassing of members was actively carried on. Clay, finding that he was not likely to be chosen, gave all his influence to Adams's election. On the 9th of February, 1825, the House proceeded to make a choice between the three highest candidates on the list; Adams received the vote of 13 States, Jackson of 7 States, and Crawford of 4 States. J. Q. Adams consequently was declared duly elected. John C. Calhoun became, also, the vice-president. Congress adjourned, March 3d, 1825, and at the same date James Monroe left the presidential chair. The fifth president's administration was certainly a successful one. There was nothing brilliant about him; he was not a man of genius evidently; his ability was certainly not above the average of men of his day; he was courteous, discreet, peace-loving, not fond of bold measures, and sincerely desirous that the hand of government should be seen and felt as little as was possible in public affairs. His foreign policy, as conducted mainly through his able secretary of state, was dignified, firm, and acceptable to the people; while at home, his administration was memorable for the acquisition of Florida, and for the steady advance of the country, despite all financial embarrassments, in its progress towards national prosperity and greatness.

Mr. Adams was inaugurated to his high office, on the 4th of March, 1825, and delivered an eloquent address, full of patriotic sentiments and earnest wishes for the advancement of our country. Henry Clay was nominated for secretary of state; Richard

Rush, secretary of the treasury; James Barbour, secretary of war; Samuel Southard, secretary of the navy; and William Wirt, attorney-general. The two latter, with Mr. McLean, postmaster-general, had held the same posts under Mr. Monroe. No objection was made to any of these names, except that of Mr. Clay, against whom the charge of bargaining and corruption was made. Twenty-seven voted for Mr. Clay's confirmation; fourteen opposed it, Andrew Jackson being one of these. The new administration had much difficulty and trouble in endeavors to arrange a treaty with the Creek Indians in Georgia, for a cession of their lands, and for their removal west of the Mississippi. A treaty was effected in February, 1825, but was not satisfactory to the larger number of the Creeks, and they resisted its being put into operation. Mr. Adams sent General Gaines to the Creek country to prevent an outbreak and investigate the whole matter. On his report that bad faith towards the Creeks, and corruption were proven against those who made the treaty, the president decided that the Indians should not be meddled with until the next session of Congress. Other treaties were made on equitable terms with Indian tribes during the summer, especially the Kansas Indians, and the Great and Little Osages.

As illustrating the activity of party politics at this date it may be noted that in October, 1825, the legislature of Tennessee, by a nearly unanimous vote, passed a resolution, nominating General Jackson for the presidency at the next election. This led to Jackson's resignation as Senator, on the ground that candidates for the presidency ought not to be members of Congress. In this connection, we may mention the fact, that immediately on Adams's election, all the friends of the disappointed candidates resolved to unite, so as to prevent his re-election, and bring in Andrew Jackson in his place. Personal differences were speedily reconciled. Benton and Jackson, who had formerly met with pistols and dirks in a duel, put their quarrels on one side, in order to work for a common object; and Crawford and Calhoun were also ranged on the side of Jackson, in opposition to the administration. The Nineteenth Congress began its first session, December 5th, 1825, and Mr. Adams's first message was sent in the next day. Able men were in the Senate, as Van Buren, Hayne, Macon, Woodbury, etc., and also in the House, as Everett, Webster, Cambreling, Polk, etc. The message was unusually long, but ably and clearly written, and containing suggestions and views which demanded attention. There was presented in it a favorable picture of the general concerns of the nation, both foreign and domestic. Yet several questions, arising out of the foreign relations of the Union, were spoken of as unsettled. It recommended the entire abolition of discriminating duties on tonnage, in respect of all nations who were willing to reciprocate the privilege; a revision of the judiciary system; a general bankruptcy law; an extension of the law of patents; internal improvements on an enlarged scale; the establishment of an observatory, a national university, and a uniform standard of weights and measures; and the promotion of voyages of discovery. The state of the finances was pronounced to be very flourishing; the entire public debt was less than $81,000,000.

The American Congress at Panama, held in 1826, through the efforts of Bolivar, president of Columbia, was looked upon with favor by Adams, and through his recommendation commissioners were appointed to take part in its deliberations. The opposition took strong ground against the whole matter, but it was evident that the heat and excitement of the dispute on this subject was due rather to political factiousness, than because there was any danger arising from this mission to the interests of the United States; so far, however, as appears by the result, neither side gained or lost anything of moment from the discussion on this question. The project of a Congress of this sort was never afterwards revived, principally because the intes tine dissensions of South America rendered it impossible to effect anything of importance, and also because no further political capital could well be made out of it. Quite a number of amendments to the Constitution were proposed, principally for the purpose of preventing the election of president by the House, as in Mr. Adams's case; but although there was a large amount of talking, no particular result was reached. A resolution was proposed in the Senate in order to bring about a reduction of the patronage in the hands of the president; but it was not successful. Daniel Webster also, as chairman of the Judiciary Committee, introduced a bill to increase the number of judges for the supreme court, mainly to facilitate the dispatch of business, especially in the West. The bill passed the House, but the Senate disagreeing, it was lost. Congress adjourned May 22d, 1826.

The present year was memorable in our annals, for the removal by death of two of those distinguished men, who had taken part in the glorious struggle for liberty, and had served in the highest office which a grateful country can entrust to any of her sons. And what rendered the event more striking was, that Thomas Jefferson and John Adams, the one by whose pen the Declaration of Independence was prepared, the other by whose powerful voice it was advocated and urged in the Continental Congress, both died on the same day, and that day the fiftieth anniversary of our national independence. During the recess of Congress, a convention of amity, commerce, and navigation, was concluded at Washington with Central America, on terms which were regarded as both liberal and reciprocal. The treaty was to continue in force for twelve years, and was ratified by the president on the 28th of October.*

* In the autumn of 1826, the abduction of Morgan took place, and gave rise to the anti-Masonic excitement, and the measures resulting therefrom. For some three or four years, the Masonic fraternity was freely denounced, and numerous politicians made use of this topic as a means o' advancing ends in which they had an interest

Congress re-assembled for its second session Dec. 4th, 1826. The president's message was not very long, and contained but few recommendations; on the whole, the state of public affairs was cheering and encouraging. An attempt was now made to introduce a uniform system of bankruptcy, but ineffectually,—the majority asserting, that though such a law would benefit the wealthy merchants of the Atlantic seaports, the rest of the community would receive from it nothing but harm. A bill for the increase of the duties on imported woolen goods, the design of which was to promote American manufactures by the operation of *protection*, was introduced early, and passed the House of Representatives; but it failed in the Senate, being thrown out by the casting vote of the vice-president. Various grants and appropriations for the promotion of internal improvements, were made in compliance with the president's recommendation. The sum of $500,000 yearly, was also granted for six years, for the gradual improvement of the navy. The proposal to bestow pensions upon the Revolutionary survivors did not meet with the success which it merited. In fact, party spirit was so strong, that less than an ordinary amount of business was accomplished. This session of the Nineteenth Congress closed, March 3d, 1827.

At this date the charge against Henry Clay was revived of bargaining and corruption, in respect to the election of Adams. It was set a going by Jackson on Buchanan's authority; and though it was slanderous and atrocious to a high degree, it had the effect of virtually blasting the political prospects of Clay. In the elections for Congress which followed, the opponents of the administration gained in strength, and were quite ready to let the fact be known.

The Twentieth Congress began its first session, Dec. 3d, 1827. There was a very full attendance of members, and in the contest for speakership the opposition gained the victory Mr. Adams's message contained various recommendations for internal improvements increase of the navy, more attention to the public lands, the increase of the judiciary, etc. During the present session, much attention was devoted to the tariff question, and the friends and opponents of protection exerted their best abilities in defence and in condemnation of the whole "American system," as it was called. Conventions were held on the subject during the summer; at Harrisburg, by the friends of Mr. Clay and the necessity of the tariff to the interests of the country; and at Columbia, in South Carolina, by those who opposed and denounced protective duties as beneficial to the capitalists at the North, but "a grievance not to be patiently submitted to, and but too well calculated to bring on the dangerous inquiry, In what manner are the southern States benefitted by the Union?" This engrossing topic occupied the House, almost exclusively, from the 1st of February to the 22d of April, 1828, when a bill passsd, much altered from that reported by the committee, but by no means conformable to the wishes of the advocates of the protective system. The Senate made a few modifications, and the bill became a law. By this act, the minimum system was extended generally to woolens; different qualities of woolen fabrics being charged *ad valorem* duties of forty-five or fifty per cent., upon the minimum of their estimated value. Unmanufactured wool was also subjected to a duty of four cents per pound, and forty per cent. *ad valorem.* Additional duties were also laid upon iron, hemp, flax, and molasses; and the minimum price of cottons was raised to thirty-five cents the square yard. The policy of this act was questioned by many of the merchants of this country, and its constitutionality by most of the people of the southern States. Unfortunately, it was a compound made up by its enemies as well as its friends, and was not really satisfactory to either. A judiciary bill, with reference to States admitted since 1789, was passed; appropriations were made for the Revolutionary veterans at last, for carrying on the Cumberland Road, etc., and the session closed May 26th, 1828.

The presidential contest became the engrossing occupation of members during the recess. Every engine known to political warfare was vigorously set in motion, and in which the shameless abuse of private character, and the slanderous imputations of every thing unworthy and disgraceful, were enough to disgust all candid, truth-loving minds, and make them almost tremble for the result of unscrupulous party movements and measures, then and thereafter. The result was what the democratic party confidently expected; Andrew Jackson received one hundred and seventy-eight of the two hundred and sixty-one electoral votes; and John Quincy Adams received only eighty-three, less than half the number of those which were given to his successful competitor. Mr. Calhoun was again elected vice-president.

Congress met again, Dec. 1st, 1828, and the same day the president sent in his message. It was long and interesting, covering the usual ground of foreign and domestic relations. The revenue was said to be in a favorable condition, and the public debt was about $58,000,000. He advocated somewhat at large the principle of protection, as embodied in the tariff act recently passed, and urged the need of fortifying the sea-coast, increasing the navy, etc. As this was the short session, little else was done than was absolutely necessary to carry on the government, soon to pass into Jackson's hands. Liberal appropriations were made for the promotion of internal improvements of various kinds; and this fruitful question was once more largely debated, and at length affirmed by considerable majorities, both in the Senate and in the House of Representatives. The continuation of the Cumberland Road, and the conditional cession of it to the States through whose boundaries it passed, occupied much of the time devoted to this section of public business. The Twentieth Congress ended March 3d, 1829, and at the same date Adams's administration reached its close. It was unfortunate, in that the retiring president had attempted, what is probably impossible in our country, *i. e.*, to do without a party, and to rise above mere party, in his course and measures. But whatever may have been the faults and failings of the administration, it certainly was conducted with purity and uprightness; and in respect to ability it compared favorably with those which had gone before. Mr. Adams himself was above reproach, in the blamelessness of his life and the patriotic devotion of his best energies to the good of his country. But he did not, at any time, possess the popular favor; he was not a man of the stamp to win popular applause; his learning, his talents, his ability, his glowing patriotism, never produced the effect which it might be supposed they would upon the community; and it need excite no surprise, that, when the contest came between him and a man such as Andrew Jackson was, that he failed entirely of a reelection; for Jackson had in large measure those qualities which attract the mass of the people; he was bold, and daring, and energetic, and had done good service in the field.

Andrew Jackson was inaugurated president of the United States, March 4th, 1829, after having delivered a brief address to the assembled audience. He appointed as his cabinet: Martin Van Buren, secretary of state; S. D. Ingham, of the treasury; J. H. Eaton, of war; J. Branch, of the navy; J. M. Berrien, attorney-general; and W. T. Barry, postmaster-general. The Senate confirmed these appointments at once. Jackson came into power under favorable auspices, and as he was known to have counselled Monroe to discard party lines and distinctions (p. 175), he now had an opportunity to mark out a truly national policy, and to conduct the government in such wise as to recognize and respect the rights and privileges of the minority as well as the majority among the people. "Retrenchment and reform," were the rallying cries of the party during the election, and retrenchment and reform the president was bound, of course, to see carried into effect wherever it was necessary. The only question to be settled was, what was meant by these terms; whether, on the one hand, the introducing of economy, prudence, simplicity, and such like, into the management and conduct of public affairs, with the utmost and stringent responsibility of public officers; or, on the other, the removing of honest, capable men, who were *not* political adherents, and the appointing of others in their places, who *were* political adherents and supporters. Jackson did not leave any one long in doubt as to what he meant by "reform." It consisted in a very extensive removal of officers who were politically considered, known, or believed to be friends and supporters of Adams at the last election, and the appointment of others in their places who had been active in securing the election of Jackson; thus opening the door to the conviction, that office under the government is to be the reward of partizanship, that "to the victors belong the spoils," and that from the highest office in the State, down to the very humblest and most insignificant, no man can be deemed qualified except he be, out and out, a member and supporter of the successful and dominant party. During the nine months recess, there were 167 removals and re-appointments, in which the Senate could have no voice; and by the end of the first year of the new administration, there had been nearly 700 changes in government officers. The meaning of "retrenchment and reform" henceforth became plain enough.* Such are the *facts* of the case, and as such they

* In contrast with this procedure on the part of Jackson, it deserves to be noted, that, although Mr. Jefferson began the system which has since been carried out so fully, (see p. 127) he removed only thirty-nine in the course of eight years; John Adams, during his four years, removed ten; Washington removed nine; Madison, five; Monroe, nine; and John Quincy Adams, two; making the sum total of removals by six presidents, only seventy-four, and most of these for sufficient cause.

Andrew Jackson

From the original painting by Chappel in the possession of the publishers.

Johnson, Fry & Co. Publishers, New York.

are presented for the reader's consideration. Jackson undertook to defend his course as wise and just, and Benton, his great admirer, argues in like strain; but, we think, it must be admitted, that in the judgment of impartial men, great mischief was set on foot when the plan of the seventh president was carried out, and when he furnished an example which later presidents have been only too ready to follow.

The Twenty-first Congress began its first session, December 7th, 1829. On the next day Jackson sent in a very long message, drawn up, evidently, with care, and filled with material for consideration and action of Congress. Among the principal measures recommended were: an amendment of the Constitution on the subject of electing the president, in order that it might be done by the people, without the intervention of electors, and that he should be ineligible for a second term; a review and alteration of the judiciary law, so as to extend the circuit court to all the States; a discontinuance of building ships of the larger classes, and the collecting and storing of materials instead; a gradual reduction of duties on articles of general consumption, which are not the production of the country; the re-organizing the department of state, etc. The public lands question came up early in the session, and led to a very ardent and important discussion. The western States, Benton being the principal leader, were greatly displeased at the course of matters, and seemed to think that their sovereignties were weakened, to say the least, if not directly interfered with by the general government's land system. Mr. Foot submitted a resolution to the Senate, December 29th, 1829, for the purpose of aiding the government plan on this subject; but it was at once attacked by Benton, on the 18th of January, 1830, with great boldness and license of speech. Hayne, of South Carolina, followed, and took even greater license, uttering sharp invectives against the eastern States, and advocating the most ultra State-rights doctrines. This brought out Daniel Webster, who, on the 20th delivered his first great speech, and on the 26th of January, followed it up by that memorable oration in defence and exposition of the Constitution. Nullification and disunion were for the time quelled; and it was reserved for the next generation to see these odious opinions break out into open and bloody rebellion. The president's appointments to office, before noted (p. 186), were, after a time, submitted to the Senate. However widely opinions differed with regard to the necessity of that kind of "reform" which Jackson had attempted, by removing so many persons from office, there was not much difference of sentiment as to the impropriety of his using the opportunities thus created for rewarding the electioneering services of his partisans. And, in consequence, several of the nominations were rejected, and in some instances, the vote rejecting them was so large as to convey a tolerably decided censure upon the course adopted by the executive. There was considerable debate on the question of retrenchment in various quarters; but no actual result followed. The Indians in the South-west memorialized Congress, claiming protection and justice in regard to their removal beyond the Mississippi; but, as Georgia was resolved that they should go, and speedily too, and as the sympathies of the executive and Congress were against the Indians, Congress made an appropriation of $500,000 towards effecting the end. In his message, Jackson, who seems to have had a special spite against the Bank of the United States, had recommended attention to the subject of its application for a renewal of its charter, which, by the way, did not expire till 1836. The matter came up in the House and the Senate, and in both, the president's views met with censure. In the eyes of most of people, the debates and action of Congress ought to have shaken the resolution of any ordinary man. But Andrew Jackson was *not* an ordinary man, and having set his mind upon a certain view of this matter, he was not to be driven from it by any doubts or hesitation as to whether he might not possibly be wrong, in a question wherein the learning, and experience, and ability of statesmen and financiers, of his own party, too, were, with scarce an exception, arrayed against him. After a busy session, Congress adjourned May 31st, 1830.

The fifth census was taken this year, with the following result: whites, 10,537,338; free blacks, 319,599; slaves, 2,009,043; total, 12,866,020.

The second session of the Twenty-first Congress began December 6th, 1830. In his message, Jackson again urged amending the Constitution in relation to electing president and vice-president. "I cannot," said he, "too earnestly invite your attention to the propriety of promoting such an amendment as will render him ineligible after one term of service." The finances were represented as in a very favorable condition; the Indian question was spoken of; and wise and harmonious action on the tariff was urged. Although the democrats were in a majority in Congress, and though it was well known that Jackson opposed all spending of money upon internal improvements, yet Congress took decided measures against Jackson's views, and virtually established the policy of our government in this respect. By large votes, appropriations were made for carrying on the Cumberland Road, and improving the navigation of the Ohio. The president, though rather fond of the *veto* power, had no alternative but to yield to the action of the national legislature.

About this time there was a serious falling out in the president's cabinet, which led to the natural result of a quarrel soon after. Calhoun and Jackson also became ill friends, and it was hoped by the "national republican" party, as they called themselves, that hey might succeed next time in electing Henry Clay to the presidency. The Twenty-second Congress began its first session, Dec. 5th, 1831, and the president's message was read to both Houses the next day. One statement of interest was made, viz., that during Jackson's three years in office nearly $40,000,000 of the public debt had been paid off. When the nominations during the recess came up before the Senate, Mr. Van Buren's name was not approved; he had been sent by Jackson to London in August, 1831, but, by the casting vote of Calhoun, he was not allowed to remain there; he came back just in time to be put on the same ticket with Andrew Jackson for vice-president, and with reasonable expectation of being Jackson's successor in the presidency. The hostility of the executive being well known towards the Bank of the United States, that institution, having good reason to fear such an enemy as this, thought it best, at an early day, to apply for a renewal of its charter; and so the great bank controversy began. Early in the year 1832 the controversy was entered upon in both Houses. The whole matter was discussed, referred to committees, reported upon, examined into in various ways, and, after weeks and months of delays, after trying the strength of friends and opponents pretty thoroughly, the Senate, on the 11th of June, passed the bill for renewing the charter, by a vote of 28 to 20. The House, after some amendment, accepted by the Senate, also passed the bill, by a vote of 107 to 85. This was on the 3d of July; for the session had been unusually protracted; but Congress arranged its adjournment so as to leave ten clear days after the bill was put into the hands of the president, lest it should be retained till the next session, as other bills had been. Jackson was all ready to meet the case. The bill was presented to him on the 4th of July, and on the 10th he returned it with his veto, a document of great length, in which the question is argued in full. Among his concluding words, he spoke very confidently: "I have now done my duty to my country. If sustained by my fellow-citizens, I shall be grateful and happy; if not, I shall find, in the motives which impel me, ample grounds for contentment and peace." Both Webster and Clay addressed the Sen ate; but, as it was not possible to obtain a two thirds vote, the bill was, of course, lost. The public lands occupied considerable attention in Congress; but, owing to the lateness of the time when they were under discussion, nothing of moment was accomplished. Internal improvements were warmly agitated, and several large appropriations were made and sanctioned by the president, having this object in view. The tariff also came under the attention of Congress, being distinctly recommended by Jackson himself, and the progress of the anti-tariff feeling in the South requiring it. The question was taken up in the House, and a tariff bill finally carried. The principle of protection was maintained by this bill, but the duties on many protected articles of domestic manufactures were considerably reduced, and it was received as a concession to the free trade party, and with the hope (a most delusive one, as it proved,) that it would have the effect of allaying the existing excitement in South Carolina. This unusually long session of Congress closed July 14th, 1832.

In the North-west fresh troubles broke out in the spring of the present year. The Sacs and Foxes, who, by treaty had agreed to remove, showed much reluctance in doing so, and the governor of Illinois was disposed to hasten their departure. He accordingly ordered the militia to use compulsion in carrying out the measure. Black Hawk was leader of the Indians at the time, and he at once resorted to the only practicable means of revenge—predatory and hostile ravages in the frontier settlements; whilst he prepared for a more formidable retaliation. In March, 1832, he assembled his own tribes, the Sacs and Foxes, with Winnebagoes, to the number of about a thousand in all, and crossed the Mississippi into Illinois. All was dismay; the settlers nearest the point of invasion fled, and a brigade of militia, ordered out for their protection, by no means appeased the alarm. By June, however, the United States troops there, together with about three thousand mounted volunteers, took the field, and Black Hawk withdrew his warriors into the swamps, which were their fortresses, and trenches, and ambuscades, at the same time; and he extended his murderous incursions over the whole of the most advanced north-western settlements. The American troops penetrated the lurking places of the Indians, and on the 21st of July defeated them on the banks of the Wisconsin, and again, August 2d, routed them completely near the mouth of the Iowa. Black Hawk and his band surrendered, and in September treaties were made, and peace restored to the North-west.

Directly after the passage of the tariff act, noted above, the representatives of South Carolina addressed their constituents on the subject, and urged upon them to sustain the sovereign rights of that State, which, they said, were invaded by the recent action of Congress. Meetings were accordingly held in South Carolina, and much excitement was manifested against the general government. The legislature was convened by Governor Hamilton, at Columbia, on the 22d of October, and the tariff question was warmly discussed. The result was, the calling of a State convention, which met on the 19th of November, 1832, at the same place. This convention proceeded to the length of recommending nullification, in the completest sense of the term. The legislature, which met on the 27th, passed ordinances to carry into effect the recommendations of the State convention, and South Carolina became thus arrayed in opposition to the laws of the United States, refusing to allow the revenue to be collected, and determining to resist by force every attempt to compel obedience This, of course, brought the question to an issue, and it remained to be seen, whether the executive would take care to have the laws of the United States enforced, and whether South Carolina would be reduced to her proper place as one of the members of the Union.

The Twenty-second Congress began its second session, December 4th, 1832. Jackson, in his message, urged the necessity of revising the tariff and putting it on a right and just foundation; "nullification" also came under his notice, and he intimated his belief "that the laws themselves were fully adequate to the suppression of such attempts as might immediately be made" to carry out the views of those who favored absolute State sovereignty. "Should the exigency arise," he continued, "rendering the execution of the existing laws impracticable from any cause whatever, prompt notice of it will be given to Congress, with the suggestion of such views and measures as may be deemed necessary to meet it." Jackson's hostility to the United States Bank was in no degree lessened. He not only recommended selling the government stock, but also begged Congress seriously to investigate the question, —"Whether the public deposits in that institution may be regarded as entirely safe." South Carolina having proceeded to the lengths mentioned above, Jackson manifested his usual decision in meeting the emergency. He gave orders to the military force at his disposal, to be ready to sustain and protect the federal officers at Charleston; and on the 10th of December, a long and energetic proclamation was issued, denouncing the movements of the nullifiers as palpable treason, and calling upon the South Carolinians to return to their loyalty to the Union.

The tariff question came up at an early day, and the discussion was entered upon at the opening of the year 1833. On the 16th of January, however, the president, by message, communicated information respecting the ordinance and nullifying laws of South Carolina, and his own proclamation thereupon, accompanied by his views of what Congress should do; and on the 21st of the month, a bill to enforce the collection of the revenue according to the law was reported by the judiciary committee of the Senate. Thus there were two bills of primary importance on the same subject, but looking in precisely opposite directions, under discussion in the Houses of Congress at the same time, —this enforcing or force bill in the Senate, to compel South Carolina to submit to the tariff of 1828, and the new tariff bill in the House of Representatives, to abolish that very tariff which the enforcing bill was to uphold. Calhoun, (who was now a senator,) offered a series of resolutions, which were in fact expansions of the old view of the State-sovereignty principle, and yet they involved the whole principle of "nullification." Starting from the definition of the Constitution, as a "compact" uniting "the people of the several States;" and of the Union, as "a union between the States" which ratified "the constitutional compact;" he proceeded to the assertions, that whilst "certain definite powers" were delegated to the general government, "to be executed jointly," each State reserved to itself "the residuary mass of powers to be exercised by its own separate government;" and that in the assumption by the general government of powers not delegated to it, its acts are "unauthorized, void, and of no effect," each State having "an equal right to judge for itself, as well of the infraction as of the mode and measure of redress," all being "sovereign parties, without any common judge." Lastly, he distinctly denied the opposite allegations, that the Union was based on a social compact of the people, "taken collectively, as individuals," and "that they have not the right of judging, in the last resort, as to the extent of powers reserved, and, of consequence, of those delegated;" because the tendency of those opinions was to "subvert the sovereignty of the States, to destroy the federal character of the Union, and to rear on its ruins a consolidated government, without constitutional check or limitation, and which must necessarily terminate in the loss of liberty itself."

Mr. Clayton proposed a resolution setting forth the real reply to Calhoun's statement. It was to this effect,—"That the people of these United States are, for the purposes enumerated in their Constitution, one people and a single nation;" "that while the Constitution does provide for the interest and safety of all the States, it does not secure all the rights of independent sovereignty to any;" "that the Supreme Court of the United States is the proper and only tribunal in the last resort for the decision of all cases in law and equity, arising under the Constitution, the laws of the United States, and treaties made under their authority;" and further, that the Senate "would not fail in the faithful discharge of its most solemn duty to support the executive in the just administration of the government, and clothe it with all constitutional power necessary to the faithful execution of the laws and the preservation of the Union."

When matters were in this critical position between South Carolina and the general government, Henry Clay came forward and proposed what was called the "Compromise Tariff" bill. The object of this was a reduction of the duties at least one-tenth directly, and a continuous reduction during subsequent years till 1841. The bill was discussed and finally adopted by large majorities in both Houses, just before the end of the session. The enforcing bill passed the Senate, February 20th, thirty-two voting in favor of it, and only one (John Tyler) against. On the 28th, it passed the House by a vote of 150 against 35. Congress adjourned on the 2d of March (the 3d being Sunday).

Jackson, though anxious to prevent any one from being president more than four years, still, like other and weaker men, made no difficulty in serving a second term. On the 4th of March, 1833, he was again inaugurated and delivered another address. Although Congress had given its judgment that the public deposits were entirely safe in the United States Bank, nevertheless, as Jackson had made up his mind to do a certain thing, he was not to be stopped by Congress. Mr. W. J. Duane was secretary of the treasury at this date, and the president supposed that he would do as the executive wished. But Mr. Duane refused to do Jackson's behest, unless authorized by Congress; he was at once removed, and on September 23d, R. B. Taney was appointed, a gentleman who had no scruples in doing what he was selected to do. On the first of October, the deposits were removed, and placed in certain selected banks in different parts of the country. For this action Jackson boldly avowed that he "took the responsibility," notwithstanding the major part of his cabinet dissented from his design. It would be difficult, in any space at our command, to give anything of an adequate description of the commercial excitement and distress which ensued upon the course adopted by Jackson. At the time, the business of the country was unusually active. The capitalists, and the merchants, and mechanics, had unlimited confidence in each other, and all the moneyed institutions in the country had extended their loans to the utmost bounds of their ability. At such a juncture, great and rigid retrenchment, attended with want of confidence, was necessarily productive of ominous consequences; private credit was deeply affected; the business of the country was interrupted; and, in short, a complete and terrible panic was produced, which seemed to be at its height when Congress met, but which was destined to last, with many fluctuations in its symptoms and violence, for some ten years.

The Twenty-third Congress began its first session, December 2d, 1833. The administration was strong in the House, but in a minority in the Senate. The great questions agitating the community came up for discussion and action. Jackson refused the request made to him to communicate to the Senate, the paper read to his Cabinet in regard to removing the deposits. This refusal was denounced as "usurpation," and led to Henry Clay's proposing, December 26th, the following resolution: "*Resolved*, That the president, in the late executive proceedings in relation to the public revenue, has assumed upon himself authority and power not conferred by the Constitution and laws, but in derogation of both." The resolution was adopted, March

28th, 1834, by a vote of twenty-six to twenty; whereupon Jackson sent in a message and long protest, denying the right of the Senate to censure his proceedings, and requesting that what he had sent be entered on the journal. A strong debate of some three weeks followed, in which Calhoun and Webster, with others, denounced the presidential tendency to high-handed exercise of executive power and patronage. On the 7th of May, by a vote of twenty-seven to sixteen, the Senate resolved, "That the protest communicated to the Senate on the 17th (of April), by the president of the United States, asserts powers as belonging to the president, which are inconsistent with the just authority of the two Houses of Congress, and inconsistent with the Constitution of the United States; and that the aforesaid protest is a breach of the privileges of the Senate, and that it be not entered on the journal."

Whilst this contest was going on in the national legislature, the people in all the great cities and towns throughout the Union, and in many of less note, held meetings, and dispatched petitions to Congress, and committees to wait in person on the president, for the purpose of representing their distress and begging him to recommend some measure of relief. As the session advanced, this popular action on the executive and Congress grew in intensity, both as to the numbers and urgency of the applications. The petitioners for relief were told, that the government could provide neither remedy nor relief; it was all in the hands of the bank, or the banks and themselves; for "they who traded on borrowed capital ought to break." In the House strong action was taken against rechartering the bank. Early in March four resolutions were proposed and passed April 4th, 1834, to this effect: That the bank ought not to be rechartered; that the deposits ought not to be replaced; that State banks ought to be used as places of deposit, but that Congress (and here the president was implicitly blamed and that with some severity) ought to prescribe the mode of selecting them, the securities, the terms, and the manner of employing them; and that a complete investigation of the affairs of the Bank of the United States should be made, for the purpose of ascertaining "the cause of the commercial embarrassment and distress, complained of by numerous citizens of the United States." Another sharp debate took place in the Senate on some of the president's proceedings; Taney's nomination as secretary of the treasury was rejected in June; and on the 30th, Congress adjourned. The closing session of this Congress was commenced Dec. 1st; but on its expiration, March 3d, 1835, it left most of the important measures unfinished; amongst which was the post-office reform bill, the custom house regulations bill, the judiciary bill, the bill regulating the deposit of the public moneys in the deposit banks, the bill respecting the tenure of office and removals from office, the bill for indemnifying the claimants for French spoliations before the year 1800, and the fortification bill.

It was an especial annoyance to a man of Jackson's temperament, that France had for so many years manifested equal negligence and unwillingness to make pro per indem nity for spoliations on American commerce. Other European powers, following this bad example, were pursuing much the same course as France. Jackson, however, resolved to have a settlement, and he took measures accordingly. In his message, Dec., 1834, he recommended reprisals, unless France paid her debts immediately. This stirred up the French blood not a little; and a nice diplomatic quarrel resulted, lasting for a considerable time. Early in 1836, however, Great Britain offered to be a mediator, and France took the necessary action by paying the indemnities without further trouble. Denmark, also, with Naples, Spain, and Portugal, speedily settled the claims against them, and these vexatious matters were disposed of.

Texas and its affairs appear cn the carpet for the first time at this date. This large province revolted from Mexico, in 1833, declared itself indeoendent, and by the decisive victory at San Jacinto in 1836, freed itself from its former owners. Its independence was recognized by the United States in 1837, with the understanding that at no distant date, it would be annexed to the Great Republic. The population, at the time, was about 20,000; but from that date it rapidly increased.

A national democratic convention having been suggested by Jackson, in a letter which was published in February, 1835, the suggestion was immediately adopted, and the convention met at Baltimore, in May. Some six hundred delegates were in attendance, and Martin Van Buren was unanimously nominated for president. Richard M. Johnson also received the nomination for vice-president. The opposition, or "whigs," as they were now called, put forward General Harrison and Daniel Webster.

The Twenty-fourth Congress began its first session, December 7th, 1835. J. K. Polk was elected speaker of the House, and the president's message was received the next day. In this document a very flattering account was given of the national finances, and the general prosperity of the country. The public debt had been extinguished, and there was a balance of some $19,000,000 in hand. The president anticipated a surplus of $6,000,000 over and above the necessary appropriations which were to be made. This surplus, it was suggested, might be laid out in navy yards, or new national works, rather than distributed amongst the States, or "reduced faster than would be effected by the existing laws." The receipt of $11,000,000 from the sale of public lands in the current year was announced; and the need of some great changes in the general land office was intimated; together with the abolition of the offices of commissioners of loans and of the sinking fund. Other topics were treated of, as the army, navy, post-office, etc. The session was a very long one; but, after all, it did not accomplish much.* One of the most important acts passed was that for regulating the deposits of the public moneys in the State banks. The majorities in its favor were unusually large, and it was approved by the president at the close of June, 1836. Thus, $37,000,000 were transferred from the national treasury to those of the States, on their pledge to keep the money safe, and repay it at some future time. The effect of this distribution of the surplus revenue among the States was what was naturally to be expected. New banks sprang suddenly into existence, with nominal capital, and the country was deluged with paper money. Speculations of the wildest character were set on foot; and it seems almost incredible, that infatuation, and folly, and greed of gain, should have seized upon nearly the entire community. No scheme seemed to be too wild or chimerical to receive attention, and so easily deluded were the people, that prodigious frauds were perpetrated without producing that shock to the moral sensibilities which is always felt in a healthy state of the body politic. A calamitous reverse was, of course, ere long, to be looked for, and it came with terrible effect within a short time. Internal improvements, the patent laws, the admission of Arkansas and Michigan, as independent and sovereign States, into the Union, and the military academy, were amongst the subjects of minor importance to which Congress devoted its time and labor now. The subject of slavery came before Congress again, and gave rise to much excitement. It was brought on by the presentation of memorials praying that slavery be abolished in the District of Columbia, over which, it was pleaded, Congress had entire authority. John Quincy Adams took an active share in this whole matter, and planted himself upon the inalienable right of petition; but the southern influence was too strong for the abolitionist memorialists to

* On the 1st of July, 1836, Congress accepted the trust offered to it by James Smithson, of London, in England, of employing £100,000 in the establishment of "The Smithsonian Institution," at Washington, "for the Increase and Diffusion of Knowledge amongst Men."

obtain anything. Congress refused to interfere with slavery in the District, and resolved to lay upon the table, without printing or reference, or taking any action whatever on them, all petitions, etc., "relating in any way to the subject of slavery, or the abolition of slavery." Congress was also called upon to consider this exciting topic in connection with the admission of Arkansas; and with a change in the boundary line of Missouri, effected through Benton's exertions, he assures us; which was "accomplished," as he writes, "by the extraordinary process of altering a compromise line, intended to be perpetual, and the reconversion of soil, which had been slave and made free, back again from free to slave." Congress closed its session on the 4th of July, 1836. On the 11th of the same month, a circular was issued by the secretary of the treasury, "by order of the president," instructing the receivers of public money to take silver and gold alone (with the exception of Virginia land scrip in certain cases) in payment for the public lands. It had been attempted, in April, to secure this object by a joint resolution of the two Houses of Congress; but the Senate refusing to entertain the proposal, it was left to Jackson to act as he thought best in the matter. The effect of this "specie circular" was, undoubtedly, to check the proceedings of the speculators in purchasing public lands; but, at the same time, it is to be noted, that it embarrassed to an almost disastrous degree the operations of the manufacturers and merchants. In several respects, no doubt, it was called for, and was salutary in its operation; but, at the same time, it was felt to be a hard and stringent measure, which would not probably have been deemed at any period necessary, had not Jackson succeeded in breaking down the United States Bank, with the consequences which followed upon that famous act (p. 188).

The presidential election took place during the autumn, and resulted as follows: Van Buren received 170 votes; Gen. Harrison, 73; and other candidates much less. R. M. Johnson received 147 votes for vice-president; F. Granger, 77; J. Tyler, 47; W. Smith, 23. As no election had been made for vice-president, the Senate, by a vote, placed Johnson in the vacant chair. Congress met for its second session on the 5th of December, 1836, and General Jackson sent in his last annual message on the following day. It gave a very favorable account of the state of affairs, and showed that a large surplus—over $41,000,000—would be in the treasury on the 1st of January, 1837. The specie circular was defended; the operation of the local banks as fiscal agents of the government was highly praised; a number of recommendations on various subjects were made; etc. Benton, the great admirer of the president, and author of the famous "expunging resolution," by unwearied labor for some three years, in season and out of season, succeeded in carrying what he proposed, by a vote of 24 to 19. The Senate, it will be remembered, had condemned Jackson for removing the deposits from the United States Bank (p. 191). The Missouri senator devoted himself to having this record of censure effaced, as if in this way the fact became any the less a fact, or the censure became any the less deserved! However, amid no little excitement, broad black lines were drawn round the resolution of the Senate, and the secretary wrote across it these words: "Expunged by order of the Senate, this 16th day of January, 1837." A vigorous attempt was made to rescind the treasury circular respecting specie payments for land sales. A resolution to this effect having been referred to the committee on public lands, a bill was reported, purporting the designation and limitation of the funds receivable for the revenues of the United States, and, in fact, providing for the reception of the notes of specie-paying banks, in certain cases. Benton, the "hard money" man, opposed it, but it passed by an overwhelming majority—41 against 5. In the House an attempt was made to amend it, so as to save the specie circular, but it failed; 143 representatives voted for the bill as it came from the Senate, and only 59 against it. On the last day but one of the session it was sent to the president, who retained it in his possession, thus preventing its becoming a law. Few acts of general interest having been passed during the session, the Twenty-fourth Congress reached its close, March 3d, 1837. At the same time, Andrew Jackson finished his eight years of occupancy of the presidential chair, and made way for his successor. It is difficult to speak of his administration, as it deserves, in the limited space at our command. The ardent admirers and partizans of the hero of New Orleans indulge in nothing less than unqualified laudation; while, on the other hand, his political enemies can hardly find language strong enough to reprobate his high-handed measures, his lawless assumption of power, his unswerving devotion to party and party purposes, and the like. We leave the reader to judge for himself, and to reflect carefully upon the probable results of men like Jackson being at the head of affairs in the United States.

On the 4th of March, 1837, Martin Van Buren was inaugurated as the eighth president of the United States, with the usual ceremonies. His address was well written, and set forth the views and principles by which he expected to be governed in the discharge of his duties. He renewed the pledge which he had given before his election, viz., "I must go into the presidential chair the inflexible and uncompromising opponent of every attempt, on the part of Congress, to abolish slavery in the District of Columbia, against the wishes of the slave-holding States; and also with a determination equally decided to resist the slightest interference with it in the States where it exists." The condition of the country, generally, in regard to commercial and business affairs was critical and even alarming. The removal of the deposits, the specie circular, and the distribution of the surplus revenue, had, in the opinion of many brought about this distressing state of things; and mercantile men in general gave expression to the conviction, that the only effectual remedy for the evils affecting the currency and commercial exchanges was to be found in the establishment of a national bank. Failures began to occur in every quarter. During the first three weeks in April, two hundred and fifty houses stopped payment in New York. In New Orleans, during two days' time, houses stopped payment, owing an aggregate of $27,000,000; and in other cities similar evidences were given of the storm that had burst over the country. The demands upon the banks increased rapidly; they could not keep their notes in circulation; the alarm grew into a panic; and a general run was made upon the banks. On the 10th of May, all the banks in New York stopped specie payments; and on the 16th, the legislature authorized this step on the part of the banks, to last for one year. The banks of other States speedily followed the example of those of New York; and all classes of the community gloomily anticipated wide-spread ruin as the inevitable result. The merchants and bankers of New York sent a deputation to Washington to beg of the president to rescind the specie circular, defer commencing suits on unpaid bonds, and to call an extra session of Congress. Other towns and cities made similar efforts to induce Van Buren to furnish some relief; but he declined acting upon their petitions, and only consented, with reluctance, to the calling an extra session of Congress. His proclamation to this effect was issued on the 15th of May, and Congress was summoned to meet in September, on account of "great and weighty matters claiming their consideration."

The extra session was begun on the 4th of September, 1837, and it became evident at once, from the tone of the president's message, that no relief was to be looked for from the government. He ascribed the state of things to overtrading speculation, fostered and stimulated by the banks, and avowed his belief, that all the government could do, or was designed to do, was to take care of itself and that it could not be expected to legislate with reference to the monetary affairs of the people. The most important recommendation which Mr. Van Buren made, was, that the government should for the future keep its money in its own hands, by the instrumentality of the scheme of a sub-treasury, or, as it was called by its supporters, the independent treasury; so that there should be an entire and total separation of the business and funds of the government from those of the banks. The finance committee of the Senate presented four bills; one, for suspending the payment of the fourth installment of the surplus revenue to the States; a second, for authorizing the issue of treasury notes equal to any deficiency which might be felt in the treasury, with an addition of $4,000,000, by way of reserve; another, for the extension of the indulgence in the payment of revenue bonds; and a fourth, for the organization of the sub-treasury system. This last proposal caused much excitement both in and out of Congress, yet it passed both Houses by small majorities. Other matters were debated, but nothing of moment was done, except authorizing the issue of $10,000,000 in treasury notes, for the immediate wants of the government. After an unsatisfactory session, Congress adjourned October 16th.

On the 4th of December, Congress again assembled, and the president sent in his first annual message. It contained various matters of public interest and concern; but, as was to be expected, the chief matter which came under discussion, was the sub-treasury scheme. Calhoun, in the Senate, supported the views of the administration, while on the other hand, Clay and Webster exerted their great powers against the plan proposed for a treasury bank. In the progress of the debate the bill was considerably modified, and a clause prohibiting the receipt of bank-paper in payment of government dues was struck out; and thus amended, it passed the Senate, in June, 1838, by a vote of twenty-seven against twenty-five. In the House it was laid on the table. Among the acts of the session, we may note here; the granting preemption rights to actual settlers; establishing the territory of Iowa; authorizing several works for internal improvements, in the way of light-boats and beacons, the navigating of certain rivers in Florida, and the like; appropriating money for suppressing Indian hostilities, etc. The following resolution also, respecting the specie circular was passed by the Senate, by a vote of thirty-four to nine, and the other House, by a hundred and fifty-one, to twenty-seven:—"*Resolved*, That it shall not be lawful for the secretary of the treasury to make, or continue in force, any general order which shall create any difference between the different branches of revenue, as to the money or medium of payment in which debts or dues accruing to the United States may be paid."

The Florida war was still in progress, and proved a source of great trouble and almost incredible expense. The removal of the Indians was a settled measure, and when they proved reluctant, collisions naturally followed. The war with the Seminoles began in December, 1835, and lasted for five years. Some of the ablest men in the army were sent against them, as Scott, Jessup, Taylor, Worth, and others; but led on by such chiefs as Osceola, Jumper, and Tiger-Tail, and with a country abounding in swamps and marshes, extensively fatal to the whites, they resisted every attempt to subdue them. No treaty stipulations were regarded by them, and they seized every occasion to inflict severe blows upon the Americans. More than once they repulsed with great loss superior numbers. In July, 1836, General Jessup officially announced the war at an end; but the restless savage could be held by no obligation. The war went on with its usual circumstances of cruelty and barbarity. There were nearly nine thousand men under arms, and the cost of the war exceeded $15,000,000. It was not till 1842, that an entire cessation of troubles in Florida took place. Resolutions in favor of annexing Texas, (p. 193), were offered in the Senate; but to no particular purpose, and Congress adjourned, July 9th, 1838.

An attempt to stir up rebellion in Canada was made in the latter part of 1837, and quite a number of the citizens of the United States sympathized with the movement, and were ready to give it assistance. Mackenzie in Upper, and Papineau in Lower Canada, were the active spirits in this revolt, and various bodies of Americans joined the rebels, so that it speedily became evident, that collision would ere long take place, in which our country's faith and honor were involved. A party of Americans, some seven hundred strong, under Van Rensselaer, of Albany, took possession of Navy Island, in the Niagara River, about two miles above the falls. Colonel M'Nab, with a body of militia, was posted opposite this island, with instructions to watch the insurgents, and not to violate the American territory. Finding that most of the supplies for the island were conveyed by a small steamer, named the "Caroline," from a landing-place on the American side, called Fort Schlosser, M'Nab dispatched some of his militia in boats, to take or destroy her. This they accomplished in the middle of the night of the 29th of December, after a short but desperate struggle, in which they killed or drove out of the vessel all the crew, and having set it on fire, let it drift down the rapids and over the Falls of Niagara. But the act, however to be regarded in itself, having been committed on American territory, caused no little excitement in the United States. The president issued a proclamation, Jan. 5th, 1838, against all persons engaging in unlawful schemes, warning them against the consequences. Gen. Scott was sent to the frontier, in January, and the Navy Island insurgents gave up their arms, etc. Other attempts of a similar character, were made at Detroit, Sandusky Bay, and the north-eastern end of Lake Ontario. Various acts of outrage were committed during the year. In November, an attempt was made to take Prescott, in Upper Canada, but failed, and about a hundred and fifty American citizens were captured and taken to Kingston, to be tried by court martial. The British authorities dealt more leniently with them than they deserved, the greater portion of them being pardoned, a very few suffering death.

The concluding session of the Twenty-fifth Congress began on the 3d of December, 1838. Few acts, however, of general interest were passed. An act was passed abolishing imprisonment for debt in certain cases; and a sharp discussion took place upon a series of resolutions, forbidding the introduction of the slavery question into Congress. The public lands question was again discussed, as also were propositions for abolishing the salt tax and the fishing bounties. Difficulties respecting the much vexed topic of the north-eastern boundary seeming to require it, the president had additional powers conferred upon him for the defence, if needed, of the United States. Congress came to an end, March 3d, 1839. At the elections, the democrats seemed to be losing strength, and they succeeded in preserving a majority in the House by refusing the five or six New Jersey whig members, on the plea that they were not elected by a majority of the votes, although they presented certificates of their election under the seal of the State.

The Twenty-sixth Congress began its first session, Dec. 2d, 1839, that is to say, the members came together at this date, and wasted three weeks in fighting over the question of the New Jersey members' seats. On the 21st, the House was organized, and the president's message received on the 24th; but the dispute about the New Jersey claimants was not settled till July, 1840. At the whig convention, in Dec., 1839, Clay, Harrison and Scott were among the principal candidates for nomination. Although Clay seemed on every account to be the best man, the convention at last settled upon Gen Harrison as their candidate; John Tyler was nominated for vice-president. The democrats, on their part, in May, 1840, renominated Van Buren for president. The sub-treasury system was long and ably discussed during the session, and its advantages and disadvantages set forth fully. The bill passed both Houses by the beginning of July, 1840, and on the 4th of the month received the president's signature and became the law of the land. The chief provisions were, that, after the 30th of June, one-fourth of all payments to the United States were to be made in gold and silver only, and so on, annually from that day, one-fourth more, until after the 30th of June, 1843, the entire amount of the revenues of every description, including payments at the post-office, would be receivable in specie alone. And similarly with regard to payments made by the United States. Four persons were very soon after the passage of the bill appointed receivers-general of the public money, for four years. A bankruptcy law was introduced by Webster, and carried through the Senate, but it was laid upon the table of the other House by a vote of a hundred and one to eighty-nine. The graduation of prices for public lands was again attempted in vain; an issue of $5,000,000 more of treasury notes was authorized; and on the 21st of July, Congress adjourned.

The sixth decennial census was taken during the year, and the result on the 1st of June, 1840, was as follows:—White males, 7,249,266; white females, 6,939,842; free colored males, 192,550; free colored females, 199,821; slaves, males, 1,240,408; females, 1,240,805; making a grand total of the population of the United States (including seamen in the national service), 17,069,453.

The presidential election was a very exciting one, and both parties used all the machinery available for such purposes to gain the victory. The result was that Harrison and Tyler were elected by very large majorities. The closing session of Congress began Dec. 7th, 1840, but was not productive of any results of moment. Another issue of treasury notes was authorized; various appropriations were made; and many schemes, which had already been much talked of in Congress, were debated anew. The matter of most interest, especially for the promise it gave of what might be done under the next administration, was a resolution proposed by Henry Clay, for the repeal of the sub-treasury law. The Senate, however, rejected the resolution. On the 3d of March, 1841, the session closed, and with it the administration of Martin Van Buren. He came into office by a very large vote; the people denied him a re-election by an equally large vote against him. It cannot but interest the reader to note, in how far the wishes and hopes of those who defeated Van Buren were gratified by this change in the administration.

On the 4th of March, 1841, Gen. Harrison was inaugurated as ninth president of the United States. His address was very long, and filled with matters at that date occupying the minds of our countrymen, and causing no little excitement throughout the country. His cabinet was an able one; Daniel Webster, secretary of state; Thomas Ewing, secretary of the treasury; John Bell, secretary of war; George E. Badger, secretary of the navy; Francis Granger, postmaster-general; and John J. Crittenden, attorney-general; the Senate having at once confirmed all the nominations. Other vacancies were filled up without delay. And a proclamation was issued on the 17th of March, summoning Congress together for an extra session, on the 31st of the following May. And this was all that Harrison was permitted to do. Though advanced in years, his physical ability seemed to give promise of energy and power of endurance; but the harassing toils of the government soon proved too much for his strength. He was beset with office-seekers; he was anxious to gratify the numerous friends and supporters who flocked about him; he gave himself incessantly to public business; and at the close of the month, he was lying on a sick bed. On Sunday, the 4th of April, pneumonia having set in, his brief career as president was brought to its close.

As this was the first instance of a president dying while in office, it produced a feeling of deep and anxious concern as to what would result therefrom. To the party who had elected Harrison, it was a terrible blow; for with him at the head of affairs, they were sure of being able to carry on the government to general satisfaction. But as respected the man who, by constitutional provision, now was to occupy the executive chair, the whig party had grave and not unnatural doubts and perplexities. John Tyler had been placed on the ticket without much thought or care as to his political principles and consistency, or his executive ability, since, in the post of vice-president these were points of comparatively little moment. When, however, by Harrison's death, he was suddenly placed in the presidential chair, with the whole term of four years before him, the successful party experienced all the pains of uncertainty as to the course Tyler would pursue in the existing state of affairs. On the 6th of April, he arrived at Washington, requested the cabinet to continue at their posts, and took a new oath of office as president of the United States. On the 16th of May, he issued an Address to the People of the United States, in which he set forth his views and sentiments, and which on the whole seemed to be satisfactory. The whigs were not without hope that Tyler would coöperate with the majority of Congress, and carry out the views and desires of those by whom he had been elected.

The Twenty-seventh Congress met for an extra session on the 31st of May, and Tyler's message was sent in the following day. Of the foreign relations of the Union, a very satisfactory account was given. A treaty with Portugal had been duly ratified. The claims upon Spain seemed in a fair way of being settled. The allusions to a national bank, and to the inexhaustible subject of internal improvements, contained in the message, were so ambiguous, that from them nothing of the president's real intentions could be divined; the party could only hope for the best. The report of the secretary of the treasury, sent with the message, warmly recommended the establishment of a national bank, as likely to "produce the happiest results, and confer lasting and important benefits on the country." The president was understood to be friendly to the plan, and Mr. Ewing, on the invitation of both Houses reported, about the middle of June, a draft of a bill for the establishment of "The Fiscal Bank of the United States." In order to obviate constitutional difficulties, it was proposed to incorporate the bank in the District of Columbia, where Congress had the power of a State legislature; and to give the bank power to establish branches only in such States as should assent to it by their legislatures. There were, of course, inserted many provisions, by which it was hoped that the abuses and corruptions alleged or proved against the former banks would be prevented. The Senate took up the bill, and after a few modifications, it was passed by a vote of 26 to 23; in the House, the vote was 128 to 97; and it was sent to Tyler, Aug. 6th. On the 9th the sub-treasury law was repealed by a large vote, and Tyler was urged to take speedy and favorable action. On the 16th of August, the president vetoed the bill, and thereby angered the party who had unintentionally placed him in power. However, as nothing could be done on this subject without Tyler's aid, another bill was prepared, submitted to the president first, and passed on the 23d. This institution was to be called "The Fiscal Corporation of the United States." The Senate passed the bill, September 3d. Tyler kept the bill for six days, and though he had already approved it, resorted to the veto again, the veto being something for which he had a remarkable proclivity. The cabinet all resigned except Webster, and the session closed Sept. 13th, 1841. Its principal acts were: a loan of $12,000,000 for the purpose of covering the deficit under Van Buren's administration; a provisional tariff act laid as much as twenty per cent. on many articles admitted free by the compromise tariff; a uniform system of bankruptcy was established; and an act was passed granting rights of pre-emption as to the public lands, and providing for the distribution of the proceeds from land sales amongst the States, substantially in accordance with Henry Clay's plan. The second session of the Twenty-seventh Congress began on the 6th of December, and continued until the 31st of August, 1842, being the longest session of the national legislature that had ever yet occurred. A very large amount of public business was transacted, there having been passed no fewer than two hundred and ninety-nine acts. Besides these bills, and the discussion arising out of them, Congress was occupied in this session by a thousand and ninety-eight reports, and above three hundred other bills, not passed. There were about a hundred private bills ready for final passage in the House, but retained till the next session, because the Senate was so much occupied by the treaty of Washington and other momentous matters. The president put his veto to four bills this session; which, of course, occasioned much debate and many protests. Tyler suggested a "board of control," instead of a bank; and, later, proposed a banking arrangement, called "the exchequer plan"; but Congress was unwilling to adopt either of these schemes. Before the adjournment, the Senate was called upon to ratify a very important treaty, usually known as the treaty of Washington. Daniel Webster was the negotiator on the part of the United States, and, in behalf of Great Britain, Lord Ashburton arrived at Washington, as special minister, on the 4th of April, 1842. Besides the boundary question, which had been so long in dispute, there were other matters of no small moment to be discussed, and, if possible, settled now; one, the indemnification or "atonement" due on the ground of the violation of the United States' territory when the Caroline was destroyed, and for that vessel, if it were not proved that its owner had acted in conjunction with the insurgents on Navy Island; and another, the right of search claimed and enforced by the British cruisers, as to ships suspected of being slavers, which arose the year preceding. Matters progressed rapidly. The Caroline business (p. 197) was soon disposed of. The other points were, the north-eastern boundary, the right of search, mutual extradition of fugitives from justice, and the taking of measures for the more effectual suppression of the slave trade. Early in August, the labors of the negotiators came to a close, and the treaty was signed August 9th, 1842. By this treaty the boundary between the State of Maine and the British provinces was at length definitely settled. On the whole, though more or less objection was made to the final arrangement, it was regarded as fair and just by sensible and reasonable men on both sides of the Atlantic. The navigation of the River St. John was declared free; all grants of lands, on whichever side of the boundary line they might be, were to be held valid; and the United States agreed to satisfy the claims of the States of Maine and Massachusetts, out of its share of the "disputed territory" fund. England and the United States both agreed to keep a small squadron on the coast of Africa, in order to crush out, if possible, the slave trade; and the reciprocal extradition of fugitives from justice was duly provided for.

The Twenty-seventh Congress began its last session, December 5th, 1842. Tyler brought forward, in his message, the "Oregon question," which was now becoming of great importance, in consequence of the unsettled boundary claims on the part of England and the United States. Various other matters, such as the tariff, currency, Tyler's scheme of an exchequer plan, etc., were urged upon the attention of Congress. Some excitement arose out of the question relative to Oregon, and it was attempted to be used largely for the purpose of making political capital. The president informed Congress, that he was about to enter into negotiations with Great Britain for the purpose of terminating the joint occupation, and fixing the boundary on mutually satisfactory terms; yet a bill was brought into the Senate, and carried by a majority of one, for taking possession of the whole of the disputed territory, the title of the United States to which it declared was certain, and would not be abandoned. The House, however, refused its concurrence. On the 3d of March, 1843, the session closed; having provided the means of future intercourse between the United States and the government of China, and having also passed an act to test the practicability of establishing a system of electro-magnetic telegraphs.

In May, of this year, Webster resigned his post, and other changes also took place in the cabinet. The elections were generally adverse to the whigs, and it was thought that Tyler helped the democrats more than any body else. In his message, at the opening of the Twenty-eighth Congress, Tyler asserted the American claim in respect to Oregon, to the parallel of 54° 40′ north latitude, but stated that no effort would be spared to effect a mutually satisfactory settlement of the question with Great Britain. The position of matters in regard to Texas was discussed at length; the finances were spoken of quite fully; a disquisition on currency, in its various ramifications, was furnished; etc. There was, however, little business transacted during the session.

John Tyler, who was sarcastically termed the "accidental" president, being anxious to distinguish himself by something of moment to the country, had sought with eagerness to bring about the annexation of Texas; and a treaty to this effect was arranged, in April, 1844, between the secretary of state and the commissioners on the part of the republic of Texas. The Senate, however, rejected this treaty, on the 8th of June, by a vote of thirty-five to sixteen. Benton, immediately after the rejection of the treaty, introduced into the Senate a bill for the annexation of Texas, provided the consent of Mexico were first obtained; and Tyler, with a rather remarkable notion of right and privilege due to the Senate, sent a messenger to the House in hope that they would help him out. That body, however, declined everything of the sort; and Benton took occasion to call Tyler himself, and his course, by some very ugly names: in fact, he denounced him as deserving impeachment.*

The national whig convention met at Baltimore on the 1st of May, and with great enthusiasm, nominated Henry Clay and Theodore Frelinghuysen for president and vice-president. The democratic convention met at the same place, on the 27th of May, and, after a number of ballotings between the names of Van Buren, Cass, Johnson, Calhoun, took a new man, James K. Polk, who received the nomination for the presidency. George M. Dallas was placed on the same ticket for vice-president. The annexation of Texas and the claim to the 54° 40′ parallel for the boundary of Oregon, were among the chief issues presented in connection with the approaching contest. The result was: Polk and Dallas received 170 electoral votes; Clay and Frelinghuysen, 105.

Congress met, Dec. 2d, 1844. Tyler's message related principally to the annexation of Texas, which, he affirmed, was urgently called for by the people. The financial statement showed a great improvement, it being estimated that a surplus of $7,000,000 would remain in the treasury at the close of the fiscal year. The message closed with some self-congratulatory words on account

* The rise and progress of that strange abomination, Mormonism, deserves fuller consideration than we can here give it. Joseph Smith, with his band of one thousand two hundred followers, in 1833, in Missouri; with his thousands in Illinois, in 1840; the murder of Smith and his brother in prison by a mob, in July, 1844; and the expulsion of the hated sect from Illinois, and their emigration beyond the Rocky Mountains to Utah; where for many years they have manifested, under Brigham Young, a dogged spirit of rebellion and resistance to law and order; these are points into which the reader may look with advantage It seems a strange thing that a vile imposture like this should prevail in our day.

of his repeated use of the veto power, and the approbation which he believed the people to have manifested in his behalf. The House, Jan. 25th, 1845, passed a series of resolutions to the effect that Congress consented to the erection of the territory "included within and rightfully belonging to the Republic of Texas" into a new State; and to the construction of a republican form of government by a convention, according to the usual plan, for the purpose of being admitted into the Union. The usual cessions of public property to the general government were made; and it was provided, that other States might be formed out of the territory, as was customary with areas of considerable extent when first admitted into the Confederation. The Senate, some weeks later, adopted the joint resolutions, and on March 1st, they were approved by Tyler. Texas thus became an integral part of the United States, although necessarily the final arrangements, and the settlement of the difficulty growing out of the complaints and menaces of Mexico, were left for future consideration. All diplomatic attempts thus far to induce Mexico quietly to yield to the necessity of the case had failed, and there was room to expect hostilities on the southwestern frontier. During the session, various appropriations were made; an act was passed by which Florida was admitted into the Union, etc. On the 3d of March, the Twenty-eighth Congress came to an end, and at the same time John Tyler retired from the office which he had attained by one of those contingencies on which all human affairs are more or less dependent.

James K. Polk was inaugurated eleventh president of the United States, March 4th, 1845. The inaugural address was long and interesting. The annexation of Texas, and the Oregon question, both of them of deep interest to the welfare of the Union, and our relations with Mexico and Great Britain, were spoken of quite fully, and in terms which commended the president's plans and purposes to the majority of the nation. Mr. Polk chose for his cabinet, James Buchanan, secretary of state; R. J. Walker, secretary of the treasury; W. L. Marcy, secretary of war; G. Bancroft, secretary of the navy; and J. Y. Mason, attorney-general. In the matter of annexing Texas, Congress had left it to Tyler's option whether to accomplish it by treaty, or to effect it immediately, according to the tenor of the resolutions passed near the close of the session. Tyler, desirous of the glory of connecting his name with the matter (p. 201), availed himself at once of the opportunity presented, and on the 3d of March, dispatched a messenger to deliver to Mr. Donelson, chargé d'affaires to Texas, the joint resolutions of Congress for the admission of Texas into the Union, instructing him to communicate to the Texan government, that he, the president, had made choice of the alternative of immediate annexation, instead of negotiating by treaty. On the part of Texas, a convention was immediately summoned, and on the 4th of July, 1845, it assented to the joint resolutions and the country thus became fully incorporated into the Union. An "army of occupation," under command of Gen. Taylor, was dispatched for defence of the frontier. The American flag was hoisted, July 26th, at the south end of St. Joseph's Island, in token that the land was now a part of the Great Republic. The Mexican minister left Washington on the 6th of March, and Mexico declared her determination to resort to arms for redress in regard to Texas. Matters remained in this unsettled condition until the breaking out of hostilities in 1846.

Oregon formed a subject of importance for the consideration of the new administration. It is to be remembered, that, in 1818, a convention was arranged between the governments of the United States and Great Britain, for the joint occupation of this region, during the next ten years; and that by a second convention, in 1827, this arrangement was indefinitely prolonged, with the provision, that, after the 20th of October,

1828, either of the contracting parties might set aside the arrangement, by giving twelve months' notice to the other. Polk had been elected with the understanding that he would insist upon the 54° 40′ parallel as the boundary of Oregon, and that the United States were to have "the whole or none" of that vast region. Nevertheless, he felt it his duty to renew the propositions of compromise, which had previously been made, by which the forty-ninth parallel was to be the northern boundary of the United States territory. Buchanan, in July, made a proposition to this effect to Mr. Pakenham, the British minister; but it was received in so unsatisfactory a manner, that, in his next communication, after giving a very full and complete *résumé* of the question as viewed by his government, Buchanan withdrew his proposal; preserving, however, the conciliatory tone of his first statement, and expressing the hopes of the president that the controversy might be speedily adjusted. There was much excitement throughout the country, and considerable hostility of feeling exhibited at the time, on this subject; but happily, the conservative spirit prevailed, and everything like fighting was frowned upon.

The Twenty-ninth Congress began its first session Dec. 1st, 1845. The president's message was long, and in it were discussed the Oregon question and the state of our relations with Mexico. A revision of the tariff was recommended, and also the establishment of a constitutional treasury for the custody of the public money. The question relative to Oregon was discussed in the Senate early in the session, and General Cass made a speech looking plainly to the chances of war with England. In the House, Stephen A. Douglas, and others, advocated similar views and claims in respect to Oregon; and at the same time, a joint resolution of the two Houses, giving the requisite notice to Great Britain for terminating the joint occupation of the territory, as the president had recommended, was pressed forward. The debates were very noisy, and appeals of various sorts were made to popular passions, and the like. Meanwhile, however negotiations had been recommenced between the secretary of state and the British minister, with good prospects of an amicable settlement of difficulties. The joint resolution, as to the giving notice to England in respect to terminating the joint occupation of Oregon, was passed, April 23d, 1846; but there proved to be no need of resorting to this step. Early in June, a convention was proposed, through the agency of the British minister, for the adjustment of the question; on the 12th, the Senate advised the acceptance of the proposal; the convention was directly agreed upon; and on the 18th, the ratification was carried in the Senate by a vote of forty-one to fourteen. By this convention, the forty-ninth parallel of north latitude was adopted as the boundary between the territory of the United States and the British possessions, but Vancouver's Island was given up to Great Britain; the navigation of Fuca's Straits, and of the Columbia River, was declared free to both American and British navigators, and rights of actual possessors of land on both sides of the boundary line were to be respected by both parties. Thus, as was expressed not long after by the American minister to England, Mr. M'Lane, there was every reason to hope "that the settlement of the Oregon question will soon come to be universally regarded as the knell of those inveterate jealousies and feuds which, it may be apprehended, have so long excited a mischievous influence over the people, if not upon the councils, of both countries."

General Taylor, who commanded the "army of occupation" in Texas, was ordered, early in the year 1846, to march to the Rio Grande, which was claimed as the western boundary of the new State. He set out for this purpose in March, reached Point Isabel on the 25th, and on the 28th encamped on the Rio Grande, opposite Matamoras. The Mexicans looked upon this advance of Taylor as an invasion of their territory, and from the indications of their feelings towards the Americans, it became apparent, that a collision must speedily follow. Taylor was waiting, in obedience to orders, for the Mexicans to strike the first blow, which they did towards the latter part of April, by attacking and capturing Captain Thornton with a squadron of dragoons. Intelligence of this rencontre reached Washington on the 9th of May. The subject was immediately taken up, and a bill was passed, by large majorities, declaring that a state of war existed between the United States and Mexico, and placing the army and navy at the President's disposal in order to prosecute the war. Polk gave his approval to the war bill, May 13th, which provided for the service of fifty thousand volunteers, and appropriated $10,000,000 for war purposes. A new tariff bill, imposing *ad valorem* duties instead of specific imposts, was passed; and also a warehousing bill, allowing public stores to be used for a limited period, without payment of duty. Congress re-established the sub-treasury arrangement, substantially as it was under Van Buren (p. 198), and this system has continued in use ever since. Near the close of the session, the "Wilmot proviso" was originated. A bill was before the House, authorizing the president to use the sum of $3,000,000, if he deemed it expedient, in negotiating a treaty of peace with Mexico, when David Wilmot, a Representative from Pennsylvania, moved to add this *proviso;* "That there shall be neither slavery nor involuntary servitude in any territory of the continent of America which shall hereafter be acquired by, or annexed to, the United States, by virtue of this appropriation, or in any other manner whatsoever, except for crimes whereof the party shall have been duly convicted; *Provided always*, that any person escaping to such territory, from whom labor or service is lawfully claimed, in any one of the United States, such fugitive may be lawfully reclaimed, and conveyed out of said territory to the person claiming his or her labor or service." The bill was sent to the Senate on the last day of the session; and so was lost. Preliminary acts were passed for admitting Iowa and Wisconsin into the Union; and by special enactments Senators and Representatives from Texas took their seats in Congress. Two bills were vetoed by the president, the river and harbor bill, and the bill for indemnifying the sufferers from French spoliations on American commerce. On the 10th of August, after an unusually long session, Congress adjourned.

The second session was begun December 7th, 1846, and most of its measures related to the war with Mexico. The House again passed the Wilmot "proviso," but the Senate refused concurrence; and, although the river and harbor improvement bill was passed again, the president vetoed it a second time. The Twenty-ninth Congress came to an end, March 3d, 1847.

Affairs in Mexico, meanwhile, were becoming very serious. Herrera had been overthrown; and Paredes was in power, and he resolved to prosecute hostilities against the United States in defence of Mexico's right to her own territory. The Mexican Congress passed a decree to support this resolve, on the 6th of July. A plan of operations was sketched out, which helped to shadow forth the uses to which it was intended to apply the anticipated results of the contest. By this plan, an "army of the west" was to be raised, and to march, under General Kearney, from its rendezvous at Fort Leavenworth, on the Missouri, against New Mexico, and thence westward to co-operate with the fleet, which was to be reinforced, against California; and an "army of the centre," under General Wool, was to invade Coahuila and Chihuahua; but these were to be subordinate to the main design (as formed by General Scott), which was, to penetrate into the interior by the line taken by Taylor, and perhaps from the coast, and to strike hard blows, and to repeat them, until Mexico should understand that her true interest consisted in making peace on such terms as should be acceptable and agreeable to the United States.

General Taylor, finding Point Isabel to be in danger from the Mexicans, made a retrograde movement to relieve it. On this, the Mexicans crossed the Rio Grande, and made some boastful demonstrations of what they proposed to do. Taylor, having arranged matters at the Point, resolved to force his way back to the Rio Grande, May 7th, 1846. At a spot called Palo Alto, the Mexican General Arista, with double the number of Taylor's army, and twelve pieces of artillery, had posted himself quite across the road, having both flanks covered by thickets of chaparral, and a reserve in his rear. At two in the afternoon, the advancing army came in sight, and the Mexican batteries opened upon them when within seven hundred yards' distance. Taylor's artillery replied with terrible effect upon the enemy's troops. The Mexicans attempted a charge with their cavalry, but were thrown into confusion before they got near our men, and retreated; another attempt failed in the same manner. They were equally unsuccessful in endeavoring to turn Taylor's right flank; and an advance of their own right was met by two eighteen-pounders, which were placed so as to enfilade their line, and caused great slaughter. After some two hours' fighting, the prairie having taken fire, the battle was intermitted, and when night fell, both sides withdrew, but neither far from the field. The gallant Major Ringgold was mortally wounded in this battle. Arista, virtually defeated, fell back on the road to Matamoras, and the next morning took up a strong position on a ravine called the Resaca de la Palma, where he was reinforced by some two thousand men. As soon as this had been ascertained, Taylor put his army in motion; in the course of the afternoon of the 9th of May, his skirmishers, advancing through the thick chaparral, came upon the enemy's forces. One battery was brought up to oppose them, and very speedily a charge of cavalry, under Captain May, swept the Mexicans from their guns and broke their line on the other side of the ravine, in spite of one or more gallant attempts to retrieve the fortune of the day; while the infantry, now fighting as skirmishers, and now forming and resorting to the bayonet, drove the enemy before them in total rout. From all parts of the field the discomfited Mexicans rushed to the river, where numbers were drowned in the vain attempt to cross. Their camp fell into the hands of the victors, with all Arista's private papers, and a large supply of arms and ammunition. Thus the Mexicans were defeated with a force little more than 2000 in number; 33 were killed and 89 wounded; the Mexican loss was estimated to be 1000. Taylor next made preparations to cross the river, and by the 17th of May everything was in readiness. Arista proposed an armistice, which Taylor refused, and the next day he crossed, and found Matamoras evacuated.

The somewhat notorious Santa Anna was living, at this time, a refugee at Havana, and our government, notwithstanding it was well known that he was an unprincipled fellow, thought he might be used to good purpose in this Mexican business. Accordingly, through help given him by our authorities, he again entered Mexico, and upset Paredes during July and August, 1846. But, as might have been expected, Santa Anna cared nothing for the United States, and sought only his own aggrandizement in what he said and did, at this time.

Taylor, meanwhile, was busily occupied; volunteers in large numbers flocked in, and it was no light matter to organize these recruits. On the 19th of July, orders were given to advance. Various important posts along the Rio Grande were occupied, and, on the 8th of August, Camargo was made headquarters. The march from this place was continued till, on September 13th, appearances of the enemy were discovered. Their outposts retired as Taylor advanced, and the whole army was concentrated on the Rio San Juan, about twenty-five miles from Monterey, on the 15th, and three days later approached the city. Monterey contained about 10,000 inhabitants, and was occupied by Ampudia, with abundance of stores, and more than 10,000 men. Taylor sent General Worth to cut off communications with Saltillo and the interior, which was successfully accomplished. During three days the attack on Monterey was carried on, beginning with September 21st, when the Mexicans, sensible that the town was doomed, and dreading an assault, proposed a capitulation early on the morning of the 24th. Ampudia was allowed to evacuate under favorable conditions; and on the 28th, the town and citadel, together with forty pieces of cannon, and a vast quantity of military stores, was given up to our countrymen. Taylor's loss was 128 killed, 368 wounded; the Mexican loss was between 500 and 1000.

At this point we may turn to other portions of the seat of war, which, in the present case, extended across the continent. Immediately on receiving the news of the commencement of hostilities on the Rio Grande, General Wool was ordered to muster and prepare the volunteers to be raised in accordance with the act of Congress declaring war. At the end of May he set out, and passing by Ohio, Indiana, Illinois, Kentucky, and Tennessee to Mississippi, met the newly-enlisted volunteers at various stations along that route, inspected them, and admitted twelve thousand of them; who, about the middle of July, were directed to join the army. About nine thousand of these were ordered to the Rio Grande, as reinforcements to Taylor's army; the rest rendezvoused at Bexar, in Texas, in readiness to march under Wool himself, as the "army of the centre," against Chihuahua. Setting out from Bexar, on the 20th of September, Wool crossed the Rio Grande at Presidis, Oct. 11th, and after a difficult march through the mountain passes and deserts, he reached Monclova. Learning of the capture of Monterey by Taylor, Wool's forces were posted at Parras, so as to be in communication with the army of occupation.

The command of the "army of the West," which was raised principally in Mississippi, was given to Colonel Kearney, who about the end of July, with less than two thousand men, was at Bent's Fort, on the Arkansas, ready to march for New Mexico. Taking in convoy the annual "caravan" of Santa Fé traders, he then set forth across the prairie; and after toils and sufferings on the part of his men quite as great as those endured by the other armies, on August the 18th he entered Santa Fé. The governor, Don Manuel Armijo, had intended to oppose him, but thought better of the matter and abandoned the place. Four days afterwards, Kearney issued a proclamation, in which he announced, that the country now having become a part of the United States, the inhabitants were to consider themselves bound to obey the laws, and submit to the regulations of the new government. The whole of New Mexico having submitted without a stroke, Kearney established a territorial government, and appointing a governor and other officers, set out, on the 25th of September, with less than a thousand men, for California. Having advanced nearly two hundred miles, he was met by an express from Captain Fremont, in California, which led to Kearney's sending back most of his troops to Santa Fé. Colonel Doniphan, early in December, left Santa Fé with eight hundred men, in three divisions, for the purpose of reinforcing Wool. The march was attended with great suffering, but our men persevered, and arrived at El Paso del Norte on the 27th, where they remained for a month waiting for news from Wool. Late in February, 1847, Doniphan left El Paso, and having met the enemy near the Sacramento, routed them, and took possession of Chihuahua on the 1st of March. After suitable rest, continuing his march, he reached Taylor's encampment late in the month of May, 1847.

Captain J. C. Fremont, of the topographical corps, set out in the spring of 1845, with an armed party, for the purpose of crossing the mountains and penetrating to the interior of California. His object was stated to be of a purely scientific character. On the 29th of Janua y, 1846, he arrived in the neighborhood of Monterey, California. Here he sought and obtained permission of De Castro, the Mexican governor, to enter the valley of the San Joaquin, in order to obtain forage for his horses, and provisions for the men. Whilst availing himself of this permission, in March, 1846, he was informed by some American settlers, that De Castro was preparing to attack him and his men upon the pretext, that, under the cover of a scientific mission, he was exciting the American settlers to revolt. Fremont then, on the plea of self-defence, took a position on a mountain overlooking Monterey, at a distance of about thirty miles, entrenched it, raised the flag of the United States, and with his own men, sixty-two in number, awaited the approach of the Mexicans for three days; but they did not molest him at all. Fremont then marched for Oregon, but having been attacked by Indians, he charged the Mexicans with inciting this, and so turned back, resolved to overthrow the enemy and capture California for the United States. Waiting for the aid of the fleet, he set matters forward rapidly, and on the 25th of July, at Sonoma, with about two hundred American settlers, proclaimed the Republic of California, with himself at the head of its affairs. Commodore Sloat, in command of the squadron of observation, had been ordered at the breaking out of the war, "to take and hold San Francisco;" but before that order reached him, on the 7th of June, he heard of the battles of Palo Alto and Resaca de la Palma, and the next day sailed for Monterey. With proclamations in Spanish and English, on July the 7th, just two days after Fremont's proclamation, Monterey was in his hands; and on the 9th, San Francisco fell, and Sloat announced, "henceforward California will be a portion of the United States." Commodore Stockton succeeded Sloat in his command, and Fremont having formed a junction with him, entered Ciudad de los Angelos, on the 12th of August, 1846, the Mexicans having fled. Stockton took possession of the country, and appointed Fremont governor. Thus the conquest of California, like that of New Mexico, was effected without the loss of a single life in battle.

General Taylor, on taking Monterey (p. 206) agreed to a suspension of arms, under the conviction, that Mexico had already been brought to that position, that she would be glad to make peace on terms agreeable to the United States, and that the home government would sanction this proceeding on his part. But "the authorities at home," as has been well said, "eager for fresh victories, or pandering to public and political taste, did not approve and confirm an act, for which General Taylor has, nevertheless, received, as he truly merits, the just applause of impartial history." The armistice at Monterey accordingly ceased, and Taylor having been informed, on the 25th of November, that Tampico was occupied by the naval forces of the United States, left Worth and Butler at Monterey and at Saltillo, and about the middle of December, set out for Victoria, the capital of Tamaulipas, where he designed to concentrate a portion of his army. While absent on this expedition, General Worth informed Taylor, that Santa Anna was making quite extensive preparations to expel the Americans from Mexico. After a careful calculation of the chances in his favor, he had judged it best to take the lead in that policy which was most popular in Mexico, viz., to resist the aggressions of the United States. He had accordingly collected an army of twenty thousand men, at San Luis de Potosi, and had he made a prompt and energetic movement he might have gained his purpose. But Taylor gathered his forces at Victoria at the beginning of January, 1847, to await the onset.

The administration, meanwhile, thought it best to make a change of operations. Taylor's line of attack was not likely to prove successful; and hence, as our ships had possession of the sea, and an army could be thrown upon any point of the coast which might seem most suitable as a base of operations, it was resolved to seize Vera Cruz, and thence to march directly upon the capital. General Scott was, therefore, once more summoned to the councils of the government, and towards the close of November, was invested with the office of "commander-in-chief of the American army in Mexico," for the purpose of carrying out this new programme of attack. Scott wrote to Taylor that he should be under the painful necessity of depriving him of the best and most efficient troops under his command. Nearly all the regulars under Worth, Patterson, Twiggs, and Quitman, were ordered to Vera Cruz; and Taylor was left to maintain himself as best he could, against the threatened attack of Santa Anna and the most effective army which Mexico could boast. The entire force which Taylor could bring into the field was four hundred and seventy-six regulars, (consisting exclusively of artillery and cavalry), and four thousand two hundred and fifteen volunteers. The enemy, according to Santa Anna's "summons," were twenty thousand strong at the time of the battle of Buena Vista; although it appears, some three or four thousand had been lost before the engagement, by death, sickness and desertion; yet, admitting this diminution, the Mexican army was more than three times as numerous as that of Taylor, and it contained the best soldiers and ablest general the country could furnish. On learning the strength of the enemy, Taylor took position at Buena Vista. The road here passed through a gorge in the mountains, and was defended on the west by a complete network of deep gullies, cut by the torrents from the heights on that side, and almost everywhere impassable, whilst on the east a narrow shelf of table-land between it and the mountains was much intersected by ravines, through which, at certain seasons, rapid streams rushed into the rivulet that meandered through the pass. The Mexican army was found to be near at hand, on the 21st of February, which led to immediate arrangements on the part of our countrymen to meet the enemy. Santa Anna had dispatched two thousand cavalry, under General Miñon, in a very circuitous route, to get into the rear of the Americans, threaten Saltillo, and cut off their retreat; at the same time, also, General Urrea had been sent in a circuit to the west of the road held by our troops, with about a thousand rancheros, to co-operate with Miñon. General Taylor, on his part, placed a battery of eight guns under Captain Washington, and properly supported, so as to command the road through the gorge; on the right of the stream, behind the gullies, he planted two guns under Captain Bragg, with supports of infantry and horse; to the left, on the narrow plateau with its steep ravines, were posted two regiments of infantry, with two guns; and on the skirts of the mountains were riflemen and cavalry. By these and other like arrangements, Taylor's force was considerably reduced in the numbers that could be employed directly against the enemy, from the wide intervals between the points he had to hold, against the Mexicans, in front, on both flanks and in his rear. Santa Anna divided his army into three columns, by means of which he was to attack on all points at once. Before commencing the attack, he sent a summons to Taylor to avoid being crushed by an instant surrender; but this of course Taylor peremptorily declined.

The battle began on the afternoon of the 22nd of February, but was of no special moment. The attack was renewed at daybreak, February 23rd, and though pressed with zeal and courage, was bravely met and sustained by our countrymen. Indeed, nothing short of the most determined bravery, and the most unflinching hardihood could have enabled our troops to make head against, and defeat, an army of the size and capability of that under General Santa Anna. At one time, when the Mexican cavalry had succeeded in turning the left of the American lines, it seemed impossible to retrieve the fortune of the day; but at this juncture, Taylor returned from a brief visit to Saltillo; his presence infused fresh vigor into the army; the impetuous riflemen of Mississippi drove back the enemy; the tide of victory was turned; and despite disasters of various kinds with the infantry, the artillery was so admirably worked and so effective, that, in fact, by it the Mexican advance was effectually stopped and the battle won. When night came, the field was covered with dead, and many an anxious hour was passed by Taylor and his men, waiting for the morrow, and preparing for a renewal of the fight. But at dawn of day, February 24th, it was found Santa Anna had retreated.

The retreat of the Mexicans was attended with intense and pitiable distresses; the sick, the wounded, the dying, and the dead were abandoned at every step. The Americans were too few in number, and too much exhausted by the conflict, to allow a pursuit; and there were the dead to be buried, and the wounded to be cared for. The total loss on the part of our countrymen was 646 killed, wounded, and missing. The Mexican loss was about two thousand five hundred, in killed and wounded; whilst in missing, and deaths during the retreat, their own authorities say, that at least ten thousand five hundred more were lost. They captured three guns in the battle; but they were defeated, completely and disastrously. By the middle of March, the American communications were completely restored; and the northern frontier of Mexico was entirely in possession of our troops. General Taylor, leaving Wool in command, reached New Orleans December 1st. He was received everywhere with marked attention, and, in consequence of that peculiar weakness of the American character, viz., admiration for military successes, he was immediately deemed, by the politicians, a first-rate man to nominate for the presidency. As we shall see, Taylor was not unwilling to serve his country in the chair of State as well as in the tented field.

General Scott (p. 208), at the earliest practicable moment, entered upon his duties, and infused new vigor into operations against Mexico. Lobos, an island to the south of Tampico, and about one hundred and twenty-five miles from Vera Cruz, was the rendezvous appointed for the armament which was to be thrown upon the coast at the nearest point to the capital; and there, in the beginning of March, 1847, were collected above twelve thousand men, and a fleet of 163 vessels to transport the army, with its guns, stores, and equipage of every kind, to its destination. On the 7th of March, the embarkation was effected; and two days afterwards the whole force was landed, without the loss of a man, at the island of Sacrificios, in close proximity to Vera Cruz. On the 18th, having, without effect, summoned the city to surrender, Scott broke ground before it; he also gave free permission to the non-combatants, such as women and children, foreign consuls, etc., to retire from the city; and on the 22d, the investment being completed, and another summons rejected, the bombardment began. Aided by the fleet, which co-operated most effectually with the land forces, Scott maintained for four days, and as many nights, such a terrific rain of fire upon the place, that it was almost converted into a heap of ruins; and the loss of life was fearfully great. The Mexicans resisted to the best of their ability, but they had neither men enough nor means to cope with their powerful assailants. Four hundred of the inhabitants had perished; and after some negotiation, the terms of surrender were arranged, and on the 29th of March, both the city and the far-famed castle of San Juan d'Ulloa, were surrendered to the victorious army. All the public stores, etc., in the city were delivered up, but perfect protection was guaranteed to the inhabitants. General Worth was appointed temporary governor of the city, and on the 8th of April, Scott took up his line of march for the city of Mexico. Having learned that Santa Anna meant to oppose his advance at Cerro Gordo, Scott hastened forward. The battle was sharply contested, but resulted in a decisive victory on the part of the Americans.

Scott's loss was more than 400. The Mexican loss, in killed and wounded, was never known, but our countrymen took 3000 prisoners, amongst whom were five generals; 4000 or 5000 stands of arms, and forty-three pieces of artillery. Santa Anna himself with great difficulty escaped to Orizaba, where he exerted himself with great diligence to get together again a force sufficient to make head against Scott's advance upon the capital. The army advanced, as soon as possible after their victory, on Jalapa and Perote, which were abandoned to them without a blow; the latter on the 22d of April, and with it a vast accumulation of warlike stores. At Amozoque, they were unsuccessfully attacked by Santa Anna; and on the 22d of May, 1847, Puebla submitted to Worth, whilst the Mexican forces retired upon the capital. This failure to retrieve the disaster at Cerro Gordo, kindled anew the flames of revolution in Mexico; and the various parties and factions in that unhappy country could agree upon no one point, except that the northern invaders were to be opposed to the last extremity, and that no peace was to be made while an enemy remained on the soil of Mexico.

Scott fixed his headquarters at Puebla, where he remained until the beginning of August, partly to recruit his troops and wait the result of certain negotiations then going on. The halt was unfortunate; for the men got sick in large numbers, and desertions became common. Into the unpleasant differences and disputes between the general-in-chief and the authorities at Washington, growing out of the scheme of superseding Scott, by the appointment of a lieutenant-general, we need not enter; neither is it material to enlarge upon the mission of Mr. N. P. Trist, who was sent by the president as commissioner, with full powers to seize upon the earliest opportunity of negotiating a peace with Mexico. The historians of the war, Ripley, Mansfield, and others, furnish all requisite details. Scott, on the 7th of August, having been reinforced, took up the line of march for the capital of Mexico, and in four days came within about fifteen miles of the city. It was found necessary to construct a new road, in order to reach the point in view, which occupied several days. Nothing can better show the exhaustion of the military power of the Mexican government, than this daring march of less than eleven thousand men, so far into a country peculiarly favorable to guerilla warfare, and in which no amount of contributions which might be levied could compensate for the destruction of its communications with the sea and the fleet. The Mexicans made vigorous efforts for defence. On every road approaching the city were strong earth-works and batteries, and around the city itself was a complete girdle of entrenchments. There was, however, an insufficiency of artillery. and the disposable troops were not above twenty thousand in number; the services of some ten thousand armed citizens might perhaps be reckoned upon, in addition to the army; and although the lines were long, the invading force was too inconsiderable to make this of any great moment. In view of all the circumstances, the plans of Santa Anna (as stated by him after the battle was lost,) appear to have been arranged with greater skill than he had shown before. It was his design to have fallen back before Scott's advance, and given battle on ground he had chosen, and in which his numbers would have told with effect upon the comparatively small army of the invaders. But the gross disobedience of General Valencia disconcerted the whole plan. With an excess of zeal, he was so anxious to attack the Americans, that he advanced to Contreras, where the ground was not tenable, and so indirectly aided Scott's movements. It involved a considerable amount of hard work and exposure to a heavy storm; but on the morning of the 20th of August, our troops reached an elevation in the rear of the Mexican position, and in seventeen minutes carried Valencia's entrenchments. The American force engaged in this brilliant action was about four thousand five hundred, whilst the enemy numbered about six thousand, and Santa Anna was sufficiently near, with double that number, to have shared in the fight if he had felt disposed. This decisive victory, however, was not all that was accomplished on that day. Whilst the divisions just mentioned were engaged on the left, Worth, by a skillful and daring movement on the right, had turned and forced the enemy's strong position at San Antonio, and then advanced directly upon a strong, well-built fortification, the *tête du pont* of Cherubusco, the other divisions hastening to the same point from the field of Contreras. In every direction the contest was furious; but the Mexicans again proved themselves unable to contend successfully with American soldiers; at every point our countrymen triumphed, and the dragoons chased the scattered and disheartened enemy to the very gates of the capital. The losses on both sides were very heavy; for this was the most sanguinary of all the engagements in the whole course of the war; but in its effect, it was certainly one of the most decisive and important.

At this point, everything seemed favorable for entering upon negotiations for peace, on terms which would be acceptable to the United States. Scott, at his head-quarters, at Tacubaya, and only three miles from the city of Mexico, arranged an armistice, with a view to a treaty, having enforced the offer by the alternative of an assault, which no one doubted would have been successful. Some pause, too, was desirable for his own men, after so long a march and such severe engagements. And for several days after the 24th of August, 1847, the commissioners appointed by the two parties attempted to ascertain the existence of some ground of agreement, whence they might start in drawing up the articles of a final treaty. But, beside the numerous factions among the Mexicans, it soon became evident that Santa Anna was not to be relied on, and that he meant to see what further he could accomplish by fighting. The armistice having now lasted for two weeks, and there appearing no probability of a treaty being arranged, Scott, on the 6th of September, notified Santa Anna that he was aware of his infractions of the armistice, and demanded satisfaction on account of them before noon on the following day, under pain of declaring the suspension of arms at an end, and proceeding with hostilities forthwith. The reply, which was sent on the 7th, accepted the latter alternative, and announced the resolution to try the fortune of war once more. Before night Scott had fully determined upon his plan of action. Having ascertained that the western side of the city seemed to be less strongly fortified than the south side, he resolved to assault it by a flank attack. But there lay directly in the line of operations, on this plan, three strong positions —El Molino del Rey, La Casa Mata, and Chapultepec; the latter a castellated height, which under ordinary circumstances could only have been reduced by a regular siege. Nevertheless, knowing the quality of his own men, and the inefficiency of the enemy, he expected to carry it, as well as the rest, by assault, and gave orders accordingly, the King's Mill—El Molino del Rey—being the first point to be carried. The attack began very early on the morning of September 8th, 1847, and it was pushed forward in so gallant a style that, in spite of the grape and canister showered upon the attacking column, in spite of a desperate rally on the part of the Mexicans, and a struggle in which eleven out of fourteen American officers fell, the place was taken, and the guns in it turned upon the fugitives, who rushed in the wildest disorder to the forts. In the meanwhile, Garland's brigade, sustained by Drum's artillery, assaulted the enemy's left, near the Molino, and after an obstinate contest drove them from their position under the protecting guns of Chapultepec. Meanwhile, an assault was ordered upon the Casa Mata, which proved to be a massive stone work surrounded with bastioned entrenchments and deep ditches, whence a deadly fire was delivered, and kept up without intermission upon the advancing troops, until they reached the very slope of the parapet surrounding the citadel. Here they were fairly mowed down by the guns of the fort, and were forced to withdraw to the left of Duncan's battery, where the remnant of the column re-formed in readiness for another assault. The Mexican cavalry threatened an attack on the American left, but were repulsed by the artillery, and by the mere appearance of the American dragoons; while new efforts were made against the Molino, which soon yielded to a desperate charge, led by Major Buchanan and Captain M'Kenzie on one side, and Captains Anderson and Ayres on the other. All the guns were now brought to bear on the Casa Mata, and the garrison, cut off from all support, and exposed to a most destructive cannonade, evacuated it. Two attempts to rally and lead their men on, for the recovery of the positions that had been lost, were made by the Mexican leaders, but they could not stand before the terrible fire of the American artillery, and by nine o'clock in the morning the battle was over. No immediate result followed this battle; but Scott was preparing to assault the capital in a few days. Chapultepec was first to be taken, and on the 12th of September, the bombardment began. It was renewed early the next morning, and at eight o'clock, a general dash of our troops was made from different points; the steep sides of the hills were rapidly climbed; and by means of scaling ladders the troops poured into the works. Chapultepec was entered on every side; the officers who were to have fired the mines were shot down before they could apply the match; and though the garrison made a stout and prolonged defence, almost at the point of the bayonet, it was all in vain, and the survivors, with their commander, General Bravo, were made prisoners. Worth and Quitman, meanwhile, had advanced upon the capital, and succeeded in attaining such positions as that there could no longer be any doubt as to the final result. Santa Anna and his adherents resolved to retreat immediately, and took the road to Guadalupe Hidalgo. A deputation of the city council came to Scott at midnight, and informed him of the flight of the government. The next morning, at nine o'clock, September 14th, 1847, Quitman was allowed the honor of hoisting the American flag on the national palace, and, immediately after, Scott and his staff rode into the vast area in front of the cathedral and palace, amid the shouts of the exulting army.

The Mexican war was now virtually at an end, and with the exception of an attack on Col. Childs at Puebla, which was repulsed, all active hostility ceased. Scott's army, which numbered 11,000 men when he left Puebla, was now reduced to less than 6,000; and above half the loss had taken place in battle; sickness, desertion, and the necessity of garrisoning some of the captured places, accounted for the rest. But the loss of the Mexicans during the same time had exceeded seven thousand, by battle alone; and besides, there were nearly four thousand prisoners in the hands of the conquerors, who had also taken more than twenty colors and standards, seventy-five guns, and fifty-seven wall-pieces, twenty thousand small arms, and an immense quantity of shot, shells, and powder.

Our naval force was occupied in several expeditions, principally in the Pacific. Guyamas was seized by Captain Lavallette, on the 20th of October, having been deserted by its garrison and its governor, and a demonstration afterwards made against it was easily defeated. Mazatlan was occupied, on the 10th of November, by Commodore Shubrick, who hoped to have made it the terminus of a line of communication with Scott or Taylor. San Blas, San José, Mulejé, San Antonio, and Todos Santos, were also the scenes of combats and skirmishes, all of them invariably ending in the success of American arms.

Mexico was now subdued, and all that remained was to settle upon terms of peace.

Scott, who was rather testy, had two or three quarrels with some of his officers and with Mr. Trist at the same time, and the dissensions and squabbles among the commanders were, and deserved to be, looked upon as simply disgraceful. Mr. Trist, though at the time not authorized to act for the United States, arranged a treaty which was completed February 2d, 1848. It was immediately dispatched to Washington, and at once sent to the Senate by Polk. It was ratified, March 10th, and subsequently by the Mexican Congress, May 30th. The principal conditions contained in the treaty were,—the restoration of peace; the cession, not only of Texas, but of New Mexico and Upper California also, to the United States; the payment, in consideration of this cession of territory, of $15,000,000 by the American government, and of the claims of the citizens of the United States against the government of Mexico, to the extent of $3,250,000; and a compact to restrain the incursions and misconduct of the Indians on the northern frontier. Peace was proclaimed by the president, July 4th, 1848.

Returning again to the consideration of home affairs, we note that the Thirtieth Congress met, December 6th, 1847. Mr. R. C. Winthrop, a whig, was elected speaker of the House, which showed a falling off in the democratic strength. A large portion of Mr. Polk's message was occupied with the Mexican war and the questions connected with it. Interesting information of a diplomatic kind was also furnished. The receipts into the treasury, during the year ending in June, 1847, had been $26,346,790; but the expenditure had reached nearly to the amount of $59,500,000. The entire public debt was said now to be $45,660,000. "Should the war with Mexico be continued," the president remarked, "until the 30th of June, 1849, it is estimated that a further loan of $20,500,000 will be required for the fiscal year ending on that day." The operation of the tariff was spoken of as decidedly beneficial, and the independent treasury was lauded in the very highest terms. In addition to these various topics, the mint, the public lands, the government of Oregon Territory, the navy, the steam marine, and the post-office, received due attention in the very lengthy message, which was concluded with a timely reference to the wise counsels of Washington against disunion, and with an invocation of the blessings of Almighty God upon the deliberations of the national legislature. During the present session there was but little accomplished, principally because of the exciting political questions, arising out of, and connected with, the approaching presidential election. The "Wilmot proviso" was again warmly debated, in connection with the bill providing a territorial government for Oregon Territory. When the bill was passing through the Senate, amongst other amendments, on the motion of Senator Douglas, the Missouri compromise amendment was appended to it; but the House refused to concur in this addition to its bill; and the Senate in consequence receded from this amendment, by a vote of twenty-nine to twenty-five, when the House accepted the others. A loan of $16,000,000 was authorized, and an act was passed giving authority to purchase the papers of Mr. Madison, fourth president of the United States. Congress adjourned on the 14th of August, 1848.

The democratic nominating convention was held in the spring of 1848. It met at Baltimore, May 22nd, and tried hard for several days to fix upon candidates who should command the vote of the party throughout the country. On the fourth ballot Gen. Cass was selected for president and Gen. W. O. Butler for vice-president. A portion of the party, not satisfied with this result, held a convention at Utica, and nominated Van Buren and C. F. Adams. The whigs, on the other hand, assembled early in June, in Philadelphia. Webster, Clay and Scott were passed over, and Gen. Taylor (p. 209), was nominated for president and Millard Fillmore for vice-president. The result was, the election of these latter to the highest offices in the gift of the people.

The Thirtieth Congress began its second session December 4th, 1848. The message of Polk was very long, and entered at large into the numerous questions of interest then occupying the public mind, although it must be confessed there was throughout rather too much of what has often been charged upon Americans, viz: an undue self-glorification. In speaking of the vast additions which had been made to the territory of the United States, and the incalculable wealth and power opened to our countrymen, he said:—"The acquisition of California* and New Mexico, the settlement of the Oregon boundary, and the annexation of Texas, extending to the Rio Grande, are results which, combined, are of greater consequence, and will add more to the strength and wealth of the nation, than any which have preceded them since the adoption of the Constitution." The president was in favor of extending the Missouri compromise line (p. 178), to the Pacific, which would have largely increased the extension of slave-holding territory. The finances were pronounced to be in good condition, the new tariff was highly praised, and the public debt was stated to be $65,778,450. Although this was the short session, considerable business was accomplished. Douglas, of Illinois, introduced into the Senate a bill to admit California as a State immediately New Mexico was subsequently included in this plan, the idea being to leave the inhabitants to determine whether they would have slavery or not; but the bill was not adopted. At the close of February, 1849, another proposition was made, viz: to extend the revenue laws over California and New Mexico, and also the Constitution of the United States, with all general laws applicable to the case. After much debate and dissension between the Houses, this proposition was agreed upon. Among the principal acts of the session may be mentioned, the establishing a territorial government for Minnesota; the making arrangements for the seventh census; the organization of the department of the interior, and the appointment of an assistant secretary of state; the running and marking off the northern boundary of the state of Iowa; and a resolution authorizing the secretary of war to furnish emigrants to Oregon, California, and New Mexico, with suitable arms and ammunition. A postal treaty also was established between the United States and Great Britain and her territories. As a matter of general interest in the progress of the slave or free issue, we may here state, that the Southern members of Congress felt called upon to meet, at the opening of 1849, and reaffirm their views on the disputed points, and also to call upon the South to present a united and immovable front, and be ready to defend their rights.

The discovery and importance of the gold region on the shores of the Pacific, gave rise to various schemes for establishing railroad communication between the eastern and western territory of our republic. Several plans were brought forward in Congress; but the only one that received attention, was that which contemplated a railroad across the Isthmus of Panama, so as to reduce the distance to California from the Atlantic States, from some seventeen thousand miles (which was the distance by way of Cape Horn), to less than six thousand miles. The bill which Mr. Benton brought forward in

* The first discovery of gold was made (in digging for a saw-mill) in February, 1848, on the grounds of Captain Suter. The rumors of the finding of El Dorado, about which the early adventurers to the western world had dreamed so frequently, immediately excited the attention of the whole community, and from not only the older portions of the United States, but from almost every part of the world, the "gold-diggings" were sought for with an avidity and eagerness which the "auri sacra fames" of the poet can hardly adequately express; within six weeks, during December, 1848, and January, 1849, more than a hundred vessels left the ports of the United States for California; and under the spur of excitement and making haste to get rich, a population was drawn to the Pacific coast with unexampled rapidity, and more various and extraordinary than had ever before gathered together in one region of country.

the Senate, to accomplish this object, did not receive the support of the majority in that body. The overland route also, though the distance was much less, was not considered at all practicable at this date.

The Thirtieth Congress came to its end, March 4th, 1849, and at the same date Polk retired from office. Senator Benton, who is probably as good a judge as any one in this matter, affirms that the faults of Polk's administration were the faults of his cabinet; the merits of it were all his own. "The Mexican war, under the impulse of speculators, and upon an intrigue of Santa Anna, was the great blot upon his administration; and that was wholly the work of the intriguing part of his cabinet. . . . . The acquisition of New Mexico and California were the distinguishing events of his administration—fruits of the war with Mexico; but which would have come to the United States without that war, if the president had been surrounded by a cabinet free from intrigue and selfishness, and wholly intent upon the honor and interest of the country." With the facts already set before him, the reader can judge for himself, in how far this laudation is deserved.

On Monday, March 5th, 1849, Zachary Taylor, the distinguished warrior, appeared before a large assemblage in Washington, and about midday delivered his inaugural address. It was a brief, plain, common-sense sort of a document, such as was to be expected from a man of his well-known character and integrity. The oath of office was thereupon taken by Taylor, and the next day he sent in to the Senate the following names of gentlemen for his cabinet, viz: John M. Clayton was appointed secretary of state; William M. Meredith, secretary of the treasury; Geo. W. Crawford, secretary of war; William B. Preston, secretary of the navy; Thos. Ewing, secretary of the interior; Jacob Collamer, postmaster-general; and Reverdy Johnson, attorney-general. The department of the interior, charged with the care of the land office, Indian affairs, patent office, census office, public buildings, etc., had been organized by the last Congress, and added another member to the cabinet. Notwithstanding Taylor's personal popularity, it soon became evident that there was about to be a majority in both Houses of Congress opposed to his administration; and from the tone and temper of the opposition press, as well as the dissatisfaction caused by the removal of democrats from office, and the appointment of whigs in their places, the president and his cabinet had reason to look forward to the approaching meeting of Congress with no little anxiety and concern. The position, also, of California and New Mexico, for which the attempt to provide territorial governments had failed, (p. 214), and the dispute stirred up by the claim on the part of Texas to jurisdiction over quite a large portion of New Mexico, demanded attention, and caused no little annoyance and vexation. Taylor took such steps as seemed to him necessary to preserve tranquillity until the boundary question could be settled by Congress. He also appointed a governor and other officers for the new territory of Oregon; and measures were taken to complete the coast survey on the Pacific shores of the United States. The rapidly increasing importance of California and the gold region caused a large increase of duty to the president, and anxious consideration on his part how best to protect the emigrants flocking thither, and how to sustain, properly and effectually, the authority of the United States in a region which had no settled government of any kind as yet provided for it. The intense application to public business began to tell upon the president's health, and the effect of the new cares and responsibilities he had assumed, was becoming evident as the summer passed away and the time for the opening of Congress approached.

The Thirty-first Congress began its first session December 3d, 1849. After some three weeks, the House succeeded in getting a speaker by a plurality vote, Mr. Cobb, of Georgia. The president's message was sent in December 24th, and proved to be a plain, clearly written and moderately long statement of the existing condition of affairs, and was marked by a spirit of earnest devotion to the best interests of our country. The slavery question now began to loom up into new importance, and to foreshadow, in measure at least, that awful struggle which ere many years came upon the Great Republic. The South naturally enough, rejoiced in the acquisition of Texas, and the enlargement of the area out of which new slave States might be formed, and it was also sanguine in the expectation that New Mexico and California might be included in the same category. The North, on the other hand, while yielding to the necessity of Texas being under the influence and guidance of slaveholders, was earnest in seeking to prevent the spread of what it deemed a great evil and stain upon our national escutcheon; and as it became more and more probable that slavery would be excluded from California and New Mexico, the North could not but exult in the prospect, and also urge in Congress measures calculated to depress Southern power and influence in our Pacific possessions. A special message was sent to the House, January 21st, 1850, in which the California and New Mexico, as well as the Texas boundary difficulty were spoken of. The subject caused considerable debate and trouble. Henry Clay, venerable for years and unquestioned patriotism, again endeavored to pour oil upon the waters of strife. On the 29th of January, he brought forward a series of eight resolutions, by which he hoped to provide a basis of compromise for the firm and lasting settlement of the slavery question. His plan in substance was, to admit California as a State; to form territoral governments in other parts of the territory acquired from Mexico; to fix the boundary of Texas and New Mexico; to propose to Texas to pay off her debt contracted previous to annexation to the United States; to declare it inexpedient to abolish slavery in the District of Columbia, while it exists in Maryland, without the consent of the people of the State and the District, and without compensating the slave-owners in the District; to declare it expedient to prohibit the slave-trade in the District of Columbia; to make more effectual provision for the recovery of fugitive slaves; and to affirm that Congress has no power to hinder the trade in slaves between the slave-holding States. Mr. Clay made an earnest and affecting speech on the points at issue, early in February, 1850; and about a month later, Calhoun stood forward, as he had always proved himself, the champion of ultra State rights and the denouncer of the aggressions and injustice of the North. Webster also took part in the debate, scorned the very name of secession, and declared that it would be, and must be, revolution. Towards the close of February, an effort was made to do something by means of a select committee of thirteen. Clay, on the 8th of May, on behalf of this committee, brought in a report of a plan of compromise, which, it was hoped, would allay existing excitement. A series of bills were presented — more generally known as the "omnibus bill" — to admit California as a State, to establish territorial governments for Utah and New Mexico, to pay Texas a sum of money sufficient to satisfy her on the subject of her boundary, to provide for the recovery of fugitive slaves, and to abolish the slave trade in the District of Columbia. Long and wearisome debates followed, week after week, even till the month of August, when it was found that the omnibus bill could not be carried, at least in its existing shape.

In the midst of this excitement and dispute, the president was suddenly called away to his account. Zachary Taylor died, July 9th, 1850, in the 66th year of his age, and before he had been able to accomplish much of any account in his high office. By this afflictive event, Millard Fillmore became president, and having taken the oath of office, July 10th, he entered at once upon his duties. Changes in the cabinet took place, Webster becoming secretary of state. On the 6th of August, Fillmore sent a message to the House, respecting the boundary question between Texas and New Mexico, the former of which had taken certain steps in the matter which were not for a moment to be tolerated. Early in the same month, the boundary between Texas and New Mexico was finally settled upon, Texas to receive $10,000,000 in consideration of relinquishment of her claims against the United States. On the 13th, the bill to admit California as a State passed the Senate by a vote of thirty-four to eighteen; on the 15th, a bill was passed to establish a territorial government for New Mexico; and on the 18th of September, a fugitive slave bill, and a bill for the suppression of the slave trade in the District of Columbia, also passed the Senate by large majorities. By the constitution of California, slavery was prohibited in that State; in New Mexico and Utah, the question was left open for future decision. Messrs. W. M. Gwinn and J. C. Fremont, senators elect from California, immediately thereafter appeared and took their seats in the great council of the nation. In this wise, so far as legislation was concerned, the bitter strife over the Wilmot proviso came to a pause; and it was hoped, by all true lovers of their country, that discord would now end in respect to that interminable, unceasing source of contention—the slavery question. But we are sorry to say, that the strife did not cease then; and, so far as men could penetrate the veil of the future, was not likely to cease for many long years to come. "The complex, cumbersome, expensive, annoying, and ineffective bill," as Senator Benton designates the fugitive slave law of 1850, gave satisfaction to neither party. The North was irritated and vexed with the mode pursued in the recovery of fugitive slaves, and with the odiousness of the whole matter, as it was now presented before their eyes; the South, on the other hand, was chagrined and exasperated to find that the difficulty of getting back their slaves was rather increased than otherwise by this new act, and that disturbances were sure to follow, and the law sure to become odious, and, consequently, next to impossible to be executed. On the 30th of September, 1850, after a session of over 300 days—the longest ever held—Congress adjourned.

The results of the seventh census, taken this year, were substantially as follows. Total white population, 19,557,271; free colored, 429,710; slaves, 3,204,093. The population of the free States was, 13,434,559. The free population of the slave States was, 6,412,151; showing a *decrease* of 778,568 since 1840; whilst the free States had in the same period increased 3,779,933, *i. e.*, rather more than half the entire population of the slave States. The grand total of the population of the United States, in 1850, was 23,191,074.

The position of the beautiful island of Cuba, and its contiguity to the United States, have naturally caused it to be looked upon with no ordinary interest by our countrymen; and, partly from good motives, and partly from the restlessness and cupidity of a large number of Americans, manifold plans and schemes have been talked of, and attempted to be carried out, so as to incorporate Cuba into the possessions of the United States. Spain, on her part, ever jealous of her powerful neighbor, has exercised great rigor in endeavoring to maintain her authority intact, and to prevent the "filibustering" schemes and plots of those who have been ready, in past years, to do all in their power to wrest this fertile island from Spain. Various piratical expeditions have been undertaken, at various times, with this purpose in view. In 1849, the impression having got abroad that the Cubans were ready for revolt, efforts began to be made, in several parts of the Union, to fit out an expedition against the Spanish powers. General Taylor, at that time president, issued a proclamation, August 11th, forbidding every outrage of the kind against the law, and warning all offenders of the punishment in store for them. Preparations, however, went on, at New Orleans, a Cuban named Lopez being the leader. About the middle of May, 1850, the "filibusters" set out under the guise of emigrants, in vessels bound for Chagres. Lopez and his company, about six hundred in number, landed at Cardenas on the 18th of May, where he issued a bombastic proclamation, but met with no encouragement. On the contrary, the people rose against the invaders, and Lopez, after a bloody skirmish, burning the governor's house, and seizing some bags of specie, re-embarked in the steamer, Creole. His men insisted on being carried to Key West, where, just as they arrived, the Spanish war steamer, Pizarro, overtook them. But its commander could get neither the money nor men; on his return, however, he found 100 men of Lopez's party on the island of Contoy, on the coast of Yucatan, and carried them to Cuba. The restless adventurer, Lopez, began to plot afresh, and was encouraged by a number of Americans in his lawless schemes. General Quitman and others were indicted at New Orleans, in July, by the grand jury, as concerned in setting on foot an unlawful expedition, and the general was arrested on the 3d of February, 1851, on this charge; he was not, however, convicted, although by many believed to be guilty. At a later date, in April, J. O. Sullivan, Captain Rogers, of the Cleopatra, and others, were arrested at New York, and the vessel which they had procured was seized by the authorities. On the 25th of April, President Fillmore issued his proclamation, in which he expressed the conviction, that the expedition against Cuba was instigated "chiefly by foreigners, who dare to make our shores the scene of their guilty and hostile preparations against a friendly power, and who seek by falsehood and misrepresentation to seduce our citizens, especially the young and inconsiderate, into their wicked schemes." And he urged upon good citizens to frown upon every such effort, as a blot upon our good name, and certain to result in loss and disgrace. Lopez, having managed to escape the vigilance of the government, sailed from New Orleans, August 3d, 1851, in the steamer Pampero. His present company numbered more than 400 men. On the 11th, he arrived off the coast of Cuba, in sight of Havana, and turning westwardly, he advanced a few miles beyond Bahia Honda, where the steamer ran aground on a coral reef. Lopez debarked on the island of Playtas with all his troops, and advanced inland with three hundred men. Colonel Crittenden, his chief officer, was left with the remainder, and, preparing to join Lopez, was attacked by a large force and routed. With difficulty he escaped to the coast, and putting out to sea in boats, he and his party of some fifty men, were taken on the 15th, carried into Havana, condemned to die, and on the 16th were shot. Lopez advanced inland about ten miles, when he was attacked by about 800 Spanish troops. After a bloody battle he fled to the mountains, was hunted by bloodhounds, and on the 26th of August was garroted at Havana as a malefactor. The men made prisoners were sent to Spain; but, in 1852, on the intercession of our government, they were allowed to return to the United States.

Union meetings were held, during the autumn of 1850, in various parts of the country, Philadelphia, Boston, Cincinnati, etc., and patriotic addresses were made, and urgent exhortations presented, so as to induce all to hold fast by the Union at all hazards. In various parts of the South, however, the evil spirit of disunion was rife, and some of the leading men were unwise enough to advise South Carolina, the leader in secession, to "bide her time," and such like stuff. The Thirty-first Congress began its second session, December 2d, 1850, and received the same day the president's message. Mr. Fillmore expressed his views, clearly and straightforwardly in regard to the tariff, internal improvements, Indian affairs, army and navy, etc. He also enlarged somewhat upon the compromise measures of the previous session, and uttered the hope that they would have the effect of quieting agitation, and uniting all Americans in love and devotion to the

Union. The total receipts into the treasury, for the year ending June 30th, 1850, were $47,422,000. Total expenditures for the year, a little over $43,000,000. The public debt was reduced nearly $500,000; and about $8,000,000 of the public debt were to be provided for within two years. The annual reports of the heads of departments were transmitted to Congress with the message, and contained elaborate and full statements of the condition and wants of various branches of the public service. During the present session there was a large amount of talking, and consequently less acting than was to be desired. A number of measures failed for want of time; others were not completed on account of violent sectional opposition. The river and harbor improvement bill was defeated by a party trick, and a joint resolution to give honor to Scott, by creating the grade of lieutenant-general, also failed. The more important bills passed were, the civil and diplomatic appropriation bill; the army and navy appropriation bill; a bill for erecting lighthouses; an act reducing postage on letters to three cents on any distance under three thousand miles; etc. Acts were also passed respecting private land claims in California; establishing a military asylum; appointing the regents of the Smithsonian Institution (p. 193); authorizing the president to send a government vessel to bring Kossuth and other Hungarian exiles to the United States, etc. While General Taylor was alive, Mr. A. D. Mann was despatched to Vienna to watch the progress of the Hungarian struggle against Austria at that date, and in case of its success to recognize the Hungarian Republic. This having become known to the Austrian government, they charged upon Chevalier Hulsemann, (*chargé d'affaires*) at Washington, to protest against any interference in Austrian affairs. Mr. Hulsemann thereupon undertook to lecture the secretary of state in pretty severe terms. This was at the end of September. Daniel Webster was delayed until December in sending his reply, but when he did send it, it proved to be such as the bellicose chevalier, as well as foreign cabinets in general, could not readily forget or attempt to evade. The reader will do well to consult this admirable letter, and see how capitally Webster asserts the entire and perfect independence of the American people to sympathize with any and every oppressed nationality, so long as they preserve the faith of treaties, and the exact neutrality in regard to European matters, which Washington advised and which has ever been the policy and course of the United States. In this connection, we may mention, that, at the close of 1851, Louis Kossuth, the famous Magyar chief, arrived in the America, and received in all quarters expressions of sympathy, subscriptions in money, public honors, etc. But these were the sentiments and evidences of good-will of the people; the government could not, and did not take any part in Kossuth's movements. Hence having received about $100,000 towards the Hungarian cause, he left for England, in May, 1852.

During the summer of 1851, political movements were active and seemed to promise democratic success in the future. The journals of the day pointed out the alarming increase of crime, and attributed it, no doubt correctly, to the fact that a very large number of emigrants had come to our shores during the past year. The proportion of native offenders to those of foreign birth was not one-fifth; and the alms-house statistics presented a similar large increase of foreigners, which had been dispatched to the United States from England and Ireland principally. The accounts from California, however, threw every thing else into the shade. There, it became a war to the knife between the citizens and organized gangs of desperadoes and villains; and, for a period, anarchy prevailed, and the "committee of vigilance" took the law and the settlement of matters into their own hands.

In October, 1851, the first Grinnell expedition reached New York in safety. It had been absent a year and a half in search of the missing Sir John Franklin; but, we regret to say, with no satisfactory result. Dr. E. K. Kane, with great enthusiasm and courage, succeeded in getting a new expedition on foot to proceed to the Arctic regions. Further on, we shall note the issue. In November, 1851, a rather unpleasant affair occurred at Greytown, which for a time seemed likely to produce serious consequences. An American steamer was forcibly stopped by a British brig-of-war, and compelled to pay port charges, etc., which the captain thought to be illegal. Happily, the British government at once disavowed the over zealous conduct of the commander of the brig, as an act of violence and in contravention of treaty engagements; and so the matter was put to rest.

The Thirty-second Congress began its first session, December 1st, 1851. The president, in his message, expressed his determination to enforce the laws of the United States, in all cases, and not to allow of interference in the concerns of foreign nations, so as to endanger the peace of the country. The receipts into the treasury during the year, amounted to $52,312,979. The expenditures had been, $48,600,000. About $7,500,000 had been paid on account of the public debt, which, on the 20th of November, was $62,500,000. The estimated receipts for the next fiscal year, were, $51,800,000; and the estimated expenditures, were, $43,000,000. Various important recommendations, on the subject of the tariff, internal improvements, protection of the frontiers, an agricultural bureau, etc., were urged upon Congress; and Fillmore again gave it as his settled opinion, that the compromise measures of 1850 ought to be adhered to by all good citizens. The question as to the fisheries off the coast of British America gave some trouble at this date; there was considerable discussion in the Senate, etc.; but, as we may here state, a reciprocity treaty was arranged in 1854, and a mutually satisfactory adjustment of the question agreed upon. On the 1st of June, 1852, the democratic nominating convention met at Baltimore, and after much disputing and balloting, concluded by putting the names of Franklin Pierce and W. R. King forward as candidates for president and vice-president. On the 16th of June, the whig convention met in the same city; there was much discussion and difference of opinion, but finally, Gen. Scott and W. A. Graham were fixed upon. The "free-soilers," on their part, nominated J. P. Hale and G. W. Julian for president and vice-president. Congress adjourned, August 31st, 1852. Considerable business was accomplished, among which were acts voting an amendment to the deficiency bill, making an additional appropriation of $25,000 for each trip to the Collins line of steamers; considerably reducing the rates of postage on printed matter; making large appropriations for the improvement of rivers and harbors in various sections of the country; granting aid to the State of Michigan in constructing a ship canal around the Sault St. Marie; etc. The French spoliation bill, and other measures of importance, were postponed until the next session.*

The presidential election took place in November, and resulted in the election of Pierce by a large majority. Some little time before Webster's death, a proposition was made by England and France to the United States to become party to a tripartite convention, in virtue of which the three powers should severally and collectively disclaim, now and for the future, all intention to obtain possession of the Island of Cuba, as well as to discountenance all attempts of a similar kind by any power whatever. In July, 1852, Mr. Crampton addressed a letter to Mr. Webster on the subject, urging the views of his government as to this matter; and the Comte de Sartiges, in behalf of France, entirely accorded with the sentiments of Mr. Crampton's letter. In consequence of Webster's death not long after,

* We may put on record here, the death of two of the most eminent patriots and statesmen of America. Henry Clay died June 29th, 1852; and Daniel Webster October 24th, 1852.

Edward Everett became secretary of state, and under date of December 1st, addressed a letter to Comte de Sartiges on the subject. It was a very long and able letter, quite worthy of Everett's reputation and ability, and it set forth, in a clear and unmistakable manner, that the United States could not and would not entertain any such arrangement. "No administration of this government," said Everett, "however strong in the public confidence in other respects, could stand a day under the odium of having stipulated with the great powers of Europe, that in no future time, under no change of circumstances, by no amicable arrangement with Spain, by no act of lawful war, (should that calamity unfortunately occur,) by no consent of the inhabitants of the island, should they, like the possessions of Spain on the American continent, succeed in rendering themselves independent, in fine, by no overruling necessity of self-preservation, should the United States ever make the acquisition of Cuba. For these reasons, which the president has thought it advisable, considering the importance of the subject, to direct me to unfold at some length, he feels constrained to decline respectfully the invitation of France and England to become parties to the proposed convention."

The second session of the Thirty-second Congress began December 6th, 1852. The president's message, clearly but in brief terms, placed before Congress the several matters of interest requiring their attention. Cuba and the tripartite convention, the Tehuantepec route, the steps taken to obtain a change in the policy of Japan, the tariff, etc., were spoken of; and it was stated that the receipts for the year were, $49,728,386; the expenditures were, $46,008,000; the balance in the treasury was, $14,632,135. The value of foreign imports during the year was estimated at $207,240,000; the aggregate exports were, $167,066,000, besides $42,507,285 in specie. In the Senate, there was much animated debate on the whole subject of the foreign policy of the United States. General Cass had a great deal to say on the subject of the "Monroe doctrine" (p. 180); Messrs. Seward, Chase, Butler, Mason, Soulé, and others, took part in the discussion; and the country generally was deeply interested in the important questions involved in dispute. Various matters of business occupied the attention of the House, and a number of acts of local interest were passed, together with a great variety of private bills. The plan of a railroad from the Mississippi to the Pacific was repeatedly discussed in the Senate, and an amendment was finally adopted to the appropriation bill, authorizing the president to use $150,000 for the expenses of surveys, explorations of the route, etc. A bill was also passed, erecting a new territorial government out of part of Oregon, to be called the Territory of Washington. The Thirty-second Congress closed its career, March 3d, 1853, and at the same date Millard Fillmore retired from the position which he had well and worthily filled for nearly three years.

Franklin Pierce, the fourteenth president of the United States, was inaugurated on the 4th of March, 1853. His address, on this occasion, was in a tone of laudation of the country and ourselves, perhaps not in the best taste, but well calculated to attract popular applause. His cabinet was selected, and confirmed at once by the Senate. William L. Marcy was made secretary of state; James Guthrie, secretary of the treasury; Robert McClelland, secretary of the interior; Jefferson Davis, secretary of war; James C. Dobbin, secretary of the navy; James Campbell, postmaster-general; Caleb Cushing, attorney-general. The vice-president, W. R. King, died on the 18th of April, by which event, Mr. Atchison, who had been elected president *pro tempore* of the Senate, was henceforth charged with the duties of the vice-president's office. A large number of diplomatic appointments were also made; among which were James Buchanan sent to England, and J. Y. Mason to France. The Mexican boundary commission, early in the year, assigned the Mesilla Valley to Mexico, which roused up Governor Lane of New Mexico, and led him to propose to resist by force of arms. Trouble seemed likely to grow out of the matter. The second Grinnell Expedition started at the end of May, 1853, (p. 220), consisting of only one vessel, under command of Dr. Kane, and seventeen hardy navigators. It was a bold and adventurous undertaking, and its issue we may state by and by. In the present connection it is proper to note that four other expeditions were fitted out, in accordance with the provisions of Congress, (p. 214), for prosecuting explorations and selecting the best route for railroad communication between the Atlantic and Pacific. The first, under Major Stevens, was to proceed from St. Paul, Minnesota, to the Great Bend of the Missouri River, thence to the most available pass in the Rocky Mountains, from the forty-ninth parallel to the head-waters of the Missouri. The second, under Lieutenant Whipple, was to proceed from the Mississippi, along the head-waters of the Canadian, across the Rio Peco, entering the valley of the Rio del Norte near Albuquerque, thence through Walker's Pass in the Rocky Mountains to the Pacific, some where on the coast of southern California. The third, under Captain Gunnison, was to pass through the Rocky Mountains near the head-waters of the Rio del Norte, thence westwardly along the Nicollet River of the Great Basin, thence north to the Lake Utah. The fourth was to operate in California, in the region west of the Colorado to the Pacific, examining the passes of the Sierra Nevada, and endeavoring to ascertain the best route between Walker's Pass and the mouth of the Gila, and from that point to the Pacific at San Diego. The case of Kostza, a Hungarian, and the course pursued by Captain Ingraham in rescuing him from Austrian power, excited considerable attention at this date. Kostza, it appears, had taken the preliminary steps to become an American citizen, but was seized by the Austrian consul-general at Smyrna, as a refugee. His release was demanded by our consul, and Captain Ingraham threatened, that unless he were given up, he should fire into the Austrian brig where Kostza was confined. Marcy, in reply to Hulsemann's note, demanding satisfaction for the outrage on Austria, entered fully into the question, set forth the grounds on which the United States government is prepared to act in all similar cases, demonstrated that Austria had no cause of complaint, and justified the course of Captain Ingraham as eminently proper under the circumstances.

On the 5th of December, 1853, the Thirty-third Congress commenced its first session. The president's message was an elaborate production; it treated fully of our foreign relations, in regard to Great Britain, Spain, Mexico, China, Japan, etc., and gave a very cheering view of domestic matters, besides reporting the finances to be in a most flourishing condition. The principal work of the session may be briefly summed up; at the beginning of 1854, Douglas introduced into the Senate his Nebraska bill, subsequently changed to include Kansas also, providing, as was his favorite notion, that when these territories should be admitted as States, they might adopt slavery or not, as they pleased. In Douglas's opinion, the compromise of 1850 (p. 217) superseded the Missouri compromise of 1820 (p. 178). Of course, sharp debate ensued on the old question of slavery extension and limit. Douglas moved an amendment, in February, to declare the Missouri compromise inconsistent with the legislation of 1850, which was adopted, thirty-five to nine; and, after a large amount of further speechifying and personal bickerings, the bill was passed, March 3d, by a vote of thirty-seven to fourteen. In the House, a similar bill was brought in and discussed. It was taken up in March, then allowed to lie by for a month, and then, after every kind of interminable discussion and dispute had taken place, was passed, on the 22d of May, by a vote of one hundred and thirteen to one hundred. The Senate adopted this bill a few days afterwards. The Gadsden treaty came before the Senate for confirmation; it settled the question of boundary with Mexico, as well as other points of interest. Near the end of the session, a bill was passed by both Houses, appropriating $10,000,000 for carrying the treaty into effect. Other matters of interest were, the discussion upon building six first-class steam frigates, and the final passage of the bill by a large vote; the president's veto of the bill appropriating ten millions of acres of public lands to the several States for the relief of the indigent insane within their limits; the holding a convention at Charleston, in April, to consider how best to set forward the interests of the Southern States; the various inklings and movements towards annexing the Sandwich Islands; the issuing of a proclamation by the president, on the 31st of May, denouncing the filibustering attempts again about to be made upon Cuba; etc. A considerable amount of public business was left unfinished, and Congress adjourned on the 7th of August, 1854.

Perry and the Japan expedition may here be noted. Perry sailed from New York on the 24th of November, 1852, in the steamer Mississippi, other vessels in the East being ordered to join him. The Cape of Good Hope was doubled during the latter part of February, 1853; Singapore was reached on the 25th of March; and Shanghai on the 4th of May. Here the commodore transferred his flag to the Susquehanna, and had now a fleet of four vessels, with two others to join him soon after. The Lew-Chew Islands were visited, and early in June, Commodore Perry directed his course to Japan. On the 7th of July, he reached the Bay of Yedo, and caused no little surprise and apprehension by steaming directly into the bay, and insisting upon carrying out the measures for which he had come so far. By his judicious firmness, the commodore succeeded in accomplishing the object of his mission; the letter of the president to the emperor was delivered; negotiations were entered into; and finally, on the 31st of March, 1854, a treaty was agreed upon and signed. Commodore Perry returned home, reaching New York early in 1855, and the treaty with Japan was duly ratified by the Senate.

During the summer and autumn, various political meetings, conventions and the like were held, and it became evident that the minds of people were by no means at rest on the subject of the Missouri compromise and the Nebraska and Kansas bill, noted above; and there seemed to be a disposition in some quarters, to form a native American party, as opposed to aliens, especially Roman Catholic, Irish and German naturalized citizens.

The Thirty-third Congress began its second session, December 4th, 1854. The message of Pierce contained the usual summary of affairs, suggestions, etc., stating, among other things, that more than $24,000,000 had been paid on the public debt, and that the balance unpaid, about $45,000,000, was redeemable at different periods within fourteen years. During the session, Pierce applied the veto on two occasions, once in regard to the appointing a commission to investigate and pay the losses sustained by Americans from French spoliation, the other in regard to increasing the annual appropriations to the Collins line of steamers for mail service. This latter, however, was added to the naval appropriation bill, and so became a law. A retired list for the navy was provided; $7,750,000 were appropriated to meet the claims of the creditors of Texas who may hold bonds for the payment of which the revenues of the State were pledged; a bill to protect emigrant passengers was adopted; a joint resolution, approved on the 15th of February, authorized the president to confer the title of lieutenant-general by brevet, in a single instance, for eminent services. General Scott was the recipient of this well-merited and distinguished honor. Just at the close of the session, Pierce commu nicated to Congress a voluminous diplomatic correspondence respecting the Ostend conference, held in October, 1854. The substance of this meeting of the American ministers to England, France and Spain, at the city of Ostend, may be briefly summed up. The point of it consisted in the value of Cuba to the United States, the almost necessity of getting possession of it, the taking measures to this end openly and fairly, the offering Spain $120,000,000 for the island, etc. Pierce hesitated rather at this last measure, which offended Mr. Soulé very much. The Thirty-third Congress came to its end, March 3rd, 1855.*

The elections, during 1855, indicated an unhealthy tendency towards attempting to draw lines of distinction between "natives" and "foreigners," and here and there disturbances and riots occurred. In the existing condition of our country, certainly this question can never be agitated with satisfaction or even safety to the body politic. In the spring of the present year, Pierce gave notice to the Danish government, in respect to the dues levied on all vessels passing the Sound, that the treaty of commerce which recognized the right to levy these dues, would be terminated at the expiration of a year; and also, that the right would no longer be recognized by the United States. The Danish government, in reply to this notification, complained that the notice was too sudden, especially as they needed the money.

The expedition in search after Sir John Franklin, we have noted already, and Dr. Kane's embarkation in 1853 (p. 222). We may briefly state here the result. On the 10th of September, the party were frozen in on the coast of Greenland, at the most northerly point ever reached. Here the party passed their first Arctic winter. The following summer was spent in exploring in every direction that was practicable, in endeavors to ascertain something through the Esquimaux, in hunting, etc. The second winter, that of 1854–55, was intensely severe and trying, and their stock of fuel became quite exhausted. The search having been prosecuted two years, with no result, and Dr. Kane deeming it impossible to spend a third winter amid the ice, the Advance was reluctantly abandoned, on the 20th of May, 1855. With sledges and in open boats, this brave party set out on their return home; and having gone through sufferings of the most bitter and severe character, they reached the Danish settlements at Upernavik at the beginning of August, completely worn down with a journey of one thousand three hundred miles in eighty-one days. Apprehensions had some time previously begun to be entertained respecting the fate of Dr. Kane and his party; and acting upon these, Lieutenant Hartstene was dispatched in May, 1855, with the bark Release and the steamer Arctic, to seek for Dr. Kane and the Advance. Early in July they reached Upernavik, and fortunately not long after fell in with the brave Arctic explorers, *i. e.*, all who survived, three of the number having died; they were gladly received on board at Disco, about the middle of September, and on the 11th of October, the expedition was welcomed back again to New York. Dr. Kane's health, however, was completely broken down; he went to Cuba in hope of relief, but died at Havana, February 16th, 1857.

The Thirty-fourth Congress began its first session, December 3rd, 1855. The House fell into a wrangle and sharp contest as to who should be speaker, whether Banks, Aiken, or somebody else. Ballot after ballot was had, day after day, and it was not till two months of the public time had been wasted, and the plurality rule had been adopted, that N. P. Banks, on the 2d of February, 1856, received one hundred and three votes for speaker, while one hundred were cast for

* During the months of January, February, and March, 1854, the Darien exploring expedition, consisting of twenty-seven men, under command of Lieut. Isaac Strain of the navy, attempted to ascertain the practicability of a route for a ship canal across the Isthmus. It was attended with dangers and difficulties, and sufferings, almost passing belief.

Mr. Aiken, of South Carolina, and eleven were scattering. President Pierce, wearied out with waiting for the organization of the House, adopted an unusual course, and, on the 31st of December, sent his message to the Senate. In this document he spoke of the views of the British government as to the interpretation of the treaty of 1850, in regard to Central American affairs; the recruiting for the Crimean war carried on by English agents in the United States; the question of the Danish Sound dues; our relations with Spain, etc. He devoted considerable space to the existing difficulties in Kansas; the State-rights question, with particular reference to the fugitive slave law; the history ot this topic; and such like; and gave it as his opinion, that the South had not "persistently asserted claims and obtained advantages over the North in the practical administration of the general government." He also undertook the defence of the Kansas-Nebraska bill.

The Kansas question from this time became a very troublesome one. The Missouri compromise was done away with, and consequently Northern and Southern men both began the contest as to which should acquire predominating influence in forming and moulding the institutions and principles of the Territory, and the State soon to grow up and demand admission into the Union. In March, 1855, an election was held for members of the Territorial legislature, and the candidates in favor of introducing slavery into the Territory received a decided majority. It was alleged, however, on the other side, that the election was carried by illegal voters having come into the territory from Missouri, and interfered with those who had a right to vote, viz., the *bona fide* residents. Governor Reeder, in a speech, not long after, said "Kansas had been invaded, conquered, subjugated, by an armed force from beyond her borders, led on by a fanatical spirit, trampling under foot the principle of the Kansas bill and the right of suffrage." The violence of party spirit increased, and riot and even bloodshed were the consequences. The settlers opposed to slavery-introduction complained, in a memorial to Congress, of the Missourians having entered the Territory and deprived them of their rights; the pro-slavery men denounced any attempt to exclude it. The election for the first legislature was held, May 22d, and the slavery ticket was carried. This body met on the 2d of July, at Pawnee, and besides accomplishing a good deal of work, showed its dislike of Governor Reeder. He was soon after displaced, and D. Woodson became governor. Very stringent acts were passed, so as to put down effectually all anti-slavery sentiment and strength; and by way of variety, now and then, the process of "lynching" was applied to persons supposed or known to hold anti-slavery opinions. A convention of settlers, some six hundred in number, met at Lawrence, August 14th, and, having passed strong resolutions against the action of the legislature, called a convention of the Territory for the 5th of September. This body met at Big Springs, and declaring that the true interests of Kansas consisted in her being a free State, called upon the people to resist, by force if needful, the action of the legislature. Reeder was nominated for delegate to Congress, and was elected by the free-soilers on the 9th of October. Whitfield, however, of the pro-slavery party, it was claimed, received a larger vote on the 1st of October, the day appointed by the legislature. This result of course threw the matter upon the House of Representatives to decide between the two contestants. The free-soil party called a convention, which met at Topeka, on the 27th of October, 1855, and closed its session on the 11th of November, after having formed a State constitution, which was to be submitted to the people on the 15th of December following, and the principal feature in which was, that slavery was not to exist in the Territory after the 4th of July, 1857. The opponents of the free-soilers held what was termed a "law and order" convention at Leavenworth, on the 14th of November. Governor Shannon was appointed president, and the main business which occupied the convention was, the expressing decided disapprobation of the course pursued by the anti-slavery men, and declaring that, if it were persisted in and sanctioned by Congress, it would certainly lead to civil war.

Brief notice may here be taken of Walker and his "filibustering" efforts in Central America. At the end of August, 1855, he landed with his party at San Juan del Sur. On the 3d of September, his force, numbering one hundred and fifty, was attacked at Virgin Bay by some four hundred government troops. After a brief but fierce contest, Walker defeated his opponents. Granada, the capital, was attacked in October; taken by surprise, but little resistance was made; General Corral surrendered; and a treaty of peace was signed. Walker was elected president of the republic, but declined in favor of General Rivas; Corral, tried by court-martial, was condemned and shot; and Colonel Wheeler, the American minister, formally recognized the government as now constituted. Reinforcements flowed in, principally from California, and the Rivas and Walker government seemed to be gaining in strength. Early in 1856, the other States of Central America determined to put Walker down and joined together for that purpose. In March, Costa Rica formally declared war against Nicaragua, to which Walker replied, by announcing his purpose to carry the war into the enemy's country. Several battles ensued. Colonel Schlessinger, with three hundred men, was totally defeated at Santa Rosa. The Costa Ricans marched into the territory of Nicaragua, some three or four thousand in number; the city of Rivas fell into their hands; and on the 11th of April a bloody battle took place, in which Walker claimed a decisive victory. Troubles soon after sprung up between Rivas and Walker; the latter was elected president in June, 1856, and undertook to make head against the States confederated to crush him or drive him out. Matters went from bad to worse, and finally, in April, 1857, he capitulated, in a state of great destitution, to Captain Davis of the St. Marys, and was conveyed, together with a part of his company, to the United States.

As to Kansas, affairs grew no better but rather the worse. Two men quarreled over the slavery question and one was killed. This stirred up the neighboring Missourians, and they rushed into Kansas to sustain their pro-slavery friends. It was with difficulty that armed collision was prevented by the governor. A free State convention was held at Lawrence, December 22d, 1855, to nominate candidates for State officers under the Constitution. Pierce, January 24th, 1856, sent a message to the Senate in regard to affairs in Kansas, containing various recommendations, etc. He also issued a proclamation against all outside armed interference. which, he said, he was prepared to suppress at once. When Reeder and Whitfield came before the House, great difficulty was found in settling which was entitled to the seat. The majority of the committee took ground against Whitfield, and asked for power to send for persons and papers. This was adopted. In the Senate, Douglas, for the committee on Territories, brought in a report claiming that the course pursued by the Territorial legislature was legal and to be sustained, and recommended, that when the population of Kansas shall amount to ninety-three thousand three hundred and forty, the number requisite to entitle her to a Representation in Congress, they be authorized to hold a convention and form a State government. The report also denounced the free-State convention at Topeka, and sharply censured the measures of the Emigrant Aid Societies. Mr. Collamer presented a minority report, taking the opposite ground, and recommended as the easiest way to settle the difficulties, that Kansas be at once received into the Union with the present constitution. The State legislature (free-soil) met at Topeka, March 14th, 1856, and addressed a memorial to Congress. In the Territory itself, during April and May, difficulties increased, and a state of almost civil war existed. The excesses to which the controversy between the advocates and the opponents of slavery led, filled the journals of the day, and gave rise to serious apprehension as to what might be the final issue. One disgraceful occurrence in Congress we may put on record here. The debates in the Senate had increased in acerbity, as was not unnatural. Douglas, Butler, Mason, and other senators, had said much respecting Kansas and kindred matters. Sumner, of Massachusetts, on the 19th of May, delivered an elaborate speech on "the Crime against Kansas," in which he did not spare Butler and others, but, with a keenness of invective rarely excelled, poured out his wrath and contempt for his opponents. Tart retorts followed, and an equally tart rejoinder came from Sumner. On the morning of the 22d, the Senate having adjourned, and while Sumner was seated at his desk, P. S. Brooks, a nephew of Butler, and a member of the House from South Carolina, came up to the Senator from Massachusetts, and pronouncing him a libeller of South Carolina, and a slanderer of his aged relative, said he was going to chastise him. Immediately on this, he struck Sumner over the head with a gutta percha cane, and repeated the blows till he had nearly killed him. Considerable noise was made in Congress by this mean, unmanly attack, and it was attempted to punish Brooks by expulsion; but those who felt the disgrace of a course of conduct such as his had been, and desired to purge our national legislature of all those persons who are willing to resort to these means of venting their anger or overcoming their opponents, were not strong enough to accomplish this end; and so Brooks, and his helpers, Keitt and Edmonson, were allowed to remain. Keitt was censured by the House, and Brooks was fined three hundred dollars by the criminal court at Washington, for his assault on Sumner.

The committee on Kansas in the House, reported against admitting either Reeder or Whitfield, and a bill was proposed to allow Kansas to enter the Union at once as a State, under the Topeka Constitution. It was lost, June 30th, 1856, by a vote of 106 to 105. The vote, however, was reconsidered, and on the 3d of July, the bill was passed by a vote of 99 to 97. In the Senate a bill was passed to secure a fair expression of the will of the people, so as to form a State constitution. Shannon was removed, and J. W. Geary appointed governor in his place. He reached Kansas in September, and entered zealously and with more or less success upon his work.

The democratic convention for nominating candidates for the presidency, met June 2d, 1856. Douglas, Pierce and Buchanan were prominent before the convention; the last named was fixed upon. J. C. Breckinridge was nominated for vice-president, Fremont and Dayton were nominated by the republicans, and Fillmore by the American party. The contest resulted in the election of Buchanan and Breckinridge. The second session of the Thirty-fourth Congress began December 1st, 1856. Pierce's message possessed more than an ordinary interest from the fact, that the president entered at large into the exciting questions on which the North and South were arrayed in hostile opposition. Pierce exerted himself to defend the views and principles on which he and his administration had proceeded with respect to the abrogating the Missouri compromise, and also with respect to the whole slavery question, and he did not scruple to lay all the blame upon the Northern men, and those who, while adhering to the compact not to disturb slavery where it lawfully existed, were determined to resist its further expansion. Benton's review of this message is very searching and severe, especially in regard to the abrogation of the Missouri compromise. The recommendations of the executive and of the several heads of the departments received due attention, and a number of acts were passed by both Houses and obtained the approval of Mr. Pierce. For the civil and diplomatic expenses of the year were appropriated nearly $17,000,000; which, added to the other necessary appropriations for carrying on the government, as the army, the navy, the post-office, etc., made the total of appropriations, about $70,000,000. The tariff, after amendment and compromise between the views of the House and the Senate, was arranged in accordance with the president's recommendation; and it was estimated, that the result would be a reduction in the revenue of about $20,000,000. The Atlantic Telegraph bill, as finally passed, provided that the sum to be paid the company should not exceed $70,000 per annum, until the net profits reached six per cent., and after that it should not exceed $50,000.*

At the December term, 1856, of the Supreme Court, an important case came before that learned body for decision, which has become well known throughout the country as the "Dred Scott Case." It excited unusual attention in every part of the United States, and the opinions of the chief-justice and the associate justices were submitted to criticism and examination far more than ordinarily keen and searching. Scott and his wife, it will be remembered, were slaves, belonging to Dr. Emerson, a surgeon in the United States army; they were taken into and resided in Illinois, and at Fort Snelling, in the territory in which, by the ordinance of 1787, slavery was forever prohibited; in 1838, Scott and his wife were taken into Missouri, where two children were born, and where, from that time, they had been held as slaves. They claimed freedom on the ground that, by the act of their master, they had been brought into free territory. The court decided against their claim, and ruled that negroes, slaves or free, are not, by the Constitution, citizens of the United States. The *political* aspects of the question, and the points argued by the court, and the views expressed, respecting the Missouri compromise, and the self-extension of the Constitution to Territories, carrying slavery along with it, gave the Dred Scott case an interest which every citizen was able to appreciate; and the decision of the court did not have the effect of quieting agitation on the slavery question, but rather added fuel to, and intensified that agitation. The official report of the decision of the Supreme Court and Benton's "Examination of the Dred Scott case," deserve to be attentively weighed by the reader and student of history. Governor Geary, in Kansas, found his position a very trying one, and so he resigned, in March, 1857, and R. J. Walker was appointed his successor. The free-State convention, and the supporters of the views which led to that convention, continued to maintain their attitude of resistance to the legislative assembly and its acts. The prospect of further difficulties was not lessened, but rather increased, as the year 1857 advanced in its course. On the 3d of March, 1857, the Thirty-fourth Congress reached its termination. At the same date, Franklin Pierce was released from the burdensome duties of president of the United States, and made way for his successor. Pierce came into office with some considerable *prestige*, as the democratic candidate and the exponent of democratic principles and purposes; he retired from his lofty position with a general feeling that he had not met the expectations of the party; his administration was to all intents and purposes a failure, and it was high time that he should be put aside.

James Buchanan, on the 4th of March, 1857, went through the usual ceremonies of inauguration, and having read his address, took the oath of office. His inaugural was of moderate length, set forth in clear language the usual democratic doctrines, claimed that popular sovereignty would settle

* In August, 1857, an attempt was made to lay the cable for the Atlantic Telegraph Company. Unfortunately the cable gave way, when some three hundred miles of length had been paid out; and the great work of connecting the old world with the new by this means had to be postponed.

difficulties in the disputed territorial questions, deprecated slavery agitation, etc. Being a long tried, almost veteran statesman; an able advocate and defender of the principles of the democratic party, who had raised him to his lofty position; and intimately acquainted with the routine of executive duties, Mr. Buchanan, so far as it was permitted to form an opinion of the future, and what it might bring forth, had every reason to felicitate himself upon a peaceful, prosperous, and satisfactory administration. Lewis Cass, of Michigan, was appointed secretary of state; Howell Cobb, of Georgia, secretary of the treasury; John B. Floyd, of Virginia, secretary of war; Isaac Toucey, of Connecticut, secretary of the navy; Jacob Thompson, of Mississippi, secretary of the interior; Aaron V. Brown, of Tennessee, postmaster-general; and Jeremiah S. Black, of Pennsylvania, attorney-general. We call attention to these names, because several of them subsequently were prominent among the secessionists and rebels, and did all the mischief they could before openly showing themselves in their true characters. R. J. Walker, governor of Kansas, was directed to see that every loyal voter have the opportunity of expressing his choice on the question, slavery or no slavery. The free-State men assembled at the polls, in October, 1857, and by a majority of nearly 4000, elected M. J. Parrott as delegate to Congress. Soon after this the Lecompton convention met, and adopted a constitution, in which it was declared, that the right of owners to their slaves was inviolable: it was also provided, that the legislature should never pass a law emancipating the slaves. On this provision alone the electors were to vote, and the ballots cast were to be endorsed, "Constitution with slavery;" or, "Constitution with no slavery;" so that, however objectionable the proposed Constitution might be, there was no alternative; it was certainly to be adopted. Walker, considering himself ill used in this matter, resigned, and J. W. Denver became his successor. At the election in December, for the adoption or rejection of the slavery clause, the vote returned was little over 6000, more than half of which came from counties along the Missouri border, where the loyal voters did not number over 1000. The legislature, at a special session, determined to submit the Lecompton constitution to the direct vote of the people, on the 4th of January, 1858, which resulted in a majority of more than 10,000 votes against it. The Kansas question occupied a large share of the attention of Congress. The Senate voted to admit the new State with the Lecompton constitution, but the House disagreed. Various plans were proposed, and finally a bill was passed which submitted the whole matter to the decision of the people of Kansas. An election was held August 3d, 1858, and the Lecompton constitution was again rejected by 10,000 majority. A little previous to this, a convention of the people of Kansas met and framed a new Constitution, which was ratified by a decided majority of the inhabitants. Denver resigned, and J. Medary was appointed his successor.

Brigham Young, the leader of the Mormons, and his sect of fanatical devotees, gave a large amount of trouble to the government at this time. He was a scoundrel bold enough to dare to undertake armed resistance to the laws of the United States, and his conduct and proceedings were such that he richly deserved the gibbet, instead of the strange toleration which was shown towards him. It is a strange thing, as we record it, that the judges of the supreme court were driven out of Utah, and that a large force of twenty-five hundred men, under a United States officer, were virtually cowed down, and in May, 1860, were withdrawn from the territory! But we shall hear of this rebellious fellow further on.

The war in China required a large increase in our squadron, in order to protect American interests, and the Hon. W. B. Reed was sent as Minister from the United States to that country. The United States agreed to pay the apportioned sum of $380,000 to Denmark, in lieu of the Sound Duties. Many of the Indian tribes also, in the extreme west, manifested great hostility, and committed several outrages requiring punishment. Financial difficulties and troubles also in the community, caused great excitement throughout the country. Stocks suddenly fell; numerous failures took place; a panic ensued in September; many of the banks failed; and specie payments were suspended. The result of all which was, a general feeling of insecurity as to money matters, and a very heavy blow to nearly all the branches of industry on which the people principally depended for means of support. Return of confidence was very slow, and the ill effects of the pressure continued far into the next year.

The Thirty-fifth Congress met for its first session, December 7th, 1857. Orr, of South Carolina, was elected speaker of the House, and the democrats were in a decided majority in both branches of the national legislature. Buchanan, in his message, spoke of financial affairs, was very severe upon the great number of State banks and the immense paper circulation throughout the country, and discussed the Mormon rebellion and impudence, and the Kansas question with its issues. As to the latter, he said, truly enough, "Kansas has for some years occupied too much of the public attention. It is high time this should be directed to far more important objects. When once admitted into the Union, whether with or without slavery, the excitement beyond her own limits will speedily pass away, and she will then, for the first time, be left, as she ought to have been long since, to manage her own affairs in her own way." In speaking of the "Latter-Day Saints," as the Mormons chose to call themselves, he stated, that he was well aware of their fanatical devoteeism to Brigham Young, and their determination to persist in rebellion against the authority of the United States. "No wise government will lightly estimate the efforts which may be inspired by such frenzied fanaticism as exists among the Mormons in Utah. This is the first rebellion which has existed in our territories; and humanity itself requires that we should put it down in such a manner that it shall be the last."* In Congress, Buchanan manifestly leaned towards the pro-slavery side of the question, and threw all the weight of his influence in favor of those who were determined to force the Lecompton constitution upon Kansas. Senator Douglas energetically opposed the views and purposes of the president, and of that part of the democratic party who agreed with him. In the House also, a considerable number of the democrats voted against the policy of the administration. After many disagreements between the two Houses, a proposition of Mr. Montgomery was adopted, April 30th, 1858, by a small majority. Valuable bounties, etc., were offered by this bill to the Kansas inhabitants, who were informed that if they adopted the pro-slavery constitution, they would be admitted as a State immediately; if not, the admission would be postponed indefinitely. As before noted, (p. 229), the people rejected the proposition most decidedly.† During the present session (May, 1858), Minnesota was admitted into the Union; and Oregon also applied, but was put off till the next session, when, February, 1859, she also was admitted. The British cruisers in the Gulf, were disposed to annoy our vessels by a sort of stopping them for search, on the plea of the laudable but officious zeal in regard to the slave-trade. This, of course, roused up our countrymen, and England took

* And yet, here in this year of grace, 1871, the Mormon rebel chief holds his own in defiance of the government, and those who insult the laws of God as well as man, are as rampant as ever!

† Walker, the "filibuster," (p. 226,) started afresh, in November, 1857, against Nicaragua. He was arrested and brought away, in December, by the commander of one of our frigates. He claimed to have large sympathy at the South, and even of the government officials. Not satisfied, he set out again, in 1860, was taken prisoner in Honduras, tried, condemned and shot, on the 12th of September..

the earliest opportunity to apologize and disclaim any purpose of offence, etc. Congress adjourned June 14th, 1858.

The attempt made to connect the Old and New World, by means of a submarine telegraph, was vigorously prosecuted during the summer. The Niagara and Agamemnon met in mid-ocean, on the 26th of June, 1858, having the cable equally divided between them, ready for paying out. A splice was made, and the Niagara headed westwardly, and the Agamemnon in the opposite direction. Various vexatious mishaps occurred; the cable broke; was mended; broke again, when the vessels were about 300 miles apart; and for the time, success was not to be attained. On the 29th of July, however, the vessels met again, and having been favored with a tolerably smooth sea, they were enabled to accomplish their eventful mission. The Niagara reached Trinity Bay, Newfoundland, on the 5th of August, and on the same day the Agamemnon reached Valentia Bay, Ireland. "Glory to God in the highest; on earth peace, good-will towards men!" were the first words sent over the wires; and, in accordance with previous arrangements, as well as evident propriety, the first dispatches which passed between the two countries, were messages of congratulation and good-will between the Queen and the President. The bright anticipations of success were not realized. Within a few weeks the wires ceased to work. The company, though by no means abandoning their design, were compelled to defer to a later day the perfecting the connection between Europe and America through the Atlantic cable. This great work of our age did not reach its entire and successful completion until the summer of 1866.

The Thirty-fifth Congress met for its second session, December 6th, 1858. Buchanan's message was very long, and touched upon several points of interest in the then existing state of affairs. Among other things, he argued strongly for the acquisition of Cuba, and urged its necessity, as the only way of stopping the slave trade, and the relieving us of the need of keeping a naval force on the coast of Africa. He asked for money, so as to be able to act promptly, if circumstances required. Buchanan also enlarged upon the miserable internal condition of Mexico, and the hardly less deplorable weakness of Nicaragua, rendering it important, he thought, to protect our frontiers on the Mexican side, and secure the safety of the routes across the isthmus by naval and land force, if needful. He gave rather a discouraging view of the finances of the government, and strongly advocated the revision of the tariff for an increase of revenue. The public debt was nearly $55,000,000, and the treasury showed a deficit, notwithstanding $20,000,000 of treasury notes had been issued. Buchanan, after urging again upon Congress the great importance and even necessity of a railroad to the Pacific, brought his long message to a close.

The Pacific Railroad question was among the first which came up in the Senate, and from the speeches which were made, it speedily became evident that a radical difference of views existed as to the route best to be adopted, and the manner of building the road. W. H. Seward, of New York, in an able speech, advocated a line from the borders of Missouri direct to San Francisco, and showed clearly its importance, in a political and military point of view, towards maintaining the union of the Pacific with the Atlantic States. He also urged that the road should be built by the government, as the only certain way to secure its completion. Iverson, of Georgia, in behalf of himself and others, expressed himself in favor of two routes, a southern as well as a northern one, and gave utterance to some significant opinions as to the need of the South securing a mode of direct communication with the Pacific, for use when the Union was (as he said it soon would be) dissolved. Other senators entered into the discussion; but as was to be expected, no action was taken at this date. Slidell, of Louisiana, in January, 1859, introduced a bill for the acquisition of Cuba, which was accompanied by an elaborate report, setting forth the policy of the United States on this subject, the necessity of our having possession of the island, and the impossibility of allowing any other power than Spain (especially England or France) to hold it. Slidell also enlarged upon the excellence of the course which he recommended, in virtually abolishing the slave trade, relieving the government of the need of maintaining a very expensive squadron on the coast of Africa, and vastly increasing our commercial advantages. The bill provided that $30,000,000 be placed in the president's hands, so as enable him to take immediate action in case negotiations with Spain for the purchase of the island were successful; the entire price to be paid it was estimated would not exceed $125,000,000. The bill was warmly discussed, and various amendments and substitutes were proposed; but with no result. Congress, on one of the last days of the session, authorized an issue of $20,000,000 treasury notes, but left the post-office and other matters to shift for themselves.

Political strifes and disputes were on the increase. The republican party, which was opposed, *toto cœlo*, to the further extension of slavery, and was striving to bring about its gradual but certain extinction by confining it to the States where it already existed, was active and energetic in its movements. The democrats, who counted on Southern help to maintain their supremacy in national affairs, were in a difficult position, being, on the one hand, many of them conscientiously opposed to slavery, and on the other, anxious to compromise matters on this perplexing subject so as to act in concert with the Southern portion of the party. At the South, however, there was little if any disguise as to the actual state of public sentiment. The re-opening of the slave trade, although that trade is declared by law to be *piracy*, was openly and boldly advocated, and in Savannah, the grand jury denounced "the sickly sentiment of pretended philanthropy and diseased mental aberration of 'higher-law fanatics." A. H. Stephens, of Georgia,—notorious subsequently for his share in the rebellion, talked about "increasing the number of the African stock," and Rhett, of South Carolina, avowed with great candor that "the South must control the government or must fall." If our rights, as he coolly assumed them to be, "are overthrown, let this be the last contest between the North and the South, and the long, weary night of our dishonor and humiliation be dispersed at last by the glorious dayspring of a SOUTHERN CONFEDERACY." Jeff. Davis,—afterwards the arch-rebel and traitor, — delivered an address in the autumn of 1859, in which he undertook to denounce the law of 1820, which declares the slave trade to be piracy, and held that nothing could "justify the government in branding as infamous the source from which the chief part of the laboring population of the South is derived." He also held, that "the normal condition of servitude" was essential for the good of the black race; that slavery ought to be protected by law in the territories; that Cuba should be secured as being important for the interests of a Southern Confederacy; and that the Union should be dissolved, if the republicans elected their candidate on the platform of putting a stop to the further extension of slavery.*

The rancorous bitterness of Southern slaveholders' feelings on the subject of their "peculiar institution" and its issues, was greatly increased by a strange, wild attempt on the part of a man named John Brown, a native of New York, to produce a rising of the slaves in Virginia. Brown, it appears from his history, had become excited beyond all

* Seward's Rochester speech, in the autumn of 1858, excited Davis's ire very greatly; in it Mr. S. said,—"The two systems (slave and free labor) are continually coming into contact, and collision results. . . . . It is an *irrepressible conflict* between opposing and enduring forces, and it means that the United States must and will, sooner or later, become either entirely a slave-holding nation, or entirely a free labor nation."

control on the slavery question, and having been a sharer in the difficulties and violent contentions in Kansas, he seemed to think himself called upon to devote his life and energies to the freeing of the slaves. Several of his sons and a small body of others (twenty-two in all, seventeen white, five black) joined him; arms and ammunition were collected; and on the night of October 16th, he made a descent upon Harper's Ferry, a town of about five thousand inhabitants, and containing the United States arsenal with 100,000 stand of arms. The buildings being unguarded, were seized upon; prominent citizens were arrested; and the workmen connected with the armory, on going to their business in the morning, were also captured. About thirty prisoners were thus made. The alarm spread rapidly, and the exaggerated reports were speedily circulated of the extent of the force, the objects had in view, the rising of the slaves, etc. About noon, on the 17th, some military companies began to arrive from the neighborhood, and two of the party having been captured, the rest were gradually driven within the arsenal grounds. A few shots were fired during the day on both sides, and the mayor of the town was killed. Brown and his party finally entrenched themselves in the engine house, where they struggled to the last; but late in the night a body of United States marines, under Colonel Lee, invested the engine house, and early on the 18th, succeeded in battering down the door and capturing the insurgents. Brown was severely wounded, and thirteen of his companions had been killed; of the citizens and soldiers seven were killed and a number wounded. Brown was tried on the charge of treason and murder, and on the 29th of October was convicted. He was sentenced to be hung, on the 2d of December, together with his companions, and at the time appointed the execution took place. Political capital was attempted to be made out of this affair, but to no particular result; whatever might be said or thought of Brown's motives, there was no man who believed in the supremacy of law and order but what repudiated all such modes of trying to obtain freedom for the blacks; and the conviction was universally entertained that, however severe the punishment, it was only such as acts like those of Brown must ever expect to meet with.

The Thirty-sixth Congress assembled at Washington, December 5th, 1859. The Senate began by appointing a committee to inquire into and report upon the Harper's Ferry affair. In the House two hundred and thirty out of two hundred and thirty-seven members were present; and the contest for the speakership immediately began. Day after day, a ballot was taken, and innumerable speeches were made on slavery in all its possible connections. Sherman, of Ohio, was the republican candidate, and, on various occasions lacked only three or four votes of an election. Mr. Bocock, of Virginia, was the democratic nominee; but neither he, nor any other who was tried, succeeded in obtaining a majority. Thus the struggle was kept up for two months; when, finally, Mr. Sherman withdrew his name, and on the forty-fourth ballot, February 1st, 1860, Pennington, of New Jersey, was elected. Buchanan, tired of waiting, sent in his message, December 27th, 1859, with the usual reports of departments. Speaking of himself as "an old public functionary," he besought his countrymen to cultivate forbearance and good will towards each other, as in the days past, and he deprecated the dangers which seemed to threaten on every hand. Congratulations were offered on the decision of the Supreme Court, that slavery was now protected in the territories; the African slave trade was discussed, against which, he said, the laws would be enforced; the foreign relations of the country were in their usual state;* Mexican affairs, however,

* Some difficulty having occurred during the year in regard to the North-west boundary line, according to the treaty of 1846, between the United States and Great Britain, and both Americans and Englishmen claiming the Island of San Juan, between Vancouver's

were spoken of at large, as being in a peculiarly vexatious condition, and it was urged, that the United States ought to interfere for redress of grievances. The purchase of Cuba, the Pacific Railroad, increase of revenues, etc., were also presented as needing speedy attention. Speech-making and political agitation seemed to be the order of the day. Nearly everybody who could speak at all, had to deliver himself on the exciting topics now before Congress. Seward,* in behalf of the republicans, made it clearly evident that, if they prevailed in the coming presidential contest, Southern supremacy in national affairs, and further extension of slavery, were at an end forever. Jefferson Davis offered a series of resolutions, strongly urging the extreme state-rights views, as they are called, and the inviolability and excellence of the institution of slavery. Other Senators from the South, not only controverted the opinions and arguments of the republicans, but gave utterance to bitter denunciations and fierce threatenings of dissolution of the Union, in the event of their being in the minority at the ballot-box. Douglas rode his hobby of popular sovereignty to his heart's content; and Sumner, who had been so brutally maltreated (p. 227,) having recovered his health sufficiently, delivered another terrible philippic on "The Barbarism of Slavery." In the House, there were more than the ordinary violence and disorder, which, indeed, at times, seemed calculated to render the national legislature a by-word and scorn in the eyes of all honest, decent men. Comparatively little business was accomplished. A homestead bill was agreed upon and passed, in June, but Buchanan vetoed it; the post-office appropriation bill was lost by want of agreement between the two Houses; and the consideration of the Pacific Railroad and the tariff was deferred till the next session. On motion of Mr. Covode, of Pennsylvania, a committee was appointed (March 5th, 1860), to inquire into charges implicating the president as having unduly interfered in obtaining the passage of laws, or having neglected to execute the laws in any State or Territory. This was aimed directly at Buchanan's course with regard to Kansas, and, notwithstanding the president's earnest protest against such a committee, as in violation of his rights, the committee vigorously prosecuted their work. Towards the close of the session a report was presented, which, among other things, brought to light a letter from Buchanan to Walker, in July, 1857, fully justifying the latter's course in Kansas, and also unearthed various frauds and abuses for which the administration was severely censured by the House. Congress adjourned, June 25th, 1860.

The party conventions were held as usual in order to fix upon candidates. The democrats met at Charleston, April 23d, but could not agree upon any name or names; they adjourned to Baltimore, and met there, June 18th; a split in the convention took place, the one portion, nominating Douglas and H. V. Johnson, the other, J. C. Breckinridge and J. Lane. A "Union" convention met at Baltimore, May 10th, and nominated John Bell and Edward Everett. The republicans met at Chicago, May 16th. W. H. Seward was a prominent man before them, but the successful nominee was Abraham Lincoln: H. Hamlin was nominated for vice-president.

The Japanese embassy, the first ever made to "outside barbarians," crossed the Pacific in the Powhatan; arrived at San Francisco on the 27th of March; thence, by way of the

Island and Washington Territory, as belonging to their respective countries, a serious collision was apprehended. The government dispatched General Scott, in September, 1859, to the Pacific coast, to look after the interests of the United States. Happily, this matter was settled without much difficulty.

* W. H. Seward, on the 29th of February, 1860, presented the memorial of the legislature of Kansas, praying for admission into the Union. We may mention here, that the House, on the 17th of April, passed a bill to admit Kansas under the Wyandot constitution; but the bill was not acted on in the Senate. Kansas was finally, after her many trials and struggles, admitted into the Union, January 28th, 1861.

Isthmus, they proceeded to Washington, in May; visited Baltimore, Philadelphia and New York, in June; and re-embarked for home in the Niagara, on the 29th of June. They were every where treated with the highest distinction, and beneficial results were expected from their visit to the United States. The results of the eighth census, taken this year, may here be noted. Total white population, 27,003,314; free colored, 487,996; slaves, 3,953,760. The population of the free States was, 18,912,454. The population of the slave States was, 8,090,860, making, with the slaves, 12,044,620. The increase of population in the free States, during ten years, was, 7,446,043. The increase of population in the slave States was, 2,428,376. The grand total of the population of the United States (including territories) in 1860, was, 31,445,080. In the new apportionment of Representatives (the number being, by law, 233) the free States gained six, making their number 149; and the slave States lost six, reducing their number to 84.

The great political struggle for the presidency took place in the autumn of 1860. There were unusual activity and excitement throughout the country, and at the South it was openly affirmed as a settled purpose on their part never to submit to the government if placed in Abraham Lincoln's hands. This was thought, at the time, to be only political talk and bluster, but subsequent events showed that the Southern disunionists were madly in earnest in their fell designs against the honor and integrity of the country. The election was held November 6th, and it resulted in the choice of Lincoln and Hamlin for president and vice-president. Southern supremacy henceforth was to be a thing of the past, and men looked anxiously to what issue all this excitement and savageness of feeling were tending. The secession leaders threatened vengeance, and all other horrible things, and they soon began to make it evident what were their long-cherished designs. Secession, a breaking up of the Union, a Southern Confederacy, a new republic, free from contamination with Northern abolitionists and mechanics, a nation founded on the absolute supremacy of the white race and the necessary perpetual slavery of the black race;—these were among the things talked of everywhere and by all; and to accomplish these the Southern aiders and abettors of treason set themselves resolutely at work. South Carolina took the lead in this insane outbreak. The governor recommended instant preparation for the contest of arms, and on the 18th of December, a convention of delegates met at Charleston; on the 20th, the ordinance of secession was reported and adopted in the following words:—"We, the people of the State of South Carolina, in Convention assembled, do declare and ordain, and it is hereby declared and ordained, that the ordinance adopted by us in Convention on the 23d day of May, in the year of our Lord, 1788, whereby the Constitution of the United States of America was ratified, and also all acts or parts of acts of the General Assembly of this State ratifying the amendments to said Constitution, are hereby repealed, and that the Union now subsisting between South Carolina and other States under the name of the United States of America, is hereby dissolved." This Convention also put forth an "Address to the People of the Slaveholding States," and a "Declaration of the Causes which justify the Secession of South Carolina from the Federal Union." The address was an attempt to justify the course which had been taken, on the ground mainly of Northern aggression, and urged especially upon the neighboring States to unite with South Carolina and form "a great slaveholding confederacy." The declaration re-affirmed the State rights theory in its most stringent form; and asserted that fifteen of the States in the Union had refused to fulfill their Constitutional obligations; that the North hated and reviled slavery; that a man had been elected president whose whole soul was hostile to slavery; that negroes, in some States, had been allowed even to become citizens; and such like. Governor Pickens, the same day, issued a proclamation, asserting, among other things, "that the State of South Carolina had resumed her position among the nations of the world, as a free, sovereign, and independent State;" and the legislature, after the various acts called for by the anomalous condition of affairs, and the need of getting ready to resist any movements on the part of the government to enforce the laws, adjourned on the 5th of January, 1861.*

The Thirty-sixth Congress met, for its second session, December 3d, 1860. Buchanan's message showed that he was in a very difficult and uncomfortable position. All his political life had been marked by partiality for the Southern views of the great questions at issue, and by a spirit of unmanly subserviency, and so he condemned the North without scruple, as the authors of the trouble now existing; at the same time he could hardly venture to stultify himself by justifying the course of the hot-headed politicians who were inaugurating armed insurrection, and so he took occasion to set forth very plainly the folly and impudence of the claim on the part of any State to secede and break up the Union, whenever it saw fit to make the attempt. "In order to justify secession as a Constitutional remedy, it must be on the principle, that the federal government is a mere voluntary association of States, to be dissolved at pleasure by any one of the contracting parties. If this be so, the confederacy is a rope of sand, to be penetrated and dissolved by the first adverse wave of public opinion in any of the States. In this manner our thirty-three States may resolve themselves into as many petty, jarring, and hostile republics, each one retiring from the Union without responsibility whenever any sudden excitement might impe them to such a course. By this process a Union might be entirely broken into fragments in a few weeks which cost our forefathers many years of toil, privation, and blood to establish." "Let us look the danger fairly in the face; *secession* is neither more nor less than *revolution*. It may or it may not be a justifiable revolution; but still it is *revolution*." But—strangely enough—having asserted all this, he seems to have become frightened at the logical conclusion, and so, very weakly, began to deny that there was any power which could *coerce* a State against her will to remain in the Union. As a sort of make-peace, however, and a sop to the fire-eaters of the South, Buchanan suggested some explanatory amendments to the Constitution, whereby slavery should be bound on the whole nation, as with bands of iron.

In the House the message received but scant courtesy from the prominent politicians with whom secession was a foregone conclusion, and Buchanan was spoken of with a mixture of pity and contempt for his weakness, vacillation, inconsistency, and the like. Still, there were those who not only believed that the Union could be preserved and secession or revolution prevented, but who were willing to make any possible concession in order to attain this desirable end. Many good men, both in and out of Congress, thus thought and hoped; and the action of the House in appointing a committee of thirty-three (one from each State), and of the Senate, in appointing a committee of thirteen, was hailed as an indication that the dark and gloomy clouds which seemed surcharged with the direst of evils would soon pass away, and that our country would be spared the unutterable trials and tribulations of war in our very midst. But, as it seemed, it was too late. Mr. Crittenden's "compromise measures," in the Senate, were lost; and no one of the large number of "peace propositions" produced any result in the House. The president sent a special message, Janu-

* The headlong precipitancy and folly of South Carolina were gladly and skillfully used by secession leaders in other States. Ordinances, similar to that above quoted, were passed by Mississippi, January 9th, 1861; by Alabama and Florida, January 11th: by Georgia, January 18th; by Louisiana, January 26th; and by Texas, February 1st.

ary 8th, 1861, to Congress, averring that "the fact cannot be disguised that we are in the midst of a great revolution," and pleading for concession to the South as necessary to save the Union. He also sent copies of a correspondence between himself and certain gentlemen from South Carolina, in which, with refreshing coolness and assurance, these gentlemen required Buchanan to disavow Major Anderson's act in taking possession of Fort Sumter in Charleston harbor, predicting terrible things if he did not, and in which also Buchanan refused to do anything of the kind demanded.

The Virginia General Assembly, January 19th, 1861, passed resolutions urging both the South and the North, and the West, to desist from all further action until the result of the peace conference be ascertained. This conference met February 4th, at Washington. Ex-president Tyler was chosen to preside; one hundred and thirty-three commissioners, representing twenty-one States, were present; it continued in session until February 27th, when it adjourned, and the result of its earnest efforts to discover a way of escape out of existing difficulties and dissensions was laid before Congress. In the Senate, the "plan of adjustment" was discussed for the few remaining days of the session, but no action resulted looking towards the settlement of the momentous question at issue.

The rebel leaders, meanwhile, were not idle. On the same day that the peace conference met at Washington, a congress of delegates from the seven seceded states (p.236) assembled at Montgomery, Alabama. Cobb, of Georgia, late secretary of the treasury, became chairman, and in his address assured his hearers that the dissolution of the Union was "a fact, an irrevocable fact; the separation is perfect, complete, and perpetual. . . . We will this day inaugurate for the South a new era of peace, security, and prosperity." Immediate steps were taken to provide for a government in place of that which they had undertaken to throw off, and to establish a Southern Confederacy. Matters were hurried forward as much as possible. The Constitution of the United States was adopted nearly as a whole, with two or three politic provisions introduced, one against the slave trade, and another against importing slaves from any state outside of the confederacy. The first of these would be good capital in seeking foreign aid and sympathy; the latter bore directly on Virginia, the great slave-breeding State in the Union. This was accomplished on the 8th of February. The next day Jefferson Davis, of Missisipi, was chosen president, and A. H. Stephens vice-president of the confederation. The former of these was a thorough politician, well versed in all matters of public life, and a man of decided ability. As an unscrupulous devotee to the scheme which had so long been coming to maturity, he was probably the best man who could have been chosen to go to any and all lengths in the attempt to break down and destroy the Union. The latter, Stephens, was also a man of ability, but of a different stamp from Davis; more yielding and impressible, and less fixed and stern in principle and determination. Less than three months before (November 14th, 1860) he had made an eloquent speech in presence of the legislature of Georgia, in which he showed the folly and wickedness of secession, and besought his countrymen never to take any part in disunion: "If the Republic is to go down, let *us* be found at the last moment standing on the deck with the Constitution of the United States waving over our heads! . . . I fear if we evince passion, and without sufficient cause shall take that step, a disruption of the ties that bind us to the Union—that instead of becoming gods, we will become demons, and at no distant day countenance cutting one another's throats!" And yet, although avowing such sentiments, he was willing to deny them all, and take the post which was offered to him. He even went so far as to glorify slavery as the greatest of blessings and privileges. "The foundations of our new government are laid, its corner stone rests upon the great truth that the negro is not equal to the white man; that slavery, subordination to the superior race, is his natural and normal condition. This, our new government, is *the first in the history of the world based upon this great physical, philosophical and moral truth!*"

Davis went through the ceremony of being inaugurated, February 18th, 1861, and also delivered an address, well written and apparently evidencing candor, love of peace and other graces. As helpers, he selected Toombs, of Georgia; Memminger, of South Carolina; Walker, of Alabama; and Mallary, of Florida. The rebel provisional Congress took such steps as they could, to secure foreign aid and recognition; to raise money; provide troops, etc. On the 16th of March, they adjourned to meet two months later at Montgomery, Alabama. It was a mean kind of thing, certainly, but it soon became evident that the rebels did not mind stealing any more than lying, and were ready to lay hands on any thing within reach. Very early demonstrations were made in reference to seizing upon the fortifications of the United States in the harbors along the southern coast, and elsewhere. The majority of Buchanan's cabinet, especially Floyd and Toucey, in the war and treasury departments, were secessionists, and were so lost to all principles of honor and integrity as to use the opportunities afforded by their official positions in advancing the cause of disunion and rebellion. Every possible facility was afforded to enable the rebels to carry out their designs; the United States troops were scattered and dispersed, so as to prevent any effective garrisoning the forts at the South; and through the connivance of the secretary of the navy, the United States ships of war were also, as far as possible, sent out of the way, or rendered unfit to do duty in behalf of law and order in our native land. In Charleston harbor, direct steps were taken to seize upon the forts, even as the work had been begun by taking possession of the custom house, the United States arsenal, etc. Fort Moultrie, a large fortress, requiring some seven hundred men to garrison it, was occupied by Major Anderson, with a force of only eighty men; and was wholly indefensible on the land side. Early alive to the critical position in which he was placed, Major Anderson begged for reinforcements, at the beginning of December, 1860; but the president, acting under the guidance of Floyd, secretary of war, refused to send them. Anderson, then, following his own judgment, on the night of the 26th of December, removed his small force to Fort Sumter, in which, being out of the way of immediate danger, and every way more favorably situated, he was confident of being able, for the present, at least, to defend the flag of his country. The Charlestonians, much excited, resolved to compel submission. The steamer Star of the West arrived with reinforcements, January 10th, 1861, but being fired into by the rebels, sailed away, and left Fort Sumter to its fate. Governor Pickens summoned Anderson to surrender, which he at once refused; whereupon he was closely besieged, and informed the war department, March 1st, that an attack on the fort might at any time be expected.

Cobb, secretary of the treasury, finding apparently that, according to the plan had in view all along by the chief traitors, there was nothing further which he could do to benefit secession and its vile purposes, resigned his post, December 10th, 1860. On the 14th, General Cass, secretary of state, refused to serve any longer in the cabinet, because the president would not strengthen the garrison at Fort Moultrie, and on the 29th, Floyd, secretary of war, having ascertained, much to his chagrin, that the president would not order Major Anderson back from Fort Sumter to Fort Moultrie, and would not evacuate Charleston harbor, resigned all further share on his part in the management of public affairs. Holt, postmaster-general, was appointed in his place, and soon gave evidence that there was to be some life and

A. Lincoln

From the original painting by Chappel, in the possession of the publishers.

Johnson, Fry & Co. Publishers, New York.

vigor in that department. Thompson, secretary of the interior, resigned, January 8th, 1861; as did also Thomas, appointed in Cobb's place, on the 14th of January. John A. Dix, was then chosen secretary of the treasury, which seemed to give assurance of more energy and decision than had heretofore marked the action of the Cabinet. By these changes it was saved from sinking qrite into public contempt. As evidence of Dix's spirit, we may mention nere, that, when he received information from New Orleans that a rebel captain of a United States cutter refused to obey orders, the new secretary telegraphed instantly: "If any one attempts to haul down the American flag, shoot him on the spot!" Holt, also, in his department, signed an order, March 1st, dismissing, with disgrace, General Twiggs from the army, because of his treachery in delivering up military posts and other property of the United States to the Texan rebel authorities. The loss to the United States (in the way of mules, horses, materials of war, etc.) was more than $1,000,000.

It was a most singular thing which took place when the members of Congress from the seceded States concluded to leave Washington and take their rightful place in open rebellion. With a degree of assurance truly wonderful, these men, the Davises, the Slidells, the Yulees, the Taylors, and the like, dared to stand up in the halls of the national legislature and avow themselves as under no obligations to obey the laws of the United States, and as determined to trample the Union under foot. With singular forbearance and lack of spirit on the part of Congress, they were listened to, and permitted to utter words as they chose, words of mingled threatenings and entreaties, words of bravado and insolence, characteristic of the men and their cause. Congress adjourned, March 4th, having accomplished almost nothing in regard to the real questions at issue. There was abundance of talking, but not much action. The rebel members, as we now know, staid up to the last moment, with the very purpose of preventing anything being done.* The loans authorized were only for temporary emergencies; and the tariff, which added to the duties some five to ten per cent., was adopted in order to gratify the manufacturing interests at the North. At the same date, Buchanan's career was ended. There was scarcely any sympathy for the "old public functionary," but rather mingled indignation and contempt. The traitors who used him, at the same time despised him; the loyal men of the country felt outraged at his culpable weakness, vacillation and inefficiency; and, altogether, he has left anything but a fragrant name behind him. As a matter of justice, however, if the reader feel so disposed, he may consult Buchanan's book, published in 1865, in defence of himself and his administration.

On the 4th of March, 1861, Abraham Lincoln went through the usual ceremonies of inauguration, and delivered his inaugural address in the presence of a crowd of deeply interested listeners. The address was a carefully prepared paper, evidently the result of Lincoln's own study and reflection, and characterized by a tone of firmness and decision, as well as by an anxious desire to avoid the dire calamities into which secessionists were hurrying the country. The president selected for his cabinet the following gentlemen: William H. Seward, of New York, secretary of state; Salmon P. Chase, of Ohio, secretary of the treasury; Simon Cameron, of Pennsylvania, secretary of war; Gideon Welles, of Connecticut, secretary of the navy; Caleb B. Smith, of Indiana, secre-

* In a letter from Yulee, of Florida, under date of January 7th, 1861, he wrote, as follows: "If we left here (Congress), force, loan, and volunteer bills might be passed, which would put Mr. Lincoln in immediate condition for hostilities; whereas, by remaining in our places until the 4th of March, *it is thought we can keep the hands of Mr. Buchanan tied, and disable the Republicans from effecting any legislation which will strengthen the hands of the incoming administration.*" This letter, which shows how deliberately secession was settled upon by Southern traitors, was found in Fernandina, Florida, when that place was captured by Union troops, March, 1862.

tary of the interior; Montgomery Blair, of Maryland, postmaster-general; and Edward Bates, of Missouri, attorney-general. Among the principal diplomatic appointments were, Charles Francis Adams to England, W. L. Dayton to France, and C. M. Clay to Russia. Sad and cheerless, for the most part, was the prospect which Abraham Lincoln had before him as James Buchanan's successor. Seven States were already ranged under the flag of rebellion (p. 236). Several others on the borders between the free and slave States were almost wild with excitement, and strongly inclined to join the disunionists in their fratricidal attempts against the life of the nation. The whole country was in a state of unparaleled ferment, not knowing what a day might bring forth. At the North and West the people, as a whole, were quite unable to realize that the Republic was on the eve of war in its direst form, and were full of anxious solicitude as to the course which the new president would adopt in the existing crisis.* At the South, the secession, revolutionary element was overriding everything, and the minds of the majority were inflamed more and more with furious eagerness to rush into the contest. The forts and strongholds and public property of the United States were seized upon everywhere, in the seceded States, without scruple or hesitation. In the loyal States there was no preparation for war; there was, with few exceptions, no belief in the near approach of war. There were thousands pledged to oppose and embarrass the incoming administration in every possible way. There was little, if any, unanimity, or concord, or agreement, as to what the emergency really was, or how it was to be met. War, it was felt, was a terrible alternative; war must be avoided, if it were possible; and even up to the very last moment, even when South Carolina stood ready to fire the first gun, and initiate the horrible struggle, there were those who would not, who could not believe, that war was the inevitable issue, and that by force only could the rightful supremacy of the Constitution be maintained.

Abraham Lincoln had never as yet been a prominent man in national affairs. He was, comparatively, little known throughout the country; and having been taken up by the republican party as their candidate, rather as a compromise than because he was the ablest man in their ranks, the people, after his election, were deeply interested in everything which tended to indicate what were his qualifications for the high office he was about to assume. They were naturally very desirous to know in how far he was fitted to take the helm of state at a time when was to be tested the ability of the Constitution and Union to weather the storm just ready to burst in every direction. Up to this date, when Lincoln became fully invested with the powers of the presidential office, his sentiments and views, so far as made known, pointed clearly to a policy of conciliation, and a desire to yield on all points where it was possible to yield, in order to preserve peace and the integrity of the Union. For a month or so, after the inauguration, the new administration gave no clear or distinct indications of its line of policy. Secession, encouraged, no doubt, by what seemed hesitation or inefficiency on the part of government, was bold, active, haughty in its course and pretensions. Not only, as we have before said, were forts, arsenals, dock-yards and public property taken possession of without scruple, but also a loan of $15,000,000 was authorized by the so-called Confederate Congress, and other measures resolved upon in view of war, which might speedily be expected. Early in April, however, Lincoln

* General Scott, in a note to Mr. Seward, March 2d, named four plans for Lincoln's consideration:—I. Adopt new party name, and carry out the compromise measures of Crittenden, (p. 236); II. Collect the duties on foreign goods outside the ports, and close and blockade them; III. Conquer the seceded States by invading armies. This was barely possible (the old general said), by having some young brilliant general, with 300,000 well disciplined men, at a cost of some $250,000,000, etc. And IV. (In Scott's own words) "Say to the seceded States, 'Wayward sisters, depart in peace!'"

and his cabinet decided upon the course to be pursued, and thenceforward, though tardily, bent all their energies to preserve the Union unbroken, and, if need be, to put down treason and rebellion by force of arms. It would be amusing, if so serious consequences were not involved, to see the coolness and effrontery with which gentlemen from the South came to Washington, insisted on recognition of their rank as ambassadors or messengers from the new government, offering to settle all points of difference in regard to what had been done, and, when plainly told by the secretary of state, that they were nobodies in reality, and their so-called government only a sham and outbreak of treason, then taking up the lofty tone of injured innocence, and retiring with indignation at the "delusions" of the government. But so it was, and in such wise, with such pretensions, the rebellion was begun. The convention of Virginia sent to Mr. Lincoln to ask a statement of his proposed policy as regarded the rebel States. On the 13th of April, he replied that, in accordance with his oath to "preserve, protect and defend" the Constitution and laws, he should "hold, occupy, and possess the property and places belonging to the government, and should collect the duties and imports." If the rebels forced the issue, as they seemed bent upon doing, he would, he said, "to the best of his ability, repel force by force."

The government having, to this extent, at least, determined upon its course, orders were given, early in April, to send vessels and men for the purpose of reinforcing Fort Sumter, (p. 237,) and also to save, if possible, Fort Pickens, at the entrance of the harbor of Pensacola, Florida. But the leaders in rebellion, knowing how important it was to them to "*strike a blow*," as some of them phrased it, and to gain a victory of some kind, resolved immediately to compel Major Anderson to surrender. On the 5th of April, Beauregard, who had traitorously deserted the flag of his country, stopped all supplies for the fort from the city, and the hot-heads called for immediate reduction of the fort. They had a number of batteries all ready, and Anderson and his brave band could not possibly long withstand an assault. He agreed to evacuate the fort on the 15th, unless otherwise ordered by the government; but this was not what the rebels wanted, and so, when a vessel arrived off the harbor, on the evening of the 10th, with supplies, they madly began the attack. At half-past four on Friday morning, April 12th, *the first gun was fired upon Fort Sumter*. The United States vessels, just outside, could give no help, owing partly to bad weather and to the batteries in all directions, but were compelled to wait the inevitable result, when the stars and stripes should be lowered. The cannonading was furious and incessant. Major Anderson and his men bravely withstood and replied to the onslaught, and the guns of the fort were served with all the vigor and spirit possible under the circumstances; but ere long, being without provisions and the fort partly in flames, surrender was the only thing left to them. They gave up the contest, so unequal and useless to continue, and having been allowed to embark on board the United States steamer Baltic, Major Anderson and his company reached New York on the 18th of April. Immediately official notice was sent to the war department, in regard to the facts of the case, as just stated. The rebel exultation over this insane act, was almost indescribable. They seemed to think that they had done a noble and stupendous thing, and that the loyal people of the country would at once give up the matter, and allow them to rejoice in and enjoy their ill-gotten gains. In the North and West, however, it was felt, that now, the deadly stab having been made, there was no longer time for hesitation or mere words. Up to this point, threats, and bravado, and pillage of public property, and such like, had been endured; but now, when traitorous sons dared assail the flag of our country and its defenders, it was felt instinctively that the life of the nation was at stake.

Action must be taken; immediate action must be had, to assert and enforce the "supreme law of the land." President Lincoln was prompt and decisive in this great emergency, and immediately issued a proclamation, calling for 75,000 militia to suppress combinations against the laws, and repossess property seized from the Union. This was under date of April 16th, 1861, and at the same time he summoned a special session of Congress for the 4th of July following. Requisitions were made upon the governors of the States for their quotas, except those in secession. The Northern and Western States sent answers promptly, evincing their loyalty and readiness to contend manfully in sustaining the Union. The governors of Virginia, North Carolina, Kentucky, Missouri and Tennessee sent replies, refusing entirely to furnish any troops, and adding violent and abusive words besides.

Jeff. Davis, on the 17th of April, issued *his* proclamation, in which he invited "all those who may desire, by service in private armed vessels on the high seas, to aid this government in resisting wanton and wicked oppression, to make applications for commissions or letters of marque and reprisal, to be issued under the seal of these Confederate States." This insolent proposition was met by another proclamation from Lincoln, April 19th, declaring a blockade of the ports of the seceded States, and subjecting the privateers in the rebel service to the laws for the prevention and punishment of piracy. Some ten days afterwards, Davis addressed the Confederate Congress, and affected to doubt whether the proclamation were authentic or not. He stigmatized Lincoln's course in no measured terms, and could not, he said, bring himself to believe that the president was prepared to "inaugurate a war of extermination on both sides, by treating as pirates open enemies acting under commissions issued by an organized government." He also stated, that there were 19,000 men in the various places seized upon by the rebels, and 16,000 more on their way to Virginia, and that in view of the present exigencies 100,000 men were to be organized and held in readiness for instant action. The last paragraph,—a memorable specimen of mingled assurance and audacity, —we give in Davis's own words:—"We feel that our cause is just and holy. We protest solemnly, in the face of mankind, that we desire peace at any sacrifice, save that of honor. In independence we seek no conquest, no aggrandizement, no cession of any kind from the States with which we have lately confederated. *All we ask is to be let alone*—that those who never held power over us shall not now attempt our subjugation by arms. This we will, we must resist, to the direst extremity. The moment that this pretension is abandoned, the sword will drop from our grasp and we shall be ready to enter into treaties of amity and commerce that cannot but be mutually beneficial. So long as this pretension is maintained, with a firm reliance on that Divine power which covers with its protection the just cause, we will continue to struggle for our inheren right to freedom, independence, and self-government." Thus far the government seemed to have some line of policy, and had begun to make some preparations for the inevitable issues at stake. How imperfect this preparation was, how inadequate the appreciation of what was before our country to do and to endure, how insufficient the sense entertained of what the rebels meant, and were able to accomplish, the rapid progress of events ere long demonstrated.

The position of Virginia, as one of the largest and most important of the border States, rendered it especially desirable for the rebel conspirators to secure control over it, and they resolved to do it by foul means, if not by fair. Virginia, naturally and properly, was proud of the Union and anxious to preserve it; and there is hardly room for doubt that could the people of the State have expressed their sentiments and wishes freely and deliberately, they would have cast their lot with the supporters of the Constitution and laws. The convention had been elected by Union votes, and the legislature had taken care, in authorizing its consideration of this matter, to provide that no ordinance of secession should have any effect without being ratified by the people. At the opening of the convention in Richmond, a majority of its members were decidedly opposed to the secession of their State; but the conspirators, stopping short at nothing, resorted to secret sessions, and to deriding the weaker members, bullying the timid, cajoling the wavering, and firing Southern pride and passion in every possible way; so that, three days after the bombardment of Fort Sumter, they gained their purpose, and Virginia was forced to secede. Although the law required the vote of the people before secession could be ratified, there was no waiting, no scruple on the part of the rebels. Troops were sent in from South Carolina and other parts; everything was assumed as being complete; members were appointed to the so-called Confederate Congress; and when the 23d of May arrived, the voting was only to support a foregone conclusion; Union men were not safe in casting their suffrages; of course, secession was carried, the actual vote being 128,884 for secession, to 32,134 against. Virginia, mad and foolish, joined the foes of law and order; and bitterly did she afterwards find occasion to repent of her action.* Within twenty-four hours after the convention had done its work, not only were the Custom House and Post Office at Richmond seized upon, but an attack on the United States arsenal at Harper's Ferry was made. The possession of this latter was of prime importance to the rebels. Situated at the junction of the Shenandoah and Potomac, some sixty miles above Washington, it constitutes the outer gate to the great valley of Virginia, and offers the readiest mode of approach from the East to Winchester and the inner region. In addition to the armory with its weapons of war, it contained a large number of shops for the manufacture of arms. The arsenal at the time was in charge of about forty riflemen under Lieutenant Jones, who, in obedience to orders, set fire to the buildings containing the arms and thus prevented the rebels from stealing them. Simultaneously with this attack on Harper's Ferry, active measures were set on foot to get possession of the Navy Yard at Norfolk. This large and very valuable depot, with its vast stores of provisions and materials for naval purposes, its shops and manufactories, was situated at Gosport, adjoining Portsmouth, on the Elizabeth river, opposite Norfolk. It covered an area of three-quarters of a mile in length and a quarter in breadth, and it had a dry-dock of granite, with ship-houses, naval hospital, etc. There were twelve vessels in the yard, but most of them were dismantled and in ordinary. The Merrimac, a first-class frigate of forty guns, was the most important of all. Her machinery needed repair, and steps had been taken to put her in order as speedily as possible. On the 17th, she was ready to be moved, and yet Commodore McCauley refused to allow her departure. His excuse was, paltry enough, too, that he relied on the honor and veracity of his junior officers, who, by the way, when they had got through at Norfolk, coolly resigned and went over to secession. Commodore Paulding was sent with the Pawnee, and some Massachusetts troops, on the 20th of April, to save what he could and destroy the remainder. When he arrived, he found that the powder magazine had fallen into the hands of the insurgents, and that the ships

* "The second secessionary movement," as the rebels termed it, which was begun by Virginia, added three other States to the Confederacy. Tennessee seceded May 6th, 1861; Arkansas, May 18th; North Carolina, May 21st. Thus, eleven States were arrayed in hostile attitude against the Constitution and laws. (See note, p. 236). In regard to Tennessee, however, it may here be stated, that she was never carried into the position of rebellion by the will of the majority of her people. On the contrary, it was only by the audacity and unscrupulousness of disunionists, that the secession act was forced upon the people. Andrew Johnson was appointed military governor, March 4th, 1862, and in September, 1863 the rebel government was quashed entirely.

were scuttled and sinking. Commodore Paulding had them set on fire, and destroying as much of the public property as was possible, he took the U. S. ship Cumberland in tow, and sailed down the river. By a strange fatuity of the government, in not making proper provision in order to save public property from the hands of thieves and robbers, the confederates gained 2,000 pieces of heavy ordnance, 300 of the guns being of the Dahlgren pattern, and in stores, furniture, etc., property to the amount of $10,000,000. All this was very mortifying, and was deservedly, as well as severely censured by the Senate committee. It added strength to the rebels, and helped to prolong the contest by turning our own guns upon us.

An attack on Washington was one of the earliest designs of the rebels. They were eager to commence it, and fancied that it would raise their credit in the eyes of the world. Doubtless, from what is now known of the defenceless condition of Washington at the time, a sudden and successful dash might have been made; but the government took steps immediately to provide for the emergency. Troops arrived from Pennsylvania, New York, and Massachusetts, and, through the exertions of General Scott, Washington was, in a few weeks, safe against assault. In attaining this end, however, it is humiliating to relate how rudely and lawlessly the Baltimoreans acted towards the troops passing through their city. A scandalous riot occurred there, on the 19th of April, and a cowardly attack was made by the mob on the Sixth Massachusetts regiment, on its way to the capital, in passing from one depot of the railroad to another. The troops behaved with great patience and forbearance; but they were compelled, in self-defence, to use their arms, and literally fight their way through. The mayor and police marshal were, or professed to be, helpless; and, for the time, secession was loudly cried up, Confederate flags raised, the United States stars and stripes trampled on, etc. The New York Seventh regiment set out, on the afternoon of April 19th, for Washington. Finding, at Philadelphia, that they could not go by way of Baltimore, they took steamer and proceeded to Annapolis. Here they found General Butler, with troops, who had got as far as the Susquehanna, and finding the bridges burned, had made their way, by the ferryboat, to Annapolis. The Seventh and the Massachusetts troops, after no little hardship, reached Washington, April 25th. Butler was very serviceable at Annapolis. He not only took post there, but he held it. He secured to the government the noble old frigate Constitution, "Old Ironsides," and saw it safely conveyed away from danger. He was prepared to enforce the rights of those called by the president to go to Washington and defend the capital from invasion. Governor Hicks protested against his landing, or remaining in Annapolis; but the general was firm and decided. The legislature of Maryland met at Frederick, on the 27th of April, and the governor endeavored to assume and claim for the State a *neutral* position, helping, as he wished, neither side, but in effect, cutting off the capital from the loyal States. On the 5th of May, General Butler advanced a portion of his command to the Relay House, about nine miles from Baltimore, and on the 14th he entered the city, took possession of Federal Hill, and issued a straightforward proclamation, insisting upon the observance of law and order, and expressing the determination of the government to sustain all good citizens in their rights and privileges. The way through Baltimore was again open from the North, and troops passed freely through the city. Union men were at liberty to express their sentiments without molestation, and to act in accordance therewith; and sedition, though not dead, was held in abeyance at least. Governor Hicks, on the 14th of May, on the last day of the meeting of the legislature, issued a call for four regiments to serve for three months in Maryland, or for the defence of Washington. The saving of Maryland from the evil designs of those who would have hurried her into secession, was due, in measure, to the active and judicious movements of General B. F. Butler,—a name, by the way, of which we shall hear more further on. General Cadwalader succeeded Butler at Baltimore, May 23d, and was equally firm and conciliatory in his action.* General Banks took command June 10th. On the 27th, he ordered the arrest of police marshal Kane, and broke up the Board of Police in Baltimore, on the ground of complicity and agreement with traitors. The two proclamations which General Banks issued, show clearly the basis and the necessity of his action in behalf of law and order. By these vigorous means Maryland was saved from the evil purposes of secession and rebellion, and retained her rightful place in the Union. General Banks being called to supersede Patterson on the Potomac, General Dix took his place in Maryland, at the close of the month of July.

Great Union gatherings began now to take place in different parts of the country. One in New York city, April 20th, was especially noteworthy for the noble spirit of patriotism then and there exhibited. But it was not in words merely, that the loyalty of the nation was manifested. Money as well as men were most liberally furnished. The subscriptions of individuals, corporations, banking institutions, towns, cities, and the legislatures of the northern and western States, freely offered for the purchase of arms, the raising and equipment of troops, and the support of the government, in a fortnight after the day of the attack upon Sumter, reached a sum estimated at over $30,000,000. The month of May was marked by active preparations for the approaching contest of arms; recruiting, forming companies, drilling, etc., were zealously carried on; and it was estimated that at least 100,000 were busily preparing for the field. On the 3d of May, the president issued a proclamation, calling for troops, to serve for three years, unless sooner discharged. Forty-two thousand volunteers were thus called for, while the regular army was directed to be increased by the addition of eight regiments of infantry, one of cavalry, and one of artillery, making an aggregate of nearly 23,000 officers and men. Eighteen thousand seamen were, at the same time, ordered to be enlisted for the naval service of the United States. Having stated that these requisitions and acts would be submitted to Congress as soon as it assembled, the president said:—"In the meantime, I earnestly invoke the co-operation of all good citizens in the measures hereby adopted for the effectual suppression of unlawful violence, for the impartial enforcement of constitutional laws, and for the speediest possible restoration of peace and order, and with those, of happiness and prosperity throughout our country."

The Southern leaders were no less active in carrying out their fell designs, and pushed forward operations in every direction. The work of public spoliation, which was begun at Charleston, Savannah, and New Orleans, was also vigorously carried on in other regions of the country. Within a few days of the fall of Sumter, the steam transport Star of the West, loaded with provisions, sent for the relief of the United States troops in Texas, was treacherously seized at Indianola by a body of insurgents, under Colonel Van Dorn; the arsenals at Liberty, in Missouri, Fayetteville, in North Carolina, and Napoleon, in Arkansas, with stores of arms and ammunition, were plundered by the rebels; Fort Smith, in Arkansas, was taken possession of by Colonel Borland, the leader of a volunteer band of secessionists. In consequence of the various acts of robbery and violence in Virginia and North Carolina defeating

* A wealthy Marylander, John Merryman, was arrested by military authority, on 25th of May, charged with treasonable practices, etc. Merryman applied to Chief Justice Taney for a writ of *habeas corpus*, to test the legality of the arrest. It was granted at once, and efforts made to enforce it against General Cadwalader; but to no purpose. Taney then delivered his opinion adverse to the president's action, condemning him and it in no measured terms.

the exercise of the proper powers of the federal government, Lincoln, on the 27th of April, by proclamation, extended the blockade of the southern coast to those States.

The government now resolved to make a forward movement into Virginia. This was accomplished on the night of the 23d of May, nuder the direction of General Mansfield. The force which crossed the Potomac consisted of some 13,000 in all, and immediate possession was taken of Arlington Heights and of Alexandria. At this latter place, Colonel Ellsworth, with his New York Fire Zouaves, arrived by water, very early in the morning of the 24th of May. Here, by an over zealous desire to show his strong feeling against rebellion, he was shot in attempting to tear down and carry off a secession flag. This determination on the part of the government to do something, in order to suppress the rebellion, alarmed the rebel leaders not a little. All the hopes and expectations based on the alliance and aid looked for from Northern sources were futile and worthless,* and Davis and his co-workers, knowing this, made strenuous efforts to urge the people to fight in his bad cause. At Harper's Ferry, Manassas, Hampton, and Richmond, the rebels were strongly posted, and it was the plan of the leaders to make Virginia, as far as possible, the battle-ground on which to test the cause they had adopted, against the force of arms wielded by Union hands. Davis knew that, on every account, it was important as well as desirable for him and his so-called government to be in Virginia; and accordingly, he made arrangements to this effect as speedily as possible. The rebel Congress met at Montgomery, Ala., at the close of April, and Davis made an elaborate apology for secession, having in view effect to be produced abroad quite as much as at home; subsequent events showed that he had calculated very shrewdly in this. On the 6th of May, war was declared against the United States, as a foreign power; an enlistment act was passed; an issue of $50,000,000 treasury notes authorized, etc. On the 21st, they adjourned to meet, July 20th, in Richmond, Virginia, which was henceforth to be the capital of the Confederate States of America. Immediately Davis left Montgomery; on arriving at Richmond, on the 28th, he was received with due honor and attention, and uttered many honeyed words of praise to the Virginians, and poured out unmingled contempt upon "the ignorant usurper," at Washington.

Beauregard (p. 241) came to Virginia to take command, and on the 5th of June issued a proclamation filled with bluster and foul-mouthed insinuations, hardly calculated to deceive the most unintelligent. Troops from every quarter were gathered, and generals and other officers of various grades, who had forsworn themselves by deserting the flag of the United States, were busily engaged in fortifying various points, and in bringing the troops into as high a state of discipline and efficiency as was in their power. The rebels saw no opportunity now of assaulting Washington, or carrying the war, as they had been led to hope, into the loyal States. Their main efforts were hence directed to the sustaining and holding the positions already occupied, and to the repulsing the advances of the Union troops. Numerous skirmishes and collisions, of no great moment, occurred at several points in Virginia; and the gunboats began to prove their value at Sewall's Point, Acquia Creek, Matthias Point, etc. On the 1st of June, Lieutenant Tompkins, with a company of cavalry made

* Franklin Pierce, formerly President of the United States, wrote—to his shame be it recorded!—to Jeff. Davis, January 6th, 1860, encouraging him and others in their base designs, in language such as this: "Without discussing the question of right, of abstract power to secede, I have never believed that actual disruption of the Union can occur without blood; and if through the madness of Northern abolitionism that dire calamity must come, the fighting will not be along Mason and Dixon's line merely. *It will be within our own borders, in our own streets,* between the two classes of citizens to whom I have referred. Those who defy law and sacred constitutional obligations, will, if ever we reach the arbitrament of arms, find occupation enough at home."

a bold dash into Fairfax Court House, and defeated a detachment of the enemy whom he found there. Two days later, a camp of some 1,500 secessionists at Philippi, Barbour County, in Western Virginia, was assaulted successfully by Union troops, under Colonels Kelly and Dumont. An Indiana regiment, under Colonel Wallace, on the 11th of June, made a rapid march across Hampshire County; a body of secessionists at Romney was dispersed and compelled to retreat. On the 9th of June, General Patterson at Chambersburg, Pennsylvania, advanced towards Harper's Ferry with a considerable force; the result of which movement was, that on the 14th, the rebels abandoned that position, after having burned the railroad bridge over the Potomac, destroyed all the property they could, and torn up the track of the Baltimore and Ohio Railroad for about twelve miles from the Ferry.

Butler, at Fortress Monroe, having about 6,000 men, undertook an expedition against the rebels at Big Bethel some twelve miles off;* but it proved a failure. General Schenck, June 17th, by order of General McDowell, marched against Vienna, a small village on the Leesburg Railroad; but was driven off by the fire of a masked battery. General Patterson crossed the Potomac at Williamsport, July 2d; and it was estimated that at the close of the month of June, there were on and near the Potomac 100,000 troops, more or less ready for active service. The rebel force was supposed to be about the same in number.

In Kentucky and Missouri at this date matters of interest and importance were transpiring. We have seen how Virginia and Tennessee fell under the power of the rebels (p. 243); it was from no lack of effort that they did not succeed equally well in Kentucky and Missouri. In the former Gov. Magoffin and others urged *neutrality*, as if that were possible. Buckner, under Magoffin, recruited all he could, and sent them to join the rebel army. The governor wished to have a convention called, a process by which secessionists had already profited much; but the legislature refused. Magoffin then issued a proclamation, calling on the Kentuckians to stand aloof from the contest, and warning all parties not to encroach on the soil, rights, honor and sovereignty of the State. Union men were roused to fresh exertion, and a small encampment of Union troops under General Nelson was formed in Garrard county. This was denounced by Governor Magoffin as a violation of the neutrality of the State, and he sent by the hands of two "commissioners" a letter to President Lincoln, demanding the withdrawal of the troops. This was under date of August 19th; a few days afterwards the president, in pretty sharp terms, declined of course to have anything to do with the Kentucky governor's commissioners, and refused to order the Union troops to leave the State. Jefferson Davis also was addressed and asked to do the same thing with the rebel troops; but Davis coolly replied, that he was sorry to say that he was compelled by necessity to seize upon points of moment, to prevent their being taken possession of by the Union forces. Previous to this, Tennessee rebels had invaded Kentucky, and carried off six cannons and 1,000 stand of arms. The legislature, which met September 2d, 1861, resolved, on the 9th, that the invading secession forces should be expelled by calling out all the troops of the State, that aid be asked from the United States, and that General R. Anderson be requested to enter upon his command immediately. Hickman and Chalk Bluffs had been seized upon and fortified by the insurgents. General U. S. Grant, alive to the importance of prompt action, marched

* The facilities afforded to the rebels by slave labor in erecting fortifications, etc., brought up a novel and rather difficult question. At Hampton, when the whites fled, the negroes came into camp near Fortress Monroe. What was to be done with them? General Butler could not think it right to send them back to their masters to work against the Union and its cause; so, with great cleverness, he pronounced them *contraband of war:* in which he was sustained by the government.

a force from Cairo, September 6th, and took possession of Paducah, where he found everything prepared for a rebel arrival instead of for him and his men. He issued a proclamation, simple and straightforward in its terms, stating that his business was to deal with armed rebellion, and nothing else would be interfered with. Columbus was occupied by the rebel General Polk, September 7th. Zollicoffer, in the eastern part of the State, had some days before seized upon Cumberland Gap, on the same plea of military necessity, and he further said he meant to hold it for the rebels. Anderson assumed command, September 20th, and called for Union volunteers. Zollicoffer met with some success in capturing a Union camp at Barboursville, but a month later, he was repulsed by Schœpf at Camp Wild Cat. A rebel force at Piketown was put to flight by General Nelson, early in November. Anderson, finding his health unequal to the task of public service, resigned, and General W. T. Sherman, in October, took command. From henceforth Kentucky showed herself to be, and remained, heart and soul in the Union.

In regard to Missouri, it deserves to be noted, that her position and influence with reference both to the older States and the vast territory of the United States beyond her limits, were of prime importance to the cause of the Union. Elements of discord, it is true, existed in her midst, and there were not a few secession agitators in the State; but, on the other hand, there were noble and active loyal men in Missouri, able and ready to meet and counteract the plans of the governor and all his helpers. Governor Jackson, like Magoffin, tried to persuade the State to join the rebels; advocated armed neutrality; got the police of St. Louis under his control; and expected to do much for secession. But Union men were not idle. Colonel F. P. Blair, raised a volunteer military guard in St. Louis, composed largely of Germans; and Captain N. Lyon, a noble, energetic officer, in command at the arsenal, St. Louis, and for the present in charge of the entire department, delivered, on the 25th of April, a large quantity of arms, some 20,000 or more, to Captain Stokes, of Chicago, who had been sent with a requisition from the secretary of war to convey these arms to Springfield, Illinois. The transfer was not effected without considerable danger from the excited crowd of secessionists in St. Louis; but by zeal and courage combined, the arms were saved from falling into the hands of these public robbers. Being entrusted with further powers by the president, to enrol 10,000 loyal men if needed for the maintenance of the authority of the United States in St. Louis and Missouri generally, Captain Lyon proceeded to vigorous measures. He resolved, with Colonel Blair's help, to break up Camp Jackson, as it was called, where the State Guard were gathered, waiting their opportunity to give help to secession and rebellion. Early on the morning of May 10th, with some 6,000 men and artillery, Lyon appeared, wholly unexpectedly, at the camp, and demanded its immediate surrender. There was no alternative. Lyon was resolute and peremptory. Everything was surrendered; twenty cannon, 1,200 new rifles, a large amount of ammunition, etc. On the return to St. Louis with the prisoners, the troops were mobbed and grossly insulted by the enraged rebel sympathizers; the soldiers were compelled to fire on the mob; and some forty or fifty persons were killed and wounded. Lyon's energy was highly approved by the government, and he was raised to the rank of brigadier-generral. General Harney, May 12th, resumed command in Missouri. He issued a proclamation, avowing his determination to maintain the authority of the United States; but a week or so later, having entered into a sort of military truce with Price, one of the rebel officers, the effect of which was to benefit treason only, his course was promptly repudiated at Washington, and General Lyon was placed in command, June 1st. Price and Jackson found at once that they had a man of uncompromising zeal and determination to deal with. Lyon insisted on disarming the State militia, and claimed the fullest right for the government to take any steps called for in order to put down armed insurrection. Jackson called these terms "degrading," and sent out a proclamation calling for 50,000 State militia to drive out the Union troops. While acknowledging that Missouri was, in some sort, one of the United States, yet the *animus* of the man was evident: "It is my duty to advise you that *your first allegiance is due to your own State*, and that you are under no obligation whatever to obey the *unconstitutional* edicts of the military despotism which has enthroned itself at Washington, nor to submit to the infamous and degrading sway of its wicked minions in this State. No brave and true hearted Missourian will obey the one or submit to the other. *Rise, then, and drive out ignominiously the invaders*, who have dared to desecrate the soil which your labors have made fruitful, and which is consecrated by your homes." Lyon did not waste any time. He moved at once on Jefferson City, which was reached June 15th; but Jackson had retreated to Booneville, cutting off the telegraph and destroying the railroad bridges. Lyon followed him, and two days afterwards defeated and dispersed the hostile forces. At the same time, in a proclamation the next day, he avowed the most liberal and conciliatory policy towards all quiet and orderly persons in Missouri.

Notwithstanding what had been done by the rebels in Virginia (p. 243), there was a large proportion of the people, especially in Western Virginia, who were fixed in loyalty and resolved to stand by the Union at all hazards. In the counties west of the Blue Ridge there were some 10,000 slaves, while in those on the east the number reached to nearly 500,000. That extensive western region, bounded by the Alleghany Mountains and the Ohio River, and bordering on the north upon Pennsylvania, had little indeed in common with the slave-holding, slave-trading interests and Southern sympathies of the eastern division. Thus socially and industrially, as well as geographically, situated, they felt the pressure of taxation to be very unequal as compared with the more favored slave-holders, and they refused to join in the work of secession. Acting on their convictions, they denounced Letcher and the rebel leaders, and took immediate steps to separate Western Virginia from any share in the evil work thus far carried on by the enemies of the Union. A convention was held at Wheeling, May 13th, 1861, at which the ordinance of secession was pronounced "unconstitutional, null and void," and another convention appointed to be held June 11th, of representatives of the people. The convention assembled on the day named. Forty counties (five to the east of the Alleghanies) were represented, and the delegates entered upon their work, first taking an oath to support the Constitution and laws of the United States. It was maintained, that the government at Richmond, having violated the Constitution of the State, its authority was thereby annulled, and that the offices of all who adhered to the usurping convention and executive were, *ipso facto*, vacant. An ordinance was passed reorganizing the State government and providing for the appointment, by the convention, of a governor, council and legislature. F. H. Pierrepont was chosen governor, and inaugurated June 20th. He delivered a straightforward, pointed loyal address, claiming that what was done, was done in defence of their just rights. The legislature met on the 22d of July; the new government was recognized by the president; two senators, Messrs. J. S. Carlisle and W. T. Willey, were chosen to take the place of the seceders, Mason and Hunter (which they did on the 13th of July); and various enactments were made suitable to the present condition of things.

General McClellan took charge of military matters west of the Alleghanies, May 26th, and issued a stirring address from Cincinnati, Ohio, urging the Virginians to join the

Union Standard. Forces were pushed forward, and McClellan took steps at once to attack the rebels, who had taken post at Laurel Hill, near Beverly. General Morris moved forward with about 4000 men in front, while McClellan, advancing from the west, with some 10,000 men, purposed attacking the enemy's left at Rich Mountain. This was on the 1st of July. Skirmishing ensued for several days, without material result. On the 11th, McClellan was in front of the enemy, but did not venture a direct attack on their strong position. Colonel Rosecrans was sent, with 3000 men, to attack in the rear; but Pegram, the rebel commander, moved off in the night, hoping to join Garnett. He failed in this, and surrendered, July 12th; and Garnett, also retreating, was hotly pursued, lost his life at Cheat River, and his entire force was routed. "Our success," said McClellan, in his dispatch, July 14th, "is complete, and secession is killed in this country." The Cheat Mountain Gaps, which formed the key to Western Virginia, were entrenched and held by a strong force of Union troops.

The people of Eastern Tennessee were entirely in accord and sympathy with the loyalists of Virginia. The inhabitants were mostly agricultural, and less dependent upon slave labor than those in the western portion of the State, and they were ardently attached to the Union and its privileges. In both Virginia and Tennessee there was a hostile, dominant power, and both were betrayed by the arts and treachery of those who held the supremacy in local affairs. Letcher, in Virginia, had accomplished secession ends; and Harris, in Tennessee, was equally unscrupulous and far more tyrannical. Coercion and terrorism prevailed; and it was a hard task for the mountaineers of the Cumberland to contend with the wealthy slave-holders on the Mississippi, and to make head against the neighboring desperadoes of Alabama, Arkansas and Louisiana. Unwilling to yield without a struggle, the loyal Tennesseeans met in convention at Knoxville, May 30th. More than 1000 representatives came together to consult as to what was to be done in this alarming crisis. Secession was denounced, and the people were besought to vote it down on the day appointed, June 8th. In the eastern counties, this was done nobly; but by the manipulation of Governor Harris, and the interposition of military power and outrage, the secession vote of the State was said to be 104,019 for separation, and only 47,238 against. The convention met again at Greenville, June 17th; set forth a declaration of grievances; exposed the conduct of rebels and traitors; and resolved to endure any sacrifice sooner than give up the Union; so far were they, however, from being able to uphold the independence of their mountain region, that after an ineffectual struggle, they were hunted, imprisoned, and driven into exile. Thousands crossed the mountains by stealth to serve in the ranks of the Union army, that they might return to their homes under the flag of the Republic, and rescue their families and friends from the intolerable tyranny which oppressed them. The brave and much enduring men of this region were compelled to bide their time;* yet it was not wholly in silence; for Eastern Tennessee had men who were able and willing to raise their voices, as well as their arms in her defence. Brownlow, Nelson, Andrew Johnson, and others stood prominently forward on the side of law and order.

Evidently, the sword was now fully drawn. The question at issue was to be settled, not by words, not by appeals on either hand, not by menaces or threatenings, not at all, in fact, but by the stern, fearful, last abitrament, that of blood. They who loved their country, and its honor and integrity, had no alternative; they had but to accept the issue

* When Gen. Schoepf repulsed the rebels at Camp Wild Cat (see p. 248), the East Tennesseeans expected him to come to their aid. Deceived by the rebel reports of their great force at Bowling Green, Schoepf, after advancing two or three days in the direction of Cumberland Gap, retreated towards the Ohio, strewing the road with wrecked wagons, dead horses, etc. and left East Tennessee to her fate.

thrust upon them, or see the Union rent in pieces, and national prosperity swallowed up in the abyss. The leaders in the Southern conspiracy had prepared themselves for this issue by many years' laborious efforts; they had forced it upon the loyal supporters of the Constitution and laws of the United States; they had driven up to the point of fury and hatred the larger portion of the people of the South, and had compelled them to face the inevitable result. And now it was to be tested, whether this great Republic was worthy of its name and place in the family of nations, or whether it was to be broken in pieces, and become a subject for scorn and contempt among those who have always sneered at freedom in America, and constantly predicted its downfall.

A glance may here profitably be taken at the relative position and capabilities of the parties concerned in this memorable struggle, big with unutterable consequences.

As regards population, according to the census of 1860, the free States and Territories contained 19,000,000, the slave States something over 12,000,000. In addition to all the free States, which were for the Union, of course, Delaware, Maryland, Kentucky and Missouri were ranked in the same connection; the population of the loyal over the seceding States was, consequently, rather more than two to one. In the arts of industry, in commerce, trade, manufactures, shipping, etc., the free States were largely superior. In these respects, and in the universally recognized claim which all established governments have upon the fealty of their people, there can be no doubt that the loyal States stood, not only before the world, but in fact, in the position best calculated to command sympathy and enforce the requirements of the supreme law of the land. But, while all this was true, and no less important than true, it must be borne in mind, that the so-called "Confederacy" had several very decided advantages over the Union and its defenders. The people of the South, principally owing to the fact of their being slaveholders, were not only bred up in aristocratic notions of superiority, and in contemptuous disregard for labor and its adjuncts, but were trained from boyhood in the use of fire-arms, and in various kinds of exercises fitting them for military life and its excitements. In the war of 1812, and in that with Mexico, the South furnished nearly twice as many soldiers as the North. So long as the system of slavery prevailed, and the class of laborers was such as rendered it degrading, in their eyes, for a white man to work, the masters were of course at liberty to devote themselves to the fascinating employments of hunting, racing, contests of skill, and the like; and "the chivalry" of the South was rarely deficient in zeal and spirit where its peculiar qualifications had room for display. At the North, on the other hand, the great mass of the population were engaged in the peaceful avocations of life, and had no time, even if they had the inclination, to devote attention to those particular things in which Southern men excelled. To this must be added the fact of the vastly superior position of the "Confederacy" for self-defence, for direct communication with each and all its parts, and for facility of intercourse by means of railroads and telegraphs. The secessionists had long been preparing for the contest; they understood thoroughly the topography of the country; they had made their calculations with great shrewdness and ability; and, counting largely upon the sympathy and co-operation of many in the North (p. 246) as well as in the old world, they were ready to enter with all their heart and soul into the war for disunion and separation from those whom they professed to, and probably did, hate and despise. The North was wholly *un*-prepared for war; the government had everything, almost, to learn; armies had to be created, in fact; and the vast distances between various points of attack, where to pierce the confederacy and break down its military power, increased immensely the difficulties in the way of Mr. Lincoln and his advisers. And further, believing, as the rebels did, that "cotton was king," they were so persuaded of its importance to the world, especially to England and France, that they expected the great powers of Europe to break up directly any blockade which might be attempted to be put in force by the United States. It is true that this result did not take place, as they confidently looked for; but it is equally true, that the South obtained a great amount of sympathy and help from abroad, and the government was very seriously hampered and injured by the doings of the partisans for disunion on the other side of the Atlantic.

The Twenty-seventh Congress met at Washington, for its first (extra) session, July 4th, 1861 (p. 242). Senators from twenty-five States were present, soon after its opening; in the House, 159 representatives answered to their names; and Mr. Grow, of Pennsylvania, was elected speaker. In both the Senate and the House, there was a large, working majority of republicans. The next day Lincoln sent in his first message to Congress. It was a document looked for with no ordinary interest in every part of the country, and was eagerly read and commented upon. In it the president discussed, at some length, the questions requiring speedy attention and action, and on account of which this extra session of the national legislature was called. A review of matters connected with the outbreak of the rebellion, and a brief statement of the policy of the new administration, was given in clear, precise terms. Inasmuch, however, as the secessionists were determined to force upon the country the issue, "immediate dissolution or blood," he stated distinctly what, in his judgment, Congress ought to do. "It is now recommended that you give the legal means for making this contest a short and decisive one; that you place at the control of the government, for the work, at least, 400,000 men and $400,000,000. . . . . Surely man has as strong a motive *now*, to *preserve* our liberties, as each had *then* (in the Revolution) to *establish* them. A right result, at this time, will be worth more to the world than ten times the men and ten times the money. The evidence reaching us from the country leaves no doubt that the material for the work is abundant; and that it needs only the hand of legislation to give it legal sanction, and the hand of the executive to give it practical shape and efficiency." The latter part of the address was devoted to arguing again the question of secession and rebellion, and the president, in his peculiar style and with equal acuteness and plainnesss, denounced the folly and wickedness of those who, for thirty years, had been drugging the public mind with the sophism, "that any State of the Union may, *consistently* with the National Constitution, and therefore *lawfully* and *peaceably*, withdraw from the Union, without the consent of the Union or of any other State." In concluding his message, Lincoln urged upon Congress the seriousness of the present eventful crisis, and hoped that there might be united, harmonious and prompt action. "And having thus chosen our course," he further said, "without guile and with pure purpose, let us renew our trust in God, and go forward without fear and with manly hearts."

The reports of the several departments accompanied the message. In regard to the army, the force was thus computed: regulars and volunteers for three months and the war, 235,000; regiments of volunteers accepted and not yet in service, 50,000; new regiments of the regular army, 25,000; making a total of 310,000. Deducting the 80,000 three months' volunteers, 230,000 would be left for the effective national army for the war, and the speedy crushing out of the rebellion.

The secretary of the navy stated that, on the 4th of March, 1861, there were 69 vessels of all classes in the navy, mounting 1,346 guns. The vessels in commission were mostly on foreign stations, with about 7,500 men, exclusive of officers and marines. The home squadron consisted of 12 vessels, carrying 187 guns, and about 2000 men; added to this was the demoralization among navy officers (259 resigned or were dismissed the service between March 4th and July 4th), although, to their honor be it recorded, the crews, like brave and loyal men, stood by the flag of the Union, and were not to be seduced into betraying or deserting it. From necessity, the department had already a number of new vessels under way, and was recruiting seamen. The effective force, at date (July 4th), consisted of the squadron on the Atlantic coast, under the command of Flag-Officer S. H. Stringham, consisting of 22 vessels, 296 guns, and 3,300 men—and the squadron in the Gulf of Mexico, under the command of Flag-Officer William Mervine, consisting of 21 vessels, 282 guns, and 3,500 men. The secretary of the treasury estimated the coming year's outlay at $300,000,000. To meet this expenditure, custom duties, direct taxes, and loans were recommended, and Chase was clear in the conviction that the people would fully sustain the government.

Congress went vigorously to work. The army was increased by authorizing the enlistment of 500,000 volunteers; the navy received its proportional increase; a loan of $250,000,000 and $50,000,000 issue of treasury notes were authorized; import duties were increased; taxes were laid, collectable at a future day; etc. Here and there, there were men like Vallandingham of Ohio, B. Wood of New York, Burnett of Kentucky, and such like, who gave some trouble, but were of small account. The army bill was very ably and warmly debated in the Senate, on the 18th of July, and members of that body gave expression to patriotic sentiments and views worthy of their position. In the House, on the 19th, Mr. Crittenden, of Kentucky, offered a resolution declaring, that the present war was forced upon the country by Southern disunionists, and that Congress, disclaiming all intention of interfering with the rights, or institutions of the States, and all purpose of conquest, would prosecute the war to defend the Constitution and preserve the Union. The resolution was laid over till Monday, the 22d, and then passed almost unanimously. The same resolution was adopted by the Senate, July 24th, on motion of Andrew Johnson. It may be set down to the credit of the national legislature, that, notwithstanding the gloomy and disheartening condition of affairs, on this memorable Monday (the day after the Bull Run repulse and humiliation) the members went on steadily with their work; and the House, unanimously,

"*Resolved*, That the maintenance of the Constitution, the preservation of the Union, and the enforcement of the laws, are sacred trusts which must be executed; that no disaster shall discourage us from the most ample performance of this high duty; and that we pledge to the country and to the world the employment of every resource, national and individual, for the suppression, overthrow, and punishment of rebels in arms." Three days later, the Senate adopted a resolution to the same effect, which lacked only one vote (Breckinridge of Kentucky) to render it unanimous. On the 24th of July, the Senate considered a bill to confiscate property used for insurrectionary purposes by persons engaged in rebellion; by which, slaves, if employed by their masters to aid in rebellion, were thenceforward free, any law to the contrary notwithstanding. Earnest debate was had over this, but it was adopted by a large vote in the Senate, and by a vote of 60 to 48 in the House. On the last day of the session, an enacting clause to the bill increasing the pay of the soldiers was added, approving and legalizing the president's acts, proclamations, etc. Congress adjourned August 6th.

The rebel Congress (p. 246) met at Richmond, July 20th, 1861. Davis's message was not very long, but was acrimonious and almost fierce in its tone towards Lincoln and his message to Congress, July 4th. There was a considerable amount of special pleading in it, in regard to what he termed the effort on the part of the government to *sub-*

jugate the seceded States, and he fairly gloried in his and their importance, because so extensive preparations had been made to put down rebellion and treason. Davis announced his purpose and plan of retaliation on account of the privateersmen captured by the United States, and on trial for piracy. With congratulations at having escaped all connection with the loyal States, he called for increase of the army, lauded the devotion of the people of the South, and wound up with a glorification of the "calm and sublime devotion" displayed on all hands. Various measures were adopted by the rebel Congress, principally looking to financial difficulties, which already began to press heavily upon the secessionists, and were among the most perplexing to manage in the existing state of affairs. Beside the "produce loan," treasury notes were authorized to the extent of $100,000,000; a war tax was imposed; etc. The army was reported at 210,000 men in the field. Davis was authorized to increase this number by 400,000 more, and also to add to the so-called navy. An act respecting alien enemies was passed, ordering them to depart out of the Confederacy, and another sequestrating their property, intended as retaliatory for the confiscation act of Congress. After a short session, the Confederate Congress adjourned, September 2d, to meet again in November.

An impression largely prevailed at this point of time, that the rebellion could be put down by prompt decisive action, and as Congress had made such liberal and large preparation, and we had so many thousand troops already in the field, it was supposed by a majority of people that a brilliant campaign of three or six months would speedily reduce the rebels to submission. Hence, the cry, "On to Richmond!" The people, impatient and in general unreasoning, were calling for action; the soldiers wished for action; action seemed one of the easiest things in the world; the enemy was undervalued; and a battle must be fought, without delay, on such a scale and in such wise, as to prove the superiority of our forces, and the insignificance of the rebel hosts. Gen. Patterson, at the beginning of July, as we have stated (p. 247), crossed the Potomac at Williamsport, with about 20,000 men. The rebels retreated, and on the 15th he occupied Bunker Hill, nine miles from Winchester. On the 17th, instead of advancing on the direct road, he turned to the left and marched to Charlestown, twelve miles eastward and near the Potomac; thus, as it turned out, leaving the road open for Johnston, the rebel general at Winchester, to carry his entire force to Manassas, and do his share in the defeat of our army at Bull Run. Patterson was sharply censured for his course, and on the 25th of July was superseded by General Banks at Harper's Ferry. General McDowell was in command of the department of North-eastern Virginia, an able and excellent officer, to whom was committed the charge of attacking the rebels under Beauregard at Manassas. He had forty-five regiments of volunteers, chiefly from New York and the Eastern States, mostly those called out for three months only. The remainder were three years' volunteers, but these had been slightly drilled, and were not fit for the battle-field. Some companies of New Jersey cavalry, and several light batteries, were a part of McDowell's force, and among his officers were some of the best in the regular army. This "Grand Army," as it was called, began its march from Washington, July 16th. General Tyler's column took the advance, and spent the night at Vienna, a few miles from Fairfax Court House. General Hunter marched with the central column, on the direct road; and General Miles advanced on the extreme left. General McDowell, who was with the centre, arrived at noon the next day, at Fairfax Court House, the enemy retiring and evidently avoiding a conflict. On the 18th, Tyler passed through Centreville and found the rebels posted at Blackburn's Ford on Bull Run; here he wasted time and men's lives in a conflict of artillery with Longstreet, the rebel Commander

McDowell, not deeming it prudent to attack the rebels in front, resolved to make a diversion and gain Manassas by an approach from the east. A flank movement was accordingly determined upon, so as to turn the enemy's position on their left with a sufficient force, which should co-operate with a direct attack on their position at Stone Bridge, and thus open the turnpike road from Centreville, and cut off the railroad communication of Manassas with the army of Johnston in and about Winchester. McDowell intended to make the attack on Saturday, July 20th, 1861, but was hindered by delays in receiving proper supplies, which did not reach him till Friday night, at Centreville, about seven miles to the north-east of Manassas. Rations were distributed and issued; and in order as far as possible to avoid marching in the heat before the fight, orders were given to move at half-past two o'clock, on Sunday morning, the 21st, expecting to open the battle at all points at six, A. M. Delays occurred, owing to the inexperience of the officers and men, so that it was some three hours later, in one of the hot July mornings in Virginia, that the troops crossed at Sudley Spring, and soon after were engaged in the battle. Details we cannot here go into, and in a brief, condensed narrative of the war the reader must not look for details. It may suffice here to state, that McDowell's plans were well laid; that the men fought well, and stood their ground nobly, from the beginning of the battle till late in the afternoon. They had been up since two o'clock in the morning; they had made a long march before fighting; and they were without food. The rebels were disheartened and broken, and in a short time probably would have taken to flight, when, at this critical moment, Johnston, who had escaped Patterson's watching, brought in some 4000 or 5000 fresh troops, and by an active, enterprising dash upon our wearied men, turned the scale, and what should have been victory, became disorder panic, rout, and sad and fearful confusion.

Davis, it seems, left Richmond by railroad on this eventful Sunday morning, and reached the field of battle about four P.M., when the contest was virtually decided. He telegraphed the welcome news to the Confederate Congress that same night, stating, truly enough, that it had been "a hard fought field," but, with needless mendacity, asserting, that the Union army was beaten by a force less than half their own number.* Davis was in favor of immediate pursuit and a dash at the capital, which course indeed was the natural one to be adopted in order to reap the fruits of victory; but it was evident that the rebels were in no condition to avail themselves of their opportunity. They were pretty thoroughly exhausted; they had no cavalry; and the attempt, in Johnston's view, would have been useless as well as dangerous. As to losses, the exact truth can hardly be obtained; in general, it may be stated: rebel loss over 2000; Union loss over 3000. Beauregard claimed as the spoils of the day, 28 pieces of artillery, about 5,000 muskets, nearly 500,000 cartridges, a garrison flag, and 10 colors captured in the field or in the pursuit; and besides these, 64 artillery horses with their harness, 26 wagons and much camp equipage, clothing, and other property left behind.

The effect of the disaster at Bull Run or Manassas was astounding. The news at first from the field of battle, as made known by reports and telegraphic communications, had been cheering, and promising certain and great victory. The next news told of utter rout and disgrace; and Monday and Tuesday, the 22d and 23d of July, saw the streets of the capital thronged with panic-stricken crowds of those who had literally fled when no man pursued. In the great cities, and throughout the country, as the wildly exaggerated telegrams made known the overthrow

* Beauregard's army numbered not less than 30,000, and was fully equal in numbers to that under command of General McDowell, and yet Davis undertook to say, as above, "Our force was 15,000; that of the enemy estimated at 35,000."

of our army, the people were in a maze, and could with difficulty credit the unwelcome reports of disgraceful defeat. The disposition now was to run into the opposite extreme, and consider what the rebels had accomplished as a virtual guarantee of final success. But the depression and discouragement, wonderful as they seemed, were only temporary. Bitter as was the lesson of that memorable week at the close of July, it was a salutary lesson. It showed loyal men what was before them; that it was no holiday undertaking of a few weeks or months to put down rebellion or treason, organized as they were on a scale of magnitude and power undreamt of heretofore; and that, if the Union was to be sustained, it must be by united, steady, unflinching energy and devotion in its behalf. The resolution and spirit of Congress we have already noted (p. 253). The people of the loyal States likewise speedily nerved themselves to avenge the losses at Bull Run, and to hold up the hands of the government at any cost, in crushing the mad and desperate attempt to destroy the life and integrity of the nation.

The position of foreign nations and the probable course to be pursued by them in regard to the United States, was a matter of very grave importance at the outbreak of the rebellion. England and France, especially, were so situated as to render their line of action of the utmost moment, whether for good or evil, to the Great Republic. If, acting out the noble, manly part, which becomes sincere friends and well-wishers of our country, they should so direct their policy, and should assume such ground, as that the weight of their influence would be given to the support of the Union and the crushing out the rebellion, the case would be rendered more easy of settlement by means of the United States power on the land, where alone the rebels had succeeded in organizing any effective resistance against the authority of the government. If, on the other hand, the great maritime nations, like England and France, should see fit, more or less openly to encourage the so-called Confederacy in its ambitious designs, and in addition to recognizing its belligerent character, should aid in furnishing it not only with supplies of various sorts but also with the means of preying upon the commerce of the United States, they certainly had the power so to do, while holding a professedly friendly attitude to the government which they were virtually helping to undermine and destroy. And, in such an event, the rebellion would be all the more likely to protract its existence, if not finally to succeed in accomplishing its end. Of course, the government was deeply interested in the position of things, and the kind and description of public sentiment abroad, and care was taken to have our country represented by able men at foreign courts, such as Adams, Dayton, Clay, Motley, Marsh, and others.

The rebel leaders were also deeply concerned in this matter, and the manner in which their present attempt at a breaking up of the Union might be looked upon by the great powers of Europe. If England and France should favor their cause, directly, or at least indirectly, it would greatly facilitate matters, and would almost ensure success to the rebellion; but if they should refuse entirely any countenance to this proposed rending in pieces of the Union, and should look upon the outbreak as an insurrection, which the lawful government of the land was able to and would in due time suppress, then, the hopes and expectations of the Confederates would be sadly curtailed of their fair proportions, and their chances of final success very considerably diminished. They had, from the beginning, agents abroad admirably adapted for the work before them, in leavening public opinion, exciting prejudice against the government, offering commercial advantages, and skillfully using the press, etc., such as Yancey, Rost, Mann, and Butler King; and there can be no doubt that by their persistency and zeal they produced a decided impression on the public mind in Europe.

Governments, however, move slowly, as becomes the gravity of their position, and in modern times, at least, they require to be well assured that the people will sustain them, before they take any step of great importance. England, for various reasons, had no special regard or affection for the United States. There is every reason to believe that England would not have grieved, had republican institutions been destroyed at this time. Yet there were noble men and clear-headed statesmen in England who saw and knew, and gave their sympathy to the cause of law and order. Hence, the English government, whatever its inclinations may have been, hesitated to venture upon a step which, if wrongly taken, would be direful indeed in its consequences. France, also, under the despotism of Louis Napoleon, was not altogether pleased at being called upon to witness our rapid strides in national wealth and power. France, too, was more or less jealous of the United States, and was quite willing to stand by, and see the Union broken up, and its power and pride humbled; but there were friends of America in France, friends who did good service by their pens as well as in other ways, in behalf of our country's honor and good name; and more than this, France was ruled by a man who, however unscrupulous as a politician, was far too sagacious to commit himself hastily to an undertaking whose success was by no means assured; he had had too large experience in the uncertainty of political scheming to give aid to experiments which, so far as he could see, were as likely to be failures as anything else. Consequently, France was not willing, or prepared, to go to the lengths which the secessionists wished or expected; and France, like England, preferred to wait awhile, and see what the future might bring forth. The general disposition in Europe was, almost certainly, to look upon disintegration of the Union as necessary results of progress in our case, there being then, as there are now, persons who have no confidence in a government of the people, conducted by and through those whom they choose for the purpose. It became the arduous duty of the secretary of state to contend against this unfriendly feeling and hostile judgment, so far as it came in the range of diplomacy and public policy; and to Mr. Seward's honor be it recorded, that he devoted himself to the task with indefatigable zeal, energy and success.

The action of the British government could hardly be called friendly or decently courteous. With unusual haste, within less than a month after the news had arrived of Fort Sumter's bombardment, and before the arrival of our minister, Mr. C. F. Adams, Her Majesty's advisers, Lord John Russell at the head, had determined that "the Southern Confederacy of America, according to those principles which seem to them to be just principles, must be treated as a belligerent." The queen's proclamation, agreed upon in Privy Council, was issued on the 13th of May, the day of Mr. Adams's arrival at Liverpool, and before he had any opportunity of speech or action on the subject. Strict neutrality, of course, was enjoined, and all the other verbiage usual in these matters was used; but the *thing* itself struck deep into many an American heart. It was felt to be very unhandsome, to say the least, and to indicate a mean and hostile spirit, especially in the hour of America's greatest of all trials. The necessity of any such action could hardly be pretended, seeing that the "Confederacy," as it styled itself, had thus far done nothing but make loud and arrogant assumptions, and had not a single port of entry at its command, free from blockade, the real effect was, and was meant to be, to open the door for the rebels to get privateers, and prey upon American commerce. As it turned out, England furnished largely the means by which the rebellion was able to lengthen its existence, and to do immense injury to our commerce. Time has already shown, and time will probably still further make manifest, what a sad blunder England made, in the attitude then assumed, and subsequently persisted in, towards our country

On the 1st of June, 1861, a royal order was issued interdicting the armed vessels and privateers of both parties from carrying prizes made by them to ports, etc., of her Majesty's colonies or possessions abroad; strict neutrality also was proclaimed, as neither the English nor the French government was willing to risk the danger of war arising out of recognizing—if either had ventured that—the so-called Confederacy. The rebel agents, Yancey & Co., were much mortified because they were unable to persuade Lord John Russell or the head of the French government to go any further in helping forward secession and its malign ends. Intercourse with M. Thouvenel was, on the whole, friendly and satisfactory, and he expressed to Mr. Dayton, our minister, generous good-feeling and good-wishes. In a note to Mr. D., Seward wrote: "Tell M. Thouvenel, with the highest consideration and good feeling, that the thought of a dissolution of this Union, peaceably or by force, has never entered into the mind of any candid statesman here, and it is high time that it be dismissed by statesmen in Europe." It is interesting, in this connection, to note the hearty sympathy of Russia in our affairs. We thought we had a right to expect offices of friendship from England and France, but had hardly counted on any special regard from Russia. In both cases we were disappointed; the former adopted a course as detrimental to our interests as was possible, short of open war; the latter gave us every assurance of good will and earnest desires for our prosperity and national honor. Prince Gortchacow wrote to the Russian minister, July 10th: "Give them (the government and others) the assurance that, in every event the American nation may count upon the most cordial sympathy on the part of our august master during the important crisis which it is passing through at present." On the subject of privateering, we may here state, that certain articles were agreed upon at Paris, in 1856, by the principal powers of Europe. The understanding between the contracting parties, Great Britain, Austria, France, Russia, Prussia, Sardinia and Turkey, was:—1st, that privateering is abolished; 2d, that the neutral flag covers enemy's goods, except contraband of war; 3d, that neutral goods, with the same exception, are not liable to capture under an enemy's flag; 4th, that blockades, to be binding, must be effective. The United States, Pierce then being president, did not accede to the propositions, desiring to have added a provision exempting the private property of belligerents from seizure on the high seas. On Lincoln becoming president, and in view of the importance of the matter at the present juncture, Seward opened the subject again, and offered to accept the original articles without the desired addition just named. England and France favored the settlement of the subject; but it was kept in abeyance some two months, when, with great coolness, these governments declared, that whatever they might now do must be *prospective*, and not invalidate anything already done. That is, having recognized the belligerent position of the rebels, they were not going to do anything which might possibly interfere with the business of privateering, which Davis was already engaged in. Seward, in calm but unmistakeable tone, put a quietus upon the whole matter, and gave foreign powers to understand, that he both knew and was prepared to maintain the rights and dignity of the United States. Privateering was of course a matter of great moment to the rebel interest, and they made the most of it. At the close of 1861, they reported having seized fifty-eight vessels of various sizes and value. One of the privateers, the Savannah, was caught, early in June, by a United States vessel, and the officers and crew were put in confinement in New York. A bill of indictment for robbery on the high seas was promptly found by the grand jury, and on the 23d of July, the prisoners, thirteen in number, were arraigned for trial, which was set down for the October term. Davis had threatened, early in July, and had taken steps to carry into effect, certain severe measures of retaliation, viz: to hang our officers and men, prisoners in his hands, in case the privateers recently captured were convicted and condemned as pirates, according to the declaration in Lincoln's proclamation (p. 242); hence, when the trial came on, it was found to involve grave questions of law, as well as expediency. The trial lasted a week and the jury disagreed. Learned jurists discussed the subject at large; it was even thought necessary to take notice of the matter in parliament; and finally, under all the embarrassments of the question, and the certainty that numbers of our officers and men in the rebels' hands would be put to death in case the piratical privateersmen were hung, the government abandoned the prosecution, and thenceforward treated them simply as prisoners of war.

We need not expend time or space over details of rebel privateering. The energetic action of the government compelled neutrality, as far as possible, on the part of foreign nations, and so the rebels met with only partial success. Here and there, pirates, like the Sumter and Nashville, were more fortunate in escaping our vessels of war, and inflicting widespread injury upon our commerce. The actual loss to our merchants was undoubtedly great, and more or less severely felt; but the chief evil result was deeper and more lasting than the destruction of property alone could produce. The course pursued by the English government, professing the strictest neutrality, and being on terms of amity with our country, was such, nevertheless, as to bring conviction to our people, that that government was not unwilling to permit, under the thinnest disguise, vessels to be built in English shipyards, and fitted out to a large extent in England, to serve in rebe hands as privateers, and prey upon the commerce of the United States. The loyal people of our country entertained strong feelings of resentment against England for what had taken place, and, at a later date, questions of grave importance came up for settlement. In this connection, although a little in advance of other parts of our narrative, we may put on record an affair which not only made some noise but seemed likely to bring on a collision with Great Britain. As previously stated (p. 258), the rebel commissioners had met with indifferent success abroad. It was consequently resolved to send others to see what they could accomplish. Two persons, J. M. Mason and John Slidell, both in former days members of the United States Senate, and well known to be ardent, thorough-going secessionists and haters of the Union, were selected for the new and difficult work to be performed, and were charged with the imposing commission of ambassadors from the "Confederate States of America" to England and France. The arrogance and presumption of Mason, on the one hand, and the bold, unscrupulous character of Slidell, on the other, gave to their appointment, and the mission they had undertaken, more than usual importance. The government resolved, if possible, to intercept them and prevent their reaching Europe. A strict watch was ordered, and several vessels detailed to keep a sharp look out for the new agents in revolution. Mason and Slidell, however, with their secretaries and a number of others, took the small steamer Theodora, and about midnight, October 11th, escaped the blockade at Charleston, and made their way safely to Nassau, New Providence. Thence, the Theodora carried the party to Cuba, where they waited for the regular West India steamer in order to proceed to England. None of the vessels sent out by government were fortunate enough to meet with the persons of whom they were in search; it was reserved for a war steamer returning from the coast of Africa to accomplish the capture of these dangerous rebels. Capt. Wilkes, of the San Jacinto, having learned that the Theodora was at Havana, resolved to seize upon these "ambassadors," so soon as they left Cuba. At the end of October, 1861, he found Mason and his co-rebel waiting for the English steamer Trent, in order to proceed to St. Thomas and thence to England. Acting on his own views of what was right in the case, Wilkes took his position so as to stop the Trent, which he did November 8th, when about 250 miles from Havana. Having relieved the English vessel of the persons required, she continued on her way. Wilkes proceeded to Hampton Roads, reported his action, November 15th, and on the 24th, consigned his prisoners to safe keeping in Fort Warren, Boston.

Captain Wilkes was much lauded for his conduct, and was thanked by Congress and the secretary of the navy. It was observable, however, that the president, in his message, early in December, said nothing about the subject, and the secretary of state, equally kept himself free from commitment, until the news from England should manifest the spirit in which that government was disposed to view the matter. The wisdom of Seward's course was soon after abundantly verified. As was to be expected, the affair produced no little excitement in England, and the rebels and their friends endeavored to make the most of it. The law officers of the crown pronounced Capt. Wilkes' act unjustifiable, and the English government determined to demand peremptorily the restoration of Mason and Slidell to British protection, with "a suitable apology for the aggression which had been committed." War preparations were begun at once, the fleet in American waters was ordered to be largely increased, etc. Our able secretary of state, in reply to Earl Russell's dispatch, went over the discussion calmly and clearly, and stated the course which the president had determined to pursue in the present instance. It was substantially this: that as Captain Wilkes had proceeded on his own convictions of duty without instructions from the government, as he had not brought the Trent in as a prize and to be judged of by the proper court, and as what was claimed by England was precisely what the United States had always been contending for, the rebel ambassadors would be placed at once at the disposal of the British minister. This was done at the close of the month of December, 1861, and the great and formidable difficulty arising out of the Trent affair was settled without resort to hostilities between England and the United States. The chagrin and disappointment of the rebels were very great, and they expressed themselves in the most violent and abusive terms, because through the wisdom and discretion of our government a war with England was avoided, and an effectual stop put to the recognition of the rebel States.

The United States navy, which was increased rapidly and successfully, became a very important element in carrying out the plans of the government to put down rebellion. During the month of August, 1861, an expedition, partly military and partly naval, was fitted out at Fortress Monroe, the destination of which, for obvious reasons, was kept secret. It consisted of nearly 900 troops, well supplied and under command of General Butler, who had, on the 13th, been relieved at the fort by General Wool; the naval portion of the expedition was three large steam-frigates and some eight or ten other vessels, with Commodore Stringham in command. Its destination, as it turned out, was Hatteras Inlet, one of the most important entrances to the extensive series of navigable waters on the river coast of North Carolina, through the long range of sand islands which here serve as a barrier against the wild waves of the Atlantic. It was here that privateers and blockade runners found easy refuge, and it was high time to drive them out. The expedition sailed from Hampton Roads, August 26th, and the next afternoon anchored off the Inlet. At daylight, on the 28th, arrangements were made for landing the troops and for attacking the forts by the fleet. A heavy swell upon the beach prevented the landing of any number of the soldiers that day. About ten A. M., the fleet opened fire on Fort Hatteras and continued it till half-past one, P. M., when both forts hauled down their flags, and the rebels deserted Fort Clark, which was taken possession of by our men and the Union flag raised

Later in the day and early the next morning, the bombardment was resumed, and told fearfully upon Hatteras. About noon, Barron, the rebel commander, surrendered, with 615 men, 1,000 stand of arms, 31 cannon, a large quantity of stores, etc. The forts were thenceforth held and garrisoned by our troops, and blockade running became a much harder work than before.

As before stated, (p. 241) the value of Fort Pickens, Pensacola, was duly estimated and Colonel H. Brown reached the fort with reinforcements, April 16th; by the end of the month, the garrison amounted to about 900 men. Other troops arrived in June, and the rebels, some 8,000, under Bragg, did not venture any attack on Pickens. But our men were not content to act simply on the defensive. Several gallant deeds were performed by parties selected for the purpose. This was in September; early in October, the rebels tried to retaliate by attacking Wilson's Zouaves, about two miles from Fort Pickens; but they met with a decided repulse and lost heavily. Colonel Brown now resolved, with the aid of the ships under McKean, to bombard the rebel batteries and works at Pensacola. This line of forts and batteries, to which Fort Pickens and the ships were now opposed, extended four miles round the bay from the navy yard, on the northeast, to Fort McRae, on the south-west. Besides the old works of Fort Barrancas and McRae there were now erected no less than fourteen separate batteries, mounting from one to four guns each, many of them ten-inch columbiads, and some twelve and thirteen-inch sea coast mortars. These powerful fortifications were defended by about 8,000 men, while Colonel Brown had under his command at Fort Pickens but one-sixth of that number. The bombardment continued till night, and, resumed again the next morning, was very effective, and silenced Fort McRae, and the navy yard, and very materially lessened the firing of Fort Barrancas and other batteries. The firing was continued till dark, and occasionally during the night with mortars, when the combat ceased. Fort Pickens was reported by Colonel Brown to be hardly at all injured.

The blockade of the mouths of the Mississippi was, from the nature of the case, very difficult, and for a considerable time it was evaded with more of less success. On the 1st of July, the famous privateer Sumter, Raphael Semmes commander, passed out, made a dozen or more captures of merchantmen, and ran into Nassau, where British sympathy and aid were freely extended. Sometime after, Semmes, continuing his devastating course, brought the Sumter into Gibraltar, where the Tuscarora found him and kept him in durance, till the privateer captain and company were tired out, and sold their vessel to escape capture. But the blockade, though by no means perfect or complete, was sufficiently so to be very vexatious to the rebels in New Orleans, and roused them to make efforts to break it if possible. A steam ram was constructed during the summer for this purpose, at Algiers, opposite New Orleans, by taking an old towboat, covering her with iron and fitting a prow of timbers and iron, very strong. Early in October, this ram Manassas set out to attack the blockading fleet, stationed at the head of the Passes, and protecting our men engaged in erecting fortifications. Late on the night of October 11th, the ram suddenly appeared, attended by fire-rafts and boats, and gave a tremendous blow to the Richmond. The other vessels slipped cables and passed down with the current, the Richmond following. Two of them grounded on the bar, and were fired on by the rebel boats; but with no special effect. The vessels next day were got afloat and escaped all injury. Captain Hollins, of the ram, wrote a bombastic account of his exploits in "peppering well" the Richmond and other vessels; but the truth soon after became known as stated above.

A large and imposing expedition was next undertaken against Port Royal, South Carolina. General T. W. Sherman was in command of the troops, about 15,000 men; while the naval portion of the expedition, consisting of the steam frigate Wabash, twenty-two first-class and twelve smaller steamers, and twenty-six sailing vessels, was commanded by Commodore S. F. Dupont, one of the ablest officers in the service. The expedition sailed on the 29th of October, from Hampton Roads, and meeting with stormy weather, did not reach Port Royal till the night of November 3d, 1861. After a reconnaissance of the rebel works, the naval part of the expedition undertook a bombardment, especially of Fort Walker, on Hilton Head, which was by far the strongest in the hands of the rebels. The Wabash led the way, the gun boats following, steaming slowly up the bay, and receiving and returning the fire of the rebel forts; then, turning southwardly, they passed nearer the stronger work, and delivered fire with fearful effect. By this arrangement, no vessel became stationary, and the rebels could not gain by experiment and practice anything like a perfect aim. At 11:30, the rebel flag was shot down, and soon after some 2,000 men gave up the contest and ran away. In the course of the afternoon, Fort Walker was taken possession of, and a large body of troops landed; and as the other fort was found to be abandoned, the stars and stripes were hoisted on its flag-staff, the next morning at sunrise. Our success was complete; and the rebels were astounded at their defeat. Beaufort was readily reached, visited and found quite deserted and given over to the negroes. The government unfortunately had not made provision for pressing any advantage which might be gained. Had General Sherman been provided with light draft steamers and other facilities, there seems no reason to doubt that, under the terror caused by the rebel defeat, a successful attack might have been made upon Charleston and Savannah; but delays occurred. General Sherman set to work fortifying his position at Hilton Head. He did not occupy Beaufort until December 6th; nor, although Tybee Island, commanding the approach to Savannah, was taken possession of by Commodore Dupont, November 25th, did General Sherman, or his successor, do anything effective for some time later. This, together with the unwillingness to use the negroes in work of every kind, for which they were much better fitted than the Northern troops, helped to delay matters, and some of the fruits of our victory were thus lost.

Efforts were made to secure, as far as possible, the cotton which was found, or might be brought within our lines. The negroes were employed in this work, and distinct plans were formed for organizing them and putting them in the way of improvement. It was a work requiring great discretion and judgment, and Secretary Chase appointed Mr. E. L. Pierce as Superintendent. The first movement of any consequence in General T. W. Sherman's department, after the occupation of Beaufort, December 6th, 1861, was a joint military and naval expedition, directed against a fortified position of the enemy on a mainland at Port Royal Ferry. Accordingly, at the end of December, a method of attack was settled upon by Sherman and Dupont, in which their forces were jointly to co-operate. The command of the naval operations was assigned to Commander C. R. P. Rodgers; the military movements were conducted by General Stevens. The preparations of both were made with the greatest skill, and carried out with remarkable accuracy. The batteries of the enemy were destroyed and the houses of the vicinity burnt.

As we have before stated (p. 249), Jackson, the rebel Governor of Missouri, had been put to flight in June, 1861, by General Lyon at Booneville, whence he retreated to the southwestern portion of the State to get aid. Lyon continued the pursuit vigorously; the rebels, however, were met in Jasper County, by a force of some 1,500 Union troops, under Colonel Franz Sigel, a brave and spirited officer, who was pushing forward to prevent a junction of Jackson's force with that which was hastening to his assistance from another quarter. Sigel, on the 4th of July, found the rebels at Brier Forks, near Carthage, with a force more than twice his in number, and professing themselves eager for a fight. They were superior in cavalry, but Sigel had better artillery. The battle was a sharp one, and Sigel was compelled to retreat to Carthage, and subsequently, the rebels having been reinforced, to Springfield, where, July 13th, he joined Lyon. This loyal soldier unfortunately had a force quite insufficient to meet the difficulties and dangers of his position and repulse the rebels, who were daily increasing in force under Price, McCulloch, and others. These encamped at Wilson's Creek, Aug. 6th, determined to capture the Union troops under Lyon. Previous to this there was an engagement at Dug Springs, in which our cavalry drove back the rebels with great energy and success. Lyon proposed to attack the enemy on the 7th of August, but it became a serious question whether, with only about 5000 men, he should endeavor to meet the rebels, numbering not less than 20,000; many of Lyon's troops, too, being fresh recruits and quite doubtful as to standing fire. The injurious effect upon the Union cause which would be produced by a retreat, was felt so keenly that Lyon resolved to make a stand and fight at any cost. Hence, on Saturday morning, Aug. 10th, at daylight, he began the battle. It was fought gallantly by our men; but the great inferiority in numbers speedily became evident. Sigel at first drove the rebels on the right, but ere long his men gave way, and the brunt of the fight fell upon Lyon's column. His horse was killed, and he was badly wounded; but mounting another, and swinging his hat in the air, called to the troops nearest him to follow. The 2d Kansas gallantly rallied around him, headed by the brave Colonel Mitchell. In a few moments the Colonel fell, severely wounded; about the same time a fatal ball was lodged in General Lyon's breast, and he was carried from the field a corpse. Major Sturgis now took command, and after a three hours' fight, the rebels were forced from their camp and the field; while our men, almost without ammunition, and considerably reduced, slowly took up their march for Springfield, which they reached at five o'clock, P. M. The enemy did not venture on any pursuit; but, as it was evident that Springfield could not be held against the force the rebels possessed, Colonel Sigel conducted the retreat to Rolla, which he reached August 19th, with the remnant of his army, his baggage train, and $250,000 in specie. Our loss in this battle was estimated at 1236; the rebel loss at 1347. Although claimed by the rebels as a victory, it was not so; it checked their operations for some time, but on the Union behalf the repulse of the rebels was dearly bought at the sacrifice of Lyon's life.

General J. C. Fremont, early in July, was ordered to take charge of the western department, embracing Illinois, and the States and Territories west of the Mississippi. It was a popular appointment, and Fremont threw himself into the work with great zeal and energy. The prospect of affairs was gloomy enough in Missouri. The State was largely hostile; the disaster at Bull Run depressed the Union men while it gave the secessionists cause for exultation; faction prevailed; the recruits were badly supplied and badly paid; and the rebels had some 50,000 men in arms on the southern frontier. General Pope was in North Missouri; General Prentiss was at Cairo with a few regiments; the troops which General Lyon had commanded were in the condition above narrated; and altogether a very unpromising scene lay before Fremont. But he lost no time in attempting to do what he could. He immediately reinforced Cairo and Bird's Point,* carrying with

* Cairo, situate in Illinois, at a point of land formed by the confluence of the Ohio and Mississippi rivers, 175 miles below St. Louis, was early seen by the Union men to be of great importance to keep possession of; Bird's Point, in Missouri, commands Cairo and could easily shell the place. Illinois troops were in Cairo as early as April 25th, and General Grant bestowed much attention in strengthening and holding it.

him for this purpose eight steamers and 3,800 men. Happily, Fremont was in time, for the rebel General Pillow had, at New Madrid, a few miles below, a force estimated at nearly 20,000, and might readily have seized upon this important strategic point. Fremont did not stand upon trifles; he declared martial law, and in a proclamation announced that the property of armed rebels would be confiscated, but, more startlingly, "*their slaves, if any they have, are hereby declared free men.*" This was going quite too fast and too far; Union men in the border States protested against it; the government had, as yet, no fixed or enlarged policy, especially of such a kind as was afterwards adopted; and the President required, in a letter to Fremont, Sept. 11th, that his proclamation or order be annulled in its most striking particulars. At Lexington, 300 miles above St. Louis, on the Mississippi, Colonel Mulligan, with about 3000 men, was besieged and compelled to surrender, Sept. 20th. Fremont now resolved to set out in pursuit of Price and his marauding forces, which he did with a force of some 30,000 men in all. He reached Springfield at the close of October, and was just about to fight the rebels when he was superseded, Nov. 2d, by General Hunter, on various grounds, extravagance, incompetency, and the like. Hunter adopted quite different plans. He repudiated fighting, and in a few days began a retreat, being followed by Price, of course. General Halleck, Nov. 18th, took command of the department. He ordered that no fugitive slaves be permitted to enter the lines of any camp, or any forces on the march. On the 23d of December, he issued an order affixing the penalty of death on all persons engaged in destroying railroads and telegraphs, and on the 25th, he declared martial law.

Price's plan was to destroy the track of the northern railroad, and cut off communication with St. Louis, but was prevented by Halleck's activity. Pope, in Northern Missouri, was successful in operating against the rebels, and the entire region between the Missouri and Osage Rivers was cleared, Price being glad to retreat to the borders of Arkansas. During the last two weeks of December, the Union army captured, in various skirmishes, 2,500 prisoners, including ten commissioned officers, 1,200 horses and mules, 1,100 stand of arms, two tons of powder, 100 wagons, and an immense amount of stores and camp equipage. As evidencing the importance of Missouri at this date to the insurgents as well as the Union cause, we may mention, that not less than sixty battles and skirmishes were fought on its soil during 1861. In this connection may be noted Grant's attempt to break up the rebel encampment at Belmont, on the Missouri side of the Mississippi, and opposite Columbus, Kentucky. This latter was the head-quarters of secession, Polk being in command. Grant was at Cairo, Illinois, and, aided by General Smith, with Union forces at Paducah, Kentucky, making a feint of attacking Columbus, he set out for Belmont. With about 4,000 men, mostly Illinois troops, he embarked, November 6th, 1861, in four steamboats convoyed by two gun-boats, to Island No. 1, within eleven miles of Columbus. The next morning he proceeded to Hunter's Point, a few miles above Belmont. The troops were landed on the Missouri shore, reached the camp at eleven o'clock, and after a sharp contest drove the rebels out, burned the tents, etc. After some hours fighting, with victory just at hand, the rebels received reinforcements in large numbers, and Grant and his men were compelled to cut their way through to their boats. This they accomplished about five P. M., and escaped with a loss of about 600. The rebel loss was computed at 800. Although forced to retreat, Grant accomplished the main result of his expedition: the camp at Belmont was broken up, and various rebel plans for operating west of the Mississippi were defeated.

Turning our attention again to Virginia, we find the Kanawha Valley freed, by the end of July, from rebel troops. Early in

September, Floyd, who was in command, occupied a high hill at Carnifex Ferry on the Gauley River. General Rosecrans, who had about 10,000 men, resolved to attack Floyd, which he did September 10th. A spirited attack was made in the afternoon, but Floyd retreated in the night, having destroyed the bridge and the ferry-boats so as to get out of harm's way. General Lee, a person subsequently of much note in the rebellion, arrived from the northward with a force of 9,000 men and some eight or ten pieces of artillery; he took command of Floyd's and Wise's troops, which raised his numbers to 20,000 men. While on his way, in August, he found General Reynolds in command at Cheat Mountain and Elk Water. His plan was, if possible, to capture Reynolds' forces by strategy, and for that purpose he pushed forward two bodies to take our men in front and rear. For three days, September 12–14th, there was skirmishing, more or less sharp, going on, but with no particular result. Rosecrans at Gauley Mount was fired at by Floyd; probably he would have flanked and surprised the rebels had not a sudden rise in the river rendered it impassable. Nov. 14th, Floyd's rear guard was driven by Benham, whereupon the rebel leader retreated some fifty miles to Peterston. General Kelly made a spirited and successful dash upon Romney, and General Milroy attempted a similar dash at Alleghany summit, but without success. On the approach of winter, Lee was ordered to take charge of the southern coast defences; Wise was ordered to Richmond; and all the rebel forces were withdrawn, except a small one under Floyd. Soon after, in December, Floyd was removed to Tennessee, for service there; and thus ended the operations of the season, the Union army being left in full possession of Western Virginia.

General McClellan (p. 250), on the call of the Government, proceeded at once to Washington, and entered upon the work of no light magnitude, in the existing crisis. "I found," he says, in a letter to the secretary of war, "no army to command; a mere collection of regiments cowering on the banks of the Potomac, some perfectly raw, others dispirited by the recent defeat (at Bull Run). . . . . The troops were not only undisciplined, undrilled and dispirited; they were not even placed in military positions. The city was almost in a condition to have been taken by a dash of a regiment of cavalry." McClellan came to his work with much *prestige*, and great things were expected of him on all hands. He began by enforcing military discipline in the camps at the capital, issuing an order to this effect, July 30th; officers of all grades were required to be at their posts and attend to their duties; and a board was appointed for examination of the officers of volunteer regiments. Congress, as we have seen, authorized the president to call for 500,000 volunteers; and the loyal States nobly responded to the call. The lesson of the defeat at Bull Run was now beginning to be learned and appreciated. McClellan was lauded to the skies, in terms which formed a painful contrast to subsequent exhibitions of popular feeling. At Lincoln's request, a "memorandum" was submitted to him by McClellan, August 4th 1861, from which an extract or two may be given. "The object of the present war differs from those in which nations are engaged, mainly in this: that the purpose of ordinary war is to conquer a peace, and make a treaty on advantageous terms; in this contest it has become necessary to crush a population sufficiently numerous, intelligent, and warlike to constitute a nation. We have not only to defeat their armed and organized forces in the field, but to display such an overwhelming strength as will convince all our antagonists, especially those of the governing aristocratic class, of the utter impossibility of resistance. Our late reverses make this course imperative. . . . . . For the main army of operations, I urge the following composition: 250 regiments of infantry, say 225,000 men; 100 field batteries, 600 guns, 15,000 men; 28 regiments of cavalry, 25,500; 5 regiments of engineer troops

7,500; total, 273,000. This force must be supplied with necessary engineer and pontoon trains, and with transportation for every thing save tents. . . . . The force I have recommended is large; the expense is great. It is possible that a smaller force might accomplish the object in view, but I understand it to be the purpose of this great nation to reestablish the power of its government, and restore peace to its citizens, in the shortest possible time. . . . . Every mile we advance carries us further from our base of operations, and renders detachments necessary to cover our communications; whilst the enemy will be constantly concentrating as he falls back. I propose, with the force which I have requested, not only to drive the enemy out of Virginia and occupy Richmond, but to occupy Charleston, Savannah, Montgomery, Pensacola, Mobile and New Orleans; in other words, to move into the heart of the enemy's country and crush the rebellion in its very heart." Several months were spent in getting the Army of the Potomac into shape, and fitting it for active operations. The new levies were recruited and pressed forward with great rapidity; arms and equipments were manufactured and supplied as fast as possible; and the general call of the people was for immediate advance. A grand review was held at Washington, October 8th; and at the close of the month, McClellan, supposing that the rebels had at least 150,000 men, well armed and disciplined (though in reality they did not number over 70,000), was unwilling to move, till he had, besides 150,000 men for advance, some 60,000 more for garrison and guard duty, and 200 additional guns. Possibly, he thought, an advance might be made by the end of November.

Banks, at the close of July, evacuated Harper's Ferry and crossed the Potomac again (p. 254). Various skirmishes took place during the summer, but they were of no great moment. Early in October, McClellan ordered a reconnaisance on the right, near the Potomac. General Stone was at Poolesville, not far from Conrad's and Edward's Ferries, between which was Harrison's Island. General McCall moved forward, October 19th, and occupied Dranesville, 17 miles west of Washington. Stone was informed of this, and ordered to keep a look-out upon Leesburg. This led to a movement which resulted, the next day, in the disaster at Ball's Bluff. The means of crossing the river to the Island and thence to the Virginia Shore, were only some flat boats from the canals, and quite unfit in the case in hand. About 2 A. M., October 21st, Colonel Baker was ordered to march to Conrad's Ferry, so as to support Colonel Devens on the other side of the Potomac. This he did, despite the wretched means of getting to Harrison's Island, and thence to the other shore; but it was not till the afternoon, six hours later than it ought to have been, that he reached the narrow and difficult ascent to the bluff. Here he found Devens already attacked by large numbers, and though all told, Baker had only 1,900 men, he concluded to fight, even at so fatal a disadvantage. For two hours or more the battle raged, with terrible loss of our men, and between 4 and 5 o'clock, Baker was killed, cheering his men to the last. A scene of disaster followed. Our men rushed down the side of the bluff, and tried to cross in a flat boat, but were shot by the rebels and drowned by the sinking of the boat. Fully one-half of Baker's entire force was lost; while the rebels escaped with a loss of about 200. This lamentable affair at Ball's Bluff was criticised every where with severity and indignation, and the question was frequently asked, who is responsible for the gross bungling and blundering which exposed our troops to almost certain destruction? Why was a force of less than 2,000 men allowed to be placed in the perilous position that this was? Why were there only such paltry means of communication as these flat boats; and why, if the movement was necessary, was it not adequately supported, when there were 40,000 of our men only a few miles distant? The subject came up before Congress for inquiry, but it was not then, nor has it been since, satisfactorily explained why this fatal result was not prevented by those in command at this time.

General Scott, on the score of age, etc., retired from active service, and McClellan was appointed by Lincoln General-in-chief, November 1st, 1861. In view of the enlarged sphere of labor imposed upon him, he addressed letters of instruction to Gen. Burnside in North Carolina, to Gen. Halleck in Missouri, to Gen. Buell in Kentucky, to Gen. T. W. Sherman in South Carolina, and to Gen. Butler, who was placed in command of the land forces to operate against New Orleans. McClellan's intention was, that the several undertakings against the enemy "should be carried out simultaneously, or nearly so, and in co-operation along the whole line;" but, various circumstances interfered, and his plan was modified and virtually given up. The coming into office of a new secretary of war, Mr. Stanton, had a marked effect upon our military operations from this date; and McClellan soon found that he had a different officer from Mr. Cameron to deal with, and one disposed to yield to the popular call for more active, speedy, forward movements. Through the efforts of General Dix, in November, the 'eastern shore" of Virginia was cleared of a body of some 3,000 insurgents, who laid down their arms and disbanded, and in March, 1862, a representative was chosen and sent to Congress. General Ord, December 20th, had a sharp engagement with the rebels near Dranesville, and in an hour's time routed them entirely. McClellan, professing his earnest desire to move against the enemy in Virginia, still both showed by his action, and gave it as his mature judgment, that the army was not sufficiently numerous, nor in the proper state of readiness to advance at the beginning of December. He preferred to wait till the winter was passed. Stanton, the secretary of war, at an early date urged upon McClellan to take immediate steps to secure the reopening of the Baltimore and Ohio Railroad, and to free the banks of the lower Potomac from the enemy's works, which seriously annoyed passing vessels. The people generally, not fathoming the causes or reasons for matters relating to the Army of the Potomac, which, according to McClellan, required "minds accustomed to reason upon military operations," were eager for some forward movement, or something which looked like it at least; and it was hard to persuade them that time was not wasted, and opportunity let to slip by without profit.

The rebel Congress met at Richmond, November 18th, 1861. Davis's message was a carefully prepared document, and took a rather lofty and self-confident tone. He was proud of what he called "glorious victories" in various quarters, and avowed, in behalf of himself and his fellow traitors, that they loathed the very idea of any possible connection with loyal men in the North and West. "With such a people we may be content to live at peace, but the separation is final, and for the independence we have asserted we will accept no alternative." The proceedings of their Congress were of no great account; but it was noticeable that the sessions were held in secret,—fit commentary on rebel pretensions to superior liberty as representatives of a free people. The present session ended, February 17th, 1862, and what was called their "permanent" Congress began next day.

The Thirty-seventh Congress commenced its second session, December 2d, 1861. In the president's message, sent in the next day, was contained a clear and exact statement of the position of the government and the progress of the war for the Union. The financial condition of affairs was spoken of in encouraging terms: "The revenue from all sources, including loans for the financial year ending on the 30th June, 1861, was $86,835,900, and the expenditures for the same period, including payments on account of the public debts, were $84,578,034. For the first quarter of the financial year ending on the 30th September, 1861, the receipts from all sources, including the balance of July 1st, were $102,532,509, and the expenses $98,239,723. . . . . . It is gratifying to know that the expenditures made necessary by the rebellion are not beyond the resources of the loyal people, and to believe that the same patriotism which has thus far sustained the government will continue to sustain it till peace and union again bless the land." The judiciary, topics of domestic policy, a scheme of colonization, army and navy operations, etc., were noted quite at large, and in closing the president said:—"The struggle of to-day is not altogether for to-day; it is for a vast future also. With a firm reliance on Providence, all the more firm and earnest, let us proceed in the great task which events have devolved upon us." The reports of the several secretaries were full and complete, and not only contained the facts in regard to government operations, but also discussed numerous questions of policy and interest, such as what was to be done with fugitive slaves in the present state of affairs, etc. Chase, secretary of the treasury, gave the probable outlay for the year, from June 1861 to June 1862, as $543,500,000; supposing that the war might continue till July 1st, 1863, he further said that the public debt would reach $900,000,000. Who could have imagined, or thought without shuddering, that, before the rebellion should be finally crushed out, the debt would mount up to *four times* that amount, or over $3,000,000,000? One of the most perplexing questions before Congress was, what course was to be pursued with regard to slavery; was it to be done away with, or was it to be upheld? The ground taken in the beginning, and persisted in for a long time, by the national authorities, was, that the insurrectionary States were to be brought to submission to the Constitution without regard to, or interference with, State institutions, and especially that the abolition or destruction of slavery was in no respect a part of the purpose of the government. The progress of events, however, and the necessity of dealing with the negroes on something of a settled plan, compelled a change or modification of public sentiment; and as we shall see on subsequent pages, slavery was doomed to universal and complete destruction. In the House, slavery was denounced as the cause of the rebellion, and a bill was introduced "to confiscate the property of rebels, to liberate their slaves, and employ or colonize the same," which was referred to the committee on military affairs. In fact, the majority were in favor of so conducting the war as to destroy slavery, root and branch. In the Senate, a motion was made to appoint commissioners to settle difficulties with the rebel States; but it was promptly laid on the table; the day had passed for any such belittling mode of settlement. A bill in regard to confiscation, like the one just noted, was introduced and referred to the judiciary committee. A resolution was offered, December 16th, 1861, to inquire into arrests made by the government, the *habeas corpus* being suspended; this was also referred to the judiciary committee.

A paragraph or two may fittingly here be bestowed upon a brief review of the state and condition of affairs at the close of the year 1861. The people of the loyal States, for the most part, entertained confident expectations in regard to the active, energetic and successful prosecution of the war for the Union. In general, excepting the few serious reverses at Bull Run, Ball's Bluff, etc., our military success was decidedly encouraging; and the brilliant exploits of the navy cheered and animated all hearts. Western Virginia was almost wholly in our hands. The prospects in the West were growing brighter. The people at large were ready and willing to any extent to furnish means, as well as men, for putting down effectually this wicked rebellion; and there was such self-reliant strength in the Union, that no resort was had to foreign aid in taking our national loans, or in finding recruits for the army and navy. McClellan was engaged in making preparations on a scale of magnitude which showed that he meant to sweep everything out of his path, when he deemed it best to set the Army of the Potomac in motion. As for McClellan, it was felt that his delaying was not only very vexatious, but also injurious to the successful carrying forward the war. *Something*, it was said on all hands, ought to be done, and done at once. He had been deluded into the belief that the rebels had from 120,000 to 150,000 in East Virginia, whereas, in fact there was not more than half that number there at any time. The autumn passed away with its fine weather; the winter settled down, and "all quiet on the Potomac" was the regular response to inquiry as to our grand army and its doings.

One question had proved perplexing and annoying in the early part of the rebellion, we mean that relating to prisoners and what to do with them. Naturally, the government was reluctant to admit, even in appearance, any belligerent right as due to the rebels by exchanging prisoners with them; yet, under the circumstances, there was no help for it, and the government can hardly be said to have acted wisely in the course which was pursued. It would not do to hang or shoot those taken on land or sea, because there were so many of our men in the hands of the rebels after the battle of Bull Run, that they could, as no doubt they would, have retaliated to the fullest extent. The government, on its part, seemed to ignore the matter, leaving exchange to be agreed upon and conducted by the commanders and officers as they deemed best. Quite a number were discharged informally on both sides, on parole. But matters did not work well in that way, where there was no agreement or concert of action: in fact, the whole subject was complicated and perplexing, and all through the rebellion there was continual annoyance and trouble with regard to prisoners. Our foreign policy was ably conducted by the secretary of state, who so judiciously settled the Trent affair (p. 260), that England had no cause of complaint; and he made it plain to foreign powers, that the rebellion was a purely domestic matter, and that no outside interference would be permitted for a moment.

The rebels, on their part, were very willing to have it thought that they were holding Washington in a sort of siege, and to give the impression of their great and powerful numbers, and of the immense risk to be run in attacking them. They had not yet enforced a general conscription, as was soon after found necessary in the rebel States; and though they helped along volunteering in a rather forcible way oftentimes, still they were in reality weaker than was supposed, and were growing weaker, while our armies were improving and becoming stronger. They were but poorly supplied with various needful articles, and the blockade, much as it was abused by fault-finders on the score of inefficiency, cut them off from obtaining aught but casual and unreliable help from abroad. They were much puffed up on account of their success at Bull Run; foreign interference, so much boasted of as certain, did not avail them at all; "King Cotton" was little better than a sham, and did not, as it was confidently said it would, "bring Europe to its knees;" and the political measures of the South amounted to almost nothing. Hence, the position of the government and people was such as to lead to cheering hope and expectation* that the war would speedily be brought to a close, especially as McClellan said, more than once, that when he *did* strike, he meant to strike at "the heart," and crush the rebellion entirely thereby. How it happened that these bright forecastings of the future were doomed to disappointment, and the rebellion was able to drag out a lengthened existence, will become evident as we proceed in our narrative.

The year 1862 opened with various encouraging evidences of activity and energy, in the West especially. The forces under McClellan were maintaining their position undisturbed, and continued to do so for some

* The financial condition of the government, it must be noted, however, was not satisfactory, More or less distrust prevailed as to public credit; and on the last day of the year 1861, the banks suspended specie payments.

time after the year began; but, in Kentucky, our army was more actively employed. General Buell, an able and energetic officer, was in command in this department, having succeeded T. W. Sherman, in November, 1861. The rebels were commanded by A. S. Johnston, formerly an officer in the United States army. He, having got together bodies of troops from various quarters, strengthened Bowling Green—a point of great importance in Kentucky—while Zollicoffer (p. 248), having secured the pass at Cumberland Gap, was taking up an important position in the midst of the rich mineral and agricultural district on the upper waters of the Cumberland. Johnston, in the latter part of December, 1861, issued a proclamation to the people of South-eastern Kentucky, in which, with considerable flourish of rhetoric, he declared that he was come to repel "those armed northern hordes who were attempting the subjugation of a sister Southern State." He asserted, also, though he himself knew that it was a slander, that the avowed object of the North was to set the slaves at liberty, and to put arms in their hands to be used against their masters. Marshall, in the eastern part of Kentucky was pursued by Colonel Garfield, who came up with and routed the enemy, January 10th, 1862, at Prestonburg. By this decisive battle, Kentucky was freed from Marshall and his force; and Generals Thomas and Schoepf were left at liberty to look after Zollicoffer. On the borders of Wayne and Pulaski County, Zollicoffer held an advantageous position on both sides of the Cumberland, which he fortified with great skill. The spot which he had selected was at Mill Springs, a bend of the Cumberland, where, at its junction with the White Oak Creek, was afforded water protection on three sides. In this area, on a range of hills several hundred feet above the river, and supporting one another, Zollicoffer had built his works, and he had encamped there some 12,000 men, with about 800 cavalry and fifteen pieces of artillery. Zollicoffer was joined, early in January, 1862, by G. B. Crittenden, who took command. In front of the rebel position was Schoepf, with about 8000 men, while General Thomas was some distance to the north with his division. This latter, in connection with Schoepf, attacked the rebels on the 19th of January, and after a severe contest of four or five hours, drove them back to their entrenchments. During the night, they made off, burning the ferryboats, and leaving behind a large amount of stores, twelve pieces of artillery, 1000 horses and mules, etc. The news of this battle was received with much satisfaction at the North, as showing what our troops were able to accomplish. This decisive victory broke up the enemy's line in Kentucky, opened the path into East Tennessee, and proved the commencement of a series of successful military operations in the progress of the war in the West. Halleck, meanwhile, was busily engaged in making preparations for operating against the left of the enemy's line on the Mississippi and the northern boundary of Tennessee. The navy department, during the autumn and winter, had pushed forward, at St. Louis and Cincinnati, the getting ready the gun boats and mortar fleet; these had gathered at Cairo for an onward movement down the Mississippi. The iron-covered gun boats were specially constructed for the service. They were broad in proportion to their length, so as to sit firmly on the water and support with steadiness the heavy batteries for which they were intended. The largest were of the proportion of about 175 feet to fifty, drawing five feet when loaded. Seven out of the twelve gun boats were iron-clad, and carried armament of the heaviest character. The mortar boats (some thirty or more in number) were about sixty feet long and twenty-five wide, and were surrounded on all sides by iron plate bulwarks six or seven feet high. The huge mortar which they carried, bored to admit a 13-inch shell, with seventeen inches of thickness from the edge of the bore to the outer rim, weighed over 17,000 pounds; while the bed or carriage on which it was placed weighed 4,500 pounds. From this formidable engine shells might be thrown a distance of two and a half to three and a half miles. Commodore Foote was placed in command of this powerful flotilla.

On the 27th of January, 1862, the President issued his "General war order, No. 1," by which the 22d of February was fixed as "the day for a general movement of the land and naval forces of the United States against the insurgent forces." Early in February, Foote and Grant resolved to attack Fort Henry, on the Tennessee River, and set out with four iron-clads and numerous transports with land forces, from Paducah, Kentucky. A body of troops under McClernand was landed about four miles below the fort, so as to take the fort in the rear, while the gunboats attacked from the water. The fight began February 6th, and as it happened, the roads being very bad, the land forces took no part in it; it was accomplished by the naval force alone. After about an hour's bombardment the rebels gave up, and the garrison, some 4000 or 5000 ran away. Directly after the surrender, Lieutenant Phelps proceeded with three gun boats about 200 miles up the Tennessee, and did good service in forcing the rebels to burn six steamers at Florence, Alabama, in capturing several vessels, seizing on lumber, rousing loyal feeling, etc. The fall of Fort Henry opened the way for an immediate advance upon Fort Donelson, on the Cumberland River. This imposing fortification was situated near the boundary of Tennessee, on the west bank of the river, about 100 miles from its mouth. It was connected by a direct road with Fort Henry, and served as an out-post or river defence of Nashville, some eighty miles above. By the aid of railroad communications, reinforcements had been hurried to Donelson, and warned by the fate of Fort Henry, the rebels determined to retain, if possible, so important a barrier against the approach of our army into Tennessee. Naturally, Donelson was a strong position, being on a sloping elevation over a 100 feet high, with other hills and ravines densely wooded all around. Two water batteries were added, supplied with heavy ordnance; on the summit were trenches, or rifle pits, protected by abattis of felled trees and interlaced brushwood; and in every suitable spot howitzers and field pieces were stationed. Its garrison amounted to nearly 20,000 men, so important was it deemed by the rebels to hold the place. Floyd, who arrived with reinforcements on the 13th of February, was chief in command, and was aided by Pillow, Buckner, etc. Grant, with about 25,000 men, set out early on the 12th of February for the land attack, while Foote, with gun boats, was to assault the water batteries. The latter was unexpectedly delayed; Grant, meanwhile, thoroughly invested the fort; and when Foote arrived, and General Wallace with 8000 more troops, February 14th, he was prepared for immediate action. The rebels, however, seeing the condition they were in, resolved early the next morning to try and fight their way out; but they were unsuccessful in this, and were driven back behind their inner works. Floyd, in the night, passed over the command to Buckner, and he and Pillow, with about 5000 men, embarked in steamboats and made their escape. The next morning early, Buckner sent a flag of truce, asking for terms, etc. Grant was short and sharp in his reply: "No terms, except unconditional and immediate surrender, can be accepted," he said. Buckner, protesting against Grant's "ungenerous and unchivalrous terms," gave up the contest, and on Sunday morning, February 16th, 1862, the Union flag waived over this stronghold of the rebellion. Our loss was severe, being over 2000 in all; the rebel loss was about 1200, beside some 14,000 prisoners. There fell into our hands also about fifty cannon, 3000 horses, 20,000 stand of arms, etc. This victory was gratifying to loyal men everywhere; but it caused much chagrin to Davis and his co-workers, as was but natural.

The fall of Fort Donelson hastened the

crisis in rebel affairs in the West. The rebel General A. S. Johnston had before this seen that Bowling Green, Kentucky, was untenable, and orders were given to evacuate it. This was done on the 14th of February, 1862, when General Mitchel took immediate possession. By a forced march of eighty miles, the rebel force reached Nashville on the 16th, and under Johnston's command passed on to Murfreesboro, thirty-two miles distant, on the Nashville and Chattanooga Railroad. Foote with his gun-boats ascended the Cumberland, destroying the extensive iron works, six miles above Dover, and reaching Clarksville on the 19th of February. The enemy had fled, and great alarm was manifested respecting the purpose of our advancing force. Of course, Nashville followed the fate of Donelson. Without the latter, it was defenceless; and hence, when the news came, on Sunday forenoon, that the fort was lost, the city was thrown into consternation. Floyd destroyed the bridges over the Cumberland, and made all speed to get away. "An earthquake," says a rebel chronicler, "could not have shocked the city more. The congregations at churches were broken up in confusion and dismay; women and children rushed into the streets, wailing with terror; trunks were thrown from three-story windows in the haste of the fugitives; and thousands hastened to leave their beautiful city in the midst of the most distressing scenes of terror and confusion, and of plunder by the mob." On the 24th of February, the Union forces reached Nashville, which was formally surrendered by the mayor into General Buell's hands. Andrew Johnson was appointed military governor of Tennessee, and early in March, 1862, he entered on his duties. He soon taught the newspapers, mayor and council, and people in general, that he both had, and knew how to use a strong hand in putting down disunion practices in Tennessee.* The taking of Nashville led to the abandonment of Columbus, by the rebels, who retreated to Island No. 10, about forty-five miles below, on the Mississippi. The successful operations of our army produced much excitement in the South, and the leaders in the rebellion began to understand better what a gigantic struggle it was in which they had engaged. Every man, young and old, was called for. Boards of police in every county of Mississippi were appointed preparatory to drafting; and the Governor of Arkansas, by proclamation, drafted into immediate service every man in the State subject to military duty, requiring him to respond within twenty days. In this way, and under such pressure, was begun that system of measures which resulted in the passing of a conscription act by the rebel Congress, April 16th, and another in September, 1862, by which, entirely irrespective of State laws and rights, every man that could be laid hold of, and even boys of eighteen, were forced into the army.

Early in February, 1862, our troops in Missouri, under command of General S. R. Curtis, pushed rapidly from Rolla towards Springfield, where the rebel leader Price had taken up his headquarters, with about 4,000 men, and had raised supplies to some extent. A sharp skirmish took place near Springfield; and Price, on the 12th of February, during the night, decamped, the United States troops entering the town early next morning. Immediately the pursuit after Price was begun, and continued a hundred miles or more from Springfield into Arkansas. On the 18th, the State line was crossed; on the 19th, Price, having had some reinforcements, attempted to make a stand at Sugar Creek; but was speedily defeated. On the 23d of February, Curtis entered and took possession of Fayetteville, capturing a number of prisoners, stores and baggage. The enemy

* General Halleck issued an order, February 22d, in which he said, among other things, "It does not belong to the military to decide upon the relation of master and slave. Such questions must be settled by civil courts. No fugitive slave will, therefore, be admitted within our lines or camps, except when specially ordered by the general commanding."

burnt part of the town before leaving on their flight over the Boston Mountains, and, as General Halleck stated in a dispatch, they were dastards enough to poison the food left behind, thus destroying between forty and fifty officers and men. The rebels had been so persistent in telling lies as to the object had in view by our troops, that General Curtis issued an address to the people of the South-west, on the 1st of March: "The only legitimate object of the war is peace, and I adhere to this legitimate object. Peaceable citizens shall be protected as far as possible. . . . . We come to vindicate the Constitution, to preserve and perpetuate civil and religious liberty, under a flag that was embalmed in the blood of our revolutionary fathers. Under that flag we have lived in peace and prosperity until the flag of rebellion involved us in the horrors of civil war." Price having been reinforced largely, was prepared to turn upon his pursuers; and so, on the 5th of March, he sent Van Dorn to attack Curtis, at or near Sugar Creek. It was a long and severe fight, beginning in the afternoon of the 6th, continuing all day on the 7th, and resumed again at sunrise on the 8th. The result was, that the rebels, though they fought desperately, were routed and driven off completely. Our loss was estimated at 1,351; the rebel loss was probably double that number. In this battle of Pea Ridge, or Elkhorn, the rebels brought forward as helpers some 2,500 Indians, under Pike, but they were not of much service to their employers; they principally succeeded in tomahawking and scalping a number of our men, to the lasting disgrace of the rebel leaders.

During the latter part of 1861, another naval and military expedition on a large scale was fitted out, to operate on the shores of North Carolina, within the waters of Pamlico and Albermarle sounds. The troops numbered about 16,000 under General Burnside; the squadron under Commodore Goldsborough consisted of eighteen light draft, steam gun-boats, with an armament of fifty

rifled cannon. The expedition set sail from Annapolis on the 9th of January, 1862. Owing to dense fogs in the Chesapeake Bay, incident to the season, it did not reach Fortress Monroe till midnight of the 10th. The next day without detention, the order was given to sail, and Sunday, the 11th, saw the fleet at sea. As had been generally supposed, while the vessels were collecting, that they would be employed inside of the capes of Virginia, but little anxiety had been felt respecting their sea-going qualities. But when exposed to the dangers of Hatteras, considerable loss and damage occurred. After much time spent in getting through the narrow and perplexing channel, the flotilla was fairly embarked on Pamlico sound, and ready for action. The rebels, meanwhile, gathered troops at Roanoke Island, a position which commanded the channel, separating the waters of Pamlico and Albermarle Sounds. On the 5th of February, the expedition set sail from Hatteras to dislodge the rebels at Roanoke. On the 7th, the troops were landed, preparatory to an attack, and when the Zouaves made a bayonet charge, the rebels abandoned their guns and ran away. This assured the entire defeat of the enemy, and though they made a stubborn resistance, they surrendered unconditionally, and Roanoke Island became ours, with its heavy guns and batteries, and eight steamers, each mounting two guns. This victory was immediately followed up by an expedition, under command of Captain Rowan, sent in pursuit of the fleet of the enemy, which had fled up the Albemarle Sound, a distance of some thirty or forty miles, into Pasquotank River, toward Elizabeth City. Captain Rowan sailed from Roanoke on the afternoon of Sunday, and arrived at the mouth of the river at night.

The following morning, the 10th of February, 1862, the fleet ascended the river, and at eight o'clock came upon the enemy's gun-boats, consisting of seven steamers and a schooner armed with two heavy thirty-two pounders, drawn up in front of the city. A brief but spirited contest ensued; the enemy set their boats on fire, and the crews escaped as best they could; the fort on Cobb's Point, mounting four guns, was abandoned; and in less than an hour the rebels were entirely defeated, and the flag-ship Delaware was moored to the wharf at Elizabeth City. The next day possession was taken of the city by our troops. Following upon this, Edenton, at the west end of Albemarle Sound, was visited and rebel vessels destroyed; as was also Winton, up the Chowan River. Goldsborough and Burnside issued a joint proclamation, addressed to "the People of North Carolina," in which they disclaimed every purpose except one, viz: restoring and sustaining the authority of the United States. Burnside next turned his attention to another part of the State. Washington, on Pamlico River, and Newbern on the Neuse, were the chief depots in this quarter for lumber, tar, turpentine and naval stores of the country. Newbern, in its size and position, was one of the chief cities in the State, and its population exceeded that of the capital, Raleigh, by several hundreds, and was second only to the seaport Wilmington. It was, moreover, by the Atlantic and North Carolina Railroad, immediately connected with Beaufort, on the ocean forty miles below, and with Goldsboro', sixty miles in the interior, the chief station on the Wilmington & Weldon Railroad. Early in March, 1862, the troops, about 8000 in number, embarked, the naval force consisting of six gun-boats, with necessary transports. On the 12th, they reached Slocum's Creek, about eighteen miles from Newbern. The next morning the troops were landed, and marched through the mud and mire to within about a mile from the rebel works. On the morning of the 14th of March the attack was made. For four hours the battle raged, but the persistence and bravery of our troops prevailed, and Newbern was taken. Other operations on the Southern coast may here be noted. In January, 1862, an exploration of an interior passage was made to the Savannah River. On the 26th of January Captain Rodgers made a reconnaissance in force up the Wright River. The rebel commodore, Tatnall, appeared with gun boats and scows; but was easily driven back. Rodgers not deeming it prudent to pass into the Savannah, near Fort Pulaski, our boats returned by the way which they went. A battery at Venus Point, on Jones Island, was erected, quietly but securely, notwithstanding the severity and tediousness of the work; another battery was planted in a similar manner on Bird Island, opposite Venus Point; so that, to the astonishment of the rebels, Fort Pulaski was cut off from communication with the City of Savannah early in February, 1862, and the stronghold in which they so confidently trusted was exposed to siege and assault by the Union forces. On the 27th of January, Captain Davis, with eight vessels, and transports carrying some 2,400 troops, under General Wright, made a reconnaissance of Little Tybee River and the adjacent waters, for the purpose of carrying out the object proposed above, viz: the isolation of Fort Pulaski. Tatnall, with five vessels, made an attack upon the expedition, when, after half an hour's fight, two of the enemy's boats were driven back, and the others ran under the guns of the fort. At the end of February, an expedition sailed from Port Royal, under Dupont and Wright, with the intention of re-occupying the principal points on the east coast of Florida. Fort Clinch, St. Mary's, and Fernandina were captured March 2d and 3d; Fort Clinch on Amelia Island was taken possession of and garrisoned. Fernandina, which was almost deserted, was occupied by the Union forces; so also was St. Mary's; at both places the preparations for defence were extensive, but the rebel troops were not there. Brunswick, in Georgia, was found in a similar condition, March 7th; and at Jacksonville and St. Augustine, Florida, no opposition was offered to the advance of our troops.

The birthday of WASHINGTON, February 22d, was observed this year throughout the loyal States with unusual honor and respect, and the hearts of the people were cheered by the memory of his life and services, the pure patriot and Christian, the bright example to us and our children in all time to come. Davis chose this day also for commencing his career as President of the so-called "Confederacy," the "provisional" arrangement having been superseded by what was called the "permanent" government in the rebel States. On this occasion Davis made an address which assumed a tone of confidence, mingled with no little bitterness and disappointment at the energy and resolution of the loyal people in the North and West. He spoke of "the malignity and barbarity of the Northern States in the prosecution of the existing war," and "the *insane* attempt to subjugate" the rebel States. He also estimated his military strength at about 500,000 men, and lauded highly the condition of his finances, asserting that the expenditure of the past year was only $170,000,000, and that the United States had wasted three times as much in vainly striving to conquer the Confederacy. With such sentiments as these, making such representations as the above, and well understanding that the struggle was no light one in which he was engaged, Davis tried to sustain his own hopes and to infuse additional life and activity into the "Confederacy." It was now a matter of life or death. It was evident that the loyal States were resolutely determined to crush the rebellion at any cost; and that Davis and those who worked with him were equally determined not to submit, so long as they were able to make any resistance whatsoever. Terrible alternative! There was no help for it; the battle had to be fought out, even to the bitter end; and the awful responsibility for shedding of blood, for carnage, cruelty, suffering, distress, and the thousand evils attendant upon war, must rest upon the men who, without any just or reasonable cause, began the rebellion of 1861, and persevered in it for four weary, desolating years.

McClellan, as we have seen (p. 268) was making large preparations for the coming campaign, and great hopes and expectations were based upon his striking, when he did strike, with tremendous and decisive effect. But McClellan very much over estimated the rebel strength, and delayed and kept on delaying to advance, lest he should not be able to cope with the enemy. The President did not pretend to know much, if anything, about military science, and the secretary of war, though bred to the law and full of zeal and spirit, was not probably better able to judge than Mr. Lincoln of the reasons which weighed so strongly with the general-in-chief against what he considered to be premature, unprepared action. The roads in Virginia, according to McClellan, were never before in so bad a condition, and he wished to attack Richmond by way of the Lower Chesapeake; but Lincoln did not approve of this, and ordered the advance towards Manassas Junction. Unhappily, for anything like prompt and energetic action, the discussion as to which was the best plan served only to waste time, and vex and anger the people. On the 8th of March, 1862, the President issued his "General War Order, No. 2;" by which it was directed that the Army of the Potomac be organized into four army corps. The first, consisting of four divisions, was assigned to General McDowell; the second, consisting of three divisions, to General Sumner; the third and the fourth, consisting each of three divisions, to Generals Heintzelman and Keyes. General Wadsworth was placed in command of the troops for the defence of Washington; and a fifth army corps, consisting of two divisions, was assigned to General Banks. On the same day, a third war order was issued, requiring that no operations be entered upon without leaving Washington entirely secure, and without clearing the navigation of the Potomac from the enemy's batteries and other obstructions. The movement upon the Chesapeake, as McClellan wished, was also ordered to move, as early as the 18th of March, or earlier, if possible. Meanwhile, several events had occurred in Virginia, which helped considerably to modify the plan of the campaign. The rebel General Jackson, early in January, 1862, moved from Winchester to the north-west, and advanced towards Hancock, about forty miles distant. He drove out some of our troops from Bath, who retreated to Hancock, where General Lander, in command, not only refused to surrender, but routed the rebels at Blue's Gap. Lander also gained a success over the enemy at Bloomery Gap, and on the 11th of February, sent word to McClellan that the district was cleared. Colonel Geary, February 24th, crossed the Potomac and took possession of Harper's Ferry. Other places were secured on the route to Winchester, which was evacuated by Jackson, March 11th, and immediately occupied by our troops. The fortifications which had been supposed to be formidable, were found to be of no value. General Banks established his headquarters here. The rebels, well aware of the large forces under way against them, resolved to decline a battle, which had been for months eagerly expected by the people of the loyal States. Retreat, at the present, was their policy, and retreat they accomplished in the coolest and most scientific manner. The heavy artillery at Manassas was leisurely removed, the railroad leading south answering the purpose of transporting men and munitions to any extent; and so skillfully was all this performed, despite McClellan's "secret service force," to give information of the rebel doings, that, when our army reached Manassas, there was not a gun left to be captured, nor hardly a straggler to be taken prisoner. On Sunday evening, March 9th, the last of the rebel force abandoned Centreville, retreating in perfect order, leaving the formidable line of fortifications on the ridge entirely empty, save a few wooden painted logs, which had been placed in the embrasures. The famous stone bridge over Bull Run, and another over Cob Run, were destroyed in the retreat. It was rather a mortifying confession, but it had to be made, that the rebels had got the better of us, and that their retreat on this occasion was equivalent to a victory. Most of persons felt sure that the number of the rebels had been greatly overestimated, and that we had given them an advantage, especially in the way of preparing for defence against our advance, which was likely to protract the contest far longer than any one as yet had contemplated.

By a war order of March 11th, 1862, McClellan was relieved of the command-in-chief, and required to remain in charge of the Army of the Potomac. Halleck, at the same time was placed in command of the Department of the Mississippi, and Fremont in command of the Mountain Department, *i. e.* the region west of the Department of the Potomac. Each and all were required to report directly and frequently to the secretary of war. At a council of the generals commanding army corps, held at headquarters, March 13th, it was deemed most expedient, Washington being properly secured against attack, and Manassas being occupied in force, to proceed to the advance upon Richmond by way of Fortress Monroe. The president and war department approved this plan of operations, and urged immediate, energetic action. At this point, however, we may properly call the reader's attention to the celebrated encounter between the Merrimac and the Monitor, not only because of its general effect upon the progress of the great contest, but also because of its marked importance in the history of naval warfare in modern times. Certainly, nothing which has ever occurred in connection with ships of war, and with attempts to render them invulnerable, is more remarkable and more significant in its results than this memorable encounter. When the rebels seized upon the Navy Yard at Norfolk, the U. S. steamer Merrimac was one of the vessels which was scuttled and abandoned by Capt. Macaulay. Subsequently, she was raised and placed in the dry dock, and special care was bestowed upon fitting her out in such wise as to be in vincible to all attack, and consequently able to act as a universal destroyer. Her hull was cut down, and a bomb-proof covering of wrought iron put over her main deck. Her bow and stern were sharpened and clad in steel, with a projecting angle of iron to pierce any adversary in her path. Her engines were stated to be 510 horse-power, and all her machinery was below the water line. Armed with ten guns, 80-pounders, rifled; with a furnace for heating shot; manned by ten lieutenants and 350 picked men; and presenting the appearance of a submerged house, with the roof only above water, the Merrimac, or as the rebels re-named her, the Virginia, was a formidable antagonist indeed for the doomed vessels then blockading the entrance to Norfolk, and the mouth of the James River. Buchanan, the commander, after forty-five years connection with the navy, had deserted the flag of his country, and was now ready to do all in his power for the new master whom he was serving. On Saturday, March 8th, the Merrimac entered upon her work. With nothing visible but her smoke stack and the Confederate flag flying from a staff, she steamed directly for the frigate Congress and the sloop-of-war Cumberland, which were stationed off James River to guard the blockade and protect the camp on the shore at Newport News. Both of these were sailing vessels, and had consequently no opportunity of manœuvring in presence of so formidable an adversary as this massive steam ram. The other vessels in the Roads, at Fortress Monroe, were signaled to the aid of the Congress and Cumberland. They were the flag-ship Roanoke, the frigates Minnesota and St. Lawrence, and some half dozen gun boats, which were employed in towing the frigates into position. The Congress and Cumberland opened fire, but their broadsides bounded harmlessly from the mailed sides of the Merrimac. Onward she came and plunged headlong into the side of the helpless frigate. The iron horn or ram, striking the Cumberland forward the main chains, made a deep gash, knocking a hole in her side near the water line as large as the head of a hogshead, and driving her back upon her anchors with great force, while the water ran into her hold. Slowly drawing back, the Merrimac poured a broadside into the sinking ship. Still the Cumberland maintained the unequal contest. Officers and men without a single voice of dissent, resolved never to surrender to the rebels; and they never left their posts till the Cumberland sank, her flag still flying at the topmast, and many were drowned. This occupied less than an hour. Next, the Congress was to suffer the same fate; but the commander ran the ship on shore. The ram then took a position astern and raked the Congress fore and aft with shells, while the latter was utterly unable to defend herself. Between 4 and 5 P. M. the Congress surrendered, was set on fire by another broadside and burned. A large proportion of the officers and men was lost. The ram proposed now to attack the Minnesota, but depth of water prevented getting near enough; so, as there was no chance of this noble ship and the St. Lawrence getting away that night, the Merrimac returned to her anchorage, waiting for the next day's light to accomplish the work of destruction.

It was a gloomy Saturday night, in view of what had been done and what was to be expected the next day; but at this point, help came by the arrival of the Monitor about ten o' clock in the evening. This remarkable vessel, untried, unknown, regarded with doubt by many, was in every way a novelty; in appearance she was not unlike what the Norfolk rebels termed her, "a Yankee cheese-box set on a raft;" and with hardly anything visible but a flat iron deck on the surface of the water, surmounted by a low round tower, pilot box, and smoke-pipe, few supposed the Monitor capable of performing what the next day fully proved her ability to do. With a hull impossible to be injured, and with a tower only ten feet high and twenty in diameter, revolving readily, and mounting two 11-inch guns, the Monitor was, in fact, a bomb-proof fort, of immense power and effectiveness. She was now emphatically on her trial trip. She had just been completed, had left New York under orders, March 6th, and had arrived, as just stated. The passage was exceedingly rough and stormy, but the Monitor proved to be a capital sea boat, and all on board of her were eager to test her capabilities in a deadly grapple with the Merrimac. Captain Worden was directed to lay the Monitor along-side the Minnesota, which he accordingly did, reaching that position at 2 A. M., Sunday, March 9th, 1862. At daylight the Merrimac started afresh, exulting in the work before her. The Monitor took position at once in front of the Minnesota, and discharged one of her 11-inch Dahlgrens upon the Merrimac. It was an astounding challenge, like a pigmy assaulting a giant; but a hundred and sixty-eight pound shot was not to be despised, come from where it might, and so the Merrimac prepared to make short work of her diminutive assailant. It was soon found, however, that the Monitor was not easily to be beaten. Broadside after broadside produced no effect upon her; it was of no avail to attempt, as the Merrimac did, to run her down, and crush her in that way; the active Monitor, with her revolving battery ever pointing full upon the ram, poured forth shot incessantly upon the sides, at the bow and the stern, seeking some vulnerable spot. The contest raged for hours, when the Monitor withdrew for a space to hoist more shot into her turret. This being done, the fight was renewed; but the Merrimac was glad ere long to retire towards Sewall's Point. It needed no words to express the fact that she was badly beaten, and compelled to stop in her career. The Monitor did not pursue the fleeing vessel; she was under orders to act on the defensive; and as the lesson just given to the rebels was a severe one, it was thought that it would probably answer for the present.*

General Shields, with his division at Winchester, having ascertained, March 19th, that Jackson was strongly posted near Mount Jackson, resolved to try and draw him out by a feigned retreat, and thus fight him to greater advantage. The troops were sent off towards Centreville, leaving Ashby's cavalry, who were on the lookout, to suppose that Winchester was being evacuated. A fight took place on the 22d and 23d, in which after a sharp struggle, the rebels were beaten with great loss. Too fatigued to pursue the enemy that night, Shields prepared for the next day's work, whether a renewal of the fight with Jackson reinforced, or a driving him into flight. On the 24th of March, the rebels retreated, and during the following week, were pursued to Woodstock, and thence to Edenburg, about twenty miles beyond Strasburg. Skirmishing was kept up by Ashby's cavalry, which protected Jackson's retreat. This victory was timely and acceptable, coming at the time it did. Troops were embarked for the Peninsula, during the latter part of March, but there was much vexatious delay in getting them to their destination. Heintzelman's corps led the way and landed, March 23d; other detachments followed. McClellan, expecting to have the support of the four army corps, directed that the first corps (McDowell's), be embarked last, intending to use it in mass on either bank of the York River, according as seemed best. He left Washington, April 1st, and arrived at Fortress Monroe the next day. Blenker's division of 10,000 men had been withdrawn, despite his protest, March 31st, to reinforce Fremont; as an offset to this, some 10,000 men, under Wool, at Fortress Monroe, were placed at McClellan's disposal, at first, but on April 3d, he was forbidden to use them without Wool's sanction. McClellan's plan

* In order to complete the history of the Merrimac's career, we may mention here, that, on the 11th of April, she appeared again in Hampton Roads, and captured a few small vessels; and, on the 11th of May, she was blown up by her officers in the Elizabeth River, to prevent her falling into the hands of the Union forces. The Monitor, to the deep regret of all loyal men, was lost in a violent gale off the coast of North Carolina, Dec. 31st, 1862.

was, as he says, by rapid movements to drive before him or capture the enemy on the Peninsula, open the James River, and press on to Richmond, before the rebels should be materially reinforced from other quarters. But McClellan's plans were not carried out as he intended, because, as he asserts, the means necessary were taken away from him. The army was put in immediate movement against the enemy's works, at various points between Fortress Monroe and Yorktown. Heavy rains had made the roads bad, and although the rebels abandoned some points, yet, when General Keyes reached Lee's Mills, he found the post too strong to be carried, as he had been directed, by assault. Heintzelman arrived in front of Yorktown on the afternoon of April 5th; both columns having been exposed to a warm artillery fire during the advance. At this point, McDowell's corps was detached from McClellan's command, greatly to his disappointment, and in fact, as he states it, rendering him powerless to turn Yorktown by West Point. It left him no choice but to attack directly in front, with such force as he had left; in short, he termed it "*a fatal error.*" Careful reconnaisances were resorted to, and advances were made through the forests, swamps, flooded roads, etc., etc. The rebel General Magruder had some 10,000 men at Yorktown, and could be reinforced at any time directly from Richmond, and was reinforced largely so soon as our army appeared. It was, therefore, prudent, if not necessary, on McClellan's part, to take the course which he did; although there were many who held, that a bold dash at the outset would have given him possession of Yorktown.

Public impatience demanded greater activity, and more evident results. The president made this plain to McClellan, in a letter of remonstrance, April 9th, in which he said, "It is indispensible to *you* that you strike a blow. . . . . The country will not fail to note—is noting now—that the present hesitation to move upon an entrenched position is but the story of Manassas repeated. *You must act.*" Siege operations were pushed forward vigorously; batteries were erected to silence the enemy's guns; reconnaisances were kept up, etc. General W. F. Smith advanced against a rebel fort, which was silenced, but he was not able to carry the entrenchments. On the 18th of April, General Augur marched upon Fredericksburg, and drove the enemy, about 3,000 in number; the town was formally surrendered. Some of Banks's force advanced and took possession of New Market, near Manassas. The rebels now saw that Yorktown must be evacuated. With their usual skill in concealing their designs, keeping up a vigorous and noisy fire, during the early days of May, they made their preparations, and on the 3d and 4th of the month abandoned all their works. The next day McClellan purposed to assault Yorktown, which now became needless. The advantage was on the rebels' side, they having stopped our progress a whole month, and having had the opportunity, meanwhile, of strengthening their position in and about Richmond. Certainly, McClellan had not acted to any great purpose or result as yet.

The rebel leaders were fully aware of the importance of the Mississippi to their plans, and, as rapidly as possible, they had carefully and skillfully fortified all the principal strategic points from the Ohio to the Gulf, a distance of nearly 1,000 miles. Beginning with Columbus in Kentucky, at Island No. 10, dividing the stream at the northern border of Tennessee, at Memphis and its vicinity, at Vicksburg, and elsewhere, to New Orleans, above and below that city, the rebels had been at work, excavating the hill-sides for batteries, throwing up trenches, mounting cannon on the heights, preparing mines on the banks and torpedoes for the channel; and using every possible means to obstruct the advance of our armies. It became, therefore, a matter of necessity to open the Mississippi as speedily as possible, and cripple the plans of the rebels most effectually. The energy and activity of our military and naval forces under Buell, Grant, Foote, etc., had driven the rebels to abandon not only Nashville and Bowling Green, but also Columbus, "the northern key to the Miss'ssippi delta," as it was called. Still, our success, great as it had been, was only a step in the onward progress down the Mississippi. Island No. 10 was the next formidable obstacle in the way of further advance: this Island, about 40 miles below Cairo, is situated at the bottom of a great bend of the Mississippi, where the stream, in a sharp curve, sweeps around a tongue of land projecting from the Missouri shore, and, pursuing thence a north-westerly course to New Madrid, on the western bank, descends past a similar narrow promontory of Tennessee soil, on its great southerly track. The distance across the upper end of the first promontory, four miles above the island, to New Madrid, is six miles, and by the river is fifteen. The passage across the second promontory is five miles, while by water it is twenty-seven. On the Tennessee shore was a great swamp, cutting off communication with the interior. General Pope, after a slow and toilsome advance, reached New Madrid, March 3d, 1862. He found the place occupied by the rebels and strongly fortified, with earthworks, lines of entrenchments, gunboats, etc., so that the approach was a matter of difficulty. Pope sent and occupied Point Pleasant, 12 miles below, and when, March 12th, he got his heavy siege guns in position, he speedily forced the rebels to run away, leaving behind them artillery, stores, etc. On the 13th, Foote left Cairo with a fleet, including seven iron-clads and ten mortar boats, and having been joined at Columbus by Col. Buford with his regiment and other troops, some 1,500 in all, he moved down the river, and took possession of Hickman, on the Kentucky shore. The next day, the expedition approached Island No. 10; reconnaissances were made along the shores; the mortar vessels were placed in position; and everything was prepared for the attack. A bombardment was begun, on Sunday the 16th; but with no particular result, except trying the range of the guns on both sides. The next day, another vigorous attempt was made by the gun-boats and mortar vessels, which kept up a continuous fire all the afternoon; but it had become evident that other help was needed to accomplish the reduction of Island No. 10. Pope's operations were expected to render this aid. In order to cut off the escape of the rebels across the Tennessee peninsula, it was only necessary to cross the river and bring his forces to bear upon the enemy from below. A canal was projected, which proved to be a very laborious operation, yet was quite successful. It was twelve miles long, six of which were through very heavy timber, requiring great exposure and privation in cutting the way through. It was completed April 4th, and was highly praised as a monument of enterprise and skill. Foote, meanwhile, was not idle or inefficient. The firing was regularly kept up, and on the night of April 1st, in the midst of a furious storm, battery No. 1 of the enemy, which had been particularly annoying to our boats, was taken by assault. The rebels, however, retreated without contesting the possession of the fort. On consideration, Foote determined to allow one of the gun boats to run the batteries. On the night of the 3d of April, in a furious storm of lightning and thunder, the gun boat Carondelet, Captain Walker, passed the entire series of rebel batteries, without returning a shot, and receiving their concentrated fire. Strange to tell, the Carondelet passed in safety, and was received with much enthusiasm by our troops at New Madrid. Three days afterwards, another gun-boat accomplished the same feat in safety. On the morning of the 4th of April, the heavy floating battery of the rebels at Island No. 10, having been fired upon for more than an hour by three of our boats, cut loose from its moorings, and drifted two or three miles down the river. The rebels, finding the case hopeless, attempted to get away; but, on the 8th of April, ascertaining that every avenue was cut off, they surrendered at discretion. Colonel Elliott took possession of the works opposite Island No. 10, saved several steamers and took some 200 prisoners. Pope, in his report, says, of what fell into his hands, there were 3 generals, 273 field and company officers, 6,700 prisoners, 123 pieces of heavy artillery, 7,000 stand of small arms, etc. Foote was visited by some rebel officers, April 7th, who surrendered to him Island No. 10.

In pushing forward operations in the South-west, it was of prime importance to effect a junction of the forces under Gens. Grant and Buell, on the upper waters of the Tennessee River, so as to cut off the rebel communications with the South and East. Nashville had been occupied, Columbus had been evacuated, and Island No. 10 was certain to be captured in a short time; hence, by advancing our forces to Corinth, in Mississippi, where was the junction of the Memphis and Charleston, and the Mobile and Ohio Railroads, the conquest of Memphis would be greatly facilitated, and another valuable point on the Mississippi River secured. In the course of a month, Tennessee being firmly held by the Union army, our energetic commanders in the West were advancing against the new lines of the enemy's defence in the States bordering on the Gulf. Beauregard, the rebel chief, concentrated his forces at and around Corinth, with Johnston, Polk, Bragg and Hardee to aid him, and with an army of more than 40,000 men. He expected to be able to rout Grant at Pittsburg Landing before Buell could reinforce him. Grant's army numbered about 30,000, and he had with him some of the best officers in the service, as W. T. Sherman, McClernand, C. F. Smith, etc. On the 11th of March, 1862, the transport steamers began to arrive at Savannah on the Tennessee River, with the advance division of the army. The gunboats, the next day, proceeded some forty miles up the river to reconnoitre, going as far as Eastport, and finding the rebels engaged in erecting fortifications wherever they could. The enemy's line of defence had for its base the Memphis and Charleston Railroad, the preservation of which was absolutely necessary to enable the rebels to hold Northern Mississippi, Alabama, and Georgia. East of Corinth were several important points on this road, as Chattanooga, Huntsville, Tuscumbia, Florence, etc.; westwardly, the road runs in a direct line to Memphis, ninety-three miles distant. The Union line was the Tennessee River, extending from Paducah in Kentucky, to Eastport in Mississippi. The gun-boats were kept moving up and down the river to prevent the erection of batteries by the rebels, and were of special service to Grant's plans. About the middle of March, the army was advanced to Pittsburg Landing. Buell was ordered to join Grant, and left Nashville, March 28th, for that purpose. Beauregard and Johnston, early in April, resolved to attack Grant alone before Buell could arrive. Pittsburg Landing is about eighteen miles from Corinth, and the assault was begun on the 6th of April, Grant being posted on the left bank of the Tennessee. Before daylight the rebel columns began to press upon our men in Sherman's brigade. Hour after hour the contest raged, and though our men as a whole fought well, yet this first day resulted in heavy loss, in prisoners, artillery, plundered camps, etc. Had not the gun-boats done excellent service, and the advance of Buell's army arrived late in the day, Grant would probably have been routed. As it was, after a night's rest, our forces now took the place of those attacking instead of being attacked. Very early on the morning of April 7th, the troops were in motion, and they went at their work with great spirit. The rebels resisted all in their power; but after a hard struggle the leaders gave up the contest. By four P. M., they were driven from the field, and were pursued until night, when our men returned to camp. The slaughter on both sides was terrible; the rebels gave as their loss 10,699; our loss was reported as 13,508. Between 2000 and 3000 of the enemy left dead on the field were buried by order of Grant. General Halleck now took command. Pope, with his division, about 25,000 in number, arrived at the Landing, April 22d, from New Madrid. With an army now of 108,000 men, Halleck placed Grant on the right wing, Buell in the centre, and Pope on the left wing, and prepared to advance at once on Beauregard at Corinth.

Congress, meanwhile, had been busily occupied in its work. The war, of course, was the engrossing topic, and everything tended to show that the war must be carried forward with energy and determination to restore the supremacy of the Constitution and laws of the United States. The republicans being in the majority kept prominently in view their opposition to slavery in all its aspects; while the Border State members contended earnestly in its favor. Trumbull's bill for the confiscation of rebel property, and giving freedom to their slaves was a decided step forward, and it was followed by others of like import. A bill for the abolition of slavery in the District of Columbia was introduced into the House, early in the session, and having been referred to the committee on the District, was reported favorably upon, March 12th, 1862. The Senate also took up the same subject, which was referred to the committee on the District, who reported a bill with amendments, in February. This was discussed during the following month. The usual arguments on both sides were gone over; the Border State members opposed it vigorously; efforts were made to fasten on to the bill a compulsory colonizing of the negroes, but to no purpose; the majority were resolved upon their course, and would not agree to any such restriction. The bill passed the Senate, April 3d, by a vote of twenty-nine to fourteen; in the House discussion was not protracted, and on the 11th, it passed by a vote of ninety-two to thirty-eight. As thus adopted by both Houses the bill declared the immediate abolition of slavery in the District; provided means for the colonization of the free blacks, if desired by them; and appropriated $1,000,000 to compensate the owners of slaves, at a rate not exceeding $300 for each. Following upon this was the passage of an act removing slavery from the Territories of the United States. It was introduced into the House, March 24th; taken up for discussion early in May; and finally adopted by large majorities. Lincoln, feeling deeply the pressure of the slavery question, and as yet not being able to see his way out of the difficulty, was anxious to make trial of a system of compensated emancipation, especially in the Border States, in the hope that through them a powerful influence might be brought to bear upon the States further south. It was his hope also, that the war would sooner come to a conclusion by adopting such a course. On the 6th of March, he sent a message to Congress, asking the following resolution to be passed: "*Resolved*, That the United States ought to co-operate with any State which may adopt a gradual abolishment of slavery, giving to such State pecuniary aid, to be used by such State in its discretion, to compensate for the inconveniences, public and private, produced by such change of system." The resolution was adopted in the House, March 11th, in the Senate, April 2d, by large majorities. The President was authorized, January 21st, to take possession of certain railroads and telegraph lines under the plea of military necessity. The bill authorizing the issue of treasury notes gave rise to long and ardent discussions. The majority argued that as money must be had, this was the safest and easiest way to obtain it. The votes in both Houses were large in favor of the measure. The issue was authorized of $150,000,000 of United States notes of denominations not less than five dollars each, not bearing interest, and creating the same a legal tender in payment of all debts public and private, within the United States, except duties on imports, and payments by the government of interest on bonds and notes, which was required to be paid in coin. This new "circulation" was to be received by the government in payment for any loans which might be negotiated by the secretary of the treasury. To fund the debt thus created and enlarged, the issue of coupon or registered bonds, to the amount of $500,000,000, bearing six per cent. interest, and redeemable at the pleasure of the United States after five years, and payable twenty years from date, was authorized. All bonds, stocks, and other securities of the United States, held within the country, were, by the act, to be exempt from taxation by or under State authority.

The rebel congress was sitting at this time at Richmond. All measures of consequence were discussed and determined on with closed doors, and no reports of speeches were made public. Some of the members urged the invasion of the North as the true pathway to success. Stonewall Jackson, among military men, strongly advocated this course. Various appropriations were made, the conscription act was passed, England and other powers were spoken of with disgust, because they had not recognized the Confederacy, etc. The session closed April 21st, 1862.

Fort Pulaski (p. 274), is a very important fortification at the mouth of the Savannah River. It has five sides or faces, including the gorge; is casemated on all sides; has walls seven and a half feet thick, and twenty-five feet high above high water; and is surrounded by a wet ditch forty-eight feet wide. At the time of the siege the fort contained forty-eight guns, of which twenty bore upon the batteries on Tybee. General Gillmore now pushed forward preparations for bombarding the fort. Rebel communications were cut off; on the 21st of March ordnance and stores began to arrive in Tybee Roads; from that date until April 9th, all the troops were occupied in the work before them; and eleven batteries with heavy guns were placed on the northern side of the island. Gillmore issued a general order, April 9th; the fort was summoned April 10th; the bombardment commenced at eight A. M., and was continued all day into the night; the next day it was resumed, and by noon the fort was so much injured that at two P. M. it surrendered. Forty-seven guns, large quantities of stores, etc., and 360 prisoners were taken. The scientific skill displayed in preparing and carrying through this attack brought prominently into notice the value of the new rifled ordnance, in all cases of a similar kind. The opinion was freely expressed, by General Hunter and others, that "no works of stone or brick can resist the impact of rifled artillery of heavy calibre." Owing to inadequacy of force, our troops did not advance upon Savannah; but the blockade was henceforth effective. About two weeks later another marked success was attained. The taking of Newbern we have already noted (p. 274). Beaufort, forty miles distant, was the next point to be secured. Fort Macon, commanding the channel to Beaufort, stood in the way; and General Parke was ordered to advance against it. As the rebels refused to surrender, siege material had to be brought from Newbern, and operations were carried on as rapidly as possible. Burnside arrived April 22d, 1862, bringing with him two barges fitted up as floating batteries, and on the 24th, the bombardment began. It was kept up for hour after hour, and about four P. M. the fort surrendered. General Reno was sent about the middle of April to make an advance upon Camden, which he accomplished with spirit and energy.

In speaking of plans for opening of the Mississippi, (p. 280,) we have noted the capture of Island No. 10. New Orleans was the next point of great moment to be secured. Ship Island, between Santa Rosa Island and the mouth of the Mississippi, near the entrance to the interior water communication with New Orleans by Lake Borgne and Lake Pontchartrain, was one of the most valuable stations along the coast. It was sixty miles distant from New Orleans, and about the same distance from the northernmost pass, at the mouth of the Mississippi. The value of this spot, as a defensive position, had been appreciated by the government, and a light-house had been erected and a fort partly completed, in 1859. The rebels destroyed these at the outbreak of the insurrection in 1861; and although some efforts were made by them to fortify the island, yet they abandoned it entirely in September. Early in December, 1861, some 2000 troops were landed on Ship Island, under General Phelps. On the last day of the year 1861, Biloxi, a small town in Mississippi, about ten miles from Ship Island, was visited by a part of the squadron and some of the troops. It was found that most of the men here had enlisted in the rebel service, leaving the women, etc., at home. Other troops arrived at Ship Island in January, 1862; and Butler, on the 25th of February, sailed from Hampton Roads to assume command of the land forces intended to operate against New Orleans. At the close of March, he had 14,000 men at the island, mostly new recruits. By the middle of April he succeeded in embarking 8000 troops for the Mississippi, which were to co-operate with the naval force which was there, and which was being pushed forward with zeal and energy. Captain Farragut reached Ship Island February 20th, and was charged with the naval operations in the Gulf. Commodore Porter was sent to aid him, with a fleet of bomb vessels and armed steamers to manage them. Farragut entered upon the work with zeal and energy; but difficulties in getting the large ships over the bars of the river delayed advance. It was not till the early part of April that the vessels of the squadron were able to move forward to their appointed stations. Farragut's force was 17 steamers and gun-boats, Porter's mortar fleet of 21 sailing vessels and 7 steamers of light draft, together with Butler's troops in the transports. The aggregate armament was about 300 guns and mortars.

The rebel preparations for guarding the approaches to New Orleans were numerous and formidable. Beside some 20 steam rams and gun-boats, they relied on two important forts, Jackson and St. Philip, on the right and left banks of the Mississippi, 25 miles from its mouth, 75 from the city. The united power of the two forts was 126 guns of long range and heavy calibre. In addition to the great strength of these forts, a strong chain was extended across the river, here half a mile wide, and fire ships, a great floating battery, and the like, were ready for defence against the loyal fleet now on its way to capture the city. The rebels were confident that New Orleans could not be taken, and they indulged in some bravado on the subject; but it was not long before they found out their mistake. The mortar boats under Porter began the bombardment on Fort Jackson, April 18th, at a distance of about 3000 yards. For six days steady firing was kept up on both sides; the chain barrier was broken up, meanwhile; and Farragut resolved to advance at once and pass the forts. The fleet was arranged in two divisions, to each of which was assigned six gun-boats. About three o'clock A. M., April 24th, the fleet got under way, Captain Bailey leading the right with his gun-boats to attack Fort St. Philip, while the other division of the ships was to aid in the attack on Fort Jackson. "The enemy's lights," says Farragut in his report, "while they discovered us to them, were, at the same time, guides to us. We soon passed the barrier chains, the right column taking Fort St. Philip, and the left Fort Jackson. The fire became general, the smoke dense, and we had nothing to aim at but the flash of their guns; it was very difficult to distinguish friends from foes." Farragut's ship, at one time was set on fire by a fire-raft; but the flames were extinguished. Fort St. Philip was soon silenced, and eleven rebel gun-boats destroyed. The forts were passed, and the victory gained, winding up with the making a total wreck of the rebel ram Manassas. Farragut sent news to Porter, and also informed Butler that the way was open for him to land his forces at Quarantine Bayou, as previously arranged. Leaving two gun-boats to protect the landing of the troops, Farragut continued his progress up the river and reached English Turn about half-past ten, on the morning of April 25th. Evidently, a panic had already seized upon the people in the city and vicinity, for cotton-loaded ships on fire came floating down, together with other indications of the greatest fright, and hasty destruction of property of all kinds. The fleet met with brief detention at the earth-work forts, six miles below New Orleans, and though annoyed by fire-rafts, etc., it anchored at one P. M. in front of the city. The levee was a scene of desolation. Ships, steamers, cotton, coal, were all in a blaze; and when Captain Bailey went on shore to demand the surrender of the city, he and his party were grossly insulted by the mob. Lovell, the rebel commander, had run away, and every one refused to pull down the Louisiana flag. Farragut was, of course, indignant, and the next morning sent plain and unmistakable word to Monroe, the mayor, that immediate submission and the hoisting the flag of the United States would be insisted on. Monroe wrote some inflated bombast to Farragut about himself and his "gallant people," but the old and true flag was hoisted nevertheless. Yet so madly fanatic were these fellows, that the flag was torn down, and Farragut threatened to fire into the city, at any moment the outrage might be repeated. Porter, who had been left with his bomb vessels to secure the reduction of the forts, proceeded actively with his work. A demand was made for their surrender, which at first was refused; Porter thereupon opened fire upon them again, and sent six of his schooners and cut off the supplies and means of escape in the rear of Fort Jackson. Butler also, having landed at Quarantine in the rear of Fort St. Philip, cut off reinforcements from that quarter. The result was, that the men in the forts showed evident signs of mutiny, and Duncan, on a second demand, concluded to accept Porter's terms. This was on the 28th of April. Porter understood that the three steamers and the Louisiana, an immense iron-clad battery of 4000 tons, which Farragut had unwittingly left behind him, had also surrendered, or were ready to surrender; but instead of that, the person in command of the vessels, named Mitchell, behaved most dishonorably, by setting fire to the battery and sending it to explode in the midst of our fleet. Providentially, the battery blew up when near Fort St. Philip, and our ships escaped without injury. Porter denounced the act of Mitchell as infamous, and on capturing the rebel steamers, he refused to parole the officers, and sent them to the North as prisoners of war. Fort Jackson was greatly injured by the bombardment, nearly 2000 shells having been thrown into it, besides some 3,000 in the ditches and outer works. Fort St. Philip was but little injured, as its fate depended on its companion across the river; when Jackson surrendered, St. Philip fell as a matter of course. By order of Butler the forts were garrisoned by the 26th Massachusetts, he himself proceeding with the rest of his troops to take possession of New Orleans; which, we may here state, he did on the 1st of May, 1862. The rebels lost six forts, besides two large earthworks above the city; 1,200 prisoners were taken; 18 gun-boats, including three iron rams, were captured; and the ram Mississippi, on which some $2,000,000 had been spent, was blown up by the rebels. The importance of this great victory over the rebels cannot be too highly estimated. Its effect was deeply felt in the loyal States, as well as in those which were in arms against the government. It taught a lesson to enemies as well as friends at home and abroad. The rebels were unwilling to credit, nay, had scouted, the possibility of the capture of New Orleans. The supporters of the Union had hoped and wished for, rather than confidently expected success. On the one side were shame, mortification, rage, hatred; on the other a lofty exhilaration, a deep and profound assurance of the ultimate if not speedy triumph of law and order. It was breaking the back-bone of the rebellion, as Porter said. It was, as the

London *Times* phrased it, "putting the tourniquet on the main artery of the confederacy." It was, as a southern writer confesses, a disaster which astounded the South, shook the confidence of the world in the boasting "confederacy," and led, by unavoidable steps, to the abandonment of the great Valley of the Mississippi. And though it is true that other strong points on the Mississppi, as Port Hudson, and especially Vicksburg, were not taken for more than a year after the fall of New Orleans, yet this was the heaviest blow of all, and this demonstrated both the energy and power of the loyal States, and their settled determination to restore and preserve the integrity of the Union at any and every cost.

McClellan entered Yorktown, May 4th, 1862 (p. 279). Although mortified at being so neatly overreached by the rebels, he was disposed to take active measures at once. He immediately sent off all his cavalry and horse artillery in pursuit, supported by infantry. "No time," he said, in his dispatch, "shall be lost. The gun boats have gone up York River. Gloucester is also in our possession. I shall push the enemy to the wall." The rebels had taken the direct road to Williamsburg, twelve miles nearer Richmond. The rebels took position at a point where the roads cross near Williamsburg. The cavalry under Stoneman began the attack, but to no particular result. Hooker came up in the night, and the next morning made an attack; but he also failed of success. Kearney and his division came up in the afternoon, and dashed into the battle. The rifle-pits were taken; the enemy's rear was gained, and they lost the day. The victory was complete, but our loss was very heavy, being 2,228. Bad roads prevented the cavalry being effective, and McClellan made slow progress towards Richmond. Despite the rain and mud, the different divisions of the army were concentrated at White House, on the Pamunkey, above West Point, May 16th. A depot was established, and by the 26th, the railroad was in order as far as the Chickahominy, and the bridge over it was nearly completed. Meanwhile, an important advantage had been gained in the capture of Norfolk. Early in May, Wool set out with an expedition from Fortress Monroe, and when he was within eight miles of Norfolk the rebels abandoned the place. Very early the next morning, May 11th, a bright light was seen in the direction of Craney Island, and about 4.30 A. M., a terrible explosion took place, which shook the land and water for miles round. Soon after it was ascertained that the ram Merrimac had been blown up, and the rebels had retreated from Craney Island after destroying all they could at the Gosport navy yard. The James River being now open, by the abandonment of the land batteries at the entrance, several United States vessels were sent to reconnoitre the river as far as was possible. Three iron-clads and two steam gun-boats pushed their way cautiously up the James, and arrived, on the 14th of May, within about ten miles of Richmond. Two miles further on, at Ward's or Drury's Bluff, resistance was made to their advance by a heavy battery and obstructions in the river. After a spirited but unsuccessful engagement, our vessels gave up the contest. The gun-boats continued to hold possession of the extended line of navigation below, but the advantage gained was for the present of less importance, while the York River, on the other side of the peninsula, was made the exclusive channel of communication with the advancing Army of the Potomac. After the retreat from Yorktown the rebels gradually withdrew within the line of the Chickahominy, with the evident purpose of making a most strenuous effort to repulse McClellan from the vicinity of Richmond. The York River and Richmond Railroad, running nearly due east and west, crossed the Chickahominy near Bottom's Bridge, about eleven miles distant from the capital of Virginia. It was on the left or southerly bank of the river, and along the line of the railroad, which separated here from the river at an acute angle, with the apex at the bridge, that several of the most important battles of the campaign were fought.

On the 15th of May, McClellan had gathered the several divisions of his army in the large plain at Cumberland, on the south bank of the Pamunkey, where a vast encampment was formed, covering some twenty square miles. White House, five miles above on the river, at the head of navigation, with a connection, by the York River Railroad, with Richmond, had been abandoned a few days before, and was thenceforward used as a permanent base for the landing of supplies during the campaign. On the 19th, our army directed its course westward towards Richmond, the capture of which was so eagerly, and in fact unreasonably longed for at the North. Davis owned that "recent disasters had spread gloom" over the rebel cause, but he affirmed that even if Richmond were taken he could carry on the contest in Virginia for twenty years or more. The left wing of the army under Keyes and Heintzelman led the way towards the Chickahominy at Bottom's Bridge; Sumner's corps in the centre following the line of the railroad; and Franklin's and Porter's corps pursued a course to the northwest. Stoneman with his cavalry crossed the river without opposition and reconnoitred. On the 20th of May, the centre and left were at the Chickahominy, and the next day the right encamped at Coal Harbor. Keyes and Heintzelman crossed on the 25th, and a reconnaissance was pushed to Mechanicsville, only about five miles from Richmond. The corps of Keyes on the left held the advance beyond the Chickahominy, being encamped on both sides of the railroad, in the vicinity of Seven Pines and Fair Oaks, and the corps of Heintzelman was in their rear, also along the railroad, in the neighborhood of Savage's Station. In the advance in this quarter, Casey held the front, with his division, about 4,000 men, nearly all raw troops. His force was stationed, the last week in May, in the immediate presence of the enemy, within six miles of Richmond, his pickets extending to within five miles of that city. Couch's division of Keyes' corps was next behind on the railroad. A line of pickets was extended across the narrow angle made by the railroad and the river, and nearly a dozen bridges were constructed, with immense toil, across the Chickahominy. The completion of these was only waited for, so as to secure entire co-operation of the whole army; and McClellan announced that a battle might be looked for at any moment, and the troops must be in readiness. Just on the eve, however, of the approaching great contest near Richmond, McClellan received information respecting a rebel force in the vicinity of Hanover Court House, which might seriously endanger his communications, or interfere with McDowell's expected, and anxiously looked for junction. By the commanding general's direction, Fitz John Porter set out, early on the morning of the 27th of May, to dislodge or defeat this force, said to consist of North Carolina troops from Newbern, under the rebel General Branch. Near Hanover Court House Porter drove the rebels, who, having been reinforced, made an attack on the rear of our force. Porter then faced about and routed them completely. It was gallantly done and relieved the right wing of the army entirely.

McClellan, as we have noted (p. 279), felt deeply the withdrawing McDowell's corps, the help of which he greatly needed in view of the proposed assault on Richmond. The government was in so much fear as to Washington, that when the rebels sent Jackson to make a raid upon Banks, they hurried McDowell, by order, May 24th, to hasten to Banks's help or rescue. This was a great blunder, to say the least, for McDowell did not help Banks at all, and McClellan was sure that, if McDowell came at once and joined him, Richmond was certain to fall. Lincoln sent McClellan word, May 25th, that he "must either attack Richmond or give up the job, and come to the defence of Washington." McClellan, though greatly annoyed, replied that he would do the best he could. Hardly had Porter and his brave band returned from Hanover Court House, when the right bank of the Chickahominy became famous for the hard-fought battle of the Seven Pines, or Fair Oaks, so called because of the localities at two important stages of the conflict, its beginning and its end. On the rebel side were the divisions of Hill, Longstreet, Huger, and Smith; and on ours, were the corps of Keyes and Heintzelman, with a portion of that of Sumner. Johnston, well aware of the critical position of affairs, and anxious to strike a blow which should be felt, took note of the advance of Casey's division, at and beyond Seven Pines; and probably supposing that the corps of Keyes, to which it belonged, was the only one which had yet crossed the Chickahominy, he thought by massing his forces in one furious onset, to break the Union lines, and destroy this section of the army before a junction could be made, by the completion of the bridges, with the troops on the other side of the stream. On the night of the 30th of May, there was a very violent storm of lightning and thunder, and torrents of rain. The roads converted into mud, the swamps flooded, and the river threatened with an unusual rise, it appeared to be a comparatively easy thing for the rebels to destroy the exposed wing of the divided army. Accordingly, orders were given by Johnston to move to the assault at daybreak, on the day appointed. With every facility of communication with Richmond, and with the various divisions occupying the roads commanding the Union position, had the rebel plan of attack been effectively carried out, backed, as it was, by a greatly superior force, it could hardly have failed of entire success. The heavy rains, however, were a great hindrance in their way, and they did not undertake operations so early as was expected. The attack, of necessity, was delayed till the afternoon. Meanwhile, Keyes had not been unobservant or inactive. Expecting an attack at any moment, he watched earnestly the indications of hostile movements brought to him on the morning of May 31st, 1862. Cars had been heard coming out from Richmond, and an aid of Johnston's had been taken prisoner by our pickets. About eleven A. M., a body of the enemy was reported approaching. Casey prepared for immediate action; and at one o'clock was assaulted by the rebels with tremendous force and energy. They endeavored to crush his division utterly before help could be brought, and the troops fell back upon the second line held by Couch's division, and with them were driven back towards Fair Oaks. The battle raged during the rest of the day, Sumner with his men coming to the rescue about six P. M., and repulsing the rebels. Very early the next morning, June 1st, the enemy renewed the attack fiercely, and with an evident determination to carry all before them by one sweeping blow. But the assault was met with unflinching steadiness on the part of our men, and by noon the rebel force was entirely defeated. They fled in confusion and haste; but, as McClellan deemed the roads unfit for pursuit of the enemy (in which many thought he was in error), nothing was really accomplished but reoccupying the lines held previous to the battle. The losses were very heavy; McClellan reported a total of some 7000; the rebel loss was probably more than 7000.

Banks, April 17th, 1862, entered Mount Jackson, pursuing the rebels beyond to New Market, of which he took possession the following day. On the 19th he went in force to see to the protection of the bridges on the south fork of the Shenandoah in the Masanutten Valley. He succeeded in his purpose, although the rebels made vigorous efforts to destroy the bridges; from such information as he could collect, he was of opinion that Jackson had left this valley. On the 22d of April, Banks wrote to Washington, announcing that "the rebel Jackson has left the Valley of Virginia permanently, and is on the way to Gordonsville, by the way of the mountains" Two days after, a recon naissance was made towards Staunton; the town was entered without opposition. The Shenandoah divided Jackson's rear guard from our forces at Strasburg and other points of the valley, and, apparently, the troublesome rebel had taken his departure. But this was not quite certain, and from all that could be learned it seemed very likely that Jackson, who had received reinforcements, giving him some 10,000 men in hand, would speedily assume the offensive. Banks thus far had not accomplished anything of moment; it was expected that he would occupy Staunton and threaten the enemy on the line of the Virginia Central Railroad; but from necessity or policy, early in May, he fell back to Strasburg. The rebels, meanwhile, were not inactive. Ewell was gathering his troops to aid Jackson, who attacked and defeated Milroy in Highland County. Fremont, however, helped to make a stand at Franklin. Jackson now, in carrying out the rebel plan (p.287), determined by a bold dash, to attempt the capture of Banks and his force. He first attacked and routed Colonel Kenly, who had about 1000 men, and then pushed on to Winchester to get in the rear of Banks. This excellent officer at once divined the purpose of Jackson, who had, as was supposed, not less than 20,000 troops with him. Banks had but one alternative left him, viz: to start at once and occupy Winchester in advance of the rebels. This was accomplished, May 24th, after some hard fighting on the road, and continuing the retreat by way of Martinsburg he reached the Potomac at sundown, May 25th, having marched thirty-five miles in one day, and fifty-three in forty-eight hours. Fortunately the rebels did not appear, and Banks and his men crossed the river in safety and with thankful hearts. The authorities at Washington, though praising Banks for his ability, were frightened anew by Jackson's being near the Potomac, and so began again to call out lustily for more troops. Possession was also taken, by military authority, of all the railroads, May 25th.

Fremont, in his Mountain department (p.276), was expected to be of great service to the good cause, in out-flanking the rebels, in cutting off the Richmond communications, etc.; but Jackson's raid led to his being called on to follow up that active rebel. His entire force, numbering 11,500 men, consisted of Blenker's division, the brigades of Schenck and Milroy, and a light brigade of Ohio and Virginia troops, under Colonel Cluseret, a French officer in the service. Fremont's army at this time was by no means in a good condition to move. They were in a region cut off from proper supplies, and their *morale* was anything but encouraging. Fremont was unwilling, however, to lose a moment's time in the present emergency, and the troops, promptly and cheerfully, took the road to Petersburg the next morning. Furnished only with ammunition and rations for three days, they pursued their way through Moorefield, by forced marches over mountain roads, rendered unusually difficult by the inclement season. In the course of a week the advance, under Cluseret, came up, near Strasburg, with Jackson's forces, already having begun their hasty retreat up the valley. Fremont came upon the rebel rear, June 1st, near Strasburg, on the road to Winchester. Jackson declined all offers of battle; his policy was to avoid fighting; and so he pushed on through Strasburg, and succeeded in passing between McDowell's advance on the one side and Fremont's on the other. Thus the rebel general proved himself too active for his pursuers. Fremont was joined at Strasburg by a body of cavalry, under Gen. Bayard, which formed a portion of McDowell's corps, and came very opportunely to his aid. Pursuing the rebels through Woodstock, Edenburg and Mount Jackson, they making every resistance possible, burning bridges, etc., Fremont crossed the Shenandoah, June 5th, on a pontoon bridge, and came up with them beyond New Market. A sharp encounter attended the arrival of our advance the next day at Harrisonburg, and the rebels were driven on, with loss, to continue their retreat. On the 8th of June, Fremont followed, with about eight thousand men and found that Jackson was ready to fight at Cross Keys, in a well selected position. The battle was fiercely contested for several hours, and our men encamped at night on the field of battle, prepared to resume the fight the next morning; but the rebels made off in the night for Port Republic, five miles distant, where is a bridge by which the south fork of the Shenandoah is crossed. The rebel commander's position was now rather critical. He must secure the bridge over the Shenandoah, nullify Fremont's further efforts by destroying all means of crossing the river, and then defeat and drive back Shields from Port Republic. Jackson's main body arrived opposite Port Republic on the night of Saturday, June 7th, and the next morning he ascertained that Shields's advance was rapidly approaching the town. Col. Carroll, with his brigade of about 1,600 men, soon after appeared, and his cavalry, with two pieces of artillery, dashed into the town and took position at the southern entrance of the bridge. Most unfortunately, Carroll did not, or could not, immediately set to work to destroy the bridge, and thus cut off Jackson's only mode of escape. With great astuteness Jackson took steps at once to secure this important bridge. He ordered a large force, June 8th, to charge upon Carroll, holding the bridge, and drove him back some two miles. Aid coming up, a stand was made, and the next morning the battle of Port Republic was fought, one of the most sanguinary of the war. The rebels compelled our men to retreat to Shields's division up the valley. Jackson and his entire force crossed the Shenandoah, June 9th, and Fremont came up the same afternoon to find the bridge destroyed and the rebels safe on the other side. There was nothing left now for Fremont but to retire, which he did almost immediately, to Mount Jackson, and subsequently to Middletown. Shields also fell back to New Market. Jackson, plainly, had outgeneralled our commanders in pursuit of him, and had obtained great advantages to the rebel cause. "Without gaining a single tactical victory," as has been said, "Jackson had yet achieved a great strategic victory, for by skillfully manœuvring 15,000 men, he succeeded in neutralizing a force of 60,000. It is not perhaps too much to say that he saved Richmond." Some army changes took place at this date. Pope was called to the command of the Army of Virginia, June 26th, including Fremont's, Banks's, and McDowell's corps. Fremont thereupon resigned.

Gen. Mitchel was active and energetic in his movements at the South. On the departure of Buell from Nashville, March 28th, 1862, he proceeded with his division of about 10,000 men, by the direct southerly line towards the main stations of the Memphis and Charleston Railroad, in Northern Alabama. The valuable points of the route in this direction were at Stevenson or Bridgeport, on the east, and Decatur on the west, at each of which places the line crossed the Tennessee River in its winding course. With the destruction of the two bridges, the communication of the rebels with the eastward would be effectually stopped. As the enemy had destroyed extensively the railroad and other bridges on the line of his march, and as it was necessary to keep open communication for obtaining supplies, Mitchel's force was employed, as he proceeded, in reconstructing the bridges. Having built 1,200 feet of heavy bridging in ten days, he reached Shelbyville, on the 9th of April, fifty-seven miles from Nashville and about the same distance from Huntsville, Alabama. Using extraordinary activity, and with the hearty co-operation of his men, Mitchel, in two days' march, arrived, on the evening of the 10th of April, within about ten miles of Huntsville. Early the next morning he took the place completely by surprise. Stevenson and Decatur were both entered the next day. The bridge at the latter place, which had been set on fire by the rebels, was saved. From Decatur, our troops advanced by the road and occupied Tuscumbia. The extension of Mitchel's lines in order to hold the railroad, rendered his situation somewhat precarious. The enemy began to gather in force and threaten him at various points. Colonel Turchin held Tuscumbia till April 24th, when he retired to Jonesborough, near Decatur. He crossed the bridge over the Tennessee at this latter point and destroyed it just in time to prevent the rebels, to whom it was of especial value, having any further use of it. Decatur was evacuated by our troops, April 27th, and by Mitchel's efforts, on the 29th, the rebels were defeated at Bridgeport and the bridge secured in our possession. Although now occupying Huntsville in safety, and though sending out expeditions in different directions, yet Mitchel was prevented, by lack of reinforcements, accomplishing what might have been done, and with terrible loss to the rebels, such as holding Chattanooga, destroying the foundries and armories at Rome, Georgia, etc. As it was, the result turned out that during May and June, our troops were compelled to retire from the positions they had gained.

Halleck meanwhile was busily engaged in making preparations for an advance on Beauregard at Corinth (p. 282). The troops were not in the best condition, many of them being sick and suffering from exposure in the late series of battles. Halleck, therefore, sent for Pope and his men at New Madrid, and summoned available forces from every portion of his wide department. The army being thus strengthened and re-organized, Halleck gave orders, April 27th, that it should hold itself in readiness for immediate movement. Pope, with his division, was on the left, Buell held the centre, and Grant, with his force, was on the right. Besides these, there were other distinguished officers, holding different positions under Halleck, such as Gens. W. T. Sherman, Thomas, McClernand, Lewis Wallace, J. C. Davis, etc. The entire army occupied a semi-circular line of six miles, and numbered over, 100,000 men. The force of the rebels was estimated to be about the same in number. The army began its advance, April 29th, gradually but steadily, and on the 3d of May, Halleck was within about eight miles of Corinth. The roads were in a wretched condition; progress was slow and toilsome; and Halleck moved cautiously. His plan was to approach the works on the front by regular siege, securing, as he advanced, all available points, and send out movable forces to cut the railroads on the enemy's flank and rear. Pope advanced his forces on the left, some ten miles, by extraordinary exertions, and ordered, May 3d, a reconnaissance towards Farmington, a commanding position, four miles to the east of Corinth, on the edge of the swamp, which was entirely successful. Corinth was invested, May 20th, on the north and east, at about four miles distant, with a gradual narrowing of the parallels, until on the 27th, our forces, well protected with batteries and heavy guns, were within 1300 yards of the rebel works. A general reconnaissance was made the next day. On the 29th and 30th of May, the batteries did their work, and the rebels succumbed; they gave up the contest, evacuated Corinth, and some two thousand prisoners and deserters fell into our hands. The same day, Colonel Elliott was sent to Boonesville, on the Mobile and Ohio Railroad, where he destroyed the track for miles, together with the depot, locomotives, cars, supplies, etc. The cavalry set off in pursuit of the rebels at once, and the same day came up with their rear-guard at Tuscumbia Creek, eight miles south of Corinth. The pursuit was continued in force for some thirty miles, and a large number of prisoners taken. The rebels retired to Tupello, fifty miles south of Corinth. Buell subsequently moved toward Chattanooga, and Grant occupied the line of West Tennessee from Memphis to Iuka, guarding the railroads from Columbus south. Halleck gave up his command, July 23d, and took position at Washington as general-in-chief.

Commodore Foote, who had done excellent service at Island No. 10 (p. 281), left New Madrid, April 12th, and proceeded down the Mississippi with his mortar boats and transports following. His purpose was to attack Fort Pillow or Wright, which was situated at the Chickasaw Bluff, near Islands Nos. 33 and 34, and about seventy miles above Memphis. A combined attack was purposed to be made by Foote with Pope's aid, but the latter was called away, to assist in operations against Corinth. The fleet remained, however, watching the enemy, with almost daily firing on and from the fort; Foote, who was suffering from a severe wound received at Donelson, was relieved of his command, May 9th, by Captain C. H. Davis. On the following morning, the rebel gun-boats and ram made an attack upon our flotilla, lying at the time tied up to the bank, three on the eastern and four on the western side of the river. The ram advanced to run down the gun-boat Cincinnati, Capt. R. N. Stembel, giving her a severe blow on the starboard quarter, and apparently uninjured by the broadsides of the gun boat. The engagement became general. The ram succeeded in damaging the Cincinnati so greatly that she soon after sunk. The other vessels did excellent service. After an hour at close quarters, one of the rebel boats being sunk and two being blown up, the enemy retired hastily under the guns of the fort. During the night of June 4th, the rebels evacuated Fort Pillow, having destroyed everything that they could before leaving. Pursuit was immediately made amid the cotton floating everywhere in the river, and on the 5th of June, the squadron arrived within two miles of Memphis. Soon after daylight, the next day, the battle began with the rebel gun-boats. Within an hour's time they were defeated, and Memphis came again under the control of the Union. Henceforth the way was open for operations against the rebels in Arkansas, by means of the principal rivers. Several expeditions were undertaken; but, as they were of no particular moment in the result, we need not dwell upon the subject.

Butler, having taken possession of New Orleans, (p. 285), soon found that he was in a position not to be envied. The great mass of the people were rampant in their insolence and outrageous conduct, and the wealthier classes hated the Union and its authority with a hatred not to be expressed in words, and which stopped at nothing to show forth their unquenchable malignity. Clearly, it required a man of nerve and sagacity and fixed purpose to crush lawlessness and revolt, who would assume rule then and there. Butler's first step was to issue a proclamation stating his views and determination in regard to maintaining order and the supremacy of the laws. "Representing here the United States, it is my wish to confine myself solely to the business of sustaining the government of the United States against its enemies." Anything like conciliation, however, the New Orleans rebels did not wish. They preferred talking in high terms about "brute force" practiced against them, and they liked their own way too well of indulging in riot and disorder, with the attendant drunkenness and street murderings; they were, in fact, savage in their fury at being put under constraint, in not being allowed to insult, spit upon, or assassinate our men; and in having a muzzle put upon the rampant, seditious newspaper press, which day by day, was striving to "fire" the Southern heart. The most pressing duty which fell upon Butler was to provide food for the starving population of a city containing 150,000 inhabitants, nearly half of whom knew not where to-morrow's bread was to come from, or whether to-morrow might not be actual starvation. The business of the city, being mostly in connection with the cotton trade, was virtually dead; the mechanics and working classes were without occupation; the wealthy rebels, with hearts of stone, as it seemed, would not contribute one cent to the relief of the poor, but were studying all the time how they might give aid to rebel bands outside the city; and Butler saw and felt that immediate action must be taken; the poor must be fed, and the rich must contribute towards doing it. The weather was hot; the streets were extremely filthy; the terrible yellow fever might soon be expected; and not a day's delay could be justified. Hence, by General Order, May 9th, he announced that, to the extent possible within his power, he would see that the hungry were fed, and the distressed relieved with provisions. As the city government purposely neglected the streets, and sanitary matters altogether, Butler next took steps by which the poor obtained work and the city was purified. Some 3000 men were set at work in sweeping the streets, purging the canals, repairing the levee, removing nuisances, and in every kind of work which could render New Orleans clean, decent and fit to live in, despite the threatened yellow fever, which, the rebels declared, with much apparent satisfaction, would make short work of their hated oppressors.

Butler's plan for obtaining funds wherewith to pay for the work thus done was ingenious as well as bold. He issued a General Order, August 4th, in which he declared that "those who have brought upon the city this stagnation of business, this desolation of the hearth stone, this starvation of the poor and helpless, should, as far as they may be able, relieve these distresses." He selected for assessment certain persons who had subscribed to a rebel loan, and such like, and compelled them to pay according to their subscriptions; so that he raised in all, for this charitable necessity, $342,000. It was bad enough to have the men behave like blackguards, whenever they dared; but when the women, the "ladies," as they called themselves, so far forgot themselves and their sex as to indulge in gross insults to our soldiers, it was plain that something must be done to put a stop to such a state of things. *How* to do this effectively was a question of some difficulty. Butler, in his General Order, No. 28, solved the matter by declaring, that every woman who should insult any officer or soldier, should "be regarded, and held liable to be treated, as a woman of the town plying her avocation;" *i. e.*, should be held liable to arrest, imprisonment for the night and a fine of five dollars. Whatever may be said of the taste of Butler, one thing is certain, it put an end at once to indecent and improper exhibitions in public of their spite and ill humor. Abating none of his zeal, Butler was diligent in enforcing the confiscation act of Congress, July 17th, 1862; he seized upon 6,000 arms of various descriptions in private hands; and he made numerous efforts to benefit the blacks—respecting whom the government had not yet adopted a definite line of policy—by enlisting many of them into the United States service, etc. Outside of the city, and in other parts of the Department of the Gulf, he strove to accomplish something; but the lack of reinforcements, and the reverses to our arms in Virginia during the summer prevented his doing all that he purposed.

Farragut, after the capture of New Orleans, proceeded to advance up the Mississippi. He sent detachments of his squadron to take possession of the principal places, and to clear the way for the opening of the river throughout its entire course. This was to be accomplished by co-operation with Commodore Davis, who was advancing from above Memphis towards Farragut's fleet below. At Baton Rouge, 140 miles above New Orleans, the national flag was raised and the arsenal and other property taken possession of on the 8th of May. On the 12th Natchez, was visited, but as it was a position of no military importance, no steps were taken to occupy it. About a week later, Commander Lee, with the advance of the squadron, arrived near Vicksburg, and under orders from Farragut and Butler, demanded the surrender of the place and its defences. This was peremptorily refused by the city authorities. Farragut arrived shortly after, with a body of troops under General Williams, and was followed by an additional naval and military force, including Porter's mortar flotilla, which had been withdrawn from its proposed theatre of operations on the Gulf. The fortifications at

Vicksburg, consisting of an extensive range of batteries on the heights, the town being built on a bluff rising to a considerable elevation above the river, were not very readily to be assailed by the guns of the squadron. In fact, the reduction of the place, which was capable of easy reinforcement from its railroad connections with the interior, was speedily ascertained to be an undertaking of no slight difficulty. Farragut determined to pass the batteries at Vicksburg. Accordingly, on the 28th of June, he did so, early in the morning, and eight out of the ten vessels under orders reached a part of Davis's fleet above, at the mouth of the Yazoo River. Davis joined Farragut at once above Vicksburg. The rebel ram Arkansas had been carried up the Yazoo River in May, and Colonel Ellet went to look after and if possible destroy her; but he was unsuccessful. On the 15th of July, the Arkansas, completely iron-clad, and with ten guns, steamed down the Yazoo, dashed in among our gunboats and other vessels, and finally arrived in safety under the fortifications of Vicksburg. As the water was falling in the river, Farragut dropped down the Mississippi and reached New Orleans, July 28th. Davis sailed up the river, and in conjunction with Curtis made a successful expedition up the Yazoo River. For the present, at least, nothing further could be done with Vicksburg, and the rebels determined to regain possession of Baton Rouge. The ram Arkansas was to attack our few gun-boats at the place, while Breckenridge from Camp Moore was to assault it by land. Our force at Baton Rouge, at the beginning of August, 1862, was weak, not more than 2000 men, Williams being in command. On the 4th, the rebels with about 6, 000 men, made a furious assault, which was kept up for five hours, under a blazing sun; but Williams and his men, with the aid of the gun-boats, defeated the rebels. The ram Arkansas, which came to take part in the fight, but did not, was destroyed by W. D. Porter, in the Essex, the next day. Butler, we may mention, was superseded by Banks, who entered on his duties at New Orleans, December 16th, 1862.

General Hunter, March 31st, took command of the department of the South, comprising South Carolina, Georgia and Florida. His force was too limited for aggressive measures, but he was watching rebel movements. In a proclamation which he issued, he astonished the government as well as others. Among other things, Hunter said, "Slavery and martial law in a free country are altogether incompatible. The persons in these three States, Georgia, Florida and South Carolina, heretofore held as slaves, are therefore declared *forever free.*" The president and his cabinet were not prepared yet to take this advanced ground, and probably the people would not have sustained him in it. Therefore, under date of May 19th, he issued a proclamation, disclaiming the action of Hunter and refusing to pronounce upon the vexed question of freeing the slaves at present. At this date, May 13th, a slave named Robert Small, accomplished a daring act which showed what the race was, occasionally, at any rate, capable of doing. Small, who had been acting as pilot for some time on board the steam-tug Planter, in the harbor of Charleston, succeeded in bringing the vessel out from under the batteries of the forts, and delivering to the Union blockading squadron a rebel gun-boat which was employed in military service in the bay. The subject of arming the negroes excited no little attention among the people generally, as well as in Congress. Hunter, in reply to a resolution of inquiry, said that this arming of the blacks was "a complete and even marvellous success." The loyal portion of the community were evidently tending to the view which finally prevailed, viz., that the necessities of war required the employment of the negro in helping to put down the great rebellion. But, in the army generally, there was a dislike to the bringing in the blacks and placing them by the side of white soldiers. In fact, the question was beset with peculiar difficulties, and it required not only a modification of popular feeling, but especially time to bring it to anything like a settlement. In June an attempt was made in the direction of Charleston. Previous to this, gradual approaches had been made by occupying Edisto Island and sending several gun-boats to Stone River. On the 2d of June, Hunter and Benham were landed on James Island, waiting the arrival of General Wright with cavalry, artillery and additional infantry from Edisto Island. Severe storms, bad roads, and insufficient means of crossing the river, delayed operations materially, and gave the rebels an opportunity to obtain reinforcements. During a week or more, sharp skirmishes were frequent; and on the 16th of June, an attack was made by order of Benham, upon the entrenched works of the enemy. Our troops fought gallantly, but after a severe struggle failed of success, having lost some 700 in killed, wounded and missing. The forces on James Island soon after returned to their quarters at Hilton Head. Mitchel (p. 271) took the place of Hunter in September, and on his arrival at Port Royal, entered zealously upon his duties. But he was not able to accomplish anything of moment for want of troops, and having been seized by the fever, he died at Beaufort, October 30th, 1862.

In Congress, on the 11th of July, an act was passed authorizing an additional issue of $150,000,000 of notes not bearing interest, similar to those described, of which $35,000,000 might be of less denominations than five dollars, but none of the fractional part of a dollar. The legal tender clause in this, as in the former act, met with much opposition in the protracted discussion on the bills in Congress; but the demands of the war were urgent, and it was adopted as the only practicable method of meeting the public necessities. Gold, as a consequence, rose in value, and the price of gold regulated the price of commodities in general. The facilities, however, given to trade and credit, lightened, for a time, at least, the financial difficulties produced by the war. To provide internal revenue, to support the government, and to pay interest on the public debt, a voluminous tax bill was passed and approved on the first of July. It embraced a comprehensive system of excise duties, licenses, special tax on articles of luxury, stamp duties, and an income tax of three per cent, for any above $600, and five per cent for any above $10,000. Besides the several acts heretofore noted, there were three bills which may be mentioned as important at this period of our national legislation. On the 20th of May, was passed "An act to secure Homesteads to actual settlers on the Public Domain." By this act any loyal person, a citizen of the United States, or one who has legally declared his intention to become such, and of the age of 21, was given the privilege of entering upon 160 acres of land, the full title to which would be secured by five year's residence and cultivation. This measure looked to a future increase of emigration, by which the wealth of the great West had been largely developed, and which at the time was proving an important aid in maintaining the war. A second important step taken by Congress was the passing, July 1st, "An act to aid in the construction of a Railroad and Telegraph Line from the Missouri River to the Pacific Ocean, and to secure to the Government the use of the same for Postal, Military and other Purposes." The third measure alluded to above, was the passing, July 1st, "An act to punish and prevent the Practice of Polygamy in the Territories of the United States, and other Places, and disapproving and annulling certain acts of the Legislative Assembly of Utah." By this act the crime of bigamy, in a Territory or other place within the exclusive jurisdiction of the United States, was to be punished by a fine not exceeding $500, and by imprisonment for a term not exceeding five years. Certain specified ordinances and all other acts of the legislative assembly of the Territory of Utah were disapproved and annulled, so far as they establish, protect or countenance "the practice of polygamy, evasively called spiritual marriage, however disguised by legal or ecclesiastical solemnities, sacraments, ceremonies, consecrations or other contrivances." As we have before noted (p. —), the head of the Mormon fanatics has successfully evaded the laws of the land up to this very date, 1871. A singular commentary this, on our efficiency in enforcing law!

In order to put the navy on its proper footing, especially as regarded the rank of its officers, Congress, on the 16th of July, passed "An act to establish and equalize the Grade of Line Officers of the United States Navy." This law provides that the active list of the officers of the United States navy shall be divided into nine grades, taking rank according to the date of their commission in each grade, as follows:—1. Rear-Admirals. 2. Commodores. 3. Captains. 4. Commanders. 5. Lieutenant-Commanders. 6. Lieutenants. 7. Masters. 8. Ensigns. 9. Midshipmen. The number of rear-admirals on the active list was limited to nine; of commodores to 16; of captains to 39; of commanders to 90; of lieutenant-commanders to 144. The act to suppress insurrection, to punish treason and rebellion, and to seize and confiscate the property of rebels, was passed on the last day of the session. This, with other action of Congress, showed that the people, through their representatives, were steadily advancing towards a practical solution of certain difficult questions, which were earnestly and ably discussed, and which, as we shall see, were in due time disposed of. The second session of the Thirty-seventh Congress was closed on the 17th of July, 1862.

Directly after the battle of Seven Pines, or Fair Oaks (p. 288), McClellan expressed his desire to move immediately upon the rebels. But he met with disappointment. The roads and the ground generally were totally unfit for active movements; the water in the Chickahominy continued so high that he could not transport the whole of his army across the river; bridges had to be built; encampments and entrenchments had to be formed in the swampy wood; and above all, probably, there was considerable uncertainty as to being able to maintain, in safety, the necessary connection with his basis of supplies at the White House. Added to this, the midsummer sun, with its intense heat, told severely upon the health of the troops, and inflamed the pestilential influences of crowded camps and noxious marshes into active and virulent diseases; and during the long weeks of inactivity in what was called the siege of Richmond, not only thousands sickened of fever and died, but the very name of the Chickahominy, with its deadly swamps, became, to the country at large, associated with suffering in its most dreaded forms. The rebels, meanwhile, were strengthening themselves in and about Richmond. R. E. Lee took command in place of Johnston, and was in hope of speedily crushing McClellan and his entire army. A bold and dashing expedition, under J. E. B. Stuart, a cavalry officer, was undertaken, and what was especially annoying, was entirely successful. Taking about 1,500 cavalry, Stuart left Richmond, June 12th, took the Charlottesville Turnpike, penetrated our lines near Hanover Court House, dashed forward, destroying all he could, and halted till midnight at New Kent Court House. Then taking an unused road, he succeeded, June 15th, in getting back among the rebels near White Oak Swamp. About 165 prisoners were taken, together with some 300 mules and horses, etc. Stuart had thus passed entirely round and in the rear of our army, having accomplished a cavalry raid which not only astonished the army and people by its audacity, but also set the example for future exploits of a similar character. Matters were now in that condition that Richmond must be taken, or McClellan withdraw his army. Lee, by a skillful use of Jackson, was able to accomplish a flank movement, and expected to be successful in cutting McClellan's communication with the White House. On the 25th of June, Heintzelman holding the advance before Fair Oaks, was ordered to push forward his pickets, and drive the enemy from the woods in his front, and in this way to relieve his men from an unwholesome position in the swampy ground, and to bring them to an open, clear space beyond. The movement was preliminary to the general action which McClellan had now resolved upon, and in the course of the afternoon was successful. Apprehending the possible approach of Jackson, he had been already considering a change of base to the James River, and had ordered supplies and stores accordingly. Being assured of Jackson's arrival at or near Hanover Court House, and divining Lee's plan and purpose in concentrating on the north bank of the Chickahominy, he hastened at once to the camp of Fitz John Porter, who was in command of the right wing of the army, and a part of whose corps held the strongly entrenched position of Beaver Dam Creek. During the afternoon of the 26th of June, the rebels crossed in several columns, in the vicinity of Mechanicsville and Meadow Bridge, and attacked McCall, who was in position at Beaver Dam Creek. Our troops were concealed by earth works, commanding the Mechanicsville road, on which the rebel divisions under Longstreet were advancing; and when the enemy had approached within short range, they opened a very destructive fire of artillery and musketry in the faces and on the flanks of the foe, driving them back in great confusion. But, as Jackson, having passed Beaver Dam Creek above, turned the position, it was of course no longer tenable for our troops.

The question now arose and had to be decided at once, what was McClellan to do? He must fight or retreat. He must advance upon Richmond, with all the risks of a battle, or he must transfer his right wing to the south bank, and make a change of base to the James River. This latter was resolved upon, although it was by no means free from danger and difficulty. The distance from Fair Oaks to the James River was about seventeen miles, and there was only a single road by which baggage and stores could be moved; but the activity and steadiness of our troops were such, that the purpose of the commanding general was nearly completed before it was at all comprehended by the rebels. The wagons and heavy guns were withdrawn during the night of the 26th of June, and united with the train which was to set out the next evening for the James River. At the same time Stoneman proceeded with a flying column to the White House, which depot, all the stores along the railroad having been re-shipped or destroyed, was evacuated. Stoneman having successfully accomplished his work, fell back upon Yorktown. The rear guard of McCall's division, consisting of Seymour's brigade, was attacked by the enemy, who, being sharply repulsed, did not attempt further to molest the movement of our men. Porter's position between Coal Harbor and the Chickahominy, was well chosen, and bravely did his men meet the attack of the rebels on the afternoon of June 27th. Porter had called for reinforcements and had only Slocum's division, making his entire force about 35,000.* The assault of Hill and Jackson was fierce and tremendous, and after a time defeat and destruction seemed to have befallen our men. Happily two brigades came up just in time, and the troops were rallied and reformed. Night prevented further movements, but the rebels expected the next morning to capture or destroy the whole army. During the night the final withdrawal of the right wing across the Chickahominy was completed, without difficulty and without confusion. Early on the morning of the 28th, the bridges were burned, and the whole army was thus concentrated on the right bank of the Chickahominy. McClellan's change of base exhibited skill and ability, and by masking the retreat of his troops, he completely de-

* In regard to this, we are told that Magruder's "great show and movement and clatter," kept all our commanders occupied, and they declared that no troops could be spared. "And thus it happened that, while on the north side of the Chickahominy 30,000 Union troops were being assailed by 70,000 Confederates, 25,000 Confederates on the south side held in check 60,000 Union troops."

ceived the rebels under Lee, who did not find out, till the night of the 28th, what was the real purpose of McClellan. Thus our men got a day's start of the enemy. In the course of the night of the 27th, Keyes was ordered to cross the White Oak Swamp with the 4th corps, and take up a position to cover the passage of the trains. Measures were also taken to increase the number of bridges across the swamp. The trains were set in motion at an early hour, and continued passing night and day until all had crossed. Porter's corps moved across the swamp on the 28th, as did also Slocum's and McCall's divisions, and the corps of Sumner and Heintzelman on the night of the 29th of June. Lee set out in pursuit on the morning of the 29th, having directed his commanders to take different routes so as to catch McClellan somewhere, if possible. Longstreet made an attack, June 30th, at Glendale, or Turkey's Bridge, in the hope of forcing our position; but without success, night putting an end to the battle. Our men thereupon quietly withdrew, and the next morning took position at Malvern Hill. Lee, finding this to be the case, determined to attack McClellan on the 1st of July, not without hope that an army which had gone through what the Army of the Potomac had, day after day for nearly a week, could be beaten in a general engagement. But the result showed how greatly he erred in his calculation. McClellan promptly placed the army in position to meet the enemy, should he again attack the left of our line; a brigade was posted in the low ground to the left of Malvern Hill, watching the road to Richmond; and the line of our troops then followed a line of heights nearly parallel to the river, and bending back through the woods nearly to the James on our right. The attack by the rebels was fierce and determined; but it was met with heroic steadiness by our troops, and our artillery fire was fearfully destructive to the enemy. Late in the evening, the rebels fell back and gave up the battle. It being necessary that the army should, as soon as possible, reach its supplies and a place of rest, McClellan left Malvern Hill, and the troops retired, during the night of the 1st and 2d of July, to Harrison's Bar, on the James River. Lee, having ascertained that McClellan was too strongly posted, to make it safe to venture further attack, took up his march some three or four days after, and returned to Richmond. The losses in killed, wounded and missing, in these Seven Days' Battles were, on the Union side, over 15,000; on that of the rebels, it was never exactly ascertained; probably, however, their loss was not short of 19,000. There was no little disappointment and vexation in the loyal States at the failure of the campaign against Richmond; at the same time, it was evident that McClellan had displayed generalship of a high order in this retreat, and accomplished successfully one of the most difficult and hazardous of the operations of war, and that the heroism of the army was worthy of all honor and praise.

McClellan's army was now in comparative security, and was enabled to spend a month or so in repose and recuperating, against further active operations. His desire and plan were, to march against Richmond by crossing the James River and advancing by way of Petersburg. He called earnestly, therefore, and constantly for reinforcements, so as to be enabled to carry out his plans. The president favored this view of McClellan in regard to the advance; but adverse influences were at work, and another plan was adopted. General Pope, who had been called from the West, for some reason or other, openly denounced McClellan's views, and as for Halleck, he did not like McC., and insisted on withdrawing the army entirely from the Peninsula. On the 3d of August, 1862, McClellan received a telegram, stating the decision which had been made, and ordering him to withdraw to Aquia Creek, and unite with Pope. Remonstrance and entreaty were of no avail; McClellan called it "a fatal blow;" but he was compelled to obey. The entire army having left Harrison's Landing, crossed the Chickahominy, marched to Williamsburg and Yorktown, and on the 20th of August, embarked for Aquia Creek, some 40 miles from Washington. Pope, in the West, (p. 281,) had shown himself active and energetic, under Halleck, and so he was pitched upon to see what he could do in Virginia. McClellan was sharply criticised, ridiculed, and condemned, and it was determined to have a general who should show a more active, aggressive, "go-a-head" spirit than McClellan had ever manifested, and who should not fail to march straight into the rebel capital. Pope seemed to be the very man, and Pope's bold style of talking, his open censuring of McClellan's course, and his avowing a purpose of conducting the war in Virginia in a way quite different from that heretofore employed, gave rise to great expectations as to what it was that he said he was about to do. Pope had been called to the command of the "Army of Virginia" in June, and while McClellan was operating against Richmond, he was at liberty to place his troops in position such as he might think best for the next campaign. He accordingly brought his troops together into such a position as that, if the enemy descended the Valley of the Shenandoah, he thought he could interpose between their advance and main army and cut off the retreat. There was also now an opportunity afforded to Pope not only to cope with the astute rebel chief, Lee, and to drive him before him, but also to test the worth of his bold words and assurances. His address to the army, July 14th, was inflated, in bad taste, and foolishly boastful. In his orders, he announced, that henceforth the troops should subsist on the country in which they were operating, compelling the people to furnish supplies. In order to put a stop to the guerrilla mode of warfare, he declared that the people in the vicinity should be held responsible for any damage done to railroads or trains; that they should be compelled to repair all such damage; that if a soldier were fired upon from a house, such house should be rased to the ground; and that any person detected in these outrages should be shot without waiting civil process. This state of affairs, gave the rebels just the opportunity they desired. There was no further danger from McClellan, by way of the James River, and so they resolved, by a rapid and energetic movement, to march upon Pope, crush him and his force by sudden and overwhelming blows, and then invade Maryland, preparatory to a general invasion of the loyal states. Never before had so advantageous an opening been presented, and Lee was not the man to let it slip away without using it to the fullest extent. Steps were taken directly for the advance, and as the entire rebel force in and about Richmond was now probably not less than 150,000 men, it was evident how fiercely and confidently the assault would be made upon Pope and his army, the only obstacle in the way of removing the battle-ground from the soil of Virginia, and of carrying fire and sword into the loyal states. Of course, it was important to strengthen Pope immediately. Burnside brought up his troops early in August; McClellan was urged to hasten forward reinforcements from his army; and Pope, with a force of between 50,000 and 60,000 took the field in person.* Other troops under Banks and McDowell were pushed forward beyond the Rappahannock, August 7th, and Buford's cavalry was advanced to Madison Court House.

Jackson, who had been reinforced by Lee, crossed the Rapidan on the 7th of August, 1862, and on the 9th, advanced rapidly to Cedar Mountain, the side of which he occupied in heavy force. Banks was instructed to take up his position on the ground occupied the previous day near Culpepper, and also to defend it. Between 5 and 6 P. M., the battle began, and for an hour and a half

* On the 4th of August, by direction of the president, it was ordered, that a draft of 300,000 militia be immediately called into the service of the United States, to serve for nine months, unless sooner discharged. The call was responded to with the usual readiness and zeal of the loyal States.

was furious and unceasing; but Banks, though at great sacrifice, was able to hold his position. Darkness put an end to the contest, although the artillery fire was continued at short range, without intermission, until midnight. Our troops rested on their arms during the night in line of battle; but the action was not resumed. For, at daylight the next morning, the rebels fell back two miles, and retired further up the mountain. Owing to fatigue and excessive heat, the men were allowed to rest and recruit on Sunday, August 10th, and the next day was spent principally in burying the dead. On Monday night, Jackson retreated, and crossed the Rapidan the next morning. A few days after the van of Lee's army joined Jackson. Pope also received reinforcements, and held the line of the Rapidan, with Sigel on the right, McDowell in the centre, at Cedar Mountain, and Reno on the left. Banks's shattered corps was at Culpepper. It being presently ascertained that the enemy were advancing in greatly superior numbers, Pope retired with his forces, on the 19th of August, to the north bank of the Rappahannock, in the vicinity of Kelly's Ford and Rappahannock station, on the railroad. Lee, having advanced his forces to the Rappahannock, attempted to cross the river, but Pope covered the fords effectually, and prevented this movement. An artillery fire was kept up for two days, the 21st and 22d, across the river, but to no material purpose. Lee then left Longstreet opposite the fords, in order to make a turning movement by Jackson on Pope's right by way of Warrenton. Pope thereupon determined to recross the Rappahannock, and "fall furiously, with his whole army," upon the flank and rear of the enemy's long column which was passing up the river. A severe storm, however, on the night of the 22d, prevented this projected attack. Jackson having been directed by Lee to get between Washington and Pope's army, and to break up his railroad communications with the capital, made a *détour*, on the 25th, for that purpose; he crossed the upper Rappahannock, and after a forced march of thirty-five miles, bivouacked at Salem, on the Manassas Gap Railroad. The next day, passing through Thoroughfare Gap, he crossed Bull Run Mountain, and before night of the same day, reached Bristow Station, on the Orange and Alexandria Railroad. Having broken up the track as extensively as possible, he sent Stuart with a body of cavalry and infantry to Manassas Junction, seven miles nearer to Washington. Besides several hundred prisoners and eight guns, Stuart obtained possession of a very large amount of commissary and quartermaster's stores, there being at the Junction supplies valued at not less than $1,000,000. Pope now determined, in this position of affairs, August 26th, to abandon the line of the Rappahannock, and throw his whole force in the direction of Gainesville and Manassas Junction, in order to crush the enemy who had passed Thoroughfare Gap, and place his army between Lee and Jackson. Pope had received additional troops from the Army of the Potomac, and was in a condition to strike a decisive blow. On the morning of the 27th, he ordered McDowell to move rapidly forward on Gainesville by the Warrenton turnpike, with the troops under Sigel and Reynolds, some 40,000 in all. Reno and Kearney were ordered to move on Greenwich to support McDowell; and Pope himself took the line of railroad towards Manassas, with Hooker's division. Porter's corps was also to follow from Warrenton, as soon as he was relieved by Banks, and to march on Gainesville. A severe engagement occured near Kettle Run, August 27th, with the rebels under Ewell, who was driven back with a loss of 300. Gainesville was reached that night and apparently there was now no escape for Jackson. Lee was two days' march distant; his position was critical and perilous; and Pope exulted in the prospect of being able to catch and destroy that shrewd commander who had done so much injury to the Union cause. "If," Pope said to McDowell, in his order of the 27th, "you will march promptly and rapidly at the earliest dawn upon Manassas Junction, we shall bag the whole crowd." Jackson, fully alive to his danger, had his choice to retire by the same way by which he came, through Thoroughfare Gap and Gainesville, or northwardly by Centreville. He preferred the latter on every account, and during the night of the 27th, and morning of the 28th of August he moved by Sudley Springs road across the Warrenton turnpike. Pope's order to McDowell was a great blunder, since he ought to have held the Warrenton turnpike at every hazard, and prevented Jackson's movement to the north of the turnpike. Consequently, when Pope felt sure of catching Jackson, he found that the rebel chief had given him the slip; and Longstreet, on the evening of the 28th of August, reached Thoroughfare Gap, and the next day effected a junction with Jackson. Pope laid all the blame upon his officers, and accused a number of them not only of negligence and want of activity and spirit, but of disobedience of orders. Serious injury resulted to our men from this mishap. Part of McDowell's troops was attacked by Jackson, who forced the way open by the Warrenton turnpike to retire or to allow Longstreet to advance. Sigel attacked Jackson at Groveton early on the morning of the 29th of August. The fight raged furiously during the day, and Sigel was saved only by reinforcements coming up just in time. Pope was very acrimonious in condemnation of Porter and his disobedience of orders; but as nearly as can be ascertained, Porter did not receive the order till dusk, and then it was simply impossible to execute it.* Pope, supposing that the rebels were retreating, determined, not wisely, to fight with Lee again, under the notion as he phrased it, that "at least he would lay on such blows as would cripple the enemy as much as possible, and delay, as long as practicable, any further advance toward the capital." Estimating his available force at this time at 40,000 men, Pope undertook, on the afternoon of the 30th of August, to fight the second battle of Bull Run or Manassas. We need not enter into details. The rebels were superior in numbers and in the general effectivensss of their force; and the day's struggles and contendings resulted in fearful slaughter and vain efforts to drive back the foe. Hour after hour the battle raged. The rebels attacked Pope's left flank with tremendous force and effect, intending to seize the Warrenton Turnpike and cut off our army's line of retreat. Towards the close of the afternoon, our troops began to give way, and only by the firmness and spirit of some battalions of regulars were they enabled to escape from rout and entire defeat. Night came on, welcome now more than ever, and under cover of the darkness the dispirited, half-starved troops made their way across Bull Run, by the Stone Bridge, and took up position on the high ground at Centreville. Lee did not attempt any pursuit that night. No official record was made of the losses in this campaign, but from all the data accessible they were not less than, 20,000. Lee sent Jackson forward immediately to cut off Pope's retreat, and on the 1st of September Jackson attacked our troops at Germantown sharply and fiercely; the rebels, however, were driven back with heavy loss. Fredericksburg was evacuated by Burnside on the 1st of September; Aquia Creek was also evacuated, and the day following, by Halleck's orders the army fell back within the defences at Washington. Pope's career in Virginia was ended, and Lee, giving up the direct pursuit, made preparations for an invasion of Mary land. Poor Pope, the only thing left for him was to retire, and so, relieved of his command, early in September, he departed for the North-west.

Turning our attention to the West again,

* Porter, a number of months subsequent to this campaign (in Jan. 1863), after having been in command of the defences of Washington, and sharing with his corps in the battle at Antietam, was tried by a court-martial at Washington for alleged disobedience of Pope's orders while under his command. The court brought in a verdict of guilty, and Porter was dismissed from the service of the United States.

we find that General Butler was in command of the main body of the army, to the east of Corinth, moving towards Chattanooga; Grant held the line from Memphis to Iuka; Curtis commanded the forces in Arkansas, and Schofield in south-western Missouri. The rebels having largely increased their forces by conscription, were resolved not only to reoccupy Arkansas, Missouri, Tennessee and Kentucky, but to invade Ohio, Indiana and Illinois, as their co-workers, under Lee, were doing in Maryland and Pennsylvania. Their purpose was to employ extensively the guerrilla system of carrying on hostilities, a system so lawless and unscrupulous as to indicate a desperate condition of affairs among those making use of it. In fact, this mode of fighting for or against a cause was denounced as a species of land piracy and highway robbery, and the men who made themselves prominent and notorious in it—the Morgans, the Forrests, the Ashbys, and the like—were looked upon as leaders of bands who hesitated not to murder as well as plunder in every direction. Bound by no law, and under no restraint, they carried fear and trembling wherever they went. Men generally of infamous characters, they would shoot down whom they pleased, drag away others, attack railroad trains, burn bridges, or fire from ambush upon wagons. By the rapidity and suddenness of their movements and attacks, these wretches were able to inflict vast injury upon the Union cause in Kentucky and other portions of the South-west, and they gave great trouble to our generals and officers on many occasions. The months of July and August, 1862, were marked by efforts of guerrilla parties along the borders of Tennessee and Kentucky, and even in the heart of the latter State. Raids and assaults of this particular description became quite common. At day-break, on the morning of July 13th, an unexpected attack was made upon the Union brigade, under command of General T. T. Crittenden, in charge of Murfreesborough, by a cavalry force over 3,000 in number, led by N. B. Forrest, a fit compeer of Morgan in these flying expeditions. Our force was about 800, who were taken prisoners, General Crittenden included. At the same time that Murfreesborough was thus surprised, there came a fresh raid into Kentucky, headed by the noted John H. Morgan. Having crossed into Kentucky from Knoxville, with about 900 men, he issued, on the 10th of July, at Glasgow, a proclamation to the inhabitants, and called upon them to give him their aid and countenance. His proclamation was full of highly wrought appeals, and the usual stuff about "Northern tyrants," "the Hessian invaders," etc. He pushed rapidly for Lebanon, and seized upon stores as well as private property. Having destroyed to a considerable extent, the railroad communication with Cincinnati, Morgan, on the 17th of July, at the head of a motley force of about 2,000, with two pieces of artillery, fell upon a body of 340 men at Cynthiana, in Harrison county—volunteers and home guards, for the most part poorly armed and undisciplined, under command of Colonel Landrum. These were soon overcome and the town fell into Morgan's hands. A body of mounted infantry was immediately gathered at Lexington and its vicinity, and placed under command of General G. C. Smith, who set out at once in pursuit of the raiders. On coming up with Morgan's cavalry near Paris, he defeated them, retaking the cannon and horses captured at Cynthiana, with a considerable portion of the stolen property. Morgan, though pursued by Smith, made his escape into Tennessee, at the close of July, boasting of his great success in his expedition. Toward the close of the month of August, a large division of the rebel troops in Tennessee threatened an invasion of Kentucky. General E. Kirby Smith, having his headquarters at Knoxville, in East Tennessee, began his advance on the 22d of August. After a very difficult and fatiguing march, Smith entered Kentucky without opposition, and on the 29th, appeared before Richmond, the capital of Madison county, forty-eight miles south-east of Frankfort. The Union troops there were about 6,500 in number, mostly undisciplined, and offered but weak resistance to Smith's assault.

The legislature of the State was at this time in session at Frankfort, and so alarmed were the members by this success of Kirby Smith, that, on Sunday evening, the 31st of August, they passed resolutions to adjourn at once to Louisville. The archives of the State, and about $1,000,000 from the banks of Richmond, Lexington and Frankfort, were transferred during the night to Louisville. A proclamation was also issued by Governor Robinson, who had recently succeeded Magoffin, and the people of Kentucky were urgently appealed to in the existing critical state of affairs. Naturally, there was not a little excitement in Louisville and Cincinnati in view of what was before them. Every effort was made to be ready to meet the advancing enemy; martial law was proclaimed; the citizens of Cincinnati worked with enthusiasm and diligence in the entrenchment of the city; and about the middle of September, the rebels finding matters in this shape gave up the purpose of attack. It was not long after the failure of Kirby Smith's attempt upon Cincinnati, that a more serious danger presented itself. This arose out of the projected invasion of the North-west by the main army of the rebels in Tennessee, under command of Bragg. Corinth, in Mississippi, it will be remembered, was evacuated by Beauregard, at the end of May (p. 291), the retreat being continued as far as Tupello, in the same State. Buell, who had been left by Halleck in command of the Army of the Ohio, after much effort and difficulty, extended his lines eastward along the Memphis and Charleston Railroad, to Huntsville, Alabama, where he established his headquarters. The rebel general, anticipating a further movement in this direction on Buell's part, sent a portion of his force to Chattanooga, thus outflanking Buell, and, with Eastern Tennessee already in possession, securing an open route in the rear of Nashville to Kentucky. Buell soon after withdrew his divisions to Murfreesborough, and the line of the Nashville and Chattanooga Railroad. Morgan made a dash upon Gallatin, August 12th, with his usual success; and on the 22d he captured General R. W. Johnson, with his force of about 800. The guerrillas became more and more audacious. Travel ceased to be safe, even near the capital; the mails were robbed; Union men were seized and dragged off; and quite frequently small detachments of Union troops were suddenly set upon and killed or made prisoners. The state of things became intolerable, and in the western part of Kentucky, they resolved to hang every guerrilla that was caught. In addition to the men who served under Morgan, Forrest, and such like, there was a class of marauders who followed or accompanied them, a desperate band, who spared neither sex nor age, and who plundered and ravaged all alike. The same process of guerrilla warfare was carried on against boats on the Mississippi, who were signaled to come near the shore, as if for passengers or freight, and then fired into from ambush, or seized and plundered. At Randolph, on the Mississippi, an outrage of this kind was perpetrated, which led General Sherman to send a force from Memphis and completely destroy the place.

Bragg, late in August, 1862, left Chattanooga and soon after entered Kentucky; Buell also marched in a northerly direction. A sharp encounter took place at Munford ville, where the railroad crosses; it resulted in the surrender of our troops, September 17th, numbering about 4500, together with ten guns. Bragg entered Bardstown on the 26th, and issued a proclamation of the usual sort produced by rebel leaders. General Morgan, who held Cumberland Gap, was cut off from his usual sources of supply by the invasion of Kentucky under Bragg. During two months from the date of the occupation of the Gap, Morgan had bravely maintained his position; but apprehension of famine, and of being finally compelled to surrender, induced him, while he had opportunity, to make good his retreat. Accordingly, on the 17th of September, he gave orders for the evacuation. The military buildings, and all the stores which could not readily be carried away, were burnt. The escape of Morgan and his troops along a wild mountain track of 250 miles, through the counties of Eastern Kentucky, by way of Manchester, Hazel Green, West Liberty, and Grayson, to the Ohio at Greenupsburg, where they arrived on the 3d of October, was one of the most perilous adventures of the war, beset, as they were, by the enemy, by Marshall's and Smith's divisions, on whose flank they were moving. Buell, following Bragg, reached Louisville, September 26th. He found a body of raw troops there, and had some difficulty in arranging matters between the officers of the Ohio and Kentucky troops. Having his army organized in three corps, Buell set out from Louisville, October 1st, with 100,000 men, in pursuit of Bragg. The battle of Perrysville occurred on the 8th, between a portion of our army and Bragg. Our troops were badly cut up, but held the field at night during which the rebels retreated. It was thought that Bragg would make a stand at Camp Dick Robinson, where Buell expected to be able to surround him; but on the night of the 11th of October, the cunning rebel made off with the spoils which he had gathered, and which he was anxious to keep. Among these spoils were 4000 wagons, with the mark "U. S." on them, and some 5000 head of cattle, 1000 mules, and as many sheep. So soon as Buell learned the fact of Bragg's retreat, he ordered immediate pursuit by the army encamped near Danville. The rebels, however, possessed such superior knowledge of the country, and were so skillful in availing themselves of every advantage, that the rear guard of Bragg was able to hold in check the advance of our troops and prevent their doing any material injury to the retreating army. Bragg kept the road toward Cumberland Gap, and retired in the direction of Crab Orchard. On the 14th of October, our army set out early for this latter place, but were delayed by sagacious manœuvres of the enemy, and their advance hindered for several hours. The pursuit was kept up as far as Loudon, and then given up. Thus, the invasion of Kentucky was successful only so far as getting supplies which the rebels wanted very much; but in every other respect it was a failure; the people of Kentucky were too loyal to be seduced into joining the so-called Confederacy.

Grant, who was now in Western Tennessee, had his lines of communication threatened by the rebels at Bolivar, August 30th, 1862, but with no result of moment. Price, however, laid his plans to break the line of communication between Grant and Buell. Iuka, a small town on the Memphis and Charleston Railroad, twenty miles south-east of Corinth, had been seized upon by the rebels, and was now occupied by Price in force. This led to steps at once, on the part of Grant and Rosecrans, who, in dislodging Price from his position, resolved to make a double attack. It was decided that a column of 18,000 men, under Grant and Ord, should move by way of Burnsville, and attack Price, while Rosecrans, moving by way of Jacinto with part of his corps, was to attack the enemy on the flank, and push forward the balance of his column on the Fulton road, so as to cut off Price's retreat, in case he should attempt it. With this understanding, on the morning of September 18th, the army began its movement, bivouacked at Jacinto, and early the next morning was within a few miles of Corinth. Word having been received from Grant as to his position, the battle was begun. The rebels were posted on a broad ridge commanding the country for some distance. The engagement speedily became general, and continued for two hours, when darkness prevented a continuance of the fight. It was a fierce contest, and brought out the bravery and spirit of the troops, who lay on their arms, expecting the next morning to enew the battle. During the night, however, the rebels evacuated Iuka, and, though pursued actively, made good their escape to Bay Spring. Having met with this repulse, they next resolved to assault Corinth. Price was joined by Van Dorn, with troops from Mississippi. Thence, the joint force proceeded northerly, and struck the line of the Memphis and Charleston Railroad, in Tennessee, in the rear of Corinth, at Pocahontas. There they were able to menace alike Grant, at his headquarters at Jackson, and Rosecrans at Corinth; and made their advance upon the latter place by way of the Chewalla road. Rosecrans, who was in command at Corinth, Grant being at Jackson, and Ord at Bolivar, had made his preparations for an attack, and had so arranged his defences that if the enemy could be drawn under them he was certain of their defeat. Early on the morning of October the 4th, the rebels were eager for the fight, and in the course of an hour, the battle was begun in earnest by a force of nearly 40,000 men. Price led one wing, Van Dorn the other. Price assaulted the right of our force with intense fury and determination; but so skillfully had Rosecrans arranged his batteries, and so bravely were the rebels met by our men, that Price's advance was repulsed before Van Dorn was able to come up on the left. The attempt was made to recover what was lost, and with valor worthy of a better cause Van Dorn's men strove for success; but in vain. They were beaten in the bloody struggle, and by noon of the same day began their retreat. Pursuit was undertaken as speedily as possible, the enemy taking the Chewalla road. After this second battle at Corinth, the troops returned to their respective positions. No immediate advance into Mississippi was undertaken by Grant, he being content to keep open his communications with Columbus, and hold his positions at Jackson and Bolivar in Western Tennessee. At the beginning of December, he took possession of Holly Springs, on the Mississippi Central Railroad, and advanced some miles beyond to confront Van Dorn, on the Tallahatchie River. To co-operate with this movement and to act on the rebel flank, an expedition set out from Helena, Arkansas, Nov. 27th, Hovey being in command of the infantry, Washburn of the cavalry. About the middle of December, Col. Dickey was sent with a body of cavalry against the Mobile and Ohio Railroad. Both these expeditions were entirely successful and of great service to Grant's plans. The rebels annoyed Grant not a little during the winter by various raids against his long line of communications. The principal effect of these attacks was to keep Grant within the borders of Tennessee. Unacquainted with the peculiar difficulties in his way, public expectation had looked for the immediate reduction of Vicksburg; but that was a more serious matter than was contemplated, and was not brought about till the middle of the following summer.

After Pope's discreditable exit (p. 301), it became a question of moment, what was to be done. Some one must take command, and that immediately, some one too who could prove himself equal to the emergency. McClellan, as it seemed, was the only man for the occasion; Halleck actually besought McClellan to "assist him in this crisis"; and, to McClellan's credit be it remembered, he promptly met the call of the government and devoted himself anew to the work. He took command of the fortifications and of all the troops for the defence of Washington, and endeavored as rapidly as possible to restore the *morale* of the army by effective drilling, discipline, etc. The success of Lee in routing Pope, as he did, seems to have persuaded the rebel authorities that it would be safe and wise to seize the present moment for invading, or, as they called it, delivering Maryland. When Lee left Richmond there was no purpose of the kind had in view, for it could hardly have been imagined what a termination of the campaign would be made by Pope, and how completely, by the abandonment of the Peninsula added to this, the way would be open for an advance into the loyal States. But the opportunity was now at hand, and though it was rather a dangerous venture, still Lee acted with promptitude and decision. He had his choice, either to make an assault upon Washington, or to cross the Potomac higher up, and so invade Maryland. The former was not to be thought of, as being entirely beyond Lee's capacity. He accordingly adopted the other alternative. Having advanced from Leesburg to the river, on the 4th of September, 1862, he managed, in two or three days, to cross his troops by fords near Point of Rocks. The advance of Lee's army, under Hill, skirting the eastern slope of Catoctin Mountains, marched towards Frederick, the capital of the State, a town of some importance, forty-four miles northwest of Washington, and sixty west of Baltimore. Much alarm was felt in Frederick, and many of the inhabitants hastily departed; the rebel troops, however, quietly entered the town and took possession on the 6th of September. Lee issued an address, two days later, appealing to the Marylanders to throw off tyranny, regain their rights in connection with their Southern brethren, etc. But he was laboring under a great mistake. His invitations and offers were treated with almost entire indifference. There was no uprising, no enthusiastic reception of the deliverers, no disposition to cast in their lot with Jeff. Davis and his company. As a whole, the State was unquestionably loyal, and adhered to the Union from motives of principle more than those of interest. In addition to all this, the miserably squalid, filthy condition of the troops under Lee did not tend to recommend them or the professed object of their coming.* Apprehensions were felt as to the probable course of advance of the rebels, whether against Baltimore or Hagerstown, according to the purpose Lee might have in view. The governors of Maryland and Pennsylvania were very active in making preparations to meet the impending danger. In this position of affairs, McClellan made his arrangements to follow Lee, and if possible defeat his probable purpose in entering Maryland. Uncertain as to the rebel general's intentions, McClellan moved cautiously from Washington. Banks was placed in command of the defences at the capital, and Heintzelman in charge of the forces on the Virginia side. The right wing consisted of the first and ninth corps, under Burnside; the centre, of the second and twelfth corps, under Sumner; and the left wing, of the sixth corps, under Franklin; the entire force being a little over 87,000. The advance was made by five parallel roads, and the columns were so disposed as to cover both Washington and Baltimore. The object of McClellan in this arrangement was, as he states, "to feel the enemy; to compel him to develop his intentions; to attack him should he hold the line of the Monocacy; or to follow him into Pennsylvania if necessary." The van of our army entered Frederick, on the 12th of September, after some severe skirmishing with the enemy's cavalry, and found that the main body of Lee's troops had left the town two days before in the direction of Harper's Ferry. McClellan had previously advised the evacuation of this place, as being of no importance to hold now that Lee had crossed the Potomac; but Halleck, with a strange obstinacy refused to allow it. Lee hence found it necessary to delay a few days to dispose of this matter. The work was committed to Jackson, who made as speedy a conclusion as was possible. Our forces there were about 13,000 in all, including some 2,000 cavalry on outpost duty. The incompetency of Miles at Harper's Ferry, and the utter lack of ability on the part of the Ford at Maryland Heights, led to our complete discomfiture after two hours' assault. The cavalry cut their way out, however; and Jackson rejoined Lee, at Sharpsburg, Sept. 16th. By a most opportune accident Mc-

* It was enough to "smell" them, as a gentleman in Frederick said, to settle the matter. Barefooted, scant in clothing, and with plenty of vermin on their persons, they certainly offered small inducement for any one to enlist in their ranks, however good they might be at hard fighting.

Clellan found, on a table at Frederick, on the day of his arrival, a copy of Lee's official order, addressed to D. H. Hill, which directed the several movements above noted. This important document revealed to McClellan Lee's whole plan of operations, and what he intended and expected to accomplish. Heretofore McClellan had moved very slowly, and Lee expected to be able to capture Harper's Ferry, and get his troops together again before he should be overtaken or interfered with. McClellan now acted with more vigor and promptitude. He ordered a rapid movement towards Harper's Ferry, but was not able to save it, as before stated, and Lee was compelled to send Hill and Longstreet in force to prevent McClellan forcing the passes of South Mountain and striking Lee's divided columns with fatal effect. McClellan's line of advance across South Mountain was for the right and centre, under Burnside, by Turner's Gap, and for the left, under Franklin, by Crampton's Gap, six miles to the southward. The South Mountain range, near Turner's Pass, is about 1,000 feet in height, and forms a strong natural military barrier. The practicable passes are not numerous, and are readily defensible, the gaps abounding in fine positions. Turner's Pass is the more prominent, being that by which the national road crosses the mountains. Crampton's Pass also was important to be secured, in order to furnish the means of reaching the flank of the enemy. Early on the morning of the 14th of September, Pleasanton, with a cavalry force, reconnoitred the position of the enemy, whom he discovered to occupy the crest of commanding hills in the gap on either side of the national road, and upon advantageous ground in the centre, upon, and near the road, with artillery bearing upon all the approaches to their position. About eight o'clock, a portion of Burnside's command moved up the mountain to the left of the main road, dividing as they advanced into two columns. They carried handsomely the rebel position on the crest in their front, and gained possession of an important point for further operations. Hooker, in the afternoon, moved up to the right of the main road. Meade was sent to attack the eminence to the right of this entrance to the gap, which was successfully carried; and other troops pressed up the mountain later and drove the rebels back. Our loss was about 1,900 in all; the rebel loss was not much less than 3,000, of which 1,500 were prisoners. Crampton's Pass, meanwhile, the carrying of which had been committed to Franklin, was vigorously attacked, and after an action of three hours the rebels were driven into flight down the other side of the mountain. During the night, Lee abandoned the position at Turner's Gap, and our right and centre, on the morning of September 15th, passed through to the west side of the mountain. McClellan ordered an immediate pursuit of the retreating enemy, which was prosecuted, however, only for a few miles, when it was discovered that Lee had resolved to make a stand at Antietam Creek. McClellan had hoped to have a fight on the 15th, and drive Lee's army into the river; but on arriving at the front and examining the position, he found it to be too late to attack that day.

Lee's position was carefully and judiciously selected. His flanks were protected by the Potomac, which here makes a sharp curve, and his front was covered by Antietam Creek. The rebel line was drawn in front of Sharpsburg, Longstreet being on the right and D. H. Hill on the left. Hood's two brigades were posted on the left to protect the road running northwardly across the Potomac to Hagerstown. Jackson held the reserve near the left. The ground chosen was well adapted for defence, and batteries were posted on the heights at various points. It was evidently a matter of necessity for Lee to check McClellan's advance, and on this battle depended the answer to the question, whether he should be in a position to carry out his ulterior designs, or abandon the attempt altogether. At daylight, September 17th, 1862, Hooker renewed the combat begun the afternoon before, when it was too late to effect anything of moment. It was a fierce and terrible struggle, hour after hour, through the day. Mansfield came to Hooker's support, and lost his life on the field. Sedgwick's, Richardson's and French's divisions of Sumner's corps took their full share in the battle, and by the efficient aid of the artillery held their ground. Burnside, who was posted opposite the rebel right, was ordered to force the passage across Antietam Creek; but, although this was of the first importance to be done promptly and thoroughly, Burnside lost several hours in the effort, and thereby enabled Lee to press severely upon Sumner's corps on his left, and arrest our men in their onward course to victory. It was one o'clock before a passage was effected, and two hours passed before the attack on the crest was made. About three o'clock this was accomplished, and the rebel battery on the Sharpsburg ridge was captured. Just then A. P. Hill, with the portion of troops under his command, arrived from Harper's Ferry by way of Shepherdstown. Reinforcing Jones on the field with over 2,000 fresh troops, the offensive was resumed, and Burnside was compelled to retire to the cover of the hill bordering on Antietam Creek. As darkness was fast approaching the battle was now brought to a close for the day, both sides being thoroughly wearied, after having spent some fourteen hours in this bloody struggle. The losses are estimated by McClellan at 2,000 killed, 9,500 wounded, 1,000 missing = 12,500. He also supposed the rebel loss to be over 25,000; some of their writers say it was less than 10,000. The battle of Antietam or Sharpsburg may be pronounced to be, on the whole, a drawn battle, although the substantial fruits of victory remained on the Union side. Lee expected and awaited an attack the next day; but McClellan, conscious of his great loss in officers as well as men, and anxiously forecasting the fatal effect of a defeat just at this time at the hands of the rebels, after much deliberation did not judge it best to resume the fight. Lee accordingly, on the night of the 18th and morning of the 19th of September, crossed the Potomac and returned into Virginia.

The invasion of Maryland occupied only two weeks. It was unquestionably a failure, and it was accompanied not only by positive loss, but by exceeding mortification and shame at the coldness, indifference and hostility manifested by the people towards the secession "deliverers." Lee was glad to get back into Virginia, and to have the opportunity of gathering up the fragments of the large and imposing force of 70,000 men, with which he had set out from Richmond. Death, wounds, desertions, straggling, and such like, had told with fearful effect upon his army; and as McClellan was not ready, if able, to follow him up, but was engaged in refitting and re-organizing his own army, Lee took post in the Shenandoah Valley, near Winchester, to recruit and prepare for the further contest, when our army should again assume the offensive. Both generals, as is usual in such cases, issued congratulatory addresses, and claimed that they had gained the victory.

McClellan's plan now was to recruit and improve the army, render Harper's Ferry secure, and watch the movements of the enemy, so as to determine the course best to be pursued in the future. The president visited the Army of the Potomac, October 1st, and spent several days with McClellan in reviewing the troops, etc. On returning to Washington, he directed Halleck, October 6th, to send a peremptory telegram, as follows: "I am instructed to telegraph you as follows: The president directs that you cross the Potomac and give battle to the enemy, or drive him south. Your army must move now, while the roads are good. If you cross the river between the enemy and Washington, and cover the latter by your operation, you can be reinforced with 30,000 men. If you move up the Valley of the Shenandoah, not more than twelve or fifteen thousand can be sent you." McClellan chose the line of the Shenandoah, and called for supplies day after day, which, he says, he could not get as fast as they were needed. Who was to blame, is not very clear, but nearly a month passed away before these troublesome matters were arranged to the commanding general's satisfaction. Meanwhile, the rebel cavalry officer Stuart, (p. 296,) carried through a raid into Pennsylvania, not unlike his previous one on the Peninsula. He crossed the Potomac near Williamsport, October 10th, and having made the entire circuit of our army, he recrossed the Potomac below the mouth of the Monocacy. The special prize gained by Stuart, was some 800 to 1,000 horses, which were seized upon at and near Chambersburg. This daring raid stirred up afresh the public impatience of delay, and McClellan was urged, by both Halleck and President Lincoln, to bestir himself and attack the rebels. Accordingly, at the close of October, 1862, the army again entered Virginia by a pontoon bridge, about five miles below Harper's Ferry. Pleasanton took the lead with a body of cavalry, and was followed by the corps of Burnside. A sufficient garrison having been left at Harper's Ferry, Sedgwick and Hancock in the lower part of the Shenandoah Valley, about Charlestown, pressed the enemy, who now began their retreat towards Richmond. The Union forces occupied the passes of the Blue Ridge. Snicker's Gap was taken possession of by Hancock, on the 2d of November, while Pleasanton, with his cavalry, was driving the enemy beyond. The last corps of the army was over the Potomac on the 5th of November, and on the 6th, the advance was at Warrenton, McClellan holding his headquarters at Rectortown, on the Manassas Gap Railroad. The movement thus far despite the inclemency of the weather promised to be successful to a high degree; for, on reaching Warrenton, on the 9th of November, while Lee had sent half of his army forward to Culpepper to oppose McClellan's advance in that quarter, the other half was still west of the Blue Ridge, and at least two days' march distant. McClellan's plan, in this state of affairs, was to march across, obliquely westward, and get between the severed portions of the rebel force, and strike a decisive and fatal blow. It seems not unreasonable to suppose that, had he been permitted to carry out his plan, he would have gained an important victory; but this was not allowed. The directors of military affairs at Washington had no liking for McClellan, and they resolved to put him out of the way as speedily as possible. This was brought about at a critical moment. Late on the night of November 7th, a dispatch arrived, displacing McClellan and putting Burnside in command. The former, we may here state, left the army within a day or two, and took no further part in the great struggle of the nation to crush the rebellion. McClellan has been extravagantly lauded and equally extravagantly vilified and defamed. We have neither time nor space to enter into the merits of the case; time will probably enable the future historian to assign him his right position in our annals.

Burnside, who thought very highly of McClellan, reluctantly accepted the difficult task before him. He did not attempt to carry out McClellan's plan, which was, by a rapid advance on Gordonsville, to interpose between Lee's divided forces and beat them in detail. He preferred endeavoring to take his army to Richmond by way of Fredericksburg, on the Rappahannock; and made his arrangements accordingly. Instead of six corps, he now made three grand divisions, of two corps each, under Sumner, Hooker and Franklin. He called for a pontoon train from Washington sufficient to admit of crossing the river. Some unwise delay took place, and the new movement was not begun till the 15th of November by Sumner's division. He reached Falmouth on the 17th, and was not only able but desirous to cross and secure Fredericksburg and the bluffs on the south bank; but Burnside would not allow it. In two days more the other divisions reached the Rappahannock, and the rebel leaders having ascertained Burnside's purpose, rapidly moved his troops to meet him. What now was to be done? The demand for *action* was not to be put off. Lee had lost not a moment in constructing defences along the crest of hills in the rear of Fredericksburg, and by the beginning of December there was a formidable array of artillery on those terraced heights, which evidenced the terrible struggle in prospect for our men, should they attempt an assault. The crossing the river, too, was by no means the easy matter which it had been at the first, for the rebels were now prepared to contest it to much better advantage, and the pontoon train, owing to some unexplained blundering, did not arrive till the last moment. Nevertheless, a demonstration of some kind was imperative, and accordingly Burnside resolved to cross the Rappahannock directly. But just where, was a grave question. He must either force a direct passage at Fredericksburg, or make the attempt above or below. So he resolved to try the crossing at Skenker's Neck, twelve miles below Falmouth, and attack Lee's left; but Lee was too watchful to allow of that. He concentrated a large body of troops at that point, and so the plan of crossing there was abandoned. Burnside now hoping to surprise Lee, determined to make the passage at Fredericksburg. There was slender ground for any such hope; but Burnside nevertheless expected to pierce Lee's lines and rout his army. For this purpose he meant to secure and occupy a military road which the rebels had constructed in the rear of the line of heights on which they were posted behind Fredericksburg. With a movement on their flank and rear, a direct attack was to be made in front, and the main works carried by storm. Such was Burnside's plan, December 10th, and during the night active preparations were made to carry the design into effect. Under cover of the batteries on Stafford Heights, five pontoon bridges were to be thrown across the stream, which was about three hundred yards wide; three immediately in front of Fredericksburg, within a short distance of each other, and the others about two miles below. Considerable work was done during the night; but the sharpshooters of the rebels became exceedingly troublesome, so much so that Burnside bombarded Fredericksburg to drive them out. This plan did not succeed, and it was found necessary to send a party across in boats, who accomplished the end. The surprise part of the plan had of course failed; but Burnside got his army across on the evening of the 11th December and the next morning. It was a great risk to attack the rebels, under all the circumstances, for Lee's position behind a long stone wall, which his artillery enfiladed on both sides, was impregnable, and no troops could stand against the fire which mowed them down. Early on December 13th, Franklin's division attacked Lee's left; but he was not successful and met with heavy losses. Sumner was ordered to assault on the right, and his men gallantly obeyed, although it was a useless and horrible slaughter to no purpose. Burnside next ordered Hooker to advance. This officer, on reconnoitring the ground and looking into the state of affairs, considered the case hopeless, and begged Burnside to give up the attack; but the commanding general insisted on the attempt being make; and the attempt *was* made. But it was in vain; out of the column of 4,000 which dashed itself against this stone wall, almost half were left on this bloody field. Happily, night was fast coming on, and the desperate conflict necessarily closed. Burnside would have made another assault the next day; but on a united remonstrance of the officers, he gave it up; and in a dark and stormy night, December 15th, he re-crossed the Rappahannock. Our entire loss was reported to be 13,321; and as there were less than 50,000 under fire, it is plain that the destruction was terrible in the extreme. The *morale* of the army was very much lowered by this most unhappy failure, and Burnside, though he made another attempt to do something, was unsuccessful, and was superseded by Hooker.

In the South-west the rebels were active and very troublesome, and Union men, under Schofield, Curtis, McNeil, Blunt and others were fully occupied in the effort to rout and disperse the guerrillas and other malicious insurgents and vagabonds. The details of the numerous skirmishes and battles we need not go into; our space is too limited for the purpose. At the close of 1862 active operations were resumed against Vicksburg (p. 305). While Grant was with his army in Northern Mississippi, having his headquarters at Holly Springs, General Wm. T. Sherman, who was in command of the army corps on the Mississippi, collected a large number of transports at Memphis, with reference to a movement against Vicksburg. Having embarked his forces here and at Helena, in number, it was stated, some 40,000 men, Sherman entered the Yazoo, December 26th, and effected a landing a few miles above the mouth on the left bank, about six miles from Vicksburg. Above and below the city, from Haines's Bluff on the Yazoo to Warrenton on the Mississippi, there was a line of hills, which with the swamps and lagoons in front afforded the rebels an excellent means of defence. Sherman sent out reconnoitring parties, who speedily ascertained and reported that, owing to its advantage of position and the defences provided by the enemy, any attempt to take Vicksburg from this direction, that is, in the rear, would be attended with very great difficulty. At the outset, the fleet was hindered in its endeavors to ascend the Yazoo, by a formidable battery at Haines's Bluff, to silence which it would be necessary to make a fresh attack upon it from the river, preparatory to an advance of the army in front. The attack was made on December 27th and 28th; it was gallantly made and pushed with energy and zeal; but it was unsuccessful and Sherman gave up the attempt. As Grant was expected to coöperate, but was not able, Sherman withdrew, January 1st, 1863, and moved down to the mouth of the Yazoo. The loss was estimated at 2,000.

Rosecrans took command of the Army of the Cumberland after the second battle of Corinth, (p. 291,) and had charge of operations in Tennessee mainly, and parts of Alabama and Georgia. He entered vigorously upon his command October 27th. The troops were drilled, disciplined and rendered effective; equipments, arms, horses and stores of every kind were collected without delay; and steps were taken to restore the broken line of communication with Nashville as speedily as was practicable. Louisville being the real base of operations, distant 183 miles from Nashville, it was necessary, particularly in the low state of the Cumberland river, to re-open and repair the railroad between the two places. Rosecrans, November 1st, moved to Bowling Green, Kentucky, and on the 5th, began the advance by this route towards Nashville, which he reached on the 10th. The rebels now determined to drive out Rosecrans, and advanced at the end of November to Murfreesborough. They numbered about 45,000, under Bragg. The plan of advance by Rosecrans was well and carefully prepared, and every step was taken to insure success over the enemy at Murfreesborough. On the 27th of December, 1862, Nolinsville and the hills in front were taken possession of by McCook. The next day a further advance was made by McCook and the other commanders, and on the 29th, being near Murfreesborough, position was taken for the fight just at hand. At daylight, December 31st, the attack was begun by the rebels. The weather was foggy, and our troops appear to have been taken somewhat by surprise. The entire front was assaulted at once, the rebels rapidly advancing in double columns; and so determined and energetic was their fighting, that, in an hour's time they captured two batteries and compelled our troops to give way. Their object was to turn Rosecrans's right flank, but they did not succeed in this. The fight was desperate, and it was with the greatest difficulty that the rebel onset was stayed. The day's contest was closed after heavy loss in artillery and men, by some changes in position on the part of Rosecrans, his extreme left resting on Stone river. On the morning of January 1st, 1863, the points opposite the ford, on Crittenden's left, were occupied with a brigade. Nothing of moment occurred till the afternoon of January 2d, when the right wing of the rebels attacked our men across Stone River, who gave way before them. The enemy followed and came within range of Crittenden's artillery. The firing was terrific, and the havoc fearfully great. In forty minutes, it was computed that they lost 2,000 men. Of course, they retreated in confusion, and had it not been dark and stormy, Rosecrans would have pursued them into Murfreesborough. The next day was stormy and no movement took place, but our men were held in readiness for battle. On the 4th of January, it was ascertained that Bragg had retreated from Murfreesborough and taken position at Tullahoma, seventy-one miles from Nashville. Rosecrans stated his loss to be nearly 9,000, besides over 3,000 missing, out of 43,400, and estimated the rebel force to be 62,000, and their loss 14,000. Bragg, on the other hand, said that he had less than 35,000 in the field, and lost about 10,000, while he estimated Rosecrans's army at 70,000. The frequent, almost perpetual contradiction, on both sides, as to numbers engaged, losses, etc., is not only vexatious, but probably can never be settled with certainty. The battle of Murfreesborough was one of the most determined and equally sustained battles of the war, and one which will be forever memorable among the great conflicts of the struggle for the Union in the West. Although it fell short of a decisive victory, it was, nevertheless, a very serious blow to the rebels, and was justly and generally hailed as a triumph to the North, securing, as it did, possession of a vast and important frontier, menaced by an active and resolute foe. During the latter part of December, 1862, General Carter made a successful cavalry expedition into Tennessee. He crossed the mountains, destroyed railroad bridges, about one hundred miles of rails on the East Tennessee road, and then made his way back into Kentucky General J. G. Foster, in North Carolina, undertook a similar expedition, in order to cut the rebel lines of communication between Richmond and the South-west. This was also in December, and was entirely successful. But, not having force sufficient to hold the advantages gained, these expeditions, gallantly carried through though they were, were of no permanent benefit.

In a brief review of 1862, it is evident that, excepting in Virginia, the national arms had been attended by lasting and important success, Forts Henry and Donelson, Pea Ridge, Fort Pulaski, New Orleans, Memphis, etc., are proofs of what had been done toward breaking down the rebel organizations, and narrowing the area of the conflict. It is true, that the virtual failure of McClellan in the campaign against Richmond, the disasters on the Chickahominy, the bunglings and misfortunes of Pope, and the ill success of Burnside, had, in great measure, neutralized the effects of the brilliant victories in the South-west and elsewhere, and prevented our securing several important advantages in various quarters. One thing became evident, and the people of the loyal States felt and acknowledged it, and that was, the necessity of increasing and rendering more effective our armies in the field. There had been great loss of life, not only in battle, but also by wounds, sickness, and other vicissitudes of war, and the territory in which operations were to be carried on, and points permanently occupied, was so vast in extent, that it was deemed not only prudent but almost imperative to call for volunteers, and add largely to the immense force already under arms. Accordingly, in July, 1862, 300,000 volunteers were called for to serve for the war. Early in August, 300,000 more, to serve for nine months, were called for, and if by the 15th, any State should not have furnished its quota, the deficiency was to be made up by a special draft. From the nature of the case, drafting was thoroughly unpopular, and though the government was resolute as to carrying it out in case of necessity, yet, happily, by the aid of liberal bounties, and the short time of service just named, there was no need of proceeding to the extreme in this matter. Early in December, 1862, the secretary of war reported, under the calls of July and August, 420,000 new troops in the field, of whom 320,000 were volunteers for three years, or during the war. According to the best estimate which can now be made, the number of troops in the service of the United States, at the close of 1862, was nearly or quite 1,000,000.* The active efforts of treasonable and disaffected persons, and the violent and malicious assaults of a portion of the press, in order to thwart the plans of the government and aid and abet the rebellion, led to the continued exercise of that power which was claimed to belong to the executive in case of manifest necessity; we refer to the suspension of the writ of *habeas corpus*. During the early period of the great struggle for national life and integrity, arrests were made by orders issued from the secretary of state; but in February, 1862, the control of this whole matter was transferred to the war department. The government thenceforward acted with promptitude and vigor. A large number of persons, known or supposed to be in complicity with the rebels, were arrested and placed in confinement, but, after longer or shorter intervals, were released, upon taking the oath of allegiance to the United States. Of course, such action was sharply criticized; outcries were made against what was denounced as tyranny in its worst form; and in some, or more cases, individuals were harshly treated, and their rights unduly invaded. Political leaders in opposition to the government made the most of all this; "peace meetings" were held in various places; the administration was vigorouly assailed; efforts were made to prevent enlistments and hinder the putting down the rebellion by force of arms; and so powerful an influence was exerted upon the State elections, near the close of the year, that the government was, in several instances, seriously worsted. Nevertheless, the energetic action of the public authorities was so far effective and salutary, that on the 22d of November, an order was issued by the war department discharging from military restraint persons charged with interfering with the draft, etc., and persons arrested for disloyalty and hostility by the commanders in rebel States, on their giving their parole. The order, however, excepted all persons who had been in arms against the government, or resisted the draft by arms, etc. When Congress met, in December, 1862, this subject occupied a large share of their attention; it was warmly and fully discussed, and the result was, that an act of indemnity was passed in behalf of the president, and those under his orders, for whatever had been done, and power was conferred giving him full authority to suspend the writ of *habeas corpus* whenever, in his judgment, the public safety required it.

The avowed object of the government, as we have several times seen, was to put down rebellion and restore the authority of the Constitution. The extravagant and vile slanders of the rebel leaders and traitors, as to lust of conquest, exciting a slave insurrection, destruction of property, etc., naturally caused the government to do all in its power to allay apprehensions, and it was announced that, "in no way or manner did the government desire to interfere with the laws constitutional-

* The numbers of the rebel force cannot be given with any exactness; some writers say there were over 400,000 in the service; but by the rigid enforcement of the conscription act in the seceded States, compelling all persons between the ages of eighteen and forty-five to do military duty, the rebel leaders managed to get together arger armies, at the end of 1862, than at any previous period, and were consequently prepared to carry on the war in 1863. The process of conscription, however, was exhausting, and could ill bear repetition. It became odious to the people of the States in rebellion; it was evaded in every possible way; and it was denounced as not only a gross violation of the much-cherished State rights' doctrine, but also as the most outrageous of military despotisms.

ly established in the Southern States, or with their institutions of any kind whatever, their property of any sort, or their usages in any respect." This was the avowed policy of the administration, so far as there was any policy, at the outbreak of the rebellion, and mainly during the years 1861 and 1862. Fremont's and Hunter's movements, in regard to the position of the slaves, and what to do with them, were repudiated, and the more radical supporters of Lincoln complained of his backwardness and lukewarmness on this subject. They urged immediate and total excision of the cursed system; but Lincoln was not prepared for that as yet. On the 22d of July, a few days after the adjournment of Congress, an order was issued in regard to the general use of rebel property in the several military departments, directing that military commanders should seize any property necessary or convenient for supplies, in any of the insurgent States; that negroes should be employed and properly compensated as laborers; and that accounts should be kept and furnished to the government in regard to these various matters. The president's favorite policy, that of compensated emancipation and colonizing the negroes, was not generally acceptable. Yet, it was evident that this question of slavery, in the present crisis, must be settled in some definite, fixed manner. It began to be felt, by both Lincoln and the people, that *something positive* must be done, and done speedily and effectively. The rebels were making use of the slaves as tillers of the ground and laborers in military operations, so as greatly to increase their capability of resistance, and enable all the white population to serve in the rebel army. The president hence was compelled to take a bold and decided stand. Accordingly, on the 22d of September, he issued his emancipation proclamation, by which the slaves of all rebels and traitors were declared to be free. This proclamation was as vigorously denounced by some, as it was lauded by others. But after all that was or could be said against this change or development of the policy of the government, the great body of the people were disposed to acquiesce in the measure, *as a war measure,* and as a military act justified by a military necessity.

The Thirty-seventh Congress began its third session on the 1st day of December, 1862. The friends and supporters of the administration were largely in the majority, both in the Senate and in the House, and the national legislature entered upon its work with becoming zeal and diligence. The president's message was a document of great length, in which Lincoln gave a review of the general condition of affairs at home and abroad, and especially argued upon the question of compensated emancipation. The condition of the finances was commended to their "most diligent consideration;" attention was called to the reports of the secretaries of war and the navy, and various interesting statements were made respecting the post office department, the public lands, the Indian tribes, etc. Attempts were made to censure the government; but failed of course. On the 4th of December, 1862, Morrill, of Vermont offered the following resolution in the House: "*Resolved*, that at no time since the commencement of the existing rebellion, have the forces and materials in the hands of the executive department of the government been so ample and abundant, for the speedy and triumphant termination of the war, as at the present moment; and it is the duty of all loyal American citizens, regardless of minor differences of opinion, and especially the duty of every officer and soldier in the field, as well as the duty of every department of the government—the legislative branch included—as a unit, to cordially and unitedly strike down the assassins, at once and forever, who have conspired to destroy our Constitution, our nationality, and that prosperity and freedom of which we are justly proud at home and abroad, and which we stand pledged to perpetuate forever." This resolution indicated clearly the sentiment which prevailed in Congress, and in the loyal States generally; it was adopted by a vote of

105 to 1. The action of Congress was prompt and energetic on the several great questions which came before it. The enlisting negroes as soldiers, the enrolling and drafting the militia, the authorizing the president to issue to private armed vessels letters of marque, the admission of the State of Western Virginia, etc., were warmly debated during the session, and afforded abundant evidence of the spirit and determination of the majority in Congress, and the lengths to which they were ready to go in support of the policy of the government. The report of the secretary of the treasury, Mr. Chase, was an elaborate and carefully prepared document, setting forth the previous financial history of the war, and the policy by which it was proposed to regulate its burdens in the future. The expenditures of the year were in excess of previous estimates some $350,000,000; and the public debt, it was stated, would by the end of the next year, amount to $1,700,000,000. The secretary urged the organization of banking associations under a general act as proposed the previous year. The central idea of the scheme was "the establishment of one sound, uniform circulation, of equal value throughout the country, upon the foundation of national credit combined with private capital. Its advantages in absorbing the public securities, providing a home market, and giving steadiness to their value, were obvious, while the measure was free from the objections of government interference formerly urged against a national bank. The action of Congress on the subject of the finances of the country was prompt and important. On the 17th of January, 1863, there was authorized the issue of $100,000,000 in United States NOTES, for the immediate payment of the army and navy; such notes to be a part of the amount provided for in any bill that might be passed during the session. The amount just named, was included in the act passed at the close of the present Congress. During the month of February, the subject of providing a sound and reliable currency for the country came up, and was fully discussed, in both the House and the Senate. The result was, the passage of "An Act to provide a national currency, secured by a pledge of United States stocks, and to provide for the circulation and redemption thereof." The vote in the Senate was ayes, 23, noes, 21; in the House, ayes, 78, noes 64. By an act, approved March 3d, 1863, there was authorized a LOAN of $300,000,000 for the current fiscal year, and $600,000,000 for the next fiscal year, for which bonds were to be issued, running not less than ten nor more than forty years, principal and interest payable in coin, bearing interest at a rate not exceeding six per cent. per annum, payable on bonds not exceeding $100 annually, and on all others semi-annually. The secretary was also authorized to issue $400, 000,000 of six per cent. TREASURY NOTES not exceeding three years to run, to be a legal tender for their face value, excluding interest, and exchangeable for and redeemable by United States notes, for which purpose alone an issue of $150,000,000, of the latter was authorized; also, a further issue, if necessary, for the payment of the army and navy and other creditors of the government, of $150,000,000, in United States notes, including the $100,000,000 authorized in January; the whole amount of bonds, treasury notes, and United States notes issued under this act not to exceed the sum of $900,000,000; also, to issue $50,000,000, in FRACTIONAL CURRENCY, in lieu of postage or other stamps, exchangeable for United States notes, in sums not less than three dollars, and receivable for any dues to the United States less than five dollars, except duties on imports; also, to receive deposits of gold coin and bullion, and to issue certificates therefor; and to issue certificates representing coin in the treasury in payment of interest, which, with the certificates of deposits issued, were not to exceed 20 per cent. beyond the amount of coin and bullion in the treasuary. A tax was also imposed on the circulation of State banks of one per cent. half yearly.

Our foreign correspondence was ably con

ducted by Mr. Seward and our ministers abroad, and it was made plain to all that the United States would allow no foreign intermeddling in our affairs, and no infraction of our rights and immunities. The course pursued by the English government was of a kind to arouse deep feeling in the United States—a feeling of mingled indignation and contempt; of indignation at the positive wide-spread injuries inflicted upon our commerce by the piratical cruisers built and fitted out in English ports; and of contempt for a government professing friendliness and neutrality, and at the same time conniving at palpable violations of law in order to favor the cause of the rebellion. The privateers, Florida and Alabama, are instances in point. Early in the year 1862, our minister called the attention of Earl Russell to the fact that a steam gun-boat was being built at Liverpool for the purposes of the rebels. Disregarding his representations, the English government allowed the vessel to leave, ostensibly for Sicily, but in reality for Mobile, where she arrived in September, and under the command of Maffitt entered upon the work of depredation and virtual piracy. In June, 1862, Mr. Adams pointed out to Russell that, in the shipyard of a member of parliament, a large war steamer was getting built, without doubt for the rebel service. This vessel, known at first as the "290," and afterwards as the Alabama, notwithstanding the urgent protest of Adams and the furnishing on his part clear and positive evidence of the design and purpose of this vessel and her owners, was allowed to depart—the Queen's advocate got sick at a *mal-a-propos* moment—July 29th, without register or clearance. She took her departure with a party of ladies and gentlemen, on the pretext of a trial trip, dismissing her visitors and well wishers on getting out of the Mersey. The United States steamer, Tuscarora, at Southampton, was telegraphed to, to intercept the "290" at sea, a risk of capture which the rebel vessel avoided by taking the channel to the north of Ireland, while her pursuer lay in wait in St. George's channel. She then proceeded, undisturbed, to one of the Azores, where according to a previous arrangement, she awaited the arrival of a bark from the Thames laden with her stores and armament. Soon after having obtained, in this way, the stores and supplies, the British screw steamer Bahama made her appearance, bringing the notorious Semmes and the late officers of the Sumter, and an additional crew and armament. Being thus equipped, Semmes mustered the crew on deck and read his commission, together with the order from Jeff. Davis to take command of the sloop of war, which was now named the "Alabama." Thus, in defiance of law and of international obligation and comity, this piratical cruiser was launched upon her career of mischief and destruction. Before the close of the year 1862, twenty-eight vessels, mostly owned at New York and in New England, fell into the Alabama's hands, the greater part of which were burned to the water's edge. Plundering and burning marked her course, and though occasionally a vessel was allowed to depart on giving heavy bonds for the ship and cargo, yet the usual practice was robbery and destruction. It need excite no wonder that strong reprobation was expressed at the course of the English government in this matter. The authorities at home sent one vessel of war after another in fruitless search of the adroitly managed cruiser, while her successive depredations, and the advantages which she obtained as a recognized "belligerent," were brought before the British cabinet, and a distinct warning was given, that England would be held responsible for the damage which this vessel had inflicted, or might hereafter inflict, on American commerce.

An attempt was made late in the year 1862, by Louis Napoleon, to get England and Russia to join him in interfering in our affairs. These governments declined, and thereupon the French emperor, as he was called, had assurance enough, early in 1863, to venture upon offering himself to help us towards settling matters with the rebels.

This offer was promptly and decisively declined; and, in an able dispatch from Secretary Seward, under date of February 6th, 1863, the ground taken and held by the United States government was set forth in language which could not be misunderstood: "This government has not the least thought of relinquishing the trust which has been confided to it by the nation under the most solemn of all political sanctions; and if it had any such thought, it would still have abundant reason to know, that peace proposed at the cost of dissolution would be immediately, unreservedly, and indignantly rejected by the American people." The effect of this dispatch was very marked, and it put an end to all further talk or offer of foreign intervention in any shape, or from any quarter. No nation was willing to incur the risk of war with the Great Republic by undertaking to recognize the rebellion. Such, in substance, was the condition of affairs at the close of 1862. There was much to hope for, and also not a little to apprehend. The people generally had made up their minds that the rebellion must and should be crushed, no matter what sacrifice might be demanded; and though discouragements of various kinds stood in the way, though a speedy return of peace was to be hoped and prayed for, rather than expected; yet there was no shrinking from the contest, there was no hesitation as to where the path of duty lay, and as to the responsibilities resting on Americans in this great crisis in our national life. The heart of the loyal people was sound and unshaken in the hour of trial.

The position of the leaders and people in rebeldom was anything but agreeable. The Masons, Slidells, Yanceys, etc., had failed utterly in obtaining recognition abroad, or any promise looking in that direction; the blockade, though not perfect, was maintained with a vigor and effectiveness which told in a marked manner upon the condition of affairs; cotton was found to be no longer the "king" which it was supposed to be, and the rebels destroyed it to a large extent, rather than suffer it to fall into Union hands; the measure adopted by the government for emancipating the slaves was tremendously severe in its effects upon the rebel States; their finances were almost hopelessly involved, and were fast approaching insolvency and bankruptcy; the conscript acts were exhausting all their strength; the Union armies were gradually and surely hemming the rebels in, always retaining important positions when once gained; and though Jeff. Davis begged and pleaded for further devotion, and for men to hasten forward, in order to keep possession of Vicksburg and Port Hudson on the Mississippi; though Stephens cried out lustily, "Never give it up!" though he exclaimed energetically, "Let the world know, and history record the fact, that we can never be conquered;" still it was evident that matters were in rather a bad way for the rebels, and that the loyal States were firmly, unalterably resolved never to allow the integrity of the nation to be broken or destroyed. The rebel congress met early in January, 1863, on which occasion Davis delivered a long and rather violent message, filled with matter adapted to the condition of affairs in the States over which he was exercising unlawful rule. He made bitter complaint against various European powers, who had recognized the blockade, and had done nothing for the benefit of the privateering interests of the rebellion. But, in his judgment, "the proudly self-reliant Confederacy," superior, as he claimed, in all respects, to its enemies, had no need to regret the lack of outside help. He branded McNeil, Milroy and Butler as guilty "of every conceivable atrocity, and as stamped with indelible infamy;" and spoke of Lincoln's emancipation proclamation with especial virulence and vindictiveness. Retaliatory measures were resolved upon; our officers and troops were to be punished who might aid in "overthrowing the institution of African slavery and bringing on a servile war" in the rebel States; a tax bill was passed, very heavy in its pressure; an impressment bill, also, etc

The condition and strength of the United States navy, at the opening of the year, was substantially as follows:—there were, as reported by the secretary of the navy, 427 vessels, carrying 3,268 guns—an increase during the year of 123 vessels, carrying 711 guns. Of these, 104, with 1,415 guns, were sailing vessels, and 323, with 1,853 guns were steam vessels. In the latter were included fifty-four iron-clad vessels of various constructions, of which twenty-eight were on the seaboard and twenty-six on the Western waters. In regard to naval operations at the beginning of 1863, we may briefly note here the capture of the Harriet Lane and the fate of the steamer Hatteras. Galveston, in Texas, had been held by Commander Renshaw, since October, 1862, by a small naval and military force at his command, consisting of the Harriet Lane and four other steamers, and less than 300, rank and file, occupying a wharf in the town. At the beginning of January, the rebels under Magruder, made an attack by land and water, in large force. The Harriet Lane was captured, and Renshaw, by a premature explosion of the vessel he was in, lost his life; a number of men were also lost; and the blockade was given up. Soon after this disaster, the privateer Alabama met the United States steamer Hatteras off the harbor, and pouring in a broadside, set her on fire and compelled a surrender. The Hatteras sunk almost immediately after the officers and crew were removed.

Burnside, as we have seen (p. 310), was superseded by "Fighting Joe Hooker," as he was commonly called in the army. On taking command, he issued a short address, and introduced various improvements. The system of grand divisions was done away with, and the army was divided into seven corps. The first corps was commanded by Reynolds; the second by Couch; the third by Sickles; the fifth by Meade; the sixth by Sedgwick; the eleventh by Howard; and the twelfth by Slocum. The cavalry was consolidated into a single corps, and was placed under command of Stoneman. Other judicious reforms were also carried into effect. Desertion and its causes were stopped; distinctive badges were given to the different corps; a system of furloughs was instituted; and as Hooker, despite his extra self-sufficiency, was highly popular with the troops, and an able administrative officer, important results were confidently looked for under his guidance. The army numbered, according to good authority, 125,000 (infantry and artillery), 12,000 cavalry, and an artillery force of about 400 guns. The rebel general was strongly entrenched on the heights south of the Rappahannock, from Skenker's Creek to U. S. Ford, a distance of about twenty-five miles, and had his troops so arranged that he could readily concentrate them on any given point. In this position Lee had only two main lines of retreat, one towards Richmond, by railroad, and the other towards Gordonsville. It was a matter of importance, therefore, for Hooker to make a movement of such a kind as to compel Lee to come out of his fortifications and fight, or to fall back to Richmond. To assist in this movement, Stoneman, with a large cavalry force, was to hasten forward, some time in advance of the army movement, and cut the railroad communications of the enemy at important points in their roads. As a direct attack on Fredericksburg was every way inexpedient, especially after former experiences, Hooker adopted a bold plan of operation against Lee's left, and on the morning of April 27th, began the carrying of it out. A strong, well-appointed column, consisting of the 5th, 11th, and 12th corps, set out for Kelly's Ford, some twenty-seven miles above Fredericksburg, intending by this wide detour to cross the Rappahannock and the Rapidan, and pass around Lee's flank to Chancellorsville. Marching on Monday, this force reached the neighborhood of Kelly's Ford on Tuesday, April 28th, and during the night and next morning, crossed at Kelly's Ford, on pontoon bridges. Early on Wednesday morning, an advance was made to Germania Ford, on the Rapidan—twelve miles distant—by the 11th and 12th corps, and to Ely's Ford, on the same stream, by the 5th corps. Celerity of movement being the chief desideratum, it was resolved immediately to put the troops over the Rapidan. Accordingly the men plunged in, many of them stripping and carrying their clothes and cartridge-boxes on their bayonets, and waded over, up to their armpits. Durring the night huge bonfires were kindled, and the remainder of the troops were passed over by the next morning. While this was going on at Germania Ford, Meade's troops were crossing at Ely's Ford. Both columns now moved, as ordered, for Chancellorsville, at the junction of the Gordonsville turnpike with the Culpepper and Orange Court House plank road, Pleasanton's cavalry keeping up the communication and protecting the right flank from the rebel cavalry attacks. This manœuvre having uncovered United States Ford, Couch's corps, which had, for three days, been lying at that point, was passed over the Rappahannock by a pontoon bridge, on Thursday, without any opposition. This force also converged toward Chancellorsville, and on Thursday night four army corps, namely, Howard's, Stevens', Meade's and Couch's, were massed at this point. That same night Hooker reached Chancellorsville, and established his headquarters at a large brick house, formerly an inn, which, in fact, constituted the entire place. The position thus secured was important, as taking in reverse Lee's entire fortified line, and by its being in direct communication with Fredericksburg by a plank road, and with Orange Court House and Gordonsville by a road through the Wilderness—a desolate region, of tangled woods—in its vicinity. The remaining corps, meanwhile, had rendered essential aid in making the flank march just noted. A feint was made of attacking Fredericksburg, on the 29th of April, after which the 3d corps joined Hooker, and Sedgwick's remained below for further orders. The success of Hocker thus far rendered him quite jubilant. On the 30th, he announced to the army that the rebels must flee, or come out and fight with the certainty of being destroyed. Lee, however, did not run away, but prepared at once to advance and give battle. On the 30th of April, at midnight, he put his troops in motion towards Chancellorsville, and, in some unexplained way, was allowed by Hooker to advance so far without opposition, as to prevent our seizing the direct communications with Richmond. Hooker, it seems, did not originally intend to remain in the tangled thicket of the Wilderness, an exceedingly bad place for the movements of a large army. The next day several columns were pushed forward to gain the open country beyond; these advance movements were quite successful and it seems plain that they should have been secured and held; but Hooker thought otherwise. He ordered the columns to fall back to Chancellorsville, and instead of marching up with his whole force, and taking the initiative in delivering battle, he strangely threw away precious advantages, and despite the remonstrances of his officers, he determined to remain on the defensive at Chancellorsville. It is difficult to account for Hooker's sudden lack of nerve and generalship at this point, since he had thus far displayed vigor and talent of a high order. On the 1st and 2d of May, Lee made various demonstrations against Hooker's front; but he had no purpose of fighting just then. He was only gaining time to allow Jackson to carry out a very bold plan of assailing Hooker's right and rear by a flank march. Taking with him about 22,000 men, Jackson set out, on the morning of May 2d, on his expedition, and worked his way with great diligence through the thickets by a path some two miles south of and parallel to the Orange plank road, where Hooker's troops were planted. Late in the afternoon, in spite of all difficulties, he reached the position aimed at for the terrible and crushing blow which he was about to inflict on Hooker's flank. From some observations which had been made of the movements of the rebel troops, it was thought that they were retreating, so Hooker expected to capture them or drive them in confusion. At 5,o'clock, P. M., however, Jackson had gained the position where he could deal the deadly blow for which he had been seeking the opportunity at so great risk. A terrific crash of musketry on Hooker's extreme right announced that the rebel general had begun his destructive operations. The preparation to meet this onslaught was very imperfect. It was supposed that Howard's corps would be able to resist the onslaught; but in vain. Between five and six P.M., Jackson burst forth with resistless impetuosity on the unprepared 11th corps. Panic stricken, taken wholly by surprise, the troops rushed forward, a disorganized mass, without arms, and anxious only to escape the rebel assault. Entreaties, threats, orders of commanders, were of no avail; they fled down the road towards headquarters, and overran the next division to the left, which was compelled to give way before the enemy even reached its position. Some resistance was made on the extreme left of the 11th corps, but in a short time the whole was in utter rout. It was now seven o'clock, and darkness was fast approaching; but Jackson had seized the breastworks, and had pushed forward within half a mile of headquarters. It was a critical moment; a new line had been formed; and as Lee was pressing his attack on Hooker's left and centre, it was the work of difficulty and danger to provide for this point. Happily, however, Pleasanton's cavalry came up at this moment, and by their noble efforts, aided by other troops, the rebel advance was checked. It was about this time, in the darkness, that Jackson was shot, singularly enough by rebel bullets. It appears, that in his eagerness, he had pressed forward beyond his own lines, and on returning was mistaken for an enemy, and fired upon, with fatal effect. His death, a few days after, removed out of the way one of the most ardent and most dangerous of the rebels.

From the position of affairs on Saturday night, May 2d, it was evident that a change of line was necessary, by which the enemy should be driven from the rear, and brought into front again. By diligent effort, during the night, this was in great measure accomplished. The new line now assumed the shape of a triangle, prolonged at the apex, the right of the line being being somewhat longer than the left. The rebels, who had been reinforcing all night, purposed to fight for the possession of the plank road, which it was necessary they should have in order to escape assaults in front and flank. At daylight, Sunday morning, May 3d, the rebels seized the crest which the day before had been occupied by the 11th corps, got 30 pieces of artillery into position thereon, and opened a heavy fire on the plain round Chancellor House. The battle soon became fierce and determined on both sides. The rebel charge was fast and furious; the steadiness and spirit of our men bravely sustained the assault; but still after a severe struggle, our troops were pressed back. Lee, meanwhile, attacked the centre and left, but he was gallantly met by our men. An order was given to fall back to Chancellor House, which was done; and for an hour or more the battle raged at the angle of the roads. Our line, however, soon began to waver; Hooker abandoned his headquarters, now on fire, and retired to a new line, about a mile nearer to the river and covering the fords. The rebels made a dash, and between ten and eleven o'clock gained possession of Chancellorsville. The position taken by Hooker was a strong one, the right flank resting on the Rapidan and the left on the Rappahannock. The corps of Meade and Reynolds were formed on the new lines, together with the troops just noted as falling back. Lee was preparing to assault with his entire force, when news from Fredericksburg compelled a pause. Sedgwick, it will be remembered, had been left some three miles below Fredericksburg to await developments of the main army at Chancellorsville. The serious injury inflicted on Hooker by Jackson's bold movement, induced the former to send orders to Sedgwick to occupy Fredericksburg, seize the heights, gain the plank road towards Chancellorsville, and move out to join Hooker, destroying any force he might meet, and reaching his assigned position by daylight, on Sunday morning. This was a movement which, if successfully carried out, was of great importance, but which also involved serious risk. Sedgwick received the order at eleven o'clock on Saturday night, and immediately set about its execution. Some hours before daylight, after sharp skirmishing, he occupied the town, and soon after, Gibbon's division crossed from Falmouth to join him. Sedgwick concluded, under all the circumstances, to carry, by assault, the heights immediately in the rear of the town, including Marye's Hill and the stone wall at its base, where our troops had suffered so severely during Burnside's campaign. Much time had already been consumed; the forenoon was fast passing, when the deadly struggle began for driving the rebels out of their position; but it was executed with a gallantry unsurpassed at any time. The rebels fled, and the road was left open for the advance, which Sedgwick immediately began. Lee, apprized of the danger from this source, sent promptly troops to assail Sedgwick, which they did, when he was about half way between Fredericksburg and Chancellorsville. A sharp encounter took place at Salem Heights, between four and five o'clock in the afternoon, and Sedgwick was unable to do more than hold his own, and hardly that, for his losses were very heavy (probably quite 5,000) and the enemy were attacking him from several different points. This was on Sunday night. The next morning, the rebels, reinforced, rushed furiously upon Sedgwick. His men resisted stubbornly, but were forced to yield ground, and under cover of the night crossed the river on a pontoon bridge. It was Lee's determination to attack Hooker, the next morning, May 6th; but during the night preceding Hooker ordered the army across the Rappahannock, and thus left the rebels masters of the field.* The losses, on our side, were very heavy, being over 17,000 in killed, wounded, and missing. The rebel loss was estimated to be about 10,000. It may be stated here that Stoneman's raid (p. 318), upon the enemy's railroad communications, though brilliant and daring, was of no material moment in a military point of view, or towards helping Hooker out of his difficulties. The army now resumed its old quarters at Falmouth, with a prospect, at no distant date, of being called upon to assume offensive operations against the foe.

On the 20th of January, 1863, General Hunter resumed command, at Port Royal, of the department of the South. Vigorous preparations were entered upon, while the monitors and iron-clads, from which much was expected in regard to conflicts with the rebels, were being completed at the North. The Passaic, with the Montauk, and the formidable battery, the New Ironsides, made their appearance at Port Royal about the middle of January. Active operations were now promised, and speedy employment in the field. General Saxton, who had been sent by the secretary of war, in June, 1862, to give attention to the abandoned plantations, and the people, especially the negroes, in the department of the South, and who was to report directly, once a week at least, to the war department, announced, about this date, the complete organization of the first (negro) regiment of South Carolina volunteers, Colonel Higginson being in command. He also expressed a very high opinion of the merit of these negro recruits. Admiral Dupont, in command of the South Atlantic squadron, for the purpose of testing the iron-clads re-

* A military critic, speaking of this badly managed affair, says: "Not the Army of the Potomac was beaten at Chancellorsville, but its commander; and Gen. Hooker's conduct inflicted a very severe blow to his reputation. The officers despised his generalship, and the rank and file were puzzled at the result of a battle in which they had been foiled without being fought, and caused to retreat without the consciousness of having been beaten."

cently arrived at Port Royal, ordered the Montauk, Commander Worden, to the Ogeechee River, opening into the Ossabaw Sound, on the Georgia coast, and through which there was an approach to within ten miles of Savannah. The privateer Nashville, which had made a number of successful trips as a blockade runner between Charleston, Wilmington and Nassau, had, in July, 1862, taken refuge in the Ogeechee, and was compelled by our fleet to remain there. To destroy Fort McAllister and capture the Nashville was the object proposed for the navy. Worden began the attack on the fort, January 27th; but though the firing on both sides was steady and constant, no result was attained. Another attempt was made February 1st, at closer quarters, *i. e.* within about 1,000 yards; but with no better success. The principal result was the testing the powers of endurance of the iron-clads and monitor class of vessels. The Nashville, we may here mention, continued concealed and protected behind Fort McAllister through the month of February to the 27th, when, at evening, she was observed in motion above the battery by Worden. He immediately moved up the river to within 1,200 yards of the Nashville, which, having grounded, was soon set on fire by Worden's fire and blown up. At the close of January, 1863, a bold movement was undertaken by the rebel vessels at Charleston. An iron-clad steamer, Princess Royal, attempted to run the blockade, but her career was arrested. She was run ashore and abandoned, and was at once taken possession of by the Unadilla. This proved to be a very valuable prize, having engines for iron-clads, rifled guns, ammunition, and stores of all kinds on board. Two days later she was taken to Port Royal, and subsequently sent to Philadelphia for adjudication. Chagrined at this loss, the rebels determined to make a bold dash, and not only to recover possession of the Princess Royal, but also to attack the blockading squadron. Accordingly, about 4 o'clock in the morning of January 31st, during the obscurity of a thick haze, two iron-clad steam rams came out of Charleston by the main ship channel, unnoticed by the squadron, and commenced an assault upon the blockading fleet, which, just at this time, was mostly composed of the light class of purchased vessels. The first onset was made upon the steamer Mercedita, formerly a merchant vessel, by the ram commanded by Ingraham, formerly of the United States service. Almost immediately the Mercedita was rendered helpless, and gave up the contest. The other ram attacked the Keystone State, at the same time, which was served much as the Mercedita had been. The other vessels on the station kept out of the way, and Ingraham and the rams retired into the Swash Channel behind the Shoals. But no real advantage was gained by all this. It is true, the rebels thought that something ought to be made by them, and so they issued a proclamation, announcing to the world, that the blockade was broken up by their superior force, and Charleston was now open and free. But this was mere braggadocio, and Dupont speedily set forth the real state of the case.

During the month of March the preliminary preparations for the attack on Charleston having been completed, the vessels of the fleet and transports were forwarded to the place of rendezvous on North Edisto River. As it was important for crossing the bar with the iron-clads, to secure the advantage of the high spring tides at the beginning of April, Dupont watched carefully the opportune moment. On the 5th of April, 1863, after several days of high wind, the sea being very smooth and the tides favorable, the fleet left its anchorage, and early in the forenoon arrived at the blockading station off Charleston harbor. Here, Commander Boutelle, of the Coast Survey, assisted in sounding and marking out the channel. These and other matters occupied the day. Early on the following morning, the 6th, the iron-clad fleet crossed the bar and was ranged opposite Morris Island, at the southern entrance of the harbor, within a mile of the shore; but that day was lost for active operations by a thick haze which prevented any observations of the shore. At noon, on the 7th of April, signal was given by the Admiral from his flag ship, the New Ironsides, for the vessels to weigh anchor, nine in number, at about a cable's length apart. The preparations made by Beauregard and his fellow laborers for the defence of Charleston were of the most extensive and formidable character. Beginning with the northern or eastern entrance by way of Maffit's Channel, there were, on Sullivan's Island, beside Fort Moultrie, two large and powerful sand batteries guarding the channel; there was Fort Sumter, built on an artificial island in the middle of the channel near the entrance of the inner harbor, a mile and a half west of Fort Moultrie, and strengthened to the very highest degree; there was Battery Bee, Mount Pleasant battery on the main land, and Castle Pinckney built on an island, about a mile from the city—all on the northerly side of the harbor. On the other side of the harbor were Wappoo battery, on James Island, near Charleston, and Fort Johnson; between this latter and Castle Pinckney was Fort Ripley, built on an artificial island in what is called the "middle ground." On Cumming's Point, Morris Islet, opposite Fort Moultrie, was Battery Gregg, and a mile south of this Fort Wagner, and a fort at Light House Island covering the landing at that place. Several hundred guns were mounted on these numerous works; and in addition, the channel between Fort Sumter and Sullivan's Island was obstructed by rows of floating casks, supporting torpedoes and other submarine obstacles. Early in the afternoon the several vessels took their assigned place in the line of battle, and special efforts were made against Fort Sumter—eight iron-clads taking up position opposite the eastern and north-eastern front, at distances of from 550 to 800 yards. Of course, the rebels were not idle or inactive in the meanwhile; on the contrary, they poured forth from their vast batteries both shells and shot in immense profusion, and with a rapidity almost beyond conception. It was of course impossible to endure long the rebel hurricane of fire. The Keokuk received her death blow within half an hour; she was struck ninety times, and had nineteen holes above and below the water line, and got away just in time to sink out of sight by evening. Others of the iron-clads began to show signs of disablement, and it became evident that the contest was too unequal to render it expedient to continue it; Dupont, therefore, about five o'clock, gave the signal to withdraw from action, intending to resume the attack next morning. On ascertaining, however, the injuries received by the several vessels, and estimating his force as quite unable to overcome the obstructions in the harbor and silence the vast works on every hand, the admiral expressed his conviction that it was utterly impracticable to take the city of Charleston, as matters now stood. The entire fleet had been able to fire only 139 shots against Sumter, with comparatively small injury to the fort; while the rebels had hurled against the iron-clads thousands of shells, shots and steel-pointed bolts, and had inflicted upon them serious damage. Dupont ordered the vessels to Port Royal for repairs, except the New Ironsides, which anchored outside Charleston bar. The casualties were very few, considering the fierceness of the rebel fire; one man died of injuries, and about 25 were wounded. Hunter and his men at Stono Inlet were waiting for an opportunity of joining in the attack; but the lack of success on the part of the fleet prevented their doing so. As to further operations against Charleston, it was thought necessary to occupy Morris Island in order to attain success. Hence Gillmore, eminent for engineering skill and ability, was sent in June to supersede Hunter.

General Banks, as has been already noted, took the place of Butler at New Orleans. This able officer was engaged in the autumn of 1862 in fitting out an expedition in the North, the destination of which was kept as secret as possible, but was supposed to be intended for the South, and especially for the benefit of Texas. Having made all his arrangements, Banks sailed from New York at the beginning of December, 1862, with some fifty vessels and about 10,000 men, and on the 16th of the same month, at New Orleans, formally assumed command of the department of the gulf. His opening proclamation was judicious, conciliatory, and to the point; and his address to the people of Louisiana, a week later, in regard to the state of things now under the Emancipation Proclamation, was marked by good sense and a just view of the rights and privileges of all concerned. In the early part of March, 1863, Banks concentrated his force at Baton Rouge, in number about 25,000 men. Twenty miles above, the rebels were strongly entrenched at Port Hudson, the most important position held by them on the Mississippi below Vicksburg. Situated on an elevated, almost perpendicular cliff, at a contracted bend of the stream, where the narrowed current ran with great violence, its formidable line of batteries threatened destruction to any hostile fleet, while on the land side the approach, easily capable of defence, was beset by swamps and other apparently invincible obstacles. The first movement of importance in this quarter was made by the navy, in aid of the operations of Grant and Porter against Vicksburg. At the beginning of February, 1863, Ellett led the way in the Queen of the West in the passage of the batteries at that place, the design being to interrupt the enemy's supplies from the west of the Mississippi. After inflicting much damage in this way, the vessel was lost by the treachery of a pilot, while ascending Red River. On receiving the news of this misfortune, Farragut determined to run past the rebel batteries at Port Hudson, and assist the operations of Porter on the river from above. The land forces of Banks were at the same time to threaten Port Hudson on the rear, and as far as possible divert their attention from Farragut's movements. This daring attempt on the part of Farragut, was made in the night of Saturday, March 14th. At nine and a half o'clock, P. M., he led the way at the head of his fleet on the flag-ship Hartford, accompanied by the gunboat Albatross, made fast to her port side. The other gun-boats followed, and six mortar vessels were brought up to shell the works. But, as it turned out, the admiral's was the only vessel that succeeded in passing. The others were too much injured, and one, having grounded, was destroyed by the rebel fire. Banks, meanwhile, had led his troops in three divisions to within about five miles of Port Hudson. There was some skirmishing with the rebel pickets, but no important advance beyond, and the next day the troops returned to Baton Rouge. Banks's attention was now turned to that part of Louisiana west of New Orleans, and bordering on the Teche River. Since the successful expedition of Weitzel in January, the rebels in that quarter had erected new fortifications and concentrated their forces, aided by a fleet of gun-boats, at several stations on the Teche River, with the intention, it was supposed, of threatening New Orleans. Banks, suspending operations for the time against Port Hudson, advanced with his forces to Berwick, where he arrived on the 11th of April, and commenced a series of active movements, which speedily swept the enemy from their strongholds throughout this central region from the Gulf to the Red River. Without dwelling upon details, we may mention that Banks, on the 8th of May, had advanced to and occupied Alexandria on the Red River, immediately after its capture by the naval force of Porter in one of his excursions from before Vicksburg. The co-operation of the two armies below and above Port Hudson was thus secured by an interior line of communication, while, what was of the utmost consequence, the rebel supplies from the west of the Mississippi were effectually cut off. In view of these various operations, under such men as Farragut, Porter, Grant and Banks, the fall of the rebel stronghold at Vicksburg and Port Hudson was looked for confidently at an early day.

Banks now moved down the Red River,

and crossing the Mississippi, he landed with a portion of his army, on the 21st of May, at Bayou Sara, a few miles above Port Hudson. On the 23d, a junction was effected with the advance of Gens. Augur and T. W. Sherman, who had brought up their forces from Baton Rouge. The Union line now occupied the Bayou Sara road at a distance of five miles from Port Hudson. Augur had an engagement with a portion of the enemy at Port Hudson Plains, on the Bayou Sara road, in the direction of Baton Rouge, which resulted in repulsing the rebels with heavy loss. On the 25th of May, the enemy was compelled to abandon his first line of works. Two days later, a general assault was made, which was kept up during the day. The rebels were driven into their works, and our troops moved up to the fortifications, holding the opposite sides of the parapet, with the enemy on the right. The great strength of Port Hudson rendered a regular investment necessary. The garrison was completely cut off from supplies, and would be ultimately starved out, if not compelled to surrender by assault. Banks, on the 14th of June, made a proposal to the rebel commander to submit to necessity and spare useless slaughter; but he refused. Several unsuccessful assaults were made by our troops, which did not, however, prevent the pushing forward the siege. A storming party was called for and rapidly filled up; but, happily, their services were not required. The rebel general Gardner, having learned that Vicksburg had fallen, on the 4th of July, felt that he too could and ought to follow such an example. Accordingly, on the 8th of July, Port Hudson was unconditionally surrendered into the hands of Banks. The surrender included 6,233 prisoners, 51 pieces of artillery, 2 steamers, 4,400 pounds of cannon powder, 5,000 small arms, and 150,000 rounds of ammunition. It was a heavy blow to the rebels and their cause, while on the other hand, loyal men rejoiced in the apparently approaching downfall of the "Confederacy."

Early in January of this year, 1863, an attack on Arkansas Post was resolved upon by Porter in conjunction with the troops under McClernard. Three iron-clads, under Porter's personal direction, with all the light draft gun-boats of the fleet, moved up the White River, about fifteen miles, when, turning to the left, they passed through a cut-off, eight miles long, into the Arkansas River. Toward the close of the afternoon, preparations were made to land about three miles below Arkansas Post, which is about fifty miles from the mouth of the river. This was accomplished during the evening and part of the next day, and the troops advanced by divisions, so as to invest the fort and be ready to join the attack on the morning of the 11th of January. Fort Hindman, against which they were marching, was a rather formidable work, being a regular square bastioned fort, the sides 300 feet in length, with casemates, and surrounded by a wide and deep ditch; it mounted twelve guns, including three Columbiads and four Parrotts, with outer defences; and there were in it about 5,000 men. Situated at a sharp bend of the river, it effectually controlled the passage of the Arkansas, protected Little Rock, the capital of the State, about 100 miles above, and sheltered the Post, where it was built, and the surrounding fertile country. On the afternoon and evening of January 10th, the attack was pressed with so much vigor and success, that, in three hours time the rebels gave up, and surrendered. Over 5,000 prisoners were taken, besides twenty pieces of cannon, ammunition, stores, etc. They were also effectually cut off from a position where they could do mischief. McClernard and his forces, and the gun-boats proceeded to join Grant at Cairo, where he had gathered his troops and was preparing in conjunction with Porter to carry out his plan for the reduction of Vicksburg.

The great strength of the defences of Vicksburg on the north, and the inutility of attempting an attack again in that direction, led Grant to the conviction that his approaches must be made from the southerly side. For this purpose, he must get his army below the city of Vicksburg a task by no means easy of accomplishment, since the vast rebel batteries would almost certainly destroy all the transports which might undertake to sail past them. In this position of affairs, work was recommenced upon the canal across the peninsula on the western side of the river; but as before, the project proved a failure, and early in March, a rapid rise in the river swept away the dam and flooded the entire vicinity. Other undertakings of a similar kind were entered upon by way of the Teusas River, Moon Lake, and Yazoo Pass; but after a great deal of toil, they were found impracticable. Porter sent an expedition through Steele's and Black's Bayou, so as to reach Haines' Bluff by Deer Creek; but this effort also proved unsuccessful. All attempts against Vicksburg from the northerly side were henceforth abandoned as inexpedient, and Grant resolved, with Porter's aid, to get his troops below the city, and make his attack from the lower or rear side, which, it is well understood, was the most easily assailable, and promised the best results. Accordingly, on the 29th of March, McClernand, with the 13th army corps, moved from Milliken's Bend toward New Carthage, about thirty-five miles below on the Mississippi. Other corps were to follow as rapidly as supplies and ammunition could be transported to them. The progress was very slow and tedious, in consequence of the bad state of the roads, the breaking of the levee at Bayou Vidal, etc., and some weeks were spent in this necessary but fatiguing work. While this movement of the army was going on, preparations were made for running transports and gun-boats past the Vicksburg batteries, these being requisite in order to give the soldiers means of crossing for operations on the Mississippi side of the river. Eight gun-boats were selected for the service, all iron-clads except one, and all furnished with such protection as could be afforded by bales of cotton and of hay, heavy timbers, etc. Three transport vessels were also added to the list. The expedition set out on its dangerous journey on the night of April 16th, and was entirely successful, except that one of the transports was burned and another injured. On the 22d of April, by Grant's orders, six additional transport steamers, with officers and crew chosen from the regiments in the vicinity, conducting as many coal barges, were sent in like manner past Vicksburg. They suffered more or less injury; but all, with one exception, got below the batteries. Two tugs with four hay barges, also, a few nights after, followed in safety. At the end of April, the army was fairly on its way from Milliken's Bend overland and past Richmond, by a military road constructed over swamps and bayous for about seventy miles to Hard Times, Louisiana, a point opposite Grand Gulf. On the 29th of April, the 13th army corps reached the Mississippi, and the 17th was not far behind. Grant embarked a portion of the troops, and moved to the front of Grand Gulf. The plan was, that the iron-clads should silence the guns of the enemy, and that the troops should land under cover of the gun-boats and carry the place by storm. The attack was begun about eight o'clock in the morning and continued during most of the day. Late in the afternoon, all the transports passed in safety. At daylight, the next morning, the troops were ferried over the river and Grant marched on Fort Gibson, twenty-eight miles from the mouth of Bayou Pierre, and between sixty and seventy south-west of Jackson, capital of the State. "We landed," says Grant in his dispatch, "at Bruinsburg, April 30th, moved immediately on Port Gibson, met the enemy, 11,000 strong four miles south of Port Gibson, at two A. M. on May 1st, and engaged him all day, entirely routing him with the loss of many killed, and about 500 prisoners, besides the wounded. Our loss was about 100 killed and 500 wounded. The enemy retreated toward Vicksburg, destroying the bridges over the two forks of the Bayou Pierre. These were rebuilt, and the pursuit has continued until the present time." Col. Grierson's great cavalry raid through the entire length of the Mississippi deserves honorable mention here. He passed between the great lines of communication, in the rear of the works at Vicksburg and Port Hudson, and came out triumphantly, May 1st, within the Union lines at Baton Rouge. Over six hundred miles were marched in less than sixteen days, and besides destroying some fifty or sixty miles of railroads and telegraph, valuable captures of stores, horses, etc., were made.

In Grant's opinion, it was of prime importance to secure his rear; by a march upon Jackson, by destroying the property of all descriptions of the enemy and the railroad; and then to march with all his force to the assault upon Vicksburg. The advance was begun, May 7th; on the 11th, McClernand reached Hall's Ferry, on the Big Black River, W. T. Sherman was at Auburn, about six miles north-east, and McPherson about eight miles further in the same direction. The next day the advance division of Sherman's corps encountered a body of the rebels, chiefly cavalry, at Fourteen Mile Creek; but after some slight skirmishing the enemy retreated toward Raymond, burning the bridge as they retired. A crossing, however, was speedily constructed, and the corps moved on its way. A battle was fought near Raymond with the rebels, about 5,000 strong; but after a two hours' contest they were routed. McPherson immediately pushed on to Clinton, some eight miles west of Jackson, where he effectually destroyed railroad and telegraph, and on the 14th, moved upon the capital of Mississippi. Grant lost no time in carrying out his plan. Jackson was assaulted by McPherson's and Sherman's troops with great spirit, and after a fight of three hours, the rebels gave up the contest, and J. E. Johnston, the rebel commander, having set fire to the buildings filled with commissary and quartermaster's stores, made a speedy retreat. The arsenal, public works, factories, bridges, etc., were effectually destroyed. We are sorry to be obliged to state, in this connection, that there was also a large amount of pillaging by the soldiers, to the disgrace of themselves and the cause in which they were engaged. Although Johnston had been unable to maintain his position, still, as Grant learned at Jackson, he had ordered Pemberton, in very positive terms, to march out of Vicksburg, and "re-establish the communications" by an assault upon Grant's rear. This Pemberton had undertaken to do, having, it was reported, some eighty regiments and ten batteries of artillery, and about 25,000 men in all. He was, however, too late to accomplish anything; Johnston had been put to flight, and Grant, by his rapid and skillful combinations, aided, as he was, by several of the best officers in the United States army, simply faced about, and advanced promptly to rout Pemberton in the same wise that he did in the case of Johnston. The troops were moved rapidly forward, and early on the morning of May 16th, the left wing of the army, under McClernand, advanced to the line of the railroad east of the Big Black River, and, in concert with Sherman's and McPherson's corps, came upon the main force of Pemberton in the vicinity of Edward's Station. Three miles south-east of this is a road which runs parallel with the railroad, crosses Champion's Hill, through which runs a small stream called Baker's Creek. Here a battle was fought, which occupied nearly the whole day; but resulted finally in driving Pemberton and his men in great confusion. Loring, the rebel commander on the right, drew off his men, in a large circuit, to Canton, where he joined Johnston. Immediately troops were sent in pursuit of Pemberton, who retreated to the Big Black, where he purposed making one more effort before betaking himself to the entrenchments of Vicksburg. It was a rather weak effort, however, for though strongly posted on both sides of the river, the rebels did not endure the assault of our men for any length of time, May 17th, but set fire to the bridge and fled, crying out "All is lost!" Seventeen cannon and about 2,000 prisoners fell into our hands by their panic-stricken conduct, and late at night the rebel troops reached Vicksburg, in a state which hardly admits of description. During the two days following, the army crossed the Big Black, and took up position, completely investing Vicksburg. Sherman held the right, McPherson the centre, and McClernand the left. Porter's share in this great movement was felt and acknowledged to be of no little value. Having destroyed the formidable works at Haines' Bluff, he sent Lieutenant Walker up the Yazoo River, with sufficient force to destroy all the enemy's property in that direction. Entire success attended the expedition, Several rams were burned, and vast quantities of stores were destroyed, amounting in all to not less than $2,000,000.

Grant supposing that Pemberton's force was almost entirely demoralized, ordered a general assault on Vicksburg, May 19th; but it did not meet with success. So also, though Grant tried the same again on the 22d, the rebels were able to hold the place against our assaults. It hence became evident that regular siege operations must be resorted to. They were commenced and carried on with vigor and perseverance, it being certain that, sooner or later, this rebel Gibraltar must be surrendered to our arms. Day by day, during the month of June, the works were pushed closer to the enemy's fortifications. Batteries and rifle-pits were erected along the entire front. Mines were constructed at several points, especially in McPherson's front, with great secrecy and under careful watch; while from the peninsula opposite the doomed city, mortar batteries poured in, day and night, without cessation, thousands of shot and shells. In addition to all this steady working, Grant had taken care to secure, at an early day, large reinforcements, so that he was in a condition not only to push forward the siege with fixed determination, but also to keep a watch upon Johnston, and be ready to repulse any effort he might venture to make for the relief of Vicksburg. The position of Grant's army, resting on the Yazoo and supported by the gun-boats, was so strong that the rebels were soon aware of the hopelessness of attempting to raise the siege. The state of things in Vicksburg, meanwhile, was far from cheering or encouraging. The women and children, in order to escape the terrible bombardment, sheltered themselves in caves excavated in the hill sides; houses and streets were ploughed by shot and shell; provisions were becoming more and more scarce; mule and dog meat, bean meal and corn coffee, were in demand; and such like; and the only possible hope of relief from Johnston outside failed entirely. It was now surrender or starving to death. The first mine which was in readiness was exploded June 25th, and our men made a gallant attack immediately; but the half-starved garrison still resisted; Vicksburg did not yet surrender. A second mine was sprung, July 1st, with tremendous effect. The case was hopeless. Pemberton, on the 3d of July, gave up the struggle, and at 10 o'clock, A. M., July 4th, our army occupied Vicksburg. Grant, in his report, stated, that there were 37,000 prisoners; 10,000 were killed and wounded; arms and munitions of war for 60,000 men were taken; etc. His total loss he estimated at nearly 9,000. Sherman was sent in pursuit of Johnston at this date, and completely destroyed Jackson and the railroads in every direction for some forty or fifty miles. Other expeditions were undertaken, on which, however, we need not dwell.

Thus the labor and toil of our army and navy were at last crowned with success. Port Hudson, as we have already narrated, followed the fate of Vicksburg, and the Great River of the West thenceforth flowed in its entire course without let or hindrance from rebel obstructions or disloyal interference. There was now good ground to hope and expect that, ere long, rebellion and its terrible evils would be stricken out of existence.

The Army of the Potomac, as we have noted, (p. 321,) was expecting soon to be led against the enemy again; but, as it turned out, delays interposed, and nothing was attempted for several weeks. The rebel general took the initiative, and prepared to strike a blow which, if successful, would tell with wonderful effect in behalf of the cause of Jeff. Davis and his fellow-traitors. The policy of defence, as the only really safe one, had been uniformly acted upon by the heads of the rebellion, except in the one instance of Lee's invasion of Maryland, in September, 1862. It was a policy exceedingly distasteful to large numbers in the army and elsewhere; Jackson had always longed to invade the North (p. 283); and there were frequent murmurings and complainings that victories, such as those at Fredericksburg and Chancellorsville, brought none of the fruits of victory. They only left matters as they were; whereas, it was urged, the conquerors ought to receive the just rewards of their brave deeds, and despoil the enemy whom they bad beaten on the field. "Carry the war into Africa" was the cry; "carry fire and sword into the Northern States; let the people there have a taste of what war is, in the destruction of their cities, and towns, and homes, and fertile fields; it must be done; and one great success would soon drive them to give up the contest and yield to our demands." Thus the discontented and hot-headed "chivalry" fretted and fumed; and they succeeded finally in having their own way in this matter. Invasion was approved at Richmond; invasion was resolved upon; and Lee had, or thought he had, good practical reasons for making the attempt, just at this time. First, there was not only the positive loss in battle, but also the demoralization consequent upon defeat. Next, there was the supposed sympathy at the North in favor of secession and its aims and ends. Again, Lee was greatly in need of horses, supplies, etc., which could easily be had by invading Pennsylvania and Maryland. Added to this, the rebel army was in high spirits, and regarded our troops as broken and quite unable to cope with them. On the 3d of June, Lee began certain movements with reference to carrying out his main design. His army having been organized into three corps, under Longstreet, Ewell and Hill, Longstreet's corps left Fredericksburg for Culpepper Court House on that day; it was followed by Ewell's corps the day after; while Hill, with his corps, occupied the lines at Fredericksburg. By the 8th of June, Longstreet and Ewell were at Culpepper, where they found Stuart with his cavalry, which had been concentrated there some time before the main movement had been undertaken. Hooker was not inattentive to what was going on. On the 6th of June, he sent Sedgwick's corps across the Rappahannock on a reconnaissance, the result of which was, that the enemy were still at Fredericksburg in force. Lee's plan was not yet discerned by Hooker. As, however, the rebel press indulged freely in significant intimations of events near at hand, and as the gathering of Stuart's cavalry at Culpepper clearly indicated some purpose of evil which ought to be looked after, Hooker resolved to send a strong force against Stuart and break up his encampment. Accordingly, on the 9th of June, early in the morning, Pleasanton, with Buford's and Gregg's divisions of cavalry, and two brigades of infantry, crossed the Rappahannock at Beverley's and Kelly's Fords. A fight ensued in regular cavalry style, and was well sustained on both sides. Pleasanton's movement was of moment, for it not only proved Lee's presence at Culpepper, but, by the capture of some rebel correspondence, disclosed clearly Lee's purpose of invading the North. On the 11th of June, Hooker advanced his right up the Rappahannock, and sent his cavalry to watch the upper forks of the river; but Lee, while Hooker was doing this, pushed forward his left into the Shenandoah Valley. Ewell's corps, on the 10th, passed the Blue Ridge at Chester Gap, crossed the Shenandoah, and marching rapidly, arrived before Winchester on the evening of the 13th, after an advance from Culpepper of seventy miles in three days. Hooker, it would seem, ought to have inflicted a blow upon Lee's long line of battle stretched out over a hundred miles; but he did not; he was compelled to regulate his movements so as to defend the approaches to Washington, and also to advance as rapidly as possible on the rebel flank, awaiting the further development of Lee's designs. He accordingly broke up camp on the Rappahannock, June 13th, moved on the direct route towards Washington, by way of the Orange and Alexandria Railroad, and reached Fairfax Court House on the evening of the 15th of June. The enemy's earliest demonstration was in the Valley of the Shenandoah, upon the outposts at Winchester and Berryville. And in regard to both they were entirely successful. Our troops gave way and retreated to Harper's Ferry, and thus the lower part of the Valley was swept of the Union forces, and the rebels captured over 4,000 prisoners, 29 pieces of artillery, 270 wagons and ambulances, and 400 horses, together with a large amount of military stores. In view of the threatened invasion, preparations were at once made for the defence of Pennsylvania. The governor issued a proclamation calling upon the people to rouse themselves in the existing emergency; and the President, June 13th, called into the service 100,000 militia to serve for six months; of these, Maryland was to furnish 10,000; Pennsylvania, 50,000; Ohio, 30,000; West Virginia, 10,000; New York also was called on for 20,000.

The success of the rebels at Winchester, above noted, was immediately followed up by the passage of a body of 1,500 rebel cavalry, under Jenkins, across the Potomac, who passed through Hagerstown and Greencastle, and then advanced to Chambersburg, which town they entered without opposition on the evening of the 15th of June. Horses, cattle, forage, goods (paid for in Confederate scrip) were freely seized upon; the bridges on the Baltimore and Ohio Railroad, from Harper's Ferry to Cumberland, a distance of a hundred miles, were destroyed by Imboden, and the road itself torn up to a considerable extent; and the rebels displayed the utmost activity in supplying their needs out of the property of the rich farmers of Pennsylvania. No wonder that an unparalleled excitement was roused in the loyal States, and intense interest manifested in the movements of that army on which rested the grave responsibility of repulsing and driving out the daring rebels. As Hooker was not to be lured away from the direct defence of the capital in order to make an attack upon Longstreet, Lee resolved at once to carry out his original purpose of invasion, and to give up the hoped-for chance of any blow against Washington. Accordingly, Ewell, having been relieved by Hill and Longstreet, began to move with the advancing column on Sunday, June 21st. On the 22d, Ewell's corps crossed the Potomac at Williamsport, passed thence to Hagerstown, and entered Greencastle early in the afternoon. On the 23d, Chambersburg was re-occupied by Rodes's division of Ewell's force. The next day, Lee, with the main body of his army, crossed into Maryland at the fords at Shepherdstown and Williamsport, and moved up the Cumberland Valley on the west side of the Cotoctin Mountains. His advance was made in two divisions, one by way of Harrisburg, the other eastward towards York and Lancaster, Pennsylvania. On the 27th of June, the main body of Ewell's, Longstreet's, and Hill's corps were encamped near Chambersburg. Early's division was detached for the purpose of crossing South Mountain, and proceeded as far east as York, while the remainder of the corps proceeded to Carlisle. Imboden, in pursuance of his instructions, had been actively engaged on the left of Ewell, during the progress of the latter into Maryland, in destroying railroad bridges, etc. On the afternoon of June 26th, several hundred of the rebel advance cavalry rode into Gettysburg, shouting and yelling, like savages from the mountains. The same afternoon, some 5,000 of the rebels entered the town. Supplies of every kind were loudly called for, and obtained to the extent of the people's ability. Hurrying forward, Early, the rebel commander, entered and occupied York, Sunday June 28th. Here also was an immediate demand for supplies and money. The authorities were called upon for $100, 000 in United States Treasury notes, 200 barrels of flour, 40,000 pounds of fresh beef, 30,000 bushels of corn, 1,000 pairs of shoes, 1,000 pairs of stockings, and 1,000 coats and caps, beside various other articles, amounting in value to not less than $150,000; but the rebels did not get more than $30,000 in cash and subsistence. At Wrightsville, on the Susquehanna, our troops there retreated across the river, and the bridge having been fired, the rebels were prevented from ravaging east of the Susquehanna. Early retreated from York on the 30th of June, and in doing so took great credit to himself and his men for their excellent conduct, seeing that they might, had they been so disposed, have retaliated "the unparalleled acts of brutality perpetrated by (our) army on (their) soil."

The Army of the Potomac, meanwhile, was slowly advancing to its work. Having crossed the Potomac, on the 25th and 26th of June, at Edwards' Ferry, the army advanced to Frederick, Maryland, where Hooker established his headquarters, and whence he might move upon Lee in the direction which seemed most advantageous. It appears to have been his purpose to menace the rebel rear by a movement towards Chambersburg, and he ordered Slocum to march with the 12th corps to Harper's Ferry, and taking with him the garrison there, under French, 11,000 strong, to push forward the proposed demonstration; but Halleck interfered. Hooker remonstrated, in earnest terms, and pointed out that the garrison at the Ferry was of no earthly use in the present state of affairs; but the general-in-chief was not to be moved; he was one of the obstinate kind; whereupon, Hooker vexed at being interfered with, requested, June 27th, to be relieved. The next morning an order came appointing Gen. George G. Meade to the command of the army of the Potomac. The appointment was an excellent one, probably the best that could have been made, and both the officers and the army felt every confidence in the judgment, courage, and skill of their new commander. His address to the army was plain, simple and straightforward, free from any nonsense or flourish, which other commanders had indulged in. At this date, Lee was preparing to cross the Susquehanna and strike Harrisburg, but having received information from a scout that Meade's army was advancing northward, and that the head of the column had reached South Mountain, he was compelled, by this rapid gathering on his flank, to concentrate his forces on the east side of the mountain, in order to preserve his communications with the Potomac. Accordingly, Longstreet and Hill were ordered to proceed from Chambersburg towards Gettysburg, about twenty miles eastward, to which point Ewell also was directed to countermarch from York and Carlisle. It was evident from the position of affairs, that a collision between the two armies could not be far distant. Meade, having compelled Lee to loose his hold upon the Susquehanna, was carefully considering where to select a position in which to receive battle on advantageous terms. The line of Pipe Creek, on the ridge between the Monocacy and the waters running into Chesapeake Bay, seemed adapted to his purpose; but no decision was yet formed, and various circumstances soon after occurring, led, providentially, to the making choice of Gettysburg as the point where the rebels were to be signally repulsed. On the 29th of June, Meade's army was in motion, and at night was in position, the left at Emmittsburg and the right at New Windsor. Buford's division of cavalry was on the left flank, with its advance at Gettysburg; Kilpatrick's division was in front at Hanover. The next day, in view of the approaching deadly struggle, Meade issued an address to the army, in which, with the utmost earnestness, he besought the officers and soldiers to bear in mind what vast interests depended on their steadiness and good conduct. "Homes, firesides, and domestic altars are involved. The army has fought well heretofore. It is believed that it will fight more desperately and bravely than ever, if it is addressed in fitting terms. Corps and other commanders are authorized to order the instant death of any soldier who fails to do his duty at this hour." On the night of June 30th, the right wing of the army was ordered to Manchester, in rear of Pipe Creek, the centre was directed towards Two Taverns and Hancock, while the left wing, consisting of the 1st, 11th, and 3d corps, under Reynolds, moved forward to occupy Gettysburg the next morning. Buford, with his cavalry, passing through the town, pushed out reconnaissances west and north, to ascertain, if possible, the movement of Lee's army. On the morning of Tuesday, June 30th, a portion of Hill's corps advanced on the Chambersburg road as far as the crest of Seminary Hill, half a mile north-west of the village, but did not remain, retiring towards Cashtown. About nine o'clock, the next morning, July 1st, Buford found himself engaged, rather unexpectedly, with the van of Hill's force, about a mile west of the town. Aware of the importance of retarding Hill's advance, Buford skillfully arranged his men and used his artillery to good effect. In less than an hour, Reynolds reached Gettysburg, and dashing through the town, hastened to Buford's support. He deployed his advance division immediately, and attacked the enemy, at the same time sending orders for the 11th corps (Howard's) to advance as rapidly as possible. Reynolds found himself engaged with a force greatly outnumbering his own, and had scarcely made his dispositions for the action, when a ball from one of the enemy's sharpshooters struck him, and he fell mortally wounded at the head of his advance. Help was sent to the 1st corp, and a part of the 11th was posted, with three batteries of artillery on Cemetery Hill, on the south of the town of Gettysburg, a most important step, and as it happened, the one which in Meade's hands secured the repulse of the rebels. In the early part of the action, the advantage was on our side; but as rebel reinforcements arrived, they pressed our men so closely that they took 2000 to 3000 prisoners, and compelled Howard to withdraw to Cemetery Ridge. It was now late in the afternoon, and our troops, coming up slowly, took position on the right and left. The rebels were quite exultant in their expressions, and held themselves ready and able to cut up Meade's army in detail, fatigued as it was, and only in part arrived. Our men had rather a gloomy prospect before them; but they faltered not and nerved themselves for battle the next day.

Meade was satisfied that Lee, on the next day, July 2d, would attack in full force, and made his arrangements accordingly. All the corps were concentrated at Gettysburg, and Meade arrived on the field about one A.M. At daylight, he inspected the position occupied, placed the several corps as he judged best, paid particular attention to the prominent ridge, Round Top, etc. About two P.M., the 6th corps, Sedgwick's, arrived, after a march of thirty-two miles since nine o'clock of the evening before. On Sedgwick's arrival, the Army of the Potomac was about equal in numbers to that of the rebels, whose line was about five miles in stretch, and was in part well concealed by a fringe of woods. Thursday morning, July 2d, did not present so bright a prospect to the rebels as the night before. It was plain now, that it would be no light matter to enter on a battle with our army; and so Lee made his arrangements leisurely and with care before beginning the attack. It was almost a special Providence that Lee thus delayed, for it afforded our troops not only full time to come up and get into position, but also to have a half day's rest, so greatly needed and beneficial.

It was about half-past 4 P. M., when Lee gave the signal for attack, when a terrible cannonading began, accompanied by an infantry charge on our left. It was intended to drive our men and gain possesion of the crest of the ridge. This work was assigned to Longstreet, while Ewell and Hill were to attack our right and centre. The struggle was fearful indeed on the left, and our men met the assault steadily, but could not endure it very long. It was a most critical moment. The rebels had thrust a portion of their force under Hood between the extreme left of Sickles and Round Top, and as Little Round Top was not yet occupied, Hood might have massed his division, pushed boldly for the rocky summit, and thus grasped the key of the battle ground. But help arrived at the opportune moment, by troops coming up and taking position on the left. Happily, Gen. Warren, chief engineer, reached Little Round Top, which was being used as a signal station, just at the time of Hood's attack. He instantly obtained a portion of the troops to seize and occupy this all important point; this was accomplished after a most furious hand-to-hand contest, in which the rebels made a desperate effort to gain the position, but were repulsed and hurled back. About six P. M., a division of the 5th corps charged the rebels most determinedly, and drove them down the rocky front of Little Round Top, across the valley below, and over the next hill into the woods beyond. On our right, the rebels did not attack till nearly sunset, when a fierce assault was made on our forces on Cemetery and Culp's Hill. The assault on the former was resolutely met, and the rebels were driven back with frightful loss. Our men on Culp's Hill, however, having been weakened by detachments sent to aid the left in its extremity, were not able to withstand the rebel attack; and hence, the enemy, after some two hours' fighting, penetrated our lines to the breastworks on the furthest right, and retained their foothold during the night. This closed the second day's struggle, in which our loss was fearfully large—some 20,000—but the real advantage was still in our hands, and Meade and his corps commanders were quite confident of being able to maintain their position, and effectually repulse the rebel host.

The rebel general's idea, on the night of July 2d, was, that Ewell should take posses of Culp's Hill and the Baltimore road, and then throw his whole force upon and break our right. This purpose, however, was defeated by Meade, who ordered a powerful artillery force against the point entered by the enemy, and opened a heavy fire, at four o'clock in the morning of July 3d. Geary with his force, having returned during the night, immediately attacked the rebels with great spirit, and having been reinforced by a brigade of the 6th corps, he succeeded, after four hours' sharp contest, in driving the rebels back and re-occupying his former position. Thus our right flank was secured, and Lee turned his attention to another point of attack. For several hours there was silence in all directions; Lee was preparing for his last great effort; Meade was waiting for the shock. The rebel artillery, nearly 150 guns, was placed on the ridge occupied by Longstreet and Hill, and a few minutes after one o'clock in the afternoon of this eventful day, the portentous silence was broken. Our artillery which crowned the left and left centre, was not so great in number as that of the enemy, but it was very effective in its important position. The cannonade, after a time, ceased without having produced any noticeable effect, and then came the "tug of war." Successive lines of rebel infantry advanced over the intervening space, resolved, if possible, to carry the heights, where our men coolly but resolutely awaited them. It was a terrible, an awfully bloody struggle. Pickett's division of Longstreet's men dashed forward with such impetuosity as fairly to mount the crest of Cemetery Ridge; but it was in vain; they were cut down, discomfited and broken. Pettigrew's division of North Carolina troops speedily broke in disorder, leaving 2,000 prisoners and fifteen stand of colors in our hands. The rebels meanwhile, showed considerable activity on their extreme right, opposite Little Round Top, from which Hood's division strove to drive our men and turn our flank; but they were not successful. A vigorous charge was made upon the enemy, and they were thoroughly repulsed, with severe loss. Thus the great battle came to its close. Lee immediately took steps for a speedy retreat. Meade, in his report, gives his reasons, at large, for not entering instantly and with his entire force, upon a vigorous pursuit of Lee and his army.* The cavalry was sent off directly, and on the 12th of July, Meade passed through South Mountain, intending to attack Lee the next day near Williamsport; but during the night the rebel general retreated into Virginia, and finally occupied the line of the Rapidan. Meade's army resumed its position on the Rappahannock. The losses in this battle were painfully great and severe, being in killed, wounded and missing, over 23,000. Lee made no report of his losses, simply stating that they were "severe;" but from the wounded, 7,540, left along the road, the prisoners taken, over 13,000, and some 20,000, probably, in killed, wounded and missing, it may be inferred that full one-third of his army was lost in this confident invasion of the loyal States. A few days later, the news arrived of the great successes on the Mississippi, at Vicksburg and Port Hudson. There was great rejoicing throughout the loyal States, and there seemed now good ground to hope that the mad struggle of the rebellion was approaching its end. President Lincoln, as was every way proper and becoming, issued a proclamation, July 15th, appointing Thursday, August 6th, as a day of national thanksgiving, which day was duly and devoutly observed.

Notwithstanding the great reverses which had recently overtaken the rebellion, the leaders in this wicked attempt were not yet disposed to yield at all. They kept up the same haughty and boastful tone peculiar to them; they were resolved that the struggle should go on, at any and every cost; and they meant to hold out, even though affairs might speedily become desperate and defeat soon crush them to the earth. On the other hand, loyal men, though surprised at the tenacity of rebel resistance, never wavered in their determination; the rebellion was to be put down, even if it took ten or twenty years to bring the war to an end. Henceforth, it began to be understood better than at an earlier date, that, so long as the leaders in this unnatural struggle could maintain organized military forces, just so long the rebellion would be able to continue its existence, and necessitate military and naval operations on our part. Of course, more money and more men were needed; both were readily to be obtained; both *were* obtained; and despite more or less of factious opposition, and sympathizing with secession and its destructive purposes, the work went bravely on towards its inevitable conclusion. In this position of affairs, and actuated by these principles and views of duty, the government steadily sought to render the army and navy as efficient as possible, and through the able and energetic officers and men to attack and subdue the rebel strongholds, and places occupied by them, so soon as the work could be accomplished. Burnside assumed command of the Department of the Ohio, March 26th 1863. This department comprised the States of Ohio, Michigan, Indiana, Illinois, Western Virginia, and Kentucky east of the Tennessee River, including Cumberland Gap, with headquarters at Cincinnati. The position was an important one, and by no means easy to fill. It required nerve, decision, and activity, all of which Burnside was thought to possess. The southern borders of Kentucky were alive with those pests of the war, the guerrillas, and the State itself was again seriously threatened with invasion. There were, too, in this department, considerable disaffection and lukewarmness toward the government; and certain noisy politicians and sympathizers with secession were doing

* As in the case of McClellan, at Antietam, so here, in Meade's case, some military critics sharply censure the not pursuing immediately the rebel army and completely routing them, as they hold to have been perfectly possible, if not quite a certainty.

all in their power to annoy, and vex, and hinder the efforts which were being put forth to break down the rebellion. These were comparatively few in number, it is true, but they were bold, loud-mouthed, and unscrupulous; and it was deemed a matter of duty to apply the proper remedy. Burnside, on the 13th of April, issued his General Order, No. 38, in which he gave all persons to understand very clearly, that he would tolerate neither unlawful deeds, nor secession, rebellious sympathizings in word and speech. Any one guilty in this wise was summarily to be sent beyond our lines into the lines of their friends. A certain member of Congress, by name Vallandingham, under the cognomen of a "peace democrat," ventured to make an abusive speech in Ohio, which brought him under Burnside's rule. He was arrested, tried and sentenced to be expelled, May 16th, which was done by sending him through the Union lines and handing him over to the rebel Bragg, as fit company under the circumstances. Burnside also brought certain rabid newspapers under his order, and forbid their circulation in his department; but he was not sustained in this by the president. It was with great regret that the head of the department found himself unable to do what he desired, because of the inadequacy of his force, and the difficulty of obtaining reinforcements. A movement on East Tennessee was prevented by this state of affairs.

Rebel notions of an aggressive policy we have already spoken of (p. 329). Lee had set out for the invasion of Maryland and Pennsylvania, and now it was thought to be a good move to cross the Ohio, plunder the southern tier of counties in Indiana and Ohio, march into Western Virginia, join Lee, etc. The leader of a projected expedition of the kind was the noted rebel raider, J. H. Morgan, a man excellently adapted for this kind of work, by his dashing energy and skill, and his utter lack of scrupulousness in seeking to attain his ends. This famous raid was remarkable in the annals of the war for the reckless zeal with which it was prosecuted, the wanton destruction of life and property which attended it, and its ultimately complete failure. Morgan having some 3,500 cavalry with a battery of artillery, set out June 27th, 1863, from Sparta, Tennessee, and by a rapid march entered Kentucky. On the night of July 2d, he crossed the Cumberland at Burkesville, and moved on Greenville, where his progress was arrested at the time by some Union cavalry. Morgan then crossed above, and the next morning reached Lebanon. Resistance being made with spirit, Morgan sacked the town and supplied himself and men with arms and ammunition. Thence he passed on, and reached Brandenburg, on the Ohio, July the 7th, and the next day, by aid of some steamboats, passed over into Indiana. Our troops, Hobson in command, arrived at Brandenburg just after Morgan had crossed. His force of cavalry and mounted infantry, with a battery, numbered 3,000. An exciting race now began. Morgan twisted and turned, in this direction and that, so as to escape pursuit, rather than from any settled plan of invasion. The alarm became general. No one knew when or where, with any precision, the bold raider would strike; but all were well aware that complete ruin, burning, robbery, pillage, and such like, followed in his train. The governors called for troops, and the calls were responded to, in order to intercept or resist the invaders. Yet, for two weeks, Morgan, by his boldness and skill, managed to keep ahead of his pursuers, traversing the highways of Indiana and Ohio, and ravaging some of the best of the southern portions of those States. Fleeing with all speed through south-east Indiana, Morgan tried several times to cross into Kentucky; but was in every case baffled. He entered Ohio, July 13th, burning the bridge over the White River behind him. Plundering every thing within reach, he crossed the Miami, at Miamiville, at which time our men were only four hours behind him. On ward the land-pirate dashed, now almost desperate; onward pressed our determined cavalry, despite the serious inconvenience arising out of the rebels having carried off the fresh horses, and left the jaded ones behind. Day and night the pursuit was kept up. Judah led his column along the roads nearest the Ohio; Hobson and Shackelford pressed forward by roads farther from the river; while the gun-boats on the Ohio were on the alert, and gave the rebels shot and shell whenever opportunity offered. Morgan burned the bridge over the Scioto, July 16th, and tried to escape over the Ohio into Kentucky; but our men came up with them at Buffington, near Pomeroy,* and the next day captured over 700 of the raiders. The noted John, however, had slipped off; whereupon, Shackelford set out immediately, and followed the raider day and night, with unflagging zeal and determination. By burning bridges, and various tricks, he escaped for a while; but on the 26th of July, when near New Lisbon, he was caught, with some 400 of his men. He was at once taken to Cincinnati and placed in the penitentiary; from which, however, he escaped about four months later to enter upon other mean and dirty work.

Burnside was now at liberty to make his contemplated advance to East Tennessee, where the trials and sufferings of loyal men were terrible beyond words to express. On the 16th of August, 1863, Burnside left Lexington, and by unfrequented roads crossed the Cumberland Mountains, so as to take the rebels by surprise; and he succeeded in accomplishing this end. Buckner, the rebel leader in this region, was astounded by the sudden appearance of Burnside's force, and not knowing what to expect, he instantly evacuated East Tennessee, and left in such a hurry as not to find time to apprise the rebels at Cumberland Gap of his movements, or to give them any orders as to the course they were now to pursue. Thus Burnside, after a very severe and trying march across the Cumberland Mountains, of some 250 miles in two weeks' time, found himself master of the situation. The advance, under Colonel Foster, entered Knoxville on the 1st of September, and two days later, Burnside was welcomed there with enthusiasm and joy rarely if ever equalled during the war. It was, in fact, a perfect ovation which met the deliverers upon their entrance. A large amount of public property claimed by the rebel authorities, as machine shops, foundries, cars, locomotives, etc., fell into Burnside's hands. About 2,000,000 pounds of salt, a large quantity of wheat (the fruits of the tithe tax), and many thousand bags were also taken. From this time East Tennessee was freed from the grinding and malignant oppression of Jeff. Davis and his abettors. Colonel DeCourcy, by order, marched on Cumberland Gap by the direct route. Learning, on the 4th of September, that the rebel force defending the Gap was strong, and likely to offer resistance, Burnside dispatched Shackelford, with his brigade, on the 5th, from Knoxville, with instructions to seize all avenues of escape to the south. He followed, himself, with another body of infantry and cavalry, on the 7th, and arrived within four miles of the Gap on the 9th, after a forced march of sixty miles. De Courcy and Shackelford had both demanded a surrender, which Frazier, the rebel commander, refused. On Burnside's arrival, the demand was renewed, and after some parleying acceded to. Fourteen pieces of artillery and 2,000 prisoners were captured at Cumberland Gap; its loss was pronounced, by a rebel journal, to be "one of the most disgraceful occurrences of the war;" and Davis groaned over the

* The scene of the action at Buffington, and all the roads in the vicinity, were literally strewn with the fruits of their raiding operations, and their army equipments. There were buggies, rockaways, spring and lumber wagons, without number; rolls of silk, muslin, calico, and other dry goods; bags full of men's clothing, hats, boots, and shoes, linen, laces, kid gloves, cutlery, men's and women's under garments—even children's petticoats—lying about in every direction, mingled with carbines, shot guns, rifles, sabres, pistols, and cartridge-boxes. Many of the latter were found to contain jewelry instead of ammunition. The woods were full of horses and mules. In places the ground was covered with pieces of greenbacks and other currency, stolen and torn by the rebels on surrendering. We are sorry to say, that very little, if any, of this spoil ever found its way back to its rightful owners.

fact, that the line of rebel communications was broken between Richmond and Middle Tennessee. During the coming two weeks Burnside was occupied in securing his position, so as to connect with the army of Rosecrans, which reached Chattanooga, September 9th; and effectual steps were taken to guard a line of 176 miles in length from the left of Rosecrans, with whom he was in direct communication, nearly to the Virginia boundary.

Rosecrans and the Army of the Cumberland were occupied for some length of time, after the battle of Murfreesborough, in preparing for an advance on Chattanooga. Various skirmishes and contests of minor importance occupied them, and the rebels annoyed our men all that they could; but this able general was not disposed unduly to hurry forward matters. He had taken time to recruit his army, to procure horses for his dismounted cavalry, and, as far as possible, to perfect all his arrangements, while he was carefully watching the dispositions of the enemy in his front. So that it was the month of June before the Army of the Cumberland was in motion. Bragg, the rebel leader, had taken line about thirty miles south of that held by Rosecrans. Bragg's force was understood to be strongly entrenched in its main positions, while in front the occupation of the roads running south from Murfreesborough, with the natural features of the country, gave it additional security against attack. It was Rosecrans's plan, in his advance, to neutralize these advantages by turning Bragg's position and making a flank attack on his right, and thus to reach his immediate base of operations at Tullahoma, on the Chattanooga Railroad. The army marched in three corps, the right under McCook, the centre under Thomas, and the left under Crittenden. By a combined movement, Rosecrans was able to deceive the rebels by threatening an advance in force on their left at Shelbyville, while the mass of his army seized Hoover's, Liberty, and other Gaps, by hard fighting. They then moved on Manchester, and having thus turned the right of the enemy's defence of Duck River, directly threatened Bragg, who was forced to fall back to Tullahoma, which he speedily abandoned, and retreated towards Bridgeport, Alabama. The advance on Chattanooga, during August, 1863, was enveloped with difficulties and trials, in endeavoring to cross the Cumberland Mountains to the upper waters of the Tennessee River, while the river, in its tortuous course, and a continuation of the mountain passes, were interposed below. The banks of the Tennessee were reached on the 20th of August, and the next day Chattanooga was shelled to some extent. Pontoon, boat, raft and trestle bridges were rapidly prepared at Caperton's Ferry, Bridgeport, the mouth of Battle Creek and Shell Mound; and, excepting the cavalry, the army made its way across the Tennessee in the very face of the rebels. Thomas, on the 8th of September, had moved on Trenton, seizing Frick's and Stevens's Gaps on the Lookout Mountain; McCook had advanced to Valley Head, and taken Winston's Gap; while Crittenden had crossed to Wauhatchie, was in communication on the right with Thomas, and threatened Chattanooga by the pass over the point of Lookout Mountain. On the 9th of September, it was found that the rebels had evacuated Chattanooga, which was immediately occupied and held by our men. Apprehensions were felt at Washington that Rosecrans might get himself into trouble, and have his right flank turned by Bragg. Halleck sent word to Rosecrans to this effect, urging caution, and ordering reinforcements from every quarter. Burnside, Sherman, Schofield, Pope, etc., were directed to hurry forward every available man. On the 14th of September, the army of Rosecrans was occupying the passes of Lookout Mountain, with the enemy concentrating his forces near Lafayette to dispute his further advance. Bragg's threatened movements, to the right and left, were merely cavalry raids to cut the line of Rosecrans's supplies, and threaten his communications with Burnside. Bragg's main army was only awaiting the arrival of Longstreet's corps, to give battle in the mountains of Georgia. It had been reinforced by troops from Johnston in Mississippi, and by the prisoners released on parole at Vicksburg and Port Hudson and declared by the rebel authorities to have been exchanged,—a course of conduct, by the way, so scandalous that Halleck denounced it in vigorous terms. By the 17th of September, our troops were brought within supporting distance, and the next day a concentration was begun, and Rosecrans's whole force was, on the 19th, on the west side of the Chickamauga. Bragg, moving his army by divisions, crossed the Chickamauga at several fords and bridges north of Gordon's Mills, near to which he endeavored to concentrate before giving battle. This was on the morning of Saturday, the 19th of September, McCook's corps forming the right of our line of battle, Crittenden's the centre, and Thomas's the left. The battle was begun about ten o'clock, when the left wing of Rosecrans was attacked by heavy masses, and vigorous efforts were made to turn our left, so as to occupy the road to Chattanooga. But in this the rebels failed entirely of success. The centre was next assailed, and temporarily driven back, but, being promptly reinforced, maintained its ground. As night approached, the battle ceased, and the combatants rested on their arms. The attack was furiously renewed on the morning of the 20th, against our left centre. Division after division was pushed forward to resist the attacking masses of the enemy, when, by an unfortunate mistake a gap was opened in the line of battle, of which the enemy took instant advantage, and striking Davis in the flank and rear threw his whole division into confusion. Pouring in through this break in our line the enemy cut off our right and right centre, and attacked Sheridan's division, which was advancing to support our left. After a gallant but fruitless effort against the rebel torrent, he was compelled to give way, but afterward rallied a considerable portion of his force, and by a circuitous route joined Thomas, who now had to sustain the whole brunt of the battle. And bravely and steadily did Thomas and his men meet and sustain the onset, way into the night. Thomas fell back to Rossville, and on the 21st he withdrew within the defences of Chattanooga. Our loss was about 16,000, and Rosecrans was sharply censured by some, although he maintained that "the battle of Chickamauga was absolutely necessary to secure our concentration and cover Chattanooga." Bragg was now able to cut off supplies from our army almost entirely.

It having been found inexpedient to have separate and independent commands, to the extent now prevailing, the government resolved to put General Grant in charge of the new "Military Divisiön of the Mississippi, embracing the Departments of the Ohio, of the Cumberland, and of the Tennessee." He arrived at Louisville, October 18th, 1863, and gave stirring notice that "the headquarters of this division will be in the field."

Bragg's plan now was to starve out Rosecrans in Chattanooga. Communication by the river, and by the railroad on the southern bank was interrupted by Bragg's force; and hence it became necessary to send supplies to Chattanooga by a circuitous and difficult road, over two ranges of mountains, by wagon transportation, upon which route the rebel cavalry had opportunity to operate with advantage. Chattanooga itself was well fortified and protected from a direct assault, but the river below was commanded by Bragg's troops at Lookout Mountain and its vicinity. Bragg occupied not only the mountain just named, but also the adjacent one, connecting Missionary Ridge, running in a south-westerly direction directly in front of Rosecrans's camps, which were thus freely exposed to view from the heights. The rebels also held Lookout Valley on the westerly side of the mountains, where a creek of the same name runs into the Tennessee; and Bragg was so confident of success as to boast that he "held the enemy at his mercy," etc. Grant, who had reached Chattanooga on the 23d of October, and ascertained the critical condition of affairs there in regard to supplies, saw plainly that the rebels must be dislodged, and communications opened, or disastrous consequences would follow. Hence, besides certain movements ordered to be made by Sherman, Palmer and Hooker to this end, another plan of relief was adopted. This was, to take a force of about 4,000 men, proceed down the river to Brown's Ferry, and seize the range of steep hills at the mouth of Lookout Valley; in this way, if the expedition were successful, Hooker's and Palmer's movements would be facilitated and rendered more secure, and the river would be open for steamboats to Brown's Ferry. This plan was promptly and thoroughly carried out during the night of the 26th of October, and Chattanooga was relieved of all fear of starvation. Hooker occupied Lookout Valley, October 26th, and the rebels were so vexed and chagrined at the success of the expedition just named, that they determined to make a desperate effort to retrieve their loss. On the night of the 28th, and morning of the 29th of October, they made their attack; but it was a failure, and Howard's corps being moved rapidly to the right, both the rebels were repulsed and the remaining crests lying west of Lookout Creek were seized and held by our troops. In carrying out his plans, Grant's next effort was to see if he could not drive out Bragg and the rebels entirely from the position they held on Lookout Mountain. He was not content with simply relieving Chattanooga; a much greater work was before him, and he devoted all his energies to its accomplishment. Happily, Bragg made a great blunder, which proved of essential advantage to Grant's purposes. The rebel general, thinking it good policy to cut off Burnside in East Tennessee, detached Longstreet from his army, early in November, to attack Burnside and take Knoxville. This, of course, weakened Bragg materially, and enabled Grant so to arrange his movements as to be almost certain of victory. Grant sent word to Burnside, explaining his purpose, and urging him to occupy Longstreet at various points, and to draw him further and further away from Bragg, only taking care to hold Knoxville at all hazards. Hooker, holding Lookout Valley, faced the enemy on the mountain, and Thomas occupied the central position, with his line of works before Chattanooga, with Missionary Ridge in front of him. Sherman was ordered, with his force, to a point on the right bank of the river above the town, with the intention of crossing and seizing the northern extremity of the ridge, which was unfortified. A cavalry force was also directed to proceed to the right and rear of the rebels, so as to cut the railroad between Cleveland and Dalton, and thus sever Longstreet's southern communications with Bragg. In this way, Hooker and Sherman would hold each flank of the enemy, while Thomas would be ready to pierce their centre. Sherman's force arrived, November 23d, and on the next day, at noon, two bridges had been laid, one, 1,400 feet long, over the Tennessee, the other, 200 feet long, over the South Chickamauga, to furnish a route for the cavalry. During the day, the remainder of his command reached the position assigned, and Sherman's men speedily rendered it unassailable by the enemy. At the same time, a brigade of cavalry, under Colonel Long, was sent to cut the railroad, which was effectually accomplished.

Grant's arrangements having been completed, he ordered a demonstration against Missionary Ridge, to develop the force of the enemy holding it. The troops marched in fine order, as if on parade, and were watched by the rebel pickets from the summits of the ridge, 500 feet above our troops. The line advanced, preceded by skirmishers, and at two o'clock, P.M., having reached our picket line, opened briskly upon the rebel pickets, who replied, and then ran into their rifle-pits Our skirmishers followed them into the pits, along the centre of Thomas's line of 25,000 troops, until we opened fire. It was a complete surprise to the rebels, in open daylight. At three P.M., the important advanced posi tion of Orchard Knoll, and the lines right and left, were secured, and arrangements were made for holding them during the night. At daylight, the next morning, November 24th, Thomas had 5000 men across the Tennessee, and established on its south bank, and commenced the building of a pontoon bridge about six miles above Chattanooga. The steamer Dunbar, formerly owned by the rebels, rendered effective aid in this crossing, carrying over 6000 men. By nightfall, Thomas had seized the extremity of Missionary Ridge nearest the river, and was busily occupied in entrenching himself. Howard, with a brigade, opened communication with him from Chattanooga on the south side of the river. Skirmishing and cannonading continued all day, on the left and centre. In carrying out his part of the work, Hooker scaled the slopes of Lookout Mountain, and from the valley of Lookout Creek drove the rebels around the point, captured some 2,000 prisoners, and established himself high up the mountain side, in full view of Chattanooga. This raised the blockade, and now steamers were ordered from Bridgeport to Chattanooga. All night the point of Missionary Ridge on the extreme left, and the side of Lookout Mountain on the extreme right, blazed with the camp fires of loyal troops. The day had been one of dense mists and rains, and much of Hooker's battle was fought above the clouds, which concealed him from view of the rest of the army, but from which his musketry made itself plainly heard. As the day dawned, November 25th, the stars and stripes were waving on the peak of Lookout Mountain, which the rebels had evacuated. Hooker moved to make a descent, and, striking Missionary Ridge at Rossville Gap, to sweep on both sides and on its summit. The rebel troops, as soon as it was light enough, hurried regiments and brigades along the narrow summit of Missionary Ridge, either concentrating on the right to overwhelm Sherman, or marching for the railroad and raising the siege. Very essential service was rendered by Sherman and his fellow commanders in stemming the attacks of rebel masses, and in judicious and effective counter-attacks. A general advance was ordered at half past three, P.M., and the storming of the ridge began with a strong line of skirmishers, followed by a deployed line of battle, some two miles in length. At a given signal the line moved rapidly and orderly forward. Our men charged the rifle pits at the foot of the ridge. The taking of these was all they had been ordered to do; but when the rebels, in large numbers, swarmed out of the rifle pits and fled before them, our brave soldiers were seized with an irresistible impulse to mount the very heights, despite the storm of shot and shell which rained down upon them from above. Onward they dashed, and officers and men, in a perfect furor of excitement, forced their way up the steep sides and broken and crumbling face of the ridge. The attempt seemed wonderfully rash and perilous, for there were not less than forty pieces of artillery on the heights, and thousands of muskets, ready to strike down the bold assailants. Nevertheless, with cheers answering to cheers, our men rushed forward and upward. Color after color was planted on the summit, while musket and cannon vomited their thunder upon them. A fierce musketry fire broke out on the left, where, between Thomas and Sherman, a mile or two of the ridge was still occupied by the rebels. Bragg left the house in which he had had his head-quarters, and rode to the rear as our troops crowded the hill on either side of him. Some of the captured artillery was put into position. Artillerists were sent for to work the guns. The rebel log breastworks were torn to pieces, carried to the other side of the ridge, and used in forming barricades across, and a secure lodgment was soon effected. The other assault to the right of our centre gained the summit, and the rebels threw down their arms and fled. Hooker, coming in favorable position, swept the right of the ridge and captured many prisoners. By sunset the ridge was taken and the day was ours. Chickamauga was avenged. Bragg decamped hastily in the night on the road to Ringgold, and thence to Dalton, firing and destroying the railroads in their flight. Our loss in killed and wounded was estimated at 5600. Some 6000 prisoners were taken, 40 pieces of artillery, 7000 small arms, etc. Thus the Chattanooga campaign resulted in rescuing Kentucky and Tennessee from the rebels, and in affording the means of immediately relieving Burnside at Knoxville. The way also was open to Atlanta, and all the rich country in its rear; in fact, the very heart of the rebellion was laid-bare, and exposed to the crushing assault which ere long was made upon it. About the middle of November, 1863, Longstreet (p. 339) advanced and crossed the Tennessee, near Loudon. The advance of his force was met with great courage and determination by our men, and was driven back two miles to the river. Following the directions of Grant, Burnside deemed it best to retire to Lenoir, and thence to Campbell's Station, twelve miles from Knoxville, a point of considerable importance to make a stand at, in order to secure the passage of the trains, and provide for the defence of Knoxville. The battle of Campbell's Station illustrated the best qualities of our officers and men, and though they were assaulted with great fury by the rebels, they succeeded in inflicting a damaging blow upon Longstreet's force. During the night of the 16th of November, Burnside drew off to Knoxville, and the next day placed his troops in position in front of the city, and prepared for the siege which was to follow. On the 18th, the rebels made a fierce attack, intending to push back our cavalry and enter the town as victors; but they were completely repulsed, after an obstinate struggle, and severe loss upon our part. Knoxville was now closely invested, the investment extending about the half the circuit of the town, on the northern, western and southern sides. Communication with Cumberland Gap was cut, November 16th, by the enemy's cavalry. Burnside took great care in strengthening his fortifications being well aware of the necessity of maintaining his position, and waiting rather anxiously promised succor from Grant. Longstreet expected to starve Burnside out; but, in consequence of Bragg's ill success at Chattanooga, his position became critical. Not at all liking to give up and leave Knoxville in our hands, he resolved to make a final effort to carry the works by assault. Early on the morning of the 29th of November, the assaulting column, composed of three brigades, made their appearance. They approached to within 100 yards of the fort unharmed. Then commenced a series of desperate and daring attacks, stubborn resistance, death, and carnage. Hour after hour it was kept up, this deadly struggle, and the ditch was piled with the dead and the dying. More than a thousand killed, wounded, and prisoners, was the cost of the assault. Our loss did not exceed 20. The rebel leader felt it necessary to give up further efforts and retire, which he did on the line of the railroad towards Virginia, December 4th. Sherman, who had been sent to Burnside's relief, arrived just as Longstreet left; but pursuit was not deemed expedient. Wilcox, who was in charge of operations in the Upper Valley, did excellent service in holding Cumberland Gap, and preventing troops from Virginia joining the rebel commander; but Longstreet continued through the winter to annoy and harass our force in Tennessee, and in the spring joined Lee for the campaign of 1864. Sherman soon after returned to Chattanooga, and Burnside, whose health was impaired, was relieved, and on the 11th of December, General J. G. Foster took command in his place.

Admiral Dahlgren was appointed to the command of the South Atlantic fleet, on the death of Admiral Foote, June 26th, 1863. He was the inventor of the gun which bears his name; and, in consequence of his scientific reputation, it was deemed advisable to send him to Charleston to co-operate with Gillmore, (p. 323) and to bring all the resources of science to bear in order to reduce that rebellious city. He proceeded at once to Port Royal, and on the 6th of July, entered upon his duties. It was now deemed most advisable, as preliminary to further offensive movements, to effect a lodgment on Morris Island, on the northern side, where batteries might be erected of sufficient force, with the new ordnance, for battering down Fort Sumter, and thus opening a way for the operations of the fleet. Concealed batteries were erected by the troops, under General Vodges, on Folly Island, adjoining Morris Island, on the south, which effectually commanded the entrance to the ship channel on that side. On the 10th of July, the needed force having arrived, the batteries opened upon the enemy, and when their guns were silenced, a charge was made by the infantry, who had crossed in boats, and the works were captured. An attempt also was made to carry Fort Wagner by assault, but it failed. The rebels in Charleston became very much alarmed at the prospect of attack on the city, and the authorities called for help, and set some 3000 negroes at work on the fortifications, so as to strengthen in every possible way the defences of Charleston. The portion of Morris Island not yet taken by Gillmore was well fortified. Fort Wagner was a very strong work; as were also Battery Gregg at Cummings's Point, Fort Moultrie, opposite Fort Sumter, on the north side of the harbor, Fort Ripley, Fort Johnson, Castle Pinckney, and numerous batteries at various points; the rebels, in fact, having in position and afloat, for the defence of Charleston, not less than 376 guns. Gillmore pushed forward operations with vigor and steadiness. Active efforts were made to bring his heavy guns into position, not only for an attack upon Wagner, but upon all the rebel works, and also to throw shells into the city of Charleston. The siege works were urged forward, and the enemy were annoyed in every way possible with sharpshooters and shells. In similar wise, the rebels threw shells, night and day, which exploded over the men at work in the trenches; and the guns of Gregg and Sumter were busily plied against the Ironsides and the Monitors, which, by their steady firing, kept Fort Wagner silent. On the 18th of July, Gillmore having placed a number of heavy guns and mortars in position, within 800 yards of Fort Wagner, determined on making another attack. The bombardment, which was to have opened at daylight, was delayed by a heavy thunderstorm during the night of the 17th, and it was not till about midday that the batteries, in concert with the fleet, opened a tremendous fire on the fort. This continued through the afternoon into the evening, the fort making little reply during the whole time. As evening set in, the impression gained ground that the rebels had run away. It was consequently resolved to send two brigades (one regiment being negroes) to take possession, or if the rebels were there, to drive them out. The assault was made with spirit and fiery energy in the night, but the rebels held the fort despite everything, and our men, about midnight, retired from the contest. Over 1500 were lost in killed, wounded and missing. Gillmore next made extensive preparations to plant new batteries, armed with the heaviest guns used in the service, so as to bombard not only Forts Wagner and Sumter, but also the city of Charleston. In the reduction of Fort Pulaski (p. 283), the heaviest gun employed was the rifle 42-pounder. Now, 200 and 300-pounder Parrott rifle guns were brought into use; and some three weeks were spent in erecting the batteries whence they were to discharge their terrible missiles. The nearest of these batteries were located a little short of two miles from Fort Sumter, about a quarter of a mile from Fort Wagner, and a mile from Battery Gregg. On the night of August 13th, our works were advanced within 420 yards of Wagner, and the first fire upon Fort Sumter, on the 15th, two and a half miles distant, sent one of these massive balls through the gorge wall, making a hole of some five feet in diameter. On the morning of August 17th, the bombardment of Fort Sumter was begun in earnest, and continued without cessation until it was, to all intents and purposes, in ruins. Dahlgren's force moved up at the same time, and attacked Forts Gregg and Wagner. The latter was entirely silenced, and the former nearly so, between nine and ten o'clock. Two of the monitors then moved to within a mile or so of the south-east front of Sumter, and opened fire upon it. In the course of the afternoon the fleet retired, keeping up, however, a fire upon Fort Wagner, to prevent the rebels remounting the guns. The result of this active and unceasing bombardment was briefly stated by Gillmore, in a dispatch, August 24th: "I have the honor to report the practical demolition of Fort Sumter as the result of our seven days' bombardment of that work. . . . . I have also, at great labor, and under a heavy fire from James Island, established batteries on my left, with effective range of the heart of Charleston, and have opened with them, after giving General Beauregard due notice of my intention to do so." Operations were now brought to a completion against Fort Wagner, which, powerful and strong as it was, was compelled to surrender on the 7th of September, when the rebels evacuated Morris Island. The army and navy now held the key of the position. That part of Charleston within the reach of the shells was greatly injured, and almost entirely abandoned by its inhabitants; there was, however, but little further progress made in the siege during the remainder of the year. Charleston was of comparatively little or no importance now, in a commercial point of view, blockade running had been effectually stopped, and whether the rebels held out for weeks or months longer or not was of no great consequence in the progress of the war for the Union and its integrity and soundness. Some further operations took place in the South and West, on which, however, we need not dwell, for the reasons just stated. The operations in the department under Grant's control, as well as in that in which the Army of the Potomac was specially concerned, were, it began to be well understood, those which would be decisive of the contest, and by which the rebellion would be ultimately crushed out of existence.

The important victories of July, 1863, at Vicksburg, Port Hudson, and Gettysburg, not only afforded to the country at large encouraging hope of the rebel military organization being speedily broken down, but also gave the secretary of state an opportunity of furnishing the principal foreign governments with some useful information in regard to the progress of the national arms. Under date of August 12th, Seward issued a diplomatic circular, addressed to the consuls of the United States abroad, for the purpose of convincing "those who seek a renewal of commercial prosperity through the restoration of peace in America, that the quickest and shortest way to gain that desirable end is to withdraw support and favor from the insurgents, and to leave the adjustment of our domestic controversies exclusively with the people of the United States." Urging with much skill the advance of our army, the steadfast support of the people, the good condition of the finances, etc., Seward was content to leave his statement of facts to make its due impression upon all concerned. By act of Congress, March, 1863, the national enrollment, preparatory to the draft, was made generally throughout the loyal States. Enrolling officers were directed to enrol all able bodied persons between the ages of eighteen and forty-five, the object being to ascertain, as far as possible, how many men liable to military duty there were, on the 1st of July, in the United States, and also to arrange, in regard to military service, how much had already been rendered, and how much was still due in the several districts. Opposition, to some extent, was made to the action of the officers, but in general it was readily and promptly repressed. The result of the enrollment, which was not completed in all the States, showed that there were considerably more than 3,000,000 men liable to military duty. For making the draft, one-fifth the number of men enrolled in the first class (*i. e.*, between the ages of twenty and thirty-five), was adopted as the quota of a district; and the boards in charge of this matter apportioned this quota among the towns and wards forming sub-districts, so as in making the draft to furnish the number of men required. Each name of this class in the sub-district was written upon a separate slip of paper, and placed in a wheel, or circular box, which was then made to revolve, and a name was drawn out and registered. This process was continued until the requisite number of names had been obtained. The person drafted was obliged to report immediately for duty, under penalty, unless he furnished a substitute, or paid $300 computation money. Of course, the draft is, and must be, from the nature of things, a rather odious affair, and demagogues and politicians took care to present it in its most repulsive features. When, in July, it was found necessary to resort to the draft, riotous demonstrations were to be apprehended, and took place in various parts of the country, but no where so fiercely and savagely as in the City of New York. Here, the drafting was begun, July 11th, without disturbance. This was on Saturday. During the next day, plans seem to have been arranged for an outbreak the following day. Accordingly a mob gathered on Monday morning, July 13th, and directly after the turning of the wheel had commenced, paving-stones and other missiles were put to use in smashing everything in the office and wounding a number of persons. With yells and shouts, they destroyed the records, tables, boxes, etc., set fire to the house, and started for further deviltry elsewhere. Being joined by gangs of thieves and scoundrels from every hole and corner of the city, the mob now entered upon a career of murder, pillage and arson. The next day, they increased in malignity and extent of outrage. Apparently, they were masters of everything; they continued their work of destruction; they threatened the city with a general conflagration; they assaulted and pursued and murdered every negro man, woman, and child who came within their reach; and they plundered stores and dwellings and private citizens with impunity. The Mayor issued a proclamation, but to no purpose; the Governor of the State did the same, and with as little effect, and begged the crowd, from the City Hall steps, to preserve peace and order. The military and police met the mob with decision wherever it attempted to make head; there was no further scruple at using ball cartridges; the rioters were frequently driven from one locality to appear again in another; and by degrees, the ringleaders having been killed or made prisoners, this disgraceful outbreak began to be subdued. During the two or three days following, the riot was pretty well reduced, and in a few days after, matters resumed their usual condition. More than fifty buildings had been burned, and property destroyed and stolen to the amount of more than $1,500,000. On the whole, however, the reaction from the riot strengthened the government, and the next month the draft was enforced in New York without opposition. The autumn elections also, were decidedly in favor of the government and its measures at this crisis of affairs.

On the 17th of October, in anticipation of the term of service of part of the volunteer troops expiring, and to provide for the probable demands of the campaign in the following spring, the president issued a proclamation, calling out 300,000 volunteers to serve for three years or the war, not, however, exceeding three years. The governors of the several States were required to raise their respective quotas, and, in case of any deficiency, a draft was ordered to be made in the States or districts, to commence on the 5th day of January, 1864. Active measures were taken to forward recruiting the volunteers whose term of service was about to expire generally re-enlisted; and when the day arrived which was appointed for the draft, it was deemed expedient that the drawing be further postponed.*

Lee, the rebel leader, after his defeat at Gettysburg (p. 344) retired in safety across the Rapidan, and Meade, with his army, took up the old line on the Rappahannock. For some time the Army of the Potomac was enjoying needed rest and an opportunity for recruiting and preparing for future operations. A considerable portion of Lee's force was sent, under Longstreet, to aid the rebel cause, just then in a rather critical condition, in Tennessee, where Bragg was in command. This was in September, 1863; and Meade, having become aware of the fact, made an advance movement, and had matured a plan, which promised well, for attacking Lee on the flank. Before, however, he could carry out his plan, the Army of the Potomac was largely depleted by the sending of the 11th and 12th corps, under Hooker's command, to the aid of our army in Tennessee. This reduced Meade to the necessity of acting on the defensive simply, until he could be supplied again with reinforcements. Early in October, Lee resolved upon an offensive movement, for the purpose of driving Meade back from the line of the Rapidan, and, by a decisive flank march, get between Meade and his communications with Washington. On Friday, October 9th, Lee crossed the Rapidan, and moved northwardly by way of Madison Court House, so as to turn Meade's right, in which movement he was quite successful. Meade, on ascertaining the rebel purpose, immediately fell back from the Rapidan and crossed the Rappahannock without molestation, and when Lee reached Culpepper, on the 11th of October, he found that our army had passed over the river some hours before. The next day, Lee advanced rapidly so as to strike Meade's line of retreat by the railroad. A retrograde movement was the immediate consequence, and during the 13th and 14th, both armies tried which could first reach the heights of Centreville. Lee, by several well planned manœuvres, expected to gain the heights of Centreville and also fall on Meade's flank and rear. But by Warren's activity and generalship in bringing up the rear, and by his repulse of the rebels at Bristoe Station, Meade obtained a strong position and stopped the rebel advance. Lee retreated again to the line of the Rapidan, and our army took up nearly the same ground as previously held. Towards the close of the year, the rebel authorities set on foot a plot to liberate some 2,500 of their officers confined on Johnson's Island, Lake Erie, and also to burn and destroy Buffalo and other lake cities. The expedition was to rendezvous in Canada, and carry on operations from thence. The American consul at Montreal, having informed the Canadian authorities on the subject, news was sent to Washington, and, through Lord Lyons, communicated to our government. Immediate steps were taken by the secretary of war, and telegrams were sent, November 11th, to Buffalo, Detroit, and other Western cities, warning them of danger and of the need of activity and vigilance. In consequence of the prompt movement of troops to the points threatened, and the measures adopted by the local authorities on the frontier, the rebel scheme came to nothing. A daring act of piracy was committed by some rebel desperadoes, early in December, 1863, by seizing the steamer Chesapeake on her way from New York to New Brunswick. They came on board as passengers, and when the vessel was off Cape Cod, they seized upon her and made prisoners of all on board. When near St. John's, they got rid of the

* The conscription act was brought up in the Thirty-eighth Congress and earnestly discussed. The chief point in the debates on the act was in reference to the propriety or necessity of retaining the $300 exemption clause. It was finally concluded to retain this, with the important restriction that the exemption thus purchased should not continue beyond a single year, when the person relieved would again be subject to draft.

prisoners by means of a pilot boat, and set out on a cruise. Their career, however, was short, for a United States gun-boat took the Chesapeake, near Halifax, where the Colonial court adjudged that the vessel be returned to her proper owners.

The Thirty-eighth Congress began its first session on Monday, December 7th, 1863, having, in both Houses, a decided majority of its members in favor of the policy of the administration, and prepared to legislate to any extent in order to put down the rebellion promptly and effectually. The Hon. Schuyler Colfax, of Indiana, was elected speaker of the House; the vice-president, Hamlin, presided in the Senate; and the Senators from West Virginia took their seats by a vote of 36 to 5. On the 9th of December, the president's message was transmitted to both Houses, and with great clearness and plainness set forth the existing condition of affairs, and the views of the chief magistrate on various questions of immediate and pressing interest. The reports of the secretaries in the several departments, which accompanied the message, exhibited a remarkable and extensive development of the resources of the country in meeting and providing for the exigencies of the war. The number and efficiency of the army, and the increase and power of the navy were duly set forth. The report on the subject of our national finances, from the secretary of the treasury, which had been looked for by the country at large with profound interest, proved to be a clear, well arranged document, and gave general satisfaction. The amount of debt had fallen short of the amount anticipated; while the receipts from all sources of income, except internal revenue, exceeded the estimates. The national debt, it was calculated, would on the 1st of July, 1864, amount to $1,686,956,641.*

Congress entered upon its work with zeal and spirit, and though various efforts were made to obtain the passage of resolutions condemnatory of the government, or negative in character, yet none succeeded; on the contrary, they became the occasion of Congress adopting clear, full, and strongly patriotic resolutions to sustain the government and push forward to the end the war against treason and rebellion. The close of 1863 showed that the condition of affairs was, on the whole, encouraging. Our armies in the West had obtained great and decisive successes; our navy was actively and efficiently useful in its sphere; and though the rebel power in Virginia was not yet broken up, the prospect was good that ere long that final blow might be struck and rebellion ended. Our shipping interests, owing to the daring and success of rebel privateers, had suffered most severely; some 200 merchant vessels, it was reported, had been destroyed, of which the aggregate tonnage was estimated to be not less than 90,000; the value of the vessels and cargoes thus destroyed was rather more than $13,500,000. Diplomatic correspondence with England and France, during the year, showed the ground taken and held by the government. As to England, her course had been felt to be illegal, unfriendly, and unhandsome, in the extreme; and more than this, our government had given a significant warning that England would be held responsible for the damage done to our commerce by lawless rovers, like the Alabama, and other vessels built at Liverpool, and allowed to set out from thence to prey upon our unprotected merchant marine. It will

* Jeff. Davis, in a very long message to the rebel congress, which met early in December, 1863, indulged himself, as usual, in charges of "consistent perfidy," "savage ferocity," "horrible barbarities," and such like, and in denouncing "the plundering ruffians" of which the army of the United States was composed. He also enlarged upon the deplorable condition of the finances of the insurgent States. All efforts by taxation, imposts, etc., had failed, and "the issues of treasury notes have been increased, until the currency in circulation amounts to more than $600,000,000, or more than threefold the amount required by the business of the country." The rebel debt was stated by Memminger, secretary of the treasury, to be, in round numbers, $1,000,000,000, of which $800,000,000 were in treasury notes; probably another year would raise the debt to more than $2,500,000,000.

be seen, by and by, that this warning was meant to be, and was, a reality, which the English ministry had to meet fully and fairly. With the French government our relations had continued to be of a friendly and cordial character, unless possibly Louis Napoleon's designs in Mexico may be thought to have given rise to some ill feeling. France disavowed any intention of establishing a monarchical government in Mexico, or taking any measures which might be considered inimical to the well-understood policy of the United States in regard to foreign interference in America. In general, then, national affairs, at the close of 1863, were in an encouraging and hopeful condition. Difficulties and trials there were, it is true; and political disputes and animosities, and sharp and bitter criminations and recriminations, were not only annoying hindrances, but productive of mischief to a large extent. Nevertheless, matters in general were in such a shape as that the people were more ready to believe the final triumph of our arms to be not far distant; and the burden on the country, in the immense expenditures and fearful mountain of debt which was being accumulated for future payment, was submitted to with a degree of readiness highly creditable to the patriotism of the people, and affording the best possible proof of their fixed convictions as to the ultimate result of the struggle through which the republic was passing.

During the early months of the year 1864, military operations were not carried on to any great extent. The winter season, except in the far South, was unfavorable, of course, to the entering upon work of any magnitude; the time, consequently, was mainly spent in preparation for the severe and even deadly struggle which the spring campaign clearly indicated. The ground was now much narrower than it was a year ago. In Tennessee, Arkansas, on the line of the Mississippi, and in Louisiana, there was good hope of being able speedily to include all these regions among the loyal supporters of the Constitution and laws of the land. Expectation, in the loyal States, no less than in those still under the control of the rebel leaders, was mainly centered upon the armies of Meade and Lee in Virginia, and Grant and Johnston in the vicinity of Chattanooga; for it was evident, from the present position of affairs, that the campaign of the spring would be of great and decisive importance, and would tax the energies and resources of the government to their fullest extent. The rebel authorities, too, conscious of their doubtful condition, were straining every nerve to resist the onward progress of the Union arms, by accumulating stores, gathering in of conscripts, strengthening their armies, etc. On the 1st of February, the president called for 200,000 men, and a draft was appointed for the 10th of March; but so successful were the efforts to enlist men by bounties, furloughs to some of the old regiments, etc., that the draft was not needed. The rebel Congress, striving to bolster up their tottering fortunes, passed a new and stringent conscription act, in February, 1864. It was provided by this, that all white men, residents of the States under their control, between the ages of seventeen and fifty, should be in the military service for the war. All in the service between eighteen and forty-five were to be retained during the war. Those between seventeen and eighteen, and between forty-five and fifty, were to form a reserve for State defence and detail duty. An act imposing additional taxes was also passed at this session, and another, in accordance with Memminger's and Jeff. Davis's recommendation, providing for the funding of the outstanding treasury notes or currency of the States in confederate bonds. This conversion was, in great measure, rendered compulsory by the refusal of the rebel authorities to receive the currency after an early day in payment of public dues and by the imposition of a tax on the notes not funded. An address was also issued to the people of the insurgent States, containing the usual topics of consolation and encouragement, and striving to excite them to renewed efforts in carrying on the war, especially by furnishing supplies to support and equip the rebel armies. Jeff. Davis, also, sent forth a proclamation to the soldiers in the field, in which he took his usual lofty tone, thoroughly abusing the loyal States and their proceedings, and asserting confidently that "assured success," awaited him and his co-laborers in secession and rebellion.

About the middle of December, 1863, Gillmore had obtained permission to send an expedition into Florida, in order to cut off rebel supplies, to procure an outlet for cotton, lumber, and other productions of the country, and to gather in for the army recruits from among the negroes. He also, in January, 1864, in accordance with Lincoln's request, inaugurated measures for restoring the State of Florida to her allegiance under the terms of the president's proclamation. Having organized an expedition for the purpose above stated, Gillmore dispatched from Port Royal, on the 5th of February, a force of about 6,000 cavalry, infantry and artillery, under command of General Seymour. They entered the St. John's River on the 7th, and the next day effected a landing at Jacksonville, without opposition, the few rebel soldiers there having taken to flight immediately. Seymour was directed to move forward his mounted force to Baldwin, some twenty miles distant, on the Central Railroad, which was accomplished by the 14th of March. A few days later, he very unwisely advanced towards Olustee, where he met with heavy loss and a severe repulse. Early in February, 1864, General W. T. Sherman, with about 30,000 men and 60 pieces of artillery, set out from Vicksburg for an expedition into the interior of Mississippi. He advanced rapidly and successfully, and reached Meridian, on the 14th, having destroyed railroads in every direction and in reach most completely, having secured ordnance and stores, destroyed the State arsenal, etc. Sherman expected to be joined by W. T. Smith with some 7,000 men; but the junction failed, and by the close of the month Sherman returned to Vicksburg. Grant sent Palmer in to Georgia, on an expedition, February 22d, but with no result. Farragut, on same date made threatening demonstrations against Mobile, but they were not pressed and were without result. The deplorable condition of the thousands of our officers and men, suffering under the inhuman treatment of the rebels at Libby Prison, Castle Thunder, and Belle Isle, roused the strongest sympathy in their behalf, and an expedition was planned, for the purpose not only of making a raid upon Richmond, but also of setting at liberty our brave countrymen who were being killed by inches by the rebels. The expedition, consisting of over 4,000 men, with a light battery of six guns, was placed under command of a distinguished young cavalry officer, General H. J. Kilpatrick; and on the evening of the 28th of February, 1864, left camp at Stevensburg; crossed Ely's Ford on the Rapidan; pushed forward rapidly the next day; crossed the South Anna at night, and on the 1st of March, was in sight of Richmond. A vigorous attack was made upon the astounded rebels; but Kilpatrick was driven off at night and forced to return without any special advantage gained. Colonel Dahlgren, who had been detached for special service, also got within sight of Richmond; but was equally unsuccessful and lost his life in attempting to cut his way through the rebel force. These operations, above spoken of, were of no great moment, and on the whole, being more favorable to the rebels than usual, afforded them opportunity of self-laudation and boasting to a considerable extent. The main current of the war, however, was very slightly affected by what had taken place, and it became evident to the careful observer, that other and far weightier trials of strength must be had, before results of any decisive character could be attained.

In the Department of the Gulf, where Gen. Banks was in command, several movements of a military kind were made in March and April, 1864, and some sharp battles fought with the rebels. Porter with his flotilla of gun-boats made an expedition up the Red

River; but, in his as in Banks's case, great labors and dangers were undergone and much loss encountered, without any adequate result gained. The rebel raider, Forrest, at the close of March, set out for an attack on our posts in West Tennessee and Kentucky. The principal result of his movement was an attack on Fort Pillow, seventy miles above Memphis, on the Mississippi, and a massacre of the garrison which must ever stamp his name with infamy. The larger part of the troops in the fort was black, and when Forrest and his savages got possession of the forts, April 12th, the slaughter of the negroes especially was marked by every circumstance of brutality that can be imagined. At least 300 were murdered in cold blood after the fort had been taken. The rebel writers and leaders rather gloried in this massacre, instead of being ashamed and humiliated at the prospect of having to bear the scorn of the world for their horrible performances.

For a long time past, there had existed in the public mind a feeling of deep dissatisfaction with the position of our army affairs. Halleck, at no time a popular man, had accomplished nothing, so far as the people could see, in his lofty post as general-in-chief; he was thought to be incompetent, probably was so. There was an evident lack of combination of effort in the operations carried on by our armies in the East and in the West; and it was continually happening that great success in one part of the field was of no advantage towards securing the ultimate end had in view. The rebels were able, by rapid movements, while holding one of the two great armies in check, to hasten to the relief of their hardly-bestead troops beaten by the other, and thus to neutralize the effect of our victories. In truth, as has been said "for three years there was presented the lamentable spectacle of a multitude of independent armies, acting on various lines of operations, and working not only with no unity of purpose, but frequently at cross-purposes; while in the military councils at Washington there ruled alternately an uninstructed enthusiasm and a purblind pedantry." There must be a head to the army; a "live" head, as the phrase was, one able to grasp the situation fully and firmly, and possessing comprehensive and administrative ability sufficient to regulate, control, and direct to the one great result, the vast military power in the hands of the government for crushing the rebellion. Grant, who had been unusually successful in his career in the West, was thought to be the man for the hour and the occasion, and Grant was accordingly elevated to the rank of lieutenant-general at the beginning of March, 1864. Immediately on assuming command of all the armies of the United States, Grant directed a re-organization of the Army of the Potomac, which, under Meade, was carried into effect at once, by order of March 24th. The united strength of this army gave Grant a movable column of about 140,000 men. The instructions given to Meade were, "that Lee's army would be his objective point; that wherever Lee went he would go also. For his movement two plans presented themselves: One to cross the Rapidan below Lee, moving by his right flank; the other above, moving by his left. Each presented advantages over the other, with corresponding objections. By crossing above, Lee would be cut off from all chance of ignoring Richmond or going north on a raid. But if we took this route all we did would have to be done whilst the rations we started with held out; besides, it separated us from Butler, so that he could not be directed how to co-operate. If we took the other route, Brandy Station could be used as a base of supplies until another was secured on the York or James River. Of these, however, it was decided to take the lower route." Grant visited the Army of the Potomac and also Butler's forces at Fortress Monroe. During the month of April, preparations of every kind were actively carried forward. Lee's army held its long established lines, formidably entrenched in his most advantageous position south of the Rapidan, with his headquarters at Orange Court House. To the north of the Rapidan with its line of communication by the Orange and Alexandria Railroad, lay the Army of the Potomac, threatening its adversary and guarding the approaches to Washington. Grant's headquarters were established at Culpepper. Owing to the weather and bad condition of the roads, operations were delayed until the beginning of May, when, everything being in readiness, and the roads favorable, orders were given for a general movement of all the armies, to take place as early as the 4th of May. Accordingly, the army broke camp and with six days' rations began its march. "Before night," says Grant, speaking of this crossing," the whole army was across the Rapidan (the 5th and 6th corps crossing at Germania Ford, and the 2d corps at Ely's Ford, the cavalry, under Major-General Sheridan, moving in advance), with the greater part of its trains, numbering about 4,000 wagons, meeting with but slight opposition. This I regarded as a great success, and it removed from my mind the most serious apprehensions I had entertained, that of crossing the river in the face of an active, large, well-appointed and ably commanded army, and how so large a train was to be carried through a hostile country and protected." Although Grant thus felicitated himself, it speedily became evident that a severe struggle must be had with the rebels before any forward movement could be made by the Army of the Potomac. The line of march, after crossing the Rapidan, led through that region known as the Wilderness, a wild and dreary tract, covered with dense undergrowth, scrub oaks, and the like, with various narrow cross-roads, thoroughly known to the rebels, and affording a capital place for deadly attack upon our men. It was along its gloomy margin that Hooker, a year before, had fought and lost the battle of Chancellorsville (p. 321). The rebel general, with a boldness and vigor unexpected, resolved to advance rapidly upon our army, and compel a battle in a region where he would have all the advantage, and where, as artillery could not be used amid the thick chapparal, our men would be at every disadvantage, and he might inflict a deadly blow upon them. Accordingly, on the morning of the 4th of May, Lee sent forward two corps of his army, to make an immediate attack. Early the next morning the rebels were in position, and the battle began about noon. Grant, in his report, says briefly, "the battle raged furiously all day, the whole army being brought into the fight as fast as the corps could be got upon the field, which, considering the density of the forest and narrowness of the roads, was done with commendable promptness." The fighting continued till late in the evening, without material advantage to either party. Both rested that night with a clear conviction that a terrible battle was to be fought on the morrow. At daylight, May 6th, the fierce struggle was resumed, and had the ground been such as to admit of manœuvring the large and well-appointed armies now arrayed one against the other, a decisive action might have been fought. As it was, the battle extended along the whole line, a distance of seven miles from Sedgwick's right to Hancock's left. Furious were the rebel assaults, and equally furious were the onsets of our men; and at night, when the fighting ceased, both armies held substantially the same positions which they occupied the evening before. Our loss on the right wing was estimated at 6,000, of which 4,000 occurred during the enemy's assault. The total loss in the two days' bloody struggle was probably not short of 15,000. The rebel loss was somewhere between 8,000 and 10,000. On the morning of the 7th of May, the bleeding combatants had little desire for renewal of the terrible struggle on the battle field. Reconnaissances, on our side, showed that the rebels had fallen behind their entrenched lines. Grant supposed Lee had had enough of fighting at present. He determined therefore to push on and put his whole force between him and Richmond; and orders were at once issued for a movement by his right flank. The immense army trains were sent during the day to Chancellorsville, there to park for the night and preparations were made for a forward movement to Spottsylvania Court House, some fifteen miles south-east. The cavalry, already in advance at Todd's Tavern, had a sharp engagement with Stuart's troopers during the afternoon, and succeeded in driving them for a considerable distance.

Previously to this, in giving Butler orders what to do, Grant stated that it was his intention to fight Lee between Culpepper and Richmond, if he would stand. Should Lee, however, fall back to Richmond, Grant purposed following him up and effecting a junction with Butler's forces on the James River, and he urged upon Butler to secure foothold as far up the south side of the river as he could, and if he could not carry Richmond, at least to detain as large a force of the enemy as possible. At this time Butler had a force of about 30,000 in all, and this officer began the ascent of the James River early on the morning of May 5th. The object had in view was the occupation of the neck of land at City Point, on the right bank, where the Appomattox empties into the James, a position about twenty miles from Richmond and ten from Petersburg, consequently threatening both places, and within easy striking distance of the important line of railroad communication between the two places. The rebels were taken completely by surprise, and the next day Bermuda Hundred was occupied and secured by our men. On the 7th of May, Butler made a reconnaissance against the Petersburg and Richmond Railroad, and after a severe contest with a body of the rebels in position covering that road from Walthal Junction north to Chester Station, he succeeded in destroying a portion of it. On the 9th, Butler sent a dispatch to Washington, summing up his operations thus far, and as it turned out, giving quite too sanguine a view of his success over Beauregard.

The Army of the Potomac pressed forward after Lee, as above stated, and on Sunday, May 8th, found that the rebels were in position at Spottsylvania Court House. By a forced march, they had gained the advantage, and barred further progress. Lee, in fact, had succeeded in placing his army across Grant's line of march; and having made Spottsylvania Ridge a bulwark of defence, he was able, for twelve days, to hold our army in check and compel a further bloody delay in the advance upon Richmond. Day after day, terrible was the fighting and slaughter. Assault after assault was made, without gaining any advantage, but only strewing field upon field with the dead. It was evident, from the tenacity and skill with which Lee offered resistance to Grant's advance, that he was not prepared to stake his fortunes upon a single great battle. Continuous fighting, within lines of defence, was his policy, and he meant, in this way, to contest every inch of ground between Grant and Richmond. The commander in chief of our armies was not, however, one to be readily turned aside from any work he had undertaken. Although the loss of life and limb had been fearful, even terrible, to contemplate, still Grant faltered not; and firmly bent on the object of his campaign, he was fully determined, at whatever cost, to continue the struggle. On May 11th, he wrote, "We have now ended the sixth day of very heavy fighting. The result, to this time, is much in our favor. Our losses have been heavy, as well as those of the enemy. I think the enemy's must be greater. We have taken over 5,000 prisoners, in battle, while he has taken from us but few except stragglers. *I propose to fight it out on this line if it takes all summer.*" The day following, May 12th, the battle was begun by capturing a whole division of the rebels, 3,000 in number, and storming successfully the line of rifle pits. The action now became general, and the bloody fray continued for fourteen hours, without cessation. Fearful was this deadly struggle, and night alone put an end to the slaughter. Grant called the enemy obstinate and said, "They seem to have found the last ditch."*

* A rebel chronicler says: "The sixth day of heavy fighting had been ended. Grant had been foiled; but his obstinacy was apparently untouched, and the fierce

Sheridan, who had been sent by Grant on a raid against the rebel line of communication with Richmond, entered upon his work with all the fire and vigor which characterized his movements as head of the cavalry of our army. His plan was to cut off the enemy's supplies in his rear, and, traversing the Peninsula, to penetrate the defences of the rebel capital. The expedition having set out, May 9th, moved towards Fredericksburg, and then, by a southerly course, turned the enemy's right, and at evening crossed the North Anna. During the night, Sheridan destroyed the depot at Beaver's Dam, a vast amount of stores, the railroad track for about ten miles, and recaptured some 400 of our men on their way as prisoners to Richmond and its horrible jails.* The next morning, May 10th, Sheridan resumed operations, and on the 11th, captured Ashland station, destroyed there, besides public stores and buildings, six miles of railroad, embracing six culverts, two trestle bridges, and the telegraph wire. The same morning, he resumed the march on Richmond. He found the rebel J. E. B. Stuart, with his cavalry, concentrated at Yellow Tavern, immediately attacked him, and, after an obstinate contest, gained possession of the turnpike, capturing two pieces of artillery, and driving his forces back across the Chickahominy. At the same time a party charged down the Brock Road, and captured the first line of the enemy's works around Richmond. During the night, Sheridan marched the whole of his command between the first and second line of the enemy's works on the bluffs overlooking the line of the Virginia Central Railroad and the Mechanicsville Turnpike. After demonstrating around the works, and finding them very strong, he gave up the intention of assaulting, and determined to recross the Chickahominy at Meadow Bridge. This was accomplished, and on the 14th, Sheridan reached the James River, where he was in immediate communication with Butler and his forces. This raid of Sheridan's had the effect of drawing off the whole of the enemy's cavalry force, and of making it comparatively easy to guard our large and important army trains. Being conducted, also, with rare address and skill, it produced upon the rebels moral effects not to be ignored, and was one of the steps in the progress towards that brilliant reputation which Sheridan attained before the close of the war.

Grant, finding the rebels hard to be driven out, now gave up operations at Spottsylvania Court House, and made a movement to the North Anna, May 21st. The rebel position was found to be very strong, and severe fighting occurred; but Sheridan secured and held Cold Harbor, May 31st. Grant, relying upon Sigel's help and co-operation in Northern and Western Virginia, and on Butler's in the South, was seriously disappointed; neither of them met his expectations. Sigel was defeated, and Butler got himself shut up in his entrenchments by the rebels, and was consequently unable to do anything. A modification of plan was necessary. Kautz's cavalry was sent on an expedition to cut the Danville Road near Appomattox station, which met with success. An attack was made by the army, June 1st, but with no advantage in the result. So, too, on June 3d, a general attack was made; it was one of the hardest contests of the war, attended by heavy losses.* Grant, who had a good share of obstinacy in him, reluctantly now moved to

and brutal consumption of human life, another element of his generalship, and which had already obtained for him with his soldiers the sobriquet of 'the butcher,' was still to continue. He telegraphed to Washington, 'I propose to fight it out on this line if it takes all summer.'"

* A contemporary writer, who is adverse to Grant's plan, criticizes him and it sharply, and says: "Grant's loss in the series of actions from the Wilderness to the Chickahominy reached the enormous aggregate of 60,000 men put *hors du combat*;" Lee's loss is estimated not to have exceeded 20,000. In a tabular statement subjoined, the killed are stated at 7,289; wounded, 37,406; missing, 9,856. To these must be added the casualties in Burnside's corps, about 5,000. The loss in officers was especially severe, being in all 3,000, a loss truly irreparable.

take position on the south side of James River. Anxious to gain possession of Petersburg before it was reinforced by the rebels, Grant ordered special efforts to be made by Gillmore and Kautz; but their attempt failed. Grant moved from Coal Harbor, June 12th, and in three days crossed the army over the river, taking the rebels quite by surprise. Hunter, who had taken the place of Sigel, entered on active operations in the region appointed him; but, the rebels proved too strong or too active for him, and he met with very little success. Sheridan went on an important cavalry raid, early in June, against the Virginia Central Railroad; but though brilliantly conducted, it was only partially successful. Grant held that the terrible loss and slaughter of our men thus far in the campaign, though dreadful to contemplate, had one encouraging aspect about it, viz., that the rebels were crippled badly, so as to prevent their undertaking offensive movements, in great measure; this, however, was at best, but doubtful consolation in the momentous crisis of our national life. A writer, whom we have before quoted, comments severely upon Grant's determination "to hammer continuously" upon the rebel forces, and says further:—"So gloomy was the military outlook after the action on the Chickahominy, and to such a degree by consequence had the moral spring of the public mind become relaxed, that there was at this time great danger of a collapse of the war. . . . . Had not success elsewhere come to brighten the horizon, it would have been difficult to raise new forces to recruit the Army of the Potomac, which, shaken in its structure, its valor quenched in blood, and thousands of its ablest officers killed and wounded, was the Army of the Potomac no more."

On the 15th of June, Smith, by Grant's order, moved against Petersburg; but delays, vexatious and ill-timed, occurred, and the advantage of surprise was lost. Grant next ordered an assault, which turned out to be a failure. Butler made a movement against the railroad; but he, too, this time, was lacking in promptitude, and met with a repulse. Grant, not yet satisfied, ordered a general assault, June 17th; but though our men fought as bravely as ever, no advantage of moment was gained. Our losses for the few days just passed amounted to 10,000. The demonstration against the Weldon Railroad was a failure; the one against the Danville Road was partially successful, though attended by heavy loss. Hunter, who had been obliged to retreat, laid open in consequence the Shenandoah Valley for rebel raids into Maryland and Pennsylvania. A large force, under Early, availed themselves of the opportunity, and took possession, very freely, of whatever they could lay hands upon. Grant was compelled by this movement of the rebels, to send troops to Washington; the militia were called out; and strenuous efforts were made to resist Early's advance. A battle was fought at the Monocacy, July 9th, which was gained by the rebels, who advanced almost to Washington, committing extensive depredations and pillaging in all directions. But, becoming alarmed at the appearance of things, they retreated. On the 25th of July, another raid was made into Pennsylvania, and Chambersburg was plundered and burned, July 30th; whereupon, the rebels again returned to Virginia. As Grant's assaults against Petersburg met with no success, a regular investment and siege was entered upon. A mine was constructed, during July, which, on the 30th, was exploded with terrible effect. As, however, the assaulting column failed to move rapidly and secure the crowning crest, no real advantage was gained. A movement was now made threatening Richmond on the north side of the James River, August 16th. Severe fighting occurred, with heavy loss; but it resulted somewhat favorably, in keeping back troops which Lee was about to send into the Shenandoah Valley to reinforce Early. Warren, on the 18th of August, moved on the Weldon Railroad, where he took position, and notwithstanding the fierce and desperate onsets of the rebels to dislodge him, was able to hold his post, with a loss of about

4,500. A battle was fought, August 25th, at Ream's station, some miles below on the road, in which Hancock's men resisted the rebels gallantly, but were forced to retire at dark, having lost 2,400 out of 8,000 men.

The political and general condition of the country at this date was far from cheering or satisfactory. The tenacity and strength of the rebel resistance, the frightful loss of life in the battles fought, the apparently small progress, the heavy, almost insupportable burdens of the war, the financial depression (gold reached 300 and over) and complaining, the cry, here and there, for "peace on any terms,"—these and the like were among the trials and troubles which the people were called upon to meet and go through with, as best they could. As the presidential election drew near, the minds of the people were filled with many anxious and perplexing considerations. On the whole, despite the complaints and abuse freely bestowed, it was deemed best to nominate Abraham Lincoln again, together with A. Johnson for vice-president. Fremont was also put forward as a candidate by the more radical republicans, and the democrats offered McClellan and Pendleton as their nominees. The action of Congress (p. 346) was, as usual, decided in support of the government. Additional measures were taken for securing increased revenues, granting new facilities for enlistments, and sanctioning the policy of the administration in regard to slavery. An ample appropriation bill, meeting the demands of the secretaries of war and the navy, was passed; new loans were authorized; a new tariff act largely increased the duties on imports, and an internal revenue law augmented licenses and taxes. Various special taxes were imposed on manufactures and articles of luxury, and the annual assessment on incomes was increased from three to five per cent. on returns between $600 and $5,000; from five to seven and a half per cent. on returns between $5,000 and $10,000, and to ten per cent. on all excess over the last sum. A specia war tax of five per cent., in addition to the three per cent. already levied, was ordered on the incomes of the year 1863. A new enrollment act, approved July 4th, 1864, supplementary to an amended enrollment bill, passed in February, had placed the whole population of the country, between the ages of twenty and forty-five, not physically or otherwise disqualified from bearing arms, at the disposal of the president. He was authorized to call, at his discretion, for any number of volunteers for one, two, or three years, and in case the quotas assigned to the several districts were not forthcoming at the end of fifty days, he was directed then to order a draft for one year, to fill such quota or any deficient portion of it. Various steps were taken with reference to the final extinction of slavery, which was now considered by the whole country to be doomed to destruction as the inevitable result of the war. The most noticeable measure on this subject before Congress, at its present session, was the proposition to submit to the action of the several States an amendment to the Constitution of the United States, prohibiting the existence of slavery within the States and Territories of the Union forever. It passed in the Senate by a very large vote, but failed in the House for lack of a two-thirds vote. The fugitive slave law was disposed of by a very decided vote of the two houses, about the middle of June. A bill in respect to reconstruction of States rescued from rebellion was passed on the last day of the session, into the details of which we need not enter, as it did not receive the president's approval. Congress adjourned the first week in July, 1864.

On the 12th of March, 1864, General W. T. Sherman was placed in command of the military division of the Mississippi, comprising the departments of the Ohio, the Cumberland, the Tennessee, and the Arkansas. General J. B. McPherson, who also ranked very highly in Grant's estimation, was assigned to the command of the department and Army of the Tennessee. Thomas was in command of the Army of the Cumberland. at Chattanooga, and Schofield of the Army of the Ohio, at Knoxville. By a subsequent order, in April, Hooker was placed in command of the 11th and 12th consolidated corps; Howard was assigned to the command of the 4th corps; and Schofield to the 23d corps. Relying on the co-operation of these and other tried officers in the field, including Blair, Palmer, Logan, Stoneman, etc., Sherman, at the beginning of the month of May, and simultaneously with the advance of the Army of the Potomac, already narrated, began that campaign destined to become famous in our annals, and fearfully crushing in its effects upon the rebellion. Next to Richmond, Atlanta—the objective point of Sherman's present campaign—was the most important position, as a centre of military operations for the rebels, and it was determined to make especially vigorous efforts to deprive them of these their last, most valuable strongholds. Atlanta, from its admirably protected situation, had been chosen at the outset, as a great military depot of supplies and materials, and a vast workshop for the purposes of war. Here were arsenals, foundries, furnaces, rolling-mills, machine-shops, laboratories, factories, which had been for three years past, and were now, busily engaged in furnishing the munitions of war for the rebels. Atlanta was not only one of the chief railroad centres in the rebel States, but it was essentially the door of Georgia, as Chattanooga of Tennessee. Atlanta once secured, it would become the new, advanced position from whence to operate, and Sherman's rear would be entirely safe. It was no light task which Sherman had before him, to pass over a track of 138 miles by the route of the railroad, and overcome the numerous obstacles in his path. Opposed to his advance was the rebel army, under J. E. Johnston, second only to that of Lee in Virginia. In point of numbers, Sherman's force was much superior. He had nearly 100,000 men, with 254 guns. The rebel force was estimated by Sherman, at 58,000, including 10,000 cavalry. But, as an offset, the rebels had every advantage of position, thorough knowledge of the ground, interior line of communication, etc.; while Sherman, at every move, departed further from his base, and risked all on the issue of the campaign. The army was set in motion at the beginning of May, 1864, in three columns, Thomas in front, Schofield on the left, and McPherson on the right. The advance was steadily onward, the rebel leader opposing such hindrance as he was able, but always compelled to give way. Sherman by his admirable strategy accomplished wonders in gaining success without any great amount of fighting. Allatoona Pass was turned towards the close of the month, and important points secured thereby. On the 9th of June, Johnston resolved to make a stand at Kenesaw Mountains, where he was attacked by Sherman and pressed for several days with vigor and success. On the 27th of June, Sherman assaulted Johnston's lines covering Marietta, but failed in carrying them and met with heavy loss, some 3,000 in all. He then turned the enemy's left, and entered Marietta, July 3d, having captured about 2,000 men. Johnston, a few days later, took alarm at Sherman's movements, and on the 9th of July, retreated to Atlanta, burned his bridges, and left Sherman master, north and west, of the Chattahoochie. Atlanta was only eight miles distant, and our army was pushed forward soon after to secure it.

The rebels, it seems, had felt very much chagrined at the fact that Johnston had done nothing but retreat before Sherman, and they clamored for a change. So, Davis removed Johnston, and appointed Hood in his place. This latter was considered the impersonation of the impetuous, dashing "chivalry" of the South; and the rebels thought he would speedily teach Sherman some bitter but needed lessons in warlike matters. On the 20th of July, all the armies had closed in, converging towards Atlanta; but Hood determined to make an attack at a point where he thought the line weak. Accordingly, in the afternoon of the 20th, he dashed forth with great fury, but only to meet with defeat and loss of probably 5,000 men. On the 22d, a bloody battle was fought, in which the rebels were met with steady and unflinching bravery. It was by far the most sanguinary battle that had as yet been fought in Georgia. Sherman's loss was nearly 4,-000; among the slain was General McPherson, a severe blow to the efficiency of the army. The rebel loss was probably doubly as great as ours. Garrard's cavalry expedition on the Augusta Road was quite successful; but Stoneman's against the Macon Road failed, and he himself with several hundred men were taken prisoners. Early in August, Sherman extended his right in order to flank Hood; but, to use Sherman's own words, in an address to the soldiers, September 8th, the rebel commander "remained henceforth on the defensive. We slowly and gradually drew our lines from Atlanta, feeling for the railroads which supplied the rebel army and made Atlanta a place of importance. We must concede to our enemy that he met these efforts patiently and skillfully, but at last he made the mistake we had waited for so long, and sent his cavalry to our rear, far beyond the reach of recall. Instantly our cavalry was on his only remaining road, and we followed quickly with our principal army, and Atlanta fell into our possession as the fruit of well concerted measures, backed by a brave and confident army. This completed the grand task which had been assigned us by our government, and your general again repeats his personal and official thanks to all the officers and men composing his army, for the indomitable courage and perseverance which alone could give success. We have beaten our enemy on every ground he has chosen, and have wrested from him *his own Gate City*, where were located his foundries, arsenals, and workshops, deemed secure on account of their distance from our base, and the seemingly impregnable obstacles supervening. Nothing is impossible to an army like this, determined to vindicate a government which has rights wherever our flag has once floated, and is resolved to maintain them at any and all costs."

Under the exigencies of the case, Sherman resolved to remove the inhabitants of Atlanta, and garrison it strictly as a military post. This was accomplished by giving the people transportation south as far as Rough and Ready, and north as far as Chattanooga. Atlanta was henceforth, in accordance with the order of September 14th, occupied simply and exclusively for warlike purposes. The well-known raider and land pirate, J. H. Morgan, we may here mention, was routed at Greenville, Tennessee, and his career of crime and outrage brought to its end by his death.

The noted privateer, Alabama, met, at last, with a deserved fate, in June, 1864. Semmes, after destroying the Hatteras, made his way across the Atlantic, and passing beyond the Cape of Good Hope, continued his depredations with very great effect upon American commerce in the eastern seas. From time to time he found refuge in sympathizing British harbors, whence, refitted and supplied anew, he sallied forth to plunder and destroy; and as the "Confederacy" had no port into which to take his prizes for legal adjudication, Semmes set up an admiralty court on the deck of his own ship, and setting fire to the merchant vessels, he took the crews prisoners and put them ashore at any place most convenient in his roving career. After a prosperous cruise in the South Atlantic, he returned to the north in the summer of 1864. The Alabama put into Cherbourg to refit, and start anew, but on the remonstrance of our minister she was ordered to leave directly. The United States steamer Kearsarge was outside, waiting for the chance of meeting the famous pirate. Semmes, finding that he was in a position where he must fight or surrender, sent word to Winslow, captain of the Kearsarge, with a sort of insolent bravado, to wait for him till he came out. Winslow, the reader may be sure, was only too glad to do this. On Sunday morning, June 19th, the Alabama sailed out, and the battle commenced when some seven miles from the shore. The day of retribution had come, and Semmes soon had enough of the Kearsarge; but Winslow would not let him escape, as he tried to do, by making for the shore. The Alabama was found to be sinking, and Winslow did all possible to save life. He asked an Englishman, named Lancaster, who was near in a yacht, to aid in this work of mercy; but this fellow, a disgrace to the English name, when he had got Semmes and some forty of the crew on board, made off for the English shore before he could be prevented. It was a mean thing every way, but he proved himself fit company for his pirate-associate, while the Alabama went to the bottom.

During the latter part of the year 1864, Farragut with his fleet was occupied in an attack upon the formidable fortifications and defences in Mobile Bay and its surroundings. He was acting in combination with General Canby and the troops under his command. The rebels relied on the strength of the forts, but even more on the immense ram Tennessee and some gun-boats. The attack was begun by Farragut and the fleet, on the morning of August 5th. The fort at the entrance, on Mobile Point, was passed in an hour's time, and the rebel ram dashed out against the Hartford, Farragut's flag-ship. The old admiral declared the fight with the ram to have been "one of the fiercest naval combats on record;" but aided by the gunboats and monitors, admirably handled as they were, the Tennessee could not hold out. About ten o'clock, the contest was closed and the Tennessee surrendered. The forts followed the fate of the ram, and in a brief space were reduced; and though Mobile was not taken, that was of minor consequence. The nest of blockade runners was broken up, and no further room was afforded to the cruisers to fit out for piratical expeditions.

After the fall of Atlanta (p. 356), the rebel cavalry made special efforts to break Sherman's extended line of railroad communication with Nashville. Forrest, one of the raiders, at the close of September, 1864, did considerable mischief in this way, and escaped before he could be caught. Hood made a move on Allatoona, October 5th, but to no purpose; he was repulsed and compelled to retreat. In September, Burbridge was sent from East Tennessee to destroy the salt-works, at Saltville, Virginia, which was not successful; but, in December, we may mention, under Stoneman, the works and place were destroyed, a loss to the rebels of immense severity and not to be repaired from any quarter. Hood moved to Dalton, and thence into Alabama, where Beauregard, October 17th, took command. Jeff. Davis, at the close of September, was at Macon, Georgia, and made a speech more unwise than was supposed possible for so astute a traitor to make. He declared that a line of policy was to be adopted in imitation of Sherman's flanking movements, by which Hood was to get into his rear and compel him to retreat into Tennessee. They greatly mistook the man, however, when they expected to beat Sherman in that way. He had formed the bold plan of cutting loose from his bases and destroying effectually the railroad to Chattanooga; thence, mainly subsisting on the rich country in the interior of Georgia, he meant to march through the State directly to the sea. All the needful preliminary steps were taken, with care and diligence, and every thing was put in readiness for the march of the army. As to Hood, we may here state, that he actually entered upon his wild scheme of invading Tennessee This was at the close of October. Thomas was at Nashville, prepared and waiting for this threatened invasion. Hood reached Franklin at the close of November, where a battle was fought, and the rebels defeated with great loss. During the night, our troops retired to Nashville, where, on the 2d of December, the rebels formed their lines in front of the city. Thomas's position was too strong to be affected by Hood's course, and soon after he assumed the offensive. On the morning of December 15th, the attack was begun on Hood's army, and it resulted in complete and thorough defeat of the enemy. Sixty-eight pieces of artillery were taken, besides about 10,000 prisoners. Pursuit was kept up for several days, and the rebels were pressed even to the Tennessee River. This famous invasion consequently ended in rout and confusion to Davis and his co-workers. As a rebel chronicler says, speaking of Hood, "he finally made his escape across the Tennessee River with the remnant of his army, having lost from various causes more than 10,000 men, half of his generals, and nearly all of his artillery. Such was the disastrous issue of the Tennessee campaign, which put out of existence, as it were, the splendid army that Johnston had given up at Atlanta, and terminated forever the whole scheme of Confederate defence west of the Alleghanies."

Sherman, on the 9th of November, 1864, issued a special order, defining his arrangements, the line of march, the mode of obtaining supplies, the course of conduct to be pursued by the troops, etc. He then effectually destroyed the railroad in his rear, and set fire to and burned all the storehouses, depots, machine-shops, and everything else in Atlanta which could be of any service to the rebels. Having concentrated at Atlanta, his troops, numbering between 50,000 and 60,000, the right wing, under Howard, moved on the 12th of November, and was followed by the left, under Slocum, on the 14th. Sherman himself accompanied the left wing. The lines of march followed generally the two lines of railroad traversing the State, the Georgia and Central, running from Savannah to Macon, and thence by a north-westerly line to Atlanta, a distance in all of nearly 300 miles; and the Georgia Railroad, running north of the former, in an easterly direction, between Atlanta and Augusta. This was connected with the southerly line by way of Waynesborough and Millen with Savannah. In the area bounded by these lines, resembling a parallelogram, with Atlanta, Macon, Augusta and Millen at the four corners, and Milledgeville at a central point in the enclosure, the important movements of Sherman's army were effected. The rebels for some time supposed that this was a mere raiding expedition into Georgia. It seemed impossible for them to grasp the boldness of Sherman's undertaking; and hence, as Grant says, "the blindness of the enemy in ignoring his movements, and sending Hood's army, the only considerable force they had west of Richmond and east of the Mississippi River, northward on an offensive campaign, left the whole country open, and Sherman's route to his own choice." Directly onward was the movement of the army and with uniform success. Howard advanced through McDonough, crossed the Ocmulgee, November 20th, struck the Georgia Central, two days later, had a sharp encounter with the rebels while destroying the track between Gordon and Griswoldsville, and occupied Milledgeville, November 21st, having travelled about 95 miles since leaving Atlanta, a week previously. The corps under Slocum marched eastwardly towards Augusta, and by the 17th of November, the road was effectually destroyed as far as Covington. One column turned southeastwardly in the direction of Milledgeville, while another continued on the line of the railroad, and destroyed it as far as Madison, sixty-nine miles east of Atlanta, and 102 west of Augusta. The cavalry were pushed on between twenty and thirty miles further, serving as a demonstration against Augusta, and thoroughly deceiving the enemy as to Sherman's real plan. From Madison, Slocum marched to Milledgeville, which was reached November 22d; and the two wings were thus brought together again. Governor Brown, and the legislature, then in session, made off as rapidly as they could, to escape from the dreaded foe. It was plain now to even the meanest capacity, that our army was marching directly and successfully through the heart of Georgia to the sea coast, and despite the calls of Beauregard and others, to destroy everything in Sherman's front, flank, and rear, that march was continued to its complete termination. On the 24th of November, the army moved, having Millen, 74 miles distant, in view. The Oconee was crossed by both Howard and Slocum on the 26th of November, although the rebels opposed such hindrance as they were able; and then, with excellent strategy, while deceiving the rebels as to an attack on Augusta, he advanced toward Millen, crossed the Ogeechee with the main body, and entered Millen, December 2d. Sherman had moved somewhat slowly, but with a purpose. As it was somewhat uncertain as to supplies when he moved on to Savannah, Sherman paid special attention to foraging, and also to the complete destruction of the railroads, including the bridge over the Ogeechee, twenty-five miles west of Millen. Savannah was now about eighty miles distant, and Sherman having left the rebel troops in his rear, where they could do no harm, advanced rapidly and regularly forward. Howard, on the 9th of December, struck the canal which connects the Ogeechee with the Savannah, about ten miles in the rear and west of the city. From this point he communicated, by means of scouts, with a gun-boat in Ossabaw Sound, and gave intelligence of his success thus far. On the 10th of December, Sherman advanced to within five miles of Savannah, where the rebels had erected the first of a line of defences. Sherman resolved to capture Fort McAllister and thus open the Ogeechee, so as to communicate with the fleet, and cut off communications between Savannah and the southern part of the State. This was accordingly done, and the Fort was carried by assault, December 13th. All the railroads into the city were destroyed and Savannah was invested. Sherman reported his army in first-rate order and equal to anything. Hardee, in Savannah, tried to hold out for a while, but on the 20th he gave it up as hopeless, fled to Charleston, and left the city to be occupied by our forces, which was done on the 21st. One hundred and fifty guns, with ammunition, etc., together with 25,000 bales of cotton, were taken, and Sherman's order, December 26th, with reference to the government of the city, was judicious and considerate.

In accordance with Grant's desire, Sheridan was, in August, placed in charge of affairs in the Shenandoah Valley. He entered on his work with spirit and energy, and on the morning of the 19th of September, Sheridan attacked Early at the crossing of the Opequan Creek, and after a most sanguinary and bloody battle, lasting until five o'clock in the evening, defeated him with heavy loss, carrying his entire position from Opequan Creek to Winchester, capturing several thousand prisoners and five pieces of artillery. The enemy rallied and made a stand in a strong position at Fisher's Hill, where he was attacked and again defeated with heavy loss on the 20th. Sheridan then took position on the north side of Cedar Creek. Early, having received reinforcements, returned to the Valley, while Sheridan was at Washington, and came very near defeating our troops at Cedar Creek. On the morning of October 19th, under cover of the darkness and fog, Early surprised and turned our left flank, and captured the batteries which enfiladed our whole line. Affairs were in a most painfully critical condition. Panic was fast demoralizing the army, and in a brief space, had not help arrived, all would have been lost. Most opportunely, that help came in the person of Sheridan himself. He was on his return from Washington, on this eventful morning, and at Winchester, thirteen miles distant, heard the booming of cannon. Instantly, aware of the importance of his presence, he set off at full speed, and never drew rein till he reached the battle field, his horse covered with foam and he himself in a state of intense excitement. The magnetism of his presence succeeded in effecting an immediate change. The men rallied, and in the course of the afternoon, completely routed Early's force, and pursued them nearly to Mount Jackson This victory brought to an end rebel attempts to invade the Shenandoah Valley.

Grant now pushed forward his plans against Richmond. Fort Harrison was taken September 28th, 1864; cavalry expeditions moved to within three miles of Richmond; reconnaissances and accompanying engagements took place early in October; and on the 27th, an attempt was made to penetrate the rebel lines at Hatcher's Run, but without success. Subsequent movements of the Army of the Potomac during the year were directed against the enemy's line for receiving supplies to the south of Petersburg. The navy having succeeded in closing the ports of Savannah, Charleston, and Mobile, the rebels had but one place left for blockade runners and the like. This was the harbor of Wilmington, N. C. It was a very valuable strategic point, and was protected by several formidable forts and batteries, especially Fort Fisher on Federal Point at the new or eastern inlet. Grant was exceedingly desirous to secure this fort, and gave the subject earnest thought. At the close of November, an armada of over seventy vessels, under Porter, was gathered in Hampton Roads, and a force of 6,500 men was added under Weitzel, Butler accompanying the expedition. The fleet arrived off New Inlet on the evening of December 15th, but a heavy gale caused delays, and it was not till the 24th, that Porter ordered an attack. Some 3,000 troops were landed and advanced very near to the fort, while the ships poured in a fearful storm of shot and shell; but, Butler interfered and ordered the troops back. Porter was much vexed and said the fort could have been taken, and Grant was so indignant that he caused Butler to be displaced and Ord put in his place. The expedition was resumed, the troops now being under command of Terry, who had some 8,000 troops landed, January 13th, 1865, ready for active work. The next day, the assault took place. Porter's heavy fire was incessant, and the army, after tremendous fighting, hand to hand conflicts, and gallant deeds of daring, succeeded at last in capturing the fort. This led to the blowing up of the other forts and destruction of batteries and defences in all directions. Porter reported the number of guns taken to be 168. Terry reported the number of prisoners to be over 2,000. Thus, by the combined efforts of the army and navy, was secured one of the most important and valuable successes of the war.

At the presidential election in November, 1864, Lincoln was chosen again to fill the high office he now held, and Andrew Johnson was also elected vice president. The Thirty-eighth Congress met for its second session, December 5th, 1864. The message contained the usual summary of foreign and domestic affairs, referring for particulars to the reports of the several departments. The debt, July 1st, was over $1,740,000,000 ; in another year, it was estimated, it would be over $2,000,000,000. The number of vessels in the navy was 671, mounting 4,610 guns, with 6,000 officers and 45,000 men. The army amounted to about 700,000 men.* Certain efforts were again made in regard to peace propositions by Mr. F. P. Blair going to Richmond and having a talk with Jeff. Davis on the subject, and then trying to induce the president to enter into negotiations with the rebels ; but, as was to be expected,

* During the summer and autumn of 1864, a commission of the highest respectability investigated the condition of our men in the horrible dens and holes called rebel prisons, at Richmond and Andersonville, Georgia. A paragraph or two from their report will show what fiendish cruelty and barbarity was systematically practiced towards our countrymen. "It is the same story everywhere:—prisoners of war treated worse than convicts, shut up either in suffocating buildings, or in outdoor enclosures, without even the shelter that is provided for the beasts of the field ; unsupplied with sufficient food ; supplied with food and water injurious and even poisonous ; compelled to live in such personal uncleanliness as to generate vermin ; compelled to sleep on floors often covered with human filth, or on ground saturated with it ; compelled to breathe an air oppressed with an intolerable stench ; hemmed in by a fatal dead-line and in hourly danger of being shot by unrestrained and brutal guards ; despondent even to madness, idiocy and suicide ; sick of disease (so congruous in character as to appear and spread like the plague), caused by the torrid sun, by decaying food, by filth, by vermin, by malaria, and by cold ; removed at the last moment, and by hundreds at a time, to hospitals corrupt as a sepulchre, there, with a few remedies, little care and no sympathy, to die in wretchedness and despair, not only among strangers, but among enemies too resentful either to have pity or to show mercy."

there could be no peace, except on the surrender of the rebel pretensions and armed resistance, or while the arch-traitor assumed the existence of two countries and expected to be treated otherwise than as a traitor and guilty of the crime of causing unutterable woes to the country at large.

Lee was appointed commander-in-chief of the rebel forces in February, 1865; he issued an urgent appeal to absentees, deserters, etc., to respond to his call; and the rebel Congress, though it was a bitter draught to swallow, yet yielding to stern necessity, voted to arm the slaves and employ them as soldiers. It was no more than a just retribution that the negroes, when invited to volunteer, declined helping the cause of those who had doomed them to everlasting bondage.

On the 31st of January, 1865, the resolution for the constitutional amendment abolishing slavery was passed. This 13th article of amendment was submitted to the legislatures of the several States, and on the 18th of December, the same year, the secretary of state announced that it had been ratified by three-fourths of the whole number of States, and was consequently valid, to all intents and purposes, as part of the Constitution of the United States. On the 4th of March, Abraham Lincoln was inaugurated for his second term of office; he delivered a brief but sensible and touching address; and so far as man could see, he had reason to hope and expect to be occupied soon in the more genial work of binding up the wounds of the bleeding nation. At the same time, Andrew Johnson took the oath of office as Vice-President, and what was very unusual and in bad taste beside, he made a speech in which he dilated upon his being "a plebeian," one of the common people, etc.

Sherman's success we have noted (p. 359). Grant called upon him now, (Dec. 28th, 1864,) to break up the railroads in North and South Carolina, and join the armies operating against Richmond as soon as he could. Having made all the preliminary arrangements, Sherman's army began its march, February 1st, 1865. It advanced across the Salkahatchie to Orangeburg, crossed the Congaree, and occupied Columbia on the 17th, the city having been pillaged and burned by the rebel cavalry. Charleston now became untenable, and Hardee made off, on the 18th of February, in the direction of North Carolina. Schofield, acting under orders from Grant, made an attack on Fort Anderson, on the Cape Fear River, guarding the approach to Wilmington. With the aid of Porter and his ships, Schofield was able to drive the rebels out, on the 18th, in consequence of which Wilmington fell into our hands and was occupied by our troops, February 22d. Further movements took place on the part of Sherman's right and left wings towards Fayetteville, N. C., which town was entered, March 11th, and all kinds of machinery, buildings for the rebel army uses, etc., were destroyed. Sherman now began to feel the need of more than usual caution. Hardee, Beauregard and Johnston had got together quite a large force in Sherman's path, and would unquestionably oppose his progress. He sent word to Terry and Schofield, at Wilmington and Newbern, to march direct for Goldsborough, which he expected himself to reach by March 20th. Hardee, having about 20,000 men, was attacked by Slocum at Averysborough, and driven out of the way of our advance. On the 18th of March, the rebel force under Johnston attacked Slocum's column, and a severe contest ensued with Sherman's army, but the enemy were repulsed and retreated. Goldsborough was taken and occupied by our army, March 23d, which rendered the obtaining of supplies easy by means of the two railroads back to the seaport of Wilmington and Beaufort, N. C. Sherman had a conference with Grant, and received directions as to the best mode of co-operating with him, so as to break up the rebellion as soon as possible. Thus, as we have seen, Sherman's army traversed the country from Savannah to Goldsborough, with an average breadth of forty miles, consuming all the forage, cattle, hogs, sheep, poultry, cured meats, corn meal, etc., and compelling the rebels to seek for food for the inhabitants from other quarters. "Of course," Sherman states, in his report, "the abandonment to us by the enemy of the whole sea-coast from Savannah to Newbern, North Carolina, with its forts, dock-yards, gun-boats, etc., was a necessary incident to our occupation and destruction of the inland routes of travel and supply. But the real object of this march was to place this army in a position easy of supply, whence it could take an appropriate part in the spring and summer campaign of 1865. This was completely accomplished on March 21st, by the junction of the three armies and the occupation of Goldsborough."

Grant's anxiety, at this date, was, lest Lee, finding the case hopeless, should abandon his position, and before he could be prevented, form a junction with Johnston, and thus protract the contest still further elsewhere. Hence Grant was very desirous to enclose Lee in, in suchwise that he would be compelled to surrender, and with his surrender the so-called Confederacy would of course fall to pieces. As a first movement, with this object in view, Sheridan was sent on a cavalry raid, starting from Winchester to cut off Lee's communications with Richmond, north of James River. This energetic officer set out, February 27th; crossed the Shenandoah and attacked Early successfully at Waynesborough; thence he marched to Charlottesville, destroying the railroads in every direction possible; but he was not able to carry out his plan fully, by crossing the James River and destroying the Southside Railroad. He next marched to White House, destroying the canal, railroads, bridges, etc., as completely as possible, and formed a junction with the army in front of Petersburg, March 27th. Lee, greatly depressed at the state of his affairs, knew that something must be done, or attempted to be done, to rouse the spirits of his men. Accordingly he ordered an assault on Fort Steadman, March 25th, which was carried forward with almost desperate energy; but it resulted in defeat, loss of 2000 as prisoners, and a further advance of our army. Grant, having in view the catching of Lee, gave instructions and orders to the army to move as speedily as possible for this purpose. On the 31st of March, Warren was pressing his entire corps on the rebel entrenched line on the White Oak Road. Lee began an attack which was pushed with great spirit and partial success; but Sheridan furnished relief in good time. The rebels, however, reinforced with cavalry, made an attack again, and the battle of Five Forks was the consequence. This was on the morning of April 1st, and during the day, after hard fighting, the rebels were driven into flight. On the same evening, Grant ordered a bombardment of Petersburg, which was kept up all night; and the next morning, Sunday, April 2d, the rebels were assaulted, driven from their lines, and forced to retreat wherever they could, in the utmost confusion. Lee sent word to Davis, that Petersburg and Richmond could no longer be held. Lee's troops retreated at once; Jeff. Davis made off directly towards the South,* and Richmond was occupied by our army on Monday morning, April 3d, 1865. The rebels had blown up and destroyed all they could, and setting fire to the buildings, a large part of the city was laid in ashes. Lee seems still to have had hopes of escaping by retreat, but Grant had taken precaution against any such result. Lee got as far as

* The fugitive arch-rebel, we may here mention, attempted to escape by way of the sea-coast. A reward of $100,000 was offered for his arrest, and the hunt was exceedingly active in consequence. He was finally caught by a portion of Wilson's cavalry, under Col. Pritchard, at Irwinsville, Wilkinson County, Ga., together with his family and a small number of attendants. This was on the morning of May 10th. Davis was brought prisoner to Fortress Monroe, and placed in close confinement. He was subsequently released on bail, under an indictment for treason. His trial was postponed several times, and finally in 1869, by a sort of general consent, the prosecution was abandoned, and with a feeling of contempt and abhorrence on the part of loyal men everywhere, he was allowed to sink into obscurity, and bear, as best he could, the gnawings of remorse.

Amelia Court House, where he confidently expected to find provisions and supplies; but they were not there, and with a half-starved army, he attempted to push on and reach the mountains beyond Lynchburg. But Sheridan and his co-laborers, pursued him with unflagging energy, and succeeded, April 6th, in getting possession of Farmville and preventing Lee from crossing the Appomattox. The next morning the pursuit was renewed, and though Lee did get across to the north side of the Appomattox, yet our men were so close that he could not destroy the bridge so as to hinder the unremitting pursuit, and exhausted, almost famished, suffering torments not to be described in words, the poor worn-out rebels were brought to the point where they must give up in sheer despair.

Grant, on the 7th of April, addressed Lee a note, and begged him to spare effusion of blood by further and useless resistance. It was hard for the rebel General thus to succumb, and he foolishly tried for two days longer to protract the contest; on the 9th, however, accepting Grant's liberal terms, Lee surrendered, and the weary, hungry, misguided men were at once supplied with food and comforts, to which they had long been strangers. The number surrendered was about 27,000, and they were allowed to depart on parole. Of course, with this decisive victory, the rebellion was crushed, and the Confederacy sunk into nothingness. Johnston surrendered to Sherman, April 26th, and Dick Taylor and Kirby Smith surrendered to Canby on May 4th and May 26th. In concluding the narrative of military operations, we may properly put on record, that, on the 1st of May, the entire army force amounted to 1,000,516, officers and men. The aggregate available force present for duty on the first of March was: Army of the Potomac, 103,273; armies in the several departments, 499,325; total, 602,598. Steps were taken immediately for mustering out the troops, so that from the beginning of May to August 7th, there were mustered out 640,806 troops; from that date to November 15th, there were mustered out 160,157; total 800,963.*

There could not but be a feeling of satisfaction and rejoicing, mingled with devout thankfulness, that the war was ended, and that now peace and concord might be allowed once more to bless the land. Although the rebellion was put down thoroughly and effectually, there were other questions and difficulties to be settled, as to the position of the seceded States, their restoration to rights under the Constitution, the kind and amount of restraint yet to be exercised, and such like. The president, we know, was greatly gratified that war was at an end, and he looked forward to the duties now devolving upon him, in the peculiar and anomalous condition of affairs, with an earnest and sincere desire to act wisely, temperately, mercifully, and yet with due regard to the dignity and majesty of the Constitution and laws violated so long and so wickedly by the rebellious States. But, alas for all human calculations! a mysterious Providence had otherwise ordered the course of events, and the sixteenth president of the United States was stricken down so suddenly, and in so horrible a manner, that, for the time, the national heart was paralyzed, and the ship of state, for the moment, appeared to be cut loose from her moorings, and, without chart or rudder, to be rushing swiftly to destruction. On Friday, April 14th, 1865, after a cabinet meeting, the president, accompanied by his family, went in the evening to a theatre in Washington. About ten o'clock, an actor, J. W. Booth, made his way from behind into the box where Mr. Lincoln was, and with deliberate aim, close by his chair, shot the president through the back of the

* As matters of interest, in this connection, it may be briefly stated, that the number of men surrendered, in the different rebel armies, was as follows: Lee's army, 27,805; Johnston's, 31,243; Dick Taylor's, 42,293; K. Smith's, 17,686; smaller organizations, in all, 55,196; making a total of 174,223. There were also in our hands nearly 100,000 prisoners of war. About 2,000 enlisted in the army; 63,442 were released; 33,127 were delivered in exchange.

head The murdered man's head fell slightly forward, and his eyes closed forever on this mortal scene. He lingered through the night, utterly unconscious, and early the next morning breathed his last. Booth, using a dagger, and rushing off across the stage, managed to escape for a time ; but was pursued and caught in a barn, near Port Royal, and on attempting to get away was shot, April 26th. Mr. Seward, this same Friday night, confined to his bed by a severe fall from his carriage, was assaulted and stabbed in several places by another assassin; but though terribly gashed in and about the throat, was not fatally wounded. It was an awful and horrible thing; assassination was utterly revolting to the American people; and these wild fanatics and murderers were looked upon with equal horror and indignation. But, whatever insane notion might have entered the brain of conspirators and traitors as to the effect of such a blow, in deranging the government and possibly benefiting the rebels and rebel sympathizers, the result showed how futile were all such calculations or vagaries of the kind. There was no political agitation or danger, no disturbance of the finances, no outbreaks, no doubt anywhere as to the stability of the government. The attorney-general officially informed Andrew Johnson, vice-president, of the facts of the case, and Johnson that same morning, April 15th, 1865, took the oath of office as president of the United States. The country was duly informed, by Secretary Stanton of what had been done, and Johnson, retaining the same gentlemen in the cabinet, the regular routine of government affairs went on as quietly and regularly as if the deplorable murder of Abraham Lincoln had never been committed.

The subsequent history of our country, during five or six years, is too near the present hour of writing to be entered upon at all at large. In fact, history cannot properly be written, with either fulness, exactness, or just appreciation of the facts and circumstances which form the staple of history, at a point of time so close to every-day chronicles of events. We shall not attempt, therefore, at the present moment, to do more than give a brief sketch or outline of what has taken place, in the History of the United States, since the accession of Andrew Johnson, and the election and inauguration into office of General Grant as president in 1869.

Among the subjects of deep and profound interest and importance which now claimed the attention of Congress and the people, were, the position, condition and legal status of the late rebellious States, and the national debt, arising out of the war, and what to do with it. The former of these led at once to difference of views and antagonism between Johnson and Congress; the latter was so enormous, being some $3,000,000,000, that it might well excite apprehensions as to the ability of the country to bear up under it, and in due time, if possible, to pay it off. Andrew Johnson was a rough specimen of a man to be elevated to the presidency. Bred to the trade of a tailor, with very imperfect means of education, in the overturnings of things produced by the rebellion he had shown unflinching steadiness, and manifested intense vigor, as a supporter of the Union and its just rights and claims. But he was like men of his stamp, very much given to one or two ideas, and was blindly and violently obstinate. When he was nominated for vice-president, it had not at all been taken into account that he might become president, and when, by that mysterious providence which removed Abraham Lincoln, so suddenly and only a month after his inauguration, Johnson took his place, it was apprehended that there would be trouble, and there *was* trouble very soon. Johnson had his theory of the position of the seceded States, that they had never been out of the Union, that nothing now was required but that they should accept their defeat and behave themselves, and all would be right and pleasant again, and that of course they had the same power as any of the loyal States to go to work, elect senators and representatives and exercise all the powers and prerogatives of Americans. Congress, on the other hand, was not willing to agree to any such mode of disposing of the matters at issue; and as the National Legislature had calculated upon having Lincoln to work with them, in harmony and concord, as to settlement of these questions, they found that there was a contest at once begun between them and the president, and that the latter was prepared to fight out the battle to the extreme. Into the particulars we cannot now go. The reader must consult the records of Congress, and the public documents which have been issued, if he desire to investigate and determine upon the merits of the subject.

Johnson, in May, 1865, issued an amnesty proclamation, under which pardon was offered to all the rebels, except in certain cases, provided they took the oath of allegiance to the United States. In July, 1868, he issued another proclamation, granting unconditionally pardon and amnesty to all except those under indictment for treason; this restriction was removed, December 25th, 1868, and amnesty was granted to all without restriction or reservation. The contest between Congress and the President grew worse as time advanced. Johnson vetoed nearly all the bills presented, and Congress on their part, passed a considerable number of bills by the two-thirds vote over his veto. This was the case with the Civil Rights Bill, which Johnson vetoed, but which was made a law by vote of Congress, April 9th, 1866. In June of the same year, the "Fenians," a secret association existing in Ireland and America, and having in view the separating of Ireland from Great Britain, made a raid into Canada from Buffalo and Vermont; but, as might be expected, met with defeat. The government interfered and the Fenians gave up the attempt. We may mention here also, that these same enemies of England, tried this plan of invading Canada to free Ireland, in 1870; but made themselves only ridiculous in the whole matter.

At the beginning of March, 1867, Congress passed a bill relative to the tenure of office held by those public servants appointed by and with the advice and consent of the Senate. It will be remembered that at the beginning of the government, under Washington, the question was raised as to whether officers appointed by the president with the consent of the Senate, could be *removed* by the president without the consent of the same body (p. 108). The construction then given was followed in all succeeding administrations; but, the Thirty-ninth Congress, brought up the subject again, and determined that the consent of the Senate was as necessary to remove as to appoint. No doubt, the condition of affairs at the time had much to do with the present settlement or decision. Mr. Stanton was secretary of war, under Mr. Lincoln, and was considered generally to be a man of excellent ability and fitness; but it was not long before Johnson became dissatisfied and out of all patience with his secretary. Stanton would not resign and leave quietly, and so Johnson resolved to compel him to go. So he notified Stanton, February 21st, 1868, that he was no longer secretary of war, and appointed another *ad interim.* It was a long and acrimonious dispute; Stanton held that he was still chief of his department, and Johnson virtually forced him out of the premises and affirmed that he was no longer a member of the Cabinet. According to the tenure of office bill Stanton could not be displaced without the consent of the Senate, and the Senate refused to give such consent. Hence, it was a nice sort of a quarrel, and neither party seemed likely to yield.

As Johnson was as pugnacious as he was obstinate, and as there were men in Congress who possessed largely the same troublesome qualities, it was resolved to try another plan to get the better of the occupant of the White House. On the 24th of February, 1868, it was resolved by the House of Representatives to impeach Andrew Johnson as guilty of high crimes and misdemeanors. The first nine articles related to the matter of Stanton's removal and forcible expulsion from office; the tenth and eleventh to Johnson's abusive language about Congress, tending to bring it into contempt, and to his declaring openly that the Thirty-ninth Congress was not a Congress according to the Constitution, etc. The Senate organized as a Court, March 5th, 1868, chief-justice Chase presiding; adjourned to the 23d, to give Johnson and his council time; met at that date and heard Johnson's answers to the charges; a replication was made the next day by the managers on behalf of the House of Representatives; during the month of April testimony was taken on both sides; and finally, after the arguments of counsel, the vote was taken, and Johnson was acquitted, May 26th, by vote of 34 to 16. Stanton thereupon resigned the war department the same day, and General Schofield took his place.

Congress refusing to admit the insurgent States to their full rights without certain guarantees, in respect to their future position and action, passed a fourteenth amendment to the Constitution, relating to the rights of voters, having in view the securing a just and equitable representation in Congress, affirming the validity and obligation of the public debt, etc. This amendment was adopted by Congress, June 16th, 1868, and ratified by the legislatures of the requisite number of States, July 20th, 1868. The fifteenth amendment was in these words; "The right of citizens of the United States to vote shall not be denied or abridged by the United States or by any State on account of race, color, or previous condition of servitude." It was adopted by Congress, on the 25th of February, 1869, and early in 1870, was ratified in the mode provided by the Constitution.

The number of States is now complete; on the basis of these amendments, and legislation of Congress, reconstruction has taken place; and the mad and wicked scheme and purpose of rebellion and treason have been defeated. God grant that the Union may be one and forever inseparable!

General Grant was elected president of the United States in the autumn of 1868, and entered upon the duties of his high office, March 4th, 1869. Public affairs have been comparatively quiet since his accession; the country is laboring hard to restore prosperity, so deeply injured by the rebellion, to get rid of taxation by liquidating the national debt, and in every way possible promote the peace and welfare of the Republic. The appointment of a joint high commission with England, early in 1871, is one of the most favorable indications of the day, inasmuch as there is every reason to hope that, by the efforts of wise, learned, patriotic, and upright men, not only the Alabama Claims will be fully and perfectly adjusted, but each and every other question or grievance or dispute with Great Britain and her people. GLORY TO GOD IN THE HIGHEST, ON EARTH PEACE, GOOD WILL TOWARDS MEN.

U. S. Grant.

From the original painting by Chappel in the possession of the publishers.

Johnson Fry & Co. Publishers, New York.

MEXICO.

CHAPTER I.

HISTORY OF MEXICO FROM THE EALLIEST ACCOUNTS TILL ITS SUBJECTION TO SPAIN.

MEXICO, in North America, is situated between 16° and 33° N. Lat., and between 86° and 117° W. Long.; being nearly 2000 miles in length, and 1,100 miles in greatest breadth. The Toltecans are the most ancient Mexican nation of which we know anything. They were expelled from their own country, which is supposed to have been *Tollan*, to the northward of Mexico, in the year A. D. 472. After leading a wandering life for more than 100 years, they settled near the City of Mexico where they built a city, called, from the name of their country, *Tollan* or *Tula*. After the final settlement of the Toltecans, the government became monarchical. Their first king began his reign in 667, and their monarchy lasted 384 years. During this period the Toltecans increased very considerably in number, and built many cities; but, when in the height of prosperity, almost the whole nation was destroyed by a famine occasioned by drought and a pestilence. The few who survived abandoned the country of Tula about 1054. A century later they were succeeded by the Chichemecas, a much more barbarous people, who came from an unknown country called *Amaquemecan*, where they had for a long time resided. They were eighteen months on their journey, and took possession of the desolate country of the Toltecans about 100 years after the famine. Though much more uncivilized than the Toltecans, they had a regular form of monarchical government, and, in other respects, were less disgusting in their manners than some of the neighboring nations. Their king, Xolotl, chose for his capital, Tenayuca, about six miles to the northward of the city of Mexico, and distributed his people in the neighboring territory; but, as most of them went to the northward, that part obtained the name of the country of the Chichemecas, in contradistinction to the rest. Xolotl found some of the Toltecans not far off, and, peacefully settled in his new dominion, entered into an alliance with them, and Nopaltzin, the son of Xolotl, married a Toltecan princess. The consequence of this alliance was the introduction of the arts and knowledge of the Toltecans amongst the Chichemecas. When Xolotl had reigned about eight years in his new territories, other bodies of people asked privilege of settlement, which was freely granted and marriages among the princes and new-comers took place. The country was peaceably divided between the princes and continued for some time to flourish, population increased greatly, and with it the civilization of the people; but, as these advanced, the vices of luxury and ambition increased in proportion. Xolotl died in the fortieth year of his reign, at a very advanced age. His son and grandsons succeeded in order, but had much trouble with rebellions which took place to a large extent. They were, however, effectually subdued. As the affairs of the Acolhuans had now begun to be connected with those of the Mexicans, it will be proper to give some account of that people.

The nation of the Aztecas, which comprised the Mexicans, dwelt till the year 1160 in a country called *Aztlan*, situated to the north of the Gulf of California, as appears by the route they pursued in their journey, but how far to the northward we are not certainly informed; probably about 2,500 miles. The Aztecas, when they left their original habitations, were divided into six tribes; but, at Culiacan, the Mexicans were left with their god (a wooden image), while the five tribes of Xochimilcas, Tepanecas, Chalcese, Tlahuicas, and Tlascalans, continued their march. The remaining tribe was divided into two violent factions, which persecuted one another, but always travelled together in order to enjoy the company of their god. At every place where they stopped an altar was erected to him; and at their departure they left behind them all their sick, and probably also all that were not willing to endure the fatigue of such journeys. They stopped in Tula nine years, and eleven more in the neighboring parts. At last, in 1216, they arrived at Zumpanco, a considerable city in the valley of Mexico, and were received in a hospitable manner by the lord of the district. He not only assigned them proper habitations, but even demanded from amongst them a wife for his son Ilhuicatl. This request was complied with, and from this marriage all the Mexican kings descended. The Mexicans continued to migrate from one place to another along the Lake of Tezcuco. Xolotl, who was then on the throne of the Acolhuans or Chichemecas, allowed them to settle in whatsoever places of his dominions they thought proper; but, some of them finding themselves harassed by a neighboring lord, were obliged in the year 1245 to retire to Chapoltepec, a mountain on the western borders of the lake, scarcely two miles distant from the site of Mexico. The Mexicans, however, did not find themselves any more secure in their new place of residence than formerly. They were persecuted by the neighboring lords, and obliged to take refuge in a number of small islands named Acocolco, at the southern extremity of the Lake of Mexico. Here for fifty-two years they lived in the most miserable manner, subsisting on fish, insects, roots, etc., and clothing themselves with the leaves of the amoxtli, which abounds in that lake. In this miserable plight the Mexicans continued till the year 1314, when they were reduced to a state of the most absolute slavery by the king of a petty state named Colhuacan. After some years a war broke out between the Colhuans and Xochimilcas, in which the latter gained such advantages that the former were obliged to employ their slaves to assist them. By their help, the Colhuans gained a complete victory. Notwithstanding, it does not appear that the haughty masters were in the least inclined to afford their slaves easier terms than before. On a certain day which the Mexicans had set apart for sacrificing to their god, the Colhuan prince attended with his nobility, not with a view to do honor to the festival, but to make a mockery. Their derision, however, was soon changed into horror, when the Mexicans, after a solemn dance, brought forth four Xochimilcan prisoners; and, after having made them dance, cut open their breasts with a knife and plucking out their hearts, offered them, whilst yet palpitating with life, to their sanguinary idol. They were immediately ordered to leave the country, and the whole nation took their route towards the north until they came to a place named *Iztacalco*, near the site of Mexico. The city of Mexico was founded in 1325 on a small island named Tenochtitlan, in the middle of a great lake, without ground to cultivate for subsistence, or even room sufficient to build habitations. To enlarge the boundaries of their island, they drove palisades into those parts of the water which were most shallow, terracing them with stones and turf, and uniting to their principal island several other smaller ones which lay in the neighborhood. The greatest effort of their industry, however, was the construction of floating gardens by means of bushes and of the mud of the lake; and these they brought to so much perfection that they produced maize, pepper, chia, French beans, and gourds. During the thirteen years that the Mexicans had to struggle, with extreme difficulty they remained at peace; but, no sooner did they begin to prosper and live comfortably, than the inveterate enmity between the two factions broke out in all its fury. About this time, the Mexicans divided their city into four parts; each quarter having now its tutelar saint, as it had formerly had its tutelar god. In the midst of their city was the sanctuary of their great god, *Mexitli*, whom they constantly preferred to all the rest. To him they daily performed acts of adoration; but, instead of making any progress in humanity, they seem to have daily improved in the most horrible barbarities, at least in their religion.

In the year 1352, the Mexican government was changed from an aristocracy to a monarchy. At first the people were governed by twenty lords, of whom one had an authority superior to the rest. This naturally suggested the idea of monarchy; and to this change they were also induced by the contemptible state in which their nation still continued, thinking that by having one leader, they would be better able to oppose their enemies. The choice fell upon Acamapitzin, a man held in great estimation amongst them, and descended from Opoclitli, a noble Aztecan, and a princess of the royal family of Colhuacan. In the meantime, the Tlatelolcos, the natural rivals of the Mexicans, likewise chose a king by applying to the king of the Tepanecos, who readily sent them his son; and he was crowned first king of Tlatelolco in 1353. In this, the Tlatelolcos seem to have had a design of humbling their rivals, as well as of rendering themselves more respectable; and, therefore, it is very probable that they had represented the Mexicans as wanting in that respect due to the Tepanecan monarch, from having elected a king without his leave, though at the same time they were tributaries to him. The consequence of this was, that he doubled their tribute, and imposed upon them many other things from which, however, they succeeded in freeing themselves. Acamapitzin governed this city, which at that time comprehended the whole of his dominions, for thirty-seven years in peace. He was succeeded by his son, who began his reign by espousing the daughter of the king of Azcapozalco. Though this princess brought him a son the first year of their marriage, the king, in order to strengthen himself by fresh alliances, married also the daughter of another prince, by whom he had Montezuma Ilhuicamina, the most celebrated of all the Mexican kings. As the Mexicans advanced in wealth and power, so did their rivals, the inhabitants of Tlatelolco. Their first king died in 1399, leaving his subjects greatly improved in civilization and the city much enlarged and beautified. The Mexicans had formed many alliances by marriage with the neighboring nations, had much improved their agriculture and floating gardens on the lake, and had built very many vessels to supply their extended commerce and fishing. In 1406, Techotlala, king of Acolhuacan, died, after a tranquil reign of thirty years. Immediately the kings of Mexico, Azcapozalco, and Tlatelolco abjured their allegiance. After a disastrous contest of three years, the rebels, designing to accomplish by treachery what they had been unable to effect by force, sued for peace and obtained it. In 1409, the King of Mexico died and his brother succeeded him. Whilst the new prince was endeavoring to secure himself on the throne, the treacherous Tezozomoc, King of Azcapozalco, employed all the means in his power to strengthen the party he had formed against the King of Acolhuacan. In this he had such success, that the unfortunate prince found himself reduced to the necessity of wandering amongst the neighboring mountains at the head of a small army, who remained faithful to him. He was persuaded to a conference and murdered. Tezozomoc next attacked and drove out the Acolhuacans. He then gave Tezcuco to Chimilpopoca, King of Mexico, and Huexotla to Tlacacotl, King of Tlatelolco; at the same time placing faithful governors in others places, and appointing Azcapozalco the capitol of his own territory, the royal residence and capital of Acolhuacan. All the rest of the Acolhuacan empire submitted; and Tezozomoc had now attained the summit of his ambition. But, instead of conciliating the minds of his new subjects, he oppressed them with fresh taxes; and, being conscious of the precarious situation in which he stood, and tormented with remorse on account of his crimes, he fell into melancholy, and at length expired in the year 1422, leaving the crown to his son Tajatzin. Tezozomoc was no sooner dead than Maxtlaton, one of his other sons, without paying the least regard to his father's will, began to exercise the functions of sovereign, and compelled his brother Tajatzin to retire to Chimilpopoca, King of Mexico. This monarch, agreeably to the character of that age and people, advised him to invite his brother to an entertainment, and then to murder him. This discourse was overheard by a servant, who in expectation of a reward, informed the tyrant of what he had heard. Maxtlaton, therefore, determined to rid himself of his brother without delay, which he accomplished by inviting his brother to an entertainment and murdering him. The King of Mexico escaped a sudden death by his absence at this time, only to perish in a manner more slow and ignominious. His revengeful foe, Maxtlaton, not content with heaping insults upon him, sent a body of troops, who, entering Mexico without resistance, carried off the king alive. Chimilpopoca was imprisoned at Azcapozalco in a strong wooden cage, the common prison for criminals.

In the meantime, the Mexicans raised to the throne Izcoatl, the son of Acamapitzin. His election was no less pleasing to the Acolhuans than it was offensive to Maxtlaton. An alliance was quickly concluded between the exiled prince and the King of Mexico; and, when the former commenced hostilities against the tyrant of Azcapozalco, the latter agreed to assist him. Maxtlaton accordingly prepared to wage war with the Mexicans. The Mexican populace, terrified at engaging so powerful an enemy, demanded that their king should submit and sue for a peace. But, Montezuma, the brave son of Huitzilihuitl, persuaded them to agree to a commencement of hostilities. Conditions of peace, however, were first sent to Maxtlaton by the hands of Montezuma. They were rejected, and the Mexican ambassador forthwith went through the ceremony of declaring war. The Mexican populace were again thrown into the utmost consternation by the news that war was inevitable, and they now requested the king to allow them to retire from their city, of which they supposed the ruin to be certain. The king encouraged them with the hopes of victory. "But, if we are conquered," replied they, "what will become of us?" "If that happen," answered the king, "we are at that moment bound to deliver ourselves into your hands to be made sacrifices at your pleasure." Nezahualcojotl was forthwith summoned to repair to Mexico with his army. On the day after his arrival, the allied forces encountered the Tepanecan troops under a general named Mazatl. After an obstinate and bloody contest which lasted till night, the Tepanecan general fell by the sword of Montezuma, and his forces were driven into their capital city. On the following day their defeat was even more signal, and resulted in the capture of Azcapozalco. Maxtlaton attempted to hide himself, but, being quickly discovered, he was beaten to death with sticks and stones. The city was plundered, the inhabitants were butchered, and the houses destroyed by the victors. This victory proved decisive in favor of the confederates. Every other place of strength in the country was quickly reduced, until the Tepanecans, finding themselves upon the verge of destruction, sent an humble embasny to the King of Mexico, requesting to be taken under his protection and to become tributaries to him. Izcoatl received them graciously, but threatened them with total extirpation if they violated the fidelity they had sworn to him. Nezahualcojotl was now seated upon the throne of Acolhuacan. Having thus accomplished the conquest of Cojohuacan, a great part of the Tepanecan country with the title of King of Tacuba was given by Izcoatl to a grandson of Tezozomoc. An alliance was then formed between the Kings of Mexico, Acolhuacan, and Tepanecan. The conditions were that they should assist each other in war, and should divide all plunder amongst themselves according to certain specified proportions. About this time the Xochimilcas, fearing lest the Mexicans should now turn their victorious arms against them, determined to commence hostilities against them, but Montezuma was sent against them and they were routed entirely.

Izcoatl died in 1436, at a very advanced age, in the height of prosperity, and was succeeded by Montezuma I., the greatest monarch that ever sat on the Mexican throne. Scarcely had he been crowned when his aid was solicited by the Tezcucans against the Chalcese. The latter were almost entirely annihilated in one desperate battle, and their city was levelled with the ground. Montezuma on his return found the King of Tlatelolcos engaged in designs against him; but Montezuma soon disposed of him. One Moquihuix was chosen in his stead; and, in the election of that chief, it is probable that Montezuma had a considerable share. This was followed by conquests of a much more important nature. He added to his dominions the province of Cuihixcas, situated to the southward, and comprehending a tract of country more than 150 miles in breadth. Then, turning to the westward, he conquered another province named Tzompahuacan. This success, however, was for a short time interrupted by a war with Atonaltzin, lord of a territory in the country of the Mixtacas, and two or three confederates. Commanding in person, he totally defeated the confederate army. By this victory, the Mexican monarch became master, not only of the dominions of Atonaltzin, but of those of many other neighboring princes, against whom he had made war on account of their having put to death some Mexican merchants or couriers without any just cause. The conquest of Cuetlachtan or Cotasta, however, which he attempted in 1457, proved a much more difficult task. This province is situated on the coast of the Mexican Gulf, and had formerly been inhabited by the Olmecans, whom the Tlascalans had driven out. The inhabitants were very numerous and fought with great valor, but were unable to resist the royal forces; and their allies were almost totally destroyed. Six thousand two hundred of them were taken prisoners, and soon afterwards sacrificed to the Mexican god of war in the barbarous manner already described. During the reign of this great monarch, a violent inundation happened in Mexico. The lake, swollen by the excessive rains which fell in 1446, poured its waters into the city with such violence, that many houses were destroyed and the streets inundated to such a degree, that boats were everywhere made use of. The inundation was soon followed by a famine. This was occasioned by the partial failure of the crop of maize in 1448, the ears whilst young and tender having been destroyed by frost. In 1450, the crop was totally lost for want of water; and, in 1451, besides the unfavorable seasons, there was a scarcity of seed. Hence, in 1452, the necessities of the people became so great, that they were actually obliged to sell themselves as slaves in order to procure subsistence. Montezuma opened the public granaries for the relief of the lower classes, but nothing could arrest the progress of the famine.

Montezuma was succeeded by Axayacatl, who pursued his predecessor's plan of conquest, in which, however, he was not very successful; many of the provinces reduced by that monarch having revolted after his death, so that is was necessary to reconquer them. The Mexicans sustained a great loss in 1469 and 1470 by the death of their allies, the kings of Tacuba and Acolhuacan. The King of Tacuba was succeeded by his son, Chimilpopoca, and the Acolhuacan monarch by his son, Nezahualpilli. A short time after the accession of the latter, the war broke out between the Tlatelolcos and Mexicans, which ended in the destruction of the former. The Tlatelolcos being thus reduced, Axayacatl next set out on an expedition against the Matlazincas, a tribe in the valley of Toluca, who still refused to submit to the Mexican yoke. Having proved successful in this expedition, he undertook to subdue Xiquipilco, a considerable city and state of the Otomies. His army gained a complete victory, carrying off more than eleven thousand prisoners, amongst whom was the chief of the Otomies himself. Axayacatl was succeeded by his elder brother called Tizoc, who was shortly afterwards murdered in a conspiracy of his subjects. Ahuitzotl, the brother of Tizoc, succeeded him in the kingdom of Mexico. His first object was to finish the great temple begun by his predecessor; and, so great was the number of workmen employed, that it was completed in four years. During the time it was building, the king employed himself in making war with different nations, reserving all the prisoners he took for victims at the dedication of the temple. The number of prisoners sacrificed at this dedication in 1486, is said by Torquemada to have been 72,324, and by other historians is estimated at 64,060. In 1487 there happened a violent earthquake; and Ahuitzotl died in the year 1502 of a disorder produced by a contusion in the head. At the time of his death, the Mexican empire had reached its utmost extent.

His successor, Montezuma Xocojotzin, or Montezuma the younger, was a person of great bravery, and was likewise a priest, and held in great estimation on account of the gravity and dignity of his deportment. But, no sooner was the ceremony of his coronation terminated, than Montezuma began to discover a pride which nobody had befoıe suspected. He deprived all the commoners of the offices they held about the court, declaring them incapable of holding any for the future. All the royal servants were now people of rank. Besides those who lived in the palace, six hundred feudatory lords and nobles came to pay court to him. In every respect he kept up, as far as was possible, an extravagant appearance of dignity, splendor, and luxury. But the reign of Montezuma, even before the arrival of the Spaniards, was far from being so glorious as those of his predecessors had been. He attempted to extort tribute from Tlascala, a small republic at no great distance from the capital, but the inhabitants had already inclosed all the lands of the republic with intrenchments, to which they now added a wall six miles in length on the west side, where an invasion was most to be apprehended. Behind these fortifications so well did they defend themselves, that, though they were frequently attacked by the neighboring States in alliance with Mexico or subject to it, they were still able to maintain their ground. Montezuma's reign was also disturbed by disastrous losses and evil omens. In 1508, an expedition against a very distant region named Amatla completely failed. By this and other calamities, together with the appearance of a comet, Montezuma was so terrified, that he applied to the King of Alcohuacan, who was reported to be very skilful in divination. Nezahualpilli told him that the comet presaged the arrival of a new people, but this being unsatisfactory to the emperor, he conferred with a celebrated astrologer, who confirmed the former interpretation.

Mexico was first discovered by Hernandez de Cordova, who, in 1517, in sailing towards the Bahamas, was driven by a succession of severe storms on the coast of Yucatan. On the 10th of February, 1519, Hernando Cortez set sail for the conquest of Mexico from Havana, and, after touching at Yucatan, arrived in Passion-week of the same year at the harbor of St. Juan de Ulloa. Here he was met by two Mexican canoes, which carried two ambassadors from the emperor of that country, and showed the greatest signs of peace and amity. Their language was translated into the Yucatan tongue by a female prisoner, whom they had recently captured; after which a Spaniard named Jerom de Aguilar interpreted the meaning in Spanish. This slave was afterwards named Donna Marina, and proved very useful in their conferences with the natives. By means of his two interpreters, Cortez learned that the object of the embassy was to inquire what his intentions were in visiting these coasts. He accordingly informed the ambassadors that he came to propose matters of the utmost consequence to the welfare of the prince and his kingdom. Next morning, without waiting for any answer, he landed his troops, horses and artillery, and began to erect huts for his men, and to fortify his camp. The day following, the ambassadors had a formal audience, at which Cortez acquainted them that he came from Don Carlos of Austria, King of Castile, the greatest monarch of the East, and was entrusted with propositions of such moment, that he would impart them to none but the emperor himself, and therefore required to be conducted immediately to the capital. This demand produced the greatest uneasiness, and in a few days Cortez was informed that Montezuma would not give his consent that foreign troops should approach nearer to his capital, or even allow them to continue longer in his dominions. In a short time a deputy named Teutile arrived with a rich present from Montezuma, and together with it delivered the ultimate orders of that monarch to depart instantly out of his dominions; and when Cortez, instead of complying with his demands, renewed his request of audience, the Mexican immediately left the camp with strong marks of surprise and resentment. Cortez, without allowing his men time for reflection, immediately set about carrying his designs into execution. In order to give a beginning to a colony, he assembled the principal persons in his army, and by their suffrages elected a council and magistrates, in whom the government was to be vested. The new settlement received the name of Villa Rica de la Vera Cruz, that is "the rich town of the true cross." Before this court of his own making, Cortez did not hesitate to resign all his authority, and was immediately re-elected chief-justice of the colony, and captain-general of his army, with an ample commission, in the king's name, to continue in force till the royal pleasure should be further known. The soldiers eagerly ratified their choice by loud acclamations; and Cortez resolved to advance into the country. Yet, as he had thrown off all dependence on Velasquez, the governor of Cuba, who was his lawful superior, he was apprehensive of his interest at court, and thought proper, before he set out on his intended expedition, to take most effectual measures against the impending danger. With this view, he persuaded the magistrates of his colony to address a letter to the king, containing a pompous account of their own services, of the country they had discovered, and of the motives which had induced them to throw off their allegiance to the governor of Cuba, and to settle a colony dependent on the crown alone, in which the supreme power, civil as well as military, had been vested in Cortez; humbly requesting their sovereign to ratify what had been done under his royal authority. A plan, however, was formed to send intelligence to Cuba; whereupon, to prevent such plots in future, Cortez, without any hesitation, burned his fleet, and thus rendered it necessary for his troops to follow wherever he chose to lead. He then began his march into the interior, with 500 infantry, 15 horse, 6 field-pieces, and with a reinforcement of native troops, consisting of 400 regulars and 200 of those Indians called Tamanes, whose office was to carry burdens and perform all manner of servile labor.

Nothing memorable happened till the Spaniards arrived on the confines of the republic of Tlascala. As the inhabitants of that province were implacable enemies of Montezuma, Cortez hoped that it would be an easy matter for him to procure their friendship; but his ambassadors were detained, a circumstance which led him to infer that the Tlascalans were hostile. He accordingly approached the city, and though opposed by immense numbers, yet in three or four battles was victorious. The Tlascalans yielded themselves as vassals to the crown of Castile, and engaged to assist Cortez in all his operations, in return for the protection which he guaranteed to extend to their republic. As soon as his troops were fit for service, Cortez resolved to continue his march towards Mexico, notwithstanding the remonstrances of the Tlascalans. But the emperor had informed Cortez that he agreed to receive his visit, and that he had given orders for his friendly reception at Cholula, the next place of any consequence on the road to Mexico. Cortez was received with much seeming cordiality; but 6000 Tlascalan troops who accompanied him were obliged to remain without the town, as the Cholulans refused to admit their ancient enemies within their precincts. In a short time Donna Marina, the interpreter, received information from an Indian woman of distinction, whose confidence she had gained, that the destruction of the Spaniards was concerted and ready for immediate execution. Cortez, alarmed at this news, resolved to anticipate his enemies. On a signal given, his troops rushed out and attacked the multitude in front, the Tlascalans at the same time assailing them in the rear; the streets were filled with slaughter, and the temples, which afforded a retreat to the priests and some leading men, were set on fire, in consequence of which they perished in the flames. At length the carnage ceased, after the slaughter of 6000 Cholulans, without the loss of a single Spaniard, and Cortez continued his march to Mexico with great circumspection and the strictest discipline.

When the Spaniards drew near the city, about 1000 persons of distinction came forth to meet them, and announced the approach of the emperor himself. Preceded by all the pomp and pageantry of an oriental monarch, Montezuma appeared in a chair or litter richly ornamented with gold, and feathers of various colors, surmounted by a canopy of curious workmanship. When he drew near, Cortez, dismounting, accosted him with profound reverence, after the European fashion. He returned the salutation, according to the mode of his country, by touching the earth with his hand, and then kissing it. Nothing material passed at this first interview. The first care of Cortez was to take precautions for his security, by planting the artillery so as to command the different avenues which led to his quarters, and by appointing a large division of his troops to be always on guard. The three subsequent days were employed in viewing the city, the appearance of which, so far superior to any place the Spaniards had beheld in America, and yet so little resembling the structure of a European city, filled them with surprise and admiration. The access to the City of Mexico or Tenochtitlan was by artificial causeways or streets, formed of stones and earth, about 30 feet in breadth. As the waters of the lake, during the rainy season overflowed the level country, these causeways were of considerable length. On the east there was no causeway, and the city could be approached only by canoes. As the approaches to the city were singular, so its construction was remarkable. Not only the temples of their gods, but the houses belonging to the monarch and to persons of distinction, were very large, and might even be termed magnificent. The habitations of the common people were mean, resembling the huts of other Indians; but they were all placed in a regular manner on the banks of the canals, which passed through the city in some of its districts, or on the sides of the streets which intersected it in other quarters. In this city, the noblest monument of the industry and the art of man whilst unacquainted with the use of iron, the Spaniards reckon that there were at least 60,000 inhabitants.

As soon as Cortez had entered Mexico, he had become sensible that, from an excess of confidence in the superior valor and discipline of his troops, he had pushed forward into a situation where it was difficult to continue, and from which it was dangerous to retire. At the same he knew that the countenance of his own sovereign was to be obtained only by a series of victories. He therefore fixed upon a plan no less extraordinary than daring. He determined to seize Montezuma in his palace, and to carry him as a prisoner to the Spanish quarters. At his usual hour of visiting Montezuma, Cortez went to the palace accompanied by five of his principal officers, and with as many trusty soldiers. Thirty chosen men followed, not in regular order, but sauntering at some distance, as if they had no object but curiosity; small parties were posted at proper intervals in all the streets leading from the Spanish quarters to the court; and the remainder of his troops, with the Tlascalan allies, were under arms, ready to sally out on the first alarm. Cortez addressed the monarch in a tone very different from that which he had employed in former conferences, reproaching him bitterly as the author of a violent assault made upon the Spaniards by one of his officers. Montezuma, confounded at this unexpected accusation, asserted his own innocence with great earnestness. Cortez replied that a declaration so respectable left no doubt remaining in his own mind; but that his followers would never be convinced that Montezuma did not harbor hostile intentions against them, unless he removed from his own palace and took up his residence in the Spanish quarters. The first mention of so strange a proposal deprived Montezuma of speech, and almost of motion, and he resented it greatly. At length, after he had been alternately coaxed and intimidated for the space of three hours, he complied with their request, and was carried off in silent pomp to the Spanish quarters. In a short time Cortez had entirely gained the ascendant over the unhappy monarch; and he took care to improve his opportunity to the utmost. He brought Montezuma to acknowledge himself a vassal of the crown of Castile; to hold his crown of him as superior; and to subject his dominions to the payment of an annual tribute. He then, at the request of Cortez, accompanied his profession of fealty with a magnificent present to his new sovereign; and, after his example, his subjects brought in very liberal contributions. Yet, although often importuned, he obstinately refused to change his religion, or abolish the superstitious rites which had been for so long a time practiced throughout his dominions. In an ebullition of zeal, Cortez led out his soldiers in order to throw down by force the idols in the great temple; but it was to no purpose. Scarcely had he escaped from this danger when he was startled by the news, that an armament sent by Velasquez, the governor of Cuba, had arrived at Vera Cruz. He afterwards learned that it consisted of 18 ships and 900 men, under a brave officer named Pamphilo de Narvaez, and that their instructions were, to seize Cortez and his principal officers, to send them prisoners to Velasquez, and then to complete the discovery and conquest of the country in his name.

After attempting in vain to induce Narvaez to share with him the glory and gain of subduing the country, Cortez resolved to trust his fate to the issue of a war. He therefore left 150 men under the command of Pedro de Alvarado, to guard the capital and the captive emperor; and marched with the remainder to meet his formidable opponent. Even after being reinforced by Sandoval, the governor of Vera Cruz, the force of Cortez did not exceed two hundred and fifty men. He hoped for success chiefly from the rapidity of his movements and the possibility of surprising his enemies. At last he attacked Narvaez in the night-time, and having entirely defeated and taken him prisoner, obliged all his troops to own allegiance to himself. A short time after the defeat of Narvaez a courier arrived from Mexico with the disagreeable intelligence that the Mexicans had taken arms, and having seized and destroyed the two brigantines which he had built in order to secure the command of the lake, had attacked the Spaniards in their quarters, and had carried on hostilities with such fury that Alvarado and his men must either have been cut off by famine or overpowered by the multitude of their enemies. This revolt had been excited by motives which rendered it still more alarming. On the departure of Cortez, the Mexicans had held a consultation for restoring their sovereign to liberty, and driving out the Spaniards. The Spaniards in the city suspected and dreaded these machinations; but Alvarado, instead of attempting to soothe or cajole the Mexicans, waited the return of one of their solemn festivals, fell upon them, unarmed and unsuspicious of danger, and massacred six hundred in cold blood. An action so cruel and so treacherous, filled not only the city, but the whole empire, with rage and indignation. Cortez advanced with the utmost celerity to the relief of his distressed companions, and entered the capital without opposition. But by this time indignation and success had so intoxicated him that he refused, with strong words of contempt, a personal interview with Montezuma. His expressions being reported amongst the Mexicans, they suddenly flew to arms, and made such a violent and sudden attack, that all the valor and skill of Cortez were scarcely sufficient to repel them. After exerting his utmost efforts for a whole day, he was obliged to retire with the loss of twelve killed and upwards of sixty wounded. When the Mexicans approached the next morning to renew the assault, Montezuma, who was still at the mercy of the Spaniards, advanced to the battlements in his royal robes, and addressed his subjects in favor of the Spaniards. But they testified their resentment with loud murmurings, and at length broke forth with such fury that they wounded him with two arrows, and struck him to the ground with a stone. The unhappy monarch now obstinately refused all nourishment, and in a short time ended his days.

Upon the death of Montezuma, Cortez having lost all hope of bringing the Mexicans to any terms of peace, prepared for retreat. But his antagonists having taken possession of a high tower in the great temple, which overlooked the Spanish quarters, and placed there a garrison of their principal warriors, the Spaniards were so much exposed to their missile weapons, that none of them could stir without imminent danger. In an attempt to capture this post Juan de Escobar, with a large detachment of chosen soldiers, was thrice repulsed, and it was only by a desperate hand to hand fight led by Cortez that the tower was taken. It was then set fire to, and towards midnight the Spaniards began their march in three divisions. But they had not proceeded far before they were suddenly alarmed with the sound of warlike instruments, and found themselves assaulted on all sides by an innumerable multitude of Mexicans. The Spaniards advanced with precipitation. At last, overborne with the numbers of the enemy, they began to give way, and in a moment the confusion was universal. More than four hundred Spanish soldiers perished, together with many officers of distinction. All the artillery, ammunition, and baggage were lost; the greater part of the horses, and above two thousand Tlascalans were killed, and only a very small part of their treasure was saved. The first care of Cortez, after he had succeeded in escaping from the city, was to find some shelter for his small shattered army. At last he discovered a temple seated on an eminence, in which he found not only the shelter he want ed, but also some provisions. For six days afterwards the Spaniards continued their march through a barren, ill-cultivated, and thinly-peopled country, where they were often obliged to feed on berries, roots, and the stalks of green maize; at the same time they were harassed without intermission by large parties of Mexicans, who attacked them on all sides. On the sixth day they reached Otumba, not far from the road between Mexico and Tlascala. Early next morning, when they reached the summit of an eminence before them, a spacious valley opened to their view, covered with a vast army of Mexicans as far as the eye could reach. Cortez advanced instantly to the charge, and a most bloody fight ensued. Cortez seized the imperial ensign and killed the general; whereupon a universal panic struck the Mexicans; every ensign was lowered, and each soldier, throwing away his weapons, fled with precipitation to the mountains.

The day after this important action, which was fought on the 8th of July, 1520, the Spaniards entered the Tlascalan territories, where they were cordially received. Cortez now set himself assiduously to prepare for a second invasion of Mexico. He drew a small supply of ammunition, and two or three field-pieces, from his stores at Vera Cruz. He despatched an officer with four ships of Narvaez's fleet to Hispaniola and Jamaica, to engage adventurers, and to purchase horses, gunpowder, and other military stores; and gave orders to prepare, in the mountains of Tlascala, materials for building twelve brigantines, so that they might be carried to the lake in pieces, ready to be put together and launched when he stood in need of their service. Without giving his soldiers an opportunity of caballing, he daily led them against the people of the neighboring provinces, who had cut off some detachments of Spaniards during his misfortunes at Mexico; and as he was constantly attended with success, his men soon resumed their wonted sense of superiority. About this period an armament fitted out by Francisco de Garay, governor of Jamaica, who had long aimed at dividing with Cortez the glory and the gain of annexing the empire of Mexico to the crown of Castile, arrived at Vera Cruz, and were soon persuaded to enlist with Cortez. About the same time a ship arrived from Spain, freighted by some private adventurers, with military stores; and the cargo was eagerly purchased by Cortez, whilst the crew, following the example of the rest, joined him at Tlascala. From these various quarters the army of Cortez was reinforced with one hundred and eighty men and twenty horses; and he mustered upwards of five hundred infantry, of whom eighty were armed with muskets or cross-bows, forty horsemen, and nine pieces of artillery. At the head of these, with ten thousand Tlascalans and other friendly Indians, he began his march towards Mexico on the 28th of December, six months after his disastrous retreat from that city.

As soon as Cortez entered the Mexican territories, he discovered various preparations to obstruct his progress. But his troops forced their way with little difficulty, and took possession of Tezcuco, the second city of the empire, situated upon the banks of the lake, about twenty miles from Mexico. For three months part of his troops were engaged in building brigantines, and the other part in reducing the towns situated round the lake. Meanwhile several of the cities tributary to Mexico were induced, through hatred to their oppressors, to make common cause with the invaders, and not only to acknowledge the King of Castile as their sovereign, but to supply the Spanish camp with provisions, and to strengthen his army with auxiliary troops. At length intelligence arrived that the materials for building the brigantines were completely finished, and they were directly brought to Tezcuco under safe convoy. Cortez determined to attack the city from three different quarters; from Tezcuco on the east side of the lake, from Tecuba on the west, and from Cuayocan towards the south. These towns were situated on the principal causeways which led to the capital, and were intended for their defence. From all the three stations he pushed on the attack against the city with equal vigor, but in a manner very different from that in which sieges are conducted in regular war. Each morning his troops assaulted the barricades which the enemy had erected on the causeways, forced their way over the trenches which they had dug, and penetrated into the heart of the city, in hopes of obtaining some decisive advantage; but when the obstinate valor of the Mexicans had rendered the efforts of the day ineffectual, the Spaniards retired in the evening to their former quarters. After this plan of attack had been followed for a month without any success, Cortez resolved to give it one trial more, and if unsuccessful, to relinquish it altogether. The assault was made furiously and determinedly, and it seemed as if they were victors; but, on a given signal, the priests in the great temple struck the great drum consecrated to the god of war; and no sooner did the Mexicans hear its solemn sound than they rushed upon the enemy with frantic rage. The Spaniards, unable to resist the fury of the onset by men maddened by religious zeal, began to retire, at first leisurely and in order, but as the enemy pressed on, and their own impatience to escape increased, the terror and confusion became general. Cortez himself would have been carried away captive by six Mexican captains, had not two of his officers sacrificed their own lives to save him. Above sixty Spaniards perished in the rout; and what rendered the disaster more afflicting, forty of these fell alive into the hands of the enemy, and were doomed to have their quivering hearts torn from their bosoms and offered up with barbarous rites to hideous idols. Cortez, even with 150,000 Indian allies, as he affirmed, found it necessary to adopt a new and more cautious system of operations. He made his advances slowly and cautiously, levelling the houses and filling up the canals as he advanced, and gradually contracting the retreat of the enemy. At length all the three divisions penetrated into the great square in the centre of the city, and made a secure lodgment there. Three-fourths of the city were now reduced and laid in ruins; and the remaining quarter was wasting fast before the attacks of famine and pestilence. At this crisis the brave Guatimozin resolved to proceed in person to rouse the distant provinces of the empire to arms. With this intent he embarked in a canoe, and was speeding swiftly over the lake when he was captured by a brigantine, and delivered into the hands of Cortez. As soon as the fate of their sovereign was known, the resistance of the Mexicans ceased, and Cortez took possession of that small part of the capital which yet remained undestroyed. Thus terminated, after it had continued for seventy-five days, the siege of Mexico, the most memorable event in the conquest of America. The exultation of the Spaniards was quickly damped by disappointment; for instead of the inexhaustible wealth which they expected, their rapacity could collect only an inconsiderable booty amidst ruins and desolation. Guatimozin, aware of his impending fate, had ordered what remained of the riches amassed by his ancestors to be thrown into the lake. The Spaniards, their cupidity unsatisfied, fell into a state of uncontrollable discontent. Some accused Cortez and his confidants of having secretly appropriated to their own use a large portion of the riches which should have been brought into the common stock. Others blamed Guatimozin for obstinacy in refusing to discover the place where he had hidden his treasure. To quiet this universal murmur, Cortez subjected Guatimozin to torture, in order to force from him a discovery of the royal treasures, which it was supposed he had concealed; but this horrid cruelty was useless. The fate of the capital decided that of the empire. The provinces one after another submitted to the conquerors. Small detachments of Spaniards, marching through them without interruption, penetrated in different quarters to the great Southern Ocean, which, according to the ideas of Columbus, they imagined would open a short and easy passage to the East Indies, and thus secure to the crown of Castile all the envied wealth of those fertile regions; and the active mind of Cortez began already to form plans for attempting this important discovery. In

CAPTURE OF THE CITY OF MEXICO BY CORTEZ.

his subsequent schemes, however, he was disappointed; but from this time until the revolutionary spirit broke out in the New World, Mexico remained in the hands of the Spaniards.

CHAPTER II.

HISTORY OF MEXICO FROM THE COMMENCEMENT OF THE REVOLUTION TO THE PRESENT TIME.

FOR nearly three centuries after the conquest of Cortez, Mexico remained quietly subject to the Spanish yoke; but the internal tranquillity thus enjoyed ceased with the invasion of Spain by the armies of Napoleon. But before proceeding to narrate the events which terminated in the separation of Mexico from Spain, it will be necessary briefly to review the system of colonial policy by which it was so long governed, and to point out the causes which ultimately led to the assertion of independence. It is to the complication of abuses, to which the old system gave rise, that we must mainly attribute those events which have changed the destiny of the New World.

The Spanish viceroy in Mexico was endowed with the prerogatives of royalty. He was commander-in-chief of the troops, and he regulated the military operations, and filled up all vacancies. All sentences of every description bore his signature, nor was there any appeal from his decision. The only checks which interposed between him and despotic sovereignty were the *residencia*, or legal investigation of his conduct, to which the king might subject him on his return to Spain, a measure which was seldom or never enforced; and the *audiencia*, or the court of appeal in the last resort. This body possessed considerable power and influence. It had control over all other tribunals, ecclesiastical as well as civil, in every case where the value of the subject in litigation did not exceed ten thousand dollars. It likewise enjoyed the privilege of corresponding directly with the sovereign and with the Council of the Indies, and might have been a very effective check on the viceroy, but he was honorary president of the body, and had thus every opportunity of conciliating the members, and attaching them to his interests and those of the Europeans. They were more easily swayed in this direction, as they were always exclusively natives of Spain. Besides the boards already noticed, the municipal corporations, called sometimes *Cabildo*, sometimes the *Ayuntamiento*, and sometimes the *City*, had a considerable influence. Their members, called *regidors*, their president, the *corregidor*, and their executive officers, the *syndics*, were chosen from the people, and originally by the people. But in a short time the situations of alcalde and regidor were disposed of to the highest bidder, the purchaser having the power of relinquishing them in favor of relatives or friends. These functionaries, however, uniformly proved the friends of the Creoles; for they were connected with them by numerous ties, and by a community of interest. The *Recopilacion de las Leys de las Indias*, or general collection of the laws of the Indies, was the name given to that chaotic mass of contradictory statutes by which the decisions of the tribunals were supposed to be determined. These statutes were originally merely decrees upon different subjects, emanating from the king or from the Council of the Indies. But it was not long before many of these decrees were annulled by others subsequently issued, so that it was scarcely possible to know which statutes were in force, and which had fallen into disuse or been suspended. It thus happened that the native American was generally the sufferer in cases in which his opponent was a European; for the difficulty of obtaining redress in any dispute was augmented by the circumstance of the latter enjoying a double or triple privilege, as a merchant, a government officer, a dignitary of the church, or at least as holding some rank in the militia. To complete the outline of that mighty fabric by which the authority of Spain in the New World was so long supported, it is necessary briefly to advert to ecclesiastical establishments. These were altogether independent of the see of Rome, and the pope could not fulminate bulls or hold any sort of intercourse with Spanish America, unless through the medium of the court of Madrid and the Council of the Indies. As might have been expected under these circumstances, a traffic in bulls became an important branch of the royal revenue. The king bought of the pope indulgences and dispensations of all kinds, and retailed them to his American subjects at an enormous profit. The business was managed with as much strictness and regularity as an ordinary commercial transaction, the monopoly of tobacco, for example; and so jealous was the king of his right, that the most severe penalties were not only enacted, but enforced against ecclesiastics who dared to infringe the regulations.

Such is the general view of the colonial system of Spain; and when we consider that all the great offices of state, not excepting the viceregal dignity itself, were open alike to Americans and Europeans, every subject of the crown being eligible, its defects, in theory at least, are scarcely so glaring as they are sometimes represented. The evils, many and grievous, consisted in the practice and in the maintenance of a system of laws by which the colonies were sacrificed to the need or greed of Spain. Every situation, from the highest to the lowest, was bestowed upon Europeans. Indeed, the colonial offices were disposed of in Madrid to the highest bidder; and at one time the proceeds, like the traffic in bulls, formed a not inconsiderable item of the royal revenue. Of the fifty viceroys who governed Mexico from 1535 to 1808, only one was an American, and even he was born in Peru. But as exclusive enjoyment of these privileges could only be preserved to the Spaniards by the ignorance of the natives, almost every species of learning was not only discouraged, but prohibited, and pains and penalties were annexed to the infringement of the laws relating to it. The Latin grammar, the philosophy of the schools, and civil and ecclesiastical jurisprudence, were the only subjects which the Inquisition allowed to be taught. No book could circulate among the people until it had been thoroughly tested and sanctioned by the monks. But whilst ignorance was ranked amongst the virtues, some branches of industry were degraded into crimes. The Americans were prohibited, under severe penalties, from raising flax, hemp, or saffron, and growing tobacco was a government monopoly. The cultivation of the olive, the mulberry, and the vine, was also frustrated by the same blind policy; and even the growth of the more precious articles of what we term colonial produce, such as cacao, coffee, and indigo, was only tolerated under certain limitations, and in such quantities as the Spanish government might require annually to import. The colonists were also forbidden to manufacture anything which could be supplied by the mother country. Notwithstanding all the efforts of Spain, the exclusion of foreign vessels from her colonies gave rise to one of the most extraordinary systems of organized smuggling which the world ever witnessed. This was known under the name of the contraband or forced trade, and was carried on in armed vessels which often bade defiance to the coast blockades of Spain, and, fighting their way to American ports, landed great quantities of European goods.

Such was the colonial system of Spain, which on all hands is admitted to have been worse even than that of the Portuguese or of the Dutch; and such were the evils to which it gave rise. When, therefore, in connection with these evils we further consider that the civil, fiscal, and criminal administration was tyrannical, unjust, or partial; that exactions in the shape of taxes, duties, and tithes, were levied with unexampled severity; that amongst the taxes was one which has justly been called "the horrible *alcavala*," and pressed heavily on all classes, being levied *in infinitum* on every transfer of goods; that nothing escaped tithes, and that every individual was compelled to purchase annually a cer tain number of papal bulls, under a penalty of forfeiting various important advantages; that every stage of legal procedure was in the most corrupt and deplorable state, and that the administration of justice had scarcely any existence whatever; that imprisonment was the grand recipe for every malady; that in the most horrible dungeons ill diet, filth, infectious diseases, and corporal punishment, including occasional torture, all combined to unhumanize the fettered victim; and, finally, that the Inquisition bound in chains of darkness the minds of all classes of the community from the viceroy downwards; —he would be a bold theorist who should venture to affirm that Spain did not deserve that fate which eventually befel her possessions in the New World.

How long an indisposition upon the part of the Creoles to assert their rights might have continued, had not the events of the year 1808 occurred, it is impossible to say; but it is generally admitted that the insurrection of Aranjuez, which led to the dismissal of Godoy, Prince of the Peace, and to the abdication of Charles VI., gave the first shock to the royal authority in America. Authentic intelligence of the resignation of the Spanish monarch arrived in Mexico on the 15th of July, 1808. The municipality and the popular party demanded the immediate creation of a *junta* in imitation of the course pursued in Spain, composed of representatives of the different corporations of the kingdom. The Audiencia were adverse to such a course; and finding that the viceroy, Don Jose Iturrigaray, was inclined to favor their opponents, they contrived to arrest him and throw him into prison. Not a few influential members of the Cabildo, who had voted for a Mexican junta, were either banished or otherwise disposed of. The viceregal authority was for the time confined to the Archbishop Lizana. In 1809, however, the archbishop was replaced by the Audiencia, to whom the central junta transferred the reins of the government. The violent and contemptuous conduct of this body only served to bring matters more speedily to a crisis. A general feeling of hostility towards the Spaniards spread throughout the country, and on the morning of the 16th of September, 1810, the standard of revolt and independence was publicly unfurled by Don Miguel Hidalgo y Costilla, curate of the village of Dolores, in the province of Guana juato. Seven Europeans, resident in Dolores, became the first victims of the revolutionary movement. They were thrown into prison, and their property seized and distributed among Hidalgo's followers. The news of this first exploit spread throughout the country with the rapidity of lightning, and was everywhere hailed as a propitious omen. His force increased so suddenly, that on the 18th, he found himself in possession of two towns, each containing 16,000 inhabitants, in both of which places the confiscated property of the Europeans enabled him to reward his partisans as well as to add to their numbers. His next object was Guanajuato, the capital of the province, and also the emporium of the Spanish treasures in that part of the country. The town was given up to pillage; the Europeans were butchered without mercy; their property eagerly seized; and before the next morning there was not left standing a single house which had belonged to a Spaniard. An enormous quantity of money, estimated at five millions of dollars, was found in the alhondiga or granary, to which the inhabitants had transported their most valuable effects. During his stay at Guanajuato, Hidalgo established a sort of government, a mint with all the appurtenances for coining money, and a foundry for casting cannon.

The intelligence of the fall of Guanajuato, whilst it gave celebrity to the name of Hidalgo, created great consternation among the Spaniards of the capital. The new viceroy, however, Don Francisco Xavier Venegas, by his judgment and firmness, preserved public tranquillity in the capital. Don Felix Maria Calleja, who headed a brigade of troops stationed at San Luis Potosi, was entrusted with a command, and ordered to pursue Hidalgo, who was excommunicated afresh. After remaining at Guanajuato until the 10th of October, Hidalgo, at the head of his army, advanced upon Valladolid, which was quietly taken possession of on the 17th of the same month. His army was now about sixty thousand strong, a force which he considered sufficient to conquer the capital, and thus, by one decisive blow to terminate the revolutionary struggle. He accordingly left Valladolid on the 19th; and at Las Cruces encountered a corps of observation under the command of Colonel Truxillo, assisted by Don Augustin Iturbide, then a lieutenant in the service of Spain. After a sanguinary contest, the royalists were defeated, and compelled to fall back upon the capital. Hidalgo, however, after appearing before the city, to the astonishment of every one, withdrew his troops without striking a blow, and retreated towards Guanajuato. On the 7th of November he came in contact with the outposts of the royal army at Aculco. A sanguinary action ensued, in which, from the superiority of their discipline and arms, the royal forces gained a complete victory. Hidalgo retreated to Valladolid, and then proceeded to Guadalaxara, where he was received with great enthusiasm. Thence he advanced to the bridge of Calderon, which is 16 miles from Guadalaxara, and having fortified himself in a strong position, he awaited the approach of the royalists. On the 16th of January, 1811, the two armies were once more in sight of each other, and on the following day a general action took place. After various attacks, which the Mexicans repulsed with spirit, Calleja at last succeeded in carrying all their batteries; and Hidalgo was forced to withdraw them from the field. He withdrew to Saltillo, followed by about 4000 men. But on the 21st of March, 1811, he was captured while setting out to the United States, and he was shot on the 27th of July.

After the death of Hidalgo, a guerrilla war was carried on in various parts of the country; but as the leaders acted without concert, and no general engagement took place, it is unnecessary to follow it in its irregular course. At this period in the history of the revolution, disaffection towards the Spaniards had become very general. Armed bands of insurgents overran the open country, and hardly a day passed without being signalized by a skirmish. Meanwhile Rayon was busily employed in furthering the scheme of a national junta, and on the 10th of September, 1811, he accomplished his purpose. A junta, or central government, was installed, consisting of five members, who were elected by the ayuntamiento, in conjunction with the principal inhabitants of the town and district. The intelligence of the formation of the junta of Zitacuaro excited enthusiastic hopes throughout Mexico; and from the first moment of its establishment, the Spaniards considered it as their most formidable enemy. Accordingly, towards the end of the year, Calleja marched with all his forces against Zitacuaro, and arrived before it on the 1st of January, 1812. On the following day he captured the town, and drove the junta to Sultepec, where it established a new seat of government; but Calleja inflicted signal and terrible vengeance on that place for affording shelter to the fugitives. In October, 1810, Morelos had been appointed captain-general of the provinces of the south-western coast, and had entered upon his duties at the head of about 1000 men. Advancing with this force upon Acapulco, he surprised and routed a well-appointed body of troops under Don Francisco Paris, the commandant of the district. Numbers from every quarter flocked to his standard, and amongst others, three persons of the name of Bravo, one of whom, Don Nicolas, afterwards became so famous. The whole of the year 1811 was spent in a series of skillful manœuvres and petty engagements, in which the insurgents were generally successful. Meanwhile intelligence reached Morelos of the arrival of the victorious royalists under Calleja; but, nothing daunted by the circumstance, he determined to await the attack at Cuautla Amilpas, which is distant about 65 miles from the city of Mexico. On the 19th of February, Calleja made a general attack upon that town, but after a conflict which lasted eight hours, he was compelled to retreat, leaving five hundred dead behind him. He erected batteries, and began to cannonade and bombard the town. Disease and severe famine soon began to diminish the numbers of the besieged, so that the commander-in-chief formed the resolution of retreating; and this he succeeded in accomplishing on the night of the 2d of May. Calleja entered Cuautla, and practiced there unheard of barbarities. Morelos, leaving Izucar, proceeded to Tehuacan, into which he made a triumphal entry on the 16th of September, 1812, having defeated three divisions of the Spanish army on his way; he also captured Acapulco in August of the following year. During the absence of Morelos everything had been prepared for the meeting of the National Congress, which took place accordingly on the 13th of September, 1813, in the town of Chilpanzingo. This assembly consisted of the original members of the junta of Zitacuaro, the deputies elected by the province of Oaxaca, and others again selected by them as representatives for the provinces in the possession of the royal troops. Exactly a month after the opening of the session, an act was published, declaring the absolute independence of Mexico.

Besides the achievements already recorded, the years 1812 and 1813 had been distinguished by several other victories gained by the insurgent generals, Don Nicolas Bravo and Matamoros. But the time had now arrived for Morelos attempting a more decisive blow than any which had yet been struck. With seven thousand men and a large train of artillery, he left Chilpanzingo on the 8th of November, and after sustaining incredible fatigue and privations, arrived before Valladolid on the 23d of December. This place was defended by a formidable force under Llano and Iturbide. Confident of success, Morelos ordered his troops immediately to advance to the attack, but they were driven back with loss, and the next morning routed entirely. He was also defeated, January 6th, 1814, and Matamoros, who was taken prisoner, was shot. Reverse after reverse followed; Morelos met with a number of defeats; and finally, he was taken prisoner, and shot by the Spaniards, December 22d, 1815. The loss of Morelos was irreparable, for he was the only patriot chief who could maintain unity of plan, concentration of purpose, and combination of movement. For several years, therefore, the history of the revolution consists only of disjointed details of a wide-spread guerrilla war, in which success on either side led to no important results.

The Congress, which had escaped under the protection of Don Nicolas Bravo to Tehuacan, was dissolved by General Teran in December, 1815. This step has been generally blamed as at least precipitate. There can be no doubt that it was attended by disastrous circumstances; for from that moment confusion became worse confounded; Victoria, Guerrero, Bravo, Rayon, and Teran, confining themselves each to his own separate circle, where they were crushed in succession by the superiority of the common enemy. Teran attempted to establish a government himself, but none would acknowledge it. Rayon, after he had commanded with great success in the mountainous parts of Valladolid, was taken prisoner, and confined in the capital until 1821. The fate of Don Nicolas Bravo was exactly similar to that of Rayon. Guerrero occupied the western coast, and here he maintained himself in the fastness of the Sierra Madre until 1821, when he joined Iturbide. Guadalupe Victoria was driven from his strongholds in his province of Vera Cruz, was deserted by all his followers, and was forced to skulk in the forest like a wild beast. When every one had thought him dead, he appeared in 1821, covered with hair and emaciated almost to a skeleton.

Some facts relative to the state of the country require to be mentioned. The cause of independence had been gradually gaining ground amongst the people, particularly since 1812, when the constitution, which was sanctioned by the Cortes of Cadiz, was extended to the transatlantic dominions of the crown. By the new constitution several important privileges had been conceded to the natives; amongst the rest, the right of electing the members of the Cabildo and the deputies to the Cortes. In law, also, matters underwent so complete a reform, that a Creole might now hope for a favorable decision, provided his cause was a good one. Thus by the new constitution the reverses sustained by the Creole leaders in the field were more than counterbalanced. Under the mild sway of Admiral Apodaca, who succeeded Calleja in the viceregal authority, all was done that could be done to secure the allegiance of the natives. The arrival of fresh troops from the Peninsula enabled him to extend his military ramifications throughout the whole country, and enforce obedience even at the most distant points.

After her last patriotic chiefs had quitted the open field and sought refuge in the mazes of the forests, a deep gloom hung over the affairs of Mexico, which remained for a long time unbroken save by the sudden inroad of Mina.* This remarkable individual landed in Mexico on the 15th of April, 1817. With about 200 men he left Soto la Marina, the place of his landing; and pushing forward to the confines of the table-land, defeated a body of 400 royalist cavalry. About the middle of June, 1817, he reached the Hacienda de Pectillos; and on a little eminence which commanded the plain he cut to pieces a royal army 2000 strong with a force of only 172 men. On the 24th of June he reached Sombrero, having in thirty days traversed a tract of country 660 miles in extent, and been three times engaged with an enemy greatly superior in numbers. In conjunction with the advanced guard of the insurgents and some recruits, he advanced upon San Juan de los Llanos, and on the 29th of June totally defeated the royalists under General Castañon On the 24th of October, at nightfall, he took Guanajuato by storm, and penetrated into the very centre of the town. At this critical moment his troops refused to advance a step farther; and time being thus allowed the garrison to arm themselves, they attacked the insurgents, who, by the general's orders, dispersed with the utmost precipitation. Mina himself was taken prisoner three days afterwards, and sent to the head-quarters of General Linan, and there he was executed on the 11th of November, in his twenty-eighth year. Not long after his death the insurgent chiefs were driven off the field, and gradually disappeared; so that in July, 1819, not one remained of those who had taken any lead in the revolution.

The cause of Mexican independence seemed now to have sunk to such a low ebb, that the viceroy wrote in great confidence to the court of Madrid, representing the country as so tranquil and submissive to the royal authority, that he would answer for its safety without the assistance of a single soldier from Europe. But the appearances on which he relied proved altogether fallacious. The disbanded insurgents, mingling freely in the ranks of the Creoles, made proselytes to the principles of the revolution even in the royal camp itself. In private the bulk of the people were as warmly attached to them as ever. About the middle of 1820 accounts arrived in Mexico of the revolution in Spain; and it soon became public that orders had been sent to Apodaca to proclaim the constitution which Ferdinand VII. had been compelled to adopt. The era of 1812 was revived, and the public mind thrown into a ferment, which the viceroy, from his restricted powers, found it impossible to allay. He took the oath to the constitution, but not sincerely, and offered the command of the army to Don Augustin Iturbide, a native Mexican, to whom allusion has already been made. The proposal was ac-

* Don Xavier Mina, a famous Spanish guerrilla chief, still more celebrated in Spain for his patriotic efforts to create a rising in favor of the Cortes of Pampeluna, subsequently to the dissolution of that assembly by the king.

cepted and Iturbide left the capital in February, 1821, with half a million of dollars, destined for embarkation at Acapulco, but with intentions very different from those by which the viceroy supposed him to be actuated. Having arrived at a town called Iguala, situated about 120 miles from the capital, Iturbide took possession of the money; and on the 24th of February, commenced the second Mexican revolution by proposing a new government, which is well known under the title of "the plan of Iguala." His force of 800 men unanimously took the oath of fidelity to the "plan," whilst a copy was transmitted to the viceroy and to all the governors of provinces. This celebrated document consisted of twenty-four articles, the principal points embodied in which were,—a declara- of Mexican independence; the recognition of the Catholic religion as the national creed; the establishment of a constitutional monarchy; the formation of a junta of government; an offer of the crown to Ferdinand VII., and in the event of his refusal, to the Infantes Don Carlos and Don Francisco de Paula, provided any of them would consent to occupy the throne in person; an abolition of castes and of the despotism of military commandants; the formation of an army for the support of religion, independence, and union, and for guaranteeing these principles, whence it was to be called the arm of the three guarantees; a general amnesty to all who should give in their adhesion to the "plan;" and other provisions of less importance.

When the viceroy learned the defection of Iturbide, he concentrated a force upon the capital for the purpose of defending it; but Iturbide having effected a junction with Guerrero, his success became certain. On his route to the Baxio, great numbers of men and officers joined his standard. Before the month of July, the whole country had recognized his authority, with the exception of the capital. On his march to invest the city of Mexico, intelligence reached Iturbide that the new constitutional viceroy and political chief, O'Donoju, had arrived at Vera Cruz. He immediately requested an interview with this functionary, and allowed him to advance as far as Cordova, where a meeting took place. O'Donoju agreed to the plan of Iguala, and in the name of his master he recognized the independence of Mexico. Such was the treaty of Cordova, which was signed by Iturbide, "as the depository of the will of the Mexican people," and by O'Donoju, as the representative of Spain, on the 24th of August, 1821. By virtue of this treaty Iturbide obtained possession of the capital, which he entered in triumph on the 27th of September. A provisional junta of thirty-six persons then elected a regency of five, with Iturbide at their head. He was at the same time created generalissimo and lord high admiral, and had assigned to him a yearly salary of $120,000. The career of Iturbide had hitherto been triumphant; but scarcely had the first Mexican Cortes met on the 24th of February, 1822, when its members split into three distinct parties: first, the Bourbonists, or those who wished to establish a constitutional monarchy with a prince of the House of Bourbon at its head; secondly, the Iturbidists, who aimed at elevating Iturbide himself to the throne; and, thirdly, the republicans, who desired a central or federal republic. The Bourbonists soon ceased to exist, the Cortes of Madrid having declared the treaty of Cordova "to be illegal, null, and void, in as far as the Spanish government and its subjects were concerned." A portracted contest ensued between the two remaining factions, and resulted in the defeat of the Iturbidists. Nevertheless, the republican party were forced to yield to the wishes of the mob and the army, and to declare Iturbide emperor on the 19th of May, 1822. The new monarch assumed the title of Augustin I.

Iturbide began his reign by demanding the right of appointing and removing at pleasure the judges of the supreme court; he claimed a veto upon all laws, not excepting the articles of the constitution then under discussion; and he recommended the estabment of a military tribunal in the capital, with powers very little inferior to those exercised by the Spanish commandants during the revolution. This attack upon their liberties the Congress indignantly repulsed. Such decisive conduct led at once to an open rupture; but Iturbide broke up the Congress by force, and appointed his own tools. Matters were brought to a crisis by the defection of Santa Anna, governor of Vera Cruz, towards the close of 1822. The far-famed Victoria, quitting his hiding-place in the mountains, was invested by the rebels with the chief command, and rallied the natives in great numbers round his standard. Echavari, who had been dispatched by the emperor to invest Vera Cruz, made common cause with the garrison of that city, and induced his whole army to follow his example. On the 1st of February, 1823, the act of Casa-Mata was signed, by which the armies pledged themselves to effect the re-establishment of the national representative assembly. Bravo, Guerrero, and Negrete now joined the republican army, and the defection became so general that Iturbide very willingly left the country. The old Congress was immediately convoked; a provisional government was established; and an executive, composed of Victoria, Bravo, and Negrete, was appointed. They conducted the affairs of the country until a new Congress was assembled in August, 1823; and in October, 1824, the federal constitution was definitively settled by the latter. Meanwhile Iturbide, the ex-emperor, had proceeded to Leghorn, had subsequently visited London, and on the 11th of May, 1824, had embarked with his family for Mexico. Disregarding the sentence of the Congress which had outlawed him, he landed about the middle of July, at Soto la Marina, where he introduced himself in disguise and under a feigned name. But he was apprehended by General Garza, and shot a few days afterwards.

The form of government adopted by the representatives of Mexico was that of a federal republic, upon the plan of that of the United States, with a few unimportant deviations. The confederation, consisting of nineteen States and four Territories, was cemented into one body politic by certain general laws and obligations, contained in the federal constitution of the 4th of October, 1824. Each State and Territory, however, retained the uncontrolled management of its own internal affairs. Victoria was elected president and Bravo vice-president. But the hopes which had been formed regarding the peace and prosperity of Mexico proved altogether fallacious. Repeated revolutions continued to disturb and agitate the country. From the moment at which the war of independence commenced the nation became divided into two parties,—natives and Guachupines, or European Spaniards. The former consisted of those who wished to establish the independence of Mexico; the latter were warmly attached to the dominion of Spain. To these two parties succeeded the Imperialists and Republicans; and, lastly, came the Centralists and Federalists, which went under the sobriquets of Escosses and Yorkinos, appellations derived from two Masonic societies, and synonymous with *aristocrats* and *democrats*.

The time was now approaching when it became necessary to find a successor to Victoria as president of the republic; and Gomez Pedraza, a very efficient member of the Mexican cabinet, was brought forward as a candidate by the Escosses party. After an arduous contest, he was elected president by a majority of two votes over Guerrero, the representative of the Yorkinos. But the disappointed party was loud in its denunciation of the successful candidate. His friends were accused of bribery and corruption, and even charged with procuring the interference of the military in some of the States. It was at this time that Santa Anna set out for Jalapa at the head of about 800 men, and took possession of Perote. There he published a manifesto charging Pedraza with having succeeded in his election by fraudulent means. He further proposed that the people and army should annul the election of Pedraza; that the Spanish residents should be banished as the primary cause of the grievances from which the Mexicans suffered, and that Guerrero should be declared president. From a feeling of hostility towards the natives of Spain, which prevailed pretty generally throughout Mexico, matters were very speedily brought to a crisis. On the night of the 30th November, 1828, a battalion of militia, headed by the ex-Marquis of Cadeña, and assisted by a regiment under Colonel Garcia, took possession of the artillery barracks at the Acordada, surprised the guard, and seized the guns and ammunition. By the 2d of December the insurrection had made alarming progress, and a sanguinary contest ensued, which ended on the 4th in the overthrow of the government troops. The city was then given up to be pillaged. Vengeance was chiefly directed against the Spaniards; but all who were supposed to possess wealth fell victims to the rapacity of an unbridled mob. These disgraceful scenes continued for two days, and property to a very great amount was destroyed or changed owners. Pedraza formally resigned his office, and was allowed to quit the territories of the republic. At a new Congress, assembled on the 1st of January, 1829, Guerrero was declared duly elected, and General Anastasio Bustamante, a distinguished Yorkino leader, was associated with him as vice-president. Santa Anna was invested with the supreme military command of the republic. The first event which disturbed the country after the elevation of Guerrero, was the arrival of an invading force from Cuba, under Barradas, in the summer of 1829. Santa Anna, however, routed the invaders, and took Barradas himself prisoner. But Guerrero was now destined to taste the cup which he had mixed for his predecessor. Early in December, 1829, Bustamante, the vice-president, flew to arms, and having placed himself at the head of the army of Mexico, which was stationed in the State of Vera Cruz, he advanced upon the capital, every where denouncing the abuses and usurpations of Guerrero. Guerrero appealed to the Congress for support; but it was all in vain; he was ultimately compelled to abdicate. The army then elected Bustamante as his successor; whilst Santa Anna, following the example of Guerrero, retired to his estates, and tranquillity was soon restored.

At this period it required no great gift of prophecy to predict that even the shadow of the constitution of 1824 would not long survive. Mexico was now beyond all doubt subjected to a military despotism; and a pretext or cause for prostrating Bustamante in his turn could not long be wanting. It was enough that the daring, crafty, and cruel Santa Anna was living in retirement and hatching new schemes of revolt. From that period Mexico has presented a kaleidoscopic exhibition of factions and parties. It would require volumes to detail the series of manœuvres, of *gritos*, and insurrections, which seated Santa Anna ultimately in power, and made him the representative of that amalgam of all parties which has been designated by a cant term in which the most incongruous ideas are jumbled together. In July, 1832, the Ayuntamiento and people of San Felipe de Austin unanimously gave in their adherence to the plan of Vera Cruz, and to the principles of the republican party, headed by Santa Anna. This example was followed by other States; and Santa Anna assumed the reins of government. In April following, he expelled the Congress; and in 1835, Gomez Farias, who had been elected vice-president, was driven into exile. Santa Anna was also successful in his new "plan;" and centralism with a *de facto* dictatorship, succeeded to the federal republic. The states were converted into departments, and the legislatures cut down to a council of five. This new order of things was acknowledged by the whole country, with the exception of Texas, which was warmly attached to federalism. It will appear, however, from the sequel, that the disaffection of this lately settled Territory led to important results.

At a meeting of the people of Texas, in

1833, a constitution had been drawn up in which, amongst other important matters, they pointed out the necessity of a separation from Coahuila. They determined also, as soon as possible to carry out their wishes. It is necessary here to premise, that the unappropriated lands, although State property, could not be granted to any one without the sanction of the general government. At this time, a great rage for land speculation existed, not only in Mexico, but in the United States, and an extensive system of fraud was the consequence. In 1834, a company of speculators, many of whom belonged to, or had come from the latter country, induced the legislature of Coahuila and Texas to grant them 400 square leagues of public land for the sum of $20,000. The transaction was disavowed and the grant annulled by the Mexican government. About the same time, an attempt to establish customs was forcibly resisted by the colonists. This, together with a demand for the persons of those who had been concerned in the grant of the 400 leagues of land, were the immediate precursors of hostilities. Proclamations and addresses were issued, calling the inhabitants of the State to arms against the encroachments of that military power which threatened their very existence, not only as a State, but as a people. Santa Anna was stigmatized as a dictator, and death was denounced against all his supporters who should enter Texas. Taxes were refused, the custom-house officers were expelled, and the laws of Mexico were set at defiance. In these circumstances, Santa Anna, who had succeeded in gaining all the other States of the republic, found it necessary to turn his attention to Texas.

In September, 1835, General Cos, the confidential friend and brother-in-law of the central chief, landed at Compano at the head of 400 men, destined to reinforce the garrison of San Antonio de Bejar. But, he was foiled in his attempt to defend that city against the Texians, and was forced to retire from the province in October. Early in March, 1836, a convention of delegates from the various settlements of Texas having assembled at Washington, issued a formal declaration of independence, setting forth the grievances which impelled the people to take that step. This declaration was signed by forty-four delegates, of whom only three or four were Mexicans by birth. When this decisive step was taken, the people of Texas undoubtedly supposed that the internal divisions of the country would afford sufficient employment for the arms of Santa Anna, forgetting that there existed in Mexico an inveterate prejudice against the United States colonists, which might induce them to overlook for a time all minor differences, and unite as against a common enemy. Early in February, 1836, Santa Anna established his headquarters on the Neuces, to the eastward of Rio del Norte. By his plan of operations, he proposed to advance in two columns; one directed against San Antonio, and the other against La Bahia, which place was lower down the coast, intending by this means to intercept all communication between the Americans and the Gulf. His troops in the first of these enterprises were repulsed; in the second they were successful, but disgraced their triumph by massacring 500 captives in cold blood. This military execution caused much excitement, and exasperated the Texians in the highest degree. They suddenly ceased to retreat, and General Houston, having rapidly countermarched a distance of about sixty miles, came up with Santa Anna. On the 21st of April, near the banks of the San Jacinto, a fierce and sanguinary conflict took place, in which the Mexicans were defeated with great slaughter, and above 700 taken prisoners, amongst whom was the commander-in-chief himself. This unexpected event totally changed the aspect of affairs, and numerous adventurers soon appeared from the United States. On the 15th of May, a convention was held at Velasco, in Texas, where it was stipulated that hostilities should cease, that the Mexican army should quit Texas, and that Santa Anna should be sent to Vera Cruz, upon condition of his agreeing neither to take up arms against the Texians, nor to exercise any influence to cause them to be taken up during the struggle for independence.

The inhabitants of Texas now set themselves to assert their distinct nationality by electing their own officers, equipping their own army and navy, and guarding their own frontiers. At the same time, their independence was publicly recognized by Great Britain, France, and the United States. For several years, Mexico was too much engrossed with internal disturbances and with the political contests of her magnates to attempt to reconquer her lost province. At length, in 1844, the commencement of negotiations for engrafting Texas on the American Union roused her from her lethargy. She protested loudly against the unjust attempt of the United States to rob her of part of her dominions. The president, Herrera, attempted, at the request of the American government, to settle the difficulty by negotiation, but, so violent was the popular indignation against such lenient measures that, on the 30th of December, 1845, he was forced to resign the presidential chair to General Paredes, the darling of the Mexican mob. The new president began his sway by raising money and levying troops for the invasion of Texas. To General Ampudia was intrusted the protection of the northern frontiers. Accordingly, on the 11th of April, 1846, he settled down with a large force at Matamoros on the Rio Grande, and confronted an American army stationed under General Taylor on the opposite bank of the river. In a short time, skirmishes between these two bodies of troops began the war, and were the signal to the United States for dispatching a large force against Mexico. An "Army of the West" and an "Army of the Centre" were organized under the respective commands of Generals Kearney and Wool. But, we need not here go into details. The narrative of the war with Mexico will be found in the history of the United States, on previous pages of this volume.

Soon after the conclusion of the war, Santa Anna, seeing that his power was on the wane, sought an asylum in Jamaica. Herrera was elected president of the republic; but, both under him and under his successor, Arista, the country continued in a state of the wildest anarchy. At length, in 1852, it had become a prevalent opinion among the Mexicans that a strong central government alone could save them from ruin. Santa Anna was allowed to be the fit instrument for effecting the desired change. Accordingly, in the same year, that dexterous politician and able general was recalled from exile by common consent. In December, 1853, he was elected perpetual president with the authority of dictator, and the title of Most Serene Highness. But, the extraordinary powers with which he was invested failed to harmonize those discordant feelings, which sprung from difference of political opinion on the one hand, and difference of race on the other. On the 22d of January, 1854, a revolution under General Juan Alvarez broke out at Acapulco, absorbed within its ranks malcontents of every description, and spread with resistless rapidity through several States in the direction of the capital. Force and policy were alike unable to check it, and at length, on the 9th of August, 1855, Santa Anna abdicated and retired to Havana. In September, Alvarez was raised to the provisional presidency, but resigned in December, in favor of Ignacio Comonfort, who received the title of president-substitute. Scarcely had the new potentate formed his ministry when he was assailed by conspiracy. Early in 1856, an insurrection headed by Haro y Tamariz enlisted in its cause a formidable number of the clergy, magistrates and destitute workmen. It was suppressed, however, by Comonfort, on the 22d of March.

Comonfort having been elected president in July, 1857, was inaugurated December 1st; within a month he was driven out by rebellion, Zuloaga taking the supreme power, and recognized by the diplomatic corps, as *de facto* the ruler. Juarez organized a constitutional government in opposition at Vera Cruz. Miramon, of the Church party, succeeded to Zuloaga's position, and became "president-substitute." Outrages and excesses of every kind prevailed; there was no real government in fact; there was no safety anywhere to person or property; and murders and assassinations were of continual occurrence. Not only citizens of the United States, but those also of England, France and Spain had abundant claims against Mexico, on the score of robbery, plundering, etc., and it became evident that some measures must be adopted to compel redress.

During 1859 and 1860, the constitutional party, with Juarez at the head, had gained strength and influence; Miramon left the country and went to Spain; and Juarez, for the time, was apparently ruler of Mexico. But the Church party gave him immense trouble and difficulty, as their interests lay in holding on to the property and power they had so long enjoyed, and were ready to fight to the death to retain. A project of interference now began to take definite shape, notwithstanding the well-known "Monroe doctrine" of our country. As we, however, just then, had the rebellion, in its threatening inception, on hand, the three nations, England, France and Spain, thought it a favorable opportunity to seek redress from Mexico, at the same time avoiding coming into collision with the Great Republic. The plan was, to send a combined fleet for the purpose of seizing upon Vera Cruz, Tampico, and other ports; then to gather the custom dues on all commerce; and thus get the funds to pay off the debts due to the contracting powers. The French military part of the expedition was then 7,000 men; the Spanish, about 11,000; the English only about 800. At the close of 1861, the Spanish troops took possession of Vera Cruz, and the other parts of the expedition arrived and took their place in the Gulf. In the country generally, the feeling against the Spaniards was bitterly hostile, and there was a resolute determination not to submit to their presence. The intervention of the French, however, under Napoleon's scheming, and the plan to establish the unfortunate Maximilian on the throne of Mexico, was of more consequence, and threatened dire evils to the nation; still, it was carried forward by means of a large army, under Marshal Bazaine, with such success as that, at the close of 1863, the French were firmly established in Mexico, held possession of the chief towns and States, and proposed to make directly new conquests north and west.

The supporters of Juarez and the republicans in general endeavored to make head against the French in Southern Mexico and on the Pacific coast. But now, as always, the inherent vice of disorder, lawlessness, want of unity and concentration of purpose and action, lack of discipline, etc., prevailed. Each general did pretty much as he pleased, and guerrillas and brigands ravaged in every direction. Santa Anna, the veteran political schemer, appeared early in 1864, at Vera Cruz, with a promise on his part to be quiet and not to meddle with politics; but having issued a proclamation which Bazaine did not like, he was sent off again much against his will. In the early part of 1864, the Mexican Deputation sent to offer the imperial crown to Maximilian, saw him again in April, at Miramar. Previously, he had scrupled about taking the crown, except appointed by the popular vote; but as that could not be obtained, he now accepted the position, April 10th, and became emperor of Mexico, so far as was possible by this act. A convention was entered into, by which the number of the French troops was to be reduced to 20,000 directly, and these were to evacuate Mexico as speedily as they could be spared.

Maximilian and Carlotta his wife, visited the Pope at Rome, to get his benediction and be told what to do so as to secure the Roman Catholic Church rights and rich possessions in Mexico; after which they embarked and reached Vera Cruz May 28th, 1864. His reception was cool and impassive on the part of the Mexicans; and though he entered the capital June 12th, with great pomp and magnificent display, there were no signs of enthusiasm or joy among the people. Maximilian entered at once on his difficult work. He earnestly sought information from all quarters; he was generous in proclaiming amnesty and release of prisoners; he was anxious to develop the resources of the country; and he even applied to Juarez and others to meet him and seek for some plan of restoring peace and establishing firmly his throne. But these latter utterly refused, and Juarez in particular maintained the unequaled contest without flinching. In appearance, the empire promised to be a success; but it was only in appearance. The country was bankrupt; the people revolutionary; feuds and discords and crimes prevailed largely; and except by the force of French bayonets, Maximilian could do nothing, and be nothing. Added to all, the pope and the Church party were thoroughly dissatisfied, and would be content with nothing less than supreme control; while Maximilian had resolved upon entire freedom of worship, and restraint upon their plans of amassing property and holding on to power over the ignorant and superstitious natives. France had at this date (end of 1865), expended $135,000,000, and lost in killed and wounded over 11,000 men. The republicans, under Juarez's government (the only one recognized by the United States), continued the struggle, and the war assumed on both sides the most ferocious shape, and was carried to excesses too horrible to mention. Attempts were made to promote immigration into Mexico, as well from the United States as from Europe, and both imperialists and republicans made efforts to raise money by loans, with very indifferent success.

The condition of affairs, during the next year (1866) was deplorable for the cause of Maximilian. He held the central portion of the country, it is true, but it was by means of French troops and foreign mercenaries (in all about 50,000); but in other parts of Mexico, though the republican armies so-called, were nearly all broken up, the guerrillas and such like kept the northern and southern States in continual disorder and distress. The first success of consequence gained by the republicans was the taking of Matamoros, in June, when Mejia, the commander of Maximilian's native troops and his force were taken prisoners. From this date, Juarez and his cause grew more and more hopeful, and the unfortunate Maximilian was soon after brought to the conviction that the experiment of the empire was a failure. Napoleon resolved to get his forces away from Mexico as soon as possible; his part of the scheme, so far as benefit to himself was concerned, had failed; his intervention was a political blunder, and he was anxious to get out of his trouble as soon as possible. The United States government gave him plainly to understand that our policy would not be departed from, and that establishing an empire was all out of place in America. Towards the close of the year 1866, Maximilian, utterly discouraged, and greatly distressed by learning that his poor wife, who had visited the pope and tried to get his approval of Maximilian's course and proceedings, but failing in this had gone crazy, was prepared to abdicate and escape utter ruin staring him in the face. Bazaine, Napoleon's head of military affairs in Mexico, declared that Maximilian must abdicate formally before he could leave the country; and so, he was persuaded, or rather driven, to hold on a while longer.

The French troops left Mexico early in 1867, and the empire of course fell speedily into ruins. Maximilian took a stand at Queretaro, with some 8,000 men, where the republican forces enclosed him in with 18,000 men; and there was no other alternative left him but to surrender at an early day. By the treachery of a fellow named Lopez, Maximilian was made prisoner at night, and his doom sealed. The ill-starred emperor and his principal generals were tried, found guilty of treason, and sentenced to be shot. Our government and that of England remonstrated and plead in vain; Juarez was immovable, unrelenting; and Maximilian was executed June 19th, 1867.

Juarez, in July, entered Mexico and resumed his position in the capital as president of the republic, after four years' absence. He was re-elected president in October, and various amendments to the constitution were proposed. Yucatan gave great trouble in an insurrection there of formidable proportion, which, however, was put down in February, 1868; and in various parts of the country gangs of robbers and plunderers were still able to make head against the government. Insurrections continued in Mexico during 1868, and disturbances and outbreaks were frequent, showing, as has for so many years been the case, that the government is not strong enough to secure protection to life and property. The record since, for the last three years, has been little else than perpetual disturbances, more or less serious, and outbreaks of passion and fighting and murdering and plundering. In fact, there is no good ground of hope for the regeneration and strengthening of Mexico, and giving it the opportunity of developing its wonderful mineral wealth and resources, without a vigorous, strong, effective government. Until that much to be desired period arrives, Mexican history will continue to be, we fear, a repetition of its past record of weakness, struggling and mortifying failure.

CHAPTER III.

STATISTICS, ETC., OF MEXICO.

Mexico is bounded on the north by California, New Mexico, and Texas; east by the Gulf of Mexico and the Caribbean Sea; south-east by British Honduras and Guatemala; and south-west and west by the Pacific Ocean. Its greatest length in a north west and south-east direction from San Diego to the extreme south part of Chiapas, is about 1,987 miles; and its greatest breadth about 1,128 miles. Its area is estimated at 829,900 English square miles, and it has a coast line of about 5,830 miles in length. A great portion of Mexico is occupied by the Cordilleras, which run through its whole length rendering the surface extremely varied. On entering this country from the south, the chain divides into two great branches; the western extending along the coast of the Pacific, and the eastern along that of the Gulf of Mexico, and afterwards subsiding into the plains of Texas. The vast tract of country between these branches, comprising about three-fifths of the entire area of the territory, consists of a central table-land called the Plateau of Anahuac, 6000 to 8000 feet in general elevation; and hence its climate, though mostly within the tropics, is decidedly temperate. This region is crossed in various directions, or divided into sub-plateaus by numerous chains of mountains—some of the peaks of which rise to a great elevation, towering far above the central plateau; the principal of these are, Popocatepetl, 17,735; Orizava, 17,388; Yxtaccihuatl, 15,700 feet above the sea-level. These and many others of the Mexican mountains are volcanoes; the first is continually burning, but for centuries has ceased to eject from its crater anything but smoke and ashes. On the western side of the city of Mexico are the volcanoes of Jorulla and Calima; the latter of which throws up smoke and ashes, but has not been known to discharge lava. Jorulla, which is situated between Calima and the city of Mexico, is of much more recent origin than any of the others. It was thrown up *en masse* from a fertile plain having an elevation of 2,890 feet, to the height of 4,149 feet above the sea-level.

While in the Old World granite, gneiss, mica schist, and clay-slate often form the central ridge of the mountain chains, these rocks seldom appear at the surface of the Cordilleras of America, being there covered by masses of porphyry, greenstone, amygdaloid, basalt, obsidian, and other rocks of the same class. The granite, which here generally forms the lowest stratum, appears at the

Benito Juarez

From the original painting by Chappel in the possession of the publishers.

surface in the little chain that borders the Pacific Ocean, and which, on the side of the Acapulco, is separated from the mass of high country by the valley of Peregrino. Farther to the east, the mountains of Mixteca and of Zapateca, in the province of Oaxaca, are formed of the granitic rock which is there traversed by veins of auriferous quartz. The great central plateau of Anahuac, between the fourteenth and twenty-first degrees of latitude, appears like an enormous dyke of porphyritic rocks, distinguished from those of Europe by the constant presence of hornblende, and by the absence of quartz. These rocks contain immense deposits of gold and silver. Basalt, amygdaloid, trap, gypsum, and primitive limestone, however, form the predominating rocks; but, hitherto, no considerable beds of rock-salt or of coal have been discovered in the plateau of Mexico. The porphyritic traps which terminate the mountains of Jacal and Oyamel appear in columns, and are crowned with pine trees and oak, which materially add to their picturesque appearance. It is from these mountains that the ancient Mexicans obtained the obsidian of which they formed their sharp-edged instruments. The Cobre de Perote is a porphyritic mountain, resembling an ancient sarcophagus surmounted by a pyramid at one end.

The mines of Mexico were wrought long before the arrival of the Spaniards, the natives of Mexico, like those of Peru, being well acquainted with the use of metals. They had also learned to dig for them, and to trace the metallic veins in the interiors of the mountains. The dependent tribes paid their tributes to the sovereign in a species of metallic currency which, though not stamped, was yet the representative of a standard value. The mines of Mexico are nearly all on the top or on the western slope of the great Cordillera, and the mining region occupies an area of about 12,000 square leagues. On the country becoming settled after the revolutionary disturbances, especially after the year 1825, the Mexican mines were eagerly seized as objects of speculation by British and American capitalists. In consequence, however, of bad management, or the wild spirit of gambling, together with the enormous expenses of getting the working of the mines under way, many of the earliest British and American speculators were ruined; but their successors are beginning to reap the benefit of their expenditure; and, throughout the republic, steam-engines and the best hydraulic apparatus are now employed. The annual average produce of the mines before the revolution was estimated at about $25,000,000. The annual produce of silver alone is estimated at about $35,000,000, and of gold, not much less. There are also some twenty-five quicksilver mines, yielding from 250,000 to 300,000 pounds of metal annually. Besides the precious metals, Mexico abounds in other ores. Iron is plentiful in the States of Valladolid, Zatatecas, and Jalisco, but has hitherto been little worked. Copper is found in a native state in Valladolid, and also, to some extent, in Guanajuato. Tin, though obtained in mines, is principally extracted from the water-carried earth found in the deep ravines. A combination of these two metals was used by the ancient Mexicans to form their tools and weapons; and they had acquired the art of tempering them so as to render them equal in utility to iron, or even to steel.

Mexico is singularly deficient in large rivers. The Rio Grande del Norte, which forms its N. E. boundary, is the largest, having a length of about 1800 miles. The principal affluents of the Rio Grande are the Conchas, the Salado and Sabinas, and the San Juan rivers. The Santander, Tampico, Panuco, and Usumasinta, are the chief of those flowing into the Gulf of Mexico; while the Rio Yompex, the Aztla, Santiago, Culiacan, and the Rio del Fuerta, fall into the Pacific. A small portion of the lower course of the Colorado is in this territory. The lakes of Mexico are numerous, and some of them are of considerable size. Lake Chapala in Jalisco covers an area of 1300 square miles, and

Lake Terminos, which, however, is more properly an arm of the sea, has an area of about 2200 square miles. The valley of Mexico contains five lakes, into which the various streams of the district flow. These cover an area of 160 square miles, and are drained by a canal cut through rock 12 miles in length, 150 feet deep, and 300 feet wide, having its embouchure in the Rio Panuco.

Mexico, as regards climate, is usually divided into the *tierras calientes*, *tierras templadas* and *tierras frias*. The first, or hot regions, include the low grounds, or those under 2000 feet elevation, on the east and west coasts. The *tierras calientes* of the west are less extensive than those of the east, as the western arm of the Cordilleras approaches nearer to the sea. The mean temperature of this region may be estimated at 77°. It is especially suited for the growth and cultivation of sugar, indigo, cotton, and bananas. The *tierras templadas*, or temperate regions, are of comparatively limited extent, and occupy the slope of the mountain chains which bound on either side the central table-land. They extend from about 2500 feet to 5000 feet in elevation, and the mean temperature is from 68° to 70°. Extremes of heat and cold are there equally unknown. The *tierras frias*, or cold regions, include all the vast plateau elevated 5000 feet and upward above the sea, and have a mean temperature of about 62°. In the city of Mexico, at an elevation of 7400 feet, the thermometer has sometimes, though rarely, fallen below the freezing point. Under the parallel of Mexico the line of perpetual snow varies from 14,000 to 15,000 feet above the sea-level. Vegetation here is not so vigorous as in the other two regions, and the plants of Europe do not succeed so well as in the *tierras templadas*. In the tropical regions, and as far north as 28° N. Lat., there are only two seasons; that of rain, lasting from June or July to September or October, and the dry season, continuing from October to the end of May. The climate of the provinces denominated *internas*, and which are situated within the temperate zone, is distinguished by a striking inequality in the temperature of the different seasons; the winters being very cold, while the summers are comparatively very warm. To this, as well as to other local causes must be attributed the aridity which characterizes a considerable portion of the plateau of Anahuac. There are few springs in the mountains; and the water, instead of collecting in little subterranean basins, filters through the earth or porous rocks, and loses itself in crevices formed by volcanic eruptions. The muriates of soda and of lime, the nitrate of potass, and other saline substances, cover the surface of the soil. Still a great part of Mexico may be classed with the most fertile countries of the earth, for there every species of vegetable production is found, or may be successfully cultivated. On the ascent from Vera Cruz, climates, to use an expression of Humboldt's, succeed each other in layers; and the traveler passes in review, in the course of two days, the whole scale of vegetation, from the parasitic plants of the tropics to the pines of the arctic regions. In some parts, however, the climate is very insalubrious. Nevertheless, excepting the seaports and some of the deeper valleys, where intermittent fever is very prevalent, Mexico ought, upon the whole, to be considered as a healthy country.

The zoology of this interesting country has only hitherto been partially explored, and what is known relates chiefly to ornithology. Of one hundred and thirteen species of land-birds ascertained to be natives of Mexico, sixty-eight seem to be peculiar to that country, eleven likewise natives of South America, and thirty-four of other parts of North America. The quadrupeds, insects, etc., are as yet little known. Deer and several varieties of antelopes are found on the table-lands, and the bison ranges in vast herds through various parts of Mexico. The domestic animals introduced by the Spaniards have increased to such a degree, that immense numbers of them run wild through the country.

From the great range of climate in Mexico, the vegetable productions must necessarily be very varied. The soil is, in many parts, of extraordinary fertility; and, where well-watered, produces abundant crops with very little labor. The most important of the agricultural productions is maize, or Indian corn, which constitutes the principal food of the inhabitants, as well as of most of the domestic animals. This valuable grain is almost everywhere cultivated with success; and, in some favorable spots, its fecundity is very remarkable. Oats are little cultivated in Mexico, but the wheat and barley of Europe have been naturalized here. The former succeeds well throughout the table-land; but, both in the *tierras calientes* and on the eastern and western slope of the Cordilleras, the ear does not form. The success of the crop on the table-land depends almost entirely upon the timely commencement of the rainy season; for, if the dry weather continue beyond the middle of June, unless the grounds can be watered by artificial means, the crops of wheat, barley, and maize are destroyed by drought. Irrigation is, therefore, the great object of the Mexican farmer; and, in the formation of reservoirs, canals, and the like, vast sums have been expended on the principal estates. The average annual produce of the whole of the corn-lands of Mexico, is estimated at twenty-five bushels for one; while in certain parts of the country, during favorable years and where the irrigation is good, from sixty to eighty bushels for one have been produced. The potato is much cultivated in Mexico. It is not an indigenous plant, but was introduced from the mountainous parts of Peru at a very early period after the conquest of that country by the Spaniards. It grows to a large size; some of those found by Humboldt having measured from twelve to thirteen inches in circumference. The banana, which flourishes up to the point where the mean temperature is 75°, produces more nutritious substance in a less space than any other plant. The same temperature necessary to the development of the banana produces also the *manioc* or *cassava*, which is also abundantly productive of aliment. Rice is but little cultivated, and not very generally known. Before the year 1810, the cultivation of the olive was prohibited lest the interests of Spain should thereby be injured. During the revolution, however, a great number of olive trees were planted; and, at present, there are several large plantations in the country. The vine was also a prohibited plant, but now flourishes in many parts. Among the other vegetable productions of Mexico are the yam, which is confined to the *tierras calientes*; the *capsicum*, which is extensively cultivated and universally used for seasoning food; and the sarsaparilla, tomato, pine-apple, pomegranate, guava, orange, lemon, melon, pear, apple, peach, etc. One of the most valuable plants of the country is the *maguey*, a species of aloe, which is, by Humboldt, designated the vine of Mexico. It furnishes a spirituous liquor called *pulqué*, which is the chief beverage of all classes of the people. Its taste is said to resemble that of cider, but its smell is disagreeable. A kind of brandy called *mexical*, very much resembling whiskey, is produced by the distillation of *pulqué*. The *maguey* plant is useful in other respects; its fibres furnish the inhabitants with a thread called *pita*, and is also employed in making ropes and paper; its juice is used as a caustic application for wounds, and its prickles serve for pins and needles. The soil of Mexico is in many parts remarkably favorable to the production of sugar, which has become one of the most valuable products of the republic. The Mexican soil has also been found well adapted for the cultivation of coffee, extensive plantations of which exist near Orizava and Cordova. The average produce of each plant is estimated at about two and a half pounds weight throughout all parts of the country where the berry is cultivated, though there are districts in Mexico in which it is said that three or four pounds are yielded. The slope of the eastern Cordillera is supposed to be best adapted for coffee estates. Tobacco is a government monopoly, and grows well in a small district near Orizava and Cordova; but the best quality comes from Simojovel in the State of Chiapas, and from some districts of Oajaca. Indigo was known and cultivated by the Mexicans previous to the conquest. It is found in Yucatan, Chiapas, and about Tehuantepec, in the State of Oajaca, and grows wild in some of the very warm districts in Tabasco. Cotton was among the indigenous products of Mexico at the time of its invasion, and formed almost the only clothing of the natives. The Aztecs possessed the art of spinning it to a very high degree of fineness, and of imparting to it beautiful and brilliant colors; but these arts have been lost. The hot regions are remarkably favorable to the growth of the plant, and it requires but little attention from the proprietor. The quantity of cotton produced in the whole country is estimated at about seven millions of pounds. Vanilla, yielding the highly esteemed spice of that name, grows wild along the eastern coast and in other parts of the republic. The *opuntia*, or Indian fig, a species of cactus, supports here an insect from whose body the well-known cochineal is made. The female alone produces the dye; and the process of rearing is complicated, and attended with much difficulty. The plantations of the cochineal cactus are confined to the State of Oajaca. Soon after the independence of Mexico was secured, the cultivation of the mulberry tree was attempted, for the purpose of feeding silk-worms, but without success. Flax and hemp have also been introduced into the country.

The chief exports from Mexico are cochineal and the precious metals. Of the latter of these products it is estimated that the one half is remitted to England, and that the other is divided equally between the United States and the continental states of Europe. The greater portion of the silver is shipped from Tampico, which is the nearest port for the mineral productions of Guanajuato, Zacatecas, San Luis Potosi, and the principal mining districts of Northern Mexico. Large quantities are also sent from Vera Cruz, as well as from Mazatlan, on the Pacific coast. The other exports are principally dyewoods, vanilla, sarsaparilla, jalap, hides, horns, and a small quantity of pepper, indigo, and coffee. The imports consist chiefly of linen, cotton, woollen, and silk goods, paper, glassware, ironware, quicksilver, cocoa, wine, brandy, and gin. The manufactures of Mexico chiefly consist of woollen, cotton, and silk goods, glass, paper, sugar, oil, wine, and brandy. The Indians excel in working jewelry, carving, sculpture, and indeed in all the ornamental arts; they are likewise good masons, painters, and musicians. They make beautiful vases, somewhat similar in form to the Etruscan, as well as toys of all kinds, wax figures, ornamental cloths of great value, and the like.

The government of Mexico is a representative federal republic. The legislative power is vested in a Congress consisting of a Senate and Chamber of Deputies. The Deputies are chosen every two years by the citizens of the States. The Senate is composed of two members from each State and the Federal District, while a number equal to that of all the States is elected by the Senate, Deputies, and Judges of the supreme court conjointly, the Deputies deciding the election in the case of the candidate not receiving a majority of all the votes. The executive power is vested in a president elected for four years. Judicial power resides in the supreme court of justice, and in circuit and district courts. Each State government is independent within its local jurisdiction, and, like the federal government, is composed of executive, legislative, and judicial departments.

The Roman Catholic religion was established here by the Spaniards, and is still maintained with rigor. At the time of the revolution the pope actively espoused the cause of Spain, and anathematized the revolutionists; but on the petition of the new government they were readmitted into favor. The ecclesiastical government is under the jurisdiction of an archbishop and nine bishops, and the revenue of the church is estimated at $20,000,000. Education is still at a low ebb, though of late years some considerable progress has been made. Several of the States have established primary schools, and many higher schools and private seminaries have been opened in the cities. In the Federal District there are 250 schools, and about 20,000 pupils. The other educational institutions are,—First, seminaries sustained and directed by the clergy; second, national colleges in the capital, sustained partly by their own funds and partly by government aid; and third, colleges and institutions in the States supported by local funds.

The republic of Mexico, according to the constitution of 1857, comprises 23 States, 1 Federal District, and 1 Territory. The Federal District comprises 87 square miles of territory, in and about the capital. The Territory comprises the peninsula of Lower California, 58,620 square miles, with only 9000 inhabitants. The entire area is about 773,144 square miles. According to the latest census, the population of Mexico amounted to 9,090,000. Of the total population, it is estimated that only about 1,000,000 are pure whites, 4,000,000 Indians, and 6000 negroes; the remainder consisting of Mestizos, Zambos, Mulattoes, Quadroons, Quinteroons, and other mixed races. The whites in Mexico are divided into two classes—Creoles, or those born in the country, and Gachupines, or native Spaniards. The Spanish population in this country still forms a numerous and important body, though the Spaniard has sunk low in the social scale. The Creole or native Mexican is commonly proud, indolent, and often vicious. An aristocratic feeling, founded on their complexion, which gives them distinction, prevents them from pursuing those kinds of labor which are deemed degrading to gentlemen. The consequence is, that their poverty is often even greater than that of the Indians; whilst from indolence, added to pride, they are prevented from following any employment beyond that of the gaming-table, or becoming the flatterers of the richer members of their own class. Throughout Mexico there is a universal predisposition to dependence upon others, or a blind reliance upon chance. The Indians form the next class of the Mexican population. They are the unmixed descendants of the aboriginal inhabitants, and consist of various tribes, resembling each other in color, and in some general characteristics which seem to announce a common origin, although differing entirely in language manners, and dress. No less than twenty languages are known to be spoken in the Mexican territory, and many of these are not dialects which may be traced to a common root, but differ as much as the languages of Sclavonic and Teutonic origin in Europe. Some possess letters which do not exist in others, and in most there is a difference of sound which strikes even the most unpracticed ear. The different tribes are scattered over the greater part of the country, and are mostly cultivators of the soil. A number of them, however, find employment in the mines; some are engaged in the manufacture of certain elegant fabrics of wool and cotton; and some in the formation of articles for domestic use. The Indian is remarkable for his patient endurance of fatigue and pain, and is exceedingly tenacious of old customs. After three centuries of constant intercourse with Europeans, he still keeps aloof from the foreigner, and continues to live in his native village. He speaks his hereditary language, delights in his old pastimes, and, according to the report of reliable travellers, occasionally worships in private his ancestral idols. Though the Mexican laws prohibit slavery, yet upon the plantations the Indians are in reality slaves. The extravagant and licentious outbursts in which they occasionally indulge bring them under pecuniary obligations, leading them to sell themselves for a number of years, or even for life, to the landlord; and this condition the latter is every ready and willing to bring about.

The middle races have, in process of time, become a very important part of the population of Mexico. In a country where rank depends more on the complexion than on those endowments which in other countries confer distinction, it is not surprising that almost every shade has its limits defined by terms which, though apparently only expressing the color, do in reality signify the rank of the individual. The son of a white, whether a Creole or European, by an Indian female, is called *Mestizo*. His color is almost a pure white, and his skin is of a peculiar transparency. If a Mestizo marry a white man, the next generation scarcely differs in anything from the European race. The issue of Negroes by Indian females bear in Mexico the singular name of *Chinos* or Chinese in common language, although by law they are named Zambos. The term Zambo, however, is generally applied to the descendants of a Negro and a female Mulatto, or of a Negro and a female Chinese. From the union of a white man and a Mulatto woman the class of Quadroons is derived. When a female Quadroon marries a white man, the children are denominated Quinteroons. The issue of a white man by a female Quinteroon is considered a white. Next to the pure Indians the Mestizos are the most numerous caste.

It was the policy of Spain to foster a spirit of rivalry between the different classes of inhabitants, by creating little imaginary shades of superiority amongst them, which prevented any two from having a common interest. Whiteness of skin was the patent of nobility; and even the Creole, whom the Spaniard depised, looked with the contempt of a European upon the rest of his countrymen. The revolution, however, put an end to castes, the differences of which were all swallowed up in the grand distinction of Americans and Europeans. The Creoles were compelled to court the alliance of the mixed classes, without whom they could make no effectual head against the Spaniards. Many of the most distinguished characters of the revolutionary war belonged to the mixed breeds; and under the system now established, all are equally entitled to the rights of citizenship, and equally capable of holding the highest dignities of the state.

Of the ancient inhabitants of Mexico some very interesting monuments remain. The work of Humboldt on New Spain first excited the curiosity of Europeans, and rescued the antiquities of Mexico from the oblivion to which they had so long been consigned; but it was only until recently, that their value as works of art, and as indications of a considerable advance in civilization, was fully appreciated. Pyramids, having even a larger base, and being otherwise scarcely inferior in magnitude to those of Egypt, are found in many parts of Mexico. Amongst the most celebrated is that of Cholula, the base of which is 1423 feet on each side, and the height 177 feet. It consists of eight graduated square towers, each rising above the other, and terminating in a species of sanctuary. Here vestiges of noble sculpture are visible, as well as at Otumba, Oajaca, Mitlan, Tlascola, and Palenque. The ruins of the latter, in particular, have attracted a considerable degree of attention, and are worthy of description. They extend for more than 20 miles along the summit of the ridge which separates the country of the wild Maya Indians from the State of Chiapas, and must have anciently embraced a city and its suburbs. The principal buildings are erected on the most prominent height; and several of them, if not all, have been provided with stone stairs. Other ruins of considerable magnitude, and distinguished by numerous sculptures, are found upon the neighboring hills. The Mountain of Tezcoca is nearly covered with ruins of ancient buildings. At Mitlan there are the remains of a large palace, the architecture of which possesses a stately grandeur, and melancholy beauty of a peculiar character. The roof of the portico is supported by plain cylindrical columns, and the facade of the palace is covered with a beautiful matwork, or basket scroll, such as is found in Egyptian sepulchral chambers. Many of the statues found at Otumba, Mitlan, Jochichalo, and the magnificent flower-temple of Oajaca, are sculptured in a purely classical style; whilst vases rivalling those of Egypt and Etruria have been discovered in sepulchral excavations. Roads are to be met with, not only in the vicinity of great cities, but at a vast distance from them, artificially constructed, like the Roman military roads, of large squared blocks of stone. These roads present a continual level, and may be called viaducts, in contradistinction to aqueducts, which were also constructed by the ancient inhabitants of Mexico. Where they traverse acclivities, they are parapeted; and the indications may still be observed, both of regular posting stations at certain intervals, and of the regular division of the distances, upon the principle of the milestones of our turnpike roads. Bridges constructed of the same durable material, and thrown across torrents, are also to be found. In these bridges there is occasionally an approximation to the principle of the arch and keystone; but in general they only display the primitive and obvious form of architraves of stones superimposed on two or more piers of the same massy character and durable materials. Every feature of these structures is at once singular, ingenious, and colossal.

With regard to the period at which these remarkable edifices were constructed, and the people to whom the labor is to be attributed, the learned are as yet not agreed. One point, however, seems pretty generally admitted, viz., that their erection must be traced to a race who inhabited the country prior to the invasion of the Mexicans, and who had attained to a considerable degree of civilization. An attempt has been made to prove that this people lived at a time prior even to the Toltecans who preceded the Mexicans by 600 years; and a close analogy between the antiquities of Mexico and those of Egypt has been shown to exist. The hypothesis advanced regarding the people is, that they were a branch of the Anakim or Cyclopean family of Syria, the shepherd kings of Egypt, the Oscans of Etruria, and the Pelasgians of Greece, the Titans or giants of classical romance, and who are recorded to have been severally expelled from Egypt and Syria. With respect to the religion and the religious rites of this ancient race, a striking analogy with those of Eygpt has likewise been traced. The gods of the Toltecans appear sculptured, as usual, in bas-relief, in the dark inner rooms of temples. He who would appear to be the chief-god is portrayed on the inner wall of the adytum of one of the sanctuaries belonging to the great temple of Palenque, and is worshipped symbolically under other forms and in other localities. He is supposed to be identical with the Osiris of Egypt and the Adonis of Syria, or the well-known classical combination of both divinities, the ancient *Adoni-Siris*. The manner in which he is enthroned, the cushion on which he reposes, the cap, the symbols, and various appurtenances, show an analogy with the Egyptian deity. But there is a column affixed to the cap which is not found on any Egyptian head-dress; it was, however, an unquestionable symbol of Osiris.

Of the temples we have already given a cursory notice. Their architecture has a theological character like that of Egypt and of Greece; and although their forms are peculiar to the country, the original type of them is extant in Syria, Palestine and Judæa. Like those of the Egyptians, they are all distinguished by architectural peculiarities, exclusively appertaining to the people by whom they were erected. A high-place of three successive terraces or steps generally constitutes the platform of the temple. The terraces are distinguished by that sloping form which the Egyptian architects peculiarly affected, and they are generally constructed of large blocks of stone, covered with stucco equally hard and durable. On the top of the high-place was an oblong rectangular court, and in the centre of this court stood the temple, divided, like the rock temples of Nubia, into three dark rooms built of stone, and having an ark or barn-shaped roof. The innermost of these rooms constitutes the sanctuary. The apartments are occasionally decorated with painted sculptures. Sometimes the staircase ascends the high-place in front, traversing the curvilinear terraces in a straight line to the door of the temple. Occasional variety was given to the square form of the area, and to the triple form of the terraces, by staircases ascending to the sanctuary from each of the cardinal points. The high-place has sometimes a circular instead of a square ground-plan, and in that case, it may remind antiquarians of the well-known *Tepes*, or high-places of Syria, which is a presumptive proof of the Syrian origin of these structures.

It appears that the creed of this ancient people was a form of deism, which permitted some varieties of symbolic representation. From the few records of their religious rites which have come down to us, and which are principally derived from the extraordinary rolls of American papyrus, formed of the prepared fibres of the *maguey*, on which their beautiful hierogyphical system is preserved, we learn that they were as simple as their creed, No human or even animal sacrifices appear to have been offered up to the presiding divinity of their temples; nothing, indeed, but fruits and flowers. Such a religious system was therefore quite different from the hideous idols and sanguinary sacrifices which were in use amongst the Mexican people.

CHAPTER IV.

POLITICAL DIVISIONS.

The republic of Mexico, as has already been stated, is divided into twenty-three States, a Federal District, and one Territory, of which we shall now proceed to give a short account. Mexico, the most populous of the whole, and which also contains the metropolitan city and the Federal District, extends from 18° 30′ to 21° 57′ of N. Lat., and from 98° to 101° W. Long., and includes an area of about 19,000 square miles. It is bounded on the W. by the State of Michoacan, S. W. by the State of Guerrero, N. by that of Queretaro, E. by Puebla, and N. E. by Vera Cruz. This State is situated on the high lands of the interior, and its surface is almost entirely mountainous. Only one of its peaks, however, attains the height of perpetual snow, namely, that of Toluca, upwards of 15,000 feet above sea level. The climate is necessarily cool and salubrious. This upland region embraces a large proportion of valuable mines. To the N. and N. E. of the central valley of the State are the great silver-mining districts of Real del Monte, Moran, and Atotonilco el Chico. Iron, lead, and carbonate of soda are also found in the State. But rich as the mines of this country are, the fertility of its soil is even more remarkable, producing every variety of plant with rapidity, and in the greatest luxuriance. The most valuable land, however, is what is called the Valley of Mexico, a splendid region, variegated with extensive lakes, and surrounded by high volcanic peaks. Its general figure is an oval of about 200 miles in circumference, and forms the very centre of the great table-land of Añahuac, elevated from 6,000 to 8,000 feet above the level of the ocean.

The most interesting object in the Valley of Mexico is the vast system of drainage by which the capital is protected against the periodical inundations of the Lake of Tezcoco, which, during the first two centuries after the conquest, threatened it repeatedly with destruction. In the centre of this valley stands Mexico City, capital of the republic and of the Federal District. Tenochtitlan, the ancient capital of the Aztecs, was built on several islands in the Lake of Tezcoco, and connected with the land by four long causeways; but the drainage of the marshes and the removal of the forests, combined with other causes, have produced a great diminution in the water of the lake; so that the modern city of Mexico, which is believed to occupy the same site, is removed from its shores by a distance of 2½ miles, although in the rainy season of the year the easterly winds occasionally cause the water to overflow the outskirts of the city, which is protected from such incursions by dykes. The city is generally reputed by travellers to be very beautiful, and never fails to excite the admiration of those who view it for the first time. It is regularly built in the form of a square, with its streets, which are both long and wide, intersecting each other at right angles. They are well paved, but not lighted, and often very imperfectly cleaned, though the town is well supplied with water brought by splendid aqueducts from the neighboring hills. The houses, built of hewn stone, have a massive and sometimes rather forbidding appearance. They generally inclose an open court, round which the different apartments are situated, the entrance being by an iron gate in front. Opposite to this is placed the staircase by which access is gained to the upper stories and to the roof, which is flat, surrounded by iron balustrades, and sometimes ornamented with bronze and mosaic work of glazed porcelain. The style of architecture in the city resembles that of southern Europe; and the public buildings are in many instances very imposing in their appearance. Mexico contains several squares, the principal of which, the Plaza Mayor, which occupies the centre of the town, is of very large extent, and is surrounded by the chief public buildings. The centre of this square was formerly occupied by a large statue in bronze of Charles IV.; but this has been removed to the quadrangle of the university. On the north side of the Plaza Mayor is the cathedral, which stands on the alleged site of the ancient *teocalli*, or temple of the Aztec war-god Mexitli, from whom the city derives its name. The cathedral is 500 feet in length and 420 in breadth; and though the style is irregular, and not in strict accordance with any architectural order, its appearance, especially in the interior, is very imposing. Besides the cathedral, Mexico is said to contain between fifty and sixty churches and convents, most of them in a mixed style of architecture, and remarkable chiefly for the richness of their ornaments. There is also a handsome theatre, and a large circular arena for the exhibition of bull-fights, called the Plaza de Toros, which has accommodation for 2000 or 3000 spectators. At the west end of the town there is a park called the Alameda, which is a great place of public resort, and has an area of ten or twelve acres, laid out in walks and labyrinths, and adorned with numerous fine trees. There are also two other promenades or *paseos*, as they are called, one on the east and the other on the west of the city. These consist of the roads leading from the town, which are raised several feet above the surrounding country, and lined with double rows of fine trees, thus affording delightful promenades, which are frequented by multitudes of the inhabitants. The one which leads to the east, called the Paseo de la Viga, skirts the Lake Chalco Canal, which adds much to the appearance of the promenade. In the city also there are several covered colonnades or arcades, which form a favorite place of resort in the evening, and are often crowded long after the other promenades are deserted. The city is supplied with water by means of two aqueducts; one of which, 11,155 yards in length, extends from Santa Fe to the Alameda, and is carried for one-third of its course on arches of stone and brick. This aqueduct supplies the city with water of an excellent quality; while the suburbs to the S. are supplied by that of Chapoltepec, which is 3608 yards in length. The manufactures carried on in Mexico are remarkable neither for quantity nor for quality; the most important being those of tobacco and plate, together with that of gold and silver lace, which is well made, and sold at a very cheap rate. The commercial as well as the manufacturing industry of Mexico is very small, and the city derives its importance almost exclusively from its being the capital of the confederation and the residence of the head of the government.

The inhabitants of Mexico City are of several different races and character. They consist of Creoles or descendants of the Spaniards, of Mestizos, of copper-colored natives, of Mulattoes, and of Europeans. Of the higher classes, many have acquired considerable wealth; but the great bulk of the people are very poor; and the lower orders, in their idleness and dirty habits, as well as in their general character, have a striking resemblance to the lazzaroni of Naples. The population of the city is estimated at about 200,000.

There are a number of other towns in the State of Mexico, as Acapulco, on the S. W. coast; Toluca, the nominal capital, situated at the foot of two steep barren hills, about 27 miles S. W. from the federal metropolis; Tezcoco, on the eastern shore of the lake of that name, 12 miles from Mexico; Otumba, once large and flourishing, but now a mere village; Lerma, which is surrounded by an extensive morass, traversed by fine raised causeways; Chalco, a pretty large town, situated in a lake of the same name, about 20 miles S. E. of the metropolis; San Augustin, at which a great annual fair is held, frequented by vast multitudes from Mexico; Tacubaya, a village about four miles from the gates of the capital, and formerly the country residence of the Bishop of Mexico; Pachuca and Cuyoacan.

To the N. W. of Mexico is the small State of Queretaro, the territories of which are divided into the six districts of Amealco, Cadereyta, San Juan del Rio, San Pedro, Toliman, Queretaro, and Jalpam. Queretaro lies entirely on the central plateau of the Cordillera, and is intersected by numerous mountain spurs and elevated hills, some of which are entirely bare, while others are covered with forests of various kinds of wood. The agricultural portions of the State are chiefly confined to the valleys, in which the soil is frequently of great fertility. The chief mining district, and the only one of any note in the State, is that of El Doctor, in the district of Cadereyta. The inhabitants, with the exception of those of the capital, are mostly employed in agriculture. Queretaro, the capital, is a finely situated and a well built town, with about 50,000 inhabitants. It contains some fine churches and convents, particularly that of Santa Clara, which is an immense building, said to resemble a little town in the interior, being regularly laid out in streets and plazas. The only other towns of importance are San Juan del Rio, San Pedro de la Cañada, and Cadereyta.

To the westward of Queretaro is Guanajuato. Large portions of the soil are of great fertility, especially the magnificent plains of the Bajio, in the southern part of the State, which extends for more than 100 miles from Apasco to beyond Leon; and in the north, where the splendid plains or *llanos* of San Felipe spread far and wide. The State contains three cities, four market-towns, and thirty-seven villages. The manufactures of wool and cotton, which formerly abounded in many of the towns, have recently much declined. Mining and agriculture now constitute the chief sources of wealth. The mineral productions are very valuable. The town of Guanajuato, in the vicinity of which the principal mines are situated, contains numerous splendid memorials of the former wealth of its inhabitants. Many of the private dwellings are magnificent, as are the churches, chapels, and other religious edifices. The town contains a cathedral, a college, a theatre, barrack, mint, university, gymnasium, and about 60,000 inhabitants. Celaya City is a considerable town, containing about 15,000 inhabitants. Salamanca is likewise a considerable place, situated in a rich part of the country, and has a population of about 15,000. San Miguel Allende, formerly San Miguel el Grande, is a pleasantly situated town on the river De la Laja, and contains about 5000 inhabitants.

To the westward of Guanajuato, and stretching along the Pacific for 480 miles, is the large State of Jalisco. It is divided into eight districts, viz., Guadalajara, Lagos, La Barca, Sayula, Etzatlan, Autlan, Tepic, and Colotlan; and these, again, are subdivided into 26 departments. The greater part of Jalisco lies on the western slope of the Cordillera; and its table-lands, which resemble those of the great plateau of Mexico, are somewhat broken up by mountain ranges. The upper regions are consequently comparatively sterile, while the low lands are rich and fruitful. The city of Guadalajara, capital of Jalisco, is situated upon an extensive plain about 450 miles from Mexico. It is built with great regularity, the streets running at right angles, being well paved, and having raised pathways on each side. The houses, with the exception of those in the suburbs, are finely built. Considerable quantities of shawls of striped calico were formerly made here; but these home manufactures have been superseded by importations from the United States. Jalisco derives little benefit from its foreign trade, San Blas, the only seaport which it possesses, being nearly abandoned. Foreign goods are introduced overland from San Luis or Mexico. The population of the capital amounts to about 70,000 souls. The town of Tepic is, next to the capital, the finest and most populous town in the State, and has a population of about 20,000. The only mining region of any note in this State is that of Bolaños.

The State of Mechoacan is bounded on the north by Guanajuato, N. E. by Queretaro, S. E. by Mexico, W. by Jalisco, and S. W., for a short distance, by the Pacific. It lies chiefly on the western slope of the Cordillera, and its surface is considerably broken by mountains and valleys. The land is abundantly watered by streams and rivers, and incloses a great number of lakes. The former riches of the State consisted almost entirely in its agricultural produce, the most ordinary manufactures being introduced from the neighboring towns of the Bajio. But the agricultural interest is by no means in so flourishing a condition as it once was, nor are the mines remarkable either for their extent or value. The whole western declivity of the Sierra Madre, comprehended within the province of Mechoacan, is noted for its insalubrity; and the sea-coast, as might be expected, is likewise very unhealthy. The *tierra caliente*, at the foot of the Cordillera, which is fertilized in part by the Rio Balsas, is rich in all the ordinary productions of the tropics; and even in the more elevated valleys sugar was grown to a very considerable extent before the revolution. The best sugar lands are now about 36 miles south of Pasquaro, the ancient capital of the Indians. At the foot of the Mountain of Jorullo there are plantations of cocoa and indigo; and in several parts of the State the various productions of the table-land can be raised in abundance. Mechoacan has been called the cradle of the revolution, from which it suffered severely. Morelia, the capital of the State, is delightfully situated at the height of 6,300 feet above the level of the sea. It consists chiefly of one long, broad street, well paved and kept in good order. The population has been estimated at 25,000.

The State of Guerrero was created by virtue of the 4th article of the Acta de Reformas, passed in May, 1847, amending the constitution of 1847. By this article it was agreed that this State should be formed of the Districts of Acapulco, Chilupa, Tasco, and Talapa, and the municipality of Coyucan,—the first three of which belonged to the State of Mexico, the fourth to Puebla, and the fifth to Mechoacan. The physical character and productions of this State correspond with those of the three States to which this region originally belonged. Its capital is Tixtly, and contains about 6,500 inhabitants.

The State of La Puebla, which is situated to the east of that of Mexico, and stretches nearly across the continent, is divided into 25 districts. The territory of the State extends beyond the western ridge of the Sierra Madre, and down to the shores of the Pacific; consequently it produces in abundance the fruits of either of the *tierras calientes*, or those common to the rest of the table-land There are, however, no mines, which uniformly create a home market; and as the foreign trade is comparatively of but little importance, the agricultural interest is in a depressed condition. Manufactures of wool and cotton are carried on to some extent in the State. La Puebla contains Popocatepetl, the loftiest mountain in North America, situated near its S. W. boundary. The capital and largest city of this State is Pueblo de los Angelos, the seat of the richest bishopric in the country, and that of the most extensive manufactures of cotton, earthenware, and wool. Glass and soap are also made; the latter to a considerable extent. The streets, like those of Mexico, are rectangular, spacious, airy, and paved with large stones in a highly ornamental manner. There are a great number of churches and convents, religious colleges, and a magnificent cathedral, richly ornamented, and held in high veneration. The principal other towns in the State are Cholula, Atlixco, Guauchinango, Tehuacan de las Granadas, Tepeaca and Huajocingo. La Puebla City contains about 75,000 inhabitants.

Tlascala, which was declared a Federal Territory in 1847, but is now a State, has an area of about 2000 square miles. It is divided into three districts called Tlaxco, Huamantla, and Tlascala. Its soil is of considerable fertility, and its climate mild and genial. Its productions are chiefly of a cereal character. The capital, of the same name, is situated on the Rio Atoyac or Papagallo, the only stream of importance in the State. It is well and regularly built, and has many relics and ruins of its former glory in the town and vicinity. At present it contains probably not more than 4000 inhabitants.

Oajaca is a very fine State, the southern boundary of which extends along the coast of the Pacific Ocean a distance of about 360 miles, from La Puebla to Guatemala. Agriculture is highly favored by the fertility of the soil and the salubrity of the climate. The Cordillera, which here forms two branches, one extending along the shores of the Pacific, the other along those of the Gulf of Mexico, incloses the beautiful and fertile region termed the Valley of Oajaça, which constitutes a great part of this State. The staple productions are, corn, chile, agave, cotton, coffee, sugar, cocoa, vanilla, tobacco, cochineal, wax, honey, and indigo; while gold, silver, copper, quicksilver, iron, rock-salt, limestone, gysum, etc. are found in the State. Oajaca, the capital, is a flourishing place, although it suffered severely during the revolution. It contains about 25,000 inhabitants. The best seaport in the State is Tehuantepec. About thirty miles from the capital, on the road leading to Tehuantepec, are the remains of what antiquarians have styled the sepulchral palaces of Mitla, lying in the midst of a rocky granitic region, and surrounded by sad and sombre scenery. According to tradition, they were erected by the Zapotecas as palaces or tombs for their princes. They consist of three edifices symmetrically arranged, the principal and finest having a front of nearly 150 feet. The walls are covered with figures and ornaments.

Vera Cruz comprises a narrow strip of land stretching along the Gulf of Mexico from the State of San Luis Potosi to that of Tabasco, a distance of 400 miles, while its breadth on an average does not exceed 50 or 60 miles. The eastern part of the State is generally level, low, and sandy; but it gradually rises inland until the country is broken into an uninterrupted series of lofty mountains and beautiful valleys. The coasts are rich in rivers, streams, inlets and lagoons, but unfortunately they are of little practical use in navigation. There are several mineral springs in the State; and at Atotonilco, near Calcahualco, in the district of Cordova, there are warm baths celebrated for their efficacy in nervous and rheumatic complaints. The State is divided into four departments, viz., Vera Cruz, Jalapa, Orizava, and Acayucam. The productions of this State are rich and varied; the differences in its altitude render it capable of yielding fruits and grains both of the temperate and torrid zone. Tobacco, coffee, sugar, cotton, corn, barley, wheat, jalap, sarsaparilla, vanilla, oranges, citrons, pine-apples, lemons, pomegranates, bananas, grapes, peaches, apricots, pears, plums, tam arinds, mahogany, ebony, cedar, oak, dye-woods, and numerous other trees, plants, and shrubs, spring almost spontaneously from the soil, and render the labor of man almost unnecessary. The city of Vera Cruz, the capital of the State, is situated on the shores of the Gulf of Mexico, in Lat. 19° 11′ 52″ N., and Long. 96° 8′ 45″ W. It is well and handsomely built of madrepore; and its red and white cupolas, towers, and battlements have a splendid effect when viewed from the sea. Many of the houses are large, being built in the Moorish or old Spanish style, and generally inclosing a square court, with covered galleries. They have flat roofs, glass windows, and are well adapted to the climate. Opposite the town, at the distance of about 800 yards, is a small island containing the strong castle of San Juan de Ulloa, which commands the town. The harbor lies between the town and the castle, and is very insecure. Vera Cruz is extremely unhealthy at all times; and during the warm season Europeans are exceedingly liable to become the victims of the *vomito prieto*, or black vomit. The city is surrounded by sand-hills and ponds of stagnant-water; there is neither garden nor mill near it; and the only water fit for use is that which falls from the clouds. The trade is very considerable; but is shared by Tampico, a port which has risen into importance within late years. It is situated about 120 miles N.N.W. of Vera Cruz, being about 312 miles from Mexico. The population of Vera Cruz amounts to about 20,000. Another town in this State is Jalapa, from which a well-known drug takes its name. Formerly it was the great mart of New Spain for European goods, as the unhealthiness of Vera Cruz compelled traders to transfer their merchandise at once to this city, where a great annual fair was held. It has now, however, little commerce of its own, and is only a sort of resting-place between Vera Cruz and Mexico. Jalapa is indebted to the peculiarity of its position for the extreme mildness of its climate. The town stands upon a little platform 4500 feet above the level of the sea, and is protected from the N.W. winds by a ridge of mountains. The population is about 25,000.

To the N.W. of Vera Cruz lies the State of San Luis Potosi, under which name, as a Spanish intendancy, were included Cohahuila and Texas, and New Leon, Tamaulipas, and San Luis. The western portion of the State is quite mountainous, but towards Tamaulipas the Cordillera is somewhat broken, and a lower hilly country stretches out towards the S.E. The climate of the mountain region and table-land is cold; while that of the lower elevations and flats towards the eastern boundary is much warmer, and at certain seasons very unhealthy. Maize, wheat, barley and fodder, are the principal agricultural productions of this State. Cattle are raised in large quantities. Wool and cotton fabrics, glass, leather, pottery, and hardwares are manufactured here to a considerable extent. In this State there are a number of rich mines, particularly those of Catorce, where a metalliferous ridge of mountains extends for many miles. With the exception of the capital, which bears the same name, it possesses no large town. San Luis, including the suburbs, contains about 35,000 inhabitants. It is well built, and contains a number of churches and monasteries and public buildings. It derives great advantage from its situation, as the natural depot for the trade of Tampico with the northern and western States. Zacatecas, Durango, and other States receive through this channel a large proportion of their foreign imports; and since the building of the new town of Tamaulipas, which, from being on a more elevated spot than the old town of Tampico, is less subject to the vomito, there is every appearance of increase in this branch of commercial intercourse.

To the W. and N.W. of San Luis Potosi is situated Zacatecas. It is a mountain country of the high plateau of Mexico, cut up by spurs of the Cordillera, and mostly arid and inhospitable. There are no rivers of any size in this State, and the country is unusually dry; water-tanks, draw-wells, and reservoirs are established on all the estates. The country, however, is particularly rich in its mineral productions, which constitute almost its sole wealth. Manufactures there are none, excepting in the capital, where there are a few cotton-spinners, as also at Aguas Calientes. Zacatecas, the capital, is situated at the foot of an abrupt and picturesque porphyritic mountain, upon the rugged summit of which is perched a neat church and a small fortress. From the inequalities of the ground on which it stands the streets are short and crooked. This town contains about 20,000 inhabitants; and Veta Grande, a village in its immediate vicinity, numbers about 6000. Aguas Calientes is a small town situated on the banks of a stream of the same name, in a broad and fertile valley, 75 miles S. of Zacatecas. It is celebrated for its woolen manufactures; and in the neighborhood are several thermal springs.

The State of Yucatan occupies the greater portion of the peninsula which separates the Gulf of Mexico from the Caribbean Sea. It is a vast alluvial plain, intersected by a mountain ridge which does not exceed 4000 feet in height. Upon some parts of this extensive territory maize, rice, cotton, pepper, tobacco, and the sugar-cane are produced, besides dyewoods, hides, and other articles. In the central parts the want of water is a very serious drawback to agriculture; the rainy season is very uncertain, and in many parts not even a stream is known to exist; so that in unfavorable years the inhabitants are compelled to have recourse for subsistence to the roots which the woods supply. The capital of Yucatan is Merida, situated on an arid plain 40 miles from the coast. It enjoys little trade, and contains only about 23,000 inhabitants. Campeachy is the principal commercial town; and here the logwood, which goes by the same name, attains its greatest perfection.

Adjoining Yucatan is Tabasco, one of the smaller States in the confederation, and previous to the revolution a province of the intendancy of Vera Cruz. A great portion of the State is extremely flat, and during the rainy season is laid under water, so that intercourse between villages has to be carried on by canoes. On the eastern boundary of Tabasco is the Laguna de Terminos, which is 45 miles long by 30 broad, and contains several large and beautiful islands. The climate of this State is extremely hot. Cacao, coffee, pepper, sugar, tamarinds, arrowroot and some tobacco are cultivated; while indigo and vanilla grow wild in the forests. Game is very abundant, and the streams are well stocked with excellent fish. The capital, San Juan Bautista, lies on the left bank of the Tabasco River, 70 miles from its mouth, and contains about 7000 inhabitants. Vessels of light draught can reach it from the sea; but its chief intercourse is carried on with the adjacent States and Guatemala.

Between Tabasco and Guatemala is situated the State of Las Chiapas, which formerly belonged to Guatemala, but which in 1833 joined the Mexican confederation. Comprehending the northern slopes of the table-lands of Guatemala, Las Chiapas is, throughout a considerable part of its territory, cut up into successions of ridges and valleys, which are rich in many of the finest tropical productions. The most important of the numerous rivers flowing from the mountains near the state of Tabasco to the Gulf of Mexico, are the Tabasco River, the San Pedro, the Usumasinta, and the Pacaitun. The climate of Las Chiapas is mild and temperate; and the chief productions are corn, cacao, sugar, tobacco, figs, apricots, and other fruits and vegetables; but a great part of the State is uncultivated and unexplored. The State is divided into four departments, and the capital is Ciudad Real, a handsome town, with a population of 8,000. The State of Las Chiapas, like that of Yucatan, contains many ancient remains.

The State of Durango is bounded on the N. by Chihuahua, W. by Sinaloa, E. by Coahuila, and S. by Zacatecas and Jalisco. The main branch of the Great Cordillera runs through this State in a N.W. direction. The north-eastern portion of the State slopes gradually downwards towards the waters of the Rio Grande, while the south-western part consists chiefly of lofty table-lands and mountain spurs. The climate is healthy and coo' and its agricultural productions are similiar to those of the other States in like circumstances. Immense quantities of horses, mules, sheep, and cattle are reared in this State; indeed, its cattle and minerals constitute its chief wealth. Iron, silver, gold, lead, and other minerals are likewise abundant. Durango, or, as it is often called, Victoria, the capital of the State, is situated 180 miles to the N.W. of Zacatecas, in the midst of a vast plain. Its population amounts to about 15,000. The principal streets, the Plaza Mayor, the theatre, and most of the public edifices, were built by Zambrano, a wealthy proprietor, who is supposed to have drawn from his mines at San Dimas and Guarisamey upwards of 30,000,000 of dollars. The towns of Villa del Nombre de Dios, San Juan del Rio, and Cinco Señores de Nazas, are almost the only considerable places in the State unconnected with the mines. The great mineral wealth of this State holds out the most encouraging prospect of ample remuneration to those who engage in mining speculations; and there can be little doubt that in time the advantages which Durango possesses will be duly appreciated by foreign and native associations of capitalists.

The State immediately adjoining Durango to the N. is that of Chihuahua. The great mountain chain of Mexico, which forms the connecting link between the Rocky Mountains of the north and the Andes of the south, is here known as the Sierra Madre, and occupies chiefly the western part of the State, where its elevation attains a great height, and at length descends abruptly till it is lost in the plains of Sonora and Sinaloa. The highest point of the Sierra Madre is said to be 8441 feet above the level of the sea. The greater portion of the State consequently lies on the plateau of Mexico, and only a small part of it on the western slope of the Sierra Madre. Large numbers of the aborigines still occupy the lonelier portions of this State, and frequently annoy the peaceful settler. Chihuahua possesses a mild and temperate climate, a fertile soil, and vast mineral resources. Agricultural operations are not much carried on here, the chief source of its wealth being the mines and cattle. The gold, silver, and copper mines are exceedingly productive. Veins of iron, cinnabar, lead, sulphur, coal, and nitre have also been found and explored. The capital of the State, Chihuahua, numbers about 12,000 inhabitants.

The State of Sinaloa is bounded on the south by Jalisco, east by Durango, south-west by Chihuahua, north by Sonora, and west by the Pacific and the Gulf of California, along the shores of which it extends for about 600 miles. The capital is Culiacan; population 10,000. It is about 540 miles in length from south-east to north-west, and has a breadth of about 150 miles. The surface is partly mountainous and partly level coast land. The coast region is little cultivated and thinly inhabited, being scorched by a burning sun; the central and eastern parts contain numerous table-lands and valleys; while the slopes of the mountains are thickly wooded with excellent timber. In the interior, the air is mild and genial. In those parts where irrigation is practiced, abundant crops of grain are raised. Wheat, Indian corn, and barley, with cotton, sugar, and tobacco, are its chief agricultural productions. This State is also rich in minerals. The principal town is Mazatlan, a seaport town and a place of considerable trade. It contains about 6000 inhabitants.

Sonora is situated on the Gulf of California to the north of Sinaloa. The western and southern portions of the State are generally flat. The eastern portion is mountainous, but contains many fine and productive valleys; this portion of the State is likewise rich in valuable mineral deposits. The climate is warm throughout the year, but in spring is subject to rapid changes in temperature. A great portion of this State is still in the possession of the Indians, most of whom are still in a wild and savage state. The trade of Sonora is principally carried on at Guyamas, which is situated in a healthy region, and possesses one of the best harbors in Mexico. It contains about 5000 inhabitants. The capital is Ures; popula ion 7000. Petic, about 120 miles north from Guyamas, is a larger town, containing about 8000 inhabitants. It is the depot for goods imported at the Guyamas, and designed for the northern district of Mexico.

The State of Tamaulipas extends along the shores of the Gulf of Mexico, southward from the Rio Grande, which separates it from Texas. It has a coast line of about 350 miles, and its breadth varies from 50 to about 160 miles. The coast is low and sandy, and fringed with lagoons varying from four to eighteen miles in width, and divided from the gulf by banks of sand. In the northern part of the State, in the neighborhood of the Rio Grande, the country is comparatively level. South of this, however, and at some distance from the coast, the surface is varied by a succession of mountains, hills, and valleys, which gradually slope westwardly to the flats and sands of the sea-coast. The climate of the interior is mild and healthy, but, on the coast, an intense heat prevails during the greater part of the year; which, combined with the rank vegetation and moisture, renders this region very unhealthy. The principal ports are Tampico and Matamoras, where a large coasting and foreign commerce is carried on to supply the middle and northern States of the republic. Matamoras is situated on the right bank of the Rio Grande, about thirty miles from its mouth, and contains about 22,000 inhabitants. Tampico stands on the northern bank of the Panuco, about five miles from its mouth. The capital of the State is Victoria, formerly Santander, and contains about 10,000 inhabitants. Numerous remains of ancient edifices etc., exist in this State.

To the westward of Tamaulipas lies the State of New Leon, which was colonized in the end of the sixteenth century by the Viceroy Monterey, who bestowed upon it the proud title of El Nuevo Reyno de Leon, or the New Kingdom of Leon. It lies among the first spurs or ridges of the Sierra Madré, and is interspersed with wide plains and fruitful valleys. The climate, except among the higher mountain ranges, is warm, but salubrious. Agriculture has not been much practiced in the State; the chief occupation of the land-holders being the grazing of cattle. Lead and silver are said to be abundant; but mining operations are only carried on at two places—Cerralvo and Valecillo. Salt is made at the salt-mines on the banks of the Tigré. The capital of the State is Monterey, estimated to contain about 15,000 inhabitants.

The State of Colima lies along the shores of the Pacific, and is bounded on the other sides by Jalisco and Mechoacan. Its surface is generally level, and here and there broken by ranges of hills. On the north-east corner of the territory is the Mountain of Colima, the most western of the Mexican volcanoes, and which rises to the height of 9,200 feet above the level of the sea. The climate is warm, and on the coast hot, but not unhealthy. Cotton, sugar, tobacco, and cacao, are its chief agricultural productions; while, on the coast, large quantities of salt are made from sea-water. Rich iron deposits have recently been found here. The chief town is Colima, about six miles south of the volcano, and containing about 30,000 inhabitants. Manzanillo, the port of Colima, is about fifty miles west of the capital, and a place of some trade.

Adjoining to New Leon and Tamaulipas is Cohahuila, which is generally elevated, and being well sheltered from the north-west winds, possesses a healthy climate. A considerable mountain chain stretches across the State in a north-westerly direction, and its surface is most luxuriantly irrigated by the numberless springs and streams which, bursting from these ridges, become tributaries to the Rio Grande. Its pastures are clothed with rich, natural grasses, and are admirably calculated for breeding, rearing, and fattening cattle; whilst its forests furnish abundance of wood, which is well calculated for every kind of construction. There are mines of saltpetre, copperas, alum, lead, tin, and copper, besides some silver in Santa Rosa, and gold in Sacramento. These mineral treasures, for want of population and of capital, have been rather ascertained than explored. The inhabitants are almost wholly of the white race, or with such slight mixture of the Indian blood as to make no distinction in color worthy of notice. The capital of the State is Saltillo, a large town containing about 20,000 inhabitants. It is situated upon the side of a hill branching off from the Sierra Madré. The inhabitants are chiefly occupied in agriculture, and produce excellent wheat and barley, and a great variety of fruits. The vines cultivated here make wine of very excellent flavor, and considerable strength.

The Territory of Lower California comprehends that long narrow strip of land which extends from the northern boundary of the republic southward to Cape St. Lucas, having on the east, the Gulf of Mexico, and on the west, the Pacific. It is about 700 miles in length, and varies in breadth from 30 to 100 miles. The surface consists of an irregular chain of rocks, hills, and mountains, which run through its entire length, and which attain a height of nearly 5000 feet. Amid these ridges there are occasionally found a few sheltered spots of productive land; but it is for the most part a barren, dreary waste, and is one of the most unattractive countries in the warm or temperate regions. Valuable mines of gold, silver, copper, and lead, are known to exist in the peninsula, and the salt-mines on the island of Carmen, in the Gulf of California, are very productive. Among the islands of the gulf immense numbers of seal are constantly found, and the whaling-grounds on the Pacific coast are of great value. The principal ports on the west coast are San Quentin, which is said to afford a secure anchorage for the largest vessels, and Magdalena, which is much resorted to by whalers during the winter season. La Paz, its capital, numbers about 1000 inhabitants; the population of the territory is almost entirely Indian or of a mixed race.

WEST INDIES.

UNDER this designation are comprised a very large number of islands, about 1000 in all, lying between North and South America, extending in two irregular lines, which join at Hayti, from Yucatan and Florida to the mouth of the Orinoco. They lie between lat. 10° and 28° north, and long. 57° and 85° west, and are divided into four groups: 1. The Bahamas, about 500 in number, being mostly low, flat islands southeast of Florida; 2. The Greater Antilles, between the Bahamas and Central America, comprising Cuba, Hayti or St. Domingo, Jamaica and Porto Rico; 3. The Lesser Antilles or Windward Islands, extending in a semicircular line, from Porto Rico to the mouth of the Orinoco; and 4. The Leeward Islands, lying off the coast of Venezuela, consisting of Margarita, Tortuga, Curaçoa, and some smaller islands. The West Indies belong to the European nations—Great Britain, Spain, France, the Netherlands, etc. The area in square miles is reckoned to be 92,223; and the population, according to the latest accounts, is about 4,000,000. The Bahamas are of coralline formation. The Antilles are volcanic, and form the peaks of a mountain chain continuous with the north-east range of Venezuela, and rising in Cuba, Hayti, and Jamaica, into summits from 6000 to 7000 feet in height. Minerals abound in the West India Islands. Gold, silver, copper, tin, iron, lead, etc., furnish sources of wealth. The forests supply mahogany, rosewood, and other woods of beautiful and useful character. The pine-apple, cocoa-nut, pomegranate, orange, lemon, banana, and other tropical fruits are found in abundance, as also spices, drugs, ginger, pepper, dye-stuffs, etc. Tobacco, coffee, and sugar, are staples in several islands, and cotton is also cultivated. Birds of beautiful plumage are frequently met with; monkeys are here and there; fish are abundant and good; and insects are so numerous and wide-spread as to become almost a pest. The population of the islands is made up of whites, negroes, and mulattoes, of which the whites are about one-third. Slavery at one time existed in all the West India islands; but Spain is the only power which has retained it to the present day.

ISLAND OF CUBA.

CUBA, the largest and richest of the West India islands, and the most important colony of Spain, was discovered by Columbus on the 28th of October, 1492, during his first voyage. It was then divided into nine independent principalities, under as many *caciques*. The aborigines are described as living in a state of happy tranquillity among themselves, and possessing a religion devoid of rites and ceremonies, but inculcating a belief in the existence of a great and beneficent Being, and the immortality of the soul. Cuba was twice visited by Columbus after its discovery—in April, 1494, and again in 1502. In 1511, his son, Diego Columbus, for the purpose of colonizing the island, fitted out an expedition consisting of about 300 men under Diego Velasquez, who had accompanied his father on his second voyage. Their first settlement was Baracoa; and, in 1514, they founded Santiago and Trinidad. In July, 1515, was planted a town called *San Cristoval de la Havaña*, which name was transferred in 1519 to the present capital. In 1538, Havana was reduced to ashes by a French privateer; and, to prevent a similar disaster in future, the *Castillo de la Fuerza*, a fortress which still exists, was built by Hernando de Soto, Governor of Cuba, and afterwards famous for his explorations in the southern and western regions of the United States, as well as for the discovery of the Mississippi. In 1554, the French again attacked and destroyed Havana. The early settlers devoted themselves principally to the rearing of cattle; but, about 1580, the cultivation of tobacco and the sugar-cane was commenced, and this led to the introduction of the system of negro slavery. Previous to 1600, two other fortresses were built for the defence of Havana—the Moro and the Punta—which are still in existence. For about a century and a half after this period, the island was kept in a state of almost perpetual fear of invasion from the French, English, Dutch, or the pirates infesting these seas; and several ineffectual efforts were made to reduce it. About 1655, the walls of Havana were commenced. In 1762, Havana was taken by an English fleet and army under Lord Albemarle. The defence was exceedingly obstinate; but, on the 14th of August, the city capitulated. The spoil divided among the captors amounted to over $3,500,000. The following year Cuba was restored to the Spaniards, and, from that time, its progress has been rapid; indeed, this restoration is regarded by native writers as the true era whence its importance and prosperity are to be dated. The administration of Las Casas, who arrived as captain-general in 1790, is represented by all Spanish writers as a brilliant epoch in Cuban history. He promoted, with indefatigable perseverance, a series of public works of the first utility; introduced the culture of indigo; extended the commercial importance of the island by removing, as far as his authority extended, the trammels imposed upon it by the old system of privilege and restriction. By his judicious administration, the tranquillity of the island was maintained uninterrupted at the time of the revolution in St. Domingo; although, as is generally believed, a conspiracy was formed at the instigation of the French among the free colored people of Cuba. For the last fifty or sixty years, the island has been presided over by a succession of governor-generals from Spain, some of whom have conducted themselves honorably, while the names of others are loaded with infamy.

The Island of Cuba is long and narrow, somewhat in the form of an irregular crescent, with its convex side towards the north. It divides the entrance to the Gulf of Mexico into two passages, that to the north-west being 100 miles wide at the narrowest part between the points of Hicacos in Cuba and Tancha on the Florida coast; and the south-west passage 114 miles wide between the Cabo de San Antonio of Cuba and the Cabo de Catoche, the most salient extremity of the peninsula of Yucatan. Cuba lies between 74° and 85° west long., and 19° and 23° north lat. Its length, following a curved line through its centre, is 790 miles; and its greatest breadth, from Cape Maternillos to Mota Cove, is 107 miles. The area is estimated at 42,383 square miles, or, including the other small islands attached to it, 44,163 square miles. The coast of Cuba is generally low and flat, and is surrounded by numerous islands and reefs, which render the approach both difficult and dangerous to those not acquainted with the proper channels. No island, however, in proportion to its size, has a greater number of excellent harbors, many of them accessible even to ships of the line. A range of mountains extends from one end of the island to the other, dividing it into two unequal portions, of which the northern is generally the narrower. The highest are those at the south-east extremity of the island, to the north-west of Santiago de Cuba, and have, according to Humboldt, an elevation of 7,673 feet. This Cordillera is one great calcareous mass, resting on a schistose formation. The summits are for the most part rocky and naked, occasionally interrupted by more gentle undulations. The central and western parts of the island contain two formations of compact limestone, one of clayey sandstone and another of gypsum. The limestone formations abound in caverns. The secondary formations, east of Havana, are pierced by syenitic and euphotide rocks united in groups. The syenite strata are interlocated with serpentine, and inclined to the north-west. In some places petroleum runs out of rents in the serpentine; and abundant springs of this fluid are also found in the eastern part of the island. The rivers in general are necessarily short, and flow toward the north and south. The largest is the Cauto, rising in the Sierra del Cobre, and falling into the Bay of Buena Esperanza on the southern coast after a course of 150 miles, for sixty of which it is navigable, though at low water obstructed by bars. On some of the rivers are beautiful cascades, while several of them flow during part of their courses under ground.

The climate of the western half of the island presents many inequalities of temperature arising from that portion of the island being situated along the northern limit of the torrid zone, and from the proximity of the American continent. The seasons are divided into rainy and dry, but the line of demarcation is not very clearly defined. The warmest months are July and August, when the mean temperature is from 82° to 84° Fahr.; the coldest are December and January, when the mean temperature is about 78°. The mean annual temperature at Havana is about 73.5° Fahr. During the rainy season the heat would be insupportable but for the regular alternation of the land and sea breezes. Snow never falls in Cuba, but hail and hoar-frost are not uncommon in the winter season; and, at an elevation of 300 or 400 feet above the level of the sea, ice is often seen several lines in thickness during the prevalence of north winds. Hurricanes are not so frequent here as in Hayti and the other West Iudia Islands, and seldom do much damage on shore. They occur during the autumn, from August to October.

The only peculiar quadruped known in the island is the *juita* or *huita*, an animal shaped like a rat, and from twelve to eighteen inches in length exclusive of the tail. It is of a clear, black color, inhabits the hollows and clefts of trees, and feeds on leaves and fruits. Its flesh is insipid, but is sometimes eaten. A few deer are found about the swamps, but they are supposed to have been introduced from the continent. The woods abound in wild dogs and cats, which are very destructive to poultry and cattle. Of domestic animals, the ox, the horse, and the pig, are the most valuable, and form a large proportion of the wealth of the island; the sheep, goats, and mules, are less numerous. The manati frequents the shores. The domestic fowls include geese, turkeys, peacocks, and pigeons. The indigenous birds are distinguished by the beauty of their plumage, and are very numerous, including upwards of 200 species. Birds of prey are few. The vulture and turkey-buzzard are protected by law and custom, on account of their service in the removal of offal. The rivers, bays, and inlets, are well supplied with fish. Oysters and other shell-fish are numerous, but of inferior quality. The reefs and shallows, and the sandy portion of the beach, abound in turtle, and the crocodile, cayman, and the iguana, are common. Among the insects may be specially noticed, the bee and phosphorescent fly. These flies are very numerous, and much used among the poorer inhabitants. Fifteen or twenty of them confined in a calabash pierced with holes are frequently used during the night to serve as a sort of lantern. The noxious insects are the nigua or jigger, a species of ant called vivajagua, the family of mosquitoes, the sand-fly, the scorpion, (less poisonous than that of Europe,) and spiders, whose bite is malignant enough to produce fever.

The forests of Cuba are of vast extent, and so dense as to be almost impenetrable. Mahogany and other hard woods are indigenous, and several sorts are well adapted for ship-building. The palm is the queen of the Cuban forests, and the most valuable tree on the island. The most common species, the *Palma real*, the cocoa tree, and the African palm, are found in all parts. The fruits of Cuba are those common to the tropics, of which the pine-apple and orange are the most esteemed. Of the alimentary plants, the *platano* or plantain is by far the most important. Next in order come the sweet and bitter *yuca* or *cassava;* the sweet root being eaten as a vegetable, and the bitter converted into bread after its poisonous juice has been extracted. The sweet potato and other farinaceous roots are also common. Indian corn is indigenous, and rice is extensively cultivated.

The mineral riches of the island have not yet been explored to any considerable extent. Though gold and silver have undoubtedly been found in the island, the quantity has never been sufficient to repay the labor of search. Gold was sent to Spain from this island by the early settlers, but it was more probably the accumulated wealth of the aborigines in previous centuries, wrested from them by tyranny and rapine at the period of the conquest, than the product of honest labor on the part of the colonists. Traces of auriferous sand are found in some of the rivers. Specimens of the finest gold have been obtained in recent times from the workings of Agabama and Sagua la Grande, but at an expense of time and labor that could not remunerate the parties engaged in it. In 1827, silver and copper were discovered in the jurisdiction of Villa Clara, and the first ores gave no less than seven ounces of pure silver to the quintal (= 107$\frac{3}{4}$ lbs.) of ore; but they have become less productive, probably from not being properly worked. The copper mines near Santiago, in the eastern part of the island, are of great extent, and very rich, employing nearly 900 persons, and yielding an ordinary average of about twenty-seven per cent. of pure metal. They were wrought with some success during the seventeenth century, but had been abandoned for more than 100 years. About the year 1830 Mr. Hardy, a landed proprietor in the island, happened, when on a visit to that part, to carry off some of the refuse of the old workings in order to subject them to analysis, the result of which was, that the metal was found so rich as amply to repay the expense of sending it to England for smelting. Several other mining companies have since been established; and the amount of copper ore exported in 1850 was about 25,000 tons Of the 35,683 tons of copper ore imported in 1851 into the United Kingdom, 20,825 tons came from Cuba. A highly bituminous substance affording a strong heat, and leaving very little solid residue in the form of ashes or cinders, is very abundant. In some places it degenerates into a form resembling asphaltum, and near the coast it is often found in a semi-fluid state like petroleum or naphtha. In the quarries near Havana, a thick slate is found, fit for floors and pavements. Marbles and jaspers of various colors, and susceptible of a high polish, are found in many parts of the island, and particularly in the Isle of Pines. It is generally believed that iron exists in various parts of Cuba, and many parts of the great Cordillera undoubtedly contain rocks of a ferruginous nature; but from the difficulty of access, the scarcity of fuel, and the want of capital, no extensive mining operations have been engaged in. Native loadstone, however, has been found in various parts, and chalybeate springs are numerous.

The chief agricultural products of Cuba are sugar, coffee and tobacco. The cultivation of these has advanced with great rapidity since 1809, when the ports of the island were more freely opened to foreigners

From 1853 to 1868, we may mention, the yearly exports of sugars were from 700,000,000 to 750,000,000 pounds. The cultivation of coffee advanced for a time with equal or even greater rapidity than that of sugar; but, in later years, from the low prices of coffee, the cultivation of sugar has become the more profitable, and in a great measure supplanted coffee. In 1840, the exportation of coffee was 54,516,988 pounds; and in 1851, only 11,907,904 pounds. Tobacco is indigenous to Cuba, and its excellent quality is celebrated in all parts of the world. Of late, 8,500,000 pounds of leaf tobacco, and 28,045,150 pounds of manufactured are annually exported. Among the other productions are Indian corn, rice, beans, plantains, cotton, cocoa, pine-apples, lemons, oranges, limes, figs, melons, etc. Of the manufactures, the principal are the making of sugar, molasses, rum, and cigars, and the preparation of coffee and wax. The foreign commerce of Cuba is very large and extensive. From 1840 to 1850, the yearly exports were valued at $25,000,000, since 1850, down to 1870, the valuation of the exports has ranged from $27,000,000 to $32,000,000, while that of the imports has averaged about the same. The discriminating and tonnage duties in favor of Spanish and Cuban vessels average about two-thirds. Despite all restrictions, one-third of the whole commerce is with the United States.

Education is in a very backward state in Cuba, although it has made decided progress since 1842. No grants in aid of public instruction are given out of the public treasury, and those who are unable to pay for education are left dependent upon private efforts. It was announced in the *Diario de la Marina* of January, 1852, that the government was about to establish nineteen primary free schools in Havana, Matanzas, and Puerto Prince, and two normal schools in Havana, but we are not aware what success they have as yet met with. The royal university of Havana has medical and law schools. A six years' study of medicine and a classical education are necessary for graduation in these sciences. There are a number of collegiate institutions and advanced schools in Havana and other cities.

The Roman Catholic is the only religion tolerated by government. An effort was made some years ago by England to obtain permission to erect a Protestant church at Havana, but without success. None can hold property or engage in any business in Cuba, without first acknowledging in writing that he is an apostolical Roman Catholic; but those who have tender consciences leave out the word "Roman," and the omission is winked at. Religion and morality, indeed, like education, are here at a very low ebb. Nowhere, probably, is presented a more dark and distressing picture of unbelief, corruption, and immorality. In 1788, Cuba was divided into two dioceses, each embracing half the island. The eastern diocese, or that of Santiago de Cuba, was, in 1804, erected into an archbishopric, while that of Havana still remains under a bishop. The revenues of the church are derived from tithes on the products of the island, the fees of christenings, marriages, deaths, etc. The total revenue of the priests and ecclesiastical authorities, is estimated at about $700,000.

The island is divided into several distinct jurisdictions, as the civil, judicial, military, ecclesiastical, etc. The military is divided into two departments, a western and an eastern, each embracing half the island. There was a third department, the central; but that was suppressed in 1851. Each department is under a commander-general, and is divided into sections, each under a commander-of-arms; the sections are subdivided into *partidos* and *cuartones*, each of the former being under a petty judge with the title of captain, and each of the latter under a leader of patrol. Politically, Cuba is divided into two provinces,—the western, or that of Havana,—and the eastern, or that of Santiago. The judicial division contains two jurisdictions—the royal pretorian audience of Havana, and the royal audience of Puerto

Prince. The maritime division comprises five provinces, which are subdivided into districts, each of the former having a commander, and each of the latter an adjutant. The captain-general is invested with almost unlimited powers, and is responsible only to the sovereign of Spain: he is the supreme head of the civil, military, and ecclesiastical jurisdictions of the island; his decisions are final, and his word is law. At Matanzas, Trinidad, Puerto Prince, and Cienfuegos, there are officers with the title of governor, whose duties, however, are of a judicial nature, extending to disputed points of every sort, civil, criminal, or military; and subordinate to them are eight lieutenancies, called *capitanais à guerra*. In all the cities and towns are municipal bodies, styled *ayuntamientos perpetuos*, exercising judicial functions. There are also in the rural districts *jueces pedaneos*, a sort of itinerant village judges or justices of the peace appointed by the local governors. All judges and other judicial functionaries are paid by fees instead of salaries; and the petty officers of the government, dependent on their fees, prey like so many wolves upon the unprotected within their jurisdiction. According to the new Spanish constitution, Cuba has the right of representation in the Spanish Cortes; but up to 1870 no representatives have been elected.

The crown revenues of the island are the *rentas maritimas*, including duties on imports, exports, and tonnage, and the local or municipal dues levied at some of the custom-houses; the *impuestas interiores*, including the tax on home manufactures, sale of papal bulls and stamped paper, the profits derived from the lottery, and the impost on cock-fights; deductions from the *rentas ecclesiasticas*, particularly those called the royal ninths and the consolidated fund, the sinking fund, the *media annata*, and the annual and monthly revenues of the clergy; personal deductions, such as from the pay of public functionaries, and the price of exemption from military service; miscellaneous receipts, as the produce of the sale of royal lands, the rents of vacant livings and unclaimed estates, the produce of vendible offices; the casual receipts, including deposits, confiscations, donations, and the recovery of arrears. The total revenue received from these sources in 1849 was $11,000,000; in 1850, $12,500,000; and in 1857, $17,368,000.

The circulating medium of Cuba is composed chiefly of the precious metals; paper money was first issued in 1857 by the Spanish Bank. The coins in use are the Spanish doblon, which is a legal tender for 17 hard dollars, and the subdivisions of the doblon, the half, the quarter, the eighth, and the sixteenth—the last being equivalent to a dollar and half a real. The Mexican, Colombian, and other South American doblons are a legal tender for 16 hard dollars, and are sometimes in demand for exportation at a premium: their divisions are worth eight, four, two, and one dollar respectively. Of silver coins, the Spanish dollar and its divisions, and also Mexican, United States, and South American dollars, are legal tenders at their nominal value.

The roads of Cuba are generally in a wretched condition. Several railways have been established: the oldest, opened in 1838, extended from Havana to Guines, a distance of 45 miles, and with branches to Ratabano, San Antonio, and Los Palos, has become the principal trunk line in the island. A railway from Regla to the mines of Prosperidad has been abandoned. There are lines in operation from Matanzas to Sabanilla, Cardenas to Bamba, Jucaro to beyond Altamisal, and Puerto Prince to Nuevitas. The coast communication is kept up by steamers which ply regularly between the different ports. The number of coasting vessels that entered the port of Havana in 1851 was 3,523. In 1852, the electric telegraph was introduced, and its lines now extend between the principal cities and towns.

It is impossible, from the conflicting accounts of the different writers upon the subject, to arrive at anything like certainty as to the number of inhabitants on the island at the time of its conquest; but it may be estimated at probably from 300,000 to 400,000. There is little doubt, however, that before 1560 the whole of this population had disappeared from the island. The first census of Cuba was taken in 1775, when the population was 170,862. In 1791 it was 272,140; in 1841, 1,007,624; in 1857, 1,107,491; in 1870, 1,515,100. This latter number was made up of 884,754 whites, 250,310 free colored, 380,036 slaves. The population of Cuba is steadily and even rapidly on the increase, and her future is a subject of deep interest to many a looker-on.

The inhabitants of Cuba are divided into four classes—the native Spaniards, who occupy nearly all the offices of power and trust; the Creoles, who are mostly planters, farmers, or lawyers, and are generally looked upon with contempt and aversion by the Spaniards, whom the Creoles hate with equal heartiness; the third class, composed of free mulattoes and free negroes in about equal parts, who are excluded by law from all civil offices; the slaves, constituting the fourth class, are divided into *bozales*, those recently brought from Africa—the *ladinos*, those imported before the law of 1821 prohibiting the slave trade—and the *criollos*, those born on the island. Cuba has long been notorious for the extent to which the slave trade has been carried on there, and the ineffectual attempts made to suppress it. The English government succeeded, in 1853, in inducing the Spanish government to pledge itself to adopt measures for its suppression; but despite all treaty pledges on the part of Spain, there are every year brought into Cuba 10,000 to 20,000 negroes from Africa.

Under a better and more liberal system of government, there can be no doubt that Cuba would speedily attain a much higher state of prosperity and importance than it has yet enjoyed. Great as is its productiveness at present, it is almost certain that under a good government it would be increased five-fold; its mineral resources would then be fully developed, and it would be able fully to take advantage of its admirable position to develop its trade. The continuance of the present oppressive line of policy in reference to Cuba must undoubtedly ere long lead to a revolution which Spain of itself will be unable to quell. Not to mention the heavy taxes with which the natives are burdened, the old exclusive system is here still in full force; officers of trust and emolument are almost without exception bestowed upon persons from Spain; the governor-general is the sole medium of communication between the colonists and the crown; his power is absolute, and from his decrees there is no appeal; and indeed the island has been under martial law since 1825. The governor-generalship is notoriously sought after and bestowed as a means of acquiring or repairing a fortune, and a five years' tenure of office is considered sufficient to realize a fortune of two or three millions of dollars. From its position, it is evident that the United States have and must have a deep interest in the prospects and future condition of Cuba. Our country can never allow it to pass into the hands of any European nation. So long as Spain can maintain her hold on Cuba, the United States will not directly interfere; but if any of the revolutions in the island turn out to be a success, or if Spain be willing to sell Cuba to the United States, then, no doubt, it would speedily be admitted into the Union. In 1848, while J. K. Polk was president, the American minister at Madrid was authorized to offer to purchase Cuba at the price of $100,000,000; but the proposal was declined very curtly by the Spanish government. The "filibustering" expeditions of Lopez, in 1850–1, we have already spoken of (p. 217–18); but there was much sympathy, especially in the South, for him and his schemes. Our government, though carrying out fully its duty in respect to the neutrality laws, did not feel called upon to go any further; and when the governments of France and England, in 1852, made a shrewd movement known as the Tripartite Convention (p. 220), by which the United States was to bind the nation, in conjunction with England and France, to guarantee Cuba to Spain in perpetuity, the president, representing popular sentiment, declined any such arrangement whatever. In August, 1854, Messrs. Buchanan, Mason, and Soulé, our ministers at London, Paris and Madrid, held a conference at Ostend, and drew up a manifesto on the subject of Cuba, arguing that the island ought to belong to the United States, that Spain had better sell it than try to keep it, that in certain contingencies (such as emancipating the slaves by Spain) we ought to seize on the island by force, etc. This sentiment in regard to Cuba, and its "manifest destiny" in connection with the United States, prevailed to a large extent, especially in the southern slave-holding States, which, feeling strongly and bitterly that the control of the government was passing out of their hands, were exceedingly anxious to add to the slave territory of the country by buying or even stealing Cuba from Spain.

But it is not simply from without that danger to Spanish rule or misrule is likely to come. For many years the Cubans have been hoping to be strong enough to throw off the yoke of Spain; and they have made various efforts at times, but never as yet with success. The Spanish forces, as a rule, have been unsparing in dealing with the Cubans, and the hatred of the inhabitants towards Spain and all belonging to her is so intense, as to lead them to wage war and fight with savage fury and vindictiveness. In October, 1866, an insurrection broke out in Cuba, and a declaration of independence was issued at Manzanillo, October 10th, giving the reasons and objects of the movement. In the eastern and central departments the movement spread rapidly, and Cespedes and the Provisional Government sought for recognition from the United States, which, however, was not granted. Numerous engagements took place between the Cuban and Spanish troops; but as the former were badly armed, and the latter soon after received reinforcements from abroad, the insurgents were unable to accomplish their purposes. During 1869 the struggle continued with unabated zeal and perseverance on the part of the Cubans; continual engagements and fights of more or less magnitude occurred; the Cubans, badly and insufficiently armed, fought to great disadvantage. Considerable help reached them from parties in the United States who sent men and military stores to the insurgents; Cespedes was elected president, and the Provisional Government strained every nerve to preserve its existence and secure independence; while, on the other hand, the new Captain-General, Rodas, by his proclamations and his acts, manifested the savage and determined spirit in which the war was to be carried on. At the close of October, 1869, a decree of the Cortes was promulgated in Cuba, whereby liberty in religion is henceforth unrestricted, and no person shall hereafter be prevented from holding office under the government by reason of his religious belief. In November, the burning of sugar plantations became quite general, and hundreds of the Cubans sacrificed them in this way to prevent the Spaniards gaining possession of these sources of wealth. During the same month the Cuban Junta was formed in New York, a body of patriots who have been and are steadily working to secure the end in view, *i. e.* Free Cuba. Our government, however, maintains the attitude above noted, and General Grant holds the view that the "political organization of the insurgents is not sufficient to justify a recognition of belligerency." Up to the present hour of writing (end of 1870), the state of affairs has not been much different from that of the previous year; and the Junta here and the Cubans at home, though hoping almost against hope, have but to work on, till the day of liberty and independence shall dawn upon the beautiful island.

HAYTI.

The Island of Hayti, or San Domingo, is second only to Cuba, among the West India Islands, both in size, beauty and wealth. It lies between Lat. 17° 36′ and 19° 59′ N. and Long. 68° 20′ and 74° 28′ W. Its length from east to west is about 400 miles; greatest width N. and S. from Cape Beata to Cape Isabella, 163 miles; area, including a few small islands, about 32,000 square miles. San Domingo is separated from Cuba and Jamaica on the W. by the Windward passage about fifty miles wide; and on the E. from the island of Porto Rico by the Mona passage, 76 miles wide. Bays and inlets indent the island in every direction, and there are numerous excellent harbors, of which that of Samana on the N.E. is especially to be noted. Three mountain chains intersect the island W. and E., on one of which Mount Cibao reaches to the height of 7200 feet. Where mountains and hills exist, there also, as in San Domingo, are numerous valleys and plains, and broad and rich pasture lands. The rivers are few in number, and of little or no value for navigation; lakes are numerous; mineral springs abound; the climate is hot and moist, but generally salubrious, and in the higher localities, perpetual spring-like beauty and attractiveness prevail. Earthquakes occasionally occur, and have at times (1751 and 1842) done great harm to life and property. Vegetation for the most part is tropical in its character. On the north side of the island are extensive forests of pine, which is much used for the purposes of ship-building; and Brazil-wood is found on many parts of the coast. The satin-wood of this island is heavier than that of the East Indies, and it takes so fine a polish that it does not require to be varnished. The cotton tree is the largest of all the vegetable productions, and is formed into the lightest and most capacious canoes. Every variety of the palm tree is found in the woods, of which they form a principal ornament. The palmetto or mountain cabbage is an erect and noble tree, which grows to the heigth of seventy feet, with esculent leaves at the top. In the congenial soil of this fertile island the sugar-cane, cotton, and coffee plants, grow in the greatest luxuriance. There is also the calabash, the fruit of which serves as a substitute for earthenware; the plantain, the staff of life in the West Indies; vanilla, which is found indigenous in the unfrequented woods; quassia or simarouba, which is a tall and stately plant, waving gracefully in the wind; sarsaparilla, indigo, tobacco, turmeric, ginger, and rice plants. The fruits and nutritive roots of San Domingo are nearly the same as those of Jamaica; but they are more abundant, and extremely fine. Of these may be enumerated the choux caraib, or Indian kale, with a variety of other vegetables that come under the same denomination; the avocato or vegetable marrow, the melon, sapadillo, guava, pine-apple, bread and jack fruit, mango, nuts, rose-apple, plums, etc., of many different species. Flowers in endless variety and splendor adorn the wild scenery of the woods, and exhale their fragrance in the desert air.

Little is known of the geological structure of this island, but a limestone containing vestiges of marine shells is the prevailing formation. Mineral springs exist in several parts. The most noted in the eastern part of the island are those of Banica, Yaya, and Pargatal; and in the west the chalybeate of St. Rose, the saline of Jean Rabel, and the alkaline sulphur waters of Dalmarie. The mineral products are various and rich, and include gold, platina, silver, quicksilver, copper, iron, tin, sulphur, manganese, antimony rock-salt, bitumen, jasper, marble, opal, lazulite, chalcedony, etc. The gold mines of the Cibao Mountains, which, in the sixteenth century, were very productive, have been abandoned, and at the present day gold is obtained only from the washings in the northern rivers. None of the mines, indeed, are successfully worked, and hence these sources of wealth are reserved for the industry of future laborers. The indigenous quadrupeds of the island were confined to four species, which the Indians called Hutia, Quemi, Mohuy, and Cory. Of these, all are believed to be extinct except the first. Horned cattle, hogs, sheep, goats, horses, mules, and asses, have been introduced from Europe, and have multiplied prodigiously in the wild and extensive pastures of the interior. Wild fowl are abundant, consisting of various species of ducks, pigeons, flamingo, the wild peacock, the mimic thrush or mocking bird, the banana bird, the Guinea fowl, the ortolan, and parrots of various species. The rivers abound with fish, some of which are very delicate. Turtle of all kinds are taken, and the land-crab is much esteemed. The serpents are not dreaded; but the centipedes, which are frequent in old buildings, are large and dangerous. The scorpion is rarely seen; but the venomous crab-spider, which is equally dangerous, is sometimes met with.

This island was discovered by Columbus in 1492, and was soon filled with adventurers, who crowded from Europe to the new world in search of sudden wealth. The natives were reduced to slavery by these settlers, who spread themselves over the island, and by their industry the colony increased rapidly in wealth and prosperity. But as it was chiefly by the desire of gold that settlers were attracted to this distant shore, San Domingo was in its turn abandoned for other regions of greater reputed wealth; and the country gradualy declined, and, instead of yielding a revenue, became a burden to Spain. About the middle of the sixteenth century the island of St. Christopher was taken possession of by a mixed colony of French and English, who being attacked by the Spaniards, were forced to fly to the barren isle of Tortuga, where they established themselves, and grew formidable, under the well-known appellation of buccaneers. They at last obtained a firm footing in San Domingo, into which they had made only predatory incursions; and by the treaty of Ryswick that part of the Island of which they had obtained possession was ceded to the King of France, who acknowledged these adventurous colonists as his subjects. The French colony languished for a while under the galling restrictions imposed on its trade, but these being removed about the year 1722, it soon attained a high degree of prosperity, and was in a very flourishing state when the French revolution commenced in 1789. The population was composed of three classes,—whites, people of color, and blacks. Of these the whites were the favored class, who engrossed all public honors and emoluments. They considered the people of color as a degraded caste, with whom it was disgraceful to associate on terms of equality. The black slaves ranked lowest in the scale, and they experienced from both classes all the evils of the most cruel bondage. A society framed of such hostile elements contained in its very constitution the seeds of hatred and contention; and in the course of the revolution which occurred in France, these were brought into full activity. The important discussions by which France was at that time agitated kindled a corresponding sensation in the colonies; and the hostile races of the whites and mulattoes were already violently inflamed against each other by the eagerness of their contests, when the National Convention, in 1791, passed the memorable decree, giving to the people of color the unlimited enjoyment of all the rights which were possessed by French citizens; thus at once breaking down all the distinctions which had prevailed in the colony, and which were sanctioned by custom and inveterate prejudice This decree excited loud and general disapprobation amongst the whites, who immediate ly adopted the most violent measures. The national cockade, the badge of their attachment to the revolution and its leaders, was openly trampled under foot, and the authority of the governor-general and the supremacy of France were equally set at nought. The several parishes proceeded to the election of a new assembly, which accordingly met on the 9th of August, under the title of the General Assembly of the French part of San Domingo. The mulattoes in the mean time, alarmed at these proceedings, were collecting in armed bodies for their defence; and the whites were so intent on the meeting of the colonial assembly that they offered no opposition to these assemblages.

Such was the state of affairs between the two hostile classes of the whites and the mulattoes, when a new and more powerful party, whom all united to oppress, now suddenly combined for their own protection and for the destruction of their enemies. On the 23d of August, reports reached the town of the Cape that the negro slaves in the neighboring parishes were in arms, and that they were destroying the plantations and massacring the inhabitants. This terrible intelligence was confirmed next day in its full extent by crowds of wretched fugitives from the neighboring country, who, having abandoned their property, were flying to Cape Town from the fury of their savage enemies. The success of this bold and deep-laid conspiracy spread universal consternation amongst the white inhabitants. The citizens in Cape Town were immediately summoned to arms, and the women and children were at the same time sent on board the ships in the harbor. Other measures were also adopted to secure the place against any sudden attack of the infuriated slaves. When these precautions had been adopted, several small detachments of troops were sent out to act offensively against the insurgents; but although partial successes were obtained in these encounters, the general result too fatally demonstrated to the white inhabitants their own weakness and the strength of their enemies. In this destructive war it was calculated that, about two months after its commencement, upwards of 2000 white inhabitants were massacred; that 180 sugar plantations and about 900 coffee, indigo, and cotton settlements were destroyed, and a thousand families reduced from opulence to misery. Of the insurgents about 10,000 are supposed to have perished in the field, and some hundreds by the hands of the public executioner; and the rebellion, which been hitherto confined to the northern parts of the island, now began to spread through the western districts, where the blacks were aided by the people of color, and where, under their united devastations, the country was laid waste for an extent of more than thirty miles. At length they approached the town of Port-au-Prince with the intention of setting it on fire; and it was with great difficulty that a treaty was concluded by which the place was saved from destruction. This treaty was ratified by the colonial assembly, which also announced its intention of granting an extension of privileges to the free people of color. But, in the mean time, the national assembly in France, under an impression of the ruinous consequences of their rash concessions to the people of color, had voted a repeal of the law which gave them the same privileges as the whites; and the intelligence of this repeal reached the colonies at the time when the colonial assembly was holding out the expectation of general equality and freedom. The mulattoes, therefore, when they heard that the national assembly had repealed their former conciliating act in their favor, knew no bounds to their indignation. All thoughts of peace were now abandoned; and the war assumed a diabolical character of cruelty, each studying to outdo the other in acts of revenge.

The national assembly, alarmed by the intelligence of these disorders, sent out three civil commissioners, with full powers to settle all disputes. But their authority soon fell into disrepute. Other commissioners were sent, and along with them 8000 troops. Unlike their predecessors, however, they adopted the most arbitrary measures; and about the beginning of the year 1793, they became absolute masters of the colony. But their severity at last provoked resistance to their authority; and having displaced the governor Galbaud, an officer of artillery, and ordered him to France, he, along with his brother, collected about 1,200 seamen, with whom they landed, and being joined by other volunteers, attacked the government house, where the commissioners were posted with their force. A fierce and bloody conflict now took place, which terminated without any decisive advantage on either side, and next day the fighting was continued in the streets of the town with various success. In the beginning of these disorders, the commissioners had sought to strengthen their party by the aid of the revolted blacks; and a body of these auxiliaries, amounting to 3000, now entered the place, which immediately became a horrid and revolting scene of conflagration and slaughter. Men, women and children were massacred by these barbarians without distinction. The white inhabitants flying to the sea for protection, were met by a body of armed mulattoes, by whom they were put to the sword without mercy; the half of the town was consumed by the flames; and the commissioners, themselves affrighted at these disorders, escaped to the sea-shore, whence, under cover of a ship of the line, they viewed with dismay the wide-spreading mischief. Ever since the commencement of these unhappy disorders, the white inhabitants had emigrated in great numbers to the neighboring islands, and to the United States; and some of the principal inhabitants having repaired to Britain, induced the British government, by their representations, to prepare an armament with a body of troops to co-operate with such of the inhabitants as were desirous of placing themselves under its protection. At this period the military force of San Domingo consisted of from 14,000 to 15,000 effective troops, and 25,000 free negroes, mulattoes, and slaves. About 100,000 blacks had retired to the mountains to enjoy a savage independence, and in the northern districts, 40,000 slaves still continued in arms. It was in these circumstances that the island was taken possession of, in September, 1793, by a British force. But though the expedition gained some partial advantages, the climate soon began to make the most dreadful havoc among the troops, and prevented them from achieving any solid success. Toussaint l'Ouverture, who was appointed general-in-chief of the black armies of San Domingo in 1797, proved himself an able and indefatigable enemy; and at length the British were obliged to evacuate the country in the year 1798. On the 1st of July, 1801, the independence of San Domingo was formally proclaimed.

But the war in Europe between Great Britain and France being by this time concluded by the peace of Amiens, Bonaparte sent out an armament, consisting of twenty-six ships of the line, and 25,000 troops, under the command of General Leclerc, his brother-in-law, for the purpose of reducing the revolted colony of San Domingo. To enter into details of the barbarous and bloody war now begun against the unfortunate inhabitants of San Domingo would be of little value. It will be sufficient to observe that the numbers and discipline of the force now landed, joined to the skill of its leaders, overpowered all open resistance in the field, so that the blacks after several obstinate conflicts, and after burning some of the principal towns, were finally compelled to retire into the inaccessible mountains of the interior, whence they carried on, under their undaunted leader, Toussaint, a desultory war against detached parties of their enemies. Elated by his success, Leclerc now threw off the mask, and rashly issued an edict proclaiming the former slavery of the blacks. Toussaint was not slow to profit by this error. Having effected a junction with Christophe, who had still 300 troops under him, and being joined by the cultivators in great numbers, who were no longer deaf to his call, he poured with this collected host like a torrent over the plain; and having everywhere forced the French posts, and driven before him their detached corps, he surrounded the town, to relieve which the French general was compelled to hasten to the spot by forced marches with all the troops he could collect. Here he had recourse to his former arts, and he was but too successful in cajoling the negro chiefs, wearied of war, into a suspension of arms. Having watched his opportunity, he privately seized Toussaint with his family and embarked him on board of a frigate for France, where, being thrown into prison, he expired in April, 1803. This act of cruel treachery spread universal alarm among the black chiefs; and Dessalines, Christophe, and Clerveaux soon appeared at the head of considerable bodies of black troops. This last contest for the possession of San Domingo was distinguished by a degree of barbarity which surpasses belief. The whites and the blacks seemed to vie with each other in deeds of cruelty and revenge. Retaliation was the plea still used to sanction every enormity, and nothing short of the extermination of one or the other party was thought of. The French, however, it was clear, were now gradually losing ground. About the year, 1803, they were confined within their fortifications by the vigorous movements of the black armies; and though reinforcements were received from France, the French general was forced to enter into a capitulation with Dessalines, by which he agreed, in 1803, to evacuate the whole island. On the 30th of November of that year, the standard of the blacks was hoisted in Cape François; and the French troops, amounting to 8000, surrendered themselves prisoners of war to the British squadron, by which they were closely watched. In 1804, a formal declaration of independence was issued, to which were attached all the names of the generals and chiefs. The ancient aboriginal name of Hayti was revived; while Dessalines, whose military talents were in great esteem, was elected governor-general for life; and in October, 1804, he was crowned emperor with great pomp. In this situation he began to display all the cruelties of a tyrant, massacring without mercy the white inhabitants, and committing the most barbarous depredations. A conspiracy was in consequence formed against him; and as he was advancing against the insurgents at the head of a few troops, he fell into an ambuscade where he was expecting his own advanced guard, and fell pierced with balls. His power was disputed by various chiefs, of whom those best known and most successful were Petion and Christophe, the former ruling over the north of the island, the latter over the southern districts. Each having a powerful body of adherents, a civil war was the immediate consequence of their rival claims. In this war, which continued for several years, many battles were fought and many lives were lost; but the issue of the struggle was still doubtful, when in the year 1810, a suspension of hostilities took place, though no formal treaty was signed. From this period civil war ceased in the island of San Domingo. Christophe was declared king of Hayti under the title of Henry I.; and, in imitation of other monarchs, he created various orders of nobility, together with numerous officers of state. He assumed to himself absolute power, and committed the greatest cruelties, according to the mere caprice of his own arbitrary will. His tyranny produced general discontent, and at last an insurrection against him. Being deserted by his troops, he anticipated his fate by committing suicide on the 20th of October, 1820. Petion died in March, 1818, greatly lamented, after having presided over the republic upwards of eleven years. He was succeeded by General Boyer, who ruled over the northern division of the island until the year 1820; when taking advantage of the death of Christophe, and the confusion occasioned by that event, he pressed forward with a considerable force, and took possession of every strong place in the island; and in this manner the whole French division of San Domingo was united under one ruler.

The Spanish division of the island had been ceded to France, in 1795, by the treaty of Basle, but it was restored to Spain by the peace of 1814. Spain, however, was no longer able to control the revolutionary spirit which prevailed in the colony; and in November, 1821, the Spanish governor was arrested by the insurgent party, headed by a lawyer of the name of Nunez, and a declaration of independence immediately issued. A strong party afterwards appeared in favor of a union of the whole island under one chief. On the 21st of January, 1822, the Haytian flag was first displayed in the city of San Domingo; and on the 9th, the keys of the city, and with them the dominion of the whole island, were surrendered to President Boyer. The independence of the new State was recognized by France in 1825, on condition that its ports should be open to the ships of all nations; that French vessels should pay only half duties; and that $30,000,000 should be paid as an indemnity, in five equal payments, the first on the 31st of December, 1825. Thus, after a series of struggles, beyond all example bloody and ferocious, the whole island of Hispaniola, with its adjacent islets, became subject to one government, under the title of the Republic of Hayti.

Boyer continued to reign over the entire island till 1843, when he was overthrown and driven from the island by a revolution headed by Riviere, who succeeded him as president. After about four months, the Spanish part of the island revolted, and Riviere marched with an army to reduce it to submission; but while on this expedition the other parts of the island revolted against him, and he was compelled to escape to Jamaica. A succession of presidents of short duration followed; and on March 1, 1846, Soulouque was elected president. Previous to his election, Soulouque was unknown to fame. Born a slave, he subsequently obtained his liberty, and became boots' cleaner to one of the illustrious black generals. He gradually rose by energy and undaunted courage, soon obtained the rank of captain, and subsequently that of general. His ambition was thoroughly aroused by his rapid promotion, and he secretly resolved to emulate the achievements of Napoleon I., whose career he studied as a model, brooding over his plans for three years. In 1849 he carried them into execution by stratagem. In April, an alleged plot to assassinate the president was made the pretext for arresting all those persons he deemed likely to oppose his views. Of these he beheaded a great number, and many fled. In Port-au-Prince, his capital, a petition was got up on the 20th of August, requesting him to accept the imperial crown. Soulouque listened graciously to this and other petitions, and received the enthusiastic salutations of the people for the Emperor Faustin I. A nobility of the first order was created, and in 1851, the sable monarch was duly and solemnly crowned. The constitution was altered and adapted to the changed condition of affairs. But Soulouque soon proved himself a tyrant and a sort of public robber, and a revolt, ere long, ensued. In January, 1859, Geffrard, one of the generals of the emperor, raised the standard of insurrection, and was supported by the whole population. Soulouque barely escaped with his life, and fled the country. The republic was again proclaimed and Geffrard became president. In May, 1865, Salnave headed an insurrection in the northern part of the republic; and for the following two or three years civil war raged with its usual fury. Geffrard was compelled to abdicate and leave the country early in 1867, and Salnave, in June, became president. A new insurrection broke out soon after, and as revolution is a chronic disorder in that region, Salnave and his various opponents and rivals kept up the contests and fightings month after month, almost to the present time. Salnave was captured at the close of 1869, and shot, and a provisional government formed, early in 1870, with Saget at the head.

The revenue of Hayti arises chiefly from customs and port-dues, territorial imposts, sale of lands, etc. In 1850, the customs' receipts amounted to $850,000; and in the same year the expenditure amounted to $1,800,000. At the present time the revenue is estimated at about $4,000,000, and the expenditures at about $3,500,000. The public debt amounts to some nine or ten millions of dollars. The established religion is Roman Catholic; but other forms of worship are not prohibited. Church affairs are superintended by a vicar-general. Education is at a low ebb; but there is room to hope that when the republic becomes settled on a firm and a stable basis, the people may have the advantages and privileges of mental and moral culture. The foreign commerce of Hayti is in the hands of foreign merchants, who are permitted to reside only at certain ports, under irksome and injurious restrictions. The foreign commerce does not probably exceed $15,000,000 of annual value. The exports are chiefly mahogany and other timber, dyewoods, coffee, tobacco and cotton. The imports are mainly from the United States; also from Great Britain and France; value, about $10,000,000. The population of the republic is estimated at 572,000; area, 10,000 square miles. The population of Port-au-Prince, the capital, is 21,000.

On the fall of Boyer, the Spaniards asserted their independence, and on the 27th of February, 1844, proclaimed the Dominican Republic. Herard Riviere, who succeeded Boyer, marched with an army of 20,000 men upon San Domingo, but was defeated at Azua by General Pedro Santana, who compelled the Haytians to retreat within their own territory. The provincial junta of the new republic now formed a constitution, and elected Santana president. He was followed by General Jimenes in 1848. Soulouque, then president of Hayti, attempted in 1849 to reconquer the territory with an army of 5000 men, but was signally defeated at Las Carreras, on the River Ocoa, 21st April, 1849, by Santana, who had only 400 men under his command. For this victory Santana received the title of "Libertador de la Patria." General Jimenes, the president, not being fitted for his task, and the invading army having been driven out of the country, Santana was called upon to restore order within the republic, and to force the president to resign. This effected, Santana directed the affairs of state until a new election had taken place, by which, upon his recommendation, Buenaventura Baez was named president. During his administration treaties of recognition and commerce with Great Britain, France, and Denmark were concluded. On the 3rd of July, 1853, Baez was banished, and Santana himself raised to the presidency. In 1857, Baez, by the aid of the clerical party, was again elected president, but in the following year, a revolutionary movement under Santana compelled him to retire. Early in 1865, Spain gave up all claim on San Domingo, and withdrew the troops from the island. Cabral was prominent in the provisional government; but in December, Baez was elected president. Another revolution broke out under Pimental, and Baez fled in June, 1866, to St. Thomas. Cabral was elected president. A treaty was formed with the United States, in February, 1867, and the Bay of Samana was offered on lease to our government for $5,000,000. In the latter part of the year another insurrection broke out in favor of Baez, who drove Cabral out of the capital, and became president. Since then there has been a contest going on between Cabral, Luperon and others, against Baez; but Baez seems to hold his own for the present. The sending a commission to San Domingo, in 1871, in reference to annexation, may lead to important results.

The Dominican Republic claims for its territory the whole of the Spanish portion of the Island. It is divided into five provinces, and has an area of about 22,000 square miles. The Dominicans are almost entirely an agricultural people. The staples of the south provinces consists chiefly of the products of the forests. In Seybo, however, the raising of cattle is the chief occupation. But by far the most industrious part is the north, generally called the Cibao, where the staple article is an excellent quality of tobacco. The articles of export are mahogany, satin-wood, fustic, lignum-vitæ and brazil-wood; tobacco, hides, etc. The imports are chiefly flour and provisions from the United States, and general merchandise from Europe.

The constitution of the republic is based on that of Venezuela. The Congress, which assembles annually, consists of fifteen deputies, three from each province, who form the Tribunado or Lower Chamber, and five senators, one from each province, constituting the Consejo Conservador or Upper Chamber. The executive power is vested in a president, who is elected for four years, and who must be a Dominican by birth, and at least thirty-five years of age. The judiciary is exercised by a supreme court and various inferior and local courts, and the French code has been adopted in legal proceedings. The value of imports is estimated at $550,000; value of exports, $800,000. No foreign debt is owing; but there exists a large home debt, on which the currency is based, and which is of low and fluctuating value. The army amounts to 16,000 men, and may be raised to 20,000. The navy consists of three corvettes and five schooners equipped as war vessels, and mounted with forty-four guns. The prevailing religion is Roman Catholic, but other denominations are tolerated. Population estimated to be about 200,000.

The chief seats of commerce are San Domingo city and Samana, a small town on a peninsula of the same name. The city of San Domingo is situated at the mouth of the Ozama, on the southern coast, in N. Lat. 18½°, and W. Lon. 70°, and is the oldest European settlement in the New World, having been built by Columbus in 1504. The population is about 14,000, and the town is defended by substantial fortifications. The cathedral is more than three centuries old. The harbor is capacious, but owing to a bar at its mouth, vessels drawing above thirteen feet of water are obliged to anchor in the open roadstead.

JAMAICA.

The Island of Jamaica lies off the Bay of Honduras, between the Caribbean Sea and Gulf of Mexico, within N. Lat. 17° 40′ and 18° 30′, and W. Long. 76° 10′ and 78° 30′, about 4,000 miles S.W. of England, 80 miles S. of Cuba, 90 miles W. of St. Domingo, and 515 miles N. of Chagres, the Atlantic port of the Isthmus of Panama. It is the most southern of that group, called the Greater Antilles, or Leeward Islands. It is the largest, and was formerly the most valuable of the British West Indies, being 160 miles in length by 50 in extreme breadth, and containing about 6,400 square miles. Within its government are comprised, besides the three small islands called the Caymanas, Balize, or British Honduras, on the mainland of Central America, with Ruatan and other islands in the Bay of Honduras. These places, though distant respectively 600 and 460 miles, have been called the dependencies of Jamaica, and are ruled by superintendents appointed by the governor.

Jamaica was discovered by Columbus on the 3d of May, 1494, while coasting along the south of Cuba during his second voyage. He called it St. Jago, after the patron saint of Spain, but it is now generally known by its Indian name, Jamaica, a word signifying the Isle of Springs. On approaching the shore, Columbus called the nearest land after his first ship, Santa Maria, a name still preserved in Port Maria. He effected a landing a little to the westward, at Ora Cabessa, where, after a slight opposition from the natives, he took possession of the country, with the usual formalities, for the King of Spain. The inhabitants were the same mild, inoffensive race as those of Cuba and Hayti. Like the Arowaks of Trinidad and Guiana, they were probably offshoots of the great Mexican stock, and very different from the fierce Caribs of the Windward Islands. After a short stay, Columbus quitted Jamaica, which remained undisturbed for nine years. In June, 1503, on his fourth and last voyage, he was driven by a tempest, in which he lost two ships, to a bay on the north side of the island, which he named Sta. Gloria (now St. Ann's Bay), where he ran his remaining vessels ashore in a small inlet still called Don Christopher's Cove.

Jamaica seems to have remained unvisited until 1509, three years after his death, when his son Diego, having established his right in the council of the Indies to the governorship of Hispaniola, which included Jamaica, sent Don Juan d'Esquirel to take possession of the island. By Esquirel the natives were treated, according to Herera, with unusual humanity. That his successors did not imitate him in this respect is proved by the astounding fact that of the Indian population, at this time estimated at from 60,000 to 100,000, not a descendant of either sex existed in 1655, when the island fell into the hands of the English, nor, it is supposed, for nearly a century before. About the year 1523, Diego Columbus, visiting Jamaica from Hispaniola, founded on the River Cobre, inland to the south of the mountain range, St. Jago de la Vega, St. James of the Plain, which gave the title of Marquis to his descendants, and is still the official capital, under the name of Spanish Town. The union of the crowns of Spain and Portugal, under Philip II., in 1580, occasioned an influx of Portuguese colonists into Jamaica, who contributed much to its strength and prosperity, but were usually on indifferent terms with the Spanish settlers. Attention had been paid at an early period to agriculture, the cotton-plant was extensively cultivated, and the sugar-cane, vine, and various kinds of corn and grass had been introduced; and whereas a small species of dog, called the alco, was the only domestic quadruped known to the aborigines, horses, horned cattle, and swine had been imported from Hispaniola, which multiplied amazingly, and a flourishing trade sprang up in lard and hides, as well as tobacco, sugar, and ginger. In 1596, during the alliance of Queen Elizabeth with the Low Countries, and the consequent war with Spain, Sir Anthony Shirley, a British admiral, invaded Jamaica with a large fleet, and landing at Passage Fort, plundered St. Jago and the neighboring territory, but made no attempt at occupation. After thirty-nine years' tranquillity, during which, under the government of Don Arnoldo de Sasi, the island rose to a high pitch of prosperity, it was again invaded in the reign of Charles I., by Colonel Jackson, who defeated the inhabitants in a severe engagement at Passage Fort, and did not retire till he had ravaged the whole country, and laid the capital under heavy contributions. The Spanish colonists never recovered from this attack.

The preposterous claim by Spain to the exclusive right of navigating the American seas, and the outrages committed upon British subjects in these parts, provoked Cromwell to send an expedition, consisting of 6,500 men, under Admirals Penn and Venables, against Hispaniola. Failing in their attempt, for which they were afterwards committed to the Tower, they attacked Jamaica, which capitulated, after a trifling resistance, on the 3d of May, 1655, after having been 161 years in possession of the Spaniards. After the capture of the island, until the restoration of Charles II., Jamaica remained under military jurisdiction. Great exertions were made by Cromwell to establish a firm and peaceable government, as well as to people the island from Scotland and

Ireland, from the Windward Islands, and from the English colonies in North America; but these efforts were for some time neutralized by the incessant attacks of the Spaniards and their negroes, who had retreated to the mountains, by the disaffection of the troops, and rapid mortality among the settlers. A better state of affairs was at length established by Colonel D'Oyley, a man of courage and capacity. A formidable armament from Hispaniola was totally defeated at Rio Nuevo, on the 8th of May, 1658, and the remnant of the Spaniards was soon after driven from the island. Their slaves, however, for the most part, remained, and maintained themselves in the mountains, where, being constantly augmented by runaway negroes, they afterwards became formidable under the name of Maroons. At this date, negro slaves began to be imported in large numbers, and about the same time Jamaica became the resort of the buccaneers, a band of freebooters composed of adventurers and outlaws of all nations, whom the war with Spain enabled to carry on their trade of piracy under the British flag. Their ill-gotten wealth was recklessly squandered in Port Royal, and their barbarous outrages applauded by the inhabitants who shared their gains. In 1670, peace was made with Spain; the title of England to Jamaica was recognized by the treaty of Madrid, and it became necessary to put down the buccaneers. This was effectually done by their own former leader, Sir Henry Morgan, who had been knighted for the capture of Panama, and was lieutenant-governor of Jamaica in 1675. He was succeeded by Lord Vaughan, during whose administration was formed in England the 4th, or Royal African Company, which established a monopoly in the slave trade. In 1678, under Lord Carlisle, an attempt was made to saddle the island with a yearly tribute to the crown, and to take away the legislative power of the House of Assembly, which was to be in future a mere instrument for voting supplies and passing those laws which, after being prepared by the governor and council, were approved at home. In consequence of the strenuous resistance of the colonists, the privileges of the Assembly were restored under Sir Thomas Lynch in 1682, but the tribute question was not settled till 1728, when £8,000 a year (currency) (about $30,000) was settled on the crown, on condition, among other things, that all the laws and statutes of England should equally apply to Jamaica: this bill, which was considered the Magna Charta of Jamaica, was passed under the administration of the Duke of Portland.

Before this event, many calamities had happened. In 1692, occurred the great earthquake, when the chief part of the town of Port Royal, built on a shelving bank of sand, slipped into the sea and was destroyed. Two years after, a powerful French armament, from St. Domingo committed the greatest cruelties and devastations on the south and east coasts, but was at length driven back by the gallantry of the militia. In 1712, and again on the same day in 1722, there were dreadful hurricanes. This last was so destructive to Port Royal that the seat of commerce was transferred to Kingston. In 1744, there was another hurricane, and no less than five in 1780 and the six following years; numerous others have occurred, at various intervals up to the present time.

In 1738, under Governor Trelawny, a pacification took place with the Maroons, after a contest of nearly forty years, during which a body of Mosquito Indians was employed against them. The Maroons are perhaps even more averse to labor than the ordinary creole negro, and certainly more thievish and dissolute; but the wild life they have led for so many generations has made them taller, and more active and vigorous. In 1760, a dangerous revolt of the slaves was speedily repressed, and punished by the most barbarous executions. In 1765, the Assembly expressed a wish to limit the importation of slaves, but the governor, by instruction, refused his consent. In 1774, a bill passed the Assembly for the same object, but was disallowed by the Board of Trade in England. From 1700 to 1786, the number of slaves imported into the island was 610,000. In 1782, Jamaica was threatened with an invasion by the combined fleets of France and Spain under De Grasse. It was saved by the victory of Rodney and Hood, off Dominica. In 1807, the slave trade was abolished, at which time there were 323,827 slaves in Jamaica. At this period, Jamaica had reached the highest pitch of prosperity. Its fields teemed with sugar, coffee, cacao, cotton, pimento, ginger, and indigo; and it was the depot of a lucrative transit-trade between Europe and the Spanish main. In 1823, the agitation in England against slavery had reached such a height that Lord Bathurst, in a despatch to the Colonial Legislature, recommended the adoption of certain measures for the amelioration of the condition of the slaves. This moderate suggestion was unfortunately rejected, and, during the following year, a proposal for the emancipation of children of a certain age shared the same fate. From this period, till the moment of emancipation, we find in Jamaica ill-advised and indefensible proceedings by the colonists, and unwarrantable interference on the part of missionaries; in England violent and unscrupulous agitation. An examination of the history of these events proves that a measure, the success of which depended upon the anxious and cordial co-operation of both parties, became at length on all sides, with few exceptions, a mere party, and too often a mere personal question. The negroes rose, in 1832, in a revolt, which was not subdued till many hundred lives had been sacrificed, property to the amount of upwards of a million destroyed, and the atrocities usually attending a servile war perpetrated on both sides. The English government passed, on the 14th May, 1833, "An Act to Abolish Slavery," but fixing an apprenticeship of twelve years, reduced afterwards to six, and eventually to four; and granting to the owners a compensation of twenty millions sterling, of which £6,162,000 was awarded to Jamaica, being rather more than £19 a head on a slave population of 309,338. All parties were determined that the apprenticeship should be a failure. The magistrates sent to protect the negroes were prejudiced against the employers, who, on their part, could not give up their power without a struggle. Their manner was more overbearing and tyrannical than in the days of slavery, and they frequently displayed the bitterness of their feelings by turning the negroes out of their houses, destroying their provision grounds, and subjecting them to every kind of annoyance. On the 1st of August, 1838, the apprenticeship was terminated by an act of the Assembly itself, and entire emancipation took place; and, in October, 1839, Sir Charles Metcalfe became governor. By a wise and conciliatory policy, he preserved the tranquillity of the colony. He brought about a better understanding between the laborers and employers, and took measures to provide religious instruction and the due administration of justice. The number of the island curates was doubled. Acts were passed for the selection of the two puisne judges from barristers of a certain standing, and for the appointment of nine chairmen of quarter sessions, also barristers. These changes were readily granted, though involving an increased expenditure of $150,000 a year. He turned his attention also to substitutes for the laborious cultivation of sugar. Agricultural societies were formed, and attempts made to develop the resources of the colony in silk, cotton, fibrous materials, tobacco, arrow-root, and copper. Silk works were established on a grand scale in St. Ann's, mines were opened, and a new prosperity seemed about to dawn upon Jamaica. None of these schemes, however, rewarded the enterprize of the promoters. They failed in succession, and from the same cause, the want of cheap and continuous labor. Fully alive to this deficiency, Sir Charles was a zealous advocate of immigration, which commenced in 1839, from Sierra Leone and the Kroo Coast; and in 1840 an

Immigration Act was passed. The result has been, thus far, an accession of some 20,000 to 30,000 coolies and other laborers.

For many years the history of Jamaica has been largely that of a succession of struggles and difficulties between the Assembly on the one hand and the Legislative Council on the other, in regard to the finances, debts, incumbrances on estates, modes of relief, etc. The constitution of Jamaica has been modified, in many important particulars, by several acts passed in the island in the years 1854 and 1856. The ruling body consists of a governor or captain-general, advised by a privy council, of a legislative council, and of an elective legislative assembly. The governor is nominated by the crown through the secretary of state for the colonies. He receives from the Imperial Government a salary of $30,000, of which about one-third is paid by the island. His privy council is appointed by himself during pleasure, without limitation of number or qualification; and its president, or senior member, administers the government during the absence of the governor, should no lieutenant-governor be appointed, though the commission is usually given to the commander of the forces. The Legislative Council is also appointed by the governor, for life. It consists of seventeen members, and forms the upper chamber, and may initiate any measures not involving imposition of taxes, or appropriation of money. The House of Assembly consists of forty-seven members, being two for each parish, and an additional one for the towns of Spanish Town, Kingston, and Port Royal. It is summoned by the governor in council; it may be adjourned, prorogued, or dissolved by the governor alone; unless so dissolved, its duration is for seven years. It forms the lower chamber, and, in conjunction with the council, and with the consent of the governor, may pass laws for the colony, provided they be not repugnant to the spirit of the English law; but all laws so passed are subject to the approval of the Imperial government. The House of Assembly had formerly the power of originating and appropriating grants of money; but by the act of 1854, this was abolished, and no grant is to originate in the Assembly except by message from the governor, or through the executive committee, a body consisting of one member of the Legislative Council, and three members of the Assembly, chosen and changed at pleasure by the governor, who are to act as his medium of communication with the Council and Assembly, and to assist him in preparing estimates, levying and disbursing money, and in the general administration of the affairs of the colony. They each receive a salary of $4000 a year and allowances. The parishes are under the government of a chief magistrate appointed for life by the governor, termed the *custos rotulorum*, who presides over the vestry, a body consisting of the rector and church-wardens, justices of the peace and ten vestrymen, who must be free-holders, tax-payers, electors, etc. The church-wardens must be also members of the established church. The vestries meet quarterly. They raise and appropriate local taxes, by authority of an annual act of the Assmbly, for the relief of the poor, and repairs of churches and public buildings; they regulate markets, and generally the affairs of the parish; and it is their duty to prepare yearly an account of the taxable and real property in the parish for the executive committee. The judicial system of Jamaica consists of a chief-justice, who must be a barrister of five years' standing, who discharges also the duties of vice-chancellor, and sits with the ordinary as surrogate; his salary is fixed at $9000 a year. Associated with him are three assistant judges, barristers of three years' standing, with salaries of $6000 a year. None of these judges are eligible to seats in the Assembly. The attorney-general discharges the duty of advocate of the admiralty, with an additional salary of $2,500 a year. The supreme court, presided over by the bench of judges, holds sittings in Spanish Town three times a year. It has an appellate jurisdiction, and out of it all process is to issue. The island is divided into four circuits,—the Home, the Cornwall, the Surrey, and the Middlesex,—in the first of which the chief-justice presides, and sits three times a year in Kingston, and three in Spanish Town. The assistant judges preside over the others three times a year. They take cognizance of crimes, insolvencies, civil causes, etc. Almost all fees are replaced by fixed salaries. Summary jurisdiction is given in small amounts to two justices of the peace. Civil cases are decided by a majority of five in a jury of seven. The same number tries criminal cases, but the verdict must be unanimous. A special jury consists of twenty-one, of which each side may strike off seven. The law of capital punishment is by this act assimilated to that of England. Within three or four years important changes have been made in the way of law-reform. District courts now exist all over the island, and judges appointed by the home government and from the bar of the mother country preside in these courts. The results thus far have been very satisfactory and justice is faithfully dispensed. The ecclesiastical establishment consists of a bishop, whose diocese includes the Bahamas and Honduras, with $15,000 a year, first appointed in 1825, previously to which the bishop of London was diocesan. There are 4 arch-deacons, 22 rectors, corresponding to the number of parishes, and 50 island or perpetual curates. There are in addition seventeen Presbyterian, sixteen Moravian, three American, forty-four Baptist, twenty-two Wesleyan, ten Independents ministers, besides Roman Catholics and Jews. The number of children in the schools is estimated at 30,000. The population of the island is about 450,000, of which 14,500 are whites, 85,000 mixed blood, and 350,000 blacks. Commerce is not in a flourishing condition. The revenue is estimated at $1,500,000; the expenditures generally are little if at all less. The principal exports are sugar, rum, coffee, pimento, ginger, etc.

On a previous page we have spoken of negro insurrections occurring at intervals, the last in 1831-2. A more recent outbreak took place in 1865, which produced great excitement not only in Jamaica, but in England and other countries. The condition of the country, for years past, had been very wretched, and the majority of the inhabitants were miserable in the extreme. Complaints of grievances were made by G. W. Gordon, a black member of the colonial legislature, to the colonial secretary in England. These complaints were made public, and much agitation was stirred up in the island in view of these serious burdens and distresses. In October, in Morant Bay, the negroes manifested an insurrectionary spirit, and burning and plundering were the results. Governor Eyre took immediate steps to crush the outbreak. Troops were ordered out and martial law proclaimed. Gordon was arrested by the governor as a conspirator, tried by court-martial and hung, October 23d. At the close of the month, those who had been shot and hung, either by the soldiery without trial, or by order of the court martial, were reported to have reached the enormous and astounding number of 2000. This indiscriminate slaughter, as it seemed, of the blacks, excited intense indignation, and the government were compelled to institute a searching inquiry in 1866. The commission in their report, shielded Eyre all that was possible; while others resolved to have him tried for the judicial murder of Gordon. The trials did not take place, and Eyre and his companions escaped; but the whole course pursued was marked by excess of zeal, savageness of spirit, and recklessness in regard to human life shocking to contemplate. Under the present governor, order exists, and the island is at peace.

CENTRAL AMERICA.

UNDER the name Central America is comprised that portion of the continent which unites North and South America. It lies between 7° and 18° north latitude, its entire length is between 800 and 900 miles, and its breadth varies from 20 to 30 miles in the narrowest to between 300 and 400 miles in the widest part, the area being about 200,000 square miles. There are five independent republics in Central America, viz., Guatemala, San Salvador, Honduras, Nicaragua, and Costa Rica. In Central America also are included the isthmus of Panama, British Honduras, parts of Mexico and Yucatan. The general surface of the country is, for the most part, mountainous. It is traversed by a part of the Rocky Mountain chain, which is marked by volcanoes, one of these, Irasu, attaining the height of 11,478 feet. The climate is warm and moist, and the soil very rich. The rainy season is in winter, and in the low districts fevers and kindred diseases prevail. Sugar-cane, tobacco and indigo are cultivated, and the forests contain very valuable woods, as mahogany, logwood, lignum-vitae, etc. Central America is important of late years, because of the several projects for connecting the Pacific with the Atlantic ocean either by railroad (as the Panama Railroad), or by ship canal. The latter, at the date of writing, is spoken of in encouraging terms and very possibly will be completed in due time. At first, when the authority of Spain was thrown off, in 1823, the five States above named formed a federal union under one government, but the confederation was abandoned in 1839. Nominally these States are under a republican form of government, but in fact, Central America has been torn and rent by internal dissensions, and the intrigues and schemes of military adventurers, even to the present day. As was said of Mexico (p. 392), so here, the greatest of all necessities is the obtaining a settled government, based on the intelligence, cultivation, industry and love of law and order of the people. Schools must be increased in number; education must be fostered; industry must be encouraged in every way possible; the spirit of the people must be roused to a due and just sense of the duties and responsibilities of free men, under a free government; the lesson must be learned, how puerile and almost destructive it is to increase, growth, development, progress, and the like, to endeavor to maintain a half-dozen or a dozen petty States, each independent of the other, each jealous of the other, each disputing, quarreling, fighting with the other, year after year, and perpetually with the same result. What, let it be supposed, would have been the fate of the Great Republic of the United States, if each one of the original thirteen had stood off by itself and spent its energies in quarreling and fighting, instead of joining all their strength together and all working together under one constitutional, free government for the common good?

GUATEMALA.

GUATEMALA is one of the five republics of Central America, bounded on the north by Mexican provinces, east by Balize, (belonging to England,) and the Bay of Honduras, south by Honduras and San Salvador, and west by the Pacific. Area, 44,500 square miles; population, according to latest estimates, nearly 2,000,000; political divisions, into sixteen departments. The principal rivers flow northward into the Gulf of Mexi co, or eastward into the Bay of Honduras. The largest is the Usumasinta, with a course of 400 miles into the Laguna de Terminos and Bay of Campeachy. Other principal rivers are, the Motagua, the Polochoc, and Cajaban. The Michatoyal is the only river flowing into the Pacific. Most of the surface of Guatemala consists of table-land, at an elevation of about 5000 feet above the sea. The products of the country, vary of course, with the variety of soil and climate. Rice, cotton, sugar-cane, tobacco, etc., flourish on the lower ground, while coffee and cochineal are obtained abundantly in somewhat higher elevations. The imports consist chiefly of wines, fancy goods, earthenware, porcelain, cutlery, hardware, silk and linens, dry goods, and British cotton. The inhabitants of Guatemala are a mixture of native Indians, Europeans, and Negroes. The natives of negro blood are principally along the N.E. coast, and in Amatitlan. With the exception of certain portions of the indigenous Indians, or northern portions of Guatemala, the people are characterized by all the vices that degrade the larger part of the inhabitants of Central America. Guatemala received its name from the Mexican word *quauhtémali*, "a decayed wooden log," because the Mexican Indians who accompanied Alvarado found near the palace of the kings of Kachiquel an old worm-eaten tree, and gave this name to the capital. In the mouth of a Spaniard the pronunciation became *guatimala*. Another derivation is from the name of *Guitemal*, the first king of Guatemala, as Quiché was named from Namaquiche, and Nicaragua from the cacique of the same name. The principal part of Guatemala was conquered in 1524 by Alvarado, who found above thirty different tribes possessing the country, each governed by its own chief, and using distinct languages and customs. The Pipil Indians still speak the Aztec or Mexican language, and dwell on the Pacific shores. Besides this there are above twenty different dialects used in the republic; but many of these are so similar that one tribe with little difficulty understands another. According to a tradition related by the historian Juarros, the Toltec Indians, the most civilized and powerful of the tribes of Guatemala, came originally from Tula in Mexico. This emigration is said to have been undertaken by the direction of an oracle in consequence of the great increase of the population in the reign of Namaquiche (*i. e.*, "Quiché the Great"), the fifth king of the Toltecas. None of the Spanish settlements were conquered with so little bloodshed as that of Guatemala; and this was mainly owing to the celebrated Dominican Las Casas, who accompanied the conquerors in their expedition into this territory. In 1524, Alvarado founded the city of Guatemala; and in 1542, a chancery and royal *audiencia* were established in this city, with authority over all the settlements and provinces from the southern boundary of Costa Rica to the northern limit of Chiapas. Hence this city became the residence of the governor and captain-general. Till his death in 1541, Alvarado had exercised authority over the Spanish settlements from their subjugation in 1524, during four years under Cortez, and subsequently by direct delegation from the crown. At this time the kingdom of Guatemala consisted of the aggregate of the settlements and districts; and under the Spaniards it formed a captain-generalship independent of the other governments and viceroyalties of Spanish America. During the fifteenth and sixteenth centuries Guatemala was severely harassed by the Dutch and English privateers, and by the inroads of the Poyaise and Mosquito Indians, who freely permitted the English to settle along their coast, while they maintained an unrelenting struggle with the Spaniards. On the 21st of September, 1821, the country became an independent State, and united itself with the Republic of Mexico; but again, on the 1st of July, 1823, it became a separate government, and eventually the confederation of the five States of Guatemala, San Salvador, Honduras, Nicaragua,

Costa Rica, with the Territory of Mosquitia, was formed. In 1840, however, this confederation was dissolved; and Guatemala, as well as each of the rest, became independent. Of late, attempts have again been made to renew the confederation, but, owing to political jealousies, without any definite result. The country has long been kept in a state of constant agitation, industry has been neglected, civil wars have been rife, and every effort to improve the condition of the inhabitants has been frustrated. Under a united and efficient system of government this country would rise into one of great importance and influence. It possesses all the elements of prosperity in the resources and advantages with which nature has so richly invested it. The government of Guatemala is rather republican in name than in fact. A few of the old nobility, and the thoroughly energetic priests and Jesuits, allow no views to find favor but their own, and take care to repress all tendencies to education and general enlightenment. The power of the president is absolute. The legislative assembly consists of forty-four deputies, with the addition of two members each from the chapter of the cathedral, the university, the high courts of justice, the economical society, and the tribunal of commerce; but the assembly is really of no moment. The revenues are estimated at $1,500,000; the expenditures, about $200,000 less. The principal cities are, New Guatemala, the capital, Old Guatemala, Quesaltenango, Flores, etc. The capital has a population of about 50,000. The commerce of the republic has been much diminished by the opening of the Panama Railroad. A tedious conflict was carried on for years with England, in regard to the territory of Balize or British Honduras, but was settled in 1859; and were it not for the curse of lawlessness and caste and intolerance, Guatemala might become not only a free but also a prosperous republic.

SAN SALVADOR.

San Salvador is a republic of Central America, lying between N. Lat.. 13° 7′, and 14° 24′, W. Long. 87° 37′ and 90° 2′, bounded on the north and east by Honduras, south by the Pacific, and west by Guatemala. Its length is 160 miles, its mean breadth 60, and its area 7,500 square miles. Population, 600,000. There are two lines of waterparting in San Salvador, one extending from east to west parallel to the Pacific coast, separating the waters that flow directly into the Pacific from the affluents of the Lempa; and the other further inland, having a parallel direction. Along the shore of the Pacific stretches a low tract of rich alluvial land, varying from 10 to 20 miles in breadth. Beyond this the ground rises abruptly to the height of 2000 feet, forming a broad table-land, above which tower many lofty volcanic peaks. From the highest portion, which forms the lower watershed of San Salvador and the southern edge of this plateau, to the chain of the *Cordilleras*, stretches the broad valley of the Lempa, about 100 miles in length, and from 20 to 30 across. The ground slopes very gradually from the south for some distance, and then descends abruptly to the proper valley of the river; on the other side it rises with a more uniform ascent, though broken and rugged, to the foot of the mountains that form the upper watershed of the country, and tower over it at a height of 6000 or 8000 feet. Besides the Lempa, San Salvador is watered by the Rio Paza in the west, separating it from Guatemala, and by the St. Miguel in the east. The whole country is remarkable for its volcanic character, and for the number of burning mountains, both active and extinct, which it contains. A line of eleven great volcanoes extends along the crest of the table-land, between the shore and the Lempa. Probably no region in the world of equal extent contains so many volcanoes, or traces of volcanic action, as this little State, where for days the traveller's road lies over beds of lava and similar substances. A consequence of this is the great fertility of the soil, and the luxuriant vegetation that covers the mountains up to their very summits. The entire soil of San Salvador is either volcanic or alluvial. The ground of the latter sort has been gradually formed, in the lapse of ages, from the ashes and stones ejected by volcanoes now extinct. It occurs for the most part in small patches, scattered over different parts of the country; the most extensive tract of alluvial ground being in the district of Gotera, in the department of San Miguel. In other places, the action of volcanic forces is most strikingly apparent, from the confused assemblage of abrupt cliffs, deep ravines, mountains, valleys, and plains indiscriminately mixed together.

The country is essentially an agricultural one, and well cultivated, the low land yielding tropical produce, and the upper regions the crops of northern climes. Indigo is the plant raised in the largest quantities. Sugar, cacao, coffee, and tobacco are also grown. Almost all the land is cultivated, very little remains unclaimed, and there are few large estates belonging to individuals. The rural population consists mostly of Indians, and the lands which they have been allowed to retain have tended to their encouragement in industrious habits. For the most part they live in villages, which stud the country in great numbers; going in the morning to and returning at night from their little patches of ground in the vicinity. Roads have been constructed throughout the most of the country. The mineral resources of San Salvador include the silver mines of Tabanco in the north-east of the State, which are easily worked, and yield from 47 to 2537 oz. per ton; and the iron mines of Petapa in the west. It is also believed that extensive beds of coal exist throughout the valley of the Lempa. A certain part of the coast of San Salvador, about 50 miles in length by 20 or 25 in breadth, between La Libertad and Acajutla, is called the Balsam Coast, because it produces what is erroneously called the balsam of Peru. This is obtained from the juice of a tree; the whole region as far inland as the mountains being covered with dense forests occupied by Indians, who make their living by selling this balsam and planks of cedar-wood. The seaports of the country are La Union, on the Gulf of Fonseca; Libertad and Acajutla further west, along the shore. Very few manufactures are carried on here, and these are chiefly articles for domestic use, such as coarse cotton cloth and hardware. The great majority of the people are Indians, belonging, in all probability, to the Nahual or Aztec race, who inhabited Mexico before the Spanish invasion. Their language is very similar to that spoken by the natives of Mexico, and they seem from the ancient traditions to have come from Nicaragua. The towns in San Salvador are generally inhabited by white men and those of mixed blood (*ladinos*), the former being generally merchants or proprietors of estates (*haciendas*), and the latter employed in mechanical pursuits. The Indians in the villages and country districts are engaged in agricultural labor.

The government of the country is republican; the executive power is in the hands of a president, elected for five years; and the legislature consists of a chamber of twenty-five members. The revenue, according to the latest estimate, amounts to nearly $1,000,000; value of exports nearly the same amount; and the prospects generally are considered to be favorable for the future progress of the republic. The capital, San Salvador, which was very greatly injured by an earthquake in 1854, now numbers in population about 20,000.

The first European who invaded San Salvador was Alvarado, one of the officers under

Cortez, in the conquest of Mexico. After having conquered the country now called Guatemala, he was informed of the existence of a powerful nation to the south-east, which he resolved also to conquer. He met with an obstinate resistance, but succeeded in penetrating as far as the capital, Cuscatlan, where, however, he only remained a few days. The country was then one of the best peopled in America, and contained many large towns as well built as those in Mexico. For a long time the inhabitants resisted the invaders; and it was only by the advantages of cavalry and fire-arms that the conquest was consummated. The country afterwards formed part of the general captaincy of Guatemala, and remained under the Spanish government till 1821, when, by a bloodless revolution, the province regained its independence. Until 1823, San Salvador, along with the other ports of the Spanish Guatemala, was united to Mexico; but in that year a confederation was formed by the five States of Guatemala, Honduras, San Salvador, Nicaragua, and Costa Rica, under the name of the Confederation of Central America. This arrangement continued until 1840, after which the component parts of the confederation became entirely independent, as they have since continued to be. Notwithstanding, there are a number of patriots in this and the other republics who look forward to a restoration of the confederation as promising to afford the most stable government, the greatest freedom, and the largest liberty of development and growth in the republic.

HONDURAS.

Honduras is a republic of Central America, lying between W. Long. 83° 20′, and 89° 30′, and N. Lat. 13° 10′ and 16°; and bounded on the N. and N.E. by the Bay of Honduras and the Caribbean Sea, S.E. by Nicaragua, S. by the Gulf of Fonseca and San Salvador, and W. by Guatemala. Area, 47,000 square miles; population, 350,000; population of its capital, Comayagua, 18,000. The general aspect of Honduras is mountainous. Ranges of mountains and hills radiate towards the N. and E. from the common base of the Cordilleras. This great chain does not in Honduras approach within fifty or sixty miles of the Pacific, and on that side presents the general appearance of a great natural wall. The northern and eastern coast of Honduras presents several bold groups of mountains, the terminations of ranges radiating from the Cordilleras. From the high plateaux of Guatemala the great range of the Cordilleras pursues a nearly eastern course to the frontier of Honduras, where it is deflected to the S.E., while a higher range, not inferior in height to the main chain, runs off E. by N. to the Bay of Honduras. Most of that wide region between the Sulaco mountains and the Atlantic, comprising nearly one-half of the territory of the State, is uninhabited except by detached Indian tribes, and is but little known, except that it is very diversified and rich in the nature of its soil and the variety of its minerals. The northern coast of Honduras presents a diversified surface. A portion is flat, and covered with vast growths of timber. In other places the mountains extend to or very near the coast. Honduras thus presents the greatest diversity of surface, fertile valleys, wide and elevated plains, and mountains terraced to their summits, affording almost every variety of soil, climate, and production. The rivers of Honduras are numerous, and some of them of large size. The principal are the Chamelicon, Ulua, Aguan or Roman, Tinto or Black River, Patuca, and Wanks or Segovia, flowing into the Atlantic; and the Choluteca, Nacaome and Goascoran, flowing into the Bay of Fonseca. The Chamelicon rises in the mountains of Merendon, and pursues a generally N.E. course to the Atlantic. It is of great length and rapid, but as it drains only a small section of country, its body of water is small. The Ulua, on the other hand, drains a vast expanse of territory, comprehending nearly one-third of the entire State, and is the largest river in Central America, the Wanks perhaps excepted. The Bay of Fonseca, the greater portion of which belongs to Honduras, is upwards of fifty miles in length, by about thirty in average breadth, with an entrance eighteen miles wide, between the volcanoes of Conchagua (3,800 feet in height) and Coseguina (3,000 feet in height). Across this entrance lie the two islands of Cochaguita and Mianguera, and a collection of high rocks called *Los Farellones*, forming four distinct channels, each having sufficient depth of water to admit the largest vessels. On the island of Tigre, near the center of the bay, is the free port of Amapala, belonging to Honduras. The principal ports of Honduras on the Atlantic are Puerto Caballo, Omoa, and Truxillo. Puerto Caballo, the first port established by the Spaniards on the northern coast is in N. Lat. 15° 49′, W. Long. 87° 57′. Cortez, in his expedition into Honduras, founded a settlement here for the purpose of making it the grand entrepôt of New Spain. For upwards of two centuries it was the principal establishment on the coast; but during the time of the buccaneers it was removed to Omoa, because of the large size of the bay, which could not be properly defended. The port of Omoa is small but secure, and is defended by a strong fort, called El Castillo de San Fernando. The town stands about a quarter of a mile from the shore, and contains about 2,000 inhabitants. Truxillo is situated on the western shore of a noble bay, in N. Lat. 15° 55′, W. Long. 86°. The population has been estimated at 2,500, of whom 1,000 were whites and Ladinos, and 1,500 Caribs. The latter are described as tall, hardy, and industrious.

The coast alluvions of Honduras are generally densely wooded, the elevated valleys of the interior spread out in broad savannahs, and the mountain plateaux are covered with forests of scattered pines, relieved by occasional clumps of oak. Of the vegetable productions of Honduras the mahogany tree stands first in importance, and, from its vast size and magnificent foliage, is deservedly entitled "king of the forest." It is to be found in nearly all parts of Honduras, in the valleys of the various streams. It is, however, most abundant upon the lower valleys of the rivers flowing into the Bay of Honduras, where the *cortes* (cuttings) are chiefly carried on by the Spaniards. A fixed sum is paid to the government for each tree cut down. Among the gum and medicinal trees, are the gum-arabic tree, copaibo tree, copal tree, liquid amber, castor oil, ipecacuanha, and the *Hevea elastica*. Among the more common of the others are the long-leaved or pitch pine, cedar, *ceiba* or silk-cotton tree, live oak, mangrove, iron-wood, calabash, various kinds of oak and palm, lime, lemon, orange, cocoa, pimento, citron, tamarind, and guava. Sarsaparilla is obtained in great abundance, and of superior quality. The sugar-cane grows luxuriantly on the plains and among the mountains, at elevations of 3,000 to 4,000 feet. Coffee, indigo, tobacco, maize, wheat, rice, and potatoes are also grown.

Honduras, in point of mineral resources, ranks first among the States of Central America. Silver, the most abundant and valuable of the ores existing in the State, is found in various combinations—with iron, lead, copper, and in some instances with antimony. Chlorides of silver are not uncommon. The silver ores are chiefly found upon the Pacific ranges or groups of mountains, while the gold washings, if not the gold mines proper, are most numerous on the Atlantic slope. There are also very valuable mines of copper; the ores containing also considerable proportions of silver. Iron ore is common, but no mines of it are worked except those of Agalteca. Platina is said to exist, but the mines have never been worked. Cinnabar has also been found in several places. Zinc, antimony, and tin also exist. The coal mines of Gracias are worked to a large extent, and have been very productive; and beds of coal have been discovered in several localities.

The Indian or aboriginal population predominates in Honduras, as in Central America generally. In the eastern portion of the State, within the district which lies between the Rio Roman and the Segovia River, an area of not less than 15,000 square miles, the country is almost exclusively occupied by native tribes, known under the general names of Xicaques and Payas. Portions of these tribes have accepted the Roman Catholic religion, and live in good understanding with the white population. Apart from these there are considerable numbers who live among the mountains, and who follow more closely their original modes of life, but who are also friendly in their intercourse with the Spaniards. They tacitly recognize the authority of the government, but it does not interfere with their modes of life. They are described as being short, but remarkably strong, and capable of carrying heavy burdens over the rocky passes of their steep mountains without appearing to suffer much fatigue. Their character for faith and honesty stands high. The coast around Carataska Lagoon, and westward as far as Brewer's Lagoon, was for many years occupied by Sambos or Mosquitos, a mixed race of Negroes and Indians; but the Caribs spreading rapidly eastward from Truxillo and Black River, have now nearly displaced them, and driven them to the southward of Cape Gracias á Dios into the Mosquito territory. The Caribs are peaceable, active and industrious, and are much employed by the mahogany cutters on the coast. Comayagua, formerly Valladolid, the capital of the republic, is situated on the southern border of the plain of the same name, in N. Lat. 14° 28′. W. Long. 87° 39′. It was founded by Alonzo Caceres in 1540. In 1827, it was taken and burned by the monarchical faction of Guatemala. It then contained about 18,000 inhabitants, and was embellished with fountains and monuments; but has never since wholly recovered. It is the seat of a bishopric, and has a large and elegant cathedral, and a university. The trade of the city is small. The coast of Honduras was discovered by Columbus in 1502. It subsequently formed part of the Spanish kingdom of Guatemala, which comprised the provinces of Guatemala, Honduras, San Salvador, Nicaragua, and Costa Rica. These threw off their allegiance to Spain in 1821, and assuming the rank of sovereign States soon after united into a confederacy called the "Republic of Central America." This union, in consequence of internal dissensions, became practically dissolved in 1839, and since that time Honduras has continued to be an independent republic. Some years ago, a claim was set up by Great Britain to a considerable portion of the coast of Honduras from Cape Comorin, near Truxillo, to Cape Gracias á Dios, on the behalf of the so-called "king of Mosquito." The matter was settled by England abandoning the claim in 1856.

Balize, often called British Honduras, is an English settlement on the east coast of Central America, and separated from Honduras by the republic of Guatemala. It has a coast line of about 200 miles in length, between the mouths of the Hondo and Sarstan, and averages about sixty miles in width. Area, about 12,000 square miles. This coast was discovered by Columbus in the year 1502, but little that can be relied upon is known of its early settlement. The abundance and fine quality of the wood, particularly mahogany and logwood, seem first to have drawn attention to it; and at a pretty early period it was occasionally resorted to by wood-cutters. But the first permanent establishment of British wood-cutters was made at Cape Catoche by some adventurers from Jamaica, whose numbers increasing, they extended as far south as the River Balize, and as far west as the neighborhood of Campeachy. The successes of the settlers aroused the jealousy of the Spaniards, and they finally succeeded in driving the woodmen from the Campeachy shore, and confining them to the limits of the present settlement. An attempt was again made, in 1718, to dispossess the British of the territory on the River Balize; but the firmness of the wood-cutters deterred the Castilians from effecting anything. In 1754, an expedition was undertaken to exterminate the colony; but by a treaty of peace concluded in the year 1763, the Spaniards were compelled to admit the right of occupancy to the British colonists, which, however, they subsequently attempted to annul. In 1784, Britain obtained from Spain a specific grant of "the lands allotted for the cutting of logwood;" and in 1790, an act of parliament conferred on Balize all the privileges of a British colony. The last attack on the settlement was made during the war in 1798, but the expedition was gallantly repulsed; and since that period the colony has remained undisturbed by foreign aggression.

The coast of the Bay of Honduras is low, and the shore is studded with a number of low islands or keys, which, however, are verdant. As we recede from the coast, the land rises into a bold and lofty country, interspersed with rivers and lagoons, and covered with gigantic forests. The lagoons or sheets of water, and the falls and rapids of the rivers, constitute sublime and beautiful features in the general aspect of the country. The Hondo River, which forms the northern boundary, is a fine stream. A few miles south of it is the New River, which has its source in an extensive lagoon. The Balize has a N.E. by E. course of above 200 miles, and discharges itself into the Bay of Honduras by two mouths about 3½ miles apart, the southern branch dividing the town of Balize into two parts. Fruits spontaneously produced, are exceedingly abundant, and consist of oranges of excellent quality, shaddocks, limes, mangoes, melons, cocoa-nuts, and many others. They are all found in the neighborhood of Balize, but are sometimes brought in large quantities from more elevated plantations. The mahogany and logwood trees are at present the staples of Honduras. The logwood is found in low swarmy grounds, growing contiguous to fresh water creeks and lakes, on the edges of which the roots, the most valuable part of the wood, ramify. There are various other kinds of wood of beautiful vein and close-texture, such as ironwood, claywood, rosewood, palmaletta, and the like. Amongst minerals, strata of fine marble and formations of alabaster are known to exist.

Balize, the capital of the settlement, stands on a low, flat shore immediately open to the sea, and guarded by numerous small islands, densely covered with trees and shrubs, and so similar as to render navigation extremely difficult. It is farther divided into two parts by the river, which is crossed by a substantial wooden bridge of 220 feet span and 20 feet in length. The houses are about 500 in number, and are in general well built, spacious, and even elegant. They are for the most part constructed of wood, and raised ten feet from the ground on pillars of mahogany. Population, about 5000. The streets are regular, and cross each other at right angles. The whole town is embowered in groves and avenues of the cocoa-nut and tamarind trees. In the neighborhood of Balize the natural heat of the climate is tempered by the sea breezes that prevail during nine months of the year, so that, even in the hottest season, the thermometer seldom rises above 83°, and during the wet season it sinks to 60°. In June, July, August and September, heavy and frequent rains fall, and these are the most unhealthy months of the year, from the decomposition of animal and vegetable matter in the adjacent lowlands and swamps. There are various classes of society in this settlement, including Europeans, colored people, Indians, and Mosquito men. The blacks of Honduras are distinct from the aborigines of the country, being of African descent. In general they are inclined to indulge those low propensities which are exhibited in a state of barbarism. The *Mosquito Indians* abound in the colony. They are remarkable for a fine muscular formation of body, but in their countenances they exhibit an utter destitution of intelligence, and their habits are most barbarous. The *Indians*, the real aborigines of the place, are a timid, inoffensive race, apparently more under the influence of instinct than of reason. They perform the most astonishing journeys through woods, as trackless as the sea, and impervious to all but themselves, with infallible correctness of direction and amazing rapidity. Although free from vindictive or malicious propensities, they are addicted to drunkenness to an excessive degree. The population of the colony is estimated at about 12,000.

NICARAGUA.

Nicaragua is a republic of Central America, and was under the Spanish dominion, one of the provinces of the captain-generalcy, called also the kingdom of Guatemala. Its boundaries are the Caribbean Sea on the east, from the lower mouth of the San Juan River to Cape Gracias á Dios; and the Pacific Ocean on the west. On the north, and separating it from Honduras, its boundary extends from the mouth of the Rio Negro, falling into the Bay of Fonseca, to the head-waters of the Rio Wanks or Segovia, following down that river to the sea at Cape Gracias. Its southern boundary, separating it from Costa Rica, starts from Punta Arenas, on the south shore of the harbor of San Juan, thence to Castillo Viejo, along Lake Nicaragua to river Japod, and thence west to the bay of Salinas on the Pacific. Nicaragua is, therefore, embraced between 83° 20′ and 87° 30′ west longitude, and 10° 45′ and 15° north latitude, and has an area of about 58,000 square miles. A large portion of this territory was claimed by England for the "king of the Mosquitos;" but in 1860, the pretension was given up, and the "Mosquito shore" now belongs to Nicaragua.

The geographical and topographical features of Nicaragua are not only remarkable, but interesting to the world at large, from the facilities which they are supposed to afford for opening a ship-canal between the Atlantic and Pacific Oceans. The northern part of the republic, embracing the whole of the district of Segovia, and a portion of Chontales, borders on the high grounds or plateau of Honduras, and partakes of its mountainous character. Here are found numerous rich mines of gold, silver, and copper, and many of the streams carry gold in their sands, whence it is washed in considerable quantities by the Indians. To the southward of this elevated district, and between it and the high mountain group or center of elevation in Costa Rica, is the great basin of the Nicaraguan lakes, lying transversely to the great range of the Cordilleras, and completely interrupting it. It is precisely this physical feature which has directed attention to Nicaragua, as probably the best point where the oceans may be connected by a canal. This great basin or valley is not far from 300 miles long by 150 miles wide, and consists in great part of broad, beautiful, and fertile plains. In its centre are spread out the Lakes of Nicaragua and Managua, which collect the waters flowing inward from every direction and discharge them through a single outlet, the Rio San Juan, into the Caribbean Sea. Some of the streams flowing into these lakes, especially those from the north, are of considerable size, and furnish a good supply of water. Lake Managua is nearly

50 miles long by 25 broad, and with an average depth of 5 fathoms of water. It approaches, at the nearest point, to within 20 miles of the Pacific Ocean. The gigantic volcano of Momotombo stands out boldly into the lake with its bare and blackened summit. Upon the northern and eastern shores of the lake, are the mountains of Matagalpa. Upon the south and west are fertile slopes and broad plains, covered with luxuriant verdure, and of almost unlimited productiveness; while in the lake itself stands the Island of Momotombita, an almost perfect cone in outline, covered with a dense forest, in the deepest recesses of which are still found gigantic idols, the rude relics of aboriginal superstition. The town of Leon was first built on the north-western shore of the lake, at a place now called Moabita, which was subsequently abandoned for its present site, in the midst of the great plain of the Marabios. The great feature of Nicaragua, however, is the lake of the same name, the Cocibolca of the aborigines. It is upwards of 100 miles in greatest length, by about 40 miles in average width. Upon its southern shore, near the head of the lake, stood the ancient city of Granada, and once the most important commercial town in the republic. Upon the same shore with Granada, but 40 miles distant, is the ancient city of Rivas or Nicaragua, the capital of a large, fertile, and comparatively well cultivated district. The water of the lake, in most places, shoals very gradually; and it is only at a few points that vessels of considerable size may approach the shore. Still, its general depth, for all purposes of navigation, is ample, except near its outlet, where for some miles it does not exceed from 5 to 10 feet. There are points, however, where the depth of water is not less than 40 fathoms. The prevailing winds on the lake, as indeed of the whole State, are from the north-east; they are, in fact, the Atlantic trades, which here sweep entirely across the continent. As already observed, the sole outlet of the great Nicaraguan basin, and of the lakes just described, is the River San Juan, debouching into the Caribbean Sea, at the now well known port of San Juan (Greytown). This river is a fine stream, but its capacities have been greatly exaggerated. It flows from the south-eastern extremity of Lake Nicaragua, nearly due east to the ocean. With its windings it is 119 miles long. The body of water which passes through it varies greatly at different seasons of the year. It is, of course, greatest during what is called the "rainy season;" that is to say, from May to October. To this variation, in some degree, may be ascribed the wide difference in the statements of the depth and capacity of the river made by different observers. The width of the river varies from 100 to 400 yards, and its depth from 2 to 20 feet. It is interrupted by five rapids,—viz., Rapides del Toro, del Castillo, de los Valos, del Mico, and Machuca. The Machuca rapids are the largest, and in many respects the worst in the river. Like the Atrato, the San Juan river has formed a delta at its mouth, through which it flows for 18 miles, reaching the sea through several channels. This delta is a maze of low grounds, swamps, creeks, and lagoons, the haunts of the manati and alligator, and the homes of innumerable varieties of water-fowl. The port of San Juan (Greytown) derives its principal importance from the fact that it is the only possible eastern terminus for the proposed inter-oceanic canal, by way of the River San Juan and the Nicaraguan lakes. It is small, but well protected, easy of entrance and exit, and has a depth of water varying from 3 to 5 fathoms. Upon the Pacific the best port of the republic is that of Realejo, anciently Possession, which is capacious and secure, but difficult of entrance.

Next to its great lakes, the most striking physical features of Nicaragua are its volcanoes, which bristle along its Pacific coast, in nearly a right line, from the Bay of Fonseca, to that of Nicoya. At the time of the conquest of Nicaragua, in 1520, the volcano of Masaya was in active eruption. It has had one or two violent eruptions since that period, and after more than half a century of quiescence, is now reported as throwing out volumes of smoke, and giving other evidences of renewed activity. Momotombo to this day sends out a constant column of smoke, and an occasional cloud of ashes. The eruption of the volcano of Coseguina in 1835 was one of the most fearful on record. It commenced on the 30th of January of that year, and continued with uninterrupted violence for four days, and then suddenly ceased. For three days the clouds of smoke and sand which it sent forth totally obscured the sun for the distance of 100 miles. Sand fell in Jamaica, in Santa Fé de Bogota, and in Mexico, over an area of more than 1,500 miles in diameter. Besides the volcanoes themselves, and the hundred yawning craters amongst the hills, there are numerous lakes of volcanic origin, shut in by vitrified, blistered, and precipitous walls of rock, without outlets, and often of great depth.

The natural resources of Nicaragua are very great. The staples of the tropics, cotton, sugar, indigo, tobacco, rice, cacao, coffee, etc., may be produced in the greatest abundance. The cotton, although as yet, from lack of sufficient labor, produced in but small quantities, is of a superior quality. Its sugar is produced from a plant slenderer, but containing more and stronger juice, than the variety cultivated in the West India Islands. Two crops, and sometimes, when the fields are irrigated, three crops are taken from the same ground annually. This cane seldom requires to be replanted oftener than once in twelve or fourteen years. The indigo is produced from an indigenous plant called *juiquilite*, and has a high reputation in commerce. Coffee flourishes well on the higher grounds, but is not extensively cultivated. The same may be said of tobacco, which is a government monopoly, and its production not allowed, except in certain quantities. Maize grows in great perfection, and, manufactured into *tortillos*, constitutes a principal article of food. Cattle are numerous, and hides form a large item amongst the exports of the country. Dye-woods, chiefly the *braziletto*, are also extensively exported. In short, nearly all the edibles and fruits of the tropics are produced naturally, or may be cultivated in great perfection. The mineral resources of Nicaragua are also very great. Gold, silver, copper, lead, and iron are found in considerable quantities in various parts, but chiefly in the districts of Segovia and Chontales. The production of these metals has greatly fallen off since the assertion of the country's independence; still the produce is considerable; but in the unsettled state of the country, it is impossible to obtain any satisfactory statistics concerning it. Sulphur may be had in inexhaustible quantities, crude and nearly pure, from the volcanoes; nitre is also abundant, as also sulphate of iron. Notwithstanding the variety of its products, and the ease with which they may be prepared for market, the commerce of Nicaragua is very small. The wants of its people are few and easily supplied.

Politically, Nicaragua is divided into five departments, each of which is subdivided into districts for municipal and other purposes. The population is estimated to be above 400,000. Of these there are 40,000 whites, 30,000 negroes, 120,000 Indians, and 200,000 Meztizos. The capital, Managua, has about 10,000 inhabitants. The people generally live in towns, and the plantations, *haciendas*, *hattos*, *huertas*, etc., are scattered over the country, being often reached by paths so obscure as almost wholly to escape the notice of the traveller. The dwellings are usually of canes, thatched with palm, many of them open at the sides, with no other floor than the bare earth, and deserving no better name than that of huts. Some of the dwellings are more pretending, are roofed with tiles, and have the canes plastered over and white-washed; and there are a few belonging to large proprietors, which are roomy, neat, and comfortable. In the towns, the residences of the better classes are built of *adobes* or sun-dried bricks, inclosing large courts, faced by broad corridors. The churches, as usual in Roman Catholic countries, monopolize nearly all that there is of architectural skill and beauty. Their leading features are Moresque; but there are a few, and conspicuously among them the great cathedral of Leon, which are of simpler and more classical styles. This cathedral is of substantial masonry throughout. It was finished in 1743, after having occupied thirty-seven years in building. The cost is said to have been $5,000,000. Nothing can better illustrate its strength than the fact that it has endured unimpaired the earthquakes and storms of more than a century. During the frequent revolutionary paroxysms of the country, it is used as a fortress, heavy guns being mounted on the roof. It has sustained several severe cannonades.

A civil war broke out in Nicaragua in 1855, the country being divided into the liberal party, having its seat in Leon, and the opposing party occupying Granada. The struggle was obstinate and severe, resulting, however, in favor of the liberals. These had called in the aid of Walker, of California, one of that class of adventurers who have a great proclivity for meddling in Cuban and South American affairs. Walker and his co-laborers succeeded in taking Granada by surprise, Oct. 13th, 1855. As was natural, dissensions soon broke out, and Walker availed himself of the opportunity and assumed supreme power, under the title of President. He made a great blunder in attempting to establish slavery, and a strong coalition was formed against him by the other States of Central America; in May, 1857, he surrendered, and his public career closed in Nicaragua, although certain partizans of his are troublesome to the country in his behalf. The republic may be said to have a reasonably bright prospect in the future, especially if, as is hoped, party disputes and contests become less acrimonious, and all the people resolve and strive to advance in industry and in mental and moral culture.

COSTA RICA.

Costa Rica is the most southern and one of the smallest of the republics of Central America, lying chiefly between Lat. 8° and 11° N., and Long. 82° and 86° W. It is bounded on the north by Nicaragua, south by New Granada, east by the Caribbean Sea, and west by the Pacific Ocean. It has an estimated area of 21,400 square miles, and a population of 135,000, of whom about 15,000 are Indians. The surface of the country is much diversified, but is chiefly occupied with mountains, some of which are volcanoes. Among these may be mentioned Irasu or Carthage, Turrialva, Chirripo, Barba, Votos, Erradura, and Miravalles. It contains two principal forests: that of Aguacate is remarkable for its rich gold mines, which were begun to be worked about 1821, and have been the means of attracting many colonists to settle there; and that of Dota which is of great extent, and through which passes the road from San José to the towns of Terrava and Borruca, leading thence into the republic of New Granada. At a point called Alto-de-Ochomogo, near Carthage, the streams which run through the principal part of the State diverge and discharge themselves respectively into the Pacific Ocean and the Caribbean Sea, so that Costa Rica may be considered as divided into two parts, a north-eastern and a south-western. This division is further borne out by the different characters of the two parts. The south-western slope is easily accessible, and its climate, throughout nearly its whole extent, varies from insupportable heat and aridity to a mild and genial temperature. On the north-eastern side the aspect is more rugged,—the number, complication, and height of the mountains, and the impetuous currents of the rivers, both large and small, attract the attention of the traveller. Among the rivers of Costa Rica are the Tempisque and Grande, falling into the bay of Nicoya; the Ucus or Macho, which afterwards takes the name of Reventason, and falls into the Caribbean Sea; the Matina, formed by the Rivers Chirripo and Barbilla; the Escudo de Veragua, dividing Central from South America; the Banana, Tiribee and Culabra, all falling into the Caribbean Sea; the Chrico Mola or Chrickam Aula, falling into the bay of Cheriqui; the Costa Rica or San Carlos, and the Sarapiqui, into the San Juan. The Baya is a canal, believed by some to be natural, and by others to have been cut by the aborigines, commencing at the port of Moin or Salt Creek, and running parallel to the coast as far as Pearl Kay Lagoon, a distance of 180 miles, being, however, stopped up in a few places. It is crossed by the river Matina and several others. Boats and canoes can come up from the port of Moin to the Matina, and up that river to the Chirripo and Barbilla, which are also navigable; so that the valuable wood on the banks of these rivers can be sent to Moin on rafts. The chief lakes are Locorra, at the head of the brook; Reventado, which supplies the city of Carthage with water; the twin lakes at Laguna, on the road from San José to the Matina; Ermosa, near the road from Barbara to the Sarapiqui; and Surtidor, at the source of the latter river.

Agricultural and pastoral pursuits constitute the principal occupation of the inhabitants. Some parts of the State afford excellent pasturage, and great numbers of cattle, hogs, goats, and sheep are reared. In the forests are the tapir, mountain cow, wild goat, wild striped boar, zahino, etc. Among its vegetable productions are coffee, sugar, maize, tobacco, cocoa, indigo, peas, beans, etc. It is also rich in various kinds of timber, as mahogany, beech, cedar, oak, chestnut, and dyewoods. The climate varies much in the different parts. In the principal inhabited places it is said to be remarkably mild and salubrious, and to have no extreme either of heat or cold, the thermometer varying between 50° and 76°; but including all places cultivated or in pasture it ranges through every degree, from the freezing point to 100°, according to the elevation of the land.

Costa Rica is divided into six departments, San José, Cartago, Heredia, Alajuela, Guanaceute, and Punta de Arenas. Its principal towns are San José, the capital, population, 25,000, and Cartago or Carthage, the former capital. The government is vested in a president and vice-president, elected for four years, and a legislative chamber composed of twelve deputies elected for three years. The chief court of justice is the tribunal of San José, which is presided over by seven judges; the State has no debt; and the revenue, derived from duties on tobacco and spirits, amounts to about 120,000 dollars. The militia consists of 5,000 men, of whom 200 are called upon periodically for active duty. The Roman Catholic is the established religion, but complete toleration is allowed by law. After the declaration of independence by the Spanish American colonies in 1821, Costa Rica formed for a short time a province of Mexico. In 1823, it became one of the States of the Central American Confederacy, but on the dissolution of that union it became an independent republic. It has, unlike the other States, been in the enjoyment of internal and external peace for several years; and the efforts of its government have been exclusively directed to the development of its internal resources. One of the latest and most important steps of the government in the right direction, has been the entering into a contract with citizens of the United States for the construction of an inter-oceanic railroad from Simon Bay to the Gulf of Nicoya.

SOUTH AMERICA.

COLOMBIA.

THE UNITED STATES OF COLOMBIA, or New Granada, is a republic of South America, in its N. W. corner, between lat. 3° 35′ S. and 12° 30′ N., and long. 65° 50′ and 83° 5′ W. It is bounded N. by the Caribbean Sea, E. by Venezuela, S. by Brazil and Ecuador, and W. by the Pacific Ocean. It comprehends the isthmuses of Chiriqui, Panama, Darien and Atrato, by one of which, probably the Darien route, the great work of inter-oceanic communication will soon be accomplished, and in successful operation. Among the large number of bays and ports on both oceans, the most important commercially, besides the free ports of Panama and Aspinwall, are Carthagena, Santa Maria, Sabanilla and Rio Hacha on the Atlantic, and Buenaventura and Tumaco on the Pacific. The natural configuration of the republic is peculiar. The Cordillera of the Andes, on entering the country, spreads out in three great ranges, the eastern, central and western, between which are the two large and beautiful valleys of Cauca and Magdalena. The east branch of the Cordillera is much the greatest in extent; it forms a series of great table-lands or plateaus, from 8,000 to 14,000 feet in elevation, cool and salubrious, where the white race flourishes especially, the African preferring the hot valleys of the coast. This plateau produces abundantly the fruits and grains of the temperate zone, and contains more than a third of the population of the republic. The most important river is the Magdalena, with its tributary the Cauca, together 2000 miles in length, and traversing nearly the entire republic from north to south. The Magdalena is navigated by steamers for 700 miles to the rapids of Honda. The Atrato is also an important river, having a length of 300 miles.

Among the various drawbacks to the more rapid and steady development of the country and increase in its population and growth, has been the almost incessant internal war, the unsettled state of the government, and the inadequate means of communication with the interior, which, for want of roads, cannot export its superabundant produce. Another great hindrance is the swampy insalubrious nature of the climate over the tracts bordering on the sea, endangering the lives of those who traverse them. So difficult of access is the valley of the Upper Cauca, which is the most fertile tract in the republic, that none of its produce can be exported except what is carried over its inclosing mountains on the backs of men. It is everywhere surrounded by lofty mountains, and the Cauca becomes unfit for navigation on issuing from the valley. The trade of the interior is carried on chiefly by mule-carriage, the roads being exceedingly bad; but of late years considerable improvement has been made in this respect.

Colombia enjoys a republican form of government, based on the written constitution of 1832, which was a close copy of the constitution of the United States. On this, however, some amendments have since been made. Every man born in the country, able to read and write, and that without distinction of class or color, is a citizen; and foreigners are naturalized at the age of twenty. The legislature consists of a chamber of deputies, elected by the people, one for every 50,000 inhabitants, and a senate of twenty-seven members, elected by provincial colleges. The president, in whom the chief executive power is vested, is chosen for four years. Justice is administered by an independent judiciary, consisting of a supreme court, and provincial and other inferior courts; and all judges are appointed by the president, with the consent of the senate. Representation is based on population, but each province must be represented by at least one deputy. All religious sects are tolerated in the State, but the Roman Catholic is the only religion that receives support from the public treasury. They do not, however, it is said, recognize the supremacy of the pope—the Archbishop of Bogota being considered the head of the church. The Bishops of Carthagena, Mompox, Neyva, Pamplona, Santa Marta, and Popayan, are his suffragans, and exercise authority in their particular dioceses. Education, formerly greatly neglected, has of late years received the attention of government, and the public generally have become alive to its great importance. Public schools, on the Lancasterian system, are established in all the large towns. In Bogota there is a university; and in the provincial capitals colleges, or high schools, have been established. Bogota has also an observatory, a public library, and several special schools; and in several places associations have been formed for the promotion of science, art and literature.

The war of the revolution bequeathed to the state a bankrupt treasury and a heavy debt. The national liabilities amount to about $44,000,000; and this sum is being constantly increased by unsatisfied interest, and a deficiency in the annual receipts. According to the latest accounts the revenue amounts to about $2,500,000; the expenditures being at least $500,000 in excess.

The United States of Colombia are nine in number, viz: Antioquia, Bolivar, Boyaca, Cauca, Cundinamarca, Magdalena, Panama, Santander, Tolima. The area of the republic is 357,000 square miles, or, admitting its claims to certain disputed territory, is 513,000 square miles. The population is estimated at 2,794,473, not including the uncivilized Indians, supposed to number about 126,000. The capital of the republic is Bogota, which is also the capital of the State of Cundinamarca; population, 40,000. The imports of the ports of Panama and Aspinwall (Colon) are valued at $35,000,000, and the exports at $67,000,000. In 1865, there arrived at Panama 353 vessels, tonnage 360,206; at Aspinwall, there arrived 556 vessels, tonnage 485,044. The value of merchandise passing over the Panama Railroad is estimated to exceed $100,000,000 annually; the number of passengers is estimated to be between 40,000 and 50,000 per annum.

New Granada was discovered by Columbus, 1498–1502. Different governments having been established throughout the country, a viceroyalty was at length, in 1732, formed of what is now the republics of Ecuador and Colombia. In 1810, the Spanish authority was thrown off, and an incessant war against that power maintained until 1824, when the Spaniards were finally vanquished. Bolivar, the most distinguished leader of the Spanish-American revolution, in 1818, proposed the union of Venezuela with New Granada; and when the Congress of Angostura met, early in 1819, the fundamental law was enacted, which established the republic of Colombia, and which was inaugurated on the 17th of December, of the same year. This union was never cordial, and lasted only ten years. In November, 1829, Venezuela seceded from it; and in May, 1830, Ecuador also withdrew. The central part of Colombia constituted itself the Republic of New Granada, November 21, 1831, or, as it is now called, the United States of Colombia. In 1832, the constitution was promulgated, and the republic divided into States. Under the constitution, New Granada became an integral State, and the powers of government were divided into legislative, judicial and executive, each independent of the other. In 1843, the constitution was reformed, but without any material change in the organization of the government. Slavery was entirely abolished, January 1, 1852. The people are hospitable, great haters of military rule, industrious, and well calculated to advance in prosperity and happiness. Into details of the disputes and dissensions of the last eight or ten years, it is not material here to enter. The most troublesome of these was the conflict in 1867, between President Mosquera and Congress, which ended in the arrest and exile of Mosquera. He had been playing the part of dictator rather freely, and on trial, in October, was condemned to imprisonment for two years and a nominal fine. The imprisonment was subsequently commuted to exile. The Darien Canal project has received much and careful attention, and a treaty with the United States been formed with reference to it. The introduction of Coolie laborers, under contract, is now fully established.

VENEZUELA.

Venezuela is a republic of South America, lying between N. lat. 1° 12′ and 12° 16′; W. long. 59° 42′ and 73° 17′; bounded on the N. by the Caribbean Sea; E. by the Atlantic and British Guiana; S. by Brazil, and W. by Colombia. Length from E. to W. 860 miles; breadth from 400 to 640; area 368,235 square miles; population, about 1,500,000; capital, Caracas, population 50,000. The name Venezuela, or Little Venice, is due to Vespucci and Ojeda, the discoverers of the lake of Maracaibo, who found the native villages there built like Venice on piles in the midst of the water. The coasts of the country are much varied both in their outline and in their character. From the Boca de Navios, the most southerly and principal mouth of the Orinoco, which makes the boundary of British Guiana, to the Gulf of Paria, the coast is occupied by the delta of the Orinoco, a low and alluvial region, intersected by the numerous branches of the river, and covered in some parts with gigantic forests. Off this part of the coast lies the British island of Trinidad, forming the east side of the Gulf of Paria. The north side of the gulf is formed by the peninsula of Paria, terminating towards the east in the promontory of the same name. From this headland westward to the Punta d'Araya extends a series of bare rocks, at some places coming close down to the sea, and at others leaving a narrow sterile plain along the shore. Opposite this part of the coast is the island of Margarita, forming a province of the republic. South of the Punta d'Araya is the opening of the Gulf of Cariaco, which runs eastward into the land, and is separated from the sea by the narrow tongue of land terminating in the Punta d'Araya. Further west, the coast, which takes a gentle curve towards the south, becomes low and sandy, and is lined with many lagoons and salt marshes. At Cape Codera, about 200 miles west of the Gulf of Cariaco, its character entirely changes; and as far as Puerto Cabello, about 155 miles, a chain of lofty mountains rises steeply from the very edge of the water This is, in fact, the termination of one branch of the Andes. At Puerto Cabello, a low and sandy tract of coast succeeds; and here it takes a curve towards the north, continuing to have this character as far as the mouth of the Lake of Maracaibo. About the middle of this tract lies the peninsula of Paraguana, joined to the mainland by a long narrow isthmus. The whole length of the coast is 1584 miles, of which about 300 are washed by the Atlantic and Gulf of Paria, the rest by the Caribbean Sea. The interior of the country is no less diversified in its character than the coast. About a fourth of the whole area is occupied by mountains, and these belong to two different chains, the Andes and their branches, which occupy the north-west; and the mountains of Parima in the south and south-east of the State. Of the former range, it is only the eastern Cordillera that enters Venezuela. That ridge traverses Colombia, and near Pamplona in that country divides into two branches. The most westerly of these extends northwards along the frontier of Colombia, and terminates near the Lake of Maracaibo. It has few summits more than 4000 feet high, and is for the most part covered with dense forests. The other branch of the Cordillera enters Venezuela, and stretches about 300 miles in a north-east direction, covering a tract of country about thirty miles broad. It consists of an enormous mass of rocks, having in general narrow plateaux called *paramos* at the summit. These *paramos* are from 10,000 to 12,000 feet above the sea; but many of the summits rise higher: the Sierra Nevada de Merida, the only one above the snow-line, being 15,342 feet, and the Pichado de Mucuchies, 14,168 feet high. The sides of the mountains have generally steep declivities, but in some places they descend by terraces which are occupied by small plains. At the point where this range terminates, the coast-range, Sierra Costanera, which may be considered as a sort of branch or continuation of it, begins. This range, which consists of several ridges nearly parallel, reaches the sea near Puerto Cabello. The first of these branches is nowhere higher than 4200 feet; the second contains the summits called Silla de Caracas, 8808 feet, and Picache de Naiguata, 9480 feet above the sea; and the loftiest points in the third are the Cerro de Platilla, 6217 feet, and the Cerro Azul, 5816 feet in height. A small portion of the N.E. of the country is occupied by a range called the Bergantin mountains. In the southern part of Venezuela, on the borders of Brazil, and nearly half way between the Orinoco and the Amazon, a range of mountains called Sierra Parima stretches from west to east, diverging from the western extremity of the Pacaraima range. This region, however, still remains unexplored; it is covered with vast and dense forests; but would probably be capable of cultivation, as the mountains do not rise above 12,000 feet from the sea.

From these mountains to the coast-range, and from the delta of the Orinoco to the foot of the Andes, the whole of Venezuela is occupied by an immense plain. The portion of this region lying north of the Orinoco and its affluent the Meta, forms what are called the *llanos* or levels of Venezuela. These plains are estimated to cover an area of 116,592 square miles, and vary considerably in their elevation; some parts being very little raised above the level of the sea, while others, near the foot of the mountains, have a height of nearly 1300 feet. The whole are characterized by the absence of forests; the trees that do grow being found either singly or in small groups. South of the Meta lies a region of a very different character; for here the country is entirely covered with dense forests, which extend as far as the boundary of Brazil, and, indeed, even beyond the equator. But in this region the frontiers of Venezuela are uncertain; for, while it claims all the country to the east of 69 degrees of W. longitude, Colombia extends its boundaries as far east as the Orinoco.

Venezuela is on the whole well watered. The principal river is the Orinoco, which is the third in size of all the South American rivers. Of rivers not belonging to its basin, there are few of any size or importance. The Cuguni rises in the east of the country, flows eastward into British Guiana, and joins the Essequibo. Further west, the Guainia, or Rio Negro, an affluent of the Amazon, crosses the south-west corner of the State. The rivers that fall immediately into the Caribbean Sea are for the most part of small size; but some of them are navigable. The lakes and lagoons of Venezuela are numerous but small; that of Maracaibo, the only one of large size, is more properly a gulf than a lake, as it communicates by a narrow channel with the sea.

The climate of the country is various in different parts, owing to their different elevation. The whole of the State is divided by the natives into three regions or zones—the hot, temperate and cold countries. The first of these comprises all the land less than 2000 feet above the sea-level; the second all lying between 2000 and 7000 feet high; and the third all above 7000 feet. The first of these divisions is by far the most extensive, including all the *llanos* and wooded plains in the country. Here the climate is quite of a tropical character. The distinction of seasons is into wet and dry; the former corresponding to the winter, and the latter to the summer of temperate countries. Immediately after the autumnal equinox the rains begin, and continue in great abundance and with few intermissions during the whole winter; while hardly any rain falls in the summer. This alternation of season produces a vast difference in the appearance of the *llanos;* for they are transformed in the winter from vast pastures into an immense sheet of water. Along the coast the seasons are subject to various modifications; and in some places there are two wet and two dry seasons annually. About the delta of the Orinoco the climate is very unhealthy, owing to noxious exhalations; and elephantiasis and *goitre* are prevalent diseases. Nearly the whole of the country, especially the regions about the coast, is liable to violent earthquakes, which have frequently proved very destructive.

The vegetable productions of Venezuela are most abundant and varied. In the whole of the temperate zone palms of various kinds abound; among which is the cocoa-palm, yielding large quantities of oil for exportation. Along with these flourish many other native plants, such as pine-apples, tamarinds, mimosas, cactuses, and the cow-tree, which yields a fluid resembling milk. Among the larger indigenous trees are the *bauhinia*, of colossal size, the bombax, or silk cotton-tree, yielding a cottony matter, and the mahogany tree; while among plants that yield valuable drugs are the sarsaparilla and dragon's-blood plants. In the more elevated and temperate regions, cinchonas, which are valuable as febrifuges, abound; and in many places form by themselves immense forests. There, too, most of the grains of temperate countries grow well. The cold regions of Venezuela are distinguished by an alpine vegetation, gradually diminishing in amount towards the snow-line. Many European fruits have been introduced into the warm regions, especially vines, figs, pomegranates, oranges, limes and lemons, which succeed well. Tobacco of excellent quality is grown in the Bergantin mountains, and in the valley of Barinas in the north-east of the country; and throughout the whole of the State maize is cultivated. Rice is only grown in a few places; wheat only at a considerable elevation; and barley only on the slopes of the Andes. Almost all kinds of pulse are raised, as well as potatoes and other edible roots. Domestic animals form, to a large extent, the riches of Venezuela. The *llanos* afford abundant pasture for cattle, horses, mules and asses; and great numbers of these animals are reared on them. Sheep and goats are not kept in large numbers, except in a few places. The chief of the wild animals are the jaguar or American tiger, hunted for its valuable skin, and the puma or lion; but both these animals are becoming rare in the country. The tiger-cat, the ounce, the tapir, varieties of the deer, and the wild hog, and many different kinds of monkeys, also abound in the forests. The birds of the country are numerous, including various species of falcons, hawks, parrots, pelicans, wild geese, etc. Two kinds of whales are frequently seen off the coast of the Caribbean Sea, and all the rivers, lakes and seas abound in fish of various kinds. The mineral resources of the country are not very great. Gold has been worked at some places in the Andes, but never with much success. Silver, tin and copper also exist, but only the last has been profitably worked. Coal occurs in the coast-range; petroleum and a kind of natron are obtained in various places; and large quantities of salt are produced in the salt-works along the Lake of Maracaibo, and on the peninsulas of Paraguana and Araya.

Manufactures in Venezuela are still in their infancy, being carried on to a very small extent, as the industry of the people is chiefly directed to agricultural and pastoral pursuits. Tocuyo, Barguisemeto, Trujillo, and Merida, are the principal manufacturing towns; and the articles made there are chiefly those required for domestic use; such as coarse cotton cloth, hammocks, straw hats and pottery. There are also a large number of tanneries in the country, as most of the leather used is of home manufacture. The commerce of Venezuela, which declined very much during the civil war that raged in the country, has since somewhat improved.

The principal seaport in the country is La Guaira, on the Caribbean Sea, near Caracas, the capital. The value of the exports from that port alone, consisting chiefly of cocoa, coffee, cotton, hides, indigo, and tobacco, amounted, according to a recent estimate, to $3,000,000; while the value of the imports in the same year was $3,380,000. At Puerto-Cabello the value of the exports was $2,900,000; and that of the imports $1,200,000; and at Bolivar and the other ports on the Orinoco, the exports were valued at $585,000; and the imports at $630,000. The most important article of export is coffee, of which Puerto Cabello, in the year 1867–8, exported 18,300,000 pounds.

The population of Venezuela, like that of the whole of what was formerly Spanish America, is of a very mixed character. There are the aboriginal inhabitants, the descendants of the Spaniards and Africans, and the various races that have been produced by the intermixture of these. The pure natives are copper-colored, some of them very dark, and others almost as fair as Europeans. They are little, and not very strong, but have large heads and limbs. Many of them are altogether independent, divided into about 100 tribes, speaking different dialects, and occupying the unexplored forests of the interior. Others are in subjection to the government of the country, but live separately, preserving their own manners and customs; while some have been entirely mixed with the more civilized races. The negroes were formerly kept in slavery, but since the prohibition of the slave-trade in 1830, the slaves had been very much reduced in number; and by a decree passed in 1854, they were emancipated. The Creoles, or people of European descent, form only about a fourth-part of the entire population; but the mixed races, Mestizos, Mulattoes, Zambos, etc., are much more numerous. The government of Venezuela is republican, being framed on the model of that of the United States. The political franchise is vested in all the people who possess a certain property qualification and are able to read and write. They choose electors, one for every four thousand, for two years; and these again appoint the president, vice-president, and members of the legislative body. This last consists of a senate, in which each province is represented by two members; and a house of representatives, consisting of one member for every twenty-five thousand inhabitants. The president and vice-president, who exercise the executive power, are elected for four years; and half of the legislative body retire biennially. Besides the central government, each province has a legislature of its own, chosen in the same way, whose acts are subject to the approval or disapproval of the central legislature. The religion of the country is the Roman Catholic; the other sects, though tolerated, are not allowed the public exercise of their religion. Education is provided for by law, but has as yet made very little progress in the country. The principal event in the history of Venezuela is the war of independence against the Spaniards, in which the famous Bolivar was the active and enterprising champion of liberty. In 1821, after securing its independence, Venezuela was united with New Granada and Ecuador to form the republic of Colombia; but this only lasted till 1830, when the three States again became independent. Since gaining its independence, the country has been in a very disturbed state, and its finances have fallen into almost total ruin, the expenditure, some years, being over three times as much as the revenue, and a large debt having been contracted. In June, 1868, the internal debt was $18,297,311; the external debt, $53,618,801. During the last year, the government issued a decree, appropriating one half of the revenue of the country for the payment of all debts; 15 per cent. of this half is to be applied to the settlement of international claims, as the American, French, English, etc. The gross revenue being estimated at $4,000,000 (Venezuela currency), would leave the sum of $300,000 for this purpose. If the country can escape the perpetual contests and fightings of military adventurers, and men ambitious of power, and can attain settled, secure and efficient government, there is room for hope in the future. At present, however, we regret to say, the prospect is anything but bright or cheering.

ECUADOR.

Ecuador is a republic in South America, lying under the equator, from which it takes its name. It corresponds, with a trifling difference, to the old Spanish province or intendancy of Quito; but formed anciently the northern portion of the empire of the Incas of Peru, and latterly the south-west province of the now dissolved republic of Colombia. It is situate between S. Lat. 6° and N. Lat. 2°, and W. Lon. 70° and 82°,—being 830 miles in length from east to west, and 560 in breadth from north to south,—and only contains an area of about 220,000 square miles. Population, 1,300,000. It is bounded on the south by Peru, on the north by Colombia, on the east by Brazil, and on the west by the Pacific Ocean; but the boundaries of the eastern portion of Ecuador are not yet very well defined. The western portion, to the extent of about a third of its area, is covered with mountains. These consist principally of a cross section of the Andes, about 7° in length, forming at the northern and southern boundaries respectively the two large mountain-knots of Loja or Loxa, and Pastos. Between these knots the range of the Andes forms a single mass, about 300 miles in length and from seventy to eighty miles in breadth, rising with a steep acclivity at the distance of about seventy to ninety miles from the shores of the Pacific Ocean, to a mean elevation of about 9000 feet, and forming on its summit a long plateau or table-land, bordered on each side by parallel ranges of mountains, which again rise several thousand feet higher, and have their peaks covered with perpetual snow. The highest, or those on the east and west sides of these ranges, are about fifty miles apart, while the lower and interior ranges occupy a breadth of several miles on each side, leaving between them a narrow belt of flat ground—from fifteen to twenty-four miles in width, and 300 miles in length from north to south—divided into three parts by three cross ridges. The southernmost portion forms the valley of Cuenca, which has an elevation of about 7800 feet; the northernmost is the celebrated plain of Quito, which has a mean elevation of about 9600 feet; and between them is the valley of Alausi and Ambato, with a mean elevation of 8000 feet. The valley of Cuenca is connected with the middle valley by the pass of Assuay, the crest of which rises to the great elevation of 15,520 feet; but the ridge between Alausi and Quito, called the *Alto de Chisinche*, rises only about 500 feet above the contiguous plains on the north, and is of inconsiderable width. Among the lofty summits that border these valleys, the following table gives the names of the principal, with their elevation in feet above the level of the sea:—

	Feet.
Chimborazo	21,424
Cayambe-Urcu	19,534
Antisana	19,137
Cotopaxi	18,875
Iliniza	17,376
Sangay	16,827
Chumbal	16,824
Carguairazo	16,663
Cotocache	16,448
Tunguragua	15,960
Pichincha	15,936

With the exception of Chimborazo, all these are active, or only recently quiescent volcanoes; and the surrounding districts are subject to frequent earthquakes, some of which have been terribly destructive.

Between the Andes and the sea the country is covered with mountains, which, however, do not seem to form continuous ridges. The shores themselves are high, rising along the Pacific with a bold and broken line of gulfs, bays, and headlands, except at the S.W., where the Gulf of Guayaquil, seventy miles wide, terminates inland, with an alluvial valley, or long plain, several miles in breadth, and so low as to be always flooded in the rainy season. In the bosom of the gulf lies the island of *Puna*, with an area of more than 200 square miles, but inhabited only by a few fishermen. To the eastward the Andes sink abruptly into the great plain which extends eastward to the Atlantic Ocean along the River Amazon and its mighty tributaries, some of which have their sources among the mountains of Ecuador. In this direction flow the waters of the valleys of Cuenca and Alausi, and Hambato, while those of Quito find their way to the Pacific through the rivers of Patias and Esmeraldas. So far as within this State, the great plain is partly wooded and partly a savannah interspersed with many lagunes and stagnant pools, and intersected by innumerable streams flowing from the Andes. Granite seems to form the basis of the whole range of the Andes, but it rarely appears on the surface. Gneiss is sometimes found in connection with the granite, but mica-schist is by far the commonest of the crystalline rocks. Quartz is likewise very abundant, and vast tracts of red sandstone with gypseous and saliferous marls occur near Quito. Porphyry and greenstone abound all over the range, and great masses of trachyte, from 14,000 to 18,000 feet thick, are visible on Chimborazo and Pichincha. Basalt, of columnar structure, inclosing olivine, and overlaid with thick beds of clay, is found on the table-land of Quito. Immense quantities of lava, tufa, obsidian, and other volcanic products, are likewise found, particularly along the western face of the Andes.

Although Ecuador lies under the equator, the great elevation of the mountain mass of the Andes renders the climate, in the elevated districts, mild and temperate. In the valley of Quito there prevails an everlasting spring, so equal in its temperature that vegetation never ceases; and the city has acquired the title of *Sempre verde* (ever-green), and *Eterna primavera* (everlasting spring). The change of seasons is scarcely perceptible, while the mean temperature of the day, all the year round, varies only from 60° to 67°, and that of night from 48° to 52°. The season between September and May is called winter, and the rest of the year summer; but the winter is only distinguishable by a somewhat greater quantity of rain, and the summer by a greater number of fine days. All the year round, however, scarcely a day passes without rain. In the mornings and evenings the sky is generally clear and serene, but in the afternoon it is generally overcast with dark clouds, which pour down torrents of rain, often accompanied with awful storms of thunder. Sometimes, however, the rain continues all night, and occasionally three or four days together. Wind blows continually along the valley, either from the north or from the south, but never with great violence. In the low country on the coasts the climate is very different. At Guayaquil the temperature is generally between 98° and 104°, and people complain of cold when it falls to 84° or 86°. In the other valleys along the coast the mean temperature of the year varies between 78° and 82°; but from December to April the heat rises to 95°, and during these months rain falls with little interruption, frequently accompanied with violent tempests. The floods of that season are so great, that in the valley of Guayaquil the country becomes one sheet of water even to the base of the Andes, to which the people betake themselves for refuge, with their herds and flocks. Fevers, diarrhœas, dysentery, vomiting, and spasms, then prevail, and the mortality is often very great. On the acclivity of the Andes, at the elevation of 3000 to 5000 feet, a soft spring temperature prevails, never varying more than 7° or 8°, and the mean temperature of the year being from 68° to 70°. The great eastern plain has a hot climate, the mean temperature being probably from 75° to 85°. The heat sometimes rises to 95°; but every day, early in the afternoon, a wind, generally accompanied with rain, begins to blow from the eastward with great force, and continues till sunset.

In the low countries that flank the base of the Andes the banana, plantain, cacao, jatropha, which produces cassava and manioc, the cotton tree, indigo, coffee, and the sugar-cane abound; beneath the elevation of 4000 feet, the plants chiefly cultivated for food are the sweet potato, manioc, yam, and banana, with rice, maize, and some legumes; but above 3100 feet most of these become rare, and thrive only in particular situations. The sugar-cane, however, has been grown so far up as 7500 feet. In some of the valleys are extensive plantations of sugar-cane, cotton, tobacco, and cocoa. The valley of Guayaquil is particularly fertile; the soil is alluvial, and there are few spots even between the tropics which can vie with it in richness and variety of vegetation. It is covered with groves of every kind of tropical fruits, either wild or cultivated, as the pine-apple, pomegranate, orange, lime, lemon, peach, apricot, granadilla, tuna, and paca. In the same region are found the olive, pepper plant, tomatoes, and sweet potatoes, gum copal, copaiba balsam, carana, dragon's blood, sarsaparilla, and vanilla. To these succeed, in the humid and shaded clefts on the slopes of the mountains, tree ferns and cinchona or Peruvian bark, the finest kind of which is obtained about eight to twelve miles south of Loja among the mountains of Uritusinga, Vallanaco, and Rumusitana, where the trees that yield it grow in a soil resting on mica-slate and gneiss, at the moderate elevation of 5756 to 7673 feet above the level of the sea. Between the elevation of 6000 and 9000 feet is the region best suited for the European cereals. Wheat will not form the ear lower than at 4500, or ripen higher than at 10,000 feet; but barley and rye grow at an elevation 2500 feet still higher. To these may be added the guinoa, a most useful production for domestic purposes. In this region also, and a little above it, grow the potato and its congeners, all of which are extensively used as food; the chick pea, broad bean, cabbage, and other European vegetables, are likewise abundant. Within the cereal limits are found the oak, elm, ash, and beech, which never descend lower than 5500 feet, and are seldom found higher than 9200 feet above the level of the sea. Higher up, the larger forest trees, except the pine, begin to disappear; and on the mountains of Quito the escallonia mark the highest limit of trees at an elevation of 11,600 feet. The bejarias, the highest of shrubs, terminate at 13,400 feet, above which in rich and beauteous verdure, rises the zone of the grasses. Above these, among the trachyte rocks, only lichens, lecideas, and the brightly colored dust-like lepraria are met with; and to these succeed the region of perpetual snow.

In some parts of the low country the air

swarms with musquitoes and other flies still more tormenting, while the ground teems with snakes, centipedes, and other reptiles. The banks of the great rivers are crowded with caymans or alligators. Bats are exceedingly numerous and of great size; the forests of the warmer regions abound with armadillos, monkeys, and cavies; and everywhere are found the jaguar, the puma, the ounce, the ocelot, and several varieties of the wild cat. The pecary and deer are likewise common, as well as that singular animal the ant-eater. The characteristic animals of the Andes are the llama, the guanaco, the vicuna and the paco or alpaca, some of which are trained as beasts of burden, while others, particularly the vicunas, run wild among the mountains, where they are hunted by the Indians. Sheep and cattle are reared in great numbers, especially the former, in the valleys of the Andes, and on the declivities of the mountains. Horses, asses, and mules, are reared in sufficient numbers to be articles of export. The chief of the birds is the condor, which is found all along the Andes southward as far as the Strait of Magellan, but nowhere to the north of the equator. The turkey, vulture, and gallinago, are frequently met with, together with many kinds of smaller birds. In some districts, particularly along the coasts, considerable quantities of bees-wax are collected; and higher up there are spots in which the cochineal insect is reared. Along the rivers of the great plain turtles are numerous; and their fat, called *manteca* butter, forms a considerable article of trade. Fishing is carried on to some extent along the coasts, and a good deal of salt-fish is prepared. A murex is also found which yields a juice used in dyeing purple.

Ecuador is less rich in minerals, especially in the precious metals, than any other of the South American States. There are indeed several mines of gold and silver, but the yearly product is inconsiderable. In some places are found lead and quicksilver, but the latter is found, as usual, in combination with sulphur, in the form of cinnabar. Near Azogue, fifteen miles N.E. by E. of Cuenca, the ore is found in an immensely thick bed of quartzose sandstone, containing fossil wood and asphalt. Sulphur is prepared in considerable quantities; gold has been washed from the sands of some of the rivers; and salt is obtained from sea-water along the coasts. The settled population is composed of Spanish creoles of pure descent, mestizos, mulattoes, and negroes, the greater part of them being agriculturists, graziers, and growers of cocoa. These form about half of the population. The other half are native Indians, of whom those that live among the mountains are mostly agriculturists, cultivating their lands with much care, and making for themselves coarse stuffs of wool and cotton. The Indians who inhabit the eastern plains are in a much lower degree of civilization. They cultivate only small patches of ground, and apply themselves chiefly to hunting and fishing. Three-fourths of the population dwell in the western or mountainous part of the State; and the total number, as above stated, is 1,300,000. The manufactures are unimportant, consisting chiefly of coarse woolen and cotton cloths and other necessary articles. The foreign trade is almost confined to Guayaquil, and is of small importance. Value of exports, 1868–9, from the port of Guayaquil, amounted to over $3,000,000. The worth of cocoa alone was estimated to be more than $2,000,000.

Till 1812, Ecuador remained a portion of the Spanish portion of the Indies. It then threw off the yoke of Spain, and in 1821 became a part of the newly constituted republic of Colombia. This union, however, lasted only till 1831, when Ecuador became an independent State. It has gone through numerous revolutions; and the democratic party having gained the ascendancy, there was a tendency to adopt the United States of America as their political model. The republic, in consequence, received a new and more liberal constitution; the Jesuits were expelled; and laws were made for the abolition of slavery. The government is vested in a president, with a vice-president and two chambers, all elective; but the constitution is still notably complicated by what has always been its principal characteristic, a predominating mixture of military despotism, the president being always the master of the State. More, perhaps, than any other country of South America, Ecuador has been slow in the development of its resources and national industry. Frequent revolutions have paralyzed its trade, and prevented the regulation of its finances. No interest has been paid on its public debt since 1826. It is emphatically the country of natural convulsions and political revolutions. In August, 1868, one of the most terrific earthquakes on record visited Ecuador; in the province of Imbalura the destruction was fearful, probably of more than 30,000 persons in all. For administrative purposes the republic is divided into the three departments of Ecuador, Guayaquil, and As suay; and these are subdivided into the seven provinces of Quito, Riobamba, Ibarra, Guayaquil, Babahoyo, Cuenca, Loja, or Loxa (Loh-ha), and Jaen de Bracamor. The State likewise claims the sovereignty of the Islas de los Galapagos, or islands of land turtles, lying under the equator at a distance of 700 to 900 miles from the mainland. The chief towns are, Quito, with from 50,000 to 80,000 inhabitants; Guayaquil, 25,000; Cuenca, 20,000; Riobamba, 15,000; Loja, Babahoyo and Ibarra, about 10,000 each. Quito is beautifully situated in the elevated plain to which it gives its name; and Guayaquil on the banks of a navigable river, opening into the spacious bay to which it gives its name.

GUIANA.

Guiana, Guyana, or Guayana, an extensive territory in the north-eastern part of South America, comprehending in its widest acceptation all that extent of country lying between the rivers Amazon and Orinoco, between Lat. 3° 30′ S., and 8° 40′ N., and Long. 50° 22′ and 68° 10′ W. It is bounded on the N. by the Orinoco and the Atlantic, E. by the Atlantic, S. by the Amazon and the Rio Negro, and W. by the Orinoco and the Cassiquiare. Its greatest length from E. to W. is about 1,200 miles, and its greatest breadth about 850 miles; estimated area 700,000 square miles. This vast territory is divided into Brazilian (formerly Portuguese) Guiana, Venezuelan (formerly Spanish) Guiana, and Colonial Guiana. The two former, comprising about five-sixths of the entire region, are now included within the limits of their respective countries; while Colonial Guiana is that to which the general term of Guiana is now commonly applied. It is subdivided into British, Dutch, and French Guiana.

Guiana, *British*, or *Demerara*, the most westerly of the three colonies, is bounded on the N. and N.E. by the Atlantic, E. by Dutch Guiana, from which it is separated by the River Corentyn, S. by Brazil, and W. by Venezuela. It lies between N. Lat. 0° 40′ and 8° 40′, and W. Long. 57° and 61°, and has an estimated area of 70,000 square miles; but the possession of much of this has been disputed by Brazil and Venezuela. It is divided into three counties, Demerara, Essequibo, and Berbice, so named from the three principal rivers which drain them. Demerara, situated between the other two, occupies the centre of the seaboard for nearly ninety miles. To the N.W. the county of Essequibo stretches along the coast towards the swamps and forests of the western frontier; and to the S.E. lies the county of Berbice. The entire coast of

British Guiana is low, and generally bordered with a sandy flat extending far out to sea, so that vessels drawing more than twelve feet of water cannot approach within two or three miles of land. The rivers, too, deposit at their mouths large quantities of mud and sand, and are thus inaccessible to vessels of large size. Extending from low-water mark to a distance of five or six miles inland, is a tract of rich alluvial soil of recent formation. This is succeeded by a flat, narrow reef of sand running exactly parallel with the present line of coast. Running parallel to this reef, at irregular distances, varying from ten to twenty miles, is a second and higher range, composed of coarse white sand; and which at a period more remote probably formed the sea-limit. In the wet seasons the intermediate tract between these two reefs becomes the bed of extensive savannahs; for the creeks being then unable to carry off the torrents of rain which fall, overflow their level banks, and inundate the surrounding country to the depth of five or six feet. On the return of dry weather the waters gradually subside, leaving behind them a thick layer of decayed grasses and aquatic plants which had floated and flourished on their surface, and these in time produce a vegetable mould of considerable thickness. The high land does not rise immediately from the plain to a great elevation, but begins with a range of sand hills of from 50 to 200 feet above the plain. Behind these the high land stretches out in level or undulating plains, rising here and there into eminences. About N. Lat. 5°, a mountain chain, an offset of the Orinoco mountains, and composed of granite, gneiss, and other primitive rocks, runs from west to east through this territory, forming large cataracts where it is crossed by the rivers, and rising frequently to the height of 1,000 feet above the level of the sea. About a degree further south is the Pacaraima chain, which, in like manner, runs from west to east, and is of primitive formation. The plains south of this range are in general level, and form extensive savannahs covered with grasses and plants. The Sierra Acarai is a densely wooded chain of mountains, forming the southern boundary of Guiana, and the watershed between the basins of the Amazon and the Essequibo. The principal river of British Guiana is the Essequibo, which rises in the Sierra Acarai, and after a course of at least 600 miles, discharges itself into the ocean by an estuary twenty miles in width, in N. Lat. 7°, W. Long. 58° 40′. In the estuary of the Essequibo are a group of beautiful islands partially cultivated, the principal of which are Varken or Hog Island, about twenty-one miles in length by three in breadth, Wakenaam and Leguan, each about twelve miles by three, and Tiger Island, about half that size. The entrance is difficult and dangerous, even for vessels of small size, on account of the banks of mud and sand. Its course lies through forests of the most gigantic vegetation. The Demerara or Demerary rises probably near N. Lat. 5°, and after a northward course, nearly parallel with the Essequibo, of more than 200 miles, it enters the Atlantic near N. Lat. 6° 50′, W. Long. 58° 20′. It is navigable for 85 miles, and at its mouth at Georgetown it is more than a mile and a half across. Farther east runs the Berbice, whose source is probably about N. Lat. 3° 40′. It joins the Atlantic by an estuary five miles in width, ten miles N. of New Amsterdam, and in N. Lat. 6° 21′, W. Long. 57° 12′. It is navigable for 165 miles from the sea, by vessels drawing seven feet water. The Corentyn, which forms the eastern boundary of British Guiana, and probably has its source in the Sierra Acarai, flows generally northward and falls into the Atlantic in N. Lat. 6°, W. Long. 57°. It is navigable for boats for 150 miles. The mineral productions of Guiana are necessarily but imperfectly known. Clays of various kinds, including excellent pipe-clay, are found near the coast. The chief rocks are granite, porphyry, gneiss, clay-slate, sandstone, etc. Traces of iron are found in various parts; and gold has been discovered in considerable quantities on the Upper Essequibo. The climate of Guiana is more healthy than that of most places in the West Indies. Its salubrity has been much increased since the occupation of the country by Europeans, the gradual clearing and cultivation of the surface having done much to mitigate those diseases so fatal in a low, marshy, and hot region. The year is divided into two wet and two dry seasons. The long rainy season sets in about the middle of April, when light showers begin to fall. The rain increases till the middle of June, when it falls in torrents; in the beginning of July these heavy rains begin to decrease; and in August the long dry season begins, and continues till November. December and January constitute the short rainy season, and February and March the short dry season. The thermometer seldom rises above 90°, and rarely falls below 75°. The mean annual temperature at Georgetown is 81° 2′; the total annual fall of rain averages about 100 inches. The vegetation of Guiana is most luxuriant. The interior is thickly wooded with valuable timber, with the exception of the swamps of Berbice and the savannahs. The trees are of great size, and many of them are valuable for their timber or their fruits, or as dye-woods. Medicinal plants, including quassia, gentian, the castor-oil plant, and many others, are abundant. The domestic animals are the same as those in England, and the wild animals are those common to tropical South America generally. Black cattle here attain a larger size than in Europe, but their flesh is not so tender and so fine flavored. The wool of the sheep is converted into hair. Game, chiefly deer, range the upper savannahs. Tigers, little inferior in size to those of Asia, but different in character, being rarely known to attack man, abound; as do also jaguars, which prey upon the herds of wild cattle and horses that graze upon the extensive plains among the mountains. Among the other animals are the tapir, armadillo, agouti, ant-bear, sloth, and a great variety of monkeys. Lizards, snakes, and alligators are numerous. There are several kinds of parrots, macaws, and humming birds; also the flamingo, Muscovy duck, toucan, spoonbill, and vampire bat. Troublesome insects are numerous, as might be expected from the swampy nature of the coast districts. The rivers and coasts abound with a great variety of fish.

The cultivated portion of British Guiana is merely a narrow strip along the sea-coast, and for a few miles up the rivers, including a portion of the islands of Essequibo. The whole surface of the coast lands being on a level with high-water mark, when these lands are drained and cultivated they consolidate and become fully a foot below it, so that the estates require to be protected from inundation by dams and sluices. Each estate has therefore a strong dam or embankment in front; while a similar erection at the back or inland boundary, as well as on each side, is requisite to keep off the immense body of water accumulated on the savannahs during the wet seasons, and which, if not repelled, would rush down to the sea, carrying everything before it. The state of his dams, therefore, requires the planter's unremitting attention; not the slightest hole or leakage is allowed to exist in them, and by law their wilful injury is considered felony. One inundation destroys a sugar estate for eighteen months, and a coffee one for six years. Inside and at the foot of these dams are trenches twelve to eighteen feet wide and five deep, running round the whole plantation, and into these, smaller trenches and open drains convey the water that falls upon the land. These large trenches discharge their contents into the sea through one or more sluices, which are opened as the tide ebbs, and shut against the returning flood. The staple productions of the colony are sugar, coffee and cotton. In proportion to the sugar obtained the quantity of molasses is large, owing partly to the defects of the common process of preparation, but chiefly to the fact that the soil is so rich an alluvium, and so abundant in alkaline and earthy saline matter. Little of the molasses is boiled down to sugar in the colony; it is chiefly made into rum, or sold to the refiners, by whom it is much prized. Although the rum produced in this colony does not equal in character that of Jamaica, it yet occupies a respectable place in the market. The quantity exported in 1851 was 15,848 puncheons. Indian-corn, rice, tobacco, indigo, sweet potatoes, yams, and arrowroot, are also cultivated.

The constitution of British Guiana still retains traces of its Dutch origin. The government is vested in a governor and a court of policy; the latter composed of ten members, five being government officers (the governor, chief-justice, and colonial secretary, attorney-general, and collector of customs), and five elected from the colonists by the College of Justice. This college is composed of seven members chosen for life by the inhabitants possessing the right of suffrage. A property qualification is required in order to become a member of the legislative assembly. Neither ministers of religion nor schoolmasters can, however, be chosen for either of the chambers. For electoral purposes the colony is divided into five districts. Electors must be in possession of an income of six hundred dollars, or pay twenty dollars per annum of direct taxes, with some other minor qualifications. The supreme civil court consists of a chief judge, two puisne judges, a secretary, registrar, and accountant. The colony is also divided into nine judicial districts, each under the charge of a stipendiary magistrate appointed and removable only by the secretary for the colonies, assisted by unpaid justices holding their commissions from the governor. The population of British Guiana is composed of aboriginal tribes and foreign settlers. The aborigines consist of six tribes of Indians, a copper-colored, lank-haired race, and evidently members of the one great family which is spread over the entire continent of America. When slavery existed these were found useful allies and auxiliaries of the planters in capturing runaway negroes who had taken refuge in the "bush." They still enjoy protection from the government, as far as is possible. Nor is their spiritual welfare neglected. Numerous schools and missions have been established by the bishop for their instruction in the remotest parts of his diocese. Religion was here in a very neglected state till 1827, when British Guiana was included in the see of Bishop Coleridge; and shortly after this it was divided into parishes. In 1838, an archdeaconry was constituted, and there were then thirteen clergymen of the Church of England in the colony. In 1842, the number had increased to twenty-eight, and the colony was erected into a bishopric, with a salary of £2,000 per annum attached. In 1851, there were one hundred and twelve churches and chapels in British Guiana; of these forty-one belong to the Church of England, the remainder to other denominations of Protestants. The Roman Catholics had three churches. The population is estimated to be 136,000, of whom 96,500 are whites, 8,000 coolies, and 15,000 negroes.

It is generally believed that this portion of South America was discovered by Vicente Yanez Pinzon, a Spanish navigator, in 1499. In 1580 the first settlement was formed by the Dutch on the rivers Pomeroon and Essequibo, and they afterwards established themselves in other places. The English began to form settlements, about 1630, in the neighborhood of the rivers Berbice and Surinam. Most of Guiana, however, remained in the hands of the Dutch till 1796, when it surrendered to the English. It was restored to the Dutch in 1802; but was again taken by the English on the breaking out of the war in 1803, and has since remained in their possession. In 1831, Demerara, Essequibo, and Berbice were formed into one colony, under the name of British Guiana. In 1834, slavery ceased in the colony, but parliament at the same time decreed that the negroes should undergo an apprenticeship: this system was abandoned in 1838. The revenue is estimated to be about $1,000,000, and the expenditures not very much less.

Guiana, *Dutch*, or *Surinam*, lies between British and French Guiana, being separated from the former on the west by the River Corentyn, and from the latter on the east by the Maroni; on the north it has the Atlantic, and on the south Brazil. It lies between north latitude 1° 30′ and 6°, and west longitude 53° 30′ and 57° 30′, being three hundred miles in length from north to south, and two hundred and sixty in extreme breadth. Area, about thirty thousand square miles. Population, fifty-three thousand, of whom five-sixths are estimated to be negroes. In physical geography, climate, productions, etc., it differs but little from British Guiana. The principal river is the Surinam, which flows northward through the center of the territory and falls into the Atlantic after a course of nearly three hundred miles. It is navigable for large ships for about twelve miles from its mouth. Along the coast and on the banks of the rivers are many settlements and plantations; and the higher parts of the country are occupied chiefly by the Maroons, the descendants of runaway negroes. In the last century they were very troublesome to the colonists, but they have now adopted more settled habits. Slavery was abolished here by the Dutch government, in 1851, but, in lieu of compensation, the slaves were to remain apprenticed and work without wages to their proprietors for twelve years. The colony is ruled by a governor appointed by the crown, and a council elected by the freeholders. Justice is administered by a supreme court, courts of minor jurisdiction, and a court of inheritance and orphans. The receipts are estimated to amount to $450,000; the expenditures to $420,000. The chief productions are sugar, rum, molasses, coffee, cacao, and cotton. Its chief trade is with Holland. Imports amount to $816,474; exports, $1,312,000. Paramaribo, the capital, is situated on the right bank of the Surinam, about ten miles from its mouth. It is built in the Dutch style, with wide and straight streets planted with orange trees; and the houses are generally two stories in height, and built of wood. Population about twenty thousand. A little north of the town is the fort of Zeelandia, where the governor resides, and where are also most of the government establishments.

Guiana, *French*, or *Cayenne*, is the smallest and most eastern of three colonies. It lies between north latitude 2° and 6°, and west longitude 51° 30′ and 54° 30′; being bounded on the north and north-east by the Atlantic, east and south by Brazil, and west by Dutch Guiana. It is about two hundred and fifty miles in length from north to south, and varies in breadth from one hundred to one hundred and fifty miles. Area, fourteen thousand square miles. It has a coast line of two hundred miles, extending from the Maroni to the Oyapoc. The low alluvial tract along the coast is of great fertility. The mountain chains run east and west, and are almost wholly of granite, but do not attain a great elevation. The country is abundantly watered; and the coast-lands appear to be less unhealthy than in British Guiana. The island of Cayenne, at the mouth of the Oyak, is about thirty miles in circumference, and is separated from the continent by a narrow channel. The roadstead at the mouth of the Oyak, though small, is the best on the coast, having everywhere from twelve to thirteen feet of water. The capital, Cayenne, is situated on the northern side of this island, and contains five thousand inhabitants. The new town is well built, and has good streets; the government house is in the old town. The harbor is protected by a fort and several batteries. The colony is divided into two districts, Cayenne and Sinnamary, and fourteen communes. The government is vested in a governor, a privy council, and colonial council composed of sixteen members elected by the colonists. Besides the staples of British and Dutch Guiana, its productions comprise pepper (including Cayenne, which is so called from the island of that name), cloves, cinnamon, and nutmegs. Trade is chiefly with France and its colonies, and is valued at more than $2,500,000. The French first settled in Cayenne in 1604; the British and Portuguese captured the colony in 1809, but restored it to the French in 1814, in whose possession it still remains. Since 1848, it has been made a place of banishment for French political offenders. Population about twenty thousand, of whom about thirteen thousand are emancipated slaves.

PERU.

PERU, a republic of South America, lies between 3° 35′ and 21° 48′ south latitude, and 68° 10′ and 81° 30′ west longitude. It is bounded on the north by the republic of Ecuador, west by the Pacific Ocean, and east and south by the territories of Brazil and Bolivia. Its extreme length from north to south is about one thousand two hundred and fifty miles, and its breadth varies from sixty to about seven hundred and fifty miles, the width increasing gradually from south to north. Area, about 509,000 square miles; population estimated at about 2,500,000.

In the chapter devoted to a General View of America, we have already given (pp. 14–17) some notices of the ancient empire of Peru, advances towards civilization, political organization, government of the Incas, religious rites and observances, Manco Capac, character of the natives, etc. We shall now present a brief *resumé* of the history and condition of Peru from the time of the Spanish invasion and conquest to the present day. Balboa, the discoverer of the Pacific Ocean, made the earliest attempt to penetrate the Peruvian empire; but without success. In 1524, an expedition was fitted out, at the head of which was Francisco Pizarro, of low birth, totally uneducated, but of a daring spirit, and able to endure the greatest fatigue. Such qualities soon brought him into notice; and he was found to be possessed of others of a higher order, fitting him to command as well as to serve. He was one of those that had accompanied Balboa on the previous expedition, and gained the esteem of that general. Associated with him on the present occasion were Diego de Almagro, a man of mean birth, but a brave soldier, and Hernando de Luque, an ecclesiastic, who acted as priest and schoolmaster at Panama. The last of these was to contribute principally to the expenses of the expedition, while the others were to give their labor and experience, with what small funds they had. A vessel was speedily got ready, and Pizarro set sail from the port of Panama about the middle of November, 1524, with little more than a hundred men, Almagro being to follow in a second vessel of inferior size, as soon as it could be fitted out. The season of the year was the most unsuitable for the enterprise, and neither Pizarro nor Almagro was able to effect anything. They saw several villages and towns along the coast and were received with hospitality by the natives; but as they were not yet strong enough to venture upon conquest they refrained from perfidy and outrage. The governor at Panama frowned upon the matter and refused help. The greed of gold was so strong that Pizarro went to Spain in 1528, and the emperor, Charles V., gave him supreme authority over any country or people he might conquer. Almagro and Pizarro quarrelled, almost of course, as the former thought himself shabbily used; but the quarrel was patched up, and so, athirst for gold, they set out anew in January, 1531, for the conquest of Peru. They mustered in all about three hundred men, and had some four or five vessels for aid along the coast. Pizarro now considered himself in a position to enter upon his nefarious purposes. He accordingly passed over to Tumbez, and there learned that the country had been for some time distracted by a civil war between the two sons of the late monarch. Huayna Capac was the reigning Inca at the time when the Spaniards first visited the coast of Peru. He is represented as a prince distinguished both in peace and war. He brought under the sway of the Incas the powerful State of Quito, and reduced to subjection many of the independent tribes on the remote borders of his territory. He likewise pursued an enlightened policy towards his subjects, encouraging agricultural and other branches of industry, opening up new roads, and introducing the civilization of the Incas among the conquered nations. He is said to have been deeply impressed with the accounts brought to him of the white men. He saw in their ships and weapons indications of a civilization and power far superior to that of his own people; and he feared that at no distant day they would return. Huayna Capac died about 1529, leaving his kingdom of Peru to his eldest son Huascar, but Quito he left to his favorite son Atahuallpa, by a daughter of the conquered monarch. The two sons, however, did not long rest contented with their respective possessions and a civil war was the consequence. Victory at length declared for Atahuallpa; and Huascar was detained a close prisoner. These events occurred in the early part of 1532, and completely diverted the attention of the Peruvians from the circumstance of a foreign invader having landed on their soil. Pizarro at once saw the importance to him and his cause of this state of the country. After some time spent in reconnoitring the country, he fixed upon a spot in the rich valley of Tangarala as a site for a settlement. Hither accordingly the Spaniards removed and set about building a town, to which they gave the name of San Miguel. Pizarro here learned that the victorious Atahuallpa lay encamped about about ten or twelve days' journey off, and he marched out of San Miguel at the head of his small body of adventurers, amounting in all to one hundred and seventy-seven men, of whom sixty-seven were cavalry. Everywhere the people received them with confiding hospitality, and as yet the Spaniards saw it to be their interest to reciprocate their friendships. In the afternoon of the 15th of November, 1532, the Spaniards reached Caxamalca, which had been vacated by the inhabitants for their reception, and immediately they sent an embassy to the Inca inviting him to visit them in their new quarters. They were graciously received by the Inca, and he promised to pay them a visit on the following day. The reception prepared for the Inca was such as he little expected when he set out with an unarmed retinue to redeem his promise. He was borne on the shoulders of his principal attendants seated on a throne or couch resplendent with plates of gold and silver, enriched with precious stones, and adorned with waving plumes of the most gorgeous hues. When he entered the plaza or great square of the town, a dominican friar, Fray Vicente de Valverde, came forward with his breviary, or, according to other accounts, a Bible in one hand, a crucifix in the other, and, approaching the Inca, expounded to him the doctrines of the Christian religion, exhorting him to embrace the true faith, and to acknowledge himself a vassal of the Spanish crown. Enraged and astonished at this extraordinary proceeding, the Inca demanded by what authority he said these things. The friar handed him the book which he held in his hand. "This," said he, holding it to his ear for a moment, "tells me nothing," and dashed it to the ground with disdain. The monk immediately ran towards Pizarro, calling out that the Christian religion had been dishonored, and at a given signal the Spaniards, who had been concealed in the adjoining buildings rushed out upon the defenceless natives. The slaughter was immense on the side of the Indians; and the murderous nature of the attack may be gathered from the fact, that not a single Spaniard was killed or wounded with the exception of Pizarro, who received a slight wound on the hand by one of his own men. Atahuallpa himself was taken prisoner; and a rich booty was found in the

EXECUTION OF THE INCA OF PERU BY PIZARRO.

From the original painting by Chappel, in the possession of the publishers.

Johnson, Fry & Co. Publishers, New York.

Peruvian camp, consisting of gold and silver, precious stones, cotton, and woollen stuffs, etc. The captive monarch soon perceived that the love of gold was the prime motive that had brought the Spaniards into the country; and as the price of his liberty, he offered to Pizarro to fill the room in which they stood with gold as high as he could reach. This room is said to have been twenty-two feet long by seventeen wide, and the height nine feet from the floor. Pizarro, charmed with the idea of so much gold, and knowing how easy a matter it was to break faith with a captive, readily entered into the agreement, and the terms of it were duly drawn up by a notary. Atahuallpa therefore, with all haste, despatched couriers to Cuzco and all the principal places of the kingdom, with orders to forward the gold utensils and ornaments of the palaces, temples, etc., to Caxamalca without delay. In the meantime, the Spaniards were not disturbed, notwithstanding their perfidious conduct, and Almagro soon after arrived with a strong reinforcement of one hundred and fifty foot and fifty horse. This was about the middle of February, 1533; and now Pizarro found himself in a position to go forward with the conquest of the country. The whole of the Inca's ransom, however, had not yet arrived; but at length they agreed to accept what had already arrived in full of the obligation. The total amount of gold, when melted down, was found to be 1,326,539 *pesos de oro*, equivalent to about $18,000,000. Besides this there were a number of articles of very delicate workmanship, which were reserved for being sent as a present to the emperor. After deducting one-fifth for the crown, the rest was divided in certain proportions among the troops, Pizarro himself and his officers receiving sums in proportion to their rank. After dividing the spoil, it came to be considered what was to be done with the Inca, who now became clamorous for his liberty; but the Spaniards made short work of him; he was executed August 29th, 1533. Early in September, the Spaniards, now amounting to about five hundred men, of whom nearly one-third were cavalry, set out from Caxamalca for the capital. Pizarro halted for some time at Xauxa, in order to found there a Spanish colony. A detachment of sixty horse, under De Soto, having been sent forward to reconnoitre the country in advance, were attacked by a body of the natives, who fought with great fury, and the issue was doubtful, till the arrival of Almagro with a reinforcement of cavalry struck terror into the natives, and prevented them from renewing the contest. Soon after this, Manco Capac arrived in great state at the Spanish camp, and, announcing his title to the throne, claimed the protection of the white men. He was received with great cordiality and assured that they had come into the country in order to vindicate the claims of Huascar to the throne, and to punish the usurpation of his rival. Taking with him the Indian prince, Pizarro now resumed his march, and on the 15th of November, 1533, entered the Peruvian capital. This city far surpassed anything that they had yet seen in the New World. The population of the city itself is said to have amounted to two hundred thousand, and that of the suburbs to as many more. Though doubtless the inhabitants had concealed much of their treasures, yet the gold obtained here is said to have even exceeded that received as the ransom of the Inca. One of the first acts of Pizarro, after dividing the spoil, was to place Manco on the throne, in order to give his acts some air of authority with the natives. He afterwards organized a municipal government, and induced his soldiers to settle in the place by liberal grants of houses and land. In March, 1534, a Spanish force, amounting to five hundred men, under Don Pedro de Alvarado, arrived in the Bay of Caraques. He had come to take possession of Quito, which he believed or pretended to believe, was not included in Pizarro's territory; but he soon after agreed to hand over his fleet, forces, and stores to Pizarro for about $500,000.

Cuzco being found to be unsuitable as the

capital of the colony, it was resolved to build another near the coast; accordingly, in January, 1535, the new capital was founded in the valley of Rimac, and was called Lima. The Spaniards applied themselves with vigor to the task of building the new city, under the eye of their chief. In the meantime, Almagro had arrived at Cuzco and taken command of that capital, and here he received intelligence from Spain that he had received a grant of all the country lying south of the southern limit of Pizarro's territory. Almagro immediately laid claim to Cuzco as being within the bounds of his territory. He accordingly proceeded to exert his independent authority, and matters were approaching an open rupture, when Pizarro managed to get him to set out on the conquest of Chili.

Manco Capac, who had hitherto so tamely submitted to be a tool of the Spaniards, was nevertheless a person of some spirit and courage; and at length, exasperated by the repeated indignities to which he was exposed, he effected his escape from Cuzco, where he then was. A rising among the natives immediately followed, and Cuzco was besieged in February, 1536, by a force amounting, it is said, to 200,000 men. To add to the distress of the Spaniards, their city was set on fire by the burning arrows and red-hot stones of the natives, and more than one-half of it was reduced to ashes. They frequently sallied out of the town, but beyond killing a number of the natives, they effected no advantage, while the natives increased in skill and bravery with each contest. The rising had been general. Several of the Spaniards living upon their estates had been massacred; and a strong force had attempted to besiege Lima, but were put to flight. Several detachments had been sent by the governor to relieve Cuzco, but they were all cut off by the natives. The siege of Cuzco had now lasted more than five months, and as the season of planting had come on, Manco, fearing a famine, sent the greater part of his followers home, with orders to return and renew the blockade as soon as their field labors were over. New and greater trouble arose. Almagro had gone on his expedition against Chili, but met with such indifferent success that he returned with his men. The contest with Pizarro led to hostilities at once. Almagro at first was the more successful, but Pizarro proved too astute for him. A battle was fought at Las Salinas, near Cuzco, June 26, 1538, a bitter, savage fight, in which Pizarro gained his end. Cuzco was given up to pillage; Almagro was taken prisoner and thrown into irons, and shortly after was condemned and executed.

Pizarro's conduct now showed that he considered himself the undisputed possessor of all this vast kingdom. Instead of attempting to conciliate Almagro's party, he treated them with undisguised contempt; while many of his own adherents he disgusted by his haughty bearing, and by the manner in which he appropriated to himself, or bestowed on his brothers and favorites, all the most valuable districts of the country. But the time had not yet come for a revolt. One of his brothers visited Spain, but was soon put in prison, and lay there for twenty years. The state of Peru was now such as to demand the immediate interposition of government; but the mission was one of extreme difficulty, for Pizarro's power was now firmly established over the country, and he was not one readily to submit to any interference with his authority. At length Licentiate Vaca de Castro, a member of the Royal Audiencia of Valladolid, was selected for this delicate mission. He was to appear before Pizarro in the capacity of a royal judge, to consult with him on the redress of grievances, especially with reference to the natives, to transmit an account of the state of the country to the court at Castile, and, in the event of Pizarro's death, to take upon himself the government of the country. Almagro's son was living at Lima, and a conspiracy was formed to kill Pizarro, who seems to have despised the warnings he received. On the 26th of June, 1541, the conspirators to the number of eighteen or twenty, sallied out from Almagro's house, headed by Juan de Herrada, shouting "Long live the king; death to the tyrant." They gained the palace without opposition, and reached the apartment where their victim was conversing with some friends, having just risen from table. Hastily enveloping one arm in his cloak, and seizing a sword, he maintained for some time the unequal contest; but at length he received a deadly thrust in the throat, and fell to the ground, when he was immediately dispatched. Thus perished the man who had acquired for Spain the richest of her possessions,—a man possessed of great abilities, but whose perfidy and cruelty have left a stain upon his character that, however much it may be extenuated by the circumstances of his early life, and the times in which he lived, can never be removed.

On the death of Pizarro, the young Almagro was placed at the head of the government, but his authority was only tardily acknowledged in places at a distance from Lima. Vaca de Castro meanwhile received the news of the death of Pizarro at Popayan. He continued his march to Quito, where he was well received, and he now produced his royal commission to assume the government. Emissaries were dispatched to the principal towns, requiring their submission, while Castro himself continued his march slowly towards the south. Almagro meanwhile had proceeded to Cuzco, where he learned of the arrival of Castro at Lima. He tried to negotiate with Castro, but to no purpose; the sword as usual was the arbiter; and accordingly a battle took place near Chupas, September 16th, 1542. Almagro was defeated, and suffered the fate of his father. Castro having now got rid of his rival, gave his attention to the settlement of the country. He laid down laws for its better government, and attempted to ameliorate the condition of the natives by in some measure protecting them from the unjust exactions of their conquerors, and by establishing schools for teaching them Christianity. But while these gradual measures were being carried out in Peru, one of a much more sweeping nature was resolved upon in Spain. This was nothing less than the proclaiming all the Indians to be vassals of the crown of Spain, and thus only to be employed in voluntary labor, for which they were to receive a fair remuneration. Slaves were declared to be free on the death of their present proprietors; but all those held by persons in public offices, ecclesiastics, or persons criminally concerned in the feuds of Almagro and Pizarro, were to be immediately set at liberty. To carry out this measure, Blasco Nuñez Vela was appointed governor of Peru, with the title of Viceroy. A royal audience, consisting of four judges, was also named to assist him in administering the law. The news of this caused the greatest excitement in Peru. The viceroy reached Tumbez on the 4th March, 1544, and immediately began to act up to his instructions by liberating a number of slaves. The country was now in the greatest consternation, and all eyes were turned towards Gonzalo Pizarro, the last in the land of the family of that name. He was invited to Cuzco, and was there invested with the title of Procurator-General of Peru. The viceroy, meanwhile, had reached Lima, where he was installed in his new office, and offered to join the colonists in a memorial to the crown, soliciting the repeal of a code which he now believed would be neither for the interests of the colony nor the crown; but in the meantime he had no warrant to suspend its execution. Gonzalo was not long in mustering a force of nearly four hundred men, and as others joined him, he was soon ready for action. The viceroy, a vain, arrogant and weak man, prepared for war. He arrested Castro on suspicion. Having resolved to retreat from Lima, the viceroy himself was arrested, and Gonzalo, per force, was invited to assume the government. He entered the city in great state, at the head of nearly 1200 followers, on the 28th of October, 1544. The first act of the new governor was to apprehend and punish those that had taken the most active part against him;

some he condemned to death, and others he sent into banishment. His next concern was to fill all the places of trust with his own partizans. Castro escaped to Spain, but was thrown into prison for twelve years, though innocent of crime. Nuñez also escaped, and prepared to contest the prize with Gonzalo Pizarro. He raised the standard of loyalty at Tumbez, and was joined by numbers. The battle was fought in January, 1546, near Quito; Nuñez was slain; and Gonzalo was hailed as a liberator of the people, being very much elated thereby.

In Spain, the news of these proceedings caused great consternation and dismay; and the government felt the greatest difficulty in coming to a decision regarding the course to be followed. At length it was resolved to try conciliatory measures, and to send out a representative who, by arguments and politic concessions, might bring back the people to their allegiance. For this difficult mission was chosen Pedro de la Gasca, an ecclesiastic who, though bred to the church, had also distinguished himself as a soldier and a diplomatist. He was a man well qualified for the management both of affairs and men; he was possessed of great abilities, of a gentle and winning manner, with at the same time, great firmness and decision of character, and of undoubted fidelity and loyalty. He received the title of President of the Royal Audience, and was placed at the head of every department in the colony, civil, military and judicial. He made few preparations, had only a small number of attendants with him, and appeared to Gonzalo and others rather a harmless visitor; but, on making known his official rank, the successful head of affairs was astounded. He soon found that Gasca was raising forces and preparing to bring Peru under the royal authority. The final contest on which all depended, was had in the plain of Xaquixagua, at the close of 1547. The two armies met, and Gonzalo found that his men openly, in troops, passed over to Gasca. He surrendered, of course, and, together with a number of others, was soon after executed. Gasca, by a judicious policy, soon reduced the country to quiet and order, and his successors had good sense enough to follow his example.

In the subsequent history of Peru there occurs little of interest to the general reader till the time of the war of independence The whole of the Spanish dominions in the New World were at first divided into two governments, one subject to the viceroy of Mexico, and the other subject to the viceroy of Peru. In 1718, the province of Quito was separated from Peru and annexed to New Granada, and in 1788, the provinces of La Plata, Potosi, Charcas, Chiquitos, and Paraguay were detached from Peru to form the government of Buenos Ayres. Each of these governments constituted a viceroyalty; while Guatemala, Venezuela, Caracas, Cumana, and Chili were severally formed into distinct jurisdictions under a captain-general. In 1780, an insurrection broke out among the Indians in Peru, under Tapac Amaro, who assumed the title of Inca, but it was at length suppressed. Peru did not join in the celebrated war of independence which broke out among the Spanish possessions in South America in 1810, and it was the last to throw off the Spanish yoke. It soon became evident, however, that the expulsion of the Spaniards from Peru was necessary to the safety of the other States; and hence a combined Chilian and Buenos Ayrean army, under San Martin, laid seige to Lima in February, 1821. After some months, a convention was agreed to, when Lascerna, the Spanish general, with his army, left Lima, and San Martin took possession of the city. On the 28th of July, 1821, the independence of Peru was declared; and a few days afterwards San Martin was proclaimed protector. Among the first legislative acts of the protectorate was a decree declaring that the children of slaves born in Peru subsequently to the 28th of July, 1821, should be free. This was followed by another abolishing the tribute, and enacting that the aborigines be thenceforth denominated Peruvians like the Creoles. On the 21st of September, the fortress of Callao surrendered to the protector. He did not long retain his popularity; deputies were summoned; and he resigned his power into their hands on 21st of September, 1822. Congress lost no time in appointing a new executive, under the title of the *Junta Gubernativa.* The proceedings of the new government were marked by feebleness and discord. It was soon expelled from power, and Gen. Don Jose de la Riva Aguero was made president of the republic. Santa Cruz, a Peruvian, who in the sequel greatly distinguished himself, assumed the chief command of the army; and it was determined in a council of war to make another effort in the Puertos Intermedios. Being unable to hold Lima, it was abandoned by the patriots, and immediately taken possession of by the royalists, who, however, soon afterwards evacuated it, after having exacted heavy contributions from the remaining inhabitants, and destroyed the mint. The cause of independence in Peru seemed hanging by a thread, which it required little exertion to break, when the celebrated Bolivar made his appearance in Lima, on the 1st of September, 1823. He was received with the greatest enthusiasm, and was immediately invested with supreme authority, military and political. Great activity was now infused into the measures of government; and acting in the capacity of dictator, Bolivar dissolved Congress, and levied an army, with which he sallied from the capital on the second week of November. Callao, however, along with the city of Lima, once more fell into the hands of the royalists. The cause of independence in Peru now seemed desperate; but the conduct of Bolivar at this critical moment is deserving of the highest praise. By his firmness, activity, and seasonable severities, he checked further defections, and obtained the respect and entire confidence of every true patriot. In the month of July, 1824, the liberating army commenced its march towards Pasco in three divisions, two of which were Colombians, headed by Generals Lara and Cordova; and one was Peruvian, under Lamar. The march was successfully accomplished; various marches and skirmishes took place during the following months; and at last a decisive battle was fought, December 9th, 1824, on the plain of Ayacucho, near the village of Quinua, a little distance in front of which lay the patriot army, not 6000 strong, that of the royalists being fully one-third more numerous. The conflict continued for about an hour, when the royalists were defeated with great loss. Indeed, their army may be said to have been almost annihilated; for 3200 rank and file, amongst whom was the viceroy, were made prisoners of war, the remainder dispersing in a state of total disorganization in all directions.

Bolivar continued dictator till the month of July, 1825, when he resigned, and placed at the head of affairs a council of government composed of his own ministers. Towards the end of 1826, he promulgated a new con stitution, according to which the executive was to be vested in an irresponsible president elected for life. This new constitution excited great discontent among the people; but it was accepted by the electoral colleges, and Bolivar was named president. The people were further incensed by the presence of the Colombian troops; and soon after, Bolivar being called away to quell an insurrection in Colombia, an open revolt broke out in Peru. The Colombian troops were expelled from the country, a Congress was assembled at Lima, and the Bolivian constitution abolished. On the 18th of June, 1827, a new constitution was promulgated, and General Lamar was named president. An increased dissatisfaction between Colombia and Peru at length led to a declaration of war between the States; and Lamar entered the Colombian territory at the head of a considerable army. A battle took place on Tarqui, near Jiron, in Quito, on the 27th of February, 1829, in which the Peruvians were defeated, and the next day preliminaries of peace were agreed to. Gamarra now became president. He retained office for the four years designated by the constitution; and at the end of this term a convention was convoked to reform the constitution. The reformed constitution was promulgated in the month of August, 1834, and General Orbegoso was named president. In January, 1835, Salaverry revolted at Callao, whereupon Orbegoso applied for aid to Santa Cruz, president of the Bolivian republic. That general accordingly entered Peru with an army, and joining forces with Orbegoso, defeated Gamarra, August 13th, 1835, and later, Salaverry himself, near Arequipa, at the end of January, 1836. Lima, Callao, and the rest of Peru immediately submitted to the conquerors. Santa Cruz having succeeded in establishing tranquillity, now assumed the supreme power; and, dividing the country into North and South Peru, he conjoined it with Bolivia, nominating himself supreme protector of the three States. This arrangement met with a powerful opposition both in Peru and Bolivia, and also brought him into collision with the republic of Chili. At length, in January, 1839, a bloody battle was fought at Yungay, in which Santa Cruz was defeated, and driven out of the country. The confederation was thus brought to a close, and the two countries, Peru and Bolivia, returned to their former limits and forms of goverment.

In Peru, a Congress was convoked, which, in November, 1839, gave out a new constitution, and nominated Gen. Gamarra, who had commanded the Chili-Peruvian troops, president of the republic. General Gamarra died in November, 1841, and on his death civil war followed, which was settled by Gen. Castilla in 1844. He was elected president, and entered upon office on the 1st of April, 1845. Castilla completed his six constitutional years of office, and under his rule the country enjoyed great peace and prosperity. His successor, General Echenique, assumed the supreme power on the 1st of April, 1851, but the people soon became dissatisfied with him; and being charged with fraud and corruption, he was driven out. Vivanco stirred up sedition and kept alive the contest for several years. The war was at length brought to a close in March, 1858, by the taking, by assault, of Arequipa, after a most obstinate defence by Vivanco and his adherents, the number of killed and wounded amounting to about 3000. Though slavery had been abolished by the charter of independence, yet it continued till put an end to by Saltilla's proclamation in 1855. He also freed the Indians from the unjust capital tax to which they had been subject since the time of the Spaniards, and the punishment of death for political offences was also abolished.

The name of Peru is not known to the early inhabitants, but was given to the country by the Spaniards; and is said to be a corruption of the word *Pelu*, the Indian name for "river," and mistaken by the Spaniards for the name of the country. The name given to it by the natives was *Tavantinsuyu*, or "four quarters of the world." The most distinguishing natural feature of Peru, and that from which the country derives its peculiar aspect and character, is the vast chain of the Andes, which traverses it in a direction from S.S.E. to N.N.W. The country is thus naturally divided into three distinct regions, differing widely from each other in their physical characteristics, and familiarly known as *La Costa*, or the region between the sea and the Andes; *La Sierra*, or the mountain region; and *La Montana*, or the wooded region to the east of the Andes, forming part of the basin of the Amazon.

La Costa, or the coast region, extends the entire length of the country, but its average breadth is not more than thirty miles. With all its extent of coast, Peru has few good harbors, probably not more than a dozen in all. The best are those of Payta, Salinas, Callao, Pisco, Islay, Arica, and Iquique. The water on the coast being almost uniformly deep, vessels are obliged to approach within a quarter of a mile of the shore before they can anchor; and as the great swell of the Pacific occasions a heavy and dangerous surf, landing with boats is both difficult and hazardous. The operation, however, is effected with ease and safety by means of *balsas* or rafts, constructed usually of cane, and supported by means of inflated seal-skins. The coast region is almost one continuous sandy waste, where no rain falls, and where neither plant nor animal can obtain subsistence. Vegetation is only to be met with along the banks of the streams that come down from the high lands. Many parts of these are dry for the greater part of the year, and only a few of them are perennial. Some of the larger streams reach the sea, but the smaller ones are absorbed by the encompassing desert, or exhausted in irrigating the cultivated patches. The insulated river valleys are thus the only inhabitable parts of the coast, and they are from twenty to ninety miles apart. The rest of the region is covered with a fine light-yellow drift sand; this is often driven about with great velocity by the wind, which, when violent, frequently raises columns of sand to the height of eighty to one hundred feet. The rainless region extends to the height of about 7000 feet above the level of the sea; but to the height of about 2000 feet above the sea the coast region is periodically refreshed by sea vapors or drizzle, called *garua*. These vapors prevail from May till November, and are most dense and abundant towards the end of June, when the *lomas* or hillocks bordering the sand-flats become covered with a luxuriant vegetation. At Lima this coast vegetation is most abundant in the months of July, August and September. The heat of this region is not so excessive as might be supposed; and during summer the thermometer rarely rises above 85°; the mean annual temperature is 72°, the maximum, 82°, and the minimum, 55°. In this district are produced most of the plants of tropical countries. The plantain, banana, pine-apple, sugar-cane, vine, cocoa, olive, coffee, cotton, as well as other fruits, some peculiar to the country, arrive at great perfection. Maize, rice, wheat, barley, and potatoes are also cultivated.

The district called *Sierra*, or highlands of Peru, commences immediately above the rainless district, at 7000 feet above the level of the sea, and extends to the eastern chain of the Andes. The Andes here consist of two main chains or cordilleras, running nearly parallel to each other, and connected in various parts by cross-ridges; but they do not in general rise to such a height as in Bolivia. The eastern cordillera from Bolivia preserves its grand character northward to 13° S. Lat., being composed of a series of snowy-peaks, which terminate in the Nevada de Sacantahi; but north of this no snow-capped mountains occur. In the western chain, near 15°, a considerable portion of the range is covered with snow; S.E. of Lima the Toldo de Nieve rises above the snow-line; and between 11° and 11° 30′ is the elevated summit of La Vinda, nearly 16,000 feet in height, and the nevadas of Pelagotas, Mayapota, and Huaylillas. Between the last mentioned and Chimborazo in Ecuador none of the summits of this chain attain the snow-line. The chains of the east and west cordilleras are usually about 100 miles apart. South of 11° S. Lat., the country between the two chains consists properly of two inclined planes sloping down from the Andes of Vilcanota and the table-land of Pasco, and separated from each other by the water-line of the Mataro, a feeder of the Apurimac, near 12° S. The southern plane lies at a great elevation, the town of Cuzco being 11,380 feet above the level of the sea; but even here wheat and Indian corn are raised, and farther north, where the country is considerably lower, the sugar-cane is cultivated. The surface is by no means level, being traversed by various ridges of hills, which rise several hundred feet above their bases. The northern plain has a very similar surface; and contiguous to the western cordillera it forms an undulating valley 40 miles wide, which is drained by the Jauja, and which, on account of its fertility, is one of the best peopled districts of Peru. In the lower part of this valley the sugar-cane suc ceeds well; while the higher produces cereals and fruits in abundance. To the north is the table-land of Pasco, which lies between 11° and 10° 30′ S., and, with the exception of a few miners' huts, in the region of permanent snow, is the highest inhabited part of the Andes. Were it not for the rich mines which it possesses, it would have remained a sheep-walk. Its surface presents several low but steep ranges of hills, with level grounds between them. These level tracts are from 13,000 to 14,000 feet above the sea, or about 1500 feet below the snow-line in this latitude. The climate is exceedingly cold all the year round, and unfavorable to any kind of cultivation. In the numerous and deep lakes which cover a considerable part of its surface, the rivers Marañon, Huallaga, and Ucayale take their rise. The northern portion of the Peruvian Andes consists of three cordilleras, of which the western contains the nevadas already mentioned. The central chain is connected with the table-land of Pasco, and runs parallel with the western chain to about 7°, their summits being about fifty miles apart; but northward of this parallel the chain runs N.E. to its termination on the banks of the Amazon. In the northern portion of this central chain a few summits occur which rise above the snow-line. The eastern cordillera is connected with the mountain system of the eastern border of the table-land of Pasco, and runs in a direction parallel with the central chain, terminating near 6° S., opposite an offset of the central range, which here comes close up to the Huallaga. The highest summits of this range are towards the south, but probably none of them much exceed 15,000 feet in height. Toward the north they sink down to mere hills. Of the two valleys inclosed by these three ranges, the western, or that of Marañon, is very narrow in its southern parts, and here the river is one continuous series of rapids and falls until it reaches 8°, where it enters a wider valley, which spreads out to 20 miles in width. This wider valley gradually subsides from 3000 to 2000 feet above the level of the sea. Its climate is consequently very hot, and its fertile soil is capable of producing all the intertropical plants and fruits. The eastern valley is drained by the Huallaga. It slopes very rapidly, from 5000 in 10° to 2000 in 9°, and in its fertility, climate, and produce resembles the valley of the Marañon. Presenting, as it does, almost every variety of climate, the vegetation of this region is extremely varied in its character, from the gigantic growth of the tropics to the dwarf plants of Lapland. In this mountainous district are situated the famous gold and silver mines of Peru. It likewise contains the sources of those vast rivers which traverse the continent of South America. Here the Marañon commences its course, and here rise its magnificent tributaries, the Ucayale, Huallaga, and others, which themselves are swelled by an innumerable multitude of streams descending from the eastern ridges of the Andes,—all being finally absorbed in the mighty Amazon. But by far the most beautiful and valuable part of the Peruvian territory is the *Montana*, or wooded region, which lies to the east of the Andes, commencing on the eastern declivity of the second chain, and stretching to the confines of Brazil and Bolivia. After crossing the Andes, and descending a few hundred feet lower in the direction of the east, the traveller beholds a country totally different from that which he has left—a country richly covered with a luxuriant vegetation. So far as we are acquainted with this region, and as yet it is only imperfectly known, it seems to rival in fertility, and in luxuriance and variety of its vegetation, even the finest parts of Brazil.

Peru is very rich in vegetable productions. The coast district has not many plants; but east of the Andes the species are very numerous. Many medicinal herbs, and a variety of balsams, oils, and gums are produced. Almonds, ginger, balsam of Copaiba, gum copal, etc., are all said to abound. On the western slopes of the Andes, the cabbage-palm is produced, as are also the cocoa-nut, the chocolate nut, cotton shrub, pine-apple, sugar cane, etc. Tobacco and jalap are abundant in the groves at the foot of the mountains; cotton is found in a wild state on the banks of the Amazon; and on the high lands which skirt the Andes for two thousand miles, at elevations from two thousand eight hundred to nine thousand five hundred feet, the different species of the cinchona or Peruvian bark are most valuable and abundant. Among the wild animals of the country are the bear, puma, jaguar, deer, fox, armadillo, etc. The Peruvian sheep are very numerous and valuable; of these there are four varieties, the llama, alpaca, guanico, and vicuna. The Spaniards brought in the European sheep, and innumerous herds are to be met with in the highlands. They also introduced horses, horned cattle and asses; all of which have increased greatly, the mule being now the ordinary beast of burden. The shores of Peru are frequented by myriads of birds, and to them we are indebted for the valuable manure called guano. The common carrion vulture is found near the towns; besides which may be noted the condor, hawks, falcons, owls, etc. In respect to agriculture, manufactures, native industry, and the like, Peru is very much below the fair average; and education has made almost no progress among the people generally. The Roman Catholic is the established religion, and by long possession the heads of the state religion have become very wealthy, and are bigoted and intolerant towards all outsiders. In theory, the government is republican, based upon representation, but in practice, it is in Peru as in so many other States, but little else than a military despotism or oligarchy. The president's term of office is six years; there are four cabinet officers, and a congress composed of a senate and chamber of deputies; two senators for every department, and one deputy for every twenty thousand inhabitants.

During the last eight or ten years, Peru has been going through contests and struggles of various sorts. Spain behaved very unhandsomely in the early part of 1864, on the plea of demanding a settlement of claims against Peru. She sent out a commissioner, who carried himself with the usual Spanish arrogance, and in March, the Spanish vessels seized upon the Chincha Islands, the most valuable possession of Peru, the worth of the guano there being estimated at some $40,000,000. Great excitement of course was stirred up, and Peru determined to maintain its rights; preparations were made for war, and an alliance was entered into with Chili; Gen. Prado was appointed dictator, and he brought to the position energy, decision, skill, and ability. In February, 1865, a treaty was made with Spain; but it proved so little satisfactory to the country, that a revolutionary movement spread in all directions, with its usual accompaniments of fighting, bloodshed, etc. Gen. Prado, the dictator, early in January, 1866, re-declared war against Spain, and joined Chili at once in the war. The Spanish fleet bombarded Valparaiso, March 30th, 1866, and thence proceeding to Callao, did the same destructive work there, May 2d. During 1867, matters continued unsettled with Spain, and in Peru several outbreaks against Prado and his government occurred. Early in the next year, Prado resigned and went to Chili, and Col. Balta being the successful leader, became president in July, 1868. Since then, various efforts have been made to induce immigration to the banks of the Amazon, to build additional railroads and lay telegraph wires in several parts of the country, to endeavor to promote fraternal feeling and combined action among the several republics of South America, and as far as possible, and as rapidly as possible, to get rid of an enormous public debt, and develop the rich resources of the country. The spirit of Peru at present is certainly progressive, and there is room to hope that despite many serious and weighty difficulties in the way, the republic may advance in genuine prosperity and true independence.

BRAZIL.

In presenting an account of this extensive and important country, the only American monarchy, we shall, *first*, give a brief historical sketch of the progressive discovery of its coasts and interior, of its gradual settlement, and of the auspices under which its social institutions have developed themselves; *secondly*, a condensed view of its physical geography, meteorology, and natural products; and, *thirdly*, a similar view of its inhabitants, their form of government, moral and intellectual culture, manufacturing, and commercial industry.

Brazil was discovered in 1499, by Vincent Yañez Pinzon, a companion of Columbus. He descried the land near Cape St. Augustine, and sailed along the coast as far as the river Amazon, whence he proceeded to the mouth of the Orinoco. He made no settlement, but took possession of the country in the name of the Spanish government, and carried home, as specimens of its natural productions, some drugs, gems, and Brazil-wood. Next year the Portuguese commander, Pedro Alvarez Cabral, appointed by his monarch to follow the course of Vasco de Gama in the east, was driven, by adverse winds, so far from his track, that he reached the Brazilian coast, April 24, and anchored in Porto Seguro (Lat. 16° south) on Good Friday. On Easter-day an altar was erected, mass celebrated in presence of the natives, the country declared an appanage of Portugal, and a stone cross erected in commemoration of the event. Cabral despatched a small vessel to Lisbon, to announce his discovery, and without forming any settlement, proceeded to India on the 3d of May. On the arrival of the news in Portugal, Emanuel invited Amerigo Vespucci to enter his service, and dispatched him with three vessels to explore the country. This navigator's first voyage was unsuccessful; but in a second he discovered a safe port, the site of which is not accurately known, to which he gave the name of All-Saints. He remained there five months, and maintained a friendly intercourse with the natives. Some of the party travelled forty leagues into the interior. Vespucci erected a small fort, and leaving twelve men, with guns and provisions to garrison it, embarked for Portugal, having loaded his two ships with Brazil-wood, monkeys, and parrots. The poor and barbarous tribes of Brazil, and their country, the mineral riches of which were not immediately discovered, offered but few attractions to a government into the coffers of which the wealth of India and Africa was flowing. Vespucci's settlement was neglected. For nearly thirty years the kings of Portugal paid no further attention to their newly-acquired territory, than what consisted in combating the attempts of the Spaniards to occupy it, and dispersing the private adventurers from France, who sought its shores for the purposes of commerce. The colonization of Brazil was prosecuted, however, by subjects of the Portuguese monarchy, who traded thither chiefly for Brazil-wood. It was convenient for these traders to have agents living among the natives; and adventurers were found who were willing to take up their abode with them. Unfortunately these were mostly criminals, and men of degraded characters and morals, generally sent out by government.

The first attempt on the part of a Portuguese monarch to introduce an organized government into his dominions, was made by John III. He adopted a plan which had been found to succeed well in Madeira and the Azores; dividing the country into hereditary captaincies, and granting them to such persons as were willing to undertake their settlement, with unlimited powers of jurisdiction, both civil and criminal. Each captain cy extended along fifty leagues of coast. The boundaries in the interior were undefined. The first settlement made under this new system was that of S. Vincente. Martim Affonso de Sousa, having obtained a grant, fitted out a considerable armament, and proceeded to explore the country in person. He began to survey the coast about Rio Janeiro, to which he gave that name because he discovered it on the first of January, 1531. He proceeded south as far as La Plata, naming the places he surveyed on the way from the days on which the respective discoveries were made. He fixed upon an island, in latitude 24½° south, called by the natives Guaibe, for his settlement. The Goagnazes, or prevailing tribe of Indians in that neighborhood, as soon as they discovered the intentions of the new comers to fix themselves permanently there, collected for the purpose of expelling them. Fortunately, however, a shipwrecked Portuguese, who had lived many years under the protection of the principal chief, was successful in concluding a treaty of perpetual alliance between his countrymen and the natives. The good understanding thus happily established was long preserved. Finding the spot chosen for the new town inconvenient, the colonists removed to the adjoining island of S. Vincente, from which the captaincy derived its name. An unsuccessful expedition was made into the interior in search of mines. Nevertheless the colony prospered. Cattle and the sugar-cane were at an early period introduced from Madeira, and here the other captaincies supplied themselves with both. The founder of the colony was soon removed from the active superintendence of its progress, by being appointed governor-general of India; but on his return to Portugal he watched over its welfare, sending out supplies and settlers, and leaving it at his death in a flourishing condition to his son. Pero Lopes de Sousa received the grant of a captaincy, and set sail from Portugal at the same time as his brother, the founder of S. Vincente. He chose to have his fifty leagues in two allotments. That to which he gave the name of S. Amaro adjoined S. Vincente, the two towns being only three leagues asunder. The other division lay much nearer to the line between Paraiba and Pernambuco. He experienced considerable difficulty in founding this second colony, from the strenuous opposition of a neighboring tribe, the Petiguares; but at length he succeeded in clearing his lands of them; and not long afterwards he perished by shipwreck.

Rio Janeiro was not settled till a later period. It was founded by Vasco Fernandes Coutinho, who having acquired a large fortune in India, sunk it in this scheme of colonization. He carried with him no less than sixty fidalgos. They named their town by anticipation, Our Lady of the Victory; but it cost them some hard fighting with the Goagnazes to justify the title. Having defeated these savages, the colonists carried on the building with spirit, planted canes, and established four sugar-works; and Coutinho, seeing everything prosperous, returned to Lisbon to enlist more colonists, and to make preparations for an expedition into the interior in search of mines. Pedro de Campo Tourinho, a nobleman and excellent navigator, received a grant of the adjoining captaincy of Porto Seguro. This, it will be remembered, is the spot where Cabral first took possession of Brazil. Tourinho and his associates fortified themselves on the place where the capital of the presidency still stands. The Tupinoquins at first offered some opposition; but having made peace, they observed it faithfully, notwithstanding that the oppression of the Portuguese obliged them to forsake the country. Sugar-works were established, and considerable quantities of the produce exported to the mother-country. It was found impossible, by reason of an endemic disorder, to rear kine in the province; but horses, asses and goats succeeded.

Jorge de Figueiredo, was the first donatory of the captaincy of *Ilhéos*. The Tupinoquins, the most tractable of the Brazilian tribes, made peace with the settlers, and the colony was founded without a struggle. The son of the original proprietor sold the captaincy to Lucas Geraldes, who expended considerable wealth in improving it; and, in a short time, eight or nine sugar-works were established. The coast from the Rio S. Francisco to Bahia was granted to Francisco Pereira Coutinho: the bay itself, with all its creeks, was afterwards added to the grant. When Coutinho formed his establishment, where Villa Velha now stands, he found a noble Portuguese living in the neighborhood, named Caramaru, who, having been shipwrecked, had, by means of his fire-arms, raised himself to the rank of chief among the natives. He was surrounded by a patriarchal establishment of wives and children; and to him most of the distinguished families of Bahia still trace their lineage.

A factory had, some time before the period at which these captaincies were established, been planted at Pernambuco. A ship from Marseilles took it, and left seventy men in it as a garrison; but being captured on her return, and carried into Lisbon, immediate measures were taken for re-occupying the place. The captaincy of Pernambuco was granted to Don Duarte Coelho Pereira as the reward of his services in India. It extended along the coast from the Rio S. Francisco, northward to the Rio de Juraza. Duarte sailed with his wife and children, and many of his kinsmen, to take possession of his new colony, and landed in the port of Pernambuco. To the town which was there founded he gave the name of Olinda. The Cabetes, who possessed the soil, were fierce and pertinacious. The Portuguese managed, however, to beat off their enemies; and, having entered into an alliance with the Tobayanes, followed up their success. Attempts were made about this time to establish two other captaincies, but without success. Pedro de Goes obtained a grant of the captaincy of Paraiba, between those of S. Vincente and Espirito Santo; but his means were too feeble to enable him to make head against the aborigines, and the colony was broken up after a painful struggle of seven years. João de Barros, the historian, obtained the captaincy of Maranhão. For the sake of increasing his capital, he divided his grant with Fernan Alvares de Andrada and Aires da Cunha. They projected a scheme of conquest and colonization upon a large scale. Nine hundred men, of whom one hundred and thirteen were horsemen, embarked in ten ships under the command of Aires da Cunha. But the vessels were wrecked upon some shoals about one hundred leagues to the south of Maranhão; and the few survivors, after suffering immense hardships, escaped to the nearest settlements, and the undertaking was abandoned.

By these adventurers, the whole line of Brazilian coast, from the mouth of La Plata to the mouth of the Amazon, had become studded at intervals with Portuguese settlements, in all of which law and justice were administered, however inadequately. It is worthy of observation, that Brazil was the first colony founded in America upon an agricultural principle, for until then the precious metals were the exclusive attraction. Sufficient capital was attracted between the year 1531, in which De Sousa founded the first captaincy, and the year 1548, to render these colonies an object of importance to the mother-country. Their organization, however, both in regard to their means of defence against external aggression and internal violence, was extremely defective. Portugal was distant, and the inhabited portions of each captaincy were too far asunder to be able to afford reciprocal assistance. They were surrounded by, and intermingled with, large tribes of savages. Behind them the Spaniards, who had an establishment at Assumption, had penetrated almost to the sources of the waters of Paraguay, and had succeeded in establishing a communication with Peru. Orellana, on the other hand, setting out from Peru, had crossed the mountains and sailed down the Amazon. Nor had the French abandoned their hopes of effecting an establishment on the coast. But the want of internal organization in the Portuguese settlements was even worse than the inadequacy of their defensive force. The governor of every captaincy exercised uncontrolled authority; the property, honor and lives of the colonists, were at the mercy of these feudal chieftains; and the people groaned under many oppressions.

The obvious remedy for these evils was to concentrate the executive power, to render the petty chiefs amenable to one tribunal, and to confide the management of the defensive force to one hand. In order to this the powers of the several captains were revoked, whilst their property in their grants was reserved to them. A governor-general was appointed, with full powers, civil and criminal. The judicial and financial functions in each province were vested in the *Ouvidor*, whose authority in the college of finance was second only to that of the governor. The chief cities received municipal constitutions, as in Portugal. Thome de Sousa was the first person nominated to the important post of governor-general. He was instructed to build a strong city in Bahia and to establish there the seat of his government. In pursuance of his commission, he arrived at Bahia in April, 1549, with a fleet of six vessels, on board of which were 320 persons in the king's pay, 400 convicts, and as many free colonists as swelled the number of adventurers to 1000. Care had been taken for the religious wants of the provinces, by associating six Jesuits with the expedition. Old Caramaru, who still survived, rendered the governor essential service, by gaining for his countrymen the good-will of the natives. The new city was established where Bahia still stands. Within four months one hundred houses were built, and surrounded by a mud wall. Sugar plantations were laid out in the vicinity. During the four years of Sousa's government, there were sent out at different times supplies of all kinds; female orphans of noble families, who were given in marriage to the officers, and portioned from the royal estates; and orphan boys to be educated by the Jesuits. The capital rose rapidly in importance, and the captaincies learned to regard it as a common head and center of wealth. The governor visited them, inspected their fortifications, and regulated the administration of justice. Meanwhile the Jesuits undertook the moral and religious culture of the natives, and of the scarcely less savage colonists. Strong opposition was at first experienced from the gross ignorance of the Indians, and the depravity of the Portuguese, fostered by the licentious encouragement of some abandoned priests who had found their way to Brazil. Next year Sousa was succeeded by Duarte da Costa, who brought with him a reinforcement of Jesuits, at the head of whom was Luis de Gran, appointed, with Nobrega, the chief of the first mission, joint provincial of Brazil. Nobrega's first act was one which has exercised the most beneficial influence over the social system of Brazil, namely, the establishment of a college on the then unreclaimed plains of Piratininga. The spot selected by him for the site of this establishment is on the ridge of the Serra do Mar, ten leagues from the sea, and thirteen from S. Vincente. It was named S. Paulo, and has been at once the source whence knowledge and civilization have been diffused through Brazil, and the nucleus of a colony of its manliest and hardiest citizens, which has sent out successive swarms of hardy adventurers to people the interior. The mode of education pursued by the Jesuits at S. Paulo was the same as that observed in all their other missions. Their good intentions were in part frustrated by the opposition of Duarte, the governor; and it was not until 1558, when Mem de Sa was sent out to supersede him, that their enlightened projects were allowed free scope. This great man, comprehending better than his predecessors the system of these missionaries, went hand in hand with the ecclesiastics during the whole of his government. Mem de Sa continued to hold the reins of government in Brazil upon terms of the best understanding with the clergy, and to the great advantage of the colonies, for fourteen years. On the expiration of his power, which was nearly contemporary with that of his life, an attempt was made to divide Brazil into two governments; but, this having failed, the territory was re-united in 1578, the year in which Diego Laurenço da Veiga was appointed governor. At this time the colonies, although not yet independent of supplies from the mother-country, were in a flourishing condition; but the usurpation of the crown of Portugal by Philip II. changed the aspect of affairs. Brazil, believed to be inferior to the Spanish possessions in mines, was considered of importance merely as an outpost to prevent the intrusion of foreign nations. It was consequently abandoned to comparative neglect for the period intervening between 1578 and 1640, during which it continued an appanage of Spain. The population increased; and domestic enterprise and foreign invasion called forth the energies of the people; but, as far as legislation was concerned, nothing was done.

No sooner had Brazil passed under the Spanish crown, than English adventurers directed their hostile enterprises against its shores. In 1586, Witherington plundered Bahia; in 1591, Cavendish burned S. Vincente; in 1595, Lancaster took Olinda. These exploits, however, were transient in their effects. In 1612, the French attempted to found a permanent colony in the island of Marajo, where they succeeded in maintaining themselves till 1618. This attempt led to the erection of Maranhâo and Para into a separate *Estado*. But it was on the part of the Dutch that the most skillful and pertinacious efforts were made for securing a footing in Brazil; and they alone of all the rivals of the Portuguese have left traces of their presence in the national spirit and institutions of Brazil. The very imperfect constitution of the United Provinces was the cause why many of the executive functions were delegated to companies of mercantile adventurers. Among the offices properly appertaining to the government, the maintenance and defence of the Spice Islands had been intrusted to the East India Company. The success of tha body suggested the establishment of a West India Company. Its charter secured to it a monopoly of the trade to America and the opposite coast of Africa, between the tropic of Cancer and the Cape of Good Hope. This body dispatched, in 1624, a fleet against Bahia. The town yielded almost without a struggle. The Dutch governor fortified his new acquisition; and his proclamation offering toleration and protection to all, collected around him a multitude of Indians, Negroes and Jews. The fleet soon after sailed, a squadron being detached against Angola, with the intention of taking possession of that colony, in order to secure a supply of slaves. The Portuguese, in the meanwhile, who had fled at first in the hope of eluding what they conceived to be merely an incursion of pirates, began to collect for the purpose of expelling the permanent intruders; and the weakening of the Dutch force by the departure of the fleet inspired them with fresh courage. The descendants of Caramaru formed a link between the aborigines and the Portuguese which existed in no other part of Brazil. The consequence was, the hearty co-operation of all the natives against the invaders. The Dutch were obliged to capitulate in May, 1625. For some years the Dutch confined themselves to depredations upon the marine of Spain and Portugal. In 1630, they attempted again to effect a settlement; and Olinda yielded after a feeble resistance. They were unable, however, to extend their power beyond the limits of the town, until the arrival of Count Maurice of Nassau, in 1630. His first step was to introduce a regular government among his countrymen; his second, to send to the African coast one of his officers, who took possession of a Portuguese settlement, and thus secured a supply of slaves. Nassau suffered repulses in several of his expeditions, and particularly in that which he undertook against Bahia.

Nevertheless, in the course of four years, the limited period of his government, he succeeded in confirming the Dutch supremacy along the coast of Brazil from the mouth of the S. Francisco to Maranhâo. He expended the revenues of the country, the booty obtained from the Portuguese, and a great part of his private fortune, in fortifying the mouths of rivers, building bridges to facilitate mercantile intercourse, and beautifying and repairing towns. He strictly observed the Dutch policy of tolerating all religions. He promoted the amalgamation of the different races, and sought to conciliate the Portuguese by the confidence he reposed in them. His object was to found a great empire; but this was a project at variance with the wishes of his employers—an association of merchants, who were dissatisfied because the wealth which they expected to see flowing into their coffers was expended in promoting the permanent interests of a distant country. Count Maurice was recalled in 1644. His successors possessed neither his political nor his military talents, and had to contend with more energetic enemies.

In 1640, the revolution which placed the house of Braganza on the throne of Portugal restored Brazil to masters more inclined to promote its interests, and assert its possession, than the Spaniards. It was indeed high time that some exertion should be made. The northern provinces had fallen into the power of Holland; the southern, peopled in a great measure by the hardy descendants of the successive colonists, who had issued on all sides from the central establishment of S. Paulo, had learned, from their habits of unaided and successful enterprise, to court independence. Adventurers had penetrated into those central mountains where the diamond is found. They had ascended the waters of the Paraguay to their sources. They had extended their limits southwards till they reached the Spanish settlements on La Plata. They had reduced to slavery numerous tribes of the natives. They were rich in cattle, and had commenced the discovery of the mines. While yet nominally subject to the crown of Spain, they had not scrupled on more than one occasion to wage war on their own account against the settlements of that country. When, therefore, the inhabitants of S. Paulo saw themselves about to be transferred, as a dependency of Portugal from one master to another, they conceived the idea of erecting their country into an independent State. Their attempt, however, was frustrated by Amador Bueno, the person whom they had selected, who utterly refused to be their king. Rio and Santos, although both evinced a desire of independence, followed the example of the Paulistas. Bahia, as capital of the Brazilian States, felt that its ascendency depended upon the union with Portugal. The government, thus left in quiet possession of the rest of Brazil, had time to concentrate its attention upon the Dutch conquests. The crown of Portugal was, however, much too weak to adopt energetic measures. The tyranny of the successors of Nassau, by alienating the minds of the Portuguese and natives, drove them to revolt, before any steps were taken in the mother country for the re-conquest of its colonies. Joao Fernandes Vieyra, a native of Madeira, organized the insurrection which broke out in 1645. He repaired to the court of Portugal, and discovering the weakness and poverty of the executive, suggested the establishment of a company similar to that which, in Holland, had proved so successful. His plan, notwithstanding the opposition of the priests, was approved of, and in 1649, the Brazil Company of Portugal sent out its first fleet. The additional impetus communicated by this new engine to the exertions of the colonists and their Indian allies, turned the scale against the Dutch. After a most sanguinary war, Vieyra was enabled, in 1654, to present the keys of Olinda to the royal commander, and to restore to his monarch the undivided empire of Brazil; and in 1661, a treaty of peace was signed with them, and they renounced their pretensions to a portion of Brazil.

After this, except some inroads on the frontiers, the only foreign invasion which Brazil had to suffer was from France. In 1710, a squadron commanded by Duclerc disembarked 1000 men, and attacked Rio de Janeiro. After having lost half of his men in a battle, Duclerc and all his surviving companions were made prisoners. The governor treated them cruelly. A new squadron with 6000 troops was entrusted to the famous Admiral Duguay Trouin to revenge this injury. They arrived at Rio on the 12th of September, 1711. After four days of hard fighting, the town was taken. The governor retreated to a position out of it, and was only awaiting reinforcements from Minas to retake it; but Duguay Trouin threatening to burn it, he was obliged, on the 10th of October, to sign a capitulation, and pay to the French admiral 610,000 crusados, 500 cases of sugar, and provisions for the return of the fleet to Europe. The same day Albuquerque, the governor of Minas, arrived with the expected reinforcement of 15,000 men. The conditions of the capitulation were, however, fulfilled. Duguay Trouin departed to Bahia to obtain fresh spoils; but having lost in a storm two of his best ships, with an important part of the money received, he renounced this plan and returned directly to France. The Portuguese henceforth governed their colony undisturbed. The approach of foreign traders was prohibited, while the regalities reserved by the crown drained the country of a great proportion of its wealth. The authority of the governors was despotic in its abuse, but limited in its corrective powers; the administration of justice was slovenly in the extreme; the pay of all functionaries, civil, ecclesiastic, and military, was so parsimonious as to render peculation inevitable; and yet, in spite of all these disadvantages, the wealth and happiness of the people continued silently and steadily to increase. The reason was, that they were left in a great measure to themselves, and had an ample field within their own land for the exertion of their industry.

We have already adverted to the important part which the inhabitants of the captaincy of S. Paulo have played in the history of Brazil. The establishment of the Jesuit college had attracted to its neighborhood a number of settlers from S. Vincente. The Indians of the district were of mild dispositions, and frequent intermarriages took place between them and the Europeans. A race of men sprung from this mixture, native to the soil, hardy and enterprising, wearing but lightly the bonds which attached them to the mother country. The first object of inquiry with the colonists was, whether the land of which they had taken possession was rich in metals. Gold was found, but not in sufficient quantities to reward the labor bestowed in search of it. The Portuguese next devoted their energies to excursions against the more remote Indian tribes, with a view to obtaining slaves. Traces of gold having been observed in the mountain ranges north of S. Paulo, successive bands of adventurers attempted to penetrate the wilderness. The spirit of enterprise was thus nourished and confirmed. At first the gold-searchers, like the slave-hunters, undertook temporary expeditions, with the view, doubtless, of returning laden with booty, and settling in their native homes. By degrees, however, as the distance of the newly discovered mines increased, and establishments for working them became necessary, new colonies were founded. Different associations of adventurers penetrated, in the years 1693, 1694, and 1695, into the district of Minas Geraes, which had been explored by the Paulists at least twenty years before. In the beginning of the eighteenth century five of its principal settlements were elevated by royal charter to the privileges of towns. In 1720, the district was separated from S. Paulo, of which it had previously been esteemed a dependency, and placed under the control of a governor-general. In 1670, the gold-searchers penetrated into Goyaz; but it was not till the commencement of the next century that, encouraged by the discovery of the mines of Cuiaba, in the province of Matto Grosso, a permanent colony was settled there.

The first attempt to regulate by legislative enactments the industry of the miners of Brazil was made as early as 1618, by Philip III. According to his code of regulations, the privileges of the discoverer were that he should have one mine of eighty Portuguese *varas* by forty, and a second allotment of sixty by thirty upon the same vein. A hundred and twenty *varas* were to intervene between the portions. Any adventurer might claim a mine, but he could only have one of the same extent as the discoverer's first portion. No one except the discoverer might have more than one original grant within the distance of a league and a half; but the purchase of another person's allotment within that distance was allowed. Mines might be sought for and worked upon private property, because they belonged to the king, but the owner of the land had a right to indemnification. Mining adventurers were entitled to turn their cattle into the lands of the municipality (*concelho*), and even into private property, without the owner's permission, upon paying the value of the pasturage. Mines might only be granted to such persons as possessed the means of peopling and working them. A grant was forfeited if not taken possession of within sixty days. The executive and judicial functions within the mining districts were vested in a *provedor* and his secretary, those of the fiscal in a treasurer. None of these officials could hold a share in a mine, or trade in its produce, under penalty of loss of office and confiscation of property. The provedor or his secretary measured out the allotments; received and inspected the samples of metal from new mines; registered the grants, with the holder's oath to pay his fifths regularly and faithfully, etc. The treasurer received the royal fifths, and superintended the weighing, registering, refining, and stamping of all the gold. A yearly account was returned of all the discoveries and produce. For many years these laws were little more than a dead letter. The Paulistas were wholly engrossed with their expeditions in quest of slaves; the government and the colonists of the other captaincies, with the Dutch and other wars. Some few gipsy-like establishments were scattered thinly throughout the gold country. By degrees the desire of gain induced the more powerful and wealthy colonists to solicit large grants. No attention was paid to the restriction of the number that might be conferred on each individual; and the consequence was, that men of influence monopolized the mines, and were obliged either to sublet them to those they had forestalled, or to leave them unopened. It was found necessary, in 1702, to alter the existing laws. The whole ordinary civil and military authority was vested in the superintendent (*Guarda Môr*). The appointment of the treasurer belonged to this officer Both were allowed a limited number of deputies. At first the salaries of all these officers were levied upon the miners, but subsequently the privilege of mining was conceded to them in lieu of a salary. No second grant was made to any person until he had worked the first. The allotments were regulated by the number of slaves which the miner employed. Besides its fifths, the crown reserved an allotment, selected after the adventurer had taken his first grant and before he had chosen his second. These regulations were enforced by strong penalties, in order to prevent frauds upon the revenue. Slaves, and all other goods except cattle, were only allowed to be introduced from Rio, and that either by the way of S. Paulo or Taboate. No idle persons were allowed to remain about the mines; no goldsmith was tolerated there, nor any settler possessed of a slave capable of exercising this craft. The same infatuated passion for mining speculations which had characterized the Spanish settlers in South America, now began to actuate the Portuguese. Adventurers crowded to the scene of action from all the captaincies; not mere "landless resolutes" alone, but men of substance also Laborers and capital were drained off to the mining districts. The sugar-mills (*Engenhos*) were either abandoned or left half-cultivated, from the inability of the proprietors to offer for slaves the ruinous prices paid by the adventurers of the mines. Brazil, which had hitherto in a great measure supplied Europe with sugar, sank before the competition of the French and English, who had no mines to distract their attention. Commerce of every kind declined along with this staple commodity. The court endeavored for a time to counteract this course of enterprise, but in vain.

A new source of wealth for Brazil, had it been properly managed, but, as matters have turned out, merely a new source of injudicious restriction, was now about to be opened up. Some adventurers who had prosecuted the business of gold-washing northwards from Villa de Principe in the captaincy of Minas, made a discovery of diamonds about the year 1710. The value of these minerals was not known till several years, when an *Ouvidor* of the *Comarca* of Serro Frio, in which they were found, who had seen unpolished diamonds at Goa, ascertained what they were. In 1730, the discovery was announced for the first time to that government, which immediately declared diamonds *regalia*. A further search showed that the district was equally rich in other gems. In 1741, its limits were described with greater precision, and the liberty to collect diamonds farmed upon a lease of forr years to two influential inhabitants, at the rate of 230,000 reis for every negro, with permission to employ six hundred. At every renewal of the lease a high rent was exacted, and the tenants indemnified themselves by conducting their operations in the most wasteful manner.

While the population of Brazil, and the cultivation of its natural products, continued thus to increase, the moral and intellectual culture of its inhabitants was left in a great measure to chance. There was a hierarchical establishment, but one altogether inadequate to the extent of the territory. There were schools, but few and far between. The colonists, thinly spread over what appeared an illimitable region, were most of them alike beyond the reach of instruction and of the arm of the law. The restrictions upon the free exercise of industry, introduced with a view to benefit the royal treasury, were little calculated to reconcile men to legal restraints which they scarcely knew in any other form. They grew up, therefore, with those robust and healthy sentiments engendered by the absence of false teachers; but at the same time they became habituated to a repugnance to legal ordinances, accustomed to give full scope to all their passions, and encouraged by their sense of ascendency over the Indians to habits of violence and oppression. From the first moment of their landing in Brazil, the Jesuits had constituted themselves the protectors of the oppressed natives. But they were strenuously opposed by the interested colonists, and by the ordinary clergy. The Jesuits were not however easily dismayed, and, by dint of the most persevering exertions, they procured from government an explicit confirmation of the freedom of the natives. Their next step was to collect their red children, as in all their other missions, into *aldeas*, over which officials of their order exercised both spiritual and temporal authority. Their intentions were pious and good, but their plan was erroneous. They attempted to teach the most recondite dogmas of the Christian faith, before either the hearts or heads of their pupils were sufficiently awakened to comprehend them. They taught observance to the rules of external decorum, without inculcating those more essential principles which are independent of all form. By depriving the Indians of the power of managing their own affairs, they effectually stifled within them the germs of human thought and action. The Indian of the aldeas was little better than a puppet, and, when separated from his tutors, he soon sunk back into hopeless and irreclaimable barbarism. The persecution of the Indians was yet more efficaciously put a stop to by the sacrifice of an equally innocent and yet more injured race. The Portuguese establishments on the coast of

Africa have ever been more extensive, and their slave dealings better organized, than those of any other nation. By this means a large number of negroes was annually imported into Brazil, and being found more active and serviceable as laborers than the native tribes, the latter were in a great measure left to enjoy their savage independence.

The Portuguese government, under the administration of Carvalho, afterwards Marquis of Pombal, attempted to extend to Brazil the effects of that bold spirit of innovation which directed all his actions. Carvalho had experienced great resistance to his plans of reform at home from the Jesuits; and his brother, when appointed governor of Maranhâo, experienced a resistance no less strenuous on their part to some measures of his government. This was enough to determine the proud minister to lessen the power of the order. With his sanction, the Jesuits and other regulars were deprived of all temporal authority over their aldeas in the State of Maranhâo and Para. These, twenty-eight in number, were converted by the edict of the governor into nine townlets, eighteen towns, and one city. The towns were to be governed by *juizes ordinarios*, to fill which offices a preference was given to Indians. The aldeas independent of towns were to be governed by their respective chiefs. The lands adjacent to the towns and hamlets were divided among the Indians, and declared heritable property. To these regulations of his brother, the minister superadded some enactments intended to supply the loss of Jesuits as teachers. The task of religious instruction was delegated to the bishop. Till such time as the Indians should be sufficiently advanced in civilization to manage their own affairs, a director was appointed to reside in each settlement; a man of integrity and zeal, and conversant with the native tongues. These functionaries were directed to combat the prejudice, that there existed a natural inferiority in the Indian character, and to promote, as far as in them lay, intermarriages between the white and red races. As a reward for the directors, they were to have a sixth part of all that the Indians reared, excepting what was specially appropriated for their own consumption.

These ordinances, originally promulgated for Maranhâo and Para, were ratified in Lisbon, and extended to the whole of Brazil. But the good which they might have done was neutralized in a great measure by some compulsory services still left binding upon the Indians, and by listlessness on the part of the white inhabitants in carrying them into effect. No good understanding could subsist between an ambitious order and the minister who had so openly braved them. Carvalho felt his new arrangement insecure as long as a Jesuit remained in Brazil. First of all, he sought to render the order suspected of being accessary to some partial revolts among the Indian troops on the Rio Negro. But it was the confession of one of the leaders of the conspiracy against the life of the King of Portugal, when put to the torture, that some Jesuits were implicated in the undertaking, that finally delivered them into his hands. In 1760, they were expelled from Brazil, under circumstances of considerable severity.

Pombal's next measure attracted more attention than his plans for the improvement of the Indians. The Brazilian Company, founded by Vieyra, which so materially contributed to preserve its South American possessions to Portugal, had been abolished, in 1721, by John V. Such instruments, however, were calculated to win the confidence of a bold spirit like that of Pombal. In 1755, he established a chartered company, with a capital of 1,200,000 crusados, in 1200 shares, to trade exclusively with Maranhâo and Para. In 1759, a similar company was chartered for Paraiba and Pernambuco. Remonstrances were made on the part of the Board of Public Good, and the British factory at Lisbon; but the members of the former body were punished, and those of the latter were disregarded. Encouraged by success, the minister established an exclusive company for the whale fishery, and bestowed upon it the monopoly of furnishing Brazil with salt. This company had its head-quarters in the island of S. Catharina. Some time after these arrangements, an extension of the facility of intercourse was granted, and Portugnse subjects, instead of being restricted to the annual fleets, were allowed to trade in single ships to Bahia and the Rio. The arrangements of Pombal extended also to the interior of the country. The claims of the original donatories in the respective captaincies were indefinite and oppressive in the highest degree. Other ministers had from time to time bought up some of these rights; Carvalho extinguished them at once, indemnifying the holders. With all his power, however, he durst not interfere in behalf of such new Christians (converted Jews) as were accused of adhering in private to their ancestral faith; but he prohibited, under strict penalties, light and malicious denunciations. He strengthened and enforced the regulations in the mining districts. Observing the profuse mode in which the treasures of the diamond district were lavished, he moved the king to take the management of it into his own hands. In 1772, an ordinance was issued, in which Pombal, as prime minister, reserved to himself, the management of this district. The details of the business were discharged by three directors in Lisbon, and three administrators in Brazil. At the head of the latter was placed an intendant-general, who, as the representative of majesty, exercised an unlimited power within his jurisdiction. He controlled the working of the diamond mines; he stood at the head of the judicial and police establishments; and he was authorized to punish every inhabitant convicted of having jewels in his possession with banishment and confiscation of goods, and even upon mere suspicion to order any individual to quit the district. The policy of many of Pombal's measures is more than questionable. His encouragement of monopolies, and his preference of the interests of the crown to those of the state, as evinced in the regulations of the mining and diamond districts, do not admit of defence. But the admission of all races to equal rights in the eye of the law —the abolition of feudal privileges, and of certain restrictions upon commerce, with the livelier spirit which he knew how to infuse even into his monopolies—powerfully co-operated towards the development of the capabilities of Brazil. The spirit of improvement must have been already awake in the bosoms of the people, otherwise even his legislative energies would have been expended in vain. Still the merit abides with him of having firmly organized the powers of the land, and marshalled their way. And yet when, upon the death of his king and patron in 1777, court intrigue forced him from his high station, and his successor was lauded to the skies for concluding a treaty of limits, in which Pombal's chivalrous bravery had rendered Spain glad to acquiesce, whilst he who had done so much for his country's institutions was reviled on all hands.

During the first thirty years after the retirement of Pombal from active life, the most important feature in the history of Brazil was the conspiracy of Minas, in 1789. In this rich district the population was increasing rapidly. Some young men began to be remarked for their literary talents, chiefly as poets. The successful issue of the recent revolution of the English colonies in North America, filled their minds with such enthusiasm, that they fancied it would be very easy to imitate them. A cavalry officer, Silva Xavier, nicknamed Tira-dentes (tooth-drawer) formed a project to throw off the Portuguese yoke and to proclaim an independent republic. He associated in his plan Colonel Freire de Andrade, commander of the military forces of Rio de Janeiro, some wealthy merchants of that town and others; but the plot was discovered. The conspirators were all condemned to be quartered, but the queen modified the sentence. Tira-dentas alone was hanged; the others were banished to Africa. As a means of adding to its popularity the government decreed the immediate abolition of the oppressive salt monopoly, as a reward for the good conduct of the people. By such means peace and tranquillity were preserved, and from that time affairs went on prosperously. The mining districts continued to be enlarged, especially in the direction of Matto Grosso and Goyaz, where diamonds had been discovered. Roads, although very imperfectly constructed, were opened to facilitate the communication with those districts. The companies of Maranhâo, Pernambuco, and Paraiba were abolished, but the impulse they had given to the agricultural industry remained. Cotton, the growth of which they had promoted in Maranhâo, was introduced into Pernambuco, and cultivated so successfully as to become in a short time the main article of export. Removed from all communication with the rest of the world, except through Portugal, Brazil remained unaffected by the first years of the great revolutionary war in Europe. Indirectly, however, the fate of this isolated country was decided by the consequences of the French Revolution. Brazil is the only instance of a colony becoming the seat of the government of its own mother country, and this was the work of Napoleon. When he resolved upon the invasion and conquest of Portugal, the Prince Regent, afterwards Don John VI., having no means of resistance, decided to take refuge in Brazil. He created a regency in Lisbon, ordered that no resistance should be offered to the French invasion, and departed for Brazil on the 29th of November, 1807, accompained by the Queen Donna Maria I., the royal family, all the great officers of state, a large part of the nobility, and numerous retainers. They arrived at Bahia on the 21st of January, 1808. The royal family was received with enthusiasm. The regent was requested to establish there the seat of his government, but a more secure asylum presented itself in Rio de Janeiro, where the royal fugitives arrived on the 7th of March. Before leaving Bahia, Don John took the first step to emancipate Brazil. By a decree dated the 28th of January, its ports were opened to foreign commerce, the merchandise being subject to a duty of 24 per cent. The exportation also of all the products of Brazil under any flag was permitted, except some royal monopolies, such as diamonds, Brazil-wood, etc.

Once established in Rio de Janeiro, the government of the regent was directed to the creation of an administrative machinery for the dominions that remained to him; and all the supreme tribunals of administration, of justice, and of finance, were established as they existed in Portugal. Besides the ministry which had come with the regent, the council of state and all the other departments of the four ministers then existing, there were in the course of one year created, a supreme court of justice and equity, which had the power to annul and revise the sentences of the other courts, the royal mint, the bank of Brazil, royal printing office, etc. The salaries of so large a number of high officials, and the maintenance of the court entailed expenses which the simple colonial administration had never required. The imposition, therefore, of new taxes, was a natural consequence. Heavy duties were successfully imposed upon tobacco, sugar, dry and salted hides, cotton, and other exports. A tax of ten per cent. upon house rents in the towns, and upon the sale of real estate, and harbor dues, were also levied. The expenses, however, continuing to increase, the government next had recourse to the reprehensible measure of altering the money standard. Gold was coined in a new form, the intrinsic value of which was not comparatively equal to the former standard, and the Spanish dollars were recoined, retaining the same weight and size, and sent into circulation with a value of 20 per cent. higher than their intrinsic and commercial value. The whole monetary system was thrown into the greatest confusion by the simultaneous circulation of three different standards of currency. From this ensued a confusion in the finances of the country, and in private transactions, as well as a fluctuation in foreign exchange, from which Brazil suffers even at the present day. The bank, in addition to its private mercantile functions, farmed many of the regalia, and was in the practice of advancing large sums to the state, sometimes in consideration of valuable deposits, sometimes upon the assignment of taxes not yet due. An extensive system of corruption, however, arose, and the breaking of the bank some years later was the consequence. Thus the government of the Prince Regent commenced its career in the New World with the most palpable and dangerous errors in the financial system.

Notwithstanding these evils, the increased activity which a multitude of new customers and an increased circulating medium, imparted to the trade of Rio, added a new stimulus to the industry of the whole nation. Immense numbers of English artisans and ship-builders, Swedish ironfounders, German engineers, and French artists and manufacturers, sought fortunes in the new land of promise, and diffused, both by example and precept, industry and ingenuity throughout the country. Useful measures were continually appearing; vaccination was introduced, various educational institutions were founded, and several arrangements were adopted in favor of commerce, such as the appointment of inspectors to prevent frauds on exported goods, and the permission to give money in bottomry, with such interest as parties might agree upon. Foreigners were permitted the free exercise of their worship; and it is worthy of remark, that while all the tribunals which existed in Portugal were established, and a See of Rio de Janeiro erected in imitation of the Patriarchal See of Lisbon, no Inquisition was established.

In the beginning of 1809, in retaliation of the occupation of Portugal, an expedition was sent from Para to the French colony of Guiana. After some fighting, the governor and garrison capitulated, and Guiana was incorporated with Brazil. Although this conquest was of short duration—for by the treaty of Vienna, in 1815, the colony was restored to France—it contributed to the improvement of agriculture in Brazil. It had been until then the policy of Portugal to prevent its colonies from enjoying the same productions. The cultivation of sugar, for instance, was reserved to Brazil and prohibited in Africa; while the cultivation of the spices of India was prohibited in Brazil, and even those which grew spontaneously (such as cinnamon), were ordered to be destroyed. Now, however, many seeds of different plants were imported not only from Guiana, but also from India and Africa, cultivated in the Royal Botanical Garden, and from thence distributed amongst private individuals. The same principle which dictated the conquest of French Guiana, dictated some attempts to seize the Spanish colonies of Monte Video and Buenos Ayres, Portugal being also at war with Spain. Here, however, a conquest by force of arms was not easy, and the chiefs of these colonies were invited to place them under the protection of the Portuguese crown. At first they affected loyalty and devotion to their king and refused the invitation; but a little after they threw off the mask, and declared themselves an independent republic. The Spanish governor was able for some time to hold the Banda Oriental in subjection, and received succors from the court of Rio de Janeiro, but was afterwards defeated by Artigas, the chief of the independents; and Monte Video met with the same fate as Buenos Ayres. The inroads made on the frontiers of Rio Grande and S. Paulo, together with the dangerous example of anarchy and of republican principles, decided the court of Rio de Janeiro to take possession of Monte Video. A force of five thousand select troops, under General Lecor, was sent from Portugal, together with a Brazilian corps under General Curado. The irregular troops of Artigas, terrible in skirmishes and surprises, were incapable of resisting disciplined troops, and were forced after a total defeat to take refuge on the right bank of the Uruguay. The garrison of Monte Video evacuated, and General Lecor took possession of the city on the 20th of January, 1817. The territory of Missiones was occupied afterwards. Artigas, however, having recrossed the Uruguay, continued master of a part of the Banda Oriental; but this province properly formed part of the Brazilian territory from 1817. Without possessing one sea-port, Artigas sent letters of marque to American privateers, which did incalculable mischief to the Portuguese commerce.

The importance which Brazil was acquiring decided the regent to give it the title of kingdom, and by a decree of the 16th of January, 1815, the Portuguese sovereignty thenceforward took the title of the United Kingdom of Portugal, Brazil and Argarves. Thus the old colonial government disappeared even in name. The national pride of the Brazilians was flattered, and for some time nothing else was heard of but addresses of thanks and congratulations, feasts and rejoicings in every district. In March, 1816, the Queen Donna Maria I. died, and the Prince Regent became king, under the title of Don John VI.

Although Brazil had now become in fact the head of its own mother country, the government was not in the hands of Brazilians, but of the Portuguese who had followed the court. This government was ignorant and profligate, and the morals of the court were far from being pure. The amiable character of the king preserved his personal popularity, but the public discontent daily increased. Justice was ill administered, and negligence, disorder, and corruption reigned in all the departments. In Portugal the discontent was still greater on account of its anomalous position, standing as it were in the relation of a colony of its own. These causes and the fermentation of liberal principals produced by the French Revolution, originated, in 1817, a conspiracy in Lisbon, which was, however, discovered in time to prevent its success. A similar result took place in the province of Pernambuco, where a regular conspiracy to establish a republican government had in fact arrived at the point of having ramifications in Bahia and other provinces; but an accident led to its bursting forth before the time, and probably was the cause of its being so promptly smothered. In Bahia the governor was able to avoid a similar outbreak, and even to detach at once a sufficient force to put down the revolution of Pernambuco, so that the republic established there scarcely lasted ninety days. Some of the chiefs fled in time; three, Martins, Mendonça, and the priest Almeida, were hung, and a great number were condemned to exile and imprisonment. Don John, fearing the progress of the republican spirit in Brazil, sent to Portugal for bodies of picked troops, which were stationed in Rio and in the different capitals of the provinces under the command of the best generals.

In Portugal the popular discontent produced the revolution of 1820. Representative government was proclaimed, and the constitution was to be framed by a congress of the representatives of the people, the Spanish constitution of 1812 being adopted provisionally. In Rio de Janeiro the Portuguese troops, with which the king had surrounded himself as a defence against the liberal spirit of the Brazilians, took up arms on the 26th of February, 1821, to force him to accept and swear to the system proclaimed in Portugal. The king attempted a modification of the Spanish constitution, adopting a chamber of peers, but the insurgents would accept no compromise. He finally submitted, took the oath, and named a new ministry. The scenes of Rio de Janeiro were repeated, or simultaneously enacted in Pernambuco, Bahia, Maranhâo, and other provinces, where the governors were deposed and provisional juntas created in their stead. The idea of a free government filled them with enthusiasm, and the principles of a representative legislature were freely adopted. From this time such use was made of the liberty of the press, that talents and knowledge of a high order were revealed, which had not been supposed to exist in Brazil. The first care everywhere was the election of deputies to the cortes of Lisbon, to take part in the framing of the new constitution of the united kingdom. Magistrates, advocates, priests, and military men, put themselves at the head of this movement and were elected. From this time great political importance was given to the existing municipal councils, which being formed by popular elections, were considered to represent the people. As the king could not abandon Portugal to itself, he determined at first to send Don Pedro, heir to the throne, to Portugal, but afterwards decided to go himself, and leave the prince in Brazil as regent and *locum-tenens.* It is now beyond doubt, that the secret instructions he left him were to oppose as far as possible the independence of Brazil, which he considered to be imminent; but if it could not be averted, to place himself at the head of the movement, and obtain the sovereignty of Brazil, so that this most considerable portion of the united kingdom might remain in the hands of the family of Braganza, rather than in the hands of adventurers. The Brazilian deputies, on arriving in Lisbon, expressed their dissatisfaction with the cortes for having commenced the framing of the constitution, and taking measures in respect to Brazil before their arrival. Brazil felt that she could not be treated as a secondary part of the monarchy. The organization which the cortes were giving to the monarchy would have the effect of reducing Brazil to its former condition of a colony. Sharp discussions and angry words passed between the Brazilian and Portuguese deputies. The news of these proceedings excited great discontent in Brazil. The tone of the discussions with regard to the prince regent irritated him, and a decree ordering his retirement to Portugal, filled the Brazilians with alarm. They saw that, without a central authority, the country would fall either into its former condition of a colony, divided into provincial governments subject to Portugal, or else into a state of anarchy. The provisional government of S. Paulo, influenced by the two Andradas, brothers of the leading deputy in Lisbon, commenced a movement for independence by asking the prince regent to disobey the cortes and remain in Brazil. The municipal council of Rio de Janeiro made a similar representation, to which the prince gave a decisive assent. The Portuguese troops assumed at first a coercive attitude, but were forced to give way before the unanimous ardor and the formidable military preparations of the Brazilians. They submitted, accordingly, to embark for Portugal. These scenes in Rio were repeated in Pernambuco, where the Portuguese, after various conflicts, were obliged to leave the country. In Bahia, however, the Brazilians succumbed, and the Portuguese troops remained masters of the city. In Maranhâo, and Para also, the Portuguese party prevailed. In Rio the agitation for independence continued. The two brothers Andradas were called to the ministry; and the municipal council conferred on the prince regent the title of Perpetual Defender of Brazil. With great activity and courage he set off to the central provinces of Minas and S. Paulo, to suppress disaffected movements and direct revolution. In S. Paulo, on the 7th of September, 1822, he proclaimed the independence of Brazil. On his return to Rio de Janeiro on the 12th October, he was proclaimed Constitutional Emperor with great enthusiasm.

Bahia was chosen by the cortes at Lisbon as a centre for resisting the independence. Thither numerous forces were sent to General Madeira, who had at his disposal, besides, militia, 12,000 of the best disciplined troops, who had served under the Duke of Wellington in the Peninsular wars. The city, however, was vigorously beseiged by the Brazilians by land, and succors were sent to them from Rio and Pernambuco. The Portuguese made many obstinate sallies, but were always repulsed; and finding their provisions fail they were obliged to embark for Portugal, July 2, 1823. Their squadron was composed of fifteen ships of war, and seventy-seven transports. The Brazilian squadron, under command of Lord Cochrane, although weaker, was better prepared for action than that of the Portuguese, which was embarrassed with so many troops. Cochrane attacked them, and took some ships. Taylor, another Englishman in the Brazilian service, followed it to the coast of Portugal, and even took some ships within the sight of land. Cochrane proceeded to reduced Maranhâo, and sent Grenfell to Para. Independence triumphed in both provinces. All resistance seemed impossible to the Portuguese after their power was destroyed in Bahia. The troops in Monte Video were abandoned by General Lecor, who declared for the independence, and they also embarked for Portugal; the Banda Oriental remaining part of Brazil, with the title of *Provincia Cisplatina.* Before the end of 1823, the authority of the emperor and the independence of Brazil were undisputed throughout the whole country. It is worthy of mention that during the whole contest the name of the king was always pronounced in Brazil with respect; all the manifestoes and proclamations were directed against the cortes, and the king was always commiserated by his Brazilian subjects as under coercion, and as a prisoner of the cortes.

In almost every part of Brazil, chiefly in the north, as soon as the Portuguese yoke was thrown off, republican movements spread. To suppress these the authorities employed the Portuguese, and, above all, the militia regiments formed of the commercial young men. These, as soon as they lost all hope of assistance from Portugal, looked to the emperor for support. The emperor, on his side, began to fear the spirit of republicanism in Brazil, and to consider the Portuguese as his firmest supporters. This disposition much influenced the course of his government and his future destiny. The contest with the troops and with the Portuguese party went on jointly with the organization of the empire. At first a council was given to the prince, composed of *Procuradores* of the provinces freed from the Portuguese yoke, which assembled in Rio de Janeiro on the 2d of June, 1822. This council immediately deliberated upon the convocation of a constituent assembly, which the prince convoked by a decree of the 6th of June. On the 3rd of May, 1823, Don Pedro, crowned emperor since 1st of December, opened this constituent assembly in Rio de Janeiro. Then commenced the discussion of a project of constitution, in which the democratic element prevailed, though not so much as in the constitutions adopted at the same time by Spain, Portugal, Naples, and Sardinia. In Brazil a chamber of senators was to be created, in whose selection the monarch would take a part; while, in the constitutions of those kingdoms, the legislative power was vested in a single chamber. The two Andradas, and their brother, at first a distinguished leader of the independence in the cortes of Lisbon, and now in the constituent assembly, encountered great opposition; while their yoke was becoming every day more insupportable to the young emperor, whom they imagined they could govern as a sovereign of their own creation. On the 16th of July, the emperor resolved to dismiss them, and a new ministry was formed. The Andradas organized a violent opposition against this and the person of the emperor, which led to the dissolution of the assembly and the exiling the Andradas, November 13, 1823. In the decree which dissolved the assembly, Don Pedro convoked another to deliberate upon a proposed constitution more liberal than the one the assembly was discussing. Public opinion, meantime, was in a state of intense fermentation. In Portugal, Spain, Naples, and Piedmont representative government had fallen. The dissolution of the Brazilian constituent assembly led to the belief that the emperor intended also to make himself absolute. In Rio S. Paulo and Minas the discontent was so strong and universal that the emperor published new decrees, proclamations and manifestoes, explaining his motives, and protesting that he wished to maintain the representative system. The proclamation of a republic in the province of Pernambuco, Ceará, and others in the north, disorders in the south, and the loss of the province of Cisplatina, were the consequences of the *coup d' état* of November 13th, 1823.

The Brazilians were universally discontented; on one side fearing absolutism if they supported the emperor, on the other they feared anarchy if he fell. The emperor, knowing the danger of an undefined position, caused the municipal council to petition him to dispense with the deliberation of a constituent assembly, and to adopt immediately as the constitution of the empire the project framed by the council of state. Accordingly, on the 25th of March, 1824, the emperor swore to the constitution with great solemnity and public rejoicings. This policy of the emperor saved him and saved Brazil. The year 1824 was a time of difficulty, but the assurance given to the Brazilians that they would not lose the representative government enabled the emperor to triumph over the rebellion of the northern provinces, and to prevent similar movements in others. On account of the continued disorders the legislative chambers were not convoked during this year. The next year found Brazil in a state of tranquillity and obedience, but still the chambers were not convoked. The cortes of Lisbon having fallen, the king fancied that the Brazilians would submit to him, and sent emissaries to Rio de Janeiro to treat with the emperor. They arrived in September, 1823, but the Brazilian ministry did not permit them to land. Afterwards preparations were begun in Portugal to fit out a squadron against Brazil; but these were finally given up, the ministers, acceding to the wishes of the king, having always opposed the war. Negotiations were opened in London between the Brazilian and Portuguese plenipotentiaries; on the 29th of August, 1825, a treaty was signed, by which the king, Don John VI., assumed the title of Emperor of Brazil, and immediately abdicated in favor of his son, acknowledging Brazil as an independent empire. Brazil was obliged to take upon herself all the debt of Portugal contracted in London=$7,500,000, and pay besides $1,000,000 as indemnification for property of Don John VI. A treaty of commerce was promised by which Portugal would be considered as the most favored nation, her merchandise paying provisionally no higher duties than 15 per cent. in the custom-houses. Finally, Brazil was to pay the sums liquidated as expenses incurred by Portugal for the transport of troops and other indemnities to private Portuguese subjects. The rebellion of the province Cisplatina (Banda Oriental), favored by Buenos Ayres, was followed by a declaration of war by the emperor against that republic. On the pretence of that war he commenced forming regiments of Germans engaged in Europe. He entered into a treaty of commerce with France, and another with England, for the cessation of the slave trade, and finally convoked the legislative chambers at Rio de Janeiro on the 4th of May, 1826.

Until the middle of the year 1823, Don Pedro had acquired in Brazil a high and well deserved popularity. He was the creator of the empire; he had delivered Brazil from anarchy, and had given her political liberty; but since the dissolution of the constituent assembly, he had entirely lost his popularity. He had given himself up to the influence of the Portuguese, preferring them in all things to the natives. He had also shown a desire to make himself absolute. The most popular men who had worked for the independence, the Andradas, were banished. The war with Buenos Ayres was considered, like the rebellion in the north, as provoked by him, and threatened disastrous consequences to the country, whose resources he should have employed in the development of its internal prosperity and its new institutions. The treaty with Portugal was not only indecorous but unjust. Brazil purchased for nearly $2,000,000 the independence which she had won by her arms, and was obliged to pay the expenses of a war in which she had been victorious. His licentious life alienated the respect and consideration of his subjects, above all, when contrasted with the high character of the empress for virtue, charity, and condescension.

The death of his father offered an opportunity to Don Pedro for regaining in some measure his popularity. He was unanimously acknowledged as king of Portugal; and representatives of the clergy, the nobility, and the people, came to Rio de Janeiro to make their submission. A suspicion immediately sprung up that the independence of Brazil would be annulled. Don Pedro, however, promptly tranquillized the public mind, by abdicating the crown of Portugal in favor of his daughter, Donna Maria, and giving it a constitution on the model of that of Brazil. This resolution, taken on the eve of opening the Brazilian legislative assembly, won him a very flattering reception from the chambers and the public.

The ministry, however, did not present any measure or system of public utility, or any regulations to give practical working to the representative government. The entire session of the chambers was passed in barren and odious accusations and recriminations. In the session of 1827, the legislative body, notwithstanding their dissatisfaction at the system of government, allowed so large a civil list that it almost absorbed a tenth part of the total revenue of the empire. The violence, however, of the opposition in the chamber of deputies was always increasing. The lavish expenditure of the public moneys, and the bad state of the finances—the currency exclusively composed of copper money and of the notes of a bank in a state of bankruptcy—the shameful manner in which the operations against Buenos Ayres, both by sea and land, were conducted; the evils suffered by commerce, the presence of mercenary soldiers and the vexation of recruiting, afforded ample subjects for public discontent and for the denunciations of the opposition. The emperor continued the same line of policy; he was constantly changing his ministers, but rarely to any profit. Unpopular treaties were made with various nations; but the chambers established by law equal custom-house duties for all nations, in order to render the treaties unnecessary. During the session of 1827, the public internal debt was consolidated and inscribed in the great book, and a department was created for the application of the sinking fund and payment of dividends.

The year 1828 was a calamitous one for Don Pedro and for Brazil. It commenced with the defeat of the Brazilian army by the Argentine forces, and this entirely through the incapacity of the commander-in-chief. In Rio de Janeiro the German and Irish regiments mutinied, and there were three days' fighting in the city between them and the Brazilian troops. Misunderstandings arose with the United States and France on account of the merchant vessels made prizes of by the Brazilian squadron blockading Buenos Ayres; and the imperial government being threatened with force, consented to pay for them. Afterwards England made a similar claim in a menacing tone, with a like result. The financial embarrassments were increasing to an alarming extent. The emperor was compelled by the English government to make peace with Buenos Ayres, renouncing the Banda Oriental, provided that it did not unite itself to Buenos Ayres, but formed an independent State with the title of the Republic of Uruguay. At length, to fill up the sum of disasters, affairs went wrong with Don Pedro even in Portugal. His brother, Don Miguel, treacherously usurped the crown, availing himself of his authority as regent, with which he had been invested. So many misfortunes were the result of a policy the responsibility of which the emperor incurred personally, as it was in opposition to the feelings of the public and of the chambers. It was under such unlucky auspices that the elections of the new deputies took place in 1829. As was expected, the result was the election everywhere of ultra-liberals opposed to the emperor, who still persevered in his course. A trifling riot in an insignificant town of Pernambuco was immediately seized as a pretext for the suspension of the *habeas corpus* in all that province, and the formation of a military commission to try even civilians. These measures caused great discontent. In October, the second wife of Don Pedro, the Princess Amelia of Leutenburgh, arrived in Rio de Janeiro. She was well received by the public. The arrival of an empress, beautiful, and adorned with so many brilliant accomplishments, encouraged a hope that the emperor would wholly abandon licentiousness and vice.

In 1830, the chamber, elected in 1829, assembled. If in the first, the opposition against the personal policy of the emperor had been violent, and led by men of the highest talent, in this, the opposition obtained almost a unanimity of votes. The democratic press every day insulted the emperor in a very unbecoming manner, and the people everywhere exhibited their disaffection. During the session of 1830, the chambers adopted a criminal code, framed according to the doctrines of Jeremy Bentham, in which punishment by death for political offences was abolished, and in the budget they included a clause which compelled the government to disband the foreign regiments. Animated by the example of France, the republican party thought that the moment had arrived to dethrone Don Pedro. Some journals suggested the idea of reforming the constitution by turning Brazil into independent federal provinces governed by authorities popularly elected, and only acknowledging the emperor as a common centre, assisted by a federal congress, as in the United States. This idea was gaining ground in the provinces, not only because it flattered local interests and passions, but because whatever tended to evince disaffection to the emperor, and limit his authority, pleased the discontented. The emperor alarmed, set off with the empress for Minas to stir up the former enthusiasm of that province in his favor, from recollections of the independence.

On his return to Rio in March, 1831, scenes of disorder occurred. Some deputies, at the time in Rio, presented a very energetic remonstrance to him, upon which he decided to form a ministry which included the most forward members of the liberal party; but men who ought to have been chosen, the most conspicuous and moderate leaders of the majority in the chamber, were excluded. The agitation and discontent continued. Don Pedro, tired of struggling, and disgusted at the opposition of his subjects, accused them of ingratitude, and resolved to try his fortune in Portugal. There, he was persuaded, he could unite Portugal and Spain under his rule; and so, early in April, he abdicated in favor of the heir apparent, then a little over five years old. The country was thus left without a government, and exposed to all the horrors of anarchy. Don Pedro immediately embarked with the empress on board an English ship of the line, leaving the new emperor, Don Pedro II., and the princesses Januaria, Francisca, and Paula. On the 13th of April he left Brazil to its fate.

Meanwhile the deputies and senators assembled to snatch the country out of the hands of the republican party. They first elected a provisional, and afterwards (May 3d) a permanent regency composed of three members. The first care of the new regent was the appointment of a ministry composed of the most influential members of the chambers. The republican party, however, enraged at seeing the power escape from their hands, excited discontent in all directions; and such horrible scenes of disorder succeeded, that it seemed as if Brazil were destined to the state of chronic anarchy which prevailed among its neighbors of the Spanish race. The regency and the ministry showed the greatest prudence and courage. To the activity and energy, however, of Feijoó, a priest, minister of justice, the country is chiefly indebted for the preservation of order and the union of the provinces. The government and its supporters adhered to the reform of the constitution, and treated to gain time, and so to modify it that the monarchy might be saved. The reform was finally decreed in 1834. Instead of a regency of three members elected by the legislative chambers, one regent only was appointed, chosen by the electors in the same manner as the deputies. The councils of provinces, which hitherto had simply a consulting vote in local matters, were replaced by legislative provincial assemblies, with power in such matters to make provincial laws, which were to be executed with the sanction of the president of the province. These reforms were well received, and immediately put into execution. They inaugurated in Brazil in reality a republican government analogous to that of the United States, for not the least difference existed between the election of the regent and that of the president of this republic. The election for the regency fell on the ex-minister of justice Feijoó, a man of small attainments and democratic principles, whose remarkable self-will and obstinacy brought him into great difficulties. The provinces, although more or less agitated, had already been reduced to obedience. Para and Rio Grande alone were in open rebellion. The former, in which great horrors were perpetrated, became pacified; but in Rio Grande the warlike habits of the people, the interest which many of the inhabitants had in a civil war, which afforded them opportunities of enriching themselves by plunder, the facility in receiving succors from the other rebels of the republic of Uruguay, and the nature of the ground, rendered the pacification of the province very difficult. The imperial forces occupied all the cities and villages, while the rebels ravaged the open country. The regent was accused of conniving at the rebels, and the opposition of the chamber of deputies became so violent, that rather than change his policy he resigned. In September, 1837, he appointed the senator Araujo Lima minister of the home department, a man of extensive abilities and experience, and who had been a candidate at all the elections for the regency. Araujo Lima appointed a ministry composed of men of the greatest note in the chambers, gave a great impulse to the war in Rio Grande, and strove to give his government the character of a monarchical reaction against the principals of democracy, which had guided the policy of Feijoó. On the new election for the regency, he was chosen by a large majority.

The experiment of a republican government in Brazil had proved so discreditable—the country was so wearied of cabals and instability, that the men known hitherto for their sympathy with democratic principles, saw that it was only by being more monarchical than the regent himself, that they would be able to seize the power. Under this impression they set to work. They maintained that as soon as the Princess Donna Januaria completed her eighteenth year, she would be entitled to the regency in the name of her brother. The article, however, of the constitution which they appealed to was not clear; and the good sense of the public perceived, that if the empire could be governed by a princess of eighteen, it would be governed far better by the emperor himself, who was then fourteen. A bill was accordingly presented to the legislature, dispensing with the age of the emperor, and declaring that he had attained his majority. It was carried after a noisy discussion, and the majority of the emperor was proclaimed in a sort of revolutionary manner on the 23d of July, 1840.

The emperor appointed a coalition ministry (including two of the Andradas), which fell before the year had expired, and was replaced by the party of the last regent, which began to be called the Saquarema party. In 1842, a rebellion broke out in the provinces of San Paulo and Minas, which was with difficulty repressed. A misunderstanding between the emperor and his ministers cast him again into the arms of the Feijoó party, which was now called the Santa Luzia party. Several ministries taken from this party governed the empire from 1843 to 1848, and the most important service rendered was the pacification of Rio Grande de Sul, obtained more through negotiation than by force of arms. In September, 1848, the emperor formed a Saquarema ministry, with the ex-regent Araujo Lima, now Visconde de Olinda at its head. The ministry commmenced with two great difficulties. Hostilities had been roused by the English government on account of neglect shown by the Brazilian authorities in putting the treaty in force for the abolition of the slave-trade. On the other hand, the governor of Buenos Ayres, General Rosas, was endeavoring to revolutionize afresh the province of Rio Grande, separate it from the empire, and in this way break up or weaken the Brazilian monarchy. The slave-trade had hitherto been impudently carried on, protected by some authorities, and tolerated by others. The number of slaves introduced in 1849 amounted to 54,000. This excess of itself, and the symptoms of insurrection which appeared, had already rendered unpopular the dealers in slaves, who enriched themselves by exacting money from the ruined planters. The appearance of the yellow fever also, until now unknown in Brazil, was attributed to the importation of slaves; so that public opinion began at last to declare against the traffic. The minister of justice, Sr. Eusebio de Queiroz, profited by this feeling to pass severe laws against slave dealing, and to secure their rigorous enforcement, so that in 1850, the importation of slaves diminished to 23,000; in 1851, to 3,280, and in 1852 to 700. In 1853 there was not a single disembarkation; so that it may now be said that the slave-trade is extinct in Brazil.

In the contest with Rosas, the success of the ministerial policy was no less brilliant. The Visconde de Olinda left the ministry, through ill health, in the beginning of 1849. He was succeeded by the Visconde de Mont Alegre, who had been one of the three regents appointed by the legislature in 1831: the secretaryship of foreign affairs was given to Sr. Paulino de Souza. This ministry entered into an alliance with the governors of Monte Viedo, Paraguay, and the States of Entre-Rios and Corrientes, for the purpose of maintaining the independence of the republics of Uruguay and Paraguay, which Rosas intended to reunite to Buenos Ayres. The troops of Rosas which besieged the city of Monte Video, and infested the frontiers of Brazil, under the command of General Oribe, were forced to capitulate. Rosas then formally declared war against Brazil. An army composed of the troops of Entre-Rios, Corrientes, Uruguay, and Brazil, commanded by General Urquiza, and assisted by the Brazilian squadron, under the command of Admiral Grenfell, marched on Buenos Ayres. Rosas was able to oppose the allies with an army of 30,000 men; but the cavalry of Urquiza and the Brazilian infantry (amounting in all to 23,000 men), completely routed them on the field of Monte Caseros, and crushed for ever the power of that bloody dictator. The Brazilian infantry took fifty pieces of cannon at the point of the bayonet, and earned a still more glorious distinction by their clemency to their prisoners.

From 1844, Brazil was free from intestine commotions and civil war, and had resumed its activity in useful undertakings. Public education received a strong impulse, and many new streets, roads, canals, improvement of ports, steam navigation, embellishment of cities, and other works of public utility were commenced. The finances rose to a degree of prosperity previously unknown, and commercial intercourse immensely increased. Of late years the prosperity of the country has been steadily on the increase, except that a protracted and obstinate struggle has been kept up with Paraguay. The government has earnestly striven to promote immigration, especially to the banks of the Amazon, where there is room for large and abundant development. According to the latest statement, the annual immigration exceeded 12,000, including Portuguese, Germans, English, etc. The great majority of these are laborers and agriculturists.

Brazil is bounded on the north by New Granada, Venezuela, and the Guianas, Brit ish, French, and Dutch; on the east by the Atlantic; on the south by the republics of Uruguay and the Argentine Confederation; a d on the west by Paraguay, Bolivia, Peru, and Ecuador. It extends from about 4° N. Lat. to 33°40′ S. Lat., and from 35° to 70° W. Long. Its greatest length is about 2600 miles, its greatest breadth about 2500; it has a sea-board of nearly 3700 miles; area estimated to be 3,000,000 square miles. The principal rivers of Brazil are the Amazon, and its tributaries the Tocantins, the Xingu, the Topajoz, from the south; and the Rio Negro and Yapura from the north. From latitude 19° to 21° south stretch the mountains of Itacolumi, 5710 English feet above the level of the sea, and of Itambi, 6900. These, and their connecting range, may be considered as the nucleus of the mountain formation of Brazil. Towards the north, and parallel to the coast, extends the Serra do Mar. Towards the S. W. a similar, or rather the same chain stretches, throwing out spurs on either side, till it gradually subsides into the high plain on the eastern side of the Parana, near its mouth. By means of the Serra dos Vertentes the Itacolumi connects with the system known under the names of Montes Pyreneos, extending in the direction of W. S. W., to the banks of the Paraguay, a little above where it receives the waters of the Parana, and thence towards the north to the sources of the Tocantins. An important arm of this latter, the Itiapomba, but of which little is yet known, runs out to the N. E., and loses itself in the northern sea-board provinces of Brazil. To the west extends the Serra Geral. To the south and the west, in the provinces of S. Paulo and Matto Grosso, these mountains attain an elevation considerably above the level of a high and extensive inland plain. From the Serra dos Vertentes, in Lat. 20° south, flow the streams which combine to form the Rio Francisco; at first in the direction of north, afterwards curving towards the east, till it reaches the ocean in Lat. 11° south. On the southern declivity of the same serra arise the highest sources of the Parana. They flow at first in the direction of due west, and then south. The Parana receiving numerous tributaries, joins the Paraguay in Lat. 27° N., and Long. 58° west. From the southern declivity of the Serra Geral, and from the western side of the Serra do Anambaty, flow the confluents of the Paraguay. From the northern side of the Serra Geral, and from the central and eastern branches of the Montes Pyreneos, descend the four great tributaries of the Amazon, which join that inland ocean from the south, and the streams that intersect the coast of Brazil between Para and the mouth of the Rio Francisco.

The great constituent of all the mountain ranges of Brazil is granite; the maritime ridge seems exclusively composed of it. The soil on the shore consists of clay, covered in many places with a rich mould, resting on a bed of granite, mixed with amphibole, felspar, quartz, and mica. In the high inland plains of Piratininga we find on the surface a red vegetable earth impregnated with oxide of iron; a mass of solid granite supports the whole. Between Rio Janeiro and Villa Rica the soil consists of a strong clay, and the rocks are composed of granite. The mountains in Minas Geraes are composed of ferruginous quartz, granite, or argillaceous schistus. Beds of limestone have been found near Sorocaba, near Sabara in Minas Geraes, and in the gold mines near S. Rita. The Itiapamba, the great chain on the northern coast, consists chiefly of granite. The northern coast from Maranhâo to Olinda is bounded by a reef of coral, in many places resembling an artificial mole. It is employed by the inhabitants in building their houses. The valley of the Amazon has been so little explored, and its impenetrable woods and luxuriant vegetation throw so many difficulties in the way of the geologist, that time must yet elapse ere we can hope for full and satisfactory intelligence. All along the banks of the main stream, and of its tributaries, as long as they continue in the plain, only two mountain rocks are discovered—the variegated and the green sandstone. Beds of marl, clays of different colors, and porcelain clay, occur frequently. On the Tapajos, gypsum occurs in one place. To the south this sandstone formation is bounded by the granite ridges of the Itiapamba, Montes Pyreneos, and Serra Geral. To the north the sandstone is bounded by the gneiss and granite of the Parimé range; to the westward, on the rivers Negro and Yapura, a quartz rock of slaty structure is the basis on which it rests.

The metallic and mineral products which occur in the geological formations above described are various. Iron is found in vast quantites in the high plains of S. Paulo and in Minas Geraes. In Goyaz and Matto Grosso whole districts are covered with formations rich in iron ore. Gold is next, in the extent of country through which it occurs, to iron. It is found in grains intermingled with the latter metal almost wherever it is worked. The chief scene of the exertions of gold-miners has hitherto been in the district of Minas Geraes, among the central mountains, and at the sources of the Paraguay. It is certain, however, that the gold country extends to S. Paulo on the south, and to the mountains among which the Tocantines arises on the north. The soil where the gold is found is ferruginous and deep in many places, resting on rocks of gneiss and granite. The gold rests on a stratum of *cascalho* or gravel, incumbent on the solid rock. It occurs sometimes in grains, sometimes in crystals, and occasionally in large masses. Lead and zinc have been found on the banks of the Rio Abaité, a tributary of the Rio Francisco; chrome and manganese in Paraopeba; platina in other rivers; quicksilver, arsenic, bismuth, and antimony, in the neighborhood of Villa Rica; and copper in Minas Novas. The diamond occurs in greatest abundance in a district of the Serra do Frio, sixteen leagues from north to south, and eight from east to west, known by the designation of the diamond district. It is found in a stratum, of variable thickness, of rounded quartzose pebbles, cemented by an earthy matter. They are found along the banks of rivers, and in cavities and water-courses on the mountains. Fine crystals of euclase are found in Matto Grosso; and no country surpasses Brazil in the size and purity of its beryls. Topazes occur in nearly the same localities as the diamond. They are found among a conglomerate of friable earthy talc, quartz, and crystals of specular iron ore; and they are of many colors, yellow, white, blue, etc. The chrysoberyl, amethyst, and green tourmaline, have been found in the Serra dos Esmeraldos. Vast quanties of culinary salt effloresce from the soil during the dry season in the upper districts of the Paraguay. In the neighborhood of Arrayal are some caves which yield annually about 2250 cwt. of saltpetre. In Piauhy quantities of alum have been found efflorescing from the sandstone. The only fossil remains of animated beings occurring in Brazil, of which we have any authentic account, are found in these caves. It is said that they correspond in every respect with the Megalonyx of Cuvier. They are scattered about in a fine greasy earth, which covers the limestone to the depth of eight inches. Bones, supposed to have formed part of a mammoth, have been found in Minas Geraes; and similar remains have been discovered in Bahia, near the Rio Solitre, and in Pernambuco. Bones resembling those of the megatherium, found in Paraguay, and now in the Cabinet of Natural History at Madrid, are said to have been seen near the Rio de Contas.

A country so extensive as Brazil, and so diversified in its surface, necessarily exhibits a considerable variety of atmospheric phenomena. The greater portion lies within the tropics, and has consequently the periodical interchange of wet and dry seasons. The narrow valleys, exposed to great heats, and surrounded by lofty mountains, have the vapours forced down upon them, and have a moist atmosphere. The high plains of the interior, the extensive level region of the northern coast, and the summits of the mountains, are comparatively dry.

Except on the loftiest mountains, and on the wide *sertaos*, the vegetation of Brazil is luxuriant beyond description. In the mountain passes in the neighborhood of the seashore, the conjoint effects of heat and moisture produce a superfluity of vegetable life, which man's utmost efforts cannot restrain. The vegetable productions of Brazil have a strong analogy with those of Guiana. The most common are the *compositæ, leguminosæ, euphorbiaceæ, rubiaceæ, aroideæ*, and ferns of the most varied forms. The vegetation of the valleys differs from that of the *campos*, as it again does from that which occurs in the *sertaos*. Along the coast, the *mangoes* are the most numerous and prominent species. They flourish from Rio Grande do Sul to Maranhâo, converting the land into a morass wherever they are allowed to flourish unmolested. Immediately behind them numerous families of palms raise their graceful heads. The underwood in the neighbourhood of Rio Janeiro consists principally of crotons. Every large river of Brazil has its own appropriate form of vegetable life, giving a peculiar character to its banks. The vegetation of the Amazon may be divided into three classes; 1, that which we find on the Islands; 2, the vegetation upon the banks overflowed at regular intervals by the stream; 3, that which stands high and dry. Representatives of the most estranged natural families grow side by side. It is only on the islands, where the willow and some other plants are found in numbers, that we are reminded of the monotony of our northern vegetation. Cocoa trees and the vanilla, *capsicum frutescens*, and different kinds of pepper, the cinnamon tree, and Brazilian cassia, abound. The flora of all the tributaries of the Amazon is similar to that just noted, until the traveller ascends above the falls, and finds himself in another region. The vegetation of the southern *campos* (corresponding to the North American *prairies*) is widely different. On the plains of the southern provinces we find scattered about strong tufts of grayish-green and hairy grasses, springing from the red clay. Mingled with these are numerous herbaceous flowers, of the most varied colors and elegant forms. A similar vegetation, but with a richer variety of plants, occurs in the diamond district. On the western declivity of the Serra do Mar, and along the upper banks of the Rio San Francisco, extends a wooded country, but of a character entirely different from that which is found in the valleys below. *Malvæ, euphorbiaceæ, mimosæ*, and such like, are the prevailing types on the Rio Francisco; cactuses, palms, and ferns, abound on the Serra do Mar. In this latter district the ipecacuan flourishes best. In the valley of the Paraguay the most striking feature is presented by the water plants, which in one river are sufficiently strong to impede the navigation of a stream both deep and broad. The forests of Brazil contain almost every species of useful and ornamental wood. The cocoa-tree is found in great quantities in the provinces on the sea-shore, and furnishes one of the most important items of internal commerce. A considerable surplus of cocoa is annually exported. One of the most valuable sorts of timber is furnished by the Ibiripitanga or Brazil-wood which yields a fine red dye. The wood itself is very hard and heavy, and takes a beautiful polish. The other trees most worthy of mention are the *jaracanda* or rosewood tree, the trumpet-tree, the laurel; the soap-tree; the tapia or garlic pear-tree, and the whole family of palms. The banana is one of the most useful of all the trees that grow in Brazil, and its fruit is the chief food of the native Indians. The fruits of Brazil are numerous and excellent. The best of these are the pine-apple, the mango, the custard-apple, the guava, and the various kinds of melons and nuts.

In an empire of such vast extent as Brazil, embracing as it does, every variety of temperature and elevation, the value and importance of the agricultural products cannot fail to be very great. The number of farmers, however, is, as yet, small compared with the extent of the soil. The chief products of

Brazil are coffee, sugar, cotton, mandioc or cassava flour, tobacco, rice, maize, fruits, and spice. Of these by far the most important now is coffee, while sugar ranks next in value, and cotton after sugar. The cultivation of sugar has not increased nearly in the same proportion with that of coffee. It is produced in greatest quantity in the districts adjoining Bahia. Cotton is found to thrive best in the dry table-lands of the northern provinces, especially in Maranhâo and Pernambuco. Its quality is considered excellent; but the rude and expensive method of its culture, and the high rates of carriage in these inland districts, operate very unfavourably for this branch of traffic. The tea plant has been recently introduced into Brazil, where it flourishes extremely well. Though not equal in quality to that of Chinese growth, it finds a ready market in Europe. Tobacco grows in greatest abundance in the neighborhood of Rio, but, from its inferior quality, it cannot compete with that of the United States, and the demand for it is annually decreasing. Rice grows in considerable quantities, and, not being much used by the natives for food, a large surplus remains for exportation. The cassava or mandioc is extensively grown, and forms the staple food of the lower classes. Tapioca is a preparation from the root of the cassava.

The varieties of animated life in Brazil are more numerous perhaps than in any other region in the world. Of beasts of prey, the most formidable are the jaguar or South American tiger, the ocelot, the tiger-cat, the puma, and the saratu, a kind of fox. Large herds of the peccary roam in the forests, in which also is to be found the tapir. This animal resembles the hog, but is many times larger, and is amphibious. It is capable of remaining a long time under water without rising to the surface to breathe. Its flesh is like that of the ox. The varieties of the monkey tribe that abound in the forests appear to be almost infinite. No less immense is the variety of birds, from the *ouira*, an eagle far larger than our most powerful birds of prey, to the humming-bird, no larger than a bee. The rhea, a species of ostrich, is found in Brazil. Snakes of every kind abound in the marshy districts, some of which, such as the rattlesnake and the jararaca, are remarkably venomous; while others, such as the boas, attain an enormous size and strength. A vast number of troublesome insects infest the margins of all the great rivers. The Brazilian birds are celebrated for the beauty of their plumage. The different species of humming birds are more numerous in Brazil than in any other country of America. The gayest butterflies flutter through the air, the blue, shining Menelaus, the Adonis, the Nestor, etc. More than ten species of wild bees have been observed in the woods; and the greater number produce honey. Lizards and caymans abound. The quantity of turtle in the Amazon and its principal tributaries is almost incredible. The waters generally swarm with fish. Of domestic animals the most important are the horse, the ox, and the sheep. Vast numbers of horses, sprung from the original European stock, roam at large over the extensive plains of the southern provinces. They are generally found in droves of twenty or thirty. Oxen are also allowed to wander half wild. They are hunted down with the *lasso* in great numbers, and are valued chiefly on account of their hides, horns, and tallow, which are exported in immense quantities.

The population of Brazil has been variously estimated at different times, and indeed even now the facilities for investigating the matter are not great. To the natural difficulties the people themselves add new causes of incorrectness. Fearing the conscription, they conceal from the authorities the number of their sons; and to avoid payment of taxes and the contribution of labor for the benefit of roads and other municipal works, they likewise conceal the number of their slaves. According to the most recent statements made by Brazilian authorities, the population of the twenty provinces of the empire, is 11,780,000; in which number are included 1,400,000 negro slaves, and 500,000 Indians.

The population of Rio Janeiro, the capital, is estimated at 600,000.

The Brazilian monarchy derives from the ancient monarchy of Portugal the principle of hereditary succession to the crown. The laws of succession are defined with great distinctness in the constitution, and are the same as in England. In Brazil there is no privileged aristocracy, but descent from the noble families of Portugal, length of time in the service of the country, or large fortune, give a certain claim to the privileges of aristocracy readily admitted by the Brazilians. The emperor rewards services according to their difficulty or importance with the titles of marquis, count, baron, or knight (mocos fidalgos). Titles are not hereditary, but if a son prove himself worthy of his father, he inherits his title. There are in the empire three orders of chivalry adopted from Portugal, those namely of Christ, Aviz, and Santiago, and two created since the declaration of independence, those namely of Cruzeiro and Rose. The senate represents the only element of aristocracy recognized by the constitution. The democratic element preponderates in the constitution of Brazil, but its action is greatly modified by the complicated system of election. The constitution established four powers, the *moderator* (what is called in England the royal prerogative), the legislative, the executive, and the judicial. The *moderator* is vested in the emperor, whom it empowers to select senators and ministers, to sanction laws, to convoke extraordinary assemblies, prorogue parliament, dissolve the chamber of deputies, grant amnesties and pardons, and suspend judges to be afterwards tried.

The legislative power is vested, for the affairs of the empire, in the general legislative assembly, with the sanction of the emperor, and for the provincial affairs in the provincial assemblies with the sanction of the president (governor) of the province. The general legislative assembly consists of two chambers, that of deputies, and that of senators. The deputies are nominated by indirect election. Citizens, and even manumitted slaves, born in the empire, who possess an income of $120, choose the electors in parochial assemblies, and these electors nominate the deputies. The qualification for an elector is an annual income of $225; that of a deputy an income of $400. The deputies are elected for four years, and must hold an annual session of four months, opening on the 3d of May. The senators are elected for life. Every province has a number of senators, equal to half its number of deputies; but they are nominated in triple lists, from which the emperor selects one-third. A senator must be forty years of age, and possess a clear annual income of $900. The allowance of a senator is one-half more than that of a deputy. The chamber of deputies has the initiative in taxes, in recruiting, and in the choice of a new dynasty. The senate has the exclusive privilege of taking cognizance of offences committed by members of the imperial family, councillors of state, senators, and deputies, during the session; of enforcing the responsibility of secretaries and councillors of state; of convoking the assembly in case the emperor fail to do so within two months after the period fixed by law; and also of calling it together on the death of the emperor.

The executive power is vested in the emperor assisted by his ministers and secretaries of state, who are responsible for treason, corruption, abuse of power, acts contrary to the liberty, security, or property of the citizens, and waste of public property. The ministers are six: one for each of the departments of home, justice, war, marine, finances, and foreign affairs. To these is superadded a council of state, composed of ten ordinary and ten extraordinary members nominated by the emperor, and the imperial prince, if of age, is by right a councillor of state. Every town and village, with the surrounding district, has a municipal counci composed of seven or twelve members, elected directly by the citizens who possess an annual income of $120. This council is charged with all that concerns the good of the district, meets four times a-year, besides extraordinary sessions. They impose fines to a certain amount, and even enforce their decrees by a penalty of thirty days' imprisonment. They annually draw up a municipal budget, which is submitted to the provincial legislative assembly for approval. Their enactments can be annulled by the provincial legislative assembly.

Each parish has four justices of peace elected for four years, but only one is actively engaged for the year. They are nominated by the citizens in the same manner as the municipal councils. Trial by jury is authorised for civil as well as for criminal cases. Each province is divided into *comarcas*, and then into municipalities. In each *comarca* there is a judge called *Juiz de Direito*, who presides at the sessions of the jury, in every municipality, twice or thrice a-year. In each municipality there is a municipal judge, who decides in civil cases, and prepares the process for the criminal. The decisions of this judge may be amended by the *Juiz de Direito*. Both must be doctors of law. The empire is divided into four appeal districts, in each of which there is a *Relacao* (court of appeal), composed of fourteen members. There is, besides, in Rio a supreme court of justice, composed of seventeen members, whose duties are to permit or refuse the revision of causes, to try its own members, or those of the court of appeal, the members of the diplomatic body, and the presidents of provinces, and to decide on disputed cases between the other courts. The civil laws, originally the same with those of Portugal, have been greatly modified by a number of new ones. A criminal code was organized in 1830, on the principles of Jeremy Bentham, and is considered very perfect and clear. The new form of procedure, and the new organization of justices, is embodied in a code decreed in 1832. Finally, a new code of commerce, nearly copied from that of France, was decreed in 1850.

To carry on the war of the independence, and to crush a subsequent revolution in the northern provinces, the government contracted two loans in 1824–5, of the nominal amount of $18,000,000; and on the recognition of its independence by Portugal, in 1825, it undertook the liability of a loan of $7,500,000. The war with Buenos Ayres, and the assistance rendered by Don Pedro to the constitutional party of Portugal, led to two farther loans in 1829, of the nominal amount of $3,800,000. Internal difficulties in 1839, compelled the regency to contract another loan of the nominal amount of $2,000,000. The debt contracted and assumed by Brazil between 1823 and 1843, therefore, amounted to $31,300,000 nominal; and throughout all its difficulties and embarrassments the imperial government punctually and honorably provided for the dividends as they became due. According to the latest information furnished by the government, the external consolidated debt of the empire amounted to $70,000,000; the internal consolidated debt amounted to $250,000,000. For a number of years there was an annual deficit in the revenue of the country, which seemed to threaten great danger to the finances, if not ultimate bankruptcy; but of late, there has been a great and marked improvement combined with growing prosperity at home, greater liberality of treatment of its produce in foreign markets, and with an improved collection of the customs' revenue, a state of chronic deficit has been changed into one of surplus. The government of Brazil has availed itself of financial prosperity to establish naval and to extend and perfect judicial means for the effectual suppression of the slave trade, has reduced the tonnage duties on shipping by two-thirds, has lowered some oppressive internal taxes, and abolished others, has already made some partial modifications of the tariff, etc. The war with Paraguay has had the effect of producing a deficit in the revenue again; but that must of course be of only temporary continuance.

For a number of years past, the annual

exports from Brazil have averaged about $60,000,000; the imports, $57,000,000. Great Britain and the United States are chiefly concerned in the foreign trade of the country, the exports to England and her dependencies being over $20,000,000 annually, those to the United States being somewhat less. France, the Argentine Republic and Portugal, also furnish markets for the products of Brazil. The standing army is reported to consist of 25,884 men. The strength of the army employed against Paraguay, was estimated recently at about 43,000, of whom, however, over 10,000 were reported as on the sick list. The total number of Brazilian troops forwarded to the war with Paraguay is given at 84,219. The navy of Brazil consists of 17 monitors and casemates, 40 wooden steamers, 8 transport steamers, and 13 other vessels of various kinds. These mount 298 cannon, and are manned by 7,353 men. Fifteen iron clads, 17 steam gun-boats, and 6 other vessels form the squadron in Paraguay, to which a number of transports is attached. Several small iron steamers have been built and are building in Europe for service on the Amazon, the exploration and settlement along the banks of which promise almost incredible results, not only to Brazil, but to the neighboring republics, and, in fact, to all maritime nations of the earth. Ten or twelve large Brazilian steamers are plying on the Amazon proper, while smaller steamers ascend to Peru and Ecuador. An international telegraph line, bringing Brazil into communication with the United States and Europe, is in course of construction, and may in the course of a year or two be in active operation.

On the whole, then, under an able and enlightened ruler, Pedro II., with decided tendency to avail herself of the advantages of progress in its manifold varieties, to extend the benefits of education to all her people, and to rid the empire of the curse of slavery, the future of Brazil may be considered as assured. If the nation be true to its mission, it cannot fail to be a great and happy nation.

BOLIVIA.

Bolivia is a republic of South America, lying between Lat. 10° 21′ and 25° 38′ S., and Long. 57° 36′ and 70° 30′ W., bounded north and east by Brazilian provinces and the Paraguay River, south by the Argentine Confederation and Chili, and west by the Pacific and by Peru. Its greatest breadth is 760 miles; its greatest length, 1100 miles; its sea coast is only about 250 miles. Area, estimated at about 600,000 square miles. It is divided into eleven departments. Population, 1,987,352, including 245,000 Indians. La Paz, the capital, has a population of 76,372.

Ever since the conquest of Peru by the Spaniards in the sixteenth century, the natives have been subjected to a system of tyranny and oppression which has few parallels in the history of the universe. They were treated little better than beasts of burthen. By their toil the gold and silver were obtained from the mines, the lands were cultivated, the flocks and herds were attended to, and all the domestic and menial offices performed. Yet the fruits of their labor, especially that of mining, which was attended with numerous privations and too often with great loss of life, were altogether devoted to enriching their cruel oppressors. While so employed they were denied all the comforts and many of the necessaries of life; they were treated as minors, and considered as incapable of attending to their own affairs and interests, nay even deprived of the means of information and improvement; while the clergy powerfully contributed to the general degradation, by keeping them in the most profound ignorance of their moral and religious duties, and substituting instead of these a few unmeaning and useless ceremonies, by means of which they plundered the Indians, without ceremony or remorse, of the scanty pittance which they were able to save from the rapacity of their civil rulers. One of their principal grievances was the *mita*, a compulsory kind of personal labor either in the working of the mines or in the cultivation of the fields, exacted from the Indians generally for the space of one year. The proprietors of mines or land to be worked or cultivated, were privileged to claim as their undoubted right, the personal services of the Indian population of the district surrounding that in which their property was situated. By the regulations of the *mita* a proportional number of the Indians of the district were annually chosen by lot for the purposes required; and some idea may be formed of the effects of such a regulation, by stating, that 1400 mines were registered in Peru alone, and that every mine which remained unworked a year and a day became the property of the first claimant. So much was the labor of the mines dreaded by those persons on whom the lot fell, that they considered it as equivalent to a sentence of death, and made all their arrangements accordingly; they were cheated in every possible manner; ground down to the earth by their accursed tyrants; and rarely escaped save by death. An estimate may be formed of the extent of this evil, by stating that 12,000 Indians were annually required by the *mita* of Potosi alone; and it is calculated that, in the mines of Peru, no less than 8,285,000 Indians have perished in this manner. Besides the *mita* for the service of the mines, the Indians were also compelled to labor for their superiors on their cultivated estates, their *estancias* or grazing farms, and also in their *obrages* or manufactories. In these latter establishments, according to Ulloa, they were obliged to work all day, and only received a pittance for their labor; the half of which was in many instances stopped to pay their arrears of tribute, and the other half was generally insufficient to pay for their necessary sustenance. The Indians were besides liable to serve as *pongos* or menial servants to the governors, and other functionaries, as likewise to the caciques and the curates; but for this service they received no recompense, excepting their food and clothing. The numbers employed in these domestic occupations in Peru and Bolivia have been estimated at 60,000. The tribute exacted by the government from every Indian between the age of eighteen and fifty-five was a capitation tax of eight dollars. This was levied with the greatest rigor, and the official persons charged with its collection too frequently committed great injustice in doing so; obliging the Indians to commence these payments at fifteen, and continue them until seventy years of age, and putting the amount of tribute for the years before and after the legal period into their own pockets. The governor of each province was responsible to the government for the amount of the tribute, which was regulated by a census of the tributary Indians, taken every seven years; and in this many frauds were practiced, the actual number being often much underrated. This tribute continued to be exacted until the year 1825, when it was finally abolished by General Bolivar on his arrival in the country; and all the Indians now enjoy the same rights and privileges as the other inhabitants of the country.

Besides all these, the Peruvian Indians were long subjected to another system of extortion no less grievous and unjust,—the law of *repartamiento*. This was originally established with the best intentions; the governors or *corregidors* of the districts being intrusted with the charge of supplying the inhabitants under their care with such articles as they might require at a fair and equitable price. But the law, which had so plausible an origin, was shamefully abused;

and it was made compulsory on the Indian population to purchase articles of the most worthless description, both in kind and quality, whether they required them or not, and at a price double or treble that for which the same article of the best possible quality might have been purchased. Thus razors were forced at an exorbitant price on Indians who had no beards to shave; and those who had never gone otherwise than barefooted were compelled to purchase velvets and silk stockings, of the use of which they were ignorant. A *repartamiento* took place in 1743, at about forty leagues from Lima, where the *corregidor* exacted the sum of $300,000 for goods which he had purchased at $70,000. The accumulated grievances at length exceeded even the powers of endurance possessed by these pacific Indians, and gave rise to the memorable insurrection of Tupac Amaru in 1780, in which torrents of native as well as Spanish blood were shed before it was finally suppressed. This event, however, gave a death-blow to the law of *repartamiento*, which was then finally abolished.

The constant and extensive operation of these demoralizing practices, although more immediately affecting the aboriginal population, could not fail to produce the most pernicious and injurious effects on the Creoles or descendants of the Spaniards; but, in addition to these causes of debasement, the latter were subjected to numerous unjust and oppressive laws, all tending to paralyze their advancement in industry, intelligence, and civilization. The raising of those vegetable productions which form the principal objects of culture in Spain, as articles of commerce, was strictly prohibited to the South Americans, however favorable the soil and climate of their native country might be for the production of them. The prosperity and happiness of the transatlantic population were of no value or importance when put in competition with the interested views and wishes of the mother country. Thus the cultivation of the vine and the olive was either prohibited, or the plants were rooted out where they had been introduced. Prohibitory decrees were issued against the manufacture of wines, brandies, vinegar, olive oil, etc.; and even the culture of almonds and raisins was interdicted. No kind of manufacture of cloth or articles of clothing was permitted which could interfere with the commerce of Spain, excepting only the coarse fabrics manufactured and worn by the Indians. And, not content with confining the commerce of South America entirely to Spain, and prohibiting it under the severest penalties with other nations, these colonies were not permitted to have any intercourse or commerce with each other. The South Americans were generally excluded from all offices of honor or emolument in their own country; and when any deviation from this law took place, it was too frequently in consequence of enormous bribes received, or a reward to some unnatural Creole for acts of cruelty and oppression committed on his own countrymen. They were systematically deprived of the means of obtaining a suitable education for their children, and every attempt at improvement on the part of the natives was resisted by the government.

The upper provinces of Bolivia and Peru were those which formed the principal scenes of the memorable insurrection of Tupac Amaru, so just in its origin, so energetic in its prosecution, and so unfortunate in its results to the Peruvian nation. From the details which have appeared of this eventful period, it is evident that a deep-rooted feeling of the oppressive and degrading servitude to which they had so long been subjected by the Spaniards, united with a lively recollection of the happiness and glory of their more fortunate ancestors, conspired to rouse the latent energies of the whole nation to accomplish their liberation from the cruel yoke under which they had groaned. And they found an able and a willing leader in Jose Gabriel Condorcanqui, cacique of Tungasuya, a lineal descendant of the Inca Tupac Amaru, whose name and title he afterwards assumed.

But although an excellent and intrepid man, and possessing the entire confidence of his countrymen, he was deficient in that knowledge, foresight and energy, so requisite for conducting to a happy determination so difficult and hazardous an enterprise. He experienced various successes and reverses, but was eventually taken prisoner, and put to death in the most barbarous manner by the Spaniards; and not long after, the superior skill and discipline of the Spaniards triumphed, and the insurrection was put down in 1782. The poor natives now sank into despondency and despair; and subsequently they viewed with apathy and indifference the rise and progress of the war of independence, the objects of which they did not rightly understand, and found it difficult to reconcile with their knowledge of the active part taken by the Creoles in the suppression of their own previous endeavors to throw off the Spanish yoke.

From the cause already stated, the war of independence was principally carried on, as regards Bolivia, by the resources of, and in concert with, the neighboring provinces of Rio de la Plata and Peru, all of which had equal cause to avenge themselves on their oppressors, but were placed in circumstances somewhat more fortunate for accomplishing their purpose. When the patriots of Buenos Ayres had succeeded in liberating, from the dominion of Spain, the interior provinces of the Rio de la Plata, they turned their arms against their enemies in possession of Upper Peru. General Antonio Balcarce was therefore sent with the forces of Buenos Ayres into that country, and succeeded in defeating the royalist General Nieto, at Cotagaita, on the 27th of October, 1810; and on the 7th November following, a similar fate overtook Colonel Cordova at Tupiza. These successes gave him possession of the country as far as the bridge of the Incas, which crosses the river Desaguadero; at which time his army had been increased by recruits to about 4000 men. Castelli was sent from Buenos Ayres as governor of Upper Peru, and to act as the commissioner of the Argentine government, with the army of Balcarce. He was a man distinguished for his great and versatile talents, but was of a restless and fiery temper. By the violence of his proceedings, and numerous acts of unjustifiable cruelty, he so far succeeded in inspiring the Spaniards with terror and dismay, that the army of Buenos Ayres was enabled, on the 25th of May, 1811, to celebrate the first anniversary of their independence among the ruins of the palace of the Incas at Tiaguanaco, on the shores of the lake of Titicaca, 2000 miles distant from Buenos Ayres. The dissolute conduct of Castelli, however, and the irregularities of the Buenos-Ayreans who accompanied him, tended greatly to alienate the affections of the inhabitants of Upper Peru from their deliverers, and considerably aided the efforts of Abascal, the viceroy of Peru, who, after some unsuccessful attempts to conclude an armistice with Castelli, in which little courtesy seems to have been observed on either side, collected all his disposable forces under his best generals. The civil administration of the provinces was neglected by the patriots; and the army became disorganized, from the dissolute conduct and negligence of Castelli and his followers. General Goyeneche was intrusted with the command of the Spanish army, which, to the amount of 4000 men, took up a position on the north side of the Desaguadero, and by an act of treachery gained a victory over Balcarce, in June, 1811. After his success Goyeneche committed great cruelties in Bolivia, particularly at Chuquisaca and La Paz; but he met with considerable opposition from the patriots, who had retired to the mountains of Cochabamba, Santa Cruz de la Sierra, and Chayanta.

General Belgrano, who succeeded to the command of the army of Balcarce, had the good fortune, at Tucuman, to defeat the royalist army, 3000 strong, under General Pio Tristan, on the 30th of September, 1812, while his own force did not amount to half that number. And, again, on the 20th of February following, he obtained another victory over the same general, who had entrenched himself in Salta with 2000 men, all of whom were either killed or taken prisoners. Belgrano generously permitted the vanquished Tristan, with his officers and men, to return to Peru, on their giving solemn pledges not to again bear arms against the republic of the Rio de la Plata. But all of them, influenced by the example of their general, and regardless of their obligation, violated their parole, and joined the army of Pezuela, which, by such dishonorable means, was augmented to 4000 men. With these he attacked Belgrano, who, with his army, had advanced into Upper Peru, and defeated him at Vilcapugio, between Oruro and Potos, on the 1st of October, 1813; and again at Ayoma, in the department of Cochabamba, on the 14th of November of the same year. Belgrano escaped with the remains of his army to Tucuman.

Notwithstanding these disasters, the cause of independence did not slumber in Upper Peru, since the numerous bands of patriots maintained themselves in Cochabamba, Santa Cruz de la Sierra, Chayanta, and Yamparaes, and obtained many advantages over the royalists, under the able command of Warnes, Camargo and Pedilla, who carried on a guerilla warfare. On the 25th of May, 1814, Colonel Arenales obtained some advantages over his opponents in the provinces of Cochabamba, and Warnes was equally fortunate on the 9th of October following, in the Quebrada of Santa Barbara. Guemes, with the irregular troops of the province of Salta, cut off the supplies of the royalists in front; whilst the guerilla parties under Warnes, Pedilla, and Muñecas, in the rear, so distressed them, that Pezuela with his army was obliged to retire upon Cotagaita. He, however, in November, 1815, defeated the patriot forces, and thus gained control of Upper Peru. Belgrano was a second time appointed to command the army stationed at Tucuman. But a spirit of disaffection and anarchy had crept into his army, which, incited by the principal officers, revolted against their general. He was deposed and made prisoner; and the officers, with such soldiers as chose to follow them, were dispersed over the provinces.

To these events succeeded, under Pumacagua, an insurrection of the Indians of the neighboring provinces of Arequipa, Cuzco, and Huamanga, in Peru; and the object being the independence of the whole country, it was joined by numerous Creoles from Bolivia and Peru. But this attempt was speedily put down by the activity of the royalist general, Ramirez. After this period Upper Peru remained tranquil for a considerable time. On the viceroy Abascal being superseded in that office by Pezuela, General Laserna was appointed commander-in-chief in Upper Peru, where he arrived in September, 1816, with 2000 fresh troops. He introduced many innovations, and very humanely prohibited the infliction of the punishment of death for political offences, without his previous permission. He made an attempt, with an army of from 4000 to 5000 men, to penetrate into the Argentine provinces, intending to march to Buenos Ayres; but he was completely foiled by the activity and intrepidity of the *Gauchos*, or irregular troops of the provinces of Salta and Jujuy, and was compelled to retire with the remainder of his army to Cotagaita.

The expedition of General Santa Cruz, prepared with great zeal and activity at Lima, landed in June, 1823, in the Puertos Intermedios, and marched in two divisions to Upper Peru: the one under Santa Cruz by the Cordillera of Iscuchaca, obtained possession of the bridge of the Incas on the Desaguadero on the 29th of July, and occupied La Paz on the 7th of August; the other division, under General Gamarra, marched by the route of Tacora and San Andres de Machaca, and reached Calemarca on the 10th of August, where it had a sharp rencontre with a division of the army of General Olañeta, and then marched to Oruro, where it was joined by Lanza with six hundred men. During six years the latter had maintained himself in the Yungas with great valor against all the efforts of the Spaniards. At this time the royalist force in Upper Peru, under Olañeta, did not exceed from two thousand to three thousand men, besides about fifteen hundred men in garrison at Puno and La Paz. But Canterac, then near Lima, hearing of the large army which had gone to Upper Peru under Santa Cruz, dispatched considerable reinforcements; Sucre also sent from Lima three thousand troops, either to co-operate with Santa Cruz, or to act separately, as occasion might require.

Santa Cruz remained in quiet possession of Upper Peru, occupying the country from Oruro to the bridge of the Incas, his head quarters being at La Paz. On the approach of the royalists, Santa Cruz took up a position near the bridge of the Incas; and at Zepita, on the 25th of August, fought an indecisive action with Valdez, who commanded eighteen hundred men, his own force being only sixteen hundred. The royalists immediately concentrated their forces at Sicuani, amounting to four thousand five hundred men, whilst those of Santa Cruz were about seven thousand men. Various movements now took place on both sides, which evinced much skill and activity on the part of the royalists, and great indecision and want of judgment on the part of Santa Cruz. In fact, the latter refused to fight at all, but kept on retreating, until his retreat became a precipitate flight. The fugitives retired by Santa Rosa and Moquegua towards Ilo, where about thirteen hundred embarked in the transports; but of an army of seven thousand men only one thousand returned to Lima. About one thousand retired from Sicasica with Lanza, but were afterwards defeated by Olañeta, and a few followers only escaped to the mountains. In May, 1824, Generals Valdez and Olañeta occupied Upper Peru, each with about five thousand men under his command, but opposed to each other on political points; the former having withdrawn his allegiance from the viceroy Lacerna, in consequence of advocating the constitutional cause of Spain, while Olañeta adhered to the principles of absolute monarchy. This dispute was useful to the cause of the patriots, as it prevented Olañeta from uniting his forces with the viceroy during the campaign which terminated in the battle of Ayacucho, so glorious to the cause of freedom. General Sucre, whose abilities and valor so much contributed to the success of that day, improved the advantages he had obtained, by his clemency and generosity to the vanquished, and by the rapidity with which he followed up his successes; so that none of the fugitives could unite with the army of Olañeta, now the only royalist general in arms in Upper or Lower Peru. A part of the army, therefore, proceeded towards Upper Peru, and in their march experienced in some instances great hardships. On hearing of the victory of Ayacucho, the patriot prisoners of war confined in the island of Chuquito, in the lake of Titicaca, rose on their guards, whom they overcame; and placing themselves under the command of General Alvarado, likewise a prisoner, they took possession of the country as far as the bridge of the Incas; a division of fifteen hundred patriots under the command of General Urdininea still occupying the quebrada of Humaguaca, on the southern frontier of the department of Potosi. General Olañeta, however, still retained his position in Upper Peru, at the head of about four thousand men, having refused to accede to the liberal and even generous terms of accommodation proposed to him by General Sucre. The latter, therefore, advanced to Oruro, and afterwards to Puno, which he reached on the 1st of February, 1825, and there obtained information that the royalist garrisons of Cochabamba, Chuquisaca, and Santa Cruz de la Sierra, had declared for the patriots, and that the city of La Paz was in possession of the indefatigable Lanza. Olañeta, with his army, diminished to two thousand, was confined to the department of Potosi, but persisted in his determined opposition, till his troops rose against him and he lost his life, in March, 1825.

General Sucre was now invested with the supreme command in Upper Peru, until the requisite measures could be taken to establish in that country a regular and constitutional government. Deputies from the various provinces to the number of fifty-four were assembled at Chuquisaca, the capital, to decide upon the question proposed to them on the part of the government of the Argentine provinces, respecting their separation or otherwise from that country. In August, 1825, they decided this question, and declared it to be the national will that Upper Peru should in future constitue a distinct and independent nation. This assembly continued their session, although the primary object of their meeting had thus been accomplished, and afterwards gave the name of Bolivia to the country; issuing at the same time a formal declaration of independence. They also voted one million of dollars to General Bolivar, as a reward for his past services; and an equal sum to those belonging to the army who had served in the campaign of 1824. The former grant, however, was only accepted by Bolivar on the express condition that it should be wholly appropriated to purchasing the freedom of about a thousand slaves still existing in Bolivia. The first general assembly of deputies of Bolivia dissolved themselves on the 6th of October, 1825, and a new congress was summoned, and formally installed, at Chuquisaca, on the 25th of May, 1826, to take into consideration the constitution prepared by Bolivar for the new republic. A favorable report was made to that body by a committee appointed to examine it, on which it was approved by the congress, and declared to be the constitution of the republic; and as such, it was sworn to by the people. General Sucre was chosen president for life, according to the constitution; but only accepted the appointment for the space of two years, and on the express condition that two thousand Colombian troops should be permitted to remain with him, which request was agreed to without difficulty by the congress.

The Bolivian constitution is founded on the strictest principles of justice, in as far as regards the civil rights and privileges of the community; but in other respects, and particularly in reference to the supreme executive authority, its provisions savor strongly of a monarchical spirit. The supreme authority is vested in a *presidente vitalicio*, or president for life, with the power of naming his successor. It guarantees to the Bolivians civil liberty, security of persons and property, and equality of rights; the free exercise and communication of thoughts and opinions, either by the press or otherwise; liberty to remain or leave the territory of the republic with their property, at their pleasure, but without prejudice to others; equality in the imposition of taxes and contributions, from the payment of which none can be exempted; and the abolition of all hereditary employments, privileges, and entails. All trials and judgments are public; and in criminal cases none can be imprisoned more than forty-eight hours without having presented to him the charges preferred against him, and being delivered over to the proper tribunal or judge. By this constitution, all legitimate power emanates directly from the people, and is in the first instance exercised by all who can justly claim the privilege of citizens. Of these, every ten nominate an elector, who exercises his delegated authority for a period of four years. At the commencement of each year all the electors assemble in the capitals of their respective provinces, and regulate their proceedings and the exercise of their various functions by a plurality of votes. They elect the members of the three legislative chambers, the number for each amounting to thirty; those for the chamber of tribunes being nominated for four years, and renewed by moieties every two years; those for the senate for eight years, and renewed by moieties every four years; and those for the chamber of censors being nominated for life. The functions of the chamber of tribunes are, to originate all laws respecting the revenue, peace and war, and to exercise an immediate inspection of those branches which are administered by the executive, with the least intervention of the legislature. This chamber also possesses the nitiative in the settlement of the territorial division of the republic; the coinage, weights and measures; the seaports, roads, bridges, and public buildings; the police, etc. The attributes and functions of the chamber of senators are, to form the civil, criminal, and ecclesiastical regulations and codes, and watch over the tribunals of justice and religion; to choose from those presented to them by the executive and by the electoral body, the prefects, governors, corregidors, judges of districts, and all others in the department of justice; to propose to the chamber of censors those who are to be members of the supreme tribunal of justice, the archbishops, the bishops, dignitaries of the church, canons, and prebends; and to examine the decision of ecclesiastical courts, bulls, rescripts, and pontifical briefs, with a view to their approval or disapproval. The chamber of censors exercise a political and moral power. It is their duty to watch that the constitution, the laws and treaties, are strictly adhered to and executed; and to express the national judgment, when such is rendered necessary by the good or bad administration of the executive government. The censors are also charged with the protection of morality, the arts and sciences, education, and the press. They exercise the important functions of condemning those who usurp sovereign power, or are guilty of high crimes and malversation; and they bestow public honors and rewards on the services and virtues of illustrious citizens. The general or collective duties and attributes of the three chambers, when united, are, to nominate the president of the republic for the first time, and to confirm his successor; to approve of the vice-president; to determine on the seat of government; to decide on any charge against members of the chambers, the vice-president, or secretaries of state; to invest the president with extraordinary powers in cases of great emergency or danger, etc. All the sessions must be public, excepting in such state cases as require secrecy. No public functionaries are capable of being members of the chambers; and the latter enjoy inviolability in their persons for opinions expressed, and are not subject to arrest.

The executive government, according to this constitution, consists of a president, vice-president, and three secretaries of state. The president of the republic is named for the first time by a majority of the collective legislature, and retains the dignity during life, with the power of naming his successor. He is the chief of the administration of the state, and is not responsible for the acts of his administration. On his death, resignation, or infirmity, the vice-president is virtually his successor. In the absence or non-existence of both of these functionaries, the three secretaries of state take charge, *ad interim*, of the administration of the government, the oldest in office acting as president until the assembling of the legislature. The constitutional privileges of the president are the most limited that have been intrusted to the supreme chief of any nation. They extend only to the nomination of the officers of the revenue, of peace and of war, and the command of the army. The president cannot deprive any Bolivian of his liberty, or inflict punishment on him, of his own accord; nor can he imprison any one longer than forty-eight hours without delivering him over to the proper judge or tribunal; nor deprive any individual of his property, unless such a proceeding be urgently demanded by the public interests; nor impede the elections or any other public functions authorized by the laws; nor absent himself from the republic or the capital without permission of the legislature. The administration belongs wholly to the ministry, which is responsible to the senate, and is subject to the zealous vigilance of the legislators, magistrates, judges, and citizens. The vice-president is proposed by the president, and approved by the legislature. He is at the head of the ministry, and, with the secretaries of state, is responsible for all the acts of the administration; while, in the name of the president and the republic, he signs all the public documents, along with these secretaries, in order to legalize the orders of the executive. Of all the magistrates intrusted with the command, the vice-president is that one whose hands are most shackled; for he has to obey both the executive and the legislature. He receives laws from the latter, and orders from the former; and between the two has often a difficult course to steer. As the expectant of the supreme command, the vice-president has the most powerful motives for the zealous and conscientious discharge of his functions, in order to secure, on the one hand, the confidence and support of the president, and, on the other, that of the legislature and the people. The three secretaries of state are for the home and foreign departments, for the finance, and for war and marine; and each is required to give in accounts of the expenses incurred in his respective department, and the estimates for each ensuing year.

The judicial power enjoys the most perfect independence, the members composing it being proposed by the people, and chosen by the legislature; a condition which insures the strict and impartial administration of the laws. Tortures and confessions are altogether abolished, as repugnant to humanity. The territory of the republic is governed by prefects, governors, corregidors, justices of the peace, and alcaldes; and the proportion of these is regulated by the population, the details to be defined by the congress; and every one in the enjoyment of office is made responsible for his actions. The armed force is composed of the regular army to garrison and defend the frontiers, of the national militia to preserve internal order, of the preventive service to protect the revenue, and of the navy, when circumstances may require the formation of such. Slavery in every form was abolished, as inconsistent with the just rights of mankind, and at variance with the whole spirit of the constitution. The exercise of religion was freed from all restraints; it being considered incompetent to legislate in matters affecting the consciences of others.

Such are the principal features of the Bolivian constitution, the merits of which will be variously estimated, according to the particular political bias of each individual. It contains in theory much that seems calculated to insure the liberty, the prosperity, and the happiness of the community. No part of it, however, has excited more criticism, or given rise to more suspicion, than that which provides for the election of a president or supreme ruler for life, with the power of nominating his successor. With such a provision, the Bolivian constitution seems to be nothing more nor less than a limited monarchy, somewhat incuriously disguised under republican forms. Had Bolivar, the lawgiver of this republic, ceased to exist, or had he retired altogether from public life, on the promulgation of the Bolivian code, his reputation as a patriot and a statesman would have been handed down to posterity as one of the brightest in the annals of history. But, unfortunately, the formation and establishment of this constitution gave rise to events in Peru, Colombia, and other parts of South America, which incontrovertibly prove that it was not dictated by that pure spirit of patriotism which his friends and admirers have attributed to Bolivar; but that under it lurked a gigantic scheme of ambition and aggrandizement, in fruitless endeavors to accomplish which much crime and misery were occasioned, whilst the glory which its author had previously earned contracted a stain which, it is to be feared, no length of time will ever efface. The project which emanated from the promulgation and establishment of this code in Bolivia, and in the prosecution of which Bolivar principally employed his active energies during the latter years of his life, was, the establishment of the same constitution in Peru and Colombia as well as in Bolivia, and the union of these three republics, either federally, or as one State, of which he was to be the president for life. The celebrated congress at Panama, which took place in June, 1826, was originally projected by him for this express object; and other expedients were also resorted to for the accomplishment of his design. But all his schemes proved abortive, and he died, December 17th, 1830, without effecting any of the objects, personal to himself, for which he had compromised his fame, and incurred the apprehension of all who were friendly to republican institutions.

The congress which sanctioned the adoption of the Bolivian code, and elected General Sucre as the president of the republic, continued its sessions, to legislate more in detail. The republic was peculiarly fortunate in its first choice of a president in the person of the conqueror of Ayacucho, whose mildness, urbanity, integrity, love of justice, and devotedness in the discharge of the important duties confided to him, endeared him to all. Under the upright administration of this officer much progress was made in organizing the various departments of the administration; the resources of the country were called forth; and effectual means were adopted for promoting the extension of education and intelligence throughout the community. Amidst these powerful inducements to tranquillity, much discontent was excited by the presence of a body of Colombian troops in the country, which, in a period of profound peace, was considered by many as derogatory to the dignity, and inconsistent with the liberty, of the republic. These succeeded in gaining over to their party the Colombian battalion of voltigeros stationed at La Paz, among whom a mutiny took place on the 23d December, 1827; but this was speedily suppressed by the Colombian cavalry under Colonel Brown, and the armed peasantry of La Paz, after a desperate resistance on the part of the mutineers, of whom eighty were killed. The battalion was consequently disbanded. This revolt was hailed with joy by the government and people of Peru, who viewed it as the first step towards the downfall of the policy of Bolivar. General Sucre, convinced that removing the principal source of discontent was essential to the stability of the constitution and the welfare of the country, applied to the government of Peru for permission to the Colombian troops to march through the territory of that State, and embark at Arica. But the Peruvian administration declined to allow this favor; subsequently, however, the troops were embarked at Arica and left Bolivia. A spirit of discord, meanwhile, had extended itself to Chuquisaca, the capital, and spread amongst the garrison. With the view of repressing this disorder, Sucre rode in amongst the mutinous soldiers, accompanied by his staff and a few other officers; but he was unsuccessful in his attempt to quell the mutiny; Colonels Lanza and Escalona were mortally wounded, and the general himself was so severely wounded as to be made prisoner. This revolt, however, was ultimately suppressed by General Lopez with some troops from Potosi, aided by the well-disposed inhabitants of Chuquisaca; and Sucre was set at liberty. But he intimated his fixed determination not to resume the office of president, except for the purpose of resigning it into the hands of congress, at its first meeting. On hearing of the affair at Chuquisaca, Gamarra called a council of war, the members of which, with only one dissentient voice, agreed as to the propriety of his marching into the Bolivian territory, with the ostensible object of preventing anarchy, and protecting Sucre from further personal violence; and this resolution was soon afterwards sanctioned by orders to the same effect from the Peruvian government. Accordingly, Gamarra and his army crossed the Desaguadero on the 1st of May; but they were coolly received by the Bolivians, whose forces being too few for resistance, retired from La Paz, and concentrated themselves towards Oruro and Potosi, under the command of General Urdininea. Ineffectual endeavours at negociation were followed by some indecisive affairs between the two armies in the province of Paria. Blanco succeeded in placing himself in communication with the Peruvian forces, and with a party of them proceeded to Chuquisaca, where he seized General Sucre, hurried him by forced marches to the head-quarters of Gamarra, and during the whole journey treated him with the greatest inhumanity and indignity. A treaty of peace was now entered into between Generals Gamarra and Urdininea at Piquisa (6th July), by which the independence of Bolivia was guaranteed, and the object of the Peruvian invasion accomplished by the retirement of General Sucre, and the removal of the few remaining Colombian troops from the territory of the republic. Accordingly, the latter embarked at Arica for Colombia on the 28th of July, under the command of Colonel Brown. Sucre was then set at liberty, and formally resigned the presidency of Bolivia on the 18th of August, 1828; on which occasion General Santa Cruz was elected as his successor. Sucre's merits in organizing Bolivia, and his impartiality in pointing out that part of the Bolivian code which he considered as most imperfect, deserve honorable mention. During the two years of his administration, colleges and Lancasterian schools were established in the capitals of each of the departments, and schools of the same description for females were instituted in three of them; besides which, other schools were multiplied throughout the country under improved regulations, and well provided with funds. Agriculture had been improved in all its branches, and no forced loan or contribution of any kind was made. Mining had increased so much, that during the preceding year one-third more of the precious metals had been extracted than in any former year. Commerce had also been promoted, and efforts were made to establish the free port of Cobija or La Mar.

Santa Cruz was now elected president of the republic; General Velasco vice-president. The new governor, who happened to be absent in Chili, found, to his surprise, on reaching Chuquisaca, that General Blanco had in the meantime usurped his functions, and appointed a new vice-president. The usurper, however, did not live long to enjoy his honors; for in a week he was assassinated, and his death left Santa Cruz in undisputed possession of the chief power. From this date till the year 1834, the president directed all his efforts to developing the internal resources of the State. The better to gain his end, and attract to his own country a share of the foreign commerce which had hitherto been almost monopolized by the neighboring States of Chili and Peru, he formed the bold design of uniting Bolivia and Peru into a confederation. The latter country was at this time in a state of anarchy. At the invitation of Orgebozo, the deposed president, Santa Cruz marched an army into Peru, gained two battles, and reinstated Orgebozo, with whose assistance he carried out his scheme, and was appointed protector of the Peru-Bolivian confederation. The two countries had just begun to prosper under his rule, when the Chilians, jealous of their commercial interests, sent an invading army, which defeated Santa Cruz at Yungay in 1839, dissolved the confederation, and compelled the protector to abdicate. He now became an exile from his country, where his influence was still dangerously great; and though he more than once tried to return, he was always intercepted. In 1843, he fell into the hands of the Peruvians, by whom he was delivered up to the Chilian government, which detained him for some time as a prisoner at Chiloe. It was at last found convenient to despatch him to Europe as Bolivian plenipotentiary; and he was, till 1852, the accredited minister of that country at the courts of London, Paris, Madrid, Rome and Brussels. After the battle of Yungay, another revolution occurred in Bolivia, which left Velasco president, and Ballivian vice-president. As the former soon showed himself incapable, the army mutinied in 1841, and endeavored to reinstate Santa Cruz. To prevent this, the Peruvians interfered, and invaded Bolivia with a large army. The vice-president hurried to meet the invaders, routed them completely at Ingavi, in his turn entered Peru, and established himself at Arica on the Pacific. Intestine troubles, however, compelled him soon after to return home, where in 1843 he was duly elected president of the republic. Despite the numerous attempts to dispossess him of his power, he retained it till 1848, when a new revolution more formidable than its predecessors compelled him to abdicate. No regular president was appointed for two years; but the administration was carried on by Manuel Isidoro Belzu, commander-in-chief of the army. These two years were signalized by the number of revolts and conspiracies, and by the bloody atrocities of a civil war. The year 1852 elapsed without a revolution, or civil commotion. It was signalized by no event of public interest, except the retirement of Santa Cruz, the death of the ex-president Ballivian, and the enactment of certain measures for the prevention of treacherous designs against the government. At the beginning of 1853, another rupture broke out between Bolivia and Peru. The principal cause of this event was asserted to be the Bolivian coinage. Since 1830, the money struck at the national mint was stated to be only 23 per cent. below the usual alloy; the Peruvians, into whose country this coinage readily found its way, maintained that it was 33, and even 40 per cent. below the legal value. The bad feeling engendered on both sides by the mutual complaints and recriminations on this subject, was further complicated by another untoward event. The Bolivian government accused M. Paredes, the Peruvian chargé d'affaires at La Paz, of communicating false intelligence to the authorities at home, and spreading alarming rumors about the intentions of the State, and demanded his recall. The Peruvians refused to comply with the demand, but to obviate difficulties M. Paredes voluntarily retired. Pending negotiations, he was seized and expelled the country by the police. His countrymen demanded reparation for this outrage, which was refused. Then began a mutual system of reprisals; the result of which was a declaration of war, and its usual results. In 1836, slavery was formally abolished in Bolivia by act of Congress, though the native Indians are still considered as in a state of tutelage, and continue to pay the capitation tax; and in 1839 the entire political constitution of Bolivia was remodelled. In 1843 it was again altered; and was not finally established till 1848. The executive is now vested in a president, who holds office for four years, and is re-eligible after an interval of the same duration. He is assisted by a council of state and four ministers. The power of legislation belongs to the congress, which consists of a senate and a chamber of deputies. The congress, whose sessions last for two months, meets annually on the 6th of August. Every department returns three senators; while the deputies are elected in the proportion of 1 to 40,000 electors. Every elector must be able to read and write, and possess a capital of 4000 piastres, or an equivalent.

Since 1854, Bolivia has had its full share of disturbances and troubles, and has suffered deeply from that same evil which we have noted in the case of other States, viz: the lack of solid and effective government. In the latter part of 1864, Melgarejo rose against De Acha, then president; the former was successful, and became provisional president. He also gained decisive victories over Belzu and other opponents in January, 1866. Bolivia joined the alliance of Chili and Peru against Spain, and, like her allies, expelled all the Spanish residents from her territory. The long dispute with Chili about the south western frontier was settled by treaty in 1866. The next year Melgarejo ordered an election for president, and convoked the national assembly in August. At the close of the year De Acha escaped from confinement, and stirred up revolution in Eastern Bolivia. A contract was entered into at this date with some Frenchmen, for the purpose of obtaining the valuable deposits of guano on the coast of Mejillones. A new congress was elected in 1868, and met in August of the same year. Melgarejo proclaimed himself dictator in February, 1869; in May he issued a decree restoring the constitution, and ordered elections for congressmen and senators. This was very acceptable to the people, although Melgarejo holds full control by means of the army being devoted to him.

Bolivia possesses many advantages from which to draw encouragement for the future. Its natural products are the potato, Indian corn, wheat, barley, etc. The finest Peruvian bark comes from the north-west of the republic. Tobacco is extensively grown, cocoa, coffee, sugar, cotton, and other valuable staples are here found, and its mineral wealth of silver, gold, lead, tin, iron, etc., is extremely abundant. The people are partly miners, partly agriculturists, and are reputed to be among the most hardy, energetic and industrious of South America. The government has for some years been occupied in efforts to develop the resources of the Amazon Valley; the internal trade amounts to $50,000,000 annually; the foreign European trade in imports amounts to some $3,000,000 annually; and the exports in Peruvian bark, guano, copper, and especially the silver product, more than offset the imports. One other thing may be mentioned, in conclusion, as decidedly encouraging, viz: that, in Bolivia, there is neither a direct tax nor a public debt, nor paper money

ARGENTINE REPUBLIC.

The Argentine Republic is a republic in South America. It is bounded on the north by Bolivia, east by Paraguay, Brazil and Uruguay, south by the Atlantic and Patagonia, and west by Chili. It lies between the 20th and 40th parallels of S. lat., and 56° and 70° W. long., covering an area of 826,828 square miles. The republic contains fourteen states or provinces, as follows:

	Population.
Buenos Ayres	550,000
Santa Fé	60,000
Entre Rios	160,000
Corrientes	115,000
La Rioja	45,000
Catamarca	110,000
San Juan	80,000
Mendoza	68,000
Cordova	165,000
San Luis	68,000
Santiago	125,000
Tucuman	105,000
Salta	105,000
Jujuy	45,000
Total	1,801,000

The population of Buenos Ayres, the captital city of the republic, is estimated to be 200,000. The federal constitution was adopted May, 1853, and revised in consequence of the re-union of Buenos Ayres with the republic, June 6th, 1860. According to this constitution the legislature consists of two chambers, a senate and house of representatives, the senate having twenty-eight and the house fifty-four members.

In the year 1516, Juan Diaz de Solis discovered the mouth of the Rio de la Plata. He took possession of the coast in the name of the king of Spain, but was slain by the natives. In 1526, Sebastian Cabot, then in the service of Spain, entered the river, and anchored opposite the site of the present Buenos Ayres. Advancing about three hundred miles upwards, Cabot discovered a fine river, the Tercero, flowing into the main stream. Up this he sailed with his fleet, and disembarking his men, built a fort, in which he left a garrison; whilst he himself, with his remaining followers, pursued his discoveries still further up the river. The Indians with whom he came in contact exhibited abundance of gold and silver plates, particularly the latter, brought by them from the eastern parts of Peru. This circumstance led Cabot to believe that mines of the precious metals existed in the country in which he then was; and accordingly he gave the name of *Rio de la Plata*, or River of Silver, to the noble stream by which it was watered. The Spaniards soon determined on colonizing this valuable acquisition; and, to prevent any interference on the part of the other nations of Europe, Don Pedro de Mendoza, with two or three thousand followers, was sent from Spain to secure the possession, and establish a relationship between it and the mother-country. He landed upon the western shore of the La Plata in the year 1535, and founded the city of Buenos Ayres, which he so named from the salubrity of the climate. Pursuing his way into the interior, he explored all the country as far as Potosi, at which mines of silver were discovered nine years afterwards. The first settlers at Buenos Ayres were most unfortunate; their town was burned by the Indians, and after suffering every privation, they were shortly afterwards compelled to abandon the place. Contentions with the Indians were frequent and bloody, for the Guarani Indians of the vast plains upon either bank of the La Plata proved much more difficult to subdue than the timid and tractable Peruvians. It was not until the year 1580, that the Europeans succeeded in their attempts to found a town upon the site chosen by Mendoza. Before this period, however, they had established themselves at Santa Fé, Mendoza, and some other places in the interior; so that the history of this part of South America differs from that of any other colony in one remarkable circumstance,—the first permanent settlement was formed in the heart of the country, and the Spaniards colonized from the interior towards the sea. But they were not permitted quietly to enjoy the success of their third attempt to found Buenos Ayres. Stimulated by the recollection of their previous triumphs in demolishing the works of the invaders on the same ground, the Indians once more attacked it; but the town was so well fortified and garrisoned as to bid defiance to their efforts. From this period the city began to prosper; and the ship which carried to Castile the intelligence of its re-foundation took home a cargo of sugar, and the first hides with which Europe was supplied from the wild cattle which now began to overspread the country, and soon produced a total change in the manners of all the adjoining tribes. The immense pampas of La Plata appear to have been originally stocked with cattle from a few which had been brought by the earliest settlers; and so rapidly had they multiplied that, about the year 1610, no less than a million is said to have been driven from the country in the neighborhood of Santa Fé into Peru.

From the first period of the colonization of this country till the year 1778, the government was dependent on that of Peru, although the chief of Buenos Ayres had the title of captain-general. The pernicious system of policy practiced by Spain towards her colonies was the main cause why this city remained for such a length of time almost entirely unknown to Europeans. Apprehensive lest commodities might be introduced into Peru by way of Buenos Ayres, and thus prejudice the sale of the cargoes imported by the fleets which they sent to Panama, the early traders solicited and obtained from the government the prohibition of every kind of commerce by the Rio de la Plata. Remonstrance and complaint produced little effect, and the provinces of the Rio de la Plata languished in indigence and obscurity. But the resources of so extensive and fertile a territory could not remain for ever concealed. As the population and wealth of the country increased, the continual remonstrances of the people at last opened the eyes of the Spanish government to the importance of the colony, and a relaxation took place in the system of commercial monopoly which had hitherto been rigorously adhered to. Indeed, the absurd restrictions had been followed by their natural consequence, smuggling; and to such a height was the contraband trade carried that, in order to put a stop to it, the government of Castile gave permission to register ships to sail under a license from the council of the Indies at any time of the year. The *flota* which hitherto had embarked from Spain once a year, and was the only legitimate means of communication with America, dwindled away from 15,000 to 2000 tons of shipping; and in 1748, it sailed for the last time to Cadiz, after having carried on the trade of Spanish America for two centuries. The register-ships now supplied the market with European commodities at a cheaper rate and at all seasons of the year; and from that time Buenos Ayres gradually rose into importance. Other relaxations in the mercantile system followed soon afterwards. In the year 1774, free trade was permitted between several of the American ports; and this was subsequently followed by additional liberties.

The improvements which took place in Buenos Ayres by this enlargement of its commercial relations were frequently interrupted by circumstances which carry us back to an early period of its history. The Spaniards and Portuguese have, by a singular coincidence, been destined to be rivals, not only in the Old but in the New World. The neighboring territory of Brazil belonged to Portugal, and bitter hostilities frequently took place between the two countries. It is computed that, in the hostile incursions which the Brazilians made into the Spanish possessions in this quarter of America, they destroyed upwards of four hundred towns and villages. These marauders, the offspring of Portuguese, Dutch, French or Italians, by Brazilian women, were called Mamelucos. Their principal object was to carry into slavery the Indians whom the Jesuits had partially civilized; and in exercising their inhuman trade they committed the most horrid enormities. In the year 1778, the provinces of the Rio de la Plata, Paraguay, Uruguay and Bolivia were erected into a vice-royalty, of which Buenos Ayres was constituted the capital. At the same time, it was thrown open to free trade of every description, even with the interior of Peru; and such was the effect of this wholesome measure that the number of vessels trading with South America was at once augmented, and kept gradually increasing from year to year.

In the year 1806, a British squadron, under the command of Sir Home Popham, appeared in the Rio de la Plata. From this armament a body of troops was landed, for the purpose of taking the capital, in which they succeeded, June 26th. They were, however, attacked and compelled to surrender, August 12th. In the meantime, British reinforcements arrived from the Cape of Good Hope, whence the original expedition had sailed; and Popham, after making an unsuccessful attempt on Monte Video, took Fort Maldonado, at the mouth of the Plata. But the intelligence of the first capture of Buenos Ayres was so well received by the British public that government resolved on maintaining possession of the banks of the Plata; and an armament was therefore fitted out for effectually reducing the country. Monte Video was taken, February, 1807, but the attack on Buenos Ayres failed, and the British forces were compelled to evacuate the country. But the events which were now passing on the continent of Europe were destined to change completely the aspect of affairs in South America. The invasion of Spain by Napoleon, in 1808, gave the colonies an opportunity of throwing off their allegiance to the mother-country. The princess-regent of Portugal, claiming the crown of Spain, despatched emissaries to La Plata to concert measures for her residence at Buenos Ayres. Her proposals were received with enthusiasm; but they were rendered abortive by the viceroy Cisneros, who was a staunch supporter of the rights of Ferdinand VII. From this period the principal supporters of the Princess Carlota changed their views, and formed plans of ultimately setting up the standard of independence. After some political struggles, they succeeded in deposing the viceroy, and, on the 25th of May, 1810, named a *junta gubernativa*, the leading member of which was Don Mariano Moreno, the secretary. He was not, however, supported, and died soon afterwards. Nearly the whole of the country was now in favor of independence; still there were continual disputes as to the form of government that should be established,—Buenos Ayres endeavoring to obtain the supreme power, while the other provinces contended for equal rights. In January, 1813, a sovereign constituent assembly was convened at Buenos Ayres. It was not until now that the Spanish flag and cockade were replaced by the bicolor. Now also the coinage bore the republican arms.

Monte Video still stoutly maintained the sinking cause of Spain; the effort was unavailing. In 1812, the town was taken, when between 5000 and 6000 royalist troops laid down their arms, and an immense quantity of military stores was likewise given up. The changes which the government of Buenos Ayres underwent we will not follow; and the civil dissensions by which the country was afflicted are equally endless and uninteresting. In 1816, a congress of deputies from all the provinces met at Tucuman, which named General Pueyrredon director of the republic, and declared the countries on the Plata independent. An army was raised and disciplined to defend the country, and to assist the people of Chili against their common enemy. The combined forces gained over the Spaniards the two decisive victories of Chacabuco (1817) and Maypu (1818). Various attempts were made by the Spaniards to regain possession of La Plata, but they were all without success; and finally their troops were totally defeated by the republicans in July, 1821. In 1824, the independence of La Plata was recognized by the British government. The internal dissensions in the country previous to the appointment of Rosas dictator in 1835, and the events which led to his downfall and flight in 1852, need not here be dwelt upon. This event, which seemed to put an end to a protracted war, was in reality but the signal for fresh contests. The people of Buenos Ayres, exulting in their newly-obtained liberty, were still animated with all their old jealousy of the other provinces, and of General Urquiza who supported their rights. Accordingly, when the governors of all the provinces, assembled by Urquiza at San Nicolas, appointed him provisory director until a general congress, which was to meet at Santa Fé, should prepare a constitution, the representative assembly of Buenos Ayres accused Urquiza of attempting to set up a new tyranny, and forbade the execution of the treaty of San Nicolas. Urquiza, in the exercise of his provisory power, dissolved the assembly, and occupied the city with his troops. While thus possessed of supreme power, the director followed a more liberal policy than Rosas, by acknowledging the independence of Paraguay, opening the La Plata to ships of all nations, and permitting free commerce in the interior of the country. But no sooner had Urquiza quitted Buenos Ayres to attend the congress at Santa Fé, than a revolution took place in the town; his troops were obliged to retire; the representative assembly again met, and appointed General Pinto provisory governor of the province. But the province of Buenos Ayres itself soon became divided, the country rising against the town; civil war raged afresh; and General Urquiza beseiged Buenos Ayres by land and sea. Meanwhile all the other provinces sent deputies to the congress of Santa Fé, which prepared a federal constitution, and published it May 1st, 1853. The representatives of Brazil and Bolivia attempted in vain to mediate between the contending parties; and afterwards the ministers of Great Britain and France interfered with as little success. On the 26th of June, 1853, Commodore Coe, the commander of Urquiza's squadron at Buenos Ayres, influenced, it is said, by a bribe, went over to the other side. Mutiny and desertion broke out in the besieging army; and Urquiza was obliged to retire to the province of Entre Rios, of which he was governor. Then ensued a separation between the contending parties. Buenos Ayres declared itself a sovereign State; while the other provinces fixed their capital at Parana, and appointed Urquiza president of the republic for six years. Two treaties were concluded in December, 1854, and January, 1855, by which the two States were to allow free commerce between their territories, to use one national flag, and to defend each other against foreign aggression. Fresh misunderstandings and aggressions however arose; and these treaties were declared null March 18, 1856. The thirteen provinces, in 1857, endeavored to lessen the preponderance of Buenos Ayres by opening up the Parana and Paraguay to commerce, and imposing extra duties of 30 per cent. on merchandise coming by Buenos Ayres. The arrangement, however, effected in 1860, by which Buenos Ayres has become and is now one of the States of the republic, has put an end to these and other troubles, and allows room for development and growth to the fullest extent.

The invasion of the province of Corrientes by a Paraguayan army, in 1865, led to a long and exhaustive struggle of several years' continuance, involving the republic in a debt for the war of $20,000,000 (gold). Nevertheless under its present ruler, Domingo F. Sarmiento, (president for the term 1868 to 1874,) the progress of the republic is very encouraging. Peace and order have been reestablished in the provinces desolated by civil war, and it is felt and believed that the Argentine republic has entered upon a new career which promises great and noble results. European immigration has been rapidly on the increase during the last ten years. Between 1858 and 1862, it averaged 5,613; during 1863 to 1867, the average was 13,000; and since that it has risen to nearly 30,000 per annum. About 10,000 of these are Italians; some 9,000 French and Swiss; together with a moderate proportion of Germans, English, etc. Towns and villages have sprung up, railroads have been built, canals have been opened, improvements in navigation adopted, and manufactures of all kinds established. More especially in this progress noticeable in the province or State of Buenos Ayres. Here there are four lines of railroad in active operation, and the city itself has grown largely in various directions. In order to give new encouragement to agriculture and immigration, Congress appropriated $200,000 for the national exhibition at Cordova, April, 1870. A sub-marine telegraph connects Buenos Ayres with Monte Video, and a telegraph line (300 miles in length) is completed between the capital and Rosario. The financial condition of the republic is now very good, its budget annually showing a gratifying increase of revenue over expenditures.

The Argentine republic has a great variety of soil and temperature, and consequently the productions and occupations of the country and people are varied and diverse to a considerable extent. Cattle forms the most valuable property, and immense numbers are herded on the luxuriant plains. Hides, skins, hair, horns, bones, salt meat, and tallow furnish a large part of the exports. Cotton, tobacco, rice, cocoa, sugar, etc., are raised, together with wheat and other grains. The fruits grown are chiefly those of southern Europe, such as the orange, fig, olive, peach, apricot, apple, pear, and grape. In mineral productions the republic is not important. The mountains occupy the western and northern portions of the country; and the fertile valleys of the rivers separate most of it into vast ranges, which are either covered with rich vegetation, or made desert by the efflorescence of salt. The south-western portion of the republic has not as yet been explored to any great extent, although promising well in the result.

PARAGUAY.

Paraguay is a republic of South America, lying between S. Lat. 27° 18′ and 21° 20′, W. Long. 54° 23′, and 58° 46′; and bounded on the north and east by Brazil, and on the south and west by the Argentine Republic. Its form is nearly that of a parallelogram: its length, from north to south, about 416 miles; average breadth, 180; area, 73,000 square miles. Population, 1,400,000; Ascuncion, the capital, has a population of 48,000.

Paraguay forms a sort of inland peninsula, being surrounded on three sides by the River Parana, and its tributary the Paraguay, which joins it at the south-west corner of the State. The centre of the country is traversed from north to south by a mountain-chain called the Sierra Anambahy, which separates itself into two at its southern extremity, forming the valley of the Tibicuary, an affluent of the Paraguay. The whole of the rivers of this country flow either into the Paraguay or the Parana; and as the central mountain-chain which divides their waters is in no place more than one hundred miles from either of these rivers, the streams of the country are more remarkable for number than for magnitude. By far the longest and most important of these is the Tibicuary already mentioned, which has a tortuous course, and waters the southern portion of Paraguay. This southern region is a rich and beautiful country, presenting a striking contrast to the adjacent parts of the Argentine Republic. It consists of broad valleys and plains affording excellent pasturage, undulating slopes, and hills covered from top to bottom with magnificent forests. The soil here is very fertile; and cultivation is more extensively carried on in this district than in any other part of the interior of South America. White cottages may frequently be seen in the midst of trees, surrounded by cultivated fields; but even here it is only scattered patches of ground that are tilled. Portions of this southern region are occupied by extensive marshes and broad but shallow lakes. The northern and eastern part of Paraguay is but little known. It seems to be a rugged and mountainous country, densely covered with forests, and watered by numerous rivers, which have many rapids and waterfalls. In the north-east there is a branch of the principal mountain-chain known by the name of the Sierra Maracaju or Maracay. To the west of the Anambahy range, the country, though mountainous, is not so rugged as that to the east; and the rivers, rapid and impetuous as they are, follow a more even course to the Paraguay. Here, as in all parts of the country, we find extensive forests; but the fertility of the soil is not so great. The climate, though tropical, is tempered by the irregularities of the surface, and by the periodical rains which fall here. The rains, though not so abundant as in countries nearer the equator, serve to fertilize the country. The heat at Asuncion, the capital, in summer averages about 85° Fahr., though it sometimes rises to 100°, and in winter it is usually about 45°; but the temperature is much influenced by the direction of the winds. In geological structure, the greater part of Paraguay belongs to the tertiary formation; but there are also some graywacke rocks in the northern and eastern portions. The productions of Paraguay are numerous, including those of tropical as well as of temperate climates. The forests abound in many kinds of timber, some of which are used for ship-building, and furnish the materials for most of the vessels that navigate the Paraguay and Parana; while there are also many dye-woods, and trees yielding valuable juices and other products; as the dragon-tree, the India-rubber tree, and the *maté*, or Paraguay tea, from which is extracted the beverage most generally used throughout South America. The last mentioned plant, which is about the size of an orange tree, grows wild in great abundance in the almost impenetrable forests in the north-east. The leaves are gathered, dried, and reduced to powder; and they afford an ample profit to the merchants of Paraguay. The pounded leaves are infused in the same way as the teas of China. Among the other natural products of Paraguay are,—indigo, cochineal, gums, wax, and medicinal plants. The principal crops raised are,—maize, rice, mandioc, tobacco, sugar-cane, coffee, and cacoa. Cotton thrives well here, and was at one time extensively grown; but its culture has now been almost entirely given up. Agriculture is not in a very advanced state in Paraguay; although this is the occupation of the greater part of the people. A large extent of the country belongs to the State, and is let out in small portions to separate families. The prairies of Paraguay, being less extensive than those of the adjacent countries, do not support very large numbers of cattle, but there are enough of horses, cattle, and sheep to supply the wants of the inhabitants. The wild animals are the same as those found in other parts of South America. The jaguar, the puma, and the ocelot are the most ferocious beasts; monkeys also abound. Of birds the largest is the cassowary; and among other remarkable species are numerous species of parrot and humming-bird, and several species of curassows and guans. Manufactures are by no means extensively carried on in Paraguay. Small quantities of sugar, rum, mandioc flour, cotton and woollen cloth, salt, lime, bricks, etc., are made for domestic use; and a few hides are tanned for exportation. At present the government monopolizes the exportation of the Paraguay tea, and nearly the whole of that of timber; so that as these articles form the principal exports of the country, nearly one-half of the whole value of goods exported belongs to the government. The imports consist chiefly of cotton and woollen goods, hardware, silk, flour, wine, sugar, and salt; and about three-fourths of these articles are of British manufacture. The imported goods are brought to Paraguay through Buenos Ayres, whence they are conveyed up the river by small schooners to Asuncion. The means of communication in the interior of the country are slow and expensive; as all goods are conveyed by means of heavy bullock carts. There are some tolerably good roads, and several of the rivers might be navigated by small steamers, to the great advantage of the commerce of the country. The port at which the greater part of the trade is carried on is Asuncion. This, with Pilar and Encarnacion, are the only ports open to foreign commerce. Pilar, on the Paraguay, is about 180 miles below Asuncion, and was, previous to 1851, the only port. At Encarnacion, on the Parana, there is no trade, as it can only be reached by boats. There are several smaller ports on the Paraguay, but these are only open to the coasting trade, and convey all their goods to Asuncion.

The constitution of Paraguay is in form republican, although there is little real liberty among the people, and no liberal policy in the government. The executive power is in the hands of a president; this office was held by Don Carlos Antonio Lopez, who was elected in 1844 for ten years, re-elected in 1854 for three, and again in 1857 for seven. The legislative body consists of a congress, which meets once every five years. The annual revenue is estimated to amount to $2,000,000, and the military forces have been raised to the number of 47,000. The navy consists of eighteen steamers. The country is divided into eight departments. The established religion is the Roman Catholic. Education is widely diffused throughout the people, and there are comparatively few who cannot read and write; but the state of morals is low. The aboriginal inhabitants of Paraguay were the Guarani Indians; and they, along with the Mestizoes, a mixed race of Spanish and Indian origin, still form the bulk of the population. In and about the principal towns, however, there are a small number of Spaniards, and there the Spanish language is coming into use, while the prevailing dialect throughout the country is the Guarani.

The estuary of the La Plata was discovered by the Spaniards in the beginning of the sixteenth century; and they soon afterwards sailed up the river and attempted to found settlements on its banks. After having been twice unsuccessful, they sent Don Pedro de Mendoza with a number of ships, in 1535, to establish a colony; and he, sailing up the Paraguay, founded the city of Asuncion, from which as a center, the Spanish extended their dominion over the countries watered by the Parana and its affluents. Paraguay then made a Spanish province, forming a part of the viceroyalty of Peru. The original settlers found the Guaranis a bold and warlike people, who offered much resistance to their arms. They were divided into numerous tribes in various stages of civilization, some living by agriculture and others by war and the chase. Their religion consisted in the worship of two deities, a good and a bad spirit; and their government was in the hands of hereditary chiefs with despotic power. These tribes, after an obstinate defence, were reduced to submission by the courage and perseverance of the Spaniards. Owing to its containing none of the precious metals, Paraguay was little attended to by the Spanish government. The Jesuits were sent into the country about the middle of the sixteenth century for the purpose of converting the natives; but they found it impossible to make much progress, or to protect the Indians against the oppression of the colonists, until the Spanish court, towards the end of the seventeenth century, granted them entire independence of the provincial authorities, along with the right to exclude all other Europeans from their settlements. After this, their labors were attended with great success; they established numerous missions or communities, in which the Indians were gradually reclaimed from their previous savage state to peaceful and industrious habits. They had thus attained to a state of some civilization, when, in 1767, the Jesuits were suddenly expelled from South America; and Paraguay again became the subject of Spanish viceroys. After this event, though some of the communities continued in existence till a later period, the greater number fell to the ground; and the inhabitants relapsed into a state of barbarism. In 1776, Paraguay became a province of the vice-royalty of Rio de la Plata, which was then formed. In 1810, Paraguay rebelled against the Spanish government; and, in the following year, without joining the confederacy of the other Spanish States, declared its independence. Its remote and isolated situation prevented any attempt being made to reduce it to subjection, and it was thus the earliest of the Argentine States that achieved its independence. The celebrated Dr. Francia, who was originally a lawyer, and afterwards secretary to the revolutionary junta, obtained such influence by his integrity and ability as to be appointed dictator in 1814, for three years, and in 1817, for life. His government, which lasted till his death, in 1840, was an absolute depotism; and has been represented by many writers as a most cruel and capricious tyranny. His measures, however, seem in many instances to have conduced to the benefit of the country: he encouraged agriculture and manufactures, composed a code of laws, established schools throughout the country, and raised a standing army. He attempted to isolate Paraguay entirely from the rest of the world, by prohibiting foreigners from entering, and detaining all who set foot in the country, a policy adopted by the Jesuit missionaries, and which he pursued probably from the same motives. In judging of the contradictory accounts given of the character of his government, we should not forget the half-savage state in which the most of the Paraguayans were at that time. After the death of Francia, the country was governed for two years by two consuls; and in 1844, the present constitution was adopted. The restrictions against foreign intercourse were not at once removed under the new system of government; but, in 1852, a treaty was signed with the Argentine Republic, and in 1853, with Great Britain, the United States, France, and Sardinia, opening up the country to the commerce of these nations. A French colony was established, in 1855, on the right bank of the Paraguay, under the name of New Bourdeaux, but it was not encouraged by the president of the republic, and had to be abandoned for want of provisions in the end of the same year.

In 1862, Don Francisco Solano Lopez assumed the presidency on the death of his father, mentioned above. Though elected nominally for ten years, Lopez is, in fact, absolute ruler of Paraguay, and unless driven out, is permitted to transmit his office to a successor. The principal feature of note in the history of Paraguay of late years, is the long, steadily maintained and desperate struggle between Lopez on the one side, and the allied powers, Brazil, Argentine Republic, and Uruguay, on the other. The war was begun in 1864, by the Paraguayans seizing a Brazilian mail steamer, and Lopez soon after invading the province of Matto Grosso. Early in 1865, Argentine vessels were captured, followed by a declaration of war, and seizing the port of Corrientes. During this and the following years, the war was carried on with varied success, at one time Lopez gaining advantages, at another the allies pressing him severely and closely. The details are neither important nor of general interest, and we shall not undertake to dwell upon them. The allies have bound themselves never to cease hostilities until Lopez is overthrown; at the same time they avow distinctly, that they shall not interfere with the independence and integrity of the republic. Of course, Lopez has no alternative but to fight it out; it is all, or nothing, with him. According to the latest information, Lopez is reduced to very nearly the last straits; but whether the contest is over and done with, or whether it will be again renewed, time alone can show. Efforts have been made to bring the struggle to a close by offers of mediation; first by Mr. Gould, English secretary of legation at Buenos Ayres, based mainly on Lopez's abdication; this was refused at once; subsequently by other parties, but without success. The American minister, Mr. Washburn, had serious difficulty with the dictator, who used him rather shabbily. McMahon, who went out as Washburn's successor, in 1868, stuck closely to Lopez; and when, in March 1869, Gen. Grant recalled McMahon, he sent a very complimentary letter to his "great and good friend," the Dictator of Paraguay. A provisional government, organized by the allies in 1869, offered free grants of land along the Upper Parana for live cattle. The monopoly on yerba, or Paraguayan tea, was also abolished.

URUGUAY.

URUGUAY, or Banda Oriental, is a republic of South America, bounded on the N. and N.E. by Brazil, S.E. by the Atlantic Ocean, S. by the river La Plata, and W. by the Uruguay River, separating it from the Argentine Republic. It lies between 30° 5′ and 34° 56′ S. lat., and 53° 10′ and 58° 20′ W. long.; and is about 360 miles in length from N.W. to S.E., by 300 in extreme breadth; area 70,000 square miles. Population, about 350,000, of whom 150,000 are foreigners; Monte Video, the capital, has a population of about 40,000.

The surface is generally elevated and undulating, consisting of extensive plains inter sected by ranges of hills of moderate elevation, and by gently sloping valleys. The principal river in the State is the Rio Negro, which divides it into two nearly equal portions. The southern portion is traversed by a range called the Cochilla Grande, which forms the water-shed between the La Plata and the Rio Negro. It enters the State from the north-east, and, after running in a south-westerly direction for some distance, it divides into two branches which terminate in the west of the State. It sends off numerous ramifications, many of which terminate rather abruptly on the banks of the Paraguay and the La Plata. In the northern portion of the State is a range called the Cochilla del Hædo, which, entering from the north, proceeds southward for some distance, and then divides into a number of arms. The country is watered by numerous streams, but none of them are of great size except the La Plata and Uruguay, which form its south and western boundaries; the Rio Negro; and the Guary, which bounds it upon the north. Little is known of the geology of the country; the prevailing rocks, however, are granite, gneiss, limestone and clay-slate. Gold and silver are said to be found, and copper has been successfully worked. The climate is mild, equable and healthy, but during the winter a good deal of rain falls in the valleys and on the low plains. The winter extends from May to October; but very little snow falls, though frost is occasionally felt in July and August. The country is fertile, but is mostly covered with rich pasture, supporting immense herds of horses and cattle, which constitute the chief wealth of the inhabitants. Timber is scarce, and chiefly to be met with on the banks of the larger rivers. Though capable of easy cultivation, agriculture is almost entirely neglected. Wheat, maize, barley, rice, cotton, flax, hemp, pease, beans, melons, the sugar-cane, vine, etc., are grown. Few or none of these products find their way out of the country, the chief exports being hides, skins, hair, horns, bones, jerked-beef and tallow. The manufactures are confined to rude articles for domestic use. Monte Video, the capital, is the centre of the foreign trade. This trade occupies about 1500 vessels, of some 300,000 tonnage. The value of exports to Great Britain and her colonies is estimated at $3,000,000; to France over $3,000,000; to the United States, something more than $11,000,000; and to other States in various proportions, making in all some $21,000,000.

Uruguay is a republic modelled after that of the United States, having a president elected for four years, a senate of ten, and a representative chamber of thirty-nine members; in point of fact, however, the government has been for many years little else than a military despotism. For administrative purposes it is divided into thirteen provinces, viz: Monte Video, Maldonado, Canelonnes, San José, Florida, Colonia del Sacramento, Soriano, Paysandu, Salto, Tacuarembo, Carro-Largo, Minas, Durazno. The revenue of the State is estimated at $2,500,000; the expenditure at $3,200,000. The total public debt amounts to some $50,000,000.

Banda Oriental was, during the Spanish rule, the name of that portion of the vice-royalty of Buenos Ayres which lay to the east of the river Uruguay, and comprehended the present Uruguay and the territory formerly known as the Seven Missions. When Buenos Ayres declared itself independent of Spain, Banda Oriental formed a part of the new republic. In 1821, however, it was taken possession of by Brazil, and united with that State under the name of Provincia Cisplatina. By the treaty of 1828 between La Plata and Brazil, the northern portion of Banda Oriental, or the Seven Missions, was united to Brazil, and the southern and larger portion formed into the republic of Uruguay. Internal dissensions led to the interference of Rosas, president of Buenos Ayres, and a long and hurtful struggle took place. Brazil, together with England and France, took matters in hand, and compelled the combatants to cease their foolish strife. Some ships of war were sent to the Plata in 1845, Monte Video was blockaded till 1849, when treaties were made with

Buenos Ayres. Fighting was not long after begun again and continued till 1851. Peace was now secured; treaties were entered into with foreign countries; and in January, 1859, Brazil and the Argentine Republic, by treaty guaranteed the neutrality and independence of the State. In 1865, and during the following years, Uruguay was one of the allied powers engaged in war with Paraguay. But here, as in other States, revolution and civil disturbances seem to be a chronic disease. In 1868, Col. Battle was elected president for the four years from 1868 to 1872.

CHILI.

The Republic of Chili occupies that long strip of land which lies on the south-western side of South America, extending from S. lat. 24° to 55° 59′; and from W. long. 69° to 72°. It is bounded W. by the Pacific Ocean, and E. by the Andes, by which it is separated from the Argentine Republic. On the N., Chili is separated from Bolivia by the extensive desert of Atacama; and it extends southwards to the extreme limits of that archipelago which embraces all the islands between Chiloë and the Straits of Magellan. Reckoning its length from the desert of Atacama to Cape Horn, it comprehends 36 degrees of latitude. Its average breadth is only 150, and where greatest, not more than 210 miles. The superficial area of Chili is computed at 132,624 square miles. Except where the Andes are intersected by ravines, which frequently expand into vales or plains fit for cultivation, these mountains, with their parallel ranges and spurs, occupy a great part of its area. Population (inclusive of Araucania, Patagonia and Terra del Fuego), 2,084,945. Santiago, the capital, has a population of 80,000.

Under the dominion of Spain, the *Capitania-General* of Chili extended from S. lat. 24° to Cape Horn; but as no settlements were actually formed beyond S. lat. 44°, the length of the Spanish possessions may be estimated at 1400 English miles. The ranges of the Andes, which, from their height and excessive coldness, are uninhabitable, cover nearly one-third of the surface of Chili. Between the Andes and the sea there are two parallel ranges, which decrease in elevation towards the coast, and are connected by several smaller ridges. Many deep basins are thus formed, some of which are filled with water from the melted snows of the Cordilleras; while in others the waters have found an outlet, and have left a fertile table-land, in which pasture may be obtained when the great droughts have destroyed the herbage in the less elevated districts.

From the foot of the lower range of the Andes the land gradually descends towards the sea, but more precipitously near the shore, which is skirted by a comparatively low tract of country. Even this district, however, is crossed by numerous spurs from the Andes, and presents a series of barren mountain plains, intersected by deep *quebradas*, or fissures, which, during the melting of the snows in summer, are watered by large and rapid streams, and form the only cultivated districts in the country. As rain rarely falls in Northern Chili, except in the two or three winter months, and as the dews are light, the districts between these fissures are almost destitute of vegetation. In the Andes, which separate Chili from the Argentine Republic, there are several passes that can be traversed in safety in summer. The most frequented are those of Dehesa, near Tupungato, to the east of Santiago; Copiapo, in Atacama; Colgüen, in Coquimbo; the Patas, in Aconcagua; and the Portillo Uspallata.

No part of South America has had its geology so well investigated as Chili. Its stupendous mountains, rising in some places to the elevation of 23,900 feet above the level of the sea,—its numerous volcanoes, three of them generally in a state of active eruption,—and its very peculiar geological structure,—make it, with the exception of Peru, the most interesting part of South America. It may be said that in Chili various geological phenomena are still in active operation. The grand range of the Cordilleras has suffered the most violent rendings and movements both upward and downward. The Cordilleras and the Andes, though often spoken of indiscriminately, are, as in Peru, different chains of mountains, running nearly parallel to each other. The former are termed in the south Cordilleras de la Costa (Cordilleras of the Coast), and between them and the Andes are extensive plateaux, which gradually sink in elevation from Central Chili to the south. For instance, Santiago, the capital, is at an elevation of 1830 feet above the level of the sea; whilst Rancagua, 63 miles further south, is 1558 feet; and Talca, 165 miles further south, is only 311 feet above the sea. Although the plain between the southern chain alters so rapidly in elevation, yet the northern chain from Aconcagua to Atacama, rising to a mean elevation of nearly 15,000 feet, displays throughout little variety in its forms; but further south, in S. lat. 33°, it assumes a different appearance, new rocks and formations showing themselves on its surface. Towards lat. 33°, volcanic masses of a modern period are first met with; cones springing up into points, covered with snow and ice, the fires of whose craters have only lately become inactive. There, rising to an elevation of 23,600 feet, is the stupendous mountain of Aconcagua, which has been generally considered as a volcano; but recent observation has ascertained that this is not the case. Although its top is far above the line of perpetual snow, yet frequently no snow is visible for many months on its surface. This is caused no doubt by the extreme dryness of the air. Further south are Tupungato, 23,000 feet high; Juncal, 19,900; the Maipo Volcano, 19,000; and El Portillo, with its immense escorias, and the volcano of San José, each rising to the height of more than 18,000 feet above the level of the sea.

The whole chain of the Cordilleras, from Terra del Fuego to Mexico, is penetrated by volcanic orifices, and those now in action are connected in great trains. In the Chilian range there are twenty-three volcanoes, some of them very ancient, without craters; some with craters, but quite extinct; others in the condition of solfataras; and others, such as Osorno, Villa Rica, and Antuco, in the south, and San José in the province of Santiago, in occasional and fierce action. The average width of the country between the Cordilleras and the sea is from 80 to 100 miles. It is crossed by various spur-like chains, the greater part of which, lying south of S. lat. 31°, range nearly north and south; but in the northern parts they run in every direction. The cultivated region of Chili may be considered to be between the river Biobio and the port of Coquimbo, that is to say, between seven degrees of latitude; and as the mean width is about two degrees of longitude, consequently the surface is equal to 7350 square Chilian leagues of twenty-five to a degree, from which must be deducted the part occupied by the Cordilleras of the Andes, forming at least one-third of this surface; therefore the actual part susceptible of cultivation is reduced to 4900 square leagues. However, several of the valleys of Huasco and Copiapo produce considerable quantities of fruit and vegetables.

There is the most positive evidence of the recent elevation of the most northern part of Chili from about 45° S. lat.; and, indeed, a similar elevation can be traced on to Peru to a distance of about 2000 miles. The marks of sea action are evident at a distance of thirty to forty miles inland, by ancient beaches, and successive and perfectly formed terraces. In Chiloe, shells are found at an ele vation of 350 feet; at Concepcion, 625; at Valparaiso, 1300; and at Coquimbo, 252 feet. At Baldera, the port of Copiapo, the present line of the railroad, to an elevation of 300 feet above the level of the sea, is cut through thick beds of shells of existing species. On examining with attention the northern part of Chili, it is seen that there have been five ascensional movements of the coast. Round the Bay of Coquimbo the surface rises like an amphitheatre in five very marked stages, forming concentric terraces. The first terrace, a mile wide, rises to an elevation of about twenty-three feet,—it consists of sand-duns, and towards the town of Serena, of salt and fresh water marshes, with shells similar to those found on the beach. A steep escarpment leads to the second terrace, about seventy feet above the level of the sea, on which the town of Serena is built, the upper part covering the third terrace at an elevation of 120 feet. The fourth terrace, which is narrow, rises 182 feet above the third; and a steep escarpment leads to the fifth, or upper terrace. Above the town, it is entirely composed of immense masses of rounded shingle, and stretches along the coast, and inland to a distance of eleven miles. About two miles from Port Coquimbo, this fifth terrace sinks about 100 feet below the surrounding level; and a few inches below the sandy surface, there is a thick stratum of calcareous matter filled with shells, which forms an excellent building-stone and good lime. On advancing northward, the same terraces are observed. On going up the valley of Huasco to the town of Ballenar, about 37 miles inland, the five terraces are perfectly defined, composed of gravel aggregated together in a matrix of clay. In the neighborhood of Valparaiso the elevation of the coast is very apparent. On the south side of that town are numerous headlands, covered with broken shells to an elevation of 230 feet; and even at an elevation of 557 feet very comminuted shells are found, similar to those which exist in the neighboring sea. The principal species are the patellæ, trochus, crepidulæ and concholepas, some of which are occasionally to be found at an elevation of 1300 feet.

North of Valparaiso, near to Concon, are immense beds of the mesodesma-donaciforme, which supply lime for the town and many leagues round. The same fossil shell is found in such abundance near Coquimbo, to the elevation of eighty feet above the sea, that an English smelting establishment at Herradura, two and a half miles from the port of Coquimbo, has frequently purchased nearly 3000 quintals in a week for the purpose of making lime; and at Sangoy, where the same English company has another smelting establishment, the quantity is so great that it is collected and delivered into the works at the low rate of two dollars per cajon of sixty-four quintals. From the indications of the action of the sea at different elevations, we may suppose that the process of elevation has been interrupted by long periods of comparative rest; and from the similarity of the distant terraces, no doubt the periods were synchronous over wide spaces of the coast.

Chili is very subject to severe earthquakes. They manifest themselves by a quick horizontal, vertical, and sometimes by a sort of rotatory vibration. They generally occur in a linear direction; but at other times partly in circles or in long ellipses. The earthquakes of 1835 and 1851 were of the latter description, the vibrations being propagated with decreasing intensity from a centre towards a circumference. It is affirmed by all miners, that the most severe shocks are not felt in deep mines, although the loud rumbling sound, like a heavy cart passing rapidly along a narrow street, which precedes the shock, is distinctly heard. It is a very general opinion, that the atmospheric pressure is disturbed on the days when earthquakes occur; but the result of seven years' barometric observations in Chili refutes this opinion, as we have observed the horary variations of the barometer to be rarely affected either before or after earthquakes. Changes of the weather, however, generally succeed earthquakes. Immediately after the great earthquake of February, 1835, torrents of rain fell in Concepcion, although in the midst of summer, when rain is nearly unknown. Experience shows, that about two desolating shocks may be expected in a century. The intensity of the shocks is supposed to be increased according to the time intervening between them, and the danger to be greatest when the volcanic vents are closed. Although they appear to be simply dynamic phenomena of motion, yet in Chili they have suddenly elevated whole districts above the ancient level. By the earthquake of February, 1835, the Isle of Santa Maria was uplifted, the southern end eight, the central part nine and the northern end ten feet; but both it and Concepcion subsided a few weeks afterwards, and even lost part of their previous elevation. The sea is generally much agitated during and for a short time after the shocks. During the earthquake which destroyed Concepcion and nearly all the towns in the south of Chili, two great waves rolled over the town of Talcahuano, and the small penal establishment of Juan Fernandez was nearly washed away; the deep sea, close in shore, was dry for a few moments, and smoke burst from the surface of the water. During an earthquake at Coquimbo, in November, 1849, the sea retired about one hundred and fifty yards, and then rolled back about twleve feet high. An English ship, anchored in seven fathoms of water, in the neighboring bay of Herradura, nearly touched the bottom from the receding of the sea, which afterwards rolled in like a bore, and the water continued to ebb and flow for an hour and a-half after the shock.

The appearance of the country is agreeably diversified by lakes, which are especially numerous in the southern provinces. In some of these, situate near the coast, such as Bacalemu, Cahuil, Vichuquen and Bolleruca, the water is brackish; but in Ranca, Villa Rica, and the lakes of the interior, it is quite fresh. They generally abound with fish; and are frequented by numerous varieties of aquatic birds. In some districts, and particularly in the Cordilleras, there are valuable thermal springs. The most celebrated for their medicinal virtues are those of Colina, Cauquenes, Panimavida and Chillan. Chili, particularly in its southern division, is abundantly supplied with rivers and streams, which, however, from the nature of the surface, have generally a short and rapid course, and are navigable only for a few miles from their mouths. The Biobio has a course of nearly 200 miles, and though not less than two miles in breadth at its mouth, is too shallow for large vessels to enter. It is navigable for river craft as far as Nacimiento, about 100 miles from the sea. The Maule is navigable for river barges for about twenty miles; and the Aconcagua, the Cauten and the Callacalla (which last is deep enough for large vessels to enter), are considerable streams. All the navigable rivers flow through that part of Chili which is south of the Maipù, where the rains fall abundantly. They are very rapid, owing to the declivity of the country, which renders them easily available for irrigation; and thus large tracts, which would otherwise be barren, are rendered rich and fertile.

In a country like Chili, extending from the tropic of Capricorn to within twelve degrees of the Antartic circle, and presenting great differences of elevation, considerable variety of climate may be anticipated. Omitting the cold and thinly inhabited region to the extreme south, and beginning with the province of Chiloë, Chili may be divided into three regions, which may be distinguished as the wet region, the corn and wine region, and the dry, or mineral region. The wet region comprehends Valdivia, Arauco and Chiloë, and is so much exposed to excessive rains, that in Chiloë it is frequently necessary to dry the wheat and barley crops by artificial means. The corn and wine region embraces the eight provinces between Arauco and Coquimbo, and in these rain falls in the months of June, July and August, with more or less abundance as they approach the south. In April, May, September and October, showers are more rare and uncertain. In the provinces south of Talca, the amount of rain being insufficient for agricultural purposes, it is necessary to resort to irrigation. The dry, or mineral region, including Coquimbo and Copiapo, is very warm, and receives only four or five showers in the whole course of the year. These, however, are so fertilizing, that an almost instantaneous change takes place in the appearance of the country. In the neighborhood of the Andes, as well as towards the south, the atmosphere is often cooled by nocturnal frosts. Spring commences in September, summer in December, autumn in March, and winter in June. The mildness and salubrity of the climate is unsurpassed by that of any other country. In a sanitary point of view, Valdivia is the most favorably situated of all the provinces; and Valparaiso and Santiago, in which are the two largest cities, are the worst. Deaths are most numerous in December, November and January; and fewest in February, March and April.

According to the constitution of Chili, the sovereignty is declared to reside in the people; but the exercise of its functions is delegated to three distinct powers: the legislative, the executive and the judicial. The legislative power is committed to the National Congress, which consists of the Chambers of Deputies and Senators. The Chamber of Deputies consists of members who are elected each for a period of three years, in the proportion of one deputy for every 20,000 inhabitants in the electoral districts. According to the eighth article of the constitution, all who exercise the right of suffrage must be twenty-one years of age if married, and twenty-five if unmarried. They must be able to read and write. They must also possess a certain amount of property, varying from $500 to $1,000 in value. Efforts have recently been made to remove all property qualifications, but without success. The Senate is composed of twenty members, who are chosen by a select body of the electors of each province; every one of whom must have a clear annual income of $500. This body must be equal to three times the number of deputies representing any particular province; and its members are chosen by the electors themselves from their own number. A senator's term of office is nine years. The house of this branch of the legislature is renewed by thirds. In each of the first two periods of three years seven new senators are chosen, and in the last only six.

The functions of the Chamber of Deputies and of the Senate, are partly discharged in concurrence with each other, and partly exclusively. The former body alone possesses the power of accusing the higher officers of government before the senate for various political offences. It originates all money bills and propositions relating to the recruiting of the military force of the country. The senate alone has the right of pronouncing judgment on those public functionaries against whom accusations have been brought by the members of the chamber of deputies. It confirms all the ecclesiastical nominations. In certain cases it gives or withholds its consent to the acts of the executive. In all the other proceedings of the legislature the concurrent voice of the two houses is necessary. Laws for the benefit of the country may originate with either body. When a law has been rejected, or the veto of the president put upon it, it cannot be brought again before the chambers till the following year. The period during which the Congress sits is limited to the three winter months; but when the affairs before it are of such a nature as to render additional deliberation necessary, the session may be prolonged by the president for fifty days. On the day before the regular session closes, the senators elect seven of their number to form the conservative committee, which replaces the Congress during the period of its prorogation. The duties of this body are, to observe the conduct of the president; to exercise in certain cases conjoint powers with him; and, generally, to see that the laws are duly obeyed.

The executive power is committed to the president, who is the supreme chief of the nation and of the administration. He is elected with the same formalities as the senators, and by electors chosen in a similar manner. The office is held for a period of five years; but the president whose term has expired may be immediately re-elected for the same period. On the termination of his second term of office, an interim of five years must elapse before he can be elected a third time. The president possesses certain exclusive powers of a very important nature. He alone can appoint and remove at will not only cabinet ministers, clerks of department, and councillors of state, but also diplomatic ministers, consuls, and the higher provincial officers. He also inducts the higher legal and judicial functionaries; but the nomination of these officers, as well as of the ecclesiastical dignitaries, must proceed from the council of state. The president has the power of distributing the army and navy according to his pleasure; and when, with the sanction of the senate, he assumes the command of the national troops in person, he alone is vested with the right of bestowing naval and military commissions. In other circumstances, the appointments of this nature which he makes must be approved by the senate. In periods of tumult and insurrection he can declare the towns and provinces of the republic in a state of siege. The president is liable to impeachment for maladministration for a year after the expiration of his authority. During that time he is not allowed on any account to leave the country, except with the permission of Congress. All the other officers of government are subject to the same law; but in their case the time is more limited.

Nearly co-ordinate with the president in the executive department is the Council of State. This body is composed of ministers in the exercise of their functions, of two members of the courts of justice, of an ecclesiastical dignitary, a general, an admiral, a chief of the administration of finances, two ex-ministers or diplomatic agents, and two former provincial intendants, governors of departments, or municipal magistrates, who must all possess the qualifications necessary for the rank of senator. The duties of the council of state are, to advise the president in the administration of the government, and to act as a check upon him in proceedings which it may consider as injurious to the interests of the country. The administrative department of the government is conducted by four cabinet ministers. One presides over home and foreign affairs; another over justice, worship, and public education; a third is a minister of war and marine; and the fourth of finance. The president has no power of enforcing obedience to orders relating to any one of these departments until they have been confirmed by the appropriate minister. The ministers are individually responsible to Congress for the due discharge of all the duties pertaining to their respective branches of the administration, and also for whatever is done by them in common as a cabinet. They are entitled to be present and to take part in all the debates of Congress; but, unless holding at the same time the office of senator or of deputy, they are not allowed to vote in that body. Any of them may be impeached by the chamber of deputies for treason against the laws of the State, or for the mal-administration of the duties of his office. An action may be brought against them even by private individuals who have suffered by any of their acts, if the Senate, to whom appeal must in the first place be made, decide that there is sufficient ground for complaint.

The tribunals of justice may be divided into three classes. Of these only two are properly judicial in their functions, the third being mainly political. The third class includes five tribunals, of which the Congress collectively and in its separate branches forms three, with parliamentary jurisdiction, and the council of state one with administrative powers. The fifth is the mixed tribunal, which was formed under the treaty with Great Britain in 1839, guaranteeing the mutual right of search in vessels suspected of slave traffic. The first of the other two classes whose functions are more strictly judicial, comprehends the supreme courts and the three courts of appeal. The supreme court has direct supervision over all the others. The courts of appeal are composed of a certain number of legal ministers or justices, with a corps of special ministers to them in certain cases. These special justices, who form a remarkable feature in the Chilian system of legal administration, are taken from the intelligent classes connected with the military, the agricultural, the mining, and commercial interests of the country. In cases on trial pertaining to their respective interests they sit on the bench, and have an equal voice with the legal judges, both as to the law and the fact. The same class comprehends four other tribunals, presided over by judges who, having been advocates, are termed, in contradistinction to the others, *learned* judges. Of these courts, one possesses the right of decision in all cases involving sums of more than $150, or in which certain government officers are the parties. Its jurisdiction extends also to criminal cases. Another decides, in connection with the provincial intendant, fiscal causes; and its decision cannot be appealed from in any suits under $200. The third of these courts, which is composed of one learned and of one commercial judge, together with the collector of customs, has the power of giving a final decision in revenue cases involving confiscation. The fourth has jurisdiction in suits for libel. There are eleven kinds of inferior tribunals, some having as important spheres of jurisdiction as the lower grades of the superior courts; but differing widely in the nature and extent of their powers. They resemble each other, and differ from the superior courts in this—that the presiding judges are educated lawyers. The ecclesiastical and military tribunals, composed respectively of dignitaries of the church and officers of the army, decide in all cases pertaining to their several spheres of duty. The Exchequer Court, over which the chief of that department presides, takes cognizance of suits arising in matters connected with that branch of the administration. The tribunals of commerce consist of members appointed by all the commercial districts except Valparaiso, and exercise jurisdiction in all cases relating to mercantile affairs. The remaining tribunals, composed of the various grades of provincial officers, have under their jurisdiction a great variety of subjects relating to mining, public roads, theatres, some domestic matters, money claims, and the lesser crimes. The Domestic Court consists of five fathers of families, summoned by the political chief of the province or department in which they reside. It hears and decides upon the complaints of minors against their parents, for refusing assent to their marriage. Complaints of this nature are of more importance in Chili than in other countries, as majority is not reached by single men till the age of twenty-five, while it is attainable through marriage at twenty-one.

For the administration of its internal affairs, Chili is divided into thirteen provinces, each with subordinate departments, sub-delegations, districts, and two settlements. The names of the provinces are,—Atacama, Coquimbo, Valparaiso, Aconcagua, Santiago, Colchagua, Talca, Maule, Nuble, Concepcion, Arauco, Valdivia, and Chiloë, and of the settlements Magallanes and Llanquihue. Each of these provinces is governed by an intendant, who is nominated by the president, and holds office for three years. The departments are under the control of governors, who hold office for a similar term. The intendant generally acts as governor in that department in which the capital of the province is situate, and is, at the same time, mayor of the municipal corporation; but the authority of this body is very limited, as it cannot dispose even of its local funds without the permission of government. The sub-delegations are directed by sub-delegadoes, who are appointed by the governors for a period of two years. Their jurisdiction extends only to minor criminal cases, and to civil suits involving sums of between $40 and $150; but they have also appellate powers from the decision of the inspector's court in actions for sums under $12. The districts are presided over by inspectors, who are chosen by the people, and hold an office similar to that of justice of the peace. They manage also the local postage arrangements. Their decision is final in all suits for sums under $12, but they also dispose of cases involving sums as high as $40, with an appeal, however, to the sub-delegado. The offices of sub-delegado and inspector are compulsory; and those who decline to undertake their duties are liable to fines equal to the sums limiting their respective legal jurisdictions.

The Roman Catholic religion is the only form of worship recognized by the constitution of Chili; and the profession of any other is prohibited by law. For the purposes of ecclesiastical administration, the country is divided into four dioceses (comprehending the archbishopric of Santiago and three suffragan bishoprics), and 157 parishes. Great efforts have been made to induce the Indians to adopt the religion sanctioned by the State. In the island of Chiloë, which is chiefly inhabited by native tribes, a propaganda has been established for this purpose; and nine missionaries have been sent to spread the faith among the Araucanian Indians. These attempts have as yet been crowned with almost no success among these fierce and untamable savages. In return for her exclusive privileges, the church in Chili furnishes a large revenue to the public finances, yielding from $250,000 to $300,000 profit annually to the state, over and above the expenses of maintaining public worship. Some few places of worship for Protestants are tacitly allowed. The power of the Roman Catholic priesthood is particularly manifested in the obstacles by which they endeavor to prevent the marriage of a Protestant and one of their own number. If a Protestant proposes to marry a Roman Catholic Chilina, he must either publically apostatize from his own faith, or purchase a *dispensa*, by making a liberal present to the bishop of his diocese; and in all such marriages it is made an indispensable condition that the children be educated in the Roman Catholic faith. The same bigotry prevails in the laws which regulate the interment of Protestants, though the stringency of these has of late been relaxed. In Santiago, adjoining the public cemetery, government has allotted a piece of ground as a burying-place for Protestants; and in Valparaiso and Coquimbo the same has been done by private individuals, with the permission of government.

Much attention is now given in Chili to the important subject of education. The first in rank of the educational establishments is the National Institute, composed of two departments—the university, and preparatory section—occupying one large edifice. The university has fifteen professors, whose salaries range from $1000 to $2000 a-year; while the average number of students is about 250. No fees are charged, and any one who has the requisite elementary knowledge may attend the classes. It is governed by five deacons, a secretary, and representatives from the faculties of science, philosophy, humanity, medicine, law, political economy, and theology; who are also charged with the superintendence of education in the provinces. The preparatory section corresponds to our grammar or high schools; and here, too, education is free. Those who reside in the school pay $150 a-year for board. The educational staff comprehends a rector, vice-rector, and twenty-six masters, whose salaries range from $2000 to $200 a-year. There are also eleven inspectors, whose emoluments vary from $200 to $400. The National Institute costs government about $50,000 a-year. In Santiago, government also supports a military academy (annual charge about $30,-

000), a school for the instruction of mechanics ($26,000), a training school for teachers ($12,500), and a seminary for the education of priests ($6000). In addition to these, an agricultural school, an academy of painting, an academy of music, a school for the deaf and dumb, and other useful institutions, are all supported at the national expense. A lyceum, on the same plan as the National Institute, is established in every provincial capital, and is supported by local taxation, government grants, and fees from pupils. Besides these, government supports throughout the country 352 schools, where poor children are taught reading, writing, arithmetic, and the Roman Catholic catechism; the municipal corporations support 100 similar schools; and over 300 schools are carried on by private individuals. The capital contains also an excellent observatory, a museum, and a public library with about 32,000 volumes. Akin to these statistics it may be added, that government contributes to twelve hospitals annually $40,000; and supports a madhouse, a penitentiary, house of correction, a convict establishment in the island of Juan Fernandez, besides prisons, a company of French Sisters of Charity, dispensaries, and vaccination establishments.

The cities and towns of Chili, with the exception of Valparaiso, are built generally upon the same plan. Their most striking peculiarity is, that they are divided into squares of equal size, the sides of which are about 400 feet in length, and inclose an area of about four acres. Within each of these quadras there are parallel rows of broad and well-paved streets, intersecting each other at right angles. The houses are also built in the form of a square, inclosing one or more courts, into which the various apartments look; and are of timber, bricks, and adobes, which are large bricks formed of mud mixed with chopped straw, and dried in the sun. The unoccupied spaces are in most cases laid out in gardens, and stocked with fruit trees and flowers. In the larger cities great taste and elegance are displayed in the furniture of the houses of the wealthy, a great part of which is supplied from abroad. The most splendid public edifice in Chili is the mint, which is built of brick, at a cost of $825,000, and contains the apartments of the president of the republic. In ecclesiastical architecture Chili is inferior to most Roman Catholic countries. The majority of the churches are very plain; and the internal decorations, paintings, and images are for the most part of a very paltry description. The Compañia and Santo Domingo, however, display considerable taste. The cathedral church has been designed on a very grand scale; and although still unfinished, has already cost $1,700,000. The cathedral of Serena is small, but much admired for the style of its architecture, which, with the light magnesian limestone used in its erection, is well calculated to resist the dangers arising from the frequency of earthquakes. In complexion the natives present considerable variety. Among the peasantry the Araucanian copper color still prevails; but in consequence of the large infusion of European blood, a greater variety of shade is to be found in the upper and middle classes. In general their complexion closely resembles that of the natives of Southern France.

Chili is rich in almost every class of metals; and of late years the silver mines have yielded enormous quantities of ore. The metals at present discovered are gold, silver, copper, lead, antimony, cobalt, zinc, nickel, bismuth, iron, molybdenum, and quicksilver; but the only ores which are worked are gold, silver, copper, and occasionally quicksilver. The metals are found in all the series of rocks between granite and trachyte, in veins generally running from N. and N.W. to S. and S.E.; in some places, however, their course is irregular; or they extend E. and W. The auriferous veins run nearly parallel to the grain or imperfect cleavage of the surrounding granite rocks. Gold is found most abundantly in the beds of detritus derived from the degradation of the upper portion of the rocks. Copper ores, containing a small quantity of gold, are generally associated with micaceous specular iron. In the hills of Altruc, about twelve miles from Rancagua, in the province of Santiago, are the only gold mines worked with any spirit, excepting some new mines near Copiapo, and they are remarkable for the variety of minerals mixed with the gold, such as galena, blende, copper and iron pyrites, and peroxide of iron. Until 1832, the only silver mines in Chili were those of Dehesa, San Francisco, San Lorenzo, Sema and San Pedro Nolazco in the province of Santiago, and Arqueros mineral district, about fifty miles from Coquimbo; but these mines now produce very little silver, and are nearly abandoned for the rich silver mines in the province of Atacama, near to Copiapo. Within a circuit of 125 miles from Copiapo there are nineteen silver mineral districts; the richest are Chañarcillo and Tres Puntas. As the mines become deeper, the silver ores are changing principally into what the natives call "metales frios" (cold ores); these contain different proportions of antimony, sulphur, and one sort a little arsenic. The dark red silver ore is a pyrargyrite, containing sulphuret of silver and antimony, with sometimes a little arsenic. The gray ore contains silver, arsenic, and antimony. Some of the mines in Chañarcillo yield nearly pure silver; the most productive are in the hands of four or five large capitalists. The ground near some of the richest mines is sometimes sold at enormous prices, the price being in some regulated by the probability of rich veins of metal running into it. A railroad runs from Caldera to Copiapo, a distance of fifty-four miles, and from that city on to Chañarcillo, a distance of about fifty miles; and a tram-road to the rich mineral district of Tres Puntas (8400 feet above the sea) has recently been completed, by which the miners are now enabled to send down the poorer silver ore which they formerly threw away.

The mines of copper may be said to occupy the first rank in the productions of Chili. It is found in more or less abundance from the province of Santiago to the most northern confines of Chili. It is generally discovered in the lower granite and metamorphic schistose series. The principal mining districts are Aconcagua, Illapel, and Tamaya, about forty miles from the coast, and seventy from Coquimbo. This last district is a mountain about 3500 feet above the sea, which produces about 150,000 quintals a-year of various kinds of sulphurets, of a produce from nine to sixty-four per cent. Tambillos, ten leagues from Coquimbo, produces principally poor sulphurets; Runeral, near the river, entirely poor carbonates; Andacollo, carbonates, oxides, oxysulphurets, and native copper; La Higuera, black sulphurets and pyrites; Herradura de Carisal and Huasco, carbonates and sulphurets of low produce. In the Cordilleras above Huasco are some mines containing ores of copper, silver, and lead combined together; but the silver does not exceed seventy marks the cajon of sixty-four quintals Spanish. Cobalt is found in the province of Santiago, near the Cordillera called Caro del Volcan; it is an arseniate containing from eighteen to twenty per cent. of cobalt. At Tambillos is found glance cobalt, and arsenite or erythrine; the former sort is frequently combined with nickel. The mines have been worked some years, and the ores shipped to England. In Huasco similar ores are found, but the mines have lately been abandoned. Nickel has been found in considerable quantities in a mine in the Cordilleras above Copiapo. The sulphuret of zinc is found in various parts; likewise antimony, lead, manganese, bismuth, mercury, and molybdena; iron ores of every description are very abundant; amongst the latter is coquimbite, or white copperas, and copiapite, or yellow copperas. It is much used by the natives for dyeing, tanning, and in the manufacture of ink. Gypsum is found in immense beds, particularly in the valley of the Pinquenes, and other places in the province of Santiago. The fine massive variety called alabaster is found at the Salto de Agua, near to Santiago, of a quality nearly equal to that of Italy. In the province of Concepcion, the coal mines have become of great importance. The Concepcion coal is excellent for the manufacture of gas and for domestic purposes; but for the smelting of copper ore it requires to be mixed with bituminous coal.

The annual value of the agricultural produce is estimated to be about $12,000,000. Irrigation is extensively practiced, without which the greater part of Chili would be unproductive. The level lands thus watered yield abundantly corn and wine, and rich pasture on which the farmers fatten the cattle bred upon the hilly portions of their estates. These hills are sparingly covered with a peculiar kind of short and wiry grass, which, after one winter of abundant rain, lasts for two seasons, even although the succeeding winter may have been dry. These arid regions likewise produce the carbon tree, which affords excellent firewood, but is used for nothing else; the carrob tree, which, in defiance of a broiling sun, stretches out his spacious limbs covered with foliage, forming a most delicious retreat to the weary traveller by day as well as by night; the espino, inferior to the carrob tree in size, hardness, and durability of its timber; and the great torch thistle, whose long, smooth spines are used by the country people for knitting-needles, and whose interior woody substance, stripped of its fleshy bark, forms the beams and rafters of their cottages. Timber is abundant in all the provinces south of Santiago, but chiefly in Arauco, Valdivia, and Chiloë, which may be termed the forest region of Chili. There are altogether above a hundred different kinds of indigenous trees, of which not more than thirteen ever shed their leaves. Several have been found serviceable in ship-building; but for purposes of house-carpentry, none afford an adequate substitute for pine. Ornamental woods are scarce, and too soft for the use of the cabinet-maker. The principal timber trees are the Chilian oak, which attains a height of forty feet; the lingue ninety feet; the cypress and the patagua forty feet; the laurel sixty feet; the luma thirty feet; the Araucanian pine, 150 feet; and the alerce, or Chilian cedar. The most valuable is the Chilian cedar, a soft but durable wood, and not liable to warp. The trunk is divided into pieces of eight feet long, and so straight are its fibres that they are split into small boards six or seven inches broad, and about half an inch thick—a single trunk yielding 500 or 600. In Valdivia and Chiloë they form the chief article of export, and are used for purposes of exchange. The Araucanian pine flourishes on the high lands south of the Biobio, and grows in pairs—the female under the foliage of the male. The fruit, which takes two years to ripen, is arranged conically, each one containing from fifty to one hundred nuts, two inches long, and which, when cooked, form more delicate eating than chestnuts. Under the governorship of O'Higgins their trunks were used for ship-masts; but the expense of bringing them to the coast prevents their being employed as such. In the gardens of Coquimbo, a fruit tree known by the name of the *Lucumo achraes* is much cultivated. Its fruit, which is about the size of a small orange, resembles somewhat a hard-boiled egg, but is too dry and insipid to form a palatable article of food.

The potato, whose introduction into Europe formed an important era in the history of agriculture, is indigenous to Chili, or, as some assert, to Peru. In the equatorial regions of South America this plant was formerly cultivated on the sides of the Cordilleras at an elevation of many thousand feet above the limits of perpetual snow in the latitudes of Europe. It is still extensively cultivated in Chili. Much attention is also bestowed on the production of the French bean. This vegetable is a standard dish with all classes, and is to the Chilian what oatmeal is to the Scotchman. The supply of the various kinds of fruit is very abundant in Chili. Apples, pears, cherries, strawberries, peaches, figs, oranges, melons, olives, quinces, and pumpkins abound. Where cultivated with care, as in some private gardens in the neighborhood of Santiago and Valparaiso, they are unrivalled in quality.

In Chili the most formidable animal is the puma. On account of its ravages in the farm-yard, it is frequently hunted with dogs, or caught by the lasso. The guanaco roams about among the lower regions of the Chilian Alps in herds numbering from twenty to one hundred. The vicuña has fixed his abode at a higher elevation. The huamul is not found in such numbers, and is unknown in the Andes beyond the bounds of Chili. Otters, wild cats, foxes, and chinchillas are numerous. The horses of Chili are inferior in strength and height, but greatly superior in point of endurance. The mule is the beast of burden, and will carry on an average a load of 355 lbs. a distance of twenty or even thirty miles per day. The breed of cattle is good; those of sheep and pigs are fast improving. Among the birds of Chili the most remarkable is the condor, which is easily recognized by the white ruff encircling its neck. As its wings on an average extend eight or nine feet, its flight has a very majestic appearance. Humboldt mentions having seen one flying at the height of 22,000 feet above the level of the sea. They scent an exposed carcase from a great distance, and soon gather round it in immense numbers. The turkey-buzzard is also very common; and when these meet the condors over the same prey, the coveted prize becomes the subject of fierce contest. These two species are most abundant in the northern districts; while eagles, hawks, and owls are more numerous in the south. The only song-birds worthy of notice are—the tenca, the thrush, the tordo (a kind of blackbird), and the molloyca (a kind of redbreast). The tenca is said to emulate the mocking-bird in imitative power. The tapaculo, a bird about the same size as the thrush, rarely flies, but runs about with great agility, emitting an odd but cheerful note. The chingol, or sparrow, has gayer plumage than his European representative. Besides these, parroquets, flamingoes, partridges, and woodpeckers abound in several localities. The pelican, the albatross, the penguin, and the shag, of which there are numerous varieties, frequent the shores.

Great varieties of fish are found off the coast of Chili, and of these the pichihuen, which is caught chiefly in the Bay of Coquimbo, is regarded as a choice delicacy. There are abundance of small sweet oysters off the coast of Chiloë; quantities of huge mussels, barnacles, and fissurellæ, off Concepcion; and large clams off Coquimbo; besides sea-eggs, cockles, limpets, etc., which are found in great plenty all over the coast. Of the reptiles of Chili, the lizards are the most numerous, and they are very harmless. Serpents are found varying from twelve to thirty inches in length. The honey-bee is propagating very fast. Of beetles, there are from 3000 to 4000 species not found in Europe.

Agriculture as a science is comparatively little known in Chili, and everything connected with the farm is still of a primitive description. The plough is a clumsy one-handed instrument, formed from the crooked trunk of a tree. In using it the peasant grasps its handle in his right hand, while in his left he wields a long sharp-pointed stick to goad on the oxen, which are invariably yoked not by the shoulder but by the horns. The operation of treading out the grain is performed by mares. For this purpose the sheaves are piled up in bundles in the centre of an extensive circus, having an empty space of from ten to twenty feet between the heap and the inclosure; and some of the bundles being spread over this space a troop of mares are made to gallop over them until all the grain has been beaten out. Winnowing is performed by throwing up spadefuls of grain into the air on windy days. Other operations of the farm are performed in an equally unskilful and tedious manner. Maize is largely cultivated in all parts of Chili, but not to such an extent as wheat. As the plant spreads out into numerous stems, half the quantity of seed used elsewhere is quite sufficient to cover the field with an abundant crop. The provinces of Aconcagua, Santiago, Talca, Nuble, Maule, and Concepcion, yield annually large crops of wheat, maize, and French beans. The lands of Aconcagua produce about fifty or sixty fanegas of wheat on every quadra, equal to about thirty or forty bushels an acre; Santiago from thirty to thirty-five fanegas on every quadra; Colchagua from twenty-five to thirty; Maule from fifteen to eighteen; Nuble, Talca, and Arauco from fifteen to twenty; and Concepcion from eight to ten. The total produce of wheat may be estimated at 1,000,000 quarters, but is increasing annually. The price of wheat has risen considerably of late years. The backward condition of agriculture in Chili is owing to the thinness and natural indolence of the population, and the absence of easy means of transportation. The government has for several years taken vigorous measures to encourage emigration from Europe into Chili, chiefly with the view of promoting the agricultural interests of the country. A great number of German agriculturists have already settled in the province of Valdivia, and every year is making additions to their number. Manufactures also, are in a backward state. In Santiago a cloth factory, commenced under the protection of government, has as yet produced only the coarser kinds of cloth, such as are used in the army. Other looms in Chili are worked by the hand, and used in the production of carpets and ponchos, some of which, made of vicuña wool, are of a very fine texture. A large portion of the population wear home-made stuffs, especially woollen. The importation of foreign goods is, however, increasing; and the facility with which stuffs from abroad can be imported has checked the establishment of important manufactures. Coarse earthenware, cordage, combs, leather, saddles, and wooden stirrups, are made in several parts of the country. In Valparaiso and Maule ship-building is carried on. In the cities and larger towns most of the mechanical trades which exist in other parts of the world are pursued.

The commerce of Chili has vastly increased since the time when the country lay torpid under the yoke of Spain. As soon as it had recovered from the unsettled condition caused by the revolution, business of all kinds required new energy, and the trade, freed from its oppressive restrictions, extended to the larger ports of the United States and Europe. A few years were sufficient to show a large increase in its export and import trade, and Valparaiso soon rose to be a flourishing port. During the years 1861 to 1865, the annual average of imports was $18,900,000; exports, $21,690,000. The commerce of the republic is steadily on the increase; in 1867, imports, $24,860,000; exports, $30,690,000; the average since has been over $25,000,000 in imports; and $32,000,000 in exports. The number of vessels entering the Chilian ports is estimated to be about 4000, making together nearly 2,000,000 tons. The merchant marine numbers over 300 vessels, together above 70,000 tons.

The revenue of Chili is, on the whole, with occasional fluctuations, in a prosperous condition. The public debt amounts to over $34,500,000. The estimates of 1869-'70, passed by both Houses of Congress, amount to $12,296,876.44, in the following form: home and foreign department, $2,576,769.76; justice, religion, and education, $1,337,005.03; finance, $5,896,257.99; war and navy, $2,486,813.66; total, $12,296,876.44. The army is composed of troops of the line (about 4000), and of the national guard, which numbers, according to the latest information, 50,618 men. The fleet consists of ten screw steamers, to which others are about to be added.

Government derives considerable profit from its monopoly of tobacco and playing-cards. To prevent the smuggling of tobacco, the authorities are obliged to maintain an expensive establishment of officers along the coast and among the mountains; and so stringent are the laws in regard to the growth of tobacco, that when it springs up, as it does, spontaneously, in the court-yards of the houses, the inhabitants are liable to a fine if it be not immediately rooted up. But for these oppressive restrictions, tobacco would undoubtedly rank high among the exports of Chili, and add greatly to the revenue.

The communication between the several cities and towns of Chili is now greatly facilitated by roads, railways, and steam-vessels. The excellent road from Santiago to Valparaiso was constructed at a great cost by General O'Higgins, when president of the republic. A road, generally kept in good repair, connects the towns of Atacama and Concepcion. A railroad has been already established between Copiapo and Caldera; and in 1852, the present M. Montt, laid the first stone on the line (about 90 miles in length), between Santiago and Valparaiso, which is now in active operation. Another has been built between Santiago and Talca; while others from Serena to the sea, from Copiapo to Tres Puntas, and from Concepcion to Talcahuano, have either been finished, or are well under way. A line of electric telegraph has also been established between Valparaiso and Santiago. Other lines also are in course of construction. In 1835, the exclusive right of steam navigation between the ports of the republic, was granted to a company, which commenced its operations in 1840. A similar privilege was afterwards extended to the same company by the governments of Peru, Ecuador, and New Granada. In May, 1868, the first steamer of the line which places Chili in direct communication with Europe, by the way of the Straits of Magellan, sailed from Valparaiso. The line receives a government subsidy of $60,000 annually, which is to be increased to $100,000, as soon as the line is permanently established, and proven to be a success.

The name Chili, is supposed to be derived from "Tchili," a word belonging to the ancient language of Peru, signifying "snow." The country first became known to Europeans in the sixteenth century. It was then, to a considerable extent, under the dominion of the Incas; but had been previously inhabited by certain tribes of Indians, of a warlike and ferocious race, who, at the period of the Spanish invasion, still maintained their independence in a great portion of the country. In the time of the Inca Yupanqui, grandfather of the monarch who occupied the throne of Peru on the arrival of the Spaniards, and the tenth in succession from Manco Capac, the reputed founder of the Peruvian empire, the first attempt was made by the Incas to extend their dominion over the territory of Chili. Yupanqui, leading his army across the desert of Atacama, and penetrating into the southern regions of the country, made himself master of a considerable portion of it. The permanent boundary of the dominions of this prince is said, by some writers, to have been determined by the river Maule; while others are inclined to think that the Rapel constituted the extreme limits of the Peruvian empire towards the south. The latter opinion is, to some extent, supported by the fact, that the remains of an ancient Peruvian fortress, apparently marking the frontier, are still found upon the banks of the Rapel; while no such remains are known to exist in any part of the country situate farther to the south. It is also worthy of remark, that this place of defence has evidently been built in the same manner as the frontier forts of Callo and Asuay, which were in all probability intended to answer a similar purpose in the province of Quito.

All the endeavors that were afterwards made by the Inca to extend his dominions further southward were unsuccessful. The better portion of the country still remained in possession of its native defenders till the arrival of the Spaniards, in the year 1535, under the command of Almagro, once the friend and companion of Pizarro. For two years, amid almost unparalleled hardships, this general endeavored to make head against the natives, who obstinately defended their soil; but at the end of that period he was obliged to retrace his steps over the Andes into Peru. Undaunted by the failure of

Almagro, Pizarro resolved to attempt the conquest of Chili. He accordingly sent forward on this expedition, 150 Spanish troops, with a body of Peruvian auxiliaries, under the command of Don Pedro de Valdivia, and was preparing to follow in person with a larger force, when he was assassinated in 1541, (p. 463).

Meanwhile, Valdivia entered Chili, overran a great part of it, and fighting his way onwards, encamped at length on the banks of the Mapocho, where he founded the city of Santiago, the present capital of the republic. For the period of twelve years he maintained his position in the country. By the end of that time he had penetrated into the southern division of Chili, where, in addition to several other cities, he founded that which is now known by his name. His life and conquests were at last brought to an end, in a desperate engagement with the Araucanian Indians.

After these events, the war continued to be carried on with various success for the long period of 180 years. At the end of that time, however, the Indians had succeeded in altogether recovering their original possessions, and all the cities founded by Valdivia fell into their hands. For another century, however, they were exposed to the constant inroads of the Spaniards, who were unwilling to give up all hope of ultimately conquering the southern part of Chili. At length, in the year 1722, this sanguinary war was brought to a termination by a treaty which defined the River Biobio as the boundary between the Indian and the Spanish territories. That part of the country which remained in possession of the Indians, lay chiefly between the River Biobio and the island of Chiloë. All the territory north of this river was entirely subject to the dominion of the Spaniards. It was divided by them into thirteen districts or provinces. Most of these provinces were very irregular in size, some of them extending from the Andes to the sea, while others, whose locality was nearer to the mountains, or upon the sea-coast, occupied only about half of that space. In the political contest between Spain and her American colonies, the inhabitants of Chili declared their independence, which, after a contest of some years, was acknowledged by the Spanish government.

A long period of profound peace followed the treaty which had been concluded with the Araucanians in 1722. During that time, however, changes of great importance were gradually developing. A new and important class of inhabitants had arisen in the country, composed of the Creoles, or natives of Chili, who were of Spanish extraction, and who spoke the Spanish language. By a perverse course of misgovernment, the authorities in Spain completely alienated the minds of this class from the mother country. It was unfortunately a maxim with the government, that the colonies existed only for the sake of Spain. The viceroys, captains-general, and officials of all grades, instead of conciliating the Chilenos, regarded them only as a means of furthering their own aggrandizement. Their insolence and tyranny, persisted in for many years, at length excited against them so bitter a feeling of hatred and discontent, that nothing but the opportunity was wanting to blow into a flame the smouldering fires of rebellion. In 1810, that opportunity occurred, when Spain was overrun by the armies of France, and no longer able to vindicate her own claims to a national existence. In July of that year, the Chilenos took the first step towards asserting their independence by deposing the president, Carrasco. A junta, which was then formed, assumed the government, with the expressed intention of conducting it according to the old system. Their real design, at first kept secret, was to declare their independence, and to separate entirely from Spain, on the first favorable opportunity.

In April, 1811, the first blood was spilt in the cause of Chilian independence. On the day appointed for the election of members to the National Congress, the Spanish rulers attempted to overawe the leaders and people of Chili, of whose dissatisfaction with their government they were fully conscious. A battalion of royal troops, which had been drawn up in the great square of Santiago, was attacked by a detachment of patriot grenadiers, and routed after a considerable loss of life on both sides. In the same year, Don Juan Jose Carrera, a young man of great talents and promise, was nominated by the junta supreme president of the Congress which was now convened, and was at the same time appointed general-in-chief of the army about to be formed. Hostilities were commenced by the Spanish troops who were sent from Lima, Coquimbo and Chiloë. In the skirmishes that took place, during the early part of the contest, the Chilian troops had generally the advantage.

In 1813, a powerful army, under the command of General Paroja, invaded Chili, but was twice defeated by the republican troops under Carrera. The royalists, however, speedily received large reinforcements; and after a severe contest, Chili was once more obliged to own for a time the sovereignty of Spain. For three years the people submitted to the old system of tyranny and misgovernment, till at length the patriot refugees, having levied an army in La Plata, and received the support of the Buenos Ayreans, marched against the Spaniards, and completely defeated them at Chacabuco, in 1817. The patriots next proceeded to organize an elective government, of which San Martin, the general of the army, was nominated the supreme director. Their arrangements, however, were not completed when they were attacked once more by the royalists, and routed at the battle of Chancharayada with great loss. Betrayed into a fatal security by this success, the royalist troops neglected the most ordinary military precautions; and being suddenly attacked by the patriots in the plains of Maipù, were defeated with great slaughter. It is believed that not more than 500 men escaped from the field of battle. This victory secured the independence of Chili.

The new republic had no sooner vindicated for itself a place among the nations of South America, than it resolved to assist the neighboring State of Peru, in achieving a similar independence. This object it at last effected, after a bloody war of six years' duration. No small share of this success, however, is to be attributed to the ability with which Lord Cochrane conducted the naval affairs.

Till 1823, General O'Higgins held the chief directorship at Santiago, but in that year, he was compelled to resign in consequence of a popular tumult. For a few weeks, a provisional triumvirate discharged the duties of an executive government. General Freire was next chosen director. During the period of three years in which he held the reins of government, the country was harassed by constant dissensions; and for the four years subsequent to his resignation continued in a state of disorder bordering upon anarchy. From 1826 to 1830, the government was administered by no fewer than six different directors, in addition to a second provisional triumvirate. In 1828, under the administration of General Pinto, a constitution was promulgated, which had the effect of temporarily reconciling political differences, and calming party spirit.

In 1831, however, when General Prieto was raised to the chief magistracy, a convention was called for the purpose of revising this constitution. The result of its deliberations was the constitution of Chili, which was promulgated on the 25th of May, 1833. Since this period, Chili has enjoyed remarkable prosperity; its government has been administered with firmness and regularity, and it has assumed a position among the nations; for, aided by the counsels of his prime minister Portales, General Prieto completely succeeded in restoring order, and in promoting the material prosperity of the republic. After holding office for ten years, Prieto retired, and was succeeded by General Bulnes, a very distinguished officer of the war of independence. Like his predecessor, he was fortunate in finding an able and intelligent minister to counsel and assist him. Manuel Montt was to him what Portales had been to Prieto, and under his guidance, Chili continued its onward march in the path of quiet and peaceful prosperity.

The insurrectionary movements which took place in Europe, in 1848, extended their influence even to the western shores of South America. Imitating the anarchists in Europe, the revolutionists formed clubs, selected emblems, and displayed banners. Their irritation was increased by the fact that for twenty years they had been deprived of all participation in the government. When the time for the presidential election of 1851 approached, they brought forward, as a candidate for the presidency, Ramon Errazaris, who had formerly belonged to the conservative party, and who was in every way unfitted for the post to which they wished to advance him. The violence of their measures at length led to serious outbreaks in the province of Aconcagua and the town of Santiago. The government at once took vigorous measures to suppress the disturbances. These places were declared in a state of siege, and order was soon restored. In 1851, the country still continued in a very agitated condition. General Urriola assumed the direction of the insurrectionary movement. On the 20th of April, serious disturbances broke out at Santiago, during the solemnities of the holy week, which were not quelled without considerable loss of life. The insurgent chief himself was accidentally killed.

The extreme liberal party next brought forward, as a candidate for the presidency, General Jose Mana de la Cruz, in opposition to Don Manuel Montt, the celebrated minister of the former president. The revolutionary party used every exertion to secure the election of their representative, but Montt was chosen president by the almost unanimous suffrages of the people. Enraged at this result, the revolutionary party resolved to throw every obstacle in the way of his regular inauguration. Insurrection was excited by their agents in the provinces of Coquimbo, Copiapo, and Valparaiso. The south was the principal seat of disturbance; and Serena, the capital of Coquimbo, was in the hands of the insurgents. General Bulnes, the former president, was appointed commander-in-chief. Having met the army of the insurgents at Longomilla, he gained a complete victory over them. A capitulation was then agreed to, the result of which was the full acknowledgement of the established government.

From that date, 1852, under the active and efficient administration of M. Montt, Chili made steady, and even rapid progress, in wealth, intelligence, and just appreciation of her position among the nations of the world. Montt was elected for a second term, in October, 1856. Having completed his allotted term, Montt was succeeded by José Joaquin Perez, who was elected president, by a unanimous vote, September 7th, 1861. Perez was again elected for the term from 1868 to 1871. Vigorous efforts have been made of late years, to extend the suffrage more largely among the people, and also to reduce the immense patronage in the hands of the president, his power being so great as to constitute him, in effect, a dictator. During the last year or two, Chili has been engaged in a renewed struggle with the wild and restive Indians in Araucania. These fight with intense fury and spare neither age nor sex. There is now a prospect of a peaceable settlement with them; but with savages like these, there is little reliance to be placed upon promises and treaties. Some $250,000 have been voted to establish military posts in their country. The great Agricultural Exhibition was held at Santiago, early in May, 1869, and proved to be a gratifying success. The action of Congress, also, in taking steps to increase and promote industry and commerce, gives assurance, as far as is possible, in sublunary matters, of the future prosperity of the republic.

As an interesting addition to the history of the South American States, we subjoin a brief narrative of the life and career of Simon Bolivar, the champion of independence in his native land. He was born in the city of Caraccas, on the 24th of July, 1783. His father was Don Juan Vicente Bolivar y Ponte, and his mother Dona Maria Concepcion Palacios y Sojo, both descended of noble families in Venezuela. After acquiring the elements of a liberal education at home, Bolivar was sent to Europe to prosecute his studies, and with this view repaired to Madrid, where he appears to have resided for several years. Having completed his education, he spent some time in traveling, chiefly in the south of Europe, and visited the French capital, where he was an eye-witness of some of the last scenes of the revolution. Returning to Madrid, he married the daughter of Don N. Toro, uncle of the Marquis of Toro in Caraccas, and embarked with her for America, intending, it is said, to dedicate himself to domestic life and the improvement of his large estate. But this plan was frustrated by the premature death of his lady, who fell a victim to yellow fever; and Bolivar again visited Europe, in order, by change of scene, to alleviate the sorrow occasioned by this bereavement. On his return home he passed through the United States, where, for the first time, he had an opportunity of observing the working of free institutions; and soon after his arrival in Venezuela he appears to have embarked in the schemes of the patriots, and pledged himself to the cause of independence. Being one of the promoters of the movement at Caraccas in April, 1810, he received a colonel's commission from the supreme junta then established, and was associated with Don Luis Lopez Mendez in a mission for communicating intelligence of the change of government to Great Britain. He took part in the first military operations of the Venezuelan patriots, after the declaration of independence on the 5th of July, 1811; and in 1812, when the war commenced in earnest, by the advance of Monteverde with the Spanish troops, he was intrusted with the command of the important post of Puerto Cabello. But the castle of San Felipe, which commanded the town, having been treacherously surrendered to the Spaniards, Bolivar was compelled to evacuate the place; and Miranda having soon afterwards made his peace with the government, Venezuela submitted to Monteverde, while those who had been most deeply committed in the revolution consulted their safety by quitting the country. On this occasion Bolivar succeeded in obtaining a passport under a fictitious name, and made his escape to Curaçoa.

But as important events were passing on the continent, he repaired to Carthagena in September, 1812, and, with other refugees from Caraccas, joined the patriots of New Grenada, who gave him a command in the small town of Baranca, under the orders of Labatut, the republican governor of Santa Martha. Not content, however, with the obscure part of a subaltern at Baranca, Bolivar undertook an expedition against Teneriffe, a town higher up on the Magdalena; and having made himself master of the place, proceeded to Mompox, driving the Spaniards before him from all their posts on the Upper Magdalena, and finally entering Ocana in triumph amidst the acclamations of the inhabitants. He then marched upon Cucuta; defeated a Spanish division commanded by Correa; and, emboldened by success, conceived the design of invading Venezuela, and expelling Monteverde. The Congress of New Grenada approved of the project, and gave him a commission as brigadier; but from the jealousy of some, the lukewarmness of others, and the procrastination of all, many disheartening obstacles were thrown in his way. By zeal and perseverance, however, he at length surmounted every difficulty, and commenced his march for Venezuela with little more than 500 men. At the head of this handful of troops he boldly entered the province of Merida; made himself master of the provincial capital, where, on learning the news of his approach, the inhabitants rose upon the Spaniards; re-established the republican authorities there; then pushed his vanguard under Jirardot upon Trujillo, where a corps of royalists under Cañas was defeated; and finally expelled the Spaniards from the provinces of Merida and Trujillo. While he was thus carrying everything before him, Bolivar obtained intelligence of the cruelty and oppression exercised by Monteverde and his subordinate officers in Venezuela; and, exasperated at their barbarity, as well as desirous to give a check to their excesses, he issued the famous decree of *guerra a muerte*, condemning to death all Spanish prisoners who might fall into his hands.

Bolivar's army increasing daily, he now formed it into two divisions, one of which he committed to the charge of Rivas, and advanced rapidly on Caraccas through the provinces of Trujillo and Varinas. After a variety of encounters, which generally terminated in favor of the patriots, a decisive battle was fought at Lastoguanes, where the flower of Monteverde's troops sustained a total defeat, and the road to Caraccas was in consequence left uncovered. Monteverde threw himself into Puerto Cabello, and Bolivar lost no time in marching on the capital, which being evacuated by the Spaniards, he entered in triumph on the 4th of August, 1813. While this operation was in progress, Mariño effected the liberation of the eastern provinces of Venezuela, of which, excepting the fortress of Puerto Cabello, the patriots regained entire possession. At this period the whole authority in Venezuela centered in Bolivar as commander of the liberating army, and a convention of the principal civil and military officers, held at Caraccas on the 2d of January, 1814, confirmed the dictatorial power which circumstances had placed in his hands. Misfortune, however, was at hand.

The contest, which had hitherto been confined to a species of partisan warfare, now assumed a more serious character. The royalists, effectually roused by the reverses they had sustained, concentrated all their means; and a number of sanguinary encounters ensued. At length, after various vicissitudes of fortune, Bolivar was defeated by Boves near Cura, in the plains of La Puerta, and compelled to embark for Cumana with the shattered remains of his forces. Caraccas was also retaken by the Spaniards in July; and before the end of the year 1814 the royalists were again the undisputed masters of Venezuela. From Cumana, Bolivar repaired to Carthagena, where he once more appeared as a fugitive, and thence proceeded to Tunja, where the Congress of New Grenada was sitting, in order to render an account of his operations. He had been unfortunate, which generally exposes a commander to misconstruction and obloquy; and his expedition, as brilliant in its outset as it proved disastrous in the issue, was severely criticised; but notwithstanding his misfortunes, and the efforts of his personal enemies, he was received and treated with great consideration; and as the Congress were then organizing an expedition against Bogota, for the purpose of compelling Cundinamarca to accede to the general coalition of the provinces, Bolivar was intrusted with the command of the forces of the union on this occasion. Accordingly, in December, 1814, he marched against Santa Fé at the head of 2000 troops. All attempts at negotiation having failed, he invested the city, drove in the out-posts, carried the suburbs by storm, and was preparing to assault the grand plaza or square, where Alvarez and the troops of Cundinamarca were posted, when the latter capitulated and acknowledged the general government of New Grenada, which was now transferred to Bogota. For this important service Bolivar received the thanks of the Congress; and even the inhabitants of the city against which he had been sent expressed their approbation of his conduct.

In the meanwhile Santa Martha had fallen into the hands of the royalists, through the incapacity of Labatut; and as the general government appreciated the importance of recovering possession of that place, Bolivar was employed on this service, with orders to receive the necessary supplies and munitions of war from the citadel of Carthagena. But the preposterous jealousy of Castillo, the military commandant, defeated all his plans. The season for action was wasted in disgraceful altercations and ruinous delays; and while Bolivar was investing Carthagena, in the hope of intimidating Castillo into submission, Morillo landed on the island of Margarita at the head of an overwhelming force of Spaniards, and put an end to dispute. Finding a check thus effectually given to any movements against Santa Martha, and satisfied that he could not be usefully employed at Carthagena, Bolivar resigned his command, and embarked for Jamaica in May, 1815. He remained at Kingston during the greater part of the year, whilst Morillo was reducing Carthagena and overrunning New Grenada almost without opposition; and in the interim narrowly escaped assassination by a Spaniard who had been hired to make an attempt on his life.

From Kingston, Bolivar repaired to Aux Cayes in Hayti, where, assisted by private individuals, and furnished with a small force by Petion, he organized an expedition, in order to join Arismendi, who had raised anew the standard of independence in the island of Margarita. In May, 1816, he reached Margarita, and sailing thence, landed on the continent near Cumana; but being attacked at Ocumare by the Spaniards, under Morales, he was compelled to re-embark. Nothing disheartened by this failure, he obtained fresh reinforcements at Aux Cayes, and in December, landed again in Margarita, where he issued a proclamation convoking the representatives of Venezuela in a general Congress. He then proceeded to Barcelona, where he organized a provisional government, and assembled troops to resist Morillo, who was then advancing at the head of a strong division. The hostile forces encountered each other on the 16th of February, 1817, when a desperate conflict ensued, which lasted during that and the two following days, and ended in the defeat of the royalists. Morillo retired in disorder, and being met on his retreat by Paez with his llaneros, experienced a new and more complete overthrow. Being now recognized as commander-in-chief, Bolivar proceeded in his career of victory, and before the close of the year had fixed his headquarters at Angostura. He presided at the opening of the Congress of Angostura on the 15th of February, 1819, when he submitted an elaborate exposition of his views on government, and also surrendered his authority into the hands of Congress. Being, however, required to resume his power, and retain it until the independence of the country should be completely established, he reorganized his troops, and set out from Angostura, in order to cross the Cordilleras, effect a junction with General Santander, commanding the republican forces in New Grenada, and bring their united means into action against the common enemy. This bold and original design was crowned with complete success. In July, 1819, he reached Tunja, which he entered after a sharp action on the adjoining heights; and on the 7th of August he gained the victory of Bojaca, which gave him immediate possession of Santa Fé and all New Grenada. Nor was this all. By the resources of men, money and munitions of war, which he found at Bogota, he was enabled to augment the effective strength of his army, and to return to Venezuela with a force sufficient to secure the expulsion of the Spaniards.

The campaign of New Grenada is unquestionably Bolivar's most brilliant achievement, and deserves much of the praise which has been lavished on it. His return to Angostura was a sort of national festival. He was hailed as the deliverer and father of his country, and all manner of distinctions and congratulations were heaped upon him. He availed himself of this favorable moment to obtain the enactment of the fundamental law of the 17th of December, 1819, by which the republics of Venezuela and New Granada were henceforth united in a single State, under his presidency, by the title of the Republic of Colombia. The seat of government was also transferred provisionally to Rosario de Cucuta, and Bolivar again took the field. Being now at the head of the most numerous and best appointed army the patriots had yet assembled, he gained important advantages over the Spaniards, under Morillo, and on the 25th of November, 1820, concluded at Trujillo an armistice of six months, probably in the hope that the Spaniards would now come to terms, and that the further effusion of blood might be spared. If such were his views, however, they were disappointed. Morillo was recalled; Torre assumed the command; and the armistice was allowed to expire without any pacific overture being made. As a renewal of the contest was therefore inevitable, Bolivar resolved, if possible, to strike a decisive blow; and this accordingly he did at Carabolo, where he vanquished Torre, and so completely destroyed the Spaniards, that the shattered remains of their army were forced to take refuge in Puerto Cabello, where two years after they surrendered to Paez.

The battle of Carabolo may be considered as having put an end to the war in Venezuela. On the 29th of June, 1820, Bolivar entered Caraccas, and by the close of the year the Spaniards were driven from every part of the country, except Puerto Cabello and Quito. The next step was to secure, by permanent political institutions, the independence which had now been conquered; and accordingly, on the 30th of August, 1821, the constitution of Colombia was adopted with general approbation, Bolivar himself being president, and Santander vice-president.

Having thus achieved the independence of his own country, Bolivar next placed himself at the head of the army destined to act against the Spaniards in Quito and Peru. The fate of Quito was decided by the battle of Pichincha, which was fought in June, 1822, and gained by the conduct and prowess of Sucre. Bolivar then marched upon Lima, which the royalists evacuated at his approach; and, entering the capital in triumph, he was invested with absolute power as dictator, and authorized to call into action all the resources of the country.

On the 6th of August, 1824, Bolivar defeated Canterac on the plains of Junin; after which he returned to Lima, leaving Sucre to follow the royalists in their retreat to Upper Peru; an exploit which the latter executed with equal ability and success, gaining a decisive victory at Ayacucho, and thus completing the dispersion of the Spanish force. In June, 1825, Bolivar visited Upper Peru, which having detached itself from the government of Buenos Ayres, was formed into a separate State, called Bolivia, in honor of the liberator. The first Congress of the new republic assembled in August, 1825, when Bolivar was declared perpetual protector, and requested to prepare for it a constitution of government.

Bolivar's project of a constitution for Bolivia was presented to the Congress of that State on the 25th May, 1826, accompanied with an address, in which he embodied his opinions respecting the form of government which he conceived most expedient for the newly-established republics. Of this code some account has already been given, (pp. 503-506,) but its most extraordinary feature consisted in the provision for lodging the executive authority in the hands of a president for life, without responsibility, and with power to nominate his successor. This alarmed the friends of liberty, and excited lively apprehensions amongst the republicans of Buenos Ayres and Chili; whilst, in Peru, Bolivar was accused of a design to unite into one State Colombia, Peru, and Bolivia, and to render himself perpetual dictator of the confederacy.

In the meanwhile the affairs of Colombia had taken a turn which demanded the presence of Bolivar in his own country. During his absence Santander had administered the government ably and uprightly; its independence had been recognized by other countries; and its territory had been subdivided into departments, defined by geographical boundaries analogously to that of France. But Paez, who commanded in Venezuela, having been accused of arbitrary conduct in the enrolment of the citizens of Caraccas in the militia, refused obedience to the summons of the Senate, and placed himself in a state of open rebellion against the general government; whilst the disaffected party, taking advantage of this collision, united with the refractory commander, and encouraged him in his opposition, by which means the northern departments became virtually separated from the rest of the republic. All, however, professed a willingness to submit their grievances to the decision of Bolivar, and equally required his return to Colombia.

Accordingly, having intrusted the government to a council nominated by himself, with General Santa-Cruz at its head, he set out from Lima in September, 1826, and hastened to Bogota, where he arrived on the 14th November, and immediately assumed the extraordinary powers which, by the constitution, the president was authorized to exercise in case of rebellion. He remained only a few days in the capital, and then pressed forward to stop the effusion of blood in Venezuela, where matters had gone on much farther than he could ever have contemplated, even supposing him to have been the mainspring of the various intrigues charged against him. On the 31st December he reached Puerto Cabello, and the following day issued a decree offering a general amnesty. He had then a friendly meeting with Paez, and soon afterwards entered Caraccas, where he fixed his head-quarters, in order to check the northern departments, which had been the principal theatre of the disturbances. In the meanwhile Bolivar and Santander were re-elected to the respective offices of president and vice-president, and by law should have qualified as such in January, 1827. In February, however, Bolivar formally resigned the presidency of the republic, at the same time expressing a determination to refute the imputations of ambition which had been so freely cast upon him, by retiring to private life, and spending the remainder of his days on his patrimonial estate. Santander combated this resolution, urging him to resume his station as constitutional president, and declaring his own conviction, that the troubles and agitations of the country could only be appeased by the authority and personal influence of the liberator himself. But distrust and suspicion of Bolivar's conduct and intentions now filled the friends of the republican institutions. A significant proof of the belief which then prevailed is the large minority in Congress who voted for accepting his resignation of the presidency. But as a majority were of a contrary opinion, and insisted on his retaining the presidency, he repaired to Bogota to take the oaths and resume his functions. Before his arrival, however, he issued simultaneously three separate decrees; one granting a general amnesty of all past offences; another, convoking a national convention at Ocaña; and a third for establishing constitutional order throughout Colombia.

His arrival was accelerated by the occurrence of events in Peru and the southern departments, which struck at the very foundation of his power. Not long after his departure from Lima, the Bolivian code had been adopted as the Constitution of Peru, and Bolivar had been declared president for life. This took place on the 9th of December, 1826, the anniversary of the battle of Ayacucho; at which time the Colombian auxiliary army was cantoned in three divisions, one in Upper, and two in Lower Peru, at Arequipa and Lima. The third division, stationed at Lima, consisted of veteran troops, commanded by Generals Lara and Sands, personal friends of the liberator But notwithstanding their known attachment to Bolivar personally, his recent conduct in Colombia had rendered them distrustful of his designs; and although they had originally no disposition to thwart his views on Peru, had his ambition been confined to that State alone, they resolved to strike a blow against his power when they conceived it employed for the subjugation of their own country. Accordingly, in about six weeks after the adoption of the new Constitution, a counter-revolution in the government of Peru was effected by this body of dissatisfied veterans. They had taken their measures so well that they arrested their general officers without opposition; placed them under the orders of Bustamente, one of their colonels; and announced to the inhabitants of Lima that their sole object was to relieve the Peruvians from oppression, and to return home to protect their own country against any attack on its liberties. Availing themselves of the opportunity thus unexpectedly afforded them, the Peruvians abjured the Bolivian code, deposed the council of ministers appointed by the liberator, and proceeded to organize a provisional government for themselves.

Intelligence of these events reached Bolivar while in the north of Colombia. He had long remained in a state of comparative inactivity; but the news of the counter revolution in Peru, effected by the very troops in whom he had most implicitly confided, called forth all his energy, and he lost no time in preparing to march to the south, in order to reduce the refractory division. But he was spared the necessity of coming to blows with these troops, who, finding the government in the hands of the national executive, had peaceably submitted to General Ovando. In the meanwhile, Bolivar had accepted the presidency, and resumed the functions belonging to his official station. But although Colombia was, to all external appearance, restored to tranquillity, the nation was divided into two parties, and agitated by their opposite views and incessant collisions. Bolivar had regained the personal confidence of the officers and soldiers of the third division; but the republican party, with Santander at their head, continued to regard, with undisguised apprehension, his ascendency over the army, and the political movements in which he was continually engaged, frequently accusing or suspecting him of a desire to imitate the career of Napoleon.

In virtue of a decree, dated Bogota, the 27th of August, 1828, Bolivar assumed the supreme power in Colombia, and continued to exercise it until his death, which took place at San Pedro, near Santa Martha, on the 17th of December, 1830. By this decree, he was authorized to maintain peace at home, to command the forces of the State by land and sea, to negotiate with foreign powers, to make peace and declare war, to enter into treaties, and in short to exercise all the functions and prerogatives of sovereign, not to say absolute power. The decree, indeed, provided that he was to be assisted in the exercise of the executive power by the council of ministers; but it is obvious, from the terms of this document, and above all, from the nature of the powers it conferred on the president, that although the council might advise, it could never control him; and that with the army at his back, he was sovereign of Colombia under a new denomination. Still his position was, in many respects, far from being an enviable one. Suspicion and distrust were excited by all his actions, and his life seems to have been embittered, if not shortened, by the incessant attacks made on his character and conduct. This seems evident from an address to the Colombian nation, which he dictated only a few days before his death; and in which, after alluding to his efforts in the cause of liberty, and asserting his disinterestedness, he complains that his enemies had abused the credulity of the people, and violated what to him was most sacred, his reputation; that he was the victim of his persecutors, who had brought him to the brink of the grave; that he had aspired to no other glory than the consolidation of Colombia; and that if his death should contribute to pacify all factions, and to strengthen the union, he would descend with tranquillity to the tomb.

PATAGONIA.

Patagonia, a large country of South America, occupies the southern extremity of that continent, from the Rio Negro to the Strait of Magellan. It lies between S. Lat. 38° 50′ and 53° 55′, W. Lon. 63° and 76°, and is bounded on the north by the Argentine Republic, east by the Atlantic, south by the Strait of Magellan, west by the Pacific, north-west by Chili. Its length from north to south, is 970 miles, its breadth varies from 200 to 420, and its area is about 300,000 square miles. The country is divided into two regions differing widely from each other in their general character. The one of these lies along the west coast, and is entirely mountainous; while the other, to the east, is in general low and flat.

In the western region, the mountains all belong to the chain of the Andes, which is here much lower than in the more northerly parts of South America, for the average height of the range in Patagonia does not exceed 3000 feet; but even here, there are some mountains upwards of 7000 feet above the sea. Southwards from the Gulf of Ancud, where the Chilian and Patagonian territories meet, the country along the shore of the Pacific presents an aspect quite different from that which is met with farther north. Instead of having a narrow strip of low land, with an almost unbroken coast extending between the mountains and the Pacific, as is generally the case on this coast, the Patagonian Andes rise abruptly out of the sea, which, frequently flowing into the deep defiles of the mountains, extends long and winding arms far into the land. Numerous high and rocky islands, rising abruptly out of the sea, line the coast. The chief of these are—Chiloe, the Chonos Archipelago, Wellington Island, the Archipelago of Madre de Dios, Hanover Island, and Queen Adelaide's Archipelago. There is also a large peninsula, called Tres Montes, lying between the Chonos Archipelago and Wellington Islands, joined to the mainland by a narrow isthmus. Near the southern extremity of Patagonia, two remarkable inlets break the continuity of the Andes chain. The first of these divides itself into two branches—Last Hope Inlet, extending to the north, and Ancon Sin Salida, or Obstruction Sound, to the south; while the second, which is much larger, spreads itself out in two sheets of water—Otway Water and Skyring Water — connected by a narrow strait. Farther to the south, not only the mountain chain, but the entire mass of the land is divided by the Strait of Magellan, extending from the Pacific to the Atlantic, and separating Terra del Fuego and the adjacent Islands from Patagonia. All the mountains of Western Patagonia, as well as those on the islands, are thickly wooded on their western declivities, but entirely bare on the side that is exposed to the ocean. The whole of the region is subject to incessant winds and rains, the breezes being generally from the west, and bringing from the Pacific an immense quantity of moisture, which is condensed on the mountains, and deluges the country with almost incessant showers. The ground is thus kept constantly wet; and there are few days in the year when rain does not fall in summer, or snow and sleet in winter. The largest river in Western Patagonia is the San Tadio, a small stream which falls into the Pacific south of the peninsula of Tres Montes. It is formed by two mountain torrents, and is navigable for about 11 miles. On the mainland opposite the island of Chiloe, there are two volcanoes, the farthest south of any that are known to have been active in modern times. These are Minchinmadiva, 8,010 feet, and Corcovado, 7,500 feet above the sea.

The eastern part of Patagonia is in its surface and climate the very reverse in many respects of the western. The land is low and flat, rising gradually in terraces from the Atlantic to the Andes. The uniformity of the surface is, however, broken by the high lands of the Espinosa, which occupy a large promontory between S. Lat. 47° and 48°, and rise to the height of 4000 feet above the sea. In the southern portion of the country, the soil consists of tertiary strata, covered with shingle, and destitute of all vegetation, except here and there scattered tufts of grass and low bushes. Although numerous salt pools occur in this region, there is a great scarcity of fresh water. North of 45° S. Lat., the country is more undulating, and not so entirely destitute of vegetation as the southern portion; for in some places the valleys and low hills are covered with grass and stunted trees, and there are even parts where good pasturage and timber may be obtained. Eastern Patagonia is traversed by several rivers, which are much larger than those that water the western region. The Rio Negro, which forms the northern boundary of Patagonia, rises in the Andes, flows first north-east, then east, and finally south-east, falling into the Atlantic. Its whole length is about 700 miles; and at a long distance from its mouth it has a breadth of 500 yards. Of the other rivers, little is known except their mouths; the Chupat, the Camerones, the Desire River, the Santa Cruz, and the Gallegos, are the most important—all falling into the Atlantic. The Santa Cruz is a river of considerable size, and is believed to flow through several lakes, one of which, Lake Capar, is 30 miles long and 10 or 12 broad. This river flows for a great part of its course in a deep valley, through an elevated plain which rises in some parts 1,800, and in others between 2000 and 3000 feet above the sea. Along the banks there are in some places, deep and extensive layers of lava.

The eastern coast of Patagonia, from the entrance of Magellan's Strait, as far northwards as 49° S. Lat., consists of cliffs of marly clay, rising 200 or 300 feet perpendicularly from the sea, and somewhat resembling, when seen from a distance, the coast of Kent. North of this, as far as 45° S. Lat., the cliffs are somewhat higher, and their prevailing structure is porphyritic. Beyond this point, the coast presents a different aspect, consisting of a shingly beach skirted by a reef of rocks. The largest gulfs of the eastern coast are those of San Matias, south of the Rio Negro; and St. George, north of Cape Blanco. There are also several harbors along this coast, such as Port San Antonio, in 41° S. Lat.; Nuevo Golfo, in 43°; Port Desire, in 47° 5′; Port San Julian, in 49° 12′; Santa Cruz, in 50° 7′; and Gallegos, in 51° 38′.

The climate of Eastern Patagonia is as remarkable for dryness as that of the western region is for its constant showers. Captain Fitzroy, who explored the Patagonian coasts between the years 1826 and 1836, thus speaks of the climate of this country:—"One naturally asks why Eastern Patagonia should be condemned to perpetual sterility, while the western side of the same country, in the same parallel of latitude, is injured by too much rain? The prevailing western winds and the Andes are the causes. The winds bring much moisture from the Pacific, but they leave it all, condensed, on the west side of the mountains. After passing the cordillera, those same winds are very dry. Easterly winds are very rare upon the east cost; they are the only ones which carry rain to the almost deserts of Patagonia. Westward of the Andes, an east wind is dry and free from clouds. All this country is exposed to severe cold weather in winter, and to excessive heat in summer. Great and sudden changes of temperature take place, when, after very hot weather, cold winds rush northwards with the fury of a hurricane." The temperature of the country south of the 45th parallel of latitude, is in general extremely cold, although during the short summer, great heat is experienced.

The vegetable products of Patagonia are very scanty, the only portion where there is a luxuriant vegetation being the country near the Rio Negro, in which the same plants are found as in the adjacent parts of the Argentine Republic. Among the forests of the west, several species of beech and many large and beautiful ferns occur. Animals are found in greater abundance than vegetables in most parts of Patagonia. Herds of guanacos, amounting to several hundreds in number, roam about the country; and the puma, the wolf, the fox, the opossum, the cavia, the armadillo, the otter, and the seal, are also met with. There are an immense number of animals of the class Rodentia — more, perhaps, than in any other part of the world. The horse is found in all parts of the country, being the invariable companion of the natives of Eastern Patagonia. The condor and the cassowary are the principal terrestrial birds; but the sea-fowl are very numerous, including several species of swans, ducks, and geese. Fish and other sea animals are plentiful along the coasts.

The aboriginal natives of Patagonia are a tall and extremely robust race of men. Their bodies are bulky, and their head and features large, but their hands and feet are small. Their limbs are neither so muscular nor so large-boned as their height and apparent bulk would lead one to suppose; they are rounder and smoother than those of white men. Their color is a rich reddish brown, rather darker than the hue of copper. The only attractive feature about their persons is their teeth, which are sound and white. Their cheek-bones are prominent, and so is their brow, which is broad but low. Their heads are furnished with a profusion of rough, lank, and coarse black hair, which is tied above the temples by a fillet of plaited or twisted sinews; and they wear no other covering upon this part of their body. The size of the Patagonians has been represented by some writers as quite gigantic; and, although the earlier voyagers have given somewhat exaggerated accounts of them, which have been improved by some subsequent authors, it seems to be the universal testimony of those who have visited the country in modern times, that they do considerably exceed the average stature of Europeans.

Captain Byron, in the middle of the last century, saw a number of men above eight feet, and some as much as nine feet in height. A recent traveller thus speaks of the natives that he saw: — "Among two hundred or three hundred natives of Patagonia, scarcely half a dozen men are seen whose height is under five feet nine or ten inches; the women are proportionately tall. I have nowhere seen an assemblage of men and women whose *average* height and *apparent* bulk equalled that of the Patagonians. Tall and athletic as are many of the South Sea islanders, there are also many among their number who are slight and of lower stature. The Patagonians seem to be high-shouldered, owing perhaps to their habit of folding their arms across the chest, in their mantles, and thus increasing their apparent height and bulk, because the mantles hang loosely, and almost touch the ground. Until actually measured, it is difficult to believe that they are not much taller than is the case."

Mr. Bourne, mate of an American vessel, who was for some time a captive in Patagonia in 1849–50, says that their average height is six and a half feet, while some nearly reach seven feet. These accounts are so precise and satisfactory that the question as to the actual size of the Patagonians may be regarded as completely set at rest. Is it more improbable that there should be races of men of *above* the European standard, than it is that there should be races whose height is *below* it? Yet we know beyond a doubt that the Esquimaux are so.

With the exception of the head, little hair grows upon their bodies; and from the face it is carefully removed by shells or pincers. They do not disfigure their naturally coarse features by piercing either nose or lip, but they bedaub their body with white, black, or red paint, forming grotesque figures, such as circles around their eyes, or great marks across their faces. This ornamental body-painting is practiced by all the different races of Patagonians, from Cape Horn to Buenos Ayres. On their feet and legs they wear boots made of the skins of horses' hind legs. Spurs made of wood, but of iron if they can get it, balls (*bolas*), or stones, attached to a long leather thong, for the purpose of catching the guanaco or the ostrich, by throwing the balls so as to wind round their legs, whilst a long tapering lance, and a knife, if it can be procured, complete their equipment. Mounted upon horses of a middle size, under fifteen hands high, and rather well-bred, the Patagonians seem to be carried no better than English dragoons, who ride eighteen stone upon horses able to carry ten; yet they go at full speed in chase of ostriches or guanacos. When hunting or making long journeys they often change horses. The women are dressed and booted like the men, with the addition of a half petticoat. They clean their hair and plait it into two tails. Ornaments of brass, beads, bits of colored glass, or such trifles, are prized by them. The huts of these wanderers are somewhat like gipsy tents. Poles are stuck in the ground, to which others are fixed. Over them are thrown the skins of animals, an irregular tilt-like hut being thus formed. It is to be observed that the inhabitants of Terra del Fuego, and of the islands to the south and south-west, wear little or no clothing.

The Patagonians appear to possess nothing like towns, but lead a wandering and unsettled life, somewhat resembling that of the Tartars. The different parts of the country are inhabited by several distinct nations, the chief of which are the following:—The Moluche, or Warrior Indians, who inhabit the Andes and neighboring regions, immediately south of the Rio Negro; the Puelche, or Eastern People, who wander about the north-east of Patagonia; the Chulian Indians, who occupy the mountainous regions south of 42° S. Lat.; the Te-huel-het, or Southern People, who inhabit the south-eastern extremity of the country; and the Fuegians, who people not only the island of Terra del Fuego, but the western coast of the mainland, as far north as the peninsula of Tres Montes. The last of these differs from the others in being of much lower stature. The various tribes into which they are divided are generally under the command of chiefs; and they subsist chiefly on the flesh of mares, guanacos, etc. They are for the most part filthy and disgusting in their habits, exceedingly vain and greatly given to lying.

Very few traces of any religious ceremonies have been observed among them. We are informed by Falconer, the Jesuit missionary, that after the dead have been interred twelve months, the graves are visited by the tribe for the purpose of collecting the bones, and conveying them to their family sepulchres, where they are set up, and adorned with all the beads and ornaments which the friends and family of the deceased are able to collect for the occasion. The ceremony is performed by certain women of the tribe, whose peculiar office it is to attend to these rites. In corroboration of the Jesuit's testimony, Captain King of the British navy, informs us, that near Port Desire he had seen the graves of the Indians upon the summits of hills, but without the bodies, which he supposes to have in all probability been removed by the Indians.

It seems highly probable that Magalhaens was the original discoverer of the southern coast of Patagonia and the northern coast of Terra del Fuego, as well as of the strait which bears his name. Sir Francis Drake passed the strait in the year 1578; and being driven by storms to the south, discovered the western and south-western coast of Terra del Fuego, and also Cape Horn; although the honor of the discovery of the latter has generally been ascribed to Jacob Le Maire, a Dutchman, in the service of the States of

Holland. In the year 1616, this navigator was the first who doubled that terminus of South America, and called it Cape Horn, after a village in Holland. Proceeding in a north-easterly direction, he crossed the strait which bears his name, and discovered Staten Island, which he so designated after the states of Holland. It is supposed that Davies, one of the companions of Cavendish in his voyage to the South Seas in 1592, was the first person who saw the Falkland Islands; but they were not, properly speaking, discovered till the year 1594, when Sir Richard Hawkins examined them, and called them in honor of his queen and himself, Hawkins' Maiden Land. The name, however was subsequently changed to Falkland Islands by Strong, another English navigator. During the early part of the eighteenth century they were re-discovered by some French navigators; and hence the origin of the French name, Malouine Islands. To Captain Cook we are indebted for the first accurate account of the south-eastern coast of Terra del Fuego, which he explored in 1774; and so little was known concerning it before this period that, when actually in sight of Cape Horn, he was unable to decide whether it was a detached island or a part of Terra del Fuego. Amongst the other distinguished names connected with the discovery or investigation of this part of the South American continent, are those of Sarmiento (whose account of a voyage down the western coast, and through the Strait of Magalhaens, has never been surpassed), Sir John Narborough, Cordova, Byron, Willis, Cateret, Bougainville, Weddel, King, Stokes, and Fitzroy. It only remains to be noticed that, although repeated attempts have been made to form permanent settlements in Patagonia, or upon the neighboring islands, particularly by the Spaniards, until recently none of these has been successful. In 1843, however, the government of Chili founded a settlement at Port Famine, on the Strait of Magellan, which was in 1850 transferred to Sandy Point, some distance to the north. This colony contained, according to the latest accounts, about twenty houses, with a chapel and sacristy. The population was 150; and they had ten horses, eighteen goats, and a number of swine. Another settlement on the strait has recently been projected; and recently, an exploring expedition was sent thither, with a view to that undertaking. The western part of Patagonia is claimed by Chili, and the eastern by the Argentine Republic. With regard to population, it must be quite obvious that no accurate idea can be formed. It has, however, been estimated at 120,000. By far the greater part of the country—that which stretches along the eastern side of the Andes, from their base to the Atlantic Ocean—is almost entirely unknown, with the exception of a very few places upon the coast. It is quite possible, therefore, that the inhabitants may be far more numerous in this region than is supposed; but the general sterility of the country holds out little prospect of any great commercial advantages to be gained by intercourse with them, except in the precious metals, which are doubtless to be found in the Patagonian Andes.

FALKLAND ISLANDS.

Falkland Islands (French *Malouines*, Spanish *Malvinas*), a group of Islands in the South Atlantic Ocean, belonging to Great Britain, and lying about 250 miles east of the nearest mainland of South America between 51° and 53° S. Lat., and 57° and 62° W. Long. The group consists of two principal islands, East and West Falkland, with several hundred others of different sizes clustered around and in the strait between them-

East Falkland is about eighty-five miles in length, by forty in breadth, and West Falkland eighty miles long by twenty-five to thirty miles wide. They are separated from each other by Falkland Sound. The other islands range in size from sixteen miles by eight, to mere islets of half a mile across. The whole group is deeply indented by numerous harbors and creeks, which, if they diminish the area, produce more than counterbalancing advantages. Very little is known of West Falkland. It is uninhabited, but at certain seasons is visited by whaling and other vessels. East Falkland is nearly divided into two unequal portions by the estuaries called Breton Sound and Choiseul Sound, the two parts of the island being connected by an isthmus not more than a mile and a half across. The northern portion is crossed by a chain of rugged hills, called the Wickham Heights, extending due east and West, from Port William to Port Sussex, and varying in height from 800 to 2000 feet. This range consists chiefly of quartz rock, which crops out with great irregularity, so that it can be crossed only at certain passes. South of this range it is one continued undulating plain, few of the heights rising to more than sixty feet above the level of the sea, and the ridges running nearly north-west and south-east. Through every little valley a stream of fresh water flows into one or other of the numerous creeks and inlets of the sea. Besides these rivulets, there are numerous fresh water ponds or lakes, varying from thirty yards to three or four miles in circumference. North of the Wickham Heights the surface is hilly, some of its elevations rising to the height of upwards of 1000 feet. The side of the heights contains slate, some of which is suitable for building and roofing purposes; and limestone has been discovered on and about the foot of Mount Usborne. From certain parts of these upper regions there descend into the valleys *streams of stones*, from twenty or thirty feet to a quarter of a mile wide, and below these stones there usually flows a stream of water. These stones are frequently of considerable size, and have not moved far, as their angles are generally but little broken. The climate is said to be very mild and salubrious. The temperature is equable, being rarely very hot in summer or very cold in winter. The ice is seldom more than half an inch thick, except in severe winters, and snow lies but a short time on the ground. Light showers are frequent, but a day of heavy rain never occurs. Excessive winds are common, but thunder-storms are extremely rare. The hottest months in the year are December and January. The soil is of a deep brown, almost black, compact, peaty quality, lying upon a strong clay subsoil, and from six inches to two feet deep.

There are few wild animals indigenous to the Falklands. The only quadruped is the warrah or wolf-fox, rather taller, but not much heavier, than the English fox. The other animals which are found in a wild state are those which have been left there by Europeans, as horned cattle, horses, sheep, wild hogs, and rabbits, all of which are very abundant. There is a plentiful supply of excellent fish in all the creeks, and of small trout in the lakes and rivulets. Hair and fur seals abound, and the black whale is still numerous about the coasts. The wild fowl are also numerous, as swans, geese, ducks, snipes, etc. There are few land birds or insects, and no reptiles.

A gigantic sedgy grass, called tussac, of the genus Carex, is very common on most of these islands. Its blade averages seven feet in length by about three-quarters of an inch in width, is extremely nutritious and admirably adapted for fattening cattle. Turnips, carrots, potatoes, and vegetables thrive well, and barley and oats have been successfully cultivated. Furze and other shrubs grow well, but there are as yet no trees. Peat is abundant, and some of it is highly bituminous.

The discovery of these islands has been by many attributed to Amerigo Vespucci, 1502; but it is more probable that they were first discovered by Davis in 1592. In 1594, Hawkins sailed along their north shore; and in 1690, Strong sailed through the channel which separates East from West Falkland, and called it Falkland Sound, whence the group afterwards took its name. During the earlier parts of the eighteenth century these islands were frequently visited by French vessels; and in 1764, a French colony was established at St Louis, on East Falkland. Two years later, the English planted a colony at Port Egmonton, West Falkland. In 1767, the Spaniards took possession of the French settlement, and three years later of the English. In consequence of this step, some negotiations were entered into, the result of which was that the sovereignty of these islands was ceded to the English, who, however, some time afterwards abandoned them. Though frequently visited by whaling vessels and others, they continued without permanent inhabitants till 1820, when they were taken possession of by the republic of Buenos Ayres. A settlement was formed at Port Louis, which rapidly increased until 1831, when, in consequence of a dispute with the United States, it was destroyed by the Americans. In 1833, the English again assumed possession of the Falklands, and stationed an officer and boat's crew at Port Louis. In 1840, the government resolved to colonize these islands, and sent out for that purpose a governor and a small establishment, who settled at Port Louis. A more advantageous situation for a settlement was subsequently found on the south side of Stanley Harbor, where, in 1844, a town was laid out. Mr. Lafone, a wealthy merchant, obtained from the government an extensive tract of land, and possession of all the wild cattle and other wild stock for six years, from 1st of January, 1848, in consideration of a payment by instalments of $300,000. Lafone's interests were purchased by a chartered company, which now possesses, in East Falkland, all the southern peninsula called Lafonia, consisting of about 600,000 acres, besides 138 islands and islets, with an aggregate area of about 200,000 acres. In 1847, the population of the colony was estimated to be less than 300. Ten years later, the governor reported that there was a steady increase in population; and according to the latest accounts, the Falkland Islands number not far from 3000 inhabitants. The commerce of these islands is of course but moderate; the exports consisting of hides, tallow, salted beef, seal skins, and fish oil; the imports being mostly timber, lime, brick, flour, sugar, coffee, and British manufactured goods. The value of the imports, as recently stated, is over $100,000 per annum, and exports about $95,000. On an average, fifty to sixty vessels touch at Stanley, which has an excellent harbor, and is supported mainly by the British government, to afford ships a place of call for water and fresh provisions in this unfrequented part of the ocean.

Painted by

Alonzo Chappel.

(KING WILLIAM OF PRUSSIA)

SUPPLEMENTARY.

THE WAR BETWEEN FRANCE AND PRUSSIA.

JULY 15TH, 1870—MARCH 3D, 1871.

AT the commencement of the narrative of this remarkable war, it seems appropriate to dwell for a moment on an occurrence in French history, that was an incidental prelude to the great drama.

For reasons that probably are not well understood by the outside world, Napoleon III. set about the experiment which was termed the *plebiscitum*—that is, a vote of the French people on the question, whether they had confidence in the Imperial Government. It was a novel proceeding. So far as the taking a vote was concerned, it was virtually the same thing as an election by the people; only, there was but one candidate for the office of Emperor: and the real point to be ascertained, was whether the election should be unanimous. Supposing the votes cast on the *plebiscitum* to be given freely, without restraint or constraint, the whole matter was an expression of opinion, merely; and why an Emperor, in the plenitude of power, should call on an entire people to express such an opinion, when it was quite certain that a vote of a *want* of confidence would lead to no definite result, is and will remain a problem. The proceeding was, at best, "fishing for a compliment" on a grand scale: and the sequel shows what the compliment was worth. As to the vote itself, it was on the whole what might have been expected. Comparatively few Frenchmen were prepared for a revolution, and they, as a mere formality, voted *yea*. Their number was 7,336,434. The minority, whose action in the premises might be called *affirmative*, set themselves in array against the Emperor, to the number of 1,502,790; a ratio one to six of the whole number. It is remarkable that in the army, where a unanimous vote was hoped for, no less than 50,000 voted *nay*. To a certain extent, what is called the popular opinion of the world regarded this vote as a proof of the strength of the empire. Others held the vote to be a proof of its weakness; and as, at least, a proof of the Emperor's own want of confidence in it: for if he felt secure in his seat, why did he wish a vote on the subject?

The vote was taken on the 8th of June. On the 11th of June, a cloud, at first no larger than a man's hand, and seemingly as remote as the poles from any connection with the *plebiscitum*, arose on the Spanish horizon. On that day, in the Spanish Cortes, Marshal Prim made a statement respecting his endeavours to provide the country with a king. But he wished his auditory to understand, that he did not seek to bring about this result by a restoration of any member of the Bourbon family. It was already rumored that a certified copy of the abdication of Queen Isabella had been received in Madrid; but the rumor proved to be in anticipation of the fact; as the formal abdication and in favor of Queen Isabella's son, Alphonso, was made in Paris on the 26th of June.

For some days following, the announcement by Marshal Prim was discussed in the Cortes, and petitions on behalf of Espartero and of the Duke of Montpensier were presented. Those petitions were rejected, and on the 5th of July, Prim made a formal offer of the crown to Prince Leopold of Hohenzollern, a prince of the reigning dynasty of Prussia, and the prince accepted the offer. The prince was the elder brother of Prince Charles of Roumania, and the eldest son of the reigning Prince of Hohenzollern, who, in 1849, surrendered to Prussia his sovereign rights. His father lived at Dusseldorf, and was considered a member of the Prussian Royal Family. The prince was thirty-five years of age, and a colonel in the Prussian foot-guards. He was married in 1861, to Marie, the sister of the King of Portugal. In religion, he was a Roman Catholic.

The news caused great excitement in Paris, where the selection was regarded as the work of Count Bismarck. In the Legislative Body, on the 6th of July, the Duke de Grammont, the Foreign Minister, said that the negotiations which led to the prince's acceptance of the offer of the crown, had been kept secret from the French Government; and he added, "We do not believe that respect for the rights of a neighboring people obliges us to suffer a foreign power, by placing a prince on the throne of Charles V., to disturb the European Equilibrium to our disadvantage, and thus to imperil the interests and the honor of France. We entertain a firm hope that this will not happen; and to prevent it, we count on the wisdom of the German nation and the friendship of the people of Spain; but, in the contrary event, with your support and the support of the nation, we shall know how to do our duty, without hesitation or weakness." M. Ollivier remarked, "The ministry is convinced that the Duke de Grammont's statement will bring about a peaceful solution; for, whenever Europe sees that France is firm in pursuance of her legitimate duty, it does not resist her desire." MM. Picard and Jules Favre asked for copies of the dispatches exchanged between the courts of Paris and Berlin, since the previous day; and when M. Ollivier, instead of complying with the request, moved an adjournment of the debate, M. Jules Favre exclaimed, "Then this is a ministry of Stock Exchange jobbers." This, of course, caused a great uproar, and the speaker was called to order. The journals of the next day asserted that, "should the Cortes vote for the Prince of Hohenzollern, the French Government will hold Prussia responsible. Stringent orders have been issued to the military authorities throughout the empire, not to grant any further leave of absence. Officers are returning to their regiments, and the frontier fortresses are undergoing a rapid inspection."

It was, at first, stated that Prim had offered the throne to Prince Leopold on his own authority, without consulting his colleagues; but later intelligence showed that there was a complete unanimity of opinion on the subject in the ministry. Prim, however, originated the nomination. It is evident that the welfare of Spain was a secondary object with her successful generals, who insisted on playing the game of revolution for their own exclusive benefit—or, what they deemed such. If they had cared to reconcile warring factions, to give the greatest attainable stability to the governnent, and to launch constitutional monarchy on the most favorable conditions, they would have fixed on a successor to Queen Isabella, in the first days of the insurrection, and thus have seated one sovereign at the same moment that they dethroned the other. But men who are selfish at home, are rarely disinterested abroad; and it is no wonder that this intriguing soldier who displayed such a philosophical indifference to the happiness of the Spanish people, should have shown himself equally careless about the maintenance of peace in Europe. A manœuvre more reckless than the choice of the Prince of Hohenzollern as the official candidate for the vacant crown, has seldom been seen. From whatever point of view it is regarded, it equally deserves condemnation. General Prim cannot but have known how intensely distasteful such a selection would be to the French nation. His offer to the prince, if made without his first securing the support of the Prussian government, was simply preparing a gratuitous humiliation for Spain: for it was idle to suppose that a candidate seriously objected to by France could make his claim good without the support of a foreign army; if, on the contrary, he had made himself acquainted with the intentions of Prussia, and found that he could rely on her support, his offer was a voluntary expedient to stir up a European war. In either case, therefore, he stands inexcusable.

The moment that the nomination of the Prince of Hohenzollern was understood in France, the French government demanded from Prussia a disavowal of the transaction. In reply, Prussia disclaimed all agency in the appointment. She further declared, that the prince was not even a relation of the family of Prussia; and that as it was General Prim who negotiated with the prince, it was he, and not Prussia, who must be held responsible. On the 12th of July the Spanish Ambassador in Paris received a dispatch from the father of Prince Leopold, stating that in consequence of the opposition to the candidature of his son, he had withdrawn it in the name of the prince. To this, France replied: "Prussia claims that she has had no agency in this candidature; if that is true, let her force the prince himself to renounce the offer. The prince is under the authority of the King of Prussia, and thus the latter has the peace of Europe in his hands." On the 14th, at Ems, as King William was walking with Count Lehndorff, his adjutant, in the Kurgarten, M. Benedetti, the French Ambassador, accosted him personally, and demanded that he, the king, should not only refuse his consent to Leopold's acceptance of the Spanish crown, but should engage, under sufficient guaranties, to resume said refusal should the prince at any future day receive the nomination. King William turned around and ordered the Count Lehndorff to tell M. Benedetti that there was no reply, and that he would not again admit M. Benedetti to an audience.

On the 15th of July, France declared war against Prussia. The causes were thus stated:

First—The insult offered to Count Benedetti, the French Minister, at Ems, and its approval by the Prussian Government.

Second—The refusal of the King of Prussia to compel the withdrawal of Prince Leopold's name as a candidate for the Spanish throne.

Third—The fact that the King of Prussia persisted in giving the prince liberty to accept the crown.

The declaration was in these words, addressed to the Senate by the Duke de Grammont:

"The manner in which the country received our declaration on the 6th of July, led us to commence negotiations with Prussia to secure her recognition of the validity of our grievances. We did not treat with Spain, whose independence we have no wish to trammel, nor with the Prince of Hohenzollern, whom we consider to be under the shadow of the king; nor have we advanced any other grievance than the candidature of the prince for the Spanish throne.

"The Prussian Minister of Foreign Affairs opposed to us a determination not to receive our representation, pretending to ignore the affair, and that he could not intervene except as head of the family; but he avowed that he had instructed Bismarck. We could not accept that answer, and we demanded that the king should influence the Prince of Hohenzollern. Resistance to our project came from the quarter where it was least expected. We then demanded that the king should give a promise for the future. This moderate demand, made in moderate terms, we declared to be without any reservation. The king declined to say that he would refuse in future to interfere with the candidature, and he refused to authorize us to transmit to you the declaration that he would in future oppose the candidature. He declared that he reserved to himself the right to consider the circumstances. Even after this refusal, we did not break off the negotiations, but adjourned our explanations to you until this date. Yesterday we were apprized that the King of Prussia had informed our ambassador that he would not again receive him; and, to render the rupture more obvious, he gave notice of his action to the cabinets of Europe. At the same time he announced that Werther might take leave, and that the armament of Prussia had commenced. On our part, we yesterday called out the reserves, and we have taken such other measures as the interest and the honor of the country demand. A copy of this declaration has been presented to the Corps Legislatif by Monsieur, the keeper of the seals. The government asks a vote of supplies and a call to arms of all classes owing the military service."

In both houses the ministerial declaration was received with great applause; but it is to be remarked, that in the Corps Legislatif a considerable minority opposed the policy of the government, at least, until they had fuller information. M. Jules Favre called on the ministry to communicate the documents which passed during the negotiations, and especially the Prussian dispatch addressed to foreign governments, admitting the refusal of the King of Prussia to receive M. Benedetti. M. Buffet opposed the demand for papers, and M. Jules Favre's motion was rejected by a vote of 164 against 83.

On the 19th of July, the North German Parliament was opened with a speech from the throne, delivered by King William in person. His majesty said, in the course of his speech—

"The candidacy of a German Prince for the Spanish throne—both in the bringing forward and withdrawal of which the Confederate Governments were equally unconcerned, and. which interested the North German Confederation only so far as the government of a friendly country appeared to found on its success the hope of acquiring for a sorely-tired people a pledge for a regular and peaceful government—afforded the Emperor of the French a pretext for a *casus belli*, put forward in a manner long since unknown in the annals of diplomatic intercourse, and adhered to after the removal of the very pretext itself, with that disregard for the people's right to the blessing of peace, of which the history of a former ruler of France affords so many analagous examples. If Germany, in former centuries, bore in silence such violations of her rights and of her honor, it was only because, in her then divided state, she knew not her own strength. To-day, when the links of intellectual and rightful community, which began to be knit together at the time of the wars of liberation, join the more slowly, the more surely, the different German races—to-day, that Germany's armament leaves no longer an opening to the enemy, the German nation contains within itself the will and the power to repel the renewed aggression of France. It is not arrogance that puts these words in my mouth. The confederate government, and I myself, are acting in the full consciousness that victory and defeat are in the hands of Him who decides the fate of battles. With a clear gaze we have measured the responsibilities which, before the judgment seat of God and of mankind, must fall on him who drags two great and peace-loving peoples of the heart of Europe into a devastating war."

Subsequently, the king received an address from the Berlin Town Council, thanking his majesty for having repelled the unheard-of attempt made on the dignity and independence of the nation, and asserting that as France has declared war against Prussia, every man in Prussia must do his duty. The king, in reply, expressed his gratitude for the sentiments contained in the address, and said:

"God knows that I am not answerable for this war. The demand sent me was one that I could not do otherwise than reject. My reply gained the approval of all the towns and provinces, the expression of which I have received from all parts of Germany, and even from Germans residing beyond the seas. The greeting which was given me here on Friday last, has animated me with pride and confidence. Heavy sacrifices will be demanded of my people. We have become unaccustomed to them, by the quickly gained victories which we achieved in the last two wars. We shall not get off so cheaply this time; but I know what I may expect from my army and from those now hastening to join the ranks. The instrument is sharp and cutting. The result is in the hands of God."

War being thus resolved on by France, nothing remained for Prussia but immediate resistance to the aggression; and the utmost energies of each nation were at once applied to the marshalling of their respective armies. The excitement in the two capitals spread, with the rapidity of telegraphic communication, throughout the two countries, and to all the civilized world. The comment of the London *Times* was—"France, without a shadow of excuse or justification, plunges Europe into a war of which no person living may see the end."

It is notable, that from the moment when the action of the French government made war inevitable, the nominal cause of the war, namely, the Prince Leopold, and even the Spanish throne itself, sank into insignificance, so far as any public interest in either was concerned.

As this war was declared by France and accepted by Prussia with the rapidity that characterize all proceedings of a period when railroads and telegraphs are the exclusive mediums of communication, each of the belligerents took its course without con sultation or negotiation with—indeed, almost without the knowledge of, the other powers of Europe; yet each was profoundly interested in obtaining for itself, at least the respect and good-will, if not the sympathy and aid of those powers. And, naturally, if either of the belligerents had at hand any means of exciting against the other the jealousy or ill-will of any of those powers, such means would be promptly used. It may, therefore, readily be supposed that Count Bismarck had some agency in promulgating the contents of a secure treaty which France had several times attempted to negotiate with Prussia. This astounding document, which exposed the real sentiments and purposes of the French Government in regard to the other European States, was published in the London newspapers of Monday, July 25th. The proposed treaty consisted of five articles, in the following words:

I. His Majesty, the Emperor of the French, admits and recognizes the requisitions which Prussia has made as the result of the last war which she sustained against Austria and her allies.

II. His Majesty, the King of Prussia, promises to facilitate the acquisition of Luxembourg by France; to that effect, his aforesaid majesty will enter into negotiations with his Majesty, the King of the Netherlands, to induce him to cede to the Emperor of the French his sovereign rights over that Duchy, in return for such compensation as shall be deemed sufficient, or otherwise. On his part, the Emperor of the French engages to bear the pecuniary charges which the transaction may occasion.

III. His Majesty, the Emperor of the French, will not oppose a federal union of the Confederation of the North with the Southern States of Germany, with the exception of Austria, which union may be founded on a common parliament, provided the sovereignty of the said States is duly respected.

IV. On his part, his Majesty, the King of Prussia, in case his Majesty, the Emperor of the French should be obliged by circumstances to cause his troops to enter Belgium, or to conquer her, will accord the succour of his arms to France, and will sustain her with all his forces of land and sea against every power, which, in that event, shall declare war upon her.

V. To ensure the complete execution of the above-mentioned arrangements, his Majesty the King of Prussia and his Majesty the Emperor of the French, contract, by the present treaty, an alliance offensive and defensive, which they solemnly engage to maintain. Their Majesties undertake beyond this, and specially, to observe it in every case where their respective States, of which they mutually guaranty the integrity, shall be menaced by aggression, holding themselves bound, in such a conjuncture, to make without delay, and not to decline on any pretext, the military arrangements which may be demanded by their common interest conformably to the clauses and provisions above set forth.

It may well be supposed, that this cool attempt on the part of Louis Napoleon, to tread in the footsteps of his illustrious predecessor by offering to give away what did not belong to him in order to obtain what belonged to others, opened the eyes of his neighboring sovereigns, and taught them how to estimate his official friendship. And, on the other hand, the fact that this treaty, though frequently pressed on the Prussian government, had been steadily rejected by them, went far toward exciting the good-will of the other powers in favor of Prussia.

The course pursued by England in the matter of neutrality, at this crisis, is worthy of a separate paragraph, and to be remembered. The point is embodied in this widely published comment: "The newspapers of all shades of opinion blame the course pursued by England, especially the unimpeded supply of coals, horses and ammunition to France, for warlike purposes, and the evasive answers of Lord Granville to the questions in the House of Lords with reference to the representations on the subject of the North German Ambassador."

The respective forces of the two nations, at the commencement of the war, may be thus stated. In the two arms of artillery and cavalry, the preponderance was but little on either side. Of infantry, France had about five hundred and fifty thousand drilled and available men; while North Germany mustered no less than nine hundred and fifty thousand, of whom almost every man had passed through his time of regular service in the army. Besides that, the troops of the line of Hesse Darmstadt, Baden, Wurtemburg and Bavaria, amounted to at least eighty battalions.

The preliminary movements of the French troops were toward a concentration in the quadrilateral formed by the towns of Nancy, Thionville, Strasbourg and Mayence. Subordinately to the general command of the Emperor, the several corps were under the leadership of Marshal MacMahon, Baron Frossard, Marshal Bazaine, Count Ladmarault, Marshal de Failly, Marshal Canrobert, and Felix Douay, General of Division. General Edmond Lebœuf was on the 21st of July appointed Major-General of the French Army.

The Prussian Army of the South was under the command of the Crown Prince, Frederic William; the Army of the Centre was led by the Prince Frederic Charles; and the right wing was commanded by Herwarth von Bittenfield. The Baron Von Moltke, in connection with the King of Prussia, was commander-in-chief of the whole Prussian force.

The first aggressive movement was made on the 20th of July, when a detachment of French troops crossed the Prussian frontier near Saarbruck, and seized the custom-house.

On the next day, Thursday, July 21st, a detachment of two hundred French soldiers crossed the Prussian frontier for a reconnaissance, and had a skirmish with a small Prussian force. The Frenchmen were finally surrounded by the Germans, and were all made prisoners. None were killed, and only a few wounded.

On Saturday, July 23d, a Prussian detachment from Saarlouis crossed the French frontier in the direction of St. Avold and Metz. After proceeding some distance, they encountered a French outpost, and a brisk skirmish ensued with a body of French chasseurs. The Prussians were driven back, leaving two men dead on the field. The loss of the French was greater. These were the first men killed in the war.

On Sunday, July 24th, the Emperor Napoleon issued the following proclamation, which is remarkable in this respect, if no other, that it assumes, on the part of France, the tone of a pacific nation, desirous of peace and unwillingly forced to resist aggression by war; whereas, the unanimous voice of the civilized world, outside of the empire, declared that France was itself the aggressor; and that she, without the slightest pretext, had forced Prussia into this terrible contest:

"FRENCHMEN: There are in the life of a people solemn moments when the national honor, violently excited, presses itself irresistibly, rises above all other interests, and applies itself with the single purpose of directing the destinies of the nation. One of those decisive hours has now arrived for France. Prussia, to whom we have given evidence during and since the war of 1856, of the most conciliatory disposition, has held our good-will of no account, and has returned our forbearance by encroachments. She has aroused distrust in all quarters, necessitating exaggerated armaments, and has made of Europe a camp where reign disquiet and fear of the morrow. A final incident has disclosed the instability of the international understanding, and shown the gravity of the situation. In the presence of her new pretensions, Prussia was made to understand our claims. They were evaded, and followed with contemptuous treatment. Our country manifested profound displeasure at this action, and quickly a war-cry resounded from one end of France to the other.

"There remains for us nothing but to confide our destinies to the chance of arms. We do not make war upon Germany, whose independence we respect. We pledge ourselves that the people composing the great Germanic nationality shall freely dispose of their destinies. As for us, we demand the establishment of a state of things guarantying our security and assuring the future. We wish to conquer a durable peace, founded on the true interests of the people, and to assist in abolishing that precarious condition of things when all nations are forced to employ their resources in arming against each other.

"The glorious flag of France, which we once more unfurl in the face of our challengers, is the same which has borne over Europe the civilizing ideas of our great revolution. It represents the same principles; it will inspire the same devotion.

"Frenchmen: I go to place myself at the head of that gallant army which is animated by love of country and devotion to duty. That army knows its worth, for it has seen victory follow its footsteps in the four quarters of the globe. I take with me my son. Despite his tender years, he knows the duty his name imposes upon him, and he is proud to bear his part in the dangers of those who fight for our country. May God bless our efforts. A great people defending a just cause is invincible. NAPOLEON."

On the same day, Sunday, July 24th, a body of Prussians crossed the frontier, near Saarbruck. After a march of several miles, they encountered a considerable French force near the town of Gersweller. On this occasion the French were driven back, leaving twelve killed or wounded on the field, while the Prussians sustained no loss. It was claimed that the result of this skirmish proved the superiority of the needle-gun over the chassepot rifle. Subsequently, a company of the Prussian Seventeenth regiment of the line captured the French custom-house at Schrecklingen, with all its officers.

On Monday, July 25th, the French government issued the following manifesto: "That, in the prosecution of the war, the commanders of the French forces shall scrupulously regard, with respect to neutral powers, the rules of international right; and that, especially, they conform to the principles of the declaration of the Paris Congress of 1856, as follows: Privateering is abolished.

A neutral flag protects the enemy's merchandise, except contraband of war. Merchandise of a neutral, except contraband of war, is seizable under a foreign flag. A blockade must be effective."

Prussia responded to this decree, and announced the adoption of its provisions.

On Tuesday, July 26th, an official decree was issued in Paris, naming the Empress Eugénie Regent, during the absence of the emperor from the capital.

On Thursday, July 28th, another skirmish took place between detachments of the two hostile forces at Volkinger. The losses were trifling, but the advantage was with the Prussians. On the same day, the emperor left Paris to join the army, and he issued the following proclamation to the soldiers:

"Soldiers: I come to take my place at your head to defend the honor of the soil of our country. You go to combat against one of the best armed of European countries; but other countries, as valiant as this, have not been able to resist your valor. It will be the same to-day. The war which now commences will be long and hardly contested, for its theatre will be places hedged with obstacles and thick with fortresses; but nothing is beyond the persevering efforts of the soldiers of Africa. You will prove once more what the French army is able to accomplish, animated by a sentiment of duty, maintained by discipline, influenced by love of country. Whatever road we may take across our frontiers we will find upon it glorious traces of our fathers, and we will show ourselves worthy of them.

"All France follows you with ardent prayers, and the eyes of the universe are upon you. Upon our success depends the fate of liberty and civilization. Soldiers, let each one do his duty, and the God of Battles will be with us. Napoleon.

"At the General Headquarters at Metz, 28th July, 1870."

On Friday, July 29th, the French fleet arrived at Copenhagen, whence it proposed to establish a blockade of all Prussian access to and from the sea, and to prepare for an aggressive movement on the Prussian ports and fortresses.

On Saturday, July 30th, the estimate of the Prussian forces, published semi-officially in Paris, was as follows: "At Treves, 300,000; in the Black Forest, 100,000; near Mayence, 200,000; in Schleswig, 100,000; near Berlin, 80,000. The triangle between Treves, Mayence, and the River Lauter, is well filled with soldiers."

It is notable, that, at this early day, while the French press was nearly unanimous in its expressions of confidence in their army and of its assured victories, and while nothing that indicated apprehensions of danger was taking place in Berlin, extensive preparations were made for the defence of Paris.

On the 31st of July and the 1st of August there were several skirmishes between the approaching hosts, which rumor magnified into important engagements; but the first encounter that in any respect deserved the name of a battle, took place on Tuesday, August 2d, on the heights of Saarbrück. These heights were occupied by a detachment of Prussians; and at about eleven o'clock in the morning, a division of the French army, commanded by the emperor in person, and accompanied by his son, made an attack on the position. The Prussians held their ground with great bravery for about two hours, when they retired from the field. The losses on each side were trifling; but the moral effect of a first victory in the campaign was important. The French emperor was so elated by this affair, that he telegraphed to the empress the following pathetic despatch:

"Louis" [that is the young Prince Imperial] "has received his first baptism of fire. He was admirably cool, and little impressed. A division of Frossard's command carried the heights overlooking the Saar. The Prussians made a brief resistance. Louis and I were in the front, where the balls fell about us. Louis keeps a bullet which he picked up. The soldiers wept at his tranquillity."

If this bombastic effusion had been a prelude to a successful and triumphant campaign on the part of France, it would still be in very poor taste; but the actual sequel of the campaign renders it intensely ridiculous.

The proclamation of the King of Prussia to his army was in very honorable contrast to the inflated sentences of Louis Napoleon. He said:

"All Germany stands unanimously in arms against a neighboring State who has surprised us by declaring war against us without any provocation. The defence of the threatened Fatherland, of our honor and our hearths, rests upon you. To-day I undertake the command of the whole army, and I advance cheerfully to a contest which, in former times, our fathers fought gloriously. The whole Fatherland trusts confidently in you, and I share their confidence. The Lord God will be with our righteous cause."

The arrangements between France and Italy for the evacuation of Rome by the French troops, were completed on the 3d of August; an event which left the Pope to adjust his affairs with the King of Italy as best he might; and which enabled Louis Napoleon to bring back to France the forces so long employed in the Pope's service, and to be now added to the French army.

Great as was the exultation of the emperor, of the French army, and, indeed, of Paris and France, over the affair of Saarbrück, the developments of a few succeeding hours sufficed to show how little actual cause there was for such demonstrations. The small force placed at Saarbrück by the Prussian commander, and its early retreat, when, had the defence of the position been intended, it could easily have been reinforced, were parts of a stratagem to draw the French divisions into an ambuscade, from which not a man would have escaped. A little behind the forests surrounding Saarbrück, a corps of 25,000 Prussians lay quietly awaiting the movements of the French troops. Had the French pursued the retreating detachment of Prussians, and undertaken to establish themselves at Saarbrück, as was expected by the Prussians, they would have been cut off. But the French seem to have suspected the trap laid for them, and they remained on the heights they had captured.

On Thursday, August 4th, the Prussian forces, under the command of the Crown Prince, moved against Wissembourg, which was held by five French regiments; namely, two of the line, and one each of Chasseurs à Pied, Zouaves, and Tirailleurs, from Algiers. The Prussian force consisted of the Fifth and Eleventh Prussian corps, and the Second Bavarian. The attack was by assault, and Weissembourg and the heights toward Geisburg were carried at the point of the bayonet. General Douay, chief in command of the French, was killed, five hundred unwounded prisoners and one gun were captured, and the entire encampment fell into the hands of the victors.

On the 5th of August, Marshal MacMahon, having learned the defeat at Wissembourg, moved rapidly toward that point with between sixty and seventy thousand men; and the Paris newspapers announced, in advance, that he had met and defeated the Prussians.

The Crown Prince marched from Weissembourg on the same day and crossed the frontier, invading the French territory to meet MacMahon, whom he encountered near Woerth on Saturday morning, August 6th, at nine o'clock. This place is about fourteen miles south-east of Wissembourg. The Prussians took post in the forest of Hagenau, and commenced a fearful artillery fire on the French columns. Turcos, Zouaves, and the troops of the line, fought heroically; but they were outnumbered, nearly three to one. The French cavalry made repeated charges, but every time without avail. The battle raged nearly the whole day, and ended by the entire defeat of MacMahon. Nearly all his staff were killed; and he himself, after having been fifteen hours in the saddle, was at length unhorsed, and fell fainting into a ditch, where he was discovered by a soldier, who revived him with some brandy from his flask. The marshal then directed the retreat of the remnant of his army, on foot. The French suffered very much from the superiority of the Prussian infantry in the steadiness and accuracy of their fire. The losses on both sides were very heavy. That of the French was 10,000 killed and wounded and 6000 prisoners; and of the Prussians, between 3000 and 4000, killed and wounded. The defeated army left behind them their entire baggage, thirty guns, two standards, and six mitrailleuses.

This was not the only disaster of the French on that day. Early in the morning, the French troops which had remained at or near Saarbrück, evacuated the place and moved toward the frontier, taking a position at Speicheren, a small village south of Saarbrück. The road from Saarbrück to Forbach runs on the western slope of the hill. The Prussians, following the French movement, charged up the hill, and a fierce contest ensued. The French, under General Frossard, held their ground on the top of the hill, where the Prussians had driven them, until dark, when they were compelled to give way. The French corps was almost entirely broken up, and its losses in killed and wounded were very heavy. The camp, a large quantity of stores, and 2000 prisoners, fell into the hands of the Prussians.

The progress of the campaign, thus far, was the reverse of what was generally looked for, and what, from tradition, might have been expected. It was the Prussians who took the aggressive, and the French who were forced to defend themselves. The Prussians moved rapidly, and in large masses; the French were easily broken, and not readily reconstructed. The excuse for their repeated defeats, as promulgated by the Paris journals, was that their armies were attacked by superior numbers; but it was the superior generalship of the Prussians which concentrated the larger masses on inferior forces.

In Paris, the news of the French reverses produced a frantic outburst of rage. The government furnished no information to the people of the defeat at Wissembourg; it first became known to them through the English newspapers. On Friday evening, August 5th, the Boulevards des Italiens and Montmartre were thronged with an immense crowd. About six o'clock in the evening the shop of a banker was assaulted and destroyed by the mob, in consequence of a rumor that he had publicly expressed his satisfaction at the French defeats. A similar demonstration was made before the office of Baron Hirsch, another banker, but the energetic action of the police saved it from destruction. Hirsch was one of the four bankers against whom proceedings had been commenced for an alleged breach of law in sending money to the enemy's country. On the night of Wednesday, August 4th, several parcels of specie belonging to the four bankers, and amounting to about three millions of dollars, were seized by the police at one of the railway stations. The money was declared to be destined for England, Italy, Holland, and Switzerland; but the authorities acted on the impression that it was really intended for Germany. On Saturday afternoon, a great revulsion in public feeling was caused by a report, at the Bourse, that MacMahon had retaken Wissembourg. For a time, the wildest excitement prevailed, and business was suspended in the law courts that the news might be read. But, on application at the government offices, it was found that the report was false. The fury of the mob, with its usual discrimination, was then turned against the Bourse, and they attempted to pull down the offending building; but, again, the influence of the police prevented the destruction. The mob then moved to the residence of M. Ollivier, who came out and assured them that the author of the false report was arrested; and that all news, of whatever complexion, should be faithfully communicated to them, as soon as it was received. On Sunday, the emperor's telegrams announced the French defeats at Woerth and Speicheren. At five o'clock in the morning the empress hurried up from St. Cloud to the Tuileries, whence she issued the following proclamation:

"FRENCHMEN: The opening of the war has not been in our favor. Our arms have suffered a check. Let us be firm under this reverse, and let us hasten to repair it. Let there be among us but a single party, that of France but a single flag, the flag of our national honor. Faithful to my mission and my duty, I come among you, and when danger threatens, you will see me the first to defend the flag of France. I call on all good citizens to preserve order; to disturb it would be to conspire with our enemies."

The Council of Ministers, in the afternoon, put forth a proclamation, which concluded as follows:

"In the face of the grave news which is received, our duty is clear. We appeal to the patriotism and energy of all. The Chambers are convoked. Let us first place Paris in a state of defence, in order to facilitate the execution of the military preparations. We declare the capital in a state of siege. Let there be no weakness, no divisions. Our resources are immense. Let us fight with vigor *and the country will be saved*."

Observe, here, that this concluding line was promulgated just twenty-three days after the declaration of war by France, against Prussia.

On Monday, August 8th, the minister issued another proclamation, in the same tone; and the state of affairs at the capital became so menacing, that the convocation of the Senate and the Legislative Body, at first appointed for Friday, the 12th, was anticipated by a change to Tuesday, the 9th of August. As soon as the Senate was assembled, M. Parrieu made a statement on behalf of the government, in which he said:

"The Emperor promised to assemble the Chamber as soon as circumstances should require. The Empress, now, did not wish to wait until the state of affairs was more compromised. We have suffered reverses, but we have not been vanquished. The greater part of our army has not yet fought, and it is ready to obtain victory for us. Our resources are intact. We ask you to authorize a levy *en masse*. Everything is ready. Paris is placed in a state of defence, and it can sustain a long siege. We shall shorten the formalities for the enrolment of volunteers. We ask you to approve a general organization of the National Guard, and the incorporation of a part of the Garde Mobile in the regular army, and to accelerate the drawing of the class for 1871. The Prussians hope to profit by our internal divisions, but that hope will be deceived. If order among us should be disturbed, we shall make use of the powers conferred upon us by the state of siege, and we shall call to our aid other forces than those of the National Guard."

In the Legislative Body, M. Ollivier attempted to deliver a similar address; but, owing to the interruptions he met with, little of what he said could be heard. M. Jules Favre declared that the military incapacity of the emperor had been fully proved, and that he ought to resign the command of the army. He proposed that the government of the country should be taken in hand by the Chamber itself. At this point there was a great uproar, in the midst of which, M. Granier de Cassagnac exclaimed that M. Jules Favre and the other members of the Left ought to be shot; notwithstanding which the Count Kérartry declared that the emperor ought to abdicate. A great tumult ensued; and the ministers nearly came to blows with some of the deputies. Ultimately, the president put on his hat and suspended the sitting. Subsequently, on the motion of M. Clément Duvernois, an order of the day, which was virtually a vote of want of confidence in the ministry, was adopted; and, shortly afterward, M. Ollivier announced that he had conferred with the empress, and that, with the consent of the emperor, General Montauban, Duke of Palikao, had been charged with the formation of a new cabinet. On Wednesday the names of the new ministry were announced: General Cousin Montauban, Minister of War; M. Chevreau, Minister of the Interior; M. Magne, Minister of Finance; M. Clément Duvernois, Minister of Commerce and Agriculture; Admiral Rigault de Genouilly, Minister of Marine; Baron J. David, Minister of Public Works; Prince de la Tour d'Auvergne, Minister of Foreign Affairs; M. Grandperret, Minister of Justice; M. Jules Brame, Minister of Public Instruction; and M. Russon-Billault, President of the Council of State.

These events in Paris already very distinctly foreshadowed a revolution, and even the nations not involved in the war, began to look aghast at its astounding developments. The power which had for some time claimed to be, and to a certain extent, was supposed to be, the first military country of Europe, had, within three weeks from the commencement of a war of its own choosing, been brought to the verge of national humiliation and disgrace. That army, which with its chassepot rifle and its unrivalled organization and discipline, assumed to control the destinies of Europe, was found, in its first hour of trial, to be almost as imbecile as the troops of Austria when led by Mack, and commanded in chief by the Aulick Council of Vienna. The explanation is to be found in the difference between the nominal and the real condition of the French army; between what its commissariat was, and was supposed to be; and between the assumed and the actual military capacity of the marshals of the empire.

The first error of Louis Napoleon was his mistaken estimate of the number of his own available troops and those of his opponents. He flattered himself that his soldiers outnumbered his enemies, when in fact, he was outnumbered by nearly two to one. And then, instead of taking the initiative of invasion, and striking a telling blow before Prussia was prepared for it, he failed to have his legions ready for action on the frontier until more than a week after the critical moment had passed.

His plan of campaign was good. Three corps at Thionville, St. Alvold and Bitche, in the front line immediately on the frontier; two corps at Metz and Strasbourg, in a second line; two corps in reserve above Nancy; and an eighth corps at Belfort. With the aid of the railways, all these troops could be massed in a few days for an attack, either across the Saar from Lorraine, or across the Rhine from Alsace, striking either north or east, as the case might require. But this was a disposition for attack. For defence, it was faulty. The first condition of a disposition of troops for defence, is to have the advance so far in front of the main body, that news of an attack can be received in time to concentrate before the enemy arrives. Thus, if one day's march is needed to bring the wings to support the centre, the advanced guard should be one day's march in front of the centre. But in this case, the three corps of Ladmirault, Frossard and De Failly, and afterward a part of MacMahon's also, were close on the frontier, and yet spread on a line from Wissembourg to Sierck—at least ninety miles. Two days, at least, were needed to bring these wings to the centre; and yet, even when the Prussians were known to be within a few miles in front, no steps were taken to shorten the line, or to push forward an advanced guard. It was almost a matter of course, that the corps so situated should be destroyed in detail. Then came the blunder of posting one division of MacMahon's corps east of the Vosges, at Wissembourg, actually inviting an attack by superior forces. Douay's defeat at Wissembourg brought on MacMahon's next blunder in trying to retrieve the fight east of the Vosges, thereby separating the right wing still further from the centre, and exposing his line of communication with it. While the right wing, MacMahon's, and portions at least of Failly's and Canrobert's corps, were crushed at Woerth; the centre, Frossard and two divisions of Bazaine, were severely beaten before Saarbrück. The remainder of the troops were too far away to render any assistance. Thus, the whole disposition, so far, indicated nothing but indecision, hesitation, vacillation in the most decisive moment of the campaign.

And all this time, what estimate of their enemies' qualities were the French soldiers permitted to have? On the last moment, indeed, the emperor informed them, that they were about to face one of the best armies of Europe; but for preceding years, they had been elaborately taught to despise the Prussians as soldiers, and to regard Prussia as unprepared for war. And this *teaching* was not limited to the rank and file of the French army. A captain in the regular service, who was a man of education, and who had been made prisoner at the "baptism of fire" affair, spent two days with the Prussian eighth corps. He was astounded at what he saw, after what he had been taught to believe. He wrote thus his first impressions on being brought to the Prussian camp:

"There were outposts under the trees, battalions massed along the roads; and, in every respect, I found what distinguishes an excellent army, as well as a nation powerfully organized for war. The demeanor of the men, the subordination of their smallest movements to chiefs maintaining a discipline far superior to ours; the patriotic expressions to which they gave vent; above all, the moral worth of the non-commissioned officers—these, and a thousand other things, which the eye of a military man catches at a glance, showed me of what this nation is capable in the hour of danger."

The same writer said, in reference to the French commissariat:

"The distribution of provisions for the campaign, did not begin until the first of August; and when it began, the men were found to be short of field flasks, cooking tins, and other camp utensils. The meat was putrid, and the bread musty," etc., etc.

This might have been expected under a regime which was forced to yield bounties to its supporters by all the known means of jobbery; for this war, according to M. Rouher's confession, was provided for long before it was declared, and the laying in of stores and equipments had been going on for many months—but, as it proved, on the system of furnishing the poorest quality for the highest price. These things, all taken together, explain the delay in the French movements and the defeats which followed them.

It is a remarkable fact, and it may be mentioned here as well as elsewhere, that General Trochu, in his well-known work "L'Armée Francaise en 1867," exposed the defects of the entire military organization of France; so that the emperor had full notice and warning of what at last proved fatal to him. General Trochu says, among other things,

"In France, after the campaigns of the republic and the empire, men whose experience was considerable, united for the purpose of furnishing the army with a system of military administration, the principles and mechanism of which had a high practical value in reference to war. . . . In the system of these great administrators the direction and control of the various services were carried on side by side, without being confounded with one another. . .

"The directors, the controllers, and the executive officers, were men of business, who had been initiated into business from the first steps in their career, and educated from an early period for the performance of their functions in the army by actual duty, by exchanges and by being specially brought into contact in every way with the details of those functions. They lived from the age of eighteen or twenty in an atmosphere of business, having special reference to the administration of the army.

"The members of the central department, and the agents of the administrative services, commenced their career as students, learning from their youth what was always to be their specialty.

"Under the system which prevails now-a-days all such functionaries, without exception, before entering upon their public business, have been through long years—the years of youth, in which men learn and study with most fruit—officers and non-commissioned officers in the army. With them a public examination takes the place of ten or fifteen years of practical and professional experience, what do I say—of thirty or forty years of such practical experience, for we see generals of brigade, not unfrequently at the last stage of their career, becoming intendant-generals, that is to say, the arbiters for the next war, of the existence of our troops in the field. It is idle, I think, to search through the whole scope of the public affairs of France for a more astounding specimen of blunder."

The same high authority says that through the failure of the intendance in the Italian campaign, whole divisions of the French army were often for days together without bread; and that in the Crimea the army must have perished but that a well-known house of business in Marseilles, stepped forward to sustain a paralyzed department. Again he says, that in consequence of being thrown upon the intendance for its supplies, the medical department of the French army, both in Italy and the Crimea, was continually at its wit's ends. The surgeon-in-chief of the guard, writing from Alexandria on the 19th of May, 1859, says:

"No litters, no ambulances, no wagons. I have begged hard for chloroform and perchloride of iron; nothing has as yet been given me."

He writes again from Valeggio on the 7th of July:

"For the last fortnight, some regiments have only once or twice had bread, and even then it was mouldy, and of a very bad quality. Wine has completely failed; there has been scarcely any issue of it."

On the 2nd of July, an officer wrote to the emperor himself from Castiglione:

"Sire, the wounded of Solferino, who were wounded here, have never yet had their wounds dressed, for want of supplies. We have lint, but no linen, no sheets, no sugar, no provisions."

Matters were quite as sad in the Crimea, perhaps worse. It is stated in the *Gazette Hebdomadaire*, in which some recent articles on the medical statistics of the French army have attracted great attention, that whereas in the English army 33.9 per cent., and in the American army 40.2 per cent. of the surgical operations in war proved fatal, in the French army, the proportions were, during the Italian campaign 63.9 per cent., during that in the Crimea 72.8; and the cause assigned for such excessive mortality, is the supremacy—the omnipotence—of the intendance militaire, which, from a medical point of view, is in a condition of absolute incapacity.

With such criticisms upon the French military service as Trochu's, unheeded, and the same errors maintained and exaggerated, which were so fatal in the Crimea and Italy, it is impossible to doubt that the French army was beaten before it saw an enemy. But it throws a strange light on the character of Napoleon III. as a ruler, to know that the publication by Trochu of his unanswerable reasons for reform, was regarded by the emperor as an insult; and was followed, not by abolishing abuses, but by withdrawing his confidence from the man who pointed them out.

Immediately after the Prussian victory at Speicheren, on the 6th of August, King William issued the following proclamation in French, to the French people:

"The Emperor Napoleon having made by land and sea an attack on the German nation, which desired and still desires to live in peace with the French people, I have assumed the command of the German armies to repel this aggression, and I have been led, by military circumstances, to cross the frontier of France. I am waging war against French soldiers, not against French citizens. The latter, consequently, will continue to enjoy security for their persons and property, so long as they themselves shall not, by hostile attempts against the German troops, deprive me of the right of according them my protection."

After the defeats and retreats of the French, as now above narrated, an official announcement showed that, on the 9th of August, Marshal Bazaine was at Metz with one hundred and thirty thousand men; Marshal MacMahon at Saverne, with fifty thousand; and Canrobert at Nancy with fifty thousand. On the same day, a general advance of the Prussians toward Metz was commenced; and the South German forces, nearly sixty thousand strong, assembled around Strasbourg, and made preparations for besieging it.

During the day, on the 10th of August, the French troops were all falling back to the line of the Mozelle, harassed by the Prussian cavalry, which had already passed Saarunion, Falquemont, and Les Etangs, capturing on their way stores of all kinds, and railway trains. They also took the small fortress of Hutzelstein, in the Vosges, which the French had evacuated, leaving the guns and provisions. MacMahon, after a brief halt at Saverne, abandoned it at night, and it was immediately occupied by the Prussians.

On the 11th of August, Strasbourg was completely invested by the Prussians; and General Beyer who commanded the garrison, was summoned to surrender; but he refused. On the same day, the *Moniteur* of Paris, gave the following account of the death of General Douay, at the battle of Wissembourg:

"The General was from the beginning in the thickest of the fight. When he saw the day was lost, after he had done all that he could to retrieve it, when not even a battalion was left him, he called his aids one by one, gave them orders and sent them away.

"As soon as the last one was gone, the general, spurring his horse, rode some distance to the front, dismounted, and taking a pistol from the holster shot the animal. Then turning around, he slowly walked towards the enemy. His soldiers vainly tried to stop him. Amid the terrible firing he deliberately walked on. The retreating soldiers, aroused by the spectacle, turned again upon the enemy, but fell in heaps around their general who still pressed forward. Another tremendous discharge from the enemy, and General Douay, almost alone, fell dead."

And also on the same day the following proceedings, among others, took place in the Corps Legislatif:

Count Palikao announced that the armament of Paris would be complete in eight days. He expressed the fullest confidence in Marshal Bazaine, and counted on a victory to efface the traces of recent reverses.

M. Glaiz-Bizoin demanded that the nation should make no treaty of peace so long as the enemy was on French soil.

Minister Magne proposed that the amount of the loan, which the government has been authorized to make, be increased from five hundred millions to a thousand millions; that the bills of the bank of France be legal tenders; that the bank shall not be obliged to redeem them in gold or silver, but that the paper circulation of the bank be limited to a thousand millions of francs, eight hundred millions to be applicable to the use of the government; that similar privileges be conferred on the bank of Algeria, whose paper circulation is limited to eighteen millions.

The minister declared the financial measure urgent, and it was carried by a vote of 251 to 1.

On the 12th of August, the *London Times* uttered this prophecy: "The pride of France is wounded and her prestige is dimmed. He who brought this on her must suffer for it. Victorious, or discrowned, is Napoleon's alternative on the next battle field." On the same day, M. Thiers said that the empire was at an end and that a republic was inevitable. And the Paris *Pays* published a letter from Charles Desmoulins, dated at

Nancy, denouncing the emperor's bad generalship. He says: "MacMahon, gallantly struggling, was beaten for lack of support, though there were multitudes of armed Frenchmen at hand eager to save him. The passage of the Rhine was undefended. The commissariat was utterly inadequate, and the soldiers were compelled to eat sour fruit and raw vegetables and take the consequences. Prussia to-day has Alsace; to-morrow she will have Lorraine. The people are desperate; the soldiers believe themselves betrayed and clamor for a leader."

Lieutenant-General Sheridan, of the United States Army, was announced, this day, as having joined himself to the Prussian staff for observation. He was courteously received and welcomed by the King of Prussia.

On the 13th of August, General Trochu assumed command at Chalons, and General Canrobert replaced D'Hilliers in command of the army at Paris. On the same day, MacMahon retreated from Nancy across the Mozelle to the fortress of Toul, and destroyed the fine bridge of seven arches, which spanned the river. The Crown Prince's army, following closely at MacMahon's heels, took possession of Nancy.

On Sunday, August 14th, at Paris, Count Palikao issued an address to the troops, in which he blames them for firing too quickly. At Wissembourg he says they used more ammunition in one day than the Prussians would in three days. The Marshal reminds the soldiers that they are now on the grand line of defence from Thionville to Metz and Nancy, and they must hold their ground. Back of this is the line of the Meuse; then that of Champagne; then the Arennes; then the line of rivers illustrated by the campaign of 1814; and behind all this is Paris; and behind Paris is all France, with 4,000,000 of armed men and 1,000,000,000 of treasure. On the same day, the *Journal Officiel* of Paris said: One of the public journals of this city still presumes to doubt that real work is going on for the armament and defence of Paris. Although it may be an act of treason to speak thus in face of the enemy, such insinuations impose the necessity of a reply, notwithstanding the danger of doing so. All the material necessary for the armament of Paris is in Paris itself. More than 600 cannon are already mounted on the walls of those forts which are likely to be first threatened with attack, and the work of placing other pieces in position continues without interruption day and night. Yesterday 7,500 workmen were engaged in cutting off the streets leading into Paris. This work has been completed, and nothing remains but to close up the openings in the walls and place drawbridges in position. Thousands of laborers are occupied outside the walls on earthworks, mines, ditches, etc., which are to connect and complete the network of fortifications around the capital.

About five o'clock in the evening of the same day, the advance guard of the Seventh Prussian army corps attacked the rear guard of the retiring French army near Metz. The latter was gradually reinforced from the fortress; and, more Prussian troops arriving to take part in the conflict, a bloody and obstinately fought battle ensued. The French were thrown back to the glacis of the outworks; when, with the approach of night, the Prussians retired to the ground where they had bivouacked the night before.

On Monday, the 15th of August, late in the afternoon, the First and Seventh Prussian army corps advanced again toward Metz and attacked the French under its walls. Again, a sanguinary conflict ensued. The French were at length driven within the city, with a loss of 4000 men. On the same day, a body of Bavarian troops, after a short bombardment, captured fortress Marsal, a small town northeast of Nancy, and found sixty pieces of artillery in the lines.

On Tuesday morning, August 16th, Marshal Bazaine, while attempting to fall back from Metz to Verdun, was attacked at Pont-à-Mousson by the Fifth Prussian Corps and forced to face about. The Prussians maintained their attack against four French corps and among them the Imperial Guard, for six hours, when they were reinforced by the First Corps. The French were again driven in upon Metz, with a loss of 2000 prisoners, two eagles and seven cannon.

The incidents of Wednesday, the 17th of August, were almost a repetition of those of Tuesday. A large body of French troops in retreat from Metz were driven as far as Gravelotte, when night put an end to the conflict.

On Thursday, the 18th, a battle was fought at Gravelotte, which, up to that time, was the bloodiest and most obstinately contested action of the war. The French were posted along the heights beyond a wide and deep ravine, whence their artillery swept every point of approach. The French, therefore, had every advantage of position, and the entire force on each side was nearly equal. King William commanded the Prussians in person, and Generals Sheridan and Forsyth watched the battle from Count Bismarck's carriage. The action lasted for nine hours, and the killed and wounded on the Prussian side were not less than 10,000. The losses of the French in the battles of the week, commencing with Sunday, August 14th, in killed, wounded, and prisoners, exceeded 50,000. The dispatch of King William at nine o'clock P. M., on Thursday, showed the result of the battle of Gravelotte. It was in these words:

"The French army, occupying a very strong position to the west of Metz, was to-day attacked under my leadership, and after nine hours' fighting, was completely defeated, cut off from its communications with Paris, and driven back toward Metz."

Bazaine with his army being thus isolated in Metz, and the Prussians having not only troops enough to hold Bazaine where he was, and also to send a separate army in pursuit of MacMachon, but having besides at least two corps ready to march upon Paris—now found the road to the French capital open before them.

On the 21st of August, General Trochu was appointed Governor of Paris, and he issued a proclamation expressive of the serious emergency in which both he and the capital were placed.

On the 22d of August, the Crown Prince of Prussia, with an army of 150,000 men commenced his march toward Paris. The London newspapers expressed the opinion that nothing, now, could interrupt his progress to the capital. On the same day, the *Journal Officiel* of Paris announced, that—

"The military situation is such that this circumstance need not alarm, still less discourage. If the enemy has happened for a moment to hold Bazaine's army near Metz, he has done so at the cost of the greatest sacrifices, and is at the same time compelled to keep there the greater part of his own army, namely the corps of Prince Frederick Charles and General Steinmetz. What in the meanwhile will the corps of the Prince Royal do? March directly on Paris? or join the other two corps in the effort to crush the army of Bazaine? The latter supposition is the more probable; but they must take into account an army re-united at Chalons or some other point, under the orders of Marshal MacMahon, an army which may place the Prussians in the same situation they boast they have put the army of Bazaine; that is to say, cut them off and block them up. Let us with confidence await events. In any case, supposing our armies are defeated at Metz or at Chalons, the Prussians may expect to encounter at Paris other and greater difficulties than any they have met with up to the present time. Paris they may be sure will defend herself to the last drop of blood, to the last cartridge. She will thus give entire France all the time it needs to come to her defence, and then there will be no hope for those who have come to brave our ramparts. Not one of them will return to his country."

On the 23d of August the following official statement of the Prussian forces was published in Berlin:

"The German forces in France have undergone a partial reorganization, and as reinforced and redistributed will go into battle in the following order:

"The first army, under the command of General Steinmetz, is composed of the First, Seventh, Eighth and Ninth Prussian army corps, amounting in all to 100,000 infantry and 28,000 cavalry.

"The second army, under the command of Prince Frederick Charles, composed of the Second, Third, Fourth, Tenth and Twelfth Prussian army corps, the corps of the Prussian Guards, the Royal Saxon corps and the division of the Grand Duchy of Hesse. This is the strongest of the three armies. It contains forty-eight regiments of infantry, with three batteries each, and four regiments of infantry, with two batteries each, and thirty-four regiments of cavalry. Aggregate in round numbers, 220,000 men and 600 guns.

"The third army, commanded by the Crown Prince, is formed into two Bavarian army corps, under Generals Tann and Hartmann, containing each eight regiments of infantry, five battalions of riflemen, and five regiments of cavalry; one mixed corps of Baden and Wurtemberg troops, commanded by General Von Werder, and consisting of eight regiments of infantry, two battalions of riflemen, four regiments of cavalry, and nine batteries of artillery, belonging to Wurtemberg, and six regiments of infantry and three of cavalry, eight batteries of artillery belonging to Baden; also the Fifth and Eleventh Prussian army corps, containing sixteen infantry and sixteen cavalry regiments and thirty batteries of artillery.

"The grand total of the German forces in France is 520,000 men, divided into sixteen army corps. Up to this time 300,000 of the Landwehr have entered Alsace and Lorraine to invest and occupy places in the rear, and relieve the regular soldiers of those duties, so that they may join their own regiments in front. Orders have been issued to disband the veteran reserves which were called out at the commencement of the war."

On the 24th of August, the Crown Prince arrived with his army at Sezanne, a town of about 5000 inhabitants, about sixty-five miles from Paris.

On the 25th, the Paris *Journal Officiel* announced that, "the sum of all the news received at the Ministry of the Interior, is that the Prussians push their reconnaisances into the Department of Marne, and even into the town of Chalons. The prefect of the Department of Upper Marne announces that a part of the northern arrondissement of Vasy is occupied by the Prussian forces.

"Orders have been given that the march of the Prussians be opposed by every obstacle which the patriotism of the people can suggest, in addition to the systematic measures which will be executed under the direction of engineer officers sent out by the government.

"The grain mills of the valley of the Seine and Marne, and all of their contents which could not be removed, have been burned. The country people are destroying the roads and doing all they can to impede the march of the Prussian armies. They will burn or destroy such provisions as they are unable to remove or store out of the reach of the Prussians. The scouts of the Prussians have made their appearance at Chalons-sur-Marne, and also at St. Menehould. The prefect of the latter town and all the railway officials have left the place."

August 26th.—There was a severe artillery battle at Kehl and Strasbourg, continued through the night. A part of the citadel and arsenal in Strasbourg were destroyed, and many fires took place from the vigorous bombardment.

General Trochu declared that all persons devoid of the means of subsistence, whether natives or foreigners, and all those whose presence contributes to the danger of public order, or is inimical to the security of persons or property, or whose acts tend to impede the measures of the authorities for the defence and general safety of the city, are to be summarily expelled from Paris. During a discussion in the Corps Legislatif, Jules Favre informed the deputies that, in his opinion, the recent French misfortunes were due to the incapacity of the leaders. After denouncing them, he demanded to know whether the army was fighting for the nation, or for a dynasty. This day, the task of removing the principal paintings and other works of art from the Louvre was begun.

August 27th.—The Prussian army which was advancing on Paris, had its head-quarters at Bar-le-Duc. The advance reached a point about midway between Chalons and Epernay. No further opposition to the march was anticipated.

August 28th.—The garrison of Vitry surrendered to the Prussians. The victors captured sixteen guns and about one thousand prisoners.

August 30th.—The Prussians, with King William in command, attacked MacMahon at Beaumont, and drove him under the walls of Sedan. Twenty pieces of artillery, eleven mitrailleurs and upward of seven thousand prisoners fell into the hands of the Prussians. In regard to all these disasters of the French, it was authoritatively stated, that the French, at the beginning of the war, were so confident of victory, that they made no systematic arrangements to save their baggage in case they were compelled to retreat; and hence, in almost every instance, it was abandoned as a matter of course. This proved a serious aggravation to the otherwise heavy losses of the French army.

From the 30th of August to the 2d of September, Bazaine, with several corps, made repeated attempts to break out from Metz in a northerly direction, with a view to cöoperating with MacMahon. Under the chief command of Prince Charles Frederic, General Manteuffel defeated all their efforts, ending in the battle of Noisseville. The French were finally driven back into Metz after sustaining very heavy losses, chiefly in killed, wounded and prisoners.

September 1st.—One day of respite was gained by the French troops, after their defeat at Beaumont and their retreat to Sedan. On Thursday, the 1st of September, the Prussian army, with King William in command, attended by Bismarck, Von Roon, Von Moltke and a numerous staff, including the American Generals Sheridan and Forsyth, lay around the village of Chevenge, about three miles from Sedan. The king and his staff occupied a hill adjoining the village; and from that elevated position they commanded a view not only of the town of Sedan, but of the valley of the Meuse for many miles around it, including, of course, the two hostile armies. The number of the Prussian troops was about two hundred and forty thousand; and that of the French about one hundred thousand. The latter were under the command of General Wimpffen, MacMahon having been severely wounded in the action at Beaumont. The Prussian, Bavarian and Saxon corps stood in the form of a crescent around Sedan, with its two horns toward the Belgian frontier. About twelve o'clock in the day, this crescent became a circle, completely enclosing Sedan and the French army,—the junction between the Prussians on the left wing, and the Saxons on the right having been by that hour effected near the road to Bouillon, and not far from La Chapelle. This circle grew smaller as the battle continued.

The battle began at six o'clock in the morning, and by nine o'clock, the batteries on each side having got within easy range of each other, the contest became animated. By twelve o'clock, the musketry fire in the valley behind Sedan had grown to one continued rattle, broken only by the loud growling of the mitrailleurs, which played with deadly effect on the advancing Saxon and Bavarian columns. General Sheridan was heard to remark that he had never before known such a well-sustained and long-continued fire of small arms. It made itself heard above the roar of the artillery.

At twelve o'clock, a Prussian battery of six guns near La Vilette, had silenced two French batteries at the foot of the hill, near the village of Floing. At ten minutes past twelve, the French infantry, no longer supported by their artillery, were compelled to retire from Floing; and, as already mentioned, the junction of the Prussian and Saxon wings, by completing the circle around the French, showed, at this moment, that all chance of escape for the French was lost. At half-past twelve, clouds of retreating French infantry were seen on the hill between Floing and Sedan, enfiladed by a Prussian battery in front of St. Menges. For a quarter of an hour, the hill was literally covered by the Frenchmen, running for their lives. At one o'clock, another French column was seen in full retreat to the right of Sedan, on the road leading from Bazeilles to the wood of La Garenne. Almost at the same moment, a third French column was seen moving up a broad grass-road through La Garenne, immediately above Sedan, to support the troops defending the Bazeilles ravine, north-east of the town. The French batteries on the edge of the wood and above it, now opened a vigorous fire on the advancing Prussian columns, whose evident intention was, to storm the hill north-west of La Garenne. The Prussians were compelled to shift their ground continually to avoid this storm of balls, until they were in sufficient strength for the final rush. Shortly afterward, the Prussian skirmishers appeared on the crest of the hill, flanking the French position. But they were few in number, and General Sheridan exclaimed, "Ah! the beggars are too weak: they cannot hold that position against all those French." And so it proved; for the French rushed upon them, at least six to one, and drove them down the hill toward the reinforcements which were hurrying to their support. In a few minutes, they returned in greater force, but still terribly inferior to the French masses. "Good heavens!" again exclaimed General Sheridan, "the French cuirassiers are there, and preparing to charge those Prussians." And, at the word, a regiment of cuirassiers, their helmets and breast-plates flashing in the bright sun, formed in squadrons and dashed down on the Prussians. Without deigning even to form in line—the Prussians never form in squares—the Prussians, at a distance of about a hundred yards, delivered one terrible volley, and proceeded to load and fire independently, on the dense mass of horsemen. The men and their horses rolled to the ground by hundreds; and the survivors, not venturing a collision with these terrible marksmen, drew bridle and retreated. The moment that they turned, the Prussians actually gave chase to them at the "double-quick;" a thing not often, if ever before, seen on a battle field. The French infantry now came forward, delivering the fire of their chassepots as they marched. The Prussians waited under this storm of bullets until their opponents were within the before mentioned distance of a hundred yards, when they again discharged that fatal volley, which stopped the French advance and drove them after their retreating cavalry. The Prussians, strengthened by reinforcements, then pressed on to the crest of the hill where they established themselves in force. It was now half-past one. Presently, a regiment of French carabiniers rode up to the Prussian position; but they met the same fate as the cuirassiers and the infantry, and the Prussians following their retreat, advanced their line about two hundred yards nearer to the French position. Suddenly, they divided themselves into two separate bodies, leaving a space of a hundred yards between them. The object of this movement was not visible at the moment, but very shortly it appeared that by some means their companions in the rear had forced up that steep height two pieces of artillery, which at once were brought into the designated space, and opened fire on the Frenchmen. Something at this point was amiss with the French infantry; for, although they still outnumbered the Prussians by at least two to one, they remained standing fast in column, sinking rapidly before the Prussian fire, and doing nothing to retrieve the day. By this time, the cuirassiers had rallied, and returning toward the crest of the hill, made straight for the two guns. The Prussians formed in line, as if on parade, and delivered a volley that destroyed almost the face of the leading squadron. The cuirassiers at once fell back and retreated, followed by their own infantry, toward Sedan. The Prussian tiralleurs now seemed to rise from the ground, so quickly did they cover the whole of the hill, and the whole mass joined in pursuit of the French. The French cavalry made one desperate attempt to check their enemies, but the day for breaking infantry with cavalry seemed to have past, and the Prussians pressed on. It is very remarkable that the French had no artillery on the hill to support their infantry. In the Bazeille ravine, however, they had both artillery and mitrailleurs, and the Bavarian divisions in that part of the field suffered fearfully from their shot. A little after two o'clock, there was a lull in the firing along the entire lines, and General Sheridan remarked that the French were hopelessly defeated. Some one inquired of Bismarck if he thought that the emperor was in Sedan. "Oh, no," was the reply: "Napoleon is not very wise, but he is not quite so foolish as to put himself in Sedan just now." It soon appeared, however, that the count had misjudged the case.

The cannonading was renewed at intervals until about five o'clock, when all firing was entirely suspended. Almost immediately afterward, a French officer, escorted by two Uhlans, came up the steep bridle-path at a hard trot, carrying a white duster on a faggot stick as a flag of truce. He proved to be a French colonel asking for terms of surrender. After a very brief conference between the king and General Von Moltke, the messenger was told that in a matter so important as the surrender of probably eighty thousand men, and an important fortress, an officer of higher rank must be commissioned to receive the terms. "You are, therefore," the reply concluded, "to return to Sedan, and tell the governor of the town to report himself immediately to the King of Prussia. If he does not arrive in an hour, our guns will open again. You may tell him that no terms other than an unconditional surrender will be accepted." At half-past six, the French General Reilly rode up with a letter for the King of Prussia. As he approached, the guard-royal of cuirassiers and dragoons drew up in line two deep behind the king. In front of the guard was the staff, and ten yards in front of them stood his majesty to receive the French general—who, to the astonishment of every one, proved to be the bearer of a letter from Napoleon to King William. The letter was in these words: "Ne pouvant pas mourir à la tête de mon armée, je viens mettue mon épée aux pieds de votre majesté:" that is, As I cannot die at the head of my army, I lay my sword at the feet of your majesty. A miserable piece of melo-dramatic affectation! and a very poor imitation of the letter addressed by Napoleon I. to the Prince Regent of England, when he surrendered himself on board the Bellerophon. *Why*, Napoleon III. "could not die," as thousands of his misguided soldiers did, sword in hand with his face to the foe, does not appear either in his brief dispatch, or on any ready reflections upon it.

A brief consultation ensued between the king, the crown prince, Bismarck, Moltke, and Von Roon. The king then sat down on a rush-bottomed chair and wrote a note on another chair held by two aides-de-camp, requesting the emperor to come to the king's head-quarters at Vendres, the next morning. The king himself handed this note to General Reilly, who stood uncovered to receive it.

Hostilities were at once suspended; and the next day the capitulation was concluded with General Wimpffen, Marshal MacMahon, being too severely wounded to act in the matter. Eighty thousand men laid down their arms and became prisoners of war. The King of Prussia sent the two following telegrams to the queen:

"Before Sedan, September 2d, 1:22 P. M. A capitulation, whereby the whole army at Sedan are prisoners of war has just been concluded with General Wimpffen, who was in command instead of the wounded Marshal MacMahon. The emperor surrendered only himself, as he had no command, and left everything to the Regency at Paris. I shall appoint his place of residence after I have had an interview with him. What a course events have taken by God's guidance!"

"Varennes, September 4th, 8 A. M. What a thrilling moment was that of my meeting with Napoleon! He was cast down, but dignified in his bearing, and resigned. I gave him Wilhelmshohe, near Cassel, as the place where he will stay. Our meeting took place in a small castle in front of the western glacis of Sedan. From there, I rode through the ranks of our army around Sedan. The reception by the troops—you may imagine it!—was indescribable. May God aid us further!"

And in a letter to the queen, King William said further—"You know by my telegrams the great historical event. It is like a dream, although we saw it. I bow before God, who alone chose my army and those of my allies, and who ordered us to be the instruments of His will."

General de Failly was killed at the battle of Sedan. It was reported that he had been shot by his own soldiers; but he was, in fact, killed by a shell.

The emperor, with a suite of about one hundred persons, and the imperial horses and carriages, arrived at Bouillon on Saturday, and on Sunday went by railway to Verviers, by way of Libramont and Liége. The King of Prussia and the emperor had jointly asked the Belgian government to authorize their passage through Belgian territory, as the emperor wished to avoid being seen by his own soldiers.

Up to Saturday night, the news of the emperor's surrender was not known to the Parisians, but statements had been made in the Chambers with the object of preparing the public mind for the worst. In the Senate, Baron Jerome David admitted that Marshal Bazaine had failed in an attempt to disengage himself from the armies which hemmed him in at Metz, and that MacMahon's attempt to extend a hand to Bazaine "has terminated in a manner unfortunate for our arms." He added, that other information had been received, but as it was from Prussian sources, the government did not deem it worthy of belief. In the Corps Legislatif, the Count Palikao said that grave events had occurred, and that for some time to come, the junction between MacMahon and Bazaine could not be effected. He said a rumour was circulated of MacMahon's being wounded, but it was not authentic. He, however, added, "The position is serious. We must no longer dissimulate. We are determined to appeal to the vigorous forces of the nation. We shall act with the greater energy, and shall cease our efforts only when every Prussian is expelled from the country." M. Jules Favre declared that all parties were unanimous in their determination to defend France to the last gasp. He concluded by attacking the imperial régime, and proposed to concentrate all power in the hands of General Trochu. Count Palikao and several of the deputies protested against the language of M. Jules Favre.

As soon as the tenor of these communications became known outside of the Chambers, the popular agitation was intense, and as yet the surrender of the emperor was not known. At eight o'clock an assemblage of about six thousand persons sent a deputation to General Trochu, to demand that he should proclaim the *déchéance* of the dynasty; but the general replied that he was a soldier, and that his oath bound him not to act against the law. He said it was for the Chamber to comply with their demands; but they might rely on his defending Paris. The crowd received his reply with shouts of "Abdication! France forever! Trochu forever!"

It was not until Sunday morning, September 4th, that the whole truth was announced in the *Journal Officiel*, which published the following proclamation, issued by the Council of Ministers:

"Frenchmen! a great misfortune has befallen the country. After three days of heroic struggles, kept up by the army of Marshal MacMahon against three hundred thousand enemies, forty thousand of our soldiers have been made prisoners. General Wimpffen, who had taken command of the army, replacing Marshal MacMahon, who was grievously wounded, has signed a capitulation. This cruel reverse does not daunt our courage. Paris is now in a state of defence. The military forces of the country are being organized. Within a few days a new army will be under the walls of Paris, and another is forming on the banks of the Loire. Your patriotism, your concord, your energy, will save France. The emperor has been made prisoner in this contest."

These statements were, however, communicated to the Corps Legislatif some hours earlier. A midnight session of the Chamber was held, when the Count Palikao related the news that was the next morning promulgated by the proclamation above quoted. M. Jules Favre then rose and submitted these propositions:

I. Louis Napoleon Bonaparte and his dynasty are declared to be divested of the powers conferred upon them by the constitution.

II. A governing commission, consisting of — members, shall be appointed by the Corps Legislatif, which commission shall be invested with all the powers of government, and which shall have for its special mission to offer every resistance to invasion, and to expel the enemy from the territory.

III. General Trochu is continued in his functions as Governor-General of the City of Paris.

The only remark on these propositions was made by M. Pinard, who said that the Chamber had not the power to decree a forfeiture of authority; and the sitting was adjourned until noon on Sunday.

As soon as the sitting was over, the ministers went to the empress, and told her that they felt themselves bound in honor to stand by the dynasty, but that, in their judgment, all hope for her and her family was over. The empress, however, desired that an effort should be made. General Trochu was consulted; but he said that he was responsible only for the defence of Paris, and that he could do nothing for the dynasty. It was then decided that Count Palikao should propose a Provisional Government, with himself at its head, which would assume power by a decree of the empress. In the meantime the deputies of the Left Centre had held a meeting, at which they agreed to support a proposal of M. Thiers, which, without saying as much in words, partially suspended the empire, and gave power to a Committee of National Defence, in which all parties would be represented. General Trochu promised to advise the Garde Nationale to go down to the Chamber and to support this combination. The Left, too, held other meetings, and agreed to insist on *déchéance*, and the nomination of a Provisional Government of nine, five of whom should be deputies of Paris. Things stood thus when, at nine o'clock, President Schneider announced that the sitting of the Chamber had commenced. General Palikao had surrounded the palace of the Corps Legislatif with troops; a body of the Gardes de Paris held the approaches of all the bridges; about three thousand troops were in the court of the Tuileries; a few regiments were stationed at their barracks, but were ready to act; and the remainder of the soldiers in Paris were left to their own inspirations. At the commencement of the session, it was evident that the Right, composed of official candidates, were awed and could not be depended on; and the troops were so thoroughly disgusted at the surrender of the emperor, that they would not act against the National Guard; they therefore fell back and were replaced by the latter. The three propositions of Count Palikao, M. Thiers, and M. Jules Favre, were then submitted to the Chamber, and they were each declared urgent, and were collectively referred to a committee. The sitting was then temporarily suspended.

On the resumption of the sitting, the galleries, and afterward the floor of the House, were invaded by the people, demanding the deposition of the emperor and the proclaiming of a republic. M. Gambetta came forward and informed the people that the Chamber was deliberating on the *déchéance.* The announcement was received with great enthusiasm, cries of "Vive la France!" and national songs. Inside the chamber there was an attempt to get through business amid cries of "Down with Bonaparte," etc., etc. President Schneider then took the chair, and addressed a few words to the members, both Right and Left, but M. Brame was the only minister who faced the storm. M. Schneider protested against the invasion of the chamber, and declared that the House could not deliberate under intimidation. There were fierce cries for the republic, and again the chamber was invaded, the benches were taken by storm, and the president was driven from his chair. M. Jules Favre then managed to get possession of the tribune, and he proclaimed the downfall of the Bonaparte family. M. Gambetta confirmed his words, and stated that in fact the *déchéance* had been voted in committee by an immense majority—the vote having been one hundred and ninety-five against eighteen.

The deputies of Paris, accompanied by the mob, then proceeded to the Hotel de Ville, which they were allowed to enter without opposition, and there M. Gambetta proclaimed the republic. The crowd afterward rushed through the streets, singing national songs, shouting "Vive la République?" and embracing and kissing each other in manifestations of exuberant joy. In this way the second empire came to an end, without bloodshed or violence. The only mischief done by the mob was the destruction of a picture of the emperor at the Hotel de Ville, and the pulling down and destroying of the busts and portraits of the imperial family, and all emblems of imperialism wherever they were seen.

As soon as the Empress Eugénie was aware of the extent and result of this revolution, she quitted the palace of the Tuileries by the entrance on the river, accompanied by but one servant, in disguise. She took a private carriage and went to the railway station in time to catch a train just starting for Belgium. The haste of her departure was shown by the appearance of the rooms, after her flight was discovered. Trunks were piled about in various places, band-boxes and articles of apparel were lying about in disorder, and the bed was not made. The official person who remained in charge of the palace said, that all those whom the empress had favored during her reign had deserted her, and not one remained to see her departure.

The circumstances attending the escape and flight of the Duc de Grammont, after he heard of the surrender at Sedan, are like some of the narratives of the old revolution. The case is thus related in the London newspapers:

"The Duc de Grammont, as Minister for Foreign Affairs, naturally heard of the emperor's surrender a day before the news was published in Paris. He saw at once that flight was necessary, as the wrath of the mob was sure to be turned against the ministry, who were responsible for the war. He accordingly went to his banker's to provide himself with money and various securities, but was informed that the partner who had charge of his affairs was in the country, whither the Duc pursued him. The partner was found engaged in burying his property in his garden, but returned to Paris and delivered up to the Duc de Grammont the papers and money which were required. On the next day the bad news was published and the minister fled. He sent off a servant in his carriage openly, and escaped himself by a private door. The mob pursued the carriage, but of course found no one in it that they wanted, and the Duc got safely to Calais. On his arrival there, however, a new cause for alarm arose. It was necessary for him to produce his passport before he could leave the country, and it was evident that in this way his identity would be discovered, and he himself, as seemed only too probable, would be arrested and sent back to Paris, never to quit it again. The risk, however, had to be encountered, and he showed his passport to the proper officer, and was, much to his relief, suffered to go on board the English steamer without remark. He at once went to the cabin, and, the better to escape notice, pretended to be very ill. In a few minutes, however, he felt an ominous tap on the shoulder, and looked around expecting to find himself a prisoner. He saw only the passport officer, who said to him, 'When you were in office you gave my son an appointment. In return for that I have to-day let you pass, and thereby in all probability saved your life.' The officer went his way, and the Duc de Grammont got safely to Dover."

In the course of Sunday, a new government, calling itself the Government of National Defence, was formed, consisting almost exclusively of members of the Left. The single exception was General Trochu, who was named president, "with full military power for the national defence," and who installed himself at the Tuileries. M. Jules Favre was entrusted with the portfolio of Foreign Affairs; M. Gambetta was Minister of the Interior; M. Picard, of Finance; General Leffo, who owed his general's commission to the government of 1848, Minister of War; M. Fourichon, of Marine; M. Crémieux, of Justice; M. Jules Simon, of Public Instruction and Religion; and M. Dorian, of Public Works. One of the first acts of the new ministry was to proclaim an amnesty for all political offences. The prisoners condemned to death for their participation in the riots at La Villette, as well as those condemned at the high court at Tours, were set at liberty. The government also decreed the dissolution of the Corps Législatif, and the suppression of the Senate and of the Presidency of the Council of State. M. Thiers was invited to join the new government, but he declined. On Monday, the *Journal of the French Republic* published the following proclamation:

"FRENCHMEN! The people have disavowed a Chamber which hesitated to save the country when in danger. It has demanded a Republic. The friends of its representatives are not in power, but in peril.

"The Republic vanquished the invasion of 1792. The Republic is proclaimed.

"The Revolution is accomplished in the name of right and public safety.

"Citizens! Watch over the city confided to you. To-morrow you will be, with the army, avengers of the country."

On Tuesday, M. Jules Favre, as Foreign Minister, issued a circular to the diplomatic agents abroad, in which he vindicated the position of the Provisional Government, and stated, somewhat broadly, the principles on which it was prepared to treat for peace. He stated that he had always been in favor of a peace policy, and of leaving Germany to manage her own affairs: that the King of Prussia had declared he made war not upon France but upon the dynasty: that the dynasty having fallen, the King of Prussia would be responsible to the world if he continued the war. He declared that "France will not yield an inch of her territory, nor a stone of her fortresses. The government will treat only for a durable peace. The interest of France is that of all Europe; but were she alone, she stands unenfeebled. Paris has a resolute army, well provided; a well-established enciente; and, above all, the breasts of three hundred thousand combatants, determined to hold out to the last. After the forts, we have the ramparts; after the ramparts, we have the barricades. Paris can hold out for three months and conquer. If she succumbs, France will start up at her appeal and avenge her. France will continue the struggle, and her aggressors shall perish."

The new government issued an appeal to

the army, explaining that the imperial dynasty had been abolished, because it was responsible for the misfortunes of France, and because the step was necessary to her preservation. The republic was proclaimed by the inhabitants of Havre, Marseilles, Nantes, Lyons, Bordeaux, and other places, with much enthusiasm. Decrees were published in Paris, abolishing the stamp duty on newspapers, and absolving all public functionaries from their oaths of allegiance to the late dynasty. The regalia and theFrench crown were deposited in the Bank of France. Alterations were made in the names of several streets which had been re-named under the empire: the Rue Dix Décembre was changed to the Quatre Septembre; the Avenue de l' Empereur, to the Rue Victor Noir; and the Rue de Morny, to the Rue MacMahon. Victor Hugo and Louis Blanc returned to Paris from their long banishment.

As soon as the arrangements connected with the capitulation of Sedan were completed, the armies of the Crown Princes of Prussia and Saxony resumed their march toward Paris. When General Uhrick, in command of Strasbourg, was informed of the surrender of Sedan, he dispatched a messenger to the head-quarters of the beseiging army, offering to surrender the fortress if he, with the garrison, were permitted to march out with the honors of war. These terms were refused by the German commander, who insisted on an unconditional surrender, and the bombardment was recommenced with increased vigor. Up to that time, the third parallel of the besiegers was completed, and their guns were within four hundred feet of the fortifications. Frequent sorties had been made by the garrison, but they were all repulsed with slaughter. The ancient library, containing many thousands of unique works, was already destroyed, and the venerable cathedral considerably damaged. King William had, however, given orders that the bombardment should be chiefly limited to the fortifications.

At this pause in the series of great battles, which until this time had been of almost daily occurrence, it is appropriate to reflect a little on the position of France. That position was intelligently described by the *Courrier des Etats Unis*, a French newspaper published in New York. That paper of September 5th, said:

"It is useless to disguise the truth. The army which has not surrendered, but has been surrendered to the enemy, was the flower ot our military population. With MacMahon destroyed and Bazaine helpless, France has left countless masses fanatical with patriotism, ready to throw themselves blindly upon the mouths of the Prussian cannon; but she has no longer an army.

"New masses, however full of confidence, are helpless against military science, discipline, and above all against modern arms. Once it was men who made war; bravery supplemented numbers; enthusiasm made heroes. Now, it is rifled cannon and perfected musketry that fight; the man is no longer more than the attendant of the weapon; he counts but for one, and courage without numbers only make victims.

"All France, with her three millions of young men from twenty to thirty years of age, rising as one, extemporized into soldiers, and hurried in full career upon the solid, intelligent, well-armed, disciplined mass of the victorious Prussians, would throw itself on butchery, and would not drive back one step the wall of steel before her.

"No doubt France will receive with a cry of fierce wrath, like the lion fallen into a ditch, the story of the surrender signed in her name; and that the first movement will be a levy of the whole people and a leap towards new combats. But this first frenzy over, cool reflection will come to throw an icy shroud on this heroism, and we doubt if any man can be found to take the lead in bringing on new conflicts, that is to say, the responsibility of new disasters.

"The people of Paris and the commanders of the besieged places, nay, every manly heart that has its hand on a flag-staff, may refuse to submit, and determine rather to die than to suffer the Prussian flag to stand on the ramparts they guard; but there will be no one to organize this resistance, which would be suicide; no political party which will risk, on this bloody resort, the future before it; no one who does not know that France has no right to commit suicide; that she belongs to the world, to civilization, to humanity, and that at least one chance of success would be necessary to justify the horrors which would result from continuing a war that could no longer be anything but an unbroken series of ravages, waste, slaughter and ruin.

"We cannot tell what counsels will prevail in the fearful embarrassments into which France is plunged. Not to-day nor to-morrow will calm and reflection come out of this chaos. Some days must be allowed to appease the hot fever of this hour. Then will come the time of great resolves. Who will take them? Doubtless the natural representatives of the country, the assembled Chambers, who will find in their patriotism the solution of the immense problem of re-establishing peace on the least sad conditions for the pride and the interest of France that can be obtained.

"The fate of the Empire is sealed. Our first defeats were the signal of its fall. Napoleon III. is no longer more than a phantom, and his dynasty dies with him. What will succeed him is the secret of the future.

"Nor is it our part to predict at a glance what changes these great events will bring to the political, moral and material condition of Europe. One prominent fact, however, seems to us to be fixed; it is that this atrocious butchery, this frightful spectacle given to a trembling world, this accursed holocaust will put an end to war. Prussia takes up the sceptre of military greatness fallen from the hands of France, but it is a broken sceptre. No longer the emblem of anything but a dead power; of glory, indeed, but glory that does not shine on the future. No longer is it arms that shall give supremacy to nations, and Germany, united by the victory of Prussia, will hereafter be neither greater nor more powerful than yesterday, if her aggrandisement is not the signal for a liberal progress of humanity. Her flag will not be more glorious, if it is only to continue to shelter effete institutions.

"The struggle henceforth is no longer between the material forces of the nations; it is in their moral development, their civilization and their liberties. Thus France, even mutilated, if it must be so, will still remain, we hope, the great leading and glorious na tion. The day when, by the fated march of events, a day, doubtless, not far distant, the destiny of the people will no longer be left to the chances of battle; the day when a less barbarous justice will settle the disputes among men; the day when armies cease to consume the brightest resources and energies of the nations, to put at risk the equilibrium of public forces, the genius of France will recover in moral power what she has lost in material power. Countries will no longer be measured by the extent of their territory and the number of their people, but by the worth of the progress they have achieved and the liberties they have conquered; on that day France, cured of her wounds, will again, in spite of the cruel way in which she is torn, take the place of honor which belongs to her in the front of civilized nations."

Those words are the more impressive, as they show that the more reflecting of the French people began themselves to understand what the rest of the world long ago knew, that the maintenance of the Imperial system and the prosecution of the ambitious projects of military glory which it entailed could never result to the benefit of France or the prosperity of Europe.

September 7th. The French engineers began to destroy the tunnels of the railroads running into Paris from the east. The Prussian advance reached Soissons. Many fine private residences and groves of trees in the suburbs of Paris were destroyed, in order to remove all obstructions between the guns of the garrison and the Prussians.

September 8th. The official report on the troops in Paris on this day gives the number at one hundred and fourteen thousand. A letter from the American Minister, Mr. Washburn, was published, announcing the recognition of the French Republic by the United States. In the afternoon, M. Jules Favre had an interview with Mr. Washburn, when the former grasping the hand of Mr. Washburn, exclaimed, "I receive this news with gratitude and profound emotion." The American Minister then solicited the liberation of the Germans who were held in prison in Paris under various charges connected with the war. Jules Favre consented, on the part of the French Government, to their discharge; and hundreds of emancipated Germans at once took their departure from Paris, provided with safe-conduct passes signed by Mr. Washburn.

M. Gambetta, the Minister of the Interior, issued a circular to the prefects of the departments, bidding them think only of war and of the restoration of calmness and security, which are alone productive of strength. "Postpone every thought," says M. Gambetta, "save that of the national defence."

The following proclamation appeared in extras and was placarded about the city:

"The country is in danger. In the presence of the enemy all differences of opinion and all opposition should disappear before the general safety. Accursed be he who can retain personal desires or prejudices in such a supreme moment. The undersigned set aside all opinions save one—that it is our duty to offer our most energetic and absolute assistance and make no condition save that the republic be maintained. Let us all be buried in the ruins of Paris rather than agree to the dismemberment of France."

Signed by Blanqui, Lacambre, the Tridor Brothers, Villeneuve, Fegnard, La Vraud, Pilhes and others.

September 9th. The German march on Paris was conducted in a systematic manner, impeded somewhat by heavy rains. The advance was in three corps. One took the route through Laon, and by the railway north and west from that place to Chauny, Noyon and Compeigne. At Laon the Prussians met with a disaster. On the afternoon of Friday, September 9th, the general in command of the fortress capitulated, to save the town and the inhabitants. The terms of capitulation had been arranged, including the setting at liberty of the garrison of Gardes Mobiles. Soon after the German staff had entered the fortress, a powder magazine exploded, and fifty Prussians, with three hundred of the Garde Mobile, were killed, and many more were wounded, including Duke William, of Mecklenburg, and the French General D'Harne. The explosion was an act of treachery on the part of the French garrison. The second German corps marched along the line of the Marne and approached Meaux on the same day. The third corps moved from the south-east by way of Montereau and Melun. Melun is about forty miles from Paris. The direct railway trains between Paris and Boulogne and Calais, were stopped on Wednesday, the 7th of September. The Director of the General Postal Administration went to Tours on the 9th, to organize the postal service for the whole of France. The Court of Criminal Justice and the Court of Cassation were transferred to Tours. M. Crémieux went with it; but the rest of the ministry and all the foreign ambassadors decided to remain in Paris. The official statement of the day reported the total number of troops—the regular army, the National Guard and the Garde Mobile—at from one hundred and eighty to two hundred thousand men. But they were indifferently armed, not half of them having the chassepot rifle; and many thousands of them had the oldest style of musket.

The government issued an official decree convoking the electoral colleges on the 16th of October, to elect a National Constituent Assembly, to consist of seven hundred and fifty members. The preamble of the decree is in these words:

"In proclaiming the Government of the National Defence, we have defined the object we had in view. The executive power had fallen to the ground; what commenced by a *coup d'état*, had ended in a desertion. We have but seized again the helm which had slipped from feeble hands. But Europe requires to be enlightened: it is necessary that she should know, by means of irrefragable proof, that the whole of France is with us. It is necessary that the invader should meet not only the obstacle of an immense city resolved to perish rather than surrender, but also a whole people, upstanding, well-organized, and represented by an Assembly capable of bearing to every place, in spite of all disasters, the living soul of the country."

Immediately on the receipt of the news, that the Republic had been proclaimed, the Duke d'Aumale, the Prince de Joinville and the Duke de Chartres, went to Paris and had an interview with two leading members of the Committee of Public Defence, who were informed that their royal highnesses considered their decree of banishment was annulled by the fall of the empire; and that, as Frenchmen, they held themselves entitled to take part in the defence of Paris. The members of the committee replied that, in their individual capacity, they fully recognized the right of the Orleans princes to return to France; but they appealed to the princes to say whether any benefit their individual services could confer on the French cause would not be more than extinguished by the probability that their presence in Paris might lead to civil disturbances. The princes, on this hint, announced their intention of quitting the capital at once, with the understanding that they would await at Calais the result of a cabinet council to be held that evening. They accordingly left Paris on the evening of the day that they arrived there; and during their brief sojourn they held no communication with any of their friends or adherents. Indeed, with the exception of the Duke de Chartres, who drove out after dark to catch a glimpse of the city, which he had not seen since he left it when a child of eight years old, the princes remained through the day in the house of the friend who accompanied them to Paris. When they reached Calais, they found waiting for them a telegram from the Council of Ministers, substantially repeating the advice given them in Paris, and requesting the princes, in courteous terms, not to delay their departure. They accordingly sailed from Calais and returned to England. Unquestionably, the ministers took a statesman-like view of that matter!

This reference to the disappointment of the Orleans princes suggests some thoughts on the fortunes and fate of the Empress Eugénie. But a few days previously, she was the most brilliant, the most powerful, the most envied and apparently the happiest woman in all Christendom—"the glass of fashion and the mould of form"—the empress of modern society and the chosen goddess of the gay world in both hemispheres. Now, she was crownless and houseless—a fugitive and an exile in a foreign land. Her departure from the Tuileries and from France was a flight as from the wild popular vengeance of another Reign of Terror, and doubtless in crossing the Belgian frontier she thought less of her imperial splendor swept away than of her personal safety secured. She was in no danger: she might have retired with deliberation and dignity; but in the midst of that fearful commotion in Paris how was she to know it? Twenty-two years before King Louis Philippe fled as precipitately in his pea-jacket from the ominous tumult of a French revolution, because he knew not that the horrible ferocities of the first French revolutionary convulsion had passed away—that the masses of the French people, through that hideous carnival of crime, had risen from the revenges of barbarism to the responsibilities of civilization.

Yet it is hard to believe that Eugénie was

not in some degree prepared for this sudden collapse of the Napoleonic empire and dynasty. She had been too active and too ambitious as a politician in the affairs of the empire, and too familiar with the reasons of Napoleon for every scheme of his, in his internal policy and in diplomacy or war, not to know the dangers that encompassed him. Yet she was, doubtless, deceived by the delusions of the *plebiscitum*, and satisfied that, from the glory of this war with Prussia, the empire would be secured for her son, as its absolute despotism had been secured for her husband, by the will of the French people. How could she believe that the French people, in ratifying the empire over and over again, had spoken under the pressure of an imperial army, and that with this army removed, they would speak for themselves without the warning of a single day?

It is all over now, and, in the light of the restored republic, it is only a matter of amazement that the shadowy empire of Louis Napoleon survived so long. For eighteen years, with the skill of a conjurer in his domestic and foreign policy, he had managed to divert the public mind of France from the outrages of his usurpation to the glories and prosperity of his government at home and abroad. But all this time, as we can now see, the French people had only submitted to the empire as a choice of evils, and that they had been impatiently awaiting their opportunity to replace the republic which he (Napoleon) betrayed and set aside, but which he had failed to extinguish.

It may be that in the glitter and splendors of her imperial court, and with emperors, kings and queens dancing attendance upon her, Eugénie really believed the republic dead, the Bourbons a mere tradition, and the empire needing only the glory of the rectification of the Rhine frontier to make its transmission to her son a scene of popular acclamation. But "how are the mighty fallen and the weapons of war perished!" We can hardly realize the stupendous events of these six weeks, or that, among them, the Emperor Napoleon is a prisoner, his prince imperial a wandering exile, and his empress a fugitive from a back door of the Tuileries, with a single attendant, and anxious only to escape with her life from the surging revolution around her. We can hardly believe that this trembling fugitive was that magnificent empress who but the other day was welcomed at Constantinople by the Sultan with a reception excelling in its oriental splendors the royal Asiatic welcome of King Solomon to the Queen of Sheba. Can it be true that this weeping exile on the Belgian frontier, pleading for information of her unhappy husband and her poor sick boy, was the same person as that glorious empress who in the grand eastern spectacle of the opening of the Suez Canal eclipsed in her radiant beauty the charms of the gorgeous Cleopatra in all her glory! Yes; the glorious empress whose presence in her imperial travels inspired the admiration and wonder of Europe, Asia and Africa, and the melancholy wanderer in search of the sick boy and his father, were one and the same person. It was only a change in the character she was called to play; and such are the ups and downs of crowns and dynasties; and so it has been from the beginning, and will be to the end.

September 10*th*. Soon after the return to Paris of Victor Hugo, he published an address to the Germans, from which the following sentences are extracted:

"You may take the fortress, you will find the rampart.

"You may take the rampart, you will find the barricade.

"You may take the barricade, and then—who knows the resources of patriotism in distress—you will find the sewers mines of powder ready to blow whole streets into the air. This will be the terrible sentence you must accept.

"To take Paris stone by stone, to slaughter Europe on the spot, to kill France in detail, in each street, in each house, that great light must be extinguished soul by soul!

"Germans, hold back! Paris is formidable!

"Think awhile before her walls. All transformations are possible for her. Her indolence gives you the measure of her energy.

"She seems to sleep. She will awake. Her thought will leap from its scabbard like a sword, and this city, which yesterday was Sybaris, to-morrow may be Saragossa."

In view of the *sequel* to the siege of Paris, that flight of the novelist is worth preserving.

On this day, Saturday, September 10th, it was announced that the Bank of France was removed to Toulouse; that all the watchmakers' and jewellers' shops were closed, and their contents removed to a place of safety; that the theatres were all closed; and that on Sunday, next ensuing, the supply of gas would be stopped. The crowd of strangers at Havre, seeking to embark from France was so great that the hotels were unable to give them lodgings. The trains arriving from Paris were several hours behind time, by reason of the number of passengers. It was announced in Berlin, that the King of Prussia, holding that the self-constituted government, which assumed to speak and act for the French nation, was destitute of even a shadow of authority, and that, in the event of the occupation of Paris by the Prussian army, he would treat for a present peace and for the future relations between France and Germany, only with the recognized Emperor, Napoleon III., he therefore gave orders that the imperial prisoner at Wilhelmshohe should be treated in every respect as the actual reigning sovereign of France.

September 11th. The corps of sappers and miners, assisted by the inhabitants, felled the forests in the departments of the Seine and Seine-et-Oise; and, as the Prussians approached, the trees were to be set on fire. The gas works had been destroyed.

September 12th. The Prussians arrived in force at Crécy and Meaux, each place about twenty-five miles from Paris, and their advanced guard reached Noisy-le-Grand, only nine miles from Paris. It was announced in Paris that M. Thiers had gone on a mission to London, and would thence proceed to St. Petersburg and Vienna, in the hope of securing such intervention from those governments as would lead to a peace.

As the Prussian forces were thus approaching the French capital, it is proper to give a brief sketch of its defences at this time.

Paris was completely surrounded by a bastioned enceinte, with a crest of nearly fifty feet high. This enceinte consisted of several main fronts, traced to suit the peculiar conformation of the ground, and formed a kind of pentagon with unequal sides. On these main fronts were traced over ninety bastions, varying in proportions, bnt maintaining a uniform shape throughout. The scarp of the works was faced with a kind of soft stone, laid in regular courses, and backed by rubble masonry. The height of the scarp was thirty-one feet, the ditch seventy-seven feet wide, and the counterscarp, eighteen feet deep, and sloping at an angle of forty-five degrees. A simple glacis, with a beam separating its crest from the top of the counterscarp, and thus forming a covered way, extended outside the ditch. The perimeter of the enceinte was over eight French leagues in length, and a considerable space was left for military purposes between the works and the city.

Inside the enceinte ran the grand military road from which the bastions and curtains of the fortifications were reached by ramps or slopes. In some of the interiors of the bastions, cavaliers of earth-work were constructed, by which a defilement of the adjoining *terre-pleins* and the military road, as well as a searching fire over the ground in front was obtained. By means of the adoption of such extended lines of front, protected by bastions constructed on the same right line, the task of approach to a besieger would be extremely difficult, as no salient point was presented which he could envelop or on which he could concentrate his attack. This is the reason why the French Government expressed their confidence in the security of Paris, as it would take an immense force to invest the place, while the besiegers would in no place be strong enough to resist the repeated *sorties en force* of the garrison.

Paris was not dependent for safety on the bastioned enceinte above described. A second and exterior line of defence had been established by which an approach to the first or interior line of works was prevented. The exterior line of defence consisted of sixteen detached forts, each one so constructed as to render it an independent defensive position, capable of resisting a siege. The town of St. Denis, on the north side, was defended by three forts, besides minor defensive works connecting the same, covering the north, east, and south sides of the town. Of these, Fort de la Briche and Fort de l'Est protected the place from attack from the north and east, while they were in turn covered by Fort d'Aubervilliers, which also protected the village of the same name.

September 13th. The Prussian advance on Paris was temporarily suspended by orders from Bismarck, and in reference to the attempts of the French officials to obtain peace. It transpired that the programme for peace entrusted to M. Thiers, included: *First*—The payment by France to Prussia of the expenses of the war. *Second*—The destruction of all the French forts in Alsace and Lorraine, excepting Metz and Strasbourg. *Third*—A temporary occupation of Metz and Strasbourg by the German troops; the occupation to continue until after a general election in France had duly authorized the complete ratification of the treaty of peace by the proper French authorities.

September 14th. Authentic information from London showed that the mission of M. Thiers was a sort of private enterprise, to ascertain the feelings and opinions of the British Government, and that he was absolutely without official instructions or authority from the new French Ministers. Of course, his *visit* came to nothing.

The termination of the temporal power of the Pope, which occurred almost simultaneously with the surrender of Napoleon, though not strictly forming any part of the history of the war between France and Prussia, was in a measure caused by that war; and a reference to the event, taken from one of the journals of the day, will not be out of place here:

"One of the most remarkable events in the wonderful transformation that Europe is undergoing through the Prussian-French war is the extinguishment of Papal sovereignty. The superstructure of the temporal power of the Pope, which has existed over a thousand years, and which has stood so long the shock of revolutions and falling dynasties, has been overturned finally by the events of the last few weeks. True, its foundations were undermined by the great French revolution at the close of the last century, and modern progress since has shaken it fearfully; but it has been propped up by the monarchies of Europe from time to time, and within the past few years it has been supported by the bayonets of the *soi-disant* modern Charlemagne—Napoleon the Third. With the fall of this aspiring emperor, this so-called eldest son of the Church, the last prop is taken away. The temporal sovereignty of the Pope and its last supporter have fallen together.

"Whatever may be the results of the war in other respects, whatever government may be established in France or transformation take place in other parts of Europe, Papal secular dominion is at end. The French soldiers have left Rome, never to return to uphold the Papacy. The republicans of France, should they hold the government, certainly will not interfere with the Italians in their rapid progress toward appropriating the Papal territory and uniting all Italy. If by any chance the Orleans dynasty should be restored, that would not make war on Italy to replace the Pope in temporal power. No, not even the Bonapartes would attempt to undo the work of Italian unity and to restore the Pope should they by any extraordinary turn of the wheel of fortune regain power in France. Under no circumstances can or will France assume again the defence or restoration of the fallen Papacy. Austria has cut loose from the Pope. Spain is too republican to think of interfering, and is powerless. Catholic Germany is too liberal, and would not raise a finger for the Pope. Of course none of the Protestant Powers will interfere. In fact, Pius the Ninth, as a temporal ruler, is without a friend—is more friendless, perhaps, than even Napoleon.

"The army of the King of Italy is meeting with little resistance in its march on Rome. The Pope has no force capable of resisting. But the Papal troops even are fraternizing with the advancing Italians. Behind all is a greater power still—the republicans of Italy. Victor Emanuel is not unwilling in the least to seize the opportunity of making Rome the capital of his kingdom, and of uniting all the Italians under one government, but if he were he could not resist the popular impulse. The agitation and enthusiasm of the people compel him to move. His own safety lies in that, if anywhere. Italy is republican to the core, and it is only by gratifying the ambition of the Italians in taking Rome that he may be able to save for a time his own crown. He is liberal and progressive and the people are willing to accept him for the time as a leader in the national movement. It is probable, however, that Victor Emanuel is but the pioneer of the Italian republic; for not only are the masses of Italy republican, but the cultivated and intelligent classes hope to restore the former liberties and glory of their country. They remember the ancient greatness of Italy and Rome under republican government, and their enthusiasm is aroused to restore the past and to march in the way of modern progress. The occupation of Rome and the destruction of the temporal power of the Pope are the first steps in the realization of their ardent and patriotic aspirations. In a few days they will see this accomplished. Long centuries of darkness and repression will yield to the enlightened spirit of the age and liberty. What a change! What a magical political transformation within a few days! So wonderful are these events that we can hardly keep pace with or realize them.

"It is said the Italian government assures the Pope that his independence will not be molested in any way. We can understand what this means, and no doubt his holiness understands it. His personal independence will not be interfered with and he may be left some authority over certain districts in Rome, embracing the Vatican and St. Peter's—something like that which a mayor has in a city; but neither the King of Italy nor the Italian republicans will consent to his retention of sovereign territorial power over the city or Papal States. That is all this soothing language about the independence of the Pope means. And why should his holiness be troubled? Why should he not be content? Has he not lately got infallibility? Is he not the chief of all mortals, with immunity from error or wrong-doing? Who can equal him? Who is so blessed? It seems providential that he should have received infallibility just before this wonderful revolution and just when he most needed it. After all, neither Victor Emanuel nor the Italian republicans can deprive him of his spiritual supremacy. He should now put himself at the head of the people and the democratic movements of the age. He could thus become more powerful than he ever has been or than any of his predecessors. The loss of his temporal power would be more than compensated by the moral influence he would exercise and the good he would do."

September 15th. The Prussians were this day camped at Croix aux Bois, Gaston Glas and Fontaine; and therefore, practically, the siege of Paris may be said to have commenced.

September 16th. The railroad trains that left Paris for the north were captured by the Prussians. The French uselessly destroyed all the works of art on highways leading out of Paris. Electric lights were placed in all the forts around Paris, to discover any attempt of the Prussians for a night attack. The Prussian advance reached Breteuil and Neuilly-sur-Marne, and their scouting parties occupied Corbeil and Clamart. At Joinville, seven miles from Paris, there were fifteen thousand Prussians.

September 17*th.* The Prussians were in force near Villeneuve, Dammartin and La Plessis. Three thousand were at Villers Cotterets and ten thousand at Nanteuil. The Paris *Gaulois* published a list of twenty bridges to the east of the capital which had been destroyed by the French to retard the Prussian advance. The scarcity of paper began to be so serious in Paris, that the newspapers were issued on half-sized sheets. No railroad trains left Paris in any direction on this day. Some of the newspapers removed their offices to Tours. The French to-day blew up the fort at Vincennes, as its position was not tenable against the Prussians. The flour mills and granaries at Carbell, fourteen miles from Paris, were burned by the Prussians.

September 18*th.* Several skirmishes took place between the Prussian advance parties and sallying parties from Paris; but they were not of importance as to numbers or results. The following opinions of General Sheridan were this day published in London:

"There seems to be but little of the war left except the siege of Paris, and that will not save France. It is possible that French troops have not done so well, as I think they are capable of doing, on one or two occasions which I witnessed, from the fact that the poor fellows found themselves so badly handled by their commanders that they could see no equivalent to be obtained by sacrificing their lives. All men like to have an equivalent for their labor, and especially is it so with soldiers, who require success where many lives have to be sacrificed. The French generalship put this out of the question in every battle which I have witnessed."

September 20*th.*—Prussia, citing the precedent of the first Napoleon, compelled the French prisoners to labor on the public works. Versailles was to-day occupied by the German Uhlans, who are somewhat like the Russian Cossacks. The government of Paris decided on constructing a complete system of barricades throughout the city. The Prussians threatened death to every man who attempted to repair the railroads which they destroyed.

The French authorities having this day announced the withdrawal of their fleet from the German Ocean and the Baltic, and the abandonment of the blockade, renders a fitting occasion for a statement of the respective naval forces of the two nations at the commencement of the war. The French fleet consisted of the following vessels:

6	large ships of the line, with	152 cannon.
14	frigates with batteries, with	228 ..
9	casemated ships, with	76 ..
5	rams, with	9 ..
2	turret ships, with	18 ..
15	floating batteries, with	198 ..
11	plated gunboats, with	22 ..
62	iron plated vessels, with	697 cannon
233	unplated vessels, with	2,618 ..
51	paddle steamers,	116 ..
100	sailing ships, with	914 ..
466	vessels of war, with	4,345 cannon.

The Prussian fleet was as follows:

3	plated frigates—Kœnig Wilhelm, Friedrich Carl, Kronprinz....with	55 cannon
1	plated corvette—Hansa	8 ..
2	plated vessels–Arminius & Prinz Adalbert	7 ..
5	covered corvettes	140 ..
5	smooth-deck corvettes	68 ..
8	gunboats, 1st class	24 ..
14	" 2d do	28 ..
1	paddle steam yacht	
2	despatch boats	6 ..
2	tug steamers	
1	transport steamer	
44	steamers	336 ..
3	frigates (eight sailing vessels)	112 ..
3	brigs (eight sailing vessels)	38 ..
2	small schooners (eight sailing vessels)	
32	armed sloops	64 ..
4	cannon jollyboats	4 ..
1	school ship	9 ..
89	vessels of war	563 ..

The reasons assigned for the withdrawal of

the fleet were, that the draught of the French iron-plated ships, from twenty to thirty feet, is too heavy for the shallow waters along the southern Baltic coast; that the guiding lights to the channels and against the shoals of that coast are extinguished and false lights substituted, rendering it difficult, if not impossible to distinguish between channels and shoals; that the Prussian inlets and river entrances are infested with torpedoes, which must be avoided, and by troublesome light-draught gunboats, or *avisos*, which cannot be pursued by heavy-draught ships, and that the regular Prussian war vessels, under the shelter of the forts and the protection of torpedoes, cannot be reached.

These reasons are sufficient in accounting for the failure of the French navy to accomplish anything in this war beyond the blockade of the Prussian ports. But had Napoleon, in his preparation for this war, studied more closely the peculiarities of the southern Baltic coast, its river mouths, its inlets, shoals, islands, etc., and studied less the strength of the Prussian navy in heavy iron-clads, the French naval operations against Prussia in this contest, instead of being useless, might have been made equal to an army in the field of a hundred thousand men. In the Crimean war England sent up in the Baltic a formidaable fleet of heavy-draught ships only to find that for aggressive purposes against Russia in that quarter they were useless. England, however, proceeded at once to repair the blunder, in building a large number of light-draught gunboats, each armed with a gun of heavy calibre, for the Baltic service; and but for the fall of Sebastopol, which brought peace, those gunboats would doubtless have tried the strength, to some purpose, even of the powerful fortifications of Cronstadt. At all events, a well appointed and numerous fleet of swift and light-draught gunboats would have enabled France in this war to give constant employment to a Prussian army on the Baltic coast of a hundred thousand men.

Napoleon, in failing to make this special provision for this war with Prussia, simply left the French navy in a condition in which it was not able to give any valuable assistance to the French army. This, too, when the navy of France numbered nearly 500 vessels of all descriptions, being very nearly on paper equal to the navy of England, even in iron-clads, and when the money expended upon a single useless but ornamental iron-plated ship would have supplied a fleet of gunboats equal to a land force of 100,000 men. Prussia had expected some formidable diversions by the French navy on the Baltic coast, and had accordingly placed an army of 100,000 men under Von Falkenstein to guard that line against the landing at any point of a French army under cover of a supporting fleet of ships or gunboats. Von Moltke, comprehending the danger of such an attack upon the rear of the Prussian army and its communications, had thus amply provided for it; but the French, in failing to make any such diversion by their navy, and in withdrawing at length from their profitless blockade, released Falkenstein's army and added its important support to the German columns operating in the heart of France.

Thus, while the developments of this war showed that the army of France was never so badly prepared for aggressive or defensive operations, it was confessed by her admiral commanding in the Baltic that his costly and formidable fleet of iron-clads in those waters were worse than useless against the Prussian fleet which was locked up, and against the Prussian seaboard towns, which, on account of flats, bars, torpedoes, false lights and light footed *avisos*, could not be approached. The whole civilized world was astonished at these revelations, in regard both to the inefficiency of the army and the navy of France, which, under the liberal expenditure of Napoleon the IIId, it was supposed, would prove equal to any possible emergency by land and sea. The facts are, however, that the empire, with all its pomp and glitter, and all its luxurious parades of abounding military strength and resources, had still, with its fearful demoralizations, brought France to the verge of ruin; that while her standing army, but yesterday the terror of Europe, was destroyed, her immense navy, pronounced useless in this conflict, was withdrawn from the field of active operations.

All telegraphic communications with Paris ceased on the 20th of September. On the same day occurred the first serious conflict since the commencement of the siege. The Prussians having passed the Seine at Choisy, six miles south of Paris, moved west and seized a low range of hills lying in front of forts Issy, Vannes, Montrouge, Bicetre, and Ivry. In the immediate vicinity of Bicetre is the village of Villejuif, where the action took place. The Crown Prince of Bavaria commanded the Prussian and Bavarian corps. The French corps was that of General Vinoy, which failed in the attempt to reach MacMahon, and after the surrender of Sedan, fell back on Paris. The engagement resulted in the total defeat of the French corps, which left seven guns and 2,500 prisoners in the hands of the Prussians, and retreated behind the forts. The condition of the country in the district between Metz, Nancy and Sedan is shown by an appeal for aid made to the United States and to England by the mayors and other civil and ecclesiastical authorities of the towns and villages in the district indicated. The appeal contains this statement:

"The people are usually dependent upon their crops and cattle for support. They have now nothing remaining; houses, stables and barns are destroyed; fields and meadows are trampled down; there is no harvest. All the cattle, sheep and swine have been seized. The laborers are pressed into the army. Not even seed-corn remains. Starvation and pestilence impend."

September 22d.—The Prussians cut the Orleans railway, and the traffic on that line was stopped at Blois. The bronze statuary of Paris was melted up to supply the foundries with material for cannon. New troubles for France were developed. A general revolt took place in Algeria, so alarming in its character that the Chasseurs d'Afrique, lately withdrawn from that country, were sent back, and many of the new Gardes Mobiles, raised in the south of France for the defence of Paris, were ordered in the same direction. Why should a French republic or a French monarchy desire to retain Algeria among its dependencies? As an attempt at colonization it was an utter failure. As a financial investment, it was worse than a disappointment, it was a constant drain. The authority of the French was established at a ruinous loss of men and money, and after all, it was maintained only over a narrow little strip of territory on the sea-coast. The productions of the country have always been considerable, but to the French they brought no revenue. In the frequent industrial expositions in Paris, especially that of 1867, they made a brave show, but every pound of cotton cost a napoleon, and every sugar cane had been produced at the expense of its weight in gold. In the towns and seaports the French opened restaurants, where idle officers drank absinthe and played billiards, and there were French barber-shops on the corners, and wretched little imitations of the gardens of the Palais Royal, where the foreign population strolled up and down after sunset—and this they called a French colony. The only purpose that Algeria served for France, during the forty years of her occupation of the soil, was as a school of war for French generals and soldiers, and a very bad school it was, judged by the light of Wœrth, Gravelotte and Sedan.

September 23d.—The Prussian *Moniteur*, official organ, published at Berlin, contained this morning two notes from Count von Bismarck to the ambassadors of the neutral powers to the North German Confederation, in relation to the propositions for peace, now under consideration.

The first of these notes is dated September 13th, in which is urged the necessity for better and more material guaranties against a new attack by France, and especially upon the States of South Germany, Bavaria, Wurtemburg and Baden. Hence the need, on the part of Germany, of possessing these fortresses, which were a perpetual menace.

In the second note Count von Bismarck denies all idea of German intervention for the reorganization of France; but says: "If Strasbourg and Metz remain in French hands, the offensive of France overpowers the defensive of Germany. *These material guaranties alone will give peace.* While France, retaining these places, will always consider a truce as enabling her to choose her own time for a renewal of hostilities, Germany asks only the passive strength to resist such attacks."

A telegram from Berlin to London stated that Count Bismarck and Jules Favre were closeted all day; the former insisting on the meeting of the Constituent Assembly to ratify any treaty that might be agreed on. Jules Favre conceded an indemnity for the cost of the war, the surrender of a part of the French fleet, and the dismantling of Metz and Strasbourg.

September 23d. The following letter from Count Bismarck, addressed to the Prussian ambassadors at the several European courts, was this day made public. It shows the views held by Prussia on the subject of peace and in reference to proposals of M. Jules Favre:

"Your Excellency is familiar with the circular which M. Jules Favre has addressed to the foreign representatives of France in the name of the men at present holding power in Paris, and who call themselves '*Le Gouvernement de la Défense National.*' I have learned simultaneously that M. Thiers has entered upon a confidential mission to the foreign courts, and I may presume that he will endeavor on the one side to create a belief in the love for peace of the present Parisian Government, and on the other side will request the intervention of the Neutral Powers in favor of a peace which shall deprive Germany of the fruits of her victories, and for the purpose of preventing every basis of peace which would make the next attack of France on Germany more difficult.

"We cannot believe in the sincerity of the desire of the present Parisian Government to make peace so long as it continues by its language and its acts at home to excite the passions of the people and to increase the hatred and bitterness of a population stung by the sufferings of war, and to repudiate in advance every basis acceptable to Germany as unacceptable by France. By such a course it becomes impossible to make peace. The people should be prepared for peace by calm words and in terms corresponding to the gravity of the situation.

"If we are to believe that negotiations with us for peace are honestly intended, the demand that we should conclude an armistice without any guaranties for our conditions of peace could be meant seriously only on the supposition that we lack military or political judgment, or are indifferent to the interests of Germany. Moreover, the hope entertained by the present rulers in Paris of a diplomatic or material intervention of the Neutral Powers in favor of France prevents the French nation from seeing the necessity of peace. When the French nation become convinced that as they have wantonly conjured up the war alone, and Germany has had to fight it out alone, they must also settle their account with Germany alone, they will soon put an end to their resistance, now surely unavailing.

"It would be an act of cruelty to the French people by the Neutral Powers to permit the Parisian Government to nourish among the people hopes of intervention that cannot be realized, and thereby lengthen the contest.

"We are far from any inclination to mix in the internal affairs of France. It is immaterial to us what kind of a government the French people shall formally establish for themselves. The government of the Emperor Napoleon has hitherto been the only one recognized by us. Our conditions of peace, with whatever government, legislating for the purpose, we may have to negotiate with, are wholly independent of the question how or by whom the French nation is governed.

They are prescribed to us by the nature of things, and by the law of self-defence against a violent and hostile neighbor.

"The unanimous voice of the Germanic governments and the German people demands that Germany shall be protected by better boundaries than we have hitherto had against the dangers and violence we have experienced from all French governments for centuries. So long as France remains in possession of Strasbourg and Metz, so long is its offensive strategically stronger than our defensive so far as all South Germany and North Germany on the left bank of the Rhine are concerned. Strasbourg in the possession of France is a gate wide open for attack on South Germany. In the hands of Germany, Strasbourg and Metz obtain a defensive character.

"In more than twenty wars we have never been the aggressors on France; and we demand of the latter nothing else than our safety in our own land, so often threatened by it. France, on the other hand, will regard any peace that may be made now as an armistice only, and, in order to avenge the present defeat, will attack us in the same quarrelsome and wanton manner as this year, as soon as it feels strong enough in its own resources or in foreign alliances.

"In rendering it difficult for France, from whose initiative alone hitherto the disturbances of Europe have resulted, to resume the offensive, we at the same time act in the interest of Europe, which is that of peace. From Germany no disturbance of the European peace is to be feared. Although France had been trying to force the war upon us for four years, we, by our care and by restraining the feelings of our national self-respect so incessantly outraged by France, had prevented its occurrence. We mean now for our future safety to demand the price of our mighty efforts. We shall demand only that which we must have for our defence. Nobody will be able to accuse us of want of moderation if we insist upon this just and equitable demand."

The French ministers, in reply to this circular of Bismarck, issued the following

"*Proclamation to France:* Before the siege of Paris, Jules Favre desired to see Count Von Bismarck, to know the intentions of the enemy. The following is the declaration of the enemy:

"Prussia wishes to continue the war in order to reduce France to a second-rate power. Prussia demands Alsace and Lorraine as far as Metz, by right of conquest. Prussia, before consenting to an armistice, demands the rendition of Strasbourg, Toul and Mont Valerien. Paris is exasperated, and will rather bury herself beneath her ruins. To such insolent pretensions we can respond but by resistance to the last extremity. France accepts the struggle, and counts upon her children."

September 24th. The incident of chief importance this day was the surrender of Toul after a bombardment of six hours. It was an important victory for the Prussians. They not only gained one hundred and ninety-seven cannon, twenty-seven hundred prisoners and five hundred thousand rations; but they captured the only remaining obstruction to their railway communication between the Prussian frontiers and Paris.

September 25th. Marshal Bazaine made a sortie from Metz; but after some hours of hard fighting, his troops were driven back with heavy losses. The Prussian prisoners which fell into his hands in the course of the action were sent back at the close of the day, as they would only be so many more to consume the provisions of the garrison. Letters conveyed from Paris to Tours by a balloon gave some particulars about the condition of Paris. The omnibuses of the capital were given up and the horses seized for the use of the garrison. Constant skirmishes took place between the besiegers and the French troops.

September 26th. The city of Orleans was evacuated to-day by the French troops on the approach of the Prussians, under Prince Albert. Advices from Tours announced that the removal of the government to a point further south was imminent. The most energetic measures for defence were resolved on. Requisitions were made for all arms in the hands of the people, and all the inhabitants were ordered to lodge and feed the troops. All men under the age of twenty-five to be called into active service. The Prussians around Paris maintained the strictest discipline.

September 28th. The event of to-day, second in importance only to the surrender of Sedan, was the unconditional surrender of Strasbourg, with its garrison of seventeen thousand men.

No city in France save Paris has greater interest for the traveller or the student of history than the capital of Alsace.

The glories of Strasbourg associate it closely with Germany. Its greatest treasure is the noble Dom or Cathedral, in which services have been conducted in the German language almost every Sunday for eight hundred years. It was built by Erwin von Steinbach in 1015, and the tower was crowned by Johann Hultz in 1413. All its architects and builders were Germans; and though it has been repeatedly struck by lightning, and the height of the spire somewhat reduced, and though in the siege the wood-work has been burned, the nave broken in, and the famous clock, the most complete in the world, perhaps destroyed, it still stands, the loftiest work of human hands on earth, rising twenty-five feet higher than the great pyramid of Egypt, and one of the chief artistic glories of the German people.

Guttenberg and Schöffer, the inventors of printing, were natives of Strasbourg, and there practiced their new art together, in a rude form, before they parted and rivalled one another in striving to perfect it. The depositions taken in the famous lawsuit between Guttenberg and Faust, in which the origin of the most important invention ever made was disputed, were contained in a manuscript volume of the time, which lay, until a few weeks ago, in the Strasbourg city library; but the library, like most of the city, is utterly destroyed, and this unique book, one of the chief antiquarian treasures of its kind in the world, has probably disappeared, together with an immense collection, no less than four thousand volumes, of books printed in the fifteenth century.

It is now nearly two hundred years since Louis XIV. seized Strasbourg, then a free city of the German empire. He marched into it in 1681, while avowedly at peace with the whole world, and immediately employed Vauban, the first engineer of his age, to make it impregnable. He built the famous citadel, and surrounded it with works so strong that it has ever since been regarded as one of the chief strongholds of France. It is, except Paris, her most important depot of military stores and manufactory of artillery, and has been strengthened and supplied from year to year by Napoleon III., as a menace against Germany.

The history of Strasbourg since the French occupation has had but one important event to record, before the siege of 1870, and that not one of such dignity as the completion of the cathedral or the invention of printing. On October 30th, 1836, Louis Napoleon Bonaparte dressed himself up with care in imitation of the well-known figure of Napoleon I; and, with a colonel of the garrison, whom he had hired to betray his trust, presented himself to the soldiers of the garrison of Strasbourg. They tried to win the troops over by a strange set of falsehoods, asserting that Louis Philippe was dead, and that Napoleon II. (not III., as afterward), had been proclaimed in Paris. But General Voirot, being awakened by the noise, coolly shut up the young would-be-emperor in prison, and in November the citizen king, considering such a hare-brained adventurer as too contemptible to treat seriously, shipped him off to America.

Of more fame and more importance than this exploit of Louis Napoleon, however, is the Strasbourg pie, known as *paté de foie gras.* Since the French flag has waved over the city, its chief manufacture, next to heavy guns, has been goose-liver pie. To produce this delicacy, the geese must be fattened in damp and dark cellars; and their food regulated so as to produce the disease which swells the liver to an enormous size. Nearly all the cellars in Strasbourg are said to have been used for this purpose; and the numbers of these pies shipped to other places, as well as of those consumed by the inhabitants, are enormous. They were so, at least, before the siege; but this had long since reduced Strasbourg to extreme want, not of luxurious *patés* so much as of rye bread, hard tack and salt bacon.

For Strasbourg was defended with a persistence and devotion, in the face of inevitable ruin, which won the applause of admirers of heroism everywhere, and gave a strong moral support to the resistance of France at all assailed points, and especially at Paris. General Uhrich continued his obstinate defence long after he was himself badly wounded, his works ruined, his guns nearly silenced, the city mostly burned, and his garrison, half of it slaughtered and the rest half starved. To do this merely as a Quixotic sacrifice to a point of honor, would have been unjustifiable, but if General Uhrich did it deliberately, with a view to afford to suffering and bewildered France a point of moral support, while preparing further resistance to the invaders, he nobly did his duty as a soldier, and is entitled to the same honor as if he had laid down his life in leading a storming party to a breach in an enemy's fortress.

September 29th.—An official statement, published at Berlin, of the captures thus far made by the Prussians since the 2d of August, showed this aggregate: prisoners, one hundred and ten thousand; horses, ten thousand two hundred and eighty; eagles, fifty-six; mitrailleurs, one hundred and two; field and fortress guns, eight hundred and eighty-seven; wagons, four hundred; and an almost incalculable quantity of small arms, ammunition, clothing, equipments, forage and provisions.

General Cluseret, to-day, headed a revolution at Lyons. He forced his way into the Hotel de Ville and harangued the people. The National Guard arrested him and his adherents. No lives were lost. Clermont was captured to-day. Three hundred Mobiles and the citizens successfully resisted the first attack of the Prussians. After the latter had been repulsed they returned with artillery and reinforcements and captured the place.

The Prussians surrounded Soissons. Shot and shell were exchanged since Saturday. The suburbs were destroyed by artillery fire. A bridge was thrown over the Aisne at that place.

Advices from Havre state that the merchandise remaining in the warehouses in that port was protected by the consuls of neutral countries, who hoisted their respective flags. A huge electric light revolved at night, lighting up the entire bay and the batteries around it. Enormous chains protected the entrance of the harbor.

September 30th.—A great number of the private documents belonging to the emperor, which were seized at the Tuileries by the officers of the new government, were made public in Tours, in the columns of the official journal of the Republic. Many noted persons under the old regime were implicated in the scandals. The provisional government at Paris had already dismissed M. Devienne, the president of the Cour de Cassation, he having been shown to be mixed up in the scandalous transactions of the ex-emperor and Marguerite Belanger. The Jecker correspondence in relation to Mexico was found, implicating the Duc de Morny and others high in the emperor's confidence. Beside these there was found a letter from Persigny to Napoleon, proving the existence of a black tribunal, and another from the Queen of Holland written directly after the battle of Sadowa, warning the emperor against the very events now occurring. Altogether the disclosures thus far made in regard to the private life of Napoleon, have substantiated all the charges that the opposition ever made, and it is thought the other letters, soon to be published, will be still more scandalous.

The following official account gives particulars of the surrender of Strasbourg:

"Since the 24th the bombardment has been terrific and almost incessant, and the breach in the walls became large enough to warrant an assault. It became evident to everybody that storming was inevitable in a few hours, unless stayed by a capitulation. On Tuesday, the 27th, near four o'clock in the afternoon, the joyful sight of a white flag was beheld flying from the cathedral. This was speedily followed by the same welcome token of surrender from the citadel. A young lieutenant of the thirty-fourth regiment was the first to discover the flag, and the firing instantly ceased. Then general attention was called to the flags by a universal cheer which rose from one portion of the besieging lines, and was soon caught up and echoed throughout the entire army.

"The scene which followed was indescribably exciting. Officers sprang to their feet and embraced each other, clasping hands. The men followed the example, and some actually cried with joy.

"The terms of the capitulation arranged have already been reported. Yesterday I was fortunately enabled to enter the city with a Baden regiment. The sight, which was impressive and sad, was relieved by the evident joy of the citizens at their release from their terrible condition of suffering and suspense.

"The commanders of the two forces, Generals Werder and Uhrich, met for the first time yesterday, after the terms of capitulation had been arranged. The meeting took place just inside the gate, on the east side. General Uhrich advanced to General Werder, and, with a voice much agitated, said:

"'I have yielded to an irresistible force when further resistance was only a needless sacrifice of the lives of brave men. I have the consolation of knowing I have yielded to an honorable enemy.'

"General Werder, much affected, placed both hands on General Uhrich's shoulders, and said:

"'You fought bravely. You will have as much honor from the enemy as you can have from your own countrymen.'

"A hasty examination of a portion of the city shows it has not suffered so much as was supposed from the bombardment. The exterior of the cathedral appears to be much injured, but not sufficiently so as to prevent its restoration in its original shape. Some fine houses in the Place de la Cathedral are burned.

"Here and there the ruins of buildings show the dangers to which the city has been exposed. In the neighborhood of the cathedral, on the east side of the city, the destruction was the greatest. A singular appearance was presented by the inhabitants, busily engaged in removing straw, bags, rags, mattresses, and every conceivable means of stopping the unwelcome visitors, from the windows. These defences, scattered in the streets, gave the appearance of a general removal of the inhabitants.

"The ruins of the theatre present a dismal appearance. Among the buildings destroyed was the fine public library. It is reported that the books were previously removed, or at least those of the greatest value.

"It does not appear that there had been much actual suffering for want of food, though the means were husbanded with the greatest care. One principal cause of anxiety was confinement and want of good water."

October 1st. The following account of the journey of an aeronaut from Paris to Tours, gives some interesting particulars:

"He started from that city at two o'clock yesterday afternoon. No Prussians were to be seen near Paris. A complete silence reigned about the city. There were no people to be seen on the roads leading to the city, and no boats of any kind on the river. On nearing Versailles the Prussians were observed in great numbers in camp. M. Tissander dropped among them great numbers of the proclamation of the government officers, which had been printed in the German language for that express purpose. The Germans opened a sharp fire on the balloon, but the range was too long, and no damage was done. On arriving over Houdan, fifteen miles south-west of Mantes, the balloon began to fall, and M. Tissander was obliged to throw out ballast. Fortunately he had several packages of newspapers which answered the purpose, and he was not obliged to throw over his letters or sacrifice anything valuable. The balloon then rose rapidly, and was carried along to a point near Dreux, in the Department of Eure-et-Loire, many miles west of the Prussian lines.

"M. Tissander descended slowly, until he came within hailing distance of a few peasants, whom he now saw for the first time. These assured him that there was no danger of capture, as no Prussians had yet been seen in the neighborhood. M. Tissander therefore alighted on reaching an open spot favorable to his project. The balloon was properly secured, and the letters, twenty-five thousand in number, were placed in sacks and taken to the post-office at Dreux, whence they will be forwarded in all directions, wherever the lines of communication are uninterrupted.

"A special locomotive was placed at the command of M. Tissander at Dreux, in which he came forward to Tours, with a large number of dispatches to the government.

"Relative to matters in Paris M. Tissander says:

"The city is admirably defended. More than 500,000 soldiers are behind the walls. These are all well-armed and disciplined. The firing from the forts has been so accurate that the Prussians have been baffled in their attempts to erect batteries.

"The city is perfectly tranquil. Nearly all the shops are open as usual, and the public squares are occupied by the troops, which are there drilled and exercised. The boulevards next to the fortifications, and the Champ de Mars, in the western part of the city, have been given up for barracks for the Garde Mobile.

"At ten o'clock in the evening all the *cafés* are closed, and a constant watch is kept throughout the night. The forts are supplied with electric lights, which are found to be admirably adapted for guarding against surprises. There is neither butter nor fruit to be had anywhere in the city, and fresh meat will soon be scarce. There is, however, no lack of salted provisions, and of flour the supply is sufficient for six months."

October 3d. Every day adds to the encroachment of the besiegers on the French capital, and they are at once closing and strengthening their lines. Thus far they have attempted no bombardment. The Canal de Lourcq has been drained by the Prussians to reduce the Parisian supply of water. A part of the besieging army of Strasbourg joined the Prussian army at Paris. On Saturday, during the sortie of the garrison of Paris, which was repelled with loss to the French, the Prussians captured 500 prisoners.

Soon after the breaking out of the war, the French authorities issued a peremptory order for the expulsion of Germans from France. The operation of this tyrannical and unprecedented edict, and the particulars of its enforcement, are thus described by a writer in Frankfort:

"The unfortunate banished Germans have been arriving during the past week by thousands from all parts of France. It has been a sad spectacle. Most were without money and food. Two workingmen came to Frankfort a few days ago in great despair. While their wives in Paris had gone to the pawnhouse to pledge enough of their furniture to procure money for the journey, the police appeared and drove them to the railroad, without allowing them to wait for their wives and children, who are now totally lost to them.

"German manufacturers have in some cities at once offered work to their countrymen, and even cities are entering into active competition for procuring the skilled labor thus thrown upon the country. Switzerland is offering temporary homes to the refugees, of whom, at the lowest estimate, 50,000 have been cast from their homes. I have heard of an old man one hundred and five years of age being seen among the refugees in Stuttgart, and in Basle an old woman of one hundred and six walked with firm step among the poor crowd. Many of them were born in France; most belong to the working and the lower classes. They say that in the French provinces a great deal of sympathy was expressed for them; but those that passed through Belgium relate that they were oftener greeted with curses and stones than with bread and water. Many of the women have broken down in confinement on the way. One woman arrived in Basle insane from the privations of the journey.

"A gentleman who saw the refugees arrive in Basle asserts that all the men were in blue blouses, the women were often in rags; little children were carried in the arms, the larger ones led by the hand. The old woman of one hundred and six had snow-white hair, was bent down, and led with great kindness by two young men. They were her grandchildren. She went to Paris ninety years ago."

In partial retaliation for this barbarous proceeding, the Prussian commanders have levied an indemnity of one hundred thousand francs in each department which they pass through, or occupy, from which the Germans were thus expelled.

Two newly organized German corps crossed the Rhine to-day, to join the invading hosts already in France. Another sortie made today from Paris, was repulsed with heavy loss to the French.

The publication and exposure, on the 25th of July, of a secret treaty proposed by France to Prussia, has already been mentioned. That exposure was so damaging to Louis Napoleon, in regard to his standing with the other European Powers, that he made haste to disavow his agency in proposing any such treaty, and he positively and distinctly denied that it originated with him. But, among other things revealed by the seizure of his private papers when the people took possession of the Tuileries, was a copy of a note from the emperor, in his own hand, containing these words:

"If France boldly places itself on the terrace of the nationalities, it is necessary to prove that the nationality of Belgium does not exist. The Cabinet of Berlin seems to be ready to enter into negotiations. It would be well to negotiate a secret *acte* which would satisfy both parties. This *acte* would have the double advantage of compromising Prussia, and of being to her a pledge of the sincerity of the emperor.

"An *acte* is wanted, and one which would consist of a regulation of the ulterior fate of Belgium in concert with Prussia, would be proving at Berlin that the emperor desires the extension as necessary to France. Since the events which have taken place in Germany there is at least a relative certainty that the Prussian government would not object to our aggrandizement."

Should the reputation for veracity of Louis Napoleon ever become a matter of public importance, the contents of that note will go far toward undermining it.

October 4th. Orders were issued to-day by Gen. Trochu to take no more prisoners into Paris, as they help to consume the stores of city. When this order was promulgated, the Prussian commander gave the same order as to the taking of French prisoners. The reason for the latter order is not obvious. The siege guns and mortars for the Prussians arrived, and were placed in position before Paris to-day. The Germans advanced from Versailles and attacked Epernay, where were posted a considerable body of Gardes Mobiles and a detachment of the line and artillery. The position was strong, and was vigorously defended; but the Germans finally succeeded in turning the flank of the French, when the latter retreated, leaving the Germans in possession of the place. The garrison at Metz continued to make daily sorties, but they were always repelled with loss. The villages around Metz were destroyed by the incessant artillery practice.

October 8th. An attempt was made by Bazaine to break through the Prussian lines around Metz; but the sortie was repulsed, and the French were driven back with a loss of 400 killed and wounded, and 600 prisoners.

October 10th. M. Gabetta, Secretary of the Interior, having made his escape from Paris in a balloon, issued the following proclamation at Tours:

"By the order of the republican government I have left Paris to transmit to you the hopes of the Parisians and others of those who are seeking to deliver France from foreigners. Paris, invested for seventeen days, presents the spectacle of two million men, forgetting their differences to withstand the invader, who expected civil discord.

"The revolution found Paris without guns or arms of any kind. 400,000 of the National Guard are now armed, and 100,000 Mobiles and 60,000 regulars are assembled. The foundries are casting cannon. The women make a million cartridges daily. Each battalion of Nationals has two mitrailleuses and field pieces, and is prepared for sorties. The forts are manned by the marines, and are supplied with artillery of the greatest excellence, and served by gunners the first in the world. Hitherto their fire has kept the enemy from erecting the smallest work. The *enceinte* on the 4th had only 500 cannon; now it has 3,800, with 400 rounds for each. Every defence has its men at their posts. The Nationals drill constantly. Behind the *enceinte* is the third line of defence—the barricades, which are adapted to the genius of the Parisians. This has all been achieved calmly and orderly, amid general patriotism. The impregnability of Paris is no illusion. It cannot be captured or surprised, and there is no danger of sedition or starvation, which the Prussians have been counting on."

October 11th. An action of importance took place to-day, at Artenay, near Orleans. About 3,500 French troops were strongly intrenched there; but the attacking force of Prussians outnumbered them, and drove them from Artenay into the forest of Orleans. Here, during the night, they were reinforced by nearly 20,000 men despatched from Orleans. But the victorious Prussians followed up their success the next morning, October 12th, drove the French from the forest into Orleans, and through it, taking possession of the town and making more than 10,000 French soldiers prisoners. The remainder of the French army at Orleans succeeded in retreating to the south bank of the Loire.

The capture of Orleans was a discouraging blow to the strength and spirit of the French defence. This ancient capital of the Franks is a centre of stirring traditions of heroism, as well as a valuable military position. Rescued from Attila by the prayers of the church, and, a thousand years later, saved from British pillage by the anointed maid whose name is linked with that of the city in history forever, it has been regarded by the French people with a reverence that is religious in its fervor, as the traditional home of the nation's patriotism, and the safe refuge of its hard-pressed valor. There is no city but Paris the occupation of which by the enemy would be more depressing to that sentimental enthusiasm which the French hoped to make a substitute for military strength and science.

Orleans is very important as a strategic position. It commands the main avenue of railway and telegraphic communication between the north and the south of France.

October 13th. Epinal, a city of about 15,000 inhabitants, in the department of the Vosges, on the Moselle, was captured by the Prussians. On the same day, the Prussians captured Breteuil.

October 16th. Soissons surrendered to-day to the Prussians. The town capitulated only after a terrible destruction of life and property. Three hundred and fifty houses are estimated to have been laid in ashes in the two Faubourgs of Rheims and of St. Christopher. The Prussians occupied the Faubourg of Rheims five days before the capitulation, and the National Guard compelled them to burn it by their incessant and destructive fire. When the Prussians attacked the Faubourg of St. Christopher for the Campiegne road, the National Guard set fire themselves to their own houses, and a terrific hand to hand encounter ensued in the streets and up to the Porte St. Christopher. The Faubourg was carried, house by house, the troops fighting in many places with clubbed muskets. Women and children flying bewildered and in fear for refuge from one side of the town to the other under the cross-fire of the combatants were struck down and killed. The Germans were driven back through the burning town four times in succession, but they were constantly reinforced and bore the French down by sheer weight of numbers. No quarter was shown in the fight of the Faubourg; the wounded were bayonetted where they fell. Women hurled furniture and stones out of the houses on the heads of the enemy. The result of this heroic resistance was an awful sacrifice of human life. The slaughter of the Germans was so terrible that the Grand Duke of Mecklenburg wrung his hands and wept. He positively refused to order an attempt to storm the town, but sent a flag to the French commander begging him to capitulate in the name of humanity. The loss of property has been only less dreadful than the loss of life. Foundries, mills, houses, refineries—the splendid glass-works of St. Gobein, where the finest mirrors in the world are made—have all been destroyed. Many beautiful villas as far as La Folie and Cervance have been demolished. The deaf and dumb asylum of St. Medard, and the convent of the Sisters of Mercy have been burned; the spires of St. Jean des Vignes, at the arsenal, the most beautiful in France, have been injured, as have also the cathedral, one of the finest in Europe, and the church of St. Leger.

October 17th. The missiles from the French forts, in some instances passing over the Prussian position, set fire to the palace of St. Cloud; and despite the efforts of the Prussians to preserve that beautiful and historic edifice, it was destroyed with all its pictures and tapestry.

St. Cloud, the ancient Novigentum, derives its modern name from Clodoald, the grandson of King Clovis. The young man escaped from the assassin hands of his uncle Clotaire to this spot, and after a life passed as a hermit in the neighboring forests was canonized by the title that the noble parks and the palace there erected in 1658 by the great capitalist, Jerome de Gondy, have since borne. The vast wealth and power of Louis XIV., which, during his reign seemed to absorb everything splendid in France, gave him possession of St. Cloud, and the grand monarch bestowed this gem upon his brother, the Duc d'Orleans. Become a royal palace it extended its hospitality to Queen Henrietta of England, who died there; and in succeeding years it witnessed the murder of Henry III.; the plottings of the First Napoleon for imperial control; the royal folly of Charles X., who dated thence the rescripts that revolted France and precipitated the revolution of 1830; and, finally, the *fêtes* of the hearty citizen-king Louis Philippe and the summer pleasures of Napoleon III. St. Cloud rivals Versailles in its memories of the lovely but unfortunate Mary Antoinette and the gayeties of Queen Victoria's sojourn in France in 1855. Some of the most imposing scenes of the reign of the First Napoleon occurred at this celebrated residence, and the shades of the gentle Josephine and of her successor the fair Austrian Marie Louise seemed, even in our day, to haunt the apartments the crowned dames once occupied, and on the walls of which their portraits smiled in the bloom of pride and beauty as limned by master hands.

None who have ever visited the delightful abode with a tourist's elegant curiosity or by imperial invitation will forget its parks stocked with rare growth and ranged by herds of English deer, its enchanting gardens, its lakes, its fountains and its cascades, the delight of the Paris Sunday throng who went a Maying in its lawns and woods.

October 18th. The French opened a heavy fire on Bagneux, before Paris. This was followed by an attack in force of the line and Garde Mobile; and, at first, the Prussians were driven back; but they soon rallied and were reinforced, and the French in turn retreated to their own lines, under a galling and destructive fire from the Prussians guns.

October 19th. Chateaudun was captured by the Prussians, after an action lasting from noon till ten o'clock at night. As usual, the French had the disadvantage of being outnumbered.

October 24th. No event of special importance took place for five days. Occasional sallies from the beseiged towns were made; and various movements were made, in several quarteri, toward an armistice or a treaty of peace. On the 24th of October, the Prussians captured Schlestadt, including twenty-four hundred prisoners and one hundred and twenty pieces of artillery. The capture of this town, a stronghold on the north-eastern frontier of France, was important, as it gave to the Prussians command of the railway from Strasbourg to Mulhausen; and thence, by Chaumont and Troyes to Paris. It also gave them full possession of Alsace.

October 27th. The great event of this day, and one which, more than anything else, except the surrender of Sedan, was fatal to France, was the surrender of Metz with Marshal Bazaine and one hundred and twenty thousand men; which included the entire remainder of the veteran French army. This capture completed the conquest of Lorraine.

The capitulation of Metz includes 67 infantry regiments, 13 battalions of foot chasseurs; 18 fort and depot battalions; 36 cavalry regiments, namely, 10 of cuirassiers, 1 of guides, 11 of dragoons, 2 of lancers, 3 of hussars, 6 of chasseurs, and 3 of Chasseurs d' Afriques; also, 6 depot squadrons; 115 field batteries; 17 batteries of mitrailleuses; 69 eagles belonging to infantry, 2 of which were captured at Mars-laTour, and 36 eagles belonging to cavalry.

Including the garrison surrendered, the army originally comprised 221 battalions of infantry and 162 squadrons of horse. The original numerical strength was 210,000 infantry, 21,450 cavalry, 690 guns and 102 mitrailleuses.

Besides the foregoing, there were three marshals—Bazaine, Canrobert and Lebœuf; three corps commanders—Frossard, De Caen and Ladmirault; forty division generals; one hundred brigadier generals; of sound prisoners, 90,000 sent to North Germany and 50,000 sent south, the sick and wounded being distributed in the same proportion.

Metz is a fortified city, the capital of the Department of the Moselle. It is situated at the confluence of the rivers Seille and Moselle, and distant 245 miles east by north from Paris. It was one of the strongest fortresses of France, ranking next after Strasbourg, and was garrisoned by 10,000 men, even in times of peace. It is surrounded by a regular system of fortifications, and entered by nine different gates, furnished with drawbridges. The most formidable and important of the works, which were commenced by Vauban and Belle-Isle, and completed by Cormontaigne, are the fort of Belle-Croix, which commands the eastern part of the city from Port des Allemands to the river; the Fort La Double Couronne, which protects the southern portion; and the Redoute du Paté, which forms an island connected with the city by a subterranean gallery. Inside the town there are many steep and narrow streets. There is also the arsenal, a cathedral, the church of Nôtre Dame de la Ronde, and the abbey of St. Vincent—religious edifices of very great antiquity. There are a military hospital, a hall of justice and public library also. Metz contains many Catholic churches, a Calvinist church, and several Israelite synagogues. The city had, before the war, manufactories of woollen goods, hosiery, plush, beer, tiles, nails, and so forth. The annual value of its products was estimated as equal to $2,000,000.

Metz was known to the Romans under the name of Dividorum. This was changed subsequently to that of Mediomatrici, the place being then the capital of Belgic Gaul. It was named Mettis in the fifth century. From this it became celebrated as the capital of Austrasia, which was afterwards called the kingdom of Metz, but which assumed the name of Lorraine in the middle of the ninth century.

Early in the tenth century, Metz fell under the power of Henry the Fowler, of Germany, but recovered its independence in the eleventh century. After that period the city became famous for its commerce with Germany, its brilliant and fascinating society, and its patronage of letters and art.

Metz was formally united to France in the year 1542.

Alsace and Lorraine comprize six French departments, the former having been divided into the departments of the Haut and Bas Rhin, and the latter into the departments of the Meuse, the Moselle, the Meurthe, and the Vosges. They are chiefly wätered by the Moselle and the Meuse, two principal tributaries of the Rhine, and are traversed by the chain of the Vosges mountains, connected with the Swiss Alps and the Black Forest. They are bounded on the east by the Rhine, on the west by the Champagne country, on the south by Switzerland, and on the north by Rhenish Bavaria. They comprise some of the most fertile territory and picturesque scenery in all the broad and beautiful land of France. Corn and wine, tobacco, pulse and fruits are raised without difficulty, and in harvests of almost fabulous plenty; timber for every useful and decorative purpose is found in the greatest abundance; and there are rich mines of silver and copper, of lead and iron. Many of their springs possess medicinal virtues of world-wide renown.

The history of both Alsace and Lorraine is singularly interesting. Alsace, as early as the time of the great Julius, was a field of battle for Celts and Germans. Cæsar himself tells the story of how the Allemanni and some other allied tribes crossed from the dim forests of Germany over the Rhine into this fertile and beautiful land, and drove out the Gauls, who had hitherto peopled it. It subsequently became a German duchy, but in 1268, the line of its hereditary dukes becoming extinct, it was parcelled out among several members of the German empire. By the peace of Munster, in 1648, a part of Alsace belonging to Austria, together with ten free cities of the empire, were ceded to France, while the remainder was still ruled by German princes owning fealty to the House of Hapsburg. The peace of Ryswick in 1697, however, gave up to France in addition the city of Strasbourg and all the territory that had been occupied by the French troops on the left bank of the Rhine. But some few square miles of territory even yet remained a fief of the empire until the beginning of the revolution, when the National Assembly, in a characteristic proclamation, declared them to be a conquest indicated by nature herself, since no foreign power could, under any consideration, be permitted to retain territory in France. Compensation was offered to the German landholders thus dispossessed, but few of them deigned to accept it, and this was one of the chief causes of the war that broke out shortly afterwards between France and Germany. It should be mentioned that the mass of the people cheerfully accepted this change of government. Alsace had long been celebrated for the freedom of its religious sentiments, and before the conquests of Louis Quatorze most of its inhabitants had embraced the principles of Luther and Melancthon. When it came under the authority of the republic it soon distinguished itself by the uncompromising extravagance of its sans-cullotism, and furnished to the National Assembly several of its most fiery and earnest demagogues.

The earliest ruler of Lorraine of whom

we have any record was Lothair, the grandson of Charlemagne, and he was succeeded by a number of princes who acknowledged fealty to the German empire. Its position, however, marked it out as the battle-field of Germany and France, and for centuries it was the scene of constant conflict. On the death of Louis XI., the last German emperor of the blood of Charlemagne, Lorraine was annexed to France, and the well-known Regnier, the hero of the satire, "Reineke Fuchs," was appointed as its duke. In subsequent contests half of Lorraine was again torn away by Germany and given to dukes receiving their nomination from the Kaiser. This state of things lasted about eighty years, when the Emperor Henry III. again united the whole of Lorraine in a single dukedom, and bestowed it upon Albert of Alsace, whom the heralds report to have been descended from the Hector of Homer. The line of princes thus founded lasted 700 years. Among them were some of the most gallant and chivalrous of mediæval celebrities, while others acquired a questionable renown for eccentricity. Simeon, the fourth of the line, after reigning twenty-two years, retired into a monastery. His nephew, Frederick, who succeeded him, was celebrated as one of the most accomplished men of his time, but perished miserably by poison at the treacherous hands of a favorite mistress. His brother, Matthew II., reigned in his stead, and lives in history as a monster of cruelty. One of his exploits was the skinning alive of the governor of some small town, who was accused of maadministration. Raoul, his successor, was killed at the battle of Cressy, and John, who followed, left his kingdom in order to follow the fortunes of his godfather and namesake, the king of France. He was captured by the Black Prince at the battle of Poictiers, and shared the captivity of the French monarch. While he was away, his dukedom was the prey of internal troubles, the unscrupulous oppression of the nobles having provoked the peasantry into insurrection. This rebellion was for a time successful, and the horrors of the revolution of 1792 were enacted on a smaller scale, much of the best blood in the duchy being poured out by the infuriated Jacquerie. Next came the war of the disputed succession, which forms so prominent a feature in Sir Walter Scott's novel, "Anne of Geirstein." Charles of Burgundy claimed the duchy for his vassal, the Comte de Vermandois, but was defeated near Nancy by the rightful heir, Duke Rene the Second, and died in a marsh just outside the city. When his body was discovered, Rene seized the cold hand and said: "May God have your soul, cousin, for you have caused me many a pain and sorrow." Rene, in all other respects, acted with the greatest magnanimity on this occasion, refusing to confiscate the lands of such of the nobility of Lorraine as had supported the pretensions of Charles, and taking only a crystal vase out of all the rich spoils of the Burgundian camp. In this vase, on the evening of the funeral of Charles, he drank to the "oblivion of vengeance." Upon his death his wife took the veil, and the ceremony of her initiation presents one of the most striking pictures in mediæval history. Her son, a boy of ten years of age, handed her the wax candle which serves as the symbol of the irrevocable vow, and then turning away wept bitterly. The whole court were in attendance, and were also affected to tears at this touching spectacle. This house reigned over the destinies of Lorraine until 1736, when Francis Stephen, who had a few years previously made quite a conspicuous figure in London fashionable society, exchanged his hereditary duchy for that of Tuscany, in order to be able to marry Maria Theresa, the Empress of Austria. Both Francis and Maria traced back their descent to Gerald of Alsace. The duchy did not immediately come within the jurisdiction of France, but was handed over to Stanislaus Leczinski, the deposed king of Poland, who reigned twenty-eight years. He was one of the most singular men of his generation. He was by turns a reckless rake and a superstitious devotee;

now he donned the cook's apron and employed himself in inventing a *ragoût* or a jelly, and again turned a few couplets or set about acquiring immortality by authorship. His death was worthy of him; as he was stooping down to light his pipe his dressing-gown caught fire and he was burned to death. After his decease, Lorraine passed into the possession of the French crown. The people, however, by no means took kindly to this forced change of masters, and various bloody riots occurred, in which women took a conspicuous part.

The moment that the news of the fall of Metz reached Tours, a government council was convened to debate the matter; on which occasion the ministers, instead of taking a common-sense view of the overwhelming calamity, waxed indignant, and endeavored to help the case by issuing the following proclamation:

"FRENCHMEN: Raise your spirits and resolution to the fearful height of the perils which have broken upon the country. It still depends on us to mount above misfortune and show the world how great a people may be who are resolved not to perish, and whose courage increases in the midst of calamity.

"Metz has capitulated. A general, upon whom France counted, even after Mexico, has just taken away (*vient d'enlever*) from the country in its danger more than a hundred thousand of its defenders. Marshal Bazaine has betrayed us. He has made himself the agent of the Man of Sedan and the accomplice of the invader; and, regardless of the honor of the army of which he had charge, he has surrendered, without even making a last effort, a hundred and twenty thousand fighting men, twenty thousand wounded, guns, cannon, colors, and the strongest citadel of France—Metz-Virgen, but for him, to the contamination of the foreigner. Such a crime is above even the punishments of justice!

"Meanwhile, Frenchmen, measure the depths of the abyss into which the empire has precipitated you. For twenty years France submitted to this corrupting power; which extinguished in her the springs of greatness and of life. The army of France, stripped of its national character, became, without knowing it, an instrument of tyranny and of servitude, and is swallowed up in spite of the heroism of the soldiers, by the treason of its chiefs.

"In the disasters of the country in less than five months two hundred and fifty thousand men have been delivered over to the enemy, a sinister sequel to the military *coup de main* of December.

"It is time for us to reassert ourselves, citizens, and under the ægis of the republic, which we have determined not to allow to capitulate, within or without, to seek in the extremity even of our misfortune the renovation of our political and social morality and manhood.

"However tried by disaster, let us be found neither panic-stricken nor hesitating. Let it be seen that we are ready for the last sacrifices, and in the face of enemies whom everything favors, let us swear never to give up so long as there remains an inch of sacred soil under the soles of our feet. Let us hold firmly the glorious banner of the French Revolution. Our cause is that of justice and of right. Europe sees it; Europe feels it. In the presence of so many unmerited misfortunes, Europe, of her own accord, receiving from us neither invitation nor encouragement, is moved and begins to act. No illusion is now left. Let us no longer languish or grow weak, and let us prove by our acts that we can ourselves maintain honor, independence, integrity—all that makes a country proud and free.

"Long live the Republic, one and indivisible!"

This unconsidered and precipitate attack upon a national general was, in the doubtful circumstances of the case, unjustifiable and unwarranted. The surrender of the French army under Bazaine, with the strongest inland fortress in the world — a fortress full of modern artillery and ammunition, with a garrison of one hundred and seventy thousand prisoners of war, is, perhaps, the greatest defeat in military history. Yet it was unavoidable. With his supplies nearly exhausted, his soldiers weakened by poor and scanty food, and decimated by pestilence, Bazaine might doubtless have held out a little longer, but to what end? There was no force to relieve him at any definite future time. Had he sacrificed half his men to get out with the rest, there was no country to feed him; only a vastly stronger force of the enemy to meet, before which he would have been more helpless than MacMahon at Sedan.

Nothing could be gained by further resistance but a short postponement of the inevitable blow which would lay France prostrate. The longer the delay, the more terrible and hopeless the shock of the country, the greater its exhaustion, its dissensions, and its anarchy. If Marshal Bazaine took the responsibility of saving scores of thousands of lives, and preventing immeasurable misery, by accepting his fixed fate a few days before it was forced upon him, the public opinion of the world will not blame him.

But there is no evidence that he could have escaped at any sacrifice, or even delayed the fall of the citadel a week. Some of his men are said to have literally died of starvation; how many must perish thus before military honor will acknowledge a necessity for surrender? Surely the Committee of Defence at Tours had no right to denounce Bazaine, unless it could show that it had a reasonable prospect of relieving him before his men were all dead, and of saving Metz at last. And of this there was no pretence, even in their proclamation condemning him for treason. Indeed, this unreasoning, frantic document gives little information as to the condition of the army which surrendered; but founds its violent denunciations upon the simple fact of the capitulation, without any inquiry into the reason which compelled it. "The 20,000 wounded," of whom it speaks, are a sufficient military defence of Marshal Bazaine's patriotism.

October 30th.—A force of 12,000 Prussians attacked the city of Dijon to-day, and, after a bombardment of several hours, the place was surrendered. It was not a fortified town. Dijon had about 40,000 inhabitants, and lies about 160 miles south-east of Paris. It is celebrated as being the birthplace of Bossuet.

November 4th.—After a long negotiation, an armistice was finally agreed upon, with the following conditions:

Its duration to be twenty-five days.

Paris to be, under certain restrictions, supplied with food taken through the Prussian lines.

Free elections to be held in all the departments.

This was signed on the part of France, by Trochu, Jules Favre, Arago, Perry, Garnier Pages, Pelletau, Picard, and Simon; and on the part of the Prussians, by Bismarck and Von Moltke.

The government of Tours, on the same day, issued the following decree:

"Whereas, the country is in danger, and it is the duty of all citizens to save her—a duty that was never more pressing and more sacred than now—it is decreed that all able-bodied married men from twenty to forty, or widowers with children, shall be mobilized and organized by the prefects, and placed at the disposition of the minister of war. The organization must be terminated on the 19th of November; all exemption based upon qualification of support of a family is abolished, even for those who have hitherto received such exemptions. The republic will provide for all families recognized as necessitous by authorities duly appointed for that purpose. The republic will adopt the children of those who die in her service. It is also desired that each department shall, within two months, have as many field batteries as it has hundreds of thousands inhabitants in the department. The prefects are entrusted with all the requisite powers to hasten the enforcement of this clause of the decree. The first battery in each department must be ready within a month."

November 7th.—Notwithstanding the formalities connected with the armistice, it finally failed of being adopted. The French government—if its disjointed members can be called a government—refused a final ratification on two points: as to the vote of Alsace and Lorraine, and as to the admission of food to Paris.

November 8th.—Verdun, to-day, capitulated and surrendered to the Prussians.

November 10th.—Briesach, to-day, surrendered to the Prussians, with its garrison of 5,000 men. It is a small, frontier village of France, of perhaps 2,000 inhabitants. The fortress dates back to Vauban, and is of the second class of fortifications in the French system.

November 11th.—After a series of attacks that continued through two days, the French succeeded in re-taking Orleans, from which the Prussians retired in good order. As it was an isolated case of French success, its moral effect on the French army was very great; yet no important results followed.

November 25th.—After a fortnight's interval, in which the privations and distress of the garrison and inhabitants of Paris continued to increase, and various movements of troops of but little importance took place elsewhere, Thionville was surrendered to the Prussians. Thionville is seventeen miles north of Metz, in the department of Moselle, near the Luxembourg border. It was the last stronghold of the French in Lorraine. The town had been on fire, from the bombardment, for three days.

November 27th.—An engagement took place to-day near Pasques, in the department of the Vosges. The French, under Garibaldi, while on their march from Pasques, came suddenly upon the outposts of the Prussian Rifles, commanded by General Werder. The Prussians at first gave way; but reinforcements being at hand, the French were, in turn, compelled to retreat, which they did in great disorder, the soldiers throwing away their arms and knapsacks in their flight.

November 28th.—General Werder took a circuit around Plombières and overtook the the French rear-guard. In the action that ensued, the French were again defeated, and the Prussian loss in killed and wounded, was but fifty men. By the capitulation of La Fere, seventy cannon fell into the hands of the Prussians.

November 29th.—Amiens was to-day surrendered to the Prussians. The following address was issued by the Prefect of the Department of the Somme, previous to the surrender:

"CITIZENS! the day of trial has arrived. In spite of all our efforts, Amiens must fall into the enemy's hands. The army of the North is retreating, and the National Guard is disarming. I leave you but will soon return. Be calm, be confident; France will be saved."

The French loss in the action which preceded the surrender of Amiens was 1000 killed and wounded, and about the same number of prisoners.

Three sorties were made to-day from Paris; but they were all repulsed with severe losses to the French.

The following dispatch from the King of Prussia was issued to-day:

"Frederic Charles reports the complete defeat of the French army of the Loire in the battle of Monday, in which the French had the Twentieth corps, probably the Eighteenth, and a portion of the Fifteenth and Sixteenth corps engaged. One thousand French were found dead on the field, and 4000 wounded, and 1000 unwounded were taken prisoners. The total German loss was 1000."

Subsequent accounts increased the number of unwounded prisoners to 2000.

December 4th.—King William sent the following despatch to Berlin: "After two days' fighting, in which the army of the Grand Duke of Mecklenburg was mainly engaged, Manstein's corps captured St. Jean, a railway station and suburb of Orleans.

Thirty guns and 1000 prisoners were taken. The Prussian loss was moderate. The Prussians found nine cannon and much ammunition on the field before Amiens."

A large number of people left Tours, fearing an attack by the Prussians, who were in great force near at hand.

December 6th.—A battle took place near Orleans between the Prussians and the French army under de Paladines, in which the latter were routed with a loss of 10,000 prisoners, seventy-seven pieces of cannon, and four gunboats on the Loire, besides the killed and wounded. De Paladines was removed from his office.

December 8th.—Gambetta, in command of the army of the Loire, succeeding de Paladines, announced that he had lost all hope of success for the French, that he could not defend Tours, and he made a formal application at the Prussian headquarters, at Versailles, for an armistice—to enable the French authorities to hold an election for members of the National Assembly, in reference to the future government of the country.

January 10th.—For more than a month, a series of military movements and partial actions took place throughout those portions of France occupied by the respective armies, with very little practical result. And during the same period, the siege of Paris was rigidly maintained. The severe weather of winter set in, and increased the hardships of the troops on both sides. Occasional sorties were made with slight results. The inhabitants of Paris, as well as the garrisons of the capital and the surrounding forts, were much straitened by want of proper food, and numerous troubles and perils were sustained by reason of the unmanageable tempers of the lower classes. At the close of the first week in January, the long threatened bombardment of Paris commenced, but with no very serious effects at first, owing to the distance of the Prussian batteries.

For several weeks preceding this date, the army of the Loire, under the command of General Chanzy had been manœuvring in front of the Prussian army by which he was opposed. Movements were initiated by General Chanzy against the Mecklenburg troops, who, at one time composed almost the entire force opposed to him, which brought to the French army success and to the sympathizers with France, hope. A glimmer of light had at length appeared on the horizon, so long dark and dreary. With many, it was thought that the day was fast approaching when Chanzy, with his 200,000 men, assaulting the German investing line outside the walls of the doomed capital, would have been the signal for Trochu to mass his forces and strike from within, cut his way out and make a junction with the army which had come to his rescue. Such a consummation was not as remote as many seemed to consider it. The forces appointed to keep watch over Chanzy and stay his advance on Paris were unequal to the task. The French commander was pressing them sorely, gaining little, it is true, but still gaining. The German commander-in-chief saw it, dreaded it, and resolved to check it. Chanzy's manœuvring so far had succeeded. It may be that the very success he attained surprised him. He rested—call it hesitation; but, whatever it may be, that delay cost him in the end defeat. There is no doubt that Chanzy's movements were the source of considerable anxiety in the German camp; for it was not until the very position of his forces as well as the strength of the army under his command, became almost threatening that the German commander-in-chief resorted to the adoption of that policy which all through the war has proved so fruitful of results for the armies of Germany. Finding the army opposed to Chanzy unequal to the task of staying the French advance, Prince Frederic Charles, with his veterans, was ordered to assume the offensive, reinforcements were hurried on from investing lines outside of Paris, and the German forces opposed to the army of the Loire were not only rendered equal in point of numbers, but made superior to it. This point gained, the results may be briefly summed up for the French in these words—checked and defeated.

These details, however, are but the preliminaries of the events which followed on the 10th of January. At nine o'clock on the morning of that day, within seven miles of the city of Le Mans, the Germans suddenly appeared in force and attacked the right wing of the French army. Sudden as was the attack the French behaved admirably. Forming line of battle they waited the struggle. Infantry, cavalry and artillery all appeared to be well handled, well posted and well supplied on the French side. It is almost needless to say that a similar remark must be applied to the Germans. It was in most respects a fair fight. On the two hills which looked down upon the valley below, clothed with a covering of snow, were arrayed the armies of France and Germany. For hours the German cannon belched forth their iron hail upon the enemy, and for hours the French replied with equal spirit to the murderous missiles. Shot and shell fairly rained on both combatants. At length the German commander ordered an advance. Then commenced the movement of the German infantry. No way loth to meet the foe, the French equally gallant, also advanced, and down the hill sides and across the plain which separated them marched the opposing forces. Midway in that valley, which but a few short hours before was covered with a mantle of spotless snow, the two armies met in hand to hand conflict. Fierce, desperate, impetuous and bloody was the struggle. Man to man the tried veterans of Germany and the hastily gathered levies of the French met. Calmly and determinedly fought the soldiers of the Red Prince; with determination equally strong, but lacking the coolness of the Germans, fought the republican soldiers of France. On the one side it was a struggle of cool, collected soldiers, directed by officers whose ability they had proved and whose tactics they understood; on the other side it was the dash of equally brave men, lacking the discipline of their opponents, but fighting with an impetuous gallantry, directed but by the individual judgment of the soldiers themselves. A contest equal in some respects, yet so unequal on the whole, could have terminated only in one way. The French were forced to retire, with a loss of 15,000 men. The German loss was comparatively small. By six o'clock in the evening the battle ended, and the snow which covered the valley in the morning served as the winding sheet of many a brave fellow that cold night of the 10th on the battle-field near Le Mans.

January 11th.– The next day General Chanzy rallied his broken columns, and, having received reinforcements, determined to try to break through the strong opposition of the Red Prince and advance to the relief of Paris. After a night of unceasing labor and anxiety daylight found the French forces ready. Their three corps, the Sixteenth, Seventeenth and Twenty-first, were commanded by Admiral Jourequiberry and Generals Colomb and Jouffroy. They consisted of about 50,000 men each, in all 150,000 men, under the command of General Chanzy. By ten o'clock in the morning Jourequiberry's corps had taken up position on the right bank of the river Huisne, General Colomb's on the plateau of Auvours, and General Jouffroy's on the right, covering the village of Brette.

The Prussians advanced along three roads, led, it is said, by Frederic Charles, and about 100,000 strong. Soon after ten o'clock a sharp fire was opened by the Prussians from well-located batteries on the left of the French. It was replied to with spirit; but the superiority of the Prussian fire soon rendered resistance useless on the part of the French; and before night the entire force of General Chanzy was disorganized and in full retreat in three different directions, with a loss of 22,000 unwounded prisoners. It was a crushing defeat for France.

One of the objects of Louis Napoleon in declaring war against Prussia, was the spoliation and dismemberment of the Prussian territory; but one of its results, was the perfect union and consolidation of the whole German empire. This political change took place while the war was at its height, and the several German States resolved themselves into an empire and designated King William of Prussia as its head. On the 18th of January, King William issued from his head-quarters at Versailles, the following proclamation of his acceptance of the imperial crown:

"In consequence of the appeal of the German princes and of the free towns for us to restore the German empire, after a lapse of sixty years, we announce that we consider it our duty to the fatherland to accept the imperial dignity. Henceforth we and our successors will bring to the title of Emperor of Germany the hope that God will vouchsafe a blissful future to the fatherland, and that under our auspices its ancient splendor may be restored.

"We partake of the dignity, conscious of our duty to preserve with German fidelity the rights of the empire and of its members to maintain peace, and to support and strengthen the independence of Germany, in the hope that the German people will reap in lasting peace within our boundaries the fruits of their bloody battles, and be safe against the renewal of French attacks. God grant that we and our successors may protect the empire, not by warlike conquests, but by works of peace, freedom and civilization."

January 22d.—A severe battle took place before St. Quentin, between the Germans under General Van Goeben, and the French army of the North, under General Faidherbe; in which the French lost six guns, 5,000 men killed and wounded, and 9,000 unwounded prisoners. The total German loss was 2,000 killed and wounded. A sortie, in force, was made by the French at Paris, which was repulsed with a loss to the French of 6,000 killed, wounded and missing.

January 25th.—Longwy, after a long siege, capitulated to the Germans, yielding to the victors 4,000 prisoners and 200 guns.

January 28th.—At last, after sustaining all the trials, privations and losses of the siege and a bombardment—and with the usual (in such cases) forgetfulness of their bombastical threats of suffering annihilation rather than surrender, and so forth, the French authorities in Paris agreed to yield to the conquering Prussians and *live* on the right side of the "last ditch." The dispatch of the Emperor of Germany to the Empress Augusta, at Berlin, dated January 29th, 1871, at Versailles, was in these words:

"Last night, an armistice for three weeks was signed.

"The regulars and Mobiles are to be retained in Paris as prisoners of war. The National Guard will undertake the maintenance of order. We occupy all the forts. Paris remains invested, but will be allowed to revictual as soon as the arms are surrendered.

"The National Assembly are summoned to meet at Bordeaux in a fortnight. All the armies in the field will retain their respective positions, the ground between opposing lines to be neutral.

"This is the reward of patriotism, heroism and great sacrifices. Thank God for this fresh mercy! May peace soon follow."

The convention for the armistice was in these words:

Count von Bismarck, Chancellor, in the name of his Majesty the Emperor of Germany, and Jules Favre, Minister of Foreign Affairs for the government of the National Defence of France, are furnished with regular power to determine the following arrangements:

Article 1. A general armistice, over all the line of military operations in the course of execution between the German and French armies, shall begin in Paris this very day, and in the Departments, within the term of three days. The duration of the armistice shall be twenty-one days, dating from to-day, and, excepting it be renewed, will be terminable everywhere on the 19th of February, at noon.

Art. 2. The armistice thus agreed upon

has for its object to permit the government for the national defence to convoke an assembly, freely elected, whether war will be continued or not. No matter what conditions of peace may be made by the Assembly to meet at Bordeaux, every facility will be given by the commanders of the German armies for the election and the meeting of the deputies who will compose the Assembly.

Art. 3. There shall be immediately surrendered to the German army, by the French military authorities, all the forts forming the perimeter and exterior defence of Paris, as well as the material of war. The communes and houses situate outside that perimeter, or between the forts, may be occupied by the German troops as far as the line drawn by the military commissioners. The ground between this line and the fortified *enceinte* of the city of Paris will be interdicted to the armed forces on the two sides. The manner of surrendering the forts by the drawing of the line already mentioned will form the object of a protocol to be annexed to the present convention.

Art. 4. During the armistice the German army will not enter the city of Paris.

Art. 5. The *enceinte* will be stripped of its guns and carriages, which will be transported to the forts designated for their reception by the commissioner of the German army.

Art. 6. The garrisons of the forts and the regiments of the line, the Mobiles and the Marines at Paris are to be prisoners of war, excepting a division of twelve thousand men, which will be under the military authority of Paris, to preserve order inside the city. The troops who are prisoners of war will lay down their arms, which will be collected at the places designated, and to be given up according to an arrangement made by the commissioner in the usual manner. These troops will remain in the interior of the city, and will not be allowed to pass the *enceinte* during the armistice. The French authorities bind themselves to take care of every individual belonging to the army. The Mobile Guard shall remain in the interior of the town. The officers of the captive troops are to be designated in a list, which is to be delivered to the German authorities. At the expiration of the armistice all combatants belonging to the army confined within the walls of Paris shall constitute themselves prisoners of war to the German army if before peace is not concluded. The officers made prisoners shall retain their side-arms.

Art. 7. The National Guard shall retain their arms, and be charged with the protection of Paris, and maintaining order. The same will be the case with the *gendarmerie*, assimilated with the troops and employed in the municipal service, such as the Republican Guard, Douanieres, Pompiers, and the whole of this category, not exceeding three thousand five hundred men. All the corps of the francs tireurs will be dissolved by an ordinance of the French government.

Art. 8. Immediately on the signature of these presents, and before taking possession of the forts, the commander-in-chief of the German armies will give every facility to commissioners of the French government to send, whether into the departments or abroad, to take steps for revictualling, and to bring into the city commodities destined for it.

Art. 9. After the surrender of the forts, and the disarmament of the *enceinte* and the garrison stipulated in Articles 5 and 6, the revictualing of Paris will be effected fairly by transit, by railways and rivers, of provisions intended for revictualment, now drawn from districts occupied by the German troops. The French government engages itself to obtain provisions outside of the line of demarcation which surrounds the position of the German armies, except in case authorization to the contrary effect is given by the commander of the latter.

Art. 10. Every person wishing to quit the city of Paris must be furnished with regular permits, delivered by the French military authorities, and submitted to the inspection of the German authorities. Free passes will be granted as a right of their position to candidates, provincial deputations, and Deputies to the Assembly. This free movement to persons who have received the authorization indicated will be permitted only between six in the morning and six in the evening.

Art. 11. The city of Paris will pay a municipal contribution of war amounting to 200,000,000 francs; the payment must be effected before the fifteenth day of the armistice. The mode of payment will be determined by a mixed French and German commission.

Art. 12. During the armistice nothing shall be taken away of public articles of value which may serve as a pledge for the recovery of the war contribution.

Art. 13. The transport into Paris of arms, munitions, and articles entering into their manufacture are forbidden by the terms of the armistice.

Art. 14. Immediate steps will be taken to exchange all prisoners of war made by the French since the commencement of the war. For this end the French authorities will hand, as promptly as possible, a list of the German prisoners of war to the German military authorities at Amiens, Le Mans, Orleans and Vesour. The liberation of German prisoners of war will be effected at the points nearest the frontier. The German authorities will deliver in exchange, at the same points, in the quickest possible time, a like number of French prisoners of war, and of corresponding grades, to the French military authorities. The exchange will extend to civil prisoners, such as captains of ships of the German merchant service and the navy, and of French civilians who may be retained in Germany.

Art. 15. A postal service, with letters unsealed, will be organized between Paris and the Departments, through the medium of the headquarters at Versailles.

In the faith of which the undersigned have appended to the present convention their signatures.

Sealed and done at Versailles, the 28th day of January, 1871. Bismarck.
Favre.

February 17th. The National Assembly, elected in conformity to the provisions of armistice, met at Bordeaux and elected M. Thiers president of the new French Republic.

February 25th. President Thiers, M. Favre, and a Committee of Consultation spent the day at Versailles in consultation with the Emperor of Germany and his advisers, and finally agreed upon a treaty of peace, embracing the following conditions:

First. The province of Alsace and the fortress of Metz to be ceded to Germany; but the fortress of Belfort, situated on the southern boundary of Alsace, to be restored to France.

Second. France to pay to Germany a war indemnity of five milliards of francs (one thousand millions of dollars).

Third. The Germans to retain possession of a portion of French territory, including a number of fortified towns, such as Sedan, until the French fulfill the conditions of the treaty of peace.

Fourth. The German army to enter Paris on Monday and to occupy the Champs Elysêes.

Fifth. As soon as the French National Assembly formally ratifies these conditions peace to be proclaimed between the two countries.

March 1st. At the session of the Assembly at Bordeaux, the Committee of Consultation made a report unanimously recommending the ratification of the preliminaries of peace as agreed on at Versailles. The Assembly assented to the ratification by a vote of five hundred and forty-six ayes against one hundred and seven nays.

The German army, at the appointed hour, ten o'clock this morning, entered within the *enceinte* under the eye of his Imperial Majesty. The Eleventh Prussian corps, thirty thousand strong, with ninety-six pieces of field artillery and a complement of cavalry, under the command of General Von Bose, advanced in two columns; one through the Porte de Neuilly and the other through the Porte du Jour. Nothing could exceed the splendid appearance of the German troops; who, despite the hard service of a seven months' campaign, appeared as fresh and in as fine condition of dress and appointments as if they had just been mustered into the service.

March 3d.—The Emperor of Germany sent the following dispatch to the Empress at Berlin:

"VERSAILLES, *March 3d.*—I have just ratified the conditions of peace, which the Bordeaux Assembly have accepted. Thus far the work is complete which was through seven months of battles to be achieved. Thanks to the valor, devotion and endurance of our incomparable army, and the sacrifices of the whole Fatherland. The Lord of Hosts has everywhere visibly blessed our enterprises, and by His mercy has permitted an honorable peace. To Him be the honor; to the Fatherland the thanks. WILHELM."

The line of demarcation between France and Germany was finally adjusted as follows:—It commences in the northwestern frontier of the Canton of Cattenom, in the Department of the Moselle; runs thence to Thionville, Briery and Gorze; skirts the southwestern and southern boundaries of the arrondissement of Metz; thence proceeds in a direct line to Chateau-Salins, and at Pettoncourt, in that arrondissement, turns and follows the crest of the mountains between the valleys of the rivers Seille and Vezouze, in the Department of Meurthe, to the canton of Schirmeck, in the northwestern corner of the Department of the Vosges; thence it runs to Saales, dividing that Commune, and after that coincides with the western frontiers of the upper and lower Rhine Departments, until it reaches to the Canton of Belfort, thence it passes diagonally to the Canton of Delle, and then terminates by reaching the Swiss frontier.

An alteration made at the last moment in these boundaries gives Belfort to France, and cedes additional territory around Metz to Germany.

Germany is to possess her acquisitions from France in perpetuity.

It is agreed that as soon as the preliminaries are ratified the Germans shall evacuate the Departments of Calvados, Arne, Gorthe, Eure-et-Loire, Loiret, Loire-et-Cher, Indre-et-Loire, and Yorme, and all territory on the left bank of the Seine. The French troops will retire behind the River Loire until peace is finally declared, except from Paris and other strongholds.

After the payment of two milliards the Germans will occupy only the Departments of Marne, Ardennes, Haut-Marne, Meuse, Vosges, Meurthe, and the fortress of Belfort.

Germany will be open to accept suitable financial instead of territorial guaranties for the payment of the war indemnity.

The evacuation of Paris by the Germans on the 3d of March, 1871, was the signal for an insurrectionary movement on the part of the Red Republicans who had gained confidence with the military license of the siege. A large body of them, with a considerable number of the National Guard, entrenched themselves on the heights of Montmartre with batteries well armed with guns. The Thiers government, unwilling to proceed to extremities, delayed to enforce the surrender of the cannon. Various riotous demonstrations in the meantime took place in different parts of the city. On the 18th, troops were sent by the government to put an end to the Montmartre demonstration. The cannon were taken possession of without resistance, and several hundred prisoners captured. A few hours afterwards several battalions of the National Guards arrived and fraternized with the insurgents, who, with increased forces, were again left in possession of the cannon. General Lecompte, who commanded the body of troops who first took the guns, and General Clermont Thomas, an eminent Republican who commanded the National Guards in Paris during the siege, were taken prisoners by the insurgents, condemned to death by an impromptu tribunal, and immediately shot. The insurrection rapidly spread, barricades were erected and the whole of Paris on the right bank of the river was abandoned to the insurgents; General Vinoy, the commander of the troops of the line, with the remnant of his forces, retired to Versailles where the government now established its headquarters. The insurgents quietly now without took possession of the Hotel de Ville, the Tuileries and the Ministry of Justice, and assumed all the authority of government within the city. A call was issued by a self-constituted "Central Committee" for the Communal elections. The government at Versailles issued a proclamation denouncing the insurrection. By the 21st, the day appointed for the election, the Committee had obtained possession of the whole city, and occupied some of the southern forts.

On the 22d an effort was made for a grand moral demonstration of the party of order. A large body of respectable citizens, entirely unarmed, proceeded to the Place Vendôme, which was occupied in force by two insurgent battalions. Fearful of the effect of any appeal which might be made, the revolutionists persistently fired upon the crowd. A number were killed, and the mass sought safety in flight. The Committee proceeded with various military and other revolutionary measures. On the 26th Communal elections were held, and resulted in a decisive triumph for the Red Republicans. The members returned, with the exception of a few notabilities, such as Pyat, Flourens, and Assy, were hitherto unknown. Two days after, the Commune was formally proclaimed in the Place de l'Hotel de Ville, where a platform covered with red cloth had been erected, on which was placed a bust, representing the Republic wearing the Phrygian cap of Liberty ornamented with red ribbon; the red flag was hoisted on all the public buildings in Paris. Funds were raised by a requisition on the Bank of France, various military positions taken outside the city, as a means of assault or protection against the Versailles troops. An effort was in fact made to advance upon Versailles, but this was defeated by the government fire from the fort at Mont Valérien, the garrison of which had been relied upon by the insurgents as friendly to their cause. Flourens who acted as General in this movement was killed. This was the commencement of a series of continued operations involving constant engagements of more or less severity, between the government troops and the insurgents, who made desperate efforts, aided by their possession of the forts, to hold the direct Versailles approaches to Paris. The military leaders of the insurgents were appointed for the occasion according to the fortune of the day. General Cluseret, acting as War Minister of the Commune, Dombrowski, a Pole, succeeding Bergeret in command of the forces outside of the city. Marshal MacMahon was called to the command of the government army, and immediately organized a series of active movements. Neuilly was the scene of the most obstinate contests, the inhabitants living in their cellars for several weeks, while their village was bombarded and reduced to ruins. The Avenue de Neuilly, with its imposing monuments, the Arc de l'Étoile, at the barrier, became the theatre of a prolonged contest. The fine residences in its vicinity suffering heavily from the bombardment. It was not till the 9th of May that Fort Issy, after an obstinate series of engagements was compelled to be evacuated by the insurgents. A deprecatory movement on the part of the latter, was finally attempted by a body of Freemasons who planted their banners on the ramparts of Fort Maillot and secured permission for two of their body to pass through the lines and proceed to Versailles. They were received by M. Thiers, who, refusing to treat with them, advised them to address the Commune if they wished to restore peace. The fall of the rebellion now depended upon the final assault on the city for which the national army had been strengthened, and the utmost precautionary measures for success taken. General Cluseret had meanwhile been succeeded in the War Ministry of the Commune by Colonel Rossel, formerly officer in the regular army.

While these military proceedings were in progress, the Commune, though mainly engrossed with the defence of the city, employed itself in various revolutionary decrees. The main political idea of the body as set forth in their official Journal was to be embraced in a charter such as their ancestors of the middle ages called their Commune. This charter was to guarantee the municipal autonomy of Paris. Paris, it was further urged, should be federated with the Communes of the other large towns of France by a treaty which the national Assembly should be called upon to accept. This, of course, was regarded by the Versailles government as an *imperium in imperio*, a virtual act of disintegration, and utterly incompatible with the now established national authority. The action of the Commune was not confined to political theories of State or local Sovereignty. At an early period it decreed the "separation of Church and State," and the confiscation of property belonging to religious communities on the ground that "the clergy had been the accomplices of the crimes of monarchy against liberty." At the same time they impeached the chiefs of the "insurgents of Versailles," as they were pleased to call them; issuing a decree summoning Thiers, Favre and other leading members of the government before the "tribunal of the people," in the mean time sequestrating their property. In pursuance of this decree the private residence of M. Thiers in the Place St. Georges, a beautiful edifice, filled with works of art, was completely destroyed. The furniture was sold at auction, the money to be given to widows and orphans of National Guards killed in this civil war; while the collection of works of art was to be distributed among the museums and public libraries of France. A special decree ordered the arrest and summary trial of every person suspected of complicity with the Versailles government. Leading personages adjudged to belong to the party of order opposed to the Commune, were ordered to be held as hostages, upon whom death was to be inflicted in retaliation for every prisoner of war or partizan of the Commune executed by order of the Versailles authorities. Large numbers of priests were arrested and confined in prison. Darbois, the archbishop of Paris, Duguerry, the curé of the Madeleine, Turct, the grand vicar of the diocese, were among the notables of the order who were imprisoned.

A dispatch dated April 23d, 1871, from the legation of the United States at Paris, from Minister Washburne to the Secretary of State at Washington, presents a memorable account of an interview with the Archbishop in prison:

"Sir: You are aware that Monseigneur Darbois, the Archbishop of Paris, was seized some time since by order of the Commune, and thrust into prison, to be held as a hostage. Such treatment of that most devout and excellent man could have but created a great sensation, particularly in the Catholic world. On Thursday night last I received a letter from Monseigneur Chigi, Archbishop of Myne, and Nuncio Apostolic of St. Liege, and also a communication from M. Lanoner Chanvins, of the diocese of Paris; Mr. Lagard, the Vicar-General of Paris, and Messrs. Bousset and Allain Chanvines, and members of the Metropolitan Chapter of the Church of Paris, all making a strong appeal to me, in the name of the right of nations, humanity, and sympathy, to interpose my good offices in behalf of the imprisoned Archbishop. I have thought that I should have been only conforming to what I believed to be the policy of our Government, and carrying out what I conceived to be your wishes under the circumstances, by complying with the request of the gentlemen who have addressed me. I therefore, early this morning, put myself in communication with General Cluseret, who seems, at the present time, to be the directing man in affairs here. I told him that I applied to him, not in my diplomatic capacity, but simply in the interest of good feeling and humanity, to see if it were not possible to have the Archbishop relieved from arrest and confinement. He answered that it was not a matter within his jurisdiction, and, however much he might like to see the Archbishop released, he thought, in consideration of the state of affairs, it would be impossible. He said that he was not arrested for crime, but simply to be held as a hostage, as many others had been; under the existing circumstances, he thought it would be useless to take any steps in that direction. I myself thought the Commune would not dare, in the present excited state of public feeling in Paris, to release the Archbishop. I told General Cluseret, however, that I must see him to ascertain his real situation, the condition of his health, and whether he was in want of anything. He said there would be no objection to that, and he immediately went with me in person to the Prefecture of Police, and, upon his application, I received from the Prefect a permission to visit the Archbishop freely at any time. In company with my private secretary, Mr. McKean, I then went to the Mazas Prison, where I was admitted without difficulty. Being ushered into one of the vacant cells, the Archbishop was very soon brought. I must say I was deeply touched at the appearance of this venerable man. With his slender person, his form somewhat bent, his long beard—for he had not been shaved apparently since his imprisonment—his face haggard with ill-health—all could not have failed to have moved the most indifferent. I told him I had taken great pleasure, at the instance of his friends, in intervening on his behalf, and while I could not promise myself the satisfaction of seeing him released, I was very glad to be able to visit him, to ascertain his wants, and to assuage the cruel position in which he found himself. He thanked me most heartily and cordially for the disposition I had manifested toward him. I was charmed by his cheerful spirit and interesting conversation. He seemed to appreciate his critical situation, and to be prepared for the worst. He had no word of bitterness or reproach for his persecutors, but, on the other hand, remarked that the world judged them to be worse than they really were. He was patiently awaiting the logic of events, and praying that Providence might find a solution to these terrible troubles without the further shedding of human blood. He is confined in a cell about six feet by ten, possibly a little larger, which has the ordinary furniture of the Mazas Prison—a wooden chair, a small wooden table, a prison bed. The cell is lighted by one small window. As a political prisoner, he is permitted to have his food brought to him from outside the prison, and in answer to my suggestion that I should be glad to send him anything he might desire, or furnish him with any money he might want, he said he was not in need at present. I was the first man he had seen from the outside since his imprisonment, and he had not been permitted to see the newspapers, or to have any intelligence of passing events. I shall make application to the Prefect of Police to be allowed to send newspapers and other reading matter, and shall also avail myself of the permission granted me to visit him, to the end that I may afford him any proper assistance in my power. I cannot conceal from myself, however, the great danger he is in, and I sincerely hope that I may be instrumental in saving him from the fate which seems to threaten him."

Simultaneously with these decrees against the clergy, the demolition was ordered of the imperial column in the Place Vendôme, erected by the first Napoleon, covered with sculptures in bronze, representing the incidents of the French victories in Germany, including the battle of Austerlitz. From the stability of this work, its destruction was a work of time, requiring considerable labor and mechanical ingenuity for its accomplishment. A large aperture was made at its base, and it was finally overthrown by ropes fastened to its summit, on the afternoon of the 16th of May. This act of vandalism was performed in the presence of the members of the Commune, or Committee of Public Safety, as the shifting local authorities were called. These officials looked from the windows of the Ministry of Justice. After various efforts, the column, one hundred and thirty-two feet in height, fell, in a straight line, on the litter prepared for it. The figure of the first Napoleon, which crowned its summit, was thrown a few feet forward, detached from the main shaft. It was expected that the fall would give a severe shock to the neighboring buildings, but, in consequence of the precautions, it proved very slight. No glass in the windows of the houses was broken; a thick cloud of dust, from the crushed and powdered masonry which formed the body of the work, rose into the air, while the crowd raised a loud shout of "Vive la Commune!" while the bands in attendance played the Marseillaise. The beautiful Chapelle Expiatoire, erected in commemoration of the first burial place of Louis XVI. and Marie Antoinette, was ordered to be destroyed, in sympathy with one of the least defensible acts in the Revolution. The motive for the demolition of the Vendôme column was proclaimed as the insult which it offered to the vanquished in its contradiction to the principle of fraternity by perpetuating the memory of the empire.

At the close of May the civil war in Paris was evidently approaching its termination. The final preparations of the Versaillists had been made for an entrance into the city, and internally, the Commune had been weakened by the dissensions of its members and the numerous disasters, in spite of the most obstinate fighting it had encountered in the field. On the night of Sunday, May 21st, an entrance into the city, contrary to expectation, was quietly effected by General Douay at the Porte de St. Cloud, while General L'Admirault took the gates of Passy and Auteuil, while General Vinoy entered by the Porte du Jour, and opened the gate of Sévres to General Cissy. Some opposition was offered by Dombrowski, at the head of a body of men, who retreated after a few hours' fighting. In the morning the Versailles troops were in position at the Arc de Triomphe, and were sweeping down the Champs Elysées and the Boulevard Haussmann. M. Thiers, who, with Marshal MacMahon, had witnessed the entry of the troops into Paris from Mont Valérien, addressing the Assembly in the afternoon, declared that "the cause of right, liberty, order and civilization was triumphant." "We will visit with the rigor of the law," he added, "those men who have been guilty of crime against France, and have not shrunk from assassination, or the destruction of national monuments. The laws will be rigorously enforced. The expiation shall be complete."

In the meantime, Paris had been completely isolated. The strictest orders were given to the German outposts to drive back all insurgents, and the advanced corps were doubled to prevent any from breaking through the circle of investment north of Paris. Dombrowski, who was wounded, attempted to pass the Prussian outposts, but was forced to go back, and was afterwards taken prisoner by the Versailles troops. Citizen Assy was also taken prisoner, and brought to Versailles. In the course of the day, however, the insurgents seemed to have recovered from their panic. New barricades were thrown up in all directions, and severe fighting went on in the streets, but the Versailles troops gradually advanced, carrying one position after another. On Tuesday morning they held the districts on the left bank of the Seine, and early in the day the insurgents' position at Montmartre was taken by two corps d'armée. A large number of insurgents were killed in the action, and about 4,000 were made prisoners. On the Place de la Concorde, and in the neighborhood of the Rue St. Honoré, there was terrible fighting during the day. A correspondent of the *Daily News* says that he looked for a moment round the corner of the Rue Faubourg St. Honoré, and had he looked for a moment longer he would have been killed. "The street," he says, "was a pneumatic tube for shell fire. Nothing could have lived in it." The losses on both sides were said to have been very heavy, and the Versaillist troops gave no quarter.

On Wednesday morning the Versaillists carried the Place de la Concorde, and also the Place Vendôme; but before they could obtain possession of the Tuileries, the palace was in flames, the insurgents having set fire to it and the Louvre, the Palace of the Legion of Honour, the Hotel of the Council of State, the Ministries of War and Finance, and the Hotel de Ville. The flames were said to have been kindled by petroleum, the fumes of which filled the air. When the news of the firing of the public buildings reached Versailles the fire brigade was dispatched to Paris, M. Thiers himself accompanying it to direct its operations. In the National Assembly on Wednesday afternoon, M. Thiers, whose voice is said to have been broken by emotion, described the terrible scenes which had occurred in Paris on that day, and implored the Assembly not to disturb the government. "When the insurrection shall have been suppressed," he said, "we shall not fail to punish according to law, but implacably." On the following day he issued a circular of information to the provinces, as follows: "We are masters of Paris, except a small portion, which will be occupied to-day. The Louvre has been saved. The Hotel of the Minister of Finance has been partially burned, and the Tuileries and the Palais du Quai d'Orsay (in which the Council of State holds its sessions) are wholly destroyed. We have already 12,000 prisoners, and shall have 20,000. The soil of Paris is strewn with insurgent corpses. Our loss is small. The army has behaved admirably. Justice will soon be satisfied, and France be happy in the midst of her own misfortunes."

The fighting was kept up on Thursday, and the Versaillists, on the evening of that day held every position but Belleville and the Buttes de Chaumont. From these strongholds the insurgents continued to rain petroleum shells on every part of Paris within reach. Here, and in the Cemetery of Pere-la-Chaise, the Communists were brought to bay, and made a desperate resistance; but, on Saturday, May 27th, these positions were carried by Generals L'Admirault and Vinoy, and the Commune was at an end. The last act of the insurrectionists was one that covered their name with infamy, and almost made men forget the horrors of the indiscriminate slaughter which the triumphant government had remorselessly wreaked upon them. On Saturday they shot the Archbishop of Paris, the Abbe Duguerry, and sixty-two other hostages remaining in their possession. The troops had previously captured La Roquette, and saved one hundred and sixty-nine hostages detained there.

The fall of the Commune was followed by the summary execution of the leaders, and of a great number of the prisoners. In the Parc de Monceaux and the Champs Elysées, the insurgents were shot in divisions of fifty or a hundred, and during the heat of the engagement no quarter had been given to the National Guards found fighting against the government. Many of the Communists who were taken had large sums of money in their possession, showing that the members of the revolutionary government had not scrupled to avail themselves of the facilities for plunder afforded by their wholesale requisitions. By June 1st order was restored, and military executions ceased.

A definitive treaty of peace between France and Prussia, was signed at Frankfort, on the 10th of May. The only important difference in the terms from those of the preliminary treaty given above, was in the retrocession of a small portion of Alsace in exchange for a strip of country near Thionville, on the borders of Lorraine, and the delay of the first payment of the indemnity until one month after the restoration of the authority of the French government in Paris.

THE END.

INDEX.

J

P

Q

R

S

T

U

V

W

X

Y

Z

www.ingramcontent.com/pod-product-compliance
Lightning Source LLC
LaVergne TN
LVHW021052110826
845150LV00001B/56